T0189859

Communications in Computer and Information Science 1052

Commenced Publication in 2007
Founding and Former Series Editors:
Phoebe Chen, Alfredo Cuzzocrea, Xiaoyong Du, Orhun Kara, Ting Liu,
Krishna M. Sivalingam, Dominik Ślęzak, Takashi Washio, and Xiaokang Yang

More information about this series at http://www.springer.com/series/7899

Juan Carlos Figueroa-García ·
Mario Duarte-González ·
Sebastián Jaramillo-Isaza ·
Alvaro David Orjuela-Cañon ·
Yesid Díaz-Gutierrez (Eds.)

Applied Computer Sciences in Engineering

6th Workshop on Engineering Applications, WEA 2019
Santa Marta, Colombia, October 16–18, 2019
Proceedings

 Springer

Editors
Juan Carlos Figueroa-García (iD)
Department of Industrial Engineering
Universidad Distrital Francisco
José de Caldas
Bogotá, Colombia

Sebastián Jaramillo-Isaza (iD)
Universidad Antonio Nariño
Bogotá, Colombia

Yesid Díaz-Gutierrez
Corporación Unificada Nacional CUN
Bogotá, Colombia

Mario Duarte-González
Universidad Antonio Nariño
Bogotá, Colombia

Alvaro David Orjuela-Cañon (iD)
Universidad del Rosario
Bogotá, Colombia

ISSN 1865-0929   ISSN 1865-0937 (electronic)
Communications in Computer and Information Science
ISBN 978-3-030-31018-9   ISBN 978-3-030-31019-6 (eBook)
https://doi.org/10.1007/978-3-030-31019-6

This Springer imprint is published by the registered company Springer Nature Switzerland AG
The registered company address is: Gewerbestrasse 11, 6330 Cham, Switzerland

Preface

The sixth edition of the Workshop on Engineering Applications (WEA 2019) was focused on applications in computer science, simulation, IoT, logistics, bioengineering, and computational intelligence. This consolidates WEA as an important conference covering different topics in engineering and applied sciences in academia/industry. WEA 2019 was one of the flagship events of the Faculty of Engineering of the Universidad Distrital Francisco José de Caldas and the Universidad Antonio Nariño in Colombia.

WEA 2019 was held at the Universidad Antonio Nariño in Santa Marta – Colombia, one of the oldest and most beautiful European-founded towns and the second most important colonial city on Colombia's Caribbean coast. We received 178 submissions from 15 countries in topics such as computer science, IoT, bioengineering, operations research/optimization, simulation systems, systems dynamics, systems modeling, power and electrical applications, software engineering, computer informatics, computational intelligence, among others. The Program Committee organized the volume into different sections to improve its readability, published by Springer Nature in the *Communications in Computer and Information Sciences* (CCIS) series. Therefore, the main topic of the conference was Applied Computer Sciences in Engineering.

All submissions were rigorously peer-reviewed by the reviewers, who provided constructive comments and as a result of their hard work, 64 papers were accepted for presentation at WEA 2019. The Faculty of Engineering of the Universidad Distrital Francisco José de Caldas, the Faculty of Mechanical, Electronics and Biomedical Engineering of the Universidad Antonio Nariño, the Corporación Unificada Nacional (CUN), the Faculty of Engineering of the National University of Colombia, and the Escuela de Infantería of the National Colombian Army made significant efforts to guarantee the success of the conference.

We would like to thank all members of the Program Committee and the referees for their commitment to help in the review process and for publicizing our call for papers. We would like to thank Alfred Hofmann and Jorge Nakahara from Springer Nature for their helpful advice, guidance, and continuous support in publishing the proceedings. Moreover, we would like to thank all the authors for supporting WEA 2019; without all their high-quality submissions the conference would not have been possible. Finally, we are especially grateful to the IEEE Universidad Distrital Francisco José de Caldas Student branch; the Institute of Industrial and Systems Engineers Chapter 985 (IISE) of the Universidad Distrital Francisco José de Caldas; the Laboratory for Automation and Computational Intelligence (LAMIC) of the Universidad Distrital Francisco José de Caldas; the groups BIOINGENIERÍA, GIBIO, and GEPRO from the Faculty of Mechanical, Electronics and Biomedical Engineering of the Universidad Antonio Nariño; the Algorithms and Combinatory (ALGOS) research group of the National

University of Colombia; and the AXON group of the Corporación Unificada Nacional (CUN) - Colombia.

October 2019   Juan Carlos Figueroa-García
                                                  Mario Duarte-González
                                                  Sebastián Jaramillo-Isaza
                                                  Alvaro David Orjuela-Cañon
                                                  Yesid Díaz-Gutierrez

Organization

General Chair

Juan Carlos Figueroa-García   Universidad Distrital Francisco José de Caldas, Colombia

Finance Chair and Treasurer

Mario Enrique Duarte-Gonzalez   Universidad Antonio Nariño, Colombia

Technical Chairs

Yesid Díaz-Gutierrez   Corporación Unificada Nacional de Educación Superior (CUN), Colombia

Julio Barón   Universidad Distrital Francisco José de Caldas, Colombia

Publication Chair

Alvaro David Orjuela-Cañón   Universidad del Rosario, Colombia

Track Chairs

Edwin Rivas   Universidad Distrital Francisco José de Caldas, Colombia

Sebastián Jaramillo-Isaza   Universidad Antonio Nariño, Colombia

Yesid Díaz-Gutierrez   Corporación Unificada Nacional de Educación Superior (CUN), Colombia

Eduyn López-Santana   Universidad Distrital Francisco José de Caldas, Colombia

Paulo Alonso Gaona   Universidad Distrital Francisco José de Caldas, Colombia

Logistics Chairs

Sebastián Jaramillo-Isaza   Universidad Antonio Nariño, Colombia

Yesid Díaz-Gutierrez   Corporación Unificada Nacional de Educación Superior (CUN), Colombia

Plenary Speakers

Carlos A. Coello-Coello	Instituto Politcnico Nacional, Mexico
Fernando Gomide	Universidade Estadual de Campinas UNICAMP, Brazil
Leonardo Bobadilla	Florida International University (FIU), USA

Program Committee

Adil Usman	Indian Institute of Technology at Mandi, India
Adolfo Jaramillo-Matta	Universidad Distrital Francisco José de Caldas, Colombia
Altagracia Carrillo Parra	Universidad Tecnológica de Xicotepec de Juárez, Mexico
Alvaro David Orjuela-Cañón	Universidad del Rosario, Colombia
Andres Ernesto Salguero	Universidad Antonio Nariño, Colombia
Andres Felipe Ruiz	Universidad Antonio Nariño, Colombia
Andres Guillermo Molano	Universidad Antonio Nariño, Colombia
Andres M. Alvarez Mesa	Universidad Nacional de Colombia, Colombia
Carlos Franco-Franco	Universidad del Rosario, Colombia
Carlos Osorio-Ramírez	Universidad Nacional de Colombia, Colombia
DeShuang Huang	Tongji University, China
Diana Ovalle	Universidad Distrital Francisco José de Caldas, Colombia
Eduyn López-Santana	Universidad Distrital Francisco José de Caldas, Colombia
Edwin Rivas	Universidad Distrital Francisco José de Caldas, Colombia
Elvis Eduardo Gaona	Universidad Distrital Francisco José de Caldas, Colombia
Feizar Javier Rueda-Velazco	Universidad Distrital Francisco José de Caldas, Colombia
Francisco García-Romero	Universidad Tecnológica de Xicotepec de Juárez, Mexico
Germán Hernández-Pérez	Universidad Nacional de Colombia, Colombia
Guadalupe González	Universidad Tecnológica de Panamá, Panama
Gustavo Puerto L.	Universidad Distrital Francisco José de Caldas, Colombia
Henry Diosa	Universidad Distrital Francisco José de Caldas, Colombia
Heriberto Román-Flores	Universidad de Tarapacá, Chile
I-Hsien Ting	National University of Kaohsiung, Taiwan
Jair Cervantes-Canales	Universidad Autónoma de México, Mexico
Jairo Soriano-Mendez	Universidad Distrital Francisco José de Caldas, Colombia
Javier Arturo Orjuela-Castro	Universidad Nacional de Colombia, Colombia

Jose Luis Villa	Universidad Tecnológica de Bolívar, Colombia
Juan Carlos Figueroa-García	Universidad Distrital Francisco José de Caldas, Colombia
Lindsay Alvarez	Universidad Distrital Francisco José de Caldas, Colombia
Mabel Frías	Universidad de las Villas Marta Abreu, Cuba
Marco A. Ramírez-Hernández	Universidad Tecnológica de Xicotepec de Juárez, Mexico
Mario Enrique Duarte-Gonzalez	Universidad Antonio Nariño, Colombia
Martha Centeno	University of Turabo, Puerto Rico
Martin Pilat	Charles University, Czech Republic
Miguel Melgarejo	Universidad Distrital Francisco José de Caldas, Colombia
Nelson L. Diaz Aldana	Universidad Distrital Francisco José de Caldas, Colombia
Oswaldo Lopez Santos	Universidad de Ibagué, Colombia
Paulo Alonso Gaona	Universidad Distrital Francisco José de Caldas, Colombia
Rafael Bello-Pérez	Universidad de las Villas Marta Abreu, Cuba
Ral Chirinos-Lechuga	Universidad Tecnológica de Xicotepec de Juárez, Mexico
Roberto Ferro	Universidad Distrital Francisco José de Caldas, Colombia
Rodrigo Linfati	Universidad del Bío Bío, Chile
Roman Neruda	Charles University, Czech Academy of Sciences, Czech Republic
Sebastián Jaramillo-Isaza	Universidad Antonio Nariño, Colombia
Sergio Rojas-Galeano	Universidad Distrital Francisco José de Caldas, Colombia
Victor Medina García	Universidad Distrital Francisco José de Caldas, Colombia
William Camilo Rodríguez	Universidad Distrital Francisco José de Caldas, Colombia
Yesid Díaz-Gutierrez	Corporación Unificada Nacional de Educación Superior (CUN), Colombia
Yurilev Chalco-Cano	Universidad de Tarapacá, Chile

Contents

Computational Intelligence

Bioengineering

Simulation Systems

Optimization

Computer Science

Solving Large Dynamical Systems
by Constraint Sampling

Omeiza Olumoye[1]([✉])(iD), Glen Throneberry[2](iD), Angel Garcia[1](iD),
Leobardo Valera[1](iD), Abdessattar Abdelkefi[2](iD), and Martine Ceberio[1](iD)

[1] The University of Texas at El Paso, El Paso, TX 79968, USA
{okolumoye,lvalera,mceberio}@utep.edu,
afgarciacontreras@miners.utep.edu
[2] New Mexico State University,
1780 E University Avenue, Las Cruces, NM 88003, USA
{gthroneb,abdu}@nmsu.edu,
http://ndehl.nmsu.edu/index.html

Abstract. The ability to conduct fast and reliable simulations of
dynamic systems is of special interest to many fields of operations. Such
simulations can be very complex and, to be thorough, involve millions
of variables, making it prohibitive in CPU time to run repeatedly for
many different configurations. Reduced-Order Modeling (ROM) provides
a concrete way to handle such complex simulations using a realistic
amount of resources. However, when the original dynamical system is
very large, the resulting reduced-order model, although much "thinner",
is still as tall as the original system, i.e., it has the same number of equations. In some extreme cases, the number of equations is prohibitive and
cannot be loaded in memory. In this work, we combine traditional interval constraint solving techniques with a strategy to reduce the number of
equations to consider. We describe our approach and report preliminary
promising results.

Keywords: Dynamical systems · Constraint solving ·
Model-order reduction

1 Introduction

The ability to make observations of natural phenomena has played a fundamental
role in our understanding of the world surrounding us. From what we observe, we
build models and we simulate them to validate them and then to understand how
these phenomena vary over time: one very important goal is to be able to predict
future behavior or features of given dynamical phenomena. Differential equations
(PDEs or ODEs) help us represent the time-dependence of these dynamic systems. Numerical approaches to solving such differential equations often require
discretization, which could involve millions of variables. As a result, so-called
high-fidelity or full-order models (FOM) yield significant CPU time issues. To

© Springer Nature Switzerland AG 2019
J. C. Figueroa-García et al. (Eds.): WEA 2019, CCIS 1052, pp. 3–15, 2019.
https://doi.org/10.1007/978-3-030-31019-6_1

overcome such issues, when given an existing large FOM, Reduced-Order Modeling (ROM) techniques can be used, which allow searching for the solutions of the given FOM in a subspace whose dimension is much smaller than the dimension of the original high-fidelity FOM model. This makes running simulations much more lightweight while maintaining high quality of the outputs.

Nonetheless, ROM techniques are not the ultimate solution to the above problem. Although the dimension of the search space is considerably smaller, the number of equations/constraints is still considerably large. In some cases, it is impossible to solve the Reduced-Order Model using Interval Constraints Solving Techniques (ICST) because of the number of constraints. In other cases, it is not even possible to load all constraints in memory. In this article, we propose a strategy to overcome this issue. We propose an iterative process in which, at each step, only a few equations/constraints are considered, and the subset of such equations changes at each step, hence addressing the abovementioned problems.

We test our approach with three examples. Two of them are classical predator-prey models that we use to test the effectiveness of our method. We then use our sampling method to solve a problem where the number of constraints makes it impossible to find the solution in the classical way. For all of these cases, we present promising experimental results.

2 Background

Modeling real-life phenomena can result in very large (most likely) nonlinear systems of equations. Solving such systems can become an issue because of their size and it is now fairly common to address this problem with techniques such as Model-Order Reduction (MOR). MOR techniques aim to reduce the dimensionality of the original problem while retaining the properties of the sought solution. In what follows, we review such techniques. We then cover the basics of interval constraint solving techniques, which are the techniques we base our approach on.

2.1 Dynamical Systems and Model-Order Reduction

Let us consider a system of equations: $F(x) = 0$, where $F : \mathbb{R}^n \to \mathbb{R}^n$. The main idea of Reduced-Order Modeling is to avoid looking for a solution of the above problem in a high-dimension space but to identify a (much smaller) subspace where the solution should lie and to look for this lower-dimension solution. As a result, we have to find a lower-dimension solution p in a subspace $W \subset \mathbb{R}^n$, whose dimension $k \ll n$.

The underlying assumption behind this principle is that when looking for x^* such that $F(x^*) = 0$, we acknowledge that:

$$\exists \, (n \times k) \text{ matrix } \Phi, \text{ with } k \ll n, \tag{1}$$

whose columns are the base vectors of W, such that x can be expressed as:

$$x = \Phi p + z$$

where $p \in \mathbb{R}^k$.

Assuming that the choice of the subspace where x^* lies is accurate, we can deduce that $z \approx 0$. As a result, we are now solving:

$$F(\Phi p) = 0 \quad \text{over } \mathbb{R}^k.$$

This is illustrated on a 3D reduced to 2D example, in Fig. 1. The solution $x \in \mathbb{R}^n$ corresponds to the non-perpendicular vector (red) not contained in the plane, which is the subspace spanned by Φ. The lower-dimension unknown $p \in W \subset \mathbb{R}^k$ corresponds to the orthogonal projection (green) of x onto the plane W. The orthogonal vector (blue) corresponds to the orthogonal component, z, that is approximately equal to zero when Φ is a "good" basis.

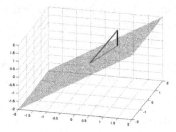

Fig. 1. Graphical Representation of ROM (Color figure online)

Let us now illustrate the workings of Reduced-Order Modeling through the following example:

Example 1. Consider the following nonlinear system of equations:

$$\begin{cases} (x_1^2 + x_1 - 2)(x_2^2 + 1) = 0 \\ (x_2^2 - 5x_2 + 6)(x_1^2 + 1) = 0 \\ (x_3^2 - 2x_3 - 3)(x_4^2 + 1) = 0 \\ (x_4^2 - 4)(x_3^2 + 1) = 0 \end{cases} \tag{2}$$

We can reduce this 4D system of equations by searching for a solution in the subspace W spanned by $\Phi = \{(2, 4, -2, 0)^T; (0, 0, 0, -4)^T\}$.

$$\begin{cases} (16y_1^2 + 1)(4y_1^2 + 2y_1 - 2) = 0 \\ (4y_1^2 + 1)(16y_1^2 + 20y_1 + 6) = 0 \\ (16y_2^2 + 1)(4y_1^2 + 4y_1 - 3) = 0 \\ (4y_1^2 + 1)(16y_2^2 - 4) = 0 \end{cases} \tag{3}$$

This new reduced system (size 2) has two solutions $Y_1 = (0.5, 0.5)^T$ and $Y_2 = (0.5, -0.5)^T$. We can obtain the solutions of (2) by plugging Y_1 and Y_2 into

$\Phi \cdot Y = X$. Note that the nonlinear system (2) has 16 solutions, but only the two contained in W are obtained by solving the Reduced Model.

Remarks: It is important to highlight that although the system of Eq. (3) has fewer unknowns than the system (2), the number of occurrences of each of the new variables is greater, which represents a challenge when the system of equations is solved using Interval Constraints Solving Techniques.

2.2   Interval Constraint Solving Techniques

Often, uncertainty in a given quantity can be expressed as an interval of possible values for this quantity. For instance, measurement instruments often come with a known maximum error. As a result, when measuring a quantity x, we instead get $\tilde{x}$, which in fact corresponds to $\tilde{x} \pm \Delta_x = [\tilde{x} - \Delta_x, \tilde{x} + \Delta_x]$, in which the true observed quantity lies. When quantities are multidimensional, we call multidimensional intervals boxes. In what follows, we start by showing how we can handle uncertainty with intervals.

In a nutshell, interval analysis, as opposed to real analysis, consists in handling every quantity as a closed interval, as opposed to a real number. The idea of interval arithmetic is as follows:

$$\forall X, Y \text{ intervals}, \ X \bowtie Y = \{x \bowtie y, \ x \in X, \ y \in Y\}, \tag{4}$$
$$\text{where } \bowtie \in \{+, -, \times, \div\}$$

More specifically, since Y might contain 0, when $\bowtie$ is $\div$, $X \bowtie Y$ would not be an interval unless we add an extra operator, $\square$, the hull, which is defined by:

$$\square(X, Y) = [\min\{\underline{X}, \underline{Y}\}, \max\{\overline{X}, \overline{Y}\}] \tag{5}$$

where $\underline{X}, \underline{Y}$ are the lower bounds of X and Y respectively, and $\overline{X}, \overline{Y}$ are the upper bounds.

The hull operator (5) ensures that all interval computations result in an interval. As a result, we in fact have:

$$\forall X, Y \text{ intervals}, \ X \bowtie Y = \square\{x \bowtie y, \ x \in X, \ y \in Y\}, \tag{6}$$
$$\text{where } \bowtie \in \{+, -, \times, \div\}$$

From there, all functions over the reals can be extended to intervals. For any mapping $f : \ \mathbb{R}^n \rightarrow \mathbb{R}$ over the reals, a mapping $\tilde{F}$ is called a valid interval extension if it satisfies the following property:

$$\forall X \in \mathbb{IR}^n, \ \{f(x), \ x \in X\} \subseteq \tilde{F}(X). \tag{7}$$

This definition allows for many interval functions to qualify as extensions of any given real function f but the goal is to identify interval functions $\tilde{F}$ that best enclose the range of the original real function f. As a result, when solving nonlinear systems of equations using interval computations, we seek to use extensions that are tight, so as to avoid overestimations as much as possible.

In this work, we use interval computations provided in RealPaver [8] and the natural extensions that this library provides.

2.3 How to Solve Nonlinear Equations with Intervals?

When solving equations with intervals, we use constraint solving techniques [12, 19]. Given an equation $f_i(x_1, \ldots, x_n) = 0$ with k occurrences of x_j in the symbolic expression of f_i, a contractor on f_i for x_j is defined by:

$$c_{i,j,l} : \mathbb{IR} \to \mathbb{IR} \text{ where: } l \in \{1, \ldots, k\}$$
$$X \mapsto c_{i,j,l}(X) = X \cap F_{i,j,l}(X_1, \ldots, X_n) \tag{8}$$

where $F_{i,j,l}$ is such that $F_{i,j,l}(x_1, \ldots, x_n) = x_j$ is equivalent to $f_i(x_1, \ldots, x_n) = 0$.

Contractors are then used (repeatedly, in a fixed-point fashion) to reduce domains of the variables of the constraint system. Contractions are alternated with bisections: when a contraction does not reduce a domain to satisfaction (either eliminating it or narrowing it to a sufficient precision), contracted domains are bisected and each of the bisected domains queued to be processed by contractors. This generic solving process (branch and prune) stops when all domains have been either eliminated or contracted to satisfaction. An example of such a process is as follows:

Example 2.
$$\begin{cases} c_1 : & x^2 + y = 1 \\ c_2 : -x^2 + y = 0 \end{cases} \tag{9}$$
where $x \in X = [-1, 1]$ and $y \in Y = [-1, 1]$.

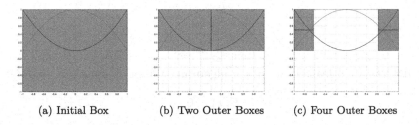

(a) Initial Box   (b) Two Outer Boxes   (c) Four Outer Boxes

Fig. 2. Outer approximations of the solutions of the system of Eq. (9)

Let us explain, step by step, how the domains of each variable, x and y, are narrowed (see [9,10] for details):

1. First, we start with the initial box, $[-1, 1] \times [-1, 1]$, containing the solution(s) of this problem, if any; see Fig. 2(a).
2. Constraint c_1 is considered and first used to define a contractor for the domain of variable y:

$$c_{1,y,1} : Y \mapsto Y \cap 1 - X^2$$

As a result, we obtain:

$$\begin{aligned} Y &= [-1, 1] \cap (1 - [-1, 1]^2) \\ &= [-1, 1] \cap (1 - [0, 1]) \\ &= [-1, 1] \cap [0, 1] \\ &= [0, 1] \end{aligned} \tag{10}$$

3. A similar step is repeated on the contractor for variable x using Constraint c_1: $c_{1,x,1}$, but this step yields not contraction for the domain of x, leaving it as $X = [-1, 1]$.
4. Moving on to Constraint c_2, and processing the domains of x and y using their respective contractors, no more contraction is obtained. The new domain after seeking a first fixed-point of contraction on the original domains yields a new domain: $[-1, 1] \times [0, 1]$.
5. If the accuracy of this new domain is deemed insufficient (which it is, in this case), then the domain is split along one of its dimension (in Fig. 2(b), it is split w.r.t. the domain of x), and the above steps 2–4 are repeated until the whole domain has been discarded (no solution) or a desired level of accuracy has been reached.
6. Repeating this process further, we reach configuration 2(c) in Fig. 2.

2.4   What Types of Problems Are We Addressing?

Let us recall that the problems we are solving in this paper are systems of first or second order differential equations. We numerically solve these problems by discretizing the domain temporally and using backward finite differences to approximate the derivatives, i.e.,

$$x'_i = \frac{x_i - x_{i-1}}{h}$$
$$x''_i = \frac{x_{i-1} - 2x_i + x_{i+1}}{h^2}$$
(11)

This discretization leads to an $n \times n$ algebraic system of equations (FOM):

$$F(x) = 0 \tag{12}$$

where $x = (x_1, x_2, \ldots, x_n)$ is the solution of (12).

If the solution x is sought in a subspace W spanned by the columns of the matrix Φ. The nonlinear system of Eq. (12) becomes to the overdetermined nonlinear system: $\tilde{F}(y) = (F \circ \Phi)(y) = F(\Phi y) = 0$.

Solving the new system is equivalent to finding the roots of the following function:

$$\tilde{F} : \mathbb{R}^k \to \mathbb{R}^n \tag{13}$$

with $k \ll n$, which is a rectangular nonlinear system of equations.

3   Our Proposed Approach

In this article, we propose a strategy to handle large-dimensional problems by constraints sampling, i.e., we work with contractors defined by taking a sampling of the original set of constraints, and when a box is splitted, each new box is contracted using a contractor defined by a new set of constraints.

The general procedure is as follows:

- Start with a system of constraints $C = \{c_1, c_2, \ldots, c_n\}$ and a initial box D_0 (search space).
- Set a candidate of solutions set $SolCand$ (will content the enough tight boxes), a set of solutions Sol, and a storage S.
- Initialize $S = \{D_0\}$
- We repeat the following process while S is not empty:
  - Select a set D of S.
  - Choose k constraints from C.
  - Contract D using the contractors defined by the previous constraints.
  - if D is enough small, then add it to the $SolCand$, otherwise, split it in two new boxes and add those new boxes to S.
- Once the set S is empty, check every set of $SolCand$ to see which of them is a solution.

---

input : System of Constraints $C = \{c_1, c_2, \ldots, c_k\}$, an Initial Box (search space) D_0; int m: the dimension of the subset of constraints to be selected at each step

output: A set Sol of boxes of size n, where n is the number of variables

1   Set $Sol = \emptyset$, $SolCand = \emptyset$
2   Stack S receives D_0
3   Select a subset $\{c_{i1}, c_{i2}, \ldots, c_{im}\}$ of m elements of C
4   **while** $Stack \neq \emptyset$ **do**
5   Take D out of $Stack$
6      $\forall j,\ l,\ D = c_{i,j,l}(D)$
7   **if** D *is still too large* **then**
8   Split D in D_1 and D_2
9   Store D_1 and D_2 in $Stack$ **Else**
10   Store D in $SolCand$
11   **end**
12 **end**
13 **while** $SolCand \neq$ **do**
14   Take S out of $SolCand$
15   **if** $\forall i,\ 0 \in c_i(S)$ **then**
16   Store S in Sol **Else** Discard S.
17   **end**
18 **end**
19 **return** Sol

Algorithm 1: Generic Sampling Constraint Solving Algorithm

4   Numerical Results

Here, we describe and report on the preliminary experiments we ran to test our proposed approach. Two of our test cases are classical predator-prey models and we used them as baseline testing. Indeed, both of them have a Reduced-Order Model that is solvable "as is". As a result, we can use these problems to check if our method allows us to obtain acceptable results compared with the traditional MOR method, and if the results are acceptable with respect to runtime and accuracy, then we can proceed and solve a more challenging problem.

4.1   Lotka-Volterra Model

Consider a classical predator-prey model known as the Lotka-Volterra model:

$$\begin{aligned} \frac{dx}{dt} &= ax - bxy, \\ \frac{dy}{dt} &= -cy + dxy. \end{aligned} \tag{14}$$

This model is represented as a system of two ordinary differential equations where the variables represent the size of the population of each species in presence of the other. x and y are respectively the number of preys and predators present at any time. a represents the rate at which the prey population increases in the absence of predators, b represents the rate at which the prey population decreases in the presence of predators, c represents the natural death rate of the predators in the absence of prey, and d represents the rate at which the predator population increases in the presence of prey.

The above system is first discretized numerically using backward finite differences. We discretize $t \in [0, 10]$ using a step size $h = 0.05$ to obtain a total of 800 constraints. The solution is sough in a three-dimensional subspace.

As described in Sect. 3, we use a sampling strategy in which we select k constraints and we contract the domain box using the contractors associated with the corresponding subset of k constraints. We select different values of k to analyze what is the best number of constraints we should take to obtain our solution. We repeat the above described procedure 100 times and we report our results in the table of Fig. 3.

The relation between the number of bisections and the runtime versus the number of constraints presented in Fig. 3, corresponds to what we expected. When k is larger, each contraction step is more efficient (but takes longer), therefore yielding fewer bisections. When k is smaller, we observe a larger number of bisection steps.

4.2   Food Chain Model

The food chain equation attempts to model an ecosystem of three species. It is a generalization of the Lotka-Volterra system. The third species only threatens

# Constraints (%)	time (secs)	Bisections
0.5	1.1213	27
1	1.0397	26
5	1.1223	21
10	1.3438	19
20	1.7106	16
30	2.1539	16
40	2.4987	15
50	2.8999	14
60	3.2955	14
70	3.6076	13
80	4.0796	13
90	4.5202	13
100	4.9551	13

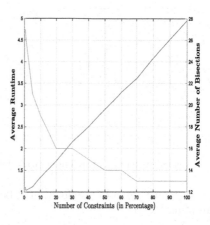

Fig. 3. Subset sampling approach in solving a particular example of the Lotka-Volterra problem

the second one. This model is represented as a system of three first-order linear differential equations.

$$\frac{dx}{dt} = ax - bxy,$$
$$\frac{dy}{dt} = -cy + dxy - eyz, \qquad (15)$$
$$\frac{dz}{dt} = -fz + gyz.$$

where x, y, and z represent different animal species such that y preys on x, and z is a predator to y; a, b, c, and d are as described in the Lotka-Volterra; e represents the rate of population decrease of the species y in the presence of species z, f represents the natural death rate of the species z in the absence of prey, and g represents the rate of population increase of the species z in the presence of prey.

Similarly to the previous case, we solve System (15) discretizing the domain and solving the algebraic system of equations using (ICST). In Fig. 5., we report the runtime and the number of bisections with respect to the number of constraints selected. The results of this experiment reinforce what we obtained in the first case: the larger k, the fewer the number of bisections, but the longer the runtime. Based on these two experiments, our approach is promising. We can not only solve our system of equations within an acceptable interval of time, but also the accuracy of the solution is highly acceptable as we can see in Fig. 4.

We are now ready to increase the complexity of the problems we address. In what follows, we attempt to solve a system of equations so large that it would even be impossible to load all the equations in memory at the same time, hence forcing us to load the constraint system only bits by bits to find the solutions.

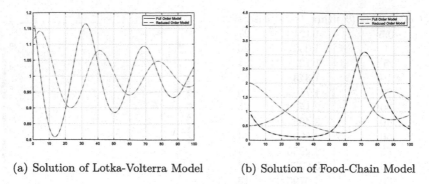

(a) Solution of Lotka-Volterra Model   (b) Solution of Food-Chain Model

Fig. 4. Comparison of the Solution of Lotka-Volterra and Food Chain Using FOM and Sampling ROM

4.3   Dynamical Modeling of Flapping Wings

In mechanical engineering, it is common to seek a system that reduces the required mechanical power to enhance the longevity of the system [23–26]. In this article, we use ICST to numerically solve the nonlinear differential equation that represents the movement of flapping wings. This is a simulation of the flapping wings of a hummingbird.

Let us assume that we want to simulate the flapping wings of a hummingbird (Fig. 6(a)) with a device represented in the diagram of Fig. 6(b). Such diagram is equivalent to a spring-mass system with a nonlinear stiffness term (Fig. 6(c)).

The spring-mass system is modeled as the second order nonlinear differential equation:

$$Mx'' + bx'|x'| + k_1 x + k_3 x^3 = F_b \cos(\omega t) \tag{16}$$

Constraints (%)	Time(secs)	# of Bisections
0.5	1.3968	23
1	1.1318	20
5	1.3325	15
10	1.6655	13
20	2.3698	11
30	3.3743	10
40	3.3868	10
50	4.0358	10
60	4.6393	10
70	5.4389	10
80	6.7846	10
90	6.8040	10
100	6.8027	10

Fig. 5. Subset sampling approach in solving a particular example of the Food Chain problem

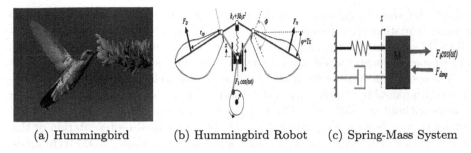

(a) Hummingbird   (b) Hummingbird Robot   (c) Spring-Mass System

Fig. 6. Dynamical Modeling. Flapping Wings Simulator

where: $x(0) = 0$, $x'(0) = 0$, $M = 0.2$, $b = 0.0556909591875$, $k_1 = 6300$, $k_3 = 10^5$, $F_b = 1.0$, and $\omega = 185$.

We solve numerically Eq. (16) by discretizing the domain with a step size $h = 0.001$ for $t \in [0, 50]$ seconds. After discretization, we obtain a nonlinear system of $50,000$ equations and $50,000$ unknowns. We are not able to solve the FOM with interval techniques. We search the solution on a subspace spanned by a basis of three elements. After reducing our search space, we obtain a system of $50,000$ equations and only 3 unknowns. Even though we are able to significantly reduce the number of unknowns, we still are not able to solve the ROM using ICST using all the constraints at once.

Starting with the initial box $[-2, 2] \times [-2, 2] \times [-2, 2]$ and taking 5 constraints at each iteration, we proceed to solve our **large dynamical system by constraint sampling**. The solving time is eight hours and returns the following solution:

$$P = \begin{bmatrix} [1.000000000000000, 1.062500000000000] \\ [1.000000000000000, 1.050483000000001] \\ [0.981992683059733, 1.023290841529867] \end{bmatrix}$$

which corresponds to the following solution (Fig. 7):

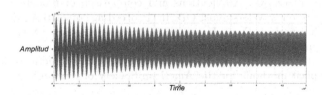

Fig. 7. Graph of the Solution of the Flapping Model

5   Conclusion

Motivated by the need to solve large dynamical systems with uncertainty and with guarantees, and realizing that ROM techniques are not sufficient to truly reduce the size of the system to be solved (in our case, the number of constraints/equations), in this article, we proposed to find solutions to large dynamical ROM systems via sampling constraints at each stage of the traditional branch and prune approach for solving continuous constraints.

We tested our approach on three dynamical models. Two of them have relatively manageable dimensions and we were able to find the solutions of their models without any difficulty. The third one, a flapping wings system, was a significantly more complex dynamical model. The numerical representation of this model consisted in a very tall nonlinear system after processing ROM techniques. We were able to find the solution of this model.

Our approach is far from being perfect though. In particular, we assumed that the parameters of our models were uncertainty-free. In our future work, we plan to explore computational strategies to help us control the uncertainty of our solutions.

References

1. Bai, Z., Meerbergen, K., Su, Y.: Arnoldi methods for structure-preserving dimension reduction of second-order dynamical systems. In: Benner, P., Sorensen, D.C., Mehrmann, V. (eds.) Dimension Reduction of Large-Scale Systems. LNCSE, vol. 45, pp. 173–189. Springer, Heidelberg (2005). https://doi.org/10.1007/3-540-27909-1_7
2. Benner, P., Quintana-Ortíz, E.: Model reduction based on spectral projection methods. In: Benner, P., Sorensen, D.C., Mehrmann, V. (eds.) Dimension Reduction of Large-Scale Systems. LNCSE, vol. 45, pp. 5–48. Springer, Heidelberg (2005). https://doi.org/10.1007/3-540-27909-1_1
3. Berkooz, G., Holmes, P., Lumley, J.: The proper orthogonal decomposition in the analysis of turbulent flows. Ann. Rev. Fluid Mech. **25**(1), 539–575 (1993)
4. Cai, L., White, R.E.: Reduction of model order based on proper orthogonal decomposition for lithium-ion battery simulations. J. Electrochem. Soc. **156**(3), A154–A161 (2009)
5. Ceberio, M., Granvilliers, L.: Horner's rule for interval evaluation revisited. Computing **69**(1), 51–81 (2002)
6. Flórez, H., Argáez, M.: Applications and comparison of model-order reduction methods based on wavelets and POD. In: Proceedings of 2016 Annual Conference of the North American Fuzzy Information Processing Society (NAFIPS), El Paso, TX, USA, pp. 1–8. IEEE (2016)
7. George, J., et al.: Idiopathic thrombocytopenic purpura: a practice guideline developed by explicit methods for the American Society of Hematology. Blood **88**(1), 3–40 (1996)
8. Granvilliers, L., Benhamou, F.: Realpaver: an interval solver using constraint satisfaction techniques. ACM Trans. Math. Softw. (TOMS) **32**(1), 138–156 (2006)
9. Hansen, E., Greenberg, R.: An interval newton method. Appl. Math. Comput. **12**(2–3), 89–98 (1983)
10. Hansen, E., Walster, G.: Global Optimization Using Interval Analysis: Revised and Expanded, vol. 264. CRC Press, New York (2003)
11. Horner, W.G.: A new method of solving numerical equations of all orders, by continuous approximation. In: Philosophical Transactions of the Royal Society of London, New York, NY (1833)

12. Jaulin, L.: Applied Interval Analysis: With Examples in Parameter and State Estimation, Robust Control and Robotics. Springer, London (2001)
13. Kerschen, G., Golinval, J.: Physical interpretation of the proper orthogonal modes using the singular value decomposition. J. Sound Vibr. **249**(5), 849–865 (2002)
14. Liang, Y., Lee, H., Lim, S., Lin, W., Lee, K., Wu, C.: Proper orthogonal decomposition and its applications, part i: theory. J. Sound Vibr. **252**(3), 527–544 (2002)
15. Lin, Y., Stadtherr, M.: Validated solutions of initial value problems for parametric ODEs. Appl. Numer. Math. **57**(10), 1145–1162 (2007)
16. Millet, A., Morien, P.: On implicit and explicit discretization schemes for parabolic SPDEs in any dimension. Stoch. Process. Their Appl. **115**(7), 1073–1106 (2005)
17. Nedialkov, S.: Computing Rigorous Bounds on the Solution of an Initial Value Problem for an Ordinary Differential Equation. University of Toronto, Toronto, Canada (2000)
18. Rewienski, M., White, J.: A trajectory piecewise-linear approach to model order reduction and fast simulation of nonlinear circuits and micromachined devices. IEEE Trans. Comput.-Aided Des. Integr. Circ. Syst. **22**(2), 155–170 (2003)
19. Sam-Haroud, D., Faltings, B.: Consistency techniques for continuous constraints. Constraints **1**(1), 85–118 (1996)
20. Schilders, W.A., Van der Vorst, H., Rommes, J.: Model Order Reduction: Theory, Research Aspects and Applications. Springer, Berlin (2008)
21. Stahl, V.: Interval Methods for Bounding the Range of Polynomials and Solving Systems of Nonlinear Equations. Johannes-Kepler-Universität, Linz (1995)
22. Willcox, K., Peraire, J.: Balanced model reduction via the proper orthogonal decomposition. Am. Inst. Aeronaut. Astronaut. AIAA J. **40**(11), 2323–2330 (2002)
23. Hassanalian, M., Throneberry, G., Abdelkefi, A.: Wing shape and dynamic twist design of bio-inspired nano air vehicles for forward flight purposes. Aerosp. Sci. Technol. **68**, 518–529 (2017)
24. Hassanalian, M., Throneberry, G., Abdelkefi, A.: Investigation on the planform and kinematic optimization of bio-inspired nano air vehicles for hovering applications. Meccanica **53**, 1–14 (2018)
25. Hassanalian, M., Throneberry, G., Abdelkefi, A.: Wing shape analysis and optimization of bio-inspired flapping wing nano air vehicles for forward flight. In: Proceeding of the SciTech 2017, AIAA Aerospace Sciences Meeting, AIAA Science and Technology Forum and Exposition 2017, Texas, USA, 09–13 January (2017)
26. Ghommem, M., et al.: Sizing and aerodynamic analysis of biplane flapping wing nano air vehicle: theory and experiment. In: Proceeding of the SciTech 2019, AIAA Aerospace Sciences Meeting, AIAA Science and Technology Forum and Exposition 2019, California, USA, 07–11 January (2019)

Scaling in Concurrent Evolutionary Algorithms

Juan J. Merelo[1], J. L. J. Laredo[2], Pedro A. Castillo[1],
José-Mario García-Valdez[3], and Sergio Rojas-Galeano[4(✉)]

[1] Universidad de Granada/CITIC, Granada, Spain
{jmerelo,pacv}@ugr.es
[2] RI2C-LITIS, Université du Havre Normandie, Le Havre, France
juanlu.jimenez@univ-lehavre.fr
[3] Instituto Tecnológico de Tijuana, Calzada Tecnológico, s/n, Tijuana, Mexico
mario@tectijuana.edu.mx
[4] School of Engineering, Universidad Distrital Francisco José de Caldas,
Bogotá, Colombia
srojas@udistrital.edu.co

Abstract. The concept of *channel*, a computational mechanism used to convey state to different threads of process execution, is at the core of the design of multi-threaded concurrent algorithms. In the case of concurrent evolutionary algorithms, *channels* can be used to communicate messages between several threads performing different evolution tasks related to genetic operations or mixing of populations. In this paper we study to what extent the design of these messages in a communicating sequential process context may influence scaling and performance of concurrent evolutionary algorithms. For this aim, we designed a channel-based concurrent evolutionary algorithm that is able to effectively solve different benchmark binary problems (e.g. OneMax, LeadingOnes, RoyalRoad), showing that it provides a good basis to leverage the multi-threaded and multi-core capabilities of modern computers. Although our results indicate that concurrency is advantageous to scale-up the performance of evolutionary algorithms, they also highlight how the trade–off between concurrency, communication and evolutionary parameters affect the outcome of the evolved solutions, opening-up new opportunities for algorithm design.

Keywords: Concurrency · Concurrent evolutionary algorithms ·
Performance evaluation · Algorithm design ·
Distributed evolutionary algorithm

1 Introduction

Despite the emphasis on leveraging newer hardware features with best-suited software techniques, there are not many papers [20] dealing with the creation of concurrent evolutionary algorithms that work in a single computing node or that

© Springer Nature Switzerland AG 2019
J. C. Figueroa-García et al. (Eds.): WEA 2019, CCIS 1052, pp. 16–27, 2019.
https://doi.org/10.1007/978-3-030-31019-6_2

extend seamlessly from single to many computers. In that sense, concurrent programming seems to be the best option if we are dealing with a multi-core multi-threaded processor architecture where many processes and threads can coexists at the same time. The latter implies applications (and algorithms) should be able to leverage those processes to take full advantage of their capabilities.

The best way to do so is to match those capabilities at an abstract level by languages that build on them so that high-level algorithms can be implemented without worrying about the low-level mechanisms of creation or destruction of threads, or how data is shared or communicated among them. These languages are called concurrent, and the programming paradigm implemented in them concurrency-oriented programming or simply concurrent programming [2].

These languages, that include Perl 6, Go, Scala and Julia, usually support programming constructs that manage threads like first class objects, including operators for acting upon them and to using them as function's input or return parameters. The latter have implications in the coding of concurrent algorithms due to the direct mapping between patterns of communication and processes with language expressions: on the one hand it simplifies coding because higher-level abstractions for communication are available; on the other hand it changes the paradigm for implementing algorithms, since these new communication constructs and the overhead they bring to processing data need to be considered.

Moreover, concurrent programming adds a layer of abstraction over the parallel facilities of processors and operating systems, offering a high-level interface that allows the user to program modules of code to be executed in parallel threads [1].

Different languages offer different concurrency strategies depending on how they deal with shared state, that is, data structures that could be accessed from several processes or threads. In this regard, there are two major fields and other, less well known models using, for instance, tuple spaces [9]:

- Actor-based concurrency [24] totally eliminates shared state by introducing a series of data structures called *actors* that store state and can mutate it locally.
- Process calculi or process algebra is a framework to describe systems that work with independent processes interacting between them using channels. One of the best known is called the *communicating sequential processes* (CSP) methodology [12], which is effectively stateless, with different processes reacting to a channel input without changing state, and writing to these channels. Unlike actor based concurrency, which keeps state local, in this case per-process state is totally eliminated, with all computation state managed as messages in a channel.

Many modern languages, however, follow the CSP abstraction, and it has become popular since it fits well other programming paradigms, like reactive and functional programming, and allows for a more efficient implementation, with less overhead, and with well-defined primitives. This is why we will use it in this paper for creating *natively* concurrent evolutionary algorithms. We have chosen Perl 6, although other alternatives such as Go and Julia are feasible.

In previous papers [21,22] we designed an evolutionary algorithm that fits well this architecture and explored its possibilities. That initial exploration showed that a critical factor within this algorithmic model is the communication between threads; therefore designing efficient messages is high-priority to obtain good algorithmic performance and scaling. In this paper, we will test several communication strategies: a loss-less one that compresses the population, and a lossy one that sends a representation of gene-wise statistics of the population.

The rest of the paper is organized as follows: next we present the state of the art in concurrency in evolutionary algorithms, followed by Sect. 3 on the design of concurrent EAs in Perl 6. Experimental results are presented next in Sect. 4; finally, we discuss our conclusions in Sect. 5.

2   State of the Art

The parallelization of nature-inspired optimization algorithms has been an active field, allowing researchers to solve complex optimization problems having a high computational cost [17]. In the literature, most works are concerned with process-based concurrency, using, for instance, a Message Passing Interface (MPI) [10], or hybrids with fine-grain parallelization by using libraries such as OpenMP [6] that offer multi-threading capabilities [15]. Recent trends in software development have motivated the inclusion of new constructs to programming languages to simplify the development of multi-threaded programs. The theoretical support used by these implementations is based on CSP. Languages such as Go and Perl 6 implement this concurrency model as an abstraction for their multi-threading capabilities. (the latter including additional mechanisms such as *promises* or low-level access to the creation of threads). Even interpreted languages with a global interpreter lock, such as Python also have included *promises* and *futures* in their latest versions, to leverage intensive multi-threading IO capabilities.

The fact that messages have to be processed without secondary effects and that actors do not share state makes concurrent programming specially fit for languages with functional features; this has made this paradigm specially popular for late cloud computing implementations; however, its reception in the EA community has been scarce [11], although some efforts have lately revived the interest for this paradigm [26]. Several years ago it was used in Genetic Programming [4,13,29] and recently in neuroevolution [25] and program synthesis [28] using the functional programming features of the Erlang language for building an evolutionary multi-agent system [3].

Earlier efforts to study the issues of concurrency in EA are worth mentioning. For instance, the EvAg model [14] resorts to the underlying platform scheduler to manage the different threads of execution of the evolving agents; in this way the model scaled-up seamlessly to take full advantage of CPU cores. In the same avenue of measuring scalability, experiments were conducted in [18] comparing single and a dual-core processor concurrency achieving near linear speed-ups. The latter was further on extended in [19] by scaling up the experiment to up to 188 parallel machines, reporting speed-ups up to 960×, nearly four times the expected linear growth in the number of machines (when local concurrency were not taken into account). Other authors have addressed explicitly multi-core architectures, such as Tagawa [27] which used shared memory and a clever mechanism to avoid deadlocks. Similarly, [16] used a message-based architecture developed in Erlang, separating GA populations as different processes, although all communication was taking place with a common central thread.

In previous papers [8,22], we presented a proof of concept of the implementation of a stateless evolutionary algorithms using Perl 6, based on a single channel model communicating threads for population evolving and mixing. In addition, we studied the effect of running parameters such as the *generation gap* (similar to the concept of *time to migration* in parallel evolutionary algorithms) and population size, realizing that the choice of parameters may have a strong influence at the algorithmic level, but also at the implementation level, in fact affecting the actual wallclock performance of the EA.

3   Design of a Concurrent Evolutionary Algorithm in Perl6

Perl 6 is a concurrent, functional language [5] which was conceived with the intention of providing a solid conceptual framework for multi-paradigm computing, including thread-based concurrency and asynchrony. It's got a heuristic layer that optimizes code during execution time. In the last few years, performance of programs written in Perl 6 has been sped-up by a $100\times$ factor, approaching the same scale of other interpreted languages, although still with some room for improvement.

The `Algorithm::Evolutionary::Simple` Perl 6 module was published in the ecosystem a year ago and got recently into version 0.0.7. It is a straightforward implementation of a canonical evolutionary algorithm with binary representation and includes building blocks for a generational genetic algorithm, as well as some fitness functions used generally as benchmarks.

The baseline we are building upon, is similar to the one used in previous experiments [22]. Our intention was to create a system that was not functionally equivalent to a sequential evolutionary algorithms, that also follows the principle of CSP. We decided to allow the algorithm to implement several threads communicating state through channels. Every process itself will be stateless, reacting to the presence of messages in the channels it is listening to and sending result back to them, without changing state.

As in the previous papers, [21], we will use two groups of threads and two channels. The two groups of threads perform the following functions:

- The *evolutionary* threads will be the ones performing the operations of the evolutionary algorithm.
- The *mixing* thread will take existing populations, to create new ones as a mixture of them.

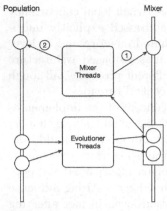

Fig. 1. General scheme of operation of channels and thread groups.

The main objective of using two channels is to avoid deadlocks; the fact that one population is written always back to the mixer channel avoids starvation of the channel. Figure 2 illustrates this operation, where the timeline of the interchange of messages between the evolver and mixer threads and evolver and mixer channels is clarified.

The state of the algorithm will be transmitted via messages that contain data about one population. Since using the whole population will incur in a lot of overhead, we use a strategy that is inspired in *EDA*, or Estimation of Distribution Algorithm: instead of transmitting the entire population, the message sent to the channel will consist of a prototype array containing the prob-

Besides, the two channels carry messages consisting of populations, but they do so in a different way:

- The *evolutionary* channel will be used for carrying non-evolved, or generated, populations.
- The *mixer* channel will carry, *in pairs*, evolved populations.

These will be connected as shown in Fig. 1. The evolutionary thread group will read only from the evolutionary channel, evolve for a number of generations, and send the result to the mixer channel; the mixer group of threads will read only from the mixer channel, in pairs. From every pair, a random element is put back into the mixer channel, and a new population is generated and sent back to the evolutionary channel.

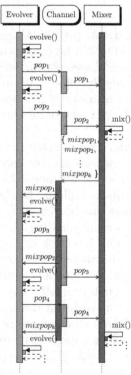

Fig. 2. Communication between threads and channels for concurrent EAs. The two central bars represent the channel, and color corresponds to their roles: blue for mixer, red for evolver. Notice how the evolver threads always read from the mixer channel, and always write to the evolver channel. (Color figure online)

ability distribution across each gene in the population. In this sense, this strategy is similar to the one presented by de la Ossa et al. in [7].

Nonetheless, our strategy differs from a pure EDA in that once the evolutionary thread have internally run a canonical genetic algorithm, it takes only the top quartile of best individuals to compute an array with the probability distribution of their genes (computed with frequentist rules) and then compose the message that is sent to the *mixer* threads.

A *mixer* thread, in turn, builds a new prototype array by choosing randomly at each gene location one probability parameter out of the two *populations* (actually, distributions), instead of working directly on individuals. While in the baseline strategy the selection took place in the mixer thread by eliminating half the population, in this new design the selection occurs in the evolutionary thread that selects the 25% best individuals to compose the probability distribution message. When the evolver thread reads the message back, it generates a new population using the mixed distribution obtained by the mixer.

4   Experimental Results

We focused on the scaling capabilities of the algorithm and implementation, so we tested several benchmark, binary functions: OneMax, Royal Road and Leading Ones, all of them with 64 bits (for function definitions see e.g. [23]).

Fig. 3. An htop utility screenshot for the used machine running two experiments simultaneously. It can be seen all processors are kept busy, with a very high load average.

However, the intention of concurrent evolutionary algorithms is to leverage the power of all threads and processors in a computer so we must find out how it scales for different fitness functions. We are setting the number of initial populations to the number of threads plus one, as the minimum required to avoid starvation, and we are using a single mixing thread. As reported in our previous papers [8, 22], we are dividing the total population by the number of threads. The population size will be 1024 for OneMax, 8192 for Royal Road and 4096 Leading Ones. These quantities were found heuristically by applying the bisection method on a selector-recombinative algorithm, which doubles the population until one that is able to find the solution 95% of the time is found.

Experiments were run on a machine with the Ubuntu 18.04 OS and an AMD Ryzen 7 2700X Eight-Core Processor at 3.7GHz, which theoretically has $8 \times 16 = 128$ physical threads. Figure 3 shows the utility `htop` with an experiment running; the top of the screen shows the rate at which all cores are working, showing all of them occupied; of course, the program was not running exclusively, but the list of processes below show how the program is replicated in several processor, thus leveraging their full power.

Observe also the number of threads that are actually running at the same time, a few of which are being used by our application; these are not, however, physical but operating system threads; the OS is able to accommodate many more threads that are physically available if the code using them is idle.

We are firstly interested in the number of evaluations needed to find the solution (see Fig. 4), since as it was mentioned previously, a tradeoff should exist between the performance of the algorithm and the way it is deployed over different threads. In this case, population size does have an influence on the number of evaluations, with bigger populations tipping the balance in favor of exploration and thus making more evaluations to achieve the same result; the same happens with smaller populations, they tend to reach local minima and thus also increase exploration.

Figure 4 shows how the overall number of populations increases slightly and not significantly from 2 to 4 threads, but it does increase significantly for 6 and 8 threads, indicating that the algorithm's performance is worsen when we increase the number of threads, and consequently more evaluations are needed to achieve the same result. This is probably due to the fact that we are simultaneously decreasing the population size, yielding an earlier convergence for the number of generations (8) it is being used. This interplay between the degree of concurrency, the population size and the number of generations will have to be explored further.

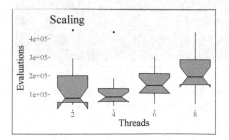

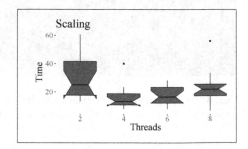

Fig. 4. OneMax: Number of evaluations vs. number of threads. Higher is better.

Fig. 5. OneMax: Total time vs. number of threads. Lower is better.

Besides, we also wanted to assess the actual wallclock time, plotted in Fig. 5. The picture shows that it decreases significantly when we go from 2 (the baseline) to 4 threads, since we are using more computing power for (roughly) the same number of evaluations. It then increases slightly when we increase the number of threads; as a matter of fact and as shown in Fig. 6, the number of evaluations per second increases

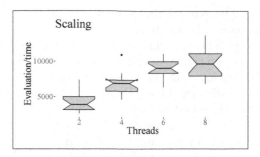

Fig. 6. OneMax: Evaluations per second vs. number of threads. Higher is better.

steeply up to 6 threads, and slightly when we use 8 threads. However, the amount of evaluations spetn overcompensates this speed, yielding in a worse result. It confirms, nonetheless, that we are actually using all threads for evaluations, and if only we could find a strategy that didn't need more evaluations we should be able to get a big boost in computation time that scales gracefully to a high number of processors.

But we were interested also in checking whether the same kind of patterns are found for other fitness functions, with a different landscape, and also how much further scaling with the number of threads could go; that is why we set up another experiment with the Royal Road function. We run the experiment as above, but in this case there were some runs in which the solution was not found within the time limit of 800 s; in the first case, for two threads, this is indicated with a lighter shade corresponding to the number of instances where it did found the solution, 6 out of 15. The number of evaluations needed to find the solution is shown as a boxplot in Fig. 7; the total time in Fig. 8 and the number of evaluations per second in Fig. 9.

Since the Royal Road function is slightly heavier than Onemax, this number reaches a lower peak of approximately 25%. Comparing also Figs. 4 with 8 we see that that Royal Road needs one order of magnitude more evaluations than OneMax to find the solution. As we capped the running time at 800 s, this causes some the lack of success for the lowest number of threads.

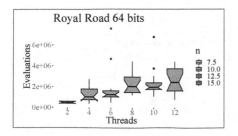

Fig. 7. Royal Road: Number of evaluations vs. num. of threads. Higher is better.

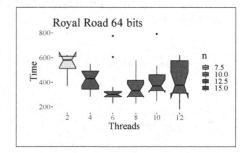

Fig. 8. Royal Road: Total time vs. number of threads. Lower is better.

The pattern these charts exhibit
is very similar to those for One-
Max. The performance scales up to
a certain range, and then it plateaus,
increasing only in speed, but not
in wallclock time. From 2 to 6
threads speed increases 2×, due to
an increase in speed with a slight
decrease in the number of evaluations needed to find the solution;
besides, success rate goes up from 2

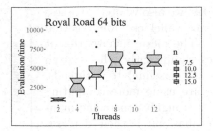

Fig. 9. Royal Road: Evaluations per second vs. number of threads. Higher is better.

to 4 threads, shifting from finding the solution 6 out of 15 times to finding it
every time. This is due to the cap in the allowed runtime, which is 800 s; it is
likely that if more time had been allowed, solution had been found.

However, we again find the same effect of increase in performance up to
an optimal number of threads, 6 in this case. This is slightly better than it
was for Onemax, which reached an optimal performance for 4 threads. The fact
that the optimal population in Royal Road is 4× that needed for OneMax will
probably have an influence. As a rule of thumb, performance will only increase
to the point that population size will make the algorithm worsen in the opposite
direction. Interestingly, it also proves that the peak performance is mainly due
to algorithmic, not the physical number of threads (around 16 for this machine).

Besides, not all problems behave in the same way and scaling in performance
and success rate is strongly problem-dependent. To illustrate that fact, we used
another benchmark function, LeadingOnes, which counts the leading number of
ones in a bitstring. Despite its superficial similarity to OneMax, it's in practice a
more difficult problem, since it has got long plateaus with no increment in fitness.
It is thus a more difficult problem which is why we had to increase the number
of generations per thread to 16 and decrease the length of the chromosome to
48, as well as the time budget to 1200 s.

Even so, results were quite different, see Figs. 10, 11 and 12 (8 threads data
not shown, because the solution was actually found with 2 and 4 threads only).
The situation is inverted with respect to the other problems. Although, as shown
in Fig. 12, the number of evaluations increases with the number of threads (and
is actually higher than for Royal Road), the success rate *decreases* and the time
to solution does the same.

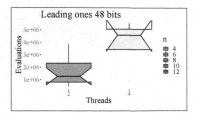

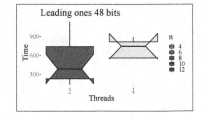

Fig. 10. Leading ones: Number of evaluations vs. num. of threads. Higher is better.

Fig. 11. Leading ones: Total time vs.
number of threads. Lower is better.

This might be due, in part, to the intrinsic difficulty of the problem, with a flat fitness landscape that only changes if a single bit (among all of them) changes when it should; this might make the short periods of evolution before sending the message inadequate for this problem. But, additionally, the message only sends a statistical representation of

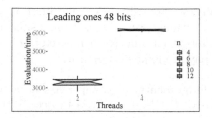

Fig. 12. Leading ones: Evaluations per second vs. number of threads. Higher is better.

the population. If there are not many representatives with the latest bits set, it can happen (and indeed it does) that the best solution in the previous evolution run is lost, and sometimes is not retrieved in the 16 generations it runs before communicating again. The latter gets worse with the increasing number of threads, since the population size decreases. As indicated at the beginning, balancing exploration and exploitation needs a population with the right size, and tipping the balance towards too much exploitation might be as negative (in terms of success rate) as too much exploration.

5   Conclusions

In this paper we studied to what extent scaling can be achieved on evolutionary concurrent algorithms on different types of problems. We observed that because OneMax simplicity requires a small population to find the solution, scaling is very limited and only means a real improvement if we use four threads instead of two. The Royal Road function with the same length is more challenging, showing an interesting behavior in the sense that it scaled in success rate and speed from 2 to 4 threads, and then again in speed through 6 threads. In this problem we measured up to 12 threads, and we noticed that the number of evaluations per second also reaches a plateau at around 6k evaluations. For 8 threads, our program uses actually 9 threads since there is another one for mixing. Since the computer only has 16 physical threads (2 threads x 8 cores), plus the load incurred by other system programs, this probably suggest a physical limit.

The experiments also indicate that creating a concurrent version of an evolutionary algorithm poses challenges such as designing the best communication strategy (including frequency and message formats) and distributing the algorithm workload, i.e. the population, among the different threads; anyway, physical features such as message size and number of threads must be considered.

As a consequence, several possible future lines of research arise. The first one is to try new algorithmic scaling strategies that consistently has a positive influence in the number of evaluations so that speedup is extended at least up to the physical number of threads. On the other hand, the messaging strategies proposed here are suitable for problem representation via a binary data structure. New mechanisms will have to be devised for floating-point representation, or other data structures. For that matter, general-purpose compressing techniques or EDAs extended to other abstract data types can be examined.

Finally, we are using the same kind of algorithm and parametrization in all threads. Nothing prevents us from using a different algorithm per thread, or using different parameters per thread. This opens a vast space of possibilities, but the payoff might be worth it.

Acknowledgements. This paper has been supported in part by projects DeepBio (TIN2017-85727-C4-2-P), TecNM Project 5654.19-P and CONACYT-PEI 220590.

References

1. Andrews, G.R.: Concurrent Programming: Principles and Practice. Benjamin/Cummings Publishing Company, San Francisco (1991)
2. Armstrong, J.: Concurrency Oriented Programming in Erlang (2003). http://ll2.ai.mit.edu/talks/armstrong.pdf
3. Barwell, A.D., Brown, C., Hammond, K., Turek, W., Byrski, A.: Using program shaping and algorithmic skeletons to parallelise an evolutionary multi-agent system in Erlang. Comput. Inform. **35**(4), 792–818 (2017)
4. Briggs, F., O'Neill, M.: Functional genetic programming and exhaustive program search with combinator expressions. Int. J. Know.-Based Intell. Eng. Syst. **12**(1), 47–68 (2008). http://dl.acm.org/citation.cfm?id=1375341.1375345
5. Castagna, G.: Covariance and controvariance: a fresh look at an old issue (a primer in advanced type systems for learning functional programmers). CoRR abs/1809.01427 (2018). http://arxiv.org/abs/1809.01427
6. Dagum, L., Menon, R.: OpenMP: an industry-standard API for shared-memory programming. Comput. Sci. Eng. (1), 46–55 (1998)
7. delaOssa, L., Gámez, J.A., Puerta, J.M.: Migration of probability models instead of individuals: an alternative when applying the Island model to EDAs. In: Yao, X., et al. (eds.) PPSN 2004. LNCS, vol. 3242, pp. 242–252. Springer, Heidelberg (2004). https://doi.org/10.1007/978-3-540-30217-9_25
8. García-Valdez, J.M., Merelo-Guervós, J.J.: A modern, event-based architecture for distributed evolutionary algorithms. In: Proceedings of the Genetic and Evolutionary Computation Conference Companion, GECCO. ACM, New York (2018)
9. Gelernter, D.: Generative communication in Linda. ACM Trans. Program. Lang. Syst. (TOPLAS) **7**(1), 80–112 (1985)
10. Gropp, W.D., Gropp, W., Lusk, E., Skjellum, A.: Using MPI: Portable Parallel Programming with the Message-Passing Interface, vol. 1. MIT Press, Cambridge (1999)
11. Hawkins, J., Abdallah, A.: A generic functional genetic algorithm. In: Proceedings of the ACS/IEEE International Conference on Computer Systems and Applications. IEEE Computer Society, Washington (2001)
12. Hoare, C.A.R.: Communicating sequential processes. Commun. ACM **21**(8), 666–677 (1978). https://doi.org/10.1145/359576.359585
13. Huelsbergen, L.: Toward simulated evolution of machine-language iteration. In: Proceedings of the First Annual Conference on Genetic Programming, GECCO 1996, pp. 315–320. MIT Press, Cambridge (1996)
14. Jiménez-Laredo, J.L., Eiben, A.E., van Steen, M., Merelo-Guervós, J.J.: EvAg: a scalable peer-to-peer evolutionary algorithm. Genet. Program. Evolvable Mach. **11**(2), 227–246 (2010)

15. Jin, H., Jespersen, D., Mehrotra, P., Biswas, R., Huang, L., Chapman, B.: High performance computing using MPI and openmp on multi-core parallel systems. Parallel Comput. **37**(9), 562–575 (2011)

16. Kerdprasop, K., Kerdprasop, N.: Concurrent computation for genetic algorithms. In: 1st International Conference on Software Technology, pp. 79–84 (2012)

17. Lalwani, S., Sharma, H., Satapathy, S.C., Deep, K., Bansal, J.C.: A survey on parallel particle swarm optimization algorithms. Arab. J. Sci. Eng. **44**(4), 2899–2923 (2019)

18. Laredo, J.L.J., Castillo, P.A., Mora, A.M., Merelo, J.J.: Exploring population structures for locally concurrent and massively parallel evolutionary algorithms. In: 2008 IEEE Congress on Evolutionary Computation, pp. 2605–2612, June 2008

19. Laredo, J.L.J., Bouvry, P., Mostaghim, S., Merelo-Guervós, J.-J.: Validating a peer-to-peer evolutionary algorithm. In: Di Chio, C., et al. (eds.) EvoApplications 2012. LNCS, vol. 7248, pp. 436–445. Springer, Heidelberg (2012). https://doi.org/10.1007/978-3-642-29178-4_44

20. Li, X., Liu, K., Ma, L., Li, H.: A concurrent-hybrid evolutionary algorithms with multi-child differential evolution and Guotao algorithm based on cultural algorithm framework. In: Cai, Z., Hu, C., Kang, Z., Liu, Y. (eds.) ISICA 2010. LNCS, vol. 6382, pp. 123–133. Springer, Heidelberg (2010). https://doi.org/10.1007/978-3-642-16493-4_13

21. Merelo, J.J., García-Valdez, J.-M.: Going stateless in concurrent evolutionary algorithms. In: Figueroa-García, J.C., López-Santana, E.R., Rodriguez-Molano, J.I. (eds.) WEA 2018. CCIS, vol. 915, pp. 17–29. Springer, Cham (2018). https://doi.org/10.1007/978-3-030-00350-0_2

22. Merelo, J.J., García-Valdez, J.M.: Mapping evolutionary algorithms to a reactive, stateless architecture: using a modern concurrent language. In: Proceedings of the Genetic and Evolutionary Computation Conference Companion, GECCO 2018, pp. 1870–1877. ACM, New York (2018)

23. Rojas-Galeano, S., Rodriguez, N.: A memory efficient and continuous-valued compact EDA for large scale problems. In: Proceedings of the 14th Annual Conference on Genetic and Evolutionary Computation, GECCO 2018, pp. 281–288. ACM (2012)

24. Schippers, H., Van Cutsem, T., Marr, S., Haupt, M., Hirschfeld, R.: Towards an actor-based concurrent machine model. In: Proceedings of the 4th Workshop on the Implementation, Compilation, Optimization of Object-Oriented Languages and Programming Systems, ICOOOLPS 2009, pp. 4–9. ACM, New York (2009)

25. Sher, G.I.: Handbook of Neuroevolution Through Erlang. Springer, Heidelberg (2013). https://doi.org/10.1007/978-1-4614-4463-3

26. Swan, J., et al.: A research agenda for metaheuristic standardization. In: Proceedings of the XI Metaheuristics International Conference (2015)

27. Tagawa, K.: Concurrent differential evolution based on generational model for multi-core CPUs. In: Bui, L.T., Ong, Y.S., Hoai, N.X., Ishibuchi, H., Suganthan, P.N. (eds.) SEAL 2012. LNCS, vol. 7673, pp. 12–21. Springer, Heidelberg (2012). https://doi.org/10.1007/978-3-642-34859-4_2

28. Valkov, L., Chaudhari, D., Srivastava, A., Sutton, C., Chaudhuri, S.: Synthesis of differentiable functional programs for lifelong learning. arXiv preprint arXiv:1804.00218 (2018)

29. Walsh, P.: A functional style and fitness evaluation scheme for inducting high level programs. In: Banzhaf, W., et al. (eds.) Proceedings of the Genetic and Evolutionary Computation Conference, vol. 2, pp. 1211–1216. Morgan Kaufmann (1999)

Sine-Cosine Algorithm for OPF Analysis in Distribution Systems to Size Distributed Generators

María Lourdes Manrique[1], Oscar Danilo Montoya[1(✉)] [ID],
Víctor Manuel Garrido[1] [ID], Luis Fernando Grisales-Noreña[2] [ID],
and Walter Gil-González[3] [ID]

[1] Programa de Ingeniería Eléctrica e Ingeniería Electrónica,
Universidad Tecnológica de Bolívar, Cartagena, Colombia
manriquemaria361@gmail.com, {omontoya,vgarrido}@utb.edu.co
[2] Departamento de Electromecánica y Mecatrónica,
Instituto Tecnológico Metropolitano, Medellín, Colombia
luisgrisales@itm.edu.co
[3] Programa de Ingeniería Eléctrica,
Universidad Tecnológica de Pereira, Pereira, Colombia
wjgil@utp.edu.co

Abstract. This paper addresses the analysis the optimal power flow (OPF) problem in alternating current (AC) radial distribution networks by using a new metaheuristic optimization technique known as a sine-cosine algorithm (SCA). This combinatorial optimization approach allows for solving the nonlinear non-convex optimization OPF problem by using a master-slave strategy. In the master stage, the soft computing SCA is used to define the power dispatch at each distributed generator (dimensioning problem). In the slave stage, it is used a conventional radial power flow formulated by incidence matrices is used for evaluating the total power losses (objective function evaluation). Two conventional highly used distribution feeders with 33 and 69 nodes are employed for validating the proposed master-slave approach. Simulation results are compared with different literature methods such as genetic algorithm, particle swarm optimization, and krill herd algorithm. All the simulations are performed in MATLAB programming environment, and their results show the effectiveness of the proposed approach in contrast to previously reported methods.

Keywords: Optimal sizing of distributed generation ·
Optimal power flow · Soft computing optimization technique ·
Sine-cosine algorithm · Radial distribution networks

This work was supported in part by the Administrative Department of Science, Technology, and Innovation of Colombia (COLCIENCIAS) through the National Scholarship Program under Grant 727-2015, in part by the Universidad Tecnológica de Bolívar under Project C2018P020 and in part by the Instituto Tecnológico Metropolitano under the project P17211.

J. C. Figueroa-García et al. (Eds.): WEA 2019, CCIS 1052, pp. 28–39, 2019.
https://doi.org/10.1007/978-3-030-31019-6_3

1   Introduction

The design of electrical networks generates nonlinear large-scale optimization problems which imply the needed of powerful optimization techniques to address these problems [1–5]. Typically, when the focus is to analyze electrical distribution networks for planning and operation always emerges a classical problem denominated: optimal power flow (OPF) problem [6,7]. This corresponds to a minimization problem that allows determining the set of voltage profiles and power generations in electrical networks with the presence of multiple generation sources by guaranteeing classical constraints of power system analysis such as energy balance, voltage regulation, and lines chargeability, and so on [8,9]. The OPF for alternating current (AC) electrical networks is nonlinear non-convex and required a combination of numerical methods such as Gauss-Seidel [10], Newton–Raphson [11] or sweep methods (only applicable for radial grids [12,13]) with combinatorial techniques in the continuous domain, i.e., particle-swarm optimization (PSO) or optimization techniques derived from it [9,14,15].

Here, we are interested in analyzing the OPF problem for AC distribution networks to address the problem of optimal dimensioning of distributed generation that can be obtained from fossil or renewable energy resources for reducing the total power loss of the network. This problem has been conventionally studied in the specialized literature embedded inside of the problem of optimal location of the distributed generation in distribution networks [9,14,16]. To do so, the OPF problem has been solved by using convex optimization approaches with semidefinite and second-order cone programming [17–19], interior point methods [20], particle swarm optimization [9,21], genetic algorithms [22], tabu search methods [23], krill herd, Firefly and bee colony algorithms [14,24,25], among others. Unlike this extensive list of previous works in this research line, here we propose a novel developed a sine-cosine optimization algorithm for solving the OPF problem in AC distribution networks focused on optimal dimensioning distributed generations. It is important to mention that this problem was previously used for solving OPF problems in power systems with mesh topologies [15]. However, that approach does not separate the problem of generation of the problem of power flow, which could be non-efficient for radial distribution networks. For this reason, a variant of that approach for radial distribution networks is proposed by using a master-slave strategy for addressing the problem of optimal dimensioning of distributed generation in radial distribution networks. In the master stage, a sine-cosine algorithm (SCA) defines the power output at each distributed generator, while in the slave stage we employ a successive approximation method based on an admittance's formulation for solving the resulting power flow set of equations [26,27]. Note that our approach has adequate performance when classical radial test feeders with 33 and 69 nodes are used, showing better performance in comparison to previously reported methods as will discussed in the results section.

The remainder of this paper is organized as follows: Sect. 2 is presented the mathematical formulation of the optimal dimensioning of distributed generators in radial distribution networks by using a classical optimal power problem formulation. Section 3 shows the proposed master-salve methodology based on a combination of the SCA with the proposed successive approximation method for power flow analysis in the slave stage. Section 4 shows the configuration of the test systems as well as the simulation scenarios considered. Section 5 presents the main conclusions and possible future works derived from this research.

2   Mathematical Modeling

Optimal location and dimensioning of distributed generations (DGs) in radial distribution networks correspond to a mixed-integer nonlinear optimization problem, which is non-differentiable and non-convex with many local minimums and non-deterministic polynomial-time, i.e., complex to be solved. The mathematical model that represents these problems is presented below

Objective function:

$$\min p_{loss} = Real\left\{\mathbf{V}^T\mathbf{Y}_L^*\mathbf{V}^*\right\};\tag{1}$$

where p_{loss} is the total power losses in all the branches of the network, $\mathbf{V} \in \mathbb{C}^{n\times1}$ is vector that contains all the complex voltage variables and $\mathbf{Y}_L \in \mathbb{C}^{n\times n}$ is the admittance matrix that contain that all the admittance effects between branches (it does not include shunt resistive connections). Note that n is the total number of nodes of the grid.

Set of constraints:

$$\mathbf{S}_{CG} + \mathbf{S}_{DG} - \mathbf{S}_D = \mathbf{D}\left(\mathbf{V}\right)\left[\mathbf{Y}_L^* + \mathbf{Y}_N^*\right]\mathbf{V}^*;\tag{2}$$

$$V^{\min} \leq |\mathbf{V}| \leq V^{\max};\tag{3}$$

$$S_{GC}^{\min} \leq |\mathbf{S}_{GC}| \leq S_{GC}^{\max};\tag{4}$$

$$S_{DG}^{\min} \leq |\mathbf{S}_{DG}| \leq S_{DG}^{\max};\tag{5}$$

$$Imag\left\{\mathbf{S}_{DG}\right\} = 0;\tag{6}$$

where $\mathbf{S}_{CG} \in \mathbb{C}^{n\times1}$ is the vector that contain all power generations in all conventional generators, i.e., slack nodes (for radial distribution system there is only one slack node); $\mathbf{S}_{DG} \in \mathbb{C}^{n\times1}$ corresponds to the vector that contains all power generation in all the distributed generation nodes; $\mathbf{S}_D \in \mathbb{C}^{n\times1}$ represents the vector of constant power consumptions. $\mathbf{D}\left(\mathbf{V}\right) \in \mathbb{C}^{n\times n}$ is a diagonal positive definite matrix of variables that contains all the voltages of the grid. $\mathbf{Y}_N \in \mathbb{C}^{n\times n}$ is the matrix of admittances related to shunt linear resistive loads connected to the nodes of the grid, this matrix is positive semidefinite or null in some cases. $V^{\min} \in \mathbb{C}^{n\times1}$ and $V^{\max} \in \mathbb{R}^{n\times1}$ are the minimum and maximum voltage bounds allowed for all nodes of the network. $S_{GC}^{\min} \in \mathbb{C}^{n\times1}$ and $S_{GC}^{\max} \in \mathbb{C}^{n\times1}$ are the minimum and maximum power generation bounds in the slack nodes; $S_{DG}^{\min} \in \mathbb{C}^{n\times1}$ and $S_{DG}^{\max} \in \mathbb{C}^{n\times1}$ are the minimum and maximum power generation capabilities in the distributed generators. The interpretation of the mathematical model given from (1) to (6) is as follows:

The objective function associated with the active power losses minimization is given in (1) which depends exclusively of the all voltage profiles of the network. In (2) is defined the power balance equation for all nodes of the networks, which is the only one nonlinear non-convex set equations in the optimal power flow model. Expression (3) defines the voltage regulation bounds of the grid; while (4) and (5) define the minimum and maximum power bounds for conventional and distributed generation. Finally, (6) shows that each distributed generator is operated with unity power factor.

Note that the mathematical model that describes the optimal power flow problem for optimal dimensioning of distributed generation in radial AC distribution network is nonlinear non-convex, which implies that numerical methods, as well as soft computing approaches, must be required to solve this problem. Here, we present a metaheuristic alternative based on sine and cosine functions to solve this problem by splitting it into two problems named the master problem and slave problem. Note that the master problem corresponds to the dimensioning of the distributed generators, while the slave problem is the classical power flow problem. These optimization problems will be formally presented and discussed in the following section.

3   Proposed Solution Methodology

To solve the OPF model defined from (1) to (6) a metaheuristic methodology is required. This combinatorial optimization approach is entrusted with defining the power output for each distributed generator in the master stage; notwithstanding once defined all power generations, a power flow method is required to determine all the voltage profiles, which allows the objective function evaluation. Each one of this stage is presented below.

3.1   Master Stage: Sine-Cosine Optimization Algorithm

The SCA is a powerful metaheuristic optimization technique for addressing continuous optimization problems [15], which is a variant of the conventional particle-swarm optimization approaches [9]. Here we will present the main aspects of this technique as follows.

Fitness Function. The main advantage of using combinatorial optimization approaches is the possibility of working in the infeasible solution space to explore some promissory regions of this space. In addition, this relaxation is possible [15], since all the constraints are included as penalties in the objective function, which transforms it into a fitness function [14]. In this paper for solving the OPF problem we employs the following fitness function:

$$z_f = \begin{pmatrix} Real\left\{ \mathbf{V}^T \mathbf{Y}_L \mathbf{V} \right\} + \alpha_1^T \max\left(0, \mathbf{V} - V^{\max}\right) - \alpha_1^T \min\left(0, \mathbf{V} - V^{\min}\right) \\ + \alpha_2^T \max\left(0, |\mathbf{S}_{DG}| - S_{DG}^{\max}\right) - \alpha_2^T \min\left(0, |\mathbf{S}_{DG}| - S_{DG}^{\min}\right) \end{pmatrix} \tag{7}$$

where $\alpha_1 \in \mathbb{R}^{n \times 1}$ and $\alpha_2 \in \mathbb{R}^{n \times 1}$ are vectors with penalty factors that allow controlling the impact of exploring the infeasible solution space. All the components of these vectors are positive numbers. There we select for each component a value of 100. Note that the fitness function can be equal to the objective function (1) if the solution space is totally feasible, i.e., all the constraints (2)–(6) must be satisfied.

It is important to mention that the capacity constraints of the conventional generators (see (4)) are not included in the fitness function, since for radial distribution systems the slack node is unique and it is assumed that this node is ideal, i.e., this node has the unbounded capability. In addition, the unity power factor requirement given by (6) is fulfilled intrinsically in the optimization process made by the SCA, for this reason, we do not consider this restriction in the fitness function (7).

Initial Population. The SCA is a population optimization technique that makes evolution this population through random controlled procedure [15]. To initialize this optimization algorithm the starting population is defined below.

$$
P^t = \begin{bmatrix} p_{11} & p_{12} & \cdots & p_{1b} \\ p_{21} & p_{22} & \cdots & p_{2b} \\ \vdots & \vdots & \ddots & \vdots \\ p_{a1} & p_{a2} & \cdots & p_{ab} \end{bmatrix}, \tag{8}
$$

where a represents the number of individuals considered and b is the number of distributed generators available for dispatching into the grid. Note that P^t is the population conformation at the iteration t.

To guarantee that the generation capability at each distributed generator satisfy the requirement defined in (4), we proposed a feasible population by calculating each component of P^t as follows.

$$
p_{ij} = GD_i^{\min} + r_1 \left(GD_i^{\max} - GD_i^{\min} \right) \ \forall i = 1, 2, ..., a, \forall j = 1, 2, ..., b; \tag{9}
$$

where ij represents the row i and column j in the matrix of the initial population and r_1 is a random number, i.e., $r_1 \in [0, 1]$.

Evolution Criterion. The sine-cosine optimization algorithm evolves by considering a simple sine-cosine rule. For doing so, let us suppose the fitness function for all individuals contained in P^t were evaluated, then, the best individual of that population is named x^t, with this individual, two possible descendants can be formulated as follows:

$$
y_i^{t+1} = x_i^t + r_2 \sin (r_3) \left| r_4 x^t - x_i^t \right|, \ i = 1, 2, ..., a, \tag{10}
$$

$$
z_i^{t+1} = x_i^t + r_2 \cos (r_3) \left| r_4 x^t - x_i^t \right|, \ i = 1, 2, ..., a, \tag{11}
$$

where r_3 and r_4 are random numbers between 0 to 1 and r_2 is entrusted of the convergence of the algorithm, and is calculated as presented below.

$$r_2 = 1 - \frac{t}{t_{\max}}, \tag{12}$$

where $t_{\max}$ is the maximum number of iterations projected for the optimization process.

Note that y_i^{t+1} and z_i^{t+1} are the potential individuals for replacing x_i^t. This substitution can be made as follows: Select y_i^{t+1} as a potential solution, if $z_f\left(y_i^{t+1}\right) < z_f\left(z_i^{t+1}\right)$; otherwise select z_i^{t+1} as a potential solution; then, replace x_i^t by y_i^{t+1} $\left(z_i^{t+1}\right)$ if its fitness function is better than $z_f\left(x_i^t\right)$; otherwise $x_i^{t+1} = x_i^t$.

It is important to point out that if one component of x_i^{t+1} violates the lower or upper bound allowed for the distributed generation, then, its value is adjusted using (9) for preserving the feasibility of the current population as defined in (5).

Stopping Criterion. The searching process of the SCA stops if one of the following criteria are attained.

- If the maximum number of iteration is reached, then, the search process of the SCA ends.
- If during $k_{\max}$ consecutive iterations the fitness does not shows any improvement, then, the search process of the SCA ends.

Pseudocode of the SCA. Algorithm 1 presents the pseudocode of the proposed SCA for optimal dimensioning of distributed generators.

Data: Read data of the network and adjust parameters of the SCA
Generate the initial population P^t;
Evaluate all the individuals P_i^t and find x^t;
for $t = 1 : t_{\max}$ **do**
$\quad$ **for** $i = 1 : a$ **do**
$\quad\quad$ Generate the potential individuals y_i^{t+1} and z_i^{t+1};
$\quad\quad$ Evaluate y_i^{t+1} and z_i^{t+1} by the slave algorithm;
$\quad\quad$ Determine which potential individual will replace P_i^t and construct the descending population P^{t+1};
$\quad$ **end**
$\quad$ Evaluate the number of non-consecutive improvements of z_f;
$\quad$ **if** $k \geq k_{\max}$ **then**
$\quad\quad$ Select the best solution contained in P^{t+1};
$\quad\quad$ Return the optimal sizing of the DGs;
$\quad\quad$ **break;**
$\quad$ **end**
end
Result: Return the optimal sizing of the DGs
Algorithm 1. Proposed optimization methodology based on the SCA

Note that in this flowchart the slave stage is essential in the evolution of the SCA since this stage allows determining the fitness function for the population and descending individuals. In next subsection will be presented this slave stage.

3.2   Slave Stage: Power Flow Method

The solution of the power flow equations given in (2) is essential in the evolution process of the sine-cosine optimization algorithm as presented in Algorithm 1. In order to solve this set of equations, let us rewrite (2) as fol lows:

$$\mathbf{S}_{CG}^{\star} = \mathbf{D}\left(\mathbf{V}_g^{\star}\right)\left[\mathbf{Y}_{gg}\mathbf{V}_g + \mathbf{Y}_{gd}\mathbf{V}_d\right], \tag{13a}$$

$$\mathbf{S}_{DG}^{\star} - \mathbf{S}_D^{\star} = \mathbf{D}\left(\mathbf{V}_d^{\star}\right)\left[\mathbf{Y}_{dg}\mathbf{V}_g + \mathbf{Y}_{dd}\mathbf{V}_d\right], \tag{13b}$$

where $\mathbf{V}_d$ and $\mathbf{V}_g$ represent the voltage profiles in the demand and slack nodes[1]. Note that $\mathbf{Y}_{gg}$, $\mathbf{Y}_{gd}$, $\mathbf{Y}_{dg}$ and $\mathbf{Y}_{dd}$ correspond to the components of the matrix $\mathbf{Y}_L + \mathbf{Y}_N$ that relates slack nodes and demands, respectively.

It is important to point out that (13a) is the power balance in the slack node, which is linear since $\mathbf{V}_g$ is perfectly known and well defined. Nevertheless, the set of equations (13b) remains being nonlinear non-convex, since $\mathbf{V}_d$ are the unknown variables. Note that $\mathbf{S}_{DG}$ are variables in the OPF problem; however, for power flow analysis, those values are considered constant, since they have been defined in the master stage.

The solution of the power flow problem it is only required to solve (13b); for doing so, let us rearrange this set of equations as follows

$$\mathbf{V}_d = \mathbf{Y}_{dd}^{-1}\left[\mathbf{D}^{-1}\left(\mathbf{V}_d^{\star}\right)\left[\mathbf{S}_{DG}^{\star} - \mathbf{S}_D^{\star}\right] - \mathbf{Y}_{dg}\mathbf{V}_g\right], \tag{14}$$

To solve (14) a recursive procedure can be added on this set of equations as presented below.

$$\mathbf{V}_d^{m+1} = \mathbf{Y}_{dd}^{-1}\left[\mathbf{D}^{-1}\left(\mathbf{V}_d^{m,\star}\right)\left[\mathbf{S}_{DG}^{t,\star} - \mathbf{S}_D^{\star}\right] - \mathbf{Y}_{dg}\mathbf{V}_g\right], \tag{15}$$

where m is the iterative counter of the power flow problem. Note that the distributed generation values depend on the t iteration of the master stage.

Note that the convergence of (15) is guaranteed, since $\mathbf{Y}_{dd}$ is diagonal dominant [26]. We can say that the power flow problem (15) is reached if and only if $\max\left|\mathbf{V}_d^{m+1} - \mathbf{V}_d^m\right| \leq \epsilon$. For power flow analysis typically the tolerance convergence ϵ is assigned as 1×10^{-10} [26], while the maximum number of iterations is defined as $m_{\max} = 25$.

4   Test Systems

In this paper, we employ two radial test feeders with 33 and 69 nodes, respectively. These test systems are classically used for optimal location and dimensioning distributed generation in electrical distribution networks. The information about those test systems is detailed below.

---

[1] $\star$ represent the conjugate operator in complex numbers.

4.1   33-Node Test Feeder

This test system is composed of 33 nodes and 32 lines with the slack source located at node 1. The operative voltage of this test system is 12.66 kV. The total active and reactive power demands for this test system are 3715 kW and 2300 kVAr, which produces 210.98 kW of active power losses. All branch data of this test feeder as well as its topological information can be consulted in [9].

4.2   69-Node Test Feeder

The base voltage for this test system is 12.66 kV, and the total demand is $3800 + j2690$ kVA [14]. In addition, the electrical parameters (electrical configuration) of this test system (resistances and inductances in all the branches as well as load consumptions) can be consulted in [9].

4.3   Simulation Scenarios

To validate the proposed approach for optimal dimensioning of distributed generation in a radial distribution test system, we employ the information provided by [14], where, five methodologies for solving the problem were studied. Notwithstanding, we are only interested in validating the optimal power flow for each technique reported in [14], which implies that we assume that the location of the generators corresponds to an input data in our approach.

5   Computational Validation

All simulations were carried-out in a desk-computer INTEL(R) Core(TM) $i7 -$ 7700, 3.60 GHz, 8 GB RAM with 64 bits Windows 10 Pro by using MATLAB $2017b$.

5.1   33-Node Test Feeder

Table 1 reports the solutions presented in [14] for all comparison methods as well as the solution reached by the proposed master-slave optimization strategy. Note that, in this test system the proposed SCA in the master stage as well as the proposed slave power flow method allows improving all the results reported in [14]. For example, see KHA method in Table 1 where is shown that the total power losses achieved by this method are 75.4120 kW, while our approach the total power losses are reduced to 73.5210 kW. This improvement (1.8910 kW), implies that the dimensioning of each generator must be changed as reported in columns 3 and 5 of Table 1.

5.2   69-Node Test Feeder

Table 2 reports the solutions presented in [14] for all comparison methods as well as the solution reached by the proposed master-slave optimization strategy.

Table 1. Numerical performance in the 33-node test feeder

Literature approaches				SCA	
Method	Location	Size [p.u]	Losses [kW]	Size [p.u]	Losses [kW]
KHA [14]	13	0.8107	75.4120	0.8018	73.5210
	25	0.8368		0.8493	
	30	0.8410		1.1014	
LSFSA [28]	6	1.1124	82.0300	1.2126	81.8680
	18	0.4874		0.4886	
	30	0.8679		0.8112	
GA [16]	11	1.5000	106.3000	0.9790	86.5282
	29	0.4228		0.4549	
	30	1.0714		0.6935	
PSO [16]	8	1.1768	105.3500	0.7378	82.9994
	13	0.9816		0.5720	
	32	0.8297		0.8690	
GA/PSO [16]	11	0.9250	103.4000	0.6899	86.1523
	16	0.8360		0.3946	
	32	1.2000		0.9537	

Table 2. Numerical performance in the 69-node test feeder

Literature approaches				SCA	
Method	Location	Size [p.u]	Losses [kW]	Size [p.u]	Losses [p.u]
KHA [14]	12	0.4715	69.6530	0.5153	69.7600
	22	0.2968		1.7425	
	61	1.7354		1.7652	
LSFSA [28]	18	0.4204	77.1000	0.5431	76.6558
	60	1.3311		1.3182	
	65	0.4298		0.4692	
GA [16]	21	0.9297	89.0000	0.5202	73.1940
	62	1.0752		1.5572	
	64	0.9925		0.1949	
PSO [16]	17	0.9925	83.2000	0.4931	71.8313
	61	1.1998		1.3153	
	63	0.7956		0.5117	
GA/PSO [16]	21	0.9105	81.1000	0.4379	72.2301
	61	1.1926		1.4859	
	63	0.8849		0.3363	

5.3   Additional Comments

Figure 1 reports the general improvement of our proposed SCA in comparison to the results presented in [14] for the 33- and 69-node test feeders. In Fig. 1(a) are presented the results obtained in the 33-node test feeder, it is possible to observe that our approach shows similar performance in comparison with the LSFSA method since our improvement is only 0.20 % better. Notwithstanding, the worst method reported in [14] is the PSO approach, since our proposed method produces 21.22 % of improvements when both are compared. In the case of the 69-node test feeder, the results are provided in Fig. 1(b), where it can be observed that the master-slave methodology proposed obtains an average reduction in the power losses of 12.19% in comparison with the comparison techniques. Just 0.11% lower than the best solution (KHA), and presenting a reduction of 0.576%, 17.76%, 13.63%, and 10.94%, when is compared with the LSFSA, GA, PSO, and the GA/PSO, respectively.

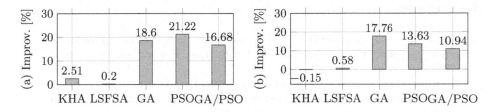

Fig. 1. Percentage of power loss improvement when the proposed approach is compared to previous reported results: (a) 33-node test feeder, and (b) 69-node test feeder

In addition, we can affirm that:

✓ The Sine-Cosine metaheuristic shows the better averaged results in contrast to the other methodologies since in the 90 % of the simulation cases analyzed it shows better performance in comparison to the results previously reported in specialized literature. The only one case (10 %), our approach shows a minimal deterioration in comparison to the KHA method for the 69-node test feeder.

✓ The results reported by GA, PSO, and the hybrid GA/PSO evidence that their methodologies were not thought to dimensioning generators, since those results are far away from KHA, LSFSA, and the proposed approach. This situation may be attributable to the parametrization of those algorithms for OPF analysis, which can be susceptible to improvements in order to increase the efficiency of those algorithms.

6   Conclusions and Future Works

In this paper was studied the problem of optimal dimensioning of distributed generation in radial distribution networks via a metaheuristic optimization technique. This methodology was designed through a master-slave optimization strategy. The master stage was a combinatorial optimization technique based on the SCA. In the slave stage, it was used as a power flow numerical method based on successive approximations. The master stage was entrusted with determining the optimal dimension of the distributed generators, while the slave stage was entrusted with evaluating the impact of these generators in terms of power losses.

Simulation results over two radial distribution test feeders with 33 and 69 nodes allowed observing that the SCA is an excellent methodology for solving OPF problems in radial distribution networks by showing better results in comparison with classical optimization algorithms.

As future work, it will be possible to embedded the SCA into a discrete metaheuristic optimization technique for locating and sizing distributed generators. These metaheuristic could be genetic algorithms, tabu search or population based incremental leaning, among others.

References

1. Keane, A., et al.: State-of-the-art techniques and challenges ahead for distributed generation planning and optimization. IEEE Trans. Power Syst. **28**(2), 1493–1502 (2013)
2. Montoya, O.D., Garces, A., Castro, C.A.: Optimal conductor size selection in radial distribution networks using a mixed-integer non-linear programming formulation. IEEE Lat. Am. Trans. **16**(8), 2213–2220 (2018)
3. Zeng, B., Zhang, J., Yang, X., Wang, J., Dong, J., Zhang, Y.: Integrated planning for transition to low-carbon distribution system with renewable energy generation and demand response. IEEE Trans. Power Syst. **29**(3), 1153–1165 (2014)
4. Li, R., Wang, W., Xia, M.: Cooperative planning of active distribution system with renewable energy sources and energy storage systems. IEEE Access **6**, 5916–5926 (2018)
5. Montoya, O.D., Grajales, A., Garces, A., Castro, C.A.: Distribution systems operation considering energy storage devices and distributed generation. IEEE Lat. Am. Trans. **15**(5), 890–900 (2017)
6. Bai, X., Qu, L., Qiao, W.: Robust AC optimal power flow for power networks with wind power generation. IEEE Trans. Power Syst. **31**(5), 4163–4164 (2016)
7. Gabash, A., Li, P.: Active-reactive optimal power flow in distribution networks with embedded generation and battery storage. IEEE Trans. Power Syst. **27**(4), 2026–2035 (2012)
8. Wang, Y., Zhang, N., Li, H., Yang, J., Kang, C.: Linear three-phase power flow for unbalanced active distribution networks with PV nodes. CSEE J. Power Energy Syst. **3**(3), 321–324 (2017)
9. Grisales-Noreña, L.F., Gonzalez-Montoya, D., Ramos-Paja, C.A.: Optimal sizing and location of distributed generators based on PBIL and PSO techniques. Energies **11**(1018), 1–27 (2018)
10. Teng, J.-H.: A modified gauss–seidel algorithm of three-phase power flow analysis in distribution networks. Int. J. Electr. Power Energy Syst. **24**(2), 97–102 (2002)
11. Zamzam, A.S., Sidiropoulos, N.D., Dall'Anese, E.: Beyond relaxation and Newton–Raphson: solving AC OPF for multi-phase systems with renewables. IEEE Trans. Smart Grid **9**(5), 3966–3975 (2018)

12. Garces, A.: A linear three-phase load flow for power distribution systems. IEEE Trans. Power Syst. **31**(1), 827–828 (2016)
13. Lisboa, A., Guedes, L., Vieira, D., Saldanha, R.: A fast power flow method for radial networks with linear storage and no matrix inversions. Int. J. Electr. Power Energy Syst. **63**, 901–907 (2014)
14. Sultana, S., Roy, P.K.: Krill herd algorithm for optimal location of distributed generator in radial distribution system. Appl. Soft Comput. **40**, 391–404 (2016)
15. Attia, A.-F., Sehiemy, R.A.E., Hasanien, H.M.: Optimal power flow solution in power systems using a novel Sine-Cosine algorithm. Int. J. Electr. Power Energy Syst. **99**, 331–343 (2018)
16. Moradi, M., Abedini, M.: A combination of genetic algorithm and particle swarm optimization for optimal DG location and sizing in distribution systems. Int. J. Electr. Power Energy Syst. **34**(1), 66–74 (2012)
17. Huang, S., Wu, Q., Wang, J., Zhao, H.: A sufficient condition on convex relaxation of AC optimal power flow in distribution networks. IEEE Trans. Power Syst. **32**(2), 1359–1368 (2017)
18. Venzke, A., Halilbasic, L., Markovic, U., Hug, G., Chatzivasileiadis, S.: Convex relaxations of chance constrained AC optimal power flow. IEEE Trans. Power Syst. **33**(3), 2829–2841 (2018)
19. Miao, Z., Fan, L., Aghamolki, H.G., Zeng, B.: Least squares estimation based SDP cuts for SOCP relaxation of AC OPF. IEEE Trans. Autom. Control **63**(1), 241–248 (2018)
20. Oliveira, E.J., Oliveira, L.W., Pereira, J., Honório, L.M., Silva, I.C., Marcato, A.: An optimal power flow based on safety barrier interior point method. Int. J. Electr. Power Energy Syst. **64**, 977–985 (2015)
21. Yang, J., He, L., Fu, S.: An improved PSO-based charging strategy of electric vehicles in electrical distribution grid. Appl. Energy **128**, 82–92 (2014)
22. Todorovski, M., Rajicic, D.: An initialization procedure in solving optimal power flow by genetic algorithm. IEEE Trans. Power Syst. **21**(2), 480–487 (2006)
23. Abido, M.A.: Optimal power flow using tabu search algorithm. Electr. Power Compon. Syst. **30**(5), 469–483 (2002)
24. Kılıç, U., Ayan, K.: Optimizing power flow of AC–DC power systems using artificial bee colony algorithm. Int. J. Electr. Power Energy Syst. **53**, 592–602 (2013)
25. Balachennaiah, P., Suryakalavathi, M., Nagendra, P.: Firefly algorithm based solution to minimize the real power loss in a power system. Ain Shams Eng. J. **9**(1), 89–100 (2018)
26. Montoya, O.D., Garrido, V.M., Gil-González, W., Grisales-Noreña, L.F.: Power flow analysis in DC grids: two alternative numerical methods. IEEE Trans. Circuits Syst. II, 1 (2019)
27. Garces, A.: Uniqueness of the power flow solutions in low voltage direct current grids. Electr. Power Syst. Res. **151**, 149–153 (2017)
28. Injeti, S.K., Kumar, N.P.: A novel approach to identify optimal access point and capacity of multiple DGs in a small, medium and large scale radial distribution systems. Int. J. Electr. Power Energy Syst. **45**(1), 142–151 (2013)

Construction of Cyclic Codes over $\mathbb{Z}_{20}$ for Identifying Proteins

Valentina Galíndez Gómez$^{(\boxtimes)}$ and Mario Enrique Duarte González

Faculty of Mechanical, Electronic and Biomedical Engineering,
Antonio Nariño University, Bogotá, Colombia
{vgalindez,mario.duarte}@uan.edu.co

Abstract. For biology, engineering and biotechnology, among others sciences related with the subject, it is essential to understand the role of proteins in the genetic information transmission process in order to conclude about evolution, changes, and connection between species. In recent work, protein synthesis process has been compared with a digital transmission system and, thus, algorithms which allow identifying biological sequences as code-words of BCH codes were developed to verify the validity of this model. Algorithms in literature are limited in respect to the length of the biological sequence, which creates restrictions when establishing taxonomic and phylogenetic inferences of living beings. In this work, we extend the number of sequences that can be analyzed by designing an algorithm that identifies, using cycling codes, biological sequences with odd length and, thus, it makes possible to find a relation between mathematical properties of cycling codes with biological properties (taxonomy and phylogeny).

Keywords: BCH codes · Proteins · Dayhoff matrix · Chinese remainder theorem

1 Introduction

In a digital communication system, error correction codes (ECC) are used for signal transmission through noisy channels, and their purpose is to reduce the error odd rate [1]. In the genetic information transmission [2], a similar phenomenon occurs during the unidirectional process named as the central dogma of molecular biology, starting with the creation of an exact copy of DNA (replication), followed by the formation of the nucleotides chain of mRNA (transcription) and the protein synthesis (translation). In those processes, there is a probability of genetic alterations caused by chemical or physical agents.

Analogously to communication systems, during these molecular processes, there is an error detection stage led by chaperones, when they detect morphology alterations in the protein by rejecting irregularly folded proteins [3]. Chaperone protein supports the folding and assembling of the protein by bounding

© Springer Nature Switzerland AG 2019
J. C. Figueroa-García et al. (Eds.): WEA 2019, CCIS 1052, pp. 40–51, 2019.
https://doi.org/10.1007/978-3-030-31019-6_4

(not merging) with the primary structure of the protein, and avoiding alien elements to be included in the protein sequence and, thus, changes in its shape and function [4]. When protein alterations are within the level of tolerance of the organism, the protein preserves its biological function and continues in the right direction [5].

The parallel between replication, transcription and translation processes with the message transmission process in a digital communication system is supported by the information and coding theory, which makes feasible the existence of an error correcting code within the genetic information transmission system [2,6]. According to ECC principles, an amino acid (AA) sequence encoding stage in DNA has been identified, which allows evolution, adaptation, and the correct functioning of the living being [7,8]. Several results support the Battail hypothesis, which suggests the presence of codes within DNA sequences. For instance, in [9,10], nucleotide sequences where identified as codewords of BCH codes over ring $\mathbb{Z}_4$ and field $\mathbb{F}_4$. In [5], cyclic codes over alphabet $\mathbb{Z}_{20}$ have been successfully used for identifying cytochrome b6-f complex subunit 6-OS proteins from different organisms within a high-affinity paraphyletic group, which was not possible through taxonomic and phylogenetic analysis [5].

In this work, an algorithm for the identification of proteins as codewords of cyclic codes over $\mathbb{Z}_{20} \cong \mathbb{Z}_4 \times \mathbb{Z}_5$ with less computational requirements than the algorithm used in [5] is introduced. The introduced algorithm does not require to compute the extended field: $\mathbb{F}_{2^r}$ or $\mathbb{F}_{5^r}$, which is a limitation by the algorithms used in [5,9,10]; thus, the protein identification process is optimized and widen. Consequently, the introduced algorithm was used to identify new proteins as codewords of cyclic codes over $\mathbb{Z}_{20}$, showing its applicability and feasibility.

The results delivered in this work, open new paths in the direction to proteins analysis and study, to look for the relationship that the found proteins have with the mathematical properties identified with the codes. It is proposed to carry out tests to implement the algorithm with other code types different from the BCH code. Regarding the mutations found during the analysis of these sequences, the question about what these mutations represent at a biological level are planned. On the other hand at the mathematical level and for the area science computer it is possible to apply specific methods that allow to quantify the computational cost savings and in this way be able to compare the presented algorithm with the one proposed in [11].

2   Overall Protein Identification Procedure

A protein is a biologically build amino acid sequence through a cellular process, and its main role is to reach a specific location within the cell, to stimulate it and allow it to play its function successfully. In this work, according to [5,12,13], a protein is called "identified" if the belonging sequence over $\mathbb{Z}_{20}$, obtained from an amino acids sequence (s_{20}), is: a codeword from an error correction code or belongs to the set of neighboring sequences with only one amino acid variation from the codeword. This set of sequences is defined as the "cloud" of a codeword

[12]. The minimum Hamming distance (d) within BCH codes building, complies the condition $d \geq 3$; thus the cloud sequences can be corrected to the proper codeword.

2.1 Mapping Proteins to Integers Modulo 20 ($\mathbb{Z}_{20}$)

The identification procedure of proteins by codewords of ECC requires the amino acid chains to be represented in the same mathematical domain in which ECCs are constructed. In order to do the representation, a mapping from biological to algebraic domain is described by using the analogy represented in the Dayhoff matrix (Fig. 1). Dayhoff matrix is a way to represent amino acids (AA) in a circular topology and has been used for elucidating the order of functional proteins and mutated proteins. Amino acids are classified according to their size and hydrophobicity and are organized in such a way that closest residues are more likely to be exchanged [14]. In order to map the sequence AA to symbols, is important to highlight the circular topology of Dayhoff matrix because ring theory allows expressing modular integers as an analytical structure geometrically similar to the matrix (Fig. 1).

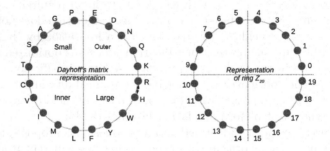

Fig. 1. The Dayhoff's matrix and its representation constrained into a circle and the geometrical representation of $\mathbb{Z}_{20}$ [5]

Figure 1 allows us to understand how the biological sequence mapping is done since each amino acid has its mathematical equivalent in the same location within the mathematical representation of $\mathbb{Z}_{20}$. The application of the Dayhoff's matrix allows obtaining the sequence as a sequence over $\mathbb{Z}_{20}$ (s_{20}), which can easily be represented as a polynomial $s(x)$.

2.2 Constructing Cyclic Codes over $\mathbb{Z}_{20}$

The obtained polynomial $s(x)$ over $\mathbb{Z}_{20}$ is said to be identified when it belongs to a ECC $\mathcal{C}_{20}$, namely, $s(x) \in \mathcal{C}_{20}$. In this process the obtained sequence $s(x)$ is factorized in two sequences $s_4(x)$ and $s_5(x)$ over $\mathbb{Z}_4$ and $\mathbb{Z}_5$ respectively, for factorizing the polynomial $x^n - 1$. $\mathbb{Z}_{20}$ factorization is possible thanks to the isomorphism between: $\mathcal{C}_4 \oplus \mathcal{C}_5 \cong \mathcal{C}_{20}$.

To obtain C_{20} through C_4 and C_5, chinese remainder theorem (CRT) is used, allowing the factor of $\mathbb{Z}_{20}$ in local ring with lower cardinality, in this case $\mathbb{Z}_4$ and $\mathbb{Z}_5$ ($\mathbb{Z}_{20} \cong \mathbb{Z}_4 \oplus \mathbb{Z}_5$) [5,14]. Hence, s_{20} can be factor in two sequences $s_4(x)$ y $s_5(x)$, such $\Psi(s_{20}) = s_4 \oplus s_5$, where Ψ is defined like [15]: $\Psi : \mathbb{Z}_{20}^n \to \mathbb{Z}_4^n \oplus \mathbb{Z}_5^n$.

In addition, CRT theorem enable to juxtapose two codes C_4 and C_5, which are linear an cyclic, in order to build a linear and cyclic code C_{20} [16,17]. In other words, is possible to build the code C_{20} through the direct sum of C_4 and C_5, as shown next: $C_{20} := CRT(C_4, C_5) := \Psi^{-1}((v_4, v_5) \,|\, v_4 \in C_4, v_5 \in C_5)$.

When juxtaposing two codes C_4 and C_5, if both of them are linear and cyclic, with parameters (n, k_4, d_4) and (n, k_5, d_5), respectively, the resulting code C_{20} has size n with cardinality: $|C_{20}| = |C_4| \cdot |C_5|$ and minimum Hamming distance $d_{20} = min\, d_4, d_5$.

For example, suppose an amino acid sequence with length $n = 9$:

$$s_A = [M\, I\, L\, K\, Y\, N\, I\, L\, I] \qquad s_{20} = [13\ 12\ 14\ 0\ 16\ 2\ 12\ 14\ 12]$$
$$s(x) = 13 + 12x + 14x^2 + 16x^4 + 2x^5 + 12x^6 + 14x^7 + 12x^8$$

Table 1. Chinese remainder theorem

$\mathbb{Z}_4/\mathbb{Z}_5$	0	1	2	3	4
0	0	16	12	8	4
1	5	1	17	13	9
2	10	6	2	18	14
3	15	11	7	3	19

Once the sequence is represented over $\mathbb{Z}_{20}$, next step is to factor the sequence into $s_4(x)$ and $s_5(x)$ by using Table 1. Each element coordinates over $\mathbb{Z}_{20}$ is passed to a tuple over $\mathbb{Z}_4$ and $\mathbb{Z}_5$:

$$s_4 = [1\ 0\ 2\ 0\ 0\ 2\ 0\ 2\ 0] \qquad s_4(x) = 1 + 2x^2 + 2x^5 + 2x^7$$
$$s_5 = [3\ 2\ 4\ 0\ 1\ 2\ 2\ 4\ 2] \qquad s_5(x) = 3 + 2x + 4x^2 + x^4 + 2x^5 + 2x^6 + 4x^7 + 2x^8$$

The Table 1 can also be used to do the reverse process, from tuple over $\mathbb{Z}_4$ and $\mathbb{Z}_5$ to $\mathbb{Z}_{20}$.

2.3   BCH Codes over $\mathbb{Z}_4$ and $\mathbb{Z}_5$

According to Sect. 2.2, it is concluded that two different cyclic codes must be constructed, such that $s_4(x)$ and $s_5(x)$ are codewords of C_4 and C_5 respectively. In this paper, BCH codes are designed and constructed for C_4 and C_5, due to their mathematical structure, implementation, construction, coding and decoding are easy and well-known [12,18]. Therefore, in the work described below, work will continue under the criteria of construction of BCH codes, such that, $s_4(x)$ and $s_5(x)$ are codewords within, where $s_4(x)$ and $s_5(x)$ are the polynomial representation of sequences s_4 and s_5.

This work uses BCH code construction procedure for C_4 and C_5 over $\mathbb{Z}_4$ and $\mathbb{Z}_5$, which allow the construction of a C_{20} over $\mathbb{Z}_{20}$ code that generates the n sized s_{20} sequence. Namely, generator polynomials ($g_4(x)$ and $g_5(x)$), which produce the BCH codes C_4 and C_5 with highest Hamming distance (d) [19], such that $g_4(x)|s_4(x)$ y $g_5(x)|s_5(x)$, are obtained.

Being β an element of order n in the ring extensions for $\mathbb{Z}_4$ or in the field extensions $\mathbb{Z}_5$ that generates a multiplicative subset with order n ($\mathcal{H}_n = \langle \beta \rangle$) [20], and $f_i(x)$ the minimal polynomial of β^i, then, $g(x)$ is the least common divisor (LCD) of β^i: $g(x) = LCD(f_1(x), f_2(x), \ldots, f_{2\delta+1}(x))$, where δ match with the BCH bound for the minimum Hamming distance of the cyclic code generated by $g(x)$ [20].

Taking into account that the generator polynomial $g(x)$, for BCH codes, is constructed as the product of some minimal polynomials, and all the minimal polynomials factorize $x^n - 1 = f_1(x) \ldots f_i(x) \ldots$, then, in this work, the multiplication of those minimal polynomial, which divide $s(x)$, results in the obtaining of a $g(x)$ and, thus, in a BCH code $\langle g(x) \rangle = C$, which contains the sequence $s(x)$; namely, $s(x)$ is a codeword of C where C is the n sized cyclic code with highest BCH bound and cardinality, containing $s(x)$ [5].

3   Proposed Protein Identification Algorithm

The proteins identification through the proposed algorithm, take s as a polynomial, denoted as $s(x)$, and look for a ECC expressed as C_n over $\mathbb{Z}_{20}$, such that $s(x)$, is a codeword that belongs to C_n [9,13].

According to Sect. 2.3, the generator polynomials $g_4(x)$ and $g_5(x)$ for codes C_4 and C_5, such that $g_4(x)|s_4(x)$ and $g_5(x)|s_5(x)$ are computed by finding the minimal polynomials over $\mathbb{Z}_4$ and $\mathbb{Z}_5$ such that divide $x^n - 1$ and the corresponding sequence $s_4(x)$ or $s_5(x)$. Finally, the Hamming minimum distance of $C_4 = \langle g_4(x) \rangle$ and $C_5 = \langle g_5(x) \rangle$ is estimated through the BCH criterion [11,17].

3.1   Factorization of Polynomial $x^n - 1$ into Minimal Polynomials over $\mathbb{Z}_4$ and $\mathbb{Z}_5$

It is important to clarify that the method selected to factor $x^n - 1$, allows to estimate the minimum Hamming distance d of the code by applying the BCH criterion directly. To above reason we used this methodology because it relates the $f_i(x)$ and the cyclotomic classes, making possible the application of the BCH criterion. This methodology excludes work with sequence sizes that are even and multiples of 5 and 4. Because the methodology used for the factorization of $x^n - 1$ does not work for multiples of 2 and 5, corresponding with $\mathbb{F}_2$ and $\mathbb{F}_5$, alphabets used in the present work. Because, when finding the minimum polynomials $f_i(x)$ in $n = 2$ or $n = 5$, there are repeated terms that do not allow the application of the BCH criterion. On the other hand, when the sequence is even the polynomial $x^n - 1$ on $\mathbb{Z}_4$ is not only decodable, that is, you can obtain different factors for $x^n - 1$ in different minimum polynomials, which implies that coding and decoding are not unique processes.

The Algorithm 1 only allows to factor the polynomial $x^n - 1$ as the product of minimal polynomials on $\mathbb{F}_p$, namely, on fields, as instance $\mathbb{Z}_5$ y $\mathbb{Z}_2$. Since $\mathbb{Z}_4$ is not a field but a commutative finite ring with identity, some additional considerations are needed to factor polynomial $x^n - 1$ over $\mathbb{Z}_4$. Starting since $\mathbb{Z}_4$ is a local ring, Hensel's lemma and Graeffe's method [20] are used to factor the polynomial as follows: The minimal polynomials over $\mathbb{Z}_4$ that factor $x^n - 1$ are obtained by applying the Graeffe's method to each one of the minimal polynomials over $\mathbb{Z}_2$ which factor the polynomial $x^n - 1$ over $\mathbb{Z}_2$.

It is important to clarify that the selected method for factoring $x^n - 1$, allows estimating the minimum Hamming distance d of the code by applying the BCH criterion. Thus, it relates the $f_i(x)$ and the cyclotomic classes, making possible the application of the BCH criterion. This methodology excludes working with sequences such that $n \pmod 5 = 0 = n \pmod 2$, since the introduced methodology does not factorize $x^n - 1$ over $\mathbb{F}_2$ or $\mathbb{Z}_5$. When the sequence is even, the polynomial $x^n - 1$ over $\mathbb{Z}_4$ is not uniquely factored, namely, which implies that coding and decoding are not unique processes, and those ECCs are nonsense.

The Algorithm 1 only allows to factor the polynomial $x^n - 1$ as the product of minimal polynomials over $\mathbb{F}_p$, namely, on fields, such that $\mathbb{Z}_5$ y $\mathbb{Z}_2$. Since $\mathbb{Z}_4$ is not a field but a commutative finite ring with identity, some additional considerations are needed to factor polynomial $x^n - 1$ over $\mathbb{Z}_4$. Starting since $\mathbb{Z}_4$ is a local ring, Hensel's lemma and Graeffe's method [20] are used to factor the polynomial as follows: The minimal polynomials over $\mathbb{Z}_4$ that factor $x^n - 1$ are obtained by applying the Graeffe's method to each one of the minimal polynomials over $\mathbb{Z}_2$ which factor the polynomial $x^n - 1$ over $\mathbb{Z}_2$.

It is important to note that there is a bijection, denoted by Γ, between each $f_i(x)$ and each $cl_p(i, n)$, according to Step 7 in the Algorithm 1. The bijection means that $\{\beta^j : j \in cl_p(i,n)\}$ are the roots of $f_i(x)$. Therefore, $\Gamma(f_i(x)) = \{\beta^j : j \in cl_p(i,n)\}$.

For $x^n - 1$ over $\mathbb{Z}_4$, factorization, Graeffe's method is used on each one of the obtained polynomials when the Algorithm 1 for the field $\mathbb{Z}_2$ is used. Is important to remark that applying the Graeffe's method the bijection Γ is preserved.

Algorithm 1. Factorization $x^n - 1$ over $\mathbb{F}_p$

Require: Data base $p(x)$, n.
1: Obtain l and r such $l \cdot n = p^r - 1$.
2: To data base, is obtain the primitive polynomial $p(x)$ degree r.
3: Compute $\beta = \alpha^l \pmod{p(\alpha)}$. Algorithm 2.
4: Multiplicative subgroup construction H_n order n: $H_n = \langle \beta \rangle \pmod{p(\alpha)}$.
5: Find cyclotomic coset:

$CL = \{cl_p(i,n) : i \geq 0\}$, where $cl_p(i,n) := \{i \cdot p^j \pmod n : j \geq 0\}$.
6: **for all** Cyclotomic coset $cl_p(i,n)$ in CL **do**
7:    minimal polynomail compute: $f_i(x) = \prod_{j \in cl_p(i,n)} (x - \beta^j)$. Now, $f_i(x)$ is a minimal polynomial over $\mathbb{F}_p$, such $f_i(x)|x^n - 1$.
8: **end for**
9: **return** $CL, F_n = \{f_i(x) : i \geq 0\}$

Finding r and l Parameters:
In this section, the Algorithm 1 is introduced. It takes as entry the size of the sequence n and a database of primitive polynomials $(p(x))$ with all possible degrees and returns the cyclotomic cosets and their correspondent minimal polynomials $(f_i(x))$.

As mentioned before in Sect. 2.3 for the code $\mathcal{C}$ obtainment, the procedure starts by choosing one primitive polynomial $p(x)$ with the appropriate degree (r), in order to do that, the equation $p^r - 1 = n \cdot l$, which have solution if, and only if: $\gcd(n, p) = 1$, must be solved. l defines the generator of the subgroup with order n $(H_n = \langle \alpha^l \rangle)$ within the extended field $\mathbb{Z}_5$ or $\mathbb{Z}_2$. r is easily solved by powering p until $p^r - 1 \pmod{n} = 0$ and then, $l = \frac{p^r - 1}{n}$.

Algorithm 2. $\alpha^l \pmod{p(\alpha)}$

Require: l, p, $p(\alpha)$.
1: Define r as the degree of $p(\alpha)$.
2: **if** $l < p \cdot r$ **then**
3:    **return** Remainder from $\frac{\alpha^l}{p(\alpha)}$ (low cost operation).
4: **end if**
5: Get l_1 and l_2, such that: $l = l_2 + (l_1)(p^m)$, $l_1 < p \cdot r$, and $m \leq \lfloor \frac{\log l}{\log p} \rfloor$, thus, $\alpha^l = \alpha^{l_2} \left(\alpha^{l_1} \right)^{p^m}$
6: Get remainder from $\frac{\alpha^{l_1}}{p(\alpha)}$ (low cost operation) i.e. $r(\alpha) = \sum_{i=0}^{r-1} a_i \alpha^i$.

7: Apply next fact: $r(\alpha)^{p^m} = r(\alpha^{p^m})$, i.e.

$$\left(\sum_{i=0}^{r-1} a_i \alpha^i \right)^{p^m} = \sum_{i=0}^{r-1} a_i \alpha^{i \cdot p^m} \qquad (1)$$

8: **for all** i such that $a_i \neq 0$ **do**
9:    Compute $\alpha^{(i+l_2) \cdot p^m} \pmod{p(\alpha)}$ (recalling the function)
10: **end for**
11: **return** $\sum_{i=0}^{r-1} a_i \left(\alpha^{(i+l_2) \cdot p^m} \right)$ $\pmod{p(\alpha)}$ (low cost operation by step 9).

Continuing the factorization of $x^n - 1$, after obtaining the $p(x)$ with degree r from a database, the next process is the identification and obtainment of all the $f_i(x)$, which has a high computational cost demand, depending on the value of r, calculated in the first step of the Algorithm 1, since in [9,10] the entire extended field $(\mathbb{F}_{p^r}^* = \langle \alpha \rangle$ for $p(\alpha) = 0$, nonzero elements of $\mathbb{F}_{p^r})$ is computed; which could make the processor to run out of RAM memory. Since the objective is to construct the multiplicative subgroup of order n $(H_n = \langle \beta = \alpha^l \rangle)$, the proposed procedure uses the Algorithm 2, which calculate $\beta = \alpha^l \pmod{p(\alpha)}$, and the needed elements for the code construction, such that, $x^n - 1 = f_1(x) f_2(x) f_3(x) \cdots$ and $x^n - 1 = \prod_{i=0}^{n-1} (x - \beta^i)$.

As previously mentioned, to obtain the minimum polynomials over $\mathbb{Z}_4$ that factor $x^n - 1$, the same polynomial is factorized over $\mathbb{Z}_2$, and then the Graeffe's method to each $f_i(x)$ over $\mathbb{Z}_2$ is applied. So, the Graeffe equation is used to each $f_i(x)$, where $e(x)$ is the sum of the terms of $h(x)$ with even exponents and $o(x)$ is the sum of the terms of $h(x)$ with odd exponents [20]: $g(x^2) = \pm(e(x)^2 - o(x)^2)$.

3.2 Finding the Generator Polynomial

The identification of the generator polynomial uses the following property: $s(x) \in C_n$ if, and only if, $g(x)|s(x)$ [21]; and uses BCH codes over $\mathbb{Z}_4$ and $\mathbb{Z}_5$ for codes C_4 and C_5, as in step 1 Algorithm 3.

After obtaining the minimal polynomials $f_i(x)$ and the cyclotomic cosets CL, the generator polynomials obtainment process for each code C_4 and C_5 starts (note that Algorithm 3 is used twice, for $C_4 = \langle g_4(x) \rangle$ and for $C_5 = \langle g_5(x) \rangle$). The initial part in Algorithm 3 identifies the generator polynomial by dividing $s(x)$ by each $f_i(x)$. Then, the polynomial $g(x)$ is formed through the product between all the $f_i(x)$ which divide $s(x)$, see equation: $s(x) \equiv 0 \pmod{f_i(x)}$.

In the third step of Algorithm 3, BCH criterion is applied in order to find the minimal Hamming distance d from $C_n = \langle g(x) \rangle$, that can be greater or equal to the highest number of consecutive roots within the multiplicative subgroup H_n.

Algorithm 3. Looking for $g(x)$

Require: F_n, CL, $s(x)$ and n.
1: Find minimal polynomials that divides $s(x)$:
    $P = \{f_i(x) \in F_n : f_i(x)|s(x), i \geq 0\}$
2: **for** $\{j \in \mathbb{N} : n > j > 0, \gcd(j,n) = 1\}$ **do**
3:    Apply BCH criterion:
      $(d, Fr_n) = BCH_{criterion}(P, CL, j)$,
      where Fr_n is the smallest set of minimal polynomials from P that are required to achieve distance d.
4:    **if** d is the largest estimation and $d \geq 3$ **then**
5:      Store Fr_n and d.
6:      Let $g(x) = \prod_{f(x) \in Fr_n} f(x)$.
7:    **end if**
8: **end for**
9: **return** $Fr_n, F_n, g(x), d$

Therefore, knowing the bijection Γ (see Sect. 3.1), the BCH criterion (Corollary 9.1 in [21]) is applied to estimate d, namely, it counts the consecutive integers in CLP_j modulus n, where $CLP_j = \bigcup_{f_i(x)|s(x)} \Gamma(f_i(x))$.

4 Results and Discussions

The new algorithm was implemented in Python. For the purpose of validating the correctness of the new algorithm, a comparison, taking into consideration the same set of protein sequences as considered in [11], is done. In this way, protein sequences, previously downloaded from the National Center for Biotechnology Information (NCBI) database [22], protein sequences were analysed according to the following criteria: not patented, not partial, not unverified, not hypothetical and by selecting only odd-sized (n) sequences. The result could not be other than achieving the same results (Table 2).

Next, some identified sequences are shown when executing the presented algorithm; it's highlighted that during validation process, was possible to identify a protein set with $n = 31, 63, 93$ that previous algorithms had not been able to identify. In Table 3, proteins are shown, and at next the names are listed.

Table 2. Parameters and Amino acid sequences of identified proteins in [11]

ID	n	Mutation	Position	$\frac{g_4(x)}{g_5(x)}$	d	s
A	1	1	$Q \rightarrow A$	$\frac{3 + 1x^1 + 3x^3 + 1x^4 + 1x^5}{4 + 3x^2 + 1x^3}$	3	QDASTKKLSECLRRIG DELDSNMELQRMIAD
B	93	56	$D \rightarrow E$	$\frac{3 + 1x^1 + 1x^3 + 3x^4 + 1x^5 + 1x^6 + 1x^7}{4 + 3x^1 + 2x^3 + 3x^4 + 1x^5}$	3	GAMALIEVEKPLYAVEVFVGETAHFEIELSEP DVHGQWKLKGQPLAASPDCEIIEDGKKHIL ILHNCQLGMTGEVSFQAANTKSAANLKVKEL

Organisms to proteins identified

A- |TFG-60187 | from *Deltaproteobacteria bacterium* organism

B- |EPC-41793 | from *Lactobacillus paracasei* organism

C- sp |NIES-970 | from *Synechococcus* organism

D- |ARO-91045 | from *Chloroplast* Flintiella sanguinaria organism

E- |OOR-26271 | from *Bacillus wiedmannii* organism

F- |WP-119627657 | from *Staphylococcus equorum* organism

G- |WP-125439530 | from *Hymenobacter perfusus* organism

H- |XP-027961683 | from *Eumetopias jubatus* organism

I- |QCQ-12957 | from *Enterococcus avium* organism

J- sp |TMED90 | from *Synechococcus* organism

K- |YP-009104816 | from *Symbiochloris handae* organism

L- |RIW-08609 | from *Vibrio harveyi* organism

M- sp |IRBG-74 | from *Rhizobium* organism

N- |YP-009395360 | from *Polysiphonia infestans* organism

O- |AYE-99184 | from *Mycobacterium paragordonae*

P- |RIB-36808 | from *Streptococcus anginosus* organism

Q- sp |SH27 | from *Dokdonia*

R- sp |ESL0225 | from *chloroplast* Lactobacillus

S- |ASF-98150 | from *Mycobacterium avium subsp paratuberculosis*

T- |AYV-11453 | from *Pseudomonas aeruginosa*

U- |RDE-16505 | from *Thaumarchaeota archaeon S14*

V- |ATU-27463 | from *Bacillus velezensis*

W- sp |YLB-04 | from *Bacillus*

X- |AAF-43609 | from *Helicobacter pylori*

Y- sp |HMWF-001 | from *Chryseobacterium*

Z- |AVQ-03452 | from *Caulobacter segnis*

The Table 4 gather the interest information for each identified sequence through error correcting codes. Is possible visualize the first attribute of each table the size of the sequence n, the position in which a mutation has been identified *Pos*, followed by modified *to* original *AA*, the polynomials generators for each field and the distance d found through the BCH criterion.

Table 3. Identified amino acid sequences with size $n = 31, 63, 93$

ID	Amino acid sequence
A	MGSVIKKRRKKMRKHKHRKLLARTRHKRKKG
B	MVNTILKEADLFCPNSVRINFTIYLFLNQAI
C	MGISDTQVLVALAIALIPGVLAFRLSTELYK
D	MEALVYVFLLIGTLMVIFFAVFFRDPPRVAK
E	MSKRRYNEKIVDISLKIADIFEKSLIYFSEY
F	MCSTLFVTIIAPIVVGVIITLFSYWLNNRDK
G	MSFATGQLKAGVYVLRLTTATGSTAQRVVRR
H	MGISTRELFLNFTIVLITVILMWLLVRSYQY
I	MRSLFQSFICPLLVGLIVALFEYWLNTKNKK
J	MESFAYILILTLAIATLFFAIAFRDPPKIGK
K	MMLSDNDVFTALFLALVTGALAVRLAIALYV
L	MWKKDWADAAVVVAWVAVWSTLVYFVPLTGL
M	MATPAGLEPATYCLEARFLCNDCEKLKTNCF
N	MSIFLSYILFVTIFMGLALGLYSSLQFIKLI
O	MRVVVNRDRCEGNAFCVNIAPEVFALDDDEYAVVITDPVPVEQETLVAQAIEACPRAALSREL
P	MSSDNIKLKYYNLQPFTKWTSGKRQLLSVLRSYMPEKYKRYFEPFVTPSSKRILANYEDLMHK
Q	MNKGTVKFFNETKGFGFITEEGVEKDHFVHISGLVDEIREGDEVEFELKEGNKGLNAVNVRVL
R	MAVPKRHTSKQKKRSRRGHIKLTVPAMHYDATTGEYRLSHRVSPKGYYKGRQVATEANSSDNQ
S	MRLMKDETVPWATGLTVTAFVAAVTGVAIVVLSLGLVRVHPLLAVGL NIVAAGGLAPTLWGWRRTPVLRWFVLGAGVGVTGAWLVLLVLAVAG
T	MRCRPSLVRGRAAQVNPGGFTTPARRPSVPHRTAGCGKSSLRPLMA GSSPSLPDGSNPSAAIVQSASDVQCSRLLKTTLYAPGALHRPQCAAV
U	MTKLVIAAKVLPTGIEVDLDALAASIGGALSDGITMRRHEKEPIAFGL FALRAEFVCEDREGQMDSLESAVRSVEGVSEFEVLNMSRSSVEMK
V	MKFLFGSINSTVLTMAGLRVLSSLIELSAAIIMLLTNDIRKAVVV NSILAIVGPLIFIITMTIGIYQIAGQLSYAKLILIFAGVVLILAGVHK
W	MEITGHTVEFLEDPFGLLAGERYEFLLDIADDEEDELYSELGTGLKV IFSVEGDAYKIAQYNFFEKDSGKVFDFALEDDEEEMVLKYCIENYQ
X	MAVSVNLGKNNLTKKGLVGFSWTTLFFGFLVPAIRGDVRWAVLMLI AQTFSLGLANIVFAFIYNKKYTTKLLEDGYEPMDEYSVGVLRSKGII
Y	MNESLDEIERFVIKRIKEIRETKGITQEELSLSIGKNIGFISQIEAP SKKAKYNLIHLNLIAIALGCSIKDFFPNEPIKEKKYDIKEIKTNKS
Z	MLQQQRTNSRGEKYVIGPTGAPLTLSDLPPPETQRWVIRRKAEVVAA VRGGLLSLDEACDRYKLTNEEFLAWQQSIDRHGLAGLRTTRLQQYR

Table 4. Code parameters for the identified proteins (size $n = 31, 63, 93$)

n	s	Mutation position	Mutation	$\dfrac{g_4(x)}{g_5(x)}$	d
31	A	15	$H \to F$	$\dfrac{3 + 2x^1 + 3x^2 + 1x^5}{4 + 1x^1 + 1x^3}$	3
31	B	17	$V \to C$	$\dfrac{3 + 1x^1 + 3x^3 + 1x^4 + 1x^5}{4 + 3x^1 + 1x^2 + 1x^3}$	3
31	C	24	$R \to W$	$\dfrac{3 + 3x^1 + 1x^2 + 3x^4 + 1x^5}{4 + 1x^1 + 1x^2 + 1x^3}$	3
31	D	15	$L \to Y$	$\dfrac{3 + 3x^1 + 1x^2 + 3x^4 + 1x^5}{4 + 1x^1 + 2x^2 + 1x^3}$	3
31	E	6	$K \to F$	$\dfrac{3 + 3x^1 + 1x^2 + 3x^3 + 2x^4 + 1x^5}{4 + 3x^1 + 4x^2 + 1x^3}$	3
31	F	28	$V \to F$	$\dfrac{3 + 2x^1 + 1x^2 + 3x^3 + 1x^4 + 1x^5}{4 + 1x^1 + 1x^3}$	3
31	G	5	$T \to D$	$\dfrac{3 + 3x^1 + 1x^2 + 3x^4 + 1x^5}{1 + 4x^2 + 1x^3 + 4x^4 + 1x^6}$	4
31	H	30	$K \to P$	$\dfrac{3 + 1x^3 + 2x^4 + 1x^5}{4 + 2x^1 + 1x^3}$	3
31	I	17	$L \to Y$	$\dfrac{3 + 2x^1 + 3x^2 + 1x^5}{4 + 3x^1 + 1x^2 + 1x^3}$	3
31	J	9	$T \to N$	$\dfrac{3 + 1x^1 + 3x^3 + 1x^4 + 1x^5}{4 + 1x^1 + 1x^2 + 1x^3}$	3
31	K	23	$V \to L$	$\dfrac{3 + 1x^3 + 2x^4 + 1x^5}{4 + 3x^1 + 4x^2 + 1x^3}$	3
31	L	9	$A \to T$	$\dfrac{3 + 1x^3 + 2x^4 + 1x^5}{4 + 3x^1 + 1x^2 + 1x^3}$	3
31	M	7	$L \to E$	$\dfrac{3 + 1x^1 + 3x^3 + 1x^4 + 1x^5}{4 + 4x^1 + 2x^2 + 1x^3}$	3
31	N	28	$I \to W$	$\dfrac{3 + 1x^1 + 3x^3 + 1x^4 + 1x^5}{4 + 3x^1 + 4x^2 + 1x^3}$	3
63	O	51	$I \to A$	$\dfrac{1 + 3x^1 + 2x^2 + 1x^4 + 1x^5 + 1x^6}{1 + 1x^2 + 3x^3 + 1x^4 + 1x^6}$	4
63	P	15	$P \to E$	$\dfrac{1 + 3x^1 + 1x^3 + 1x^4 + 2x^5 + 1x^6}{1 + 1x^2 + 3x^3 + 1x^4 + 1x^6}$	3
63	Q	28	$F \to E$	$\dfrac{1 + 1x^1 + 1x^2 + 2x^4 + 3x^5 + 1x^6}{1 + 2x^1 + 2x^2 + 3x^3 + 2x^4 + 2x^5 + 1x^6}$	3
63	R	42	$V \to I$	$\dfrac{1 + 1x^1 + 1x^2 + 2x^4 + 3x^5 + 1x^6}{1 + 2x^1 + 3x^2 + 3x^4 + 2x^5 + 1x^6}$	3
93	S	89	$L \to A$	$\dfrac{3 + 3x^1 + 3x^2 + 1x^3 + 3x^4 + 3x^6 + 1x^7}{1 + 1x^1 + 1x^2 + 3x^3 + 4x^4 + 1x^6}$	3
93	T	50	$P \to L$	$\dfrac{3 + 1x^1 + 2x^2 + 2x^3 + 1x^4 + 1x^5 + 2x^6 + 1x^7}{4 + 4x^1 + 3x^2 + 1x^5}$	3
93	U	66	$S \to W$	$\dfrac{3 + 2x^1 + 3x^2 + 1x^7}{4 + 1x^2 + 3x^3 + 2x^4 + 1x^5}$	3
93	V	58	$I \to H$	$\dfrac{3 + 2x^1 + 3x^2 + 1x^7}{1 + 1x^1 + 1x^2 + 3x^3 + 4x^4 + 1x^6}$	3
93	W	13	$D \to T$	$\dfrac{3 + 3x^1 + 3x^2 + 1x^3 + 3x^4 + 3x^0 + 1x^7}{4 + 2x^1 + 1x^2 + 3x^3 + 1x^5}$	3
93	X	44	$M \to Q$	$\dfrac{3 + 1x^5 + 2x^6 + 1x^7}{1 + 4x^1 + 3x^2 + 3x^5 + 1x^6}$	3
93	Y	67	$C \to G$	$\dfrac{3 + 2x^1 + 3x^2 + 3x^3 + 2x^4 + 2x^5 + 3x^6 + 1x^7}{4 + 4x^1 + 3x^2 + 1x^5}$	3
93	Z	23	$L \to E$	$\dfrac{3 + 1x^1 + 1x^3 + 3x^4 + 1x^5 + 1x^6 + 1x^7}{4 + 3x^1 + 2x^2 + 4x^3 + 1x^5}$	3

5   Conclusions

In this work an algorithm for identifying proteins as codewords of BCH codes over alphabet $\mathbb{Z}_{20}$ is proposed and implemented. The algorithm uses information theory and abstract algebra and is capable to overcome several computational limitations related with protein identifications, as reported in previous works. Therefore, it allowed to identify a larger number of proteins with length $31, 63, 93$, which had not been possible to identify.

Understanding the usefulness of identifying algebraic properties in proteins in an information theory framework, is possible to expand the research field implied in the behavior of the genetic information transmission, and at the same time, all the cellular processes which are triggered by this process. Future works are related with finding a relation of proteins with the mathematical properties identified with the codes, as showed in [5].

Also, it is necessary to continue working in the improvement of the algorithm effectiveness for a larger number of sequences sizes. We propose to make tests to implement the algorithm with non BCH codes.

Acknowledgment. Authors thank Universidad Antonio Nariño (project number: 2017224) and Pontificia Universidad Javeriana - Bogotá (project ID: 7830).

References

1. Pérez, E.M., Mandado, E., Mandado, Y.: Sistemas electrónicos digitales. Marcombo (2007)
2. Battail, G.: Information theory and error-correcting codes in genetics and biological evolution. In: Barbieri, M. (ed.) Introduction to Biosemiotics, pp. 299–345. Springer, Dordrecht (2008). https://doi.org/10.1007/1-4020-4814-9_13
3. Gierasch, L.M., Horwich, A., Slingsby, C., Wickner, S., Agard, D.: Structure and Action of Molecular Chaperones: Machines that Assist Protein Folding in the Cell. WorldScientific (2016)
4. Calabrese, R.L.: Channeling the central dogma. Neuron **82**(4), 725–727 (2014)
5. Duarte-González, M., Echeverri, O., Guevara, J., Palazzo Jr., R.: Cyclic concatenated genetic encoder: a mathematical proposal for biological inferences. Biosystems **163**, 47–58 (2018)
6. Barbieri, M.: Code biology-a new science of life. Biosemiotics **5**(3), 411–437 (2012)
7. Nelson, D.L., Lehninger, A.L., Cox, M.M.: Lehninger Principles of Biochemistry. Macmillan, London (2008)
8. Liu, Y., et al.: Impact of alternative splicing on the human proteome. Cell Rep. **20**(5), 1229–1241 (2017)
9. Faria, L., Rocha, A., Kleinschmidt, J., Palazzo, R., Silva-Filho, M.: DNA sequences generated by BCH codes over GF (4). Electron. Lett. **46**(3), 203–204 (2010)
10. Rocha, A.S.L., Faria, L.C.B., Kleinschmidt, J.H., Palazzo, R., Silva-Filho, M.C.: DNA sequences generated by Z4-linear codes. In: 2010 IEEE International Symposium on Information Theory Proceedings (ISIT), pp. 1320–1324. IEEE (2010)
11. Duarte Gonzalez, M.E.: Modelagem da síntese de proteínas e sua estrutura organizacional através de códigos corretores de erros. [recurso eletrônico]. Ph.D. dissertation (2017)
12. Brandão, M.M., Spoladore, L., Faria, L.C., Rocha, A.S., Silva-Filho, M.C., Palazzo, R.: Ancient DNA sequence revealed by error-correcting codes. Sci. Rep. **5**, 12051 (2015)
13. Faria, L., Rocha, A., Palazzo Jr., R.: Transmission of intra-cellular genetic information: a system proposal. J. Theor. Biol. **358**, 208–231 (2014)
14. Taylor, W.R.: The classification of amino acid conservation. J. Theor. Biol. **119**(2), 205–218 (1986)
15. Guenda, K., Gulliver, T.A.: Construction of cyclic codes over $\mathbb{F}_2 + u\mathbb{F}_2$ for DNA computing. Appl. Algebra Eng. Commun. Comput. **24**(6), 445–459 (2013)

16. Blake, I.F.: Codes over certain rings. Inf. Control, **20**(4), 396–404 (1972). http://www.sciencedirect.com/science/article/pii/S0019995872902239
17. Dougherty, S.T., Harada, M., Solé, P.: Self-dual codes over rings and the Chinese remainder theorem. Hokkaido Math. J. **28**(2), 253–283 (1999). https://doi.org/10.14492/hokmj/1351001213
18. Faria, L.C., et al.: Is a genome a codeword of an error-correcting code? PloS One **7**(5), e36644 (2012)
19. Palazzo Jr., R.: Álgebra e Códigos de Bloco. Universidade Estadual de Campinas (UNICAMP) (2013)
20. Huffman, W.C., Pless, V.: Fundamentals of Error-Correcting Codes. Cambridge University Press, Cambridge (2010)
21. Peterson, W.W., Peterson, W., Weldon, E., Weldon, E.: Error-Correcting Codes. MIT Press, Cambridge (1972)
22. Geer, L.Y., et al.: The NCBI BioSystems database. Nucleic Acids Res. **38**(Suppl. 1), D492–D496 (2009)

Evaluation of Stencil Based Algorithm Parallelization over System-on-Chip FPGA Using a High Level Synthesis Tool

Luis Castano-Londono[1,3(✉)], Cristian Alzate Anzola[1], David Marquez-Viloria[1], Guillermo Gallo[2], and Gustavo Osorio[3]

[1] Department of Electronics and Telecommunication Engineering,
Instituto Tecnológico Metropolitano ITM, Medellín, Colombia
{luiscastano,davidmarquez}@itm.edu.co,
cristianalzate224500@correo.itm.edu.co
[2] Rynova Research Group,
Rymel Company, Medellín, Colombia
guillermogallo@rymel.com.co
[3] Department of Electrical, Electronics and Computing Engineering,
Universidad Nacional de Colombia, Manizales, Colombia
gaosorio@unal.edu.co

Abstract. Iterative stencil computations are present in many scientific and engineering applications. The acceleration of stencil codes using parallel architectures has been widely studied. The parallelization of the stencil computation on FPGA based heterogeneous architectures has been reported with the use of traditional RTL logic design or the use of directives in C/C++ codes on high level synthesis tools. In both cases, it has been shown that FPGAs provide better performance per watt compared to CPU or GPU-based systems. High level synthesis tools are limited to the use of parallelization directives without evaluating other possibilities of their application based on the adaptation of the algorithm. In this document, it is proposed a division of the inner loop of the stencil-based code in such a way that total latency is reduced using memory partition and pipeline directives. As a case study is used the two-dimensional Laplace equation implemented on a ZedBoard and an Ultra96 board using Vivado HLS. The performance is evaluated according to the amount of inner loop divisions and the on-chip memory partitions, in terms of the latency, power consumption, use of FPGA resources, and speed-up.

Keywords: Stencil computation ·
Field programmable gate array (FPGA) · System-on-a-chip (SoC) ·
High-Level Synthesis (HLS)

1 Introduction

Iterative stencil computations are present in scientific and engineering applications such as: numerical integration of partial differential equations [11,18,26],

J. C. Figueroa-García et al. (Eds.): WEA 2019, CCIS 1052, pp. 52–63, 2019.
https://doi.org/10.1007/978-3-030-31019-6_5

image processing [3, 22], Particle-in-Cell simulation [22], graph processing [15], among others. The acceleration of stencil codes using parallel architectures has been widely studied [2, 6, 13, 17, 18, 25–28]. One of the most important limitations of the stencil computation is its small operational intensity [23, 26], which makes it difficult to take advantage of the supercomputers that have a large number of processing units (microprocessors and GPUs) [23].

In the last years, FPGA based accelerators has been proposed to improve stencil computation performance with low power consumption [5–7, 10, 16, 21, 23, 26]. FPGAs have a large number of registers, which facilitates the transfer of data between the iterations of a computation without the need to access an external memory. This leads to an increase in operational intensity and processing speed [26]. In a previous work, we presented an evaluation of architectures for stencil computation, in which it is shown that it is possible to reach execution times similar to those of a CPU used as a reference using registers and on-chip memory [1]. However, these architectures were experimentally tested for small mesh sizes due to the resource limitations of the FPGA used.

FPGA accelerators are usually implemented by means of a hardware design language (HDL) [9, 10, 19, 26]. However, HDL designs require extensive knowledge of the hardware [26]. In order to raise the level of abstraction of designs and facilitate implementation, some High-Level Synthesis tools (HLS) has been used as in [8, 14, 19, 20, 24, 28]. The HLS tools allow to ignore some hardware details, but often deliver solutions less efficient compared to those obtained using HDL [19]. In these cases it is necessary to manually rewrite the code to optimize, for example, memory access [8].

There have been attempts to improve the performance of HLS solutions. For example, in [6], a set of design options have been explored to accommodate a large set of constraints. Most literature works achieve high performance by evading spatial blocking and restricting the input size. On the other hand, in [28], spatial and temporal blocking are combined in order to avoid input size restrictions. It is well known that one of the bottlenecks in the HLS solutions is access to data [4, 8]. In this way, it is necessary to optimize memory management. In [8], graph theory is used in order to optimize the memory banking. In [4], a non-uniform partition of the memory is proposed in such a way that the number of memory banks is minimized. Loop pipelining is another key method for optimization in HLS [13]. However, the performance level of the solutions may not be optimal when complex memory dependencies appear. In [12–14], loop pipelining capabilities are improved in order to handle uncertain memory dependencies.

In this document, it is presented a strategy that attacks the HLS optimization problem on two fronts: memory management and loop pipelining. To achieve the task, it is proposed a method to split the mesh in such a way that total latency is reduced using on-chip memory partitioning and pipeline directives. As a case study is used the two-dimensional Laplace equation implemented for two different development systems, the ZedBoard using Vivado Design Suite and the Ultra96 board using Vivado SDx. The performance is evaluated and compared according to the amount of inner loop divisions and the memory partitions in terms of the latency, power consumption, use of FPGA resources, and speed-up. The rest of the document is organized as follows. In Sect. 2, it is presented the two-dimensional Laplace equation and the approach to its numerical solution by means of finite difference method. In Sect. 3, the details of the implemented stencil computing system are presented. Results are presented in Sect. 4. Finally, the conclusions are given in Sect. 5.

2   Case Study: Two-Dimensional Laplace Equation

Suppose Ω as a domain of R^2 with boundary defined as $\partial\Omega$. The partial differential equation shown in (1) is considered elliptical for all points $(x, y) \in \Omega$.

$$\frac{\partial^2 u}{\partial x^2} + \frac{\partial^2 u}{\partial y^2} = 0 \tag{1}$$

This expression is known as two-dimensional Laplace equation and it is used to describe the stationary temperature distribution in a two-dimensional region given some boundary conditions. An approach to the numerical solution of this equation is obtained using the finite difference method. The Ω region is discretized in the two dimensions x and y by defining a number of points I and J respectively. This approach is obtained for the iteration $n + 1$ as in (2), considering a uniform distribution of the points in the domain of the solution.

$$u_{ij}^{n+1} = \frac{1}{4}(u_{i+1,j}^n + u_{i-1,j}^n + u_{i,j+1}^n + u_{i,j-1}^n) \tag{2}$$

The implementation of this approach is known as the Jacobi algorithm. For Dirichlet boundary conditions, it is described for a number of iterations N as shown in Algorithm 1.

Algorithm 1. Stencil for the Laplace equation using the Jacobi algorithm.

Input: initial and boundary conditions, mesh size, number of iterations
Output: temperature $u(x, y)$ at iteration N
1 Loop 1: **for** $n \leftarrow 0$ **to** $N - 1$ **do**
2 | Loop 1.1: **for** $j \leftarrow 1$ **to** $J - 2$ **do**
3 | | Loop 1.1.1: **for** $i \leftarrow 1$ **to** $I - 2$ **do**
4 | | | $u_{i,j}^{n+1} \leftarrow 0.25(u_{i+1,j}^n + u_{i-1,j}^n + u_{i,j+1}^n + u_{i,j-1}^n)$
5 | | **end**
6 | **end**
7 **end**

---

3   System Implementation

The implementation was performed for two different development systems, the ZedBoard using Vivado Design Suite and the Ultra96 board using Vivado SDx. In both cases, the Zynq processing system (PS) interacts through of AXI interface and DMA with a custom IP created in Vivado HLS using C language for the programmable logic (PL) section. The ARM core is the host processor where the main application runs over a PetaLinux terminal, and the custom IP core executes the algorithm based on the stencil scheme. This application includes the generation of initial values and the boundary conditions which are stored in BRAM. Then, the number of iterations is defined and the stencil computation function is called. When the stencil algorithm execution is finished, the results become available in the DDR3 RAM and these can be read and saved in a text file with 15 significant digits in decimal format. The block diagram of the system is shown in Fig. 1.

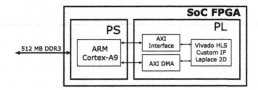

Fig. 1. Block diagram of the system implemented using *Vivado Design Suite.*

3.1   Baseline Architecture of the Custom IP Core

The sequential implementation of the code, defined as architecture A_1, was used as reference to compare against the performances of the parallel implementations. Given that the data arrive to the main function as a vector, the line code for stencil operation in Algorithm 1 is implemented as shown in Algorithm 2.

The maximum size that can be used for a square mesh is determined by the amount of BRAM memory blocks in the FPGA device (*BRAM_Blocks*). Considering a BRAM block size of 18 Kb, the use of simple floating point format, and that the algorithm requires two arrays to store the values of the last two iterations, the mesh size is calculated as shown in (3).

$$mesh\_size_{max} = \sqrt{\frac{RAM\_Blocks \times 18000}{32 \times 2}} \tag{3}$$

3.2   Parallelization

The acceleration of the algorithm execution, defined as architecture A_2, was achieved using a pipeline directive in Loop 1 of the stencil code. In addition, some modifications are made to the stencil code implementation to reduce the latency.

Algorithm 2. Stencil computation algorithm for N iterations using vectors.

Input: initial values and boundary conditions, mesh size, number of iterations (N)
Output: temperature at iteration N

1 **Function** *stencil_2D(u[65536], v[65536]: float)* **is**
2   Loop 1: **for** $j \leftarrow 1$ **to** $J - 2$ **do**
3   Loop 1.1: **for** $i \leftarrow 1$ **to** $I - 2$ **do**
4              $v[j * X_I + i] \leftarrow$
                $0.25\, (u[j * X_I + i + 1] + u[j * X_I + i - 1] + u[(j + 1) * X_I + i] + u[(j - 1) * X_I + i])$
5   **end**
6   **end**
7 **end**
8 **Function** *Laplace_2D() : void* **is**
9   Loop 1: **for** $n \leftarrow 0$ **to** $N - 1$ **do**
10   stencil_2D(u,v)
11   Loop 1.1: **for** $j \leftarrow 1$ **to** $J - 2$ **do**
12   Loop 1.1.1: **for** $i \leftarrow 1$ **to** $I - 2$ **do**
13                 $u[j * X_I + i] \leftarrow v[j * X_I + i]$
14   **end**
15   **end**
16   **end**
17 **end**

A first approach makes the most of the Loop 1.1 of the Laplace function, considering the transfer operations used when the vector u is updated with the vector v to calculate a new iteration. Thus, the upper limit of the external loop is reduced by half as shown in Algorithm 3.

Algorithm 3. Pseudocode of the stencil computation algorithm implementation reducing the number of iterations of the external loop to N/2.

Input: initial and boundary conditions, mesh size, number of iterations (N)
Output: temperature $u(x, y)$ at iteration N

1 **Function** *Laplace_2D() : void* **is**
2   Loop 1: **for** $n \leftarrow 0$ **to** $N/2$ **do**
3   stencil_2D(u,v)
4   stencil_2D(v,u)
5   **end**
6 **end**

To improve performance, a method for splitting the mesh into three blocks on the y axis is proposed, as shown in Fig. 2. The distribution is made so that the number of divisions in block B2 is a power of 2, and considering that the number of rows in blocks B1 and B3 is odd because of the rows of boundary conditions. This distribution allows the application of the parallelization directives in such a way that the synthesis time, the amount of resources and the latency are reduced. The memory partition directive allows the different blocks to access the corresponding data concurrently, which are distributed in a number of smaller arrays defined by the partition factor. The approach, defined as architecture A_3, is described as shown in Algorithm 4.

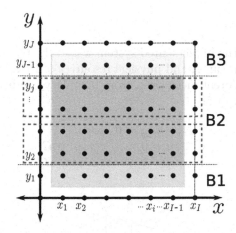

Fig. 2. Distribution of blocks for processing.

Algorithm 4. Pseudocode of the algorithm based on stencil with two-dimensional arrangement of 256 × 256 for N iterations.

Input: initial and boundary conditions, mesh size $(I \times J)$, iterations (N), divisions of $B2$ (PY), rows in B1 (PYF), rows in each subdivision of B2 (PYI), rows in B1 and B2 (PYL)

Output: temperature $u(x, y)$ at iteration N

```
1  Function stencil_2D(u[65536], v[65536]: float) is
2      for j ← 1 to PYF-1 do
3          # pragma pipeline
4          for i ← 1 to I − 2 do
5              s1 ← u[j * X_I + i + 1] + u[j * X_I + i − 1]
6              s2 ← u[(j + 1) * X_I + i] + u[(j − 1) * X_I + i]
7              v[j * X_I + i] ← 0.25 (s1 + s2) ;              // Stencil for block B1
8          end
9      end
10     for j ← 1 to PY do
11         for i ← 1 to I − 2 do
12             # pragma pipeline
13             for k ← 1 to PYI − 2 do
14                 s1 ← u[(j + PYF + PY * k) * X_I + i + 1]
15                 s2 ← u[(j + PYF + PY * k) * X_I + i − 1]
16                 s3 ← u[(j + PYF + PY * k + 1) * X_I + i]
17                 s4 ← u[(j + PYF + PY * k − 1) * X_I + i]
18                 v[(j + PYF + PY * k) * X_I + i] ← 0.25 (s1 + s2 + s3 + s4) ;   // Stencil
                       for block B2
19             end
20         end
21     end
22     for j ← 1 to PYF do
23         # pragma pipeline
24         for i ← 1 to I − 2 do
25             s1 ← u[(j + PYL) * X_I + i + 1] + u[(j + PYL) * X_I + i − 1]
26             s2 ← u[(j + PYL + 1) * X_I + i] + u[(j + PYL − 1) * X_I + i]
27             v[(j + PYL) * X_I + i] ← 0.25 (s1 + s2) ;       // Stencil for block B3
28         end
29     end
30  end
```

4   Results

The performance of the implemented system was evaluated according to numerical results, execution times, and physical resources of FPGA. Numerical results were obtained for different mesh sizes, from boundary conditions and initial values defined as shown in (4).

$$\begin{cases} u_{xx} + u_{yy} = 0 \\ \qquad u = 0, \qquad \forall(x,y) \in \Omega \\ \qquad u = 1, \qquad \forall(x,y) \in \partial\Omega \end{cases} \qquad (4)$$

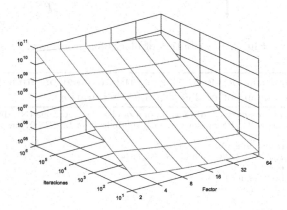

Fig. 3. Latency for 4 processing blocks of the middle division according to number of iterations and partition factor of on-chip memory.

Performances of the implemented architectures are obtained measuring execution time. The architecture A_3 has several configurations, therefore, a design space exploration is performed based on two parameters: number of subdivision in the middle block and the memory partition factor. For this purpose, latencies are obtained in terms of clock cycles for different combinations of both parameters and the number of iterations. The latency measurements are performed for block sizes of 4, 8, 16, 32, and 64 for the middle block, and assigning values of 2, 4, 8, 16, 32, and 64 as memory partition factor. For each combination of these parameters the simulation is carried out for 10^1, 10^2, 10^3, 10^4, 10^5, y 10^6 iterations. In Fig. 3 are shown the latencies for 4 subdivisions of $B2$ based on number of iterations and memory partition factor. It is observed that the performance improves with the increase of this last parameter. Latencies obtained are used for the execution time calculations considering a 100 MHz clock frequency.

Table 1 show the speed-up achieved using the A_3 with 4 processing blocks in relation to the base architecture A_1 and to the sequential execution on CPU. It is observed a number of iterations from which the acceleration tends to a constant value.

Table 1. Speed-up with regards to the base architecture A1 based on number of iterations and memory partition factor.

		Factor											
		t_{A_1}/t_{A_3}						t_{CPU}/t_{A_3}					
		2	4	8	16	32	64	2	4	8	16	32	64
N	10^1	20,44	33,11	49,48	65,72	78,61	87,19	0,87	1,41	2,10	2,79	3,34	3,77
	10^2	23,78	43,15	76,27	123,73	179,63	232,24	0,84	1,53	2,70	4,37	6,35	8,21
	10^3	24,18	44,51	80,67	135,82	206,36	279,03	0,79	1,46	2,64	4,45	6,76	9,14
	10^4	24,22	44,65	81,14	137,16	209,48	284,77	0,79	1,45	2,63	4,45	6,79	9,24
	10^5	24,23	44,66	81,19	137,30	209,80	285,36	0,78	1,44	2,61	4,41	6,74	9,17
	10^6	24,23	44,66	81,19	137,31	209,83	285,42	0,78	1,44	2,62	4,42	6,76	9,19

The best performance was determined making a plot of the latency based on the number of subdivisions in the block $B2$ and memory partition factor for a number of 10^6 iterations, as shown in Fig. 4. The lowest latency was observed using a combination of 4 subdivisions and memory partition factor of 64.

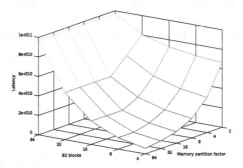

Fig. 4. Latency for 10^6 iterations based on the number of processing blocks and the partition factor of on-chip memory.

Execution times were measured experimentally for the architectures implemented on the ZedBoard and an Ultra96 board. Table 2 shows execution times according to the number of iterations for the implemented architectures.

Table 2. Execution times in microseconds for different number of iterations with the different architectures implemented.

Iterations	ZedBoard				Ultra96	
	A_1	A_2	$A_{3(16 \times 16)}$	$A_{3(4 \times 32)}$	$A_{3(4 \times 64)}$ 100 MHz	$A_{3(4 \times 64)}$ 200 MHz
10^1	158.212	16.199	3.710	2.086	1.928	993
10^2	1.552.677	150.163	25.259	9.008	7.011	3.561
10^3	15.497.303	1.489.794	240.753	78.231	57.877	29.250
10^4	154.943.576	14.886.115	2.395.667	770.466	566.516	286.139
10^5	1.549.406.305	148.849.317	23.944.818	7.692.819	5.652.881	2.854.981
10^6	15.494.033.580	1.488.481.343	239.436.321	76.916.319	56.516.436	28.543.256

The speedup achieved for the implemented architectures calculated in relation to the baseline and the sequential implementation on CPU is shown in Table 3.

Table 3. Speed-up achieved for the implemented architectures in relation to the sequential implementation on CPU.

Iterations	ZedBoard					Ultra96	
	t_{A_4}/t_{A_1}	A_1	A_2	$A_{3(16\times16)}$	$A_{3(4\times32)}$	$A_{3(4\times64)}$ 100MHz	$A_{3(4\times64)}$ 200 MHz
10^1	75,85	0,04	0,43	1,86	3,31	3,59	6,96
10^2	172,37	0,04	0,38	2,26	6,34	8,15	16,04
10^3	198,10	0,03	0,35	2,20	6,76	9,14	18,08
10^4	201,10	0,03	0,35	2,18	6,79	9,24	18,29
10^5	201,41	0,03	0,35	2,17	6,74	9,17	18,16
10^6	201,44	0,03	0,35	2,17	6,76	9,20	18,21

The consumption of hardware resources for each architecture is shown in Table 4.

Table 4. Hardware resources required on ZedBoard and Ultra96. The entire system includes processing modules.

Resource	ZedBoard				Ultra96	
	A_1	A_2	$A_{3(16\times16)}$	$A_{3(4\times32)}$	$A_{3(4\times64)}$ 100 MHz	$A_{3(4\times64)}$ 200 MHz
LUT	5.644	25.574	16.776	34.277	64.540	64.540
Flip Flop	6.599	22.836	17.689	39.204	69.256	86.570
Slices	2.267	9.100	6407	12.415	–	–
DSP48	5	17	36	97	144	144

The power consumption for the implemented architectures is shown in Table 5.

Table 5. Power consumption for the implemented architectures. The entire system includes processing modules.

	ZedBoard				Ultra96	
	A_1	A_2	$A_{3(16\times16)}$	$A_{3(4\times32)}$	$A_{3(4\times64)}$ 100 MHz	$A_{3(4\times64)}$ 200 MHz
Core Power (W)	0,297	1,005	1,037	1,535	1,349	4,989
Total Power (W)	1,87	2,592	2,617	3,599	3,539	5,341

5   Conclusions

This paper presents a strategy for the implementation of algorithms based stencil on SoC-FPGA using Vivado HLS, addressing the problem of optimization in terms of memory management and parallelization of cycles. The general scheme of the implemented architectures involves the use of an ARM Cortex-A9 microprocessor that acts as master, on which the main application is executed. The processor interacts through an AXI interface with an IP created in Vivado HLS, which performs the execution of the algorithm based on stencil. The architectures are implemented on a ZedBoard Zynq Evaluation and Development Kit under the Vivado Design Suite environment and on an Ultra96 board using Vivado SDx. The source code of the main application is made in C and executed under PetaLinux on the PS using a terminal console. The communication is done using an AXI interface and direct access to memory (DMA).

To improve performance in terms of execution time a method is proposed to split the mesh into three parts on the y-axis. The distribution is done so that the number of rows in block B2 is a multiple of a power of 2, considering that blocks B1 and B3 have one row less because they include contour conditions. An unrolling of the internal cycle is proposed so that the latency of the intermediate cycle is reduced according to the number of subdivisions of B2. Additionally, the on-chip memory partition is made in such a way that each subdivision can access the corresponding data concurrently.

An exploration of the design space for the generalized architecture is performed, based on the number of B2 processing subdivisions and the factor used for the memory partition. For this, latencies are obtained in terms of clock cycles for different combinations of both parameters and number of iterations. It is observed that the performance improves with the increase of the memory partition factor. It is found that the configuration that provides the best performance and that can be implemented in the ZedBoard is with 4 divisions of B2 and 32 partitions of memory. For this configuration we obtain an acceleration of approximately $209.83\times$ in relation to the base architecture and $6.76\times$ in relation to the CPU used as reference. The power consumption with this configuration is approximately 3.6 watts. For the Ultra96 the A3 architecture is implemented with a configuration of 4 divisions of B2 and 64 memory partitions. In this case an acceleration of $9.2\times$ to 100 MHz and $18.21\times$ to 200 MHz is achieved in relation to the sequential execution on CPU.

Acknowledgements. This study were supported by the AE&CC research Group COL0053581, at the Sistemas de Control y Robótica Laboratory, attached to the Instituto Tecnológico Metropolitano. This work is part of the project "Improvement of visual perception in humanoid robots for objects recognition in natural environments using Deep Learning" with ID P17224, co-funded by the Instituto Tecnológico Metropolitano and Universidad de Antioquia.

References

1. Castano, L., Osorio, G.: An approach to the numerical solution of one-dimensional heat equation on SoC FPGA. Revista Científica de Ingeniería Electrónica, Automática y Comunicaciones **38**(2), 83–93 (2017). ISSN 1815–5928
2. Cattaneo, R., Natale, G., Sicignano, C., Sciuto, D., Santambrogio, M.D.: On how to accelerate iterative stencil loops: a scalable streaming-based approach. ACM Trans. Archit. Code Optim. (TACO) **12**(4), 53 (2016)
3. Chugh, N., Vasista, V., Purini, S., Bondhugula, U.: A DSL compiler for accelerating image processing pipelines on FPGAs. In: 2016 International Conference on Parallel Architecture and Compilation Techniques (PACT), pp. 327–338. IEEE (2016)
4. Cong, J., Li, P., Xiao, B., Zhang, P.: An optimal microarchitecture for stencil computation acceleration based on non-uniform partitioning of data reuse buffers. In: Proceedings of the 51st Annual Design Automation Conference, pp. 1–6. ACM (2014)
5. Deest, G., Estibals, N., Yuki, T., Derrien, S., Rajopadhye, S.: Towards scalable and efficient FPGA stencil accelerators. In: IMPACT 2016 - 6th International Workshop on Polyhedral Compilation Techniques, Held with HIPEAC 2016 (2016)
6. Deest, G., Yuki, T., Rajopadhye, S., Derrien, S.: One size does not fit all: implementation trade-offs for iterative stencil computations on FPGAs. In: 2017 27th International Conference on Field Programmable Logic and Applications (FPL), pp. 1–8. IEEE (2017)
7. Del Sozzo, E., Baghdadi, R., Amarasinghe, S., Santambrogio, M.D.: A common backend for hardware acceleration on FPGA. In: 2017 IEEE International Conference on Computer Design (ICCD), pp. 427–430. IEEE (2017)
8. Escobedo, J., Lin, M.: Graph-theoretically optimal memory banking for stencil-based computing kernels. In: Proceedings of the 2018 ACM/SIGDA International Symposium on Field-Programmable Gate Arrays, pp. 199–208. ACM (2018)
9. de Fine Licht, J., Blott, M., Hoefler, T.: Designing scalable FPGA architectures using high-level synthesis. In: Proceedings of the 23rd ACM SIGPLAN Symposium on Principles and Practice of Parallel Programming (PPoPP 2018), vol. 53, pp. 403–404. ACM (2018)
10. Kobayashi, R., Oobata, Y., Fujita, N., Yamaguchi, Y., Boku, T.: OpenCL-ready high speed FPGA network for reconfigurable high performance computing. In: Proceedings of the International Conference on High Performance Computing in Asia-Pacific Region, pp. 192–201. ACM (2018)
11. László, E., Nagy, Z., Giles, M.B., Reguly, I., Appleyard, J., Szolgay, P.: Analysis of parallel processor architectures for the solution of the Black-Scholes PDE. In: 2015 IEEE International Symposium on Circuits and Systems (ISCAS), pp. 1977–1980. IEEE (2015)
12. Liu, J., Bayliss, S., Constantinides, G.A.: Offline synthesis of online dependence testing: parametric loop pipelining for HLS. In: 2015 IEEE 23rd Annual International Symposium on Field-Programmable Custom Computing Machines (FCCM), pp. 159–162. IEEE (2015)
13. Liu, J., Wickerson, J., Bayliss, S., Constantinides, G.A.: Polyhedral-baseddynamic loop pipelining for high-level synthesis. IEEE Trans. Comput.-Aided Des. Integr. Circ. Syst. **37**, 1802–1815 (2017)

14. Liu, J., Wickerson, J., Constantinides, G.A.: Loop splitting for efficient pipelining in high-level synthesis. In: 2016 IEEE 24th Annual International Symposium on Field-Programmable Custom Computing Machines (FCCM), pp. 72–79. IEEE (2016)
15. Mokhov, A., et al.: Language and hardware acceleration backend for graph processing. In: 2017 Forum on Specification and Design Languages (FDL), pp. 1–7. IEEE (2017)
16. Mondigo, A., Ueno, T., Tanaka, D., Sano, K., Yamamoto, S.: Design and scalability analysis of bandwidth-compressed stream computing with multiple FPGAs. In: 2017 12th International Symposium on Reconfigurable Communication-centric Systems-on-Chip (ReCoSoC), pp. 1–8. IEEE (2017)
17. Nacci, A.A., Rana, V., Bruschi, F., Sciuto, D., Beretta, I., Atienza, D.: A high-level synthesis flow for the implementation of iterative stencil loop algorithms on FPGA devices. In: Proceedings of the 50th Annual Design Automation Conference, p. 52. ACM (2013)
18. Natale, G., Stramondo, G., Bressana, P., Cattaneo, R., Sciuto, D., Santambrogio, M.D.: A polyhedral model-based framework for dataflow implementation on FPGA devices of iterative stencil loops. In: 2016 IEEE/ACM International Conference on Computer-Aided Design (ICCAD), pp. 1–8. IEEE (2016)
19. de Oliveira, C.B., Cardoso, J.M., Marques, E.: High-level synthesis from C vs. a DSL-based approach. In: 2014 IEEE International Parallel & Distributed Processing Symposium Workshops, pp. 257–262. IEEE (2014)
20. Reagen, B., Adolf, R., Shao, Y.S., Wei, G.Y., Brooks, D.: Machsuite: benchmarks for accelerator design and customized architectures. In: 2014 IEEE International Symposium on Workload Characterization (IISWC), pp. 110–119. IEEE (2014)
21. Reiche, O., Özkan, M.A., Hannig, F., Teich, J., Schmid, M.: Loop parallelization techniques for FPGA accelerator synthesis. J. Signal Process. Syst. 90(1), 3–27 (2018)
22. Sakai, R., Sugimoto, N., Miyajima, T., Fujita, N., Amano, H.: Acceleration of full-pic simulation on a CPU-FPGA tightly coupled environment. In: 2016 IEEE 10th International Symposium on Embedded Multicore/Many-core Systems-on-Chip (MCSoC), pp. 8–14. IEEE (2016)
23. Sano, K., Hatsuda, Y., Yamamoto, S.: Multi-FPGA accelerator for scalable stencil computation with constant memory bandwidth. IEEE Trans. Parallel Distrib. Syst. 25(3), 695–705 (2014)
24. Schmid, M., Reiche, O., Schmitt, C., Hannig, F., Teich, J.: Code generation for high-level synthesis of multiresolution applications on FPGAs. arXiv preprint arXiv:1408.4721 (2014)
25. Shao, Y.S., Reagen, B., Wei, G.Y., Brooks, D.: Aladdin: a pre-RTL, power-performance accelerator simulator enabling large design space exploration of customized architectures. In: ACM SIGARCH Computer Architecture News, vol. 42, pp. 97–108. IEEE Press (2014)
26. Waidyasooriya, H.M., Takei, Y., Tatsumi, S., Hariyama, M.: Opencl-based FPGA-platform for stencil computation and its optimization methodology. IEEE Trans. Parallel Distrib. Syst. 28(5), 1390–1402 (2017)
27. Wang, S., Liang, Y.: A comprehensive framework for synthesizing stencil algorithms on FPGAs using OpenCL model. In: 2017 54th ACM/EDAC/IEEE Design Automation Conference (DAC), pp. 1–6. IEEE (2017)
28. Zohouri, H.R., Podobas, A., Matsuoka, S.: Combined spatial and temporal blocking for high-performance stencil computation on FPGAs using OpenCL. In: Proceedings of the 2018 ACM/SIGDA International Symposium on Field-Programmable Gate Arrays, pp. 153–162. ACM (2018)

Path Tracking Control for Micro-robots with Helmholtz-Maxwell Coils Actuation

Daniel F. Murcia Rivera$^{(\boxtimes)}$ and Hernando Leon-Rodriguez$^{(\boxtimes)}$

Industrial and Mechatronics Engineering Departments, Faculty of Engineering,
Nueva Granada Military University, Bogota, Colombia
{u1802440,hernando.leon}@unimilitar.edu.co

Abstract. This work is dedicated to present a proposed control system for tridimensional and planar position of a magnetized micro-robot on a high viscous medium with electromagnetic actuation. Detailed process for control derivation, simulation and experiments are exposed.

Keywords: Micro-robot · Path tracking · Electromagnetic actuation · Discrete control

1 Introduction

The physics at low-level scale can become weird compared to macro-scale because the appearance of forces and effects that where despised on macro-scale. Micro robots are systems that deal with this type of forces, and for many or partially all applications, it is required the control of position of them. Because of that, a prototype of a micro-robot relatively big with an electromagnetic actuator was developed.

The most highlighted application of these tiny systems, are related to health. Micro robots can treat blocked vessels due to bad feeding or poor physical activity [1]. They can also deliver medicine into specific locations increasing the effectiveness of the medicine and reducing secondary effects in other body parts [2]. Endoscopy is another area of application, [3] and [4] develop electromagnetic systems for specialized endoscopy micro robots. Comparing with traditional methods, this technology can overcome issues of infection due to surroundings [5] and risks due to competence [6].

The first thing to consider at these scales is the dominance of viscous forces. The Reynols number in this domain become small and by its definition, it indicated that it can be despised the inertial forces. The movement of the robot becomes no past dependent, and only determined by forces applied at the instant [7]. The system of this article is not fully at micro-scale, so perhaps consideration of its forces is necessary.

Another issue of these tiny systems is how to implement the actuator that generates the movement. Firstly, the power supply, in macro-scale batteries are used but using this at tiny scale results on big complexity [8]. Second, if is actually fulfilled the energy issue, how the actuator can transform its supply into kinetic energy? Complex machining processes are necessary for creating the actuator. A system for delivering medicine show on [9] uses a micro-hydraulic pump actuator.

© Springer Nature Switzerland AG 2019
J. C. Figueroa-García et al. (Eds.): WEA 2019, CCIS 1052, pp. 64–77, 2019.
https://doi.org/10.1007/978-3-030-31019-6_6

The approach in the presented system is to manage the actuation by an electromagnetic generator exercising forces over a magnetized robot. The complexity of tiny actuators is simplified but control becomes complex because of nonlinearities. Electromagnetic actuation systems are diverse, categorizing them there are two class of actuation: gradient and rotatory magnetic field [10]. In case of the type of electromagnetic generator, there are permanent magnet and coil magnet types [11]. Figures 1 and 2 shown the used actuation system based in coils generators producing both class of actuation, [12] presents a similar system.

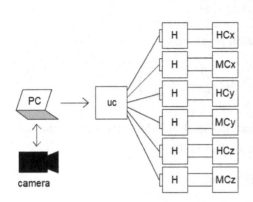

Fig. 1. Schematic micro-robot system diagram uc: microcontroller H: h bridge circuit HC: Helmholtz coil MC: Maxwell coil

Fig. 2. Implemented electromagnetic actuation system

2   System and Equipment

The based equipment used to evaluate the trajectory of the micro robots are one Camera Canon EOS Rebel T3 1100D with Macro Lens 100 mm; 6 DC Power supply Versatile Power BENCH 100-10XR. Table 1 is showing the geometry and parameter of each coil placed in the axis x, y, z; and also the number of coil's turns

Table 1. System geometry and coils parameters.

Coils	Axis	Diameter (mm)	N turns
Helmholtz	x	200	196
	y	121.5	234
	z	65	221
Maxwell	x	172	240
	y	114	320
	z	61	165

3 Modelling

3.1 Three-Dimensional Space Model

Equations (1) and (2), presented by [12], govern the way an intensity magnetic field $\vec{H}$ influence over the dynamics of a permanent magnet.

$$\vec{F} = \mu_0 V (\vec{M} \cdot \nabla) \vec{H} \tag{1}$$

$$\vec{T} = \mu_0 V \vec{M} \times \vec{H} \tag{2}$$

Rewriting (1) by expanding the operation result in:

$$\vec{F} = \mu_0 V \left(M_x \frac{\partial \vec{H}}{\partial x} + M_y \frac{\partial \vec{H}}{\partial y} + M_z \frac{\partial \vec{H}}{\partial z} \right)$$

By using the principle of superposition, the total H field is the sum of the field produced by Maxwell ($\overrightarrow{H_m}$) and Helmholtz ($\overrightarrow{H_h}$) coils.

$$\vec{H} = \overrightarrow{H_m} + \overrightarrow{H_h} \tag{3}$$

Please note that the first paragraph of a section or subsection is not indented. The first paragraphs that follows a table, figure, equation etc. does not have an indent, either.

Subsequent paragraphs, however, are indented.

3.2 Independence of Force Under the Influence of Helmholtz Coils

Defining a new vector $\overrightarrow{\partial_p H_m}$ the H field is:

$$\overrightarrow{H_m} = \overrightarrow{\partial_p H_m} \circ [x \quad y \quad z]^T \tag{4}$$

Because $\overrightarrow{H_m}$ is a gradient field, and $\overrightarrow{H_h}$ is a uniform field, only $\overrightarrow{H_m}$ has incidence over the actuation force.

$$\frac{\partial \overrightarrow{H_m}}{\partial v} = \left[\frac{\partial \overrightarrow{H_m}}{\partial x} \quad \frac{\partial \overrightarrow{H_m}}{\partial y} \quad \frac{\partial \overrightarrow{H_m}}{\partial z} \right]^T$$

$$\frac{\partial \overrightarrow{H_m}}{\partial v} = \overrightarrow{\partial_p H_m} \qquad \frac{\partial \overrightarrow{H_h}}{\partial v} = 0$$

Using (3) and the expand form of (1), the actuation force is:

$$\vec{F} = \mu_0 V [M_x \partial_x H_{mx} \quad M_y \partial_y H_{my} \quad M_z \partial_z H_{mz}]^T$$

$$\vec{F} = \mu_0 V \left(\vec{M} \circ \overrightarrow{\partial_p H_m} \right) \tag{5}$$

Note that v express a system coordinate variables (x, y, z) and that $\circ$ corresponds to the Hadamart product.

3.3 Planar Space Model

In planar space, the actuation force $\vec{F}'$ is given by replacing with local variables $\vec{M}'$ and $\overrightarrow{\partial_p H_m'}$ on (5) that are characterized for having zero components on $\hat{z}'$. The actuation torque is simply the z component of (2) with local variables.

$$\vec{F}' = \mu_0 V \left(\vec{M}' \circ \overrightarrow{\partial_p H_m'} \right)$$

$$T' = \mu_0 V [0 \quad 0 \quad 1] \vec{M}' \times \vec{H}'$$

Introducing dynamics of the magnetic body and its medium, the proposed dynamic model is:

$$I \ddot{\theta}' = T' - B_i \dot{\theta}' \tag{6}$$

$$m \ddot{\vec{p}}' = \vec{F}' - B_f \dot{\vec{p}}' - \vec{W} \tag{7}$$

Depending on size, weight ($\vec{W}$) can be despised.

3.4 Coils Field as Function of Currents

Theory exposed in [12] relates the coils current and the H field generated for both Helmholtz and Maxwell coils.

$$\vec{I_m} = \begin{bmatrix} i_{m1} \\ i_{m2} \\ i_{m3} \end{bmatrix} \tag{8}$$

For Maxwell case, defining a current vector (8) for enclosing coils current in one variable is necessary to rewrite equations in matrix form.

$$\overline{C_m} = 0.6413 \begin{bmatrix} n_{m1} r_{m1}^{-2} & 0 & 0 \\ 0 & n_{m2} r_{m2}^{-2} & 0 \\ 0 & 0 & n_{m3} r_{m3}^{-2} \end{bmatrix} \tag{9}$$

$$\bar{G} = \begin{bmatrix} 1 & -0.5 & -0.5 \\ -0.5 & 1 & -0.5 \\ -0.5 & -0.5 & 1 \end{bmatrix} \tag{10}$$

From these matrix variables the equations relating current and gradient field for Maxwell coils are:

$$\overrightarrow{g_m} = \overline{C_m}\overrightarrow{I_m} \tag{11}$$

$$\overrightarrow{\partial_p H_m} = \bar{G}\,\overrightarrow{g_m} \tag{12}$$

Helmholtz coils equations can also rewritten into matrix form, where its current vector is $\overrightarrow{I_h}$.

$$\overrightarrow{H_h} = 0.7155 \begin{bmatrix} \frac{n_{h1}}{r_{h1}} & \frac{n_{h2}}{r_{h2}} & \frac{n_{h3}}{r_{h3}} \end{bmatrix}^T \circ \overrightarrow{I_h} \tag{13}$$

3.5 Maxwell Coils Influence on Orientation

As [12] mentioned, the orientation of the magnet is controlled by Helmholtz coils. From (6) the result system is:

$$I\ddot{\theta}' = \mu_0 VM\left(H_y' cos(\theta') - H_x' sin(\theta')\right) - B_i \dot{\theta}'$$

Making dynamic variables zero the steady condition of the system is:

$$H_y' cos(\theta') = H_x' sin(\theta')$$

$$\left|\overrightarrow{H'}\right| sin(\theta_d') cos(\theta') = \left|\overrightarrow{H'}\right| cos(\theta_d') sin(\theta')$$

$$\theta_d' = \theta'$$

Which means that actual magnet's orientation will match H field orientation if is applied a magnitude of field different to zero. However considering (3) the $\overrightarrow{H'}$ will include $\overrightarrow{H_m'}$ that is not constant and is function of the actual position, causing an undesirable deviation of the induced orientation by the Helmholtz coils.

3.6 About Approximations

The exposed model for the calculation of the H field generated by the coils is valid along some limits of operation. It is important to take into account these restrictions for understanding the parameters of the controller.

$$\oint \vec{H} d\vec{s} = I + \iint \vec{D} d\vec{f} \tag{14}$$

The physical law for electromagnetics is mainly Maxwell's equations, from where Biot-Savart's law can derived from (14) by approximating D to zero, which is valid for DC current [13]. This statement points out limits of frequency for the actuator signals, been slow changes more accurate than fastest.

$$B(z) = \frac{\mu_0 I n r^2}{2} \left[\frac{1}{\left(r^2 + \left(z - \frac{d}{2}\right)^2\right)^{3/2}} \pm \frac{1}{\left(r^2 + \left(z + \frac{d}{2}\right)^2\right)^{3/2}} \right] \tag{15}$$

The magnetic field of a point along the z-axis of a coil pair exposed by [14] is compacted on (15), where the plus sign correspond to Helmholtz and minus to Maxwell coil. The model expressions (12) and (13) are obtained evaluating the function of the magnetic field at z = 0, in the case of Maxwell coil the approximation is done by Taylor series expansion (order one) for the function at point z = 0. Therefore, the model operation point is [0 0 0] and is valid for points near to it.

The estimates constants are computed as follow:

$$\mu_0 = 2.3709 * 10^{-8} \; \frac{H}{m}$$

$$V = 2.5133 * 10^{-8} \, m^3$$

$$M = 50 * 10^6 \; \frac{A}{m}$$

$$B_f = 0.1964 \; \frac{Ns}{m}$$

$$B_i = 4.0 * 10^{-6} \; \frac{Nms}{rad}$$

4   Control

4.1   Variable Planar Space

A variable planar space is proposed for simplify the tridimensional position control. In this approach the actual position and the actual desired point resides in a plane. The initial magnetization vector $\overrightarrow{M_0}$ and the target vector $\overrightarrow{T_A}$, that aims the desired position $\overrightarrow{P_d}$, defines the basis vectors for the planar subspace.

$$\vec{T_A} = \vec{P_d} - \vec{P_0} \tag{16}$$

$$\hat{x}' = \frac{\vec{M_0}}{\left\|\vec{M_0}\right\|} \qquad \hat{z}' = \frac{\vec{M_0} \times \vec{T_A}}{\left\|\vec{M_0} \times \vec{T_A}\right\|} \tag{17}$$

Rotating $\hat{x}'$ by 90° over the $\hat{z}'$ axis by applying Rodrigues rotation formula, the final basis is then:

$$\hat{y}' = \hat{z}' \times \hat{x}' + \hat{z}'(\hat{z}' \cdot \hat{x}') \tag{18}$$

An indeterminate of the basis can be presented when the direction of $\vec{M_0}$ and $\vec{T_A}$ matches.

4.2   Maxwell Field

Finding $\overrightarrow{\partial_p H'_m}$ from the planar space model:

$$\overrightarrow{\partial_p H'_m} = \frac{\vec{F}'}{\mu_0 V} \circ \left(\vec{M}'\right)^{\circ - 1}$$

By considering that robot's orientation is already the desired one then:

$$\angle \vec{F}' = \theta' \ \left|\vec{F}'\right| = F''$$

Defining a direction vector $\vec{a}$

$$\vec{a} = cos(\theta')\hat{x}' + sin(\theta')\hat{y}'$$

Transforming into global coordinate system

$$\overrightarrow{\partial_p H_m} = \frac{F''\vec{a}}{\mu_0 V} \circ (M\vec{a})^{\circ - 1}$$

Making the Hadamart power and product respect to the global basis vectors

$$\overrightarrow{\partial_p H_m} = \frac{F''}{\mu_0 VM}(\hat{x} + \hat{y} + \hat{z}) \tag{19}$$

If direction vector $\vec{a}$ has zero components, the corresponding component on $\overrightarrow{\partial_p H_m}$ is undefined and thus it can take any value, making (19) valid for any $\vec{a}$.

4.3   Gravity Compensation

The total force applied to the robot must compensate gravity for correct position control.

$$\vec{F} = \vec{F}' + \vec{W}$$

In consequence, on (19) is added an additional term

$$\overrightarrow{\partial_p H_m} = \frac{1}{\mu_0 VM} \left[F''(\hat{x} + \hat{y} + \hat{z}) + W \left(\hat{z} \circ (\vec{a})^{\circ - 1} \right) \right]$$

Simplifying by discomposing vector $\vec{a}$, the resulting equation is only defined if z-component of $\vec{a}$ is different from cero.

$$\overrightarrow{\partial_p H_m} = \frac{1}{\mu_0 VM} \left[F''(\hat{x} + \hat{y} + \hat{z}) + W a_z^{-1} \hat{z} \right] \tag{20}$$

4.4   Maxwell Currents

Using (11) and (12) the necessary current is:

$$\overrightarrow{I_m} = \left(\overline{GC_m} \right)^{-1} \overrightarrow{\partial_p H_m}$$

A problem finding current is that $\overline{G}$ is not invertible, so that cannot be achieved an arbitrary actuation force. Nevertheless, if movements are only at planes x-y, x-z or y-z, $\overline{G} \, \overline{C_m}$ can be reduced to a submatrix ensuring the forces in plane and allowing neglecting the perpendicular force because components of $\vec{M}$ cancel its influence.

$$\overrightarrow{I_m} = \left(\overline{GC_{sub}} \right)^{-1} \frac{1}{\mu_0 VM} \left[F''(\hat{x} + \hat{y} + \hat{z}) + W a_z^{-1} \hat{z} \right] \tag{21}$$

4.5   Helmholtz Currents

$$\vec{H}' = \overrightarrow{H_m} + \overrightarrow{H_h} \tag{22}$$

For compensating Maxwell influence over the orientation of the robot, $\overrightarrow{H_h}$ should be set as (22) making local H stay in a desirable angle as $\overrightarrow{H_m}$ changes, as expressed on (4).

$$\angle \vec{H}' = \angle \overrightarrow{T_A'}$$

The requirement for this compensation is that direction must be corrected in continuous time because disorientation is also continuous. Therefore discrete control may not totally compensate Maxwell influence.

$$\overrightarrow{I_h} = 0.7155^{-1} \overrightarrow{H_h} \circ \left[\frac{r_{h1}}{n_{h1}} \quad \frac{r_{h2}}{n_{h2}} \quad \frac{r_{h3}}{n_{h3}} \right]^T \tag{23}$$

Increasing the magnitude of the field should reduce the undesired disorientation.

4.6 Discrete Control

$$m\ddot{p}'' = F'' - B\dot{p}'' \tag{24}$$

The model in the line that contains the actual and desired points is show on (24). Setting a state feedback discrete controller and if guaranteed desired orientation, the position of the robot is controlled.

$$q[k+1] = Gq[k] + Hu[k] \tag{25}$$

$$y[k] = Cq[k] + Du[k] \tag{26}$$

Equations (25) and (26) are the discrete state space representation of system (24), where: 'q' is the states vector, 'u' the input signal, and 'y' the output of the system.
Algorithm 1

$$u[k] = K_i v[k] - K\tilde{q}[k] \tag{27}$$

Algorithm 2

$$u[k] = sign(T_a \cdot T_{aa}[k]) abs(K_i v[k] - K\tilde{q}[k]) \tag{28}$$

An observer outputs an approximation for the state vector, this is denoted with $\tilde{q}$.

In one-dimensional space, the state vector 'q' includes velocity and position at this dimension. Distance from initial point to actual point (that is the position at this dimension) is always positive, so if disturbances make position go less than the inverse of the reference, Algorithm 1 will make unstable the system. Algorithm 2 takes into account actual target vector T_{aa} making system stable.

$$u[k] = F''[k] \tag{29}$$

$$v[k] = R[k] - y[k] + v[k-1] \tag{30}$$

$$\tilde{q}[k] = Hu[k-1] + Ly[k-1] + (G - LC)\tilde{q}[k-1] \tag{31}$$

With a settling time of 5 s and sampling time of 0.7 s the constants of the controller are:

$$K_i = 0.0486$$

$$K = [-0.0037 \quad 0.1808]$$

State observer constants:

$$L = \begin{bmatrix} 0 \\ 1 \end{bmatrix}$$

4.7 Point-to-Point Control Algorithm

Define initial $\overrightarrow{M_0}$, $\overrightarrow{P_0}$ vectors and calculate target vector $\overrightarrow{T_A}$. Define planar subspace basis defined on (17), (18). If $\angle \vec{M} \neq \angle \overrightarrow{T_A}$ orientation actuation is started using (23) and setting $\overrightarrow{H_h} = \widehat{T_a}$. When desired angle is reach, one-dimensional position control starts with (21) and (28). As desired orientation sets very fast, position control start in same time with orientation control. At each time step correct orientation by measuring the actual position, for compensating orientation disturbances. When desired position $\overrightarrow{P_d}$ is reach, move to next point starting again the control algorithm. When its position is inside a tolerance range, position $\overrightarrow{P_d}$ is reach.

5 Simulation

Simulation in Figs. 3 and 4 use 6-DOF equations of motion with respect to body axes, so a transformation from global to relative axes is necessary to convert forces to relative ones. Direction cosine matrix defines this transformation. Compensators are included to coincide the rigid body global system with used global system.

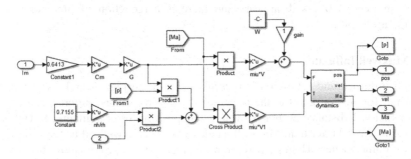

Fig. 3. Plant model. Current-forces conversion and gravity influence.

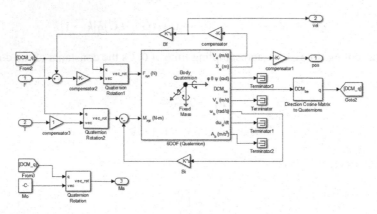

Fig. 4. Model. Dynamics of rigid body relating input forces-torques to position-orientation.

5.1 Saturation

Testing with saturation effect is presented in Figs. 5 and 6 as follows: Actual position [x, y, z] → [yellow, purple, aquamarine]; Reference position [x, y, z] → [red, green, blue].

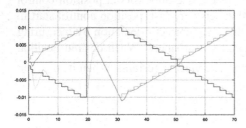

Fig. 5. Path 1 y-z plane. Position (m) versus time (s). (Color figure online)

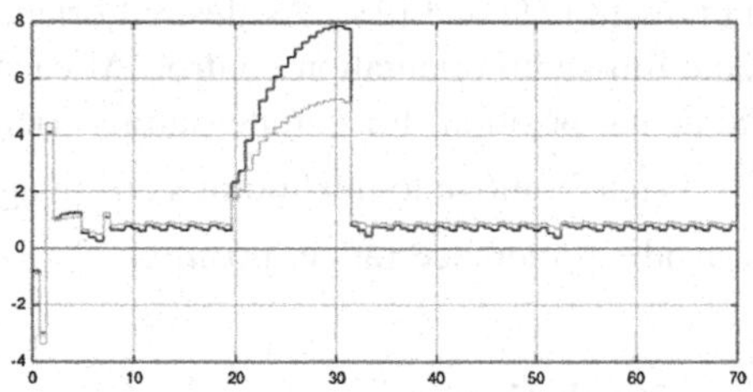

Fig. 6. Path 1. Current (A) versus time (s). Maxwell currents before saturation. (Color figure online)

Saturation is set to −2 and 2 A for the Maxwell currents. Relating Fig. 6 with 5, values that surpasses the saturation not fulfill gravity compensation on some intervals and spikes appear. On the other hand is expected, with no limits disturbance due to gravity on interval 0–5 s disappears and there is a reduction of time for reaching reference at 20–30 s.

5.2 Maxwell Influence

Maxwell influence and saturation is present and show in Figs. 7 and 8 can make the system not follow that good to the reference, by putting spikes. Reference changes as one-dimensional distance is reach even when position error remains. If Helmholtz currents are much larger than Maxwell's a decrease of Maxwell influence is done. The problem comes when Helmholtz current increase its approximation become less accuracy, Helmholtz coils begin to influence the actuation force showing in Fig. 8

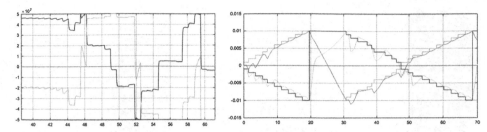

Fig. 7. Path 1. Orientation vector M (A/m) versus time (s)

Fig. 8. Path 1. Position (m) versus time (s). Duplicated Hh magnitude.

5.3 Model Constants Error

Other errors of constants of model will affect control but the main constant that relates current and force will be priority as it determines the error of the control as show on Figs. 9 and 10, Which showing a result of axis error.

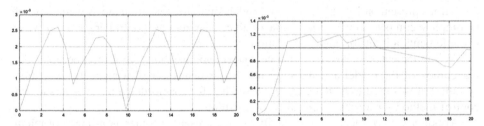

Fig. 9. Path 2. Position (m) versus time (s). Model constant uo*V with +10% of error

Fig. 10. Path 2. Position (m) versus time (s). Model constant Bf with +10% of error.

6   Results

Tested were carry out on x-y plane and these are represented as follow: Actual position [x, y] → [red, green]; Reference position [y, z] → [yellow, purple].

Figure 11 is showing a sequence of micro-robot trajectory and target positions. The blue crosses show some of the principal points set to be reach by the micro-robot creating a "S" trajectory.

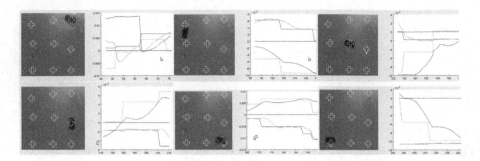

Fig. 11. Controller test. 'S' shape trajectory. Position (m) versus time (s). (Color figure online)

7 Conclusions

One of the limitations of the controller is that there is no correct gravity compensation while rotation occurs, only when desired orientation is reach compensation is correct. Also Maxwell influence sometimes causes high disorientations that cause spikes, plus quantization error and the saturation makes path tracking noisy. This a reason for little distortions present on Fig. 8. In addition, spikes on robot's position are as well cause of incomplete compensation at orientation z-values near zero the controller can improve if it implements a limit for angle orientation.

At implementation, spikes conduce system to instability probably because the inaccuracy of the model and the high non-linear behaviour of a magnetic levitating system that was tried to be done on 'z' axis. Therefore, is needed a more sophisticated control method for a robust control of 'z' position.

About x-y movement where gravity is not present, another non-linear problem emerges. Friction between robot and walls as well as changes on viscosity because wall-effects makes model observer not follow correctly the actual position causing that control do not work also at x-y when robot is at the bottom. By choosing a robot that can float in the surface of the medium, x-y control works well as presented.

On general 3D movement as explained on derivation of (21), allowed movements with its algorithms are only for certain planes. Also because disturbances and the lack of other feedback for full position measurement, 3D movement will tend to be incorrect as disturbances and errors accumulates. Also is important to remark the importance of characterization because model constants error will affect the effectiveness of the controller.

For future works and for enabling a full 3D path a solution can be from taking multi-point approximations and variable controller constants as well a more accurate and sophisticated observer that takes in account non-linear disturbances affected the robot.

Acknowledgement. This research was supported by the project Inv-Ing-2106 Nueva Granada Military University of Colombia.

References

1. Park, S., Cha, K., Park, J.-O.: Development of biomedical microrobot for intravascular therapy. Int. J. Adv. Robot. Syst. **7** (2010). https://doi.org/10.5772/7260
2. Nelson, B., Kaliakatsos, I., Abbott, J.: Microrobots for minimally invasive medicine. Ann. Rev. Biomed. Eng. **12**, 55–85 (2010). https://doi.org/10.1146/annurev-bioeng-010510-103409
3. Yim, S., Sitti, M.: Design and rolling locomotion of a magnetically actuated soft capsule endoscope (2012)
4. Ciuti, G., Valdastri, P., Menciassi, A., Dario, P.: Robotic magnetic steering and locomotion of capsule endoscope (2009)
5. Cowen, A.: The clinical risks of infection (2001)
6. Romagnuolo, J., Cotton, P., Eisen, G., Vargo, J., Petersen, B.: Identifying and reporting risk factors for adverse events in endoscopy (2011)
7. Purcell, E.M.: Life at Low Reynolds Number. AIP Publishing (1976)
8. Choi, H., et al.: Electromagnetic actuation system for locomotive intravascular therapeutic microrobot (2014)
9. Ha, V.L., et al.: Novel active locomotive capsule endoscope with micro-hydraulic pump for drug delivery function (2016)
10. Jeong, S., Choi, H., Young, S.K., Park, J.-O., Park, S.: Remote controlled micro-robots using electromagnetic actuation (2012)
11. Xu, T., Yu, J., Yan, X., Choi, H., Zhang, L.: Magnetic actuation based motion control for microrobots (2015)
12. Lee, C., et al.: Helical motion and 2D locomotion of magnetic capsule endoscope using precessional and gradient magnetic field (2014)
13. PHYWE series of publications: Magnetic field of paired coils in Helmholtz arrangement, Göttingen, Germany
14. Youk, H.: Numerical study of quadrupole magnetic traps for neutral atoms: anti-Helmholtz coils and a U-chip. Can. Undergraduate Phys. J. **3**, 13–18 (2005)

Visualization of Emotions Experienced in the Use of Immersive Augmented Reality Technologies for the Real Estate Sector

Daniel Esteban Casas-Mateus
and Nicole Valentina Chacon-Sanchez[✉]

Universidad Distrital Francisco José de Caldas, Bogotá, Colombia
{decasasm, nvchacons}@correo.uditrital.edu.co

Abstract. In this study an emotional analysis was made using a brain-computer interface called Emotiv Epoc+, in order to improve the access to real estate sector using immersive environments build through AutoCAD and Unity tools where from construction plans a real estate contour is made with the help of AutoCAD to later generate a 3D model thanks to the Unity tool with which the model real estate is represented; it was found that using this kind of environments increase 4 out of 5 emotions normalized levels, being these emotions Engagement, Frustration, Instantaneous Excitement y Long-Term Excitement, it is conclude that the costs of real estate enterprises could be decreased because they would not need to build a model house, additionally with the results of emotional analysis the user experience can be improved modifying the features of the immersive environment at the user's pleasure.

Keywords: Brain activity · Brain-computer interface · Emotional analysis · Emotions · Immersive environment · Modeling · Real estate · Simulation · Three-dimensional spaces · Virtual reality

1 Introduction

Throughout history, humanity has had the need to build and obtain housing as expressed by Barrio, García and Solis in their article (Barrio et al. 2011), even at present, this need is a social problem in which politics has been involved as explained by Rincon and Campo in his article (Camelo Rincon and Campo Robledo 2016). Real estate construction projects being defined as goods that cannot be transported from one place to another such as houses, apartments, buildings, among others (Editorial Cultura 2002), can be a complex task for the real estate sector, for the time of development and changes in demand, prices, costs, investment, among others (Forcael et al. 2013). Finally, a solution to these tasks according to studies developed by Govea and Maldonado (AutoDesk 2018) is to avoid the construction of real estate models of real estate projects by promoting the use of virtual reality, that it is called any technology that allows to simulate three-dimensional spaces and visualize them through a device (AutoDesk 2018).

J. C. Figueroa-García et al. (Eds.): WEA 2019, CCIS 1052, pp. 78–88, 2019.
https://doi.org/10.1007/978-3-030-31019-6_7

Additionally, the use of virtual reality technologies stimulates the behavioral activation (Herrero et al. 2013) of the user, for this reason a brain-computer interface is used to graphically visualize this behavior, these types of interfaces measure brain activity and is able to describe the interactions of humans with their environment (Minguez 2010), in this way register the user's brain activity. According to the above, the real estate sector can be benefited by involving in its projects the virtual reality to expose its model buildings, in this way to reduce costs, reduce construction times and analyze the connection that the end user has with the property.

In the following section, the characteristics of selection of tools and methodologies for the project that are used for the development of the proposal, which is explained in the section of materials and methods, that give way to the measurement of the immersive environment in where the tests and related results are described, delivering an analysis and quantifying them, to finally establish the future works and conclusions of this study.

2   Materials and Methods

2.1   General Approach

Figure 1 shows the general approach of the scenario to be worked, in which the AutoCAD tool is used to model the contour of the property to export it and work it in Unity, which is used as a tool for the implementation of the immersive environment where the end user You can enter, move and visualize the property, finally through Emotiv EPOC + an emotional analysis is made about the experience of the end user with the visualization of real estate.

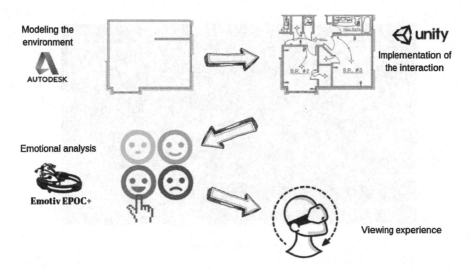

Fig. 1. General approach

2.2   Modeling the Contour of Real Estate

Through the modeling software AutoCAD, which is a 2D and 3D modeling software developed by Autodesk (AutoDesk 2019; Mora Ortiz and Medinilla Martinez 2015), the 3D model of the property is developed. Parameter is collected as square area, height of walls, number of rooms, number of bathrooms, number and location of windows, number and location of doors, among others, which establishes the scale of the model with these characteristics, which are specified in construction plans. The construction plans are always necessary and these are previously established in the construction, therefore no additional expenses are incurred.

For the modeling in this project, layers of walls, doors, windows and floor plans are taken into account with which AutoCAD works, as shown in Fig. 2.

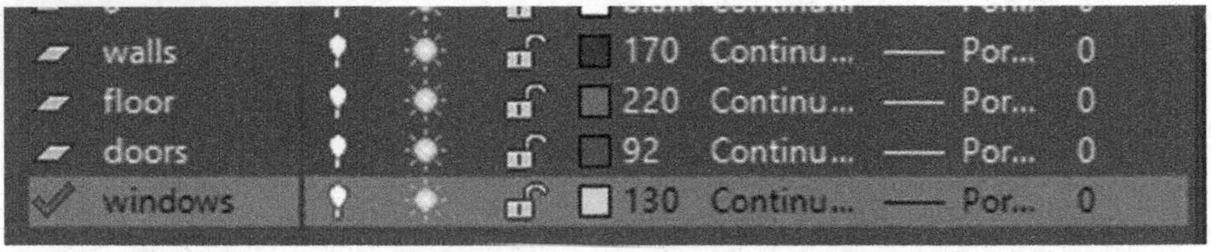

➤	walls	♀	☀	☐	☐	170	Continu...	—— Por...	0
➤	floor	♀	☀	☐	☐	220	Continu...	—— Por...	0
➤	doors	♀	☀	☐	☐	92	Continu...	—— Por...	0
✓	windows	♀	☀	☐	☐	130	Continu...	—— Por...	0

Fig. 2. AutoCAD features

These layers grant the privilege of creating, inserting, and modifying objects within each layer used to associate objects according to their function or location (AutoDesk 2018). For each layer the floor plan is modeled, the walls, windows and doors respectively, for this a 2D model is generated as shown in Fig. 3.

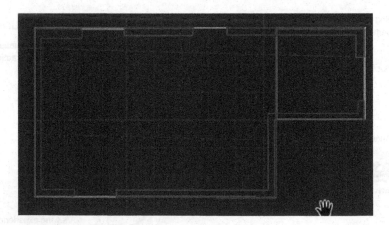

Fig. 3. AutoCAD contour

Finally the 2D drawings are taken to 3D modeling, climbing walls, locating doors and windows as shown in Fig. 4. Additionally these changes are seen in simultaneous modeling 2D to 3D since AutoCAD allows multiple windows and each window has configuration of views.

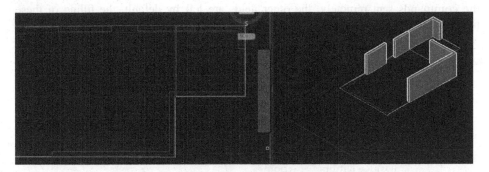

Fig. 4. AutoCAD 3D modeling

2.3 Implementation of the Interaction with Real Estate

With the model of the real estate made in AutoCAD, the implementation is carried out in Unity, which is a multiplatform video game engine created by Unity Technologies, for this specific case it is used in Microsoft Windows, it is important to clarify that after imported the model from AutoCAD to Unity no modification can be made to it, this model is presented in Fig. 5.

Fig. 5. Final 3D model

Regarding the development of the immersive environment, two tasks are carried out, the first the implementation of the keys or commands with which the movement is executed, and second the activation of the collisions in the imported model with the objective of not crossing walls and increasing reality in the user's experience.

For the implementation of movement commands in Unity we proceed to the creation of the two axes in which the end user can move, these are the vertical and horizontal, each of them are assigned to main and alternative navigation buttons, the type is button or mouse button, the Axis for the horizontal is "X axis" and for the vertical "Y axis", the Joy Num is "Get motion from all joysticks" so that later it detects the commands sent remotely, the other fields are left by default, the filling of these fields is seen in Fig. 6 for the case of the horizontal axis.

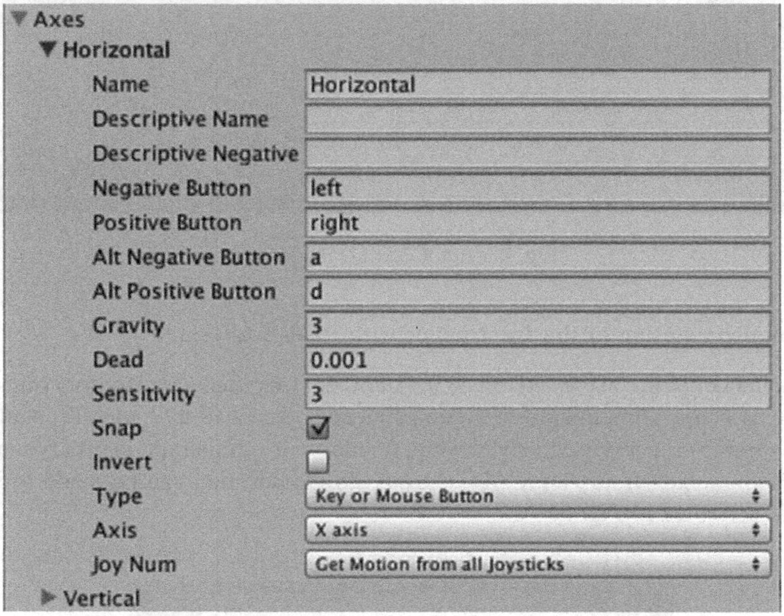

Fig. 6. Axes configuration

Now we proceed to the activation of the collisions for the imported model of AutoCAD, for this we must add a Mesh Collider to the object already mentioned, which is assigned the material and mesh as shown in Fig. 7.

Fig. 7. Collision configuration

With this, the Unity implementation for the immersive environment is finalized, which is seen as shown in Fig. 8, which shows a one-story building with doors and windows complemented by the lower flat, which for this case is the floor.

Fig. 8. Immersive environment

2.4   Emotional Analysis of the Viewing Experience

To carry out the visualization of the environment, we look for a tool with which we can have feedback, in such a way that there is a result both for the end user, who will see the property in the immersive environment and for the real estate who implements it to know the level of impact of the technology implemented.

To do this, a brain-computer interface is used, called Emotiv Epoc +, this is a non-invasive tool that aims to capture data related to the emotions experienced by the bearer, this device can be seen in Fig. 9.

Fig. 9. Emotiv Epoc+

In this case, the device is used in two moments, the first in which the end user visits a real model house carrying the brain-computer interface, where the real-time data of the emotions experienced is captured, for this capture and recording of data using the Zendesk tool, called Emotiv Xavier SDK, which allows to verify certain features of the device such as battery level and signal in addition to the emotions already mentioned.

Then the same exercise is done to visualize the model house through the immersive environment, where the same data is recorded to later perform an analysis.

3   Mesurement of the Inmersive Environment

Once the implementation has been completed, the tests are carried out, which are carried out in two stages, as shown in the presentation of Fig. 10.

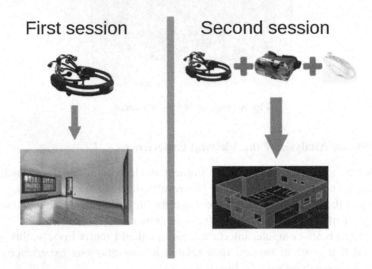

Fig. 10. Test scenario

Before carrying out the tests, the target group, the place of execution and the model implemented to perform the same dimensions as the real one are determined. As a place of execution is taken a building with apartments for sale where they had the authorization to use one of them, previously the model was developed to have it already installed in the application, externally 13 participants were summoned, who had no knowledge prior to the procedure that was carried out and they did not know each other.

In the first session the visit to a model home is made using the Emotiv Epoc+, where the user's feelings are captured from the detected brain waves, this process is visualized through the Emotiv Xavier SDK, which provides this option to see in real time and simultaneously perform the recording of data in flat files, these files are stored with time in milliseconds in which the capture is made and the normalized value, i.e. from 0 to 1, of each of the emotions, being these Engagement, Frustration, Meditation, Instantaneous Excitement and Long-Term Excitement.

In the second session the implementation developed in Unity is taken and exported in an APK (Android Application Package) to be installed in a cell phone with a minimum of 3 Gb of RAM (Random Access Memory) and 192 Mb of space either in internal storage or in memory SD (Secure Digital). Then via Bluetooth connects the cell phone with the device that performed the interaction, that for this case the joystick included with the augmented reality glasses is used, we proceed to open the application and install the cell phone inside the glasses for viewing, the installation is as shown in Fig. 11.

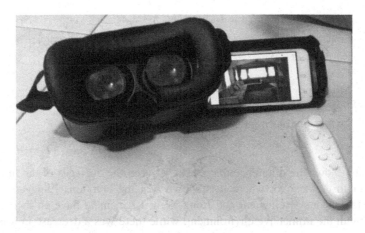

Fig. 11. Installation App and VR glasses

As in the previous session, the capture and visualization of the emotions is performed, graphically these are visualized in histograms, where the emotions to be displayed are selected and the update of each record is made in real time while parallel recording in flat files, in Fig. 12 an example of the histogram with some of the emotions is shown.

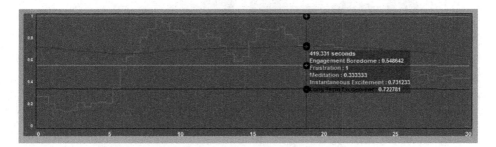

Fig. 12. Emotions histogram

It is important to clarify that none of the participants had knowledge of what was done by the others, in order to improve the final experience, and capture the records of the emotions without the participants being predisposed.

4   Results Analysis

After the tests are carried out, the captured data is analyzed individually, that is, first an analysis is carried out by each of the participants in their two experiences, separating each one of the experienced emotions, then all experiences are averaged. house real model and in another field for those experienced in the immersive environment for each emotion, obtaining the results presented in Table 1.

Table 1. Emotions averages

Emotion	Average first part	Average second part
Engagement	0.4899230	0.5289932
Frustration	0.4534791	0.4893909
Meditation	0.2353921	0.1896281
Instantaneous excitement	0.7380932	0.7583913
Long-term excitement	0.7201043	0.7303309

Figure 13 shows the difference that exists between the averages of the first session with respect to the second, where it is shown that the emotions Engagement, Frustration, Instantaneous Excitement and Long-Term Excitement have an increase when performed with the immersive environment, while there was a decrease in Meditation.

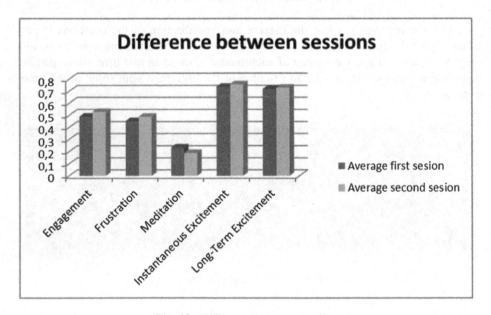

Fig. 13. Difference between sessions

On the other hand, the analysis is made by each individual where the difference value is found for each emotion and it is determined whether it increases or decreases, these results are expressed in Table 2.

Table 2. Emotion level movement

Emotion	Increment	Decrement
Engagement	8	5
Frustration	10	3
Meditation	4	9
Instantaneous excitement	9	4
Long-term excitement	8	5

Figure 14 shows through circular graphs the percentage of participants who had increased interaction with certain emotions and those who had a decrease for it, this process is performed for the five emotions.

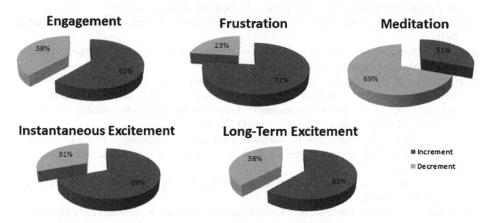

Fig. 14. Performance analysis

5   Conclusions and Future Works

As can be seen in the work presented for 4 of the 5 emotions, there is an increase when performing the activity with the brain-computer interface, with which it is seen that the impact on both instantaneous and long-term excitement has good results, based on these two emotions it is said that by using immersive technologies you can increase the connection of the property with the client as well as reduce costs for real estate if the model house does not exist and is created by technological means.

Regarding future works, studies are taken into account in which tools such as Sweet home 3D are implemented for the addition of objects with which the end user experience can be improved and thus generate more impact, as proposed in (Gonzalez Iparraguirre and Sanchez Vargas 2016) the creation of elements for the home so that the user can modify certain characteristics such as color and texture, on the other hand in (Ozakar and Ortakci 2017) the Sweet Home 3D add-on with web applications is used in which an analysis of the electricity consumption in real estate before being built using web information systems to obtain data directly, this analysis is done both quantitatively and graphically.

References

AutoDesk: 33 consejos que todo usuario de AutoCAD debe conocer (2018). https://damassets. autodesk.net/content/dam/autodesk/www/campaigns/mexico-lp/autocad/autocad-2019_33Tip s_Ebook_a4-landscape-es.pdf

AutoDesk: AutoCAD for Mac and Windows (2019). https://www.autodesk.es/products/autocad/ overview

Barrio, D., Garcia, S., Solis, J.: Management model for technological innovation in real estate. Revista ingeniería de construcción, pp. 353–368 (2011)

Camelo Rincon, M., Campo Robledo, J.: An Analysis of Housing Policy in Bogotá: A Supply and Demand Perspective. Revista Finanzas y Política Económica (2016)

Editorial Cultura, S.A.: Diccionario de Contabilidad de Finanzas. Editorial Cultura, S.A., Madrid (2002)

Forcael, E., Andalaft, A., Schovelin, R., Vargas, P.: Application of the real options valuation method to estate projects. Obras y Proyectos (2013)

Garcia Barreno, P.: Realidad Virtual: Nuevas experiencias sensoriales. Ediciones Nobel, S.A. (n.d.)

Gonzalez Iparraguirre, M., Sanchez Vargas, R.A.: Simulación web 3D de un departamento domotizado del grupo algol s.a.c para medir el consumo energético del aplicativo luminaria. Universidad Privada Antenor Orrego – UPAO (2016)

Herrero, R., Castillo, D., Vizcaiono, Y.: Analisis en el tratamiento psicologico de la fibromalgia: El uso de la realidad aumentada. Red de Revistas Científicas de América Latina y el Caribe, España y Portugal (2013)

Minguez, J.: Tecnologia de Interfaz Cerebro - Computador. Grupo de Rob otica, Percepcion y Tiempo Real (2010)

Mora Ortiz, L., Medinilla Martinez, N.: Herramienta para el diseño de escenografías en grupos de teatro universitario. Escuela Técnica Superior de Ingenieros Informáticos Universidad Politécnica de Madrid (2015)

Ozakar, K., Ortakci, Y.: A low-cost and lightweight 3D interactive real estate-purposed indoor virtual reality application. GeoAdvances (2017)

An Educational Strategy Based on Virtual Reality and QFD to Develop Soft Skills in Engineering Students

Bellanire Pinzón-Cristancho(iD), Hebert Alberto Calderón-Torres(iD),
Camilo Mejía-Moncayo(✉)(iD), and Alix E. Rojas(iD)

Universidad EAN, Calle 79 # 11-45, Bogotá, Colombia
{bpinzonc5764,hcaldero2890,cmejiam,aerojash}@universidadean.edu.co

Abstract. This work exposes an educational strategy based on gamification for the development of soft skills in engineering students, through the simulation of the process of product development based on QFD (Quality Function Deployment) in a virtual reality environment using "Second Life". The steps carried out in this work are explained starting from the proposal design process, followed by the development of the proposal and the evaluation. Finally, the findings showed that the proposal achieved their goals; thanks to that, the virtual environment furnished conditions very close to the QFD implementation in a company, which helped to promote positive interactions among students who overcame the apathy and fear among them and finished with a positive perception of the process.

Keywords: Virtual reality · Educational strategy · Gamification · Soft skills · QFD Quality Function Deployment · Engineering education

1 Introduction

The labor market in all fields of knowledge requires that professionals can achieve organizational objectives, overcoming difficulties, conflicts, and communication problems. However, this process goes beyond the hard skills which are generally developed in the curricula. Therefore, to achieve this is necessary the development of soft skills like integrity, communication, courtesy, responsibility, social skills, positive attitude, professionalism, flexibility, teamwork, and work ethic as is described by Robles [11]. These skills have been taking more importance in the curricula, due to their significant impact on projects success and organizations [7,10].

Soft skills could be difficult to learn and teach, due to exceeds the scope of traditional classes as is described by Pulko and Parikh [10], because soft skills requires the students in the event of activities where they must communicate, reach agreements, work as a team and interact positively to achieve the proposed objective, and clearly this scheme has no place in a master class. In this

© Springer Nature Switzerland AG 2019
J. C. Figueroa-García et al. (Eds.): WEA 2019, CCIS 1052, pp. 89–100, 2019.
https://doi.org/10.1007/978-3-030-31019-6_8

sense, it is necessary to use different methodologies and strategies to achieve their development. In particular, in the case of the training of engineers [7,10], which traditionally has been characterized by giving greater relevance to the development of hard skills, it is necessary to consider other strategies like gamification.

The gamification proposes the use of games to stimulate and have a direct interaction of the user with the environment in situations in which it does not commonly apply [8]. Allows optimizing the participation of users, involving participants in a more agile way concerning achieve the goals and increase the indicators of progress and improves the processes necessary for the success of the implementation of good practices in organizations [4].

In this sense, to facilitate its adoption, Oprescu et al. [9] propose that the gamification should be oriented to locate the user as the center of the experience, including active elements based on psychological and sound behavioral theories. Focusing work on the knowledge acquisition, skills development, motivation or behavior change, on personal and organizational well-being, in which experiences generate fun and attractive emotions, including elements of humor, play, and fun as part of work processes, balancing collaboration and competition in order to transform the existing work processes in the organization, to achieve collaborative efforts for the future and using knowledge either as a result and feedback for a justifiable and predictable return on investment.

Gamification complemented with virtual reality (VR), produces CVE (Collaborative Virtual Environment) which makes it possible to use methods of instruction different from traditional direct instruction, which allows students to develop more conventional notions. In which social interaction and collaborative work favor cognitive development, as well as the management of social skills [3]. CVE represents a unique means of communication, a predominantly visual technology that brings together people and remote objects in spatial proximity that facilitates interaction [13].

Another CVE advantage is that participants attention keeps in the task, without reality distractions, fostering much more focus on the job, compared to real life; scenarios are more straightforward than real life, because all objects fulfill a specific task [12].

In CVE each user uses an avatar (a graphic representation in the virtual world), by mean of which can to interact in the CVE. In a multiuser situation, the avatar is also the means that allows users to be aware of the presence of other [2]. On the other hand, with the use of an avatar, participants acquire absolute anonymity. The appearance of people is standardized in some way, and this could facilitate the interaction and the treatment among the participants avoiding the fear of face to face contact [12].

Quality Function Deployment QFD is a methodology developed in Japan in the late 1960s by Professors Shigeru Mizuno and Yoji Akao. QDF is a systematic planning process in which the voice of customers is considered translating their demands into design targets and quality assurance points [1]. Also, QFD helps to integrate and manage the elements necessary to define, design, and produce a product (or deliver a service) that could meet or exceed the client's needs [5]. The process set for QFD methodology has 4 phases:

- Phase I - Product planning: Consider the customer's requirements matrix versus the quality characteristics.
- Phase II - Design Planning: Consider the quality characteristics versus the characteristics of the components.
- Phase III - Process planning: Consider the characteristics of the components versus the characteristics of the process.
- Phase IV - Production planning: Considers the characteristics of the process versus the production requirements.

QFD estimates several aspects that should be considered concerning communication, product improvement, and documentation to achieve to obtain databases for future design and modifications. It provides a systematic process for designing and modifying products and services, reducing costs, and launch times for products or services, since errors and reprocesses are avoided in critical stages. Finally, customer satisfaction is increased by responding quickly and accurately to their needs and requirements [5]. The above processes require from participants' soft skills like teamwork, leadership, conflict managing, communication, achievement orientation, and others. Whereby QFD is an excellent tool to establish situations in which develop soft skills.

This paper exposes an educational strategy based on a virtual reality environment and gamification to the development of soft skills in engineering students by mean of the simulation of the design of products under the QFD methodology (Quality Function Deployment). Besides, the use of a virtual platform such as Second Life is more familiar to current students and reduces the difficulties associated with distance, time, and fear of face-to-face contact.

2   Proposal Design Process

The proposal design process carried out in this work was based on the method proposed by Gómez Alvarez et al. [6], and took into consideration a set of objectives and rules to establish the methodological steps which allow us to define the schedule for participants in the implementation, the design of the virtual reality environment, and the evaluation process. The methodology is summarized in the following steps:

- Step 1 - Initial identification: the primary purpose of this phase is identifying the qualitative and quantitative elements which allow focussing the proposal and determine the measurement instruments of it, considering the pedagogical objectives.
- Step 2 - Proposal design: considering the previous step, the main elements of the proposal are decided. Regarding the following aspects:
  - Process: What will be done? Nature of the action.
  - Object: About what? About what the process will work.
  - Location: Where? Geographic or local location.
- Step 3 - Phase of implementation or execution: the implementation of the actions proposed in the previous stage from the implementation of the developed in a virtual reality application.

- Step 4 - Final evaluation: analyze and evaluate the improvement of students' abilities once they complete the process through the developed application.

In order to develop the first methodological step, the following pedagogical objectives were considered:

- Understand the importance of defining a plan for the development of a project.
- Recognize the importance of collaborative work, taking into account the need to establish standards or conditions before the execution stage.
- Strengthen teamwork by assigning roles and responsibilities (selecting roles) based on the recognition of environmental conditions, and also knowing the importance of ongoing communication between the members of the team.
- Identify the characteristics and strengths of each team member to assign roles and responsibilities.

Besides, a set of rules was considered in this proposal to promote and encourage collaboration among the participants. In it, each of the participants is part of a board of directors of a company in Second Life that wants to develop a new audio technology product but does not know how to do it according to the needs of customers. Considering those as mentioned earlier, the first house of QFD methodology is implemented, and the sections in which the teamwork enters into participate are described as follow:

- Setting the goal: characteristics must meet the product.
- Establish the list of WHAT?: characteristics of the product that customers want.
- Assign weight coefficients to WHAT?: values in order of importance.
- Evaluation of the competition: evaluate the degree of excellence achieved by the competitors in each of the WHAT? (Benchmarking competitive market).
- Identify the possible HOW?: look for a way to achieve WHAT? (technical characteristics)
- Analysis of the HOW?: analyze how the "HOWs" influence and the correlations that exist between them.
- Assignment of relationship coefficients: assign coefficients of the relationship between the "WHATs" and "HOWs."
- Hierarchize the HOW?: rate each of the "HOW'S" and rank them.
- Technical competitive Evaluation. evaluate the degree of excellence achieved by competitors in each of the HOW?

The schedule established for participants in the implementation include 5 min to choose the role (see Table 1) they will play during the meeting of the board of directors and can communicate orally or through the platform chat to define strategies, criteria and decision making to follow in terms of: activities to be carried out (assignment of coefficients, definition of HOWs, among others) and leader assignment or responsible for the team. The participants have the following times according to each stage:

- Assign weight coefficients to the WHAT ?: 10 min
- Identify the possible HOW?: 10 min
- Analysis of the HOW: 20 min
- Assignment of coefficients of relationship: 15 min
- Hierarchy the HOW: 5 min

Table 1. Participants roles

Role	Skills	Functions
Leader 1	Leadership, Communication, Proactivity, Organization, Empathy, Assertiveness, Respect	To orient the activity. Evaluate the performance of the participants and the development of the event. Provide technical support during the development of the game
Leader 2	Leadership, Communication, Proactivity, Organization, Empathy, Assertiveness, Respect	It moderates the implementation of the proposal. It indicates the rules to be into account for the implementation of the plan, such as times, media, and others. It manages the documentation loaded on the platform, updating the matrix during each of its stages
Financial Manager	Critical Thinking, Communication, Discipline, Creativity, Initiative, Intuition, Planning and negotiation capacity, Teamwork, Leadership	It participates in the board of directors as a commercial or financial manager, focusing their decisions to the strategic planning of the company that evaluates the viability of the proposals according to administrative, economic, business and operational criteria
Marketing Manager	Leadership, Assertive communication, Respect, Creativity, Teamwork	It participates of the board of directors as marketing manager, focuses their decisions towards the traditional target market and the potentials to which the product can be offered, validating its feasibility, viability, market behavior and the means under which marketing and advertising can be carried out effectively and with results

(continued)

Table 1. *(continued)*

Role	Skills	Functions
Production Manager	Leadership, Assertive communication, Respect, Conciliator, Teamwork, Attention to detail to ensure that the product check is optimal, Ability to prioritize and manage different projects, Ability to analyze and resolve process-related problems, Decision-making under pressure situations	It participates in the board of directors as production manager, the focus of its decisions must be oriented towards production planning, taking into account criteria such as supply and demand, types of processes, projections, machinery and technology, capacity, process times, production strategies, bottlenecks, facility layout, location, labor, costs, equilibrium point and inventories
Supplies Purchase Manager	Organization, Negotiation, Leadership, Assertive communication, Empathy, Negotiation, Analysis, Respect, Critical thinking, Teamwork	To participate in the board of directors as supplies purchase manager, need the focus of its decisions should be oriented towards planning, management, procurement supplies, specifically raw material, and other resources Require for the production process, control of suppliers and flow of money and information
Logistics Manager	Organization, Leadership, Teamwork, Analytical capacity, Adaptability, Assertive communication, Critical thinking, Decision-making under pressure situations	It participates in the board of directors as a logistics manager, focuses their decisions must be oriented towards the management and control of inventories, distribution, delivery of products, planning, and costs
Quality Assurance Manager	Organization, Leadership, Teamwork, Analytical capacity	It participates in the board of directors as a quality assurance manager, focus their decisions must be oriented towards the fulfillment of the requirements and requirements of the products as requested by the clients, customer satisfaction, measurement and Evaluation of the processes, and continuous improvement of the productive process of the Organization in general

Fig. 1. Virtual environment

3   Development of the Proposal

The process carried out by the participants initially included determining a base product, an objective market, and a market study. Once this has been carried out, the results of this last one are the scenario where the different participants interact to make decisions based on previous activities such as the identification and analysis of data and technical and strategic aspects of both types. Quantitative as qualitative, since the aim is to dimension an environment as close as possible to the real business and labor life in the industrial and productive world.

The explanation of the case, rules, methodology, and objectives was made before the activity through audio on the platform. The participants start visualizing the virtual environment and the layout of the first house of the QFD matrix with their respective sections. The virtual environment and the QFD matrix can be seen in Figs. 1 and 2.

The participants start by choosing a humanoid avatar according to the role it will have within the proposal (see Fig. 3), which will be its graphic representation within the platform, then its user name; Next they must download and install the software on the computer (if applicable), enter the platform with their username and password, perform the basic travel tutorials. Once the above is done, they can communicate through a chat, which allows them to socialize and make decisions about the action plan to be executed. When the previous activities have been carried out, the virtual scenario of the proposal begins.

The avatar of the users is in the first person, that is, the participants can not see themselves, just as it happens in real life, the participant can only observe their extremities (arms and legs). The user-name is displayed in the top of the avatar to facilitate identification (see Fig. 4).

In the scenario, users can carry out different actions: select objects, manipulate selected objects, navigate and talk, among others. The different types of

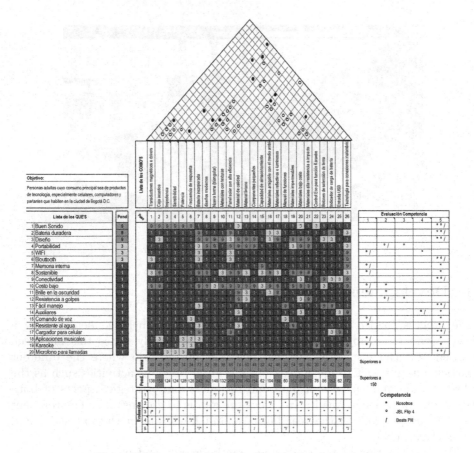

Fig. 2. QFD matrix developed in the implementation

navigation of the avatars are: (a) walking, that is, when the user is on the ground, (b) flying, that is, when the user is in the air, (c) swimming, that is, when the user is in the water, (d) teleporting through portals, (e) displacement to specific places through the main browser or through a particular URL. These movements are executed employing the mouse and the arrows of the keyboard.

During the process, users will have access to the rules of the game, the explanation of virtual platform, the explanation diagram of how the matrix should be completed and the virtual scenario seen from different perspectives to identify the area of work and the parts of the matrix.

Participants developed the matrix on the platform by verbal communication and once completed the completion of the matrix; it will be possible to evaluate the members of the work team and compare the plan of the strategy initially proposed with the activities that were carried out (development/execution).

Fig. 3. Avatars

Fig. 4. Participants meeting at CVE.

4   Evaluation

The evaluation had two approaches. Firstly, the soft skills of participants demonstrated during the activity in the developing of its role is assessed quantitatively. Secondly, the participants evaluate the activity and the contributions that it gave them qualitatively.

A rubric was developed for assessing the participants. It includes the skills defined for the role and a scale to asses the performance from the perception of the leaders 1 and 2 and comments; an example is described in Table 2. In the activity evaluation, each participant exposes their opinions and feelings about the process, self-evaluation, and provide recommendations to improve the activity.

Table 2. Example of role evaluation

Role: Quality Assurance Manager	
Qualify the performance of the participant in the role from 0 to 10 Taking into consideration that:	
If not is possible, identify evidence of the skill in the participant [0]	
It is deficient the skill level demonstrated by the participant [1–3]	
It is medium the skill level demonstrated by the participant [4–6]	
It is competent the skill level demonstrated by the participant [7–9]	
It is excellent the skill level demonstrated by the participant [10]	
Skill	Performance
Organization	
Leadership	
Teamwork	
Analytical capacity	
Comments:	

5   Findings

Once the activity finished and the evaluation tests were carried out, it was possible to find the following findings:

The participants were pleased by the work produced, and a positive perception of them was registered, there was clarity in the subject, and the communication was excellent under an atmosphere of respect and coordination in which pedagogical objectives were fulfilled.

The leader was chosen among the participants, and its plan for the activity was assertive, due to its constant accompaniment during the event. In the same way made the performance evaluation of the participants, to measure their participation and commitment assumed throughout the exercise.

The time was similar to the scheduled (one hour and 10 min) since in some stages it took more time than established, which generated decision making under pressure. However, each one of the steps described previously up to the evaluation was made. Take into account that this work was planned to develop the first house of the QFD matrix through a collaborative virtual reality environment, in the case to cover complete QFD matrix it is necessary to consider several sessions.

It is recommended to do more tests with this type of media as it allows to simulate real-life situations saving costs and promoting teamwork and the use of new technologies in business and industrial environments.

6   Conclusions

An educational strategy is exposed in this work, which, by mean of a collaborative virtual environment and the implementation of the QFD methodology, achieves the development of soft skills in engineering students.

The CVE had visual elements that allow students to simulate a real-world situation such as the design of a product. In a way that is closer to them.

Besides, the CVE implemented in "Second Life" allows the students to carry out the activity in a stable, safe, practical, reliable, and charming way. The event generated benefits for the participants, promoting learning and the interest of them for wanting to know more about the subject.

QFD is an advantageous methodology to design products or services. Due that QFD contemplates from the needs of the client to the design quality plan of the production system. Also, their characteristics forced to a constant interaction of the participants.

The results obtained during the execution of the activity was as expected, and the proposed objectives were achieved.

References

1. Akao, Y.: Quality Function Deployment: Integrating Customer Requirements into Product Design. Productivity Press (1990)
2. Çapin, T.K., Pandzic, I.S., Thalmann, D., Thalmann, D., Thalmann, N.M.: Realistic avatars and autonomous virtual humans in VLNET networked virtual environments (1998)
3. Chittaro, L., Ranon, R.: Web3D technologies in learning, education and training: motivations, issues, opportunities. Comput. Educ. **49**(1), 3–18 (2007). https://doi.org/10.1016/j.compedu.2005.06.002
4. Dorling, A., McCaffery, F.: The gamification of SPICE. Commun. Comput. Inf. Sci. **290 CCIS**, 295–301 (2012)
5. Franco, C.A.: La integración de las necesidades del cliente en los productos y servicios de la empresa. Estudios Gerenciales **73**, 33–42 (1999)
6. Gasca-Hurtado, G.P., Peña, A., Gómez-Álvarez, M.C., Plascencia-Osuna, Ó.A., Calvo-Manzano, J.A.: Realidad virtual como buena práctica para trabajo en equipo con estudiantes de ingeniería. RISTI - Revista Iberica de Sistemas e Tecnologias de Informacao (16), 76–91 (2015). https://doi.org/10.17013/risti.16.76-91
7. Kumar, S., Hsiao, J.K.: Engineers learn "Soft Skills the Hard Way": planting a seed of leadership in engineering classes. Leadersh. Manag. Eng. **7**(1), 18–23 (2006)
8. Lee, J., Hammer, J.: Gamification in education: what, how, why bother? Acad. Exch. Quart. **15**(2), 1–5 (2015)
9. Oprescu, F., Jones, C., Katsikitis, M.: I PLAY AT WORK-ten principles for transforming work processes through gamification. Front. Psychol. **5**, 14 (2014). https://doi.org/10.3389/fpsyg.2014.00014
10. Pulko, S.H., Parikh, S.: Teaching 'Soft' skills to engineers. Int. J. Electr. Eng. Educ. **40**(4), 243–254 (2013). https://doi.org/10.7227/ijeee.40.4.2
11. Robles, M.M.: Executive perceptions of the top 10 soft skills needed in today's workplace. Bus. Commun. Quart. **75**(4), 453–465 (2012). https://doi.org/10.1177/1080569912460400

12. Schroeder, R.: Being There Together: Social Interaction in Virtual Environments. Oxford University Press, Oxford (2011)
13. Wolff, R., et al.: Communicating eye gaze across a distance without rooting participants to the spot. In: 2008 12th IEEE/ACM International Symposium on Distributed Simulation and Real-Time Applications, pp. 111–118. IEEE, October 2008. https://doi.org/10.1109/DS-RT.2008.28

Rotation of Sound Fields Which Are Represented by Means of a Plane Wave Expansion

Diego Mauricio Murillo Gómez[1]([⊠]) and Filippo Maria Fazi[2]

[1] Universidad de San Buenaventura, Medellín 08544, Colombia
diego.murillo@usbmed.edu.co
[2] University of Southampton, Southampton SO17 1BJ, UK
http://www.usbmed.edu.co

Abstract. The synthesis of sound fields by means of planes waves is a widely used approach in auralization. In this paper, two methods for rotating acoustic fields, which are represented by this propagating kernel are investigated. For this, numerical simulations of acoustic fields that satisfy the homogeneous Helmholtz equation are performed. From this data, rotation algorithms are derived based on a spherical harmonic transformation and vector base amplitude panning functions. The results indicate that both methods are suitable for the generation of a rotation operator when the sound field is represented by means of plane waves. Nevertheless, the use of spherical harmonics leads to more accurate sound field reconstruction as long as the number of coefficients is equal to the number of plane waves considered in the expansion.

Keywords: Plane wave expansion · Rotation · Spherical harmonics · VBAP

1 Introduction

Auralization is a subject of high scientific interest due to its extensive applications in areas such as research and consultancy [1–3]. In that sense, the development of new methods for interactive spatial sound reproduction that allows a more realistic hearing experience is desired. Binaural reproduction can be achieved by using headphones or loudspeakers with crosstalk cancellation [4]. Arrays of loudspeakers can be also implement to synthesize the acoustic field based on spatial reproduction techniques such as Ambisonics or Wave Field Synthesis [5].

A methodology commonly used to reconstruct acoustic fields that satisfy the homogenous Helmholtz equation is based on a Plane Wave Expansion (PWE) [6]. This mathematical representation allows for the use of multiple sound reproduction techniques and the generation of interactive auralizations in which the listener can interact with the virtual space [7]. For example, translation can be

© Springer Nature Switzerland AG 2019
J. C. Figueroa-García et al. (Eds.): WEA 2019, CCIS 1052, pp. 101–113, 2019.
https://doi.org/10.1007/978-3-030-31019-6_9

simply achieved by the application of delays that modify the phase of the planes waves according to the listener's movement [8].

In terms of rotation, several methods can be implemented for a plane wave expansion. The interpolation of Head Related Transfer Functions (HRTFs) is a widely used methodology by the scientific community, but it is restricted only for binaural reproduction [9]. Other approaches that enable multiple sound reproduction techniques are spherical harmonics [10] and Vector Base Amplitude Panning [11]. An analysis of these two last methods as rotation operators is presented in this paper.

The paper is organized as follows: the theoretical bases of the plane wave expansion and the derivation of the rotation operators are described in Sect. 2. Section 3 addresses the methods and experiments. An analysis of the outcomes is carried out in Sect. 4. Finally, in Sect. 5, the conclusions are presented.

2   Theoretical Bases

2.1   Plane Wave Expansion

A sound field that satisfy the homogenous Helmholtz equation can be described in terms of plane waves as [7]

$$p(\mathbf{x},\omega) = \int_{\widehat{\mathbf{y}}\in\Omega} e^{jk\mathbf{x}\cdot\widehat{\mathbf{y}}} q(\widehat{\mathbf{y}},\omega) d\Omega(\widehat{\mathbf{y}}), \tag{1}$$

where j is the imaginary unit, k is the wavenumber, $\mathbf{x}$ corresponds to the evaluation point, $\widehat{\mathbf{y}}$ is a unit vector identifying the direction of arrival of each plane wave, q is the amplitude density function and Ω denotes a sphere of unitary radius. This continuous distribution can be related to an infinite number of loudspeakers that are located far from the listener's location. Nevertheless, in terms of implementation, the use of an infinite number of loudspeakers is not feasible so Eq. 1 must be discretized in a finite number of L plane waves leading to

$$p(\mathbf{x},\omega) = \sum_{l=1}^{L} e^{jk\mathbf{x}\cdot\widehat{\mathbf{y}}_l} q(\widehat{\mathbf{y}}_l,\omega) \Delta\Omega_l, \tag{2}$$

in which $\Delta\Omega$ is the area attributed to each direction $\widehat{\mathbf{y}}_l$. A consequence of discretizing equation is the local dependency on the accuracy of the reconstructed acoustic field. In that sense, [12] propose the following relation between the number of plane waves, the frequency of the field and the area of accurate reconstruction

$$L = \left(\left\lceil 2\pi \frac{R}{\lambda} \right\rceil + 1 \right)^2, \tag{3}$$

where $\lceil \cdot \rceil$ is the ceiling round operator, L is the number of plane waves, λ is the wavelength and R is the radius of a sphere within which the reconstruction is accurate. Finally, it is important to point out that the use of plane waves as kernel of propagation imposes constrains such as the reconstruction of near acoustic fields.

2.2   Rotation Operators

Spherical Harmonics

The spherical harmonics are the angular component of the solution of the wave equation when it is expressed in spherical coordinates. For an interior case, in which there are not acoustic sources inside of the reconstructed area, the acoustic pressure is given by [13]

$$p(\mathbf{r}, \omega) = \sum_{n=0}^{\infty} \sum_{m=-n}^{n} A_{nm}(\omega) j_n(kr) Y_n^m(\theta, \phi), \tag{4}$$

where j_n is the spherical Bessel function of the first kind of order n and $Y_n^m(\theta, \phi)$ are the spherical harmonics defined by as

$$Y_n^m(\theta, \phi) = \sqrt{\frac{(2n+1)}{4\pi} \frac{(n-m)!}{(n+m)!}} P_n^m(\cos\theta) e^{jm\phi}, \tag{5}$$

in which P_n^m is the Legendre associated function. The discretized plane wave expansion, namely Eq. (2), can be described in terms of spherical harmonics using the Jacobi-Anger expansion as [14]

$$\sum_{n=0}^{\infty} \sum_{m=-n}^{n} A_{nm}(\omega) j_n(kr) Y_n^m(\theta, \phi) =$$

$$4\pi \sum_{l=1}^{L} q_l(\omega) \sum_{n=0}^{\infty} j^n j_n(kr) \sum_{m=-n}^{n} Y_n^m(\theta, \phi) Y_n^m(\theta_l, \phi_l)^* d\Omega(\widehat{y}_l), \tag{6}$$

where $(\cdot)^*$ denotes the complex conjugate. Based on the orthogonality relation of the spherical harmonics, Eq. (6) can be simplified as

$$A_{nm}(\omega) = 4\pi \sum_{l=1}^{L} \sum_{n=0}^{\infty} \sum_{m=-n}^{n} j^n q_l(\omega) Y_n^m(\theta_l, \phi_l)^* d\Omega(\widehat{y}_l). \tag{7}$$

Equation (7) describes the plane wave expansion in terms of complex spherical harmonic coefficients. Based on this representation, it is possible to implement a sound field operator and return to the plane wave domain after the rotation has been performed. A shifting in the azimuthal plane of ϕ_0 can be expressed as

$$p(r, \theta, \phi - \phi_0, \omega) = \sum_{n=0}^{\infty} \sum_{m=-n}^{n} A_{nm}(\omega) j_n(kr) Y_n^m(\theta, \phi - \phi_0). \tag{8}$$

Expanding the right side of Eq. (8)

$$p(r, \theta, \phi - \phi_0, \omega) =$$

$$\sum_{n=0}^{\infty} \sum_{m=-n}^{n} A_{nm}(\omega) j_n(kr) \sqrt{\frac{(2n+1)}{4\pi} \frac{(n-m)!}{(n+m)!}} P_n^m(\cos\theta) e^{jm\phi} e^{-jm\phi_0}, \tag{9}$$

yields

$$p(r, \theta, \phi - \phi_0, \omega) = \sum_{n=0}^{\infty} \sum_{m=-n}^{n} j_n(kr) Y_n^m(\theta, \phi) A_{\phi_0 nm}(\omega), \qquad (10)$$

in which

$$A_{\phi_0 nm}(\omega) = A_{nm}(\omega) e^{-jm\phi_0}. \qquad (11)$$

Equation (11) indicates that the rotation of the sound field in the azimuthal plane can be performed by taking the product between the complex spherical harmonic coefficients and a complex exponential, which argument depends on the angle of rotation. A decoding approach can be performed to return to the plane wave domain after the rotation has been conducted [14]. This is achieved by truncating the spherical harmonic series, namely Eq. (7), to an order N.

$$A_{nm}(\omega) = 4\pi \sum_{l=1}^{L} \sum_{n=0}^{N} \sum_{m=-n}^{n} j^n q_l(\omega) Y_n^m(\theta_l, \phi_l)^* d\Omega(\hat{\mathbf{y}}_l), \qquad (12)$$

for $n = 0...N$ and $|m| \leq n$. This is a finite set of linear equations that can be solved in terms of the least squares solution by formulating an inverse problem [14]. In order to have at least one solution, the number of spherical harmonic coefficients $(N+1)^2$ is required to be lower than, or equal to, the number of plane waves, namely $L \geq (N+1)^2$. Equation (12) can be written in matrix notation as

$$\mathbf{a} = \mathbf{Yq}. \qquad (13)$$

The relation between the number of spherical harmonic coefficients and the number of plane waves defines the dimensions of matrix $\mathbf{Y}$. For the case of $L > (N+1)^2$, the problem is overdetermined yielding a matrix that is not squared. The solution for $\mathbf{q}$ is given by

$$\mathbf{q} = \mathbf{Y}^{\dagger} \mathbf{a}, \qquad (14)$$

where $(\cdot)^{\dagger}$ indicates the Moore-Penrose pseudo-inverse (L2 Norm).

Vector Base Amplitude Panning (VBAP):
VBAP is a sound reproduction technique based on the formulation of amplitude panning functions as vectors and vector basis. It allows the incoming direction of a wave to be controlled over a unit sphere. For 3D sound reproduction, a set of three loudspeakers closest to the target incoming direction are selected to reproduce the sound. In that sense, the sound field generated by a PWE can be rotated in the azimuthal plane by ϕ degrees simply by shifting the plane waves in the opposite direction of the orientation of the listener.

$$p(\mathbf{x}_{\text{rotated}}, \omega) = \sum_{l=1}^{L} e^{jk\mathbf{x} \cdot \hat{\mathbf{y}}_{(l-\phi)}} q(\hat{\mathbf{y}}_{(l-\phi)}, \omega) \Delta\Omega_{(l-\phi)}, \qquad (15)$$

These rotated plane waves can be recreated by using multiple sets of three different plane waves, whose incoming directions are restricted to the directions established by the original discretized plane wave expansion. This means that for each plane wave of the PWE, a set of three planes waves must be used to generate the rotated version. The amplitude weightings of each set of three plane waves are estimated by means of an inverse method. The formulation to rotate one plane wave is presented as follows (same principle applies for the remaining plane waves) [15].

The direction of the target "rotated" plane wave direction is determined by the unit vector $\widehat{\mathbf{y}} = [y_1, y_2, y_3]^T$. Likewise, the amplitude weightings of the three plane waves used to generate this "rotated" plane wave are represented by the vector $\mathbf{q} = [q_1, q_2, q_3]^T$. Finally, the matrix that contains the direction of the three selected plane waves closest to the target incoming direction is denoted as $\mathbf{L} \in \mathbb{R}^{(3 \times 3)}$, in which the coordinates of each plane wave are determined by each column of the matrix i.e. $\mathbf{l}_1 = \mathbf{L}(:, 1)$. Therefore, the following relation is established

$$\widehat{\mathbf{y}} = \mathbf{Lq}, \tag{16}$$

whose solution for $\mathbf{q}$ is given by

$$\mathbf{q} = \mathbf{L}^{-1}\widehat{\mathbf{y}}. \tag{17}$$

In addition, the amplitude weightings are normalized based on a coherent summation in which the sum lead to unity, namely,

$$\mathbf{q}_{\text{normalized}} = \frac{\mathbf{q}}{q_1 + q_2 + q_3}. \tag{18}$$

3   Methods and Results

Numerical simulations have been conducted in Matlab to evaluate the performance of the rotation operators. Firstly, a sound field corresponding to a plane wave of 250 Hz coming from an elevation ($\theta = 90$) and azimuth angles of ($\phi = 45, 170$) were analytically synthesized in a free field domain with dimensions of $5\,\text{m} \times 10\,\text{m} \times 3\,\text{m}$. Samples of the sound fields were extracted by using a cubic virtual microphone array with linear dimensions of 1.6 m and a spatial resolution of 0.2 m (729 microphone positions). This information was used to estimate the complex amplitude of a PWE by means of an inverse method. The number of plane waves was chosen to be ($L = 64$) because it corresponds to the number of complex spherical harmonic coefficients for an order ($N = 7$), which facilitates the implementation and assessment of the rotation operators.

Figure 1 shows the comparison between the real part of the analytical (A) and the reconstructed (B) acoustic pressure (Pa) in a cross-section of the domain ($z = 1.5\,\text{m}$). The black circle corresponds to the area of expected accurate reconstruction by solving Eq. (3) for R. The results indicate that the plane wave expansion is able to accurately synthesize the target acoustic field, but as expected, only within a specify area of the domain. Good match between the area of accurate reconstruction and the radius predicted by Eq. 3 was also found.

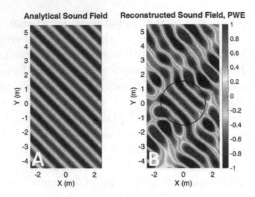

Fig. 1. Acoustic field reconstructed by means of a plane wave expansion ($L = 64$). Target field corresponds to a plane wave coming from ($\theta = 90$) and ($\phi = 45$).

Two cases have been evaluated. The first corresponds to the plane wave incoming from $\theta = 90$ and $\phi = 45$, which is rotated by $\phi_0 = 45°$. The second case is the plane wave incoming from $\theta = 90$ and $\phi = 170$, which is rotated by $\phi_0 = 60°$.

3.1 Rotation by Means of Spherical Harmonics

Based on the reconstructed acoustic field illustrated in Fig. 1B, a shift of 45° and 60° in the azimuthal angle was carried out to evaluate the rotation of sound fields using a description in terms of spherical harmonics. Figure 2 illustrates a diagram of the implementation.

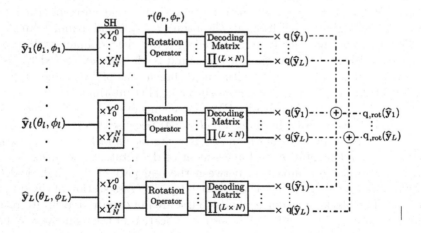

Fig. 2. Diagram of the implementation of the spherical harmonic rotation operator.

Figures 3 and 4 show the reconstructed acoustic pressure compared to their analytical references. (A) corresponds to the initial reference sound field, (B) is the reconstructed sound field by the plane wave expansion, (C) is the reference rotated sound field and (D) is the reconstructed and rotated sound field by the implementation of a spherical harmonic transformation.

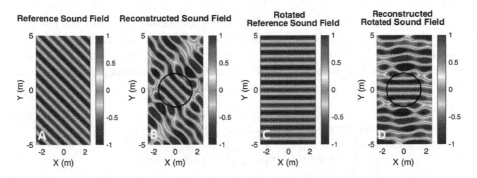

Fig. 3. Rotation of an acoustic field by means of spherical harmonics. The reference sound field is a plane wave coming from ($\theta = 90$) and ($\phi = 45$). The rotation angle corresponds to ($\phi_0 = 45$).

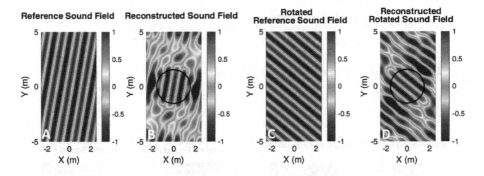

Fig. 4. Rotation of an acoustic field by means of spherical harmonics. The reference sound field is a plane wave coming from ($\theta = 90$) and ($\phi = 170$). The rotation angle corresponds to ($\phi_0 = 60$).

Results confirm the suitability of the spherical harmonic transformation to rotate the acoustic field. No relevant differences were found between the acoustic fields of the plots (B) and (D) close to the central point of the expansion, which indicates that rotation of the sound field using spherical harmonics does not affect the initial accuracy achieved by discretized plane wave expansion, namely the radius predicted by Eq. (3). However, this statement is true only if the number of spherical harmonic coefficients is equal to the number of plane waves, $(N+1)^2 = L$. Otherwise, the area of accurate reconstruction is reduced according to the number of spherical harmonic coefficients implemented.

3.2   Rotation by Means of VBAP

An implementation based on VBAP has been carried out to rotate the acoustic field in the plane domain directly. Figure 5 describes the signal processing flow of the algorithm. A comparison between rotated acoustic fields using VBAP and their analytical references is presented in Figs. 6 and 7. Same angles implemented for the spherical harmonic case has been considered.

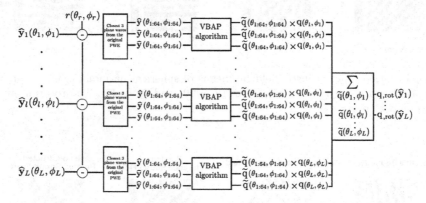

Fig. 5. Diagram of the implementation of the VBAP rotation operator.

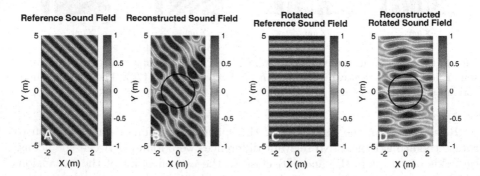

Fig. 6. Rotation by means of VBAP. The reference sound field is a plane wave coming from $(\theta = 90)$ and $(\phi = 45)$. The rotation angle corresponds to $(\phi_0 = 45)$.

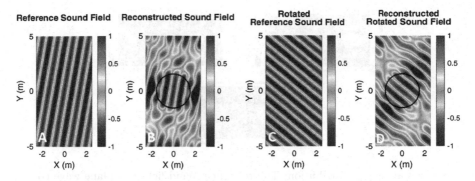

Fig. 7. Rotation of an acoustic field by means of VBAP. The reference sound field is a plane wave coming from ($\theta = 90$) and ($\phi = 170$). The rotation angle corresponds to ($\phi_0 = 60$).

The results indicate that VBAP is also a suitable approach to perform the rotation of acoustic fields, which are described by a plane wave expansion. Nevertheless, a more robust analysis is performed in the following section to compare both approaches.

4   Metrics for Performance

In this section, a comparison of the rotation methods is conducted by means of the spatial distribution of the energy in the plane wave expansion, the energy required for the synthesis of the acoustic field and normalized error.

4.1   Spatial Distribution of the Energy

An analysis of the spatial distribution of the energy has been conducted to assess whether the rotation operator affects its integrity. The PWE is discretized by means of an "uniform" sampling so it is expected that this spatial distribution should not change. Figures 8 and 9 show the interpolated energy density function q plotted over an unwrapped unit sphere for the two cases considered. (A) corresponds to the initial spatial energy distribution of the PWE, (B) is the spatial energy distribution of the PWE after rotation has been performed using spherical harmonics and (C) is the spatial energy distribution of the PWE after rotation has been performed using VBAP.

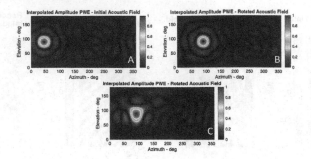

Fig. 8. Spatial energy distribution. The reference sound field is a plane wave coming from $(\theta = 90)$ and $(\phi = 45)$. The rotation angle corresponds to $(\phi_0 = 45)$.

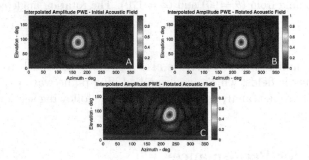

Fig. 9. Spatial energy distribution. The reference sound field is a plane wave coming from $(\theta = 90)$ and $(\phi = 170)$. The rotation angle corresponds to $(\phi_0 = 60)$.

Outcomes indicate that the energy is mainly focused on the direction in which rotation has been performed. Nevertheless, the spatial distribution of the energy of the PWE tends to remain unmodified in the case of the spherical harmonic rotation operator. In contrast, for VBAP, a change in the spatial energy distribution is found. This suggests that the relation in terms of amplitudes and phases between the plane waves is modified yielding to a rotated, but different synthesized sound field.

4.2   Energy Required for the Synthesis of the Rotated Sound Field

An evaluation of the total energy required by the plane wave expansion to synthesize the acoustic field when rotation operators are implemented is carried out. The total energy of the PWE is estimated from Eq. (19).

$$E(\omega) \sim \sum_{l=1}^{L} |q_l|^2 (\omega). \tag{19}$$

Table 1 illustrates the values of energy corresponding to the PWE before and after rotation operators are implemented. The results indicate that the energy is similar for the spherical harmonic operator. However, the energy is lower when VBAP is implemented. The reason is because the reference acoustic field corresponds to a single plane wave. This means that only 3 plane waves of the PWE are generating the sound field for the case of VBAP. It is expected that in more complex acoustic fields in which all the plane waves are used, the energy gets higher.

Table 1. Energy of the plane wave expansion before and after rotation of the acoustic field.

Frequency/method	Case 1				Case 2			
	125 Hz	250 Hz	500 Hz	1 kHz	125 Hz	250 Hz	500 Hz	1 kHz
PWE	1.2250	1.0401	0.5476	0.0516	1.0464	0.8671	0.7204	0.0091
SH	1.0023	1.0079	0.6329	0.0605	0.9294	0.8682	0.7204	0.0094
VBAP	0.3877	0.3680	0.2553	0.0176	0.6177	0.5613	0.5070	0.0050

4.3 Normalized Error

A normalized error is implemented to compare the rotated reconstructed acoustic field respect to the target one. This allows to evaluate if the area of accurate reconstruction given by the PWE is affected by the rotation operators. The normalized error is defined as:

$$e(\mathbf{x}, \omega) = 10 \log_{10} \left[\frac{|p(\mathbf{x}, \omega) - \tilde{p}(\mathbf{x}, \omega)|^2}{|p(\mathbf{x}, \omega)|^2} \right], \tag{20}$$

where $p(\mathbf{x}, \omega)$ is the target acoustic pressure and $\tilde{p}(\mathbf{x}, \omega)$ is the reconstructed acoustic pressure. Figures 8 and 9 show the normalized errors in a cross-section of the domain ($z = 1.5$ m) for both rotation algorithms. The white contour defines the region within which the normalized error is smaller than -20 dB. Figures 10 and 11 for both approaches, spherical harmonics and VBAP, respectively.

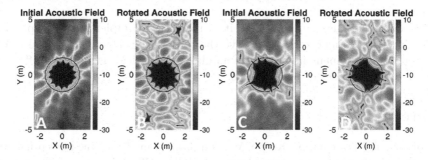

Fig. 10. Normalized error for the spherical harmonic case. (A) is the reference sound field ($\phi = 45$), (B) is the rotated sound field ($\phi_0 = 45$), (C) is the reference sound field ($\phi = 170$) and (D) corresponds to the rotated field ($\phi_0 = 60$).

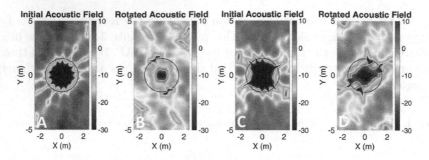

Fig. 11. Normalized error for the VBAP case. (A) is the reference sound field ($\phi = 45$), (B) is the rotated sound field ($\phi_0 = 45$), (C) is the reference sound field ($\phi = 170$) and (D) corresponds to the rotated field ($\phi_0 = 60$).

An analysis of the acoustic errors indicates that the area of accurate reconstruction is similar when the spherical harmonic operator is used. In contrast, the outcomes show that the implementation of VBAP as a rotation operator reduce the area in which the synthesis of the sound field is correct. These findings suggest that a lower order of spherical harmonics is required to achieve the same accuracy as VBAP for use as rotation operators.

5   Conclusions

Two different methodologies have been evaluated to perform the rotation of acoustic fields based on a plane wave representation. The suitability of these approaches extent the use of the PWE as kernel for interactive auralizations. Applications of this method can be real-time sound field processing for video games, listening tests, among others.

An implementation of VBAP as an interpolation tool validates the suitability of this method to rotate sound fields in the plane wave domain. However, a comparison with the rotation operator based on a spherical harmonic transformation reveals that the latter approach is more accurate in terms of sound field reconstruction.

The outcomes also support that it is required to implement the spherical harmonic rotation operator to preserve the initial accuracy given by the PWE. However, this statement holds as the number of spherical harmonic coefficients is equal to the number of plane waves.

References

1. Forssen, J., Hoffmann, A., Kropp, W.: Auralization model for the perceptual evaluation of tyre-road noise. Appl. Acoust. **132**, 232–240 (2018)
2. Tenenbauma, R., Taminatoa, F., Meloa, V., Torres, J.: Auralization generated by modeling HRIRs with artificial neural networks and its validation using articulation tests. Appl. Acoust. **130**, 260–269 (2018)

3. Vigeanta, M., Wanga, L., Rindel, J.: Objective and subjective evaluations of the multi-channel auralization technique as applied to solo instrument. Appl. Acoust. **72**, 311–323 (2011)
4. Møller, H.: Fundamentals of binaural technology. Appl. Acoust. **36**, 171–218 (1992)
5. Daniel, J., Nicol, R., Moreau, S.: Further investigations of high order ambisonics and wavefield synthesis for holophonic sound imaging. In: 114th Convention of Audio Engineering Society, Amsterdam, vol. 5788, pp. 1–18 (2003)
6. Menzies, D., Al-Akaidi, M.: Nearfield binaural synthesis and ambisonics. J. Acoust. Soc. Am. **121**, 1559–1563 (2006)
7. Murillo, D., Astley, J., Fazi, F.: Low frequency interactive auralization based on a plane wave expansion. Appl. Sci. **7**, 1–22 (2017)
8. Winter, F., Schultz, F., Spors, S.: Localization properties of data-based binaural synthesis including translatory head-movements. In: Proceedings of the Forum Acusticum, Krakow, pp. 7–12 (2014)
9. Langendijk, E., Bronkhorst, A.: Fidelity of three-dimensional-sound reproduction using a virtual auditory display. J. Acoust. Soc. Am. **107**, 528–537 (2000)
10. Murillo, D., Fazi, F., Astley, J.: Spherical harmonic representation of the sound field in a room based on finite element simulations. In: Proceedings of the 46th Iberoamerican Congress of Acoustics, Valencia, pp. 1007–1018 (2015)
11. Pulkki, V.: Virtual sound source positioning using vector base amplitude panning. J. Audio Eng. Soc. **45**(6), 456–466 (1997)
12. Ward, D., Abhayapala, T.: Reproduction of a plane-wave sound field using an array of loudspeakers. IEEE Trans. Audio Speech Lang. Process. **9**(6), 697–707 (2001)
13. Williams, E.: Fourier Acoustics, 1st edn. Academic Press, London (1999)
14. Poletti, M.: Three-dimensional surround sound systems based on spherical harmonics. J. Audio Eng. Soc. **53**(11), 1004–1025 (2005)
15. Murillo, D.: Interactive auralization based on hybrid simulation methods and plane wave expansion. Ph.D. thesis, Southampton University, Southampton, UK (2016)

Displacement Dynamics and Simulation for Overhead Gantry Crane Using Servo Control System

Zuly Alexandra Mora P.[1], Andrés Camilo Castaño Rivillas[1],
James Guillermo Moncada B.[1], Deisy Carolina Páez[1],
and Paolo Andres Ospina-Henao[2](✉)

[1] Facultad de Ingeniería Mecatrónica, Universidad Santo Tomás,
Carrera 18 No. 9 - 27, Bucaramanga, Colombia
deisy.paez@ustabuca.edu.co
[2] Departamento de Ciencias Básicas, Universidad Santo Tomás,
Carrera 18 No. 9 - 27, Bucaramanga, Colombia
paolo.ospina@ustabuca.edu.co

Abstract. This paper presents an alternate form for the dynamic modelling of a mechanical system that simulates in real life a gantry crane type, using Euler's classical mechanics and Lagrange formalism, which allows find the equations of motion that our model describe. Moreover, it has a basic model design system using the SolidWorks software, based on the material and dimensions of the model provides some physical variables necessary for modelling. The force is determined, but not as exerted by the spring, as this will be the control variable. The objective is to bring the mass of the pendulum from one point to another with a specified distance without the oscillation from it, so that, the answer is overdamped. This article includes an analysis of servo system control in which the equations of motion of Euler-Lagrange are rewritten in the state space, once there, they were implemented in Simulink to get the natural response of the system to a step input in F and then draw the desired trajectories.

Keywords: Euler Lagrange Formalism · Space of States · Controllability · Servo system control

1 Introduction

The cranes are used as support for heavy loads in various industrial applications such as shipyards, ports, constructions, factories, among others. Generally, the control of these devices is done manually by operators with wide knowledge, practice and dexterity [1]. In industries involving cranes, the punctuality and effectiveness of the handling system are important contributors to the productivity of the process or industry. It is for this reason that the implementation of

J. C. Figueroa-García et al. (Eds.): WEA 2019, CCIS 1052, pp. 114–125, 2019.
https://doi.org/10.1007/978-3-030-31019-6_10

a control strategy to the gantry crane can bring several advantages, such as support to the operator, safety, automatic operation and rejection or compensation of disturbances. Port cranes are subject to the presence of external disturbances, such as wind or carriage movement, these external forces can cause the load to oscillate. In most applications these oscillations have negative consequences; the load balancing makes the positioning more difficult, thus increasing the discharge time and operator inefficiency; when the payload is dangerous or fragile, the oscillations can cause load damage and insecurity [2,3]. Some examples are the neural networks [4], Proportional Derivative Control (PD) [5], State feedback [6], fuzzy logic [7], Nonlinear adaptive control [8], Hybrid control (nominal characteristic trajectory (NCT) with Proportional Integral Control (PI)) [9], H infinite [10], Linear Quadratic Regulator (LQR) [10], Output-Delayed feedback control [11], among other strategies that feed the state of the art of these systems. Despite the study of different control strategies, the technique known as state feedback is undoubtedly one of the most used by researchers to mitigate position errors and oscillations. Over the years, engineers have sought to improve ease of use, increase operational efficiency and mitigate crane safety issues by tackling three very important issues; Motion- induced oscillation; Disturbance-induced oscillation; And positioning capability. During the present work several aspects of study were taken into account, starting in the Sect. 2 by the dynamic modeling of the system through the Euler-Lagrange equations in a conservative way. Next, in Sect. 3, the system was modeled taking into account the non-conservative forces and the trajectory was defined for the future simulations. The simulations were performed to compare these results, these are shown in Sect. 4. The Sect. 5 shows each of the steps, criteria and discusses about the crane with for the design of the servo system and finally in the Sect. 6 we present the conclusions of the work.

2   Symbolic Model

The crane type modeling system started from a model in which intervenes a spring at the point where the force is applied for the movement of the carriage on the rail, as shown in Fig. 1 and the real gantry crane as shown in the Fig. 2. For this system the Lagrangian model was developed, in which initially the kinetic and potential energies are calculated.

The Lagrangian of any system is defined,

$$\mathcal{L} = T - U, \tag{1}$$

where, T is the kinetic energy and U the potential, therefore, for this model it is,

$$
\begin{aligned}
\mathcal{L} = \ & T_1 + T_2 + T_3 + T_4 + T_5 - U_1 - U_2 \\
= \ & \tfrac{1}{2} M \dot{x}^2 + \tfrac{1}{2} m_2 \left(\tfrac{1}{4} l^2 \dot{\theta}^2 + l \dot{\theta} \dot{x} \cos \theta + \dot{x}^2 \right) \\
& + \tfrac{1}{2} m_1 (l^2 \dot{\theta}^2 + 2 l \dot{\theta} \dot{x} \cos \theta + \dot{x}^2) \\
& + \tfrac{1}{24} m_2 l^2 \dot{\theta}^2 + \tfrac{1}{2} m_1 \dot{\theta}^2 \left(\tfrac{2}{5} r^2 \right) \\
& + g l \cos \theta \left(m_1 + \tfrac{m_2}{2} \right) - \tfrac{1}{2} K x^2 .
\end{aligned}
\tag{2}
$$

Fig. 1. Initial system image   **Fig. 2.** Gantry crane

In the Euler-Lagrange equations, q, represents the degrees of freedom (DOF) generalized, in this case, there are two DOF, θ and x, therefore,

$$\frac{d}{dt}\left(\frac{\partial \mathcal{L}}{\partial \dot{\theta}}\right) - \frac{\partial \mathcal{L}}{\partial \theta} = 0 \tag{3}$$

$$\frac{d}{dt}\left(\frac{\partial \mathcal{L}}{\partial \dot{x}}\right) - \frac{\partial \mathcal{L}}{\partial x} = 0. \tag{4}$$

From (3) and (4), the Euler-Lagrange equation, is obtained,

$$\ddot{\theta} l^2\, A + (\ddot{x}\, l \cos\theta + g\, l \sin\theta)\, B = 0 \tag{5}$$

$$\ddot{x} C - (\ddot{\theta} l \cos\theta - l\dot{\theta}^2 \sin\theta) B + K\, x = 0, \tag{6}$$

where,

$$A = \left(m_1 + \frac{m_2}{3}\right) + \frac{2}{5} m_1\, r^2 \tag{7}$$

$$B = m_1 + \frac{m_2}{2} \tag{8}$$

$$C = m_1 + m_2 + M \tag{9}$$

The solution for θ is shown in Fig. 3 and x for in Fig. 4.

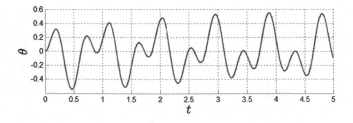

Fig. 3. θ solution for the first 5 s.

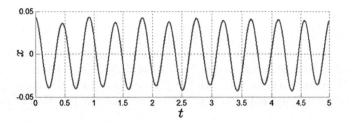

Fig. 4. x solution for the first 5 s.

3   Non-conservative Model

To control the system described above, the spring is deleted, which exerts a force on the mass placed on the rail. The force is determined, but not as exerted by the spring, since this will be the variable being monitored. The objective is to bring the mass of the pendulum from one point to another with a specified distance it to oscillate, so the answer is overdamped. From the system described in Fig. 5, the dynamic model is determined from the Euler-Lagrange equations for generalized force, this is

$$\frac{d}{dt}\left(\frac{\partial \mathcal{L}}{\partial \dot{q}_i}\right) - \frac{\partial \mathcal{L}}{\partial q_i} = Q_i, \qquad i = 1, 2 \tag{10}$$

where $q_1 = \theta$, $q_2 = x$, $Q_1 = Q_\theta$ and $Q_2 = Q_x$; these last two represent the generalized forces over the system, which will no longer be conservative, due to the existence of an external force F and friction is assumed in the pendulum axis $(b_1\dot{\theta})$ and carriage contact with the rail $(b_2\dot{x})$, according to Fig. 5. With this variation, the new Euler-Lagrange equations, are

$$\ddot{\theta} D + (\ddot{x} l \cos\theta + g l \sin\theta) B = -b_1 \dot{\theta} \tag{11}$$

$$\ddot{x} C + (\ddot{x} l \cos\theta + g l \sin\theta) B = F - b_2 \dot{x} \tag{12}$$

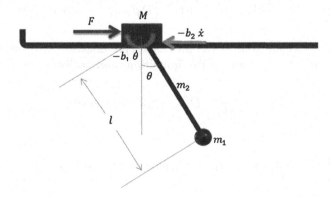

Fig. 5. Non-conservative model variables.

where

$$D = \left(\frac{2}{5} m_1 r^2 \right),$$ (13)

and B, C are the same terms in the Eqs. (8) and (9), respectively.

A suitable trajectory for the variable x is that in which the speed starts and ends at zero, the trigonometric function tanh, so that the function of the desired trajectory is,

$$x = \frac{d}{2} \tanh \left[\alpha \left(t - \frac{T}{2} \right) \right] + \frac{d}{2},$$ (14)

where d is the distance to travel, t represents time, T the time and α a factor to vary the slope of the curve. The function type proposed is more than twice differentiable, this ensures a continuous acceleration along the way. Having defined the trajectory to x, these values are entered into Eq. (11), and trajectories for θ y $\dot{\theta}$ are found.

3.1 Matrix Representation of Dynamic Model

Starting from [12], despite the complexity of the dynamic equation (15) that the behavior of manipulative robots, this equation and its formant terms have properties that are of interest in themselves. In addition, these properties are of particular value in the study of control systems for manipulators.

$$M(\mathbf{q})\ddot{\mathbf{q}} + C(\mathbf{q}, \dot{\mathbf{q}})\,\dot{\mathbf{q}} + G(\mathbf{q}) + f(\dot{\mathbf{q}}) = \tau,$$ (15)

so that (15) is the dynamic equation for mechanical systems of n degrees of freedom (DOF). Where M, is the inertia tensor of the system, C, is the centrifugal forces and Coriolis matrix, G the vector of gravity, f, the friction matrix and τ, the external forces. The equations of motion (11) and (12) in matrix form are as follows,

$$\begin{bmatrix} Bl\cos\theta & D \\ Bl\cos\theta + C & 0 \end{bmatrix} \begin{bmatrix} \ddot{x} \\ \ddot{\theta} \end{bmatrix} + \begin{bmatrix} 0 & 0 \\ 0 & 0 \end{bmatrix} \begin{bmatrix} \dot{x} \\ \dot{\theta} \end{bmatrix} + \begin{bmatrix} Bgl\sin\theta \\ Bgl\sin\theta \end{bmatrix} + \begin{bmatrix} 0 & b_1 \\ b_2 & 0 \end{bmatrix} \begin{bmatrix} \dot{x} \\ \dot{\theta} \end{bmatrix} = \begin{bmatrix} 0 \\ F \end{bmatrix}$$

Clearing the accelerations of the previous representation (16), we obtain the equations that will be used for future simulations and perform the control of the system.

$$\ddot{x} = \frac{1}{det(M)} [-D(F - b_2\dot{x} - Bgl\sin\theta)],$$ (16)

and

$$\ddot{\theta} = \frac{1}{det(M)} [(-Bl\cos\theta - C)(-b_1\dot{\theta} - Bgl\sin\theta) + (Bl\cos\theta)(F - b_2\dot{x} - Bgl\sin\theta)],$$ (17)

where, $det(M) = -D(Bl\cos\theta + C)$.

4   Simulation

To validate the linearization obtained, we proceeded to simulate the nonlinear model (Euler-Lagrange equations) and the state space model (Matrix A, B, and $\widetilde{C}$), putting them to respond to the same input $F = 0.1$ of 2 s.

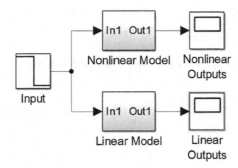

Fig. 6. Block diagram with both models.

The Fig. 6, shows the general scheme of both simulated models, the scheme containing the nonlinear model is shown below (Fig. 7).

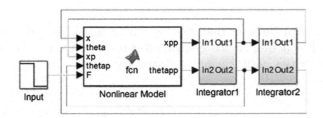

Fig. 7. Nonlinear model block diagram.

The block that is called Non-linear model is a function of Matlab, which contains the Euler-Lagrange equations of motion. The system response for the conditions given above is shown in Fig. 8, 9, 10 and 11.

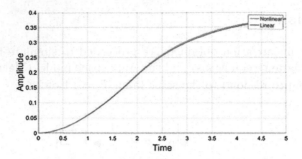

Fig. 8. Cart position for both models

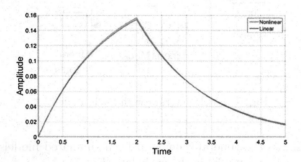

Fig. 9. Cart speed for both models

In Fig. 9, it can be seen that the system increases its velocity while the external force F is acting on the system, after the external force is not present, the velocity decreases until reaching a stationary zone.

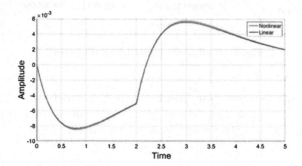

Fig. 10. Pendulum position for both models

In Figs. 8, 9, 10 and 11, the red line represents the response of each of the corresponding variables of the nonlinear model, while the blue line is the behavior of the linearized model.

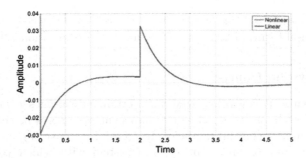

Fig. 11. Pendulum speed for both models

5 System Control

For the design of controllers by state feedback it is necessary to work with the subsystem of minimal realization [13], this subsystem is characterized by complete controllability and observability, because the non-controllable part of a system is independent of inputs, it is not possible to modify the subsystem by any state feedback acting on this. Therefore, it is necessary to verify the complete controllability of the system to be able to design the controller by feedback [14]. For the design of the state feedback controller, it is necessary to verify that the system has a subsystem of minimal realization, for this it is assumed that all states are physically measurable, So the system is fully observable, besides this, it is necessary to know if it is totally controllable or not, For this the controller $Q = [B\ AB\ A^2B\ A^3B]$, matrix is calculated, this matrix has a range equal to 4, while the matrix A has a range of 3, therefore, the system is fully controllable (oversized system).

5.1 Transformation to Phase Variables

For the design of the controller by state feedback it is convenient to express the matrices of the system in its controllable canonical form, which require a transformation matrix T, which is defined as $T^{-1} = [e; eA; eA^2; eA^3]$, where, $e = Q^{-1}(n)$, being n, is the last row of the inverse of the matrix Q.

So that $A_f = T^{-1}AT$ and $B_f = T^{-1}B$, where,

$$A_f = \begin{bmatrix} 0 & 1 & 0 & 0 \\ 0 & 0 & 1 & 0 \\ 0 & 0 & 0 & 1 \\ 0 & -10174 & -19020 & -7075.1 \end{bmatrix}, \tag{18}$$

$$B_f = \begin{bmatrix} 0 \\ 0 \\ 0 \\ 1 \end{bmatrix}, \tag{19}$$

here, A_f and B_f, are the representation of the system in phase variables (controllable canonical form). The vector $\widetilde{C}$, is already in the canonical form.

5.2   Servo System Control

The servosystem is a controller that has certain advantages over other classic controllers, such as its good performance in systems sensitive to disturbances and with modeling inaccuracies, in addition to ensuring a zero position error. It is necessary to know the type of system with which you are working, there are several ways to know the type of a control system, among the most common is to calculate the transfer function or find its own values which give us information from the poles of the system, in this case the own values $VP = [-1.95, -7077, 0, -0.737]$, were calculated, observing that there is a system type 1, so the first feedback constant k_1, will be 0.

5.3   Poles Allocation

The design of the controller was done by means of pole assignment, also known as poles location technique. In this case it starts by analyzing the eigenvalues of the system, these eigenvalues represent the poles of the closed-loop system. Next, the desired poles of the system are located with the criterion of $t_s = 4T$ (previously defined a $T = 5\,\mathrm{s}$, in the defined path), therefore, the desired poles will be located at 20. It suffices that $b_0 \neq 0$, to place the desired poles anywhere, being in this case $b_0 = 1$, since it is the first value of vector $\widetilde{C}$. For the calculation of the vector K and the proportional action K_0 we start from,

$$A_r = A_f + B_f K_f - K_0 B_f \widetilde{C} \tag{20}$$

being, A_r, the feedback matrix,

$$A_r = \begin{bmatrix} 0 & 1 & 0 & 0 \\ 0 & 0 & 1 & 0 \\ 0 & 0 & 0 & 1 \\ -160000 & -32000 & -2400 & -80 \end{bmatrix}. \tag{21}$$

The A_r matrix contains the polynomial resulting from locating the desired poles $P_d = (s + 20)^4$. Clearing the feedback vector K_f and the proportional constant K_0 from (20), we obtain,

$$K = [0, -1.0727, -13.406, -3.3737]$$
$$K_0 = 160000,$$

being, $K = K_f T^{-1}$.

The matrix A and B represented in physical variables.

The Fig. 12, shows the system block diagram with the proposed path, the feedback vector K and the proportional action K_0.

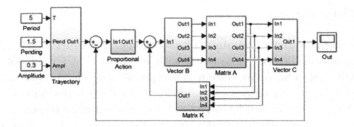

Fig. 12. Block diagram with controller

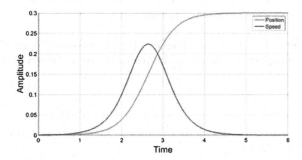

Fig. 13. Cart outputs

The Fig. 13, shows the position and speed of the cart under the action of the controller, it is observed that the cart arrives at the desired position by the trajectory defined in a non-abrupt way and without going back. As for the speed, we see that this increases when the cart is starting and decreases when it is reaching its stationary zone, so that the car remains with a null position error. As for the position and velocity of the pendulum shown in Fig. 14, it can be seen that the controller tries to keep the pendulum at its equilibrium point, it can be seen in the red line that the position has few oscillations, with a maximum amplitude of 0.014 radians (0.8063°) and minimum of 0.0185 radians (−1.0588°).

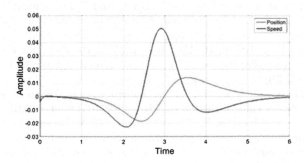

Fig. 14. Pendulum outputs

6   Conclusions

Because the defined control required a linear model, it was necessary to linearize the system, which allowed us to work with a model that would not go away largely to the real. The servo system is a type of controller in state space that responds well to perturbations. In addition, this driver guarantees us a null position error. It can be seen from Fig. 8, that the controller responds correctly, since it takes the carriage to the desired position in a good way following the path defined in Eq. (14). The criterion selected for the pole assignment gives good results, since the controller obtained guaranteed all the requirements of position, trajectory and oscillations in the system.

Acknowledgments. Deisy Carolina Páez and P. A. Ospina-Henao, gratefully acknowledge the permanent support of Vicerrectoría Académica de la Universidad Santo Tomás.

References

1. de Moura Oliverira, P.B., Boaventura Cunha, J.: Gantry crane control: a simulation case study. IEEE (2013)
2. Sorensen, K.L., Singhose, W., Dickerson, S.: A controller enabling precise positioning and sway reduction in bridge and gantry cranes. Control Eng. Pract. **15**, 825–837 (2006)
3. Khalid, A., Singhose, W., Huey, J., Lawrence, J.: Study of operator behavior, learning, and performance using and input-shaped bridge crane. In: Proceedings of the 2004 IEEE International Conference on Control Applications (2004)
4. Fernández Villaverde, A., Santos Peñas, M.: Control de una grúa pórtico mediante redes neuronales. In: XXVII Jornadas de Automática, Almeria (2006)
5. Fang, Y., Dixon, W.E., Dawson, D.M., Zergeroglu, E.: Nonlinear coupling control laws for a 3-DOF overhead crane system. In: Proceedings of the 40th IEEE Conference on Decision and Control (Cat. No. 01CH37228) (2004)
6. Kim, Y.S., Hong, K.S., Sul, S.K.: Anti-sway control of container cranes: inclinometer, observer, and state feedback. Int. J. Control Autom. Syst. **2**(4), 435–449 (2004)
7. Liu, D.T., Guo, W.P., Yi, J.Q., Zhao, D.B.: Double-pendulum-type overhead crane dynamics and its adaptive sliding mode fuzzy control. In: Proceeding of the Third International Conference on Machine Learning and Cybernetics, Shanghai (2004)
8. Yang, J.H., Yang, K.S.: Adaptive control for 3-D overhead crane systems. In: Proceedings of the 2006 American Control Conference, USA (2006)
9. Ahmad, M.A., Raja Ismail, R.M.T., Ramli, M.S., Hambali, N.: Investigations of NCTF with input shaping for sway control of double-pendulum-type overhead crane. IEEE (2010)
10. Burul, I., Kolonic, F., Matusko, J.: The control system design of a gantry crane based on H infinity control theory. In: MIPRO 2010, Croatia (2010)
11. Dey, R., Sinha, N., Chaubey, P., Ghosh, S., Ray, G.: Active sway control of a single pendulum gantry crane system using output-delayed feedback control technique. In: 11th International Conference Control, Automation, Robotics and Vision, Singapore (2010)

12. Kelly, R., Santibáñez, V.: Control de Movimiento de Robots Manipuladores, p. 327. Pearson Education, S.A., Madrid (2003)
13. Domínguez, S., Campoy, P., Sebastián, J.M., Jiménez, A.: Control en el Espacio de Estados, 2nd edn, p. 440. Pearson Education S.A., Madrid (2006)
14. Ogata, K.: Ingeniería de Control Moderna, 3rd edn, p. 1015. Pearson Education S.A., México D.F. (1998)

Performance Evaluation of SoC-FPGA Based Floating-Point Implementation of GMM for Real-Time Background Subtraction

Luis Javier Morantes-Guzmán[1,2]([✉]), Cristian Alzate[1], Luis Castano-Londono[1], David Marquez-Viloria[1], and Jesus Francisco Vargas-Bonilla[2]

[1] Faculty of Engineering, Instituto Tecnológico Metropolitano ITM, Medellín, Colombia
{luismorantes,luiscastano,davidmarquez}@itm.edu.co,
cristianalzate224500@correo.itm.edu.co
[2] Faculty of Engineering, Universidad de Antioquia UdeA, Medellín, Colombia
jesus.vargas@udea.edu.co

Abstract. The embedded systems continue to display as solutions of smart surveillance systems. Background subtraction using Gaussian Mixture Model (GMM) is often portrayed as a common step for video processing. This work discusses the implementation of an embedded vision system on system-on-a-chip (SoC) device that integrates both a processor and an FPGA (Field Programmable Gate Array) architecture. The conventional Register Transfer Level (RTL) design, typically used for FPGA programming is slow, and the use of floating-point arithmetic is complex. However, the use of High-Level Synthesis (HLS) tools allows describing algorithms using high-level programming languages. Three background subtraction algorithms with floating-point arithmetic were developed using a hardware-software co-design methodology. The paper presents the details of the implementation on a ZedBoard Zynq Evaluation and Development Kit, considering requirements as hardware resources and power consumption used. Also, performance comparisons among a PC-based, ARM, FPGA and SOC-FPGA implementations are presented. The results showed that frame rates needed for real-time video processing were reached.

Keywords: Background subtraction ·
Gaussian Mixture Model (GMM) ·
Field Programmable Gate Array (FPGA) · System-on-a-chip (SoC) ·
High-Level Synthesis (HLS)

1 Introduction

The video surveillance applications over embedded vision systems have had a rapid growth in recent years. These systems make use of background subtraction as one of the key techniques for automatic video analysis. The state of the

© Springer Nature Switzerland AG 2019
J. C. Figueroa-García et al. (Eds.): WEA 2019, CCIS 1052, pp. 126–134, 2019.
https://doi.org/10.1007/978-3-030-31019-6_11

art methods make use of GMM estimators as background subtraction approach
but it has a high computational cost for real-time implementation [6,7]. Hardware implementations of GMM algorithm on FPGA has been proposed in some
works to deal with the computational burden requirements. An architecture for
real-time segmentation and denoising of HD video on Xilinx and Altera FPGAs is
presented in [5]. The authors describe the implementation and performance evaluation of OpenCV based GMM algorithm and morphological operations applied
to a sequences of 1920 × 1080 frame size. In a latter work [6], authors present
implementation and evaluation of architectures based on the OpenCV GMM
algorithm for HD video over FPGA and ASIC technologies. In both cases, the
FPGA based implementations were developed using VHDL. Fixed-point representation is used to achieve required performance for HD video resolution. An
FPGA based implementation of GMM for offline background subtraction using
fixed point arithmetic is presented in [1]. The block diagrams of the implemented
system modules are shown. Moreover, qualitative results for a group of 360 × 240
frames selected from a sequence of 1250 are presented. The implementation of
other FPGA based approaches of background subtraction techniques are found
in some works. A performance evaluation of two multimodal background subtraction algorithms implemented on a ZedBoard is presented in [3]. A performance
comparison of GMM, ViBE, and PBAS algorithms implementation on CPU,
GPU, and FPGA is presented in [2]. In [8], is presented a summary of several
FPGA based implementations of background modelling algorithms, developed
by these authors in previous works. Additionally, the authors present the evaluation of the PBAS implementation using the SBI dataset. An FPGA based
implementation of the codebook algorithm on a Spartan-3 FPGA is presented in
[9]. The authors describe the system architecture and performance for sequences
of 768 × 576. Hardware acceleration for real-time foreground and background
identification based on SoC FPGA is presented in [10]. The proposed architecture was implemented on a Zynq-7 ZC702 Evaluation Board and is evaluated
using datasets of real-time HD video stream.

The main contribution of this paper is a implementation that allows major
flexibility in comparison to previous works with fixed-point representation and
conventional RTL description. In this paper is presented an FPGA based implementation of the GMM algorithm on a ZedBoard using floating-point arithmetic. The OpenCV GMM function code is adapted for the Vivado-HLS, and
parallelization directives are used for optimization. Taking advantage of the SoC
architecture of the Artix-7 FPGA device, the generated HLS custom IP core is
integrated with a Zynq processing system allowing the development of a complete embedded vision system. The hardware resources and power consumption
are presented for the HLS custom IP core and the complete embedded vision
system. Moreover, performance comparison with CPU software-based implementation for sequences at three different resolutions is presented in frames per
second (fps). The experimental results show that the developed system is suitable for real-time at 768 × 576 resolutions with low-power consumption. The
paper is organized as follows. In Sect. 2 the implemented algorithms and system

architecture are described. Results and performance analysis are presented in Sect. 3. Finally, conclusions are drawn in Sect. 4.

2 Proposed Method

The algorithm implementations were developed using a hardware-software co-design methodology. The first stage is the software design that starts with the coding of the algorithms using C++ language and OpenCV libraries to take advantage of the rapid prototyping, visualization, and easy re-coding. The BGSLibrary (Background Subtraction Library) [13], covers a collection of algorithms from the literature. We selected three classic background subtraction algorithms: Frame Difference, Gaussian Mixture Model (GMM1) [11], and Efficient Gaussian Mixture Model (GMM2) [14]. The common steps of the GMM methods may be summarized in Algorithm 1.

Algorithm 1. Gaussian Mixture Model

Input: Frame Image I. Max. Gaussian distributions = 3
 1: **for** each I **do**
 2:    **for** each pixel j in I **do**
 3:       Select number of Gaussians
 4:       Represent j by sum of weighted Gaussian distributions
 5:       Update all distributions
 6:       Check for match with current pixel
 7:    **end for**
 8: **end for**
Output: Foreground Mask, Background Model.

The hardware implementation stage proposes two steps. The first step is the acceleration of the Algorithm 1 using Vivado HLS. Parallelization directives are applied in the code to improve the performance of the algorithm following the diagram showed in Fig. 1. Finally, HDL code generated by Vivado HLS is

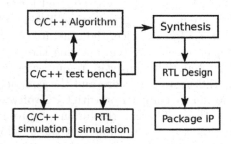

Fig. 1. HLS flow design used for FPGA implementations of the algorithms.

synthesized and downloaded to the FPGA. Figure 2 shows the code generated with the name HLS Custom IP Core inside of the SoC-FPGA architecture.

The algorithms were implemented on a ZedBoard Zynq Evaluation and Development Kit, which is a heterogeneous architecture based on FPGA. The integrated development environment (IDE) for HDL synthesis named Vivado® Design Suite was used for the synthesis of each design. Vivado® High-Level Synthesis (VHLS) is included in the suite, and it is responsible for transformation of the code written in C/C++ to HDL using a software-based approach, see Fig. 1.

The Operating System (OS) named PetaLinux was used on the ARM. This OS is a Linux distribution customized for SoC Kit boards and it facilitates the management of the peripherals on the development board such as Ethernet, USB, and HDMI ports. The communication between the processor and the FPGA is performed using AMBA AXI4-stream protocol. This is a data flow handler that offers several end-to-end stream pipes for the data transport of the applications. AXI4-stream works as a data transmission channel between the processing system (PS) and the programmable logic (PL). In the PS side, it works as a memory access control executed from a C++ function in PetaLinux. In the PL side, the communication is done using AXI Master. AXI Master maps the memory to stream conversion, and it performs the low-level transmission tasks, allowing to the designer to read/write the DRAM in Linux, and read/write from FPGA to DRAM using a high level approach. AMBA AXI4-Lite is an interface for data transmission between PS and PL for simple communication because it has a low-throughput memory-mapped communication and this interface is used for the control signals and status registration of the data, see Fig. 2.

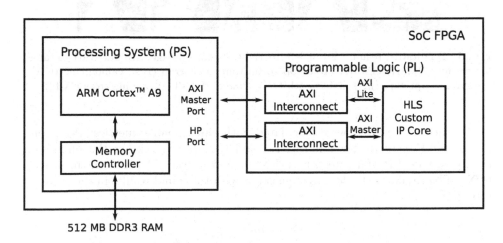

Fig. 2. Architecture of embedded vision system on SoC-FPGA.

3   Experiments and Results

We compared implemented algorithm quantitatively and qualitatively on the Wallflower dataset [12]. The results show that the proposed architecture can compute the foreground of the scenarios in the first column of the Fig. 3.

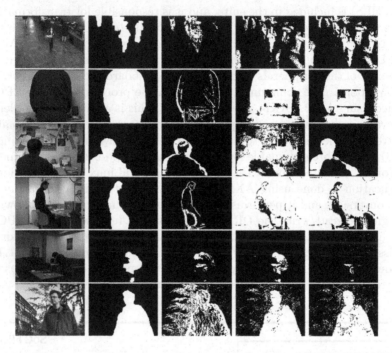

Fig. 3. Qualitative results. From left to right: original image, ground truth, Frame Difference, GMM1, GMM2. From top to bottom: bootstrap (BS), camouflage (CA), foreground aperture (FA), lightswitch (LS), time of day (TD), waving trees (WT).

Quantitative results were calculated with three quality metrics: Precision, Recall and F-score, as shown in Eqs. 1, 2 and 3, which are based on the amount of false positives (FP), false negatives (FN), true positives (TP) and true negatives (TN). The results in Table 1 are consistent with the found results in the state of the art.

$$Precision = \frac{TP}{TP + FP} \quad (1)$$

$$Recall = \frac{TP}{TP + FN} \quad (2)$$

$$F\text{-}score = \frac{2 \cdot Precision \cdot Recall}{Precision + Recall} \quad (3)$$

Table 1. Performance using Wallflower dataset [12].

Algorithm	Sequence						
	Metrics	BS	CA	FA	LS	TD	WT
Frame Difference	Precision	0.834	0.721	0.754	0.888	0.823	0.626
	Recall	0.686	0.557	0.601	0.630	0.622	0.643
	F-score	0.753	0.629	0.669	0.737	0.709	0.635
GMM1 [11]	Precision	0.654	0.836	0.579	0.213	0.967	0.911
	Recall	0.675	0.807	0.602	0.389	0.796	0.945
	F-score	0.664	0.822	0.591	0.276	0.873	0.928
GMM2 [14]	Precision	0.626	0.895	0.839	0.310	0.895	0.913
	Recall	0.676	0.897	0.736	0.322	0.550	0.938
	F-score	0.652	0.896	0.784	0.316	0.682	0.925

The complete embedded vision system proposed is based on a heterogeneous architecture composed of a SoC-FPGA, as seen in Fig. 2. The complete system transmits information between ARM and FPGA, for this reason the maximum performance of the different implementations is limited for the maximum bandwidth of communication channels. However, the complete system facilitates management of peripherals and data using the operating system. Moreover, HLS custom IP vision core running in the standalone FPGA can be used in applications with direct connection to the FPGA. Table 2 shows both main hardware resources and power consumption in the algorithm implementations. This table compares the data for the HLS custom IP vision core on FPGA and the complete embedded vision system on the SoC-FPGA. The latter uses an amount greater of hardware resources due primarily to the drivers for the management and the transmission of data provided by the ARM.

Table 2. Hardware resources required on a ZedBoard FPGA after place and route. The whole system includes processing modules.

Algorithm	LUT	Flip Flop	Slice	DSP48	Power (W)
HLS custom IP vision core (FPGA)					
Frame Difference	1667/53200	2341/106400	701/13300	4/220	0.025
GMM1 [11]	18452/53200	56265/106400	9473/13300	25/220	0.446
GMM2 [14]	18872/53200	57698/106400	9623/13300	47/220	0.375
Complete embedded vision system (SoC-FPGA)					
Frame Difference	4452/53200	5275/106400	1739/13300	4/220	1.593
GMM1 [11]	32336/53200	68875/106400	12860/13300	25/220	2.102
GMM2 [14]	34056/53200	72059/106400	13249/13300	47/220	2.046

The performance of the SoC-FPGA and standalone FPGA were compared against a PC, as can be seen in Table 3. The ZedBoard Zynq is a SoC that contains a dual core ARM Cortex-A9 and one Artix-7 FPGA, with a FPGA clock period of 10 ns (100 MHz). The PC is equipped with a processor AMD Quad-Core A10-9620P running to 2.5 GHz. The average frame rate in PC, ARM and SoC-FPGA is computed as in Eq. 4. For FPGA we need to compute a frame rate as in Eq. 5. The performance measures for SoC-FPGA are better than the measured for the PC, and SoC-FPGA allows the real-time implementation in all cases. The standalone FPGA has the best performance because it does not have the limitation of the communication channels. Additionally, a comparison against the standalone ARM of the SoC-FPGA is included. An ARM processors is one of a family of CPUs based on the RISC architecture that is typically used over microprocessor boards and mobile devices used for real-time embedded system applications. The performance of FPGA in the most of the cases exceeds by 10× the performance of ARM, achieving over 40× in the best cases.

$$fps = \frac{1}{(\text{elapsed time per frame})} \tag{4}$$

$$fps = \frac{1}{(\text{FPGA cycles per frame}) \cdot (\text{clock period})} \tag{5}$$

Table 3. Performance comparison for sequences at three resolutions, in fps.

Resolution	Algorithm	PC	ARM (PS)	FPGA (PL)	SoC-FPGA (PS+PL)
160 × 120 [12]	Frame Difference	2459	597	5019	4947
	GMM1 [11]	284	30	1295	519
	GMM2 [14]	623	77	1728	613
352 × 288 [13]	Frame Difference	483	137	1277	1269
	GMM1 [11]	63	6	246.3	128
	GMM2 [14]	152	14	328	153
768 × 576 [4]	Frame Difference	141	28	224	220
	GMM1 [11]	19	2	56	22
	GMM2 [14]	38	3	75	26

4   Conclusions

This work presented implementation of three background subtraction algorithms in real-time using floating-point arithmetic. The HLS implementations permit a fast design and implementation of several architectures with different parallelization directives, in this way, it is possible to improve the performance of complex algorithms with a standard floating-point precision. The performance measures of the proposed architecture shown better computational times compared to PC-based implementation, and the parallelization of the GMM algorithms reached the frame per seconds needed for real-time video processing with a low power consumption. For these reasons, the heterogeneous architectures based on FPGA shown to be an effective tool for the video surveillance applications over embedded vision systems.

Acknowledgements. This study was supported by the AE&CC research Group COL0053581, at the Sistemas de Control y Robótica Laboratory, attached to the Instituto Tecnológico Metropolitano. This work is part of the project "Improvement of visual perception in humanoid robots for objects recognition in natural environments using Deep Learning" with ID P17224, co-funded by the Instituto Tecnológico Metropolitano and Universidad de Antioquia. L. J. Morantes-Guzmán is under grants of "Convocatoria de Doctorados Nacionales 617 - COLCIENCIAS 2013".

References

1. Arivazhagan, S., Kiruthika, K.: FPGA implementation of GMM algorithm for background subtractions in video sequences. In: Raman, B., Kumar, S., Roy, P.P., Sen, D. (eds.) Proceedings of International Conference on Computer Vision and Image Processing. AISC, vol. 460, pp. 365–376. Springer, Singapore (2017). https://doi.org/10.1007/978-981-10-2107-7_33
2. Bulat, B., Kryjak, T., Gorgon, M.: Implementation of advanced foreground segmentation algorithms GMM, ViBE and PBAS in FPGA and GPU – a comparison. In: Chmielewski, L.J., Kozera, R., Shin, B.-S., Wojciechowski, K. (eds.) ICCVG 2014. LNCS, vol. 8671, pp. 124–131. Springer, Cham (2014). https://doi.org/10.1007/978-3-319-11331-9_16
3. Cocorullo, G., Corsonello, P., Frustaci, F., Guachi, L., Perri, S.: Multimodal background subtraction for high-performance embedded systems. J. Real-Time Image Proc. (2016). https://doi.org/10.1007/s11554-016-0651-6
4. Ferryman, J., Shahrokni, A.: Pets 2009: dataset and challenge. In: 2009 Twelfth IEEE International Workshop on Performance Evaluation of Tracking and Surveillance, pp. 1–6, December 2009. https://doi.org/10.1109/PETS-WINTER.2009.5399556
5. Genovese, M., Napoli, E.: FPGA-based architecture for real timesegmentation and denoising of HD video. J. Real-Time Image Proc. **8**(4), 389–401 (2013). https://doi.org/10.1007/s11554-011-0238-1
6. Genovese, M., Napoli, E.: ASIC and FPGA implementation of the Gaussian mixture model algorithm for real-time segmentation of high definition video. IEEE Trans. Very Large Scale Integr. VLSI Syst. **22**(3), 537–547 (2014). https://doi.org/10.1109/TVLSI.2013.2249295
7. Goyal, K., Singhai, J.: Review of background subtraction methods using gaussian mixture model for video surveillance systems. Artif. Intell. Rev. **50**, 241–259 (2017). https://doi.org/10.1007/s10462-017-9542-x
8. Kryjak, T., Gorgon, M.: Real-time implementation of background modelling algorithms in FPGA devices. In: Murino, V., Puppo, E., Sona, D., Cristani, M., Sansone, C. (eds.) ICIAP 2015. LNCS, vol. 9281, pp. 519–526. Springer, Cham (2015). https://doi.org/10.1007/978-3-319-23222-5_63
9. Rodriguez-Gomez, R., Fernandez-Sanchez, E.J., Diaz, J., Ros, E.: Codebook hardware implementation on FPGA for background subtraction. J. Real-Time Image Proc. **10**(1), 43–57 (2015). https://doi.org/10.1007/s11554-012-0249-6

10. Safaei, A., Wu, Q.M.J., Yang, Y.: System-on-a-chip (SoC)-based hardware acceleration for foreground and background identification. J. Frankl. Inst. **355**(4), 1888–1912 (2018). https://doi.org/10.1016/j.jfranklin.2017.07.037. Special Issue on Recent advances in machine learning for signal analysis and processing
11. Stauffer, C., Grimson, W.E.L.: Adaptive background mixture models for real-time tracking. In: 1999 Proceedings of the IEEE Computer Society Conference on Computer Vision and Pattern Recognition (Cat. No. PR00149), vol. 2, p. 252 (1999). https://doi.org/10.1109/CVPR.1999.784637
12. Toyama, K., Krumm, J., Brumitt, B., Meyers, B.: Wallflower: principles and practice of background maintenance. In: Proceedings of the Seventh IEEE International Conference on Computer Vision, vol. 1, pp. 255–261 (1999). https://doi.org/10.1109/ICCV.1999.791228
13. Vacavant, A., Chateau, T., Wilhelm, A., Lequièvre, L.: A benchmark dataset for outdoor foreground/background extraction. In: Park, J.-I., Kim, J. (eds.) ACCV 2012. LNCS, vol. 7728, pp. 291–300. Springer, Heidelberg (2013). https://doi.org/10.1007/978-3-642-37410-4_25
14. Zivkovic, Z., van der Heijden, F.: Efficient adaptive density estimation per image pixel for the task of background subtraction. Pattern Recogn. Lett. **27**(7), 773–780 (2006). https://doi.org/10.1016/j.patrec.2005.11.005

Maze Solution Device with Stewart's Platform and OpenCV

Joseph Mauricio Gutierrez Valero[✉] and Hernando Leon-Rodriguez[✉]

Electronics Engineering Department, Universidad El Bosque, Bogota, Colombia
{jgutierrezv,hefrainl}@unbosque.edu.co

Abstract. This article presents the analytic study of the kinematics model for a Stewart's platform; its includes the derivation of closed-loop expressions for the inverse Jacobian matrix of the mechanism and its derived time domain. A physically prototype platform was implemented to generates control with an artificial vision system executed in OpenCV library. The results includes the estimation of behaviour of the mobile platform and its mathematical relationship. The mathematical model and simulations of OpenSource were evaluated initially in Matlab, to finally perform an automatic maze labyrinth solution on top of the platform.

Keywords: Stewart platform · Kinematics analysis · Parallel robot · Artificial vision system

1 Introduction

The Stewart platform mechanism is mainly associates as a hexapod prismatic robot. It is a parallel kinematic structure that can be used like basic machine for motion control with 6 degrees of freedom [1]. The mechanism itself consists of a stationary platform with one base platform and mobile platform which are connected via six prismatic actuators on universal joints (See Fig. 1). The Stewart platform, also known as the "Gough-Stewart" platform, was first introduced by Gough in 1956 as a tire testing machine [2]. Such an application has been motivated by the excellent mechanical characteristics of the mechanism in terms of its higher rigidity and strength-to-weight ratio when it is compared with serial link manipulators; and also, its greater maneuverability when compared to conventional machine tool structures. The introduction of industrial robot was the beginning of a new era in many fields; the serial manipulators became an invaluable tool for a broad range of applications. The advantages of machines and mechanisms developed the needs of higher precision, robustness, stiffness and load-carrying capacity arise, which its parallel manipulators begin to show-up.

The completely parallel link mechanisms, which include the Stewart platform, show kinematic characteristics different from those of the series link mechanisms. The inverse kinematic solution for the Stewart platforms is the determination

© Springer Nature Switzerland AG 2019
J. C. Figueroa-García et al. (Eds.): WEA 2019, CCIS 1052, pp. 135–146, 2019.
https://doi.org/10.1007/978-3-030-31019-6_12

of joint's position on the space where the six link lengths gives position and orientation of the mobile platform with respect to the base's position represented in the Cartesian space [3]. The determination of mobile platform's position on Cartesian space in a given position is the most computationally demanding. However, closed-form solutions and numerical iterative schemes are used, with simpler closed-form solutions for special arrangements [4]. The kinematic solutions of forward speed and forward kinematics, on the other hand, are linear, requiring a system solution of linear equations that involve the inverse Jacobian matrix and its time derivative. Closed-form expressions for these matrices are necessary for dynamic transformation.

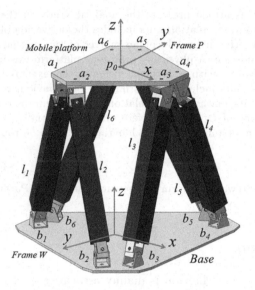

Fig. 1. Stewart platform mechanism

In this article, we present a kinematic and dynamic analysis of a structure called the Stewart platform, as shown in Fig. 1. This is the organization of the system, observing that it is a hexapod system, with six degrees of freedom, using the solution of Newton Euler formulation the structure of the machine tool is closely related to the octahedral hexapod manufactured by Ingersoll. The kinematic study includes the determination of closed form expressions for the inverse Jacobian matrix and its time derivatives [5]. The effects of having different configurations of strut end joints in the kinematics and dynamics of the mechanism are modeled more accurately.

2 OpenCV Artificial Vision

The project has work with OpenCV, an open source library of computer vision and documentation in C, Java and Python. Although, it is not the first choice of using Python; the main reason is the shell facilitates and the rapid developed of projects in the terminal. The bash command terminal also makes the library and prerequisites easy to download in Linux distributions such as Raspbian. However, having also played with Java libraries for Android is it maybe the most robust and reliable system, but at the beginning, it may take longer to start.

Computer Vision: It is the study of machines that have the ability to extract information from an image that is important to address some tasks. In the research discipline, computer vision deals with the hypothesis of artificial systems that extract information from images. The image information can take many structures, for example, video sequences, views of different cameras or multidimensional information like medical scanner.

Color Recognition: Colors can be measured in different ways; Undoubtedly, the human impression of colors is a subjective procedure by which the mind reacts to the shocks that are created when the approaching light responds with few kinds of conical cells in the eye [6].

HSV Color Model: HSV refers to Hue, Saturation and Value. The HSV color model was introduced by Alvy Ray Smith in 1978 and it is used as part of computer graphics applications. In HSV, the tone represents a saturated color on the outer edge of the color wheel. The amount of white added to the color defines the saturation. 0% means that the color (in V = 100%) is totally white; whereas, 100% means totally saturated without bleaching. Value means brightness of color. 0% indicates pure black or totally dark; 100% speaks of total brightness, where hue and saturation determine the current color [7].

3   Coordinate System Assignment

The first step is to define a generalized coordinate vector, whose elements are the six variables chosen to describe the position and orientation of the platform, such as [8]:

$$q = (X, Y, Z, \phi, \theta, \psi)^T \tag{1}$$

The joint space coordinate vector l is defined as:

$$l = (l_1, l_2, l_3, l_4, l_5, l_6)^T \tag{2}$$

where l_i for $i = 1, \ldots, 6$ are the lengths of the six numbered links of the Stewart Platform. In the following sections, the mapping between these two sets of coordinates and their time derivatives will be presented. Thanks to the angles of Euler that give a set of three angular coordinates, it will serve us to specify the orientation of a reference system of orthogonal axes, since it is a mobile system, with respect to another reference system of orthogonal axes normally fixed. The concept of Fig. 2 was introduced by Leonhard Euler in rigid solid mechanics to describe the orientation of a solidary reference system with a rigid solid in motion.

The Euler angles constitute a set of three angular coordinates that serve to specify the orientation of a reference system of orthogonal axes, normally mobile, with respect to another reference system of orthogonal axes normally fixed.

The intersection of the chosen coordinate planes xy and XY is called line of nodes, and is used to define the three angles as shown in Fig. 3.

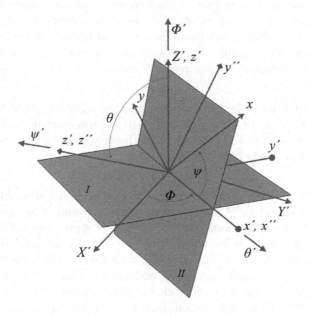

Fig. 2. Representation of Euler angles z-x-z.

4   Kinematics of the Moving Platform

The rotation matrix involving the three Euler angles and is given for the uses of angular representation as follow:

$$
{}^{W}R_{P} = \begin{pmatrix} c\psi c\phi - c\theta s\phi s\psi & -s\psi c\phi - c\theta s\phi c\psi & s\theta s\phi \\ c\psi s\phi + c\theta c\phi s\psi & -s\psi s\phi + c\theta c\phi c\psi & -s\theta c\phi \\ s\psi s\theta & c\psi s\theta & c\theta \end{pmatrix} \tag{3}
$$

Before proceeding to the inverse kinematic solution, it is useful to express the angular velocity $\omega = (\omega_X, \omega_Y, \omega_Z)^T$ and angular acceleration $\alpha = (\alpha_X, \alpha_Y, \alpha_Z)^T$ of the moving platform with reference to frame W as functions of the first and second time derivatives of the Euler angles $(\dot{\phi}, \dot{\theta}, \dot{\psi})$ and $(\ddot{\phi}, \ddot{\theta}, \ddot{\psi})$ Referring back to Fig. 2, the moving platform has an angular velocity component $\dot{\phi}$ along the Z'

axis, an angular velocity component $\dot{\theta}$ along the X' axis, and an angular velocity component $\dot{\psi}$ along the Z'' axis. Resolving these components along the axes of frame W we obtain.

$$\omega = \begin{pmatrix} \omega_X \\ \omega_y \\ \omega_Z \end{pmatrix} = \begin{pmatrix} 0 & c\phi & s\phi c\theta \\ 0 & s\phi & -c\phi s\theta \\ 1 & 0 & c\theta \end{pmatrix} \begin{pmatrix} \dot{\phi} \\ \dot{\theta} \\ \dot{\psi} \end{pmatrix} \tag{4}$$

The angular acceleration of the moving platform is obtained from (Eq. 4):

$$\alpha = \begin{pmatrix} \alpha_X \\ \alpha_Y \\ \alpha_z \end{pmatrix} = \begin{pmatrix} 0 & c\phi & s\phi s\theta \\ 0 & s\phi & -c\phi s\theta \\ 1 & 0 & c\theta \end{pmatrix} \begin{pmatrix} \ddot{\phi} \\ \ddot{\theta} \\ \ddot{\psi} \end{pmatrix} + \begin{pmatrix} 0 & -\dot{\phi}s\phi & \dot{\phi}c\phi s\theta + \dot{\theta}_s\phi c\theta \\ 0 & \dot{\phi}c\phi & \dot{\phi}s\phi s\theta - \dot{\theta}c\phi c\theta \\ 0 & 0 & -\dot{\theta}s\theta \end{pmatrix} \begin{pmatrix} \dot{\phi} \\ \dot{\theta} \\ \dot{\psi} \end{pmatrix} \tag{5}$$

5   Inverse Kinematics

The inverse kinematic solution of the Stewart platform refers to the determination of the displacements of the six links and their time derivatives corresponding to a given Cartesian position of the mobile platform in terms of three positional displacements and three angular displacements of Euler and its derivatives of time [9]. In the following sections, closed-form solutions are presented for inverse position kinematics, velocity and acceleration.

5.1   Inverse Position Kinematics

Referring back to Fig. 1, the coordinates of the ith attachment point a_i on the moving platform, given with reference to frame **P** as $^P a_i = (x_{ai}, y_{ai}, z_{ai})^T$, are obtained with reference to the world coordinate system W by using:

$$a_i = x + {}^W R_P^P a_i \tag{6}$$

Once the position of the attachment point a_i is determined, the vector L_i of link i is simply obtained as

$$L_i = a_i - b_i \tag{7}$$

where b_i is a known 3-vector that represents the coordinates of the base attachment point b_i with reference to frame W. The length l_i of link i will be simply computed from

$$l_i = \sqrt{L_i \cdot L_i} \tag{8}$$

Equations (6)–(8) represent the solution to the inverse position kinematic problem involving the determination of the six link lengths for a given Cartesian coordinate vector q representing the position and orientation of the moving platform. The unitary vector along the prism link union axis is calculated from

$$n_i = L_i/l_i \tag{9}$$

5.2 Inverse Rate Kinematics

The velocity of point ai is obtained by differentiating Eq. (6) with respect to time

$$\dot{a}_i = \dot{x} + \omega \times {}^{W}R_P^P a_i \tag{10}$$

The projection of this velocity vector on the axis of the prismatic joint of the bond produces the rate of expansion of the bond i

$$l_i = \dot{a}_i \cdot n_i = \dot{x} \cdot n_i + \omega \times \left({}^{W}R_P^P a_i \right) \cdot n_i \tag{11}$$

or

$$l_i = \dot{x} \cdot n_i + \omega \cdot \left({}^{W}R_P^P a_i \right) \times n_i \tag{12}$$

Where, for a triple scalar product a × b · c, the point and cross products can be interchanged resulting in a · b × c, as long as the order of the vectors is not changed. For the purpose of deriving the inverse Jacobian matrix of the Stewart Platform, it is useful to write Eq. (12) for the six links, in matrix form, as

$$i = J_1^{-1} \begin{pmatrix} \dot{x} \\ \omega \end{pmatrix} \tag{13}$$

where

$$J_1^{-1} = \begin{pmatrix} n_1^T & \left({}^{W}R_P^P a_1 \times n_1 \right)^T \\ \vdots & \vdots \\ n_6^T & R_P^P a_6 \times n_6)^T \end{pmatrix} \tag{14}$$

Now substituting Eqs. (4) into (13) yields

$$i = J_1^{-1} J_2^{-1} \dot{q} = J^{-1} \dot{q} \tag{15}$$

Where Eq. (16) presents the solution to the inverse rate kinematic

$$J_2^{-1} = \begin{pmatrix} I_{3\times3} & O_{3\times3} & & & \\ & & 0 & \cos\phi & \sin\phi\sin\theta \\ O_{3\times3} & & 0 & \sin\phi & -\cos\phi\sin\theta \\ & & 1 & 0 & \cos\theta \end{pmatrix} \tag{16}$$

For the assignment of the coordinate system of Fig. 3 and the formulation of the Euler angle z-x-z, this type of singularity will occur for all horizontal positions of the platform. Since the formulation of the Euler angle z-x-z allows us to directly identify the direction of orientation. By changing the orientation of the fixed coordinate system W, as shown in Fig. 3, the singularity of the formulation will now occur when the platform is in a vertical position. This is very far from the normal operating configurations of the system.

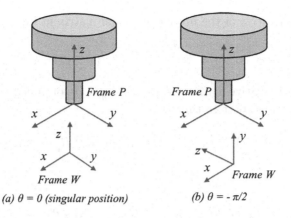

(a) $\theta = 0$ (singular position)   (b) $\theta = -\pi/2$

Fig. 3. Coordinate system assignments

5.3   Inverse Acceleration Kinematics

The acceleration of point ai is obtained by differentiating Eq. (10) with respect
to time

$$\ddot{a}_i = \ddot{x} + \alpha \times {}^W R_P^P a_i + \omega \times \left(\omega \times {}^W R_P^P a_i \right) \tag{17}$$

Now, l_i is simply obtained by differentiating with respect to time.

$$\ddot{l}_i = \ddot{a}_i \cdot n_i + \dot{a}_i \cdot \dot{n}_i \tag{18}$$

where n_i is given by

$$\dot{n}_i = \omega_i \times n_i \tag{19}$$

where ω_i for $i = 1, \ldots, 6$ are the angular velocities of the links, expressions
for which will be derived in Sect. 6. It is possible to avoid computing ω_i for
$i = 1, \ldots, 6$ in order to evaluate Eq. (19), since n_i can also be determined by
differentiating Eq. (9) with respect to time, to obtain

$$\dot{n}_i = \left(\dot{L}_i - \dot{l}_i n_i \right) / l_i \tag{20}$$

Now, l_i in Eq. (20) is found by differentiating Eq. (8) with respect to time
which results in

$$\dot{l}_i = \frac{L_i \cdot \dot{L}_i}{l_i} \tag{21}$$

and $\dot{L}_i$ is found by differentiating Eq. (7) with respect to time and substituting
Eq. (10) to yield

$$\dot{L}_i = \dot{x} + \omega \times {}^W R_P^P a_i \tag{22}$$

An alternative solution for the kinematic problem of inverse acceleration in
terms of the inverse Jacobian matrix is obtained by differentiating Eq. (15) with
respect to time

$$\ddot{l} = J^{-1}\ddot{q} + \frac{dJ^{-1}}{dt}\dot{q} \tag{23}$$

The time derivative of the inverse Jacobian matrix in Eq. (23) is given by

$$\frac{dJ^{-1}}{dt} = \frac{dJ_1^{-1}}{dt} J_2^{-1} + J_1^{-1} \frac{dJ_2^{-1}}{dt} \tag{24}$$

where the time derivative matrices $\frac{dJ_1^{-1}}{dt}$ and $\frac{dJ_2^{-1}}{dt}$ are obtained by differentiating J_1^{-1} and J_2^{-1} with respect to time as

$$\frac{dJ_1^{-1}}{dt} = \begin{pmatrix} (\omega_1 \times n_1)^T \left(\left(\omega \times {}^W R_P^P a_1 \right) \times n_1 + {}^W R_p^P a_1 \times (\omega_1 \times n_1) \right)^T \\ \vdots \\ \vdots \\ (\omega_6 \times n_6)^T \left(\left(\omega \times {}^W R_p^P a_6 \right) \times n_6 + {}^W R_p^P a_6 \times (\omega_6 \times n_6) \right)^T \end{pmatrix} \tag{25}$$

$$\frac{dJ_2^{-1}}{dt} = \begin{pmatrix} I_{3\times3} & O_{3\times3} & \\ & 0 & -\dot{\phi}s\phi & \dot{\phi}_c\phi s\theta + \dot{\theta}_S\phi c\theta \\ O_{3\times3} & 0 & \dot{\phi}c\phi & \dot{\phi}s\phi s\theta - \dot{\theta}c\phi c\theta \\ & 0 & 0 & -\dot{\theta}_s\theta \end{pmatrix} \tag{26}$$

Furthermore, we can replace $\omega_i \times n_i$ by $\dot{n}_i$ can be computed from Eqs. (20)–(22).

6   Forward Kinematics

In this section, we will use the numerical iterative technique, based on the Newton-Raphson method, to solve the direct kinematic problem. The Newton-Raphson method can be used to find the roots of the single-variable and multivariable equations [10]. Next, the procedure presented produces accurate results based on the specified tolerance. This will be demonstrated by a numerical example. For a certain position of the mechanism, we will define a function. F(q) *as*

$$F(q) = l(q) - l_{given} \tag{27}$$

where l(q) is the coordinate vector of the joint space calculated from the inverse kinematic solution that uses a coordinate vector of the Cartesian space, and is the known coordinate vector of the joint space. If q is the required forward kinematic solution, l(q) will be equal to l, and F(q) will be zero. A numerical solution using the Newton-Raphson method is given by:

$$\tilde{q}_i = \tilde{q}_{i-1} - \left(\frac{\partial F\left(\tilde{q}_{i-1} \right)}{\partial q} \right)^{-1} F\left(\tilde{q}_{i-1} \right) \tag{28}$$

where q_i is the approximate solution obtained after the ith iteration. It can be shown that the matrix $\frac{\partial F(\tilde{q}_{i-1})}{\partial q}$ is same as the inverse Jacobian matrix $J^{-1}\left(\tilde{q}_{i-1} \right)$ given by Eq. (15). Hence, Eq. (28) may be written as

$$\tilde{q}_i = \tilde{q}_{i-1} - J\left(\tilde{q}_{i-1} \right) \left(l\left(\tilde{q}_{i-1} \right) - l_{given} \right) \tag{29}$$

Starting with an initial conjecture $\tilde{q}_0$, Eq. (29) is used interactively until an acceptable solution is reached. Since there are many solutions, it is very important to start with an initial estimate close to the current position of the platform.

7   Analysis and Results

Figure 4 is showing the prototype arrange with the based components used like, camera on top, some light to avoid shadows and fake data, the maze labyrinth object, the target ball and reference coin placed on maze labyrinth and bellow the Stewart platform powered by 6 lineal servomotors.

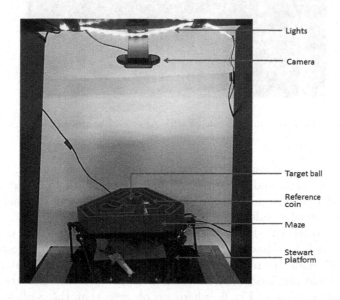

Fig. 4. Prototype of Stewart's platform with maze labyrinth

The first step was to obtain useful data in the frame from the camera so that it can be easy identify the target objects. It would be easy to identify the unfiltered pixel artifacts in our frame as an objective, however, for us to have a reliable system, we must also minimize the possibility of any "false positive" (a common term in computer vision) as any background. Objects with a similar coloration that can confuse the system. To minimize this possibility, it is better to choose an objective that is easy to discriminate. The other way to minimize false positives is to use a profile in a primitive way. In this specific case, we will use a spherical lens to be able to use the circle search functions available in OpenCV to identify the target object among the remaining artifacts in the captured frame.

The values of X and Y give us directly our values of Cartesian coordinate axis in unprocessed pixels; then we can normalize these values by using the total width and height of the table to obtain a usable index of −1 to 1 and a normalized radius of 0 to 1. The normalization of values makes the code more usable for different camera resolutions as well as making the X, Y axes more mathematically useful.

Fig. 5. Camera view of HSV filter and target object

The Cartesian position X, Y of the ball through the labyrinth, it would be uses to find the angle and magnitude to identify the path that surrounds it in a Polar coordinate system. Figure 5 shows what is seen from the raspberry and the system of interdependent coordinates.

Once its selected the shapes and the bodies to be represent, we use the Sim-Mechanics in order to draw the animated representation during the simulation. Now we can simulate the model. Viewing our model during the simulation makes it easy to see that our model simulates faster than clock time in a standard PC, its final result is seen in Fig. 6, where we observe that the z-plane generates

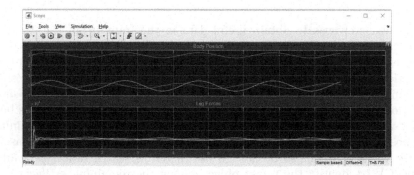

Fig. 6. Position and actuation force

less oscillations with respect to the x-axis of the system. The friction effect is considered significant for realistic friction levels, which suggests that friction compensation should be an explicit control objective.

To see the significance of the different terms in the obtained dynamic equations, computer simulation is used to calculate the inverse dynamics of the combined system including actuator dynamics. Inertial, velocity terms of the combined system as reflected on the machine prismatic joint axes are evaluated. The project when estimating the necessary force by the motors in the possible positions of the platform, representing in Fig. 6. It was finished that it would be constant. With a starting peak that later stabilizes.

8 Conclusions

Combining several representations of the problem of advanced kinematics with optimization techniques, an efficient method was found to solve the problem. For the purposes of real-time simulation, several mobile platforms were mathematically predefined [11].

The task of an advanced method of kinematic resolution was, then, to track the position and orientation of the mobile platform, knowing the initial position. The resolution method was able to determine the exact position and orientation of the mobile platform within negligible error margins. Problem of the equivalent trajectories: due to the existence of multiple solutions for the advancement of the kinematics, there may be more than one route that the mobile platform can follow and have exactly the same support lengths at each point of the road.

The resolution algorithm may, in some circumstances, jump to an equivalent path at certain division points. It has been said that each route represents an equally correct solution of advanced kinematics, but only one of them represents the true trajectory of the mobile platform. An empirical algorithm was designed that increased the probability of finding the correct solution and was successful in all test cases. Unfortunately, it can not be shown that it is present in every imaginable movement of the mobile platform [12].

The resolution method will always find the correct solution if the change in the position or direction of movement of the mobile platform. If that condition is met, the described method can be used in the resolution of advanced kinematics in real time.

Acknowledgements. This work is supported by Universidad El Bosque and the Research Vice-rectory with the research project PCI-2017-8832.

References

1. Jakobovic, D.: Forward kinematics of a Stewart platform mechanism. Faculty of Electrical Engineering and Computing, pp. 1–3, May 2002
2. Grosch, P.: Universal tyre test machine. In: Automatic Control, Robotics and Computer Vision, pp. 117–137, June 1962

3. Song, S.-K., Kwon, D.-S.: New direct kinematic formulation of 6 D.O.F Stewart-Gough plataform using the tetrahedro approach. Trans. Control Autom. Syst. Eng. **4**(3), 1–7 (2002)
4. Nategh, M.J., Karimi, D.: A study on the quality of hexapod machine tool's workspace. Int. J. Mech. Mechatron. Eng. **4**(3), 438–443 (2009)
5. Müller, A.: Closed form expressions for the sensitivity of kinematic dexterity measures to posture changing and geometric variations. In: IEEE International Conference on Robotics Automations (ICRA), pp. 3–7, June 2014
6. Pathare, P., Opara, U., Al-Said, F.A.-J.: Colour measurement and analysis in fresh and processed foods: a review. Food Bioprocess Technol. **6**, 36–60 (2013)
7. Wang, H., Li, R., Gao, Y., Cao, C., Ge, L., Xie, X.: Target recognition and localization of mobile robot with monocular PTZ camera. J. Robot. **2019**, 1–12 (2019)
8. Donald, B.R.: Algorithms in Structural Molecular Biology, 7th edn. MIT Press, Cambridge (2012)
9. Rodriguez, E., Jaimes, C.I.R.: Conceptual design and dimensional optimization of the linear delta robot with single legs for additive manufacturing. Proc. Inst. Mech. Eng. Part I: J. Syst. Control Eng. (2019). https://doi.org/10.1177/0959651819836915
10. Lafmejani, A.S., Masouleh, M., Kalhor, A.: Trajectory tracking control of a pneumatically actuated 6-DOF Gough-Stewart parallel robot using back stepping-sliding mode controller and geometry-based quasi forward kinematic method. Robot. Comput.-Integr. Manuf. **54**, 96–114 (2018)
11. Marcos, M., Machado, J.T., Perdicolis, T.A.: A multi-objective approach for the motion planning of redundant manipulators. Appl. Soft Comput. **12**, 589–599 (2012)
12. Irvine, R.: The GEARS conflict resolution algorithm, November 1997

Analysis of the Adverse Events and Incidents Reported to Departmental Technosurvillance Program of Medical Devices in Antioquia, Colombia During 2016 and 2017

Mabel Catalina Zapata[1,2]([envelope]), Juan Guillermo Barreneche[1,2] [ID],
Jhon Eder Mosquera[2], and Sebastián Londoño[2]

[1] Bioinstrumentation and Clinical Engineering Research Group - GIBIC,
Universidad de Antioquia UdeA, Calle 70 No. 52-21, Medellín, Colombia
mcatalina.zapata@udea.edu.co
[2] Bioengineering Department, Engineering Faculty,
Universidad de Antioquia UdeA, Calle 70 No. 52-21, Medellín, Colombia

Abstract. The study analyzes the causes of the adverse events reported to technosurveillance program of medical devices in the department of Antioquia in Colombia for the years 2016 and 2017. This paper identifies the main medical equipment involved in the reports and proposes possible improvements that could allow the decrease of the adverse events; having as reference the advances of the *Instituto Nacional de Vigilancia de Medicamentos y Alimentos* (known in spanish as INVIMA) and international institutes. The three main medical equipment involved in these reports are infusion pumps, dialysis machines and negative pressure wound therapy systems, which represent more than 30% of the reports. The principal causes of events are device usage errors, alarms failure and pressure problems. According to the results of the analysis, it is not only necessary to improve the correct use of these technologies through of proposed training model. In order to achieve a reduction of the adverse events in the department of Antioquia, also is necessary to standardize the equipment and processes whenever possible and to implement usability tests. Through this measure, reliability can be increased, the need for crossed training can be minimized and can be identified potential problems and unintended consequences of the use of technology, like related with alarms failure and pressure problems.

Keywords: Adverse events · Biomedical equipment · Infusion pumps · Dialysis machine · Negative pressure system

1 Introduction

Currently, medical technology is considered a pillar for health care, since its implementation can improve the diagnosis and treatment of patients in any

J. C. Figueroa-García et al. (Eds.): WEA 2019, CCIS 1052, pp. 147–158, 2019.
https://doi.org/10.1007/978-3-030-31019-6_13

health institution [1]. The use of this technology implies in the majority of cases improvement in the efficiency of the processes, however, the risks and adverse events that accompany this new generation of technology are a growing trend at the global level [2].

The Pan American Health Organization, together with the GHTF (Global Harmonization Task Force) reported that between 50% and 70% of incidents with medical devices are related to errors in the assembly, suppression of alarms, wrong connections, incorrect clinical use, incorrect selection of usage parameters, incorrect programming and monitoring failure [3]. For its part, the Medicines and Health Care Regulatory Agency in the United Kingdom (MHRA) during the period from 2011 to 2012 reported 11.970 adverse incidents related to medical devices [4].

Additionally, an international benchmark is the ECRI institute, which is a non-profit organization that provides information and research services in the area of health and annually makes a report listing the 10 technologies or medical practices that it considers should be receive priority in its security. By the end of 2016 it's necessary to take into account the infusion errors that cause uncontrolled flows in the infusion pumps, the risk to which the patients are exposed when the alarms of the ventilators are damaged and the misuse and operation of surgical staplers [5]. By the end of 2017, it is important to highlight risk situations such as the misuse of drug delivery systems with bar codes, the low adoption of safer lines for enteral feeding and electrosurgical active electrodes without coating [6].

In Latin America there is a study on the safety of patients in hospitals called IBEAS about the prevalence of adverse events (EA by its acronym in Spanish) in Latin American hospitals. This was carried out in collaboration with WHO, PAHO, and the ministries of health of Costa Rica, Mexico, Peru and Colombia, in which 58 health service institutions from these 5 countries participated and a total of 11.555 hospitalized patients were analyzed. From which it was concluded that more than 60% of the adverse events analyzed were avoidable [7].

Other researchers have also been commissioned to perform similar studies on a smaller scale, performing analysis and monitoring in particular services in different institutions of the country, where they have identified that adverse events independently of the type of medical device and the place of incidence, have as main cause the incorrect use of the device, as stated by Alfonso Marín et al. [8].

In Colombia, the national regulatory technosurveillance program is implemented through resolution 4816 of 2008, which is a postmarketing surveillance strategy for the technology, in order to reduce the risks and adverse events that result from its use [9]. Through this program in the country, different epidemiological surveillance methodologies have been implemented, ranging from passive surveillance to intensive surveillance. Technosurveillance in the country relies on the active surveillance or mandatory notification of problems related to the use and quality of medical devices, carried out by the actors at the local level such as health professionals, importers, manufacturers, patients, operators and users [10].

Therefore, in the country since 2011 by INVIMA has been promoting and focusing efforts towards proactive surveillance (to anticipate to) and intensive as part of the new surveillance trends epidemiological of the 21st century, where it is sought to implement administrative interventions, action policies and educational type in accordance with the problems identified in each institution [11].

The technosurveillance program has four levels of operation, which are the national, departmental, local level and users of medical devices [12]. This study analyzed the incidents and adverse events that were presented to the departmental program of technosurveillance in Antioquia during the period 2016–2017 (departmental level) and the results were compared with the national and local levels. To compare with the national level, the reports presented by INVIMA on the national technosurveillance program were taken into account. Regarding the local level, the technosurveillance reports of a third-level health care institution of the department were taken into account.

The main objective of the study was to identify the biomedical equipment involved in the events and incidents with a major incidence and the main causes of failure associated with them. Finally, possible solutions were proposed to help to prevent situations and actions that lead to adverse events and incidents with this equipments particularly. It was based on the progress made by INVIMA and international authorities in this area.

2 Materials and Methods

2.1 Study Material

This study was conducted based on the data of the technosurveillance reports in the department of Antioquia during 2016–2017. The nature of this information is confidential, therefore, the professionals of the Sectional Secretariat of Health and Social Protection of Antioquia, responsible for the management of this data, previously carried out a work of supervision of the pertinent information to protect the privacy of the institutions, professionals and patients involved in them. The technosurveillance reports of a local department institution were also taken into account for the analysis. This is a third level institution of health care, which has an installed capacity of 596 beds and a total of 81 health services enabled according to the data of the special registry of health providers (REPS by its acronym in spanish) [13].

2.2 Techniques and Statistical Analysis

Initially a descriptive analysis is carried out by means of which the number of events and adverse incidents consolidated in the database are quantified, both in total in the period analyzed and for each of the years. The nature of the institution that carries it out is also identified, that is, public or private nature.

Subsequently, each of the types of reports in four large groups is quantified, which are defined in resolution 4816 of 2008 and are: adverse events and incidents of a serious and non-serious nature [9].

Subsequently, the procedure consists of analyzing the type of medical device involved in the reports as follows: initially a filter is made according to the type of sanitary registry of the device, where it is that those that relate the acronym DM (medical devices) have a classification of risk I and IIa and those with the acronym EBC (controlled biomedical equipment) have a risk classification IIb and III according to decree 4725 of 2005 [14], generating two lists or groups. After this classification, all those devices that were not biomedical equipment were eliminated from the list of medical devices, in order to consolidate the information with the biomedical equipment, object of this study. This process was carried out in the first instance by means of the generic and commercial names of the device and its use. Later, with the devices that could not be identified by means of the above parameters, an additional parameter was taken into account, which was the review of the description of the event or adverse incident. It is important to mention that for the case of the list of devices with type of EBC registry, it was also necessary to resort to the description of the event or incident given that some registers under the acronym EBC also cover accessories and spare parts of the biomedical equipment.

Finally, having the list of biomedical equipment involved in the database, we proceed to quantify the incidence of the same on the total of the reports and for the equipment which had more than 5% of incidence in the biomedical equipment list, the failure causes are analyzed. These causes of failure are analyzed according to the probable cause registered in the database, which are those contemplated in the Colombian Technical Standard 5736 that establishes the structure of the coding for types of adverse events and their causes. This standard is an adoption of ISO 19218: 2005 [15]. Once was identified the failure causes for this equipments, a Pareto analysis [16] was made, taking as hypothesis that the 20% of the failure causes, generate the 80% of the adverse events and incidents.

According to the consolidated information for biomedical equipment, its possible causes of failure and the Pareto analysis, comparison is made with the national level according to the reports of the technosurveillance program for 2015 and 2018 [17], and with the local level according to the technosurveillance database from the institution mentioned above. Subsequently, a review of the progress of INVIMA is made regarding the prevention of this type of events in the equipments identified, and also with international entities such as the FDA, NPSA, ECRI, among others, to finally propose improvement actions, focused in preventing events. This methodology is summarized in the diagram of Fig. 1.

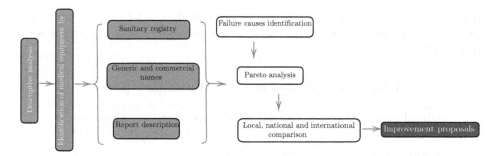

Fig. 1. Methodology

3   Results

3.1   Classification of the Report Type

In the database a total of 3011 reports were presented, of which 1302 and 1709 corresponded to the years 2016 and 2017 respectively. Additionally, it was identified that 333 of them were reported by public institutions, 2432 by private institutions and for 6 reports it is not identified the nature of the institution that presented it. Regarding the type of report, a distribution of the same was found as illustrated in Table 1, from which it can be seen that the highest type of report is given for non-serious adverse incidents (NSAI) with 82%, followed by the non-serious adverse events (NSAE) with 13.3%. It is also shown that serious adverse events (SAI) present a 3.2% incidence and serious adverse events (SAE) present a 0.9%

Table 1. Percentage of reports according to their classification

Type of report	SAE	SAI	NSAE	NSAI	Non Id
Percentage of report	0.9 %	3.2 %	13.3 %	82.0 %	0.5 %

3.2   Biomedical Equipment Involved and Associated Causes of Failure

In relation to total reports related with the identified biomedical equipment, it was found that the total number of these was 300, which corresponds to 10% of the total of the reports presented during the period analyzed. Of this amount, 69.1% were found that correspond to biomedical equipment with risk classification IIb and III, and 30.6% correspond to biomedical equipment with risk classification I and IIa. This reports (300) correspond with a total of 64 different technologies or medical equipments. The equipments that were involved in a greater number of reports (with significant incidence) were three, which are infusion pumps, dialysis machines and negative pressure systems, as can be seen in Table 2.

Table 2. Biomedical equipment involved in the reports

Medical equipment	Amount	Percentage	Risk	Classification
			I and IIa	IIb and III
Infusion pump	48	15.9 %		x
Dialysis machine	34	11.3 %		x
Negative pressure system	22	7.3 %		x
Total	**104**	**34.5 %**		

Of all the equipments involved in the reports, the equipments with more than 5% of incidence in this are infusion pumps, dialysis machines and negative pressure systems. For these three technologies the causes of associated failure are illustrated in Tables 3, 4 and 5 respectively. The rest 61 technologies associated with 196 reports do not have a relevance incidence, and present randomly occurrence.

Table 3. Failure causes for infusion pumps

Code	Failure cause	Amount	Percentage
950	Use error	21	43.8%
930	Non-identified	8	16.7%
790	Others	4	8.3%
520	Alarm failure	4	8.3%
850	Quality assurance	3	6.3%
540	Calibration	3	6.3%
500	Abnormal use	2	4.2%
870	Software	1	2.1%
710	Labelling and use instruction	1	2.1%
610	Electric circuit	1	2.1%
Total		48	100.0%

Note: Code and failure cause established on the Colombian Technical Standard, 5736

From Table 3, the main cause of failure for the infusion pumps was "use error", however this cause is followed by 8 reports where there is no cause of failure. For these reports where a cause of failure is not identified, a revision of the description of the same is made and it is found that within the same they relate to possible causes such as failure in alarms and electrical circuit of the equipment.

From Table 4 it has been that the main cause of failure of the dialysis machines was "others". A particular review of these reports was made and causes of failure were found that can be reclassified to have a better observation of the possible causes of the event or incident. Within this reclassification made according to the reading of the description of the report there are three possible associated causes which are: failure in alarms, mechanical components and electrical circuit of the equipment.

Table 4. Failure causes for dialysis machines

Code	Failure cause	Amount	Percentage
790	Others	17	50.0%
540	Calibration	7	21.0%
520	Alarm failure	7	21.0%
730	Maintenance	1	3.0%
740	Manufacturing	1	3.0%
720	Leak	1	3.0%
Total		34	100.0%

From Table 5, it is observed that for the negative pressure systems there was only one cause of associated failure which was "alarms failure". A review of these reports was made and it was verified that although most of these were related to the lack of activation of the alarms due to different circumstances, there are also reports in which only the negative pressure mechanism or generation of vacuum is related.

Table 5. Failure causes for negative pressure systems

Code	Failure cause	Amount	Percentage
520	Alarm failure	22	100.0%
Total		22	100.0%

Finally, the Pareto analysis was made with the total failure causes presented above (104) and is found that, approximately 30% of the failure causes (520, 950, 790, 540 or Alarm failure, Use error, Others and Calibration respectively), generated the 82% of the adverse events and incidents related with medical equipment, this results are showed in the Fig. 2.

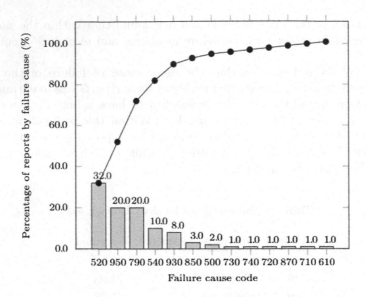

Fig. 2. Pareto analysis of failure causes

4   Discussion

4.1   Classification of the Report Type

From the departmental level reports, there is a greater incidence tendency in the non-serious adverse incidents which correspond to 82% of the total of the reports, followed by the non-serious adverse events that represent 13.3% which together represent 95.3% of total reports. These trends for these two types of notifications are analogous to those reported by INVIMA at the national level for 2015, where the total of 6478 reports was that 58% corresponded to NSAI and 36% to NSAE, representing 93% thereof [18]. Regarding the local situation of classification of the reports of adverse events and incidents, a higher incidence tendency is followed in incidents followed by non-serious events.

However, although serious events and incidents represent a low percentage of reports (4.17%) it is important to follow up on them since the serious nature of these implies an event or potential risk that could have led to death or serious deterioration of the patient health, operator or anyone who might be involved in the event [19].

4.2   Biomedical Equipment Involved and Associated Causes of Failure

Of the total of reports related to biomedical equipment, 69% of them are related to equipment that has risk classification IIb and III, that is, a classification of high and very high risk respectively. This implies special attention to these equipments because they are intended to protect or sustain life or to prevent the deterioration of human health [19]. Situation that is very important to take measures that reduce the incidence of these in adverse events and incidents.

The results of the Pareto analysis are so useful because it was found that by focusing on to reduce four causes of the failure (30% of the total), is possible to obtain a reduction of approximately 80% of adverse events and incidents related with the medical device with major incidence in the department reports.

Particularly, at the departmental level, infusion pumps have the highest incidence in technosurveillance reports and their main cause of failure is associated with errors of use. When compared with the national level, it is also the biomedical equipment that is most related to adverse events and incidents. This situation is reflected in the national report of technosurveillance for the year 2018 in which within the top 10 of medical devices most reported, are the infusion pumps as the biomedical equipment most related to the reports. This situation has been addressed by the intensive technosurveillance strategy in the country, because within the non-implantable medical devices of difficult traceability "signaled and prioritized" by the centinel network are the infusion pumps. Additionally, there is a study material available that allows each referent to identify the risks in the use of this particular equipment, where one of the most prevalent recommendations is the training of personnel in the use of these [17].

Additionally, regarding the infusion pumps, the FDA developed an initiative to improve infusion pumps and proposed tasks such as improving user knowledge regarding these equipments and facilitating the improvement of the design since its manufacture [20].

It also has that, according to the problems reported by the ECRI institute related to infusion pumps, 48% of them are related to concentration errors and programming errors of the device [21]. This points to possible failures in the use of technology and engineering design problems of the equipment that can increase the risk of errors of personnel operating the equipment, as proposed by Johnson et al. [22] in their study of attitudes towards the errors of use in medical devices and prevention of adverse events [22]. Regarding the dialysis machines, which represent the second biomedical equipment with greater presence in the departmental level reports as illustrated above, and although its main failure rate was associated with "others", it has a high incidence of failure in alarms according to the analysis described. It has that at a national level these equipments have also had a high incidence in the reports, because they are also within the 6 types of biomedical equipment marked and prioritized with a "high" signal level that have been involved in alerts, recall or security reports [17]. For this reason, the INVIMA proposes the development of intensive surveillance in renal units and the application of the failure analysis methodology and its effects for these equipments.

A study on safety in the dialysis facility states that, while dialysis machines rarely have a high mortality, human errors related to the machine interface and lack of communication between health professionals are common sources of mistake [23]. Additionally, a study on patients dialyzed in Pennsylvania in 2010, reported that more than 12% of adverse events were triggered by breaches of the protocols by the professionals in charge of the procedures [24].

The project for patient safety of the renal association in conjunction with the National Patient Safety Agency (NPSA) of England had the objective of formulating and sharing solutions to clinical incidents and risks. During this project, both manufacturing faults and equipment technical failures were identified as well as causes of failure in the hemodialysis machines derived from use errors (programming errors). Failures generally are caused when the personnel is not related to all types of machines, therefore as a recommendation there is training for new personnel and for those who change equipment [25].

Negative pressure systems were presented as the third biomedical equipment with the highest number of reports at departmental level with a greater cause of failure associated with "alarm failure". At a national level, these have not been within the equipments with high prevalence. Internationally, there are several reports of this type of equipment in the database of adverse events of the FDA for a period from 2014 to 2019, where there have been 53 problems with alarms, 12 pressure problems and have that the largest number of reports (394) does not have enough information to classify the equipment's problem [26].

When comparing the results obtained at departmental level with the national level in terms of infusion pumps and hemodialysis machines, a high relation was obtained between them. Additionally, a broad international overview was illustrated in which similar problems have been addressed in relation to these equipments and improvements such as those mentioned have been proposed. However, when comparing the results with the local level, that is, with the reports from the department's third-level institution, a high relation was not found between the types of biomedical equipment involved. Situation that can be associated with the fact that although it is true that this institution has a large number of services enabled, the safety conditions of one institution to another change, as well as factors of workloads and the type of professionals that operate the technology.

The Research Health Care Quality Agency (AHRQ) through the human factors engineering states that usability tests of technology can identify potential problems and unintended consequences of the use of technology. Also one of the main pillars of this discipline is standardization, or the reduction of the variability of brands and equipment models in an institution as much as possible [27].

According to the biomedical equipments and the identified causes of failure, a proposed strategy to mitigate the incidence of adverse events and incidents takes into account several aspects that contribute to these. In the first instance it is recommended for infusion pumps and dialysis machines, reduce the variability of brands, models and/or references of the equipment of the institutions, in such a way that the professionals only need to be aware of the handling of a type of technology. Have an effective training model, where the knowledge acquired by the people during the teaching process can be validated through performance tests. Improve the interface of the technology by means of a design with an easy to use and intuitive structure for the professional, which can be achieved by implementing the usability test by the equipment manufacturers.

There are many training models in the use of medical devices, in particular it is pertinent to review the model proposed by Echeverry et al. [28], in which a diagnosis is made prior to the learning stage to identify the knowledge of the staff and then focus training in identified gaps or weaknesses. Additionally, it has the use of virtual tools where people have an individual interaction with the study material and later it is complemented with practical and theoretical sessions where the time is optimized. Finally, a final validation is carried out in which the knowledge and/or skills acquired in the use of a certain medical device are evaluated.

5   Conclusions

It was found that the situation of the Antioquia department, regarding the reports of adverse events and incidents reported to the departmental program of technosurveillance is similar to the national situation in terms of the type of notifications made with a high prevalence of no serious events and incidents. Additionally, the two biomedical equipments that present the most reports are also among the most reported equipments nationwide. From these two situations it is concluded that there is a high relationship between these two levels of the program, which is useful due to the applicability at the departmental level of the advances, guidelines and recommendations made by INVIMA at the national level. Additionally, the events related to these technologies are not exclusive to the country but are also related to adverse events at an international level. Therefore it is useful and relevant that infusion pumps and dialysis machines are within the interest of agencies, institutions and researchers because they constantly analyze their failure causes and design and implement strategies to mitigate the undesirable consequences of their use.

Regarding the failure causes associated with infusion pumps and dialysis machines, for which INVIMA has recommended personnel training in the use of technology to strengthen all stages of the life cycle of the same, it is recommended to implement a training model like the one proposed, where you can measure its efficiency by means of evaluations at the end of it and optimize the time by means of previous checks. It is also important to note that in conjunction with the training, measures must be taken, such as the standardization of equipment in the institutions and the promotion of usability tests of the technology.

Acknowledgements. The authors would like to thank to the Sectional Secretariat of Health and Social Protection of Antioquia, for provide the information about the adverse events and incidents reported to technosurveillance program in Antioquia, 2016-2017. This study has been partially supported by Universidad de Antioquia through the Grant FIT18-1-02 - SISTEMA DE MEDICIÓN DE PRESIÓN FLEXI-BLE and Ruta N Medellín, through the CTI project 248C-Desarrollo de un dispositivo biomédico flexible.

Conflicts of Interest. The authors declare that they have no conflicts of interest.

References

1. OMS. Medical devices: managing the mismatch. Technical report (2012)
2. Arias, D., Camacho, J.E., Osorno, J.: Skill improvement in patient safety through training strategy implementation in health-care workers. Rev. Ingeniería Biomédica **10**(20), 21–25 (2017)
3. Hernández, A.: Techno surveillance, perspective of the Pan American Health Organization. Technical report (2008)
4. Medicines and Healthcare products Regulatory Agency (MHRA). Medical devices, adverse incidents reported to MHRA 2011 to 2013. Technical report, April 2014
5. ECRI. Top 10 Health Technology Hazards for 2017. Technical report 1 (2016)
6. ECRI. Top 10 Health Technology Hazards for 2018. Technical report (2017)
7. OMS. IBEAS design: adverse events prevalence in Latin American hospital. Technical report Prevalencia, eventos, adversos (2010)
8. Alfonso Marín, L.P., Salazar López, C.: Incidence of adverse events associated with medical devices within a health institution in Colombia. Rev. Ingeniería Biomédica **4**, 71–84 (2010)
9. Ministry of social protection. 4816 Resolution of 2008 (2008)
10. INVIMA. National Techno Surveillance Program (2012)
11. INVIMA. The post-marketing surveillance in Colombia. Technical report (2018)
12. INIVMA. Niveles de operación y responsabilidades de los actores del programa de tecnovigilancia (2012)
13. Colombian Government. Database of special registry of health service providers (2019)
14. Ministry of social protection. Decree 4725 of 2005 (2005)
15. ICONTEC. Technical Standard 5736 (2009)
16. Izar, J., González, J.H.: Chapter IV 4.1 Pareto chart, p. 8, May 2004
17. INVIMA. Sentinel Hospitals Network in Technosurveillance (2018)
18. INVIMA. ABC of Technosurveillance, Bogotá (2012)
19. INVIMA. Statistics of 2015. Technical report, Bogotá (2015)
20. FDA. Infusion pump. Technical report (2010)
21. Camacho, J.: Mechanisms for risk prevention with infusion pumps (2018)
22. Johnson, T.R., et al.: Attitudes toward medical device use errors and the prevention of adverse events. Jt. Comm. J. Qual. Patient Saf. **33**(11), 689–694 (2007)
23. Kliger, A.S.: Maintaining safety in the dialysis facility. Clin. J. Am. Soc. Nephrol. **10**(4), 688–695 (2010)
24. Pennsylvania Patient Safety Advisory. Hemodialysis administration: strategies to ensure safe patient care. Pennsylvania Patient Safety Advisory, pp. 87–96 (2015)
25. Rylance, P.B.: Improving patient safety and avoiding incidents in renal units. J. Ren. Nurs. **6**(1), 24–28 (2014)
26. FDA. Total Product Life Cycle (2019)
27. Agency for Healthcare Research and Quality. Human Factors Engineering (2019)
28. Echeverri, L.B., García, J.H., Barreneche, J.G.: Training model design in healthcare services involving medical devices. Rev. Ingeniería Biomédica **10**, 27–34 (2016)

Teleagro: Software Architecture of Georeferencing and Detection of Heat of Cattle

Paola Ariza-Colpas[1](✉), Roberto Morales-Ortega[1],
Marlon Alberto Piñeres-Melo[2], Farid Melendez-Pertuz[1],
Guillermo Serrano-Torné[3], Guillermo Hernandez-Sanchez[3],
Hugo Martínez-Osorio[3], and Carlos Collazos-Morales[4]

[1] Universidad de la Costa, CUC, Barranquilla, Colombia
{parizal, rmoralesl, fmelendel}@cuc.edu.co
[2] Universidad del Norte, Barranquilla, Colombia
pineresm@uninorte.edu.co
[3] Extreme Technologies, Barranquilla, Colombia
{gserrano, ghernandez, hmartinez}@extreme.com.co
[4] Universidad Manuela Beltran, Bogota, Colombia
carlos.collazos@docentes.umb.edu.co

Abstract. The systems of livestock production contribute in a preponderant way to improve the quality of life of the communities, since it allows to support the production of the daily sustenance of the communities, to conserve the ecosystems, to promote the conservation of the wild life and to satisfy the values and traditions cultural Latin America, with its large wilderness areas, and a privileged climate favors the maintenance of livestock, to meet the demands of food and ensure regional and global food security. In Colombia, the agricultural sector contributes approximately 11.83% of the national GDP at current prices, according to the Bank of the Republic. Likewise, the livestock industry participates with 3.6%, in comparison with other sectors of the agricultural economy, the production of Colombian cattle doubles and triples to other sectors, such as poultry, coffee and floriculture. In addition, it contributes to the generation of employment in more than 25% of the total jobs generated in the agricultural sector and approximately 7% of the total employment of the Colombian economy (http://www.banrep.gov.co/is/pib). Within agricultural production, livestock occupy 38 million hectares, being 9 times larger than the area dedicated to agriculture. However, agriculture contributes 63% of the value of agricultural production, while livestock, mainly extensive, contributes 26% (FEDEGAN, Strategic Livestock Plan 2019). The large proportion of the area with agricultural vocation dedicated to precarious extensive livestock has explained the low agricultural productivity in Colombia, with very serious consequences for human and sustainable development. This document shows the results of the communications, software and hardware platforms to help the livestock sector to manage production.

Keywords: Tecnhnological system · Georreferenced detectioni · Zeal of bovine cattle

© Springer Nature Switzerland AG 2019
J. C. Figueroa-García et al. (Eds.): WEA 2019, CCIS 1052, pp. 159–166, 2019.
https://doi.org/10.1007/978-3-030-31019-6_14

1 Introduction

An indicator of productivity that allows making comparisons is the extraction rate and the percentage of the herd that is sacrificed. In Colombia it is approximately 14%, a value that has remained stable in recent years, indicating the few advances in productivity. This rate is well below the world average of 21%, and even more against countries such as Argentina 25% or the United States 38%. If the extraction rate in Colombia were equal to the world average, it would produce more than five million heads per year, instead of the nearly four million that are currently slaughtered; and if the extraction average were that of Argentina, more than six million heads would be produced per year for slaughter [1].

The bovine cycle can also be taken as an indicator of the technological level of the activity. The greater the duration of the cycle, the lower the technological level and the profitability of the livestock activity [2]. Econometric measurements of the livestock cycle in Colombia show more marked and deeper cycles than other herds, and have shown that from the moment the gestation begins until the steers are slaughtered there is a period of five years, which reflects a period of maturation of very extensive investment.

Regarding investment in the agricultural sector, there are "growth bottlenecks" that inhibit investment in the agricultural sector, such as insecurity, lack of definition of property rights, inadequate infrastructure, lack of innovation and development technology and the lack of access to financing, among others. With a view to the future in the short and medium term, it is worth asking how the Colombian agricultural sector can take advantage of the opportunity of the high prices of agricultural commodities in international markets and the entry into operation of Free Trade Agreements signed by the country, to make a leap in production and productivity, taking into consideration principles of economic, social and environmental sustainability [3].

Economic sustainability refers to the fact that the sector must be able to generate income based on the comparative and competitive advantages of its productions; [4] Social sustainability refers to the fact that the income generated by the sector must be at least sufficient to guarantee a decent life for all farmers in the field, and environmental sustainability refers to the fact that agricultural activity must preserve the environment.

The article is organized in the next section. First, the problem of livestock sector in Colombia is shown. Second, we explain the software applications. Third, each of the components of the hardware architecture is detailed. Fourth, the conclusions of the experimentation are shown and future works. Finally, the researchers thank all those who supported the development of this project.

2 Problems of Livestock Sector in Colombia

Livestock producers in Colombia represent 80.7% of the farms currently [5] in the department of Cesar. It is important to define that this production is fundamentally based on family-type production. The small livestock production can and generates an important part of the necessary food for the internal market of the department. The family or backyard livestock production contributes to the growth of the gross domestic product, could help boost exports of livestock products, generates jobs, besides being a source that generates nutrients for consumption and is a key factor in the fight against insecurity food and sustainable. rural development.

The potential contribution of this sector to the agricultural economy of the Department of Cesar and to food security depends, in most cases, on the timely receipt of animal and veterinary health services, technical assistance and other support needed for guarantee sustainability of their production systems. Small-scale producers require not only access to better and new technologies, but also innovations in production systems that guarantee their access to markets and improve the contribution of self-consumption to the requirements of diets [6, 7].

Livestock can also protect households from crises such as those caused by drought and other natural catastrophes. Possession of animals can increase the ability of households and individuals to fulfill their social obligations and improve cultural identity.

Livestock is also a basic source of guarantees for the poor and allows many households to obtain access to capital and loans for commercial purposes. Thus, livestock is an important asset of capital that, with careful attention, can give a boost to households to get out of extreme poverty and benefit from market economie, the incentives for investment in any industry are given in the security of recovery and generation of profit from the resources invested and combined with a return in the short and medium term of this investment, when in the bovine production the adequate techniques are not used to production, the return on investment is slow and in the department of Cesar [8], this slow return has traditionally been managed especially in the small producers who represent the majority in the sector.

On the other hand, insecurity in the region, kidnappings, extortion, cattle rustling and armed conflict, do not provide the guarantees to increase investment in the cattle production of the department, so in the last decade, investment in the sector in the department has been decreasing [9]. The small producers of the cesar department do not have the economic capacity to access the technologies that have already been developed and successfully tested in bovine production, which does not allow them to compete with the producers who have access to them, so that every day its profitability decreases, the lack of technological resources, technical assistance and capacity to take on challenges such as those of climate change, increasingly opens the existing gap in the region. The efficiency of a productive sector is measured at the regional level by the capacity to supply the domestic market fully and generate surpluses that allow it to export, currently Colombia has three free trade agreements that would allow it to export meat, with the United States, the European Union and Canada, however we are talking about economies with a sector of bovine production technified, in some cases with the basket compensated, or subsidized production, with a superior infrastructure and an exchange rate in its favor, therefore the technological backwardness in the department the possibility of accessing international markets would be increasingly remote.

One of the causes of the crisis of livestock in the department of Cesar is the productive cycle of a cow, which includes all the phases and events through which the cows pass, between a birth and the next birth, to reduce to the appropriate minimum, it is necessary to perform heat detection efficiently, which requires a visual observation of certain behaviors that the cows present during this period, which does not guarantee the success of this, which has placed the periods open in the department months, when a cow under normal conditions its open period is 12 months. With the decrease in the open period, the small producer would obtain a profit of approximately 680 thousand pesos per year, by incorporating the technology for the detection of heat and with a percentage of efficiency of 50% of the cattle females of the cattle inventory of the region. Amounting to 500 thousand copies, annual income for producers would amount to 170 billion pesos, which represents 1.6% of the GDP of the department [10].

Although there are technological solutions, small producers in the department of Cesar have several obstacles to a greater use of information technology. These include the following: insufficient development of communications infrastructure; high costs of acquiring computers, telecommunication equipment and related computer programs, as well as the costs of exploiting communications; deficiency of human capital to develop and manage new technology, and lack of a private market capable of offering infrastructure, developing computer programs and promoting applications. On the other hand, the investment costs in technology is affected by the fear of the investor for the insecurity that plagues the country's fields, are factors that undoubtedly affect sustainable growth of livestock, one of these manifestations of insecurity is that of cattle rustling or cattle theft, according to the National Federation of Cattle Ranchers-FEDEGAN, The municipalities with the highest incidence of cattle theft, after Valledupar, are Codazzi, La Jagua de Ibirico and Astrea. It is a recurring theme, there are times when it increases, in others it decreases but it has never stopped showing up [11].

The research and transfer of technical knowledge and processes to producers and workers of livestock companies, are fundamental pillars for regional development and would be crucial to solve the problems of the sector, however for the department of Cesar, no research has been conducted that seek to reduce the cost of computer applications that could generate an impact on productivity and that are accessible to small producers, who represent the majority of the population dedicated to livestock production. With the development of a technological product commercially accessible to small producers, in addition to the contribution to economic development, a viable and scalable enterprise will be generated [12].

The present article shows the results of a project that was framed in the national public policies, this is how in the document bases of the National Development Plan "All for a new country", it is indicated as the objective of the national government To promote the inclusive economic development of the country and its regions, To achieve a more equitable and inclusive society through a greater articulation between the policies of economic development and those of social development. It seeks to enhance the contribution of Science Technology and Innovation in the development of business initiatives that contribute to reducing the gaps of the population.

The same objective points to the need to strengthen agricultural competitiveness to consolidate the countryside as a generator of employment and wealth for rural inhabitants. In order to increase rural productivity and profitability, it requires the provision of sectoral goods and services, as well as integral interventions in the territories, that allow optimizing production conditions, consolidating domestic markets and taking advantage of access to new markets. One of the strategies achieved in the document is to implement a system of comprehensive technical assistance, which is articulated with the National Agricultural Innovation System and has as a starting point the needs of producers and market conditions.

The low productivity of the agricultural sector and the gaps between agricultural research and technical assistance, explains in part the low effectiveness of technological packages in the sector. The pillar that supports the productivity of agricultural activity is the research and transfer of technical knowledge and processes to producers and workers of livestock enterprises.

With the transfer of technology to the sector we have an opportunity, a resource and we must work in this line, technology is the engine of change and every future scenario must be thought in terms of human development, social, economic and environmental sustainability.

3 Software Architecture of Teleagro

This section provides information on the infrastructure architecture of the platform that will be used for the implementation of the TELEAGRO project See Fig. 1.

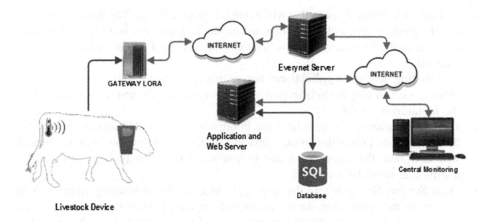

Fig. 1. General operation of the solutions

3.1 Local Operation of the Solution

Each animal will have an intrauterine device that will monitor the temperature of the cow and wirelessly transmit the data periodically and/or event, it must have an energy autonomy of the same duration of the main device located on the neck of the animal, from which it will be sent to the server along with the other parameters or variables. See Fig. 2.

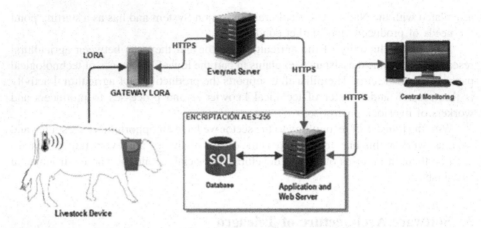

Fig. 2. Local operation of the solutions

3.2   Description of Components

- **Devices:** Electronic devices that will monitor livestock status. The devices will have an RF interface that will allow them to connect to the Lora Gateway, which sends the data to the Everynet server so they can be consulted and stored in the central database.
- **Monitoring Server (Application):** Server that contains the service that will be in charge of consulting the information of the Everynet servers and sending the data to the monitoring center.
- **Central database:** Server where the information of the platform in general, the different guilds, productive units, farms and all their configurations will be stored. It will also store the information that is monitored from the pomegranate and the alarms that could be generated.
- **Web Server:** Server where the web application of the monitoring center will be hosted. In the application the monitoring of the livestock of each productive unit will be carried out as well as the visualization of the alarms that may be generated. In addition to all the basic functionalities of the platform.
- **Server Application:** Corresponds to the instances where the services that update the monitored values of the animals are kept in real time. Initially this scheme will support up to 20,000 devices (cattle) reporting approximately every 15 min.
- **Database:** Corresponds to the instance where the database system that supports the platform is hosted. Initially it will support 20,000 devices (cattle) reporting approximately every 15 min.

4   Results

The transmission of the data that is collected through the devices through LORA protocols are sent by the Lora Gateway through the HTTPS protocol with Authentication by a Secret Token. All communication with the servers is done through the HTTPS communication protocol. In addition, for web applications authentication will be performed using a token (cookie) to avoid the CSRF (Cross Site Request Forgery) (Forgery of inter-site requests).

The system contemplates the control of inactivity times of sessions of up to 15 min, once this time has elapsed, users must authenticate on the platform again. The databases can only be accessed from the servers on which the applications and interfaces of the TeleAgro platform are installed.

The information stored in the application and database servers will be encrypted with unique 256-bit keys through the AES-256 encryption algorithm. The passwords will be stored in an encrypted way, with a mechanism for stretching passwords using the PBKDF2 algorithm with SHA256 hash.

5   Conclusions

Through the implementation of this platform it is possible to have a communications system that responds to the requirements of the livestock farmers of the department of Cesar in Colombia, since it manages to identify the different variables that begin in the processes of: fertilization, productivity and variable management to support decision making in this sector.

Acknowledgment.   To the company extreme tecnologies for the development of the information platform and to the company Fegacesar, for allowing the piloting of this solution.

References

1. Pérez, L.A.Q., Romero, J.A., Rojas, R.L.: Evaluación de dos protocolos de inseminación artificial a término fijo (IATF) con dos inductores de ovulación (benzoato de estradiol y cipionato de estradiol) en vacas raza criollo caqueteño en el departamento del Caquetá. REDVET: Rev. Electrónica de Vet. **16**(9), 1–11 (2015)
2. Gaignard, L., Charon, A.: Gestion de crise et traumatisme: les effets collatéraux de la «vache folle». De l'angoisse singulière à l'embarras collectif. Travailler (2), 57–71 (2005)
3. de la Rosa, C.A.: An inexpensive and open-source method to study large terrestrial animal diet and behaviour using time-lapse video and GPS. Methods Ecol. Evol. **10**(5), 615–625 (2019)
4. Desiato, R., et al.: Data on milk dioxin contamination linked with the location of fodder croplands allow to hypothesize the origin of the pollution source in an Italian valley. Sci. Total Environ. **499**, 248–256 (2014)
5. Iwashita, H., et al.: Push by a net, pull by a cow: can zooprophylaxis enhance the impact of insecticide treated bed nets on malaria control? Parasit. Vectors **7**(1), 52 (2014)

6. Bhattarai, N.R., et al.: Domestic animals and epidemiology of visceral leishmaniasis, Nepal. Emerg. Infect. Dis. **16**(2), 231 (2010)
7. Doherr, M.G., Zurbriggen, A., Hett, A.R., Rüfenacht, J., Heim, D.: Geographical clustering of cases of bovine spongiform encephalopathy (BSE) born in Switzerland after the feed ban. Vet. Rec. **151**(16), 467–472 (2002)
8. Palechor, M., Enrique, F., De La Hoz Manotas, A.K., De La Hoz Franco, E., Ariza Colpas, P.P.: Feature selection, learning metrics and dimension reduction in training and classification processes in intrusion detection systems (2015)
9. De-La-Hoz-Franco, E., Ariza-Colpas, P., Quero, J.M., Espinilla, M.: Sensor-based datasets for human activity recognition–a systematic review of literature. IEEE Access **6**, 59192–59210 (2018)
10. Palechor, F.M., De la Hoz Manotas, A., Colpas, P.A., Ojeda, J.S., Ortega, R.M., Melo, M.P.: Cardiovascular disease analysis using supervised and unsupervised data mining techniques. JSW **12**(2), 81–90 (2017)
11. Mendoza-Palechor, F.E., Ariza-Colpas, P.P., Sepulveda-Ojeda, J.A., De-la-Hoz-Manotas, A., Piñeres Melo, M.: Fertility analysis method based on supervised and unsupervised data mining techniques (2016)
12. Calabria-Sarmiento, J.C., et al.: Software applications to health sector: a systematic review of literature (2018)

Optical Mark Recognition Based on Image Processing Techniques for the Answer Sheets of the Colombian High-Stakes Tests

Oscar Espitia[1], Andres Paez[1], Yuri Mejia[2(✉)], Mario Carrasco[1], and Natalia Gonzalez[1]

[1] Instituto Colombiano para la Evaluación de la Educación (ICFES), Bogotá D.C., Colombia
[2] Universidad Antonio Nariño, Bogotá D.C., Colombia
ymejia43@gmail.com

Abstract. Optical Mark Recognition (OMR) is the process of electronically extracting intended data from marked fields, such as squares and bubbles fields, on printed forms. OMR is useful for applications in which large numbers of hand-filled forms need to be processed quickly and with a high degree of accuracy, for instance, reading the answer sheets of high-stakes tests. Nowadays, image processing techniques and advancement in computing could help to read the answer sheets, quickly and reducing operational costs. This work introduces a systematic procedure of image processing with two segmentation steps that conclude in the extraction and recognition of marks of answer sheets of Colombian High-Stakes Tests. Some preliminary results show that the accuracy is 99.83%, on average, in the first calibration stage, with 4 blocks of about 400 images, each one. A sampling procedure was performed to determine an adequate number of images to verify the performance of the method in the scenario of the application Saber 11 in the second semester of 2018. The conclusion of the exercise, with around 65.000 images, was 99.7% of accuracy, which was run in an 8 logical processors pc architecture, getting an average speed of 8 sheets per second. Thus making it suitable for real applications or for performing a labeling process for deep learning training.

Keywords: OMR · Image processing · High-Stakes Tests

1 Introduction

Optical Mark Recognition (OMR) tools are currently used to automate the grading for a large number of exams. However, there are requirements for specialized mechanical equipment with practical difficulties [3]. Currently, image processing techniques can promote a way to mitigate the difficulties and requirements for reading exam answer sheets.

© Springer Nature Switzerland AG 2019
J. C. Figueroa-García et al. (Eds.): WEA 2019, CCIS 1052, pp. 167–176, 2019.
https://doi.org/10.1007/978-3-030-31019-6_15

Some approaches have been proposed for OMR by using image processing techniques. For instance, Nguyen et al. propose the classification of multiple option-exam sheets by using an efficient and reliable camera, i.e. with high-quality images. First, the edges of the answer sheets are detected with the Hough transform algorithm as a reference for generalized processing, and in this way, the marks can be recognized by locating the coverage of the answers areas [5].

Additionally, Sattayakawee [7] proposes a scoring algorithm for a grid-type answer sheet, which uses a method based on profile projection and thresholding techniques. Rakesh et al. proposed system consists of an ordinary printer, scanner, and a computer to perform the whole process from the design of forms, and in this way, the marked forms are scanned and processed to recognize the source format, which results in a spreadsheet [2].

On the other hand, Marakeby presents a low-cost OMR solution that takes advantage of the computational architecture of multiprocessing. In this approach, answer sheets are digitized using a regular camera. Initially, the edges are located and then the bubbles with the answer categories, without correcting the rotation of the image. This method uses an adaptive binarization to mitigate the effects of light on images taken with regular cameras [4].

In that way, this paper presents a procedure based on image processing techniques, which are applied over scanned images, and therefore, taken in relatively steady conditions. In general, the method consists of two segmentation steps. In the first one, the answers regions are detected (bubble blocks), and in the second one, the marks within the areas detected in the first step are recognized by locating marks in a hypothetical grid.

The document is organized as follows: Sect. 2 describes the different parts of the form inside the sheets and the firsts steps of the procedure, denote as preprocessing, and the segmentation of the answer regions. Section 3 shows the mark recognition process over the segmented regions. Section 4 shows the results of the experiments performed for testing the proposed procedure. Finally, the conclusion is established.

2   First Segmentation Step: Extraction of the Bubble Blocks

This section presents a procedure for extracting the areas of interest from a form, as the one describe the Sect. 2.1, there are some preprocessing steps in Sect. 2.2 for preparing the image for the bubble blocks extraction in Sect. 2.3. These treads belong to the first segmentation step.

2.1   Description of the Answer Sheet

Fig. 1 shows the structure of an answer sheet of a high-stakes test in Colombia. The top section corresponds to the data related to the identification of the examinee. The bottom section has the answers form with six bubble blocks. An examinee answer the test by filling a single bubble for each item.

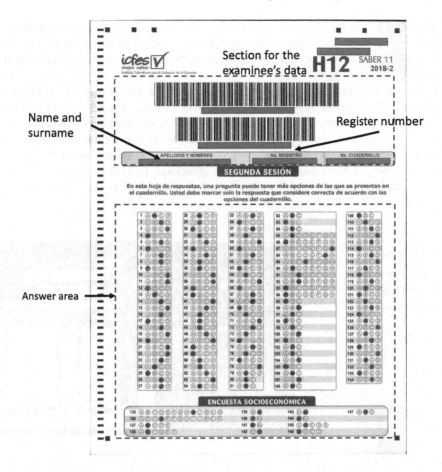

Fig. 1. An example of an answer sheet for the high-stake test Saber 11. There are two main sections: the top corresponding to the examinee's data (name, surname, and identification numbers in bar-codes and text) and the bottom section that is the answer area

2.2 Preprocessing

In the first stage of preprocessing, images must be read as matrices, 3 per image, because they have the 3 bands (RGB), however, to simplify the processing, it is recommended to perform a grayscale transformation, which can be done by performing a weighted average of the 3 bands, or as in this case, by selecting the band with more information, green. The next step of the procedure is the search for a threshold to transform the matrix into a binary one. This process is called thresholding and is the simplest way to separate objects from the background in an image. The Otsu method is a common method used for selecting a global threshold [6], it consists of finding the value (threshold) that minimizes the variance within the class objects and the class background. The variance within classes is the weighted sum of the two variances classes, and the weight values are the sum of the pixel intensities of the class divided by the total number of pixels in the image. The threshold is obtained by exhaustive search. Figure 2(a) and (b) shows an example of an original image for an answer sheet and after the thresholding step, respectively.

In order to identify the regions with objects in the image, it is required to expand those ones, results from the thresholding. There are some imaging morphological operations for performing the task known as hole filling [1]. Figure 2 (c) shows the image after filling the holes for connecting the areas. The algorithm consists in invading the complementary of the shapes in input from the outer boundary of the image, using binary dilations [1]. Holes are not connected to the boundary and are therefore not invaded. The result is the complementary subset of the invaded region.

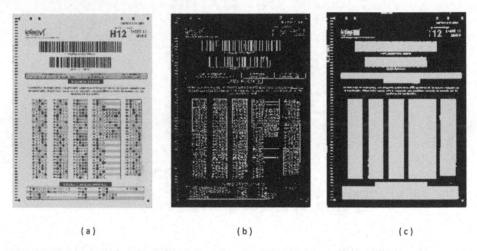

(a)   (b)   (c)

Fig. 2. Stages of the preprocessing: (a) Original image, (b) thresholding, and (c) Hole filling.

There are two regions of interest on the answer sheet. First, the identification of the examinee placed in the three horizontal blocks on the top of the answer sheet (see Fig. 2(c)). Both require pattern recognition algorithms. Second, the answer region, which corresponds to the parallel vertical blocks and the horizontal block of the bottom of the answer sheet (see Fig. 2(c)). The interest of this approach is focused on reading the marks. Algorithms available in Python libraries are used to read text and bar-codes. In this way, areas that are not currently of interest are excluded by taking into account their pixels densities.

2.3 Segmentation

The segmentation is performed in three stages: object removal, region labeling, and region extraction. The object removal keeps the regions with the biggest areas by using a thresholding operation that computes the number of pixels in each region and removes the ones smaller than a given threshold (see Fig. 3(a) for result). After that, the labeling of each region (see Fig. 3(b)) is required for identifying each one separately. In this way, we can compute measurements over the regions, such as areas, the boundary pixels, centroids, etc [6].

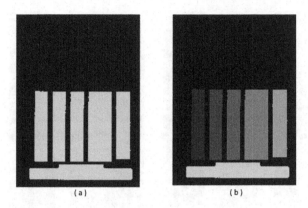

(a)   (b)

Fig. 3. First two stages of the segmentation: (a) Object removal and (b) region labeling.

The whole process described above is summarized in Algorithm 1, where the arrray that represents the image is denoted by $I_{[\cdot]}$; $I_{[R,G,B]}$ is the original RGB image;

$$T(I(x,y)) = \begin{cases} 1, & \text{if } I(x,y) \geq t, \\ 0, & \text{if } I(x,y) < t \end{cases}$$

is the thresholding function, with t as the Threshold; $\oplus$ is the dilation operator, such that $I \oplus S = \{(x,y) | [(S)_{(x,y)} \cap I] \in I\}$, with S as the structuring element [1]; and t_{Area} is the threshold for excluding small regions.

Result: $I_{R1}, \cdots, I_{Rn}$ %Separated bubble blocks
initialization $I_{[R,G,B]}$;
$I_{[G]} = I_{[R,G,B]}[G]$ %green channel selection;
$I_{BW} = T(I_{[G]})$ %Thresholding;
$I_{HF} = I_{BW} \oplus S$ %Hole filling;
$[R_1, R_2, \cdots, R_n] = \text{labeling}(I_{HF})$;
for $i = 1$ *to* n **do**
    $Prop_i = \text{Region\_props}(I_{HF}[R_i])$ %Measurements computation;
    if $I[Prop_{i-Area}] > t_{Area}$ **then**
        $I_{Ri} = I_{[G]}[Prop_i]$ %Region extraction;
    end
end

Algorithm 1. Bubble blocks extraction

Finally, the regions can be selected from the original image by using the boundary pixels found as the result of the procedure described above. The outcome of the segmentation must be the separated bubble blocks, such as in the region extraction, for extracting each bubble block in a single image as is shown in Fig. 4.

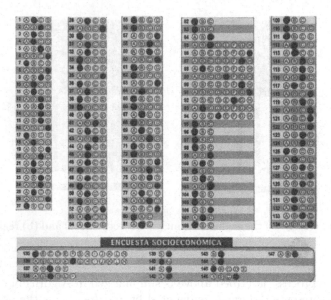

Fig. 4. Region extraction. Each bubble block is extracted as a single image.

3   Second Segmentation Step: Mark Recognition

After extracting each bubble block, the mark recognition is performed. A hypothetical grid setting for codification of possible answers $\{\emptyset, A, B, C, \cdots\}$ is assumed by calibrating the size of the grid with the marked bubbles that fit to a square. This is shown in Fig. 5(left).

Following the grid, a bubble block can be split by rows, which corresponds to the answer categories for each item. In this way, each item row can be processed separately by identifying classes in small segments: objects, i.e. marked bubble; and background, including unmarked bubbles. Again, the separation of the classes can be done by thresholding, as is shown in Fig. 5(Right). The last step in the mark recognition is to find the centroid of the marked bubble and to assign the label to the corresponding codification region.

This last procedure could be summarized as follows. Let $I_{Ri} \in \mathbb{R}^{M \times N}$ be a bubble block; $I_{Rij} \in \mathbb{R}^{\delta \times N}$ and $I_{Rik} \in \mathbb{R}^{M \times \delta}$ a row and a column segment from the bubble block, respectively, where δ is the size of the square that contains a bubble. Thus, a cell from the grid mentioned before could be a partition of

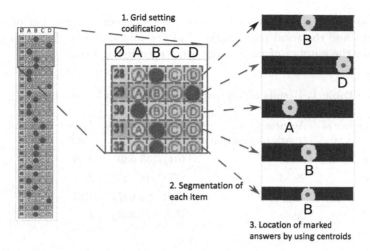

Fig. 5. Steps in the mark recognition process: 1. generate a hypothetical grid setting for codification, 2. each item is segmented (one by one), and 3. the marked bubbles are detected by using centroids.

pixels $\{(x,y)|(x,y) \in (X_j, Y_k)\}$ such that $X_j = \{x|x \in [(\delta j - \delta), \delta j]\}$ and $Y_k = \{y|y \in [(\delta k - \delta), \delta k]\}$, with $j(\in \mathbb{N}) = 1, \cdots, \frac{M}{\delta}$ and $k(\in \mathbb{N}) = 1, \cdots, \frac{N}{\delta}$. After thresholding, the marked bubbles can be treated as the regions in Sect. 2.3, in this case, the required measurement is the location of the objects, the centroid of a bubble could give a reliable location of the answers, then, let c be the centroid of an arbitrary marked bubble, the match between the mark and the category answer will be find by locating c in a I_{Rik} column segment. Notice that $\frac{N}{c} \in Y_k$ and Y_k is related to the actual columns in the grid, i.e. $\{Y_1, \cdots, Y_{\frac{N}{\delta}}\} = \{\emptyset, A, B, C, \cdots\}$.

4   Results

In order to test the proposed algorithm, a preliminary experiment was performed to calibrate the parameters such as threshold, the size of the bubbles, with some sets of images, selected randomly from a bank; and a test with a greater number of answer sheets was performed with the parameters established in the calibration stage.

4.1   Calibration

The simulation scenario is the set of answer sheets from the high-Stake exam Saber 11, applied in the second semester of 2018. For the calibration of parameters, we selected 4 folders, each one with around 400 images. Some preliminary results are shown in Table 1. The accuracy was greater than 99.83%, and the time the algorithm takes to recognize the marks of each sheet is 0.38 seconds per sheet. Notice that the accuracy is the relation between the number of correctly read marks and the total read marks, and the mistakes are related to the type 1 error, i.e. the number of marks that were read incorrectly.

Table 1. Results of four experiment scenarios for calibration

Number of sheets	Accuracy [%] (mark recognition)	Mistakes/items	Time consuming [min]
426	99.83	(91)/(53 530)	2.69
366	99.84	(77)/(48 125)	2.35
490	99.89	(70)/(63 637)	3.12
369	99.88	(55)/(45 833)	2.47

Additionally, it was found that the average size of the bubbles is 25×25 pixels and that the thresholding algorithm gives a result close to the expected to differentiate the bubble blocks, adjustable with less than 5 iterations (increasing or decreasing the initial threshold by adding or subtracting a value $= 5$), with the number of regions detected, which must be between 3 and 5, as the stopping criterion.

On the other hand, the mistakes were independently reviewed and found to be caused by irregularities in the images, such as those shown in the Fig. 6, in which can be noticed some gaps and marks that are confusing to the algorithm.

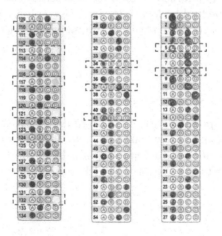

Fig. 6. Some causes of mistakes in the mark recognition.

4.2   Testing

For the test of the algorithm with the parameters previously found, a sampling was designed for selecting a set from the image bank of 2.575.583 images, having into account the different types of answer sheets. Notice that the types of sheets are different because of the setup of the bubble blocks. Table 2 shows the initial sizes of the samples per each type of answer sheet.

Table 2. Sample sizes per type of answer sheet

Type of answer sheet	Total
01	20 001
02	874
03	13 079
10	875
11	13 444
12	20 001
Total	68 274

Finally, from the expected sample, 64.940 images were found to perform the procedure. By the other side, the algorithm was implemented in Python 3.7, the Scikit image library [8], which processes images as arrays of the Numpy library, was used. To reduce the time the algorithm takes to execute the procedure with a large amount of data, the Multiprocess library was used for managing 8 logical processors in a pc, such that several images were processed simultaneously. The results of this test are summarized in Table 3.

Table 3. Results of a test with 64940 answer sheets.

Scenario	Number of sheets	Accuracy [%] (mark recognition)	Mistakes	Time consuming [s]
Saber 11 2018-2	64 940	99.7	(23 377)/(7 792 386)	0.1 per sheet

5   Conclusion

An OMR procedure based on image processing is proposed. The main steps are a preprocessing stage with segmentation and region extraction, and a mark recognition stage based on finding the marked objects centroids in a hypothetical codification grid. The results show an accuracy of at least 99.7% with a time consuming of about 0.1 seconds per sheet. A test with 64940 sheets from different types for the second-semester application of 2018 of Saber 11 exam was conducted. The type 1 error is trackable to different irregularities in the sheets, due to the image capture, or the wrong manipulation by the examinees, But still, there is a work to do in order to mitigate the mistakes. In this way, future work concerns deeper analysis in those errors, and also other approaches based on deep learning algorithms, because the proposed procedure can be used mixed with a classification model, either in training, as annotator, or in one of the stages.

References

1. Gonzalez, R.C., Woods, R.E.: Digital Image Processing, 3rd edn. Pearson Prentice Hall, Upper Saddle River (2006)
2. Rakesh, S., Atal, K., Arora, A.: Cost effective optical mark reader. Int. J. Comput. Sci. Artif. Intell. **3**(2), 44–49 (2013)
3. Kubo, H., Ohashi, H., Tamamura, M., Kowata, T.: Shared questionnaire system for school community management. In: 2004 International Symposium on Applications and the Internet Workshops, pp. 439–445, January 2004. https://doi.org/10.1109/SAINTW.2004.1268671
4. Marakeby, A.: Multi-core processors for camera based OMR. Int. J. Comput. Appl. **68**(2), 62–66 (2013)
5. Nguyen, T.D., Manh, Q.H.: Efficient and reliable camera based multiple-choice test grading system. In: 2011 International Conference on Advanced Technologies for Communications (1979)
6. Otsu, N.: A threshold selection method from gray-level histograms. IEEE Trans. Sys. Man Cybern. **9**(1), 62–66 (1979)
7. Sattayakawee, N.: Test scoring for non-optical grid answer sheet based on projection profile method. Int. J. Inf. Educ. Technol. **3**(2), 273–277 (2013)
8. van der Walt, S., et al.: Scikit-image: image processing in python. PeerJ **2**, e453 (2014). https://doi.org/10.7717/peerj.453

Computational Intelligence

Towards a Deep Learning Approach for Urban Crime Forecasting

Freddy Piraján$^{(\boxtimes)}$, Andrey Fajardo$^{(\boxtimes)}$, and Miguel Melgarejo$^{(\boxtimes)}$

Laboratory for Automation and Computational Intelligence,
Universidad Distrital Francisco José de Caldas, Bogotá, Colombia
1@evocom.com.co, lafajardof@correo.udistrital.edu.co,
mmelgarejo@udistrital.edu.co

Abstract. This paper presents a deep learning approach for urban crime forecasting. A deep neural network architecture is designed so that it can be trained by using geo-referenced data of criminal activity and road intersections to capture relevant spatial patterns. Preliminary results suggest this model would be able to identify zones with criminal activity in square areas of $500 \times 500\,\mathrm{m}^2$ in a weekly scale.

Keywords: Deep learning · Convolutional neural networks ·
Environmental criminology · Crime forecasting

1 Introduction

Recent advances in environmental criminology rely on pattern recognition, urban factors identification and crime prediction based on temporal patterns [1]. Urban factors may include employment status and home living locations around the cities. In fact, some of them involve relationships between urban areas with high marginalized zones, inequality conditions and poverty with the motivation of people to get involved in criminal activities. For instance, local related neighborhood interactions like house burglary are considered as local crime-related factors [2].

Some traditional methods use time series from historical records to study criminal activity at a local neighborhood area with little or no consideration of the spatial distribution of urban crime data whereas others focus only on the geographic determination of crime clusters [3]. More recently, criminology experts have developed interest to adopt deep learning techniques in their work in order to generate policies to combat criminal activity [4–6].

Environmental criminology has increased its interest in the relationship between crime activity and the urban backcloth associated with it [7]. Experts focus on crime as a complex phenomenon [8] whereas conventional methods study crime activity based on data information like individual economical status, level of education and past crime occurrences [9]. Therefore, information like spatial patterns from spatio-temporal crime signals has received considerable attention [10]. Particularly, in Bogotá city (Colombia, South America), theoretical tools from criminology have been adopted in order to gain a better under-

© Springer Nature Switzerland AG 2019
J. C. Figueroa-García et al. (Eds.): WEA 2019, CCIS 1052, pp. 179–189, 2019.
https://doi.org/10.1007/978-3-030-31019-6_16

standing of criminal activity. This approach has been useful to direct police patrolling efforts to zones where criminal activity is highly plausible [11].

There upon environmental criminology perspective, data contributions can be integrated with data visualization techniques [12] and artificial intelligence methods [13,14] to study spatial and temporal features [15] altogether to provide additional statistics related to crime activity. In this work, this particular phenomenological approach is used to compute spatial-temporal signals that might reveal useful information about thefts events in Bogotá city. In addition, strengths and weaknesses of a deep learning architecture for crime prediction are presented using some statistics to assess model performance in conjunction with data visualization while keeping a convenient number of parameters.

This paper is organized as follows: Sect. 2 presents our method: data preprocessing, model architecture, experimental setup, deep learning training strategy and validation scheme. Section 3 presents preliminary results and findings. Finally, we draw conclusions and comment about recommendations for upcoming research in Sect. 4.

2   Materials and Methods

2.1   Data Base

The database[1] contains reports of mobile phone thefts in Bogota City, Colombia. It was collected privately, therefore it is not available online. These data cover a time frame from January 10th, 2012 to May 31st, 2015, which corresponds to 1273 days (176 weeks) characterized by a daily average crime count of 19 thefts.

Formally, the database is composed by two sets: $C = \{c_1, \ldots, c_L\}$ is the set of crime[2] events and $R = \{r_1, \ldots, r_M\}$ which is the set of road intersections (or road nodes). Each crime event is reported as a triplet $\{D_q^c, X_q^c, Y_q^c\}$. For an event c_q, with $q = 1...L$, D_q^c is its date, X_q^c is its horizontal coordinate in the cartographic system for Bogotá city and Y_q^c is its vertical coordinate. In the case of R, each road node r_s, with $s = 1...M$, is reported as a duplet $\{X_s^r, Y_s^r\}$, where X_s^r and Y_s^r correspond to the geographic coordinates of the node in the same cartographic system of crime events.

2.2   Data Preprocessing

Spatio-Temporal Resolution: Spatio-temporal resolution for crime analysis and visualization is selected according to [16]. A crime mass is the counting of crime events in a given square areal unit (i.e. box) over a defined time interval. The signal of crime masses in Bogotá city corresponds to a multifractal process where information scaling remains constant over different spatial resolutions as the time scale increases. In fact, the informational self-similarity of this signal is preserved for a spatial resolution $\delta_{xy} \geq 500 \times 500\,\mathrm{m}^2$ over a weekly temporal scale.

---

[1] The database was provided by *Fundación Ideas para la Paz*.
[2] The words *theft* and *crime* are used indistinctly throughout the document.

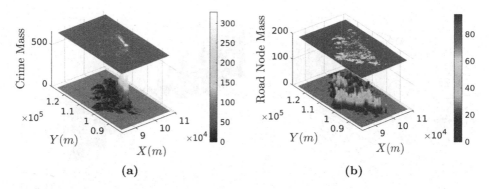

Fig. 1. Data visualization at a spatial resolution of $500 \times 500\,\mathrm{m}^2$: (a) aggregate crime masses for 1273 days, (b) road-node masses.

Data Exploration: Figure 1a presents aggregate daily crime masses for 1237 days computed over $500 \times 500\,\mathrm{m}^2$ boxes. Road-node masses computed with the same spatial resolution are depicted in Fig. 1b. Regarding theft masses it can be noticed that most of the historical activity concentrates in very few regions, which configure strong hotspots. Also note the majority of boxes exhibit little to no theft events. On the other hand, boxes with significant road-node masses are frequent across the study area.

Input Volume Generation: Data selection and data representation are very important criteria to feed models correctly. Thus, the sets C and R are transformed in such a way that can be used to feed in a convolutional neural network. In fact, data are represented as a real-valued tensor $\mathbf{T}$ of order D such that $\mathbf{T} \in \mathbb{R}^{A_1 \times \cdots \times A_D}$, where A_d corresponds the d-th direction of the input tensor.

Input data are set up as a three dimensional volume, as shown in Fig. 2a. The input volume is assembled by stacking bi-dimensional maps[3]. Each map has dimensions $(\Delta y\,bins \times \Delta x\,bins)$, where $\Delta y\,bins$ and $\Delta x\,bins$ correspond to the number of boxes in the abscissa and ordinate directions respectively.

Available data are configured as an input volume $\mathbf{T}$ composed of twelve bi-dimensional maps $(depth = 12)$, as depicted in Fig. 2a and described in Table 1. More specifically, with one map of crime masses $E(k)$ where k corresponds to the time index, 8 maps of crime masses taken from the first order Moore neighborhood around mass box $e_{i,j}$ at time k $(N_1(k), \ldots, N_8(k))$, one map of crime masses at previous time $E(k-1)$, one map with aggregate crime masses (i.e. crime masses history) H and one map with road-node masses RN. Then, the model architecture is fed by three-dimensional volumes and fetches out a bi-dimensional crime masses map $\hat{E}(k+1)$ for every given input $\mathbf{T}(k)$, which represents the model prediction of $E(k+1)$, as shown in Fig. 2b.

The content of each input channel is inspired based upon dynamic and static features in urban areas commonly found in the context of environmental

---

[3] Each bi-dimensional map corresponds to a single channel from the input volume $\mathbf{T}$.

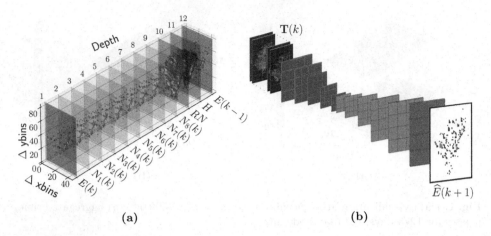

(a)   (b)

Fig. 2. Organization of training data (a) Input volume composed by 12 channels. (b) Input to output data processing.

Table 1. Channels used to form Input volume **T**.

Description	Time dependent		Description	Time invariant	
	Map (channel)	Elements		Map (channel)	Elements
Crime masses at time k	$E(k)$	$e_{i,j}(k)$	Crime masses history	H	$H = \sum_{k=1}^{T_{end}} E(k)$
Moore Neigborhood at time k	$N_1(k)$	$e_{i-1,j-1}(k)$	Road node masses	RN	$rn_{i,j}$
	$N_2(k)$	$e_{i,j-1}(k)$			
	$N_3(k)$	$e_{i+1,j-1}(k)$			
	$N_4(k)$	$e_{i-1,j}(k)$			
	$N_5(k)$	$e_{i+1,j}(k)$			
	$N_6(k)$	$e_{i-1,j+1}(k)$			
	$N_7(k)$	$e_{i,j+1}(k)$			
	$N_8(k)$	$e_{i+1,j+1}(k)$			
Crime masses at time $k-1$	$E(k-1)$	$e_{i,j}(k-1)$			

criminology [12]. Dynamic features are related to crime distribution at the neighborhood level and they correspond to channels $E(k), N_1(k), N_2(k), \ldots, N_8(k)$ in the input volume **T**. Equally important, the temporal dependence is taken into account by adding the input channel with the map of crime masses for the immediately previous time $E(k-1)$. On the other hand, static features are those with almost zero time dependency. In this case, the road-node masses map channel RN represents the geographical canvas scenario where crime phenomena take place. In addition, crime masses history H characterizes the past of criminal activity in the city. It can also be interpreted as the aggregate memory of the phenomenon that provides spatial information from a coarse temporal scale.

2.3   Model Architecture

Crime features exploration started with state of the art deep neural network architectures like LeNet, AlexNet, VGGNet moving forward with encoder decoder deep convolutional neural networks [17]. Then, a systematic iterative implementation over different architecture configurations led to a convolutional-deconvolutional architecture with an extra pooling layer on top of it. This architecture is depicted in Fig. 3a. Here, convolutional layers (in purple) match with deconvolutional layers (in green) in number and size. The pooling layer (in red) is plugged in on top of that architecture when predictions are required at different spatial resolutions. In addition, Rectified Linear Units [18] nonlinearities were interspersed with model's layers along the convolutional-deconvolutional architecture.

2.4   Experimental Set-Up

The number of filters f in convolutional layers was chosen to be $f = 2^p$, for $p = 1, 2, \ldots 10$, with an odd number of neurons per filter. Also, *valid* zero-pad and *one strided* convolutions were applied. In the same fashion, the upsampling layers are based on transposed convolutions [19] with the same number of filters as in convolutional layers. Then, followed by a pooling layer on top of the architecture with a zero-strided 2×2 max-pooling operation.

Experiments were scheduled in a parallel infrastructure with Intel(R) Xeon(R) CPU's E31225 @ 3.10 GHz and Nvidia Quadro P1000 GPU's running experiments in TensorFlow 1.3.0 [20]. The reason behind this approach was to take advantage of the fast data flow offered in online grid computing to distribute tasks that involve the computation of matrix-matrix and matrix-vector operations with data processing in the margin of big data. Hence, this implementation simplified the computation graph related to the analytic gradient computation during the model training iterations.

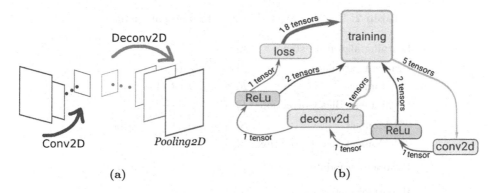

Fig. 3. Architecture and training: (a) Convolutional (purple) - Deconvolutional (green) - Pooling (red) architecture. (b) Data flow during training. (Color figure online)

Operations and data flow during the training process were programmed as a computational graph (See Fig. 3b). Here the model output is fetched by streaming the input data through the nodes that represent model's architecture during the forward pass. Then, the loss function is computed and the analytical gradient is sent backwards to update model's trainable neurons. The matrix-matrix and matrix-vector operations are computed in parallel as indicated by the training algorithm.

2.5 Training Strategy

An adaptive moment estimation algorithm called Adam [21] was used during the learning process. It computes individual learning rates for different parameters from estimates of first and second moments of the gradient. Thus, gradient estimation, bias correction of moments, update of moments and parameters update were computed as presented in Table 2. In this case, the training algorithm hyper parameters values were: learning rate $\alpha = 1e^{-3}$, first gradient moment coefficient $\beta_1 = 0.9$, second gradient moment coefficient $\beta_2 = 0.999$ and avoiding zero-division coefficient $\varepsilon = 1e^{-7}$.

In regard of used data, weekly input volumes $\mathbf{T}(k)$ were generated, where $k = 1...12$ for training and $k = 13...16$ for validation. These weeks correspond to the last four months of the database. In addition, H was configured as the aggregation of crime masses of the other 160 weeks.

Training was carried out with a loss function $L(\hat{E}(k+1), E(k+1))$ selected as the Mean Square Error, where $\hat{E}(k+1) = f(\mathbf{T}(k), W)$ and W is the weight matrix of the network. In order to overcome the stochasticity of random initialization, 33 independent runs were scheduled during 500 epochs allowing the model to overfit the training data. The intuition behind this process consists on picking the best model, saving its parameters values at every single epoch and then evaluating its performance at different training steps. Hence, the best model was reserved for further consideration during the model assessment stage.

Table 2. Learning algorithm updates and parameters

Learning algorithm step	Action
Gradient estimation	$dx_t = \nabla f(x_t)$
1st Moment	$F_{t+1} = \beta_1 F_t + (1 - \beta_1) dx_t$
1st Moment Bias Correction	$F_{t+1}^{corrected} = \frac{F_{t+1}}{1 - \beta_1^t}$
2nd Moment	$S_{t+1} = \beta_2 S_t + (1 - \beta_2)[dx_t]^2$
2nd Moment Bias Correction	$S_{t+1}^{corrected} = \frac{S_{t+1}}{1 - \beta_2^t}$
Parameters update	$x_{t+1} = x_t - \alpha \frac{F_{t+1}^{corrected}}{\sqrt{S_{t+1}^{corrected}} + \varepsilon}$
Hyperparameters	$\alpha, \beta_1, \beta_2, \epsilon$

2.6   Deep Learning Architecture for Crime Forecasting

In order to assess the model performance, four statistics were chosen. As per [22]: "No one measure is universally best for all accuracy assessment objectives, and different accuracy measures may lead to conflicting conclusions because the measures do not represent accuracy in the same tray".

Figure 4 shows a comparison between the model output and actual data. For a $500 \times 500\,\mathrm{m}^2$ resolution there are 4080 values in these maps with more than 3000 zero boxes (i.e. no relevant values) and just tens of non zeros boxes (i.e. boxes with crimes or changes in crime counting). Statistics used to assess the model output have been chosen with the class-imbalanced data set challenge in mind (Precision, Recall and F1 score) [23,24].

While accuracy, as measured by quantitative errors, is important, it may be more crucial to accurately forecast the direction of change of crucial variables [25]. In particular, crime masses directional accuracy can be used in a binary evaluation fashion. Thus, either increase or decrease of crime predictions were considered as upward (1 if $e_{i,j}(k + 1) > e_{i,j}(k)$) or downward ($-1$ otherwise) disregarding its quantitative values.

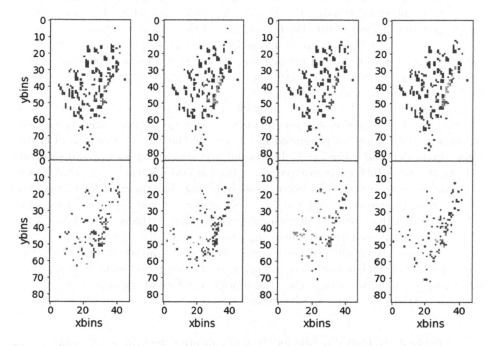

Fig. 4. Comparison between predicted and actual crime masses. Upper row: model output, lower row: actual data. The model outputs crime masses maps where the majority of predictions fall into the region surrounding crime hotspots during the four weeks of validation. Note expected output crime maps are class-imbalanced.

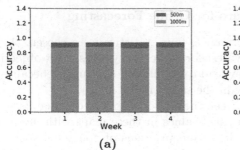
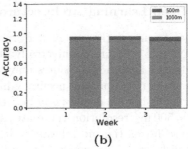

(a)   (b)

Fig. 5. Results for the four validation weeks: (a) model accuracy, (b) model directional accuracy.

3   Results

Accuracy results are presented in Fig. 5 for the four validation weeks. A high level of accuracy was obtained for two spatial resolutions $\delta_{xy} = 500 \times 500\,\text{m}^2$ and $\delta_{xy} = 1000 \times 1000\,\text{m}^2$. However, this statistic is not reliable given the data imbalance. This can be observed through the $B_R = (B_{nz}/B_z)$ ratio, where B_z corresponds to the number of Zero Crime Boxes and B_{nz} is the number of Non-zero Crime boxes. The average B_R over the four validation weeks is approximately 80/4080 for the former resolution and 80/924 for the latter. Therefore when the model reports a mass of zero crimes there is a high probability that its prediction falls in the zero crime region.

The main interest for crime mass predictions is in regions where crime activity occurs. Thus, precision and recall statistics averaged over the four validation weeks were introduced as presented in Table 3. In the case of precision of crime mass prediction and precision of directional accuracy the model presents better results at $1000 \times 1000\,\text{m}^2$ compared with those at $500 \times 500\,\text{m}^2$. Note that precision values were very poor in both cases. Implying that the model's perception about crime occurrence is not reliable. This problem might be solved including a loss function that focus in more local performance at the neighborhood level of crime occurrences during the learning process. Regarding recall of crimes, the model shows better results for the coarser resolution for all weeks whereas in the case of recall of tendency of crime occurrences it is for most weeks higher at the finer resolution, which means that the model is not good when stating that at certain locations are going to be crimes.

Table 3. Additional results for the four validation weeks in percentage.

Resolution	Crime masses						Directional accuracy					
	Precision (%)		Recall (%)		F1 score (%)		Precision (%)		Recall (%)		F1 score (%)	
	Mean	Std	Mean	Std	Mean	Std	Mean	Std	Mean	Std	Mean	Std
$500 \times 500\,\text{m}^2$	12.87	0.07	31.51	3.40	18.23	0.56	9.55	1.64	14.71	3.32	11.57	2.22
$1000 \times 1000\,\text{m}^2$	24.30	3.62	36.91	2.70	29.22	3.21	17.91	3.27	17.01	2.07	17.43	2.62

In addition, F1 score was introduced to consider the trade-off over results between precision and recall, as well as the database imbalance for model assessment. In this case, the F1 scores reported in Table 3 along with the visual results (see Fig. 6) between the perception of the model $\hat{E}(k+1)$ and the ground truth map $E(k+1)$ favor to understand that the trained model is hitting a very low portion of rare crimes developing at multiple locations in the city. It may be improved by using filters of different shapes. The intuition behind this is that given the multi-scale nature of the crime masses $E(t)$, the usage of filters of multiple sizes in a similar fashion to *Inception Modules* [26] will allow the top level layers to squeeze out information from each region involving dynamics at different spatial resolutions as the filters raster across the maps. In other words, it may be helpful to capture better not only the dynamics at hot spot zones but also to hit rare crimes that distribute across the urban area.

Results show that evaluating the model output at higher resolutions than the one it was trained for increases its performance in most statistics. In fact, the low precision and recall values came out because the model does not predict exactly the same (X, Y) coordinates for most of expected crime masses but in the boxes located around the actual position. Therefore the model prediction

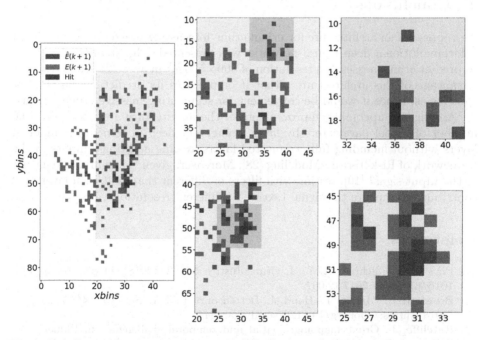

Fig. 6. Left figure depicts an example of the model output (red boxes), expected output (green boxes) and their intersection (blue boxes). It is shown in upper rigth figures that even if the model predictions do not match the expected values, their positions are close to actual crime boxes in a radius ε_{xy} at a local neighborhood level. In lower right figures, it can be noticed that the model identifies crime hotspots zones in the city. (Color figure online)

capacity will improve as it will be better to predict true positive values at a spatial resolution very close to the one it was trained for. This may be achieved by using the tendency of crimes as expected output during the training stage instead and batch normalization [27] for cases with a very deep architecture setup.

On the other hand this model has also some good advantages. Even if it might not predict the exact (X, Y) coordinates of the expected crime mass, actual criminal activity is likely to happen in boxes located in a small radius $(X \pm \varepsilon_x, Y \pm \varepsilon_y) > (0, 0)$ around predicted $\hat{e}_{i,j}(k+1)$ in the neighborhood region as shown in Fig. 6. Note that the model is able to identify crime hotspots regions. Similarly, this network architecture allows the designer to gain intuition about the kernels that might be used to extract features in correlation operations with the incoming inputs at convolutional and deconvolutional layers. In addition, this model has a very reduced number of parameters when compared with a traditional deep convolutional network where the number of parameters is at the order of millions while the explored architecture has a maximum of $3 \times 3 \times 2^5$ parameters in the biggest configuration.

4   Conclusions

A proposal of an architecture for urban crime forecasting based on convolutional - deconvolutional deep neural networks was presented. The architecture allows to predict crime masses at a resolution of $500 \times 500 \,\mathrm{m}^2$ in a weekly scale. Another advantage of this architecture is that it emphasizes its predictions on the hot spot zones, hence it would be convenient for segmenting massive crime regions.

Among the upcoming improvements of the architecture are: increasing the number of model parameters by layer, going very deep in terms of number of layers without including fully connected layers, testing additional inputs in the framework of Risk Terrain Modeling [28]. Moreover, given the multi-scale nature of the input signal [16], testing with filters of different shapes at each layer may contribute to capture the signal texture at different resolutions.

References

1. Piza, E.L., Gilchrist, A.M.: J. Crim. Justice **54**, 76 (2018). https://doi.org/10.1016/j.jcrimjus.2017.12.007
2. Brelsford, C., Martin, T., Hand, J., Bettencourt, L.M.A.: Sci. Adv. **4**(8), eaar4644 (2018). https://doi.org/10.1126/sciadv.aar4644
3. Ratcliffe, J.: Crime mapping: spatial and temporal challenges. In: Piquero, A., Weisburd, D. (eds.) Handbook of Quantitative Criminology, pp. 5–24. Springer, New York (2010). https://doi.org/10.1007/978-0-387-77650-7_2
4. King, T.C., Aggarwal, N., Taddeo, M., Floridi, L.: Sci. Eng. Ethics (2019). https://doi.org/10.1007/s11948-018-00081-0
5. Mohler, G., Brantingham, P.J., Carter, J., Short, M.B.: J. Quant. Criminol. (2019). https://doi.org/10.1007/s10940-019-09404-1

6. Stalidis, P., Semertzidis, T., Daras, P.: Examining deep learning architectures for crime classification and prediction (2018)
7. Brantingham, P.J., Valasik, M., Mohler, G.O.: Stat. Public Policy **5**(1), 1 (2018). https://doi.org/10.1080/2330443X.2018.1438940
8. Nobles, M.R.: Am. J. Crim. Justice (2019). https://doi.org/10.1007/s12103-019-09483-7
9. Aaltonen, M., Oksanen, A., Kivivuori, J.: Criminology **54**(2), 307 (2016). https://doi.org/10.1111/1745-9125.12103
10. Rumi, S.K., Deng, K., Salim, F.D.: EPJ Data Sci. **7**(1), 43 (2018). https://doi.org/10.1140/epjds/s13688-018-0171-7
11. Blattman, C., Green, D., Ortega, D., Tobón, S.: Hotspot interventions at scale: the effects of policing and city services on crime in Bogotá, Colombia. Technical report, International Initiative for Impact Evaluation (3ie) (2018). https://doi.org/10.23846/DPW1IE88
12. Bruinsma, G.J.N., Johnson, S.D.: The Oxford Handbook of Environmental Criminology. Oxford University Press, Oxford (2018). Google-Books-ID: qPdJD-wAAQBAJ
13. LeCun, Y., Bengio, Y., Hinton, G.: Nature **521**, 436 (2015)
14. Adamson, G., Havens, J.C., Chatila, R.: Proc. IEEE **107**(3), 518 (2019). https://doi.org/10.1109/JPROC.2018.2884923
15. Quick, M., Li, G., Brunton-Smith, I.: J. Crim. Justice **58**, 22 (2018). https://doi.org/10.1016/j.jcrimjus.2018.06.003
16. Melgarejo, M., Obregon, N.: Entropy **20**, 11 (2018). https://doi.org/10.3390/e20110874. http://www.mdpi.com/1099-4300/20/11/874
17. Su, J., Vargas, D.V., Sakurai, K.: IPSJ Trans. Comput. Vis. Appl. **11**(1), 1 (2019). https://doi.org/10.1186/s41074-019-0053-3
18. Macêdo, D., Zanchettin, C., Oliveira, A., Ludermir, T.: Expert Syst. Appl. **124**, 271 (2019). https://doi.org/10.1016/j.eswa.2019.01.066
19. Gao, H., Yuan, H., Wang, Z., Ji, S.: IEEE Trans. Pattern Anal. Mach. Intell. 1 (2019). https://doi.org/10.1109/TPAMI.2019.2893965
20. Abadi, M., Barham, P., Chen, J., Chen, Z., Davis, A., Dean, J., et al.: Proceedings of the 12th USENIX Conference on Operating Systems Design and Implementation, OSDI 2016, pp. 265–283. USENIX Association, Berkeley (2016)
21. Kingma, D.P., Ba, J.: arXiv:1412.6980 [cs] (2014)
22. Stehman, S.V.: Remote Sens. Environ. **62**(1), 77 (1997). https://doi.org/10.1016/S0034-4257(97)00083-7
23. Tharwat, A.: Appl. Comput. Inform. (2018). https://doi.org/10.1016/j.aci.2018.08.003
24. Wang, X., Jiang, X.: Sig. Process. **165**, 104 (2019). https://doi.org/10.1016/j.sigpro.2019.06.018
25. Pierdzioch, C., Reid, M.B., Gupta, R.: J. Appl. Stat. **45**(5), 884 (2018). https://doi.org/10.1080/02664763.2017.1322556
26. Szegedy, C., Vanhoucke, V., Ioffe, S., Shlens, J., Wojna, Z.: Proceedings of IEEE Conference on Computer Vision and Pattern Recognition (2016). arXiv:1512.00567
27. Wu, S., et al.: IEEE Trans. Neural Netw. Learn. Syst. 1–9 (2018). https://doi.org/10.1109/TNNLS.2018.2876179
28. Caplan, J.M., Kennedy, L.W. (eds.): Risk Terrain Modeling Compendium for Crime Analysis, Rutgers Center on Public Security (2011)

Binary Optimisation with an Urban Pigeon-Inspired Swarm Algorithm

Sergio Rojas-Galeano[⊠]

Universidad Distrital Francisco José de Caldas, Bogotá, Colombia
srojas@udistrital.edu.co

Abstract. In this paper we introduce a metaheuristic for optimisation of discrete binary problems, derived from a recently proposed particle swarm algorithm inspired on the foraging behaviour of urban pigeons. The new variant of the algorithm is obtained by mapping the real–valued search space of the original version into a discrete binary–valued encoding. We illustrate the feasibility of the method on several binary benchmark problems and we study the impact of different running parameters such as problem dimension, population size and maximum number of evaluations. The potential of the method and possible extensions for improvement are also discussed.

Keywords: Metaheuristics · Particle Swarm Optimisation · Binary optimisation benchmarks

1 Introduction

The homing and foraging behaviour of populations of pigeons (from the rock [7], passenger [6] or feral kind [1,10]) and other species of urban birds [3,10,11,15], have recently provided a rich source of inspiration for a number of optimisation methods for unconstrained continuous–domain optimisation. All these approaches can be interpreted under the common framework of Particle Swarm Optimisation algorithms [8,17], where the location of each agent (particle) from a population represents a candidate solution to a given optimisation problem; the particle's location is iteratively improved using rules accounting for direction and speed depending on the locations of the best particle in the population and the preceding trajectories of individual and surrounding particles.

In a previous study a simplified urban pigeon–inspired model was proposed (the PUPI algorithm [1]), obtaining effective performances in several real–valued benchmarks functions, despite the simplicity of its updating rules. The question arises about how to extend such model to operate on discrete search spaces, in particular, binary–valued problems, given that these kind of domains have important practical applications in engineering. The goal of this paper is precisely to address this question.

The adaptation to discrete domains of other pigeon–inspired models have been elsewhere attempted: in [10] the AFB algorithm is used to solve problems

© Springer Nature Switzerland AG 2019
J. C. Figueroa-García et al. (Eds.): WEA 2019, CCIS 1052, pp. 190–201, 2019.
https://doi.org/10.1007/978-3-030-31019-6_17

of binary–valued logic circuits by optimising the real–valued weights of a neural network, whereas in [2] a binary version of the PIO algorithm is applied to the multidimensional knapsack problem by constraining the values of the pigeons' location array to the 0–1 coordinates. Similarly, a PIO algorithm with mixed binary/real representation was reported in [16] to address optimisation of power generation from an economic and fuel consumption viewpoints, integrating novel costs caused by the load of electric vehicles charging. In contrast to these approaches, here we resorted to define an explicit mapping expressing real–valued locations as binary–valued strings, that is, a genotype–to–phenotype encoding. The latter is more closely related to the binary version of the original particle swarm algorithm (see [9]).

The paper is organised as follows. We initially revise the main aspects of the real–valued PUPI model, then we define a genotype–to–phenotype mapping that yields its binary version and lastly, we report experiments in a number of binary benchmarks as a proof–of–concept of the feasibility of the new variant. The paper closes with a discussion of avenues for further research.

2   Algorithm Description

2.1   Overview of the PUPI Optimiser

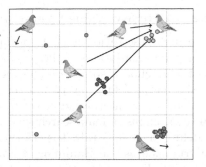

Fig. 1. Illustration of the two kinds of movements on PUPI (taken from [1]).

Urban pigeons are opportunistic foragers whose feeding habits have been classified into two modes, flock feeding and solitary feeding [14]. The latter is exhibited by individuals that wander around their habitat in search for food, whereas the former occurs when other pigeons start chasing a solitary feeder that has found a source of food, thus forming a flock. These are the core ideas of the *Population–based Urban Pigeon Inspired* (PUPI) algorithm [1] for continuous-domain optimisation: firstly, that during the flocking formation pigeons are able to overflight other potential richer sources of food, and secondly, that solitaries are exploring the habitat preventing the entire population to converge to a single supply of food. These ideas are illustrated in Fig. 2.1.

In the PUPI model the landscape of food distribution is associated with the function to be optimised, i.e. $f : \Re^d \rightarrow \Re$, with $f(\mathbf{x})$ representing the concentration of food at the coordinate $\mathbf{x} \in \Re^d$. The population of pigeons $\mathcal{P}$ is split into a flock feeding subset and a solitary feeding subset. The flock chooses a single leader, the pigeon located at the richest source of food at a given time; the remainder pigeons in the flock will try to follow the leader to that location. On the other hand, the solitaire pigeons are simply walking around (although they may become a leader if they find better food sources). Thus $\mathcal{P} = \ell \cup \mathcal{F} \cup \mathcal{W}$, where each subset correspond to pigeons behaving in the roles of leader, followers and walkers. Besides, the fitness of pigeon P_i would be $f_i = f(\mathbf{x}_i)$.

Now, the search operators of the algorithm are applied to each pigeon depending on the subset they belong to, followers following the leader and walkers walking randomly. In other words, given two random vectors $\mathbf{u}_i \sim N(\mathbf{0}, 1)$ and $\mathbf{v}_i \sim N(\mathbf{0}, 0.01)$, the location of each pigeon in the population at each iteration is updated as $\mathbf{x}_i = \mathbf{x}_i + \Delta\mathbf{x}_i$, where:

$$\Delta\mathbf{x}_i = \begin{cases} \alpha(\mathbf{x}_\ell - \mathbf{x}_i) + \mathbf{v}_i & P_i \in \mathcal{F} \\ \sigma\mathbf{u}_i & P_i \in \mathcal{W} \end{cases}$$

The parameters $0 < \alpha < 0.1$ and $0 < \sigma \leq 1$ are the stepsizes of the two types of updates. The random component of the followers move, $\mathbf{v}_i$, is intended to simulate the effect of wind or collisions with other pigeons during their flights towards the leader $\mathbf{x}_\ell$, whereas the random direction vector $\mathbf{u}_i$ is intended to account for the errant behaviour of walker pigeons. Notice that these updates should be confined to the boundaries of the search space, in order to ensure the feasibility of the solution. Finally, at any time the algorithm reports $\mathbf{x}_\ell$ as the current candidate solution and a memory of the best leader ever would be kept as the final solution found by the swarm.

2.2 A Binary–Valued Version

The first observation is that the update rules of the PUPI model are in fact geometric translations of the pigeons' locations carried out as gradual "jumps" on the Euclidean space defining the landscape of the cost function (the extent of the jumps defined by parameters α and σ). Hence, the current location of a pigeon can be interpreted directly as the coordinates of a candidate solution in the continuous–domain search space. In binary–valued spaces it would possible to redefine the update rules to perform a geometric translation using an appropriate metric such as the Hamming distance; however, the induced Hamming space does not allow gradual but steep jumps (it is not possible to flip, say, half a bit), rendering the stepsizes of the update rules useless, and consequently the ability of discovering better sources of food during the flights of pigeons forming the flock, the main motivation of the algorithm.

In order to preserve the essence of the algorithm, we resort to separate the search space of real–valued vector of pigeon locations from the solution space of binary-valued variables of the optimisation problem. This can be done by means of an encoding function, a technique known as genotype–to–phenotype mapping (or gpm()) widely used in evolutionary algorithms [13]. We remark that this approach is reminiscent of the adaptation of the original particle swarm algorithm to its binary version [9]: in there, the mapping is performed by considering each particle location as a probability distribution that maps every coordinate to a binary value. Our proposal in contrast, defines the following mapping function $\mathrm{gpm} : \Re^d \to \{0, 1\}^d$ with threshold $0 < \tau < 1$:

$$\mathbf{b} := \mathrm{gpm}(\mathbf{x}; \tau) = (x_1 > \tau, x_2 > \tau, \ldots, x_d > \tau)$$

where the condition $a > b$ evaluates to 1 if true or 0 otherwise. Hence, the binary vector $\mathbf{b}$ becomes the phenotype expression of genotype $\mathbf{x}$ at threshold τ.

In the following, without loss of generality, we will constrain the search space to $\mathbf{x} \in [0,1]^d$ and will set the threshold parameter $\tau = 0.5$. The resulting algorithm is depicted below.

Algorithm 1. PUPI-bin (maxisation problems)

Input: $f(\mathbf{b}), \mathbf{b} \in \{0,1\}^d$: cost function,
$n > 0$: pigeon population size,
$0 \le \eta_\omega \le 1$: proportion of walkers in population,
$0 < \alpha, \sigma \le 1$: follower, walker move step
$0 < t < T$: starvation and abundance periods
Output: $\mathbf{b}^\star$, best solution found

1 $\mathcal{P} \leftarrow \{\mathbf{x}_i : \mathbf{x}_i \sim U(\mathbf{0}, \mathbf{1})\}_{i=1}^n$ /* initialise pigeons */
2 $\mathcal{W} \leftarrow \mathrm{choose}(\mathcal{P}, \eta_\omega)$
3 $\mathcal{F} \leftarrow \mathcal{P} \setminus \mathcal{W}$
4 $\mathbf{b}^\star \leftarrow \mathrm{gpm}(\mathbf{x}_1)$ /* genotype-to-phenotype mapping */
5 **while time available do**
6      $\quad \mathbf{x}_\ell = \arg\arg\max \{f(\mathrm{gpm}(\mathbf{x}_i))\}_{i=1}^n$ /* leader */
7      $\quad \mathbf{b}^\star = \arg\max \{f(\mathrm{gpm}(\mathbf{x}_\ell)), f(\mathbf{b}^\star)\}$ /* find best */
8      $\quad$ **for each** $\mathbf{x}_i \in \mathcal{F}$ **do**   /* move followers */
9          $\quad\quad \mathbf{v}_i \sim N(\mathbf{0}, 0.01)$
10         $\quad\quad \mathbf{x}_i = \mathbf{x}_i + \alpha(\mathbf{x}_\ell - \mathbf{x}_i) + \mathbf{v}_i$
11     $\quad$ **for each** $\mathbf{x}_i \in \mathcal{W}$ **do**   /* move walkers */
12         $\quad\quad \mathbf{u}_i \sim N(\mathbf{0}, \mathbf{1})$
13         $\quad\quad \mathbf{x}_i = \mathbf{x}_i + \sigma \mathbf{u}_i$
14     $\quad \mathcal{P} \leftarrow \mathcal{P} \cup \mathbf{x}^\star$ /* elitism */
15     $\quad$ **if** t **steps elapsed then**   /* walkers-only */
16         $\quad\quad \mathcal{W}, \mathcal{F} \leftarrow \mathcal{P}, \emptyset$
17     $\quad$ **if** T **steps elapsed then**   /* walkers+followers */
18         $\quad\quad \mathcal{W} \leftarrow \mathrm{choose}(\mathcal{P}, \eta_\omega)$
19         $\quad\quad \mathcal{F} \leftarrow \mathcal{P} \setminus \mathcal{W}$

---

3   Experiments

The algorithm and benchmark functions were implemented in the Python programming language (version: 2.7.10) using the numerical computation **numpy** library (version: 1.14.0). The code is available on request. The experiments were executed on a 1.4 GHz Intel Core i5 running Mac OS X version 10.13.6.

3.1   Sanity Test

We initially conducted a sanity test to verify the feasibility of the new algorithm on a typical instance of each of the benchmark problems described in Table 1. We chose a medium problem size of $d = 64$ and set the algorithm parameters to

Table 1. Benchmark binary problems

Problem	Definition	Description
OneMax	$f(\mathbf{b}) = \sum_{i=1}^{d} b_i$	Counts the total number of ones in the vector $\mathbf{b}$. The optimum is: $f(\underbrace{1,1,\ldots,1}_{\leftarrow\, d\,\text{times}\,\rightarrow}) = d$
SquareWave	$f(\mathbf{b}) = \sum_{i=1}^{d} \left(1 - \text{abs}\left(b_i - \left(2\lfloor\frac{i}{T}\rfloor - \lfloor\frac{2i}{T}\rfloor\right)\right)\right)$	Computes the similarity of vector $\mathbf{b}$ to a binarised version of a sinusoidal wave with period $T = \sqrt{d}$. The optimum is: $f(\underbrace{0,0,0,1,1,1}_{\leftarrow\,\frac{d}{T}\,\text{bits}\,\rightarrow},\ldots,\underbrace{0,0,0,1,1,1}_{\leftarrow\,\frac{d}{T}\,\text{bits}\,\rightarrow}) = d$
BinVal	$f(\mathbf{b}) = \sum_{i=1}^{d} b_i \times 2^{i-1}$	Computes the decimal value of the binary vector $\mathbf{b}$. The optimum is: $f(\underbrace{1,1,\ldots,1}_{\leftarrow\, d\,\text{times}\,\rightarrow}) = 2^d - 1$

the default values of $n = 30, \eta_\omega = .25, \alpha = 0.1, \sigma = 0.1$, with a maximum number of 40000 evaluations per experiment. The results are summarised in Table 2.

It can be seen that for the problems OneMax and SquareWave the algorithm was able to discover the optimum at roughly half the number of allocated evaluations mark. There seems no particular pattern was followed to find the solution, as the bits are set on or off scattered around the phenotypic space. However, the algorithm clearly correctly discovers the hidden structure of each problem as soon as the 6000 evaluations (which is particularly more evident in SquareWave).

The case of the BinVal problem was a little different, as it happened to be harder to solve. Although the optimum for this problem is the same as OneMax the algorithm failed to obtain the global maximum at the end of the execution (6 bits remained off after 39600 evaluations). It is noticeable however, that the solution is evolved following a pattern where the most significant bits are set on first, whereas the phenotypic subspace corresponding to the least significant bits are let to explore at the final stage of the execution. The figure shows that a solid block of the first three rows of bits are set on as early as the 6000 evaluations; then the block grows larger by setting on the subsequent significant bits at a slow rate as the evaluations progress. The algorithm is thus biased to explore the subspace of most significant bits as their contribution to the fitness value heavily overrides the contribution of the least significant bits.

The latter argument is further stressed in higher–dimensional problems; it can be seen in this case that for $d - 64$, the contribution to the fitness value of the bits that are off in the final panel ($t = 39600$) correspond to $1 + 2^3 + 2^4 + 2^5 + 2^8 + 2^{17} = 131385$, which is a tiny 0.0000000000007% of the $1.844674407370929 \times 10^{19}$ fitness value of the optimal solution. Thus, we may say that the pigeons do not bother exploring those dimensions as they turn out to be an negligible source of food.

3.2 Further Experiments

In order to examine the behaviour of parameter tuning on the effectiveness of the algorithm, we carried out a deeper empirical study on the same benchmark

Table 2. PUPI-bin algorithm sanity test on binary benchmarks. Size for the three problems is $d = 64$. The best solution $\mathbf{b}^\star \in \{0,1\}^d$ at time t of a single algorithm execution is shown as a 8×8 binary matrix, with the most significant and least significant bits at coordinates $(0,0)$ and $(7,7)$ respectively. Time t is measured in number of function evaluations out of a 40000 limit. See Table 1 for problem definitions and optimal solutions. The parameters used for the three experiments were: $n = 30, \eta_\omega = .25, \alpha = 0.1, \sigma = 0.1$.

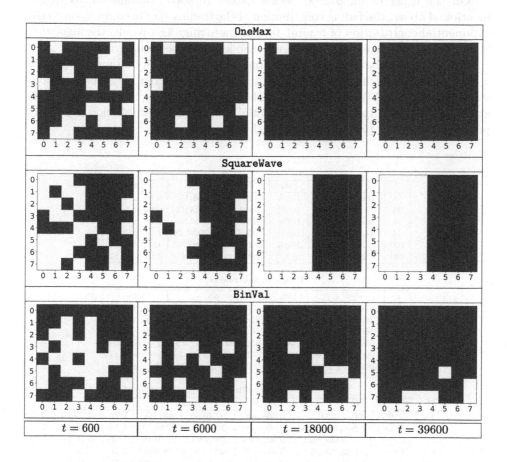

problems of Table 1; results are reported as averages over 100 repetitions per experiment.

To begin with we wanted to assess the impact of increasing problem size, $d \in \{16, 25, 36, 64, 100, 400\}$. The results are summarised in Fig. 2. In OneMax and SquareWave the *exact* optimum is hit in 100% of the repetitions, for dimensionalities $d \leq 100$ (except $d = 100$ in SquareWave which reaches 99%); for $d = 400$, an approximate optimum with a tolerance of 16 bits is achieved in 36% and 38% respectively. In fact, the average best fitness approaches the 383 mark for both problems indicating that those sub-optimal solutions missed the tolerance bits (the optimals being 400). Besides, the execution times is roughly invariant with respect to problem size (except for the largest problem, which incur a reasonable increase due to the evaluation time taken by its larger bit-strings); the latter contrast to the number of evaluations needed to reach the optimal, which increases steadily with the number of dimensions, approaching the allocated 40000 evaluations in the largest problem.

On the other hand, `BinVal` seems harder to solve, because of, as it was mentioned above, the fading contribution of the trailing bits in comparison to the exponential contribution of leading bits in the string; as a result, the algorithm is less prone to explore the subregions encoded in those trailing bits.

For this particular problem, the optimal solutions were found for $d \leq 36$ with a zero *Mean Average Error* (MAE). In larger sizes, higher average deviations starting with a MAE of 531 for $d = 64$ up to 8.39×10^{113} for $d = 400$, hints at the harsh difficulty that the exponential scale of the cost function of `BinVal` poses to the search procedure used by the algorithm.

Problem: `OneMax`

d	f^*	hits	evals	t
16	16.00 ± 0.00	100%	1149.80 ± 786.14	0.95 ± 0.11
25	25.00 ± 0.00	100%	2609.60 ± 1043.02	0.96 ± 0.09
36	36.00 ± 0.00	100%	4599.60 ± 1866.53	0.99 ± 0.10
64	64.00 ± 0.00	100%	10404.00 ± 3940.78	1.05 ± 0.14
100	100.00 ± 0.00	100%	18155.80 ± 5592.60	1.11 ± 0.07
400	382.98 ± 4.54	36% †	39031.00 ± 837.41	1.67 ± 0.12

Problem: `SquareWave`

d	f^*	hits	evals	t
16	16.00 ± 0.00	100%	1203.80 ± 894.88	1.24 ± 0.16
25	25.00 ± 0.00	100%	2582.80 ± 1157.06	1.40 ± 0.34
36	36.00 ± 0.00	100%	4625.60 ± 2183.37	1.30 ± 0.03
64	64.00 ± 0.00	100%	9582.80 ± 3017.35	1.37 ± 0.04
100	99.99 ± 0.10	99%	17336.40 ± 5145.14	1.45 ± 0.11
400	383.53 ± 3.28	38% †	39160.20 ± 929.16	2.15 ± 0.19

Problem: `BinVal`

d	f^*	MAE	evals	t
16	65535.00 ± 0.00	0.00e+00	1540.80 ± 851.38	1.26 ± 0.50
25	3.36e+07 ± 0.00e+00	0.00e+00	3000.80 ± 1244.86	1.16 ± 0.28
36	6.87e+10 ± 0.00e+00	0.00e+00	5069.80 ± 2710.16	1.06 ± 0.19
64	1.84e+19 ± 2.79e+02	5.31e+02	10759.60 ± 3856.54	1.16 ± 0.26
100	1.27e+30 ± 1.94e+13	3.86e+13	14411.00 ± 4754.89	1.54 ± 0.83
400	2.58e+120 ± 7.85e+114	8.39e+113	32490.00 ± 5558.21	2.19 ± 0.51

Fig. 2. Summary of results varying problem size $d \in \{16, 25, 36, 64, 100, 400\}$. Algorithm parameters were set as $n = 20, \eta_\omega = 0.25, \alpha = 0.1, \sigma = 1$ with 40000 evaluations allocated per each of a total 100 repetitions. (**Legend** → d: dimensions; f^*: cost function of best solution found; **evals**: evaluations taken to reach best solution; t: execution time (secs); **hits**: percentage of repetitions that found the exact optimum; †: percentage of repetitions that found an approximate optimum to a tolerance of up to 2 bytes; **MAE**: mean average error of the best fitness value compared to the optimum problem value.)

Secondly, we investigated the role of population size, $n \in \{20, 40, 80\}$; these results are reported in Fig. 3. Here we can see a pattern occurring in the three problems: a small population size ($n = 20$) seems to be the most appropriate setting for this parameter (OneMax hits: 100%, SquareWave hits: 100%, BinVal MAE: 2.99×10^{13}). Higher values of this parameter decrease the effectiveness.

The above mentioned behaviour is explained because as the population increases the actual exploration phase of the algorithm is cut short due to more pigeons spending the evaluation budget faster (recall that the evaluations quota for these experiments is constant, max_eval = 40000); hence the solutions obtained are sub-optimal. Execution times and evaluations needed to reach best solution behaved as discussed before.

Lastly, we wanted to assess the importance of the maximum number of evaluations allocated to the algorithm during optimisation. We tried different problem sizes; here we report results for $d = 64$ and $d = 100$ (see Fig. 4). In this case, since the population size is kept constant ($n = 20$) a significant advantageous impact is evident on the algorithm when the allocated number of evaluations is increased; therefore at least a budget of max_eval = 40000 is recommended.

Now, from a different angle, we also decided to evaluate by means of a distance metric the effectiveness of the algorithm in discovering the desired phenotypic solution to each of the benchmark problems. In this direction, in order to re-examine the difficulty posed by the BinVal problem regarding the exponential contribution to the fitness by the most significant bits in high dimensional prob-

Problem: OneMax

n	f^*	hits	evals	t
20	100.00 ± 0.00	100%	18777.00 ± 6543.94	0.98 ± 0.01
40	99.95 ± 0.22	95%	25765.20 ± 6375.36	0.86 ± 0.02
80	99.91 ± 0.29	91%	29824.00 ± 5712.02	0.79 ± 0.02

Problem: SquareWave

n	f^*	hits	evals	t
20	100.00 ± 0.00	100%	18122.20 ± 5162.78	1.34 ± 0.12
40	99.96 ± 0.20	96%	24976.00 ± 5837.79	1.13 ± 0.03
80	99.89 ± 0.31	89%	30158.40 ± 5504.67	1.04 ± 0.05

Problem: BinVal

n	f^*	MAE	evals	t
20	$1.27e+30 \pm 1.93e+13$	$2.99e+13$	15161.40 ± 5406.78	1.14 ± 0.02
40	$1.27e+30 \pm 2.94e+19$	$2.95e+18$	20964.40 ± 6791.12	0.99 ± 0.05
80	$1.27e+30 \pm 2.02e+13$	$3.34e+13$	23383.20 ± 5226.34	0.85 ± 0.13

Fig. 3. Summary of results varying population size $n \in \{20, 40, 80\}$ for problems with $d = 100$ averaged over 100 repetitions. Algorithm parameters were set as $\eta_\omega = 0.25, \alpha = 0.1, \sigma = 1$ with 40000 evaluations allocated. (**Legend** → n: popsize; f^*: cost function of best solution found; **evals**: evaluations taken to reach best solution; t: execution time (secs); **hits**: percentage of repetitions that found the exact optimum; **MAE**: mean average error of the best fitness value compared to the optimum problem value.)

.... $d = 64$ ....

Problem: OneMax

max_eval	f^*	hits	evals	t
10000	63.75 ± 0.50	78%	7080.40 ± 1614.45	0.25 ± 0.01
20000	63.99 ± 0.10	99%	8703.60 ± 2584.87	0.59 ± 0.10
40000	64.00 ± 0.00	100%	9624.80 ± 3133.80	1.27 ± 0.49

Problem: SquareWave

max_eval	f^*	hits	evals	t
10000	63.86 ± 0.35	86%	7114.00 ± 1541.78	0.39 ± 0.10
20000	64.00 ± 0.00	100%	8858.60 ± 2706.09	0.75 ± 0.14
40000	64.00 ± 0.00	100%	10024.80 ± 3274.41	1.45 ± 0.20

Problem: BinVal

max_eval	f^*	MAE	evals	t
10000	1.84e+19 ± 1.76e+12	1.98e+11	7089.20 ± 1571.77	0.31 ± 0.12
20000	1.84e+19 ± 1.07e+08	1.08e+07	9516.20 ± 3304.31	0.61 ± 0.12
40000	1.84e+19 ± 2.71e+02	4.49e+02	10744.60 ± 3649.13	1.26 ± 0.27

.... $d = 100$ ....

Problem: OneMax

max_eval	f^*	hits	evals	t
10000	98.10 ± 1.29	12%	8632.40 ± 950.13	0.28 ± 0.04
20000	99.82 ± 0.46	85%	14612.20 ± 2943.16	0.73 ± 0.25
40000	100.00 ± 0.00	100%	17754.80 ± 5428.90	1.35 ± 0.44

Problem: SquareWave

max_eval	f^*	hits	evals	t
10000	98.48 ± 1.13	23%	8913.00 ± 1015.46	0.48 ± 0.20
20000	99.83 ± 0.40	84%	14827.20 ± 2783.68	0.66 ± 0.02
40000	100.00 ± 0.00	100%	17522.00 ± 5077.86	1.38 ± 0.21

Problem: BinVal

max_eval	f^*	MAE	evals	t
10000	1.27e+30 ± 1.54e+25	1.68e+24	8339.00 ± 1177.22	0.35 ± 0.09
20000	1.27e+30 ± 1.92e+24	1.94e+23	12131.80 ± 3255.98	0.57 ± 0.06
40000	1.27e+30 ± 2.04e+13	3.68e+13	15456.20 ± 5590.63	1.30 ± 0.24

Fig. 4. Summary of results varying the maximum number of evaluations max_eval $\in$ $\{10000, 20000, 40000\}$ for problems with $d = 64$ (top) and $d = 100$ (bottom) averaged over 100 repetitions. The algorithm parameters were set as $n = 20, \eta_\omega = 0.25, \alpha = 0.1, \sigma = 1$. (**Legend** → same as Fig. 3)

lems, we applied a log-transformation to the definition of its cost function. This adjustment yields a fitness function that is expressed as the sum of the exponents of the powers of two, associated to the loci that are set to one in the bitstring: $f(\mathbf{b}) = \sum_{i=1}^{d} b_i \times \log_2 2^{i-1}$. The optimal solution of the new problem, that we have termed PowSum, is the all-ones vector whose fitness value is $\sum_{i=1}^{d}(i-1)$, likewise that of BinVal.

Therefore, we completed the empirical analysis by running experiments with the four problems and evaluating the phenotype of the solutions found by means of two different metrics: Hamming distance and Euclidean distance. We set the parameters to $n = 30, \eta_\omega = 0.1, \alpha = 0.1, \sigma = 0.1,$ max_eval $= 40000$ varying $d \in \{16, 25, 36, 64, 100\}$ for 100 repetitions. The results are shown in Fig. 5.

Let us observe initially the panel on the top, reporting the average fitness; it is clear that the algorithm approximates the solution with low variability in the four problems and moreover, it is also evident the decrease of fitness value in the PowSum problem compared to the BinVal problem, due to the logarithmic transformation that was applied.

Next let us focus on the panel in the middle, which reports the average Hamming distances to the desired solution of each problem with respect to the solutions found in each repetition. The first observation here is that for all the

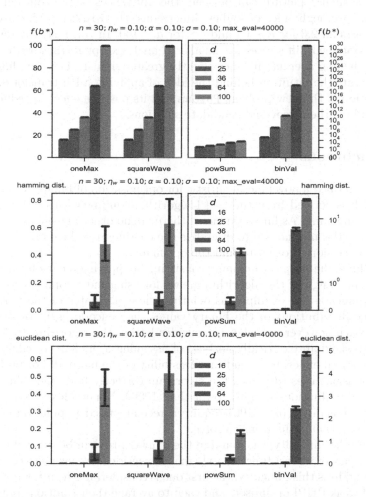

Fig. 5. Distance metrics analysis of the phenotype of solutions found by the algorithm on four benchmarks: OneMax, SquareWave, BinVal, PowSum. **Top:** Average fitness value for each dimensionality is reported for reference; notice the linear scale of the problems in the left panel versus the semilog scale of the problems in the right panel. **Middle:** Hamming distance results; the scales in the panels are linear (left) and logarithmic (right). **Bottom:** Euclidean distance; here, both axis are in linear scale.

problems when $d \leq 36$ the difference (distance) to the optimal is negligible. Besides, when $d \geq 64$, for OneMax and SquareWave the average difference including variability is lower than one bit. The case of BinVal, as it was noticed previously, exhibits an increased difference of around 10 bits in average for these high dimensions. However, it is interesting to see that in the case of PowSum, for $d = 64$ the average difference is lower than a single bit, whereas for $d = 100$ the average difference is around three bits.

Finally, regarding the panel on the bottom where the Euclidean distance is reported, a similar picture can be seen: the differences of the solutions in low dimensions are negligible; in higher dimensions, the BinVal problem exhibits distances around 2.3 for $d = 64$ and 4.8 for $d = 100$. In contrast, the remainder problems obtained differences are smaller than 1, except PowSum with $d = 100$ which reached an average distance slightly greater than 1. These findings seem to corroborate the intuition behind the idea of applying a log transformation in the definition of the new problem PowSum and its positive effect in reducing the inexactitude of the discovered candidate solutions.

4   Conclusions

We have described a novel metaheuristic for optimisation of binary–valued problems, which is derived from the PUPI algorithm equipped with a genotype-to-phenotype mapping. As far as we know, there are no other pigeon–inspired algorithms using this mechanism to discretise the continuous-valued explored by the real–valued version in order to find the optimal.

We defined the simplest mapping consisting of applying a cut-off threshold of $\tau = 0.5$. The design of the algorithm allows for using more sophisticated gpm() mappings, such as for example, associating the coordinates of the particles to probability distributions of the binary values they encode [4,9]. Before trying that approach however, we plan to consider letting the algorithm to *learn* the cut–off threshold automatically, instead of assigning a predefined value.

The reported experiments indicate feasibility of the method. For problems of lower dimensionalities ($d \leq 64$), the algorithm correctly finds the solution with a number of evaluations roughly lower than 10000. Nonetheless, instances with higher dimesionalities ($d \geq 100$) require a recommended population size of 20 pigeons and 40000 evaluations to solve.

A particular difficulty was found in the BinVal problem because of the exponential increase of its cost function in higher dimensions. We visualise two avenues to further address this difficulty: the first one is considering executing not one but a series of weak PUPI optimisers and then to average their solutions in the hope of finding a most accurate optimal, much in the spirit of the widely–known ensemble methods of machine learning such as boosting or bagging predictors [5]. The second one in the same vein, is again to execute several weak PUPI optimisers *concurrently*, enabling channels to interchange partial solution information in order to scale up the effectiveness of the search procedure, as it has been reported recently with other kind of evolutionary algorithms [12].

References

1. Blanco, A., Chaparro, N., Rojas-Galeano, S.: An urban pigeon-inspired optimiser for unconstrained continuous domains. In: 8th Brazilian Conference on Intelligent Systems (BRACIS). IEEE Xplore Digital Library (2019)
2. Bolaji, A.L., Babatunde, B.S., Shola, P.B.: Adaptation of binary pigeon-inspired algorithm for solving multidimensional Knapsack problem. In: Pant, M., Ray, K., Sharma, T.K., Rawat, S., Bandyopadhyay, A. (eds.) Soft Computing: Theories and Applications. AISC, vol. 583, pp. 743–751. Springer, Singapore (2018). https://doi.org/10.1007/978-981-10-5687-1_66
3. Brabazon, A., Cui, W., O'Neill, M.: The raven roosting optimisation algorithm. Soft Comput. **20**(2), 525–545 (2016)
4. Crawford, B., Soto, R., Astorga, G., García, J., Castro, C., Paredes, F.: Putting continuous metaheuristics to work in binary search spaces. Complexity **2017**, 19 (2017)
5. Dietterich, T.G.: Ensemble methods in machine learning. In: Kittler, J., Roli, F. (eds.) MCS 2000. LNCS, vol. 1857, pp. 1–15. Springer, Heidelberg (2000). https://doi.org/10.1007/3-540-45014-9_1
6. Duan, H., Qiao, P.: Pigeon-inspired optimization: a new swarm intelligence optimizer for air robot path planning. Int. J. Intell. Comput. Cybern. **7**(1), 24–37 (2014)
7. Goel, S.: Pigeon optimization algorithm: a novel approach for solving optimization problems. In: 2014 International Conference on Data Mining and Intelligent Computing (ICDMIC), pp. 1–5. IEEE (2014)
8. Kennedy, J., Eberhart, R.: Particle swarm optimization. In: IEEE International Conference on Neural Networks, vol. 4, pp. 1942–1948. IEEE (1995)
9. Kennedy, J., Eberhart, R.C.: A discrete binary version of the particle swarm algorithm. In: 1997 IEEE International Conference on Systems, Man, and Cybernetics, vol. 5, pp. 4104–4108. IEEE (1997)
10. Lamy, J.-B.: Artificial Feeding Birds (AFB): a new metaheuristic inspired by the behavior of pigeons. In: Shandilya, S.K., Shandilya, S., Nagar, A.K. (eds.) Advances in Nature-Inspired Computing and Applications. EICC, pp. 43–60. Springer, Cham (2019). https://doi.org/10.1007/978-3-319-96451-5_3
11. Meng, X.B., Gao, X.Z., Lu, L., Liu, Y., Zhang, H.: A new bio-inspired optimisation algorithm: bird swarm algorithm. J. Exp. Theor. Artif. Intell. **28**(4), 673–687 (2016)
12. Merelo, J.J., Laredo, J.L.J., Castillo, P.A., García-Valdez, J.-M., Rojas-Galeano, S.: Exploring concurrent and stateless evolutionary algorithms. In: Kaufmann, P., Castillo, P.A. (eds.) EvoApplications 2019. LNCS, vol. 11454, pp. 405–412. Springer, Cham (2019). https://doi.org/10.1007/978-3-030-16692-2_27
13. Rothlauf, F.: Representations for Genetic and Evolutionary Algorithms, pp. 9–32. Springer, Heidelberg (2006). https://doi.org/10.1007/3-540-32444-5_2
14. Spennemann, D.H., Watson, M.J.: Dietary habits of urban pigeons (columba livia) and implications of excreta PH-a review. Eur. J. Ecol. **3**(1), 27–41 (2017)
15. Torabi, S., Safi-Esfahani, F.: Improved Raven Roosting Optimization algorithm (IRRO). Swarm Evol. Comput. **40**, 144–154 (2018)
16. Yang, Z., Liu, K., Fan, J., Guo, Y., Niu, Q., Zhang, J.: A novel binary/real-valued pigeon-inspired optimization for economic/environment unit commitment with renewables and plug-in vehicles. Sci. China Inf. Sci. **62**(7), 070213 (2019)
17. Zambrano-Bigiarini, M., Clerc, M., Rojas, R.: Standard particle swarm optimisation 2011 at CEC-2013: a baseline for future PSO improvements. In: 2013 IEEE Congress on Evolutionary Computation, pp. 2337–2344. IEEE (2013)

Control of a Microturbine Using Neural Networks

Helbert Espitia[1](✉), Iván Machón[2], and Hilario López[2]

[1] Universidad Distrital Francisco José de Caldas, Bogotá, Colombia
`heespitiac@udistrital.edu.co`
[2] Universidad de Oviedo, Oviedo, Spain
{`machonivan,hilario`}`@uniovi.es`

Abstract. In many distributed generation applications, microturbines are used for energy conversion. On the other hand, neural networks are a suitable option for the control of complex non-linear systems. Thus, in this article is shown the speed control of a microturbine using neural networks. For this process, the identification of the microturbine using a neural network is carried out in order to subsequently perform the optimization of the other neural network used for control.

Keywords: Control · Neural networks · Microturbine

1 Introduction

Distributed resources of energy are an important alternative to supply electric power, the approach of distributed generation may allow the costs of generators and the production of electricity to be cheaper [1]. Some distributed resources of energy are: eolian generation, fuel cells, microturbines and photovoltaic systems [2]. According to [3] and [4], using appropriated control schemes is possible to improve the reliability and the power quality.

A microturbine (MT) generation system belongs to the type of thermal generation due to characteristics like lower cost, higher efficiency, more reliability and convenience; thus, MT system is considered one of the best forms of distributed generation. However, a microturbine is a complex thermal dynamic system which makes complicated to establish a precise model because of the manifested non-linearities and uncertainties [2,5]. Some investigations addressing proper modeling for a MT can be seen in [2,5–7] and [8].

Conventionally, a MT shows controls of velocity, acceleration, temperature, and fuel. According to [5], a microturbine is mainly adjusted by velocity which is regulated to a constant value close to nominal velocity in conditions of normal operation.

Meanwhile, neural networks (NN) offer an acceptable control alternative when having a highly complex system given by non-linearities, parameter variance, and saturation, among others [9].

© Springer Nature Switzerland AG 2019
J. C. Figueroa-García et al. (Eds.): WEA 2019, CCIS 1052, pp. 202–213, 2019.
https://doi.org/10.1007/978-3-030-31019-6_18

A system of control to a microturbine using NN is proposed in this paper; the work is mainly focused on velocity controls, leaving the possibility of studying other control variables in further papers.

2   Microturbine Model

In relation of development models for a microturbine, in [6] a modular model of sixth order to a microturbine is presented. Moreover, [7] describes a simple model based on a transfer function.

According to [8], assuming the microturbine operates always close to its nominal velocity, and ignoring the start and off processes, it is then possible the construction of a simple model. In this regard, it is necessary to bear in mind that suppositions may arise uncertainties in the model [5].

2.1   Microturbine Operation

In general, the following process are involved in the operation of a microturbine:

1. Air at atmospheric pressure enters to the gas turbine through the compressor.
2. Air is compressed to achieve the conditions to combustion.
3. The fuel (gas) is mixed with the air in the combustion chamber.
4. Then, combustion takes place. Hot gases are expanded through the turbine to generate mechanic energy.

During the combustion process, the chemical energy present in the combustion reagents is transferred to the gas flux. This energy is given by gas enthalpy such that it becomes into mechanic work by the gas expansion through the turbine. It also occurs that in the last stage of the combustion process a part of the flux is derivate to activate the compressor [10]. Figure 1 displays the interaction of these systems. From this view three components can be seen to a MT:

1. Combustion system.
2. Turbine and compressor system.
3. Thermal system.

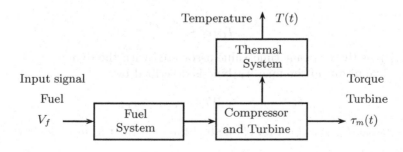

Fig. 1. Microturbine systems.

Fuel System. Figure 2 shows the fuel system parts. Main components are the valve positioner and the flux dynamic behavior. In this figure V_f is the fuel input signal, this is amplified via K_f (gain) and compensated using F_0 which are the fuel flux without load in nominal velocity. Then, the signal passes through the valve and actuator positioner to produce the fuel flow signal W_f [2].

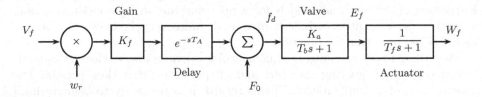

Fig. 2. Fuel subsystem.

According to [11] and [12], the transfer function associated to the valve is:

$$E_f = \frac{K_a}{T_b s + 1} f_d \tag{1}$$

Regarding the flux dynamics the respective transfer function is:

$$W_f = \frac{1}{T_f s + 1} E_f \tag{2}$$

where K_a represents the gain associated with the valve positioner, T_b and T_f are time constant values for the valve positioner and the fuel system. Meanwhile, f_d, E_1 are the input and output positioner of the valve, and W_f is the flux signal fuel.

Turbine and Compressor Systems. Figure 3 displays the block diagram of the gas turbine. Turbine input signals are the fuel flux W_f and the angular velocity $w_r(t)$. Output signals are the turbine torque $\tau_m(t)$. According to [11] and [12], the transfer for the gas turbine is:

$$W_C = \frac{1}{T_{CD} s + 1} W_{fC} \tag{3}$$

where T_{CD} is the constant time value associated with the dynamics of the gas turbine. The torque of the microturbine is described by:

$$F_C = a_C - b_C W_C + c_C (1 - w_r) \tag{4}$$

As observable, F_C is a function of the fuel flux and the turbine velocity.

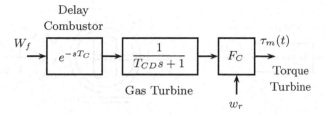

Fig. 3. Turbine and compressor systems.

Thermal System. The fuel burnt (fuel flux) in the combustion chambers generates torque of the turbine and the gas escape temperature [11]. Figure 4 shows the block diagram of the thermal system.

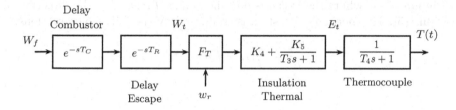

Fig. 4. Thermal system.

According to [11] and [12], the escape temperature of the gas is given by:

$$F_T = T_{ref} - a_t(1 - W_t) + b_t(1 - w_r) \qquad (5)$$

where F_T is a function whose entries consist of fuel flux with delay W_t, and the turbine velocity $w_r(t)$. Escape temperature is measured using a set of thermocouples which are assigned in the radiators.

On the other hand, K_4 and K_5 are constant values associated with the insulation transfer function (opposing to the radiation). T_3 and T_4 are values of constant time of the transfer functions of both the insulation and the thermocouple. In addition, T_{ref} represents the escape temperature (reference temperature) [5,8].

3   Permanent Magnet Synchronous Generator

In energy generation systems, the Permanent Magnet Synchronous Generator (PMSG) is widely used to obtain transformation from mechanical to electrical energy [13]. According to [14] and [15], permanent magnet synchronous generators need no feeding of direct current (DC) for the excitation circuit, neither have contact brushes.

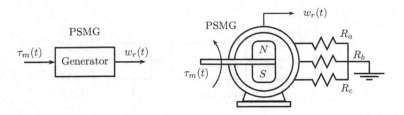

Fig. 5. Scheme of a PSMG.

The scheme for PMSG is shown in Fig. 5, where the input of the generator is the torque $\tau_m(t)$ and the output the angular velocity $w_r(t)$. Related works using PMSG and neural systems are presented in [16] and [17].

The dynamic model of a PMSG is composed of two parts, one mechanical and the other electrical that is obtained of the mobile synchronous framework of two signals $d - q$, where the axis q is 90° ahead axis d regarding the direction of rotation [15]. The mechanical system is composed by the following equations:

$$\frac{dw_r}{dt} = \frac{1}{J}(\tau_c - Fw_r - \tau_m) \tag{6}$$

$$\frac{d\theta}{dt} = w_r \tag{7}$$

where w_r rotor angular velocity, θ angular position, J is the rotor inertia, F rotor viscous friction, and τ_m mechanical torque. For the electrical part the model equations in the coordinates $d - q$ are:

$$\frac{di_d}{dt} = \frac{1}{L_d}v_d - \frac{R}{L_d}i_d + \frac{L_q}{L_d}pw_ri_q \tag{8}$$

$$\frac{di_q}{dt} = \frac{1}{L_q}v_q - \frac{R}{L_q}i_d - \frac{L_d}{L_q}pw_ri_d - \frac{\lambda pw_r}{L_q} \tag{9}$$

$$\tau_e = 1.5p[\lambda i_q + (L_d - L_q)i_di_q] \tag{10}$$

in these equations i_d, i_q are the currents, v_d, v_q voltages, L_d, L_q the inductances, R stator resistance, λ amplitude of the flux induced by the permanent magnets, p number of pole pairs, and τ_e electromagnetic torque. For current and voltage conversions is used the parameter $\gamma = 2\pi/3$. The current conversion from $d - q$ to abc axis is:

$$\begin{bmatrix} i_a \\ i_b \\ i_c \end{bmatrix} = \begin{bmatrix} \cos(\theta) & -\sin(\theta) \\ \cos(\theta - \gamma) & -\sin(\theta - \gamma) \\ \cos(\theta + \gamma) & -\sin(\theta + \gamma) \end{bmatrix} \begin{bmatrix} i_d \\ i_q \end{bmatrix} \tag{11}$$

The voltage conversions from abc to $d - q$ corresponds to:

$$\begin{bmatrix} v_d \\ v_q \end{bmatrix} = \frac{2}{3} \begin{bmatrix} \cos(\theta) & \cos(\theta - \gamma) & \cos(\theta + \gamma) \\ -\sin(\theta) & -\sin(\theta - \gamma) & -\sin(\theta + \gamma) \end{bmatrix} \begin{bmatrix} v_a \\ v_b \\ v_c \end{bmatrix} \tag{12}$$

4   Neural Networks

According to [18,19] neural networks are a suitable alternative for the identification and control of dynamic systems when the system presents non-linearities. One of the advantages of neural networks is the flexibility of adaptation, association, evaluation and recognition of patterns [20].

The information is processed through inputs, a weight per connection and an output associated with an activation function as corresponds to equation (13), where each input x_n is weighted using w_n and added to be later evaluated by an activation function f to obtain the output y. Some activation functions are: sigmoid, gaussian, linear, saturated linear, and hard limit. The addition of network layers allows the increase of the adaptation capabilities [21].

$$y = f \left(\sum_{n=1}^{N} w_n x_n \right) \tag{13}$$

In applications of identification and control can be used feed forward or backward networks. In recurrent networks (feed-backward networks) feedback is present among neurons as well as from the output to the inputs. In feed-forward the signals move forward only, therefore, it is necessary an additional feedback from the output to the inputs [22].

5   Neural Control System

Neural control system is proposed as an alternative to identify and to control dynamic systems, using its capacity as approximator for general functions [9]. Figure 6 shows the neural network control model.

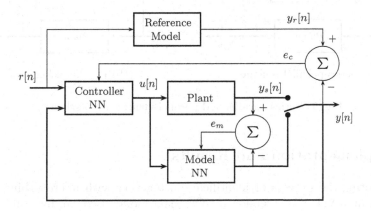

Fig. 6. Neural network control reference model.

In Fig. 6 it is shown two neural networks used for the neural control system, where $y[n]$ is the measured signal of the process, $u[n]$ is the control signal, $r[n]$

the reference for the controller, $y_s[n]$ the simulated plant output, and $y_r[n]$ the desired output (reference-model).

The considered architecture uses two neural networks, one for the control and another to estimate the plant model. Thus, the identification of the plant is first carried out and subsequently the controller training. The plant identification is made using the Backpropagation algorithm, after carrying out the identification, the controller training is performed using the algorithm Dynamic Backpropagation in which it incorporates in a closed loop the dynamics of the neural-model plant and the dynamic behavior of the controller, thus, the parameters of the controller are optimized so that the output has the desired behavior (reference-model). After being trained the controller is put into operation with the plant [23, 24].

5.1 Identification Using Neural Networks

According to [25], when using neural networks, the classic methods for identifying dynamic systems are series-parallel and parallel, shown in Fig. 7. In the series-parallel identification scheme are directly used the inputs and outputs of the plant; under this approach, the Backpropagation method can be used as a training algorithm [26]. On the other hand, in the parallel identification scheme, inputs of the plant are used and the output of the network being feedback to the inputs, with this perspective, the Dynamic Backpropagation is employed as training algorithm [24]. In this paper is used series-parallel identification.

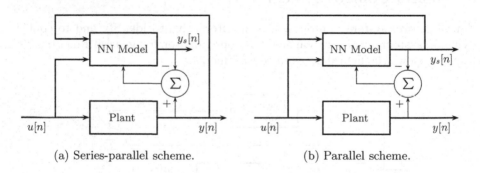

(a) Series-parallel scheme.   (b) Parallel scheme.

Fig. 7. Series-parallel and parallel identification scheme.

6 Implementation and Results

Implementing the process of identification, together with microturbine control are made in MATLAB® (version 7). The plant model used can be seen in Fig. 8; it can be noted that the input corresponds to the flux of fuel and the output to the angular velocity. A random signal is employed to obtain the data used in plant identification which allows to describe the different behaviors present in the system output (velocity). Figure 9 permits to see the neural controller architecture using MATLAB®.

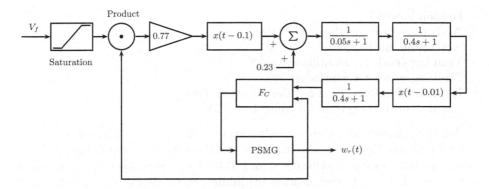

Fig. 8. Microturbine model used.

The general expressions for neural networks used for identification are given by f_p and for control by f_c functions. Taken p as the output delays, q as the input delays, m as reference delays, then the equations for plant model $y_s[n+1]$ and the control signal $u[n+1]$ are:

$$y_s[n+1] = f_p(y[n], y[n-1], ..., y[n-p+1], u[n], u[n-1], ...$$
$$, u[n-q+1]) \tag{14}$$

$$u[n+1] = f_c(y[n], y[n-1], ..., y[n-p+1], r[n], r[n-1], ...$$
$$, r[n-m+1], u[n-1], ..., u[n-q+1]) \tag{15}$$

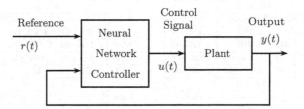

Fig. 9. Neural control system scheme.

For control and identification process, different neural networks are used taking 2, 3, and 4 delays for the input as well as to output feedback. The neural networks used have two hidden layers, the first layer is set using 2, 3, and 5 neurons, and the second layer one neuron. For plant identification is used the function "TRAINLM" that implements the Levenberg-Marquardt Backpropagation, and for controller training is used "TRAINBFGC" corresponding to the BFGS (Broyden-Fletcher-Goldfarb-Shanno) quasi-Newton Backpropagation method. The additional configurations of neural controller are:

- Hidden layers: 2
- Activation functions layer 1: sigmoid
- Activation function layer 2: linear
- Training epoch for identification: 300
- Training epoch for controller: 50
- Number of training data for identification: 6000
- Number of training data for controller: 1000

Each configuration is respectively executed 20 times to identification and control training; thus, obtaining the values of the Mean Squared Error (MSE) as shown in Table 1a for identification, and Table 1b for controller training. These tables present for each configuration the minimum, maximum, average and standard deviation (STD) values. To perform the controller training is used the configuration of 2 delays and 5 neurons obtained from the identification process (neural-model). Part of data used for identification can be seen in Fig. 10a; this figure also displays the results of the identification process made with the neural network.

Table 1. Results for identification and controller training.

(a) MSE training process values obtained for identification.

Delays: 1			
Value	Neurons: 2	Neurons: 3	Neurons: 5
Min	1.49E-04	1.36E-04	1.17E-04
Max	3.72E-03	3.68E-03	7.95E-04
Mean	1.54E-03	7.86E-04	1.79E-04
STD	1.66E-03	1.04E-03	1.50E-04
Delays: 2			
Value	Neurons: 2	Neurons: 3	Neurons: 5
Min	2.33E-05	1.38E-05	1.15E-05
Max	2.44E-03	2.30E-03	1.11E-03
Mean	1.50E-03	5.58E-04	1.89E-04
STD	9.24E-04	8.42E-04	3.66E-04
Delays: 3			
Value	Neurons: 2	Neurons: 3	Neurons: 5
Min	2.17E-05	1.86E-05	1.14E-05
Max	1.68E-03	1.59E-03	1.39E-03
Mean	1.11E-03	5.44E-04	2.78E-04
STD	5.74E-04	5.97E-04	4.26E-04

(b) MSE values obtained for controller training.

Delays: 1			
Value	Neurons: 2	Neurons: 3	Neurons: 5
Min	2.65E-02	1.20E-02	3.21E+00
Max	7.63E+01	2.28E+01	2.07E+02
Mean	1.52E+01	6.25E+00	3.60E+01
STD	2.56E+01	7.85E+00	5.59E+01
Delays: 2			
Value	Neurons: 2	Neurons: 3	Neurons: 5
Min	4.92E-03	4.30E-02	1.25E-01
Max	2.28E+01	9.17E+01	2.28E+02
Mean	1.24E+01	1.50E+01	5.32E+01
STD	9.67E+00	2.29E+01	7.23E+01
Delays: 3			
Value	Neurons: 2	Neurons: 3	Neurons: 5
Min	6.35E-03	4.85E-02	1.18E-02
Max	2.20E+01	2.28E+01	1.34E+02
Mean	6.60E+00	9.12E+00	2.69E+01
STD	7.83E+00	8.41E+00	3.22E+01

Figure 10b shows the control system response after the training, as an example, it is taken a configuration using 1 delay and 3 neurons. This process includes the identified model (with the neural network) to train the controller which is implemented with another neural network.

Finally, the results of the simulation of the neural controller with the plant model can be seen in Fig. 11; in this case, the microturbine model is used for simulation.

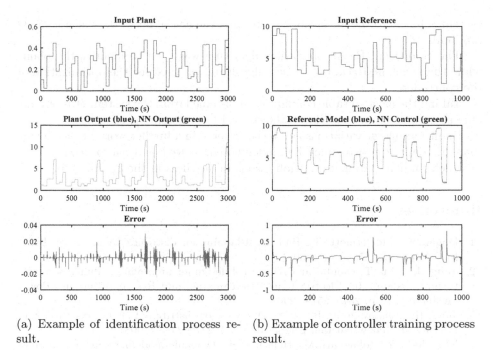

(a) Example of identification process result.

(b) Example of controller training process result.

Fig. 10. Graphical results for identification and controller training. (Color figure online)

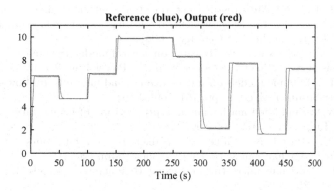

Fig. 11. Simulation for microturbine control. (Color figure online)

These simulations allow to see the system behavior when it is performing the controller training and also the controller response operating with the microturbine model.

7 Conclusions

In this work, the identification and control of a microturbine were achieved using a neural network scheme. Observations show that the performance of the system is linked to the initial configuration of the neural network, which is made randomly.

The traditional Backpropagation algorithm was used to identify the plant, while the Dynamic Backpropagation algorithm was used for the optimization of the controller.

Taking the most suitable configuration obtained from the system, it is observable that the system can achieve the control for different speed values.

Plant parameter variations can be considered in a further work in such a way that an adaptive process may be implemented, as well as a neuro-fuzzy system in which random parameter initializations be needless in the neural system.

References

1. Dugan, R., McDermott, T., Ball, G.: Planning for distributed generation. IEEE Ind. Appl. Mag. **7**, 80–88 (2001)
2. Tong, J.P., Yu, T.: Nonlinear PID control design for improving stability of microturbine systems. In: Electric Utility Deregulation and Restructuring and Power Technologies, pp. 2515–2518 (2008)
3. Jiayi, H., Chuanwen, J., Rong, X.: A review on distributed energy resources and MicroGrid. Renew. Sustain Energy Rev. **12**, 2472–2483 (2008)
4. Khorshidi, A., Zolfaghari, M., Hejazi, M.A.: Dynamic modeling and simulation of microturbine generating system for stability analysis in microgrid networks. Int. J. Basic Sci. Appl. Res. **3**(9), 663–670 (2014)
5. Yu, T., Tong, J.P.: Auto disturbance rejection control of microturbine system. In: IEEE Power Energy Society General Meeting - Conversion and Delivery of Electrical Energy in the 21st Century (2008)
6. Li, Z., Wang, D.H., Xue, Y.L.: Research on ways of modeling of microturbine (part 1): analysis of dynamic characteristic. Chin. J. Power Eng. **25**, 13–17 (2005)
7. Lasseter R.: Dynamic models for micro-turbines and fuel cells. In: Power Engineering Society Summer Meeting, pp. 761–766 (2001)
8. Rowen, W.J.: Simplified mathematical representation of heavy duty gas turbines. ASME J. Eng. Power **105**, 865–869 (1983)
9. Nguyen, H., Prasad, N., Walker, C., Walker, E.: A First Course in Fuzzy and Neural Control. Chapman & Hall/CRC, Boca Raton (2003)
10. Jurado, F.: Modeling micro-turbines using Hammerstein models. Int. J. Energy Res. **29**, 841–85 (2005)
11. Guda, S., Wang, C., Nehrir, M.: Modeling of microturbine power generation systems. Electr. Power Compon. Syst. **34**(9), 1027–1041 (2006)
12. Wanik, M., Erlich, I.: Dynamic simulation of microturbine distributed generators integrated with multi-machines power system network. In: 2nd IEEE International Conference on Power and Energy, PECon 2008 (2008)
13. Chen, J., Wu, H., Sun, M., Jiang, W., Cai, L., Guo, C.: Modeling and simulation of directly driven wind turbine with permanent magnet synchronous generator. In: IEEE Innovative Smart Grid Technologies-Asia (ISGT Asia) (2012)
14. Rolan, A., Luna, A., Gerardo, V., Aguilar, D., Azevedo, G.: Modelling of a variable speed wind turbine with a permanent magnet synchronous generator. In: IEEE International Symposium on Industrial Electronics (ISIE), pp. 734–739, 5–8 July 2009

15. Patil, K., Mehta, B.: Modeling and control of variable speed wind turbine with permanent magnet synchronous generator. In: International Conference on Advances in Green Energy (ICAGE), pp. 17–18 (2014)
16. Espitia, H., Díaz, G.: Identification of a permanent magnet synchronous generator using neuronal networks. In: Workshop on Engineering Applications - International Congress on Engineering (WEA) (2015)
17. Espitia, H., Díaz, G., Díaz, S.: Control of a permanent magnet synchronous generator using a neuro-fuzzy system. In: Figueroa-García, J.C., López-Santana, E.R., Rodriguez-Molano, J.I. (eds.) WEA 2018. CCIS, vol. 915, pp. 89–101. Springer, Cham (2018). https://doi.org/10.1007/978-3-030-00350-0_8
18. Torres, N., Hernandez, C., Pedraza, L.: Redes neuronales y predicción de tráfico. Revista Tecnura **15**(29), 90–97 (2011)
19. Martinez, F., Gómez, D., Castiblanco, M.: Optimization of a neural architecture for the direct control of a Boost converter. Revista Tecnura **16**(32), 41–49 (2012)
20. Pérez, F., Fernández, H.: Las redes neuronales y la evaluación del riesgo de crédito. Revista Ingenierpias Universidad de Medellín **6**(10), 77–91 (2007)
21. Arrieta, J., Torres, J., Velásquez, H.: Predicciones de modelos econométricos y redes neuronales: el caso de la acción de SURAMINV. Semestre Económico **12**(25), 95–109 (2009)
22. Heaton, J.: Introduction to Neural Networks with Java, pp. 41–49. Heaton Research Inc., St. Louis (2008)
23. Hagan, M., De Jesús, O., Schultz, R.: Training recurrent networks for filtering and control. In: Medsker, L.R., Jain, L.C. (eds.) Recurrent Neural Networks: Design and Applications, pp. 325–354. CRC Press, Boca Raton (2000)
24. De Jesús, O., Hagan, M.T.: Backpropagation algorithms for a broad class of dynamic networks. IEEE Trans. Neural Netw. **18**(1), 14–27 (2007)
25. Garrido, S.: Identificación, estimación y control de sistemas no-lineales mediante RGO. Tesis para optar al título de Doctor, Departamento de Ingeniería de Sistemas y Automática, Universidad Carlos III, Madrid, España (1999)
26. Singh, M., Singh, I., Verma, A.: Identification on non linear series-parallel model using neural network. MIT Int. J. Electr. Instrum. Eng. **3**(1), 21–23 (2013)
27. Li, Y., Zhao, X., Jiao, L.: A nonlinear system identification approach based on neurofuzzy networks. In: Proceedings of ICSP (2000)

Hybrid Metaheuristic Optimization Methods for Optimal Location and Sizing DGs in DC Networks

Luis Fernando Grisales-Noreña[1]($\boxtimes$) (iD), Oscar Daniel Garzon-Rivera[1](iD),
Oscar Danilo Montoya[2](iD), and Carlos Andrés Ramos-Paja[3](iD)

[1] Departamento de Electromecánica y Mecatrónica,
Instituto Tecnológico Metropolitano, Medellín, Colombia
luisgrisales@itm.edu.co, oscargarzon220554@correo.itm.edu.co
[2] Programa de Ingeniería Eléctrica e Ingeniería Electrónica,
Universidad Tecnológica de Bolívar, Cartagena, Colombia
omontoya@utb.edu.co
[3] Facultad de Minas, Universidad Nacional de Colombia, Medellín, Colombia
caramosp@unal.edu.co

Abstract. In this paper is proposed a master-slave method for optimal location and sizing of distributed generators (DGs) in direct-current (DC) networks. In the master stage is used the genetic algorithm of Chu & Beasley (GA) for the location of DGs. In the slave stage three different continuous techniques are used: the Continuous genetic algorithm (CGA), the Black Hole optimization method (BH) and the particle swarm optimization (PSO) algorithm, in order to solve the problem of sizing. All of those techniques are combined to find the hybrid method that provides the best results in terms of power losses reduction and processing times. The reduction of the total power losses on the electrical network associated to the transport of energy is used as objective function, by also including a penalty to limit the power injected by the DGs on the grid, and considering all constraints associated to the DC grids. To verify the performance of the different hybrid methods studied, two test systems with 10 and 21 buses are implemented in MATLAB by considering the installation of three distributed generators. To solve the power flow equations, the slave stage uses successive approximations. The results obtained shown that the proposed methodology GA-BH provides the best trade-off between speed and power losses independent of the total power provided by the DGs and the network size.

This work was supported by the Instituto Tecnológico Metropolitano, Universidad Tecnologica de Bolívar, Universidad Nacional de Colombia, and Colciencias (Fondo nacional de financiamiento para ciencia, la tecnología y la innovación Francisco José de Caldas) under the National Scholarship Program (call for applications 727-2015), the Scholarship Program (Joven investigador ITM); and the projects P17211, C2018P02 and "Estrategia de transformación del sector energético Colombiano en el horizonte de 2030 - Energética 2030" - "Generación distribuida de energía eléctrica en Colombia a partir de energía solar y eólica" (Code: 58838, Hermes: 38945).

© Springer Nature Switzerland AG 2019
J. C. Figueroa-García et al. (Eds.): WEA 2019, CCIS 1052, pp. 214–225, 2019.
https://doi.org/10.1007/978-3-030-31019-6_19

Keywords: Direct-current networks · Distributed generation ·
Metaheuristic optimization · Genetic algorithm ·
Particle swarm optimization · Optimal power flow

1 Introduction

Due to the importance of the DC networks and the need of integrating renewable resources on the electrical systems for reducing the negative impact associated to the fossil fuels [1], different authors have evaluated the integration of distributed generators (DGs) in DC grids. Multiple methods have been proposed to evaluate the DC power flow, such as Gauss-Seidel, Newton-Raphson, linear approximations, successive approximations, among others [1,2]. To evaluate the impact of the power supplied by the DGs into the DC grid, in literature have been proposed optimal power flow methods for finding the power level to be injected by each generator, with the purpose of improving different technical indicators, such as power losses or voltage profiles [3]. An example of this is presented in [4], where a second order cone programming formulation is proposed to solve the problem of optimal power flow (OPF) in stand-alone DC microgrids. In addition, in [5] is proposed a convex quadratic model for solving the OPF problem using, as objective function, the reduction of the power losses. The main problem of those methods is the requirement of specialized optimization software for solving the OPF problem. For this reason, different authors have proposed methodologies based on sequential programming by using metaheuristic optimization techniques; hence solving the OPF problem without specialized software. This is the case of the work presented in [6], where it is proposed a hybrid method with a master-slave structure that uses a continuous approach for the genetic algorithm (CGA) and the Gauss-Seidel method to solve the OPF problem. Similarly, in [7] is addressed the OPF problem in DC microgrids by using a combinatorial optimization technique known as black hole optimization (BHO), where the results shown the effectiveness and robustness of that method. Finally, in [8] is used a PSO algorithm to solve the OPF problem in DC grids by considering DGs and batteries in the electrical network.

To the best of the authors knowledge, the problem of optimal location and sizing of DGs in DC networks has not been explored in the specialized literature. Nevertheless, this problem has been addressed by different authors in AC systems by proposing optimization techniques based on sequential programming and other optimization methods [9]. The effectiveness and robustness of those methods have been evaluate considering different technical and operatives criteria, such as the power losses and voltage profiles, and the processing time required by the solution methods.

The previous review shows that it is necessary to propose optimization methods for solving the problem of optimal location and sizing of DGs in DC networks. Those methods must to ensure an acceptable quality in the solution and short processing times. For those reasons, in this paper is presented a mathematical formulation for solving the problem of optimal integration of DGs in DC grids by using the reduction of power losses as objective function and all the typical constraints associated to this type of electrical networks [5]. In this work the GA is selected as solution method for the optimal location of the DGs, this based on the satisfactory results obtained with this method in AC grids [10]. For solving the OPF problem in DC networks were selected three different metaheuristic techniques: PSO [8], CGA [6] and BH [7]. The main objective of the work is to find the hybrid methodology that presents the best balance between objective function minimization and processing time. The three hybrid solution methods are evaluated in two test systems with 10 and 21 buses, respectively, in which three DGs can be located. All simulations were carried out in MATLAB by using the successive approximation reported in [1] for solving the multiple power flows required in the sizing stage.

The paper is organized as follows: in Sect. 2 is presented the mathematical formulation used for the optimal location and sizing of DGs in DC networks. Section 3 shows the master-slave methodology formed by a GA and the three continuous optimization methods. In Sect. 4 is presented the simulation results and their discussion. Finally, Sect. 5 reports the conclusions and some possible future works.

2   Mathematical Formulation

The mathematical formulation of the problem of locating and sizing DGs in DC networks is described below.

Objective function:

$$\min P_{Loss} = \sum_{i \in \mathcal{N}} \left[\left(\sum_{j \in \mathcal{N}} G_{ij} v_i v_j \right) - G_{i0} v_i^2 \right] \tag{1}$$

Set of constraints:

$$P_i^g - P_i^d = \sum_{j \in \mathcal{N}} G_{ij} v_i v_j \quad \{\forall i \in \mathcal{N}\} \tag{2}$$

$$v_i^{min} \leq v_i \leq v_i^{max} \quad \{\forall i \in \mathcal{N}\} \tag{3}$$

$$I_{ij} \leq I_{ij}^{max} \quad \{\forall ij \in \mathcal{B}\} \tag{4}$$

$$P_i^{g,min} x_i^{DG} \leq P_i^g \leq P_i^{g,max} x_i^{DG} \quad \{\forall i \in \mathcal{D}\} \tag{5}$$

$$\sum_{i \in \mathcal{N}} x_i^{DG} \leq NDG_{max} \tag{6}$$

$$\sum_{i \in \mathcal{N}} P_i^g x_i^{DG} \leq P_{DG}^{max} \tag{7}$$

$$x_i^{DG} \in \{0, 1\} \quad \{\forall i \in \mathcal{D}\} \tag{8}$$

In the previous model, Eq. (1) minimizes the power losses on the electrical system associated to the energy transportation, $\mathcal{N}$ is the set of buses that form the DC network, G_{ij} is the ij^{th} component of the matrix of conductances, G_{i0} is the conductance associated to the resistive load connected at bus i, v_i and v_j are the voltages in the buses i and j, respectively. Note that the power losses were selected as objective function, since it is highly used in the specialized literature for evaluating the performance of different methodologies in AC networks [11–13]. The set of restrictions in the problem are shown from (2) to (8). The power balance at each bus is defined in (2), where P_i^g and P_i^d are the power generated and consumed at the bus i, respectively. In (3) are presented the maximum (v_i^{max}) and minimum (v_i^{min}) bounds for the nodal voltages. Expression (4) presents the thermal current bound of each branch in the electrical system, were $\mathcal{B}$ is the set of branches that form the electrical network, i_{ij} the current of the line ij and I_{ij}^{max} the maximum current allowed in that line. The maximum and minimum power bounds to be injected by the DG connected at bus i are show in (5), where x_i^{DG} is a binary variable that takes the value of 1 when a DG is located at bus i, and it takes a value of 0 otherwise; the binary nature of x_i^{DG} is defined in (8), and $\mathcal{D}$ represents the set of buses selected for locating DGs. Finally, constraint (6) limits the maximum number of DGs that can be introduced (NDG_{max}), while constraint (7) imposes the maximum level of penetration (P_{DG}^{max}) allowed into the DC grid.

3 Proposed Methodology

The problem of optimal location and sizing of DGs in DC networks is solved using a master-slave methodology. In the master stage a Chu & Beasley genetic algorithm is used [14], which defines the location of the DGs. In the slave stage are employed three different continuous methods: PSO [8], CGA [6] and BH [7], which solve the OPF problem. In addition, it is used the power flow method based on successive approximations for evaluating all the power flows required in the OPF solution [1]. The master and slave stages are detailed below.

3.1 Master Stage: Chu & Beasley Genetic Algorithm

The master stage is implemented with a GA to determine the best location of the DGs for reducing the total power losses in all the branches of the DC network. This optimization technique works with selection, recombination and mutation operators, to generate each offspring during the searching process [14]. These operators allow replacing the worst individual of the population by the offspring, this in the case that the fitness function is improved, and only for new solutions different from all individuals of the population (diversity criterion). The parameters and characteristics selected for this optimization technique are taken from [10]: population size (40), selection method (tournament), cross over (simple), mutation (random binary simple). In addition, the stop criterion is a maximum generational cycles (iterations) equal to 40 or 10 iterations without improving the fitness function.

3.2   Slave Stage: Continuous Optimization Method

The slave stage is used for dimensioning the DGs and to evaluate the fitness function of the individuals in the initial and descending populations generated by the master stage at each iteration. This process is performed with three different continuous optimization techniques: PSO, CGA and BH. Those methods were selected since they have been used in literature for OPF analysis in DC networks. On the other hand, with the objectives of reducing the processing time and provide a fair comparison between the continuous methods, the successive approximation method reported in [1] was used for solving the power flows required in the evaluation of each continuous optimization method for OPF analysis. The description of each continuous method is presented below.

Particle Swarm Optimization (PSO): the PSO is a bio-inspired meta-heuristic algorithm based on the behavior of the flocks of fish and birds, and it was proposed by Eberhart and Kennedy in 1995 [15]. This method takes advantage of the mode used by the groups of animals for exploring a region to find a common source of food for all individuals of the group. By modeling each individual as a particle, it is possible to transform the group of individuals in a particle swarm dispersed over a solution space. This particle swarm is limited by a set of constraints associated with each problem. In the PSO algorithm each step or iteration takes into account the information of each particle, as well as the particle swarm information, for generating the next movement, this to find a good solution for the problem. The application of PSO for solving the OPF problem in DC grids is described in [8].

Continuous Genetic Algorithm (CGA): This optimization method, proposed in [6], is a continuous approach of the conventional GA proposed by Che & Beasley in [14]. It uses the selection, recombination and mutation operators with a continuous representation in order to generate the population representing the sizes of the DGs defined by the master stage.

Black Hole Optimization Method (BH): This is a nature-inspired optimization technique based on the dynamic interaction between stars and black holes [16]. This technique has been used for solving nonlinear optimization problems by implementing a particle swarm (stars) as well as a criterion of elimination and generation of stars through a heuristic approach (event horizon radius). The iterative process of this optimization method for solving the OPF problem in DC grids is reported in [7].

The parameters selected for the sizing techniques are shown in Table 1. Those equivalent values are assigned with the aim of providing a fair comparison between the continuous methods.

Table 1. Parameters of the sizing techniques

Method	CGA	BH	PSO
Number of particles	30	30	30
Selection method	Tournament	Event horizon radius	Cognitive and social component: 1.4
Update population method	Cross over: averaging	Cognitive and social component	Speed/Inertia (max-min): (0.1–0.1)/(0.7–0.001)
Mutation	Random population	Random population	R1 = R2: Random
Stopping criterion	Max. iterations: (200) Iteration without improving: (50)	Max. iterations: (200) Iteration without improving: (50)	Max. iterations: (200) Iteration without improving: (50)

4   Simulation Scenarios and Results

The combination of the GA with the three continuous optimization algorithms produce the following hybrid methodologies: GA/PSO, GA/CGA and GA/BH. The simulations of those methods were carried out on a Dell Precision T7600 Workstation with 32 GB of RAM memory and with an Intel(R) Xeon(R) CPU ES-2670 at 2.50 GHz.

Two DC test systems with 10 and 21 buses were considered for evaluating each hybrid method [17]. These systems have been previously proposed for addressing OPF problems in [6], and [7]. However, some modifications were made to the test systems: a unique slack generator is considered for each system, and only constant power loads are considered, which implies that all the DGs and batteries of the conventional test systems have been replaced by constant power loads. Note that 100 kW and 1 kV are used as power and voltage bases, respectively.

To guaranteed a fair comparison among all of the hybrid optimization approaches, the following assumptions were made: (i) All the nodes are candidates for locating DGs, except the slack node. (ii) A maximum of three DGs can be installed $NDG_{max} = 3$. (iii) Three levels of penetration for the DGs are considered: 20%, 40% and 60%. Finally, (iv) the minimum and maximum power levels able to be generated by each DG in both test systems are 0 and 1.5 p.u, respectively [5]. The previous assumptions are typically used for the optimal location and sizing of DGs in AC grids [10,11].

The fitness function (FF) used in those algorithms is given in (9). This function penalizes when the total power injected by the set of DGs is higher than the maximum power allowed (P_{DG}^{Max}). The expression for penalty (P_{en}) is reported in (10), where P_i^g is the power generated at the bus i.

$$FF = \min\left(P_{Loss} + P_{en}\right) \tag{9}$$

where

$$P_{en} = \max\left[0, \left(\sum_{i \in N} P_i^g x_i^{DG}\right) - P_{DG}^{\max}\right] \tag{10}$$

The validations were carried out by testing the same cases with each hybrid optimization technique. The simulation results are presented in Tables 2 and 3, which reports, from left to right, the following information: the hybrid method, the DGs location and size, the power losses (P_{loss}), the square voltage error (V_{error}), the worst voltage profile and the associated bus, and finally, the processing time ($Time$). For the analysis of the results, the scenario without DGs for both test systems is used as reference (base case).

4.1   10 Bus Test System

In this subsection are presented the simulation results associated with the 10 bus test system reported in Table 2. By analyzing the reduction of power losses with respect to the base case (without DGs), it is observed that the GA/PSO method provides the best solution, with an average reduction of 63.18%, i.e. 0.54% and 4.01% higher than GA/CGA and GA/BH, respectively. With respect to the processing time, the shortest time is obtained by the GA/BH, with an average time of 21.98 s, presenting an average reduction of 43.25% and 72.61% when it is compared with the GA/PSO and GA/CGA. In addition, the impact of the optimization methods on the voltage profiles is analyzed using the V_{error}, presented in Eq. (11), and the worst voltage profiles [10]. In Eq. (11) V_{base} is the base voltage assigned to each test system.

$$SVE = \sum_{i \in \mathcal{N}}^{n} (V_i - V_{base})^2 \tag{11}$$

For the reduction of the V_{error} with respect to the base case (0.0075 p.u), the best results are provided by the GA/PSO, with an average reduction of 64.56%; it also exhibiting an additional reduction of 1.99% over the other hybrid methods, with an average worst voltage profile of 0.9823 p.u. The worst result, in terms of voltage profiles, is provided by the GA/BH, with an average reduction of V_{error} of 61.23% and an average worst voltage profile of 0.9814 p.u. Nevertheless, the different methodologies present a voltage absolute error lower than 2% when they are compared with the base voltage (1 p.u), hence satisfying the constraint of +/−5% around the nominal voltage. This limit is selected according to the load and type of network in order to guarantee a secure and reliable operation [18].

4.2   21 Bus Test System

The results obtained for this test system are presented in Table 3. The highest average reduction of the power losses is achieved again by the GA/PSO with a value of 72.74%, the GA/CGA is at second placed with 71.42%, while the lower impact is given by GA/BH with an average reduction of 65.51%. Concerning the processing time, it was obtained an average time of 28.09 s, 73.78 s and 148.15 s for the GA/BH, GA/PSO and GA/CGA, respectively. The GA/BH method takes the first place, presenting a reduction of 61.92% and 81.03% with respect

Table 2. Results for the 10 bus test system

Method	Location/size [kW]	P_{loss} [kW]	V_{error} [p.u]	Min. vol. [p.u]/bus	Time [s]
Without DG	—	14.3628	0.0075	0.9690/9	—
Maximum level of power injected by the DGs: 20%					
GA/PSO	5/0.3435 9/0.5628 10/0.0879	8.8690	0.00448	0.9768/8	32.26
GA/CGA	4/0.2907 5/0.2095 9/0.4909	8.9117	0.00454	0.9764/8	62.85
GA/BH	5/0.4250 7/0.2035 8/0.3645	8.9262	0.00448	0.9765/9	20.66
Maximum level of power injected by the DGs: 40%					
GA/PSO	5/0.5263 9/0.8744 10/0.5876	4.8656	0.00239	0.9828/4	38.19
GA/CGA	3/0.3586 5/0.8599 9/0.7697	4.9337	0.00243	0.9824/10	75.07
GA/BH	3/0.0225 5/0.9997 8/0.9370	5.2157	0.00238	0.9817/10	21.41
Maximum level of power injected by the DGs: 60%					
GA/PSO	4/1.2347 9/0.9113 10/0.8365	2.1286	0.00106	0.9883/8	45.75
GA/CGA	3/0.8556 4/1.2402 9/0.8860	2.2207	0.00110	0.9882/10	102.86
GA/BH	5/1.1674 6/1.1925 8/0.2745	3.6121	0.00170	0.9843/10	23.88

to the GA/PSO and GA/CGA, respectively. Moreover, the maximum average reduction of the V_{error} was obtained by the GA/PSO with a value of 81.70%, while the minimum average reduction is provided by the GA/BH (76.98%). With respect to the bus voltage profiles, the average absolute error, with respect to the base voltage, is 0.027, 0.029 and 0.033 p.u for the GA/BH, GA/PSO

Table 3. Results for the 21 bus test system

Method	Location/size [kW]	P_{loss} [kW]	V_{error} [p.u]	Min. vol. [p.u]/bus	Time [s]
Without DG	—	27.6034	0.0567	0.9211/17	—
Maximum level of power injected by the DGs: 20%					
GA/PSO	17/0.4979 18/0.4477 21/0.2175	12.8878	0.02100	0.9591/12	68.27
GA/CGA	16/0.9583 20/0.1560 21/0.0494	13.1250	0.02161	0.9591/12	142.10
GA/BH	15/0.1211 18/0.6031 20/0.4143	13.5089	0.02227	0.9547/17	20.45
Maximum level of power injected by the DGs: 40%					
GA/PSO	12/0.8326 15/0.7950 17/0.6987	6.2049	0.00767	0.9747/20	74.18
GA/CGA	11/0.9560 16/0.9338 17/0.4333	6.5654	0.00800	0.9736/20	148.54
GA/BH	12/0.3929 15/0.7937 21/1.0045	8.2473	0.00892	0.9686/17	27.88
Maximum level of power injected by the DGs: 60%					
GA/PSO	8/0.5928 11/1.5 16/1.3968	3.4763	0.00244	0.9834/20	78.89
GA/CGA	11/1.4791 17/0.9870 19/0.9939	3.9743	0.00147	0.9823/9	153.81
GA/BH	11/1.0660 13/0.8375 17/0.7886	6.8031	0.00796	0.9713/18	35.94

and GA/CGA, respectively. It is worth highlighting that the voltage profiles present a voltage absolute error lower than 5%, satisfying the voltage constraint associated with this type of systems. The previous results show that, in both test systems, the GA/PSO obtained the best results in terms of the technical aspects considered in this paper: Power losses and voltage profiles; and the fastest technique is the GA/BH, followed by the GA/PSO and GA/CGA. Furthermore, as the level of power injected by the DGs increases, the technical aspects are improved and the processing time is increased for all the hybrid methods.

Figure 1 was developed to analyze the trade-offs provided by each method, in terms of power losses and processing time, for any network size and level of power injected by the set of DGs. In this figure the Y-axis reports the average value of power losses, in percentage, with respect to the base cases (without DGs); and the X-axis reports the average processing time required by each method, also in percentage, with respect to the hybrid method requiring the longest processing time in all test systems, i.e. GA/CGA. In both axes, the average values were calculated considering the results obtained in all the test systems. In this figure, the best solution is the origin $(0, 0)$, since it represents power losses and processing time equal to zero. Analyzing the global results shown in Fig. 1, it is concluded that the GA/BH is the fastest method, with an average processing time of 23.52%, but with the worst average power losses (37.84%). In this way, the worst solution in terms of processing time is the GA/CGA method, with an average processing time of 114.20s (100%-Base case), obtaining the second place in terms of power losses (32.93%). The GA/PSO is the second faster method with an average value of 49.32%, it also providing the best results in terms of power losses with an average value of 32.03%. On the base of those results it is concluded that the best balance between power losses reduction and processing time is obtained by the GA/BH, followed closely by the GA/PSO.

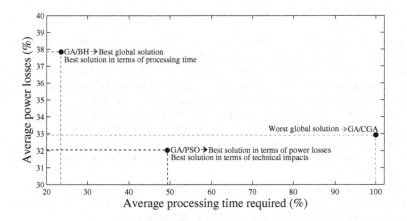

Fig. 1. Average impact of the hybrid methods in all test scenarios proposed

5   Conclusions and Future Works

In this paper was proposed a hybrid method employing a master-salve structure, based on sequential programming, for solving the problem of location and sizing of distributed generators in DC networks. In the master stage a GA was used to define the optimal location of the DGs; while the slave stage was implemented with continuous optimization methods (PSO, CGA and BH) to define the size of each distributed generator. The location and sizing methods were combined to find the hybrid method that provided the best results in terms of power losses and processing times. To evaluate the impact of each hybrid method was proposed a mathematical formulation that analyzed the impact of the distributed generation into the grid. The results shown that as the level of power injected by the DGs grows, the power losses are reduced and the processing time are increased. In addition, the GA/PSO provided the best results in terms of technical impact (reduction of power losses and voltage profiles) with the second shorter processing time. The GA/PSO presented the second and third place in relation to the technical impacts and processing time, respectively; and the GA/BH presented the best performance with respect to the processing time and the worst results in terms of technical impact. Finally, the GA/BH provides the best trade-off in terms of power losses reduction and processing time for locating and sizing distributed generators in DC networks, followed closely by the GA/PSO. As future works it will be considered the evaluation of other location methods applied in AC networks, and the use of parallel processing methods for reducing the processing time.

References

1. Montoya, O.D., Garrido, V.M., Gil-González, W., Grisales-Noreña, L.: Power flow analysis in DC grids: two alternative numerical methods. IEEE Trans. Circuits Syst. **II**, 1 (2019)
2. Garces, A.: Uniqueness of the power flow solutions in low voltage direct current grids. Electr. Power Syst. Res. **151**, 149–153 (2017)
3. Gil-González, W., Montoya, O.D., Holguín, E., Garces, A., Grisales-Noreña, L.F.: Economic dispatch of energy storage systems in dc microgrids employing a semidefinite programming model. J. Energy Storage **21**, 1–8 (2019)
4. Li, J., Liu, F., Wang, Z., Low, S.H., Mei, S.: Optimal power flow in stand-alone DC microgrids. IEEE Trans. Power Syst. **33**(5), 5496–5506 (2018)
5. Montoya, O.D., Gil-González, W., Garces, A.: Sequential quadratic programming models for solving the OPF problem in DC grids. Electr. Power Syst. Res. **169**, 18–23 (2019)
6. Montoya, O.D., Grisales-noreña, L.F.: Optimal power dispatch of DGs in DC power grids: a hybrid Gauss-Seidel-Genetic-Algorithm methodology for solving the OPF problem. WSEAS Trans. Power Syst. **13**, 335–346 (2018)
7. Velasquez, O., Giraldo, O.M., Arevalo, V.G., Noreña, L.G.: Optimal power flow in direct-current power grids via black hole optimization. Adv. Electr. Electron. Eng. **17**(1), 24–32 (2019)
8. Wang, P., Zhang, L., Xu, D.: Optimal sizing of distributed generations in DC microgrids with lifespan estimated model of batteries. In: 2018 21st International Conference on Electrical Machines and Systems (ICEMS), pp. 2045–2049, October 2018

9. Grisales Noreña, L.F., Restrepo Cuestas, B.J., Jaramillo Ramirez, F.E.: Ubicación y dimensionamiento de generación distribuida: Una revisión. Ciencia e Ingeniería Neogranadina **27**(2), 157–176 (2017). https://revistas.unimilitar.edu.co/index.php/rcin/article/view/2344
10. Grisales-Noreña, L.F., Gonzalez Montoya, D., Ramos-Paja, C.A.: Optimal sizing and location of distributed generators based on PBIL and PSO techniques. Energies **11**(4), 1018 (2018)
11. Mohamed Imran, A., Kowsalya, M.: Optimal size and siting of multiple distributed generators in distribution system using bacterial foraging optimization. Swarm Evol. Comput. **15**, 58–65 (2014)
12. Mahmoud Pesaran, H.A., Huy, P.D., Ramachandaramurthy, V.K.: A review of the optimal allocation of distributed generation: objectives, constraints, methods, and algorithms. Renew. Sustain. Energy Rev. **75**, 293–312 (2017)
13. Grisales, L.F., Grajales, A., Montoya, O.D., Hincapié, R.A., Granada, M.: Optimal location and sizing of distributed generators using a hybrid methodology and considering different technologies. In: 2015 IEEE 6th Latin American Symposium on Circuits Systems (LASCAS), pp. 1–4, February 2015
14. Chu, P., Beasley, J.: A genetic algorithm for the generalised assignment problem. Comput. Oper. Res. **24**(1), 17–23 (1997)
15. Kennedy, J., Eberhart, R.: Particle swarm optimization. In: Proceedings of ICNN 1995 - International Conference on Neural Networks, vol. 4, pp. 1942–1948, November 1995
16. Bouchekara, H.: Optimal power flow using black-hole-based optimization approach. Appl. Soft Comput. **24**, 879–888 (2014)
17. Montoya, O.D., Grisales-Norena, L.F., González-Montoya, D., Ramos-Paja, C., Garces, A.: Linear power flow formulation for low-voltage DC power grids. Electr. Power Syst. Res. **163**, 375–381 (2018)
18. Montoya, O.D.: On linear analysis of the power flow equations for DC and AC grids with CPLs. IEEE Trans. Circuits Syst. **II**, 1 (2019)

A New Approach to Improve Learning in Fuzzy Cognitive Maps Using Reinforcement Learning

Frank Balmaseda[1]([✉]), Yaima Filiberto[1], Mabel Frias[1], and Rafael Bello[2]

[1] Universidad de Camagüey, Carretera de Circunvalación Norte entre Camino Viejo
de Nuevitas y Ave Ignacio Agramonte, Camagüey, Cuba
{frank.balmaseda,yaima.filiberto,mabel.frias}@reduc.edu.cu
[2] Central University of Las Villas, Carretera Camajuaní km 5.5, Santa Clara, Cuba
rbellop@uclv.edu.cu

Abstract. Fuzzy Cognitive Maps (FCM) are dedicated to modeling complex dynamic systems and has been widely studied. One of those studies probed that Computing with Words (CWW) is very effective to improve the interpretability and transparency of FCM. Learning methods to calculate the weight matrix in a map are the target of hundreds of studies in various parts of the world. These methods allow the map to learn or evolve towards a better state, but always taking into account that the output must be evaluated and compared using a real scenario. Reinforcement Learning has, within its performance, one of the possible answers to this problem, aimed at improving the classification capacity of the map and thus improving the learning of its weights. This paper presents a new learning method for Fuzzy Cognitive Maps. The proposal was evaluated using international databases and the experimental results show a satisfactory performance.

Keywords: Fuzzy Cognitive Maps · Reinforcement learning · Weight matrix

1 Introduction

Cognitive maps were presented for the first time in 1976 by [3], their main objective being to represent social scientific knowledge through designated digraphs where the arcs are causal connections between the nodes. Fuzzy Cognitive Maps (FCM) [18], were introduced as an extension of Cognitive Maps theory, and they are recurrent structures modeled through weighted graphs. In this representation, each node or concept of the graph may represents a variable, an object, entity or state of the system that is intended to be modeled; while the weights in the connections determine the causality between these concepts. There are two fundamental strategies to build FCMs: manual and automatic. In the first variant, the experts determine the concepts that describe the system, as well as the direction and intensity of the causal connections between the neurons. In the

© Springer Nature Switzerland AG 2019
J. C. Figueroa-García et al. (Eds.): WEA 2019, CCIS 1052, pp. 226–234, 2019.
https://doi.org/10.1007/978-3-030-31019-6_20

second variant, the topology of the map and the weight matrix are constructed from historical data, or representative examples that define the behavior of the system. Regardless of the strategy, domain experts need to define the architecture that best fits the system that is intended to model, as well as the restrictions inherent in the model [20]. The formulation of learning algorithms to estimate the causality of the system (matrix of causal weights that regulate the interaction between the concepts) is still an open problem for the scientific community [22]. The learning algorithms that are dedicated to the classification of the weights in FCM still present gaps, both in the efficiency and in the results that they offer. For instance, in [4] authors recognize that using Ant Colony System outperforms RCGA, NHL and DD-NHL algorithms in terms of model error, but only when multiple response sequences are used in the learning process, not so when one response sequence is used. Other studies like in [16] and [25], shows the proposals are a little bit slow because for computing every weight it is necessary to consider the other concepts involved in the causal-effect relation for a target concept. The broad attention of the authors to the subject reinforces the premise of its importance. Within this framework, there is a clear need to improve the methods used (or, as is the case of this paper, to create new ones) up to now to carry out the learning of the FCM.

2   Fuzzy Cognitive Maps and Computing with Words

In a FCM the inference can be defined mathematically using a state vector and a causality matrix. The state vector A_{1xN} represents the activation degree of the concepts, and the causal weight matrix W_{NxN} defines the interaction between the concepts. The activation of C_i will depend on the activation of the neurons that directly affect the concept C_i and the causal relationships associated with that concept. The process of inference in an FCM is then summarized in finding the value of the state vector A through time for an initial condition A^0 as can be seen in the Eq. (1)

$$A_i^{(t+1)} = f(\sum_{j=1}^{N} A_j^{(t)} W_{ji}), i \neq j \tag{1}$$

The causal relationships between the concepts can occur in 3 ways. For two concepts C_i and C_j it is fulfilled that:

- $W_{ij} > 0$: Indicates a positive causality between the concepts C_i and C_j, which means an increase (decrease) in the value of C_i leads to the increase (decrease) in the value of C_j.
- $W_{ij} < 0$: Indicates a negative causality between the concepts C_i and C_j, that is, the increase (decrease) in the value of C_i leads the decrease (increase) in the value of C_j proportional to the absolute value of W_{ij}.
- $W_{ij} = 0$: Indicates the non-existence of a causal relationship between C_i and C_j. It can also occurs when W_{ij} is very close to zero.

On the other hand, CWW [29] was presented as a methodology that allows introducing linguistic variables with the objective of performing computational operations with words instead numbers. Linguistic variables describe situations that can not be clearly defined in quantitative terms and allow a very particular type of translation from natural language to numerical or numerical sentences. Some models inspired in his technique are briefly described below:

- *Linguistic Computational Model based on membership functions.* The linguistic terms are expressed by fuzzy numbers, which are usually described by membership functions. This computational model makes the computations directly on the membership functions of the linguistic terms by using the Extension Principle [8].
- *Linguistic Computational Symbolic Model* [5]. This model performs the computation of indexes attached to linguistic terms. Usually, it imposes a linear order to the set of linguistic terms $S = \{S_0, ..., S_g\}$ where $S_i < S_j$ if and only if $i < j$.
- *The 2-tuple Fuzzy Linguistic Representation Model* [14]. The above models perform simple operations with high transparency, but they have a common drawback: the loss of information caused by the need of expressing results in a discrete domain. The 2-tuple model is based on the notion of symbolic translation that allows expressing a domain of linguistic expressions as a continuous universe.

3   FCM and Reinforcement Learning

The main problem of reinforcement learning methods is to find an optimal policy of actions that is capable of reaching a goal maximizing the rewards. Starting from an initial state, the agent chooses an action in each iteration, which is evaluated in the environment and receives penalties or rewards according to the results [26]. The Fig. 1 shows a general performance of this technique.

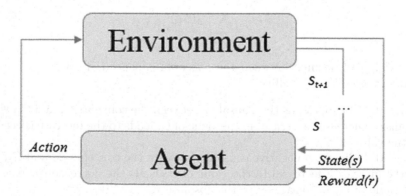

Fig. 1. Behavior of a reinforcement learning problem.

The learning methods for FCM in the literature formulate several hypotheses and most of them have application results that improve the classification of FCM. Below, some of these approaches are briefly described:

- *Differential Hebbian Learning* [7] is based on the following principle: if the cause concept C_i and the effect concept C_j change the activation value simultaneously, then the causal weight W_{ij} will increase with a constant factor, otherwise the causality will not be modified in that iteration, see Eq. 2.

$$W_{ij}^{(t+1)} = \begin{cases} W_{ij}^{(t)} + \gamma^{(t)}[\Delta A_i/\Delta A_j - W_{ij}^{(t)}] \; if \; \Delta A_i \neq 0 \\ W_{ij}^{(t)} \qquad\qquad\qquad\qquad\quad if \; \Delta A_j = 0 \end{cases} \qquad (2)$$

- *Balanced Differential Algorithm* [16] proposes to use the activation degree of the nodes that are simultaneously modified during the weight matrix updating. This algorithm assume it is a FCM without concepts using auto-connections and that it is adjusted iteratively.
- In [19] the authors proposes a method based on Evolutionary Strategy to adjust the structure of the map using historical data, where each instance is composed of a pair of vectors. The first vector encodes the activation degree of the input concepts, while the second vector denotes the response of the system for the specified configuration.
- In [23] the authors applied Particle Swarm Optimization to estimate the appropriate structure of the system from a sequence of multiple state vectors. The peculiarity of this method lies in its learning scheme: the response of the system is defined by decision-making nodes.
- A new automated approach based on Genetic Algorithms with Real Coding can be found in [25]. The idea of the method is to maximize the objective function $(x) = 1/(1 + \alpha * (x)$, reducing the global error of the map.
- In [4] the authors presented a novel algorithm inspired in Ant Colony Optimization to adjust maps with dozens of concepts. In this model, each weight is encoded as a sequence of discrete states. During the search process, each ant constructs a solution. In the next step, each discrete solution is transformed to its continuous equivalent, resulting in a matrix of causal weights.

3.1 Learning Algorithm

The method proposed in [9] uses a Learning Automata (LA) [21,27], which are simple reinforcement learning components for adaptive decision making in unknown environments. An LA operates in a feedback loop with its environment and receives feedback (reward or punishment) for the actions taken. The general update scheme is given by Eqs. 3 and 4:

$$p_m(t+1) = p_m(t) + \alpha_{reward}(1 - \beta(t))(1 - p_m(t)) - \alpha_{penalty}\beta(t)p_m(t) \quad (3)$$

$$if \; a_m \; is \; the \; action \; taken \; at \; time \; t$$

$$p_j = p_j(t+1) - \alpha_{reward}(1 - \beta(t))p_j(t) + \alpha_{penalty}\beta(t)\left[(r-1)^{-1} - p_j(t)\right] \quad (4)$$

$$if \ a_m \neq a_j$$

where $p_i(t)$ is the probability of selecting action i at time step t. The constant α_{reward} and $\alpha_{penalty}$ are the reward and penalty parameters. When α_{reward} = $\alpha_{penalty}$, the algorithm is referred to as linear reward-penalty (L_{R-P}), when $\alpha_{penalty} = 0$, it is referred to as linear reward-inaction (L_{R-I}) and when $\alpha_{penalty}$ is small compared to α_{reward}, it is called linear $reward - \varepsilon - penalty$ ($L_{R-\varepsilon P}$). $\beta(t)$ is the reward received by the reinforcement signal for an action taken at time step t. r is the number of actions [28].

In [9] authors propose the use of RL in decision making problems specifically in Personnel Selection. Basing in this approach, in this paper it is proposed using RL as a learning method to adjust the weight matrix of a FCM+CWW. To reach this objective define a FCM+CWW as the environment over which the agent must make the decisions. The parameters to be used in the environment are defined as follows:

- Firstly, the size of the list of terms that are used in the map: For this proposal a study is included in [10] that sates, through a transfer function, the use of linguistic terms instead numerical methods traditionally used to represent the weights in the causal relationships of the maps. This list may vary depending on the needs of precision in the domain, therefore, it can be simplified to three terms (Low, Medium, High), however, the author suggests to use fifteen terms as described in [10].
- Length of the relations list: A FCM contains a list of relationships used to determine the connections between each concept involved in the map.
- Training set: These instances are necessary for the classification algorithm to train with that set and to return the best individual. The training set is crated from the cross validation technique used to perform the data validation.

From this point, the environment continues with obtaining the reward and updating the weight matrix, as is shown in Algorithm 1.

Algorithm 1. Establishing classification

1: Create map (concepts and relationships).
2: Assign matrix weights to the map using FCM+CWW+RL.
3: Assign to each concept C_i, the value of each feature of the object to be classified.
4: Assign the linguistic term "NA" to each decision concept.
5: Calculate the activation value of the concepts.
6: Classify a new object O_c using Eq. 5.

$$O_c = F(\arg \max_{A_k \in A^D} \{A_k\}) \tag{5}$$

where F returns the value of the class D_k and A^D is the activation set of the decision concepts. It is worth mentioning that our symbolic model based on

FCM conserves its recurrent nature. This implies that the FCM will produce a state vector composed by linguistic terms in each iteration until it discover a fixed point or reach a maximum number of iterations. The new method suggests using the classification accuracy value as a reward. This value tends to 1 when the reward is high an Eq. (6) we formalize the expression used to calculate the reward once the classification is done, where r_i is the reward in the i-th iteration, δ_i is the number of well-classified objects for the same iteration, and T is the total instances of the data set:

$$r_i = \frac{\delta_i}{T} \tag{6}$$

With this value, the agent performs the updating of the weight matrix and the reward is calculated in each iteration, which substitutes the time T commonly used for this type of problem. Below, the steps of the method are detailed presented in Algorithm 2.

Algorithm 2. FCM+CWW+RL

1:    $\forall\, i = 1...n,\ \forall\, j = 1...n,\ M_{ij} = 1/n$
2: Obtain reward $r_i = \frac{\delta_i}{T}$
3: Update M using r_i.
4: Repeat from step two until reach the stopping condition.

Modifying the reward function on each iteration allows finding a new state of the map and evaluating it in order to determine improvements in the classification, otherwise, this state will not be visited again through the iterations.

4   Experimental Results

This section present the experimental framework that uses 13 data-sets from [2]. The cross-validation method [6] was used to validate the results that subdivided the data set into k subsets of equal size (in this experimental frame k = 10), of which one part makes up the set of tests and the other part the set of training. When using this technique the number of subsets with which we worked was taken into account, because with higher values for k, the trend of the real error range of the estimate is reduced. In addition, the estimate will be more precise, the variance of the error range real is greater and the necessary computation time also increases as the number of experiments to be performed increases. For the statistical analysis were used the hypothesis test techniques in [12,24], Friedman and Iman-Davenport for multiple comparisons [17] in order to detect statistically significant differences in a group of results. Holm test [15] is used in these experimental studies to find significantly higher algorithms. These tests are suggested in [6,13], [12] and [11], where the authors agree in the relevance of using them for validating results on the reinforcement learning area. KEEL module Non-Parametric Statistical Analysis was also used in this work for the statistical processing of the experimental results [1].

Experiment 1: Compare the method proposed (FCM+CWW+RL) with 3 algorithms: MLP, NB and ID3 which are implemented in WEKA tool.
Goals: Determine if the accuracy of the propose method FCM+CWW+RL is significantly superior to accuracy of MLP, ID3 and NB. In Tables 1 and 2 are shown these results.

Table 1. Results of accuracy for each method

Datasets	MLP	NB	ID3	FCM+CWW+RL
apendicitis	82.09	85.09	70	88.72
blood_tranfussion	75.81	75.81	75.14	76.03
echocardiogram	90.02	90.82	85.43	90.91
heart-5an-nn	72.95	84.8	65.55	77.03
iris	94.67	94.67	89.33	96.66
liver_disorders	53.59	62.88	49.82	62.96
planing-relax	63.27	60.94	53.27	71.37
saheart	62.77	67.97	49.57	67.99
yeast3	91.3	91.29	88.8	92.12
pima_5an-nn	67.03	74.22	59.51	75
acute_inflammation	100	100	100	100
yield	51.78	62.5	53.57	65
phoneme	81.1	76.62	80.6	78.07

Table 1 shows the list of all datasets used to compare the accuracy of this proposal with a well-known classification algorithms.

Table 2. Holm test for $\alpha = 0.05$ for classification accuracy, taking as control FCM+CWW+RL

i	Algorithms	$z = \frac{(R_0 - R_i)}{SE}$	p	Holm	Null hypothesis
3	ID3	4.557327	0.000005	0.016667	Rejected
2	MLP	2.582485	0.009809	0.025	Rejected
1	NP	1.97482	0.048286	0.05	Rejected

In Table 2 can be observed the results of applying the Holm test, and how the null hypothesis is rejected for all the algorithms with which this proposal is compared to.

5 Conclusions

In this article has been studied a new learning method which improves the classification in the FCM+CWW where the concepts activation values and the causal weights are described by linguistic terms. The obtained results show the effectiveness of using RL as a learning method to adjust the weight matrix in FCM. According to results presented in this work, the proposal is statistically best than MLP, NB and ID3 in terms of classification accuracy.

References

1. Alcala, J., Fernandez, A.: Keel data-mining software tool: data set repository, integration of algorithms and experimental analysis framework. J. Mult. Valued Logic Soft Comput. **17**, 255–287 (2010)
2. Asuncion, A., Newman, D.: Uci machine learning repository. A study of the behaviour of several methods for balancing machine learning training data. SIGKDD Explor. **6**, 20–29 (2007)
3. Axelrod, R.: Structure of Decision: The Cognitive Maps of Political Elites. Princeton University Press, Princeton (1976)
4. Chen, Y., Mazlack, L., Lu, L.: Learning fuzzy cognitive maps from data by ant colony optimization. In: Genetic and Evolutionary Computation Conference (2012)
5. Delgado, M., Verdegay, J.L., Vila, M.A.: On aggregation operations of linguistic labels. Int. J. Intell. Syst. **8**, 351–370 (1993)
6. Demsar, J.: Statistical comparisons of classifiers over multiple data sets. J. Mach. Learn. Res. **7**, 1–30 (2006)
7. Dickerson, J.A., Kosko, B.: Virtual worlds as fuzzy cognitive maps. Presence **3**, 173–189 (1994)
8. Dubois, D., Prade, H.: Fuzzy Sets and Systems: Theory and Applications. Academic Press, New York (1980)
9. Filiberto, Y., Bello, R., Nowe, A.: A new method for personnel selection based on ranking aggregation using a reinforcement learning approach. Computación y Sistemas **22**(2) (2018)
10. Frias, M., Filiberto, Y., Nápoles, G., García-Socarrás, Y., Vanhoof, K., Bello, R.: Fuzzy cognitive maps reasoning with words based on triangular fuzzy numbers. In: Castro, F., Miranda-Jiménez, S., González-Mendoza, M. (eds.) Advances in Soft Computing, pp. 197–207. Springer International Publishing, Cham (2018)
11. Garcia, S.: Advanced nonparametric tests for multiple comparisons in the design of experiments in computational intelligence and data mining: experimental analysis of power. Inf. Sci. **180**, 2044–2064 (2010)
12. García, S., Herrera, F.: Evolutionary under-sampling for classification with imbalanced data sets: proposals and taxonomy. Evol. Comput. **17**, 275–306 (2009)
13. Herrera, F., García, S.: An extensionon statistical comparisons of classifiers ove-multiple data setsfor all pairwise comparisons. J. Mach. Learn. Res. **9**, 2677–2694 (2008)
14. Herrera, F., Martínez, L.: A 2-tuple fuzzy linguistic representation model for computing with words. IEEE Trans. Fuzzy Syst. **8**(6), 746–752 (2000)
15. Holm, S.: A simple sequentially rejective multiple test procedure. J. Stat. **6**, 65–70 (1979)

16. Huerga, A.V.: A balanced differential learning algorithm in fuzzy cognitive maps. In: 16th International Workshop on Qualitative Reasoning (2002)
17. Iman, R., Davenport, J.: Approximations of the critical region of the Friedman statistic. Commun. Stat. Part A Theory Methods **9**, 571–595 (1980)
18. Kosko, B.: Fuzzy cognitive maps. Int. J. Approximate Reasoning **2**, 377–393 (1984)
19. Koulouriotis, D.E., Diakoulakis, I.E., Emiris, D.M.: Learning fuzzy cognitive maps using evolution strategies: a novel schema for modeling and simulating high-level behavior. IEEE Congress on Evolutionary Computation pp. 364-371 (2001)
20. Nápoles, G.: Algoritmo para mejorar la convergencia en Mapas Cognitivos Difusos Sigmoidales. Master's thesis, Universidad Central "Marta Abreu" de las Villas (2014)
21. Narendra, K., Thathachar, M.: Learning Automata: An Introduction. Prentice-Hall, Upper Saddle River (1989)
22. Papageorgiou, E.I.: Learning algorithms for fuzzy cognitive maps - a review study. IEEETrans. Syst. Man Cybern. B Cybern. **42**, 150–163 (2012)
23. Parsopoulos, K.E., Papageorgiou, E.I., Groumpos, P.P., Vrahatis, M.N.: A first study of fuzzy cognitive maps learning using particle swarm optimization. In: IEEE Congress on Evolutionary Computation, pp. 1440–1447 (2003)
24. Sheskin, D.: Handbook of Parametric and Nonparametric Statistical Procedures. Chapman & hall, Boca Raton (2003)
25. Stach, W., Kurgan, L., Pedrycz, W., Reformat, M.: Genetic learning of fuzzy cognitive maps. Fuzzy Sets Syst. **153**, 371–401 (2005)
26. Sutton, R.S., Barto, A.: Reinforcement Learning: An Introduction, 2nd edn. The MIT Press, London (2017)
27. Thathachar, M., Sastry, P.: Networks of Learning Automata: Techniques for Online Stochastic Optimization. Kluwer Academic Publishers, Dordrecht (2004)
28. Wauters, T., Verbeeck, K., De Causmaecker, P., Vanden Berghe, G.: Fast permutation learning. In: Hamadi, Y., Schoenauer, M. (eds.) LION 2012. LNCS, pp. 292–306. Springer, Heidelberg (2012). https://doi.org/10.1007/978-3-642-34413-8_21
29. Zadeh, L.A.: Outline of a new approach to the analysis of complex systems ad decision processes. IEEE Trans. Syst. Man Cybern. B Cybern. **3**(1), 28–44 (1973)

Vortex Search Algorithm for Optimal Sizing of Distributed Generators in AC Distribution Networks with Radial Topology

Oscar Danilo Montoya[1]([✉])[iD], Luis Fernando Grisales-Noreña[2][iD],
William Tadeo Amin[1], Luis Alejandro Rojas[3][iD], and Javier Campillo[1][iD]

[1] Programa de Ingeniería Eléctrica e Ingeniería Electrónica,
Universidad Tecnológica de Bolívar, Cartagena, Colombia
{omontoya,jcampillo}@utb.edu.co,witambu@gmail.com
[2] Departamento de Electromecánica y Mecatrónica,
Instituto Tecnológico Metropolitano, Medellín, Colombia
luisgrisales@itm.edu.co
[3] Escuela de Diseño e Ingeniería, Fundación Tecnológica Antonio de Arévalo,
Cartagena, Colombia
luis.rojas@unitecnar.edu.co

Abstract. This paper proposes a vortex search algorithm (VSA) optimization for optimal dimensioning of distributed generators (DGs), in radial alternating current (AC) distribution networks. The VSA corresponds to a metaheuristic optimization technique that works in the continuous domain, to solve nonlinear, non-convex, large scale optimization problems. Here, this technique is used to determine the optimal power generation capacity of the DGs from the top-down analysis. From the bottom-up, a conventional backward/forward power flow is employed for determining the voltage behavior and calculate the power losses of the network, for each power output combination in the DGs. Numerical results demonstrate that the proposed approach is efficient and robust for reducing power losses on AC grids by optimally sizing the capacity the DGs, compared with other approaches found on literature reports. All the simulations were conducted using the MATLAB software.

Keywords: Electrical distribution networks · Distributed generation · Optimal power flow · Metaheuristic optimization · Vortex search algorithm

This work was supported in part by the Administrative Department of Science, Technology, and Innovation of Colombia (COLCIENCIAS) through the National Scholarship Program under Grant 727-2015, in part by the Universidad Tecnológica de Bolívar under Project C2018P020 and in part by the Instituto Tecnológico Metropolitano under the project P17211.

J. C. Figueroa-García et al. (Eds.): WEA 2019, CCIS 1052, pp. 235–249, 2019.
https://doi.org/10.1007/978-3-030-31019-6_21

1 Introduction

Recent advances in power electronics allow reducing distributed generation costs, thus, facilitating mass integration of those power sources in modern electrical systems [1,2]. This integration mainly takes place by adding photovoltaic and wind power plants at distribution system levels [3,4]. These distributed generators offer several advantages, for instance: power losses reduction [5], voltage profile improvement and important reductions in greenhouse emissions [6,7], etc. Nevertheless, not all aspects are positive; as an example, integration of those devices can often overcharge distribution lines [8,9], induce overvoltages in sensible nodes [10], produce undesired firing in protective devices [11] and cause reverse power flow problems [8], among others.

In this paper, authors approach the problem of optimal dimensioning of distributed generation in radial AC distribution networks from the utility's point of view [5,12]. This problem has been widely explored in specialized literature with multiple optimization techniques, such as: genetic algorithms [13], tabu-search [14], loss-sensitivity factors [15], particle swarm optimization [6,13], krill-herd algorithms [5], bee colony optimization [16], bat and fish algorithms [17,18] among others. In spite of this, those approaches are mainly focused on determining the location and sizing of the distributed generators by using hybrid metaheuristic optimization techniques, which combine discrete methods in the location problem and continuous methods for solving the sizing problem. For instance, this approach has been proposed by [6], where a population-based incremental learning algorithm is combined with a conventional particle swarm optimization method. Note that the dimensioning problem is typically left for a conventional methods, without considering their importance inside the location problem, since it is the core of the technique in terms of calculating the objective function.

By taking the sizing problem of the distributed generation in AC distribution systems into account, this paper addresses this issue from an optimal power flow (OPF) analysis point of view, by using a master-slave optimization strategy. On the master stage, a vortex search algorithm for defining the size of each distributed generator is proposed [19], while in the slave stage, a conventional backward/forward power flow calculation is employed [20]. Note that the vortex search algorithm has been used previously in OPF analysis for transmission systems [21] and active filter design [22]; nevertheless, after the revision of the literature, the authors did not find evidence about its application to the problem addressed in this paper, which becomes a research gap for the specialized literature that this paper tries to address.

It is important to point out, that the OPF problem is a nonlinear non-convex optimization problem that requires using numerical methods to be solved; to achieve this, there are two common approaches found in specialized literature, one of them is focused on exact mathematical optimization, while the other one is oriented to combinatorial optimization. In the case of the exact methods, their main contributions fall within the line of convex optimization with semi-definite programming approaches [23–25], second order cone programming [26], sequential quadratic programming [27] and interior point methods [28], among others. The main disadvantage of these approaches is the requirement of specialized software to carry out their implementations. In the case of combinatorial methods, more common approaches use particle swarm optimization methods which allows solving the problem of optimal sizing of DGs in a pure-algorithmic sense [6, 12, 13]. These is an important advantage of the proposed vortex search algorithm, since it can be easily implemented in any programming language with free access. Note that these advantages can be exploited by utilities and researchers to develop their own software for power grid applications.

The remainder of this paper is organized as follows: Sect. 2 shows the compact formulation of the optimal power flow problem in AC distribution networks by using a complex domain representation. In Sect. 3, the proposed master-slave methodology for solving the problem of optimal sizing of distributed generation by highlighting the advantages of combining the vortex search algorithm with the classical back/forward power flow, is presented. Section 4 shows the configuration of the tests systems as well as the main features of the simulation. Section 5 presents the numerical results and their discussion. Finally, in Sect. 6 the main conclusion derived from this work are presented, as well as the possible future research work.

2 Optimal Power Flow Formulation

The OPF problem is a nonlinear non-convex optimization problem that represents the best combination of voltage profiles and power output in all the generators in order to achieve the minimal power losses for a particular load condition [12, 27]. The formulation of the OPF problem is presented below.

Objective function:

$$\min p_{loss} = real\left\{ \sum_{i=1}^{n}\sum_{j=1}^{n} \mathbf{V}_i \mathbf{Y}_{ij}^{\star} \mathbf{V}_i^{\star} \right\}, \tag{1}$$

where p_{loss} quantifies the total power losses in all the branches of the network, $\mathbf{V}_i$ and $\mathbf{V}_j$ are the complex voltage profiles associated to the nodes i and j, respectively; $\mathbf{Y}_{ij}$ represents the admittance component of the nodal admittance matrix that relates the nodes i and j, respectively. Note that $(\cdot)^{\star}$ and $(\cdot)^{T}$ are the conjugate and transposed operations, respectively. In addition, $real\{\cdot\}$ obtains the real value of a complex number.

Set of constraints:

$$\mathbf{S}_i^{cg} + \mathbf{S}_i^{dg} - \mathbf{S}_i^{d} = \mathbf{V}_i \sum_{j=1}^{n} \mathbf{Y}_{ij}^{\star} \mathbf{V}_i^{\star}, \quad i = 0, 1, \dots, n-1 \tag{2}$$

$$V^{\min} \leq |\mathbf{V}_i| \leq V^{\max}, \quad i = 0, 1, \dots, n-1 \tag{3}$$

$$\mathbf{S}_i^{cg,\min} \leq \mathbf{S}_i^{cg} \leq \mathbf{S}_i^{cg,\max}, \quad i = 0, 1, \dots, n-1 \tag{4}$$

$$\mathbf{S}_i^{dg,\min} \leq \mathbf{S}_i^{dg} \leq \mathbf{S}_i^{dg,\max}, \quad i = 0, 1, \dots, n-1 \tag{5}$$

$$imag \left\{ \mathbf{S}_i^{dg} \right\} = Q_i^{dg} = 0, \quad i = 0, 1, \dots, n-1 \tag{6}$$

$$\mathbf{V}_i = 1.0 \angle 0, \quad i \equiv 0 \,(\text{slack node}), \tag{7}$$

where $\mathbf{S}_i^{cg}$, $\mathbf{S}_i^{dg}$ and $\mathbf{S}_i^{d}$ are the power generation in the conventional and distributed generators as well as the power consumption on each node i, respectively; $V^{\min}$ and $V^{\max}$ are the minimum and maximum voltage deviations allowed at the nodes. $\mathbf{S}_i^{cg,\min}$ and $\mathbf{S}_i^{cg,\max}$ represent the minimum and maximum power outputs in each conventional generator connected at node i; while $\mathbf{S}_i^{dg,\min}$ and $\mathbf{S}_i^{dg,\max}$ are the minimum and maximum power outputs permitted for each distributed generator connected at node i. Q_i^{dg} represents the reactive power generation capability at each distributed generator connected to the node i.

The interpretation of the mathematical model defined from (1) to (7) is as follows: in (1), the objective function related to the total active power losses minimization, is defined; (2) defines the complex power balance equality constraint at each node (Kirchhoff's laws in combination to the first Tellegen's theorem); in (3), the voltage regulation constraint per node is defined; expressions (4) and (5) represent the minimum and maximum power outputs in all the conventional and distributed generators interconnected to each node, respectively; with (6) the condition that the power output at each distributed generator is only active power, i.e., each distributed generator operates with unity power factor, is guaranteed. Finally, in (7), the regulated voltage profile in the slack node of the network, is presented. This corresponds to the conventional generator node (this value is valid in per unit representation where the slack voltage is assumed as the base of the voltages).

The solution of the model (1)–(7) requires numerical optimization techniques, since the complex balance set of equations defined by (2) is non-convex and the authors did not find specialized literature where an analytical solution of these equations is used [27]. For this reason, numerical methods such as Gauss-Seidel [29], Newton-Raphson [25], convex approximations [23, 24, 30] or graph methods [20] are developed for solving this set of equality constrains (e.g., typically known as power flow problem in AC grids). In the next section, a master-slave strategy to solve the OPF problem above is described by using a combination between the vortex search algorithm and the conventional backward/forward power flow method.

3   Proposed Methodology

In this section, the OPF problem is addressed by implementing a master-slave methodology composed as follows: in the master stage, the vortex search algorithm defines the active power output at each distributed generator. In the slave stage, the power flow model is solved using a sweep method known as backward/forward power flow method. Each component of the master-slave methodology is discussed below.

3.1   Master Stage: Vortex Search Algorithm

The Vortex search algorithm is physical inspired in a metaheuristic optimization technique for a single-based numerical optimization of nonlinear non-convex functions [22]. This technique was inspired in the vortical behavior of stirred fluids [19]. The VSA provides an adequate balance between the exploration and exploitation of the solution space by modeling the search behavior as a vortex pattern, using an adaptive step size adjustment scheme [31]. In the exploration step the VSA uses a wide solution space region to increase the global search ability of the algorithm; once the algorithm attains a near sub-optimal solution its search works in an exploitative manner to tune the solution to an optimal value.

To present a graphical interpretation of the VSA behavior, let us consider a bi-dimensional optimization problem. In this example a vortex pattern can be modeled by a number of non-concentric circles, where the outer (higher diameter) circle of the vortex in centered on the solution space, where its initial center can be attained as

$$\mu_0 = \frac{x^{\max} + x^{\min}}{2}, \tag{8}$$

where $x^{\max}$ and $x^{\min}$ are $d \times 1$ vectors that define the upper and lower bounds in an optimization problem contained into a d dimensional space. The number of neighbor solutions is named as $C_t(s)$, where t represents the iteration number. In the beginning process, $t = 0$, $C_0(s)$ are generated by a random process using a Gauss distribution in the d-dimensional space. Here, $C_0(s) = \{s_1, s_2, ..., s_n\}$, where n represents the number of candidate solutions. Note that a general Gauss distribution in meta-variable space is defined as follows

$$p(x|\mu, \Sigma) = \left((2\pi)^d |\Sigma| \right)^{-\frac{1}{2}} exp \left\{ -\frac{1}{2} (x - \mu)^T \Sigma^{-1} (x - \mu) \right\} \tag{9}$$

where $x \in \mathbb{R}^{d \times 1}$ is a random vector of variables, $\mu \in \mathbb{R}^{d \times 1}$ is a sample mean (center) vector, and $\Sigma \in \mathbb{R}^{d \times d}$ is a covariance matrix.

Remark 1. Note that if the elements of the covariance matrix are equal and if the off-diagonal elements of this matrix are zero, then, the resulting shape of the Gaussian distribution will be spherical or circular for bi-dimensional spaces [19].

A sample form of calculating Σ using equal variances and zero covariances is presented below

$$\Sigma = \sigma^2 \mathcal{I}_{d \times d}, \tag{10}$$

where σ^2 represents the variance of the Gaussian distribution and $\mathcal{I}_{d \times d}$ is an identity matrix. Note that the standard deviation of the Gaussian distribution (i.e., σ_0) can be defined as:

$$\sigma_0 = \frac{\max\left\{x^{\max}\right\} - \min\left\{x^{\min}\right\}}{2}, \tag{11}$$

where σ_0 can be considered as radius of the hypersphere in a d-dimensional space, for our bi-dimensional example, σ_0 corresponds to the radius of the circle (r_0). Note that in order to attain an adequate exploration in the space of solution, initially, σ_0 is the biggest possible circle; then, during the search process, its radius is decreased to be closer to the optimal solution. In the selection stage, the best solution $s^{0,*} \in C_0(s)$ is selected and memorized to replace the current center of the circle μ_0. Each solution s_k^l needs to lie within its bounds before the selection step, to achieve this, the following rule is used

$$s_k^l = \begin{cases} \left(x_l^{\max} - x_l^{\min}\right) r_l + x_l^{\min}, & s_k^l < x_l^{\min} \\ s_k^l, & x_l^{\min} \leq s_k^l \leq x_l^{\max} \\ \left(x_l^{\max} - x_l^{\min}\right) r_l + x_l^{\min}, & s_k^l > x_l^{\min} \end{cases} \tag{12}$$

where $k = 1, 2, \ldots, n$, $l = 1, 2, \ldots, d$, and r_l represent an uniformly distribution of random number between 0–1. Note that the best solution $s^{t,*} \in C_t(s)$ is updated if and only the current solution is better, which produces an updating of the center μ_t and its radius r_t.

The most critical process in the VSA is the adaptive adjustment of the radius by using a variable-step approach [22]. Here, we consider the lower incomplete **gamma** function as recommended in [19] for performing this task.

$$\gamma(z, a) = \int_0^x e^{-t} t^{a-1} dt, \tag{13}$$

where $a > 0$ is known as shape parameter and x is a random variable, and z is the upper integration limit. Here, we are interested to the incomplete inverse **gamma** function for determining the adaptive radius size at each iteration as presented below.

$$r_t = \sigma_0 \gamma^{-1}(z, a_t), \tag{14}$$

in MATLAB the incomplete inverse gamma function for the variable radius calculation can be computed as follows

$$r_t = \sigma_0 \frac{1}{z} gammaincinv(z, a_t), \tag{15}$$

where the a_t parameter is defined as $a_t = 1 - \frac{t}{t_{\max}}$, being $t_{\max}$ the total number of iterations. In addition, the z parameter is selected as 0.1 as reported in [22].

3.2   Slave Stage: Radial Power Flow Solution

The implementation of the VSA requires the evaluation of the objective function to advance through the solution space. Notwithstanding, the OPF formulation given from (1) to (7) holds an equality constraints, associated to the power balance per node (see Eq. (2)) that requires to be solved before the objective function calculation. Here, this set of equations is solved by using a classical backward/forward method [20]. For doing so, let us consider a conventional radial distribution networks as presented in Fig. 1.

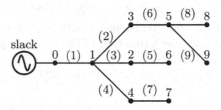

Fig. 1. Radial configuration of an AC distribution network

Figure 1 shows the nodes as well as the number associated to the lines in the parenthesis. Now, by using a graph formulation, it is possible to relate the currents through the lines $\mathbf{J}_{\mathcal{E}}$ and the net currents injected to the nodes $\mathbf{I}_{\mathcal{N}}$. Note that the $\mathcal{E}$ set contains all the branches of the radial network, while the $\mathcal{N}$ set contains all nodes of the network only by excluding the slack bus (renamed here as the node 0). The matrix that relates these currents takes the following form

$$
\begin{pmatrix} J_1 \\ J_2 \\ J_3 \\ J_4 \\ J_5 \\ J_6 \\ J_7 \\ J_8 \\ J_9 \end{pmatrix} = \begin{bmatrix} 1\,1\,1\,1\,1\,1\,1\,1\,1 \\ 0\,0\,1\,0\,1\,0\,0\,1\,1 \\ 0\,1\,0\,0\,0\,1\,0\,0\,0 \\ 0\,0\,0\,1\,0\,0\,1\,0\,0 \\ 0\,0\,0\,0\,1\,0\,0\,0\,0 \\ 0\,0\,0\,0\,1\,0\,0\,1\,1 \\ 0\,0\,0\,0\,0\,0\,1\,0\,0 \\ 0\,0\,0\,0\,0\,0\,0\,1\,0 \\ 0\,0\,0\,0\,0\,0\,0\,0\,1 \end{bmatrix} \begin{pmatrix} I_1 \\ I_2 \\ I_3 \\ I_4 \\ I_5 \\ I_6 \\ I_7 \\ I_8 \\ I_9 \end{pmatrix} \Leftrightarrow \mathbf{J}_{\mathcal{E}} = P\mathbf{I}_{\mathcal{N}}, \tag{16}
$$

where P is the current flow matrix. In addition, the voltage drop at each line can be calculated as follows

$$
\mathbf{V}_{\mathcal{E}} = \mathbf{Z}_{\mathcal{E}}\mathbf{J}_{\mathcal{E}}, \tag{17}
$$

where $\mathbf{Z}_{\mathcal{E}}$ is the primitive impedance matrix that contains the series impedance of each branch in its diagonal.

If we apply Kirchhoff's second law to each closed loop trajectory starting at node 0 and ending at each node, the following expression is obtained

$$V_{\mathcal{N}} = 1_{\mathcal{N}}V_0 - P^T V_{\mathcal{E}}, \tag{18}$$

Note that, if expressions (16) and (17) are substituted into (18), the following formulation is reached

$$V_{\mathcal{N}} = 1_{\mathcal{N}}V_0 - P^T Z_{\mathcal{E}} P I_{\mathcal{N}}, \tag{19}$$

From (19) it is important to mention that the term $P^T Z_{\mathcal{E}} P$ can be interpreted as the nodal impedance matrix, i.e., $\mathbf{Z} = P^T Z_{\mathcal{E}} P = \mathbf{Y}^{-1}$.

Now, it is possible to define a relationship between the nodal injected current and the voltages of the nodes as a function of the complex power flow as follows

$$I_{\mathcal{N}} = diag(\mathbf{V}_{\mathcal{N}}^{\star})^{-1} \left[\mathbf{S}_{\mathcal{N}}^{dg} - \mathbf{S}_{\mathcal{N}}^{d} \right]^{\star}, \tag{20}$$

were $diag(\cdot)$ generates a diagonal square matrix of the argument.

If we substitute (20) on (19) and add an iterative counter m, then, the power flow problem can be solved iteratively as presented below

$$V_{\mathcal{N}}^{m+1} = 1_{\mathcal{N}}V_0 - Z_{\mathcal{E}} diag(\mathbf{V}_{\mathcal{N}}^{m,\star})^{-1} \left[\mathbf{S}_{\mathcal{N}}^{dg} - \mathbf{S}_{\mathcal{N}}^{d} \right]^{\star}, \tag{21}$$

The stopping criteria of the backward/forward power flow method is the delta variation of the nodal voltages between two continuous iterations, i.e., $\max\left\{ \left| V_{\mathcal{N}}^{m+1} - V_{\mathcal{N}}^{m} \right| \right\} \leq \epsilon$, where ϵ can be assigned as 1×10^{-10}.

Note that when (21) converges, the power flow balance equations defined in (2) are successfully solved; in addition, the objective function of the OPF problem given in (1) can be rewritten from (17) as follows

$$\min p_{loss} = real \left\{ \mathbf{J}_{\mathcal{E}}^{T} \mathbf{Z}_{\mathcal{E}}^{T} \mathbf{J}_{\mathcal{E}}^{\star} \right\}. \tag{22}$$

3.3   Flowchart of the Master-Slave Proposed Approach

The master-slave methodology proposed in this paper for solving the OPF in radial distribution networks is composed in the master stage by the VSA method and in the slave stage by the radial power flow method. Algorithm 3.3 presents the pseudo-code of the proposed methodology [19,22].

Note that the application of the VSA only requires the evaluation of the objective function (radial power flow problem for OPF analysis in our case); notwithstanding its philosophy, it is extensible to any continuous optimization problem [22]; this characteristic makes this metaheuristic algorithm attractive for multiple engineering problems, since its search steps (exploration and exploitation) allows reaching high quality results in a pure-algorithmic sense [19,22], which permits avoiding the usage of commercial software for solving optimization problems being it one of the main advantages of the VSA.

4   Test Systems

Here, we consider the possibility of using two conventional and large-used radial distribution networks with 33 and 69 nodes. These systems are classically employed in optimal location and dimensioning of distributed generation [5,6]. The information of those system is shown below.

In the first system is the 33-node test system, which is composed of 33 nodes and 32 lines with the slack source located at node 1. The operative voltage of this test system is 12.66 kV. The total active and reactive power demands for this test system are 3715 kW and 2300 kVAr respectively, generating 210.98 kW of active power losses. The electrical configuration of this test feeder as well as all branch data can be consulted in [6]. The second test feeder is the 69-node test system, which operates with a voltage of 12.66 kV, and the total demand is $3800 + j2690$ kVA [5]. The single line diagram of this test system as well as the

---

Algorithm 1. Proposed master-slave optimization based on the VSA and the backward/forward power flow

---

1: **Inputs:**
2: Initial center μ_0 calculated from (8);
3: Initial radius r_0 (or the standard deviation σ_0) as calculated in (11);
4: Set the initial best fitness function as $p_{loss}(s_{best}) = \infty$ (minimization problem);
5: Make $t = 0$;
6: **while** $t \leq t_{max}$ **do**
7:     Generate candidate solutions by using Gaussian distribution around the center μ_t with a standard deviation (radius) r_t as defined in (9) to obtain $C_t(s)$ with d-dimension in rows and b columns (b are the number of DGs considered in the OPF problem);
8:     If $C_t(s)$ overpass any upper or lower bound, put it within its bounds by using (12);
9:     Evaluate the slave problem (see Eq. (21) for each s_k in If $C_t(s)$ and calculates its corresponding objective function $p_{loss}(s_k)$ as (22);
10:    Select the best solution s^* as the argument that produces the minimum of $p_{loss}(s)$ contained in $C_t(s)$;
11:    **if** $p_{loss}(s^*) < p_{loss}(s_{best})$ **then**
12:        $s_{best} = s^*$;
13:        $p_{loss}(s_{best}) = p_{loss}(s^*)$;
14:    **else**
15:        Keep the best solution attained so far s_{best};
16:    **end if**
17:    Make the center μ_{t+1} being equal to the best solution s_{best};
18:    Update the current radius r_{t+1} as (15);
19:    $t = t + 1$;
20: **end while**
21: **Output:**
22: Best solution found s_{best} as well as its objective function $p_{loss}(s_{best})$;

---

electrical parameters of this test system (resistances and inductances in all the branches as well as load consumptions) can be consulted in [6].

4.1 Simulation Scenarios

To validate the proposed approach for optimal dimensioning of distributed generators in AC radial distribution systems, the information provided by [5] is used, where, five methodologies for solving the problem were studied. Notwithstanding, since the purpose of this work is to validate the optimal power flow for each technique, it implies that the location of each generators corresponds to an input data in the approach presented here. In order to confirm the power losses reported in [5], the power generation provided by this reference is evaluated in order to provide a fair comparison of the approach presented here in comparison with literature reports.

5 Numerical Results

All simulations were carried-out in a desk-computer INTEL(R) Core(TM) $i7 -$ 7700, 3.60 GHz, 8 GB RAM with 64 bits Windows 10 Pro using MATLAB $2017b$. The parametrization of the VSA method considered 1000 iterations, 4 individuals in the population (d-dimension equal to 4); while the radial power flow takes the error of convergence about 1×10^{-10} with 100 iterations as maximum. Note that the per-unit representation in Tables of this section uses a power base of 1000 kW as reported in [5].

5.1 33-Node Test Feeder

In the simulation results that will be provided for this test system, each generator located on the network has been set in the range of 0.20 p.u to 1.20 p.u; which implies that the initial center of the sphere for this 3-dimensional problem (three distributed generators) is $\mu_0 = (7, 7, 7)$ with an initial standard deviation of $\sigma_0 = 5$.

Table 1 presents the numerical performance of the proposed master-slave VSA in conjunction with the radial power flow approach for optimal dimensioning of DGs in the 33-node test system. Results are compared with the krill-herd algorithm (KHA) [5], loss-sensitivity factor with simulated annealing (LSFSA) [15], genetic algorithms (GA) [13], particle swarm optimization (PSO) [13] and a hybrid GA/PSO [13].

In Table 1 it is possible to observe that the VSA algorithm provides a better power losses performance in comparison with each literature reported approach; e.g., Observing the solution provided by the KHA method, the VSA manages to reduces the power losses by around 1.9048 kW; while in the case of the GA/PSO method the VSA reduces the power losses in 35.3284 kW. The reduction percentage of the proposed approach in comparison with the literature methods evaluated is listed in the last column of the Table 1. This column shows that

Table 1. Numerical performance in the 33-node test feeder

Method	Literature approaches			Vortex search algorithm		
	Location	Size [p.u]	Losses [kW]	Size [p.u]	Losses [kW]	Improv. [%]
KHA [5]	13	0.8107		0.8116		
	25	0.8368	75.3977	0.8712	73.4929	2.5263
	30	0.8410		1.0741		
LSFSA [15]	6	1.1124		1.2000		
	18	0.4874	82.0418	0.4913	81.8747	0.2037
	30	0.8679		0.8051		
GA [13]	11	1.5000		0.9668		
	29	0.4228	106.0682	0.5398	86.5031	18.4458
	30	1.0714		0.6255		
PSO [13]	8	1.1768		0.7498		
	13	0.9816	105.3296	0.5629	82.9583	21.2391
	32	0.8297		0.8376		
GA/PSO [13]	11	0.9250		0.6682		
	16	0.8630	121.3259	0.3713	85.9975	29.1186
	32	1.2000		0.9284		

there is a technical tie between the proposed VSA method in comparison with the LSFSA approach, since 0.2 % difference represents a very small improvement that can be attributed to the parametrization of the algorithms.

Figure 2 reports the numerical performance of the proposed VSA when used for solving the OPF problem considering the location of the generators reported in each one of the comparative methods as inputs. Note that the radius behavior (see Fig. 2(a)) shows the importance of exploration of the solution space during the first iterations of the algorithm; notwithstanding when number of iterations increase, then, the VSA focuses in the exploitation of the solution space. This exploration and exploitation behaviors are confirmed in the objective function performance (see Fig. 2(b)), as shown, during the first 50 iterations the objective function decreases fast, but after this number of iterations, its values remain quasi-constants.

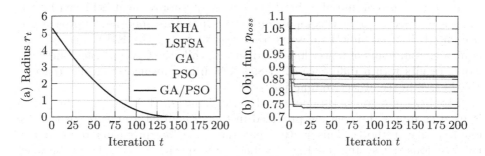

Fig. 2. Behavior of the proposed master-slave methodology for the 33-node test feeder: (a) radius behavior and (b) objective function performance

5.2   69-Node Test Feeder

In the simulation, the location of each generator on the network is assumed to be set in the range of 3.00 p.u to 20.0 p.u; which implies that the initial center of the sphere for this 3-dimensional problem is $\mu_0 = (11.5, 11.5, 11.5)$ with an initial standard deviation of $\sigma_0 = 8.5$.

Table 2. Numerical performance in the 69-node test feeder

Method	Literature approaches			Vortex search algorithm		
	Location	Size [p.u]	Losses [kW]	Size [p.u]	Losses [kW]	Improv. [%]
KHA [5]	12	0.4962	69.7144	0.4958	69.7144	0
	22	0.3113		0.3114		
	61	1.7354		1.7352		
LSFSA [15]	18	1.1124	77.2461	0.5271	76.6155	0.8164
	60	0.3113		1.3608		
	65	1.7354		0.4539		
GA [13]	21	0.9297	89.0286	0.4899	73.1045	17.8864
	62	1.0752		1.4628		
	64	0.9925		0.3000		
PSO [13]	17	0.9925	83.9634	0.5307	71.6494	14.6659
	61	1.1998		1.4808		
	63	0.7956		0.3002		
GA/PSO [13]	21	0.9105	84.7498	0.4864	72.0992	14.9270
	61	1.1926		1.4884		
	63	0.8849		0.3002		

Table 2 presents the numerical performance of the proposed master-slave VSA in conjunction with the radial power flow approach for optimal dimensioning of DGs in the 69-node test system when it is compared to the literature approaches reported in [5]. Note that for this test system, the KHA and the proposed VSA method attains the same objective function (69.7144 kW) with small differences in the generation power outputs, i.e., the KHA method in the nodes 12, 22 y 61 requires generation of 0.4962 p.u, 0.3113 p.u and 1.7354 p.u, while the proposed VSA needs a generation of 0.4958 p.u, 0.3114 p.u and 1.7352 pu. On the other hand, in the last column of Table 2 percentage of improvement achieved by our proposed VSA method in comparison to the literature reported approaches is presented; it is possible to observe that the VSA and the KHA methods are equivalents in terms of power losses reduction; while the GA approach offers the worst results with a difference of 17.89% which is equivalent to a difference of 15.924 kW in the objective function.

Finally, Fig. 3 shows the numerical performance of th VSA algorithm when is used as inputs the location provided in the specialized literature for the five comparative methods. This picture has the same interpretation presented in the previous test system for Fig. 2, which confirms the strong relation between exploration and exploitation advantages of the VSA for nonlinear continuous optimization.

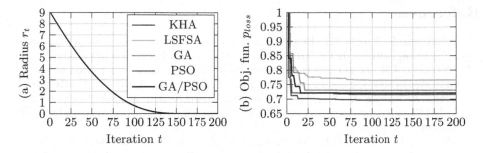

Fig. 3. Behavior of the proposed master-slave methodology for the 69-node test feeder: (a) radius behavior and (b) objective function performance

6   Conclusions and Future Works

This paper presented a new hybrid optimization algorithm for optimal dimensioning of distributed generation in radial AC distribution networks. The proposed algorithm uses a master-slave optimization approach. In the master stage, an emerging vortex search algorithm was implemented, while in the slave stage, a classical radial power flow method was employed. Numerical results confirmed the applicability and efficiency of the proposed optimization method in comparison with classical approaches such as genetic algorithms and particle swarm approaches as well as emerging methods such as krill-herd algorithms.

The main advantage of the VSA optimization method corresponded to the combination between the exploration and exploitation characteristics over the solution space by implementing a variable radius search, since in the first iterations, a wide region of the solution space is analyzed (exploration), while as the iterations progress, this radius decreases and promissory solution areas are intensively analyzed (exploitation).

The classical radial power flow method employed in the slave stage was the essential tool in the OPF analysis, since it allowed the evaluation of the objective function by solving the resulting power flow model when distributed generations are assigned by the VSA. This method confronts the non-convexities owns in the analysis of power flow through the use of a graphical model without resorting in large matrix investments. In addition, the combination of this power flow method in conjunction to the VSA approach allowed proposing a pure-algorithmic methodology for optimal sizing of distributed generation in AC radial networks, which was an important advantage, since this methodology can be implemented in any free software.

As future works, it will be possible to address the problem of optimal location of distributed generation in AC radial distribution networks by embedding the VSA approach in a new master-salve optimizer by using modern discrete optimization techniques such as the population-based incremental learning or the ant-lion optimizer, and so forth. It will be also interesting to analyze the OPF problem in direct current networks by using the VSA as optimizer.

References

1. Blaabjerg, F., Kjaer, S.B.: Power electronics as efficient interface in dispersed power generation systems. IEEE Trans. Power Electron. **19**(5), 1184–1194 (2004)
2. Carrasco, J.M., et al.: Power-electronic systems for the grid integration of renewable energy sources: a survey. IEEE Trans. Ind. Electron. **53**(4), 1002–1016 (2006)
3. Zhao, X., Chang, L., Shao, R., Spence, K.: Power system support functions provided by smart inverters a review. CPSS Trans. Power Electron. Appl. **3**(1), 25–35 (2018)
4. Hossain, M.J., Pota, H.R., Mahmud, M.A., Aldeen, M.: Robust control for power sharing in microgrids with low-inertia wind and PV generators. IEEE Trans. Sustain. Energy **6**(3), 1067–1077 (2015)
5. Sultana, S., Roy, P.K.: Krill herd algorithm for optimal location of distributed generator in radial distribution system. Appl. Soft Comput. **40**, 391–404 (2016)
6. Grisales-Noreña, L.F., Gonzalez-Montoya, D., Ramos-Paja, C.A.: Optimal sizing and location of distributed generators based on PBIL and PSO techniques. Energies **11**(1018), 1–27 (2018)
7. Montoya, O.D., Grajales, A., Garces, A., Castro, C.A.: Distribution systems operation considering energy storage devices and distributed generation. IEEE Lat. Am. Trans. **15**(5), 890–900 (2017)
8. Sgouras, K.I., Bouhouras, A.S., Gkaidatzis, P.A., Doukas, D.I., Labridis, D.P.: Impact of reverse power flow on the optimal distributed generation placement problem. IET Gener. Transm. Distrib. **11**(18), 4626–4632 (2017)
9. Mahat, P., Chen, Z., Bak-Jensen, B., Bak, C.L.: A simple adaptive overcurrent protection of distribution systems with distributed generation. IEEE Trans. Smart Grid **2**(3), 428–437 (2011)
10. Chao, L., Yongting, C., Xunjun, Z.: Analysis and solution of voltage overvoltage problem in grid connection of distributed photovoltaic system. In: 2018 China International Conference on Electricity Distribution (CICED), pp. 1114–1117, September 2018
11. El-khattam, W., Sidhu, T.S.: Resolving the impact of distributed renewable generation on directional overcurrent relay coordination: a case study. IET Renew. Power Gener. **3**(4), 415–425 (2009)
12. Attia, A.-F., Sehiemy, R.A.E., Hasanien, H.M.: Optimal power flow solution in power systems using a novel Sine-Cosine algorithm. Int. J. Electr. Power Energy Syst. **99**, 331–343 (2018)
13. Moradi, M., Abedini, M.: A combination of genetic algorithm and particle swarm optimization for optimal DG location and sizing in distribution systems. Int. J. Electr. Power Energy Syst. **34**(1), 66–74 (2012)
14. Abido, M.A.: Optimal power flow using Tabu search algorithm. Electr. Power Compon. Syst. **30**(5), 469–483 (2002)
15. Injeti, S.K., Kumar, N.P.: A novel approach to identify optimal access point and capacity of multiple DGs in a small, medium and large scale radial distribution systems. Int. J. Electr. Power Energy Syst. **45**(1), 142–151 (2013)
16. Balachennaiah, P., Suryakalavathi, M., Nagendra, P.: Firefly algorithm based solution to minimize the real power loss in a power system. Ain Shams Eng. J. **9**(1), 89–100 (2018)
17. Kumar, Y.A., Kumar, N.P.: Optimal allocation of distribution generation units in radial distribution systems using nature inspired optimization techniques. In: 2018 International Conference on Power, Energy, Control and Transmission Systems (ICPECTS), pp. 1–6, February 2018

18. Sudabattula, S.K., Kowsalya, M.: Optimal allocation of solar based distributed generators in distribution system using Bat algorithm. Perspect. Sci. **8**, 270–272 (2016). Recent Trends in Engineering and Material Sciences
19. Ozkıs, A., Babalık, A.: A novel metaheuristic for multi-objective optimization problems: the multi-objective vortex search algorithm. Inf. Sci. **402**, 124–148 (2017)
20. Marini, A., Mortazavi, S., Piegari, L., Ghazizadeh, M.-S.: An efficient graph-based power flow algorithm for electrical distribution systems with a comprehensive modeling of distributed generations. Electr. Power Syst. Res. **170**, 229–243 (2019)
21. Aydin, O., Tezcan, S., Eke, I., Taplamacioglu, M.: Solving the Optimal power flow quadratic cost functions using Vortex search algorithm. IFAC-PapersOnLine **50**(1), 239–244 (2017). 20th IFAC World Congress
22. Dogan, B., Olmez, T.: Vortex search algorithm for the analog active filter component selection problem. AEU - Int. J. Electron. Commun. **69**(9), 1243–1253 (2015)
23. Huang, S., Wu, Q., Wang, J., Zhao, H.: A sufficient condition on convex relaxation of AC optimal power flow in distribution networks. IEEE Trans. Power Syst. **32**(2), 1359–1368 (2017)
24. Venzke, A., Halilbasic, L., Markovic, U., Hug, G., Chatzivasileiadis, S.: Convex relaxations of chance constrained AC optimal power flow. IEEE Trans. Power Syst. **33**(3), 2829–2841 (2018)
25. Zamzam, A.S., Sidiropoulos, N.D., Dall'Anese, E.: Beyond relaxation and Newton-Raphson: solving AC OPF for multi-phase systems with renewables. IEEE Trans. Smart Grid **9**(5), 3966–3975 (2018)
26. Miao, Z., Fan, L., Aghamolki, H.G., Zeng, B.: Least squares estimation based SDP cuts for SOCP relaxation of AC OPF. IEEE Trans. Autom. Control **63**(1), 241–248 (2018)
27. Garces, A.: A quadratic approximation for the optimal power flow in power distribution systems. Electr. Power Syst. Res. **130**, 222–229 (2016). http://www.sciencedirect.com/science/article/pii/S037877961500276X
28. Nejdawi, I.M., Clements, K.A., Davis, P.W.: An efficient interior point method for sequential quadratic programming based optimal power flow. IEEE Trans. Power Syst. **15**(4), 1179–1183 (2000)
29. Teng, J.-H.: A modified gauss-seidel algorithm of three-phase power flow analysis in distribution networks. Int. J. Electr. Power Energy Syst. **24**(2), 97–102 (2002)
30. Montoya, O.D., Gil, W.J., Garces, A.: Optimal Power Flow for radial and mesh grids using semidefinite programming. Tecno Logicas **20**(40), 29–42 (2017)
31. Ramli, M.A.M., Bouchekara, H.R.E.H.: Estimation of solar radiation on PV panel surface with optimum tilt angle using vortex search algorithm. IET Renew. Power Gener. **12**(10), 1138–1145 (2018)

Assessment of Metaheuristic Techniques Applied to the Optimal Reactive Power Dispatch

Daniel Camilo Londoño⬤, Walter Mauircio Villa-Acevedo⬤,
and Jesús María López-Lezama$^{(\boxtimes)}$⬤

Universidad de Antioquia, Calle 67 No 53-108, Medellín, Colombia
{daniel.londono,walter.villa,
jmaria.lopez}@udea.edu.co

Abstract. The optimal reactive power dispatch (ORPD) problem consists of finding the optimal settings of several reactive power resources in order to minimize system power losses. The ORPD is a complex combinatorial optimization problem that involves discrete and continuous variables as well as a nonlinear objective function and nonlinear constraints. From the point of view of computational complexity, the ORPD problem is NP-complete. Several techniques have been reported in the specialized literature to approach this problem in which modern metaheuristics stand out. This paper presents a comparison of such techniques with a Mean-Variance Mapping Optimization (MVMO) algorithm implemented by the authors with two different constraint handling approaches. Several tests with the IEEE 30 bus test system show the effectiveness of the proposed approach which outperforms results of previously reported methods.

Keywords: Optimal reactive power dispatch · Metaheuristic techniques ·
Power loss minimization

1 Introduction

The Optimal Reactive Power Dispatch (ORPD) is a vital process in the daily operation of power systems. The main objective of the ORPD is the minimization of power losses, although other objectives such as minimization of voltage deviation and improvement of voltage stability limits can also be considered [1]. These objectives are sought by finding the optimal settings of available reactive power sources. The ORPD involves integer decision variables such as transformer tap settings and reactive power compensations, as well as continuous decision variables such as generator set points. Also, the ORPD features nonlinear constraints and nonlinear objective function, which makes it a challenging optimization problem. Early attempts to approach this problem resorted to conventional optimization techniques; however, their main disadvantage is their convergence local optimal solutions given the non-differential, non-linearity and non-convex nature of the ORPD problem. From the standpoint of mathematical optimization the ORPD problem is NP-complete. These type of problems are better handled by metaheuristic techniques than by classic optimization methods.

J. C. Figueroa-García et al. (Eds.): WEA 2019, CCIS 1052, pp. 250–262, 2019.
https://doi.org/10.1007/978-3-030-31019-6_22

Several metaheuristic techniques have been proposed to address the ORPD problem. In [2] the authors proposed a Differential Evolution (DE) technique. DE is a population-based algorithm similar to a genetic algorithm (GA) that implements crossover, mutation and selection operators. The main difference between DE and GA are the selection and mutation schemes. In [3] the authors present a Chaotic Krill Herd Algorithm (CKHA) to solve the ORPD problem. CKHA was proposed in [4] and is based on the herding behaviour of krill swarm when searching for food in nature. This metaheuristic technique combines a random and a local search to account for diversification and intensification, respectively. The authors considered three objective functions: minimization of power losses, minimization of voltage deviation and enhancement of voltage stability. In [5] the authors proposed a a particle swarm optimization (PSO) algorithm for reactive power and voltage control considering voltage security assessment. This latter objective is reached through a continuation power flow and contingency analysis. Other variants of this technique such as hybrid PSO [6], turbulent crazy PSO [7], comprehensive learning PSO (CLPSO) [8], and PSO with aging leader and challengers (ALC-PSO) [9] have also been applied to solve the ORPD problem. In [10] a gravitational search algorithm (GSA) is proposed to solve the ORPD problem. This technique was initially proposed in [11] and is a swarm-based metaheuristic inspired in the Newtonian gravitational law. Variants of this technique applied to the ORPD, namely improved gravitational search algorithm (IGSA) and opposition-based gravitational search algorithm (OGSA) are presented in [12] and [13], respectively. A bunch of other metaheuristic techniques such as firefly algorithm (FA) and hybrid firefly algorithm (HFA) [14], biogeography-based optimization (BBO) [15] and moth-flame optimization (MFO) [16] have also been applied to solve the ORPD problem. A detailed description of such techniques is out of the scope of this paper; however, a classification and comparison of them can be consulted in [17].

In this paper several metaheuristic techniques applied the ORPD are compared with an adaptation of the Mean-Variance Mapping Optimization (MVMO) algorithm proposed by the authors. The contributions of this paper are threefold: (1) a novel adaptation of the MVMO is implemented to approach the ORPD problem; (2) two constraint handling approaches are developed and compared for the proposed algorithm, and (3) comparison is provided with several metaheuristic techniques reported in the specialized literature showing the effectiveness and robustness of the proposed approach.

Several tests were performed with the IEEE 30 bus test system to show the applicability of MVMO for dealing with the ORPD problem. Better results than those previously reported by other metaheuristics are obtained with the proposed methodology.

The remaining of this paper is as follows. Section 2 presents the mathematical modeling of the ORPD problem, Sect. 3 describes the solution approach, Sect. 4 presents the tests and results, and finally conclusions are presented in Sect. 5.

2 Mathematical Modeling

2.1 Objective Function

The objective function of the ORPD problem approached in this paper consists of minimizing power losses as expressed in (1). In this case, N_K is the set of lines, *Ploss* represents power losses, g_k is the admittance of line k (connected between nodes i and j), V_i and V_j are voltage magnitudes at buses i and j, respectively; and θ_{ij} is the angle between buses i and j.

$$Min\,Ploss = \sum_{k \in N_K} g_k \left(V_i^2 + V_j^2 - 2V_iV_j \cos\,\theta_{ij} \right) \tag{1}$$

2.2 Constraints

Constraints of the ORPD are given by Eqs. (2)–(9). Equations (2) and (3) represent the active and reactive power balance required in any conventional power flow. In this case, N_B is the set of buses, G_{ij} and B_{ij} are the real and imaginary values of the admittance matrix in position i, j, respectively. P_{gi} and P_{di} are the active power generation and demand at bus i, respectively. Q_{gi} and Q_{di} are the reactive generation and demand at bus i, respectively. Equations (4)–(9) represent the inequality constraints of the ORPD. Upper indexes *min* and *max* stand for minimum and maximum limits of the corresponding variables. Equation (4) represents voltage limits of generators. In this case, V_{gi} is the voltage magnitude set point of the ith generator while N_G is the set of generators. Equation (5) represents the limits of tap positions of transformers. T_i is the tap position of transformer i, and N_T is the set of transformers available for tap changing. Equations (6) and (7) account for reactive power limits supplied by capacitor banks and reactors, respectively. In this case, Q_{ci} and Q_{Lj} are the reactive power injections of capacitor bank i and reactor j, respectively. N_C and N_L are the sets of capacitor banks and reactors, respectively. Voltage limits in load buses (denoted with subindex *PQ*) are given by Eq. (8), where V_{PQi} is the voltage magnitude at the ith load bus and N_{PQ} is the set of load buses. Finally, Eq. (9) indicates the limits of apparent power flow in branch l, given by S_{li}.

$$V_i \sum_{j \in N_B} V_j \left[G_{ij} \cos\,\theta_{ij} + B_{ij} \sin\,\theta_{ij} \right] - P_{gi} + P_{di} = 0 \tag{2}$$

$$V_i \sum_{j \in N_B} V_j \left[G_{ij} \sin\,\theta_{ij} - B_{ij} \cos\,\theta_{ij} \right] - Q_{gi} + Q_{di} = 0 \tag{3}$$

$$V_{gi}^{min} \leq V_{gi} \leq V_{gi}^{max}, \quad i = 1, \ldots, N_G \tag{4}$$

$$T_i^{min} \leq T_i \leq T_i^{max} \quad i = 1, \ldots, N_T \tag{5}$$

$$Q_{ci}^{min} \le Q_{ci} \le Q_{ci}^{max} \qquad i = 1,\ldots,N_C \tag{6}$$

$$Q_{Lj}^{min} \le Q_{Lj} \le Q_{Lj}^{max} \qquad j = 1,\ldots,N_L \tag{7}$$

$$V_{PQi}^{min} \le V_{PQi} \le V_{PQi}^{max}, \qquad i = 1,\ldots,N_{PQ} \tag{8}$$

$$S_{lk} \le S_{lk}^{max}, \qquad k = 1,\ldots,N_K \tag{9}$$

2.3   Codification of Solutions

Control variables of the ORPD are given by the set points of generators, tap positions of transformers, and reactive power injections provided by capacitor banks and reactors. Such variables are limited by constraints (4)–(7), respectively. Enforcement of these constraints is provided directly in the codification of candidate solutions. Every set of variables is randomly initiated within their respective limits. For example, voltage set points of generators are considered within the range $[V_{gi}^{min}, V_{gi}^{max}]$ using a fine grained discretization. Similarly, other limits are considered for tap positions, capacitor banks and reactors. Every variable is coded according to specific system data. Figure 1 depicts the codification of a candidate solution.

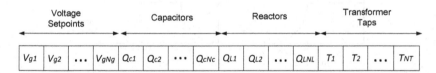

Fig. 1. Codification of solution candidates for the ORPD problem (Source: Authors)

2.4   Constraint Handling of the ORPD

Constraint enforcement of Eqs. (2) and (3) is provided through the power flow solution. Enforcement of constraints (4)–(7) is provided through the codification of solution candidates as indicated in the previous section. The remaining constraints given by Eqs. (8) and (9) can be handled by penalizing deviations from established limtis. In this case, a fitness function labeled as F_1 is defined as the power losses plus penalizations on voltage deviations (VD) and power flow deviations (PFD) as indicated in Eqs. (11)–(13). In this case, μ_V and μ_{Pf} are penalization factors for voltage and power flow deviations, respectively.

$$F_1 = Ploss + \mu_V VD + \mu_{Pf} PFD \tag{10}$$

$$VD = \sum_j max\left\{0, \left(V_j^{min} - V_j\right)\right\} + max\left\{0, \left(V_j - V_j^{max}\right)\right\} \tag{11}$$

$$PFD = \sum_k max\{0, (S_{lk}^{min} - S_{lk})\} + max\{0, (S_{lk} - S_{lk}^{max})\} \qquad (12)$$

An alternative constraint handling approach, that also serves as a stopping criterion is presented in Eq. (13) [18]. This consists of a product of subfunctions that has three components: voltage limits on load buses f_{VN}, power flow limits on branches f_{CR}, and a goal on total power losses f_{loss}. Every subfunction is deviced in such a way that if the corresponding variable is within specified limits, its value is 1; otherwise, its value is lower than one (see Fig. 2). A goal on power losses is previously defined and established as another subfunction as indicated in Fig. 2c. Such goal must be set by the system planner based on the knowledge of the power system. Note that the product of all subfunctions is equal to 1 only if the ORPD problem is both feasible and optimal (according to a specified goal). This represents an advantage from the standpoint of optimization since the value of F_2 can be used as a stopping crieterion. Further details in the implementation of F_2 to the ORPD problem can be consulted in [18].

$$F_2 = \left[\prod_{i=1}^{N_L} f_{VN}(i)\right] \left[\prod_{j=1}^{N_K} f_{CR}(j)\right] f_{loss} \qquad (13)$$

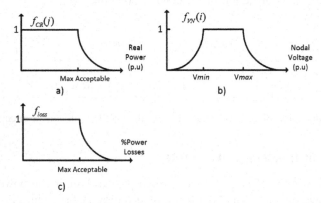

Fig. 2. Subfunctions for: (a) enforcement of power flow limits; (b) enforcement of voltage limits in load buses; and (c) identification of an optimal solution with respect to power loses (Source: Authors)

3 Solution Approach

MVMO was initially conceived and developed by Erlich in 2010 [19]. The basic concept shares several similarities with other evolutionary algorithms; however, its main feature is the use of a special mapping applied for mutating the offspring, which is based on the mean and variance of the n-best population. The swarm version of this algorithm, described in [20, 21] is implemented in this paper.

As in most evolutionary algorithms, the classic MVMO operates over a set of solutions, its objective is to execute a correct and accurate optimization with a minimum quantity of objective functions evaluations. The inner search space of all the variables within MVMO is restricted to [0, 1]. Thus, the minimum and maximum limits of the variables must be normalized in this range. During each iteration, it is not possible that any vector solution component violates the corresponding limits. To achieve this objective, a special mapping function was developed. The inputs of this function are the means and variance of the best solutions that the MVMO has found so far. Note that the output of this mapping function will be always within the range [0, 1], avoiding violation of variable limits during the search process. The shape and mapping curves are adjusted according to the progress in the search process and the MVMO updates the candidate solution around the best solution in each step of the iteration [19]. In the same way, MVMO is able to search around the best local solution with a small possibility of being trapped in a local optimal solution. The basic considerations of the classic MVMO are detailed below.

3.1 Fitness Evaluation and Constraint Handling

The chi-squared test is applied for each candidate solution. The feasibility of the solution is checked and a fitness valued is assigned. The static penalization approach is used to handle constraints. Since the control variables are self-limited, all depending variables are restricted by applying the fitness function as indicated in Eq. (14) where f is the original objective function, n is the number of constrains, β is the order of the penalization term, vi is the penalization coefficient of the ith constraint and g represents the inequality constraints.

$$\min f' = f + \sum_{i=1}^{n} v_i max[0, g_i]^{\beta} \tag{14}$$

3.2 Enhanced Mapping

The mapping function transforms a variable x_i^* varied randomly with unity distribution to another variable x_i, which is concentrated around the mean value. The new value of the ith variable is determined by Eq. (15). Where h_x, h_1 and h_0 are the outputs of the mapping function based on the different inputs given by Eq. (16). The mapping function (h-function) is parameterized as indicated in Eq. (17), where s_1 and s_2 are shape factors that allow asymmetric variations of the mapping function. Finally, the shape factor is calculated as indicated in Eq. (18). In this case, f_s is a scale factor that allows controlling the search process during each iteration, while $\bar{x_i}$ and v_i are the mean and variance of the solution archive, respectively. A more detailed description on how to adjust shape and scale is presented in [22].

$$x_i = h_x + (1 - h_1 + h_0)x_i^* - h_0 \tag{15}$$

$$h_x = h(x = x_i^*), h_0 = h(x = 0), h_1 = h(x = 1) \tag{16}$$

$$h(\bar{x}, s_1, s_2, x) = \bar{x}(1 - e^{-x \cdot s_1}) + (1 - \overline{x_i})e^{-(1-x)s_2} \tag{17}$$

$$s_i = -ln(v_i)f_s \tag{18}$$

3.3 Solution Archive

This archive constitutes the base knowledge of the algorithm to guide the search direction. Therefore, the n best individuals that the MVMO has found so far are saved in this archive. The fitness value for each individual is also saved. The following rules are adjusted to compare the generated individuals in each iteration and the existing archived solutions aiming to avoid losing high quality solutions: (i) any feasible solution is preferred over any unfeasible solution, (ii) between two feasible solutions, the one with the best fitness value is preferred, (iii) between two unfeasible solutions, the one with the lowest fitness value is preferred. The update is only done if the new individual is better than those that are currently in the archive. Feasible solutions are located in the upper part of the archive. These solutions are organized according to their fitness value. Unfeasible solutions are organized according to their fitness and located in the lower part of the archive. Once the archive is complete with n feasible solutions, any unfeasible solution candidate would not have the chance to be saved in the archive.

3.4 Offspring Generation and Stopping Criterion

The first positioned solution in the archive (the best so far), named as *xbest*, is assigned as the parent. For offspring generation a variable selection is performed. MVMO searches the mean value saved in the solution archive for the better solution only in m selected directions. This means that only these dimensions of the offspring will be updated while the $D - m$ remaining dimensions take the corresponding values of *xbest*, being D the dimension of the problem (number of control variables). Then, mutation is carried out, for each m selected dimension. Finally, the search process of the MVMO stops after a predetermined number of fitness evaluations.

In its swarm variant, MVMO is initiated with n particles. In this case, each particle, or candidate solution has its own solution archive and mapping function. In the process each candidate solution executes m steps to identify an optimal set of independent solutions. Later, the particles exchange information. In some cases, some particle are very close to each other, which means that there is information redundancy. This redundancy is eliminated by discarting redundant particles. As with PSO, a local and global best solution are defined. Also, the normalized distance between each particle to the local best and global best solutions are calculated.

A particle is discarded from the process if its normalized distance is less than a certain predefined threshold. If such threshold is zero, all particles are taken into account in the whole process; otherwise, if the threshold is one all particles are discarded except from the global best. After independent evaluation, and if the particle is further considered, its searching will be directed toward the global solution by assigning global best instead of local best solution, as parent for the particle's offspring. The remaining steps are identical with those of the classical MVMO. A detailed description of swarm MVMO is presented in [21, 23].

4   Tests and Results

The IEEE 30 bus test system was used to show the effectiveness of the proposed approach. This system comprises 6 generators, 4 transformers with tap changers and 9 capacitor banks adding up 19 control variables. The data of this systems can be consulted in [2]. One hundred runs were executed using penalizations $\mu_V = 10000$ and $\mu_{Pf} = 1000$. Table 1 presents the results in p.u considering a base of 100MVA. For implementing fitness function F_2 a goal of 0.0448 pu of power losses was considred. A comparison is presented with different metaheuristic techniques applied to the same problem and reported in the specialized literature. İn order to guarantee the reproducibility of the results presented in this paper, the specific values of all control variables are shown in Table 1a and b. Note that power losses before optimization are 0.05833 pu as indicated in the second column of Table 1a. The best reduction of power losses is obtained using the proposed MVMO algorithm using fitness function F_1 which results in power losses of 0.0045626 pu, representing a reduction of 21.48% with respect to the base case. Note that when applying fitness function F_2 MVMO is slightly outperformed by DE and BBO; however, its performance is still superior to that of the other metaheuristics. Figure 3 allows a quick comparison of the results obtained with the different methodologies. It can be observed that the performance of MVMO is similar to that of MFO, DE and BBO. Figures 4 and 5 illustrate the convergence of the proposed approach for fitness functions F_1 and F_2, respectively. In this case, four runs of the algorithm are randomly selected. Note that regardless of the initial condition all runs converge to approximately the same value; also, F_2 converges to -1 since the problem is set for minimization.

Table 2 presents some statistical results of the performance of MVMO for 100 runs with the power systems under study. Note that better solutions are obtained when implementing a classic penalization (F_1). However, such difference is small (0.5%). The main advantage of implementing F_2 lies on its lower computational time as can be observed in the last row of Table 2. It is worth to mention that both constraint handling approaches are effective since voltage and power flow deviations are cero. Also, all solutions obtained in the runs are very similar, as can be inferred from the standard deviations.

Table 1. Best control variable settings for power loss minimization of the IEEE-30 bus test system with different algorithms

(a)

Control variable (pu)	Initial [2]	ABC [14]	FA [14]	CLPSO [8]	DE [2]	BBO [15]
V_{G1}	1.05	1.1	1.1	1.1	1.1	1.1
V_{G2}	1.04	1.0615	1.0644	1.1	1.0931	1.0944
V_{G5}	1.01	1.0711	1.07455	1.0795	1.0736	1.0749
V_{G8}	1.01	1.0849	1.0869	1.1	1.0736	1.0768
V_{G11}	1.05	1.1	1.0916	1.1	1.1	1.0999
V_{G13}	1.05	1.0665	1.099	1.1	1.1	1.0999
T_{11}	1.078	0.97	1	0.9154	1.0465	1.0435
T_{12}	1.069	1.05	0.94	0.9	0.9097	0.9012
T_{15}	1.032	0.99	1	0.9	0.9867	0.9824
T_{36}	1.068	0.99	0.97	0.9397	0.9689	0.9692
Q_{C10}	0	0.05	0.03	0.049265	0.05	0.049998
Q_{C12}	0	0.05	0.04	0.05	0.05	0.04987
Q_{C15}	0	0.05	0.033	0.05	0.05	0.049906
Q_{C17}	0	0.05	0.035	0.05	0.05	0.04997
Q_{C20}	0	0.041	0.039	0.05	0.04406	0.049901
Q_{C21}	0	0.033	0.032	0.05	0.05	0.049946
Q_{C23}	0	0.009	0.013	0.05	0.028004	0.038753
Q_{C24}	0	0.05	0.035	0.05	0.05	0.049867
Q_{C29}	0	0.024	0.0142	0.05	0.025979	0.029098
P_{loss}	**0.05833**	**0.048149**	**0.047694**	**0.046018**	**0.045417**	**0.045435**
VD	0.0097	0	0	0.001456	0	0
PFD	0	0	0	0	0	0

(*continued*)

Table 1. (*continued*)

(b)

Control variable (pu)	HFA [14]	MFO [16]	IGSA [12]	MVMO (F_1)	MVMO (F_2)
(b)					
Control variable (pu)	HFA [14]	MFO [16]	IGSA [12]	MVMO (F_1)	MVMO (F_2)
V_{G1}	1.1	1.1	1.081281	1.1	1.09925
V_{G2}	1.05433	1.0943	1.072177	1.094	1.09325
V_{G5}	1.07514	1.0747	1.050142	1.0745	1.07225
V_{G8}	1.08688	1.0766	1.050234	1.07675	1.0745
V_{G11}	1.1	1.1	1.1	1.1	1.0985
V_{G13}	1.1	1.1	1.068826	1.1	1.097
T_{11}	0.9801	1.0433	1.08	1.052	1.038
T_{12}	0.9500	0.9	0.902	0.9	0.934
T_{15}	0.9702	0.97912	0.99	0.984	0.996
T_{36}	0.9700	0.96474	0.976	0.968	0.977
Q_{C10}	0.04700	0.05	0	0.05	0.046
Q_{C12}	0.04706	0.05	0	0.05	0.0415
Q_{C15}	0.04701	0.04805	0.038	0.05	0.0295
Q_{C17}	0.02306	0.05	0.049	0.05	0.047
Q_{C20}	0.04803	0.04026	0.0395	0.043	0.039
Q_{C21}	0.04902	0.05	0.05	0.05	0.048
Q_{C23}	0.04804	2.5193	0.0275	0.027	0.041
Q_{C24}	0.04805	0.05	0.05	0.05	0.047
Q_{C29}	0.03398	0.021925	0.024	0.0245	0.0255
P_{loss}	**0.04753**	**0.04541**	**0.04762**	**0.045399**	**0.045626**
VD	0.0061	0	0	0	0
PFD	0	0	0	0	0

Table 2. Statistical results for power loss minimization for the IEEE 30 bus test system based on 100 trials.

IEEE Case	30	
Fitness function	F_1	F_2
Best solution, $_{pu}$	0.045399	0.04562
VD, $_{pu}$	0	0
PFD, $_{pu}$	0	0
Worst solution, $_{pu}$	0.045791	0.04570
Mean, $_{pu}$	0.045514	0.04568
Standard deviation	0.0092	0.0014
Average computing time (seconds)	1.8917	1.7687

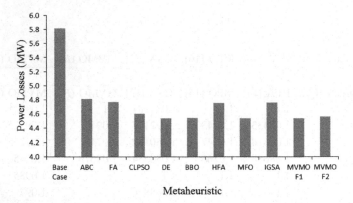

Fig. 3. Power losses obtained with different metaheuristic techniques for IEEE-30 bus test system (Source: Authors).

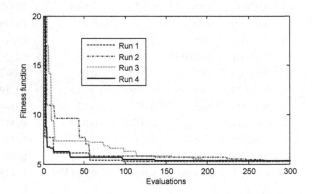

Fig. 4. Convergence of MVMO with F_1 for the IEEE-30 bus test system (Source: Authors)

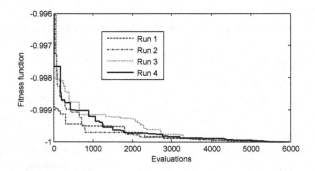

Fig. 5. Convergence of MVMO with F_2 for the IEEE-30 bus test system (Source: Authors)

5 Conclusions

This paper presented an implementation and adaptation of penalty functions within the MVMO metaheuristic to solve the ORPD problem. MVMO is a population-based stochastic optimization technique. The distinctive feature of this algorithm lies on the use of a mapping function applied for mutating new candidate solutions based on the mean and variance of the n-best population attained. Two different constraint handling approaches are implemented: a conventional penalization of deviations from feasible solutions and a product of subfunctions that serves to identify both when a solution is optimal and feasible. Although slightly better solutions were obtained with the classic constraint handling approach; the second one is faster, which makes it more suitable for online applications.

It was found that the proposed adaptation of the MVMO to approach the ORPD problem is able to find better results than those previously reported for the IEEE 30 bus test system. The values of control variables are presented so that results can be verified by researchers for future comparison with other metaheuristics.

Acknowledgements. The authors acknowledge the sustainability project of Universidad de Antioquia and Colciencias (Project code 1115-745-54929; contract 056-2017) for the economic support in the development of this work.

References

1. Mohseni-Bonab, S.M., Rabiee, A.: Optimal reactive power dispatch: a review, and a new stochastic voltage stability constrained multi-objective model at the presence of uncertain wind power generation. Transm. Distrib. IET Gener. **11**, 815–829 (2017). https://doi.org/10.1049/iet-gtd.2016.1545
2. Ela, A.A.A.E., Abido, M.A., Spea, S.R.: Differential evolution algorithm for optimal reactive power dispatch. Electr. Power Syst. Res. **81**, 458–464 (2011). https://doi.org/10.1016/j.epsr.2010.10.005
3. Mukherjee, A., Mukherjee, V.: Solution of optimal reactive power dispatch by chaotic krill herd algorithm. Transm. Distrib. IET Gener. **9**, 2351–2362 (2015). https://doi.org/10.1049/iet-gtd.2015.0077
4. Gandomi, A.H., Alavi, A.H.: Krill herd: a new bio-inspired optimization algorithm. Commun. Nonlinear Sci. Numer. Simul. **17**, 4831–4845 (2012). https://doi.org/10.1016/j.cnsns.2012.05.010
5. Yoshida, H., Kawata, K., Fukuyama, Y., Takayama, S., Nakanishi, Y.: A particle swarm optimization for reactive power and voltage control considering voltage security assessment. IEEE Trans. Power Syst. **15**, 1232–1239 (2000). https://doi.org/10.1109/59.898095
6. Esmin, A.A.A., Lambert-Torres, G., de Souza, A.C.Z.: A hybrid particle swarm optimization applied to loss power minimization. IEEE Trans. Power Syst. **20**, 859–866 (2005). https://doi.org/10.1109/TPWRS.2005.846049
7. Gutiérrez, D., Villa, W.M., López-Lezama, J.M.: Flujo Óptimo Reactivo mediante Optimización por Enjambre de Partículas. Inf. Tecnológica. **28**, 215–224 (2017). https://doi.org/10.4067/S0718-07642017000500020

8. Mahadevan, K., Kannan, P.S.: Comprehensive learning particle swarm optimization for reactive power dispatch. Appl. Soft Comput. **10**, 641–652 (2010). https://doi.org/10.1016/j.asoc.2009.08.038

9. Singh, R.P., Mukherjee, V., Ghoshal, S.P.: Optimal reactive power dispatch by particle swarm optimization with an aging leader and challengers. Appl. Soft Comput. **29**, 298–309 (2015). https://doi.org/10.1016/j.asoc.2015.01.006

10. Duman, S., Sonmez, Y., Guvenc, U., Yorukeren, N.: Optimal reactive power dispatch using a gravitational search algorithm. Transm. Distrib. IET Gener. **6**, 563–576 (2012). https://doi.org/10.1049/iet-gtd.2011.0681

11. Rashedi, E., Nezamabadi-pour, H., Saryazdi, S.: GSA: a gravitational search algorithm. Inf. Sci. **179**, 2232–2248 (2009). https://doi.org/10.1016/j.ins.2009.03.004

12. Chen, G., Liu, L., Zhang, Z., Huang, S.: Optimal reactive power dispatch by improved GSA-based algorithm with the novel strategies to handle constraints. Appl. Soft Comput. **50**, 58–70 (2017). https://doi.org/10.1016/j.asoc.2016.11.008

13. Shaw, B., Mukherjee, V., Ghoshal, S.P.: Solution of reactive power dispatch of power systems by an opposition-based gravitational search algorithm. Int. J. Electr. Power Energy Syst. **55**, 29–40 (2014). https://doi.org/10.1016/j.ijepes.2013.08.010

14. Rajan, A., Malakar, T.: Optimal reactive power dispatch using hybrid Nelder-Mead simplex based firefly algorithm. Int. J. Electr. Power Energy Syst. **66**, 9–24 (2015). https://doi.org/10.1016/j.ijepes.2014.10.041

15. Bhattacharya, A., Chattopadhyay, P.K.: Biogeography-based optimization for solution of optimal power flow problem. In: ECTI-CON2010: The 2010 ECTI International Conference on Electrical Engineering/Electronics, Computer, Telecommunications and Information Technology, pp. 435–439 (2010)

16. Mei, R.N.S., Sulaiman, M.H., Mustaffa, Z., Daniyal, H.: Optimal reactive power dispatch solution by loss minimization using moth-flame optimization technique. Appl. Soft Comput. **59**, 210–222 (2017)

17. Rojas, D.G., Lezama, J.L., Villa, W.: Metaheuristic techniques applied to the optimal reactive power dispatch: a review. IEEE Lat. Am. Trans. **14**, 2253–2263 (2016). https://doi.org/10.1109/TLA.2016.7530421

18. Villa-Acevedo, W.M., López-Lezama, J.M., Valencia-Velásquez, J.A.: A novel constraint handling approach for the optimal reactive power dispatch problem. Energies **11**, 2352 (2018). https://doi.org/10.3390/en11092352

19. Erlich, I., Venayagamoorthy, G.K., Worawat, N.: A mean-variance optimization algorithm. In: IEEE Congress on Evolutionary Computation, pp. 1–6 (2010). https://doi.org/10.1109/CEC.2010.5586027

20. Erlich, I.: Mean-variance mapping optimization algorithm home page. https://www.uni-due.de/mvmo/

21. Rueda, J.L., Erlich, I.: Optimal dispatch of reactive power sources by using MVMOs optimization. In: 2013 IEEE Computational Intelligence Applications in Smart Grid (CIASG), pp. 29–36 (2013). https://doi.org/10.1109/CIASG.2013.6611495

22. Cepeda, J.C., Rueda, J.L., Erlich, I.: Identification of dynamic equivalents based on heuristic optimization for smart grid applications. In: 2012 IEEE Congress on Evolutionary Computation, pp. 1–8 (2012). https://doi.org/10.1109/CEC.2012.6256493

23. Rueda, J.L., Erlich, I.: Evaluation of the mean-variance mapping optimization for solving multimodal problems. In: 2013 IEEE Symposium on Swarm Intelligence (SIS), pp. 7–14 (2013). https://doi.org/10.1109/SIS.2013.6615153

Memberships Networks for High-Dimensional Fuzzy Clustering Visualization

Leandro Ariza-Jiménez[1](✉)[iD], Luisa F. Villa[2][iD], and Olga Lucía Quintero[1][iD]

[1] Mathematical Modeling Research Group, Universidad EAFIT, Medellín, Colombia
{larizaj,oquinte1}@eafit.edu.co
[2] System Engineering Research Group, ARKADIUS, Universidad de Medellín, Medellín, Colombia
lvilla@udem.edu.co

Abstract. Visualizing the cluster structure of high-dimensional data is a non-trivial task that must be able to deal with the large dimensionality of the input data. Unlike hard clustering structures, visualization of fuzzy clusterings is not as straightforward because soft clustering algorithms yield more complex clustering structures. Here is introduced the concept of membership networks, an undirected weighted network constructed based on the fuzzy partition matrix that represents a fuzzy clustering. This simple network-based method allows understanding visually how elements involved in this kind of complex data clustering structures interact with each other, without relying on a visualization of the input data themselves. Experiment results demonstrated the usefulness of the proposed method for the exploration and analysis of clustering structures on the Iris flower data set and two large and unlabeled financial datasets, which describes the financial profile of customers of a local bank.

Keywords: Fuzzy clustering · Clustering visualization · Membership network · High-dimensional data

1 Introduction

Practical problems and applications related to data clustering not only can benefit from organizing data into unknown groups, but also from understanding how groups are constituted and related to each other [27]. One way to obtain this information is by using methods to visualize clustering results [16,17]. Since most data of interest are high-dimensional, the visualization of the clustering structure of such data is a non-trivial task that must be able to deal with the large dimensionality of the input data.

For clustering structures obtained from the application of hard clustering algorithms on high-dimensional data, an indirect and straightforward solution to show these cluster structures is projecting the original data down to two- or three-dimensional spaces [21,23]. Then, different colors or symbols can be

© Springer Nature Switzerland AG 2019
J. C. Figueroa-García et al. (Eds.): WEA 2019, CCIS 1052, pp. 263–273, 2019.
https://doi.org/10.1007/978-3-030-31019-6_23

used to represent how data objects were clustered in a scatter plot of the data. Traditional methods to obtain this low-dimensional spaces are principal component analysis (PCA), multidimensional scaling (MDS), and self-organizing maps [2,25]; or new methods like the t-Stochastic Neighbor Embedding algorithm [18,19]. However, due to these methods reduce somehow the data dimensionality, an accurate representation of the original cluster structure is not guaranteed [29].

On the contrary, the visualization of fuzzy clusterings is not as straightforward as in the case of crisp clustering results. Indeed, unlike the output of a hard clustering algorithm, which is just a list of clusters with their corresponding members, soft clustering algorithms yield complex clustering structures, wherein data objects can belong to one or more clusters with probabilities [30].

So far, several works have addressed the problem of visualizing high-dimensional fuzzy clusterings. In [1,5], a method is proposed to visualize fuzzy clustering results by performing an iterative process based on an MDS method that maps the cluster centers and the data into a two-dimensional space taking into account the membership values of the data. In [3], a method is presented for the interactive exploration of fuzzy clusters using the novel concept of neighbor-grams, which is not well suited for medium-sized data sets. In [12], a technique is introduced to represent high-dimensional fuzzy clusters as intersecting spheres, and it is suitable for larger datasets; however, it heavily depends on the use of a three-dimensional visualization to preserve the overlapping regions appropriately in the original space. In [26,31], Radviz, a radial non-linear visualization tool that displays multidimensional data in a two-dimensional projection, is used for developing a visualization that expresses the overall distribution of the membership degrees of all data points in a fuzzy clustering; however, as [31] pointed out, scalability is a problem for the Radviz-based visualizations when the number of clusters is large. In [24] fuzzy partitions from data are visualized by using MDS to map the degree of belongingness of data objects to clusters into a metric vector space which has mathematical dimensions.

In this work is proposed a straightforward representation of the fuzzy clustering results from high-dimensional data based on a simple network-based scheme, without relying on a visualization of the data itself. To this end, here is introduced the concept of membership network, which is an undirected weighted network constructed based on the fuzzy partition matrix that represents a particular fuzzy clustering.

The remainder of this paper is organized as follows: Sect. 2 briefly presents a theoretical background for data clustering and networks. Section 3 introduces the proposed network-based method to represent fuzzy clustering structures in high-dimensional data. Results and discussion are presented in Sect. 4, and finally, the concluding remarks can be found in Sect. 5.

2   Theoretical Background

As mentioned before, this work deals with a network-based representation of fuzzy clusterings on multidimensional data. Consequently, we first introduce here the basics for data clustering and networks.

2.1   Data Clustering

Clustering is the term used for methods whose objective is to partition a given set of unlabeled data objects into groups, known as clusters, such that data objects in the same group are similar and those in different groups are dissimilar to each other [4].

Suppose that $\mathbf{X} = \{\mathbf{x}_1, \mathbf{x}_2, \dots, \mathbf{x}_N\}$ is a set of N d-dimensional data objects, where $\mathbf{x}_j \in \mathbb{R}^d$. There are two broad forms of clustering, namely hard clustering and soft clustering, also referred to as crisp and soft clustering, respectively. In the first case, clustering methods obtain a K-partition of $\mathbf{X}$, $C = \{C_1, C_2, \dots, C_K\}$, $K \leq N$, such that $C_i \neq \emptyset$, $C_1 \cup C_2 \cup \dots \cup C_K = \mathbf{X}$, and each data object belongs to exactly one cluster, i.e. $C_i \cap C_j = \emptyset$, for $i, j = 1, \dots, K$ and $j \neq i$.

On the contrary, soft clustering considers that the boundaries between clusters are ambiguous, so that a data object $\mathbf{x}_j$ can belong to more than one cluster C_i with a degree of membership $u_{ij} \in [0, 1]$, such that

$$\sum_{i=1}^{K} u_{ij} = 1, \ \forall j = 1, \dots, N \tag{1}$$

and

$$0 < \sum_{j=1}^{N} u_{ij} < N, \ \forall i = 1, \dots, K. \tag{2}$$

Based on the above membership degrees, a fuzzy clustering can be represented by a $K \times n$ matrix $U = [u_{ij}]$, known as the fuzzy partition matrix.

The most representative algorithms for hard and soft clustering are the K-means and the Fuzzy c-Means (FCM) algorithms, respectively. Both these algorithms are center-based clustering algorithms, that is, algorithms that look for a predefined number of clusters. These algorithms assume the existence of clusters by using the distances of data points from the cluster centers. Then, these algorithms perform an iterative optimization procedure to seek an optimal clustering of data. FCM is considered the fuzzy counterpart K-means and uses a parameter $m \in [1, \infty]$ that controls the "fuzziness" of the resulting clusters. In particular, when m is close to 1, the entries of the fuzzy partition matrix U converges to 0 or 1, and clusters become crispier; whereas when m increases, the entries of the same matrix decreases and clusters become fuzzier [30].

2.2   Networks

A network is a set of items, which we will call nodes or vertices, with connections between them, called links or edges [22]. Network nodes can be organized into groups, commonly called communities, that have a higher probability of being connected between them than to members of other groups [6].

Formally, a network can be denoted as $G = (V, E)$, where V is the set of nodes and E is the set of links such that $E \subseteq V \times V$. The pair (p, q) is the link connecting the node p with the node q. Links can be undirected, i.e. if $(p, q) \in E$ then $(q, p) \in E$. In addition, links can be associated with a real number, called its weight, by defining a weight function $\omega : E \to \mathbb{R}$. Finally, $|V|$ and $|E|$ represent the number of nodes and links, respectively.

Importance of networks lies in its ability to represent and facilitate the study and analysis of the interactions between real-world entities [22]. Network visualization can improve the understanding of the structure of those interactions [10]. To this end, layout algorithms that automatically arrange the nodes and links in an aesthetically pleasing way are used (see [10,13] for a recent review of these algorithms). For visualization purposes, the family of force-directed algorithms is commonly used today [7,11,14]. These algorithms model a network as a physical system where nodes are attracted and repelled according to some force [10]. Some of the algorithms included in this family are Fruchterman-Reingold [8], GRIP [9], OpenOrd [20], and ForceAtlas2 [15].

3   Membership Networks

Here is introduced a novel method to visualize clusterings obtained from the application of soft clustering algorithms on high-dimensional data. Rather than using the original data itself, the cluster memberships are used as a clue to link the data objects to the resulting clusters and revealing the similarities among the formers through a membership network. Moreover, this kind of visualization facilitates the understanding of the uncertainties present in the data without any *a priori* knowledge or assumptions.

Consider a set of N data objects, $\mathbf{X} = \{\mathbf{x}_1, \ldots, \mathbf{x}_N\}$, $\mathbf{x}_j \in \mathbb{R}^d$. Let $A = \{A_1, \ldots, A_C\}$ be a clustering provided by a center-based soft partitioning clustering algorithm, e.g. FCM, represented by a C-by-N fuzzy partition matrix $U = [u_{ij}]$ and let a_i be the center of the partition A_i for $i = 1, \ldots, C$.

An undirected weighted membership network, $G_U = (V, E)$, that represents the above fuzzy clustering can be constructed as follows:

1. Consider each data object $\mathbf{x}_j$ and each cluster center $\mathbf{a}_i$ as node of G_U, i.e. let $V = \{\mathbf{x}_1, \ldots, \mathbf{x}_N\} \cup \{a_1, \ldots, a_K\}$.
2. Link each data object $\mathbf{x}_j$ with every cluster center a_i to represent the belonging of $\mathbf{x}_j$ to more than one cluster, i.e. let $E = \{(\mathbf{x}_j, \alpha_i), i = 1, \ldots, C; j = 1, \ldots, N\}$.
3. Associate to each link $(\mathbf{x}_j, \mathbf{a}_i)$ a weight $\omega(\mathbf{x}_i, \alpha_j)$ equal to the degree of membership of $\mathbf{x}_j$ in the cluster A_i, i.e. let $\omega(\mathbf{x}_j, \mathbf{a}_i) = u_{ij}$.

A mathematical property of the obtained membership network is that it allows computing a cluster validity index for fuzzy clusterings, called partition coefficient (PC) [28], as $PC = (2|V|)^{-1}\text{Tr}(W^2)$, where W is the symmetric $|V|$-by-$|V|$ matrix obtained when all of the weight edges of the graph G_U are recorded in a single matrix.

Figure 1 provides an example to illustrate the proposed method for fuzzy clustering visualization. Eight multidimensional data objects were clustered into two groups using a fuzzy clustering algorithm. The clustering result is a fuzzy partition matrix U. The undirected weighted membership network that represents this fuzzy clustering has as many data objects as nodes. Two additional nodes, nodes 9 and 10, represent the centers of the fuzzy clusters. Data object nodes are connected to the cluster center nodes using links having weights given by the entries of the matrix U. For clarity, the color and the thickness of the links between data object nodes and cluster center nodes is proportional to the degree of membership of each data object to the different clusters. Darker and thicker links indicate a higher degree of membership.

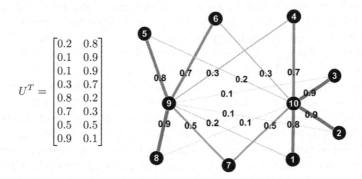

Fig. 1. Representing a fuzzy clustering result (left) as an undirected weighted membership network (right) using the proposed method.

Once a network membership is built, it can be visualized using a layout algorithm that automatically arranges the nodes and links in an aesthetically pleasing way. In particular, the OpenOrd algorithm [20] is used here for this task, since it is an algorithm suitable for drawing undirected weighted networks, and able to provide layouts for large-scale real-world networks wherein clusters can be better distinguished.

4   Results and Discussion

Experiments were performed to demonstrate the feasibility of the network-based approach for visualizing soft clusterings obtained from different datasets. As the purpose of this paper is mainly on presenting a clustering visualization method, the traditional FCM algorithm was used to obtain fuzzy clusterings from the data sets. In particular, the number of clusters C and the fuzzification parameter m were manually set depending on the case.

4.1   Iris Flower Dataset

The proposed visualization method is first demonstrated using the widely known Iris flower data set. This multidimensional data set consist of four morphological measurements taken on 50 samples from three different species of Iris flowers: setosa, versicolor, and virginica. In particular, it is known that all the samples of Iris setosa are linearly separable from the samples of the other two species, while the latter species are not linearly separable from each other.

Three soft clusters for the Iris data set were initially obtained using FCM with $m = 2$. Figure 2A shows the membership network constructed based on the fuzzy partition matrix that represented the resulting clustering. Three groups of nodes representing the 3-cluster structure are visible in this network-based representation. Groups at the top of the figure represent two clusters that contain virginica and versicolor samples, while the remaining group represents a cluster with setosa samples. Each group of nodes has an anchor node which represents the cluster center, and, for clarity purposes, the size of the cluster center node is larger than the nodes representing data objects. Darker and thicker links indicate a higher degree of membership. As expected, intra-cluster links have a greater membership weight in comparison with extra-cluster links when clusters are well separated from each other. However, as the boundary between the clusters of virginica and versicolor samples is ambiguous, there exist nodes in this boundary belonging both clusters with a no well-defined degree of membership, and thus they are linked to both cluster center nodes with darker and thicker connections.

Since m is a crucial parameter of FCM, membership networks representing fuzzy clusterings obtained after running FCM on the Iris data set for different values of m were also constructed. Figure 2 also shows the behavior of the built membership networks under these conditions. As stated before, when m is close to 1 the entries of matrix U converge to 0 and 1, i.e., clusters become crispier. This is represented as well-separated groups whose nodes are compactly arranged around the cluster center node, except for those nodes which are in the boundary of two overlapping clusters (Fig. 2B). As m is increased, the cluster fuzziness also increased, and thus groups start to overlap each other due to the strength of the association between the nodes, and the clusters are not clearly defined (Fig. 2C and D).

4.2   Financial Datasets

The applicability of the proposed visualization method on large real-world data with unknown clustering structure is demonstrated using two datasets which describe the financial behavior of 18.583 customers of a local bank, during a particular time window. The first data set describes each customer using four

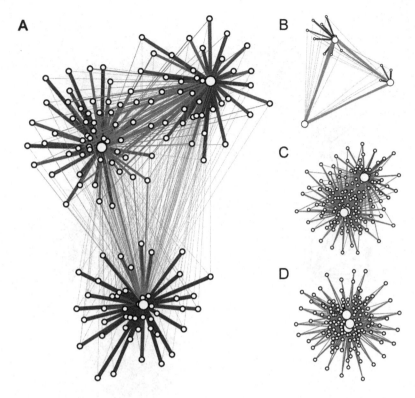

Fig. 2. Membership network representing a 3-cluster fuzzy structure discovered by the FCM algorithm on the Iris flower data set for different values of the fuzzification parameter m. (A) $m = 2$. (B) $m = 1.1$. (C) $m = 5$. (D) $m = 8$.

variables which characterize its transactions with other customers, and the second data set consists of ten variables describing the financial statements of each customer.

Since these datasets have an unknown underlying structure, they were arbitrarily clustered into ten groups of customers using the FCM algorithm with $m = 2$. Figures 3 and 4 show the resulting network-based representation for each soft clustering.

Data exploration based on organizing both datasets into ten arbitrarily soft clusters and using the network-based approach to visualize both clustering results demonstrate how different are their corresponding underlying structures. The clustering structure provided by FCM on the first data set consist of both large and predominant groups, and small groups (Fig. 3), while the same algorithm partitioned the second data set into regular size clusters (Fig. 4). Furthermore, larger groups discovered in the first data set are more closely connected in comparison with the smaller groups (Fig. 3), which could indicate that the former groups represent data objects lying in large regions with almost uniform data density, while the latter groups consist of data objects that are outliers. A

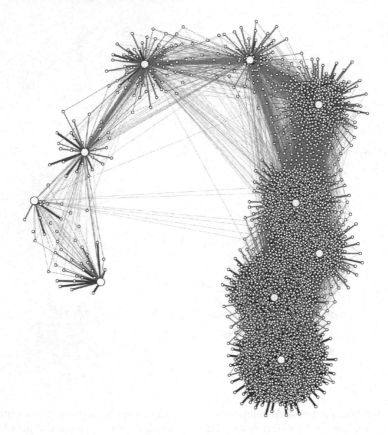

Fig. 3. Membership network representing a 10-cluster fuzzy structure discovered by the FCM algorithm on the first financial data set for $m = 2$.

subsequent examination of these group of outliers indicated that they correspond to clients who participate in numerous and large transactions, and thus these clients could be of interest for receiving special banking services related with financial transactions. On the other hand, the well-connected groups of nodes discovered in the second data set (Fig. 4) may also consist of data objects sharing the same feature like the larger groups in the first data set (Fig. 3). However, this result could also be interpreted as there is no evidence of the existence of natural groups in the second data set, and thus, the FCM algorithm only performed segmentation of the bank customers. Finally, the closeness between the three cluster center nodes in the middle of Fig. 4 could indicate that a cluster has been wrongly split into three clusters, as FCM necessarily must partition the data into a given number of clusters.

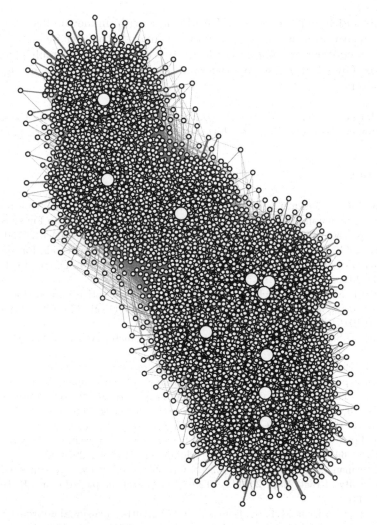

Fig. 4. Membership network representing a 10-cluster fuzzy structure discovered by the FCM algorithm on the second financial data set for $m = 2$.

5 Conclusions

In this work is presented a method to visualize clustering structures obtained from the application of fuzzy clustering algorithms on high-dimensional data. The proposed method uses undirected weighted membership networks to represent fuzzy partition matrices. This simple network-based method allows understanding visually how elements (data objects and clusters) involved in this kind of complex data clustering structures interact each other, without relying on a visualization of the input high-dimensional data itself. The proposed visualization method provides a means to represent near-crisp and very fuzzy clustering structures and to explore large real-world data with unknown clustering structure. As future work, we plan to extend our analysis to other methods, besides FCM, that consider the notion of data objects belonging to multiple groups, such as the Gustafson-Kessel algorithm and the Possibilistic c-Means algorithm, among others.

Acknowledgements. This research work was supported by Centro de Excelencia y Apropiación en Big Data y Data Analytics -Alianza CAOBA- and Universidad EAFIT.

References

1. Abonyi, J., Babuska, R.: FUZZSAM - visualization of fuzzy clustering results by modified Sammon mapping. In: IEEE International Conference on Fuzzy Systems, vol. 1, pp. 365–370 (2004). https://doi.org/10.1109/FUZZY.2004.1375750
2. Bécavin, C., Benecke, A.: New dimensionality reduction methods for the representation of high dimensional 'omics' data. Expert Rev. Mol. Diagn. **11**(1), 27–34 (2011). https://doi.org/10.1586/erm.10.95
3. Berthold, M.R., Wiswedel, B., Patterson, D.E.: Interactive exploration of fuzzy clusters using neighborgrams. Fuzzy Sets Syst. **149**(1), 21–37 (2005). https://doi.org/10.1016/j.fss.2004.07.009
4. Everitt, B.S., Landau, S., Leese, M., Stahl, D.: Cluster Analysis. Wiley, Hoboken (2011)
5. Feil, B., Balasko, B., Abonyi, J.: Visualization of fuzzy clusters by fuzzy Sammon mapping projection: application to the analysis of phase space trajectories. Soft Comput. **11**(5), 479–488 (2007). https://doi.org/10.1007/s00500-006-0111-5
6. Fortunato, S., Hric, D.: Community detection in networks: a user guide. Phys. Rep. **659**, 1–44 (2016). https://doi.org/10.1016/j.physrep.2016.09.002
7. Francalanci, C., Hussain, A.: Influence-based Twitter browsing with NavigTweet. Inf. Syst. **64**, 119–131 (2017). https://doi.org/10.1016/j.is.2016.07.012
8. Fruchterman, T.M., Reingold, E.M.: Graph drawing by force-directed placement. Softw. Pract. Exp. **21**(11), 1129–1164 (1991). https://doi.org/10.1002/spe.4380211102
9. Gajer, P., Goodrich, M.T., Kobourov, S.G.: A multi-dimensional approach to force-directed layouts of large graphs. Comput. Geom. **29**(1), 3–18 (2004). https://doi.org/10.1016/j.comgeo.2004.03.014
10. Gibson, H., Faith, J., Vickers, P.: A survey of two-dimensional graph layout techniques for information visualisation. Inf. Vis. **12**(3–4), 324–357 (2013). https://doi.org/10.1177/1473871612455749
11. Heberle, H., Carazzolle, M.F., Telles, G.P., Meirelles, G.V., Minghim, R.: Cell NetVis: a web tool for visualization of biological networks using force-directed layout constrained by cellular components. BMC Bioinform. **18**(S10), 395 (2017). https://doi.org/10.1186/s12859-017-1787-5
12. Höppner, F., Klawonn, F.: Visualising clusters in high-dimensional data sets by intersecting spheres. In: Proceedings of 2006 International Symposium on Evolving Fuzzy Systems, EFS 2006, vol. 2, no. 2, pp. 106–111 (2006). https://doi.org/10.1109/ISEFS.2006.251180
13. Hu, Y., Shi, L.: Visualizing large graphs. Wiley Interdiscip. Rev. Comput. Stat. **7**(2), 115–136 (2015). https://doi.org/10.1002/wics.1343

14. Ishida, Y., Itoh, T.: A force-directed visualization of conversation logs. In: Proceedings of Computer Graphics International Conference - CGI 2017, pp. 1–5. ACM Press, New York (2017). https://doi.org/10.1145/3095140.3095156
15. Jacomy, M., Venturini, T., Heymann, S., Bastian, M.: ForceAtlas2, a continuous graph layout algorithm for handy network visualization designed for the Gephi software. PLoS ONE **9**(6), 1–12 (2014). https://doi.org/10.1371/journal.pone.0098679
16. Leisch, F.: A toolbox for K-centroids cluster analysis. Comput. Stat. Data Anal. **51**(2), 526–544 (2006). https://doi.org/10.1016/j.csda.2005.10.006
17. Leisch, F.: Neighborhood graphs, stripes and shadow plots for cluster visualization. Stat. Comput. **20**(4), 457–469 (2010). https://doi.org/10.1007/s11222-009-9137-8
18. van der Maaten, L.: Accelerating t-SNE using tree-based algorithms. J. Mach. Learn. Res. **15**, 3221–3245 (2014). http://jmlr.org/papers/v15/vandermaaten14a.html
19. van der Maaten, L., Hinton, G.: Visualizing high-dimensional data using t-SNE. J. Mach. Learn. Res. **9**, 2579–2605 (2008). http://www.jmlr.org/papers/v9/vandermaaten08a.html
20. Martin, S., Brown, W.M., Klavans, R., Boyack, K.W.: OpenOrd: an open-source toolbox for large graph layout. In: Proceedings of SPIE, p. 7868, January 2011. https://doi.org/10.1117/12.871402
21. Metsalu, T., Vilo, J.: ClustVis: a web tool for visualizing clustering of multivariate data using Principal Component Analysis and heatmap. Nucleic Acids Res. **43**(W1), W566–W570 (2015). https://doi.org/10.1093/nar/gkv468
22. Newman, M.E.J.: The structure and function of complex networks. SIAM Rev. **45**(2), 167–256 (2003). https://doi.org/10.1137/S003614450342480
23. Pison, G., Struyf, A., Rousseeuw, P.J.: Displaying a clustering with CLUSPLOT. Comput. Stat. Data Anal. **30**(4), 381–392 (1999). https://doi.org/10.1016/S0167-9473(98)00102-9
24. Sato-Ilic, M., Ilic, P.: Visualization of fuzzy clustering result in metric space. Proc. Comput. Sci. **96**, 1666–1675 (2016). https://doi.org/10.1016/j.procs.2016.08.214
25. Serra, A., Galdi, P., Tagliaferri, R.: Machine learning for bioinformatics and neuroimaging. Wiley Interdisc. Rev.: Data Min. Knowl. Discov. **8**(5), 1–33 (2018). https://doi.org/10.1002/widm.1248
26. Sharko, J., Grinstein, G.: Visualizing fuzzy clusters using RadViz. In: Proceedings of International Conference Information Visualisation, pp. 307–316 (2009). https://doi.org/10.1109/IV.2009.74
27. Wang, K.J., Yan, X.H., Chen, L.F.: Geometric double-entity model for recognizing far-near relations of clusters. Sci. China Inf. Sci. **54**(10), 2040–2050 (2011). https://doi.org/10.1007/s11432-011-4386-5
28. Wang, W., Zhang, Y.: On fuzzy cluster validity indices. Fuzzy Sets Syst. **158**(19), 2095–2117 (2007). https://doi.org/10.1016/j.fss.2007.03.004
29. Xu, R., Wunsch, D.: Survey of clustering algorithms. IEEE Trans. Neural Netw. **16**(3), 645–678 (2005). https://doi.org/10.1109/TNN.2005.845141
30. Xu, R., Wunsch, D.C.: Clustering algorithms in biomedical research: a review. IEEE Rev. Biomed. Eng. **3**, 120–54 (2010). https://doi.org/10.1109/RBME.2010.2083647
31. Zhou, F., et al.: A radviz-based visualization for understanding fuzzy clustering results. In: Proceedings of 10th International Symposium on Visual Information Communication and Interaction, pp. 9–15. ACM, New York (2017). https://doi.org/10.1145/3105971.3105980

Speed Estimation of an Induction Motor with Sensorless Vector Control at Low Speed Range Using Neural Networks

Martin Gallo Nieves, Jorge Luis Diaz Rodriguez[(⊠)],
and Jaime Antonio Gonzalez Castellanos

Universidad de Pamplona, Pamplona, Colombia
martingallo6@gmail.com, jdiazcu@gmail.com,
gcjaime@gmail.com

Abstract. This paper deals with the study, design and implementation of a speed estimation technique, using an Artificial Neural Network (ANN), for a three-phase induction motor type Squirrel Cage. The main objective of this technique is to estimate the speed of the engine from its own conditions at low speed, with the purpose of applying vector control without the use of a traditional speed sensor that supplies the control loop with the speed of rotation the motor. When replacing the traditional sensor with RNA, a sensorless control loop is obtained. The training of the RNA was done collecting data in different ranges of engine speed, both empty and loaded. The simulation of the system is carried out in the Simulink platform, from the Matlab software package and the implementation of the control strategy is done using the Raspberry Pi 3B card.

Keywords: Induction motor · Speed estimation · Vector control · Sensorless control · Artificial neural networks

1 Introduction

Squirrel-cage three-phase electric motors are the most commonly used in industrial processes for mechanical power supply. This is due to its characteristics compared to other types of electric motors, such as: lower weight, low cost, low physical robustness (weight/power ratio) and fewer parts [1].

However, a large part of the equipment and applications used in the industry must operate at variable speeds and controlled in an agile and precise way for its good performance.

Within the control strategies of the induction motors and especially the indirect vector control it is necessary to measure the rotor speed. This measurement was made from analog speed meters that present noise problems. Then appeared digital speed meters such as encoders, resolvers and photoelectric meters that allowed to solve most of the disadvantages of analog sensors but with a higher cost.

In the present work, a speed estimation strategy based on artificial intelligence is used, using neural networks that achieve excellent results by applying a novel strategy based on the use of delays in the data, applying it to a Sensorless vector control algorithm.

© Springer Nature Switzerland AG 2019
J. C. Figueroa-García et al. (Eds.): WEA 2019, CCIS 1052, pp. 274–284, 2019.
https://doi.org/10.1007/978-3-030-31019-6_24

2 Induction Motor

If a three-phase voltage is applied to an induction motor, three three-phase currents will circulate; these currents produce a magnetic field Bs that rotates counterclockwise [1].
The rotation speed of the magnetic field is given by the following equation:

$$n_s = 120 f_e / p \tag{1}$$

Where:

n_s: speed of the magnetic field [revolutions per minute or simply *rpm*].
f_e: frequency of the input voltage (power source) [Hz].
p: number of motor poles.

2.1 Induction Motor Analysis

Figure 1 shows a diagram of a three-phase induction machine. This type of machines has cylindrical magnetic structures in both the rotor and the stator. These structures are the same in each of the parts of the electric motor, with a phase difference between them [2]. Additionally, the cage rotor induction machine is also symmetrical, for the same reasons. However, the number of rotor phases is greater than three. In fact, each bar of the cage constitutes a phase.

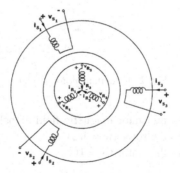

Fig. 1. Schematic representation of a three-phase induction motor.

2.2 Mathematical Model of the Three-Phase Induction Motor

The voltage model of a induction motor is defined by the sum of the voltage drop plus the magnetic flux equations. It is represented through the following equations [2]:

$$V_S = R_S I_S + L_{SS} \frac{dI_S}{dt} + L_{SR}(\theta) \frac{dI_R}{dt} + \frac{\partial L_{SR}(\theta)}{\partial \theta} I_R \frac{d\theta}{dt} \tag{2}$$

$$V_R = R_{RR} I_R + L_{RR} \frac{dI_R}{dt} + L_{RS}(\theta) \frac{dI_S}{dt} + \frac{\partial L_{RS}(\theta)}{\partial \theta} I_S \frac{d\theta}{dt} \tag{3}$$

In these equations, V_S represents the voltages at the stator terminals and V_R is the voltage at the rotor terminals which, in the case of the squirrel-cage motor, is equal to zero. R_S and R_R are the matrix representation of the stator and rotor resistances, respectively.

2.3   Simulation of the Three-Phase Induction Motor

Figure 2 shows the model of the three-phase induction motor resulting from the equations of voltages (1) and (2) projected on the d-q axes, and referred to the stator and the rotor respectively. It also shows the block that generates the voltages from the maximum voltage, the frequency and establishing a phase difference of 120° electric degrees between each phase. This model is implemented using Matlab/Simulink blocks that allows to simulate the electric motor in the following axes reference frames:

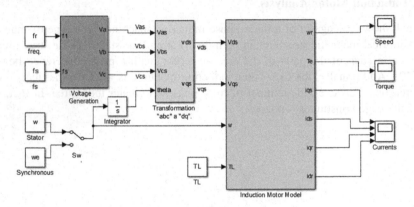

Fig. 2 Induction motor model.

- Reference frame fixed to the stator magnetic field (synchronism speed) ($w = w_e$).
- Reference frame fixed to the rotor ($w = w_R$).
- Reference frame fixed to the stator ($w = 0$).

2.4   Simulation Results

The motor data used in the simulation are presented in Table 1.

Table 1. Induction motor parameters.

Parameter	Value	Parameter	Value
P	2 poles	L_R	144.6 [mH]
R_S	1.0 [ohm]	L_M	136.0 [mH]
R_R	1.3 [ohm]	Jm	0.022 [Kg m^2]
L_S	35.4 [mH]		

The resulting rotor speed of the electric motor model is shown in Fig. 3. It can be verified that the motor speed reached 377 rad/sec in more than 1.5 s.

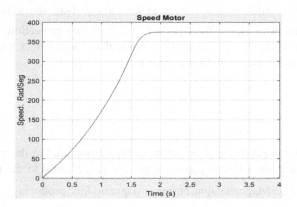

Fig. 3. Rotor speed at no load condition.

3 Vector Control of the Induction Motor

Vector control, also called Oriented Field Control (FOC), was proposed Hasse [3] and Blaschke [4]. This control strategy allows independent control of magnetic field flux and electromagnetic torque. This is achieved by reducing the non-linear model of the motor to a model referred to two orthogonal axes d-q, which allows the induction motor to be modeled in the same way as a separate excitation DC motor [5]. Transforming from a three-phase system to a two-phase system, using space vectors and the transformation α-β to a system of axes d-q. Allowing to control the magnetic flux by means of the regulation of the current component of the direct d axis, while the torque is controlled by regulating the current associated with the quadrature q axis.

Figure 4 shows the vector diagram, with the axes of coordinates α and β stationary, and d and q the components of the vector axes, which are rotated by an angle λ.

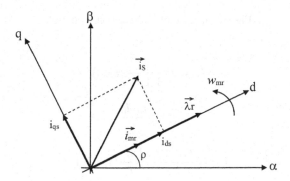

Fig. 4. Vector diagram of the axes d-q.

The Field Oriented Controller (FOC) is responsible for positioning the magnetic flux vector directly on the axis d, so that the quadrature current is zero ($i_{Sq} = 0$). The magnetic flux must also be kept constant so that the electromagnetic torque is proportional to the variation of the current in the axis q. Thus the motor is controlled indirectly through the stator current ($\overrightarrow{i_S}$). Through its two projections on the axes d-q provide two components, real part (i_{Sd}) controls the magnetic flux and the imaginary part (i_{Sq}) controls the electromagnetic torque.

$$\overrightarrow{i_S} = i_{Sd} + ji_{Sq} \tag{4}$$

Where:

$i_{Sd}\angle\lambda$: Stator current in the d-axis component proportional to the magnetic flux.
$i_{Sq}\angle T_e$: Stator current in the q-axis component proportional to the torque.
$\overrightarrow{i_{mR}} = \overrightarrow{\lambda_R}\big/L_M$: Magnetization current (magnetic flux producing).

3.1   Indirect Vector Control Method

The angle λ for the indirect vector control method is obtained through the slip calculation, applying Eq. 7. Figure 5 shows the general indirect scheme of vector control, the inputs of said system being the i_{Sd} currents (reference values of magnetic flux) and i_{Sq} (electromagnetic torque reference values).

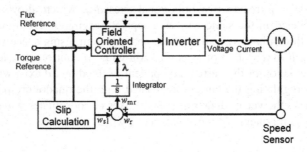

Fig. 5.   Scheme of indirect vector control.

$$\lambda_r(s) = \frac{L_m}{1 + \tau_r\,s}\,i_{ds}(s) \tag{5}$$

$$w_{sl} = \frac{L_m\,i_{qs}}{\tau_r \cdot \lambda_r} \tag{6}$$

$$w_{sl} = \frac{L_m\,i_{qs}}{\tau_r \cdot \lambda_r} = \frac{1}{\tau_r}\frac{i_{qs}}{i_{ds}}(\tau_r\,s + 1) \tag{7}$$

4   Implementation of the Estimator Using Neural Networks

The artificial intelligence technique used to estimate the electric motor speed was the Artificial Neural Networks (ANN). This choice is due to the good results obtained using this technique in systems with nonlinear dynamics [6]. The type of neural network chosen is *"feedforward"* with automatic back-propagation and supervised learning [7].

The designed RNA has 6 inputs, which correspond to 3 voltage signals and 3 current signals, that is, a voltage sensor and a current sensor for each phase of the motor. Figure 6 shows the block diagram of the proposed estimator.

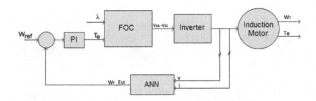

Fig. 6. Block diagram of the proposed estimator.

The implementation of the Artificial Neural Network to carry out the estimation of the speed will be executed in a Raspberry Pi development card, in conjunction with the Simulink/Matlab programming environment. In this environment, the necessary algorithms were developed, which were then turned over to the development card, from which they were executed autonomously. On the other hand, the signals delivered by the current and voltage sensors enter the development card by means of the GPIO pins, and are handled, within the Simulink environment, by means of the I/O blocks.

Figure 7 shows the blocks that conform the vector control loop to be used with the real electric motor.

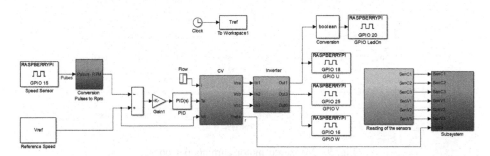

Fig. 7. Simulink model of the vector control for tests. (Color figure online)

GPIO blocks are used to send and/or receive data to/from the Raspberry Pi development card. In this case, the GPIO 15 block is the port through which the pulses delivered by the speed sensor are received. These input pulses are translated at a speed in rpm by means of a conversion block. Figure 7 shows the mention block highlighted in red.

The block corresponding to the inverter is highlighted in orange, and is responsible for receiving the signals from the vector control strategy and transforming them into PWM signals, which drive the power circuits, and which are sent to the development card by means of GPIO blocks 16, 18 and 25.

The reading of the voltage and current sensors was done using an Arduino development card, by means of the Analog/Digital converter. Thus, the signals from the sensors are converted into binary data and sent to the Raspberry Pi card.

Figures 8 and 9 show the voltage and current signals taken from the real electric motor. In this case, the signals obtained at three different speeds are shown: 200 rpm, 500 rpm and 800 rpm. These will later be used for the training of the neural network.

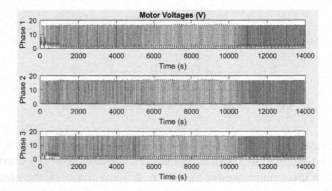

Fig. 8. Measured motor voltages per phase.

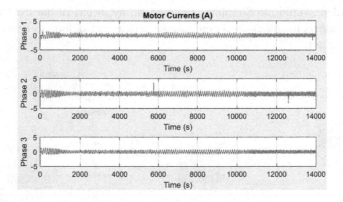

Fig. 9. Measured motor currents per phase.

The voltage and current data are sent to the Matlab Workspace, and are stored in the matrices V_S and I_S respectively. Subsequently, these matrices are concatenated in a single matrix called Inp.

Once the training is done, we proceed to generate the block in Simulink that contains the trained RNA, using the *gensim* function.

5   System Validation

To implement the speed control strategy of the induction motor, the following components are used:

- Raspberry Pi Model 3B card.
- Electric power inverter.
- Current sensors.
- Voltage sensors.
- Arduino UNO card.
- Induction motor.

Figure 10 shows a photograph of the entire test bench used to carry out the experiments concerning the development of the project.

Fig. 10. Experimental setup.

The following figure shows the block diagram of the neuronal estimator, where the RNA block (blue block) is added, which is in charge of estimating the speed of the motor, depending on the voltages and currents of each phase of the machine. This estimated speed signal will be used to close the indirect control loop (Fig. 11).

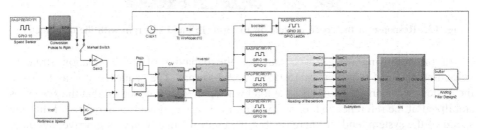

Fig. 11. Block diagram of the neuronal estimator. (Color figure online)

5.1   Estimator Results Using Neuronal Networks

The results obtained from the implementation of the vectorial control loop. The tests made with different speeds and how the system behaves both in vacuum and under load are shown. The robustness of neural networks for Sensorless vector control is also evidenced when load is applied to the engine.

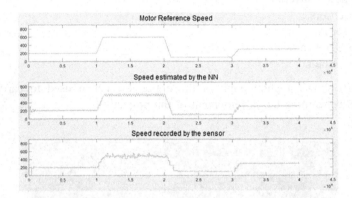

Fig. 12. Response of the speed estimation for 100, 200, 300 and 600 rpm.

The above image shows the reference velocity (up), the velocity estimated by the ANN (center) and the velocity measured by the horseshoe sensor (down). It starts with a speed of 200 RPM, then changes speed to 600 RPM, then lowers the reference speed to 150 RPM and finally sets the speed to 300 RPM.

To validate that the motor speed is correct, a manual tachometer was used to corroborate the speed of the three-phase motor.

Fig. 13. Response of the speed estimation for 300, 150 and 400 rpm with the tachometer.

In the following images you can see the behavior of the estimation strategy, velocities obtained with load at 150, 200 and 300 rpm. The sequence was as follows: the system was started and at 15 s the load was applied, it is observed that the system is stabilized at the reference value; at 25 s the load was removed, it is observed that the speed of the system tends to increase, but the control strategy makes it arrive, again, at the reference value.

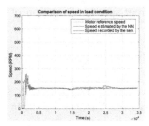
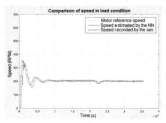
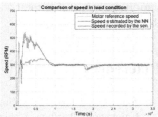

Fig. 14. Load at 150 rpm.   **Fig. 15.** Load at 200 rpm.   **Fig. 16.** Load at 300 rpm.
(Color figure online)

Figure 14 shows the comparison of the speed in load condition. The red line is the control response applying the estimate with neural networks and the blue line is the real speed given by the sensor. It is observed that the estimated value tends to follow the real value after a few tenths of seconds showing a fairly good convergence.

From 1.5 s the vector control response is evaluated using the estimated speed. It is observed that the vector control responds adequately, i.e. both the estimation and the control are operating correctly. At 2.5 s the load is removed and the system responds again correctly. This indicates that the motor speed estimate is correct.

The behavior of the estimate at 200 rpm, for which it was not trained, shows the learning of the network and its satisfactory response as shown in Figs. 14 and 15 the robustness of the estimation strategy tends to decrease in the transient of the response, but instead continues to converge in the rest of the estimate, indicating that the response in its entirety is considered satisfactory.

6 Conclusions

It was demonstrated, by means of this work, that it is possible to close a control loop for a three-phase squirrel cage type induction machine, using, instead of a speed sensor, an ANN that estimates the motor speed using the currents and voltages of each of the phases of the machine. This is evidenced in the analysis of Figs. 13, 14 and 15, which show the comparison between the simulated system, the estimated ANN speed and the actual motor speed.

Efforts were concentrated on controlling the machine in an RPM range below 500. This was to demonstrate that the Sensorless vector control technique is effective even in this speed range. Again, Figs. 12, 13, 14, 15 and 16 show positive results in this scenario.

It was demonstrated that the set SIMULINK - Raspberry Pi 3B, is a solution, at hardware level, valid for the problem presented: to control a three-phase induction machine, at low speeds, using the Sensor-less vector control strategy.

It was demonstrated, through the work done, that it is possible to design and train an ANN that estimates the speed of an induction machine, using as training data various patterns of current and voltage, characteristic of different speeds of rotation of the machine.

References

1. João, C., Palma, P.: Accionamentos Eletromecânicos de Velocidade Variável. Fundação Calouste Gulbenkian, Lisboa (1999)
2. Barbi, I.: Introdução ao Estudo do Motor de Indução. Universidade Federal de Santa Catarina (1988)
3. Hasse, K.: Zur Dynamic Drehzahlgeregelter Antriebe mit stromaschinen, techn, Hoschsch. Darmstadt, Dissertation (1969)
4. Blaschke, F.: The principle of field orientation as applied to the new "Transvektor" close-loop control system for rotating-field machines. Siemens Rev. **39**(5), 517–525 (1972)
5. Kakhim, A.H., Rezak, M.J.A., O'Kelly, D.: A PWM inverter using on-line control algorithms. In: UPEC 1991, pp. 333–336 (1991)
6. Pyne, M., Chatterjee, A., Dasgupta, S.: Speed estimation of three phase induction motor using artificial neural network. Int. J. Energy Power Eng. **3**(2), 52–56 (2014)
7. Ponce Cruz, P.: Inteligencia artificial con aplicaciones a la ingenieria. Alfaomega, México (2010)
8. González, J., Azevedo, M., Pacheco, A.: Control vectorial del Motor de Inducción para el Control de Velocidad del Rotor por cambio de Frecuencia, II Congreso Venezolano de Ingeniería Eléctrica, Mérida (2000)
9. González, J., Silveira, M., Pacheco, J.: Comparación de la red neuronal y el filtro de Kalman en la estimación de velocidad del motor de inducción (2004)
10. Gallo, M., Duran, C.: Integrated system approach for the automatic speech recognition using linear predict coding and neural networks. In: IEEE Electronics, Robotics and Automotive Mechanics Conference, CERMA 2007 (2007)
11. Quintero, C.M., Rodríguez, J.L.D., García, A.P.: Aplicación de redes neuronales al control de velocidad en motores de corriente alterna. Revista Colombiana de Tecnologías de Avanzada **2**(20), 113–118 (2012)

A Preliminary Study on Symbolic Fuzzy Cognitive Maps for Pattern Classification

Mabel Frias[1]($\boxtimes$), Gonzalo Nápoles[2], Yaima Filiberto[1], Rafael Bello[3], and Koen Vanhoof[2]

[1] Universidad de Camagüey, Carretera de Circunvalación Norte entre Camino Viejo de Nuevitas y Ave Ignacio Agramonte, Camagüey, Cuba
{mabel.frias,yaima.filiberto}@reduc.edu.cu
[2] Universiteit Hasselt, Agoralaan gebouw D, Diepenbeek, Belgium
{gonzalo.napoles,koen.vanhoof}@uhasselt.be
[3] Central University of Las Villas, Carretera Camajuaní km 5.5, Santa Clara, Cuba
rbellop@uclv.edu.cu

Abstract. Within the neural computing field, Fuzzy Cognitive Maps (FCMs) are attractive simulation tools to model dynamic systems by means of well-defined neural concepts and causal relationships, thus equipping the network with interpretability features. However, such components are normally described by quantitative terms, which may be difficult to handle by experts. Recently, we proposed a symbolic FCM scheme (termed FCM-TFN) in which both weights and activation values are described by triangular fuzzy numbers. In spite of the promising results, the model's performance in solving prediction problems remains uncertain. In this paper, we explore the prediction capabilities of the FCM-TFN model in pattern classification and concluded that our method is able to perform well when compared with traditional classifiers.

Keywords: Fuzzy Cognitive Maps · Computing With Words · Classification

1 Introduction

Pattern classification tries to identify the right category, among a predefined set, to which an observed pattern belongs. These observations are often described by a set of predictive attributes of numerical and/or nominal nature called features [14]. Some successful classifiers include: Multilayer Perceptron (MLP) [21], Naive Bayes (NB) [10], Support Vector Machines (SVM) [16], Ensemble Learners, Random Forests and Deep Neural Networks [26]. In these models, the term "successful" refers to their ability to reduce the number of misclassified observations, which translates in models with high generalization capabilities. However, most of these models perform like black-boxes, which means that they cannot explain how decisions are made or allow for the injection of human knowledge into the reasoning modules.

© Springer Nature Switzerland AG 2019
J. C. Figueroa-García et al. (Eds.): WEA 2019, CCIS 1052, pp. 285–295, 2019.
https://doi.org/10.1007/978-3-030-31019-6_25

Recently, a research field dedicated to understanding how computational models operate has (re)emerged. Explainable Artificial Intelligence (XAI) [12] aims to bridge the gap between the prediction ability of Machine Learning (ML) algorithms and interpretability, transparency, fairness, accountability, etc. This proposal is mainly concerned with building transparent prediction models. But another alternative to bridge the gap between comprehensibility and accuracy is to improve the prediction power of models able to naturally explain their reasoning mechanism. For example, combining Fuzzy Cognitive Maps (FCMs) [11] with Computing with Words (CWW) [27], to describe the concepts' activation values and the causal relations between them.

FCMs are recurrent neural networks which allow to model a complex system in terms of causal relationships and well-defined concepts where the knowledge is usually expressed by means of numerical values. In the FCM literature, some attempts to expanding the action field of fuzzy cognitive mapping combine its graphical nature with a natural language. For example, in [23] the authors proposed a FCM-model based on CWW to improve the interpretability of diagnostic models of cardiovascular diseases. Gónzalez et al. [9] employed a representation model based on linguistic 2-tuple for modeling project portfolio interdependencies. Likewise, Rickard et al. [18] introduced another symbolic model based on interval type-2 fuzzy membership functions and the weighted power mean operator, [5,19,20]. More recently Dodurka et al. [4] analyzed the causal effect for fuzzy cognitive maps designed with non-singleton fuzzy numbers. While in [8], the authors explore a reasoning mechanism for FCMs where numerical concepts and relations are replaced with triangular fuzzy numbers into the qualitative reasoning process attached to the model.

In this paper, we propose a symbolic FCM-based model for pattern classification. The main learning goal in this model is to compute the weight matrix using the Genetic Algorithm, CHC [6]. When a new instance arrives, we activate the symbolic input neurons attached with the *FCM-TFN* model [8] and next the symbolic reasoning process is performed. Finally, the decision class is derived from the symbolic activation values of output neurons. The numerical simulations have shown that our model is able to obtain competitive prediction rates with respect to state-of-the-art classifiers such as ID3 [17], NB, MLP and SVM. More importantly, the whole classification model is described by means of linguistic terms instead of numbers.

The paper is organized as follows. Section 2 goes over some important concepts related with FCM-TFN model, whereas Sect. 3 describes the linguistic FCM for classification problems proposed. The experiment results are presented in the Sect. 4, while Sect. 5 provides the concluding remarks.

2   Background About FCM-TFN

In this section, we briefly introduce the FCM-TFN reasoning model [8]. This method replaces the numerical components of the FCM reasoning (i.e., the concepts' activation values and the causal weights) with linguistic terms. Figure 1

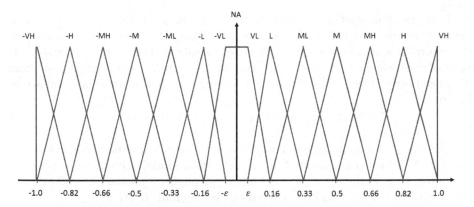

Fig. 1. Linguistic terms and their membership functions.

illustrates the membership functions associated with these terms. The negative terms will only be used to describe a negative causal weights w_{ij} between two concepts since the concept's activation values $C = \{C_1, C_2, \ldots, C_N\}$ are always positive.

Equation 1 shows the aggregation of the N_i linguistic terms impacting the ith concept, which produces a triangular fuzzy number (TFN) [25],

$$\tau(M_i^{(t+1)}) = \sum_{j=1}^{N_i} I_j(w_{ji}, A_j^{(t)}) \tag{1}$$

such that the aggregation between $(w_{ji}$ and $A_j^{(t)})$ is the defined as follows:

$$I(w_{ji}, A_j^{(t)}) = \tau(w_{ji})\tau(A_j^{(t)}). \tag{2}$$

where $\tau(w_{ji})$ and $\tau(A_j^{(t)})$ are TFNs for w_{ij} and $A_i^{(t)}$, respectively. A TFN can be defined as follows. Let $\hat{a} = [a^L, a^M, a^U]$, where $a^L \leq a^M \leq a^U$, then $\hat{a}$ is called a TFN, where a^L and a^U stand for the lower and upper values of $\hat{a}$, and a^M is the modal value. There are many papers related to the fuzzy number arithmetic (e.g., [24,25]). In this paper, we adopted the notation introduced by [25] that defines the multiplication between two TFNs $\hat{a} = [a^L, a^M, a^U]$ and $\hat{b} = [b^L, b^M, b^U]$ as follows: $\hat{a} \times \hat{b} = [min(a^L \times b^L, a^L \times b^U, a^U \times b^L, a^U \times b^U), a^M \times b^M, max(a^L \times b^L, a^L \times b^U, a^U \times b^L, a^U \times b^U)]$.

The next step in the reasoning process is devoted to recovering the linguistic term attached to $\tau(M_i^{(t+1)})$. So each calculated TFN is compared to the TFNs defined for the linguistic terms of Fig. 1. With this goal in mind, it is use the deviation between two TFNs as a distance function [2], which can be defined as follows:

$$\delta(\hat{a}, \hat{b}) = \sqrt{\frac{1}{3}\left[(a^L - b^L)^2 + (a^M - b^M)^2 + (a^U - b^U)^2\right]}. \tag{3}$$

Equation 4 shows how to compute the symbolic activation value for the i-th neural concept, where S is the domain set of linguistic terms used to activate the neurons and represent the causal relationships. Being more precise, this symbolic reasoning rule determines the linguistic term reporting the minimal distance between its TFN and the one resulting after performing the calculations in Eq. 1.

$$A_i^{(t+1)} = \underset{S_k \in S}{\arg\min}\{\delta(\tau(M_i^{(t+1)}), \tau(S_k))\} \tag{4}$$

However, the linguistic term computed in this step could be defined by a negative TFN, which is not allowed in this activation model. Aiming at overcoming this issue, it relies on a transfer function for symbolic domains. Figure 2 displays the transfer function which is inspired on the sigmoid function.

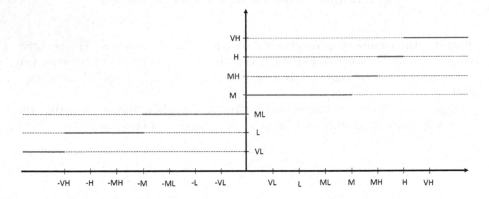

Fig. 2. Transfer function for symbolic domains

It should be highlighted that this function ensures computing positive linguistic values for concepts, yet causal relations defining the interaction among concepts could be described by using either positive or negative terms.

3   Symbolic FCM for Pattern Classification

The inherent ability of FCMs to model complex systems has encouraged their use in solving pattern classification problems, having appropriate input and output concepts and appropriate interconnections between them [15].

In this section, we propose a symbolic reasoning model for solving pattern classification problems based on the FCM-TFN approach. The structure of this map—termed ClassFCM—consists of input concepts $C = \{C_1, C_2, \ldots, C_N\}$ that represent the features and decision concepts $D = \{D_1, D_2, \ldots, D_N\}$ that denote decision classes. Therefore, S is the domain of the linguistic terms set used to activate the concepts and represent the causal weights. Moreover, the relation among decision concepts is always negative since in standard pattern classification problems the decision classes are mutually exclusive. On the other hand, each input concept has a relationship with all decision concepts that might be either positive or negative.

After building the network topology, the immediate challenge is to compute a weight matrix able to produce the proper decision class for a new instance. To do that, we need a supervised learning algorithm able to support symbolic values.

3.1 Learning Algorithm

In this section, we present a learning algorithm to estimate of the symbolic relationships among concepts. Roughly speaking, when building FCM-based models we can rely on the human expertise or use data-driven learning approaches [7]. The former regularly ensures to have authentic causal models while the latter often leads to more accurate models, even when they might lack of a straightforward causal meaning. On the other hand, the stochastic nature of population-based algorithms make them more likely to find a weight configuration leading to improved prediction rates.

That is the reason why we use the CHC Algorithm (Cross-generational elitist selection, Heterogeneous recombination, and Cataclysmic mutation), proposed by Eshelman in 1991 [6], to compute the symbolic weight matrix in our model. In this search method, each individual represents a candidate weight matrix, while each chromosome represents a *TFN* encoding a linguistic term. Despite the various modifications made to CHC algorithm, it is still used in its original form. For example, in [22] the authors used CHC to optimize the processing of sign language data because is an algorithm easy to implement, with relatively low execution times and high performance. It goes without saying that any other discrete optimizer might be used as well.

CHC uses an elitist selection method that preserves the best individuals (see Algorithm 1). The HUX (Half Uniform Crossover) crossing operator is used to maximize the genetic distance between individuals, the reproduction only occurs if the Hamming distance (genetic difference between the parents) is greater than the incest threshold (1/4 of the size of the chromosome). The distance is decreased for each generation without improvements, when the amount of different bits among the selected parents is less than the threshold, means that the individuals are too similar. This indicate a stagnation of the algorithm, so the search should be restarted [13].

In the pseudo-code, L is the number of symbolic weights to be estimated, the number of individuals p is set to 100, while the incest threshold d is set to $L/4$. Equation 5 shows the objective function to be maximized,

$$Acc(X) = \frac{1}{E}\sum_{e=1}^{E} \begin{cases} 1, & \phi(A_{De}^T) = L_e \\ 0, & \phi(A_{De}^T) \neq L_e \end{cases} \tag{5}$$

where X denotes the weight matrix, E is the number of training instances, $\phi(.)$ is the decision model to be used for determining the class label, while L_e represents the expected decision class for the e-th training instance.

3.2 Classification Approach

Once a weight matrix is generated, we need to evaluate its discriminatory power on the training set. To do that, each concept C_i of the map is activated with its corresponding feature value, for each object of the training set. The activation values of concepts are taken from a dataset. Later on, the symbolic reasoning process is preformed and the decision concept having maximal activation value is compared with the expected decision class. The steps to classify a new object are summarized below:

Algorithm 1. CHC algorithm

L : chromosome length
p : population size
d : incest threshold

1: $d = L/4$
2: **while** not stop **do**
3:     create new child population
4:     **for** i = 1 to $p/2$ **do**
5:         select P1, P2 from population without replacement
6:         **if** hamming distance (P1, P2) > d **then**
7:             C1, C2 = HUX crossover(P1, P2)
8:             insert C1, C2 into child pop
9:     **if** child pop is empty **then**
10:         $d = d - 1$
11:     **else**
12:         take best p individuals from union of parent and child populations as next population
13:     **if** $d < 0$ **then**
14:         keep one copy of best individual in population
15:         generate p-1 new population members by flipping 35% of the bits of best individual
16:         $d = L/4$

---

1. Assign to each concept C_i the value of each feature for the object to be classified.
2. Assign the linguistic term "NA" to each decision concept D_i.
3. Calculate activation value of decision concepts according to FCM-TFN.
4. Determine the decision class using the following equation,

$$\phi(A^D) = \operatorname{argmax}_k\{A_k\}, A_k \in A^D \tag{6}$$

such that $\phi(.)$ returns a decision class, whereas A^D represents the set of activation values for decision concepts. It is worth mentioning that the FCM-TFN will produce a state vector comprised of linguistic terms at each iteration-step until either a fixed-point is discovered or a maximal number of iterations is reached. On the other hand, since a state vector is a permutation of the linguistic terms, we can ensure that chaotic situations are not possible, however, cycles might show up.

4   Experimental Results

For simulation purposes we have adopted 13 datasets from the UCI repository[1], which were partitioned using 10 k-fold cross validation [3]. Table 1 summarizes the number of instances, the number of attributes and the number of classes. The reader can notice that such datasets are rather small. The reason behind our choice is that pattern classification problems defined on the basis of expert knowledge (e.g., FCM-based models) regularly involve a limited number of instances.

The ClassFCM method is compared against 4 algorithms implemented into WEKA: Multilayer Perceptron (MLP), Naive Bayes (NB), Decision Trees (ID3) and Support Vector Machines (SVM). In all cases we used the default parameter settings, thus the experimental analysis is formulated on the basis of the algorithms' performance when their parameters have not been optimized. Concretely, the configuration for MLP can be summarized as: the number of hidden layers is set to $(attribs + classes)/2$, the learning rate is 0.3, the momentum is 0.2, while the number of epochs is set to 500. The Kernel Estimator and the Supervised Discretization for NB were not used. On the other hand, the configuration for SVM is: the epsilon value for the round-off error is $1.0E-12$ and the exponent for the polynomial kernel is set to 1.0 (linear kernel). The ID3 method does not have parameters to be adjusted in WEKA.

Table 1 shows the accuracy of the classification models for each dataset. The best results are highlighted in boldface.

Table 1. Accuracy reported for each classifier.

Datasets	Instances	Attributes	Classes	MLP	NB	ID3	SVM	ClassFCM
apendicitis	106	8	2	82.09	85.09	70.00	84.04	**87.91**
iris	150	5	3	94.67	94.67	89.33	95.99	**96.00**
blood transfusion	748	5	2	75.81	75.81	75.14	75.66	**77.27**
echocardiogram	132	12	2	90.02	**90.82**	85.43	89.22	90.05
new-thyroid	215	6	2	93.89	**95.33**	90.66	93.89	**95.33**
planning-relax	182	13	2	63.27	60.94	53.27	59.93	**70.84**
saheart	462	10	2	62.77	67.97	49.57	70.77	**72.73**
glass0	214	10	2	77.18	76.27	**78.69**	76.72	77.71
pima-10an-nn	768	9	2	66.90	72.78	56.62	**73.04**	72.14
haberman	306	4	2	68.96	74.84	67.95	**77.04**	75.52
vertebra-column-2c	310	7	2	75.44	71.60	65.47	**78.70**	72.48
yield	56	9	3	47.66	62.66	61.00	57.99	**66.66**
parkinsons	56	9	2	87.68	78.10	**87.68**	84.52	84.63

The Wilcoxon signed rank test and different post-hoc procedures were used as suggested by Benavoli et al. [1]. Table 2 reports the unadjusted p-value computed by the Wilcoxon signed rank test and the corrected p-values associated with each pairwise comparison using ClassFCM as the control method. A null hypothesis will be rejected if at least one of the post-hoc procedures indicates a rejection.

---

[1] http://www.ics.uci.edu/~mlearn/MLRepository.html.

Table 2. Adjusted p-values according to different post-hoc procedures using the Class-FCM algorithm as the control method.

Algorithms	p-value	R^-	R^+	Bonferroni	Holland	Holm	Null hypothesis
MLP	0.02148	13	78	0.08592	0.08319	0.08592	Rejected
NB	0.00341	4	74	0.01367	0.08319	0.08592	Rejected
ID3	0.00170	4	87	0.00683	0.08319	0.08592	Rejected
SVM	0.09424	21	70	0.37696	0.09424	0.09424	Rejected

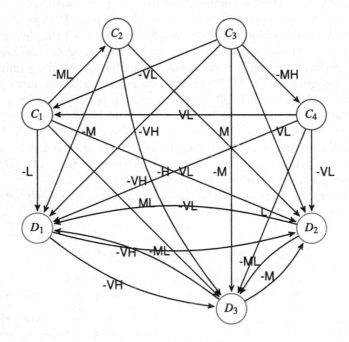

Fig. 3. Symbolic weight matrix computed by the CHC algorithm.

The results of the ClassFCM model are statistically superior to the other classifiers for a 90% of the confidence interval. If we assume a 5% significance level, then such classifiers are comparable with each other in terms of prediction rates, for the datasets adopted for simulation purposes. However, the distinctive feature of our proposal relies on its transparency. Being more specific, the synergy between graphical nature of FCM-based architectures with the flexibility of using linguistic terms allows obtaining a neural reasoning model with increased transparency.

Aiming at illustrating the transparency of our model, we use the "Iris" dataset as a proof of concept. This dataset is comprised of 4 attributes and 3 decision classes. Figure 3 shows the weight matrix computed by the CHC algorithm. Concepts C_1 and C_2 are the length and width of the sepal leaf, while concepts C_3 and C_4 are the length and width of the petal leaf, respectively.

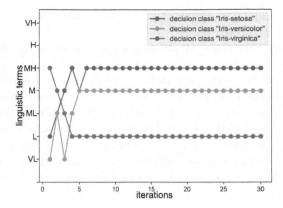

Fig. 4. Convergence of ClassFCM for an instance labeled as "Iris-setosa".

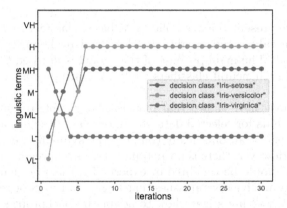

Fig. 5. Convergence of ClassFCM for an instance labeled as "Iris-versicolor".

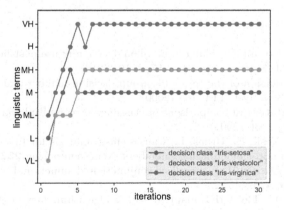

Fig. 6. Convergence of ClassFCM for an instance labeled as "Iris-virginica".

Concepts D_1, D_2 and D_3 represent the decision classes Iris-setosa, Iris-versicolor and Iris-virginica, respectively.

In order to illustrate the symbolic reasoning process of our recurrent neural classifier, we have randomly selected three instances. Figures 4, 5 and 6 show that the neural system converges very fast, in less than 10 iterations in all cases.

In these three examples, the decision classes were correctly classified but in the first two examples, the algorithm alternatively produces different decision classes until it converges. In the third example the proposal correctly classified the instance since the first iteration. This brings to life a sensitive topic: FCM-based classifiers should converge, otherwise we might end up with an incorrect decision class, even when the model was capable of producing the proper one in previous iterations.

5   Conclusions

In this paper, we presented a symbolic FCM-based classifier in which both concepts' activation values and weights are described by linguistic terms such as *low, medium, high*. The main purpose of this model is devoted to increasing the transparency of such neural classifiers while computing competitive prediction rates.

The simulations have shown that our classifier is able to outperform state-of-the-art algorithms for selected datasets. In our case, we have adopted an evolutionary approach to automatically compute the symbolic weight matrix from historical data. However, there is no guarantee that such weights have any causal meaning as they should be validated by experts. On the other hand, population-based algorithms involve several issues that might lead to poor results. As a feature research, we will investigate how to adapt the backpropagation algorithm to the symbolic context.

References

1. Benavoli, A., Corani, G., Mangili, F.: Should we really use post-hoc tests based on mean-ranks? J. Mach. Learn. Res. **17**, 1–10 (2016)
2. Chen, C.: Extension of the topsis for group decision-making under fuzzy environment. Fuzzy Sets Syst. **114**, 1–9 (2000)
3. Demsar, J.: Statistical comparisons of classifiers over multiple data sets. J. Mach. Learn. Res. **7**, 1–30 (2006)
4. Dodurka, F., Yesil, E., Urbas, L.: Causal effect analysis for fuzzy cognitive maps designed with non-singleton fuzzy numbers. Neurocomputing **232**, 122–132 (2017)
5. Dujmovic, J., Larsen, H.: Generalized conjunction/disjunction. Int. J. Approximate Reasoning **46**, 423–446 (2007)
6. Eshelman, L.J.: The CHC adaptive search algorithm: how to have safe search when engaging in nontraditional genetic recombination. Found. Genet. Algorithms **1**, 265–283 (1991)
7. Felix, G., Nápoles, G., Falcon, R., Froelich, W., Vanhoof, K., Bello, R.: A review on methods and software for fuzzy cognitive maps. Artif. Intell. Rev. (2017)

8. Frias, M., Filiberto, Y., Nápoles, G., García-Socarrás, Y., Vanhoof, K., Bello, R.: Fuzzy cognitive maps reasoning with words based on triangular fuzzy numbers. In: Castro, F., Miranda-Jiménez, S., González-Mendoza, M. (eds.) MICAI 2017. LNCS (LNAI), vol. 10632, pp. 197–207. Springer, Cham (2018). https://doi.org/10.1007/978-3-030-02837-4_16

9. Gónzalez, M.P., De La Rosa, C.G.B., Moran, F.J.C.: Fuzzy cognitive maps and computing with words for modeling project portfolio risks interdependencies. Int. J. Innov. Appl. Stud. **15**(4), 737–742 (2016)

10. John, G.H., Langley, P.: Estimating continuous distributions in Bayesian classifiers (1995)

11. Kosko, B.: Fuzzy cognitive maps. Int. J. Man-Mach. Stud. **24**, 65–75 (1986)

12. Lipton, Z.: The mythos of model interpretability. arxiv preprint arxiv:160603490 (2016)

13. Molina, D., Pandolfi, D., Villagra, A., Leguizamón, G.: Applying CHC algorithms on radio network design for wireless communication. In: XX Congreso Argentino de Ciencias de la Computación (Buenos Aires 2014) (2014)

14. Nápoles, G., Mosquera, C., Falcon, R., Grau, I., Bello, R., Vanhoof, K.: Fuzzy-rough cognitive networks. Neural Netw. **97**, 19–27 (2018)

15. Papakostas, G., Koulouriotis, D.: Classifying patterns using fuzzy cognitive maps. In: Glykas, M. (ed.) Fuzzy Cognitive Maps, vol. 247, pp. 291–306. Springer, Heidelberg (2010). https://doi.org/10.1007/978-3-642-03220-2_12

16. Platt, J.: Fast training of support vector machines using sequential minimal optimization. In: Schoelkopf, B., Burges, C., Smola, A. (eds.) Advances in Kernel Methods- Support Vector Learning. MIT Press, Cambridge (1998)

17. Quinlan, R.: Induction of decision trees. Mach. Learn. **1**(1), 81–106 (1986)

18. Rickard, J.T., Aisbett, J., Yager, R.R.: Computing with words in fuzzy cognitive maps. In: Proceedings of World Conference on Soft Computing, pp. 1–6 (2015)

19. Rickard, J., Aisbett, J., Yager, R., Gibbon, G.: Fuzzy weighted power means in evaluation decisions. In: 1st World Symposium on Soft Computing (2010)

20. Rickard, J., Aisbett, J., Yager, R., Gibbon, G.: Linguistic weighted power means: comparison with the linguistic weighted average. In: IEEE International Conference on Fuzzy Systems (FUZZ-IEEE 2011), pp. 2185–2192 (2011)

21. Rosemblatt, F.: Principles of Neurodynamics. Spartan Books, New York (1962)

22. Rosero-Montalvo, P.D., et al.: Sign language recognition based on intelligent glove using machine learning techniques. In: 2018 IEEE Third Ecuador Technical Chapters Meeting (ETCM), pp. 1–5 (2018)

23. Saleh, S.H., Rivas, S.D.L., Gómez, A.M.M., Mohsen, F.S., Vá zquez, M.L.: Knowledge representation using fuzzy cognitive maps and hesitant fuzzy linguistic term sets. Int. J. Innov. Appl. Stud. **17**(1), 312–319 (2016)

24. Su, W., Peng, W., Zeng, S., Pen, B., Pand, T.: A method for fuzzy group decision making based on induced aggregation operators and euclidean distance. Int. Trans. Oper. Res. **20**, 579–594 (2013)

25. Van, L., Pedrycz, W.: A fuzzy extension of Saaty's priority theory. Fuzzy Sets Syst. **11**, 229–241 (1983)

26. Witten, I.H., Frank, E., Hall, M., Pal, C.: Data Mining: Practical Machine Learning Tools and Techniques (2017)

27. Zadeh, L.A.: Outline of a new approach to the analysis of complex systems ad decision processes. IEEE Trans. Syst. Man Cybern. **SMC–3**(1), 28–44 (1973)

Prediction and Decision Making System Through Neural Networks for Investment Assets: Gold, Euro Dollar and Dow Jones

Cesar Hernando Valencia Niño[✉], Alfredo Sanabria, Carlos Pinto, and David Orjuela

Floridablanca, Colombia
cesar.valencia@ustabuca.edu.co

Abstract. The problem is to test the weak hypothesis of efficient markets through three neural networks that can predict the trends of investment assets such as: The Dow Jones, gold and Euro dollar, according to theories of technical analysis to automate positions of both long and short investment in the Spot market.

With regard to forecasting time series, multiple approaches have been tested, through statistical models such as [1–3], where forecasts are made from different information sources with characteristics differentiated (sasonality, tendency, periodicity), however, other actors have begun to gain strength by getting the first places in international competitions, this is the case of Neural Networks, in works published as [4–6] the results have shown that this type of model offers a real opportunity to work with time series of different characteristics.

Keywords: Neural networks · Decision making · Invesment · Assests · Prediction and decision

1 Introduction

Technical analysis is the study of market movements, mainly through the use of charts with the purpose of forecasting future price trends [7].

This type of analysis based on the theory of Dow Jones in 1882, states that the trends and prices of the past can be repeated in the future, is a cyclical analysis that is based on the psychology of the investor, that by observing the same pattern in the past infers that it will repeat itself in a cyclical way when awakening the same feelings in the investors, fear, euphoria, security etc.

According to [7] within the technical analysis there are 2 subsets called technicians and Chartists. The first one is more statistical and quantitative analysis that will be the center of this investigation. The second one is more of pattern analysis, it is more subjective.

This type of analysis will be used in the investment assets Eur/usd, Gold and Dow Jones, to study their historical behavior.

The investors aim to maximize profits with the occurrence of risks. In the absence of reliable predictive systems, inferences are made in the short time about the behavior

© Springer Nature Switzerland AG 2019
J. C. Figueroa-García et al. (Eds.): WEA 2019, CCIS 1052, pp. 296–308, 2019.
https://doi.org/10.1007/978-3-030-31019-6_26

of prices. Currently there are some tools but they work in isolation, that is, they are not flexible enough to include the 3 investment assets addressed in this project. [8] using a neural network managed to predict the price of call options of the Spanish Telefónica company with a 98% accuracy, with this we can argue the high potential of the neural network applied to financial structured products. The justification decreased the risk through a technological tool of artificial intelligence. As a support system allows support to the person or people in charge of buying and selling, an additional advantage is the ability to be re-trainable, this means that they allow flexibility to adapt to changes in behaviors of the variables to work.

The justification for this research is the high volatility presented in the financial markets and its importance in predicting trends in the most relevant assets in the world market, the Dow Jones, which is the world benchmark for measuring the economy. The strongest pair of currencies traded in the forex market is the euro dollar and commodities refuge in times of crisis is gold, through the theories of technical analysis and the construction of a system that allows us to analyze and make decisions in the Spot market in a period of high continuity and difficult operation as a result of sudden changes in prices.

The origin of the stock market technical analysis arises, at the beginning of the big exchanges, when the companies were not obliged, to publish their financial information and the slates began, to observe that the prices that the market shouted at certain specific moments began to repeat itself, and we begin to talk about market cycles, starting the technical analysis which is based on the historical prices of the financial assets used to predict the future.

The most recent theoretical developments on the stock markets were made based on the hypothesis of efficient markets emerged in the 70s in the Chicago school, postulated by Eugene Fama Nobel Prize in economics 2013, where he defined efficiency in markets as: "Where the prices of the assets reflect all the information available in the market" Fama 1970. According to this maxim, the market price of the assets is equal to their theoretical value, they are negotiated at equilibrium prices making it impossible for there to be assets over valued or undervalued, to the market to reflect all the possible information, prices would have random behavior, its prediction is not possible and you can not obtain higher yields than the market because the prices contain all the available information.

1.1 Dow Jones

Dow theory was born in the late nineteenth century, and its bases are presented in the 5 postulates of Dow in which it is emphasized that the market has a cyclical component and was the origin of Chartism, exposed by [9]:

(1) The indices discount everything.
(2) The market has three trends.
(3) The main trends have three phases.
(4) The stockings must be confirmed between them.
(5) The volume should confirm the trend (Fig. 1).

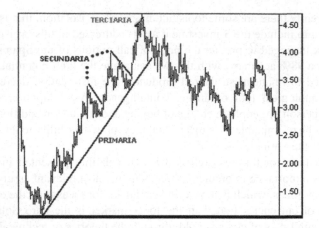

Fig. 1. Dow Jones theory.

Raphl Elliot after the financial crisis of 1929, begins an exhaustive study on the behavior of prices and begins to observe certain patterns of trends that he calls waves, identifiable, concludes that these can be repeated in market cycles, in five waves bullish and after these there would be a bearish trend (Fig. 2).

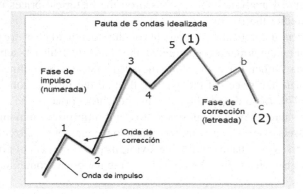

Fig. 2. Elliott waves.

1.2 Theoretical Research

There are approximate studies such as the one conducted by [10] entitled: "Technical analysis of financial markets based on artificial intelligence techniques." Where the author proposes, the design of a neural network that predicts the behavior of a robot according to the The current situation of the market and its neuronal learning will be according to the historical events faced by the robot.

[11] through technical analysis of the RSI, Stochastic, Macd, and Williams indicators, create investment portfolios with signals of purchase and sale of the Euro, IGBC, S & P500 and Dow Jones to maximize profitability by calculating a profitability

index to this portfolio named by dynamic authors. Making the bench mark, with the creation of a portfolio of these securities without using technical analysis, calculating a profitability index called by static authors. Where they concluded that the dynamic index was several times higher than the static one according to each indicator, maximizing the profitability of this portfolio (Table 1).

Table 1. Cost effectiveness.

	Rentabilidad a diciembre de 2009											
	IGBC			Euro			S&P500			Dow Jones		
	Dinámica	Estática	Var%	Dinámica	Estática	Var%	Dinámica	Estática	Var%	Dinámica	Estática	Var%
RSI	152,73	108,67	41%	133,11	119,32	12%	121,34	90,25	34%	129,72	96,13	35%
MACD	142,80	108,67	31%	123,95	119,32	4%	102,10	90,25	13%	109,19	96,13	14%
Estocástico	120,15	108,67	11%	116,63	119,32	−2%	120,73	90,25	34%	119,40	96,13	24%
Williams	107,56	108,67	−1%	113,35	119,32	−5%	84,86	90,25	−6%	121,10	96,13	26%

In [12] Design a neural network to forecast the Japanese yen, including relevant economic fundamental indicators, concluding that the inclusion of the fundamental indicators decreased the prediction errors for the next 3 weeks.

In [13] he analyzes the obtaining in the general index of the Madrid Stock Exchange of profitability by means of: Technical analysis, neural networks, genetic algorithms, genetic programming and analogous occurrences.

In [14] they constructed a neural network Back propagation by contrasting it with an Arima and Garch econometric model using the Colombian stock index, concluding the high predictability of the artificial intelligence system vs the econometric model.

In [15] the authors propose by means of the technical analysis of the indicators: Macd, Rsi and moving averages Japanese candlesticks and Bollinger Bands, in the Euro/Dollar, using the Metatrader Negotiation platform to obtain the data and Matlab for the processing of neural networks, they carry out purchase and sale operations according to the signals provided in matlab.

This oscillator called in English Relative Strength Index created by mechanical engineer J. Welles Wilder Jr., published in his research New concepts in technical trading systems.

This oscillator measures the forces of supply and demand to determine if prices are over-bought (expensive) or over-sold (cheap). It is calculated used Eq. 1.

$$IFR = 100 - \frac{100}{1 + FR} \tag{1}$$

The most used period is 14 sessions that may be days or weeks at a shorter period, the more sensitive the indicator and the wider the amplitude and the opposite happens if the sessions are increased the indicator is softened and the amplitude is smaller. This indicator has values between 0 and 100 and an average line of 50. According to Welles Wilder, if the indicator exceeds the limit of 70, it is considered that prices are over bought and if it falls below 30, they are over-sold, the average line of 50 represents indecision for operators.

The work of [16] mentions that a value of about 80 purchase and one over sale of 20 will give more security to the analysis in 14 sessions.

MACD (Moving Average Convergence Divergence): this indicator belongs to the family of oscillators created in 1979 by the administrator of investment funds Gerard Apple, is composed: by two lines one called Macd. which is the difference between two moving averages of 12 and 26 sessions and a signal line with an exponential average of 9 sessions. Accompanied by a histogram to confirm the trends of the macd lines. The purchase signals are produced by crossing the Macd line to the signal line or both lines cross from bottom to top, confirmed with the beginning of the formation of the histogram greater than zero, confirming the overselling zone. Otherwise, it would produce a sales signal.

OVB (On-Balance Volumen): The volume indicator reflects the transactions made in the market, and precedes the price according to Charles Dow volume must confirm the trend, otherwise there is a high probability of presenting a market divergence.

1.3   Neural Networks Forecasting

A neural network, as humans do based on acquired knowledge generate solutions to different problems, the network takes as a reference the resolved problems in order to make decisions and perform data classification. They base their operation on the extraction of data from tables, experimental data or databases that are then used as inputs (voltage, current, system variables) of the network and output the established signals (boolean variables, speed, temperature, etc.).

Multilayer networks are based on sets of single-layer sensory units and were created to solve various problems with higher difficulty with supervised training, are constituted by the entrance of the layer, one or more hidden layers and the output layer of the net.

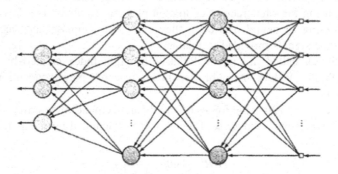

Fig. 3. MLP network.

Figure 3 shows the organization of a neural network that has 4 input signals, two hidden layers and three output signals. The input layer lets pass the information required for further processing in the hidden layers, finally, the output layer that allows the classification of the information, the final result will be delivered by the output signals. In the first hidden layer, the link between the input signals and their output can be analyzed, that is, all the network inputs reach each neuron of the hidden layer together with a synaptic weight and the output is directed to all the neurons of the next layer, in the same way for each neuron of the hidden layers and the output layer.

The learning or training can be classified as supervised training (the required response is known and the adjustment of the weights in the synaptic connections reduces the error generated by them) and unsupervised (the answer is unknown). There is another type of training called Hebb's rule in which inhibitory or excitatory functions are used, that is, if two processed signals (input and output) are active their synaptic weight is reinforced, if on the contrary these signals are inactive their weight remains same; the training may or may not be supervised.

In order to forecast a time series using neural networks, it is necessary to take into account the temporal relationship that exists between the data for periods of time, this means that constant time slots must be maintained in the values presented as inputs, in order to achieve This effect uses a sample window that can vary in size and that would involve the historical ones to be considered to make the forecast.

For forecasting processes of time series, two procedures are used, the first one that makes the forecast in a single iteration for the necessary values, the second procedure is multi-step where a cyclical forecast is made where the predicted values can enter or not in the forecast sliding window like a Fig. 4.

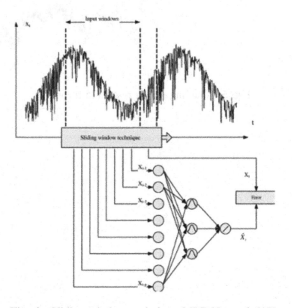

Fig. 4. Sliding window technique MLP Network [17].

2   Forecasting Results

The database available to perform the forecast tests consists of 1325 records that comprise the time period from September 3, 2012 to September 29, 2017, to have different perceptions of the forecast results were generated 5 sub bases of data, which are organized according to the size of the test set, for this case are 5, 10, 15, 20 and 45 records.

2.1   Euro/Dollar Database

The Eurodollar indicator refers to the ratio of dollars deposited in the foreign currency, that is, those that are outside the banking system of the United States, this means that it does not contain any close relationship with the euro but with European banks where they are deposited.

It is considered one of the most important sources of funding and there is no exact amount that can quantify its size in part to the lack of regulation and the large number of participants worldwide, it is estimated that the influence of this index is highly important in the financial world.

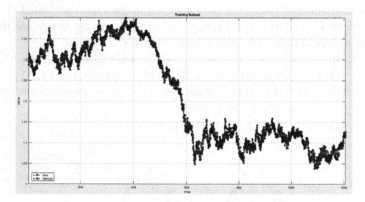

Fig. 5. Training subset result (45 records).

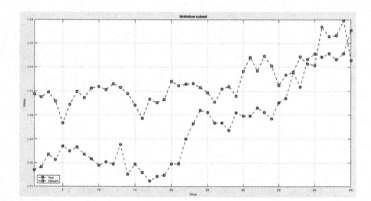

Fig. 6. Validation subset result (45 records).

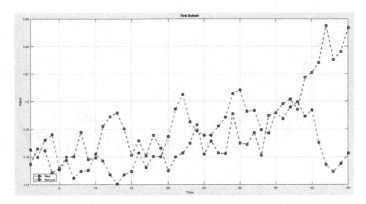

Fig. 7. Test subset result (45 records).

In Figs. 5, 6 and 7, it is possible to notice the behavior of the network response for the euro/dollar database with a test window of 45 records, in Table 2 the error metrics for the data are presented (sub databases used in this series).

Table 2. Euro/Dollar results

	5	10	15	20	45
MAPE	1.3209	1.7613	**0.6963**	0.8113	0.9633
RMSE	0.0176	0.0245	**0.0100**	0.0121	0.0142

The results presented are from the test set, that is, outside the sample.

2.2 Gold Database

Being one of the most precious metals since many centuries, the negotiations based on this are characterized by being very desirable since their value remains stable despite moment of movement in the financial market, has been known as a "quotable asset" and denominated in some parts like "refuge".

In Figs. 8, 9 and 10, it is possible to notice the behavior of the network response for the gold database with a test window of 10 records, in Table 3 the error metrics for the data are presented (sub databases used in this series).

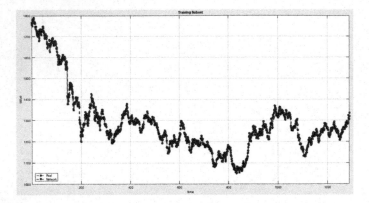

Fig. 8. Training subset result (10 records).

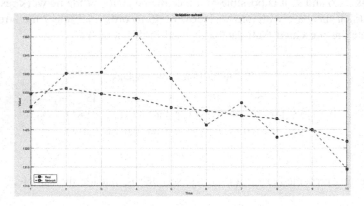

Fig. 9. Training subset result (10 records).

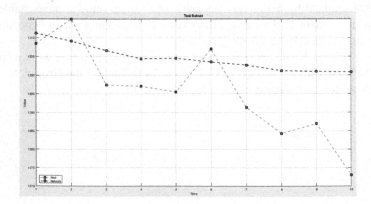

Fig. 10. Training subset result (10 records).

Table 3. Gold results

	5	10	15	20	45
MAPE	0.8985	0.8615	1.3969	**0.6111**	0.7903
RMSE	0.0125	0.0128	0.0198	**0.0092**	0.0117

The results presented are from the test set, that is, outside the sample.

2.3   Dow Jones Database

Denominated as a stock market index, it is composed of 30 of the most important shares of all the listed companies in the Nasdaq and the New York Stock Exchange, however, transportation and public services actions are not included, without being the stock exchange index. of New York, is one of the most used to monitor the behavior of this, also stands out because it is one of the oldest indices used to determine the behavior of important actions.

It is known as a balanced index, which represents the movement of the most important stocks in the New York Stock Exchange.

In Figs. 11, 12 and 13, it is possible to notice the behavior of the network response for the Dow Jones database with a test window of 15 records, in Table 4 the error metrics for the data are presented (sub databases used in this series).

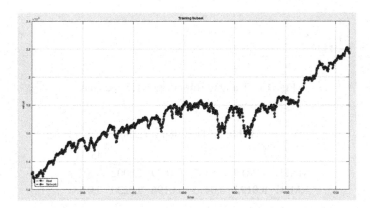

Fig. 11. Training subset result (15 records).

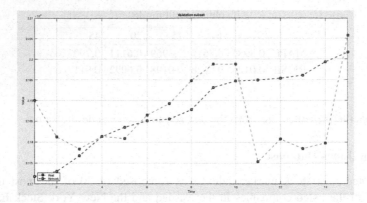

Fig. 12. Training subset result (15 records).

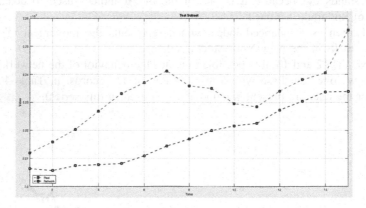

Fig. 13. Training subset result (15 records).

Table 4. Dow Jones results

	5	10	15	20	45
MAPE	**1.3816**	3.5482	1.4679	1.8002	3.5104
RMSE	**0.0193**	0.0475	0.0196	0.0230	0.0470

3   Conclusions

For the tests carried out on the three intelligent systems, multiple configurations of their most relevant parameters were tested, presenting several databases and still yielding the same results presented in Sect. 2; this is mainly due to the non-stationary properties of the myoelectric signals making the classification more complex despite being two gestures only, and forcing to use robust intelligent systems.

The results presented show the efficiency that RNA handles in the portable embedded system, which lends itself to multiple applications in various areas. The success of the device was to train the neural network in a separate computer, since the computational expense that requires a training is high, and to program in the embedded system only the structure of the neural network leaving space to the synaptic weights and the biases, since which are the data that is acquired from training, thus making the embedded system suitable for processing the RNA.

References

1. Singh, S., Taylor, J.H.: Statistical analysis of environment Canada's wind speed data. In: 2012 25th IEEE Canadian Conference on Electrical and Computer Engineering (CCECE), Montreal, QC, pp. 1–5 (2012)
2. Asami, A., Yamada, T., Saika, Y.: Probabilistic inference of environmental factors via time series analysis using mean-field theory of ising model. In: 2013 13th International Conference on Control, Automation and Systems (ICCAS), Gwangju, pp. 1209–1212 (2013)
3. Shenoy, D.S., Gorinevsky, D.: Stochastic optimization of power market forecast using non-parametric regression models. In: 2015 IEEE Power & Energy Society General Meeting, Denver, CO, pp. 1–5 (2015)
4. Han, M., Xi, J., Xu, S., Yin, F.L.: Prediction of chaotic time series based on the recurrent predictor neural network. IEEE Trans. Sig. Process. **52**, 3409–3416 (2005)
5. Cherif, A., Cardot, H., Boné, R.: SOM time series clustering and prediction with recurrent neural networks. Neurocomputing **74**, 1936–1944 (2011)
6. de Aquino, R., Souza, R., Neto, O., Lira, M., Carvalho, M., Ferreira, A.: Echo state networks, artificial neural networks and fuzzy systems models for improve short-term wind speed forecasting. In: 2015 International Joint Conference on Neural Networks (IJCNN), Killarney, pp. 1–8 (2015)
7. Murphy, K.: Executive Compensation. Marshal School of Business (1999)
8. Orjuela-Cañón, A.D., Posada-Quintero, H.F., Valencia, C.H., Mendoza, L.: On the use of neuroevolutive methods as support tools for diagnosing appendicitis and tuberculosis. In: Figueroa-García, J.C., López-Santana, E.R., Rodriguez-Molano, J.I. (eds.) WEA 2018. CCIS, vol. 915, pp. 171–181. Springer, Cham (2018). https://doi.org/10.1007/978-3-030-00350-0_15
9. Estévez, P.G.: Aplicaciones de las Redes Neuronales en las Finanzas. Facultad de Ciencias Económicas y Empresariales, Universidad Complutense (2002)
10. Murphy, J.: Análisis técnico de los mercados financieros. Gestión, Barcelona (2003)
11. Pina, A.: Análisis técnico de mercados financieros basado en técnicas de inteligencia artificial (2014)
12. Roncancio Millán, C.A., Valenzuela Reinoso, A.F.: Desarrollo de un modelo de Trading algorítmico para índices bursátiles y divisas (2010)
13. Villa, F., Muñoz, F., Henao, W.: Pronóstico de las tasas de cambio. Una aplicación al Yen Japonés mediante redes neuronales artificiales. Scientia et technica (2006)
14. González Martel, C.: Nuevas perspectivas del análisis técnico de los mercados bursátiles mediante el aprendizaje automático: aplicaciones al índice general de la bolsa de Madrid (2003)
15. Cruz, E.A., Restrepo, J.H., Varela, P.M.: Pronóstico del índice general de la Bolsa de Valores de Colombia usando redes neuronales. Scientia et technica (2009)

16. Castellanos Vargas, O.E., Jaramillo Jaramillo, J.M.: Cuantificación de riesgo en estrategias de análisis técnico del mercado de divisas usando redes neuronales (2007)
17. Kaufman, P.J.: Trading Systems and Methods. Wiley, Hoboken (2005)
18. Paoli, C., Voyant, C., Muselli, M., Nivet, M.: Forecasting of preprocessed daily solar radiation time series using neural networks. Solar Energy **84**, 2146–2160 (2010)
19. Valencia, C.H., Quijano, S.N.: Modelo de optimización en la gestión de inventarios mediante algoritmos genéticos. Iteckne **8**(2), 156–162 (2011). ISSN 2339-3483

Using Data-Mining Techniques
for the Prediction of the Severity of Road
Crashes in Cartagena, Colombia

Holman Ospina-Mateus[1,2][✉] [iD],
Leonardo Augusto Quintana Jiménez[2],
Francisco José López-Valdés[3] [iD], Natalie Morales-Londoño[4] [iD],
and Katherinne Salas-Navarro[5] [iD]

[1] Department of Industrial Engineering, Universidad Tecnológica de Bolívar,
Cartagena, Colombia
Hospina@utb.edu.co
[2] Department of Industrial Engineering, Pontificia Universidad Javeriana,
Carrera 7 # 40-62, Bogotá, Colombia
lquin@javeriana.edu.co
[3] Instituto de Investigacion Tecnológica (IIT), ICAI Engineering School,
Universidad Pontificia de Comillas, c/Alberto Aguilera 25, 28250 Madrid, Spain
fjlvaldes@comillas.edu
[4] Projects Construction and Effective Management - PCEM SAS, Cartagena,
Colombia
nmorales@pcem.com.co
[5] Department of Industrial Management, Agroindustry and Operations,
Universidad de la Costa, Barranquilla, Colombia
ksalas2@cuc.edu.co

Abstract. *Objective*: Analyze the road crashes in Cartagena (Colombia) and
the factors associated with the collision and severity. The aim is to establish a set
of rules for defining countermeasures to improve road safety. *Methods*: Data
mining and machine learning techniques were used in 7894 traffic accidents
from 2016 to 2017. The severity was determined between low (84%) and high
(16%). Five classification algorithms to predict the accident severity were
applied with WEKA Software (Waikato Environment for Knowledge Analysis).
Including Decision Tree (DT-J48), Rule Induction (PART), Support Vector
Machines (SVMs), Naïve Bayes (NB), and Multilayer Perceptron (MLP). The
effectiveness of each algorithm was implemented using cross-validation with
10-fold. Decision rules were defined from the results of the different methods.
Results: The methods applied are consistent and similar in the overall results of
precision, accuracy, recall, and area under the ROC curve. *Conclusions*: 12
decision rules were defined based on the methods applied. The rules defined
show motorcyclists, cyclists, including pedestrians, as the most vulnerable road
users. Men and women motorcyclists between 20–39 years are prone in accidents with high severity. When a motorcycle or cyclist is not involved in the
accident, the probable severity is low.

Keywords: Road crashes · Prediction · Data mining · Severity

© Springer Nature Switzerland AG 2019
J. C. Figueroa-García et al. (Eds.): WEA 2019, CCIS 1052, pp. 309–320, 2019.
https://doi.org/10.1007/978-3-030-31019-6_27

1 Introduction

According to the World Health Organization WHO [1], approximately 1.4 million people died in traffic accidents in 2016, and it is estimated that more than 50 million people suffered severe injuries Traffic accidents in 2016 were the eighth cause of death, and the main causes of death for people between the ages of 15 and 29 years old. In addition, such accidents affect pedestrians, cyclists, and motorcyclists. Half of the road deaths occur among motorcyclists (28%), pedestrians (23%), and cyclists (3%). Mortality rates in low-income countries are 3 times higher than in high-income countries. Although only 1% of motor vehicles are in emerging countries, 13% of deaths occur in these nations [1]. Colombia in 2016 obtained a rate of 18.5 fatalities per 100,000 inhabitants. This figure is close to the global average (18.2) and the average middle-income countries (18.8). Between 2012–2018 in relation to the road users involved, the motorcyclists correspond to 50% of the victims. Pedestrians with 24%. The users of vehicles with 17%. The cyclists with 5% of accidents. The objective of this research was to analyze the road crashes in Cartagena (Colombia), and the factors associated with the collision and severity. Cartagena has 1.2 million inhabitants and more than 120,000 motor vehicles. Cartagena in the last two years (2017–2018) has remained in the top positions for fatal accidents in capital cities. In the last 8 years, Cartagena has been considered the fifth most dangerous city in road safety after Medellin, Cali, Bogota, and Barranquilla.

2 Method

The method is based on official information from the control entities, which allowed for the application of data mining and machine learning techniques. The method is based on the application of Decision Tree, Rule Induction, Support Vector Machines, Naïve Bayes, and Multilayer Perceptron with WEKA software. The decision tree constructs classification models in the form of trees. Rule Induction is an iterative process that follows a divide-and-conquer approach. Naïve Bayes is a classification algorithm based on Bayesian theorem. Multilayer Perceptron creates a feed-forward artificial neural network. Support vector machines are learning algorithms for classification and regression analysis. In the prediction of road accidents, data mining techniques have been implemented, such as: regressive models [2], neural networks [3], artificial intelligence [4], decision trees [5], Bayesian networks [6], SVM [7], and combined methods. The aim is to establish a set of decision rules for defining countermeasures to improve road safety. The effectiveness of each algorithm was implemented using cross-validation with 10-fold. The methodological process of this investigation is presented in four steps: (a) Pre-processing of accident dataset; (b) application of data mining techniques through Weka Software; (c) analysis of results and metrics; (d) definition of decision rules and analysis of associated factors.

2.1 Data Sources (Include Sample Size)

The registration of traffic accidents corresponds to the Cartagena database from January 2016 to December 2017. The dataset corresponds to the reports by the Administrative Department of Traffic and Transport (DATT). In total, 10,053 traffic accidents were reported by agents and police. The data records information about temporality, road users, gender and age. For the pre-processing of the data set, 27 categorical variables were defined (see Table 1). The variables were classified into four categories: (1) road actors involved in the crash, (2) individuals involved, (3) weather conditions and timing, (4) accident characteristics. The levels of injury severity were determined as low-level-of-injury (material damages, minor, non-incapacitating injury) or high-level-of-injury (injured victims and fatality).

Table 1. Definitions and values of traffic accident variables from four categories in the dataset.

Categories	Description	Label	Definition [Code] (Value)
Road actors	Number of cars	NLV	[0] Without vehicle; [1] one vehicle and [2] more than two vehicles
	Number of buses	NB	[0] Without vehicle; [1] one vehicle and [2] more than two vehicles
	Number of motorcyclists	NM	[0] Without motorcycle, [1] One motorcycle and [2] more than two motorcycles
	Number of cyclists	NC	[0] Without bicycles; [1] one bicycle; and [2] more than two bicycles
	Number of heavy vehicles	NHV	[0] Without vehicle; [1] one vehicle and [2] more than two vehicles
	Number of others (pedestrians, Non-register)	NOT	[0] Without; [1] one road actors; and [2] more than two road actors
	Relationship of road actors	RAV	[1] Solo motorcycle; [2] motorcycle-car; [3] motorcycle-heavy-vehicle; [4] motorcycle-bicycle; [5] Solo Cars; [6] Car-heavy-vehicle; [7] Solo-heavy-vehicle; [8] Solo bicycle; [9] Car-bicycle; [10] heavy-vehicle-bicycle; [11] others non-register
	Relationship type of service	RTS	[1] Particular; [2] particular-public; [3] public; [4] official-particular; [5] official-public; [6] official and [7] unidentified
Individuals	Gender of driver cars	GC	[1] Male; [2] female; [3] UNISEX; and [4] not defined
	Gender of the motorcyclist	GM	
	Gender of the bus driver	GB	
	Gender of the cyclists	GC	
	Gender of drivers of heavy vehicles	GHV	
	Driver's age	YC	[1] (0–19); [2] (20–39); [3] (40–59); [4] (60–79); [5]
	Motorcyclist's age	YM	(< 79)
	Bus driver's age	YB	
	Cyclist's age	YC	
	Heavy vehicle driver's age	YHV	
	Victim's age injured	YV	

(continued)

Table 1. (*continued*)

Categories	Description	Label	Definition [Code] (Value)
Weather/timing	Month	MON	[1] January–March; [2] April–June; [3] July–September; and [4] October–December
	Day of the week	DW	[1] During the week and [2] weekend
	Type of day	TD	[1] Holiday and [2] working day
	Type of commercial day	TCD	[1] Normal, [2] biweekly salary and [3] monthly salary
	Weather conditions (Precipitation, unit: mm)	WC	[1] (0–15); [2] (15–30); [3] (30–60); [4] (60–90); and [5] (< 90)
Accident characteristic	Accident class	CLA	[1] Collision; [2] falling from the vehicle; [3] run over; [4] dump Vehicle; [5] fire and [6] Others
	Injured or dead victim	VID	[0] Not recognized; [1] one injured/dead; and [2] two injured/dead or more
	Severity	SEV	[1] Low-level-of-injury and [2] high-level-of-injury

3   Results

The software WEKA contributed to the purification of the information by means of the Remove Misclassified method and duplicated instances. The dataset was reduced to 7,894 instances. Table 2 summarizes the variables used and their relationship to the severity. The analyzed data was divided into 16% of low, and 84% high-level-of-injury. In the descriptive analysis of the data, the greatest number of accidents occurs between cars (45%), followed by cars-heavy vehicles (28%), and finally between cars-motorcycles (14%). Accidents between private and public vehicles are prevalent (44%). Accidents involving motorcyclists (76%) and bicycles (88%) are more severe. The most frequent type of crash is the collision (99%), and the most severe are being run over (100%) and falling off the vehicle (93%).

Table 2. Statistics of road crashes for Cartagena in 2016–2017.

Label	Definition [Code] (Value)	% Total	Severity [1]	Severity [2]
NLV	[0] Without vehicle	12%	57%	43%
	[1] One vehicle	49%	81%	19%
	[2] More than two vehicles	39%	96%	4%
NB	[0] Without vehicle	77%	82%	18%
	[1] One vehicle	21%	90%	10%
	[2] More than two vehicles	2%	95%	5%
NM	[0] Without motorcycle	81%	94%	6%
	[1] One motorcycle	17%	42%	58%
	[2] More than two motorcycles	2%	12%	88%
NC	[0] Without bicycles	99%	84%	16%
	[1] One bicycle	1%	17%	83%

(*continued*)

Table 2. (*continued*)

Label	Definition [Code] (Value)	% Total	Severity [1]	Severity [2]
NHV	[0] Without vehicle	85%	82%	18%
	[1] One vehicle	14%	92%	8%
	[2] More than two vehicles	1%	97%	3%
NOT	[0] Without	91%	85%	15%
	[1] One road actors	9%	77%	23%
	[2] More than two road actors	0%	71%	29%
RAV	[1] Solo motorcycle	3%	14%	86%
	[2] Motorcycle-car	13%	47%	53%
	[3] Motorcycle-heavy-vehicle	2%	30%	70%
	[4] Motorcycle-bicycle	0%	4%	96%
	[5] Solo Cars	45%	95%	5%
	[6] Car-heavy-vehicle	28%	96%	4%
	[7] Solo-heavy-vehicle	6%	93%	7%
	[8] Solo bicycle	0%	0%	100%
	[9] Car-bicycle	0%	27%	73%
	[10] Heavy-vehicle-bicycle	0%	19%	81%
	[11] Others non-register	0%	79%	21%
RTS	[1] Particular	37%	75%	25%
	[2] Particular-public	44%	88%	12%
	[3] Public	17%	92%	8%
	[4] Official-particular	1%	83%	17%
	[5] Official-public	1%	85%	15%
	[6] Official	0%	58%	42%
	[7] Unidentified	0%	85%	15%
GC	[1] Male	74%	87%	13%
	[2] Female	6%	88%	12%
	[3] UNISEX	7%	97%	3%
	[4] Not defined	13%	58%	42%
GM	[1] Male	18%	39%	61%
	[2] Female	0%	18%	82%
	[3] UNISEX	0%	0%	100%
	[4] Not defined	81%	94%	6%
GB	[1] Male	22%	90%	10%
	[2] Female	0%	0%	0%
	[4] Not defined	77%	82%	18%
GC	[1] Male	1%	18%	82%
	[2] Female	0%	10%	90%
	[4] Not defined	99%	84%	16%
GHV	[1] Male	15%	93%	7%
	[2] Female	0%	100%	0%
	[3] UNISEX	0%	100%	0%
	[4] Not defined	85%	82%	18%

(*continued*)

Table 2. (*continued*)

Label	Definition [Code] (Value)	% Total	Severity [1]	Severity [2]
YC	[0] Without registration	14%	60%	40%
	[1] (0–17)	1%	96%	4%
	[2] (18–35)	26%	85%	15%
	[3] (36–45)	28%	90%	10%
	[4] (46–55)	20%	89%	11%
	[5] (56–69)	9%	87%	13%
	[6] (<70)	1%	85%	15%
YM	[0] Without registration	82%	94%	6%
	[1] (0–17)	0%	16%	84%
	[2] (18–35)	11%	37%	63%
	[3] (36–45)	4%	42%	58%
	[4] (46–55)	2%	45%	55%
	[5] (56–69)	1%	37%	63%
	[6] (<70)	0%	50%	50%
YB	[0] Without registration	78%	82%	18%
	[1] (0–17)	0%	100%	0%
	[2] (18–35)	10%	89%	11%
	[3] (36–45)	7%	90%	10%
	[4] (46–55)	4%	92%	8%
	[5] (56–69)	2%	91%	9%
	[6] (<70)	0%	100%	0%
YC	[0] Without registration	99%	84%	16%
	[1] (0–17)	0%	0%	100%
	[2] (18–35)	0%	19%	81%
	[3] (36–45)	0%	10%	90%
	[4] (46–55)	0%	9%	91%
	[5] (56–69)	0%	33%	67%
	[6] (<70)	0%	0%	100%
YHV	[0] Without registration	85%	82%	18%
	[1] (0–17)	0%	50%	50%
	[2] (18–35)	4%	92%	8%
	[3] (36–45)	5%	94%	6%
	[4] (46–55)	4%	94%	6%
	[5] (56–69)	2%	93%	7%
	[6] (<70)	0%	94%	6%
YV	[0] Without registration	99%	84%	16%
	[1] (0–17)	0%	0%	100%
	[2] (18–35)	0%	0%	100%
	[3] (36–45)	0%	0%	100%
	[4] (46–55)	0%	0%	100%
	[5] (56–69)	0%	0%	100%
	[6] (<70)	0%	0%	100%

(*continued*)

Table 2. (*continued*)

Label	Definition [Code] (Value)	% Total	Severity [1]	Severity [2]
MON	[1] January–March	22%	89%	11%
	[2] April–June	28%	82%	18%
	[3] July–September	30%	82%	18%
	[4] October–December	20%	84%	16%
DW	[1] During the week	74%	85%	15%
	[2] weekend	26%	81%	19%
TD	[1] Holiday	4%	84%	16%
	[2] working day	96%	84%	16%
TCD	[1] Normal	52%	84%	16%
	[2] Biweekly salary	16%	82%	18%
	[3] Monthly salary	33%	84%	16%
WC	[1] (0–15)	37%	86%	14%
	[2] (15–30)	9%	81%	19%
	[3] (30–60)	12%	82%	18%
	[4] (60–90)	8%	82%	18%
	[5] (<90)	33%	83%	17%
CLA	[1] Collision	99%	84%	16%
	[2] Falling from the vehicle	0%	7%	93%
	[3] Run over	0%	0%	100%
	[4] Dump Vehicle	0%	73%	27%
	[5] Fire	0%	100%	0%
	[6] Others	0%	89%	11%
VID	[0] Not recognized	66%	100%	0%
	[1] One injured/dead; and [2] two injured/dead or more	17%	0%	100%
	[2] Two injured/dead or more	18%	0%	100%

After descriptive statistical analysis, an inferential and correlational analysis of the variables proposed in the prediction of severity was proposed. The proposed analyzes were the Spearman and Friedman ANOVA correlation. Table 3 summarizes the results.

Table 3. Statistical analysis of the results for the prediction of the severity.

	Spearman RC		Friedman ANOVA		
	R^2	P-Value	Mean square	F-Ratio	P-Value
NLV	−0.3123	0	110.886	1384.45	0
NB	−0.094	0	74.247	927	0
NM	0.5924	0	197.696	2468.29	0
NC	0.1837	0	26.7644	334.16	0
NMH	−0.1053	0	7.59372	94.81	0
NOT	0.0608	0	0.000874166	0.01	0.9168
RAV	−0.4131	0	2.15764	26.94	0
RTS	−0.1788	0	0.546751	6.83	0.009
YD	−0.1843	0	0.674626	8.42	0.0037

(*continued*)

Table 3. (*continued*)

	Spearman RC		Friedman ANOVA		
	R2	P-Value	Mean square	F-Ratio	P-Value
YM	0.5697	0	0.315334	3.94	0.0472
YB	−0.0946	0	0.100419	1.25	0.2628
YHV	−0.1042	0	0.015438	0.19	0.6606
YC	0.1765	0	0.0846726	1.06	0.3039
YVC	0.1989	0	13.7402	171.55	0
GC	0.173	0	0.479928	5.99	0.0144
GM	−0.5852	0	2.69317	33.63	0
GB	0.0942	0	0.507256	6.33	0.0118
GHV	0.1045	0	0.104282	1.3	0.2538
GC	−0.1801	0	0.286762	3.58	0.0585
MON	0.048	0	1.91877	23.96	0
DW	0.0451	0.0001	0.0695317	0.87	0.3515
TD	−0.0006	0.9591	0.18272	2.28	0.1309
TCD	0.0104	0.3555	0.142195	1.78	0.1827
WC	0.0369	0.0011	0.264161	3.3	0.0494
CLA	0.1109	0	0.797542	9.96	0.0016

The variables NOT, YB, YHV, YC, GHV, DW, TD, and TCD do not evidence a significant statistical association with the direct prediction of the severity of the accident (p-value > 0.05). The variables with a statistical association on the prediction will be represented in the definition of the rules (p-value < 0.05).

After the data pre-processing, the selected data mining techniques are applied and parameterized (See Table 4) with the 10-fold cross-validation technique. The results are compared with the metrics: precision, accuracy, recall, and area under the ROC curve (See Table 5). The results show a high consistency and similarity in the prediction metrics in the applied techniques.

Table 4. Parameters settings for all classifiers.

Method	Parametrization
DT-J48	weka.classifiers.trees.J48 -C 0.25 -M 2
PART	weka.classifiers.rules.PART -M 2 -C 0.25 -Q 1
NB	weka.classifiers.bayes.NaiveBayes;Use kernel estimator F, Use supervised; discretization
SVM	weka.classifiers.functions.SMO -C 1.0 -L 0.001 -P 1.0E-12 -N 0 -V -1 -W 1 -K "weka.classifiers.functions.supportVector.PolyKernel -E 1.0 -C 250007" - calibrator "weka.classifiers.functions.Logistic -R 1.0E-8 -M -1 -num-decimal-places 4"
MLP	weka.classifiers.functions.MultilayerPerceptron -L 0.3 -M 0.2 -N 500 -V 0 -S 0 -E 20 -H a

Table 5. Comparison of all prediction results and performance metrics based on 10-fold cross-validation

Method	Classified instances		Accuracy	Precision	Recall	ROC Area	Time (seg)
	Correctly	Incorrectly					
DT-J48	7059	835	89.4%	89.1%	89.4%	83.0%	0.11
PART	6972	922	88.3%	87.6%	86.9%	86.4%	0.21
NB	6969	925	88.3%	89.5%	88.3%	86.8%	0.02
SVM	7002	892	88.7%	89.7%	88.7%	83.1%	46
MLP	6976	915	88.4%	88.2%	88.4%	86.2%	386

From the best results of each of the techniques, 12 priority decision rules for road safety were defined (See Table 6).

Table 6. List of rules identified with all methods applied.

Number	Identified rule (decodified)
1	If (NM $\geq$ 1) then Severity = High
2	If (NM: 0 & NC:0) then Severity = Low
3	If (NM > 1 & GM: Male, NVL:1, MON: July–December) then Severity = High
4	If (NM > 1 & GM: Male, NVL:1, MON: April–June, WC > 30 mm) then Severity = Low
5	If (NC > 1) then Severity = High
6	If (NM > 1 & GM: Male, NVL:1, MON: 2, WC > 90 mm, TD: Working day, YM: 20–39 years, TD: Weekend, GC: Male, TDC: biweekly and monthly salary) then Severity = High
7	If (GM: Male or Female, YM: 20–39 years) then Severity = High
8	If (NM $\geq$ 1, NVL:1, GM: Males, YM: 40–79 years) then Severity = Low
9	If (CLA: Collision, NM = 0, NC:0) then Severity = Low
10	If (CLA: Collision, NLV = 2, WC < 30 mm) then Severity = Low
11	If (CLA: Runover) then Severity = High
12	If (RAV: motorcycle-heavy-vehicle, WC > 60 mm) then Severity = High

4 Discussion

The results show cyclists and motorcyclists as the most vulnerable road users. Motorcyclists men and women between 20 and 39 years are predictive of high severity accidents. When there are no motorcycles or cyclists involved in the accident, the probable severity is low. Also, the collision between two motorcycles is considered of high severity. If the crash is a runover the severity is high, and it is inferred that the victim is a pedestrian. Finally, if the crash is between vehicles with rigid protection systems such as cars, buses or carriages, the accident decreases its severity.

This investigation allowed analyzing the accident records of Cartagena (Colombia) with data mining techniques. The rules contribute to the definition of strategies for the reduction of the severity of accidents. The presence of vulnerable road users (motorcyclists, cyclists, and pedestrians) were predictive variables on the severity of the accidents, as well as the results of [4, 8].

Rules 1, 2, 3, 4, 6, 8 and 12 show that more than 50% of the rules are related to the users of motorcycles. Motorcyclists are a population with significant growth due to the conditions for mobility, transportation, sports and other economic activities [9–11]. Subsequently, some countermeasures are exemplified by the defined rules. These rules are based on findings in the United States and the European Union on vulnerable users that can be replicated to reduce and eliminate road accidents. Among the policies, strategies and countermeasures to improve the road safety of the motorcyclist and the recommendations of WHO [12], are: Promote culture and education in road safety [13]. Analysis and monitoring of accident reports [14]. Road safety campaigns on the most vulnerable users in the ages of 15 to 30 years [15]. Promote the use of protective elements [16]. Restrict and punish driving under the influence of drugs and alcohol [17]. Control the speed according to the road type [18]. Improve the quality of roads, or design exclusive lanes [19]. Improve mechanical conditions and maintenance [20]. Improve the visibility of the motorcyclist [21]. Improve road safety conditions such as lighting, and infrastructure [22]. Forbid the transport and exposition of children on motorcycles [23]. Penalize violations and risky behaviors [24]. Restrict the manipulation of electronic devices while driving [25].

Finally, some additional countermeasures based on the rules are: Define road safety control plans according to the season. Rules 3 and 4 contrast that there are more demanding months in road control. Define speed limits conditioned by the intensity of rainfall. Rules 6 and 12 show that moderate and intense rains increase the possibility of accidents. Motorcyclist accidents can be avoided if interaction with other users is reduced. This is achieved from single circulation lanes. Rules 1, 3, 4, 6, 8 and 12 relate cars when the motorcycle interacts with another vehicle (e.g. Trucks and Cars). Finally, rules 7 and 8 confirm that the age of the motorcyclist influences the severity of the accident. These rules allow you to define license plans according to age. For example, in Europe, there are restrictions on circulation, speed, displacement, and violations according to age. Rule 11 is closely related to the high severity of the abuses. To define effective countermeasures from these rules it would be good to include new variables. These should be focused on additional aspects such as accident location, interception, location of the road, type of road, signaling, lighting, time, among others.

5   Conclusion

In this study, motorcyclists at young adult ages are related to predictive factors of severity at a level of injury or fatality. Global records in 2016 placed Colombia in the tenth position worldwide, the third in the region and second in South America in motorcyclist accident. In 2018 Colombia has 8.3 million motorcycles registered. In the last 7 years (2012–2018) the proportion of dead and injured motorcyclists is close to 50% of road users. Analyzing the accident rate of motorcyclists in Colombia and their causality are future investigations essential to improve road safety. The limitations of the study are the sub-registration of data by traffic control entities. If more causal variables are included, the creation of significantly more strategic rules for road safety can be achieved (for example, state and road conditions).

This investigation allowed analyzing the accident records of Cartagena (Colombia) with data mining techniques. The rules contribute to the definition of countermeasures, focused on vulnerable users for the reduction of the severity of accidents. The definition of rules from data mining is more effective than analyzing information with a simple descriptive statistical analysis. Because the analysis of the information is done in a correlational way, this contributes to obtain results that are easier to understand and apply. Techniques such as multivariate analysis or black-box techniques require additional steps for the analysis of information.

Acknowledgements. Funding for first author was covered by (CEIBA)—Gobernación de Bolívar (Colombia). We thank the Administrative Department of Traffic and Transportation (DATT) in the accompaniment and support of the information required for this investigation.

References

1. World Health Organization (WHO): Global status report on road safety 2018 (2018). https://apps.who.int/iris/bitstream/handle/10665/276462/9789241565684-eng.pdf?ua=1
2. Savolainen, P., Mannering, F.: Probabilistic models of motorcyclists' injury severities in single- and multi-vehicle crashes (in English). Accid. Anal. Prev. **39**(5), 955–963 (2007)
3. Abdelwahab, H., Abdel-Aty, M.: Development of artificial neural network models to predict driver injury severity in traffic accidents at signalized intersections. Transp. Res. Rec.: J. Transp. Res. Board **1746**, 6–13 (2001)
4. Hashmienejad, S.H.-A., Hasheminejad, S.M.H.: Traffic accident severity prediction using a novel multi-objective genetic algorithm. Int. J. Crashworthiness **22**(4), 425–440 (2017)
5. Sohn, S., Shin, H.: Data mining for road traffic accident type classification. Ergonomics **44**, 107–117 (2001)
6. Huang, H., Abdel-Aty, M.: Multilevel data and Bayesian analysis in traffic safety. Accid. Anal. Prev. **42**(6), 1556–1565 (2010)
7. Li, Z., Liu, P., Wang, W., Xu, C.: Using support vector machine models for crash injury severity analysis. Accid. Anal. Prev. **45**, 478–486 (2012)
8. Delen, D., Tomak, L., Topuz, K., Eryarsoy, E.: Investigating injury severity risk factors in automobile crashes with predictive analytics and sensitivity analysis methods. J. Transp. Health **4**, 118–131 (2017)
9. Balasubramanian, V., Jagannath, M.: Detecting motorcycle rider local physical fatigue and discomfort using surface electromyography and seat interface pressure. Transp. Res. Part F **22**, 150–158 (2014)
10. Shafiei, U.K.M., Karuppiah, K., Tmrin, S.B.M., Meng, G.Y., Rasdi, I., Alias, A.N.: The effectiveness of new model of motorcycle seat with built-in lumbar support (in English). Jurnal Teknologi **77**(27), 97–103 (2015)
11. Ospina-Mateus, H., Jiménez, L.A.Q.: Understanding the impact of physical fatigue and postural comfort experienced during motorcycling: a systematic review. J. Transp. Health **12**, 290–318 (2019)

12. World Health Organization (WHO): Seguridad de los vehículos de motor de dos y tres ruedas: manual de seguridad vial para decisores y profesionales (2017). https://apps.who.int/iris/bitstream/handle/10665/272757/9789243511924-spa.pdf?sequence=1&isAllowed=y

13. Segui-Gomez, M., Lopez-Valdes, F.J.: Recognizing the importance of injury in other policy forums: the case of motorcycle licensing policy in Spain (in English). Inj. Prev. Short Surv. **13**(6), 429–430 (2007)

14. Schneider Iv, W.H., Savolainen, P.T., Van Boxel, D., Beverley, R.: Examination of factors determining fault in two-vehicle motorcycle crashes (in English). Accid. Anal. Prev. **45**, 669–676 (2012)

15. Ivers, R.Q., et al.: Does an on-road motorcycle coaching program reduce crashes in novice riders? A randomised control trial (in English). Accid. Anal. Prev. **86**, 40–46 (2016)

16. Donate-López, C., Espigares-Rodríguez, E., Jiménez-Moleón, J.J., de Dios Luna-del-Castillo, J., Bueno-Cavanillas, A., Lardelli-Claret, P.: The association of age, sex and helmet use with the risk of death for occupants of two-wheeled motor vehicles involved in traffic crashes in Spain. Accid. Anal. Prev. **42**(1), 297–306 (2010)

17. Albalate, D., Fernández-Villadangos, L.: Motorcycle injury severity in Barcelona: the role of vehicle type and congestion (in English). Traffic Inj. Prev. **11**(6), 623–631 (2010)

18. Clabaux, N., Brenac, T., Perrin, C., Magnin, J., Canu, B., Van Elslande, P.: Motorcyclists' speed and "looked-but-failed-to-see" accidents (in English). Accid. Anal. Prev. **49**, 73–77 (2012)

19. Sager, B., Yanko, M.R., Spalek, T.M., Froc, D.J., Bernstein, D.M., Dastur, F.N.: Motorcyclist's lane position as a factor in right-of-way violation collisions: a driving simulator study (in English). Accid. Anal. Prev. **72**, 325–329 (2014)

20. Rizzi, M., Strandroth, J., Holst, J., Tingvall, C.: Does the improved stability offered by motorcycle antilock brakes (ABS) make sliding crashes less common? In-depth analysis of fatal crashes involving motorcycles fitted with ABS (in English). Traffic Inj. Prev. **17**(6), 625–632 (2016)

21. Clarke, D.D., Ward, P., Bartle, C., Truman, W.: The role of motorcyclist and other driver behaviour in two types of serious accident in the UK (in English). Accid. Anal. Prev. **39**(5), 974–981 (2007)

22. López-Valdés, F.J., García, D., Pedrero, D., Moreno, J.L.: Accidents of motorcyclists against roadside infrastructure. In: IUTAM Symposium on Impact Biomechanics: From Fundamental Insights to Applications, vol. 124, pp. 163–170, Dublin (2005)

23. Brown, J., Schonstein, L., Ivers, R., Keay, L.: Children and motorcycles: a systematic review of risk factors and interventions. Inj. Prev. **24**(2), 166–175 (2018)

24. Elliott, M.A., Baughan, C.J., Sexton, B.F.: Errors and violations in relation to motorcyclists' crash risk (in English). Accid. Anal. Prev. **39**(3), 491–499 (2007)

25. Truong, L.T., Nguyen, H.T., De Gruyter, C.: Mobile phone use while riding a motorcycle and crashes among university students. Traffic Inj. Prev. **20**, 1–7 (2019)

Bioengineering

Validation of Parametric Models in Microelectrode Recordings Acquired from Patients with Parkinson's Disease

Sebastian Roldan-Vasco[1]([✉]), Sebastian Restrepo-Agudelo[1],
Adriana Lucia Lopez-Rios[2], and William D. Hutchison[3]

[1] Instituto Tecnológico Metropolitano, Medellín, Colombia
sebastianroldan@itm.edu.co
[2] Hospital Universitario San Vicente Fundación, Medellín and Rionegro, Colombia
[3] Division of Neurosurgery, Department of Surgery and Physiology,
University of Toronto, Toronto, Canada

Abstract. The Deep Brain Stimulation (DBS) has become one of the most common therapies applied to patients with Parkinson's disease (PD). Microelectrode recordings (MER) are taken invasively to measure the electrical activity of neurons in the basal ganglia during DBS procedures. The modeling of the MER signals can help to characterize the electrical behavior of the different nuclei along the surgical trajectory. In this paper, we applied linear and nonlinear parametric structures to model MER signals in 19 patients with PD undergoing DBS in two targets of the basal ganglia. We compared the fits obtained by different orders of pure autoregressive (AR) and AR-moving average (ARMA) models, as well as three models with exogenous input – ARX, ARMAX and BoxJenkins. Furthermore, we evaluated the performance of a nonlinear ARX – NARX - model. All comparisons were made in both right and left hemispheres. We found that exogenous input reduces the fit of the model significantly. The best performance was achieved by the AR model, followed by ARMA. Although NARX had better behavior than ARX, ARMAX and BoxJenkins, it did not surpass the fit of the AR and ARMA. Furthermore, we could reduce the order of the AR reported previously by increasing the database considerably. These results are an approach to characterize the MER signals, and could serve as a feature for pattern recognition-based algorithms intended for intraoperative identification of basal ganglia.

Keywords: Microelectrode recordings (MER) ·
Deep brain stimulation (DBS) · Signal modeling · Parametric study ·
Parkinson's disease · Subthalamic nucleus

1 Introduction

Parkinson's disease (PD) represents the most frequent neurodegenerative disorder after Alzheimer's disease. Its cause is still unknown [1]. Throughout the

© Springer Nature Switzerland AG 2019
J. C. Figueroa-García et al. (Eds.): WEA 2019, CCIS 1052, pp. 323–334, 2019.
https://doi.org/10.1007/978-3-030-31019-6_28

last 60 years, several treatments have been used to relieve the symptoms caused by this disorder. Those treatments can be categorized as: (1) surgical ablative strategies (pallidotomy, thalamotomy), (2) pharmaceutical treatments (L-Dopa) and, (3) non-ablative surgeries, specifically deep brain stimulation (DBS) [2]. DBS uses an implanted neurostimulator to apply electrical pulses (typically $\sim 60 - 90\,\mu s$) at a given amplitude ($\sim 2 - 4\,V$) and frequency ($\sim 130 - 185\,Hz$), in specific brain structures affected by the abnormal neurophysiological behavior related to PD [3]. A wealth of evidence in patients with PD show that stimulation of the subthalamic nucleus (STN) and globus pallidus internus (GPi) ameliorates parkinsonian motor symptoms [4].

A fundamental task for the localization of optimal surgical target in DBS procedure, is the visualization of neuroelectrical activity by microelectrode recording (MER). MER signals allow the discrimination of electrical behavior from individual neurons [5]. Their average firing rate can vary between 0 and 500 Hz, with tonic, irregular or bursty firing patterns and occasionally show periodic oscillations in firing rate at theta, alpha, beta and gamma frequency bands [6,7]. Inaccurate location of the stimulator may result in adverse events, it decreases the effective voltage range for therapeutic effects and may increase the risk of morbidity and mortality [8]. Modeling strategies seek to support the functional neurosurgeon not only in the identification of specific neuronal structures related to motor dysfunctions, but also in the automatic detection of the STN borders.

MER signals based methods have been proposed for improving the intraoperative target localization. Most of them have applied traditional pattern recognition schemes, in which the classification rate seems to be highly dependent on the feature space. Several authors have used wavelet transform based features. However, the selection of a proper mother wavelet could be problematic because similar behavior could be present in different basal ganglia [9]. Furthermore, most of them are based only on the information given by the spikes, ignoring the background noise, which is a good indicator of the presence of the STN [10].

Pinzon-Morales et al. applied optimal wavelet feature extraction and three classical classifiers in two databases of MER signals [11]. They obtained a maximum accuracy below 87% for combined databases. Afterwards, they improved the classification rate by using adaptable spectral features obtained from wavelet transform and a filter bank method [9]. Cagnan et al. used noise level, compound firing rate and measures based on power spectral density as feature space, and they achieved 88% agreement in detection of STN [10]. The two last works used rule-based detection methods, which fail to generalize the behavior of different nuclei [12].

The relatively new concept of spike-independent features results in a robust feature space that can be extracted from MER signals, reducing effects of the inter-subject physiological variability and of intermittent artifacts [13]; however, feature proliferation could lead to irrelevant or redundant features [14]. Chaovalitwongse et al. extracted spike detection-dependent and independent features from MER signals in 17 patients. They could detect STN, zona incerta and substantia nigra (SNr) with an accuracy around 90%. However, with frequency-based features the accuracy decreased to 50% [15]. Feature selection methods improve the performance for STN detection of both spike dependent- and independent features, independently of the classifier [14].

Although complex models have been proposed [16], more simple classification schemes have shown to be reliable. Moran et al. used the normalized root mean square (NRMS) and the estimated distance to target in order to detect STN borders, achieving an error below 0.5 mm [17]. Valsky et al. proposed a new feature named the ratio of high-low frequency power. They used it together with the trajectory history to detect STN-SNr border (97% hits) [12]. Thompson et al. used NRMS and power spectral density, with an agreement on the optimal track of 84% [18]. It is evident that there is a high variability of results between reported papers.

Modeling techniques have been studied in the analysis of the neuronal behavior. These methods include parametric [19] and nonparametric [20] structures. It is widely accepted that parametric structures are reliable to model dynamic characteristics of several systems even in presence of noise sources [21]. Despite of this, few studies were found in MER signals. Pukala et al. applied autoregressive (AR) structures to thalamic and STN signal modeling, in order to identify specific brain structures from three patients. They found that the distribution of the model coefficients and percentage of correct classification were different for each patient's basal ganglia [22]. Furthermore, the number of patients used for this study was limited, so the model confidence was low and there is lack of generalization.

Parametric models, specifically AR, have shown to have better frequency resolution than traditional spectral characterization for short data windows [23], and they are suitable for analysis of tremor data [24]. Furthermore, parametric techniques are better than nonparametric methods to distinguish between neuronal states using spectral information from cerebral recordings [25].

This paper presents a methodology based on parametric modeling, both linear and non-linear in order to characterize microelectrode recordings acquired from 19 patients undergoing DBS procedures. This characterization is the first stage of a wider scheme oriented to MER-based identification of basal ganglia, as a support tool for functional neurosurgery. The goal of the current work is to characterize MER signals through parametric models instead to classify basal ganglia.

2   Materials and Methods

2.1   MER Signals Recording

The modeling scheme was applied retrospectively to a database of 19 patients with advanced Parkinson's disease undergoing standard DBS surgery of bilateral STN. The medical staff registered up to four channels per microelectrode. All recordings were obtained while the patients were awake, at rest, and monitored for alertness. The STN was localized anatomically on preoperative imaging (MRI) and then intra-operatively by its firing pattern and background activity. The MER signals were acquired with the Frederick Haer LP+ microTargeting system (FHC, Inc.). The recorded signals of the local field potentials (LFP) were obtained from basal ganglia along the intra-operative trajectory. Signals were recorded at the points of interest of the functional neurosurgeon, and the location was given by the distance from the electrode to the pre-established surgical target in Z-axis.

The signals were acquired with sampling frequency of 48 kHz, 16 bits resolution and digital band-pass filter with cutoff frequencies between 0.03 and 2.5 kHz (by default) and a line noise adaptive filter. These cutoff frequencies were modified by the surgeon during the acquisition process, aiming to obtain the optimal visualization of the spikes according to the expected neural activity. In most cases the filter bandwidth was set from 5 to 3000 Hz in order to attenuate low frequency noise. If this did not produce suitable noise suppression, then one of the 3 open channels was grounded. This study was conducted according to the protocol approved by the local ethics committee of Centros Especializados San Vicente Fundación (Rionegro, Colombia). The characterization and modeling techniques were computed offline in Matlab (The Mathworks, Inc.).

2.2 Signal Processing

The signals were exported in .plx format and later converted into Matlab format. The analyses were performed using custom scripts. Although the recording equipment has its own stopband filters, we performed a digital notch filter in cascade with center frequency at 60 Hz and its harmonics (120, 180, 240, 300, and 360 Hz). A 10th order Butterworth topology was used. The same bandpass filter implemented intraoperatively was used.

2.3 Linear Parametric Modeling

The most used parametric structures for brain signals modeling are the auto-regressive with moving average (ARMA) [26] and the pure auto-regressive (AR) [27]. In this study, we considered models defined by AR structures, ARMA, ARX (AR with exogenous input), ARMAX (ARMA with exogenous input) and Box-Jenkins models (BJ). Considering an input stimulus $u(n)$ and an output (MER signal) $y(n)$, a general model of a discrete-time dynamic system can be written as follows [28]:

$$y = f(\phi(n), \theta) \tag{1}$$

The function $f(\bullet)$ represents the time series, θ is the vector of parameters, and $\phi(n)$ is the regression vector given by:

$$\phi(n) = [y(n-1) \cdots y(n-n_y) \ u(n) \cdots u(n-n_u)] \tag{2}$$

The Eq. 1 can be expressed as follows [29]:

$$A(q)y(n) = \frac{B(q)}{F(q)}u(n) + \frac{C(q)}{D(q)}e(n) \tag{3}$$

Where $e(n) \sim N(0, \sigma_e^2)$ is the moving average variable, a background noise normally distributed with zero mean and standard deviation σ_e; the terms that depend on q represent a polynomial of backward shift operators of the system's difference equation, in which $q^{-1}y(n) \equiv y(n-1)$. The coefficients of the polynomials represent the parameters of the system θ. The configuration of these polynomials depends on the parametric structure. In AR, $B(q) = F(q) = 0, C(q) = D(q) = 1$; in ARMA, $B(q) = F(q) = 0$; in ARX, $F(q) = C(q) = D(q) = 1$; in ARMAX, $F(q) = D(q) = 1$; in BJ, $A(q) = 1$. The selection of the appropriate model structure depends on the number of parameters, i.e. the dimension of θ (model's order) and the optimization method as well. For the AR and ARMA cases, we made an exhaustive evaluation of orders ranged between 5 and 20, which give a good performance according to [30, 31]. The goal of the parametric modeling is to find the parameters θ that minimize the loss function [28]:

$$V(\theta) = \frac{1}{N} \sum_{n=1}^{n_{max}} (y(n) - f(\phi(n), \theta))^2 \qquad (4)$$

Where N is the signal's length and n_{max} is the model's order. For the ARX, ARMAX and BJ models, we applied the model proposed by Santaniello et al. aiming to generate the exogenous input [32]. We used also the Akaike's information criterion (AIC) as estimator of the optimal model's order. The AIC is given by [33]:

$$AIC = -2\ln V(\theta) + 2n \qquad (5)$$

This criterion allows to do a selection of the minimum order that guarantees the best fitness between the generated and the sampled signals. We made a comparison between the fit given by the assessed models via hypothesis test. Since the amount of data is large, we applied the student t-test.

2.4   Non-linear Parametric Modeling

Nonlinear ARMAX models (NARMAX) were introduced in 1985, gaining interest and development since [34]. A simplification of this model is the NARX, applied when the error can be assumed as Gaussian noise. The NARX model has the same form as Eq. 1. However, $f(\bullet)$ is a nonlinear function of the regressors expressed in forms such as $y(n-1)^2, u(n-1)y(n-2), \tan(u(n-2))$, etc. In this case, we assessed two neural network based functions, a wavelet network (wavenet) and a sigmoid network (sigmoidnet). Ten units (neurons) and one hidden layer were used for both functions. Similarly to the linear case, the student t-test was implemented for comparison between models.

3   Results and Discussion

The bandwidth of the signals was selected in order to capture the gamma oscillations (60–200 Hz) and the high-frequency oscillations (200–500 Hz) of the STN

[6,7]. We analyzed 1029 signals from right hemispheres and 1139 from left ones. Time windows of 1 s were chosen for model estimation. A different window with the same length was randomly chosen for validation, avoiding superposition of data with the estimation segment. Three samples ahead were used as prediction horizon. This process was applied for both linear and nonlinear models. The accuracy of all models was computed by the Euclidean distance. The goodness of fit was obtained for each assessed order in every signal, and it was computed from the validation segment. Mean and standard deviation of the fit was computed per structure and hemisphere (see Fig. 1).

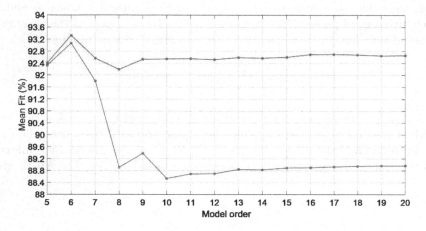

Fig. 1. Fit per model order. Blue and red lines indicate results obtained from right and left hemispheres, respectively. (Color figure online)

Let AR(n) denote an AR model of order n. The maximum selected order $n = 20$, was set as a limit value for modeling, because the fits for orders above $n = 15$ tend to a plateau. Although there are two different plateau levels (92% for left and 88% for right hemisphere), we found that the optimal parametric structure was AR(6) in both hemispheres (Fig. 1). The differences in the plateau might be due to that the left side is usually recorded first, and systematic like anesthetic effects could appear (less effect on the right side). The fit for both hemispheres were not statistically significantly different ($t = -0.93, p = 0.355$). The main advantage of the found model is the simplicity, which reduces the computational cost.

The reported mean of fit can be complemented with the analysis of the median. Figure 2 shows the median fits obtained from the estimation of AR(6) in the whole dataset. There were patients with fits in only one hemisphere, because the bandwidth in the missing hemisphere was discarded for analysis, i.e. low cutoff frequencies attenuated components lower than 100 Hz. The box-plot confirms that the fits of AR(6) models in every patient were around the same value, most of them above 90%, which gives a reliable scenario for modeling of

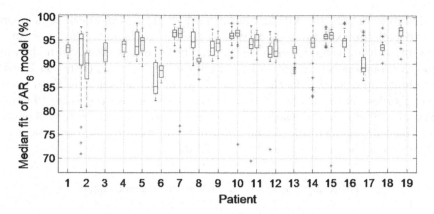

Fig. 2. Box-plot of the median fits computed for the MER recordings of all patients. Blue and red boxes indicate results obtained from the left and right hemispheres, respectively. (Color figure online)

MER signals acquired during DBS procedure. On a previous work with signals of two patients, we reported that the optimal model of basal ganglia signals was AR(13). However, the present work reduces the optimal order value until 6 and subsequently the complexity of the model, which generates an acceptable fit validated with a higher database, and agrees with the fact that increasing the model order incorporates additive noise into the AR model [24].

Let ARMA(na,nc) denote an ARMA model. with orders na for $A(q)$, and nc for $C(q)$ (see Eq. 3). We found that the best parameter configuration was ARMA(20,20) (Table 1). Although the best ARMA structure used the maximum order allowed, the obtained fits were below of the accuracy estimated with AR(6) model ($t = 8.01, p < 0.001$). Additionally, the dispersion of the accuracy was higher for all combinations of ARMA orders than for AR(6) (Table 1).

Table 1. Fits for AR and ARMA models.

Model	Order	Left hemisphere	Right hemisphere
AR	6	**93.33 ± 4.97**	**93.07 ± 5.16**
	20	92.66 ± 8.49	88.96±11.87
ARMA	10,10	92.44 ± 8.72	88.91±11.91
	5,10	92.33±8.80	88.0 ± 12.0
	10,5	92.44±8.66	88.90 ± 11.90
	20,20	92.52±8.66	89.03 ± 11.78

For ARX, ARMAX and BJ models, we used three information criteria for estimation of the order: AIC, AIC corrected and the Bayesian Information Criterion. However, we did not find differences in terms of the fit value, thus we decided to work with the AIC for simplicity. For all cases and both hemispheres, the order of the exogenous input was 1, i.e. the polynomial $B(q)$ was always constant with no backward shift operator. The order associated with the auto-regressive component was 3.56 ± 1.27 (right) and 3.60 ± 1.20 (left). Both orders were similar and it remarks the independence of the hemisphere. Even though rational orders have no mathematical sense, in this case the value illustrates the mean and standard deviation of the global data-set, but for each signal the model has only integer orders. The order of the auto-regressive component that best represent the most of records was 4 (Table 2).

Table 2. Mean fits for models with exogenous input.

Model	Right hemisphere	Left hemisphere
ARX	84.15 ± 7.56	84.34 ± 8.02
ARMAX	82.98 ± 7.95	83.61 ± 8.62
Box-Jenkins	72.49 ± 8.00	73.0 ± 8.18

Although the optimal order found for ARX, ARMAX and BJ is lower than the order for AR and ARMA, the fit decreases considerably when an exogenous input is applied (between 9% and 20%). The difference between AR and ARX fits ($t = -38.95, p < 0.001$), and between ARMA and ARMAX fits ($t = -21.14, p < 0.001$), is statistically significant. This does not mean necessarily that the time series could not be modeled with an exogenous input, but maybe the chosen signal in this case was not appropriate. Table 2 shows the results for both hemispheres and the three structures with exogenous input.

Notably, according to the Tables 1 and 2, the moving-average component (MA) reduces the accuracy of the model. In both AR-ARMA and ARX-ARMAX cases, the reduction is near to 1%. However, this difference was not statistically significant ($t = 3.19, p = 0.0014$). The complexity of the MER signals (non-regular spikes, phase-amplitude coupling, nested oscillations, and abrupt changes in time domain) could be the factor that limit the capability of representation of the MA component. This could explain the lowest accuracy of the BJ model (Table 2). In this case, it is remarkable that if complexity of the model increases, the capability of representation of the MER signals decreases.

For the non-linear case, we applied two NARX structures for each signal. The chosen nonlinearity functions were sigmoid and wavelet. We found the order by means of the AIC scheme and we applied subsequently a hypothesis test for nonlinearity with the obtained orders. However, the number of non-linear regressors was null for all cases. After having tested several alternatives for orders, we found that $na = 4$, $nb = 4$, and $nk = 1$, satisfied the hypothesis of nonlinearity. The fit obtained with the last values was better than with orders given by AIC (Table 3). When the order (4,4,1) is applied, the fit improves around 2.5% and 3.5%. This difference is statistically significant for right (sigmoid – $t = -9.17, p < 0.001$; wavelet – $t = -8.66, p < 0.001$) and left hemisphere too (sigmoid $- t = -7.14, p < 0.001$; wavelet $- t = -6.83, p < 0.001$). There are not statistically significant differences between nonlinearity functions in both hemispheres for Sig-AIC ($t = -1.87, p = 0.061$), Wav-AIC ($t = -1.86, p = 0.063$), Sig-441 ($t = 1.23, p = 0.219$), and Wav-AIC ($t = 1.07, p = 0.286$). Although the nonlinear modeling achieves better results than linear structures with exogenous input, when comparing with the simplest model AR, and even ARMA, they are overcome.

Additionally, spectral analysis of the modeled and real signals was done. The median peak frequency for all signals were around 12 Hz. Additionally, mean and standard deviation of the error of peak frequency were computed for each structure: AR (0.08 ± 14.30 Hz), ARMA (0.48 ± 14.29 Hz), ARX (0.48 ± 14.25 Hz), ARMAX (1.25 ± 15.06 Hz), BJ (0.62 ± 14.33 Hz), Sig-AIC (0.55 ± 13.81 Hz), Wav-AIC (0.37 ± 13.94 Hz), Sig-441 (0.55 ± 13.67 Hz), and Wav-441 (0.35 ± 13.57 Hz). Although AR process achieved the lowest error, with all models the spectral behavior is conserved. Furthermore, We assessed the residuals of all parametric structures, and we found that such residuals are reasonably normally distributed and uncorrelated, a basic condition to determine whether parametric models are suitable to describe the dynamics of a time-series [35].

Previous works have reported that the optimal order for modeling of basal ganglia signals is AR(13) or superior [31]. With a more robust database in terms of the amount of signals and points recorded, we found that with the simplest model, i.e. the AR, and a low order $n = 6$, we can get a good representation of the complex behavior of the MER signals.

Table 3. Fits for NARX models. Sig: sigmoidnet, Wav: wavenet, AIC: Akaike's Information Criterion.

Model	Right hemisphere	Left hemisphere
Sig-AIC	85.0 ± 6.63	84.33 ± 7.83
Wav-AIC	85.0 ± 6.59	84.40 ± 7.80
Sig-441	87.45 ± 7.90	87.90 ± 7.37
Wav-441	87.39 ± 7.87	87.78 ± 7.48

A limitation of this work is that the signals were passed by the modeling block independently of the depth in the Z-coordinate, i.e., the signals were not labeled with specific anatomical points. For future work, we must analyze the dependency of the given order from specific points of the intracerebral trajectory. We must to acquire and record signals at specific planned points for all future patients, in order to find a correspondence between depth and mathematical descriptors of the models.

Since AR coefficients have been widely used for characterization of other biomedical signals, these parameters could serve as features for machine learning algorithms. In MER signals, other feature such as power band ratio, peak to average power ratio, phase amplitude coupling, interspike interval, etc, have been used in characterization oriented to classification and prediction [36]. We propose as future work the use of the parameters of AR model as an additional feature for classification purposes in MER. This could be extended with a VAR model (vector autoregressive), in order to process the whole dataset instead of each individual signal, giving a wide panorama of the surgical track. This may have potential use in the intraoperative environment as a tool for detection of basal ganglia during DBS procedures.

4   Conclusions

MER signals recorded from patients with PD in DBS implantation surgery, were modeled by parametric linear and nonlinear structures. We assessed both the optimal order and the fit for different models structures. The presence of exogenous input in the models ARX, ARMAX and Box-Jenkins decreases the fit. Although nonlinear ARX has an acceptable fit, AR has the highest one, above 90%. We could reduce the order of the AR model to 6 and validate the results of a previous reported work. This result is more statistically significant because it was computed in a bigger database. Our approach is useful for analysis, simulation and characterization of basal ganglia signals.

Acknowledgments. This work was supported by Instituto Tecnológico Metropolitano (code P14222), Medellín, Colombia, with co-execution of Universidad de Antioquia and Hospital Universitario San Vicente Fundación (Medellín and Rionegro).

References

1. Diazgranados Sánchez, J.A., Chan Guevara, L., Gómez Betancourt, L.F., Lozano Arango, A.F., Ramirez, M.: Description of parkinson disease population in a neurological medical center in Cali, Colombia. Acta Neurológica Colombiana **27**(4), 205–210 (2011)
2. Benabid, A.L., Chabardes, S., Mitrofanis, J., Pollak, P.: Deep brain stimulation of the subthalamic nucleus for the treatment of Parkinson's disease. Lancet Neurol. **8**(1), 67–81 (2009)
3. Brittain, J.S., Brown, P.: Oscillations and the basal ganglia: Motor control and beyond. Neuroimage **85**, 637–647 (2014)
4. Deep-Brain Stimulation for Parkinson's Disease Study Group: Deep-brain stimulation of the subthalamic nucleus or the pars interna of the globus pallidus in Parkinson's disease. N. Engl. J. Med. **345**(13), 956–963 (2001)
5. Basha, D., Dostrovsky, J.O., Rios, A.L.L., Hodaie, M., Lozano, A.M., Hutchison, W.D.: Beta oscillatory neurons in the motor thalamus of movement disorder and pain patients. Exp. Neurol. **261**, 782–790 (2014)
6. Beudel, M., Brown, P.: Adaptive deep brain stimulation in Parkinson's disease. Parkinsonism & Relat. Disord. **22**, S123–S126 (2016)
7. Yang, A.I., Vanegas, N., Lungu, C., Zaghloul, K.A.: Beta-coupled high-frequency activity and beta-locked neuronal spiking in the subthalamic nucleus of Parkinson's disease. J. Neurosci. **34**(38), 12816–12827 (2014)

8. Patel, D.M., Walker, H.C., Brooks, R., Omar, N., Ditty, B., Guthrie, B.L.: Adverse events associated with deep brain stimulation for movement disorders: Analysis of 510 consecutive cases. Operative Neurosurg. **11**(1), 190–199 (2015)
9. Pinzon-Morales, R., Orozco-Gutierrez, A., Castellanos-Dominguez, G.: Novel signal-dependent filter bank method for identification of multiple basal ganglia nuclei in Parkinsonian patients. J. Neural Eng. **8**(3), 036026 (2011)
10. Cagnan, H., et al.: Automatic subthalamic nucleus detection from microelectrode recordings based on noise level and neuronal activity. J. Neural Eng. **8**(4), 046006 (2011)
11. Pinzon-Morales, R.D., Orozco-Gutierrez, A.A., Carmona-Villada, H., Castellanos, C.G.: Towards high accuracy classification of mer signals for target localization in parkinson's disease. In: 2010 Annual International Conference of the IEEE Engineering in Medicine and Biology Society (EMBC), pp. 4040–4043. IEEE (2010)
12. Valsky, D., et al.: S top! border ahead: Automatic detection of subthalamic exit during deep brain stimulation surgery. Mov. Disord. **32**(1), 70–79 (2017)
13. Wong, S., Baltuch, G., Jaggi, J., Danish, S.: Functional localization and visualization of the subthalamic nucleus from microelectrode recordings acquired during dbs surgery with unsupervised machine learning. J. Neural Eng. **6**(2), 026006 (2009)
14. Rajpurohit, V., Danish, S.F., Hargreaves, E.L., Wong, S.: Optimizing computational feature sets for subthalamic nucleus localization in dbs surgery with feature selection. Clin. Neurophysiol. **126**(5), 975–982 (2015)
15. Chaovalitwongse, W., Jeong, Y., Jeong, M.K., Danish, S., Wong, S.: Pattern recognition approaches for identifying subcortical targets during deep brain stimulation surgery. IEEE Intell. Syst. **26**(5), 54–63 (2011)
16. Chan, H.L., Wu, T., Lee, S.T., Lin, M.A., He, S.M., Chao, P.K., Tsai, Y.T.: Unsupervised wavelet-based spike sorting with dynamic codebook searching and replenishment. Neurocomputing **73**(7–9), 1513–1527 (2010)
17. Moran, A., Bar-Gad, I., Bergman, H., Israel, Z.: Real-time refinement of subthalamic nucleus targeting using bayesian decision-making on the root mean square measure. Mov. Disord. Official J. Mov. Disord. Soc. **21**(9), 1425–1431 (2006)
18. Thompson, J.A., et al.: Semi-automated application for estimating subthalamic nucleus boundaries and optimal target selection for deep brain stimulation implantation surgery. J. Neurosurg. **18**, 1–10 (2018)
19. Li, P., et al.: Autoregressive model in the Lp norm space for EEG analysis. J. Neurosci. Methods **240**, 170–178 (2015)
20. Jerger, K.K., et al.: Early seizure detection. J. Clin. Neurophysiol. **18**(3), 259–268 (2001)
21. Mignolet, M., Red-Horse, J.: Armax identification of vibrating structures-model and model order estimation. In: 35th Structures, Structural Dynamics, and Materials Conference, p. 1525 (1994)
22. Pukala, J., Sanchez, J.C., Principe, J., Bova, F., Okun, M.: Linear predictive analysis for targeting the basal ganglia in deep brain stimulation surgeries. In: Proceedings of the 2nd International IEEE EMBS Conference on Neural Engineering, pp. 192–195. IEEE (2005)
23. Cassidy, M., et al.: Movement-related changes in synchronization in the human basal ganglia. Brain **125**(6), 1235–1246 (2002)
24. Spyers-Ashby, J., Bain, P., Roberts, S.: A comparison of fast fourier transform (FFT) and autoregressive (AR) spectral estimation techniques for the analysis of tremor data. J. Neurosci. Methods **83**(1), 35–43 (1998)
25. Faust, O., Acharya, R., Allen, A.R., Lin, C.: Analysis of EEG signals during epileptic and alcoholic states using AR modeling techniques. IRBM **29**(1), 44–52 (2008)

26. Duque, G.J., Munera, P.A., Trujillo, C.D., Urrego, H.D., Hernandez, V.A.: System for processing and simulation of brain signals. In: IEEE Latin-American Conference on Communications, LATINCOM 2009, pp. 1–6. IEEE (2009)
27. Tseng, S.Y., Chen, R.C., Chong, F.C., Kuo, T.S.: Evaluation of parametric methods in EEG signal analysis. Med. Eng. Phys. **17**(1), 71–78 (1995)
28. Gomis, P., Lander, P., Caminal, P.: Parametric linear and non-linear modeling techniques for estimating abnormal intra-GRS potentials in the high resolution ECG. WIT Trans. Biomed. Health **3** (1970)
29. Likothanassis, S., Demiris, E.: Armax model identification with unknown process order and time-varying parameters. In: Procházka, A., Uhlíř, J., Rayner, P.W.J., Kingsbury, N.G. (eds.) Signal Analysis and Prediction. Applied and Numerical Harmonic Analysis, pp. 175–184. Springer, Cham (1998). https://doi.org/10.1007/978-1-4612-1768-8_12
30. Roldán-Vasco, S.: Linear and non-linear autoregressive modeling in subthalamic nucleus for patients with movement disorders. comparison and critical analysis. In: 2014 XIX Symposium on Image, Signal Processing and Artificial Vision (STSIVA), pp. 1–5. IEEE (2014)
31. Restrepo-Agudelo, S., Roldán-Vasco, S.: Time domain reconstruction of basal ganglia signals in patient with parkinson's disease. In: 2015 20th Symposium on Signal Processing, Images and Computer Vision (STSIVA), pp. 1–5. IEEE (2015)
32. Santaniello, S., Fiengo, G., Glielmo, L., Catapano, G.: A biophysically inspired microelectrode recording-based model for the subthalamic nucleus activity in Parkinson's disease. Biomed. Signal Process. Control **3**(3), 203–211 (2008)
33. Stoica, P., Selen, Y.: Model-order selection: A review of information criterion rules. IEEE Signal Process. Mag. **21**(4), 36–47 (2004)
34. Worden, K., Becker, W., Rogers, T., Cross, E.: On the confidence bounds of gaussian process NARX models and their higher-order frequency response functions. Mech. Syst. Signal Process. **104**, 188–223 (2018)
35. Tomlinson, G., Worden, K.: Nonlinearity in Structural Dynamics: Detection, Identification and Modelling. CRC Press, London (2000)
36. Kostoglou, K., Michmizos, K.P., Stathis, P., Sakas, D., Nikita, K.S., Mitsis, G.D.: Classification and prediction of clinical improvement in deep brain stimulation from intraoperative microelectrode recordings. IEEE Trans. Biomed. Eng. **64**(5), 1123–1130 (2017)

Self-Organized Maps for the Analysis of the Biomechanical Response of the Knee Joint During Squat-Like Movements in Subjects Without Physical Conditioning

Andrea Catalina Plazas Molano[1], Sebastián Jaramillo-Isaza[1(✉)], and Álvaro David Orjuela-Cañón[2]

[1] Antonio Nariño University, Bogotá, Colombia
sebastian.jaramillo@uan.edu.co
[2] Universidad del Rosario, Bogotá, Colombia

Abstract. Biomechanical analyses provide an extensive source of data that are deeply explored by physicians, engineers and trainers from the mechanical and physiological point of view. This data includes kinetic and kinematic parameters that are quite useful to study human locomotion. However, most of these analyses stay on a very superficial level. Recently data and computational science expanded their coverage to new areas and new analysis tools are available. These analyses include the use of machine learning tools for data mining processes. All of these new tools open a total new level of data analysis, thus newer and deeper questions are proposed in order to provide more accurate prediction results with strict decision support. On the other hand, Squat is an exercise widely used for physical conditioning since it puts into operation various muscles at the same time of the lower and upper train. However bad squatting could drive to injuries at the back and knee level. These injuries are especially common in patients without physical conditioning. In this study, squat data is analyzed using Self-Organizing Maps (SOM) to identify possible relevant parameters from the subjects that could affect the movement performance especially at the knee joint.

Keywords: Biomechanics · Self-Organizing Maps · Kinematics · Squat · Knee-biomechanics

1 Introduction

The Self-Organizing Maps (SOM) were presented by Teuvo Kohonen in 1982, so they are also called Kohonen's Self-Organized Maps or Kohonen's Neural Networks. These maps are inspired by the ability of the human brain to recognize and extract relevant traits or characteristics of the world around them. This method has a learning level of greater evolution, since the network, in some way, is able to find autonomously the structure of the data, without need to give ordered pairs where it is necessary to define an output to its corresponding input [1]. In addition, SOM offers a similar mapping as principal component analysis does, but in a nonlinear mode [2]. This allows visualizing

© Springer Nature Switzerland AG 2019
J. C. Figueroa-García et al. (Eds.): WEA 2019, CCIS 1052, pp. 335–344, 2019.
https://doi.org/10.1007/978-3-030-31019-6_29

undiscovered relation between data that previously linear methods did not provide in spite of dataset size.

The SOM method has been used in the area of biomechanics to perform more exhaustive analysis of the obtained data, since it allows removing redundancies in the input data while allowing analyzing multivariate information in a single plane, without lose proximity information in the initial space of multiple variables that are taken as inputs [3]. Among the applications it is important to highlight its use to identify specific movement patterns [4, 5] and to define functional groups [6, 7].

On the other hand, squat movement is a widely used resistance exercise. When it is executed correctly it promotes mobility and balance of different joints of the body [8]. This exercise consists of the flexo-extension of the knee and hip obtaining a descent angle of approximately 90° [8–10]. This articulated movement makes the squat one of the most used exercises for body training [8]. Physical conditioning plays an important role in the muscular development of the human being, giving greater stability and less risk of injury [11, 12]. Knowing that the knee is the largest synovial joint in the body, it has the greatest risk of injury [13]. However, in most of the cases not special attention is given to this joint when performing an exercise routine for the first time, especially in people who are just starting training programs. For these subjects in particular, any type of extra load or bad execution of some movement bring with it greater repercussions in the stability of the knee and therefore lesions of medium and high complexity [14].

This paper presents the results of a study that aims to use innovative tools to estimate the stability of the knee when performing the Squat movement. This will be done by observing the flexion angle and the variation of movement in the transverse axis under different loading conditions provided by different types of dumbbells. This type of analysis allows one to better understand the behavior of vulnerable joints such as the knee during the execution of movements where it is strongly requested and the possible consequences on the subjects who perform these movements. Additionally, the present work employs (SOM) models to analyze the squat movement in an alternative way. For this, SOM makes a mapping from ten different input variables, allowing observing the same data in two dimensions, maintaining similarities and differences between these variables. This transformation is useful to develop clustering techniques supported by a visual understanding of data, as in the present case, given for the proposed scenarios.

2 Materials and Methods

2.1 Equipment and Software

In this study three video cameras Basler AG scA640-70gc with a Sony ICX424 CCD sensor and 70 frames per second acquisition rate were used. In addition, four different software were employed for the collection and processing of the biomechanical data. Among them, MaxTRAQ 2D (Innovision-Systems) was used for the recording of the movement and the markers labeling. Then, MaxTRAQ 3D (Innovision-Systems) was applied for the digitization and creation of the 3D model. Next, Mokka Biomechanics was used to reconstruct the biomechanical model, for the kinematic analysis and the data export and finally, MatLab software (Campus License UAN) to analyze the data using the Self-Organized Maps.

2.2   Subjects and Load Elements

The squat movement was analyzed in a group of 10 volunteers (5 women and 5 men Table 1) without clinical symptoms, without history of previous lower limb injuries any without physical conditioning. Three dumbbells were included to perform the movement under different loads. Each of them has different shape and weight: (1) Roman (6.1 kg), (2) Adjustable (5.9 kg) and (3) Horizontal (5.3 kg) (see Fig. 1).

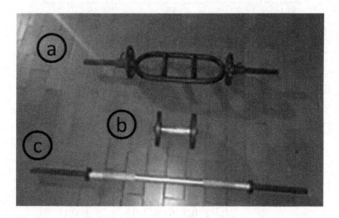

Fig. 1. Dumbbells used to perform the movement (a) Roman, (b) Adjustable and (c) Horizontal.

2.3   Markers and Experimental Protocol

Ten passive markers were located at the level of the lower train specially in the involved joints, such as hip, knee and ankle (see Fig. 2). Then, the movement to be performed was explained to each subject. They were asked to bend the knees at a 90° angle with the back as straight as possible, with the arms extended upwards under four different conditions: 1free (without load) and then using the three different dumbbells involved in this study. Each subject performed several trial movements until they were comfortable and able to couple the gesture without problem.

2.4   Clustering Analysis

The information obtained can be interpreted as multidimensional because there are ten variables (sex, age, weight, height and information of right and left leg in x, y and z). Being able to group them in a space of so many dimensions is an impossible task for the human brain. However, some approximations, such as the Konohen Self-Organized Maps (SOM), allow one to reduce the number of variables to a map of neurons without losing the proximity information between data [1, 2]. In this way, the data obtained was used to train a SOM network, which provides proximity information on a map. A later step for that analysis was the use of the *k-Means* algorithm to group the neurons in regions of interest ready for analysis [15]. The proposed SOM and the k-Means analysis were performed on the four proposed movements (free, Roman dumbbell, adjustable dumbbell and horizontal bar) and then a comparison was made based on the grouped maps that represent each of the movements. Some of the advantages of the SOM map are that it is a very useful tool for representing multivariate data and it can be used to search the influence of each input variables in the global response of the study.

Table 1. Information of each volunteer involved in the test and their mean±SD

Subject	Age (years)	Weight (Kg)	Height (m)
Women			
Subject 1	22	55	1,58
Subject 2	21	60	1,50
Subject 3	20	53	1,52
Subject 4	21	57	1,58
Subject 5	24	47	1,55
	21,6 ± 1,5	54,4 ± 4,9	1,55 ± 0,04
Men			
Subject 6	21	83	1,87
Subject 7	21	58	1,70
Subject 8	21	53	1,68
Subject 9	22	85	1,80
Subject 10	22	60	1,72
	21,4 ± 0,5	67,8 ± 15	1,75 ± 0,1

2.5 Statistical Test

Basic comparisons using Test-t method were performed between groups for both men and women to identify statistically significant differences ($p < 0.05$) between the joint amplitudes and the values of joint displacement in the transverse axis.

2.6 Informed Consent

In agreement with the recommendations established in the Declaration of Helsinki and the Colombian resolution 8430 of 1993 for experimental research in health topics, each of the subjects was requested to provide a signed informed consent expressing their voluntary participation in the present study and confirming to have understood the entire procedure, as well as the treating and use of the resulting data.

3 Results and Discussion

By means of the reconstruction in the Mokka Biomechanics software and MatLab calculi routines, the values of knee flexion angle are collected for each of the subjects, they are divided by gender and summarized in Table 2.

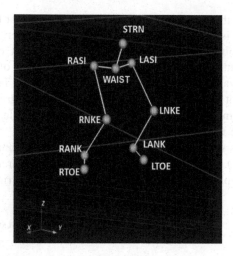

Fig. 2. Markers location on different joints of the lower body

Table 2. Knee joint amplitude and displacement for each subject and load condition

	Type of load	Knee flexion angle (°)	Displacement in the transverse axis (cm)			Knee Flexion Angle (°)	Displacement in the transverse axis (cm)	
			Right Knee	Left Knee			Right Knee	Left Knee
Women					Men			
Subject 1	Free	81	3	10	Subject 6	90	7	10
	Roman	78	4	12,8		90	6	12
	Adjustable	78	4,7	12		87	8	12
	Horizontal	73	5,5	12		90	2	10
Subject 2	Free	94	1	5	Subject 7	99	6	8
	Roman	94	1	5		94	6	8
	Adjustable	89	1,5	5		96	6	9
	Horizontal	87	1,3	5		98	6	10
Subject 3	Free	90	2,5	8	Subject 8	72	10	10
	Roman	85	1	8,5		75	12	6
	Adjustable	86	1	9		72	10	13
	Horizontal	83	3	8,5		79	13	18
Subject 4	Free	76	5	13	Subject 9	99	1	5
	Roman	65	9	7		85	1	5
	Adjustable	75	3	7		90	1	5
	Horizontal	65	9	8,5		97	2	10
Subject 5	Free	100	2	10	Subject 10	83	1,5	14
	Roman	92	2	9		85	2	15
	Adjustable	93	2	10		88	2	16
	Horizontal	96	2,5	9		90	7	10

In Figs. 3A and B the displacement in the transverse axis for the knee joint for one of the female subjects is represented. All subjects including men and women followed the same behavior pattern (see Table 2). In these images it can be seen that the transverse displacement, which is associated with the stability of the knee, presents a smaller displacement value for the right leg than for the left leg. This may be associated with the dominant foot of the subjects which tends to allow greater loads during the execution of the movements. However, a kind of abnormal displacement can be seen in the results of the knee for the right leg for all subjects.

Statistical analyzes show no significant differences in joint amplitude between men and women ($p > 0.05$). However, statistically significant differences ($p < 0.05$) were found between the displacements of the knee of both left and right leg.

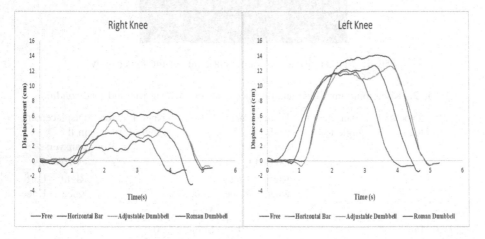

Fig. 3. Displacement at the knee joint in the transverse axis for the different load conditions

Figure 4 shows the trained maps which has been grouped by means of the k-Means algorithm. In that figure is possible to observe each of the variables for each movement achieved for every subject involved in this study.

In addition, from the results found it is possible to evaluate the flexion-extension, displacement in the transverse axis, speed and acceleration, allowing identifying the instability in the knee joint as the main object of study in the Squat movement.

From data presented in Figs. 3 and 4 it is possible to affirm that lack of physical conditioning generates a marked instability in the knee joint. This could be due to absent of physical conditioning since soft tissues such as muscles, tendons and ligaments apparently don't have the necessary training to support this solicitation.

This hinders the correct execution of the gesture, being reflected in both an abnormal patron of displacement in the knees and in the difference of the flexion angles (in many cases the subjects did not reach the aimed 90° flexion angle).

Another important fact to consider during squatting performance is muscle activation. It has been reported that greater or lesser activation of the muscles is generated depending on the knee angle of flexion. The muscles that differ in their activation are

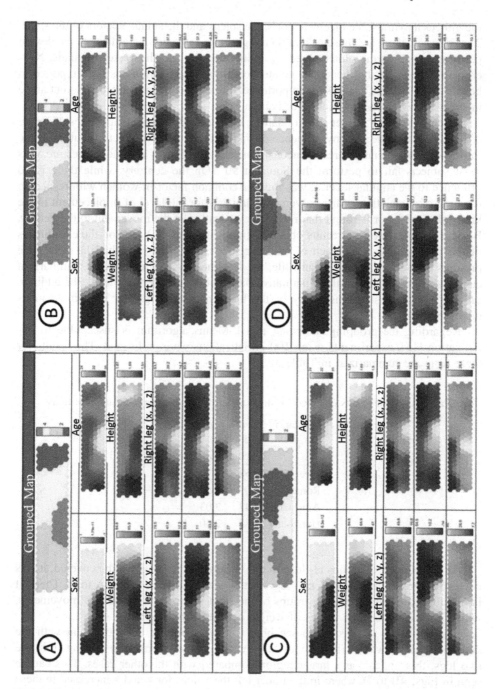

Fig. 4. Grouped maps with input variables for: (a) Free movement, (b) Roman dumbbell, (c) Adjustable dumbbell and (d) Horizontal bar.

the gluteus maximus, the biceps femoris, the soleus and the spinal erectors of the spine. That is to say, there are muscles that do not generate activation regardless of the flexion performed such as the gluteus medius, vastus lateralis and the vastus medialis. Nevertheless, the angle that generates greater total muscle activation has been reported to be 90° [16, 17]. This justifies the importance to reach the recommended 90° joint angle in order to have maximal muscle activation.

After performing gender discrimination, there is no difference that defines the angle of flexion of the knee or any influence of this variable on the correct execution of the movement. Both genders present inconsistencies at the time of execute the gesture, thus most subjects fail to perform the Squat at 90°. On the contrary, while there is no influence to the angular level, it was found a common factor in women with respect to the time of completion of the movement; similarly for the level of di placement in the knee joint, no factor is found that relates the execution of the movement to the gender. Besides, by means of the results obtained graphically Fig. 3, based on the coordinates of the transverse axis for each of the knee joints, it can be seen that the right knee presents greater instability, meanwhile, the left knee is a bit more stable. Similarly it can be analyzed based on the quantitative data that at the kinematic level, the addition of weight increases the instability of the knee, reaching a greater magnitude in its displacement.

Regarding the grouping, knowing that k-Means algorithm is susceptible to initialization [15], experiments using 100 initializations were performed. The results for these tests are summarized in Table 3.

Table 3. SOM results obtained for the number of groups using 100 initializations.

Movement	Number of groups	
	Media	Variance
Free	2.58	1.70
Roman	4.09	2.59
Adjustable	4.47	3.03
Horizontal	5.88	2.40

As the number of groups is close to five, where all the cases will be covered, it was decided to group the map into five regions that were shown in Figs. 4A to D. There, it is possible to observe how the groups of the right part prevail in the five movements, which are related to high values of weight and masculine height.

In addition, it is possible to see how when performing the movement with the dumbbell greater values (light tones) are evident in the information coming from the two legs, this appears as a larger region compared with the other cases. This can be seen in Figs. 4B to D, where in the upper left the values for x and z increased in these movements for both legs, this region being clearer. These results show differences between two groups of movements: free and with the adjustable dumbbell, and another with Roman and horizontal bar which is also visualized by grouped maps and their similarity between groups. This may be due to the fact that the subject tends to move with more freedom during free squatting (without weight) and with the adjustable dumbbell, compared to when using any of the others bars, causing that in these directions (x and z) more force is used to perform the exercise.

4 Conclusions

According to the results, the joint solicitation and its apparent stability depend on the angle and weight with which the movement is executed. This fact supports the findings of many reported papers dealing with squat biomechanics [18–22]. Therefore, new ways for quantifying and representing the influence of different variables in the response of the involved joints is priceless for better understand human motion.

The use of the Self-Organizing Map (SOM) allows one to observe similarities between free and dumbbell movements, as well as another group given by movements that used Roman and horizontal bars. This was observed by the increase in movement in the x and z axes that were observed when visualizing the data with this technique.

Finally, the outcomes from SOM analyses are constructed based on a static and user-defined map size. According to the literature, this kind of imposition on feature map formation could compromise the accurate representation of the topology of an input space. Nevertheless, the results presented in this paper has shown that SOM is a strong option for the analysis of biomechanical data. However, further work could be carried out to make more concrete statements about the influence of these parameters in the correct performing of the squat like movements.

Acknowledgments. Authors want to thank to the Universidad Antonio Nariño for all the financial support to this work under Project number 2017217.

References

1. Caicedo Bravo, E.F., Lopez Sotelo, J.A.: Una Aproximación Práctica a Las Redes Neuronales Artificiales. Cali, Colombia (2017)
2. Lamb, P., Bartlett, R.: Self-organizing maps as a tool to analyze movement variability. Int. J. Comput. Sci. Sport. **7**, 28–39 (2008)
3. Rodrigo, S.E., Lescano, C.N., Rodrigo, R.H.: Application of Kohonen maps to kinetic analysis of human gait. Rev. Bras. Eng. Biomédica **28**, 217–226 (2012)
4. Serrien, B., Blondeel, J., Clijsen, R., Goossens, M., Baeyens, J.-P.: Analysis of 3D motion patterns with self-organising maps (SOM) and statistical parametric mapping (SPM): a methodological proposal. Comput. Methods Biomech. Biomed. Eng. **17**, 162–163 (2014)
5. Hoerzer, S., Jacob, C.: Defining functional groups in biomechanics using self-organizing maps, pp. 1–11 (2015)
6. Hoerzer, S., von Tscharner, V., Jacob, C., Nigg, B.M.: Defining functional groups based on running kinematics using self-organizing maps and support vector machines. J. Biomech. **48**, 2072–2079 (2015)
7. Chulvi Medrano, I.: Revisión narrativa del rol de la sentadilla en los programas de acondicionamiento neuromuscular y rehabilitación TT - Narrative review of the role of the squatting in neuromuscular conditioning and rehabilitation programs (2009)

8. Braidot, A.A., Brusa, M.H., Lestussi, F.E., Parera, G.P.: Biomechanics of front and back squat exercises. J. Phys. Conf. Ser. **90**, 012009 (2007)
9. Mirzaei, B., Nia, F.R., Saberi, Y.: Comparison of 3 different rest intervals on sustainability of squat repetitions with heavy vs. light loads. Brazilian J. Biomotricity **2**, 220–229 (2008)
10. Escamilla, R.F., et al.: Effects of technique variations on knee biomechanics during the squat and leg press. Med. Sci. Sports Exerc. **33**, 1552–1566 (2001)
11. Escamilla, R.F.: Knee biomechanics of the dynamic squat exercise. Med. Sci. Sports Exerc. **33**, 127–141 (2001)
12. Miguel, A., Pereira, N.V.: Comparación entre la Sentadilla y la "Sentadilla a una pierna con Pié lastrado" con respecto a la Actividad Electromiográfica, la Fuerza Resultante y la Sobrecarga (2006)
13. Ariel, B.G.: Biomechanical analysis of the knee joint during deep knee bends with heavy load. Biomechanics **IV**, 44–52 (2016)
14. Myer, G.D., et al.: The back squat: a proposed assessment of functional deficits and technical factors that limit performance. Strength Cond. J. **36**, 4–27 (2014)
15. Kanungo, T., Mount, D.M., Netanyahu, N.S., Piatko, C.D., Silverman, R., Wu, A.Y.: An efficient k-means clustering algorithm: analysis and implementation. IEEE Trans. Pattern Anal. Mach. Intell. **24**, 881–892 (2002)
16. Slater, L.V., Hart, J.M.: Muscle activation patterns during different squat techniques. J. Strength Cond. Res. **31**, 667–676 (2017)
17. Gullett, J.C., Tillman, M.D., Gutierrez, G.M., Chow, J.W.: A biomechanical comparison of back and front squats in healthy trained individuals. J. Strength Cond. Res. **23**, 284–292 (2009)
18. Ostermann, M., et al.: How to squat? Effects of various stance widths, foot placement angles and level of experience on knee, hip and trunk motion and loading. BMC Sports Sci. Med. Rehabil. **10**, 14 (2018)
19. Diggin, D., et al.: A biomechanical analysis of front versus back squat: injury implications kinematic differences occurring between both front squat and back squat techniques using 2D video analysis. Biomech. Sport. **11**, 643–646 (2011)
20. Lander, J.E., Bates, B.T., Devita, P.: Biomechanics of the squat exercise using a modified center of mass bar. Med. Sci. Sports Exerc. **18**, 469–478 (1986)
21. Gawda, P., Zawadka, M., Skublewska-Paszkowska, M., Smołka, J., Łukasik, E.: Biomechanics of the squat in rehabilitation and sports training. Med. Sport./Polish J. Sports Med. **24**, 87–96 (2017)
22. Schoenfeld, B.J.: Squatting kinematics and kinetics and their application to exercise performance. J. Strength Cond. Res. **24**, 3497–3506 (2010)

Is It Possible to Correlate Age Related Time-Dependent Micro Mechanical Properties of Cortical Bone and Its Physico-Chemical Data?

Sebastián Jaramillo-Isaza[1]([⊠]), Pierre-Emmanuel Mazeran[2], Karim El-Kirat[2], and Marie-Christine Ho Ba Tho[2]

[1] Antonio Nariño University, Bogotá, Colombia
sebastian.jaramillo@uan.edu.co
[2] Sorbonne Universities – University of Technology of Compiègne, Compiègne, France

Abstract. Correlational models between mechanical and physico-chemical properties are of interest for bone modeling and numerical simulations of bone growth and remodeling. Therefore, the aim of this work was to determine if it is possible to correlate mechanical and physic-chemical properties of cortical bone.

Micro-mechanical and physico-chemical data were assessed in a rat cortical bone life-span model including samples aged of 1, 4, 9, 12, 18 and 24 months old. Time-dependent mechanical properties at the micro scale including elasticity, viscous properties and hardness were determined using nanoindentation tests. Meanwhile, physico-chemical properties include tissue micro-porosity, mineral, phosphates, carbonates and collagen content were determined using specific techniques for each property. Then, both properties were correlated and the highest matched were used to propose correlational models using multivariable-linear regressions.

These initial results show good determinant and correlation coefficients in high agreement with the experimental data. These results could provide new evidences of how physico-chemical properties affect the mechanical response of bone material.

Keywords: Bone biomechanics · Nanoindentation · Physico-chemical properties · Mechanical properties · Correlations

1 Introduction

Ageing is a natural process inducing variation of bone properties and is widely investigated in literature [1–7]. However, assessments on human bone models are rarely reported mostly due to ethical issues. Therefore, animal models such as rabbit or rat models are commonly used to investigate bone structural, mechanical and physico-chemical variations. Most of those studies include the effects of diseases, dietary conditions or single physical activity [8–10]. Rat and rabbit models are useful in such

© Springer Nature Switzerland AG 2019
J. C. Figueroa-García et al. (Eds.): WEA 2019, CCIS 1052, pp. 345–356, 2019.
https://doi.org/10.1007/978-3-030-31019-6_30

investigations thanks to the availability of young specimens (with only a few days of birth) and to the possibility to include the complete life span from growth to senescence.

Mechanical properties at the micro-scale are commonly assessed using nanoindentation. Mazeran et al. [11] proposed a new four stages protocol (load-hold-unload-hold) combined with a time-dependent mechanical model allowing the calculation of the elastic, viscoelastic, plastic and viscoplastic properties from a single nanoindentation test. This method has been successfully tested on polymers [11] and cortical bone [12, 13].

In order to describe the evolution of the structural and physic-chemical properties through ageing, it is necessary to perform measurements i.e. tissue micro-porosity, mineral, phosphates, carbonates and collagen content over a longer period (from birth to death). For this aim, a previous study performed in our laboratory by Vanleene et al. [14, 15] provides the data of the micro structural and physico-chemical properties.

To have a better understanding of how mechanical and physico-chemical properties are related and how they can affect each other, different correlations can be performed. In this work, linear regressions between physico-chemical properties and mechanical properties are quantified allowing the construction of correlational models for the evolution of mechanical properties due to bone ageing from growth to senescence.

2   Materials and Methods

2.1   Bone Samples

Femoral cortical bones of male rats RJHan:WI Wistar covering ages from growth to senescence (ages 1, 4, 9, 12, 18, 24 months old) were used. All the samples were cut transversely at the proximal and distal end of the femoral diaphysis. It is important to highlight that each bone sample coming from different specimens. Physico-chemical and mechanical properties were assessed at different moments of this study. Thus, two different samples size per age was used for each assessment. The first group of six samples per age was used for physico-chemical analyses. Meanwhile a second group of five samples per age was used to determine mechanical properties.

2.2   Mechanical Properties

Mechanical properties were assessed using nanoindentation tests. The time-dependent mechanical properties have been computed according to the model proposed by Mazeran et al. [11]. This model composed of different mechanical elements (spring for elasticitic modulus (E_{elast})), two Kelvin-Voigt elements for viscoelasticity (E_{ve1} and E_{ve2}; η_{ve1} and η_{ve2}), slider for plasticity-hardness (H) and dashpot for viscoplasticity (η_{vp})) is used to fit the experimental indentation depth versus time curves. All these elements have a quadratic response (square root of the load proportional to displacement and/or displacement velocity). Then the experimental nanoindentation curves have been correctly fitted by the mechanical model.

2.3 Physico-Chemical Properties

Physical and chemical characteristics were measured using different methods that are described here below.

ESEM Images and Micro-Porosities
Micro porosities were analyzed from complete images of proximal cross sections of femurs which were first reconstructed from about 10 partial images (pixel resolution: 2 μm) using an ESEM (Environmental Scanning Electron Microscope) (Philips XL30 ESEM-FEG, Royal Philips Electronics, the Netherlands). Then, ESEM images were analyzed using QWinStandard image analysis software V2.7 (Leica Microsystems Imaging Solution Ltd., UK). Percentage of micro porosity (% porosity) was calculated from the total pore area, including canals and lacunae, divided by the total cross sectional area.

Fourier Transformed InfraRed (FTIR)
Spectroscopy analyses were performed on six samples per age group (1760- X FTIR Spectrometer, PerkinElmer Inc., MA, USA). The spectra were curve-fitted in the ν4 PO_4, ν2 CO_3 and collagen amide band domains (Galactic GRAMS software, NH, USA).

Chemical Test for Carbonates and Nitrogen
Two chemical analyses were performed on samples. Carbonates weight percentage (CO3W%) was measured on six samples per age group using a CO2 Coulometer (Coulometrics Inc., Co, USA). Protein nitrogen weight content was analyzed on three samples per age group using an Elemental Analyzer EA 1110 CHNS (Thermo Fisher Scientific Inc., MA, USA).

X-ray Diffraction
As previous analyses consumed most of sample powder, specimens were pooled in each age group. X-ray diffraction was recorded with a X-ray diffractometer (Inel CPS 120, Enraf Nonius SA, France) using Co radiation (X-ray wave length = 1789 Å). Two peaks at 30° and 45° (2θ) were identified respectively as [002] (c-axis of apatite lattice) and [310] diffraction planes of the apatite crystals.

2.4 Correlational Models

The correlation and the determination coefficients were computed for both mechanical and physico-chemical properties using the statistical analysis and graphics software SYSTAT version 2012 (SYSTAT Software Inc.). Multivariable regressions were computed in the non-normalized experimental data. These regressions were carried out using the physico-chemical properties with high correlation coefficients and could fit very well the mechanical response. In the present study, all physico-chemical variables were considered as independent even if they are strongly correlated. They are different only when multicollinearity is detected.

These regressions were performed to obtain the best fit of the experimental data and to assess the relevance of each physico-chemical property to increase or decrease the mean value of the mechanical response. The Eq. 1 represents the model used for these regressions:

$$M_{property} = Constant \times \left(1 + A \times X_{Property} + B \times Y_{property}\ldots\ldots\right) \qquad (1)$$

Where, M is the mechanical property, A, B, are coefficients and X, Y are the higher correlated physico-chemical properties and the sign positive or negative indicates their effect in the mechanical response.

The model considers linear relationships between the different physico-chemical properties and the different mechanical properties. This simple model is sufficient to generate very good correlation between most of the mechanical properties.

3 Results and Discussion

3.1 Time-Dependent Mechanical Properties

The mean values and standard deviation of the mechanical properties are summarized in Table 1.

Table 1. Values of the mechanical properties computed from the nanoindentation experiments in the longitudinal direction of the rat femoral cortical bone [12] (Copyright© Reprinted with permission). Mean ± standard deviation

Age (Months)	E_{elast} (GPa)	E_{ve1} (GPa)	$\eta_{ve1} \times 10^2$ (GPa.s)	E_{ve2} (GPa)	$\eta_{ve2} \times 10^3$ (GPa.s)	H (GPa)	η_{vp} (GPa.s)
1	26.4 ± 3.4	43.2 ± 6.1	17.6 ± 3.3	79.0 ± 12.3	48.0 ± 9.9	0.70 ± 0.09	250.9 ± 28.8
4	40.7 ± 6.7	57.6 ± 16.9	19.3 ± 4.6	114.8 ± 15.8	64.0 ± 13.6	0.93 ± 0.06	334.6 ± 27.9
9	35.9 ± 3.8	75.6 ± 17.7	28.3 ± 8.2	140.1 ± 23.0	73.6 ± 12.1	0.97 ± 0.10	364.3 ± 43.0
12	39.8 ± 6.3	78.2 ± 18.4	23.6 ± 9.6	150.1 ± 25.9	57.4 ± 13.5	1.04 ± 0.12	357.6 ± 45.5
18	38.4 ± 6.8	75.1 ± 19.1	28.2 ± 8.4	150.4 ± 25.9	71,5 ± 15.1	1.06 ± 0.10	381.6 ± 35.8
24	34.6 ± 4.6	71.4 ± 15.4	22.6 ± 9.6	146.0 ± 18.6	68.6 ± 18.2	1.13 ± 0.09	408.5 ± 43.1

3.2 Physico-Chemical Properties

The values of the micro structural and physico-chemical properties are summarized in Table 2. They were reported for a similar set of samples by Vanleene et al. [14, 15].

Table 2. Variation of the physico-chemical properties of Wistar rat femoral cortical bone with age

Age (Months)	Porosity%	CO_3W%	PO_4%	Ca%	N%	Collagen%
1	8.1	4.1	20.7	42.2	4	21.4
4	3.1	4.9	18.2	39.2	3.6	19
9	3.3	6.1	17.9	39.4	3.3	17.6
12	2.6	6.1	18	39.7	3.3	18.3
18	3.6	6	18	39.3	3.3	17.8
24	4	6	18	39.3	3.3	17.4

3.3 Correlations Between the Mechanical and Physico-Chemical Properties

Mechanical properties obtained by nanoindentation tests were correlated with microstructural and physico-chemical properties. The correlational coefficients (R) are presented in Table 3.

Table 3. Simple correlation coefficient R for the mechanical and physicochemical properties of rat bone

Mechanical properties	Porosity%	CO_3W%	PO_4%	Ca%	N%	Collagen%
E_{elast}	−0.949	0.608	−0.867	−0.878	−0.703	−0.673
E_{ve1}	−0.828	0.992	−0.885	−0.780	−0.981	−0.919
η_{ve1}	−0.576	0.842	−0.682	−0.597	−0.810	−0.778
E_{ve2}	−0.842	0.981	−0.914	−0.837	−0.991	−0.948
η_{ve2}	−0.679	0.744	−0.822	−0.844	−0.794	−0.884
H	−0.799	0.900	−0.899	−0.864	−0.937	−0.940
η_{vp}	−0.781	0.903	−0.908	−0.886	−0.942	−0.974

3.4 Correlational Models

The correlational models were computed using the multivariable linear regressions method and the highest coefficients calculated in Sect. 3.3. Then, each equation was compared and analyzed to its corresponding experimental mechanical property. The equations proposed for each mechanical property are described hereafter.

Elastic Response
The equation that relies the elastic modulus to the structural and physico-chemical properties obtained from the multivariable regression is:

$$E_{elast} = 73.7 \times (1 + (0.109 \times PO_4\%) - (0.06 \times Porosity) - (0.0571 \times Ca\%))$$

$$R^2 = 0.971 \tag{2}$$

The values obtained from the experimental data and by means of the correlational equation are presented in Fig. 1.

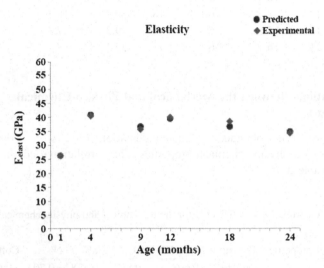

Fig. 1. Values show the elastic modulus from the experimental data "♦" and the correlational model "•" computed as a function of bone porosity, phosphate and calcium content with $R^2 = 0.971$.

Elastic modulus reacts positively to the increase of phosphate, more precisely, a decrease of the phosphate composition during the life-span leads to decrease of the elastic modulus (of about 30%) but negatively to the increase of porosity (values vary by about 33%), and calcium (variation of about 17%). According to Vanleene et al. [15] porosity decrease with age and affects the elastic response of bone. In addition, excess of calcium is associated with bone pathologies [16] and could decrease the stiffness of bones.

Globally, porosity affects the elastic response of bone but not the properties linked to permanent deformation and viscosity. The porosity measured in this study is not the genuine microporisity but an apparent one. This fact could explain why R value for the elastic response is lower than values of other correlations. However, the results obtained here are in good agreement with previous works which have reported a strong relationship between this structural characteristics and the elastic response of bone [15, 17, 18].

Viscoelasticity
For the elastic component of the two viscoelasticities, the following equations were calculated:

$$E_{ve1} = 110 \times (1 - (0.5 \times N\%) + (0.0661 \times CO_3W\%) + (0.0524 \times Collagen\%))$$

$$R^2 = 0.997 \tag{3}$$

$$E_{ve2} = 1278 \times (1 - (0.31 * N\%) - (0.0471 \times CO_3W\%) + (0.0148 \times PO_4\%) + (0.00876 \times Collagen\%))$$

$$R^2 = 0.999 \tag{4}$$

The values obtained from the experimental data and by means of the correlational equations are presented in Fig. 2.

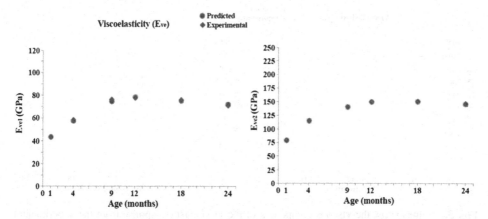

Fig. 2. Values show the elastic component of the viscoelastic response from the experimental data "♦" and the correlational model "•" computed for the elastic component E_{ve1} with bone carbonates, nitrogen, collagen and phosphates with $R^2 = 0.997$. and E_{ve2} with bone nitrogen, carbonates and collagen with $R^2 = 0.999$.

These results suggest that physico-chemical properties have not the same effects in the two elastic components. According to the correlational equation, the elastic component E_{ve1} reacts positively to the increase of carbonates (variation about 13%) and collagen (21%) but negatively to the increase of nitrogen (35%). Meanwhile the second elastic component reacts positively to the increase phosphate (variation close to 4%) and collagen (about 4%) but it is affected by the increase of nitrogen (22%) and carbonates (10%). Taking into account the information proposed by the correlational equations, nitrogen content is a critical parameter that affects the elastic response of viscoelasticity. According to Jarvis et al. [19], nitrogen content present in human bone decreases with burial age and acts as an inhibitor of decomposition during the initial period of interment.

For the viscous components of viscoelasticity, the determination coefficients were low for all the physico chemical properties. Nevertheless, the following equations were computed with those that are lightly correlated and are able to reproduce the chaotic aspect of the curve:

$$\eta_{ve1} = -10236 \times (1 + (0.267 \times N\%) + (0.107 \times CO_3W\%) - (0.0156 \times Collagen\%))$$

$$R^2 = 0.740 \tag{5}$$

$$\eta_{ve2} = 420 \times (1 + (0.0412 * PO_4\%) - (0.0307 \times Ca\%) - (0.0205 \times Collagen\%))$$

$$R^2 = 0.874 \tag{6}$$

The values obtained from the experimental data and by means of the correlational equations are presented in Fig. 3.

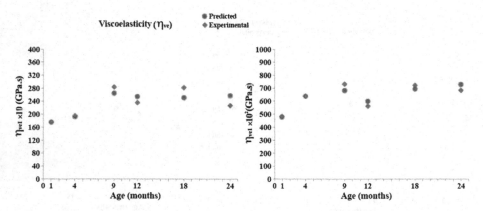

Fig. 3. Values show the viscous component of the viscoelastic response from the experimental data "♦" and the correlational model "•" computed by multivariable regression analyses: for the viscous component η_{ve1} bone nitrogen, carbonates and collagen with $R^2 = 0.740$. For the second viscous component η_{ve2} bone phosphate, calcium and collagen with $R^2 = 0.874$.

According to these results, the first viscous component, η_{ve1} of viscoelasticity reacts positively to the increase of nitrogen (19%) and carbonates (21%) and negatively to collagen (6%). Meanwhile the second viscous component η_{ve2} reacts positively to the increase of phosphate (12%) and negatively to the increase of calcium (9%) and collagen (8%).

Hardness
For hardness of bone material, the following equation was computed:

$$H = 18.3 \times (1 - (0.337 * N\%) - (0.0902 \times CO_3W\%) + (0.0201 \times Ca\%) - (0.00426 \times Collagen\%))$$

$$R^2 = 0.991 \tag{7}$$

The values obtained from the experimental data and by means of the correlational equation are presented in Fig. 4.

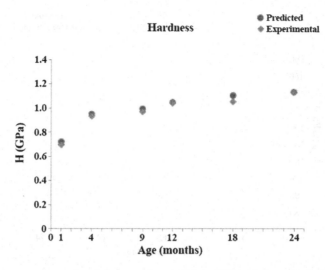

Fig. 4. Hardness response from the experimental data "♦" and the correlational model "•" computed as a function of bone carbonates, nitrogen, calcium and collagen with $R^2 = 0.991$.

Hardness is related to bone strength. According to our results, this property reacts positively to the increase of calcium (6%). This calcium is an essential mineral involved in bone mass and structure. Meanwhile the increase of nitrogen (24%), carbonates (18%) and collagen (2%) seem to have a negative effect in bone toughness.

Viscoplasticity
The viscoplastic response of bone could be described the following equation as:

$$\eta_{vp} = 4810 \times (1 - 0.303 * N\% - 0.0869 \times CO_3W\% + 0.0203 \times Ca\% - 0.0111 \times Collagen\%)$$

$$R^2 = 0.999 \tag{8}$$

The values for Viscoplasticiy (η_{vp}) obtained from the experimental data and by means of the correlational equation are presented in Fig. 5.

Viscoplasticity is related to the evolution of permanent deformation of the bone structure when a constant stress is hold during a given time. According to our results, this property reacts positively to the increase of calcium (6%); meanwhile it is affected negatively by the increase of nitrogen (21%), carbonates (17%) and collagen (4%).

It could be notice that hardness and viscoplasticity are correlated to the same properties (CO3W%, PO4%, nitrogen% and collagen %) and they are poorly correlated to porosity. The organic components of bone such as collagen fibrils take part in the elastic recovery of bone. This could justify why the increase of collagen can negatively affect the viscoplastic response of bone. It is clear from Eqs. (7) and (8) that the evolution of hardness and viscoplasticity obeys to the similar laws suggesting that these two properties are intrinsically dependent.

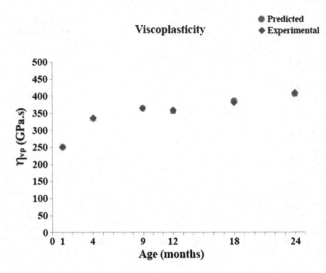

Fig. 5. Visco-plastic response from the experimental data "♦" and the correlational model "•" computed as a function of bone carbonates, nitrogen, calcium and collagen with $R^2 = 0.999$.

Table 4 summarizes the influence of the physical properties on the different mechanical properties. It appears from the analysis of the data that the different behaviors are sensitive to different physical properties. Indeed, Elastic modulus is mainly sensitive to porosity, phosphate and calcium, whereas plasticity and visco-plasticity are mainly sensitive to carbonate, nitrogen and calcium. Considering the visco-elastic behaviors, the two elastic components are mainly sensitive to carbonates, nitrogen and collagen composition. Nevertheless, the influence is different: an increase of carbonates percentage generates an increase of the first elastic component, whereas it generates a decrease of the second elastic component. Plasticity and viscoplasticity have very similar behavior and could be considered as similar.

Table 4. Influence of the physical properties on the different mechanical properties.

Mechanical properties	Porosity	$CO_3W\%$	$PO_4\%$	$Ca\%$	$N\%$	Collagen%
E_{elast}	−33%		31%	−17%		
E_{ve1}		13%			−35%	21%
η_{ve1}		11%			27%	−2%
E_{ve2}		−9%	4%		−22%	4%
η_{ve2}			12%	−9%		−8%
H		−18%		6%	−24%	−2%
η_{vp}		−17%		6%	−21%	−4%

The selected correlational variables were chose on the fact that they provide a good R^2 coefficient. This does not mean that other physico-chemical variables cannot affect the mechanical properties of bone. In fact, even if the selection of the variables was extensive, there is always the probability of new variables that have not been considered or even defined yet as being critical to the outcome. Nevertheless, this information could be useful to understand how and which mechanical properties of bone are affected by the variation of some physico-chemical properties. Most of the mechanical properties were negatively correlated with the compositional properties. The Pearson's correlation show that all the high correlated physico-chemical properties have significant statistical level ($p < 0.05$).

Finally, it is important to notice that physico-chemical properties vary with aging, the correlational model proposed in this work does not predicts the variation of the mechanical properties with aging but the value of mechanical properties for specific physico-chemical conditions.

4 Conclusions

The correlational method used in this study allows one to identify the influence of dietary or metabolic factors, diseases or other variables in the structural and material properties of bone. This information could be useful to better understand the variation of the mechanical properties of cortical bone with aging.

Lineal regressions are a simple way to determine connections among the data. However, if more information, for example new physicochemical data, is added to the equations proposed here, those equations could change. This is why, if others computational methods or data processing techniques are used, they could be providing more information about how these properties are linked.

References

1. Currey, J.D., Brear, K., Zioupos, P.: The effects of ageing and changes in mineral content in degrading the toughness of human femora. J. Biomech. **29**, 257–260 (1996)
2. Bailey, A.J., Paul, R.G.: The mechanisms and consequences of the maturation and ageing of collagen. Proc. Indian Acad. Sci. Chem. Sci. **111**, 57–69 (1999)
3. Mosekilde, L.: Age-related changes in bone mass, structure, and strength–effects of loading. Z. Rheumatol. **59**(1), 1–9 (2000)
4. Danielsen, C.C., Mosekilde, L., Svenstrup, B.: Cortical bone mass, composition, and mechanical properties in female rats in relation to age, long-term ovariectomy, and estrogen substitution. Calcif. Tissue Int. **52**, 26–33 (1993)
5. Fukuda, S., Iida, H.: Age-related changes in bone mineral density, cross-sectional area and the strength of long bones in the hind limbs and first lumbar vertebra in female Wistar rats. J. Vet. Med. Sci. **66**, 755–760 (2004)
6. Willinghamm, M.D., Brodt, M.D., Lee, K.L., Stephens, A.L., Ye, J., Silva, M.J.: Age-related changes in bone structure and strength in female and male BALB/c mice. Calcif. Tissue Int. **86**, 470–483 (2010)
7. Burket, J., Gourion-Arsiquaud, S., Havill, L.M., Baker, S.P., Boskey, A.L., van der Meulen, M.C.H.: Microstructure and nanomechanical properties in osteons relate to tissue and animal age. J. Biomech. **44**, 277–284 (2011)

8. Indrekvam, K., Husby, O.S., Gjerdet, N.R., Engester, L.B., Langeland, N.: Age-dependent mechanical properties of rat femur. Measured in vivo and in vitro. Acta Orthop. Scand. **62**, 248–252 (1991)
9. Akkus, O., Adar, F., Schaffler, M.B.: Age-related changes in physicochemical properties of mineral crystals are related to impaired mechanical function of cortical bone. Bone. **34**, 443–453 (2004)
10. Isaksson, H., Malkiewicz, M., Nowak, R., Helminen, H.J., Jurvelin, J.S.: Rabbit cortical bone tissue increases its elastic stiffness but becomes less viscoelastic with age. Bone **47**, 1030–1038 (2010)
11. Mazeran, P.-E., Beyaoui, M., Bigerelle, M., Guigon, M.: Determination of mechanical properties by nanoindentation in the case of viscous materials. Int. J. Mater. Res. **103**, 715–722 (2012)
12. Jaramillo Isaza, S., Mazeran, P.-E., El Kirat, K., Ho Ba Tho, M.-C.: Time-dependent mechanical properties of rat femoral cortical bone by nanoindentation: an age-related study. J. Mater. Res. **29**, 1135–1143 (2014)
13. Jaramillo Isaza, S., Mazeran, P.-E., El-Kirat, K., Ho Ba Tho, M.-C.: Heterogeneity of time-dependent mechanical properties of human cortical bone at the micro scale. J. Musculoskelet. Res. **18**, 1550017 (2015)
14. Vanleene, M., Mazeran, P.-E., Ho Ba Tho, M.-C.: Influence of strain rate on the mechanical behavior of cortical bone interstitial lamellae at the micrometer scale. J. Mater. Res. **21**, 2093–2097 (2006)
15. Vanleene, M., Rey, C., Ho Ba Tho, M.C.: Relationships between density and Young's modulus with microporosity and physico-chemical properties of Wistar rat cortical bone from growth to senescence. Med. Eng. Phys. **30**, 1049–1056 (2008)
16. Dent, C.E., Smellie, J.M., Watson, L.: Studies in osteopetrosis. Arch. Dis. Child. **40**, 7–15 (1965)
17. Currey, J.D.: The mechanical consequences of variation in the mineral content of bone. J. Biomech. **2**, 1–11 (1969)
18. Ho Ba Tho, M.-C., Mazeran, P.-E., El-Kirat, K., Bensamoun, S.: Multiscale characterization of human cortical bone. Comput. Model. Eng. Sci. **87**, 557–577 (2012)
19. Jarvis, D.R.: Nitrogen levels in long bones from coffin burials interred for periods of 26–90 years. Forensic Sci. Int. **85**, 199–208 (1997)

A Methodology for Driving Behavior Recognition in Simulated Scenarios Using Biosignals

Juan Antonio Dominguez-Jimenez⬤, Kiara Coralia Campo-Landines⬤,
and Sonia Helena Contreras-Ortiz(✉)⬤

Universidad Tecnológica de Bolívar, Cartagena de Indias, Colombia
scontreras@utb.edu.co

Abstract. The recognition of aggressive driving patterns could aid to improve driving safety and potentially reduce traffic fatalities on the roads. Driving behavior is strongly shaped by emotions and can be divided into two main categories: calmed (non-aggressive) and aggressive. In this paper, we present a methodology to recognize driving behavior using driving performance features and biosignals. We used biosensors to measure heart rate and galvanic skin response of fifteen volunteers while driving in a simulated scenario. They were asked to drive in two different situations to elicit calmed and aggressive driving behaviors. The purpose of this study was to determine if driving behavior can be assessed from biosignals and acceleration/braking events. From two-tailed student t-tests, the results suggest that it is possible to differentiate between aggressive and calmed driving behavior from biosignals and also from longitudinal vehicle's data.

Keywords: Driving behavior · Acceleration patterns ·
Feature extraction · Biosignals

1 Introduction

Human behavior and cognitive processes are affected by emotions that are often difficult to handle. Emotions are accompanied by physical and physiological responses [2]. They are produced by the effect of hormones and prepare the body to face various situations. There are different emotions that can be identified by behavioral patterns, physiological responses and facial expressions [4]. Examples of emotions include: anger, fear, enjoyment, sadness and disgust, among others. These emotions can be classified by two features: valence (pleasantness) and arousal (activation) [9]. According to Reeve, emotions involve both biological and cognitive domains [18]. The biological domain explains the emotions from genetic events and facial expressions prior to some vital event. On the other hand, the cognitive domain states that there will not be physiological response to a stimulus if it is not assessed first from what it represents for the individual.

© Springer Nature Switzerland AG 2019
J. C. Figueroa-García et al. (Eds.): WEA 2019, CCIS 1052, pp. 357–367, 2019.
https://doi.org/10.1007/978-3-030-31019-6_31

Thus, this position declares that the emotion is caused by the subject's interpretation to events and it depends on his judgments. There are several models of emotions [16, 20, 21]. The majority of these models organize emotions regarding their valence and arousal.

Although emotions have an adaptive and survival function, the levels in which they occur also seem to have a negative impact on people's driving behavior. The 2018 global status report on road safety provided by the World Health Organization (WHO) stated that the number of road traffic deaths on the world's roads continues unacceptably high [14]. The nature of the human being predisposes him to show aggressive behaviors that help him to survive [10]. However, there is not an explanation of in what extent emotions contribute to the number of road accidents yet, since emotions are not considered causes of them [11]. Only very intensive events such as extreme violence or road rage are registered as causes of accidents. Road rage refers to when a driver is angry, or is involved in situations that evokes anger, including overtaking, cutting in the lane, driving too slowly, and honking among others [15, 23, 24]. This phenomena is one of the most frequently experienced on the roads [12]. According to the study carried out by Qu et al., aggressive driving behaviors accounted for approximately 94.4% of all traffic deaths in China [17]. Some emotions that are elicited by very intense events, including anger, happiness, surprise, stress and anxiety, can potentially affect perception and judgments of the person. Therefore, in order to ensure road safety, drivers should stay calmed during driving, even if they are angry or frustrated [6].

Recent studies on driving behavior recognition have been developed while driving in simulated scenarios or in real driving conditions. The main problem with the experimentation during real driving is that there are several factors that cannot be controlled including weather, traffic, road conditions, among others. The use of simulators allows to control these factors as much as possible, and the driver safety is guaranteed. In the last decade, several studies have been developed on the recognition of driving behavior. Wang et al. carried out a cross-cultural study to assess the driving behavior during critical situations in the commercial SILAB simulator. Their founds suggest that driving behaviors are sensitive to cultural aspects. For example, they observed that Chinese participants maintained higher speeds and their reaction time was longer than Germans' in the stated scenario [22]. Hongyu et al. carried out a study on twelve young drivers under angry emotion. They used standardized videos to induce the driver's anger emotion previous to the driving test. By using an independent sample t-test, they found that anger produces unstable longitudinal and lateral operation of the vehicle [5].

The variations in the levels of human stress may vary heart rate among other physiological responses [19]. These responses can be recorded using sensors such as electrocardiography (ECG), galvanic skin response (GSR), photoplestymography (PPG), temperature, etc. Lanata's et al. evaluated the ANS variations from driving style changes with incremental stressing conditions by collecting ECG, GSR and RSP from fifteen subjects. They found high compatible results in HRV (mean of R-R intervals and peak frequency in HF band), GSR (first four statistical moments) and vehicle's features (steering wheel angle correction and vehicle velocity difference) [8]. In Ooi's study, the authors proposed a framework for driver emotion recognition based on GSR in simulated scenarios. Their results show that his approach can accurately recognize stress and anger from neutral emotion [13].

Most of the studies conducted in this matter have focused on physiological signal processing and vehicle performance. This work presents a more subject-centered methodology for driving behavior recognition from two domains: the vehicle's performance and the psycho-physiological, where the subject's opinions are considered to confirm that the target driving behavior was reached. The biosignals were acquired using an instrumented glove and analyzed using the methods described in a previous work [3]. The data was analyzed using two tailed t-test comparisons.

The rest of the paper is organized as follows. Section 2 explains the information related to the physiological signals. Section 3 describes the driving simulator, the experimental protocol and data acquisition. Section 4 presents the analysis of the results. Finally, Sect. 5 summarizes the main results from this work.

2   Physiological Signals

The driving task involves physiological responses that are controlled by the autonomous nervous system (ANS). Some examples are: muscle contraction, heart rate, sweat secretion, and respiration rate, among others. These physiological signals can be recorded using sensors to obtain information related to the driver's emotional state. In this work, we used galvanic skin response (GSR) and heart rate (HR) for emotion recognition. Below, there is a description of these signals.

– **Galvanic skin response.** It is related to the electrical conductance of the skin, which varies with the amount of sweat due to environmental events and the subject's psycho-physiological state. It has been used as an indicator of arousal, attention, stress, and also for lying detection in polygraphs.
– **Heart rate.** It is controlled by the by the ANS and varies with the subject's emotional state. It is used on the psychological domain as arousal indicator. HR can be collected by attaching electrodes on the chest/arms to acquire ECG, and by measuring variations in light absorption on the skin with photoplethysmography (PPG).

3   Methodology

We analyzed variations in two biosignals (PPG and GSR) and vehicle's longitudinal data during driving behavior experiments on fifteen participants using a driving simulator. For this study, two driving behaviors were considered: calmed and aggressive. Both were elicited by giving instructions to the volunteers, and by modifying environmental conditions in the simulator. Signal acquisition was performed using and custom-made instrumented glove [3] and the vehicle's data was acquired via image processing from a driving simulator.

3.1 Participants

Fifteen subjects (14 male, 1 female) aged 19 to 24 years old (22.08 1.45) were invited to participate in the study. All subjects were healthy volunteers and gave their written informed consent. The consent stated that the purpose of the study was to analyze behaviors while driving in a driving simulator. A survey was carried out to collect basic information from the volunteers. All subjects had a standard driving license for conventional drivers in Colombia (B1). They stated that the mean distance they traveled per day was 15 km approximately. Three subjects declared that had used a driving simulator before. Seven subjects had five or more years of driving experience (46.6%), seven subjects had two to four years of driving experience, and one subject had only one year of experience. Before the test, thirteen volunteers stated that felt relaxed and one that felt anxious.

3.2 Data Acquisition and Signal Processing

The vehicle's data was extracted from a driving simulator running on a desktop computer with an external speaker. We used a Logitech MOMO force-feedback steering wheel in front of a 21 in. screen with 1280×720 resolution. Longitudinal vehicle's data was acquired by recording the screen at 30 frames per second to further implement basic image processing techniques to extract data from the tachometer and the braking and throttle pressure bars. Figure 1 shows a binarized screenshot of them.

On the other hand, the PPG and GSR signals were acquired using an instrumented glove through USB using terminal emulator PuTTY (Release 0.7, Simon Tatham). Then, they were filtered with FIR filters to reduce noise. The PPG signal was filtered with a band-pass filter with corner frequencies of 0.1 Hz and 10 Hz, and the GSR signal was low-pass filtered with cutoff frequency of 1 Hz [3]. The signals were analyzed using time and frequency domain methods in MatLab (Mathworks).

3.3 Driving Scenarios

We designed simple driving scenarios to ensure data acquisition in conditions as close as possible to real driving. Each participant was allowed to practice freely with the simulator to get familiar with it. Only when they showed that they can easily control the system, the test started. Two driving scenarios were simulated: calmed and aggressive. They were carried out in a four kilometers motorway with four lanes.

- **First scenario.** The participant was asked to drive as he/she does it in real life. In this scenario, the subject was not informed of the destination or the duration of the test to avoid eliciting physiological changes due to time pressure.

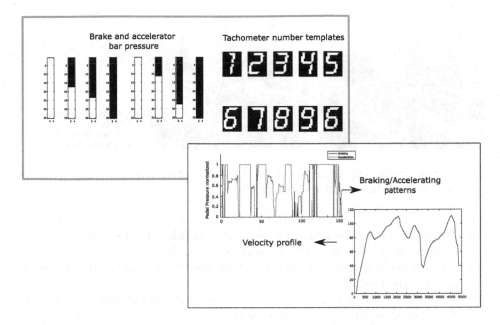

Fig. 1. Extracted features from the driving simulator

- **Second scenario.** The subject was asked to follow the same trajectory that he did in the first scenario, but faster. In this case, aggressiveness was induced in participants by controlling some events related with the external driving environment that includes: increased traffic, elevated noise levels due to horns, and a limited time to complete the task. A timer showing the remaining time was used to increase stress levels. Figure 2 illustrates the two listed scenarios.

3.4   Experimental Protocol

A block diagram of the methodology is shown in Fig. 3. The experimental procedure is described next.

1. The volunteer arrived to the laboratory.
2. The researcher described the procedure of the experiment and answered the questions of the subject.
3. The subject signed an informed consent.
4. The volunteer was asked to fill in an anonymous survey prior to the experiment about his/her driving experience and current emotional state.
5. The instrumented glove was carefully placed by the researcher on the left hand of the subject. The researcher had an informal chat with the participant to help him/her to relax.
6. Baseline data from the sensors was collected for two minutes.
7. The subject was informed that he/she has to maintain both hands on the steering wheel during the test.

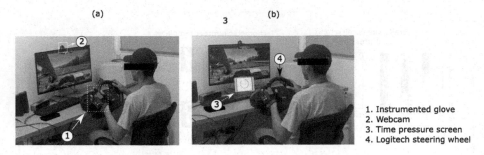

1. Instrumented glove
2. Webcam
3. Time pressure screen
4. Logitech steering wheel

Fig. 2. Proposed driving scenarios. First scenario (to induce calmed driving) (a), Second scenario (to induce aggressive driving) (b).

8. To avoid any learning bias, the subject was asked to drive in a practice scenario to get familiar with the simulator and the glove.
9. The subject was asked to drive as he/she usually does in the real life with no time constraints.
10. The subject was asked to drive the second scenario. He/she was told to drive faster to arrive by the time limit.
11. The purpose of the experiment was explained by the researcher and an spontaneous conversation was established with the volunteer to know his/her thoughts on the experiment.

The whole experiment lasted 40 min approximately per subject.

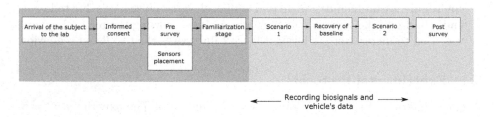

Fig. 3. Block diagram of the proposed experimental protocol

3.5   Features Extraction

Driving styles significantly affect the vehicle's performance. Both existing technologies: internal combustion engine (ICE) either battery (BEV), or fuel cell-powered (FCV) vehicles, are affected by harsh acceleration and deceleration and poor anticipation [7]. The main factor that generates these patterns is driving behavior. Even though the variables related to cognitive processes, including perception and thoughts, are not easy to measure, the responses associated to them, such as HR and sweat secretion, can be measured with biosensors. Therefore, the selected biosignals and data from the vehicle's performance were analyzed to extract several features in time and frequency domains to characterize the two target driving behaviors. For the GSR signal, we used features such as: mean, dynamic range, energy and zero-crossing ratio of the first five modes obtained with empirical mode decomposition (EMD), and ratio of negative values of the first difference of the GSR over the total number of samples. The PPG signal was analyzed with the FFT to obtain the HR in 5-seconds windows. Then, features such as total harmonic distortion, root mean square, root mean square differences of successive R-R intervals, among others, were calculated. The complete list of features is in Table 1.

Table 1. Features extracted from biosignals and braking/acceleration events

Domain	Divisions	Features
Biological	GSR	Mean, Standard Deviation, Dynamic Range, Variance, Energy and zero crossing rates of the first five EMD modes, Ratio of negative values over the total number of samples
	PPG	HR Mean, HR Standard Deviation, HR Variance, HR dynamic range HR total harmonic distorsion (THD), HR Root Mean Square, HR Root Mean Square of Successive Differences RR, Frequency activity in low (LFnu), high (HFnu) frequencies and their normalized ratio (LF/HF nu)
Vehicle	Acceleration/Velocity	Mean, Std, Variance, Max and Min
	Braking/Throttle	Mean, Std, Variance, Max, Min, Skewness, and Frequency of both normalized pedal pressures

4   Results

4.1   Survey Results

In the second survey, 86% of the subjects (13) declared that they identified differences between the two driving scenarios including higher traffic, higher noise and time limitations. 73% of the subjects (11) stated that felt relaxed/quiet during the first scenario, and the rest declared that felt excited. With respect to the second scenario, 73% of the participants declared felt anxious, and the rest stated felt neutral. 93% of the volunteers declared that felt a change in their driving style between the two proposed scenarios. Some of the subject's statements were: *"I had to drive faster"*, *"I accelerated in more aggressive way because of the time pressure"*, *"I made more abrupt movements"*.

Figure 4 illustrates how often participants felt anxiety during the second scenario. Most of the volunteers (79%) stated felt anxiety. 93.33% (14) of the participants identified the first scenario as calmed, and 80% (12) identified the second scenario as aggressive.

From the self-assessment manikin test [1], we extracted information regarding valence and arousal. From the valence domain, 66.66% of the volunteers felt something very positive regarding their driving style for the first scenario, while for the second scenario 46% declared felt something very negative. The reason that the second scenario was not considered negative for a number of participants may be that they consider that their usual driving style is aggressive. From the arousal domain, the mean for the first scenario was 3.56 ± 2.12 while for the second scenario it was 7.08 ± 2.0. Figure 5 illustrates the score for the ratings of the scenario. It was expected that the scores were located in the LAHV quadrant for calmed driving and in the HALV for aggressive driving. However, the scores are spread out, and the reason may be related to subject's perceptions and thoughts about which facts account for aggressive and calmed behaviors while driving.

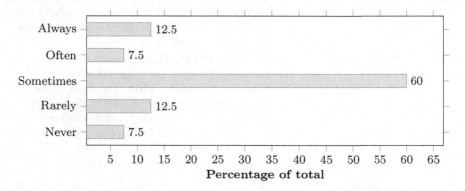

Fig. 4. Histogram for the frequency of anxiety felt by the subjects during the last scenario

4.2   Statistical Analysis

The hypothesis of this work is that there will be significant variations on the features extracted from the signals, obtained from the subject and the vehicle, for the two driving scenarios. Therefore, it will be possible to assess the driving behavior from these signals. Table 2 shows the student t-test results for biosignals and vehicle's data. The differences between the two scenarios are as expected, but not all differences are statistically significant. Information marked with asterisk means that p-values are less than 0.05. It is notable that variables extracted from GSR and vehicle are statistically significant with an 95% of certainly. From the biosignals, the ratio of negative values of the first difference of the GSR is the only statistically significant. However, the mean values of heart rate during aggressive scenarios were higher than during calmed driving but the difference was not statistically significant. The reason may be that some subjects are used to drive in an aggressive way and feet comfortable with that. Thus, in these subjects physiological signals had no significant variations between the two scenarios.

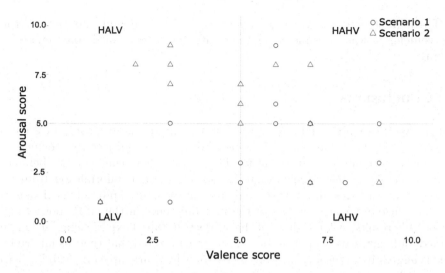

Fig. 5. Scatter plot for the volunteer's ratings of each scenario. Each quadrant denotes the levels of arousal and valence where H is High and L is Low.

Table 2. Two tailed-independent t-test results analyzing the difference in the features for each driving behavior, C: calmed, A: aggressive.

Variable	μ	t	p value	95% CI of the difference
Heart rate mean		−1.4886	0.1479	[−13.45, 2.13]
C	79.9730			
A	85.6358			
Ratio of negative values of the GSR		−2.1842	< 0.05*	[−0.14, −0.04]
C	0.3664			
A	0.4380			
Mean velocity		−2.3721	< 0.05*	[−18.10, −1.26}
C	78.2325			
A	87.9166			
Mean of the braking pedal pressure			< 0.05*	[−0.019, −0.0007]
C	0.01759			
A	0.02761			
Standard deviation of the braking pedal pressure		−1.88	0.070	[−0.059, 0.0025]
C	0.08510			
A	0.11367			
Mean of the throttle pedal pressure		−2.5758	< 0.05*	[−0.2152, −0.0243]
C	0.4847			
A	0.6045			

On the other hand, from the vehicles features, mean velocity, mean of the braking pedal pressure, and mean of the throttle pedal pressure differ statistically with 95% of certainly.

Through student-t test, we observed that, with GSR and information from the vehicle, it was possible to differentiate between calmed and aggressive driving.

5   Conclusions

In this work, we proposed a subject-centered approach to elicit and analyze calmed and aggressive driving behaviors. We used the subject's statements to confirm the driving style in scenario. The results show that driving behavior recognition is possible using biosignals and longitudinal information from the vehicle. The statistical analysis showed that, in the case of physiological signals, only the ratio of negative values of the first difference of the GSR showed high compatible results. A large share of the subjects declared experiencing driving in calmed and aggressive scenarios, but most of them stated that their usual driving style is aggressive. This fact may be the reason why heart rate compatibility with the prior hypothesis was not as high as we expected.

The second survey showed that aggressive drivers are aware about their driving style. Thus, a recommendation for future work is to identify the participant's driving behavior previous to the test, to adapt the stimuli and simulated environmental conditions according to that. The next stage of this research is to integrate an object-oriented library designed for estimating electric vehicles range to assess the impact of different driving behaviors on the battery pack from velocity profiles and braking/acceleration events.

Furthermore, future work includes

- To assess driving behavior considering battery state of charge (SOC), traveled distance, power converters' demand among others.
- To increase the sample size and to include other biosignals such as electromyography, respiration, etc.
- To use machine learning techniques for driving behavior classification.

References

1. Bradley, M.M., Lang, P.J.: Measuring emotion: The self-assessment manikin and the semantic differential. J. Behav. Ther. Exp. Psychiatry 25(1), 49–59 (1994)
2. Cooper, C.L., Dewe, P.J.: Stress: A Brief History. Wiley, Chichester (2008)
3. Domínguez-Jiménez, J., Campo-Landines, K., Martínez-Santos, J., Contreras-Ortiz, S.: Emotion detection through biomedical signals: A pilot study. In: 14th International Symposium on Medical Information Processing and Analysis, vol. 10975, p. 1097506. International Society for Optics and Photonics (2018)
4. Ekman, P.: An argument for basic emotions. Cognit. Emot. 6(3–4), 169–200 (1992)
5. Hongyu, H., Zhou, X., Zhu, Z., Wang, Q., Xiao, H.: A driving simulator study of young driver's behavior under angry emotion. Technical report, SAE Technical Paper (2019)
6. James, L., Diane, N.: Road Rage and Aggressive Driving: Steering Clear of Highway Warfare. Prometheus, Amherst (2000)

7. Knowles, M., Scott, H., Baglee, D.: The effect of driving style on electric vehicle performance, economy and perception. Int. J. Electr. Hybrid Veh. **4**(3), 228–247 (2012)
8. Lanatà, A., et al.: How the autonomic nervous system and driving style change with incremental stressing conditions during simulated driving. IEEE Trans. Intell. Transp. Syst. **16**(3), 1505–1517 (2014)
9. Lang, P.J.: The emotion probe: Studies of motivation and attention. Am. Psychol. **50**(5), 372 (1995)
10. Lang, P.J., Bradley, M.M.: Appetitive and defensive motivation: Goal-directed or goal-determined? Emot. Rev. **5**(3), 230–234 (2013)
11. Mesken, J.: Determinants and consequences of drivers' emotions. Stichting Wetenschappelijk Onderzoek Verkeersveiligheid SWOV (2006)
12. Mesken, J., Hagenzieker, M.P., Rothengatter, T., de Waard, D.: Frequency, determinants, and consequences of different drivers' emotions: An on-the-road study using self-reports,(observed) behaviour, and physiology. Transp. Res. Part F Traffic Psychol. Behav. **10**(6), 458–475 (2007)
13. Ooi, J.S.K., Ahmad, S.A., Chong, Y.Z., Ali, S.H.M., Ai, G., Wagatsuma, H.: Driver emotion recognition framework based on electrodermal activity measurements during simulated driving conditions. In: 2016 IEEE EMBS Conference on Biomedical Engineering and Sciences (IECBES), pp. 365–369. IEEE (2016)
14. Organization, W.H., et al.: Global status report on road safety (2018)
15. Peng, Z., Wang, Y., Chen, Q.: The generation and development of road rage incidents caused by aberrant overtaking: an analysis of cases in China. Transp. Res. Part F Traffic Psychol. Behav. **60**, 606–619 (2019)
16. Plutchik, R.: A general psychoevolutionary theory of emotion. In: Theories of Emotion, pp. 3–33. Elsevier, Amsterdam (1980)
17. Qu, W., Ge, Y., Jiang, C., Du, F., Zhang, K.: The dula dangerous driving index in China: An investigation of reliability and validity. Accid. Anal. Prev. **64**, 62–68 (2014)
18. Reeve, J.: Understanding Motivation and Emotion. Wiley, Chichester (2014)
19. Rodgers, M.M., Pai, V.M., Conroy, R.S.: Recent advances in wearable sensors for health monitoring. IEEE Sens. J. **15**(6), 3119–3126 (2015)
20. Russell, J.A.: A circumplex model of affect. J. Pers. Soc. Psychol. **39**(6), 1161 (1980)
21. Sacharin, V., Schlegel, K., Scherer, K.R.: Geneva emotion wheel rating study (2012)
22. Wang, W., Cheng, Q., Li, C., André, D., Jiang, X.: A cross-cultural analysis of driving behavior under critical situations: A driving simulator study. Transp. Res. Part F Traffic Psychol. Behav. **62**, 483–493 (2019)
23. Wu, X., Wang, Y., Peng, Z., Chen, Q.: A questionnaire survey on road rage and anger-provoking situations in China. Accid. Anal. Prev. **111**, 210–221 (2018)
24. Zhang, T., Chan, A.H.: The association between driving anger and driving outcomes: A meta-analysis of evidence from the past twenty years. Accid. Anal. Prev. **90**, 50–62 (2016)

Using Machine Learning and Accelerometry Data for Differential Diagnosis of Parkinson's Disease and Essential Tremor

Julián D. Loaiza Duque[1,2] , Andrés M. González-Vargas[1,2]([✉]) ,
Antonio J. Sánchez Egea[3]([✉]) , and Hermán A. González Rojas[3]

[1] Universidad Autónoma de Occidente, Santiago de Cali, Colombia
amgonzalezv@uao.edu.co
[2] Grupo de Investigación en Ingeniería Biomédica G-BIO, Santiago de Cali, Colombia
[3] Universidad Politécnica de Cataluña, Barcelona, Spain
antonio.egea@upc.edu

Abstract. Parkinson's disease (PD) and Essential Tremor (ET) are the most common tremor syndromes in the world. Currently, a specific Single Photon Emission Computed Tomography (^{123}I-FP-CIT SPECT) has proven to be an effective tool for the diagnosis of these diseases (97% sensitivity and 100% specificity). However, this test is invasive and expensive, and not all countries can have a SPECT system for an accurate differential diagnosis of PD patients. Clinical evaluation by a neurologist remains the gold standard for PD diagnosis, although the accuracy of this protocol depends on the experience and expertise of the physician. Wearable devices have been found to be a potential tool to help in differential diagnosis of PD and ET in early or complex cases. In this paper, we analyze the linear acceleration of the hand tremor recorded with a built-in accelerometer of a mobile phone, with a sampling frequency of 100 Hz. This hand tremor signal was thoroughly analyzed to extract different kinematic features in the frequency domain. These features were used to explore different Machine Learning methods to automatically classify and differentiate between healthy subjects and hand tremor patients (HETR Group) and, subsequently, patients with PD and ET (ETPD Group). Sensitivity of 90.0% and Specificity of 100.0% were obtained with classifiers of the HETR group. On the other hand, classifiers with Sensitivity ranges from 90.0% to 100.0% and Specificity from 80% to 100% were obtained for the ETPD group. These results indicate that the method proposed can be a potential tool to help the clinicians on differential diagnosis in complex or early hand tremor cases.

Keywords: Parkinson's Disease · Essential Tremor ·
Machine Learning · Accelerometry · Wearable device

© Springer Nature Switzerland AG 2019
J. C. Figueroa-García et al. (Eds.): WEA 2019, CCIS 1052, pp. 368–378, 2019.
https://doi.org/10.1007/978-3-030-31019-6_32

1   Introduction

Tremor is an involuntary, rhythmic and oscillatory movement of a part of the body [1]. It is not seen during sleep and its effects are commonly observed in the fingers, hands, legs, head and voice [2]. The limbs and head, when not supported, show a slight tremor called physiological tremor, which is generally of low amplitude and interferes only with fine motor control [1,3]. Physiological tremor is usually not visible or symptomatic, unless it is increased by fatigue or anxiety, whereas pathological tremor is usually visible and persistent [1].

Parkinson's disease (PD) and Essential Tremor (ET) are the most common tremor syndromes worldwide [4,5]. The differentiation between PD and ET can sometimes be difficult at early stages or patients without a family history of PD, and misdiagnosis rates can reach up to 25%, even when they are handled by a specialist in movement disorders [4,7–9]. Typically, PD is characterized by resting tremors and ET by postural or kinetic tremors [5]. However, some PD patients may have postural tremor [5] and some ET patients may have resting tremors during disease progression [10,11]. Accordingly, an early and accurate diagnosis is fundamental for treatment selection [4,5,10]. Early treatment of PD reduces or prevents disability and the need for support to maintain the quality of life, whereas incorrectly prescribing PD medication to ET patients is ineffective and exposes them to potential and serious side effects [5]. Nowadays, dopamine transporter (DAT) imaging using Single Photon Emission Computed Tomography (SPECT) with appropriate tracers (^{123}I-FP-CIT) has proven to be an efficient tool for diagnosing PD [4,5,12]. This technique is a high cost test and its use is limited to a few developed countries worldwide. Additionally, it is an invasive test with a radioactive fluid that requires patient compatibility, which may present limitations for its use.

Wearable devices are currently being widely investigated in the movement disorder field, because they can help clinicians in the differentiation between PD and ET. Several works have been published on this topic. Uchida et al. [11] used a triaxial accelerometer to measure the intensity and frequency of hand tremor in resting, posture, writing and walking conditions in subjects with ET and PD patients. They stated that tremor is attenuated during walking in ET subjects with resting tremor and increased in PD patients. Recently, Bernhard et al. [13] studied the gait and balance deficit by using wearables at the lower back and the ankle. They denoted that wearable devices let us assess the progression of movement disorders and response to treatment. Additionally, Wile et al. [14] made a classification of patients with PD and ET via calculation and analysis of the Mean Harmonic Power by using a smartwatch accelerometer. Thanks to that, they noted that compared to an analog accelerometer, a smartwatch device can provide accurate and relevant information for differential diagnosis between PD and ET subjects, based on postural tremor. Locatelli et al. [5] recorded hand tremors during resting, postural and kinetic tasks using a wearable sensor to differentiate PD and ET patients. They observed that, in the frequency domain, the execution of resting tasks showed a predominance of PD over ET tremors, while the data provided by postural and kinetic tasks stand out in

ET subjects. On the other hand, some researchers have used Discrete Wavelet Transforms and Support Vector Machines to differentiate between the two hand tremor conditions. Woods et al. [3] developed an offline application that uses a mobile phone accelerometer to perform the diagnosis and classification of PD and ET patients. Also, Surangsrirat et al. [9] classified PD and TE patients based on temporal angular velocity fluctuations, recorded with a 6-DOF inertial measurement unit. Additionally, Kramer et al. [15] recorded electromyography (EMG) and accelerometry (ACC) signals to distinguish between different types of tremor through Wavelet Coherence Analysis (WCA). They stated that WCA is superior to a standard coherence analysis and could be a useful additional tool for discriminating between tremor types, when the result obtained with other methods is inconclusive. Furthermore, Nanda et al. [8] used the Wavelet transform to extract EMG and ACC signal features. These features combined with an Artificial Neural Network were used to perform a quantitative classification of ET and PD. Finally, Raza et al. [16] compared the diagnosis obtained by using wearable devices with respect to the early diagnosis made by a specialist. In this work, machine learning methods were used to perform the differential classification between PD patients and patients with other movement disorders.

In previous works [4,6], methods for the differential diagnosis of subjects with movement disorders using the built-in accelerometer of a mobile phone were proposed. The proposed method in [4] allows to characterize and recognize the discriminatory features of hand tremor in patients with PD and ET. The present work uses the same data to implement several machine learning algorithms and kinematic indexes that could enhance the discrimination features and, ultimately, improve the sensibility and specificity not only between PD and ET, but also other types of tremor. We expect this method will be extremely useful to aid physicians in the differential diagnosis of complex or early cases.

2   Materials and Methods

Figure 1 shows the different steps of the method we use. These include signal recording using a smartphone, signal processing classification methods using Matlab.

The demographic characteristics of the subjects, the method for recording and preprocessing of the acceleration data used in this study is described in [4]. Data preprocessing, kinetic feature extraction, training and validation of classifiers were carried out using Matlab v. R2017b (Mathworks Inc., USA). Figure 2 summarizes all the tasks performed for the data structuring. Recorded data were initially preprocessed to remove noise components associated with respiration, pulse, or any sudden high-frequency movement. In addition, Power Spectral Density was calculated for each acceleration signal, from which six kinetic features were extracted. Finally, the set of kinetic features of each subject was properly labeled to structure the data.

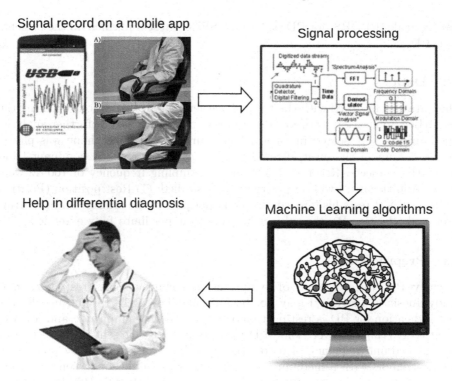

Fig. 1. Schematic of differential diagnosis system for PD and ET subjects.

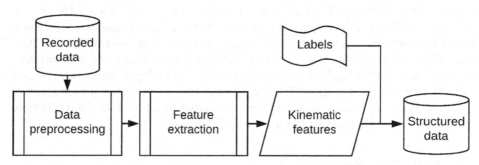

Fig. 2. Data structuring process: recording, preprocessing, featuring and labeling.

2.1 Subjects

A total of 52 subjects (17 patients with PD, 16 patients with ET, 12 healthy subjects and 7 patients with inconclusive diagnosis) were recorded in the Movement Disorders Unit of the Hospital Clínic of Barcelona between October 2015 and December 2016 [4]. All the patients had visually evidences of hand tremor and were diagnosed or had strong indications of PD or ET. Patients had scores of 1 or 2 on the Fahn-Tolosa-Marín scale for ET and Unified Parkinson's Disease

Rating Scale (UPDRS) for PD patients, a SPECT test confirmed all the patients with PD.

2.2 Data

The data was recorded with the triaxial accelerometer of an iPhone 5S using the SensorLog application software [17], and sent to a computer for further analysis. The subjects were seated in an armrest chair and the smartphone was placed on the dorsum of the most affected hand in patients or in the dominant hand in healthy subjects. Records of 30 s with a sampling frequency of 100 Hz were taken. Additionally, two arm positions were studied: (1) Rest position (Position A): the subject rests his forearm on the upper part of the armrest and (2) Arms stretched (Position B): the subject keeps both upper limbs fully extended.

2.3 Preprocessing

In early PD, the full triad of symptoms and clinical signs (resting tremor, bradykinesia and rigidity) may not be fully manifested [18,19] and usually the first indication for PD is resting tremor with moderate amplitude and low frequency (4–6 Hz), however, some PD patients may also present postural tremor with a medium frequency of 6 to 8 Hz [5]. ET is characterized by posture or kinetic tremors with medium frequency (5–8 Hz) [5], although some patients may have tremors at rest during disease progression [10,11]. Besides the preprocessing described in the aforementioned study, the signals were filtered using a 10th order Butterworth filter with cut-off frequencies of 1 and 16 Hz [20], in which the PD and ET frequencies are found. Breathing, pulse or any sudden high frequency movement during recordings were also removed with this filter. Since the analysis was performed in the frequency domain, Power spectral density was calculated using Welch's periodogram by averaging 3s segments of signal recording with 50% overlap of Hanning's windows. The average power spectral densities of the linear accelerations were calculated to find the kinematic indices that allow us to differentiate hand tremor differences.

2.4 Feature Extraction

Figure 3 exhibits a Normalized Power Spectral Density (PSD) of tremor of an ET subject. It also illustrates the kinetic features calculated from the spectral power analysis: Median Power Frequency (MPF), Power Dispersion (PD), Peak Power Frequency (PPF), Harmonic Index (HI), Relative Power Contribution to the first harmonic (RPC) and Relative Energy (RE) to compare PD and ET subjects.

- **MPF:** Frequency at the power distribution center.
- **PD:** Frequency band, centered on MPF, which contains 90% of the total power.
- **PPF:** Frequency at which the maximum power is found.

- **HI:** Quotient between the area under the power spectral density curve and a rectangle bounded on the sides by the frequency band of interest (0–20 Hz) and vertically from 0 to PPF.
- **RPC:** Quotient between the power spectral density of harmonics found between a frequency division threshold (f_{th}) and 20 Hz and the total normalized power spectral density between 0 and 20 Hz.
- **RE:** Quotient between the normalized power spectral densities of resting (PSD_r) and posture (PSD_p) in the frequency range 0 to 20 Hz.

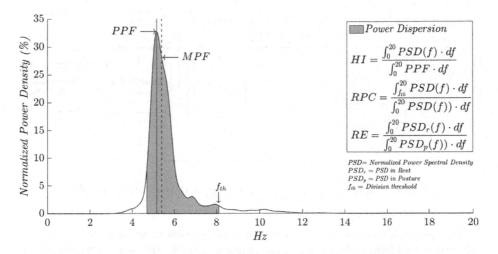

Fig. 3. A normalized spectral power density of tremor in an ET subject

In particular, RE and RPC features were added to enhance the differentiation between PD and ET [4], since their tremor frequency components are different in resting or posture conditions. Theoretically, PD patients should present a higher total spectral power of resting tremor than postural tremor, and in the opposite way for ET patients. The set of features extracted from the data of each subject were respectively labeled according to two classification groups:

1. **HETR** Group:

- Tremor patients - **TR** (Positive Class)
- Healthy subjects - **HE** (Negative Class)

2. **ETPD** Group:

- Parkinson's Disease - **PD** (Positive Class)
- Essential Tremor - **ET** (Negative Class)

Therefore, it is possible to classify subjects between HE and TR and, within subjects identified as TR differentiate between PD and ET patients.

2.5   Training, Validation and Selection of Classification Models

Figure 4 shows all the tasks performed in the process of training, validation and selection of classification models. All data were randomly divided into two sets (training set and validation set) with a proportion of 70-30. For the training set, a total of 63 combinations of features and classification methods were tested with Machine Learning algorithms with and without Principal Component Analysis (PCA), 23 with PCA + 23 without PCA.

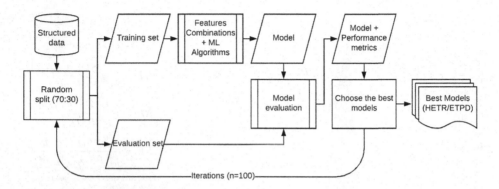

Fig. 4. Training, validation and selection of Classification Models

The performance of the classification models was evaluated by using a 6-fold cross validation. For each classification model, the accuracy and Area Under the Curve (AUC) for non-parametric receiver operating characteristic were estimated from the classification probabilities resulting of cross validation. Afterwards, validation sets were used to calculate Sensitivity (Eq. 1), Specificity (Eq. 2) and SSMean (Eq. 3), which is the average value of specificity and sensibility. In this context, Sensitivity defines the ability of a classification model to detect a positive case, that is, to detect patients with tremor in the group of HETR or patients with PD in the group of ETPD. Furthermore, Specificity defines the ability of the classification model to identify negative cases, being healthy subjects in the group of HETR Group or patients with ET in the group of ETPD.

$$Sensitivity = \frac{TP}{TP + FN} \tag{1}$$

$$Specificity = \frac{TN}{TN + FP} \tag{2}$$

$$SSMean = \frac{Sensitivity + Specificity}{2} \tag{3}$$

Validation and training processes were iterated 100 times for the same feature combinations and classification methods. This ensured that the training was carried out with a varied set of data, so that classification models with different performance levels were considered. After all iterations, Sensitivity, Specificity and SSMean were calculated for each classification model. Classification models with the highest average values of SSMean in the groups of HETR and ETPD were identified. The best 10 classification models after these 100 iterations process were listed and studied in the results section.

3   Results

The output results after applying the iteration methodology is listed in Table 1. All the results reported here are obtained by testing on validation sets. The 10 best classification models come from a total of 2898 classification models, due to the feature and classification methods combinations. The average column represents the mean behavior during 100 iterations (in which training and validation data were randomized), whereas the best case column shows the best performance among all iterations.

Table 1. Healthy vs. Trembling subjects discrimination. Top 10 Classification Models with the highest SSMean values in the HETR group. **PCA:** Principal Components Analysis, **Sen:** Sensitivity **and Spe:** Specificity

Features	Method	PCA	Averages			Best Case		
			Sen	Spe	SSMean	Sen	Spe	SSMean
PPF + MPF	Quadratic Discriminant	No	71.5	99.4	85.4	90.0	100.0	95.0
MPF + HI	Quadratic Discriminant	No	71.3	99.5	85.4	90.0	100.0	95.0
PPF + MPF + PD	Quadratic Discriminant	No	71,2	99.0	85.1	90.0	100.0	95.0
MPF	Quadratic Discriminant	No	70.7	99.4	85.0	90.0	100.0	95.0
MPF	Quadratic Discriminant	Yes	70.7	99.4	85.0	90.0	100.0	95.0
PPF + MPF + HI	Quadratic Discriminant	No	73.2	96.9	85.0	90.0	100.0	95.0
PPF + MPF	Quadratic Discriminant	Yes	70.2	99.8	85.0	90.0	100.0	95.0
PPF + MPF + PD	Quadratic Discriminant	Yes	70,2	99.8	85.0	90.0	100.0	95.0
MPF + PD	Quadratic Discriminant	Yes	70.2	99.4	84.8	90.0	100.0	95.0
MPF + PD + HI	Quadratic Discriminant	No	70.5	98.9	84.7	90.0	100.0	95.0

It is noticeable that all the models used the Quadratic Discrimination method, and the common kinematic feature for all of them was MPF. This suggests that the MPF feature may provide a significant differentiation between HE and TR. The classification model with the highest SSMean average was obtained using both MPF and PPF features. In other words, compared to the other models, this classification model had the best performance in most of the 100 iterations. The models that presented the maximum SSMean values are considered on the top of the table, because of the combined good results in sensibility and specificity. Note that for all classification models the best cases had an SSMean value of 95.0% (90.0% Sensitivity and 100.0% Specificity). Moreover, Table 2 shows the best 10 classification models with the highest SSMean values

Table 2. Parkinson's Disease vs. Essential Tremor patient discrimination. Top 10 Classification Models with the highest SSMean values in the ETPD group. **PCA:** Principal Components Analysis, **Sen:** Sensitivity **and Spe:** Specificity

Features	Method	PCA	Averages			Best Case		
			Sen	Spe	SSMean	Sen	Spe	SSMean
RPC + RE + HI	Logistic Regression	No	69.2	85.4	77.3	100.0	90.0	95.0
RPC + RE + MPF + HI	Logistic Regression	No	69.5	83.0	76.3	100.0	90.0	95.0
RPC + RE + PPF + HI	Logistic Regression	No	67.7	84.5	76.1	100.0	80.0	90.0
RPC + RE	Logistic Regression	No	66.7	84.8	75.8	100.0	100.0	100.0
RPC + RE + PPF	Logistic Regression	No	66.4	84.9	75.7	90.0	90.0	90.0
RE + PPF + HI	Logistic Regression	No	66.6	83.9	75.3	100.0	100.0	100.0
RE	Medium KNN	No	73.8	76.4	75.1	100.0	100.0	100.0
RE	Cubic KNN	No	73.8	76.4	75.1	100.0	100.0	100.0
RE	Medium KNN	Yes	73,8	76.4	75.1	100.0	100.0	100.0
RE	Cubic KNN	Yes	73.8	76.4	75.1	100.0	100.0	100.0

for the group of ETPD, where it can be noted which method and kinematic are essential to distinguish between PD and ET subjects.

The first six classification models used the Linear Regression method, whereas the last four used different types of KNN algorithms. Note that the kinematic feature RE is used in all the classification models to differentiate between the two groups. This is consistent with the results obtained in [4], since with this feature a significant differentiation was obtained between patients with PD and ET (84.4% discrimination accuracy). RPC is a feature that also had significant performance in the previous paper. Classification models that use these two features are on the top five. The present work found that the best case of the classification model that combines the Logistic Regression method and these two kinematic features (RPC and RE) obtained a SSMean value of 100.0% (100.0% Sensitivity and 100.0% Specificity). Table 2 shows five other cases in which an SSMean value of 100.0% was obtained. These are promising results to develop a helpful tool for clinicians for the differential diagnosis of PD and ET. However, a larger database will be needed in order to further validate these results.

4   Conclusion

The potential benefits of using Machine Learning for classification of patients with hand tremor was investigated in this paper. The main findings drawn from this research are, firstly, that the linear acceleration is able to provide significant information for an appropriate classification of healthy subjects and patients with tremor and, ultimately, differentiate between PD and ET subjects. The effectiveness of such differentiation depends substantially on the correct selection and evaluation of the classifier to be implemented. Secondly, during the training of the classifiers, it was possible to identify outstanding performance of kinetic features combinations and classification methods. In particular,

Quadratic Discriminant method combined with MPF feature were the most relevant combination to differentiate healthy from pathological subjects, whereas Logistic Regression method combined with RE and RPC features were crucial to differentiated PD from ET subjects.

As future work, the methodology presented in this paper will be implemented to analyze the angular velocity signal of the gyroscope built-in the mobile device. In this way, it will be possible to determine if the angular velocity assess a higher performance level than that obtained with the linear acceleration analysis. Finally, a low-cost app will be developed to provide relevant information to clinicians to help in clinical evaluation of the patients with hand tremor in the first stages.

Acknowledgements. This work was supported by Dirección de Investigaciones y Desarrollo Tecnológico (DIDT) of Universidad Autónoma de Occidente, Project 19INTER-308: "Herramienta no invasiva de bajo costo para el diagnóstico diferencial temprano en pacientes con Parkinson y Temblor Esencial" and by the Serra Húnter program (Generalitat de Catalunya) reference number UPC-LE-304.

References

1. Bhatia, K.-P., et al.: Consensus statement on the classification of tremors. From the task force on tremor of the International Parkinson and Movement Disorder Society. Mov. Disord. **33**, 75–87 (2018). https://doi.org/10.1002/mds.27121
2. Bhavana, C., Gopal, J., Raghavendra, P., Vanitha, K.-M., Talasila, V.: Techniques of measurement for Parkinson's tremor highlighting advantages of embedded IMU over EMG. In: 2016 International Conference on Recent Trends in Information Technology (ICRTIT), pp. 1–5. IEEE (2016)
3. Woods, A.-M., Nowostawski, M., Franz, E.-A., Purvis, M.: Parkinson's disease and essential tremor classification on mobile device. Pervasive Mob. Comput. **13**, 1–12 (2014). https://doi.org/10.1016/j.pmcj.2013.10.002
4. Barrantes, S., et al.: Differential diagnosis between Parkinson's disease and essential tremor using the smartphone's accelerometer. PLoS ONE **12**, e0183843 (2017). https://doi.org/10.1371/journal.pone.0183843
5. Locatelli, P., Alimonti, D.: Differentiating essential tremor and Parkinson's disease using a wearable sensor – a pilot study. In: 2017 7th IEEE International Workshop on Advances in Sensors and Interfaces (IWASI), pp. 213–218. IEEE (2017)
6. González Rojas, H.-A., Cuevas, P.-C., Zayas Figueras, E.-E., Foix, S.-C., Sánchez Egea, A.-J.: Time measurement characterization of stand-to-sit and sit-to-stand transitions by using a smartphone. Med. Biol. Eng. Comput. **56**, 879–888 (2018). https://doi.org/10.1007/s11517-017-1728-5
7. Miller, D.-B., O'Callaghan, J.-P.: Biomarkers of Parkinson's disease: present and future. Metabolism **64**, S40–S46 (2015). https://doi.org/10.1016/j.metabol.2014.10.030
8. Nanda, S.K., Lin, W.-Y., Lee, M.-Y., Chen, R.-S.: A quantitative classification of essential and Parkinson's tremor using wavelet transform and artificial neural network on sEMG and accelerometer signals. In: 2015 IEEE 12th International Conference on Networking, Sensing and Control, pp. 399–404. IEEE (2015)

9. Surangsrirat, D., Thanawattano, C., Pongthornseri, R., Dumnin, S., Anan, C., Bhidayasiri, R.: Support vector machine classification of Parkinson's disease and essential tremor subjects based on temporal fluctuation. In: 2016 38th Annual International Conference of the IEEE Engineering in Medicine and Biology Society (EMBC), pp. 6389–6392. IEEE (2016)
10. Papengut, F., Raethjen, J., Binder, A., Deuschl, G.: Rest tremor suppression may separate essential from Parkinsonian rest tremor. Parkinsonism Relat. Disord. **19**, 693–697 (2013). https://doi.org/10.1016/j.parkreldis.2013.03.013
11. Uchida, K., Hirayama, M., Yamashita, F., Hori, N., Nakamura, T., Sobue, G.: Tremor is attenuated during walking in essential tremor with resting tremor but not Parkinsonian tremor. J. Clin. Neurosci. **18**, 1224–1228 (2011). https://doi.org/10.1016/j.jocn.2010.12.053
12. Algarni, M., Fasano, A.: The overlap between essential tremor and Parkinson disease. Parkinsonism Relat. Disord. **46**, S101–S104 (2018). https://doi.org/10.1016/j.parkreldis.2017.07.006
13. Bernhard, F.-P., et al.: Wearables for gait and balance assessment in the neurological ward - study design and first results of a prospective cross-sectional feasibility study with 384 inpatients. BMC Neurol. **18**, 114 (2018). https://doi.org/10.1186/s12883-018-1111-7
14. Wile, D.-J., Ranawaya, R., Kiss, Z.-H.-T.: Smart watch accelerometry for analysis and diagnosis of tremor. J. Neurosci. Methods **230**, 1–4 (2014). https://doi.org/10.1016/j.jneumeth.2014.04.021
15. Kramer, G., Van der Stouwe, A.-M.-M., Maurits, N.-M., Tijssen, M.-A.-J., Elting, J.-W.-J.: Wavelet coherence analysis: a new approach to distinguish organic and functional tremor types. Clin. Neurophysiol. **129**, 13–20 (2018). https://doi.org/10.1016/j.clinph.2017.10.002
16. Raza, M.-A., Chaudry, Q., Zaidi, S.-M.-T., Khan, M.-B.: Clinical decision support system for Parkinson's disease and related movement disorders. In: 2017 IEEE International Conference on Acoustics, Speech and Signal Processing (ICASSP), pp. 1108–1112. IEEE (2017)
17. Sensorlog (Version 1.9.4) Mobile application software. http://itunes.apple.com. Accessed 24 Apr 2019
18. Brooks, D.-J.: Parkinson's disease: diagnosis. Parkinsonism Relat. Disord. **18**, S31–S33 (2012). https://doi.org/10.1016/S1353-8020(11)70012-8
19. Arvind, R., Karthik, B., Sriraam, N., Kannan, J.-K.: Automated detection of PD resting tremor using PSD with recurrent neural network classifier. In: 2010 International Conference on Advances in Recent Technologies in Communication and Computing, pp. 414–417. IEEE (2010)
20. Jeon, H., et al.: Automatic classification of tremor severity in Parkinson's disease using a wearable device. Sensors **17**, 2067 (2017). https://doi.org/10.3390/s17092067

A Wireless, Modular and Wearable System for the Recognition and Assessment of Foot Drop Pathology

Santiago Noriega[ID], Maria C. Rojas[ID], and Cecilia Murrugarra[(✉)][ID]

Electronic Engineering Program, Faculty of Engineering, Universidad El Bosque,
Bogota, DC 110111, Colombia
{snoriega,mcrojass,cmurrugarra}@unbosque.edu.co
http://www.unbosque.edu.co

Abstract. In this paper, a portable, low cost and non-invasive real-time signals processing prototype was designed and developed for the diagnosis and continuous monitoring of the physiopathological condition of foot drop. The behavior of the electrical activity of the Tibialis Anterior (TA) and Peroneus Longus (PL) muscles through bipolar surface electromyography (sEMG), together with the angular measurement of the joint complex of the ankle-foot in the sagittal and frontal planes using an Inertial Measurement Unit (IMU) sensor system, are monitored from a mobile interface. This prototype consists of five modules capable of performing functions of sensing, signal processing, data storage, and transmission. The Central Processing Unit (CPU) process the sEMG signals from the two-channel amplifier with 10 bits of resolution at a sampling frequency of 1ksps; the IMU Sensor System operates at a sample rate of 1ksps with 16 bits of resolution. Both sEMG and angular displacement data registers are transmitted wirelessly via Bluetooth communication protocol to a mobile interface designed for smartphones/tablets and PC. Data verification was made using a commercial electromyograph and a goniometer. The observations regarding the health status of the patient on a statistical, mathematical analysis of the collected data, exhibiting a mean-square-error of 5,27% for the sEMG as well as an average error of $\leq \pm 2°$ in the angular displacement measurements. The prototype designed and developed establishes a new perspective in the recognition and elaboration of profiles of physiopathological disabilities in humans, development of clinical applications, and databases for future studies of the disease.

Keywords: Foot drop · Rehabilitation · EMG · Sensors ·
Real time, signal acquisition

This work was supported by a grant from the Faculty of Engineering and Electronic Engineering Program of Universidad El Bosque, with the research project number PFI-2017-EL-011.

© Springer Nature Switzerland AG 2019
J. C. Figueroa-García et al. (Eds.): WEA 2019, CCIS 1052, pp. 379–393, 2019.
https://doi.org/10.1007/978-3-030-31019-6_33

1   Introduction

There are usually several ways in which biomedicine and electronics overlap to generate a benefit, for example, rehabilitation through stimulation [1] or equipment for the prevention of physiological conditions or diseases [2]. There are several physio-pathological scenarios for clinical monitoring. However, foot drop pathology has been selected to research and assess. This condition can be generated through various causes, frequently is attributed to accidents that compromise the dorsal extensor muscles of the foot and toes that are innervated by the deep peroneal nerve [3]. A person suffering from this condition finds it involved, depending on the degree of involvement, to move the foot through the joint complex of the ankle in the sagittal and frontal planes. Accurately perform the dorsiflexion and plantar flexion movements, which correspond to tilt the instep of the foot up and down respectively (these movements occur in the sagittal and frontal planes). This phenomenon results in a deficiency of the Tibialis Anterior (TA) and Peroneus Longus (PL) muscles, muscular entities responsible for carrying out these movements. Bearing in mind that in most cases of foot drop there is an insufficiency of the TA and PL muscles and deficient performance of the ankle joint complex, it has been tried to assess and reckon foot drop through electromyography systems [4] or by making angular measurements of the joint involved [5]. However, currently, the foot drop pathology diagnoses and evaluated by independently measuring these two physiological variables.

The study and research of surface electromyography, commonly denoted as sEMG, is based on surface electrodes located over the muscles of interest. This approach in the detection of muscular activity is know as *bipolar sEMG* [6]. There are several reasons to perform the sEMG procedure, the most common considerations are: (i) in rehabilitation protocols, where it is imperative to know the activation characteristics of the muscles [7]. (ii) in studies of muscular force distribution and definition of muscular systems [8]. (iii) in medical applications focused on sports where it is needed to limit and optimize the energy expenditure of an athlete [9]. (iv) in the activation and control of prostheses through muscle signals [10]. Regardless of the application, the success of the bipolar sEMG depends directly on the attributes and features of the person's neuromuscular system, as well as on the techniques and cares when placing the surface electrodes over the muscle. Concepts such as muscle characteristics (structure, size, location) [11], type of electrodes (either superficial or intramuscular) [12] and additional considerations (electric transmission gel, shave of the application area, the distance between the electrodes) [13] have direct impacts on the efficiency and effectiveness of the bipolar sEMG.

Even though the technological dynamic that the world is adopting a few years ago in the measurement of physical variables such as angular displacement is evolving, non-electronic instruments (e.g., mechanical goniometers) continue to position themselves as the first and most reliable option when assessing the physiological state of a patient. However, the evolution regarding more technological and versatile tools is becoming increasingly pronounced, fast, and visible. There are various techniques to measure the angular displacement of a given joint complex, mainly, there are three ways to do this: (i) encoders systems,

(ii) flexible sensors and (iii) IMU sensors. The first of these methods is about systems based on encoders [14], while this option offers high accuracy in measurements of angular displacement, it requires additional mechanisms around the joint to be studied; this generally negatively affects the user experience in terms of comfort and maneuverability. The second technology, flexible sensors or *flex sensors*, are transducers that act as variable resistors, changing their resistance value as a result of the bend grade over their surface [15]. Flex sensors are commonly used to estimate the angular displacement regard to a reference plane, in the prosthesis control according to a given joint angular movement, in physiotherapy and orthopedics applications [16]. However, flex sensors have some disadvantages (average error and mandatory use of conditioning circuits) that make them inferior to other alternatives [17]. The third alternative to measuring the angular displacement is the Inertial Measurement Unit, also known as IMU sensors. The IMU sensors are embedded circuits generally consisting of precision gyroscopes, accelerometers, magnetometers, and pressure sensors. One of the significant characteristics of the IMU sensors is the capability to estimate angular displacement values from a series of angulation and rotation measurements from the sensors inherent to the IMU system, which provides greater precision and lower average error when sensing [18]. The IMU sensors have the advantage of being able to be placed on any part of the body that reflects the angular displacement produced by some joint (for example on the instep of the foot instead of the ankle). This attribute makes IMU sensors extensively used in virtual immersion devices [19]. The overall panorama of the angular displacement measurement shows that the encoder systems have an average error of 3.25°, the flex sensors 6.92° and the IMU systems 0.08° [17].

In this paper, a wireless, modular, and wearable prototype of an electronic system focused on the diagnosis and continuous monitoring of the physiopathological condition of foot drop is presented. This device has properties that allow it to assess in real-time the behavior of the electrical activity of the TA and PL muscles, together with the angular measurement of the joint complex of the ankle in the sagittal and frontal planes. The sensed data is sent to a mobile interface, allowing to issue observations regarding the health status of the patient based on a mathematical analysis of the collected data, besides of generating databases for future studies of the condition. This prototype is presented as a new tool in the identification and assessment of foot drop pathology, integrating the measurement of its most determinate and revealing physiological variables.

2   General System Architecture

The global system consists of three stages to perform the task of detection, conditioning, processing, storage and transmission of physiological signal data of the TA and PL muscles and the angular displacement of the ankle-foot joint complex. These stages have been classified as (Sect. 2.1) Location of the peripherals of the system in the body of the user, (Sect. 2.2) Platform of the electronics device, and (Sect. 2.3) Mobile interface in a smartphone/tablet for real-time visualization. Figure 1 shows general system configuration, where, Fig. 1(a) shows the human body representation, with the location of the system's peripherals in the user's body. Figure 1(b) shows the platform of the electronics modules of the system, once the data registers of sEMG and the angular displacement are received, the CPU unit performs the appropriate signal processing, to then execute the functions of storage and data transmission. Figure 1(c) shows the data packets are sent to a mobile interface on a smartphone/tablet for real-time visualization. Table 1 shows the general technical specifications of the system.

Table 1. General technical specifications of the system.

Description	Nomenclature	Value
sEMG Channels	$sEMG_{ch}$	2
sEMG bandwidth	$sEMG_{bw}$	10 Hz–450 Hz
Max. Gain	G	10000 V/V
Commom Mode Rejection Ratio	CMRR	130 dB
sEMG ADC Resolution	$sEMG_{ADC}$	10 bits
sEMG Sampling Frequency	$sEMG_{fs}$	1 ksps/ch
IMU Sensor Resolution	IMU_{res}	16 bits
IMU Sensor sampling frequency	IMU_{fs}	1 ksps
Range of Motion Arc	MOV_{ARC}	±90° in each plane
Communication Protocol	——	Bluetooth
Reciever	——	Smartphone/tablet
Max. Transmission Distance	d_{TX}	9 m
Power Supply	V_S	3 Ah 5-cell Lithium
Autonomy of the System	——	8 h
Dimensions	——	$15.5 \times 9 \times 11$ cm
Weight	——	600 g

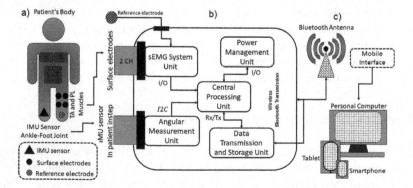

Fig. 1. General system configuration: (a) Location of the system's peripherals in the user's body, (b) Platform of the Electronics Device: five modules of the system, and (c) Mobile interface on a smartphone/tablet for real-time visualization.

2.1   Location of the Peripherals of the System in the User Body

The EMG detection is performed through surface electrodes installed over the Tibialis Anterior (TA) and Peroneus Longus (PL) muscles; the reference electrode must be fixed on the person's ankle, over the malleolus. The IMU sensor is installed on the side of the instep of the person, using a velcro fastening system.

2.2   Platform of the Electronics Device

This system is composed into five units or modules liable for performing the task of conditioning and processing of signals, storage, and data transmission. This system is conceived around a *Central Processing Unit* and four modules: *sEMG Detection Unit, Angular Measurement Unit, Power Supply Unit*, and *Data Transmission and Storage Unit*, each one with different and specific functionalities described the following subsections.

sEMG Detection Unit is a conditioning circuit segmented in stages of: (a) instrumentation, (b) amplification (at the input and output of the circuit), (c) filtering (as a high pass filter and low pass filter), (d) rectification and (e) integration. The sEMG signals are captured by the surface electrodes and conditioned to obtain the (i) raw signal, the (ii) rectified signal and the (iii) envelope of the signal. The first is the instrumentation/differential stage, elaborated around an instrumentation amplifier with adjustable gain. This stage estimate the voltage difference between two points of the muscle and the reference, for later be amplified. The amplification stages were established both at the beginning/input and at the end/output of the sEMG Detection Unit; this allows a pre-amplification before filtering the signal, as an amplification at the end of the circuit; the maximum gain tunable is 10000V/V. The sEMG Detection Unit incorporates an active second order band pass filter composed of a second order high pass filter and a second order low pass filter; the cutoff frequencies of these filters are 10 Hz and 450 Hz respectively, due the frequency distribution of the information of the TA and PL muscles. These two filters were designed in a Chebyshev topology (Notch filter was not implemented due to the loss of relevant information). The rectification stage was implemented; this part of the circuit oversees rectifying the signal to be later able to obtain the envelope of the EMG signal. Finally, the signal is integrated through an amplifier in an integrator configuration; this type of configuration works similarly to a low pass filter with a low cutoff frequency 2 Hz. Figure 2 shows the block diagram of the sEMG Detection Unit, with three general EMG outputs: raw, rectified and envelope of the EMG signal. These outputs offer sufficient information for the observation and assessment of the electrical activity of the TA and PL muscles in the time domain.

Angular Measurement Unit is built around an Inertial Measurement Unit (IMU), model *MPU6050*, which allows obtaining variables such as acceleration, speed or position with 16 bits of resolution at a sampling frequency of 1 ksps.

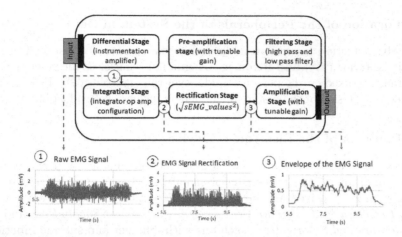

Fig. 2. sEMG Detection Unit block diagram. As general characteristics, tunable gains, second-order Chebyshev filters, and cutoff frequencies 10 Hz to 450 Hz. In the lower part of the figure shows the raw, rectified, an envelope of the signals captured by the sEMG.

For foot drop pathology, we want to estimate the angular position and measure the *arc* of movement of the ankle-foot joint complex. The angular position in the sagittal and frontal planes is searched in the IMU sensor registers to be read and processed by the CPU through an I^2C communication protocol. This communication protocol allows to establish up to four maximum transmission speeds, from 100 kbps (standard mode) to 5 Mbps (ultra fast mode). For this case, speed of 400 kbps (fast mode) was configured. Additionally, the I^2C communication protocol operates synchronously in a serial configuration, allowing up to 1008 number of slaves (there is no limit to the number of masters).

The angular displacement is obtained as an indirect measurement from the data of the accelerometer and gyroscope sensors inherent to the IMU system, and the mathematical algorithm is realized in the *Central Processing Unit*. Using the values of the accelerometer, it is possible to estimate the angular displacement of the Eqs. 1 and 2, where acc_x and acc_x, represent the acceleration values in the respective planes.

$$\theta_x = tan^{-1} \frac{acc_x}{\sqrt{acc_y^2 + acc_z^2}} \tag{1}$$

$$\theta_y = tan^{-1} \frac{acc_y}{\sqrt{acc_x^2 + acc_z^2}} \tag{2}$$

Similarly, it is possible to calculate the angle sensed by the gyroscope data through Eqs. 3 and 4, where the angular displacement values are calculated taking the initial angle (θ_{xo}) and the difference in time of the rotation data.

$$\theta_x = \theta_{xo} + \omega_x \triangle t \tag{3}$$

$$\theta_y = \theta_{yo} + \omega_y \triangle t \tag{4}$$

Finally, it is possible to estimate the angular displacement in terms of the angles calculated by the accelerometer and gyroscope. The Eqs. 5 and 6 represent the angular displacement in terms of the information sensed by the accelerometer and gyroscope; these expressions are known as the complementary filter (CF). The main benefit of using the CF model is the high precision in the measurements. The CF can be modeled as a low pass filter for the accelerometer and a high pass filter for the gyroscope (X and Y in Eqs. 5 and 6 are the filter coefficients). These filters allow reducing the fast variations of acceleration and the detection of sudden gyroscope rotations.

$$Angle[0] = X(Angle[0] + Gyro_{angx}dt) + Y(Acc_{angx}) \tag{5}$$

$$Angle[1] = X(Angle[1] + Gyro_{angy}dt) + Y(Acc_{angy}) \tag{6}$$

Central Processing Unit (CPU) is designed around a *ATmega328P* microcontroller (μC) which receives the information of the envelope sEMG signals of the TA and PL muscles, and the angular variation of the ankle-foot joint in both sagittal and frontal planes. To digitize an analogous signal, it is fundamental to fulfill the *Nyquist-Shannon*[20], with $F_s \geq 2F_{max}$, where: F_s, is the sampling frequency and F_{max}, is the maximum analogue frequency of the signal. The Fs of the data acquisition system is 1 ksps (10 bits ADC of the μC). The TA and PL muscles signals are in the 10 Hz to 450 Hz frequency spectrum; therefore using a sampling rate of 1 ksps, to ensure a good signal processing and treatment. The registers from the IMU sensor require an I^2C communication protocol to be processed by the μC. The μC request information about the angular displacement through the values of acceleration and rotation in the three axes, searching in the IMU sensor registers, each value is stored in a specific address. The CPU also executes the protocols and algorithms of storage and data transmission. The format of the data storage is vector columns containing volts for sEMG and degrees for IMU sensor (as well as μC code execution time); the data packets are sent via Bluetooth to a mobile interface on a smartphone/tablet for real-time visualization (only when the two variables are sensed to guarantee synchronization).

Data Transmission and Storage Unit is responsible for receiving the information issued by the CPU and, in sequential order, storing and transmitting it. The data storage is accomplished through a 16 GB *micro-SD card*, which allows storing the information. The stored data are amplitudes in volts and angular displacements in degrees. Once the data packets are stored and organized in vectors, the data transmission is carried out through the Bluetooth communication protocol. Due to the type of information, and the real-time visualization goal, a baud rate of 125200 was chosen. The information is transmitted encoded, so the smartphone/tablet must decode the data segment to understand which data has been sent. Figure 3, shows the algorithm behind this process. Figure 3a, shows the data transmission protocol. The data packets of sEMG and IMU sensor are encrypted sent to identify the type and class of physiological variable that is being transmitted, and the Fig. 3b shows the data reception algorithm. Within the mobile interface, a segment header reader is used to identify and classify the information transmitted; once the mobile interface identifies the packet header, it proceeds to real-time visualize the respective information.

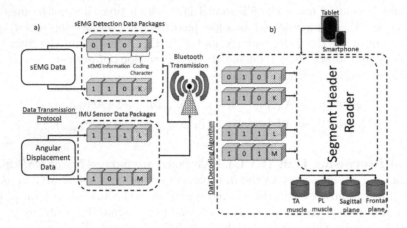

Fig. 3. (a) Data transmission protocol. (b) Data reception algorithm.

Power Supply Unit the system uses a Lithium Lion battery, accompanied by a *Battery Management System* (BMS) which protects against overload, over discharge and short circuit scenarios. After the BMS, the battery voltage is supplied to a single to dual rail circuit in order to achieve dual voltage, necessary for the sEMG Detection Unit which has mandatory information within negative signals. In this case, we used 18.5 V–3 Ah battery. The battery ensures 8 h autonomy; however, lower voltage batteries can be used with similar results.

2.3   Mobile and Desktop Interfaces

The Mobile Interface was developed on the Java programming language for smartphones or tablets; this tool can graph in real-time the values of the sensed physiological variables. The display device is prepared to receive four different data segments at specific times. The Fig. 3 explains the algorithm used to receive and visualize the data. Similarly, an interface for PCs called *desktop interface* was designed. This application allows to deploy a much more in-depth statistical analysis; this feature also grants the system the ability to estimate a clinical diagnosis to the specialist, establishing the patient's health status based on purely mathematical analysis.

3   Results

3.1   Electronic Device

All subsystems of the development electronic device have been designed to be joined by connectors with each other. Figure 4 shows the integration of all the electronic cards and their functioning tests is confirmed once the assembly has been completed. Figure 4(a) and (b) shows the top and lateral view of the assembly electronics cards of the prototype developed, and the Fig. 4(c), shows the electronics cards developed with the connectors of the sensors of the system.

(a) Top view for assembly electronics card developed.

(b) Lateral view for assembly electronics card developed.

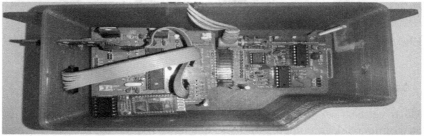

(c) Portable box with electronics cards developed inside, and wired connectors from the sEMG and IMU sensors.

Fig. 4. Complete integration of the electronics cards, connectors, and sensors for the prototype device developed.

3.2 Assembly of the Electronic Device and Integration of Sensors

The surface EMG electrodes needs gel to make a good impedance coupling; they also need to be installed in accordance with the SENIAM [21] regulations or recommendations for both muscles. The assembly was made in a portable box adjustable to the user's waist through a belt, emulating a waist bag. The ankle clamp is fixed to the user's leg through velcro straps; it provides an installation surface for the IMU sensor, and has holes as reference points for the location of the surface electrodes. To avoid erroneous readings or incorrect IMU sensor installation, a 3D printed piece that serves as an enclosure for the IMU board was used; also a velcro hook system was provided to ensure that the sensor is always installed in the same way. The Fig. 5 shows the electronic prototype fully installed on the patient's body. This device was developed as a passive sensing tool, transparent to the user, which does not limit or affect the movement of the user, basic security and protection mechanisms were taken into account, such as the characteristics provided by the BMS. The orange piece is the electronic card container; it houses all the electronic cards with the exception of the IMU sensor located on the side of the instep. The person's leg is covered with an extended ankle brace, which gives firmness to the experimental setup and supports the installation of the surface electrodes, through the ankle brace holes.

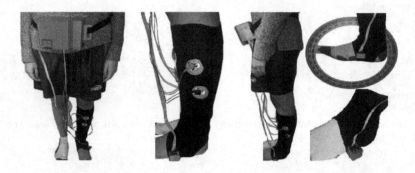

Fig. 5. Disposition of the system in the patient's body with the ankle clamp

3.3 Angular Displacement Data Verification

The data verification was based on the comparison of the measurement made with a commercial goniometer and the calculated value by the IMU sensor of the system prototype. We used a certified mechanical goniometer[1]. According to Nordin [22], the normal movement *arc* for motions in the sagittal plane (dorsiflexion and plantar flexion) is 75°, while for movements in the frontal plane (eversion and inversion) it is 40°. This suggests that the IMU sensor fully meets the functional requirements due to its capability of measuring movements *arcs* of maximum 180° in each plane (−90° to 90°). Table 2 shows the measurements realized. Figure 6 shows an experimental measurement between the mechanical goniometer and the IMU sensor of the developed prototype. The Fig. 6(a), shows simultaneous measurements between goniometer and the IMU sensor of our device in sagittal and frontal planes, without exceeding 2° of average error in both planes. This can be due to a correct calibration of the sensor and proper installation of the card in the patient's foot. The angles to compare the samples were chosen arbitrarily, and five simultaneous measurements were made between the mechanical goniometer and the IMU sensor. Figure 6(b) and (c), shows the comparison in bar graphs between the goniometer and the IMU sensor in the sagittal and frontal planes correspondingly, and the error of each measurement.

---

[1] Ez Read Jamar Goniometer-Manual medical goniometer.

Table 2. Statistical analysis goniometer vs IMU sensor. Angular displacement data

Plane	Test	Goniometer	IMU sensor	Error
Sagittal	1	27°	29,2°	−2,2°
	2	17,5°	17,3°	0,2°
	3	36°	37,9°	−1,9°
	4	90°	87,5°	2,5°
	5	0°	0,7°	−0,7°
	Avg error	–	–	**1,5°**
Frontal	1	14°	14,3°	−0,3°
	2	25°	26,3°	−1,3°
	3	82°	80,4°	1,6°
	4	70°	72,5°	−2,5°
	5	43°	41,8°	1,2°
	Avg error	–	–	**1,38°**

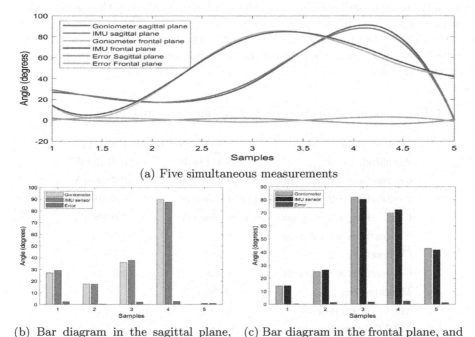

(a) Five simultaneous measurements

(b) Bar diagram in the sagittal plane, and the error of each measurement

(c) Bar diagram in the frontal plane, and the error of each measurement

Fig. 6. Experimental measurements between the mechanical goniometer and the IMU sensor of the developed prototype.

3.4   SEMG Detection Data Verification

The envelope signal of the TA muscle was captured by a commercial electromyograph[2] and the prototype, with the aim of making a statistical comparison of both tool's signals. The Fig. 7, shows the sEMG detection data verification, setup, and results obtained for the tests realized. Was necessary to parallel the TA muscle signals to the inputs of both devices while the ground reference was the same for both instruments, the Fig. 7(a), shows the experimental setup. The patient performed three muscle contractions, each one of around 1.5s to 2s with a separation of around 2s. As can be seen in Fig. 7(c), the muscle contractions were recorded by both devices. Figure 7b show the bar diagram the contraction times recorded by the prototype and the commercial electromyograph. In the statistical analysis presented in Table 3, parameters such as the Mean Square Error (MSE), average amplitudes of contraction, the maximum amplitude of each contraction and contraction time intervals are estimated. The MSE measures the difference between the estimator and what is estimated, we obtained MSE of *0.96%*, *6.84%* and *16.17%* for the first, second, and the third contraction respectively. However, the hole record presented an MSE of *5.05%*. The first two contractions are broadly similar in both instruments; however, the third contraction presents a delay in the data collected by our device; This may be due to the order and types of filters used in the sEMG Detection Unit. Likewise, the data presented in the measurement of contraction times are very positive, presenting a maximum difference of 150 ms in the contraction #3.

Table 3. Statistical Analysis - sEMG, amplitude, contraction and % MSE

Measurement	Commercial EMG	Prototype
Amplitude Average	0.3118mV	0.3618 mV
Contraction #1 max amplitude	0.9286 mV	0.9856 mV
Contraction #2 max amplitude	1.0998 mV	1.0691 mV
Contraction #3 max amplitude	1.0663 mV	1.0998 mV
Contraction #1 interval	1.65 s	1.644 s
Contraction #2 interval	1.649 s	1.696 s
Contraction #3 interval	1.908 s	1.756 s
Measurement	% MSE	
MSE Contraction #1	0.96%	
MSE Contraction #2	6.84%	
MSE Contraction #3	16.18%	
Total MSE	5.05%	

---

[2] ADInstruments Powerlab recording unit, Teaching Series-26T model.

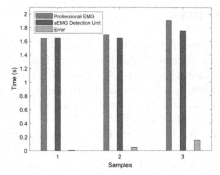

(a) Setup for the sEMG detection data verification

(b) Bar diagram the contraction times

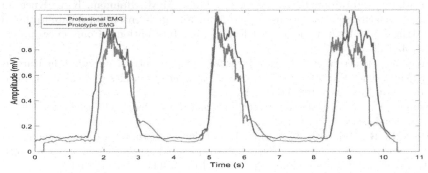

(c) Results obtained from the measurements and comparison of sEMG registers

Fig. 7. sEMG Detection data verification between *ADInstruments Powerlab recording unit, Teaching Series-26T model* and the developed prototype

4   Conclusions

The development of a device to support the recognition and assessment of the pathology condition of foot drop was realized. The precision and portability attributes make the device suitable for use in patients and to help the specialist when making decisions in a faster and more accurate way, related to diagnosing and control of foot drop condition. All the results collected and shown in this document were made in healthy patients. However, the collected measurements were used to verify the accuracy and fidelity of the prototype, obtaining robust results; these results and the design of the equipment show that it is feasible to use the device in real patients, thus opening a new perspective when designing rehabilitation protocols by strictly assessing the pathological conditions of a patient. The system attributes allow to open a much more in-depth picture, not only to diagnose and to monitor the pathology, but also to generate databases which allow the researcher to know the impact of any physical disease through the behavior of inherent physiological variables.

References

1. Borbajo, T.J., Casil, R., Cruz, J.V., Peñaflor, T., Musngi, M.M.: Electromyography controlled functional electrical stimulation data acquisition system for leg rehabilitation. In: DLSU Research Congress 2017, p. 5 (2017)
2. Koydemir, H.C., Ozcan, A.: Wearable and implantable sensors for biomedical applications. Ann. Rev. Anal. Chem. 11(1) (2018). https://doi.org/10.1146/annurev-anchem-061417-125956
3. Aldemir, C., Duygun, F.: New and unusual causes of foot drop. Med. Sci. Int. Med. J. 6(3), 491–495 (2017). https://doi.org/10.5455/medscience.2017.06.8602
4. Mashhadany, Y.I.A., Rahim, N.A.: Real-time controller for foot-drop correction by using surface electromyography sensor. Proc. Inst. Mech. Eng. 227(4), 373–383 (2013)
5. Masdar, A., Ibrahim, B.S., Hanafi, D., Jamil, M.M., Rahman, K.A.: Knee joint angle measurement system using gyroscope and flex-sensors for rehabilitation. In: BMEiCON 2013–6th Biomedical Engineering International Conference, pp. 5–9, October 2013
6. Stegeman, D., Hermens, H.: Standards for surface electromyography: the European project surface EMG for non-invasive assessment of muscles (SENIAM). Enschede Roessingh Res. Dev. 108–112 (2007)
7. Neblett, R.: Surface Electromyographic (SEMG) biofeedback for chronic low back pain. Healthcare 4(2), 27 (2016)
8. Merletti, R., Rainoldi, A., Farina, D.: Surface electromyography for noninvasive characterization of muscle. Electromyographie superficielle pour une caracterisation mesuree du muscle. Exer. Sport Sci. Rev. 29(1), 20–25 (2001)
9. Massó, N., Rey, F., Romero, D., Gual, G., Costa, L., Germán, A.: Surface electromyography applications in the sport. Apunts Med. Esport. 45(165), 121–130 (2010)
10. Kutilek, P., Hybl, J., Kauler, J., Viteckova, S.: Prosthetic 6-DOF arm controlled by EMG signals and multi-sensor system. In: Proceedings of 15th International Conference MECHATRONIKA, pp. 1–5, March 2017
11. Day, S.: Important Factors in Surface EMG Measurement. Bortec Biomedical Ltd., pp. 1–17 (2002)
12. Melaku, A., Kumar, D.K., Bradley, A.: Influence of inter-electrode distance on EMG, pp. 1082–1085, May 2005
13. Ghapanchizadeh, H., Ahmad, S.A., Ishak, A.J.: Effect of surface electromyography electrode position during wrist extension and flexion based on time and frequency domain analyses. Int. J. Cont. Theo. Appl. 9(5), 2643–2650 (2016)
14. Zhang, Z., Dong, Y., Ni, F., Jin, M., Liu, H.: A Method for Measurement of Absolute Angular Position and Application in a Novel Electromagnetic Encoder System (2015)
15. Aneri, M., Rutvij, H.: A review on applications of ambient assisted living. Int. J. Comput. Appl. 176(8), 1–7 (2017)
16. Manoj, S., Priti, N., Nandnikar, D.: Sensorized glove for rehabilitation purpose. Int. J. Eng. Res. Gen. Sci. 3(3), 189–194 (2015)
17. Khayani, S.B.: Development of wearable sensors for body joint angle measurement, p. 70, May 2011
18. Desa, H., Zul Azfar, A: Study of Inertial Measurement Unit Sensor, May 2014
19. Kumar, K., et al.: An improved tracking using IMU and vision fusion for mobile augmented. 6(5), 13–29 (2014)

20. Adcock, B., Hansen, A., Roman, B., Teschke, G.: Generalized sampling **48**(9), 187–279 (2014)
21. Stegeman, D., Hermens, H.: Standards for surface electromyography: The European project Surface EMG for non-invasive assessment of muscles (SENIAM). Surface Electromyography Application Areas and Parameters. In: Proceedings of the Third General SENIAM Workshop on surface electromyography, Aachen, Germany, pp. 108–112, January 1998
22. Nordin, M.: Biomecanica Basica del Sistema Muscoesqueletico-Nordin.pdf (2004)

Proposal of a Model of a Hexapod Robot of Hybrid Locomotion (Extremities-Wheels)

Brayan Contreras[(✉)], Natalia Sánchez[(✉)], Rubén Hernández[(✉)], and Marco Jinete[(✉)]

Piloto University, Bogotá, Colombia
{brayan-contrerasl, natalia-sanchez,
marco-jinete}@upc. edu. co,
ruben. hernandez@unimilitar. edu. co

Abstract. This research work analyzes the selection criteria (criteria or criteria) for mobile robots according to the characteristics of each of the existing general locomotion systems (wheels, extremities, tracks in the robots and their integrations), as well as the CAD model and the simulation of a mobile robot with hybrid locomotion (wheels-extremities). Therefore, the description of each one of the kinematics derived from the locomotion systems used was made. However, the simulation of the robot was carried out simultaneously using the software add-in SIMULINK-MATLAB "SIMSCAPE MULTIBODY". As a result, the positioning control of the robot was developed in its differential wheel locomotion system where the linear and angular velocity graphs can be appreciated, as well as a 0% control error, that is, the reference and the end point the displacement is the same. On the other hand, the movement graphs of the robot were obtained in each of its links (coxa, femur and tibia) while executing a linear movement routine. This prototype is an innovative design, since it has different types of locomotion, said previously.

Keywords: Hexapod robot · Locomotion · Kinematics · Differential · Modeling · Simulation

1 Introduction

Mobile robotics is currently considered an area of advanced technology [1], in which it develops autonomous vehicles that are capable of moving in known or unknown environments. Nowadays there are robots with designs and characteristics of locomotion that allow them to adapt, whether in aerial, terrestrial or aquatic environments; these characteristics influence directly in the mobility, manoeuvrability, versatility and capacity of evasion in obstacles of the robot [2].

Locomotion systems are a key factor for the transition and adaptation from one environment to another, as they give the robot the ability to adapt in unstructured environments, even when changing different ways of moving, this is the case of articles such as: "Robotics Amphibious Salamander With Bio-Inspired Locomotion", in which presents an amphibious robot bio-inspired in the locomotion of the salamander, this has the capacity to adapt in terrestrial and aquatic environments [3], "A Hybrid Flying and

© Springer Nature Switzerland AG 2019
J. C. Figueroa-García et al. (Eds.): WEA 2019, CCIS 1052, pp. 394–405, 2019.
https://doi.org/10.1007/978-3-030-31019-6_34

Walking Robot For Steel Bridge Inspection", in which proposes an innovative design of locomotion for the inspection of steel bridges in a three-dimensional space using a hybrid locomotion system for the transition from the land to the air [4] and "Hybrid Aerial And Aquatic Locomotion In Anat-Scale Robotic Insect", which presents a set of computational and experimental theoretical studies that precede the first robot of an insect that is capable of making a transition of air-aquatic environment [5]. However, hybrid locomotion systems do not only focus on the transition of means of displacement, but they can also be subcategorized to adapt specifically in any of the means of displacement previously mentioned, despite being a single environment, they have a great variety of forms and/or alternatives of mobility.

This research paper proposes a hexapod robot with hybrid locomotion (extremities-wheels (differential setting)) that integrates the individual characteristics of each of these types of displacement; it also presents an analysis of the advantages and disadvantages of each of the locomotion systems using tools that identify the characteristics that influence the design and construction of these types of robot. This research paper will be useful as a preliminary point of reference for those who want to design a hybrid mobile robot, for this reason, the research paper will be divided in the following sections (2) Description of the systems of terrestrial locomotion, (3) Selection criteria and design of locomotion, (4) Proposal of a hybrid robot extremities-wheels, (5) Mathematical model of the resulting CAD design, (6) Results of the model (7) conclusions.

2 Description of Terrestrial Locomotion Systems

Land mobile robots are widely used today as they have a wide variety of applications, these are usually commercial, industrial, security or for the exploration of hostile environments [6] Land mobile robots are generally classified into approximately four categories: wheeled robots, limb robots, track robots and hybrid locomotive robots [7]. Wheeled robots tend to have a better performance in terms of energy consumption and speed, as long as they move on flat surfaces that do not imply the need for high traction on its wheels. Due to the fact that this types of robots present several difficulties in terms of operation on unstructured surfaces that have obstacles and discontinuous surfaces [8], limb robots tend to have greater stability and adaptability on irregular surfaces, although among its drawbacks there is complexity in its designs and control systems, in addition to a high energy consumption and low mobility speed in relation to wheel robots [8], track robots have a larger contact with the surface, which gives them a greater traction with the surface, however its speed is limited and its energy consumption is higher than in wheel robots but is lower than limb robots [8], hybrid locomotion robots are integrations of one or more terrestrial locomotion systems; the purpose of these robots is the development of an suitable, stable and low energy consumption movement mechanism for any land, whether structured or unstructured. Among these robots, there are others with extremities-wheels [7, 15], extremities-worms [8, 16], worm wheels [8, 17] and extremities-wheels-worms robots [8, 18] as it is shown in Fig. 1.

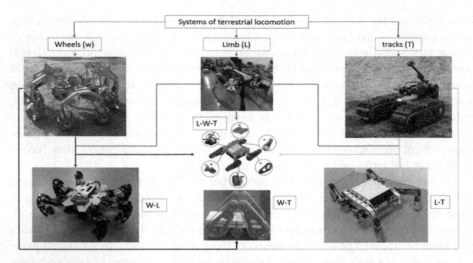

Fig. 1. Visual description of land mobile robots according to their category and integration (Source: W [19], L [20], T [21], WL [7], WT [17], LT [16], LWT [18])

2.1 Types of Locomotion Systems and Development of Conceptual Design

For the conceptual development of a mobile robot, it is essential to know the environment and the application that is going to be developed, since this allows to select the fundamental characteristics of the robot, but also its systems that will optimize the performance and operation of each, inside these robots, the locomotion system is perhaps the most important of all since this influences directly the mobility, manoeuvrability, versatility and capacity of evasion of obstacles of the robot.

Therefore, the steps to follow the development of an suitable terrestrial robot for its applicability were structured and designed. First of all, it is recommended to carry out a historical investigation of locomotion systems or robots that perform or have similarity in the execution of activities such as the desired one, since this allows to recognize the characteristics that the design under development must have. Secondly, a transmission system must be designed in such a way that the number of elements does not affect the operation in the locomotion [22].

According to "The Mexican Association of Mechatronics A.C.", the strategy of designs for new robots focuses on using several locomotion systems that adapt the mechanism to the different types of the environment [22]. This strategy is called hybrid or multimodal locomotion systems [23, 24]. Within this strategy there are three design approaches: Additive Design, Semi-Additive Design and Integral Design.

Table 1 shows a qualitative and quantitative comparison of the most relevant aspects that must be taken into account in the construction of a terrestrial locomotion robot. This comparison was based on the characteristics proposed by García and Arias' article "*Prototipo Virtual De Un Robot Móvil Multi-Terreno Para Aplicaciones De Búsqueda Y Rescate*" [2] which allows identifying some of the most relevant aspects that must be taken into account when selecting the locomotion system(s) for the robot.

Table 1. Evaluation criteria

Locomotion systems	Nomenclature	Criterion	Evaluation	Characteristics	Definition
		High	1		
		High/medium	2		
		Tall short	3	Mechanical complexity and control	Level of complexity of the control system (Hardware and Software)
		Median	4	Technology provision	Level of maturity in the technologies used to carry out the system
Wheels	W	Medium/High	5	Maximum speed	Maximum speed on flat surfaces in the absence of obstacles
Tracks	T	Medium/Low	6	Energy efficiency	Energy efficiency under normal operating conditions, on flat and compact land
Extremities	L	Low	7	Crossing of obstacles	Ability to cross obstacles with random shapes in unstructured environments
Hybrid	L-W	Low/Medium	8	Climb steps	Ability to climb individual steps and stairs in structured environments for human beings
Hybrid	L-T	Low High	9	Stairs	Ability to climb slopes with a coefficient of friction greater than 0.5
Hybrid	W-T	Complete	10	Climb earrings	Ability to operate on uneven terrain (grassy terrain, rocky terrain)
Hybrid	L-W-T	Complete in progress	11	Irregular ground operation	Ability to operate on soft terrain (sand)

That hybrid locomotion systems in mobile robots are more effective and efficient for some applications since they are capable of providing better results in aspects such as dynamics, kinematics and mobility. Based on this, the locomotion of extremities-wheels is chosen to carry out the design of the robot, considering that when joining these two locomotion's it has greater efficiency when taking a linear trajectory.

3   CAD Model of Hybrid Robot Extremities-Wheels

The CAD model is based on a hybrid locomotion robot determined by the configuration of extremities-wheels. For the locomotion with extremities, the characteristics of the hexapod robots were selected, this is due to its mechanical distribution of manoeuvrability, performance in irregular surfaces and stability.

The stability of this type of robot is determined from the support of the polygon formed from the extremities that are used during the operation or the stability phase. In general, when hexapod robots are moving, they use three support extremities, these provide support, while the other three extremities are responsible for the new positioning keeping the robots in the same place. In general, when hexapod robots are moving, they use three support extremities, these provide support, while the other three extremities are responsible for the new posture, keeping the robot in the same location, the polygon formed by the support extremities used indicates whether or not the robot is stable with respect to the support surface, the polygon formed by the support of the extremities indicates whether or not the robot is stable with respect to the support surface, this is determined from the location of the robot's centre of gravity. The robot is stable if the projection of the mass centre is inside the support polygon, and this is at the stability limit if the projection of the mass centre is outside the support polygon [25]. Figure 2 shows the CAD model of the robot which uses the extremities of the locomotion system in the phase of stability.

Fig. 2. (A) CAD design Hybrid robot locomotion extremities. (B) CAD design Hybrid robot locomotion wheels differential configuration (Source: Authors)

For locomotion with wheels, the characteristics of differential robots were selected. The steering is given by the difference in speed of the wheels. Traction is also achieved with these same wheels. These are mounted on a single axle, however, each one is independently propelled and controlled, which provides traction and steering for each wheel. This system is very useful is the ability of the movement of the mobile is considered, having the possibility of changing its orientation without movements of translation. The control variables of this system are the angular speeds of the left and right wheels. This design is one of the least complex locomotion systems. The robot can go straight, can turn on itself and draw curves. An important problem is how to solve the equilibrium of the robot since it is necessary to look for additional support to the two existing wheels, this is achieved through of one or two support wheels in a triangular or rhomboidal design. The triangular design may not be sufficient depending on the weight distribution of the robot and the rhomboid design because it may cause unsuitability to the ground if the ground is irregular it may require some kind of suspension.

4   Result of the Mathematical Model of CAD Design

After designing the hybrid robot extremities-wheels, it is necessary to develop the mathematical model. Therefore, the investigation was made from the design that it was proposed in order to compare the mathematical models implemented in different robots and also to make a description of the main characteristics that must be taken into account when making the kinematics of the locomotion of legs and wheels.

For manipulator robots (open kinematic chains) the Denavit - Hartenberg coordinate assignment method is used [26]. In the case of self-guided vehicles, however, since there are multiple closed kinematic chains, there is ambiguity when choosing the order of the joints. To avoid this problem, the Sheth - Uicker [26, 27] assignment method is used, implementing coordinate systems.

Taking into account the mathematical models of each type of wheel mentioned, the authors L. Enrique and O.E. Ramos obtained the same results using different methods [28, 29]. Figure 3 shows the schemes used for each of the articles.

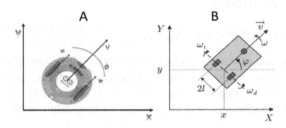

Fig. 3. (A) Track tracking with a mobile robot of differential configuration and (B) Trajectory Tracking in a Mobile Robot without Using Velocity Measurements for Control of Wheels (Source: A [28], B [29])

According to several authors and sources of information [30–34] the robots of extremities usually use the method of assignment of coordinates of Denavit - Hartenberg, since its implementation is simpler in models with multiple degrees, besides relating the parts and parameterizing them [30], however, for the robots of locomotion with wheels direct kinematics is used, this is because the kinematics of a robot can be obtained from different methods, each method is more efficient depending on the model to study.

5   Simulation

The simulation design was developed by using the Matlab "Simscape Multibody", this provides a simulation environment for 3D systems, which is represented from block diagrams, which are built up from the equations of motion of the mechanical system.

The blocks used in the simulation can represent bodies, joints, constraints, force elements and sensors. However, this complement has the ability to import 3D assemblies, which contain each of the properties assigned to the original assembly including masses, inertias, joints, constraints and geometries. The obtained solutions are presented below in Fig. 4.

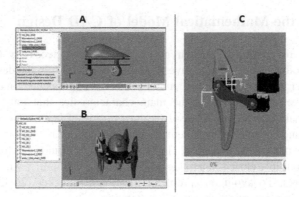

Fig. 4. (A) Differential model assembly (B) Hybrid robot assembly front view (C) Extremity assembly (Source: Authors)

6 Results of the Model

6.1 Differential Robot Position Control

To control the position of the locomotion robot with wheels, the differential kinematic model was used, where the control point is located at a distance (a) from the centre of the axle of the wheels. In addition, the graphs of the speeds and the error with respect to the transition of the trajectory were obtained the nomenclature used is:

u	ω	φ
Linear speed	Velocidad angular	Angular position

6.1.1 Differential Model Control Point Wheel Axle

The basic differential model is used to contrast the positioning and speed equations of differential robots (Fig. 5).

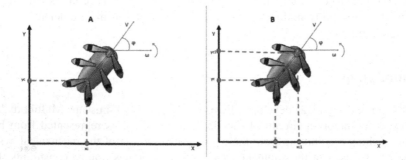

Fig. 5. (A) Differential model control point in the center of the wheel axle (B) Differential model control point at a distance (a) from the center of the wheel axle (Source: Authors)

In Eq. 1, the position and velocity of the system with the control point on the axis of the wheel is presented

Positioning equations
$$xr = xc$$
$$yr \doteq yc$$

Speed equations
$$\dot{x}r = \dot{x}c = u\cos(\varphi)$$
$$\dot{y}r = \dot{y}c = u\sin(\varphi) \qquad (1)$$

$$xc = Centro\ del\ vehiculo\ eje\ x$$
$$yc = Centro\ del\ vehiculo\ eje\ y$$

In Eq. 2, the position and velocity of the system is presented with the point at a distance a from the center of the wheel axis

Positioning equations
$$xr = xc + a\cos(\varphi)$$
$$yr = yc + a\sin(\varphi)$$

Speed equation
$$\dot{x}r = \dot{x}c - a\omega\sin(\varphi)$$
$$\dot{y}r = \dot{y}c + a\omega\cos(\varphi) \qquad (2)$$
$$\dot{x}r = u\cos(\varphi) - a\omega\sin(\varphi)$$
$$\dot{y}r = u\sin(\varphi) + a\omega\cos(\varphi)$$

Once the kinematic model of the differential control point robot has been obtained at a distance (a) from the centre of the wheel axis, the position control of the robot is developed.

6.2   Position Control

In Fig. 6(A), it is possible to appreciate the actions of control of the linear speed and the angular speed obtained from the model, thanks to them, it was determined that the actions of control for the linear speed are scarce since there are no sudden changes of the linear speed within the displacement. However, the angular speed has sudden changes at the beginning of the displacement, which indicates that the actions of control for the angular speed are high in the first stage of the displacement of the differential robot, this allows to infer that the robot is suitable in linear surfaces, however in surfaces with changes of direction, it will tend to destabilize.

In Fig. 6(B), it shows the control error of the robot displacement, however, although, the model tends to destabilize in sudden changes of speed or curves, the control actions are sufficient to bring this error to 0% and stabilize the system.

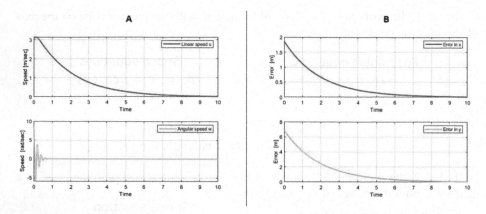

Fig. 6. (A) Linear and angular speed of the proposed differential model under suitable conditions (B) Control errors obtained from the differential model under optimum conditions (Source: Authors)

6.3   Robot Stabilization Routine in Locomotion of Extremities

Within the results of the model, the displacements of each one of the parts that form the leg of the robot were obtained; these are coxa, femur and tibia, these can be appreciated in Fig. 7.

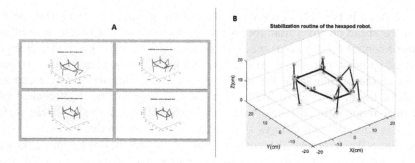

Fig. 7. (A) Frames of the proposed stabilization routine (B) Final position of the proposed stabilization routine (Source: Authors)

The Figs. 7(A) and (B) show some of the movements made by the robot when executing the established routine.

In Fig. 8 it can be seen that the transitions made by the tibia are stable while the transitions made in the sections of the femur and the coxa have sudden changes of positioning this indicates that the coxa and the tibia are the links of the robot that more changes of address effected.

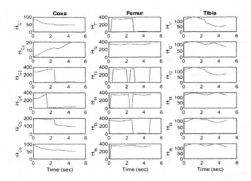

Fig. 8. Displacement of each of the parts of the hexapod robot when executing the displacement routine (Source: Authors)

7 Conclusions

In conclusion, the robot model was designed for safety applications in industries with two types of surfaces. First, that they have smooth surfaces inside, where the differential locomotion will be implemented maintaining a low energy consumption and lastly in irregular surfaces, the extremities model is used, this type of surface can be exterior which presents the complexity of movement.

Consequently, a research was carried out in which the types of mobile robots were described according to its category and integration. By proposing the most relevant models and characteristics of each type of locomotion, this will allow researchers to select the most suitable model for the application that they wish to supply.

The differential wheel locomotion system is a simple model of basic control and programming, but its applicability is very limited, for this type of locomotion, smooth movements must be carried out since sudden changes of direction or sudden rotation conversions can cause over current peaks and wear in the motors.

The control actions of the differential locomotion model. It was determined that the model tends to be destabilized when making turns. However, the control actions are sufficient to take this error to 0% and stabilize the system.

On the other hand, the simulations used in the locomotion system with extremities showed smooth transitions in the tibia, while the transitions of the coxa and the femur are more abrupt.

References

1. Bermúdez, G.: Robots móviles, pp. 6–17 (2002)
2. Adrian, R., García, G.: Prototipo virtual de un robot móvil multi-terreno para aplicaciones de búsqueda y rescate. ResearchGate, October 2016
3. Aguilar, W.G., Luna, M.A., Moya, J.F., Abad, V.: Robot Salamandra Anfibio Con Locomoción Bioinspirada. Ingenius **17**, 51 (2017)
4. Ratsamee, P., et al.: A hybrid flying and walking robot for steel bridge inspection. In: SSRR 2016 - International Symposium on Safety, Security and Rescue Robotics, pp. 62–67 (2016)

5. Chen, Y., Helbling, E.F., Gravish, N., Ma, K., Wood, R.J.: Hybrid aerial and aquatic locomotion in an at-scale robotic insect. In: IEEE International Conference on Intelligent Robotics and Systems, vol. 2015, pp. 331–338, December 2015
6. Historia, O.: Robots móviles terrestres, vol. 12, pp. 3–12 (2015)
7. Zhai, Y., et al.: Gait planning for a multi-motion mode wheel-legged hexapod robot. In: 2016 IEEE International Conference on Robotics and Biomimetics, ROBIO 2016, pp. 449–454 (2016)
8. Bruzzone, L., Quaglia, G.: Review article: locomotion systems for ground mobile robots in unstructured environments. Mech. Sci. 3(2), 49–62 (2012)
9. Wei, Z., Song, G., Zhang, Y., Sun, H., Qiao, G.: Transleg: a wire-driven leg-wheel robot with a compliant spine. In: 2016 IEEE International Conference on Information and Automation, ICIA 2016, pp. 7–12. IEEE, August 2017
10. Tedeschi, F., Carbone, G.: Towards the design of a leg-wheel walking hexapod. In: MESA 2014 - 10th IEEE/ASME International Conference on Mechatronic and Embedded Systems and Application Conference Proceedings (2014)
11. Lu, D., et al.: Mechanical system and stable gait transformation of a leg-wheel hybrid transformable robot. In: 2013 IEEE/ASME International Conference on Advanced Intelligent Mechatronics, AIM 2013, Mechatronics Hum. Wellbeing, pp. 530–535 (2013)
12. Zhong, G., Deng, H., Xin, G., Wang, H.: Dynamic hybrid control of a hexapod walking robot: experimental verification. IEEE Trans. Ind. Electron. 63(8), 5001–5011 (2016)
13. Endo, G., Hirose, S.: Study on roller-walker - energy efficiency of roller-walk. In: Proceedings - IEEE International Conference on Robotics and Automation, pp. 5050–5055 (2011)
14. Lu, D., Dong, E., Liu, C., Xu, M., Yang, J.: Design and development of a leg-wheel hybrid robot HyTRo-I. In: IEEE International Conference on Intelligent Robot and Systems, pp. 6031–6036 (2013)
15. Bingham, B., et al.: J. F. Robot. 28(6), 950–960 (2011). vol. 28, no. 6, pp. 1–16 (2010)
16. Fujita, T., Tsuchiya, Y.: Proceedings of the ASME 2015 International Design Engineering Technical Conferences & Computers and Information in Engineering Conference IDETC/CIE 2015 DETC2015- 47982, pp. 1–8 (2017)
17. Fei, Y., Wu, Q., Zhu, Y.: Study on climbing slope of wheel-track hybrid mobile robot. In: M2VIP 2016 – Proceedings of 23rd International Conference on Mechatronics and Machine Vision in Practice (2017)
18. Michaud, F., et al.: Multi-modal locomotion robotic platform using leg-track-wheel articulations. Auton. Robot. 18(2), 137–156 (2005)
19. Kim, J.-H., Myung, H., Lee, S.-M. (eds.): RiTA 2018. CCIS, vol. 1015. Springer, Singapore (2019). https://doi.org/10.1007/978-981-13-7780-8
20. Gao, J.S., Li, M.X., Hou, B.J., Wang, B.T.: Kinematics analysis on the serial-parallel leg of a novel quadruped walking robot. Opt. Precis. Eng. 23(11), 3147–3160 (2016)
21. Guarnieri, M., Takao, I., Debenest, P., Takita, K., Fukushima, E., Hirose, S.: HELIOS IX tracked vehicle for urban search and rescue operations: Mechanical design and first tests. In: 2008 IEEE/RSJ International Conference on Intelligent and Robotics System IROS, Fig. 2, pp. 1612–1617 (2008)
22. Manuel, J., Arreguín, R.: Ingeniería Mecatrónica en México 2016 (2016)
23. Poungrat, A., Maneewarn, T.: A starfish inspired robot with multi-directional tube feet locomotion, p. 5 (2017)
24. Saranya, R.: Octapod spider-gait-walking robot implementation using nano processor, pp. 16–19 (2016)
25. Sorin, M.O., Mircea, N.: Matlab simulator for gravitational stability analysis of a hexapod robot. Rom. Rev. Precis. Mech. Opt. Mechatron. 39, 157–162 (2011)

26. Ramos-silvestre, E.R., Morales-guerrero, R., Silva-ortigoza, R., De Posgrado, D., De Mecatrónica, Á.: Modelado, simulación y construcción de un robot móvil de ruedas tipo diferencial (2010)
27. Ramos, O.E.: La cinematica de robots móviles es cuando poseen diferentes tipos de locomocion (2017)
28. Ramos, O.E.: Cinemática de Robots Móviles (2017)
29. Enrique, L., Alejandro, M., Leonardo, E.: Seguimiento de trayectorias con un robot móvil de configuración diferencial path-following with diferential mobile robot suivi de trajectoires en utilisant un robot mobile à, vol. 5, no. 1, pp. 26–34 (2014)
30. Rodríguez-calderón, J.P., Ramos-parra, M.F., Peña-giraldo, M.V.: Simulación de un Robot Hexápodo Bioinspirado en el Tenebrio. Lámpsakos **14**, 33–39 (2015)
31. Gorrostieta, E., Soto, E.V.: Algoritmo Difuso de Locomoción Libre para un Robot Caminante de Seis Patas. Comput. y Sist. **11**(3), 260–287 (2008)
32. Profesional, U., Lopez, A., Para, Q.U.E., El, O., Maestro, G.D.E., Ciencias, E.N.: Análisis Cinemático de un robot metamórfico tipo hexápodo (2017)
33. Sucar, L.E.: Introducción a la Robótica (2016)
34. Mauricio, J., et al.: Diseño de sistema, pp. 1–129 (2011)

Decoupling Method to Solve Inverse Kinematics for Assistant Robot

Yeyson Becerra[(✉)] ⓘ and Sebastian Soto[(✉)] ⓘ

Corporacion Unificada Nacional de Educacion Superior, Bogota, Colombia
{yeyson_becerra,sebastian_soto}@cun.edu.co

Abstract. Inverse kinematics solution for a six degree of freedom assistant robot will be presented in this work. Denavit-Hartenberg parameters and decoupling method will be used to find a closed solution for the robot. Novel approach to analyze torso and arm assistant robot will be described and inverse kinematics solution will be detailed. Arm Workspace and augmented work-space (including torso) will be compared. Experiments, simulations and results of the proposed algorithm will be presented as well as a discussion of them.

Keywords: Inverse kinematics · Decoupling method · Workspace

1 Introduction

This research is oriented to the kinematic analysis of an assistant robot composed by a humanoid robot -NAO- [20] and a mobile robot -Robotino-. The assistant robot main task is to manipulate objects over table's surfaces; therefore, it is necessary to enable an additional degree of freedom located in the hip of NAO, achieving an inclination that allows it to perform actions over the table that otherwise they would not be possible.

Inverse kinematics use various methods for solving trajectories of integrated robotic manipulators such as those found in many models of assistants. To perform multiple tasks by a robot in a efficient way, it is necessary to use mathematical methods to execute its movements with autonomy and precision [1].

This work presents the inverse kinematics solution trough decoupling method for an assistant robot, which divide the inverse kinematics problem into two subproblems. The first three joints are calculated through Denavit-Hartenberg parameters and the end-effector position; the last three, instead of position, it is used end-effector orientation. It is also necessary to identify a wrist point in the kinematic model in order to separate both subproblems [3].

Inverse kinematics solution for a humanoid robot have been presented in diverse papers [12,15,17–19], even for some different platforms or methods [2,4,6, 8–10,16]. This research use an extra degree of freedom as it is mention previously

---

Supported by Corporación Unificada Nacional de Educación Superior.

J. C. Figueroa-García et al. (Eds.): WEA 2019, CCIS 1052, pp. 406–415, 2019.
https://doi.org/10.1007/978-3-030-31019-6_35

and two links located in torso's robot. Thus, the assistant robot enlarge its work-space.

Section 2 of this article presents the problem declaration and general description of the assistant robot as well as its work-space; Sect. 3 offers a brief explanation of inverse kinematics using D-H parameters and develops the inverse kinematics solution through decoupling method; Sect. 4 analyzes the results; and finally Sect. 5 presents conclusions.

2   Problem Statement

In order to pick up an object located over a table, the assistant robot should bend to the front as shown in Fig. 1; it is mainly because the robot is not able to reach the object just moving its arm, which is a 5-DOF robotic arm. Therefore, it is used an extra degree of freedom to reach the targets, which is located in the hip area of the robot; thus, the kinematics analyzed in this paper refers to a 6-DOF robot.

This new configuration allows to enlarge the assistant robot workspace. This work is focused in the inverse kinematic solution through decoupling method based on Denavit-Hartenberg parameters.

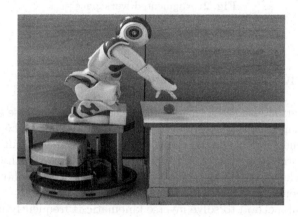

Fig. 1. Assistant robot

2.1   5-DOF vs 6-DOF

To analyze the assistant robot workspace, it is used Matlab®. As it is stated before, forward and inverse kinematics have been studied in some other papers [17,18] for a NAO robot [20] but it has not been studied the robotic arm inverse kinematics (5-DOF) with an extra joint located in hip area, creating a 6-DOF robotic arm. Regarding this extra joint, it is possible to define an augmented work-space as it is mentioned in Becerra [19].

The augmented work-space simulation can be seen (Fig. 2); the front, side and top view are presented. Black lines describe the robotic arm workspace, while red and blue dash lines describe the augmented work-space. The simulation shows when the assistant robot tilts to the front 12°.

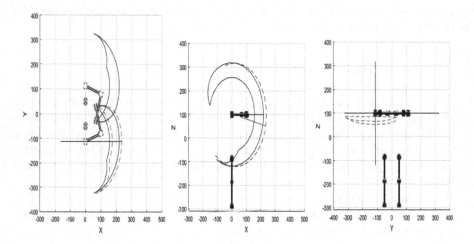

Fig. 2. Augmented workspace

3   Inverse Kinematics Solution

The Denavit-Hartenberg (D-H) algorithm is used to solve inverse kinematics for a 6-DOF assistant robot. D-H is a systematic method to describe and represent the spatial geometry of kinematic chain elements. This method utilizes a Homogeneous Transformation Matrix (HTM) to describe the relationship between two adjacent rigid elements. HTM relates spatial localization of robot end effector, regarding to coordinates system of robot base [22].

Conventional method to solve inverse kinematic is frequently used to obtain the position of a 3-DOF robot, even though it may be equally used for a 6-DOF robot with a higher complexity. Therefore, it is used decoupling method to solve inverse kinematics for a 6-DOF assistant robot. The inverse kinematics problem is divided into two parts; the first one is to obtain the D-H parameters and asses its forward kinematics solution, the second one is to use decoupling method based on D-H parameters and asses its inverse kinematics solution.

To find the forward kinematics solution, it is used the D-H convention [21], that is represented as a product of four basic transformations, see Eq. (1). Where R_z and R_x are rotation matrices; T_z and T_x are translation matrices; and θ_i, d_i, a_i, α_i are the D-H parameters associated with $link_i$ and $joint_i$. Hence, A_i is a matrix that states robot's localization (translation and orientation); further, this a matrix that relates robot's end-effector with reference system robot's base.

$$A_i = R_{z,\theta_i} T_{z,d_i} T_{x,a_i} R_{x,\alpha_i}$$

$$= \begin{bmatrix} c_{\theta_i} & -s_{\theta_i} & 0 & 0 \\ s_{\theta_i} & c_{\theta_i} & 0 & 0 \\ 0 & 0 & 1 & 0 \\ 0 & 0 & 0 & 1 \end{bmatrix} \begin{bmatrix} 1 & 0 & 0 & 0 \\ 0 & 1 & 0 & 0 \\ 0 & 0 & 1 & d_i \\ 0 & 0 & 0 & 1 \end{bmatrix} \begin{bmatrix} 1 & 0 & 0 & a_i \\ 0 & 1 & 0 & 0 \\ 0 & 0 & 1 & 0 \\ 0 & 0 & 0 & 1 \end{bmatrix} \begin{bmatrix} 1 & 0 & 0 & 0 \\ 0 & c_{\alpha_i} & -s_{\alpha_i} & 0 \\ 0 & s_{\alpha_i} & c_{\alpha_i} & 0 \\ 0 & 0 & 0 & 1 \end{bmatrix}$$

$$= \begin{bmatrix} c_{\theta_i} & -s_{\theta_i}c_{\alpha_i} & s_{\theta_i}s_{\alpha_i} & a_i c_{\theta_i} \\ s_{\theta_i} & c_{\theta_i}c_{\alpha_i} & -c_{\theta_i}s_{\alpha_i} & a_i s_{\theta_i} \\ 0 & s_{\alpha_i} & c_{\alpha_i} & d_i \\ 0 & 0 & 0 & 1 \end{bmatrix} = \begin{bmatrix} n_x & o_x & a_x & p_x \\ n_y & o_y & a_y & p_y \\ n_z & o_z & a_z & p_z \\ 0 & 0 & 0 & 1 \end{bmatrix} = \begin{bmatrix} n & o & a & p \\ 0 & 0 & 0 & 1 \end{bmatrix} \tag{1}$$

As it is indicated in the D-H algorithm [20,21]; the first step is to define coordinates frames in every joint for the 6-DOF assistant robot as shown in (Fig. 3), the second step was to generate the D-H parameters (Table 1), in order to know the forward kinematics solution and start working in the inverse kinematics solution.

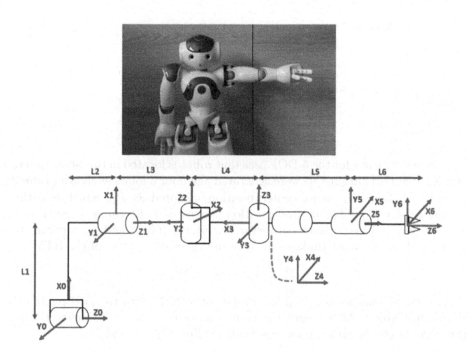

Fig. 3. Coordinate frames

Table 1. D-H parameters for the 5-DOF humanoid robot arm

Joint	θ	d	a	α
1	θ_1	l_2	l_1	0
2	$\theta_2 - \pi/2$	l_3	0	$-\pi/2$
3	$\theta_3 + \pi/2$	0	$-l_4$	0
4	$\theta_4 - \pi/2$	0	0	$\pi/2$
5	θ_5	l_5	0	0
6	θ_6	l_6	0	0

3.1 Decoupling Method

To find a inverse kinematics solution for the 6-DOF assistant robot, it is necessary to split the problem into two parts, position and orientation. To do this, wrist center is identified to separate position from orientation and thus, getting two sub-problems. Moreover, inverse kinematics problem starts setting desired position and desired orientation.

Table 2. D-H parameters for 3-DOF - kinematic decoupling

Joint	θ	d	a	α
1	$\theta_1 + \pi/2$	l_2	l_1	$\pi/2$
2	θ_2	0	0	$-\pi/2$
3	θ_3	l_3	0	0

The wrist center for the 6-DOF assistant robot is located in the elbow (joints 4 and 5). The D-H parameters were generated again for 3 joints as shown (Table 2), in order to know the wrist center position, denoted as $\vec{P}_w$, which is a three dimensional vector. The desired position for the end effector is denoted as $\vec{P}_e$, which is also a three dimensional vector, see Eq. (2). The l_4 and l_5 are parameters associated to the robot (links) and $\vec{z}_5$ is an orientation vector of the HTM.

$$\vec{P}_w = \vec{P}_e - (l_5 + l_6)\vec{z}_6 \qquad (2)$$

Inverse kinematics is solved for a robot of 3 DOF, with the D-H parameters shown in Table 2. As a result, the equations listed below that define the first three joints (θ_1, θ_2 and θ_3) are obtained, see Eqs. (3), (4) and (5).

$$\theta_1 = \arctan\left[\frac{l_4 \sin\theta_3(P_{w_y}\sin\theta_2 + P_{w_x}\cos\theta_2) + P_{w_y}l_1}{l_4\sin\theta_3(P_{w_x}\sin\theta_2 - P_{w_y}\cos\theta_2) + P_{w_x}l_1}\right] \qquad (3)$$

$$\theta_2 = \arcsin\left[\frac{P_{w_x}^2 + P_{w_y}^2 - l_4^2\sin^2\theta_3 - l_1^2}{2l_4\sin\theta_3 l_1}\right] \qquad (4)$$

$$\theta_3 = \arccos\left[\frac{(P_{w_z} - l_2 - l_3)}{l_4}\right] \tag{5}$$

Once the three first joints are defined for the robot arm, it is necessary to define the last three joints (θ_4, θ_5 and θ_6). To do this, it is used the orientation matrix $[n\ o\ a]$ of HTM, that is represented by R_6^0, see Eq. (6).

$$R_6^0 = \begin{bmatrix} n\ o\ a \end{bmatrix} = \begin{bmatrix} n_x\ o_x\ a_x \\ n_y\ o_y\ a_y \\ n_z\ o_z\ a_z \end{bmatrix} = R_3^0 R_6^3 \tag{6}$$

R_6^0 is the desired orientation for the end effector, which had been already known since the beginning of the inverse kinematics problem. R_3^0 is determined from the values of θ_1, θ_2 and θ_3; R_6^3 is the matrix from which joints (θ_4, θ_5 and θ_6) are obtained. The equations are listed below (7), (8).

$$\theta_4 = \arccos\left[\sin(\theta_1 + \theta_2)\sin\theta_3 a_x - \cos(\theta_1 + \theta_2)\sin\theta_3 a_y + \cos\theta_3 a_z\right] \tag{7}$$

$$\theta_5 + \theta_6 = \arccos\left[\cos(\theta_1 + \theta_2)o_x + \sin(\theta_1 + \theta_2)o_y\right] \tag{8}$$

4   Experimentation and Results

To test the effectiveness of inverse kinematics algorithm presented in the previous section, it is evaluated 7 different robot's positions for Forward Kinematics Solution (FKS) and Inverse Kinematics Solution (IKS). There are six links that define the kinematic chain: L1 = 185 mm, L2 = 83 mm, L3 = 15 mm, L4 = 105 mm, L5 = 55.95 mm and L6 = 57.75 mm; and six rotational joints.

Results are summarized in (Tables 3, 4, 5, 6, 7, 8 and 9), FKS returns end-effector's position and orientation and IKS returns joints positions. To understand results, it is necessary to check again (Fig. 3), where the assistant robot is in its initial position. Results of FKS are given in millimeter and results of IKS are given in grades.

Table 3. Position 1

Analyzed Position	Forward Kinematics			Inverse Kinematics
	Position Vector		Orientation Matrix	
	Px	Py	PZ	NOA	$(\theta_1\ \theta_2\ \theta_3\ \theta_4\ \theta_5\ \theta_6)$
	185	0	316.7	0 1 0 −1 0 0 0 0 1	0;0;0;0;0;0

Table 4. Position 2

Analyzed Position	Forward Kinematics				Inverse Kinematics
	Position Vector			Orientation Matrix	
	Px	Py	PZ	NOA	$(\theta_1\,\theta_2\,\theta_3\,\theta_4\,\theta_5\,\theta_6)$
	185	218.7	98	0 1 0 0 0 1 1 0 0	0;0;-90;0;0;0

Table 5. Position 3

Analyzed Position	Forward Kinematics				Inverse Kinematics
	Position Vector			Orientation Matrix	
	Px	Py	PZ	NOA	$(\theta_1\,\theta_2\,\theta_3\,\theta_4\,\theta_5\,\theta_6)$
	185	105	- 15.7	0 1 0 1 0 0 0 0 −1	0;0;-90;-90;0;0

Table 6. Position 4

Analyzed Position	Forward Kinematics				Inverse Kinematics
	Position Vector			Orientation Matrix	
	Px	Py	PZ	NOA	$(\theta_1\,\theta_2\,\theta_3\,\theta_4\,\theta_5\,\theta_6)$
	185	113.7	203	0 1 0 0 0 1 1 0 0	0;0;0;-90;0;0

Table 7. Position 5

Analyzed Position	Forward Kinematics			Inverse Kinematics
	Position Vector		Orientation Matrix	
	Px	Py	PZ	NOA	$(\theta_1\,\theta_2\,\theta_3\,\theta_4\,\theta_5\,\theta_6)$
	298.7	0	203	0 0 1 0 −1 0 1 0 0	0;-90;0;-90;0;0

Table 8. Position 6

Analyzed Position	Forward Kinematics			Inverse Kinematics
	Position Vector		Orientation Matrix	
	Px	Py	PZ	NOA	$(\theta_1\,\theta_2\,\theta_3\,\theta_4\,\theta_5\,\theta_6)$
	0	185	316.7	1 0 0 0 1 0 0 0 1	90;0;0;0;0;0

Table 9. Position 7

Analyzed Position	Forward Kinematics			Inverse Kinematics
	Position Vector		Orientation Matrix	
	Px	Py	PZ	NOA	$(\theta_1\,\theta_2\,\theta_3\,\theta_4\,\theta_5\,\theta_6)$
	-218.7	185	316.7	0 0 −1 0 1 0 1 0 0	90;0;-90;0;0;0

5   Discussion

The assistant robot presented in this work is composed by a mobile robot called robotino and a humanoid robot called NAO.

Some other works about forward and inverse kinematics for a NAO robot had been developed previously [15,17,18] but these were focused in arms, legs and neck of the robot. The results presented in this work, provide a inverse kinematics solution for a 6-DOF assistant robot, assessing the robotic arm with an extra joint. Moreover, an extra joint allows to enlarge the assistant robot workspace, which is usufull to manipulate farther objects.

Inverse kinematics solution obtained, shows θ_5 and θ_6 in a same equation, it can be understood that these two variables are dependent of each other and further, one of these two joints is redundant for the robotic arm.

Future research can be oriented to humanoid robots that having different kinematics models; in the other hand, this research can be used as a manipulate subsystem to create autonomous systems supported by a computer vision algorithm.

6   Conclusions

It was possible to solve inverse kinematics problem through decoupling method for a 6-DOF configuration of an assistant robot.

Taking advantage of the robot's mechanical characteristics, it was possible to increase efficiency in its work-space.

An augmented work-space was identified, achieving to manipulate objects located over a table's surface.

An extended inverse kinematics solution for a humanoid robotic arm allows to maximize the assistant robot's reach.

Iterative method, neural networks and fuzzy logic can be used to solve the kinematic chain proposed in this work.

References

1. Jin, Y., Chen, M., Yang, G.: Kinematic design of a 6-DOF parallel manipulator with decoupled translation and rotation. IEEE Trans. Robot. **22**(3), 545–551 (2006)
2. Goldenberg, A., Lawrence, D.: A generalized solution to the inverse kinematics of robot manipulator. J. Dyn. Syst. Measur. Control (1985)
3. Iliukhin, V., Mitkovskii, K., Bizyanova, D., Akopyan, A.: The modeling of inverse kinematics for 5 DOF manipulator. Proc. Eng. **176**, 498–505 (2017)
4. Kurt, S.: Augmentable multi-vertebrated modular space station robot. Proc. Soc. Behav. Sci. **195**, 2612–2617 (2015)
5. Pataky, T., Vanrenterghem, J., Robinson, M.: Bayesian inverse kinematics vs. least-squares inverse kinematics in estimates of planar postures and rotations in the absence of soft tissue artifact. J. Biomech. **82**, 324–329 (2019)
6. Ram, R., Pathak, P.M., Junco, S.: Inverse kinematics of mobile manipulator using bidirectional particle swarm optimization by manipulator decoupling. Mech. Mach. Theory **131**, 385–405 (2019)
7. Zhai, G., Zheng, H., Zhang, B.: Observer-based control for the platform of a tethered space robot. Chin. J. Aeronaut. **31**, 1786–1796 (2018)
8. El-Sherbiny, A., Elhosseini, M., Haikal, A.: A comparative study of soft computing methods to solve inverse kinematics problem. Ain Shams Eng. J. **9**, 2535–2548 (2018)

9. McEvoya, A., Corrella, N.: Distributed inverse kinematics for shape-changing robotic materials. Proc. Technol. **26**, 4–11 (2016)
10. Sancaktar, I., Tuna, B., Ulutas, M.: Inverse kinematics application on medical robot using adapted PSO method. Eng. Sci. Technol. Int. J. **21**, 1006–1010 (2018)
11. Mohana, R., Tan, N., Tjoelsen, K., Sosa, R.: Designing the robot inclusive space challenge. Dig. Commun. Netw. **1**, 267–274 (2015)
12. Atique, M., Sarker, R., Ahad, A.: Development of an 8DOF quadruped robot and implementation of Inverse Kinematics using Denavit- Hartenberg convention. Heliyon **4**(12), e01053 (2018)
13. Somov, Y., Butyrin, S., Somova, T.: Control of a free-flying robot at preparation for capturing a passive space vehicle. IFAC-PapersOn Line **51**, 72–76 (2018)
14. Frisyras, E., Moulianitis, V., Aspragathos, N.: ANNs to approximate all the inverse kinematic solutions of non-cuspidal manipulators. IFAC-PapersOn Line **51**, 418–423 (2018)
15. Wen, S., Ma, Z., Wen, S.: The study of NAO robot arm based on direct kinematics by using D-H method (2014)
16. Moin, A., Rahman, A.: Inverse kinematics solution for a 3DOF robotic structure using Denavit-Hartenberg convention. In: International Conference on Informatics, Electronics and Vision, ICIEV 2014, pp. 1–5 (2014)
17. Orfanoudakis, E., Lagoudakis, M., Kofinas, N.: Complete analytical inverse kinematics for NAO. In: 13th International Conference on Autonomous Robot Systems, pp. 1–6 (2013)
18. Kofinas, N., Orfanoudakis, E., Lagoudakis, M.: Complete analytical forward and inverse kinematics for the NAO humanoid robot. J. Intell. Robot. Syst. **77**, 251–264 (2015)
19. Becerra, Y., Leon, J., Orjuela, S., Arbulu, M., Matinez, F., Martinez, F.: Smart manipulation approach for assistant robot. In: Zelinka, I., Brandstetter, P., Trong Dao, T., Hoang Duy, V., Kim, S.B. (eds.) AETA 2018. LNEE, vol. 554, pp. 904–913. Springer, Cham (2020). https://doi.org/10.1007/978-3-030-14907-9_87
20. Gouaillier, D., Blazevic, P.: A mechatronic platform, the Aldebaran robotics humanoid robot. In: 32nd Annual Conference on IEEE Industrial Electronics, IECON 2006 (2007)
21. Barrientos, A.: Fundamentos De Robótica, 2nd edn. McGRAW-HILL, New York (2007)
22. Denavit, J., Hartenberg, R.S.: A kinematic notation for lower-pair mechanisms based on matrices. J. Appl. Mech. **22**, 215–221 (1955)

Hyperthermia Study in Breast Cancer Treatment Using Three Applicators

Hector Fabian Guarnizo Mendez[1]([✉]),
Mauricio Andrés Polochè Arango[2], John Jairo Pantoja Acosta[3],
Juan Fernando Coronel Rico[1], and Juan Sebastian Amaya Opayome[1]

[1] Universidad El Bosque, Bogotá, Colombia
{hguarnizo,jcoronelr,jamayao}@unbosque.edu.co
[2] Universidad de San Buenaventura, Bogotá, Colombia
mpoloche@usbbog.edu.co
[3] Universidad Nacional de Colombia – Sede Bogotá, Bogotá, Colombia
jjpantojaa@unal.edu.co

Abstract. This paper assesses the initial collateral effects which result from the use of electromagnetic (EM) hyperthermia treatment. In this particular case, the focus of study is breast cancer treatment by means of an electromagnetic simulation model. A breast model was created by using the electrical properties to tissues, and it was radiated with three applicators at 2.45 GHz to generate increased of temperature, analyzing the distribution of power density inside the breast. The third applicator, it is a new applicator developed in the Groove Gap Waveguide technology (GGW). A comparison between the power density in the tumor and other breast tissues (fat and lobes) is presented. Results show that the location of the microwave applicator is a factor that determines the unwanted overheating of tissues closed tumor. The preliminary results indicate that with the new applicator developed in the Groove Gap Waveguide technology (GGW) is possible to focus the EM energy. Moreover, the tissues close to the tumor obtain a lower concentration of power density.

Keywords: Heat flow · Hyperthermia · Radiation · Applicator

1 Introduction

In the world the breast cancer is the second most common cancer and it is the most common cancer in women [1]. The breast cancer treatment depends on the cancer stage, sensitivity to hormones and the type of breast cancer, among other. The main treatment options are surgery (lumpectomy, mastectomy, and axillary lymph node dissection), radiotherapy, chemotherapy, and immunotherapy, stem cell transplantation and targeted medicine therapies. Along with the mentioned methods, another method known as hyperthermia (or thermal therapy) is being evaluated in clinical studies. Hyperthermia is a method in which body tissues that present tumors are exposed to high temperatures in order to destroy the tumor or cancer cells, but without significantly affecting healthy tissues. This technique is currently under study in human patients [2] and in human breast cancer cell lines [3]. In the non-invasive electromagnetic (EM) hyperthermia one

© Springer Nature Switzerland AG 2019
J. C. Figueroa-García et al. (Eds.): WEA 2019, CCIS 1052, pp. 416–427, 2019.
https://doi.org/10.1007/978-3-030-31019-6_36

of the constant challenges is to focus the EM energy at the target (cancerous tissue) while avoid damage to surrounding tissues [4, 5]. In the cancer treatment based on hyperthermia, the human body is exposed to high temperatures (up to 45 °C). For this reason, it is important to know the temperature and power density distributions in order to obtain a more effective microwave heating and avoid unwanted heating in other tissues. In [4, 6], the temperature distribution over to 3D breast model is presented.

On the other hand, in the context of the health problems associated with microwave radiation some studies have been done. In the case of an electroencephalogram (EEG), slight changes in cerebral metabolism and cerebral blood are observed during exposure; however, these slight changes do not exceed the range of normal physiological variations [7]. At the molecular level, in V79 in vitro and in cultures of human lymphocyte cells, a significant increase in the number of specific lesions of the chromosome is observed in the exposed cells [8]. With regard to the heart, it has been observed that due to the location of the heart and the skin effect (poor penetration) the heart is not subject to high microwave fields. It has also been pointed out that an increase in heart rate cannot be related to temperature variations produced by pulsed or continuous electromagnetic waves. On the other hand, it is mentioned that the heartbeat could be regulated with the repetition frequency of the appropriate pulse [9]. In [10] it is mentioned that the organs of the body most susceptible to the thermal effects produced by microwaves are the testicles and the eyes. Nathanson mentions in [11, 12] that treatment with hyperthermia causes changes in the microvascular tumor function, these changes can potentiate the detachment of tumor cells in the heated site. In [13] it is mentioned that local hyperthermia only improves the metastatic rate of melanoma B16. When the treatment with hyperthermia and radiotherapy was implemented, the metastasis decreased. Based on the above and in other studies, it can be said that there is no conclusive evidence from preclinical models or trials in humans that local-regional hyperthermia causes an increase in metastasis. With respect to the studies done in the context of the treatment of breast cancer using the hyperthermia technique, in [14] a therapeutic program was implemented combining concurrent taxol, hyperthermia and radiotherapy followed by mastectomy. Within the results obtained, it was observed that hyperthermia may be a strategy to improve tumor reoxygenation. Vujaskovic in [15] presents a neoadjuvant combination treatment of paclitaxel, liposomal doxorubicin, and hyperthermia. In this work it was observed that the treatment is a feasible and well tolerated strategy in patients with locally advanced breast cancer (LABC). In [16] Tamer Refaat shows that hyperthermia and radiation therapy are effective for locally advanced or recurrent breast cancer. In his work he showed that when implementing hyperthermia, an increase of 50% in the effectiveness of the treatment was obtained.

In the electromagnetic (EM) hyperthermia treatment currently energy is coupled into tissues through waveguides or applicators (antennas) like: array tapered microstrip patch antenna, array antipodal tapered slot, array of rectangular patch elements, antipodal Vivaldi antennas, Miniaturized cavity-backed patch antenna, Antenna with an Embedded EBG Structure, and applicators based on metamaterial technology, that emit microwaves [17–21]. The use of a radiation frequency of 2.45 GHz is justified based on the electrical properties of the breast tissues [6] and allowed the design of small applicators.

In this paper, the power density distribution dissipated in a breast radiated by microwaves at 2.45 GHz is analyzed to determine overexposure zones, the influence of the applicator position, and the possible undesired effects by increases of temperature in the others parts of the breast. In particular, three different applicators are presented in this work, the first applicator is a waveguide, the second applicator is developed in SIW (*substrate integrated waveguide*) technology and the third applicator is a new applicator developed in GGW (*Groove Gap Waveguide*) technology. The characteristics used in the electromagnetic simulation are presented in detail. The power density was obtained for two cases, first the applicator is located at 2 cm away the breast, and 90° above the breast; Second the applicator is located at 2 cm away the breast, and 135° above the breast.

2 Methodology

The electromagnetic simulation was carried out using the finite element method (FEM) solver of ANSYS Electronics® as show in [22]. The breast was modeled by the skin, fat, lobes and muscle [21, 23, 24]. The breast model radius was of 6.5 cm and the tumor was modeled like a cube wide, high and large of 0.8 cm and the simulation setup is presented in the Table 1.

Table 1. HFSS Configuration setup

Properties	Values
Maximum number of passes	10
Maximum delta S	0.01
Maximum converged passes	3
Order of basis function	Mixed order

The maximum delta S values and maximum converged passes values were chosen in order to improve the mesh accuracy and to improve the convergence of the simulation. Mixed order basis function was chosen because the breast has different tissues and different electrical properties (permittivity (ε) and conductivity (σ)). Mixed order assigns base function elements based on the need greater precision in different parts of the model. Mixed order uses a higher order where more precision is required, and a lower order where the fields are weaker. The flow chart of the simulation process carried out in HFSS is presented in [22].

Table 2 shows the electrical properties of the breast tissues used in the electromagnetic simulation based in the properties reported in [25] and [26] for a frequency of 2.45 GHz.

Table 2. Electrical properties of the breast tissues

Tissue	Relative permittivity	Conductivity (S/m)
Muscle	52.7	1.7
Tumor	56	1.8
Fat	5.3	0.3
Skin	38	1.5
Lobes	35	1

3 Applicators at 2.45 GHz

The first applicator is a waveguide WR340. The Fig. 1 shows the second applicator. For the design of this applicator the SIW (*substrate integrated waveguide*) technology was used. The SIW technology applicator was designed based on the design procedure presented in [27].

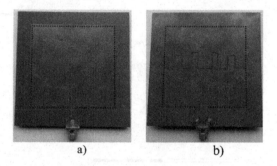

a)   b)

Fig. 1. SIW technology applicator at 2.45 GHz. (a) Top view, (b) Bottom view

Figure 2 presents the third applicator. For the design of this applicator the GGW (*Groove Gap Waveguide*) technology was used. The GGW technology applicator was designed based on the design procedure presented in [27–29]. The radiation system of the GGW technology applicator is not shown in Fig. 2 because it is in patent process.

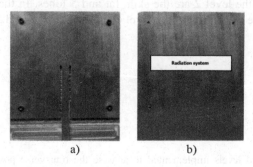

a)   b)

Fig. 2. GGW technology applicator at 2.45 GHz. (a) Top view, (b) Bottom view

4 Results

Two applicator locations were considered. First, the applicator was placed at 90° over the breast (Fig. 3) to consider the case where the location of the tumor is not aligned with the applicator. Then, the applicator was placed at 135° over the breast as show in Fig. 8 to consider alignment between the applicator and the tumor. The three applicators were exited with a power of 1 W. Figure 3 shows the case when the applicators are 90° over the breast.

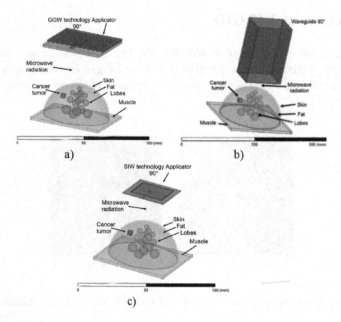

Fig. 3. 3D model for the applicators at 90° over the breast, the tumor is not aligned with the applicators. (a) GGW technology applicator, (b) Waveguide applicator (c) SIW technology applicator.

The breast was split in 4 levels to obtain the power density. In the level 1 are the fat, skin and a lobe. In the level 2 are the skin, fat and 5 lobes. In the level 3 are the fat, skin, 5 lobes and the tumor and in the level 4 are the skin, fat and 5 lobes (see Fig. 4).

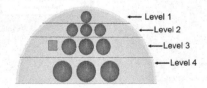

Fig. 4. 3D model and levels implemented to analyse the transverse power density inside the breast.

Figures 5, 6 and 7 show the first case, that is, the applicator is 90° over the breast.

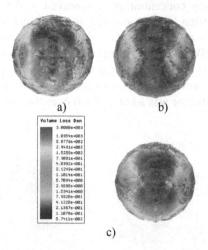

c)

Fig. 5. Power density [kW/m^3] in the level 3 (Fig. 4). The applicators are located 2 cm over the breast, the tumor is not aligned with the applicators. (a) GGW technology applicator at 90°, (b) waveguide applicator at 90°, (c) SIW technology applicator at 90°.

Figure 5 shows the power density obtained on the fat in the level 3 (Fig. 4) at 2.45 GHz when the applicator was located 2 cm over the breast.

As shown in Fig. 5, the highest power density concentration is obtained with the SIW technology applicator and the waveguide applicator. However, the power density is more focused on the fat with the GGW technology applicator.

Figure 6 shows the power density obtained on the lobes and tumor in the level 3 (Fig. 4) at 2.45 GHz when the applicator was located 2 cm over the breast, and it is 90° over the breast.

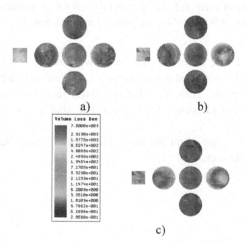

c)

Fig. 6. Power density [kW/m^3] in parts of the level 3 (Fig. 4). The applicators are located 2 cm over the breast, the tumor is not aligned with the applicators. (a) GGW technology applicator at 90°, (b) waveguide applicator at 90°, (c) SIW technology applicator at 90°.

Figure 6 shows that the highest power density concentration is obtained on the lobes. This power density concentration is observed in the Fig. 5 too. The highest power density concentration is obtained with the SIW technology applicator and the waveguide applicator. However, the highest power density concentration on the tumor is obtained with the GGW technology applicator and the lowest power density concentration on the lobes is obtained with the GGW technology applicator also.

Figure 7 shows the power density obtained on the fat in the level 4 (Fig. 4) at 2.45 GHz when the applicator was located 2 cm over the breast, and it is 90° over the breast.

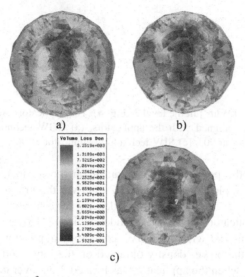

Fig. 7. Power density [kW/m^3] in the level 4 (Fig. 4). The applicators are located 2 cm over the breast, the tumor is not aligned with the applicators. (a) GGW technology applicator at 90°, (b) waveguide applicator at 90°, (c) SIW technology applicator at 90°.

In the Fig. 7, it can be observed that the power density is more focused with the GGW technology applicator. This power density focalization is important because most of the tissues below level 3 (Fig. 4) will have lower levels of irradiation.

Now, Figs. 9, 10 and 11 present the second case, that is, the applicator is 135° over the breast.

Figure 8 shows the case when the applicator is 135° over the breast, the tumor is aligned with the applicators.

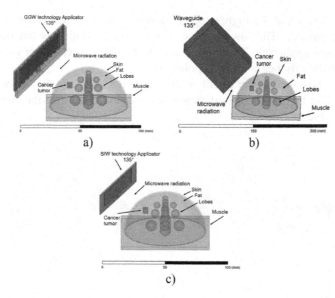

Fig. 8. 3D model for the applicators at 135° on the breast, the tumor is aligned with the applicators. (a) GGW technology applicator, (b) Waveguide applicator (c) SIW technology applicator.

Figure 9 shows the power density obtained on the fat in the level 3 (Fig. 4) at 2.45 GHz when the applicator was located 2 cm over the breast, and it is 135° over the breast.

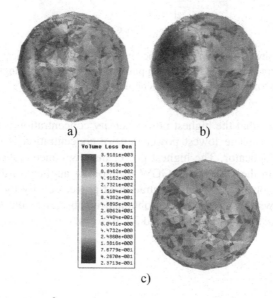

Fig. 9. Power density [kW/m³] in the level 3 (Fig. 4). The applicators are located 2 cm over the breast, the tumor is aligned with the applicators. (a) GGW technology applicator at 135°, (b) waveguide applicator at 135°, (c) SIW technology applicator at 135°.

424   H. F. Guarnizo Mendez et al.

Figure 9 shows that the highest power density concentration is obtained with the waveguide applicator. The lowest power density concentration is obtained with the SIW technology applicator. The highest power density concentration is found in the tissue located directly below of the applicator.

Figure 10 shows the power density obtained on the lobes and the tumor in the level 3 (Fig. 4) at 2.45 GHz when the applicator was located 2 cm over the breast, and it is 135° over the breast.

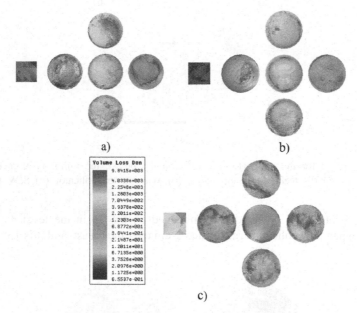

a)   b)

c)

Fig. 10. Power density [kW/m^3] in parts of the level 3 (Fig. 4). The applicators are located 2 cm over the breast, the tumor is aligned with the applicators. (a) GGW technology applicator at 135°, (b) waveguide applicator at 135°, (c) SIW technology applicator at 135°.

Figure 10 shows that the highest power density concentration is obtained with the waveguide applicator. The lowest power density concentration is obtained with the SIW technology applicator. The highest power density concentration is found in the tumor. However. In the case of the GGW technology applicator, the tissues that are close to the tumor obtain a high concentration of power density too (see Fig. 9).

Figure 11 shows the power density obtained on the fat in the level 4 (Fig. 4) at 2.45 GHz when the applicator was located 2 cm over the breast. and it is 135° over the breast.

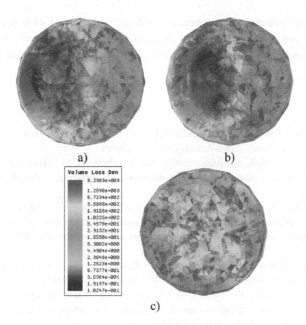

Volume Loss Den
3.2983e+003
1.2596e+003
6.7234e+002
3.5888e+002
1.9156e+002
1.0225e+002
5.4578e+001
2.9132e+001
1.5550e+001
8.3002e+000
4.4304e+000
2.3648e+000
1.2623e+000
6.7377e-001
3.5964e-001
1.9197e-001
1.0247e-001

a)   b)

c)

Fig. 11. Power density [kW/m^3] in the level 4 (Fig. 4). The applicators are located 2 cm over the breast, the tumor is aligned with the applicators. (a) GGW technology applicator at 135°, (b) waveguide applicator at 135°, (c) SIW technology applicator at 135°.

In the Fig. 11, it can be observed that the power density is more focused with the GGW technology applicator. This power density focalization is important because most of the tissues below level 3 (Fig. 4) will have lower levels of irradiation.

5   Conclusions

This paper presented the power density concentration on a breast with a cancerous tumor when is radiated with three applicators. From the presented results can be concluded that the fat and the lobes are the tissue that dissipates the highest power density.

The results indicate that with the new GGW technology applicator, it is possible to obtain the best EM energy focus for the two cases, that is, the applicator is 90° over the breast and it is aligned with the tumor and the second case, the applicator is 135° over the breast and it is aligned with the tumor. Moreover, in the case when the new GGW technology applicator is used, the tissues that are close to the tumor obtain a lower concentration of power density in comparison with the concentration of power density in the tumor.

Additionally, in the 2 cases, it is observed to improve the effectiveness of the treatment with hyperthermia, the location of the applicator is a relevant variable because with suitable locating obtained, the electromagnetic radiation in healthy cells can be avoided.

Currently, the process for the miniaturization of the new GGW technology applicator is carried out. Then, an array of miniaturized new GGW technology applicator will be carried out with the aim of improving the focus of electromagnetic energy.

References

1. W. International, "World Cancer Research Fund," Breast cancer statistics. https://www.wcrf. org/dietandcancer/cancer-trends/breast-cancer-statistics
2. Chicheł, A., Skowronek, J., Kubaszewska, M., Kanikowski, M.: Hyperthermia - description of a method and a review of clinical applications. Reports Pract. Oncol. Radiother. 12(5), 267–275 (2007)
3. Lee, T.H., Bu, J., Kim, B.H., Poellmann, M.J., Hong, S., Hyun, S.H.: Sub-lethal hyperthermia promotes epithelial-to-mesenchymal-like transition of breast cancer cells: implication of the synergy between hyperthermia and chemotherapy. RSC Adv. 9(1), 52–57 (2019)
4. Nguyen, P.T., Abbosh, A.M.: Focusing techniques in breast cancer treatment using non-invasive microwave hyperthermia. In: ISAP 2015, pp. 1–3 (2015)
5. Iero, D.A.M., Crocco, L., Isernia, T., Korkmaz, E.: Optimal focused electromagnetic hyperthermia treatment of breast cancer. In: 2016 10th European Conference on Antennas Propagation, EuCAP 2016, pp. 1–2 (2016)
6. Merunka, I., Fiser, O., Vojackova, L., Vrba, J., Vrba, D.: Utilization potential of balanced antipodal Vivaldi antenna for microwave hyperthermia treatment of breast cancer. In: 8th European Conference on Antennas Propagation, EuCAP 2014, vol. 6, pp. 706–710 (2014)
7. Vander Vorst, A., Rosen, A., Kotsuka, Y.: RF/Microwave Interaction with Biological Tissues. Wiley, Hoboken (2006)
8. Garaj-Vrhovac, V., Fucic, A., Horvat, D.: The correlation between the frequency of micronuclei and specific chromosome aberrations in human lymphocytes exposed to microwave radiation in vitro. Mutat. Res. 281, 181–186 (1992)
9. Tamburello, C.C., Zanforlin, L., Tiné, G., Tamburello, A.E.: Analysis of microwave effects on isolated hearts.pdf, pp. 804–808 (1991)
10. Ely, T.S., Goldman, D.E., Hearon, J.Z.: Heating characteristics of laboratory animals exposed to ten-centimeter microwaves. IEEE Trans. Biomed. Eng. BME-11(4), 123–137 (1964)
11. Nathanson, S.D., et al.: Changes associated with metastasis in B16-F1 melanoma cells surviving heat. Arch. Surg. 125(2), 216–219 (1990)
12. Nathanson, S.D., Nelson, L., Anaya, P., Havstad, S., Hetzel, F.W.: Development of lymph node and pulmonary metastases after local irradiation and hyperthermia of footpad melanomas. Clin. Exp. Metastasis 9(4), 377–392 (1991)
13. Gunderson, L.L., Tepper, J.E.: Clinical Radiation Oncology, 4th edn. Elsevier Inc., Philadelphia (2016)
14. Jones, E.L., et al.: Thermochemoradiotherapy improves oxygenation in locally advanced breast cancer. Clin. Cancer Res. 10(13), 4287–4293 (2004)
15. Vujaskovic, Z., et al.: A phase I/II study of neoadjuvant liposomal doxorubicin, paclitaxel, and hyperthermia in locally advanced breast cancer. Int. J. Hyperth. 26(5), 514–521 (2010)
16. Refaat, T., et al.: Hyperthermia and radiation therapy for locally advanced or recurrent breast cancer. Breast 24(4), 418–425 (2015)
17. Chakaravarthi, G., Arunachalam, K.: Design and characterisation of miniaturised cavity-backed patch antenna for microwave hyperthermia. Int. J. Hyperth. 31(7), 737–748 (2015)

18. Yong-Xing, D., Xiao-Li, X., Li-Li, W.: The analysis and simulation of planar spiral antenna for microwave hyperthermia, pp. 1–4 (2007)
19. Bt Lias, K., Narihan, M.Z.A., Buniyamin, N.: An antenna with an embedded EBG structure for non invasive hyperthermia cancer treatment. In: Proceedings of the 2014 IEEE Conference on Biomedical Engineering and Sciences, IECBES 2014, "Miri, Where Engineering in Medicine and Biology and Humanity Meet," pp. 618–621, December 2014
20. Vrba, D., Vrba, J.: Applicators for local microwave hyperthermia based on metamaterial technology. In: 8th European Conference on Antennas and Propagation, EuCAP 2014, pp. 68–71 (2014)
21. Curto, S., Ruvio, G., Ammann, M.J., Prakash, P.: A wearable applicator for microwave hyperthermia of breast cancer: performance evaluation with patient-specific anatomic models. In: Proceedings of the 2015 International Conference on Electromagnetics in Advanced Applications, ICEAA 2015, pp. 1159–1162 (2015)
22. Guarnizo Mendez, H.F., Polochè Arango, M.A., Pantoja Acosta, J.J.: Hyperthermia study in breast cancer treatment. In: Figueroa-García, J.C., Villegas, Juan G., Orozco-Arroyave, J.R., Maya Duque, P.A. (eds.) WEA 2018, Part II. CCIS, vol. 916, pp. 256–267. Springer, Cham (2018). https://doi.org/10.1007/978-3-030-00353-1_23
23. Nguyen, P.T., Abbosh, A.M., Crozier, S.: Realistic simulation environment to test microwave hyperthermia treatment of breast cancer. In: IEEE Antennas and Propagation Society AP-S International Symposium, pp. 1188–1189 (2014)
24. Korkmaz, E., Isık, O., Sagkol, H.: A directive antenna array applicator for focused electromagnetic hyperthermia treatment of breast cancer. In: 2015 9th European Conference on Antennas and Propagation, vol. 1, pp. 1–4 (2015)
25. Porter, E., Fakhoury, J., Oprisor, R., Coates, M., Popovic, M.: Improved tissue phantoms for experimental validation of microwave breast cancer detection. In: 2010 Proceedings of the Fourth European Conference on Antennas and Propagation (EuCAP), pp. 4–8 (2010)
26. Nikita, K.S. (ed.): Handbook of Biomedical Telemetry. Wiley, Hoboken (2014)
27. Bohórquez, J.C., et al.: Planar substrate integrated waveguide cavity-backed antenna. IEEE Antennas Wirel. Propag. Lett. **8**, 1139–1142 (2009)
28. Boria, V.E., Sánchez-Escuderos, D., Bernardo-Clemente, B., Berenguer, A., Baquero-Escudero, M.: Groove gap waveguide as an alternative to rectangular waveguide for H-plane components. Electron. Lett. **52**(11), 939–941 (2016)
29. Nawaz, M.I., Huiling, Z., Kashif, M.: Substrate integrated waveguide (SIW) to microstrip transition at X-Band. In: 2014 International Conference on Circuits, Systems and Control, pp. 61–63 (2014)

Design and Implementation of a Data Capture and Consultation System, Using a Drone that Identifies Disease Time Gray Rot by Botrytis in a Strawberry Crop in Sibate Cundinamarca

Edgar Krejci Garzon[1(✉)], Paula Perez[1(✉)], Yesid Diaz[1(✉)],
Sandra Moreno[1(✉)], and Edgar Andres Krejci Bautista[2(✉)]

[1] Corporación Unificada Nacional de Educación Superior CUN,
Bogotá, Colombia
{edgar_krejci, Paula.perezc, yesid_diaz,
sandra.moreno}@cun.edu.co
[2] University of Cundinamarca, Bogotá, Colombia
ekrejci@ucundinamarca.edu.co

Abstract. In the current context, technology drives solutions to problems that normally affect productivity in the field, the AXON Research group, from the CUN Systems Engineering program, through the HORUS research center is implementing a solution via web, so that the farmer can consult in a timely manner problems generated by a disease called Botrytis cinerea that affects strawberry crops in the savannah of Bogotá, data capture tests have been performed using Vehicles unmanned aerial calls drones, these images are processed and analyzed for according to the results obtained send the alert to the farmer of the main areas that are affected by this disease and can be prevented from spreading to the entire crop generating large losses to the farmer.

Keywords: Multispectral · Drones · Agroindustry · Technology

1 Introduction

Precision agriculture in the current context to have great progress in all countries of the world, the main goal is to improve the quality of agricultural products that are being harvested in different regions of the country.

In previous research it was found that in Europe, especially in Spain, solutions have been implemented for large farmers in crops with high profitability such as grapes for winemaking or beet, applying these technologies shows a great improvement in the quality of the final product and minimizes possible losses due to damage caused by diseases that damage the crop.

The implementation of modern machinery helps to make the work of the farmer more efficient and faster and achieve a production where the quantity of final product of good quality was maximized. The use of drones is important to obtain data in a fast, accurate and efficient way to locate possible insect pests or problems in the soil,

© Springer Nature Switzerland AG 2019
J. C. Figueroa-García et al. (Eds.): WEA 2019, CCIS 1052, pp. 428–439, 2019.
https://doi.org/10.1007/978-3-030-31019-6_37

applying different methods of study such as the use of multi-spectral cameras, analysis can be performed to demonstrate in a timely manner a disease that affects the crop and all agricultural production.

On the other hand, the researcher and director of the national precision agriculture program of the INIA (National Institute of Agricultural and Food Research and Technology) and agronomist Stanley Best, indicates that the use of drones (unmanned aerial vehicles) in agriculture is an increasingly common practice, and that good results in terms of efficiency are confirmed by farmers, as well as researchers. Stanley Best recognizes its help for the maximization of yields, since unlike the farmer who must move through the field, looking "at eye" for deficiencies that may exist in the crop, the drone flies over the field and manages to gather information about the state of the crops, with greater precision, thanks to the aerial capture of thermal and multispectral photographs. According to Best, "the producer needs to have accurate information to take action, and today, the technology allows us to tell the producer what he has to do and how, efficiently" [1].

An important example is a study that was carried out on a corn crop in Zaragosa Spain, which, using a multispectral chamber, conducted several studies on the level of nitrogen in corn grown in sprinkler irrigation in Zaragoza (ZAR) and Albacete (ALB). The level of nitrogen available in the different experimental plots was variable due to different levels of initial mineral nitrogen in the soil and in those that also applied different doses of nitrogen fertilizer (Irrigation).

According to this study, flights with a drone with a camera (SPAD-502, Minolta Camera Co., Ltd., Japan) were carried out, and very variable indices between one crop and another were obtained as a result.

The results in this study show that the use of this technology does benefit agricultural production, both because of its correlation with chlorophyll content and grain yield, the digital level (ND) in green (540–560 nm).

Obtained from commercial multispectral images in intermediate stages (V15) of the corn crop seems promising to evaluate the nutritional status of the crop. Its real feasibility as a decision tool requires a lower cost, so it would be necessary to perform work in commercial farming plots with lower spatial resolution images (Irrigation).

For the analysis that was carried out, a strawberry crop was chosen located in the municipality of Sibate San Rafael village Finca Villa Andrea owned by Agronomist Javier Prieto, where a disease called gray fungus (Botrytis cinerea), which is a fungus, was found that affects the crops and other plantations considerably damaging a plantation, affecting significantly the fruit, this disease is known as strawberry rot, which is one of the most complex pathogens to solve when the environmental conditions for its proliferation are suitable for infecting a whole crop, that's why it is important to detect this disease in time and with the use of UAVs, with a high definition camera you can show the damage in a quick way, also with this same technology we can use the chemical that is needed exactly to attack this type of fungus.

1.1 Problem Detected in the Crop

The previous analysis that was made to the crop shows a significant loss in the production due to factors that affect the efficient growth of the strawberry, the factors that most affect the strawberry are:

1.1.1 Control of weeds: It is vitally important to identify quickly where this type of weeds can be generated that can affect the growth of the plant in a crop larger than 10 ha. It is important to send this information so that they can be removed manually or with a mechanical system.

1.1.2 Excess of chemical products: if there is no control in the quantity of chemical products, a high level of deterioration of the soil is reached, affecting future plantings of crops.

1.1.3 Gray fungus (Botrytis cinerea): the most common disease of strawberry plantations affects the fruit significantly and damages production.

1.1.4 Meteorological Factor: The location zone of the crop to study is very prone to sudden changes in humidity, according to the IDEAM (Institute of Hydrology, Meteorology and Environmental Studies), the average rainfall in the area is 7000 to 9000 mm per year [3] (Fig. 1).

Fig. 1. Annual precipitation map in Colombia

2 Application of RPA and Chambers to Detect Problems in Crops

The use of drones and cameras for agriculture are the basis for obtaining data quickly and efficiently, and according to Eija Honkavaara "this new technology is highly relevant, because it opens up new possibilities for measuring and monitoring the environment, which is becoming increasingly important for many environmental challenges" [8].

In this study we used a drone from the DJI Phantom 4 brand, and a camera adapted to the drone of the Parrot Sequoia brand, this camera analyzes the vitality of the plants by detecting the light they absorb.

This sensor is compatible with any type of drone, the data that is obtained helps the farmer to make decisions about the health of his crops. This camera works with two sensors the "multispectral" sensor, located for taking photos in front of the plants, captures the light reflected by the plants in four different parts, green, red, as well as two infrared bands invisible to the human eye. The "sunshine" sensor, located above the drone, memorizes the intensity of the light that emanates from the sun in these same four light bands.

The Parrot Sequoia multispectral sensor integrates a GPS module that significantly increases the accuracy of the collected data without having to resort to the data memorized by the transport platform, be it an airplane, drone, tractor, etc. Its different internal components allow you to know at all times your altitude, your flight speed and your situation to adapt your capture speed accordingly [6].

Thanks to the amount of data that can be obtained with this camera, they can be efficiently processed by applying it to the strawberry crop and feeding the platform so that this information can be received in a timely manner by the farmer (Tables 1 and 2).

Table 1. Parrot camera technical features

10 MPX RGB camera	Definition: 4608 × 3456 pixels HFOV: 63.9° VFOV: 50.1° DFOV: 73.5°
4 cameras with global shutter on a single 1.2 MPIX band	Definition: 1280 × 960 pixels HFOV: 61.9° VFOV: 48.5° DFOV: 73.7°
4 different bands	Green (550 BP 40) Red (660 BP 40) Red border (735 BP 10) Near infrared (790 BP 40)
Dimensions and characteristics	59 mm × 41 mm × 28 mm 72 g (2.5 oz) Up to 1 fps Built-in 64 GB storage IMU & magnetometer 5 W (peak ~ 12 W)
Solar sensor	4 spectral sensors (the same filters as the body) GPS IMU & magnetometer Slot for SD card 47 mm × 39.6 mm × 18.5 mm

Table 2. Characteristics drone table

Variables	Drone multirotor	Drone fixed wing
Coverage area	Maximum coverage of 10 ha	Coverage of more than 1000 ha
Battery life	Minor by greater number of engines	More coverage
Resolution of the photographs	Depends on the camera and flight height	Depends on the camera and flight height
Stability in flight	Excellent stability	Less stability
Equipment cost	Less	Greater
Piloting ability	Less	Greater
Flight time	Up to 2 h	Greater than 2 h depending on the type of fixed wing that is operating

3   Processing Captured Images

To understand well the UAV drone that was used in this study, it is important to know the differences between each of the different models that exist, the multi rotor and the fixed-wing drone, each of them is used according to the study to be performed, in the specific case of the strawberry crop, since it is not a large area, the multi-rotor drone of the DJI Phantom 4 brand was used, due to its stability and precision in the capture of the images, but it is important to be clear that for a study of crops whose land is very extensive it is advisable to use another type of drone that has a wider area coverage, the following table shows the specific differences of each type of drone.

The photos taken by the drone camera are processed using a software called Qgis, the great advantage of this program is that it is a professional GIS application that is built on Free Software and Open Source (FOSS).

QGIS is an Open Source Geographic Information System (GIS) licensed under the GNU General Public License. QGIS is an official Open Source Geospatial Foundation (OSGeo) project. It runs on Linux, Unix, Mac OSX, Windows and Android and supports numerous formats and functionalities of vector data, raster data and databases [4].

The processed images give us some results that can be interpreted to see the health of the crop, in the specific case of the research that is being carried out, we look at the ranges of colors that are generated in healthy plants and compare them with plants with the disease of gray rot called Boytritis (Fig. 2).

Fig. 2. Strawberries with gray rot disease (Botrytis).

Observing the Image taken by the drone, you can see a fruit with the fungus disease, which can be easily demonstrated, with the help of the Qgis software, you can generate results that can be quantified to perform an analysis of the quantity of affected plants and their exact location in the crop (Fig. 3).

Fig. 3. Image generated by the Qgis software.

According to this image we see in the range of RGB bands some results that show a series of colors where each pixel can be analyzed according to that result to show where the disease is in the fruit of the plant.

With these images we can determine the way to process them and add the types of processes with images that can be made.

Taking into account the previous basic utilities of the images in a GIS, the operations on these images can be divided into three main groups:

- Correction, the equipment used to collect the images can incorporate errors, noise, or distortions. Eliminating or treating these so that their effect is less is a prior process that in most cases is an essential requirement before the analysis.
- Improvement, improvement is the next step to correction. Once the images have been corrected, the information they contain can be made more explicit through different types of modifications. In the visual analysis, the improvement of an image makes it easier to perceive the content of it and give it a direct use. The characteristics of the plant or its own shape can be seen more clearly. When these processes of identifying elements and characteristics are carried out automatically by means of algorithms and not manually, it is also important to prepare the images to improve them in the face of this process. Improving an image, we also improve the ability of these algorithms to "see" the information we intend to obtain, in a way very similar to what happens with a human observer [7].

Extraction of information. The values of the different bands of an image can be used to derive new ones, such as variables of physical type or belonging to predefined classes that can identify the elements present in the field. These processes imply an interpretation of the image in question [7].

By analyzing what can be done with the image, we look at the respective bands with the software and obtain more precise results (Fig. 4).

Fig. 4. Fruit with the Botrytis disease.

The software shows us some results which are interpreted by the agronomist, these results generated by the Qgis program, are sent through the platform that was designed for storage of information, interpretation and online consultation that the farmer can carry out with the health data of the crop (Fig. 5).

Fig. 5. Results rendering of bands.

With the information already processed of the images, the database of the application via the web is fed.

4   Via Website Software

The software used to manage the images and results interpreted by the agronomist is developed in the PHP programming language, using the database management system Postgresql, the objective of the study obtained from the images loaded to the application is to make the results of the analysis obtained by the processing previously done by the Qgis software, the different roles created, each role has a different access and a specific function, the drone operator feeds the database with the obtained images, the agronomist goes up the processed images to be consulted by last to the last role of the application, the farmer owner of the crop will proceed to take the pertinent actions to prevent the disease from spreading throughout the crop and damaging all strawberry production.

The design of the front-end, is very easy to use it has the general information of the application, and the option to access quickly with a username and password (Fig 6).

Fig. 6. Front-end web application

The scheme that is implemented for the storage of the data, is done through the application in an easy way by means of forms with graphs and schedules to follow the sequence of how the crop is improving every month according to the measures taken by the farmer (Fig. 7).

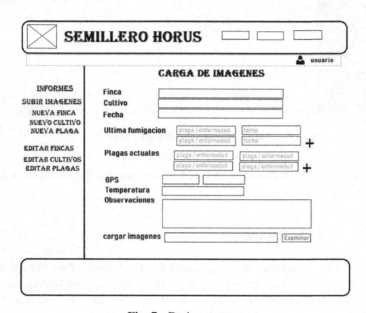

Fig. 7. Design moqups

5   Process Model 1

The process performed by the drone for the collection of photos for the study, has several phases of execution, these phases of the process are:

1. Flight Route is programmed
2. The photos are captured automatically
3. The drone returns to the starting point.
4. The data taken by the drone is collected
5. The pilot of the drone uploads the photos to the web application (Fig. 8).

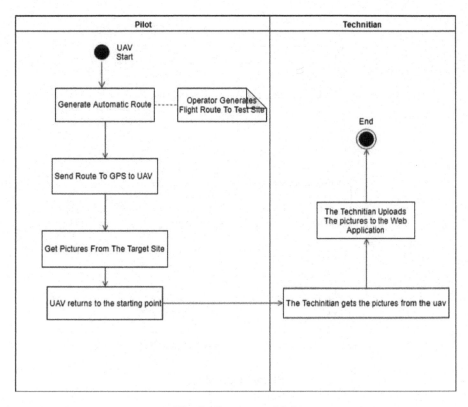

Fig. 8. Process model 1

6   Case of Use

The process for capturing and processing images using a drone with an RGB or multispectral camera is obtained thanks to the work of the three roles involved in the process, which are the drone pilot, the agronomist, and finally the farmer who receives the results of the image processing to apply the corrective measures that are necessary so that the crop is not affected in its entirety by the fungus Botrytis (Fig. 9).

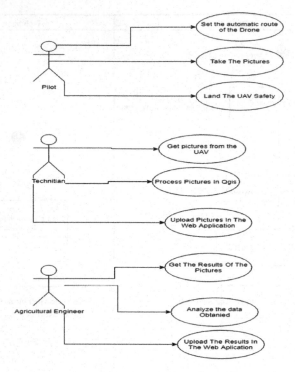

Fig. 9. Case of use

7 Results

The use of drones to capture images using RGB or multispectral cameras is an accurate and efficient way to locate problems in strawberry crops.

The processing of images using Qgis shows that the photos taken by the drone can be processed efficiently, the RGB and multispectral cameras like the parrot SEQUOIA + captures everything that we cannot see and facilitates the identification of some of the problems in a culture of Strawberry.

The application developed for the sending of the information shows that the use of the web facilitates the opportune sending of the information to the farmer with the results interpreted by the agronomist with all the recommendations so that they are applied in the crop, the importance of agriculture Precision to optimize the technical processes is fully proven not only for a strawberry crop but for any type of agricultural process.

8   Conclusions and Recommendations

The gray rot disease called Boytritis is a big problem for strawberry crops in Sibate Cundinamarca, the use of new technologies such as unmanned aerial vehicles are an excellent solution for a quick way to detect these diseases, the use of software that efficiently and quickly sends the results to be easily consulted using any mobile device.

It is important to clarify that this technology especially multispectral type cameras give us better results and precision than a RGTB camera, it is recommended to use fixed-wing drones and multispectral camera of the parrot brand.

Currently, it is possible to find free satellite images, drones of not so high cost and, in the same way, more powerful and more comfortable price sensors, from which it is possible to extract more information from the electromagnetic spectrum and with more precise resolutions per band, discriminating in greater detail the visible spectrum, infrared and thermal, among others; thus, the realization of compositions and appropriate uses of these spectral bands is possible to specify the current state of the crop and identify some types of problems suffered by the plants or otherwise estimate the possible productivity of the land in the future [2].

References

1. García-Cervigón, D., José, J.: Estudio de Índices de vegetación a partir de imágenes aéreas tomadas desde UAS/RPAS y aplicaciones de estos a la agricultura de precisión (2015)
2. González, A.: Drones Aplicados a la Agricultura de Precisión. Publicaciones e Investigación (2016)
3. IDEAM (s.f.): Mapas de Precipitación promedio en Colombia. IDEAM, Bogota
4. Qgis: Obtenido de Qgis.org, 15 de 02 de 2019. https://qgis.org/es/site/about/index.html
5. Riegos, U.D. (s.f.): Utilización de imágenes aéreas multiespectrales para evaluar la disponibilidad de nitrógeno en maíz
6. Sequoia, P.: Grupoacre. Recuperado el 17 de 03 de 2019, de Grupoacre, 18 de 02 de 2018. https://grupoacre.co/catalogo-productos/cámara-multispectral-sequoia/
7. Volaya: Obtenido de Volaya-Libro SIG, 18 de 1 de 2019. http://volaya.github.io/libro-sig/chapters/Imagenes.html
8. Honkavaara, E., et al.: Processing and assessment of spectrometric, stereoscopic imagery collected using a lightweight UAV spectral camera for precision agriculture. 5006–5039 (2013). https://doi.org/10.3390/rs5105006

Human Atrial Electrophysiological Models Under Fractional Derivative: Depolarization and Repolarization Dynamics During Normal and Fibrillation Conditions

Juan P. Ugarte[1]([✉]) and Catalina Tobón[2]

[1] GIMSC, Facultad de Ingenierías, Universidad de San Buenaventura,
Medellín, Colombia
juan.ugarte@usbmed.edu.co
[2] MATBIOM, Facultad de Ciencias Básicas, Universidad de Medellín,
Medellín, Colombia

Abstract. Atrial fibrillation (AF) is the most common arrhythmia within the clinical context. Advanced stages of the AF involve several difficulties in its management and treatment. This occurs mostly because the initiation and perpetuation mechanisms of the AF are still not fully understood. Cardiac scientific computation has become an important tool in researching the underlying mechanisms of the AF. In this work, an equation of action potential propagation that implements fractional order derivatives is used to model the atrial dynamics. The fractional derivative order represents the structural heterogeneities of the atrial myocardium. Using such mathematical operator, the Courtemanche and Maleckar human atrial electrophysiological models, during healthy and AF conditions, are assessed. The results indicate that, through the fractional order variations, there are electrophysiological properties whose behavior do not depend on the cellular model or physiological conditions. On the other hand, there are properties whose behavior under distinct values of the fractional order, are specific to the cellular model and to the physiological condition and they can be characterized quantitatively and qualitatively. Therefore, the fractional atrial propagation model can be a useful tool for modeling a wide range of electrophysiological scenarios in both healthy and AF conditions.

Keywords: Fractional calculus ·
Human atrial electrophysiological models · Atrial fibrillation ·
Myocardium structural heterogeneity

1 Introduction

Atrial fibrillation (AF) is the most common and among the most complex supraventricular arrhythmias. It is associated with high rates of cardiovascular

© Springer Nature Switzerland AG 2019
J. C. Figueroa-García et al. (Eds.): WEA 2019, CCIS 1052, pp. 440–450, 2019.
https://doi.org/10.1007/978-3-030-31019-6_38

morbidity and mortality, where the cerebral stroke is its most critical complication [28]. In episodes of AF lasting less than 7 days (paroxysmal AF), current therapeutic strategies achieve success rates of approximately 80% [11]. When the episode exceeds 7 days, it is considered persistent AF, and if it continues for a period longer than 12 months it is considered as long-standing AF [13]. At these advanced stages, the management of the arrhythmia involves several difficulties. The AF is characterized by rapid and asynchronous activations of atrial muscle cells that is manifested through irregular ventricular rhythms and contractile dysfunction [7]. The fibrillation propagation pattern results from an electrical and structural process of the myocardium known as remodeling. The electrical remodeling presents, at a microscopic level, alterations in the repolarization [4,26]; and, at the mesoscopic level, abnormalities in the adaptation of the refractory period and the duration of the action potential (AP) to rhythm changes [15,20]. The structural remodeling is characterized by dilatation, hypertrophy of the myocytes and fibrosis, the latter being a hallmark in the arrhythmogenic processes [11,14]. Although it is recognized that the electrophysiological and structural remodels contribute synergistically to the substratum of the AF [3,30], the knowledge of the AF dynamics of genesis and perpetuation remains incomplete.

In silico studies have addressed the problem of reproducing the propagation of AP over the atrial tissue under conditions of electrophysiological remodeling due to AF, including structural remodeling [19,24]. Through the computational approach, conditions that are complicated or currently impossible to assess experimentally can be implemented and analyzed. The mathematical formulation representing the cardiac dynamics can have a deep influence over the obtained results. The mathematical formalism of the human atrial membrane kinetics have been described mainly by two classical models: the Courtemanche [8] and the Nygren [22] models. While the former has been widely used, it has been not further developed, while the latter has been upgraded through the Maleckar atrial formulation [18]. The Courtemanche and Maleckar mathematical formalisms constitutes the main atrial cellular representations in cardiac scientific computation [27]. On the other hand, most of the investigations performed out to date implement the standard diffusion equation to model the AP propagation [6]. However, such approach assumes that the cardiac tissue is homogeneous while in reality, the myocardium is a complex and heterogeneous medium.

Bearing this ideas in mind, in this work the Courtemanche and Maleckar atrial models are assessed through a novel mathematical formulation of AP propagation based on fractional order derivatives. Fractional calculus is a field of growing interest within applied research [17]. Therefore, a fractional order diffusion equation is implemented to describe the atrial AP propagation. The fractional order represents the structural heterogeneity of the tissue: as the derivative approaches to 2 (which is the standard diffusion equation) the tissue is more homogeneous, and as the derivative order approaches to 1, the tissue increases its structural heterogeneity. Under such scheme, the above mentioned atrial cellular formalisms are assessed under sinus rhythm (healthy) and persistent AF conditions. The electrophysiological properties are analyzed and discussed respect to experimental observations.

2 Methodology

2.1 Model of Atrial Propagation

The transmembrane ionic current of an atrial cell is implemented using the Courtemanche [8] and Maleckar [18] mathematical formalisms. Both formulations include time- and voltage-dependent ionic currents that contribute to the generation of the human atrial AP: the Na^+ current (I_{Na}), the L-type Ca^{2+} current (I_{CaL}), and the K^+ currents I_{to}, I_{Kur}, I_{K1}, I_{Kr}, and I_{Ks}. They also include electrogenic pump and exchanger currents: the sarcolemmal Ca^{2+} pump current (I_{CaP}), the Na^+/Ca^{2+} exchanger current (I_{NaCa}), and the $Na^+ - -K^+$ pump current (I_{NaK}), which are responsible for the maintenance of intracellular ion concentrations. The Na^+ and Ca^{2+} time-independent or background currents (I_{bNa} and I_{bCa}, respectively) are also included. The total transmembrane ionic current is given by:

$$I_{ion} = I_{Na}+I_{K1}+I_{to}+I_{Kur}+I_{Kr}+I_{Ks}+I_{CaL}+I_{CaP}+I_{NaK}+I_{NaCa}+I_{bNa}+I_{bCa}. \tag{1}$$

The Maleckar model reformulates the repolarizing currents I_{Kur} and I_{to} using updated experimental data. Furthermore, an acetylcholine-activated K^+ current I_{KACh} is added to simulate the effects of vagal stimulation. Although these two models are based on similar data, they exhibit fundamental differences. The primary is related with the assumed baseline action potential shape, and, consequently, the sizes of the underlying ionic currents. The Courtemanche model generates a spike–and–dome type of AP; in contrast, the Maleckar model generates a triangular AP. The AP propagation is modeled using the unidimensional (1D) fractional diffusion equation:

$$\frac{\partial V_m}{\partial t} = D\frac{\partial^r V_m}{\partial x^r} - \frac{1}{C_m}I_{ion}, \tag{2}$$

where $r \in (1,2]$ is the order of the fractional derivative, V_m is the transmembrane potential, D is the diffusion coefficient, I_{ion} is the transmembrane ionic current, t and x are temporal and spatial variables. Standard diffusion is a particular case of Eq. (2) when $r = 2$. Sinus rhythm electrophysiological conditions correspond to the basal parameters for the Courtemanche [8] and Maleckar [18] models. The persistent AF electrical remodeling is known to affect the conduction properties of the ionic channels [9]. Therefore, the persistent AF conditions are implemented by varying the of ionic conductances as previously reported [25,27].

2.2 Numerical Methods, Simulation Protocol and Electrophysiological Measures

The Eq. (2) is numerically solved by applying Neumann boundary conditions and using a semi-spectral method in which. The temporal derivative is discretized using the Euler method and the spatial fractional approximated using a spectral representation [29]. Atrial strands are designed as 1D domains of 2 cm in length discretized in 130 nodes. The spatial discretization step is $\Delta x \approx 154\,\mu$m and the temporal discretization step is $\Delta t = 0.1\,$ms. The fractional order r is tested through values ranging from 1.1 to 2 in steps of 0.1. To generate propagation, the stimulation is applied at one end of the atrial strand, with a strength twice the diastolic threshold and 2 ms of duration. A train of 10 stimuli is applied at a basic cycle length of 1000 ms. The electrophysiological measures are observed during the propagation generated by the tenth stimulus. A simulation of 10 s takes approximately 13 min on a computer with a 2.3 GHz i7 quad-core processor and 16 GB DDR3 RAM.

The action potential duration (APD) is measured as the time interval from the maximal value of the AP upstroke derivative (activation time) to the 90% of repolarization. The APD dispersion is defined as the range of APD values within the strand. The diffusion coefficient D is adjusted for each value of r in order to obtain a conduction velocity of 63 cm/s during sinus rhythm conditions. The conduction velocity is estimated as the slope of the linear curve that relates the discrete spatial nodes with the activation times during a propagation wave. Restitution properties are measured by applying a S1–S2 stimulation protocol. The S1 is a train of 10 stimuli at a basic cycle length of 1000 ms. The S2 is a single stimulus that occurs after S1 at decreasing time intervals respect to the last stimulus of S1. The time interval between the last S1 stimulus and S2 is known as the coupling interval. The coupling interval is decreased until no propagation is generated. For each value of the coupling interval, an APD value is recorded at two-thirds the length of the strand from the stimulation point. In this manner, an APD restitution curve for each variation of r is generated.

3 Results

In order to simulated the episodes during sinus rhythm and persistent AF, the diffusion coefficient D is adjusted for both models. The Table 1 shows the D estimations for each value of the derivative order r. For both models, as r decreases, the value of D increases. This means that, in order to sustain the conduction velocity constant under the decreasing variations of r, the value of D must increase. Here, the Maleckar model has D values greater than those for the Courtemanche model, for all test values of r.

3.1 Action Potential Depolarization and Repolarization

Figure 1 left shows the action potential for the Courtemanche (top) and Maleckar (bottom) models. Sinus rhythm conditions are shown in the left column and AF

Table 1. Adjusted values of D (cm^2/s) for generating a conduction velocity of $63\,\text{cm/s}$ during sinus rhythm

r	2	1.9	1.8	1.7	1.6	1.5	1.4	1.3	1.2	1.1
Courtemanche	1.60	2.21	3.05	4.20	5.80	7.60	10.54	13.23	18.01	23.00
Maleckar		2.31	3.13	3.65	5.40	6.70	9.30	12.00	15.30	20.00	25.00

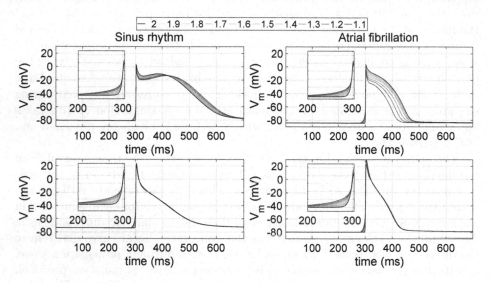

Fig. 1. The Courtemanche (first row) and Maleckar (second row) AP recorded at the center of the atrial strand. The color waveforms represent the AP for the r test values. The first and the second columns correspond to sinus rhythm and AF, respectively.

in the right column. The measures are obtained from the central point in the atrial strand. The Courtemanche model presents the lower resting membrane potential and the longer APD. The Maleckar model presents a triangular shape. It can be seen that the order r has a strong effect in modulating the depolarization dynamics. The inset in each plot shows a zoomed view of the AP foot, which is the transition from the resting to the activation state. The standard diffusion ($r = 2$) generates an abrupt AP foot, while for $r < 2$ the AP foot is ralentized, depicting a slower transition as r decreases towards 1.1. Such depolarization behavior is common to both models during sinus rhythm and AF. Measures of the depolarization dynamics are shown In Fig. 2. The maximum derivative of the AP upstroke is shown in the left plot. It can be seen that, as r increases, the maximum derivative value increases. The Maleckar (dashed line) model generates significant differences of the maximum derivative during sinus rhythm (cross marks) and AF (circle marks), while with the Courtemanche model (continuous line) both physiological conditions present similar behavior. The middle plot in Fig. 2 shows the maximum peak value of the sodium current. In this case, as r

decreases the sodium peak value increases. Important differences of the sodium maximum peak in both models during sinus rhythm and AF can be seen.

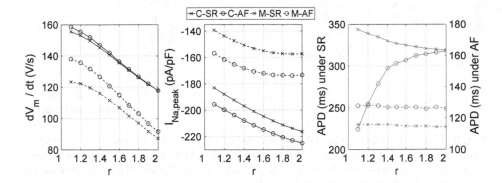

Fig. 2. Left: variation of the maximum derivative during depolarization respect to r. Middle: sodium current maximum peak values for the r testing values. Right: the APD corresponding to the AP in Fig. 1. In all plots, the continuous and dashed lines correspond to the Courtemanche (C) and Maleckar (M) models, respectively. Circle and cross marks depict sinus rhythm (SR) and AF (AF) conditions, respectively. (Color figure online)

In Fig. 1, the course to repolarization for the Courtemanche model is strongly modulated by the order r during sinus rhythm and AF. However, the Maleckar remains practically invariant against changes of r. To study this behavior the APD values are obtained and they are plotted in Fig. 2 right. As observed in the AP waveforms, the Courtemanche model (continuous line) present important variations to the changes of r. Moreover, the APD increases as r decreases during sinus rhythm (blue line) and the APD increases with r during AF (orange line). On the other hand, the APD of Maleckar model is approximately constant when r varies during both physiological conditions.

3.2   Atrial APD Dispersion and Restitution Properties

The effect of r on the APD dispersion is shown in Fig. 3 left. For both models, the APD dispersion increases as r decreases. In both conditions, the standard diffusion case ($r = 2$) generates the lowest APD dispersion. Two regimes generated by r can be identified for the Courtemanche model (continuous line): for $1.7 < r \leq 2$ the APD dispersion values during AF (circle marks) are greater than those during sinus rhythm (cross marks), and for $1.7 \leq r$ such relation is interchanged. For the Maleckar model (dashed lines) the opposite occurs: for $1.7 < r \leq 2$ the larger values of the APD dispersion correspond to sinus rhythm, while for $1.7 \leq r$ the larger values correspond to AF. Overall, the Maleckar model during AF generates the largest increment of the APD dispersion from standard diffusion ($r = 2$) to $r = 1.1$.

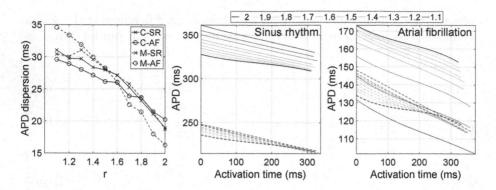

Fig. 3. Left: variations of the APD dispersion respect to the r values for both models. Sinus rhythm and AF conditions are shown. Middle: APD family of curves of vs activation time, generated by the r test values under sinus rhythm. The r variations are represented by distinct colors. Right: APD family of curves vs activation time generated with the r test values, under AF. The continuous and dashed lines represent the Courtemanche and Maleckar models, respectively. (Color figure online)

The relation between the APD of each cardiomyocyte within the strand and the corresponding activation time is shown in Fig. 3 middle (sinus rhythm) and right (AF). A family of curves is generated through the variations of r. It can be seen that the Courtemanche model (continuous line) generates a broader variation of the APD vs activation time in comparison to the Maleckar model (dashed line). Moreover, the Courtemanche model under both electrophysiological conditions behaves in different manner against the variation of r: during sinus rhythm, the APD values over the strand increase as r decreases, while during AF the APD values decrease with r. Such opposite properties generated under distinct physiological conditions are not observed for the Maleckar model: during sinus rhythm and AF, the APD increase as r decreases.

The APD restitution curves for both models (top is the Courtemanche model and bottom is the Maleckar model) are shown in Fig. 4. The restitution curves family corresponding to the test values of r, has a greater variation for the Courtemanche than for the Maleckar model. The insets in each plot present the minimum-coupling-interval APD against r (blue lines), where the Courtemanche model present a monotonic decrease as r decreases, and the Maleckar model trends to increase a r decreases during sinus rhythm and it decreases with r during AF. The insets also shown the minimum coupling intervals against r (orange lines). In this case, the Courtemanche model evinces a monotonous increment of the minimum coupling interval as r decreases during sinus rhythm and a monotonous decrement of such feature as r decreases during atrial fibrillation. On the other hand, the Maleckar model evinces a monotonous increment of the minimum coupling interval as r decreases during both physiological conditions.

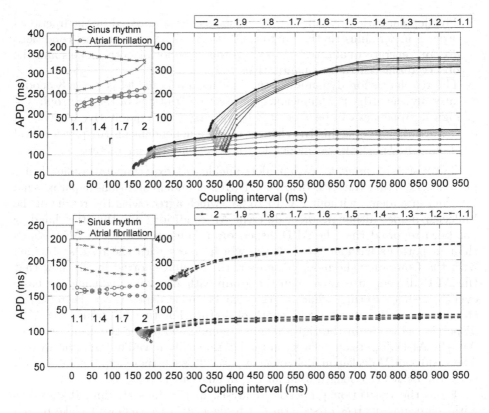

Fig. 4. The APD restitution curves under for the Courtemanche (top, continuous line) and Maleckar (bottom, dashed line) models. The circle and cross marks represent sinus rhythm and AF conditions, respectively. The insets depict the variations of the minimum-coupling-interval APD (blue) and the minimum coupling interval (orange) respect to the r test values. (Color figure online)

4   Discussion

In this work, the two principal models of human atrial electrophysiology are implemented separately under a fractional-order spatial derivative as 1D diffusion operator. The fractional order r represents the structural complexity of the atrial strand. Sinus rhythm and persistent AF conditions are implemented in the Courtemanche and Maleckar models and the depolarization and repolarization properties of both models are studied. The electrophysiological properties, whose response to the variations of r do not depend on the cellular model or physiological conditions, are identified. On the other hand, those properties whose behavior under different values of r are specific to the cellular model and to the physiological condition, have been characterized quantitatively and qualitatively. The main findings are described as follows:

- The depolarization dynamics of both models are modulated by the fractional order r under sinus rhythm and persistent AF. The physiological conditions do not generate qualitative changes in the behavior of both models and the observed differences are quantitative.
- The repolarization dynamics of the Courtemanche model is strongly modulated by the order r. Significant quantitative variations of the electrophysiological properties can be generated by varying r. The qualitative behavior of the atrial system agains the changes of r are dependent on the physiological condition. The Maleckar model does not present such characteristics.

The results obtained for each model coincide with experimental studies. It has been observed that the APD dispersion is greater under conditions of paroxysmal FA than in patients without FA [10,16,23], which agrees with the results of the Maleckar model, although under different AF conditions. On the other hand, it has been reported that the APD dispersion in humans is lower in AF patients than in patients without AF [1,2,12], which agrees with the results obtained with the Courtemanche model. However, the results reported by [2] show that the APD dispersion is greater in the group with AF when reducing the basic cycle length to 400 ms, while in [12] such behavior depends on the region of the atrium, with a basic cycle length of 400 ms. For the AF group, the APD dispersion is larger in the right atrium appendix, while for the group without AF, the APD dispersion is larger in the lateral medium wall of the right atrium. The results of Maleckar model coincide partially with these experimental data, since the basic cycle length used for the simulations is 1000 ms.

From the restitution properties analysis, under sinus rhythm, the strands with increasing degrees of structural heterogeneity (decreasing r) make propagation difficult by premature stimulation. Such feature is cellular-model independent. However, the Courtemanche model presents a wider range of restitution dynamics and larger APD reductions for decreasing degrees of structural heterogeneity. The Maleckar model describes atrial strands with reduced variability of the APD restitution dynamics against increasing structural heterogeneities. During AF conditions, the Courtemanche model generates strands whose increasing degree of structural heterogeneity (r approaching to 1.1) facilitates the AP generation and propagation from premature stimulation. On the contrary, the Maleckar model describes atrial strands whose high degree of heterogeneity hinders stimulation by premature stimuli.

The distinct responses of both models to the variations of r may represent regional differences in the atrium, as well as the inherent heterogeneity of the human atrial cardiomyocytes [27]. The quantitative differences between both models under the same physiological condition have been described in previous works [5,21,22,27,31]. However, the qualitative changes described in this work have not been described in previous in silico studies.

5   Conclusions

In this study, the fractional diffusion equation is assessed using the Courtemanche and Maleckar human atrial models. Through the variation of the fractional derivative order r, several electrophysiological dynamics with distinct properties can be generated. While the depolarization dynamics of both models are strongly modulated by the r values, such modulation of the repolarization dynamics is only achieved for the Courtemanche model. Thus, the fractional atrial propagation model studied in this work can be a useful tool for modeling a wide range of electrophysiological scenarios during healthy and AF conditions.

References

1. Bode, F., Kilborn, M., Karasik, P., Franz, M.R.: The repolarization-excitability relationship in the human right atrium is unaffected by cycle length, recording site and prior arrhythmias. J. Am. Coll. Cardiol. **37**(3), 920–925 (2001)
2. Boutjdir, M., et al.: Inhomogeneity of cellular refractoriness in human atrium: factor of arrhythmia? L'hétérogénéité des périodes réfractaires cellulaires de l'oreillette humaine: Un facteur d'arythmie? Pacing Clin. Electrophysiol. **9**(6), 1095–1100 (1986)
3. Burstein, B., Nattel, S.: Atrial fibrosis: mechanisms and clinical relevance in atrial fibrillation. J. Am. Coll. Cardiol. **51**(8), 802–9 (2008)
4. Caballero, R., et al.: In humans, chronic atrial fibrillation decreases the transient outward current and ultrarapid component of the delayed rectifier current differentially on each atria and increases the slow component of the delayed rectifier current in both. J. Am. Coll. Cardiol. **55**(21), 2346–2354 (2010)
5. Cherry, E.M., Evans, S.J.: Properties of two human atrial cell models in tissue: restitution, memory, propagation, and reentry. J. Theor. Biol. **254**(3), 674–690 (2008)
6. Clayton, R.H., Bernus, O., Cherry, E.M., Dierckx, H., Fenton, F.H., Mirabella, L., Panfilov, V., Sachse, F.B., Seemann, G., Zhang, H.: Models of cardiac tissue electrophysiology: progress, challenges and open questions. Prog. Biophys. Mol. Biol. **104**, 22–48 (2011). https://doi.org/10.1016/j.pbiomolbio.2010.05.008
7. Corradi, D.: Atrial fibrillation from the pathologist's perspective. Cardiovasc. Pathol. Off. J. Soc. Cardiovasc. Pathol. **23**(2), 71–84 (2014)
8. Courtemanche, M., Ramirez, R.J., Nattel, S.: Ionic mechanisms underlying human atrial action potential properties: insights from a mathematical model. Am. J. Physiol. **275**(1 Pt 2), H301–H321 (1998)
9. Dobrev, D.: Electrical remodeling in atrial fibrillation. Herz **31**(2), 108–112 (2006)
10. Hertervig, E., Li, Z., Kongstad, O., Holm, M., Olsson, S.B., Yuan, S.: Global dispersion of right atrial repolarization in healthy pigs and patients. Scand. Cardiovasc. J (SCJ) **37**(6), 329–333 (2003). https://doi.org/10.1080/14017430310016207
11. Jalife, J.: Mechanisms of persistent atrial fibrillation. Curr. Opin. Cardiol. **29**(1), 20–7 (2014)
12. Kamalvand, K., Tan, K., Lloyd, G., Gill, J., Bucknall, C., Sulke, N.: Alterations in atrial electrophysiology associated with chronic atrial fibrillation in man. Eur. Heart J. **20**(12), 888–895 (1999)
13. Kirchhof, P., et al.: 2016 ESC guidelines for the management of atrial fibrillation developed in collaboration with EACTS. Europace **18**(11), 1609–1678 (2016)
14. Kottkamp, H.: Human atrial fibrillation substrate: towards a specific fibrotic atrial cardiomyopathy. Eur. Heart J. **34**(35), 2731–2738 (2013)
15. Lalani, G.G., et al.: Atrial conduction slows immediately before the onset of human atrial fibrillation a bi-atrial contact mapping study of transitions to atrial fibrillation. JAC **59**(6), 595–606 (2012)

16. Li, Z., Hertervig, E., Yuan, S., Yang, Y., Lin, Z., Olsson, S.B.: Dispersion of atrial repolarization in patients with paroxysmal atrial fibrillation. Europace **3**(4), 285–291 (2001)
17. Machado, J.A., Kiryakova, V.: The chronicles of fractional calculus. Fract. Calc. Appl. Anal. **20**(2), 307–336 (2017). https://doi.org/10.1515/fca-2017-0017
18. Maleckar, M.M., Greenstein, J.L., Giles, W.R., Na, T.: K+ current changes account for the rate dependence of the action potential in the human atrial myocyte. Am. J. Physiol. Heart Circ. Physiol. **297**, H1398–H1410 (2009)
19. McDowell, K.S., Zahid, S., Vadakkumpadan, F., Blauer, J., MacLeod, R.S., Na, T.: Virtual electrophysiological study of atrial fibrillation in fibrotic remodeling. PLoS ONE **10**(2), e0117,110 (2015)
20. Narayan, S.M., Kazi, D., Krummen, D.E., Wj, R.: Repolarization and activation restitution near human pulmonary veins and atrial fibrillation initiation a mechanism for the initiation of atrial fibrillation by premature beats. J. Am. Coll. Cardiol. **52**(15), 1222–1230 (2008)
21. Niederer, S.A., et al.: Verification of cardiac tissue electrophysiology simulators using an N-version benchmark. Philos. Trans. R. Soc. A Math. Phys. Eng. Sci. **369**(1954), 4331–4351 (2011)
22. Nygren, A., Leon, L.J., Giles, W.R.: Simulaations of the human atrial action potential. Philos. Transsactions R. Soc. A **359**(1783), 1111–1125 (2001)
23. Ogawa, M., Kumagai, K., Gondo, N., Matsumoto, N., Suyama, K., Saku, K.: Novel electrophysiologic parameter of dispersion of atrial repolarization: comparison of different atrial pacing methods. J. Cardiovasc. Electrophysiol. **13**(2), 110–117 (2002)
24. Trayanova, N.A., Boyle, P.M., Arevalo, H.J., Zahid, S.: Exploring susceptibility to atrial and ventricular arrhythmias resulting from remodeling of the passive electrical properties in the heart: a simulation approach. Front. Physiol. **5**, 435 (2014). https://doi.org/10.3389/fphys.2014.00435. http://journal.frontiersin.org/article/10.3389/fphys.2014.00435/abstract
25. Ugarte, J.P., Tobón, C., Orozco-Duque, A.: Entropy mapping approach for functional reentry detection in atrial fibrillation: an in-silico study. Entropy **21**(2), 1–17 (2019)
26. Voigt, N., et al.: Enhanced sarcoplasmic reticulum Ca^2+ leak and increased Na^+-Ca^2+ exchanger function underlie delayed afterdepolarizations in patients with chronic atrial fibrillation. Circulation **125**(17), 2059–2070 (2012)
27. Wilhelms, M., Hettmann, H., Maleckar, M.M., Koivumäki, J.T., Dössel, O., Seemann, G.: Benchmarking electrophysiological models of human atrial myocytes. Front. Physiol. **3**, 487 (2013)
28. Xu, Y., Sharma, D., Li, G., Liu, Y.: Atrial remodeling: new pathophysiological mechanism of atrial fibrillation. Med. Hypotheses **80**(1), 53–6 (2013)
29. Yang, Q., Liu, F., Turner, I.: Numerical methods for fractional partial differential equations with Riesz space fractional derivatives. Appl. Math. Model. **34**, 200–218 (2010)
30. Yue, L., Xie, J., Nattel, S.: Molecular determinants of cardiac fibroblast electrical function and therapeutic implications for atrial fibrillation. Cardiovasc. Res. **89**(4), 744–53 (2011)
31. Zhang, H., Garratt, C., Zhu, J., Holden, A.: Role of up-regulation of IK1 in action potential shortening associated with atrial fibrillation in humans. Cardiovasc. Res. **66**(3), 493–502 (2005)

Comparative Analysis Between Training Methods for a Fuzzy Inference System Potentially Applicable to the Assessment of the Health Status of the Spine in Military Personnel

Fabián Garay[1]([✉]) [iD], Daniel Gutiérrez[2], Fabián Martínez[1],
David Lombana[2], Hammer Ibagué[1], and José Jiménez[1]

[1] Escuela de Infantería – Ejército Nacional de Colombia, Bogotá, Colombia
cienciatecnologia.esinf@cedoc.edu.co,
fsgarayr@correo.udistrital.edu.co
[2] School of Medicine, University Foundation Juan N. Corpas, Bogotá, Colombia
daniel-gutierrez@juanncorpas.edu.co

Abstract. The Colombian Army personnel are exposed to long training and work periods, which involve abrupt, sudden and unexpected body movements together with carrying excessive loads on their backs. That leads to the development of spine disorders on the short, medium and long term. It also affects the soldier's quality of life, and has a great economic impact on their families, the Army and the State due to absenteeism, incapacity for work and specialized medical attention. In traumatology, orthopedics and physiatry, pelvic parameters are used to check the sagittal balance and to evaluate the erect position and the spinal function. These parameters also are important in the prevention, diagnosis and treatment of diseases such as scoliosis, spondylolisthesis, herniated discs and others. This work presents and compares various training methods for a computer-assisted system able to assess and classify spinal health status among military personnel. Different methods were used: diffuse inference system designed from experience, supervised learning obtained from a previous study by the 'Backpropagation' algorithm, computational evolution by the simple genetic algorithm and automatic learning algorithms and their combinations in classifiers sets with neuronal networks and fuzzy classifier from other previous researches on this topic. The system was trained with a collection of data taken from the UCI's automatic learning repository, which includes sagittal balance parameters data (pelvis incidence or PI, pelvis inclination or PT, lumbar lordosis angle or LL, sacrum slope or SS). The system was validated by the evaluation of its computational performance and by diagnostic utility measurements. Results show that the simple genetic algorithm brings the highest performance, is the best solution to the problem, and is an excellent tool to help health professionals to leave the zone of diagnostic uncertainty.

Keywords: Backpropagation · Classifiers · Computer-assisted diagnosis · Diffuse inference system · Sagittal balance · Simple genetic algorithm · Spine

J. C. Figueroa-García et al. (Eds.): WEA 2019, CCIS 1052, pp. 451–471, 2019.
https://doi.org/10.1007/978-3-030-31019-6_39

1   Introduction

Musculoskeletal disorders of the spine are one of the main causes of loss of time of service, temporary incapacity for work and long-term disability in military organizations worldwide. In the United States, a study found that out of 87% of military personnel evacuated due to musculoskeletal injuries, 86% were due to spinal pain and could not return to military activity [1]. In developing countries such as Latin American countries, up to 85% of military personnel have been reported suffering from some type of musculoskeletal disorder of the spine [2]. Therefore, it is not surprising that primary prevention of these disorders and pain, their most common symptom, is a research priority in military populations since they have a great economic and social impact [3]. The studies that have been carried out to prevent these disorders have identified that main biomechanical risk factors are heavy physical work, stiff work positions and uncomfortable dynamics, the vibration of the whole body and lifting of loads. Identified psychosocial risk factors are negative affectivity, low level of labor control, high psychological demands and high job dissatisfaction, conditions that usually occur in military personnel [2].

In physiatry, traumatology and radiology, sagittal balance has been studied as an indicator of the health status of the spine. In normal conditions, this balance optimizes both, standing and walking position, allowing for the lowest possible energy expenditure. When this situation of normality is absent due to a musculoskeletal disorder, both spine and pelvis use compensatory mechanisms (pelvic retroversion, lumbar retrolisthesis, thoracic hyperkyphosis, knee flexion, ankle extension, etc.) to overcome this issue [4]. This results in an increase in muscular effort, use of accessory muscles and greater energy expenditure. It also generates fatigue and pain, which make standing and walking inefficient, increasing disability and decreasing the quality of life of patients [5]. Taking this into account, it is of critical importance to know and describe the variations in the parameters that determine the sagittal balance in the prevention, diagnosis and treatment of diseases such as scoliosis, lordosis, spondylolisthesis or herniated disc among others [6]. Currently, bioinformatics systems have become important diagnostic support tools in health sciences. Studies reveal that the medical community is increasingly trusting these tools that provide support in clinical decision-making [7].

This document presents the design of a diffuse inference system for classification of the health status of the spine, a system that can help to draw a conclusion on the normality or abnormality of the spine, based on four entries (PI, PT, LL and SD). For the diffuse modeling of this problem, three techniques were proposed: diffuse inference system created from experience, supervised learning (backpropagation) and finally through the simple genetic algorithm. Finally, a comparison was made between the best of the results obtained with a previous study that used automatic learning algorithms and their combinations in sets of classifiers with neural networks.

2   Background

A wide search of scientific articles, unpublished research results, databases and journals reveal a growing interest in the scientific community on the development of intelligent systems to support the diagnosis in different fields of medicine. For this study case, mainly the applications of these systems are evidenced in medical spine image analysis. For example, the study of Ellingson, Ulmer, & Schmit title "Gray and White Matter Delineation in the Human Spinal Cord Using Diffusion Tensor Imaging and Fuzzy Logic" which the objective was to improve the delineation of gray and white matter in the spinal cord by applying signal processing techniques to the eigenvalues of the diffusion tensor and a fuzzy inference system (FIS) to delineate between gray and white matter in the human cervical spinal cord [8]. A most recent study about the Spine detection in Computed Tomography (CT) and Magnetic Resonance (MR) using iterated marginal space learning, present a novel method that combines Marginal Space Learning (MSL), for efficient discriminative object detection and the detection of multiple objects, in this research was used to simultaneously detect and label the spinal disks [8].

2.1   Classifiers with Neural Networks for Study on the Vertebral Column

Research carried out by Neto & Barreto is restated, where they report the results of a comprehensive performance comparison between independent machine learning algorithms Support Vector Machines (SVM), Multilayer Perceptron (MLP) and Generalized Regression Neural Network (GRNN). The evaluation consisted of determining the ability of these net to discriminate patients who belong to one of three categories: normal, herniated disc and spondylolisthesis. Previously, three sets were created from the set T = 310 of available samples: a set W free of outliers, a set N containing only outliers, and a third set S related to the first and the second set. For each classifier, 50 rounds of training and testing were carried out, the training samples were randomly selected from the third data set (S), and the rest were used for the test. After the 50 rounds of training and testing, corresponding to a specific P-value, the mean success rate and the standard deviation of the success rates observed during the tests were determined [9]. They were randomly separated from the data set of the repository, in the proportion 80% for training and 20% for testing [9]. The values obtained in this investigation for the rate of the average adjustment in the test and the respective standard deviations, as a function of P, can be seen in Table 1.

Table 1. Results for the SVM, MLP and GRNN classifiers.

P(%)	SVM	MLP	GRNN
0	96,51 ± 3,65	98,70 ± 1,76	96,51 ± 3,46
20	88,68 ± 7,39	93,39 ± 3,90	90,00 ± 4,94
40	86,33 ± 7,25	90,02 ± 4,27	84,79 ± 5,72
60	85,47 ± 7,03	87,90 ± 4,63	80,94 ± 5,18
80	83,47 ± 5,06	83,53 ± 5,99	78,98 ± 4,70
100	82,16 ± 4,95	83,03 ± 5,70	75,41 ± 5,58

Taken from: [9].

These results show that the performance of the 3 classifiers is maximum when the outliers are not present in the data (i.e. P = 0%). The MLP classifier had the best performance with a success rate of 98.70 ± 1.76, which was higher than the others. However, in this same research it is stated that although for P = 100% the average adjustment rates of the SVM and MLP classifiers were higher than 82%, these values were considered good by the orthopedic physician consulted [9].

Other study about the Neural Network in this topic, it was titled "Artificial Neural Network for Supporting (ANNs) Medical Decision Making: A Decision Model and Notation Approach to Spondylolisthesis and Disk Hernia", focuses on the impact of ANNs on the Decision-Making Process (DMP) for a special kind of medical diagnosis called Spondylolisthesis and Disk Hernia. Through the Decision Model and Notation standard (DMN), in this way, ANNs supported decision making for Spondylolisthesis and Disk Hernia diagnosis improve efficiency and quality of health service, especially in developing countries. This research used the advantages of Levenberg–Marquardt to a different approach of optimization, which is slower as algorithm but with great accuracy, this appreciable on the result obtained of 96,1% accuracy [10].

A study used back-propagation neural network (BPNN), rough set theory GA Algorithm (RST-GA) and rough set theory Johnson Algorithm (RST-JA) to test a medical database of vertebral columns from UCI, showed that the BPNN is superior to RST-GA and RST-JA for the medical diagnosis of vertebral column with a classification accuracy of 90.32%, and under the ROC curve (AURC) of 99.42% [11]. Finally, a study published in 2015 into the 4th International Conference on Instrumentation, Communications, Information Technology, and Biomedical Engineering (ICICI-BME) use the combination of genetic algorithm and bagging technique for classification on spinal disorders; in this case, proposed method is applied to three classifier algorithms, namely naïve bayes, neural networks and k-nearest neighbor, as a result they had, that the best algorithm was k-nearest neighbor with an accuracy of 89.03% [12].

2.2   Fuzzy Classifiers for the Study on the Vertebral Column

An available study in the IEEE Latin America Transactions of 2014, describes the training and application of a fuzzy singleton classifier that is used for the diagnosis of pathologies of the vertebral column, the data set used is too from University of California Irvine UCI Machine Learning Repository. In this case each input variable is partitioned into triangular membership functions so that consecutive fuzzy sets exhibit and specific overlapping of 0.5, the singleton consequents are employed and least square method is used to adjust the consequents. However, the accuracy obtained in the training was 86.2903% and in the validation of 90.3226% [13]; values very under of the obtained in our study, even in the second method with the better result. The main contribution of this research is the comparison it makes between its results and the classification methods related in the scientific literature, applied to the data set of the UCI Machine Learning Repository, as can be seen in the Table 2. Comparison with other methods.

Table 2. Comparison with other methods.

Method	Maximum accuracy (%)
ARTIE model [14]	83.87
MUSCLE model [14]	85.81
SVM [15]	89.03
Babalik et al. [15]	91.61
Multilayer Perceptron (MLP) [9]	83.03
Generalized Regression Neural Network (GRNN) [9]	83.03
Fuzzy classifier [13]	90.32

Modified from: [13].

3 Preliminaries

3.1 Sagittal Balance

To evaluate the sagittal balance, there are a series of angles and measurements that can be evaluated with precision in a spinogram, that can, in turn, characterize the shape and orientation of the pelvis. Some of the most commonly used and targeted measures in this study are: Pelvic Incidence (PI), PT Pelvic Tilt, Lumbar Lordosis Angle (LL) and Sacred Slope (SS) [16].

Pelvic Incidence (PI). It is defined by the angle formed between the line perpendicular to the sacred slope SS (Sacral Slope), the upper face of the sacral inclination S1 at its midpoint and the line connecting this point with that corresponding to the bicox-ofemoral axis. Tebet ensures that its normal value is 51.8°; however, its value has been found to vary within a range comprised between 45° and 60° (Fig. 1).

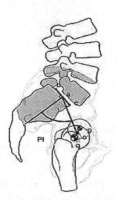

Fig. 1. Pelvic incidence is the intersection from the center of the femoral head to the midpoint of the sacrum (o-a) and a line perpendicular to the center of the end of the sacrum (a). Taken from: [16].

Sacral Slope (SS). The Sacral Slope corresponds to the angle between the sacral plate and the horizontal plane, its normal value is 39.7° and can vary in a range from 36° to 42° [16] (Fig. 2).

Fig. 2. The sacral slope (SS) is the intersection of the horizontal reference line (HRL) and the final sacral plate (b–c). Taken from: [16].

Pelvic Tilt (PT). The PT (Pelvic Tilt) corresponds to the angle between the line joining the midpoint of the sacral plate to the bicoxofemoral axis and the vertical plane, its normal value is 12.1° [16]; however, it can be between 12° and 18° (Fig. 3).

Fig. 3. The pelvic tilt (PT) being the intersection of a vertical reference line, starting at the center of the head of the femur (o) and the midpoint of the final sacral plate (a). Taken from: [16].

Lordosis Lumbar (LL). It is the parameter measured between the upper plate of the Lumbar vertebral and the lower plate of V. lumbar 5; its normal value is between 43° and 61° (Fig. 4).

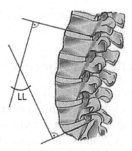

Fig. 4. Lumbar lordosis (LL) calculated from L1 to S1. Taken from: [17].

3.2   Fuzzy Inference Systems

They are non-linear systems that can be of the Mamdani type like the one in Fig. 5, in which three main elements can be found: fuzzification, diffuse inference engine (MID) and defuzzification; there are other configurations such as the one of the Sugeno type, which differs in the way in which the output is calculated [18]. These systems can be of the MISO (Multiple Input Single Output) or MIMO (Multiple Input Multiple Output) type, based on the theory of fuzzy sets and fuzzy logic [19].

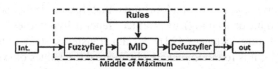

Fig. 5. Architecture of the Mamdani type diffuse system proposed for the evaluation of the proposed classification systems.

The fuzzifier is responsible for mapping the input within the fuzzy sets, that is, assigning a membership value of an input variable to each set, to activate the rules that are set in terms of linguistic variables and that are used to draw an interpretation. The MID or inference engine generates a mapping of the antecedent sets in the consequent sets, through the combination and calculation of the rules. Finally, the defuzzifier seeks to obtain an entire output from the composition of the diffuse outputs of the MID [20].

As mentioned by Villate, to obtain a compact description of a diffuse system, a non-linear equation known as Diffuse Base Function Expansion (EFBD) is used, which is based on Zadeh's extension principle [21]. The equation is presented in (1).

$$y(x) = f_s(x) = \frac{\sum_{l=1}^{m} y_l \left(\prod_i^p a_i^l exp \left(-\frac{\left(x_i - x_i^l\right)^2}{\left(\delta_i^l\right)^2} \right) \right)}{\sum_{l=1}^{m} \left(\prod_i^p a_i^l exp \left(-\frac{\left(x_i - x_i^l\right)^2}{\left(\delta_i^l\right)^2} \right) \right)} \tag{1}$$

Where the subscript s refers to a singleton fuzzifier, p refers to the number of entries and M refers to the number of rules [20].

3.3 Fuzzy Inference System Based on Experience

The fuzzy sets, as well as the rules used in a fuzzy system, are proposed to solve the problem by connecting inputs and outputs. The systems of diffuse inference based on experience seek to extract the rules that are set in terms of linguistic variables for expert in the topic of application. These variables are extracted from numerical, theoretical or information data provided by sensors, which are intended to resemble the human interpretation of the problem for instance, if sizes were used, labels such as small, medium and large would be used, that is to say that it tries to extract the day-to-day way of appreciating the environment.

The way in which an entry is reflected on an exit must be fixed, so it is done through the experience of the expert and his prior knowledge of the behavior of the system, generally using the Mamdani structure of yes-then. However, some authors claim that the use of these systems based on experience, reduce the need for intervention by experts in the interpretation of results [22].

3.4 EFBD (Fuzzy Base Function Expansion) by Supervised Learning

Supervised learning makes use of algorithms that reason from externally supplied instances (known data or training) to produce general hypotheses, which then make predictions about future instances [23]. A data transfer system is translated into an indication of Eq. (1), it is required that are chosen and the values of (xi, δi, yi), which is difficult, and a specific behavior of the system is sought. However, this task is simplified through the use of media in neural networks and knowledge in the algorithm. Among existing limitations, there is no guarantee that an optimal solution is found since the search space is usually very large and there is not the computational resources to observe it in its entirety, which makes it necessary to initialize several times the EFBD parameters to be able to observe a greater number of solutions.

3.5 Genetic Algorithm

The genetic algorithm is based on the conception of evolution and biological behavior described by Charles Darwin. It consists of the initialization, the aptitude function, the selection, the crossing and the mutation. To ensure a uniform distribution in the solution space, initialization is random, the individuals are evaluated through the objective function and the fitness function, indicating the performance of each one, through the selection by roulette, the crossing is made and the mutation generating new populations and greater diversity, the crossing mixes the genetic information of two individuals producing a new one; within the classification problems, diffuse inference systems optimized through Genetic Algorithms are used [24].

4 Methodology

From Eq. (1), the inference system was synthesized considering a singleton type fuser, Mamdani implication for each product, T product norm, Gaussian membership functions and defuzzifier by center average. Subsequently, the training was carried out so that it can classify and determine the health status of the spine based on the data obtained from a specialized repository. For their training, three methods were used: diffuse inference system built from experience, supervised learning through the backpropagation algorithm and computational evolution by means of the simple genetic algorithm. Regarding the data used, all the attributes were normalized in the range of 0 to 1. Finally, for each of the training methods, their computational performance was evaluated, given the classification error, as well as their utility as a diagnostic test in terms of its sensitivity, specificity, positive predictive value, negative predictive value and likelihood positive and negative ratios. To give an added value to the study, the behavior of the algorithm with better performance was compared with the results of a previous study that made use of sets of classifiers with neural networks and Fuzzy Classifier.

4.1 Database

A database "Vertebral Column Data Set" of the UCI Machine Learning Repository is used. This is a compilation of databases, domain theories and data generators used by the machine learning community for the empirical analysis of the machine learning algorithms [25]. The database was initially organized into three categories: normal (100 patients), herniated disc (60 patients) or spondylolisthesis (150 patients). Subsequently, hernia and spondylolisthesis disc categories were merged into a single category called "abnormal" (210 patients). For the first method evaluated, all the normalized data was taken; for the two remaining methods a preprocessing was carried out, they were normalized, and they were divided in 70% for system training and 30% for validation of this, leaving the data as shown in Table 3. Out of the six parameters evaluated in the database, only four were taken, on the advice of the orthopedic expert consulted.

Table 3. Treatment of the data used for training and validation in the three methods.

Data organization	Training	Validation
The experience	N/A	310 (100 normal and 210 abnormal)
Supervised learning	218 (147 abnormal and 71 normal)	92 (63 abnormal and 29 normal)
Genetic algorithm	218 (47 abnormal and 71 normal)	92 (63 abnormal and 29 normal)

4.2   The Experience

To define a solution through experience, it was established that the number and form of membership functions are chosen based on the trends of the data. It is intended that membership functions delimit the greatest amount of data and give more opportunity to trigger the data that present greater deviations. The output sets are left as widely separated as possible and then related by the rules. The fuzzy sets shown in Fig. 6 are presented. The Mamdani product implication method, the aggregation method by standard t and the centroid defuzzifier are applied.

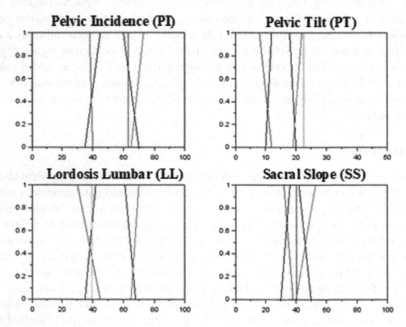

Fig. 6. Membership functions for each of the entries.

The implementation of this solution is developed using the Matlab *fuzzy* tool, which allows the adjustment of each parameter, calculates the classification results for each input data and allows the export of said solution as a function within the *workspace*.

4.3   Supervised Learning: Backpropagation

Backpropagation was used as a supervised learning method, through the application of the algorithm visible in Fig. 7.

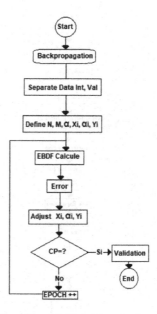

Fig. 7. Flow diagram algorithm: backpropagation.

To find the appropriate values of learning rate (alpha) and number of rules (M), an alpha was chosen that produced a minimum number of validation errors with M = 8 that was found from the knowledge of the experts (analysis of the supplied database), after accepting alpha = 0.001, 1000 tests were made each with 500 epochs and the validation error was observed, leaving as a result the minimum classification error histogram of Fig. 9(a). The results obtained regarding the training error and the validation error can be seen in Table 4.

Table 4. Training errors, validation and total for the backpropagation algorithm.

Case	Period	Training error	Validation error	Total error
Min. validation	71	49,1% (107/218)	**17,4% (16/92)**	39,7% (123/310)
Min. training	14	30,3% (66/218)	68,5% (63/92)	41,6% (129/310)

4.4   Computational Evolution: Genetic Algorithm

For the application of computational evolution on the diffuse inference system, the genetic algorithm is used; the design is described in the flow diagram of Fig. 8, the parameters of the cyclic algorithms with the stop criterion, evaluating the lower validation and training errors. Within the algorithm, elitism was implemented to find a local minimum more quickly. The algorithm parameters are described in Table 5.

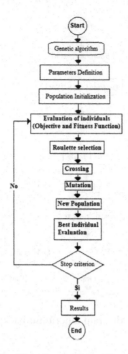

Fig. 8. Genetic algorithm flow chart.

Table 5. Parameters used in the genetic algorithm.

Parameters	Value
Parameters	4
Input	8
Rules	32
Population	64
Intermediate population	0.01
Selective pressure	0.7
Probability of crossing	0.1

A multi-objective cost function was built in Eq. (2). It is a classification error, sensitivity and specificity, this function is sought through the weighting method. The fitness function is represented in Eq. (3) and indicates the adaptation of the individual to the problem, ensuring that the selected individuals have the best characteristics. The best individual is assigned a set of means and deviations from the functions of belonging to the antecedents and the consequents. The tests were performed with 6000 generations and with 40 runs.

$$Fobj = 0,9Error_c + \frac{0,1}{0,5(Sensitivity + Specificity)} \qquad (2)$$

$$F_{itness} = (1 - press) * \frac{(fobjmax - fobj)}{([fobjmax - fobjmin, eps])} + press \qquad (3)$$

4.5   Classifiers with Neural Networks

The research carried out by Neto & Barreto is restated, where they report the results of a comprehensive performance comparison between independent machine learning algorithms Support Vector Machines (SVM), Multilayer Perceptron (MLP) and Generalized Regression Neural Network (GRNN), the evaluation consisted of in determining the ability of these, to discriminate patients who belong to one of three categories: normal, herniated disc and spondylolisthesis. Previously three sets were created from the set T = 310 of available samples: a set W free of outliers, a set N containing only outliers, and a third set S related to the first and the second set. For each classifier, 50 rounds of training and testing were carried out, the training samples were randomly selected from the third data set (S), and the rest were used for the test. After the 50 rounds of training and testing, corresponding to a specific P-value, the mean success rate and the standard deviation of the success rates observed during the tests were determined [9].

4.6   Computational Performance Evaluation and Diagnostic Utility

To evaluate the solutions obtained by each of the methods, it is necessary to previously establish the metric that should be used. In this case, it is appropriate to use different criteria designed to evaluate the performance of classification systems and the utility of diagnostic tests. The classification error gives us a metric of the proportion of the total of the data poorly qualified by the system and is calculated by means of expression (4), where Ec is the classification error, NE number of erroneous or misclassified data and ND number total data evaluated.

$$E_c = \frac{NE}{ND} \qquad (4)$$

The utility of diagnostic tests is usually described and/or quantified in terms of their sensitivity, specificity, positive predictive value, negative predictive value and positive and negative likelihood ratios [26].

Sensitivity and specificity are measures that describe how well a clinical test is performed. They describe the diagnostic performance of the test in a group of patients, comparing for each patient their test result with whether they have the condition of interest (diagnosis or result). Sensitivity is the proportion of people who have the condition of interest that was correctly identified with the test with a positive result. On the other hand, specificity is the proportion of people who do not have the condition of interest and who are correctly identified by the test [27]. These metrics are given by the equations represented in Table 6.

Table 6. Calculation of sensitivity, specificity, positive and negative predictive values of a test using the 2 × 2 table.

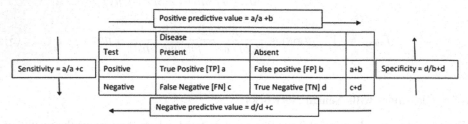

Taken from: [28].

Sensitivity and specificity are important measures of the diagnostic accuracy of a test, but they cannot be used to estimate the probability of disease in an individual patient. This limits the possibility of intuitive clinical interpolations for each patient.

The positive predictive (PPV) and negative (NPV) values provide estimates of the probability of the disease and are calculated with the equations represented in Fig. 11. It amounts to the probability that the diagnostic test delivers the correct diagnosis, be it positive or negative [26]. However, their results are highly influenced by the prevalence of the disease in the study being analyzed. Thus, the higher the prevalence of the disease, the higher the PPV and the lower the NPV of the diagnostic test. Therefore, it is necessary to have alternative statistical approaches to summaries the diagnostic strength of a particular test and that yields a specific clinical utility [29].

To measure the clinical benefit of a diagnostic test independently of the prevalence, the application of the likelihood ratio (LR) is more useful. The LR or likelihood ratios are defined as how many times a patient with the disease is more likely to have a certain test result than patients without the disease. Put another way, the odds ratio is a specific outcome in patients with disease versus those who do not. In the case of dichotomous results, the positive LR takes values between 1 and infinity, while the negative LR takes values between 1 and 0 [26]. The use of LR is a very useful tool for taking clinical decisions when requesting a diagnostic test, because they are values inherent to it and independent of the prevalence of the disease. Although its calculation derives from conditioned probabilities based on Bayes' theorem, it can be estimated based on parameters of sensitivity and specificity with Eqs. (5) and (6). Its impact on clinical utility is reflected in Table 7 [29].

$$LR(+) = \frac{Tasa\ de\ verdaderos\ positivos}{Tasa\ de\ falsos\ positivos} = \frac{Sensibilidad}{1 - Especificidad} \tag{5}$$

$$LR(+) = \frac{Tasa\ de\ falsos\ positivos}{Tasa\ de\ verdaderos\ negativos} = \frac{1 - Sensibilidad}{Especificidad} \tag{6}$$

Table 7. Ranges of likelihood ratio values and their impact on clinical utility.

LR positive	LR negative	Utility
10	<0.1	Highly relevant
5–10	0.1–0.2	Useful
2–5	0.5–0.2	Regular
<2	>0.5	Wrong

Taken from: [29]

As a general term, it should be remembered that a positive LR higher than 10 and a negative LR lower than 0.1 indicates a relevant change in the probability of the preliminary test, which determines with high certainty a change in clinical behavior. Therefore, a diagnostic test will be more useful insofar as its LR (+) is of greater magnitude, since it allows to confirm with certainty the presence of disease, and in cases where its LR (–) has a low value, since the disease is ruled out. This reflects the ability of a diagnostic test to change a pretest probability to a new posttest probability and has been simplified using the Fagan nomogram, it consists of three columns parallel to each other, graded in order to estimate the probability posttest, known the pretest probability and an LR of the test to be tested [29].

5 Results and Discussion

From the histograms in which a statistical characterization of the total classification error is represented in the solutions found by the algorithm of supervised learning (backpropagation algorithm) and computational evolution (genetic algorithm) in Fig. 9, it is found that the average error found of the solutions in the genetic algorithm is 3.23% (success rate of 96.77 ± 0.09), which is lower than the solutions found with backpropagation algorithm that is equivalent to 27.1%, which indicates that the simple genetic algorithm provides a better solution for this classification problem.

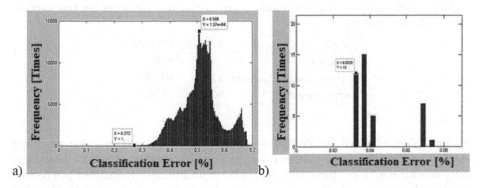

Fig. 9. (a) Histogram error classification algorithm backpropagation. (b) Histogram error classification genetic algorithm.

When comparing the results of the solutions obtained by the three methods presented in Table 8, it is found that the solution with the lowest total error of computational classification is generated by the simple genetic algorithm (3.23%), which is a 23.97% better than the one generated by the backpropagation algorithm and 80% better than the solution found from the experience. The algorithm based on experience, presents a too high computational error (80%) therefore, its reliability is minimal.

The sensitivity for each of the training methods applied to the best solution found by the system is shown in Table 8. This shows that the genetic algorithm and backpropagation algorithm are the ones that tend to classify diseased vertebral columns with values of abnormal sagittal balance. However, it had previously been found that the backpropagation algorithm has a very high computational classification error (27.20%), which is inferred, its performance is low compared to the genetic algorithm. On the other hand, it was found that the genetic algorithm is the one that best tends to classify healthy columns with normal sagittal equilibrium values when presenting a specificity of 78.57.

Table 8. Results total error (TE), training error (TrE), validation error (EV), specificity and sensitivity for the best solutions in the three methods.

Method	TE [%]	TrE [%]	EV [%]	Specif [%]	Sens [%]
Experience	80	–	80	17.02	20.48
Backpropagation algorithm	27,20	30,3	17,4	71,43	99,0
Genetic algorithm	3,23	2.03	4.8	78,57	98,28

The results of the PPV and PNV found for each of the training methods are presented in Table 9. In the case of the genetic algorithm, the probability that the patient has the vertebral disease since the diagnostic test is positive is 90, 47% and the probability that the patient does not have the disease since the diagnostic test was positive is 95.66%.

Table 9. Results positive predictive values, negative predictive values for the best solutions found in the three methods.

Method	PPV [%]	PNV [%]
Experience	33,81	9,36
Backpropagation algorithm	87,76	97,18
Genetic algorithm	90,47	95,66

The values obtained for the LR + and LR – are presented in Table 10. When interpreting these, it can be said that, for the genetic algorithm, it is 4.59 times more likely that a patient with abnormal values in the sagittal balance is qualified as a column vertebral disease that a patient with normal values has the same result. On the other hand, it was found that the genetic algorithm is highly relevant in clinical utility when obtaining an LR – less than 0.1, the result value was 0.02, and it means that finding a healthy spine is 50 times (1: 002) more frequent in those who do not have vertebral disease than in those who have it.

Table 10. Results positive likelihood ratio (LR +), negative likelihood ratio (LR –), later positive and negative Odds for the best solutions found in the three methods.

Method	LR + (95% CI)	LR – (95% CI)	Posterior Odds + [%] (95% CI)	Posterior Odds - [%] (95% CI)
Experience	0.25 (0.18, 0.35)	4.67 (2.78, 7.86)	34% (27%, 42%)	91% (85%, 94%)
Backpropagation algorithm	3.47 (2.4, 5.01)	0.01 (0.00, 0.07)	88% (83%, 91%)	2% (0%, 13%)
Genetic algorithm	4.59 (2.94, 7.16)	0.02 (0.01, 0.07)	90% (86%, 94%)	4% (2%, 13%)

The Fagan nomogram represented in Fig. 10 allows comparing the change of the pretest probability with a new posttest probability using the genetic algorithm. With a pretest suspicion of 67% (prevalence) of vertebral disease, the posttest possibility of having this entity increased to 90%. On the contrary, in the case of a healthy spine, the posttest possibility decreases to less than 4%.

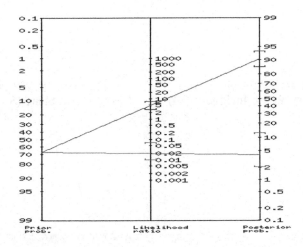

Fig. 10. Fagan Nomogram with graphical representation of the pre- and post-test probabilities of reference for the genetic algorithm. Retrieved from: [30].

Table 11 shows the parameters that characterize the fuzzy system with the best solution found among the three methods used, in this case, it corresponds to the genetic algorithm.

Table 11. Values of means and deviation for the best solution of the simple genetic algorithm.

	Averages							
	Rule 1	Rule 2	Rule 3	Rule 4	Rule 5	Rule 6	Rule 7	Rule 8
PI	−1,83	0,20	−2,92	−1,79	2,29	0,77	−2,13	−0,06
SS	−1,30	−1,09	−2,67	−1,04	−1,28	0,75	−2,45	0,13
PT	−0,78	0,31	1,27	−1,72	−1,73	−0,42	1,01	1,14
LL	−0,26	0,44	−0,77	−2,83	−2,59	0,57	0,75	0,48
	Deviation							
PI	2,29	−2,71	−1,16	−2,54	1,74	−2,25	0,02	−1,53
SS	2,79	2,51	2,37	1,25	−0,16	−2,59	−1,46	0,74
PT	−2,98	0,71	−1,48	2,87	−1,45	−2,36	−0,94	−2,20
LL	1,77	2,84	0,57	2,70	2,75	−2,52	−2,11	−0,56

The representation of the fuzzy sets for said solution can be seen in Fig. 11, where it is evident that the mean of the fuzzy sets tends to the average value of the data of each entry for each subject.

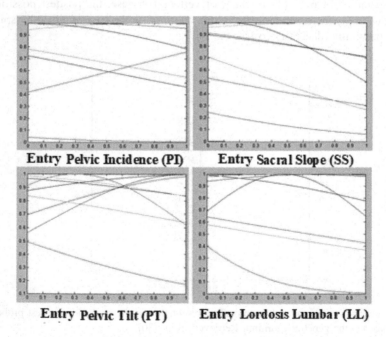

Fig. 11. Fuzzy sets of the best subject

6 Conclusions

From the data found in this research, it can be concluded that the implementation of a diffuse inference system to find a solution to the problem of classification of the health status of the spine from the values of the sagittal balance, presented a good performance, when obtaining with the genetic algorithm a minimum total classification error of 3.21% and with a median number of rules (M = 8), which implies a computational cost not so high for what is considered to be computationally useful as a tool support for the diagnosis.

The simple genetic algorithm implemented has the lowest computational classification error and therefore the best performance compared the backpropagation algorithm and training from experience, when finding the best solution to classify the health status of the spine based on the values of the sagittal balance.

In terms of sensitivity, with a value of 98.28, the genetic algorithm is more useful when it comes to detecting truly dysfunctional vertebral columns and therefore clinically important in the diagnosis, treatment and prevention of risk of disease extension.

On the other hand, based on the LR values, it is concluded that the genetic algorithm is highly relevant in clinical utility to rule out the presence of vertebral disease and regular to confirm it. In other words, it is an excellent tool to help the clinician leave the area of diagnostic uncertainty.

In comparison with the best result obtained by the MLP classifier (98.70 ± 1.76) and the simple genetic algorithm (96.77 ± 0.09), it can be said that the genetic algorithm performed better than the SVM and GRNN classifiers and even though was slightly lower than that of the MLP, considering the deviations, both classifiers have comparable behaviors. According to the classification methods related in the scientific literature and as evidenced in Table 2, the results are better for the method proposed in this study with the genetic algorithm.

References

1. Burgio, M., Onyejekwe, O.E.: Degenerative disc disease in the active military special forces and the financial benefits of early detection using a quadruple blind-study. J. Bioequiv. Availab. **10**, 1–6 (2018). https://doi.org/10.4172/jbb.1000366
2. Moscoso, C., Grace, V., Macías, M., Danny, D.: Incidencia de lesiones músculo esqueléticas en columna vertebral en militares en servicio activo que pertenecen a la ESFORSE - Ambato. Universidad Técnica de Ambato - Facultad de Ciencias de la Salud - Carrera de Terapia Física, Ambato (2017)
3. Childs, J.D., Wu, S.S., Teyhen, D.S., et al.: Prevention of low back pain in the military cluster randomized trial: effects of brief psychosocial education on total and low back pain–related health care costs. Spine J. **14**, 571–583 (2014). https://doi.org/10.1016/j.spinee.2013.03.019
4. Guiroy, A., Gagliardi, M., Sícoli, A., et al.: Spino-pelvic sagittal parameters in an asymptomatic population in Argentina. Surg. Neurol. Int. **9**, S36–S42 (2018). https://doi.org/10.4103/sni.sni_365_17
5. Nguyen, N.-L.M., Baluch, D.A., Patel, A.A.: Cervical Sagittal Balance. Contemp. Spine Surg. **15**, 1–7 (2014). https://doi.org/10.1097/01.CSS.0000441214.29279.d0

6. Roussouly, P., Nnadi, C.: Sagittal plane deformity: an overview of interpretation and management. Eur. Spine J. **19**, 1824–1836 (2010). https://doi.org/10.1007/s00586-010-1476-9

7. Oulas, A., Minadakis, G., Zachariou, M., et al.: Systems bioinformatics: increasing precision of computational diagnostics and therapeutics through network-based approaches. Brief. Bioinform. (2017). https://doi.org/10.1093/bib/bbx151

8. Michael Kelm, B., Wels, M., Kevin Zhou, S., et al.: Spine detection in CT and MR using iterated marginal space learning. Med. Image Anal. **17**, 1283–1292 (2013). https://doi.org/10.1016/J.MEDIA.2012.09.007

9. Neto, A.R.R., Barreto, G.A.: On the application of ensembles of classifiers to the diagnosis of pathologies of the vertebral column: a comparative analysis. IEEE Lat. Am. Trans. **7**, 487–496 (2009). https://doi.org/10.1109/TLA.2009.5349049

10. Servadei, L., Schmidt, R., Bär, F.: Artificial neural network for supporting medical decision making: a decision model and notation approach to spondylolisthesis and disk hernia. In: Ciuciu, I., Debruyne, C., Panetto, H., Weichhart, G., Bollen, P., Fensel, A., Vidal, M.-E. (eds.) OTM 2016. LNCS, vol. 10034, pp. 217–227. Springer, Cham (2017). https://doi.org/10.1007/978-3-319-55961-2_22

11. Huang, M.-L., Hung, Y.-H., Liu, D.-M.: Diagnostic prediction of vertebral column using rough set theory and neural network technique. Inf. Technol. J. **13**, 874–884 (2014). https://doi.org/10.3923/itj.2014.874.884

12. Prasetio, R.T., Riana, D.: A comparison of classification methods in vertebral column disorder with the application of genetic algorithm and bagging. In: 4th International Conference on Instrumentation, Communications, Information Technology, and Biomedical Engineering (ICICI-BME), pp 163–168. IEEE (2015)

13. Contreras, J., Claudia Bonfante, M., Quintana, A., Castro, V.: Fuzzy classifier for the diagnosis of pathology on the vertebral column. IEEE Lat. Am. Trans. **12**, 1149–1154 (2014). https://doi.org/10.1109/TLA.2014.6894013

14. Kotti, M., Diamantaras, K.I.: Towards minimizing the energy of slack variables for binary classification. In: 20th European Signal Processing Conference (EUSIPCO 2012). EURASIP, Bucharest, pp. 644–648 (2012)

15. Babalık, A., Babaoğlu, İ., Özkış, A.: A pre-processing approach based on artificial bee colony for classification by support vector machine. Int. J. Comput. Commun. Eng. 68–70 (2013). https://doi.org/10.7763/IJCCE.2013.V2.139

16. Tebet, M.A.: Conceitos atuais sobre equilíbrio sagital e classificação da espondilólise e espondilolistese. Rev. Bras. Ortop. **49**, 3–12 (2014). https://doi.org/10.1016/J.RBO.2013.04.011

17. Sasani, M., Aydin, A.L., Oktenoglu, T., et al.: The combined use of a posterior dynamic transpedicular stabilization system and a prosthetic disc nucleus device in treating lumbar degenerative disc disease with disc herniations. Int. J. Spine Surg. **2**, 130–136 (2008). https://doi.org/10.1016/SASJ-2008-0008-NT

18. Espitia, H.E., Soriano, J.J.: Sistema de inferencia difusa basado en relaciones Booleanas. Ingeniería **15**, 52–66 (2010)

19. Long, L., Zhao, J.: Adaptive fuzzy output-feedback dynamic surface control of MIMO switched nonlinear systems with unknown gain signs. Fuzzy Sets Syst. **302**, 27–51 (2016). https://doi.org/10.1016/J.FSS.2015.12.006

20. Villate, A., Rincon, D.E., Melgarejo, M.A.: Sintonización de Sistemas Difusos utilizando Evolución Diferencial. In: XVIII International Congress of Electronic, Electrical and Systems Engineering, Lima, pp 1–8 (2011)

21. Zadeh, L.A.: Fuzzy sets. Inf. Control **8**, 338–353 (1965). Zadeh, L.A.: Similarity relations and fuzzy orderings. Inf. Sci. **3**, 177–200 (1971). Goguen, J.A.: J. Symb. Log. **38**, 656–657 (1973). https://doi.org/10.2307/2272014
22. Baquero Hernández, L.R., Rodríguez Valdés, O., Ciudad Ricardo, F.Á.: Lógica Difusa Basada en la Experiencia del Usuario para Medir la Usabilidad. Rev. Latinoam. Ing. Softw. **4**, 48 (2016). https://doi.org/10.18294/relais.2016.48-54
23. Osisanwo, F.Y., Akinsola, J.E.T., Akinjobi, J., et al.: Supervised machine learning algorithms: classification and comparison. Int. J. Comput. Trends Technol. **48**, 128–138 (2017). https://doi.org/10.14445/22312803/IJCTT-V48P126
24. Celemín-páez, C.E., Martínez-gómez, H.A., Melgarejo, M.: Fuzzy classifiers tuning using genetic algorithms with FCM-based initialization. Ing. y Compet. **15**, 9–20 (2013). https://doi.org/10.25100/iyc.v15i1
25. Dheeru, D., Karra Taniskidou, E.: UCI Machine Learning Repository: Vertebral Column Data Set (2017). http://archive.ics.uci.edu/ml. Accessed 8 June 2017
26. Bravo, S., Cruz, J.: Estudios de exactitud diagnóstica: Herramientas para su Interpretación Diagnostic accuracy studies: Tools for its Interpretation. Rev. Chil. Radiol. año. (2015). https://doi.org/10.4067/S0717-93082015000400007
27. Hancock, M., Kent, P.: Interpretation of dichotomous outcomes: risk, odds, risk ratios, odds ratios and number needed to treat. J. Physiother. **62**, 172–174 (2016). https://doi.org/10.1016/j.jphys.2016.02.016
28. Gogtay, N.J., Thatte, U.M.: Statistical Evaluation of Diagnostic Tests (Part 1): Sensitivity, Specificity, Positive and Negative Predictive Values Introduction to Screening and Diagnostic Tests (2017)
29. Silva Fuente-Alba, C., Molina Villagra, M.: Likelihood ratio (razón de verosimilitud): definición y aplicación en Radiología. Rev. Argentina Radiol. **81**, 204–208 (2017). https://doi.org/10.1016/j.rard.2016.11.002
30. Schwartz, A.: Diagnostic Test Calculator (2006)

Internet of Things

From a Home-Area-Network to a Secure Internet of Things Application

Maryori Sabalza-Mejia⑩, Luz Magre-Colorado⑩, Ivan Baños⑩,
and Juan Carlos Martínez-Santos⁽✉⁾⑩

Program of Electrical and Electronics Engineering,
Universidad Tecnologica de Bolivar, Cartagena, Bolivar 130010, Colombia
maryorism730@gmail.com, luz0928@gmail.com, ivanalejandrobanos@gmail.com,
jcmartinezs@utb.edu.co

Abstract. In this paper, we present a secure system to control devices at home through the web, which we implement based on the Do It Yourself (DIY) culture. We use a model based on the Goal Question Metric approach to evaluate the quality of our system. Given that we are now in the era of the Internet of Things (IoT), security must be at the same level or even in a higher priority than other aspects such as speed, size, and power consumption. The objective of this work is to verify that acceptable levels of confidentiality, integrity, availability, access control, authentication and non-repudiation can be guaranteed in open platforms such as Arduino, Galileo, Energia, Tiva C, among others. Taking into account these platforms, we developed a system with access control that implements motion detection, light control, and generates a power consumption record. The results show a comparison between our security implementation and other authors' implementation.

Keywords: Security · Internet of Things · Home area network · TDES · Open source

1 Introduction

Nowadays there are more "things" than people connected to the Internet. People have opted to control their home from a computer or cellphone because they want to turn on/off the lights, setup the air conditioning, review the status of their alarms, among other things, at any time.

In the rising of the Internet of Things (IoT), developers have designed and implemented secure systems to ensure that our home will be protected even though it is connected to the Internet. Moreover, people can connect devices to the Internet in their own homes, to monitor their house using a physical IP address, but they do not take security as a critical aspect. Without security, there is no protection of the information sent from the sensors and anyone could have control of the household. An attacker gets access to the network after

© Springer Nature Switzerland AG 2019
J. C. Figueroa-García et al. (Eds.): WEA 2019, CCIS 1052, pp. 475–486, 2019.
https://doi.org/10.1007/978-3-030-31019-6_40

participating in the routing structure. From there, the intruder can send messages to any network node depending on where the attacker is. With that kind of access, such attacker may delay, reorder or drop legitimate packets [8]. This scenario is shown in Fig. 1. Until today different alternatives for IoT have been designed targeting the security issue, it is worth mentioning the Framework for Cyber-Physical Systems for IoT [23]. This framework recommended assurance of confidentiality, integrity, and availability.

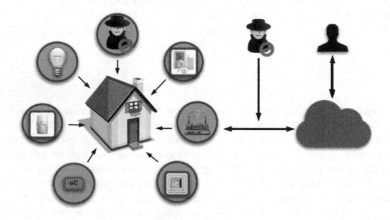

Fig. 1. A non-secure scenario

For this reason, the problem revolving around this work is how to ensure that a low-cost hardware/software system meets acceptable security levels. Could a microcontroller-based system withstand the levels of encryption needed to handle information through a network? This research borne of a previous work [24].

Our project proposes a DIY low-cost hardware/software system, based on micro-controllers that ensures the user satisfactory levels of security. It provides the user the ability to control their devices from anywhere in a secure way. We used open source platforms such as Arduino (UNO and Galileo) and Energia (Tiva-C Launchpad). These devices have an affordable cost. We also used HyperText Markup Language (HTML) to design the web application. Besides that, we used an Structured Query Language (SQL) server [6] in order to create our database and store the information collected by the system.

This article is organized as follows. In Sect. 2, we explain why to use TDES. In Sect. 3, we present the system requirements for the design of our system. Section 4 introduces the details of our implementation. Section 5 depicts the results of this project. Section 6 presents the related work. Finally, Sect. 7 concludes our paper.

2   Encryption Algorithm: Why TDES?

TDES is a triple data encryption algorithm and is classified as symmetric because it uses 3 keys in the Encrypt-Decrypt-Encrypt (EDE) mode so the combined key size is 168 bits. For the encryption in the system, we used TDES encryption instead of AES. We chose TDES because it is easy to implement, so for DIY projects it is appropriate. Because even though AES is faster than TDES, there is almost no difference in performance in this case, given that the information that is sent from the sensors is very small, and we could not possibly reach the 32 GB of information threshold. Also, the availability of the library was an important factor when deciding which algorithm to use.

3   System Requirements

There are many elements, such as sensors, actuators, and other devices, that can be used to control our home's gadgets from the Internet, and multiple micro-controllers are there to implement it. However, what you should never miss in these systems, is security. So it should be noted that there are security standards and requirements for these systems in order to ensure that only authorized users can monitor and control these home systems. Below, we give an overview about the meaning of each necessary requirement.

In order to obtain a low-cost hardware/software system that ensures the users can connect devices to the Internet securely, our system has to meet both the FIPS 199 [1] and ISO 7498-2 [12] requirements. These standards establish the definitions of confidentiality, integrity, availability, authentication, access control and non-repudiation. We used these requirement definitions as reference in our final design.

4   Implementation Details

Figure 2 shows a diagram of our system. The main components of our system are the "*things*", the *web application*, and the *users*. The "*things*" are sensors and actuators controlled by micro-controller-based boards like Arduino (UNO R2, Arduino, Italy) or Tiva C (Series TM4C123G, Texas Instruments, Texas) that are connected to the Internet through an Arduino Ethernet Shield (W5100, WIZnet, Silicon Valley). Our system requires at least one Ethernet module to be connected and considered an IoT application. The *web application* is developed using Bootstrap [5] and it allows us to handle our SQL server-based database, our authentication system, and the user interface using HTML language and .NET (Open Source Cross Platform Development). Finally, the *users* are people who have the authorization to access the system. As we can see, the deployment is divided into four stages.

4.1   Stage 1 - Basic Setup

We check the connection between a "thing" and a local server through a LAN. At this stage, we just set up the interconnection between a microcontroller, an Ethernet shield, a router, a computer, and a sensor/actuator. The interface between

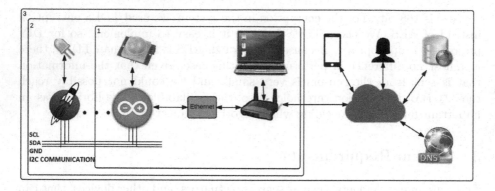

Fig. 2. Diagram of the system.

the Ethernet module and micro-controller is through libraries designed for the Arduino Ethernet shield that comes with the test of Dynamic Host Configuration Protocol (DHCP). It allows the user to know what is the IP address assigned to the "thing" [4]. Box 1 of Fig. 2 shows a "thing" with a sensor/actuator. However, our approach can support multiple sensors and actuators connected to the same board as well as many things connected directly to the router.

4.2   Stage 2 - Network Sensor Communications

The next step was to set up a network sensor communication. We decided to establish an Inter-Integrated Circuit (I2C) interface. This is a multi-master, multi-slave, single-ended, serial computer bus. Then, "things" (digital sensors and actuators) send information to a Board-Slave that later is forwarded to a Board-Master, that is responsible for loading the information to the local web server. The information is visible to the user upon request. We implemented communication between platforms using the *Wire.h* library [3] that supports both Arduino and the Tiva C boards, this allows them to use the I2C communication protocol. At this point, we are able to connect an Arduino UNO, an Arduino Galileo [7], and a Tiva C board[1]. See Box 2 of Fig. 2.

4.3   Stage 3 - Cloud Service

In this stage, we migrated our web server to the cloud, see Box 3 of Fig. 2. We used Ormuco Cloud Hosting[2]. We set up our Windows Server 2012 R2 on a virtual machine with one VCPU, 2 GB of RAM, 50 GB of storage, and a physical IP address that makes it available from anywhere. The Bootstrap's framework allows us to design a responsive web application. The server also supports our SQL server-based database.

---

[1] Tiva C Series TM4C123G LaunchPad Evaluation Board.
[2] Ormuco: The Connected Cloud.

4.4   Stage 4 - Security Implementation

In the following paragraphs, we present a summary for each security requirement and how we assure each one of them.

In the web application with the server, confidentiality is assured by using an encryption algorithm through the communication channels. To navigate through the web application, the HTTPS protocol is used by installing and configuring a SSL certificate on the Internet Information Server where the web application is deployed. Integrity is ensured by validating the data introduced by the user in the web application, in the client browser, and in the server, to mitigate the human error while filling any form in the application. To provide non-repudiation (the information is encrypted using the user's password), the system creates a registry with an action log table in the database for every action done while a session is active. The server checks if the authenticated user's role has the permission to navigate to a particular page before it's loaded to the browser. There are two different roles: administrator and regular users. Authentication is ensured by giving each user a unique user name.

In the communication between the server and the master (gateway) like at Fig. 3, confidentiality is assured by encrypting the messages between the things and the server using the TDES algorithm with a key established earlier in the process. To check the data integrity in the end of the communication channel, we used the SHA-1 hash function. Even though it has security vulnerabilities, it's faster than other SHA hash functions and the purpose of using this function is to ensure integrity, not confidentiality.

The "things" authenticate using Encrypt and Sign Mutual Authentication protocol depicted in Fig. 4, the authentication system only accepts passwords with at least 8 characters and containing one digit, one lower-case letter, one upper-case letter and one special character. The passwords are encrypted and stored using the SHA256 hash function and a random alphanumeric salt. The I2C communication protocol between the master and the slaves, the data taken from the sensors, and the actions that the user makes are stored in the database using the same encryption algorithm TDES, with an asymmetric key established by the user's and the thing's password. This is also used to check integrity and non-repudiation. For each "thing", an identification number is generated while they are created.

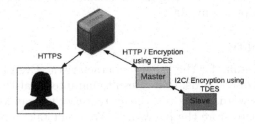

Fig. 3. Communication protocols

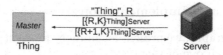

Fig. 4. Encrypt and Sign Mutual Authentication. Based on protocol shown by Stamp in [10].

5   Results

We demonstrated that is indispensable to guarantee security requirements such as: confidentiality, integrity, availability, authentication, access control and non-repudiation, using the model based on the Goal Question Metric approach (GQM) in DIY projects.

The GQM method is that the metric for the measurement must be oriented to objectives, this measurement model has three levels. The conceptual level (goal), the operational level (question), that is a set of questions used to characterize the way of assessment of an specific goal, and the quantitative level (metric) that is a set of data associated with every question in order to answer it in a quantitative way [16], the data could be either objective or subjective.

We have followed the main recommendations to secure our web application against many types of attacks that unintended users can use to gain control of other users' accounts, delete accounts and/or change data [2]. This approach mixes data filtering, encryption, and other methods to make any attack more difficult to succeed. We tried defending the system against SQL Injections, because the main problems of sql injections affect confidentiality, authentication and integrity of the user because all the information stored in the database is affected. We have tried to cover all the well-known vulnerabilities. So far; Session Hijacking, Network Eavesdropping, Cross Site Scripting, Brute Force Attacks, Covert Timing Channel Attacks.

The model expressed in [15], set as goals the security requirements, giving as a result six different goals. The metrics are mostly subjective. However, it gives us an understanding of our system and where to focus to improve in the future. Using the model, we obtained the following values. To calculate these values, a set of questions were answered giving each question a value from 0 to 1. The percentage was calculated by adding and dividing the result by the number of questions and multiplying by 100.

5.1   Confidentiality

In Table 1 are the results for the privacy characteristic. Even though there is an effort to have strong passwords, that doesn't guarantee that the users will surely choose a secure password. Moreover, the system uses the random .NET function to generate the salt to store the passwords. We don't take into account characteristic seven because no data is required to comply with any legal requirements. The total percentage is 83%.

Table 1. Results for confidentiality

Characteristic	Result
1. Data transmission security	1
2. Password strength	0,8
3. Password storing	1
4. Data classification	1
5. Critical data management	0,5
6. Critical modules management	1
7. Data compliance with any legal requirement	NA
8. Random numbers generation	0,5
Total	83%

5.2   Integrity

In Table 2 are the results for the Integrity characteristic. The problem is that the system only does two validation checking out of more than 10 set of inputs. Moreover, the system doesn't have a proper way to protect itself against a malfunction and doesn't ensure synchronization. The percentage is 67%.

Table 2. Results for integrity

Characteristic	Result
1. Validation process for a set of inputs	0,5
2. Authentication method	1
3. Integrity assurance	0,5
4. Error checking and exception handle management	1
5. Numbers of critical class or module that process data	0,5
6. Synchronization management	0
Total	67%

5.3   Availability

The availability requirement is mostly delegated to the cloud provider, that guarantees a 99,9% availability. Nevertheless, there is an interaction between the application and the gateway of the controllers that could be a point of failure depending on the internet connection on the gateway side.

5.4   Identification, Authentication and Authorization

In Table 3 are the results for the identification, authentication and authorization characteristic. The issue with authorization is that we only have two roles and they can access all the resources they have authorization for. The percentage is 86%.

Table 3. Results for identification, authentication and authorization

Characteristic	Result
1. User identification	1
2. Authentication method	1
3. Authentication session management	1
4. Total failed login attempts	1
5. User authorization method	0,5
6. Resources and level of use management	0,5
7. Number of authentication/authorization layers	1
Total	86%

5.5   Non Repudiation

In Table 4 are the results for the characteristic of non repudiation. The only problem here is that we post a table with the logs, but there is no filters by date, making the search annoying. The percentage is 93%.

Table 4. Results for non repudiation

Characteristic	Result
1. Attributes considered for proof of transaction	1
2. Log file access	1
3. Interaction entry in log checking	0,8
Total	93%

In our point of view, a system requirement has good quality if its percentage is over 80%. However, that doesn't mean that a lower percentage gives a bad qualification, but it gives us points for improvement. In our case, we have to focus on the integrity requirement.

6   Related Work

There are several secure approaches out there, we will compare the security requirements applied to some of these to our proposed system.

6.1   Commercial Systems

Existing companies such as: Devicehub.net, Nearbus.net, Ubidots.com and Temboo.com that provide services that allow users to connect and monitor their household objects through their platforms in exchange for a monthly fee.

The Nearbus platform replicates a small part of the microcontroller's memory into the Cloud. This system uses its own communication protocol between the platform and the device. This platform only monitors the connectivity between a microcontroller and the cloud. Our application instead, allows to control devices and visualize the collected data from sensors.

Devicehub.net offers a Platform as a Service (PaaS) in which the hardware/mobile developers can connect and remotely manage multiple devices. This platform offers control and visualization of digital/analog sensors, map sensors and digital/analog actuators. Our application does not offer the mapping of the sensors but the user administrator has its own control panel to add devices or assign users to each room.

Ubidots is a platform that allows to control, monitor and automate hardware solutions connected to the internet, in 2018 it was deployed in education so that people who study IoT can build, develop and test their solutions.

Temboo is a platform that integrates embedded systems such as Arduino, Raspberry pi to implement/execute automated systems over the internet, in order to connect any type of sensor to the cloud.

This platforms use a login to authenticate a user, and the user will get an ID for each device that registers into the system. Also, they use encryption in their communication protocol to guarantee confidentiality. They don't mention anything about non-reputation and access control.

6.2   Non-commercial Systems

Pirbhulal et al. [17] developed a secure home and automation system based on IoT using wireless sensor networks (WSN), encrypting the data from the proposed algorithm: Triangle-based security algorithm (TBSA), which is based on an efficient key generation mechanism. According to this work, the requirements for a secure IoT system are: Authentication, Trustworthiness, Data Freshness, Confidentiality and privacy, Sensor localization, Integrity, Non-repudiation, Availability, Access control.

Han et al. [18] proposes security conditions for a smart home, which are based on meeting the requirements of confidentiality, integrity and availability. For confidentiality, sending data from the smart device at home to another device must be done with encrypted text and a password of more than 8 characters.

They use the 128 bit encryption algorithm to prevent an intruder from replicating and modify the data. Likewise, passwords of domestic devices must be configured to be highly secure and changed periodically. To ensure integrity, it is recommended to include access control and mutual authentication in the sensors through the domestic gateway. Verification of firmware integrity is recommended for availability.

A solution presented by Henze et al. [9], satisfies confidentiality and access control due to their focus on the implementation of privacy for cloud-based services of the IoT. Here, they introduce the Privacy Enforcement Points (PEP), these act as a representative of each user and allows them to remain in control over security and privacy requirements. This implementation provides confidentiality and prevents unauthorized access. However, they make no mention to the integrity, availability, authentication, and no-repudiation requirements.

The solution of Li et al. [13] provides confidentiality, integrity, and authentication because they use an authentication and encryption mechanism. They also control users access, because only trusted users can authenticate themselves with the server synchronously.

The solution proposed by Li et al. [14], satisfies confidentiality and access control by adopting an ABE encryption system to send information to the control server from the devices. Using the digital signature technology and a hash function, they can guarantee authentication and integrity. Availability is assumed by the author.

Lounis [11], uses the Attribute-Based Encryption (ABE). ABE ciphers the data before uploading them to the cloud. They don't need to trust the server to prevent unauthorized access, because the access policies are already embedded in the ciphered text. This solution, satisfies all the security criteria that we are looking for. However, this solution is for medical applications and may vary according to the Healthcare Authority (HA) policies. Our system, besides fulfilling all the criteria, is a low-cost approach for home automation.

Other proposals for secure smart home by Stergiou et al. [19] and Santoso et al. [20] use asymmetric cryptography AES so that it is only the user that configures, accesses and controls the system of their house. However, other methods have been implemented like Simon/Speck [22], these are cryptographic algorithms for devices limited in processing, memory and resources which can be used in I2C or 1-wire protocols. For example in the solution presented by Magre et al. [21], where they implement this protocol to secure a home automation system.

These projects contribute to the security implementation on information systems. They try to focus on specific features. However, almost one of those cover all the secure features neither were developed for low-cost platforms.

7   Conclusions and Future Work

This paper describes a low-cost DIY hardware/software system that meets both the FIPS 199 and ISO 7498-2 standards.

For confidentiality, we used both symmetric and public key encryption. Encryption also helps us to ensure integrity and non-repudiation of the data stored on the database as the transmissions between the actors of the system. To guarantee availability, we rely on good coding practices in conjunction with hosting services that provide infrastructure such as firewalls, proxies, caches, redundancy, etc. That helps us to mitigate Denial-of-Service attacks and related attacks. An authentication system allows us to set up an identification and password to each user and thing connected to our system as well as the database. We also set up different roles that allow to handle our system.

Given that the result of the quantitative evaluation does not reach 100%, the system still has room for improvement in future implementations.

Acknowledgments. We would like to thank the anonymous WEA reviewers for their comments and feedback on the ideas in this paper and Tecnologica de Bolivar University for their support.

References

1. FIPS Pub: Standards for security categorization of federal information and information systems. NIST FIPS 199 (2004)
2. Nixon, R.: Learning PHP, MySQL, JavaScript, and CSS: A Step-by-Step Guide to Creating Dynamic Websites. O'Reilly Media Inc., Beijing (2012)
3. Nicholas Zambetti: Wire.h library (2006)
4. Margolis, M.: Arduino Cookbook: Recipes to Begin, Expand, and Enhance Your Projects. O'Reilly Media Inc., Sebastopol (2011)
5. Bootstrap framework. https://uxplanet.org/how-to-customize-bootstrap-b8078a011203. Accessed 8 Apr 2016
6. Bulger, B., Greenspan, J., Wall, D.: MySQL/PHP Database Applications. Wiley, New York (2003)
7. Ramon, M.C.: Intel Galileo and Intel Galileo Gen 2. Intel® Galileo and Intel® Galileo Gen 2, pp. 1–33. Apress, Berkeley, CA (2014). https://doi.org/10.1007/978-1-4302-6838-3_1
8. Hummen, R., Hiller, J., Wirtz, H., Henze, M., Shafagh, H., Wehrle, K.: 6LoWPAN fragmentation attacks and mitigation mechanisms. In: Proceedings of the Sixth ACM Conference on Security and Privacy in Wireless and Mobile Networks, pp. 55–66. ACM, April 2013
9. Henze, M., Hermerschmidt, L., Kerpen, D., Huling, R., Rumpe, B., Wehrle, K.: User-driven privacy enforcement for cloud-based services in the internet of things. In: 2014 International Conference on Future Internet of Things and Cloud, pp. 191–196. IEEE, August 2014
10. Stamp, M.: Information Security: Principles and Practice. Wiley, Hoboken (2011)
11. Lounis, A., Hadjidj, A., Bouabdallah, A., Challal, Y.: Secure and scalable cloud-based architecture for e-health wireless sensor networks. In: 2012 21st International Conference on Computer Communications and Networks (ICCCN), pp. 1–7. IEEE, July 2012
12. International Organization for Standardization: Technical Committee ISO/TC 97: ISO7498-2: Information processing system, open system interconnection, basic reference mode. Part 2: security architecture. International Organization for Standardization (1989)

13. Li, X., Xuan, Z., Wen, L.: Research on the architecture of trusted security system based on the internet of things. In: 2011 Fourth International Conference on Intelligent Computation Technology and Automation, vol. 2, pp. 1172–1175. IEEE, March 2011

14. Li, D., Sampalli, S., Aung, Z., Williams, J., Sanchez, A.: Fine-grained encryption for search and rescue operation on Internet of Things. In: Asia-Pacific World Congress on Computer Science and Engineering, pp. 1–9. IEEE, November 2014

15. Islam, S., Falcarin, P.: Measuring security requirements for software security. In: 2011 IEEE 10th International Conference on Cybernetic Intelligent Systems (CIS), pp. 70–75. IEEE, September 2011

16. Van Solingen, R., Basili, V., Caldiera, G., Rombach, H.D.: Goal question metric (GQM) approach. In: Encyclopedia of Software Engineering (2002)

17. Pirbhulal, S., et al.: A novel secure IoT-based smart home automation system using a wireless sensor network. Sensors 17(1), 69 (2017)

18. Han, J.H., Jeon, Y., Kim, J.: Security considerations for secure and trustworthy smart home system in the IoT environment. In: 2015 International Conference on Information and Communication Technology Convergence (ICTC), pp. 1116–1118. IEEE, October 2015

19. Stergiou, C., Psannis, K.E., Kim, B.G., Gupta, B.: Secure integration of IoT and cloud computing. Future Gener. Comput. Syst. 78, 964–975 (2018)

20. Santoso, F.K., Vun, N.C.: Securing IoT for smart home system. In: 2015 International Symposium on Consumer Electronics (ISCE), pp. 1–2. IEEE, June 2015

21. Magre Colorado, L.A., Martíincz Santos, J.C.: Leveraging 1-wire communication bus system for secure home automation. In: Solano, A., Ordoñez, H. (eds.) CCC 2017. CCIS, vol. 735, pp. 759–771. Springer, Cham (2017). https://doi.org/10.1007/978-3-319-66562-7_54

22. Beaulieu, R., Treatman-Clark, S., Shors, D., Weeks, B., Smith, J., Wingers, L.: The SIMON and SPECK lightweight block ciphers. In: 2015 52nd ACM/EDAC/IEEE Design Automation Conference (DAC), pp. 1–6. IEEE, June 2015

23. Griffor, E.R., Greer, C., Wollman, D.A., Burns, M.J.: Framework for cyber-physical systems: volume 1, overview (No. Special Publication (NIST SP)-1500-201) (2017)

24. Sabalza, M.M., Santos, J.C.M.: Design and construction of a power meter to optimize usage of the electric power. In: 2014 III International Congress of Engineering Mechatronics and Automation (CIIMA), pp. 1–5. IEEE, October 2014

A Personal Activity Recognition System Based on Smart Devices

Harold Murcia[✉] and Juanita Triana

Facultad de Ingeniería, Universidad de Ibagué, Ibagué 730002, Colombia
harold.murcia@unibague.edu.co

Abstract. With the continuous evolution of technology, mobile devices are becoming more and more important in people's lives. In the same way, new needs related to the information provided by their users arise, making evident the need to develop systems that take advantage of their daily use. The recognition of personal activity based on the information provided by the last generation mobile devices can easily be considered as an useful tool for many purposes and future applications. This paper presents the use of information provided from two smart devices in different acquisition schemes, assessing conventional supervised classifiers to recognize personal activity by an identification of seven classes. The classifiers were trained with a generated database from eight users and were evaluated in offline mode with other two generated databases. The prediction experiments were qualified by using F1-score indicator and were compared with the native prediction from the cellphone. The obtained results presented a maximum F1-score of 100% for the first validation test and 80.7% for the second validation test.

Keywords: Activity recognition · Machine learning · Wearable devices · Cell phone data · Myo armband

1 Introduction

Colombia the latest years has been highly influenced by the intelligent devices use like the global trend, from applications for home tasks to industry processes. Nonetheless, the majority of users and developers, use their smart devices generally with communication or entertainment purposes, ignoring the big potential offered by the different sensors and small elements that this device incorporates, and how this subsystems combination could offer additional benefits variety, for example, the personal activity recognition, which is a new study field [1,2] that pretends to provide intelligent systems users with new perception tools, so they can be the fundamental inputs of different software elements that ease the devices use, perform specific actions by themselves, or carry out automatic tasks that favour daily activities, i.e: help people with special needs, furthermore permits to device some autonomy. An example of this technology consist in the task and states activation in function of automatic recognition activities, e.g: disable the

© Springer Nature Switzerland AG 2019
J. C. Figueroa-García et al. (Eds.): WEA 2019, CCIS 1052, pp. 487–499, 2019.
https://doi.org/10.1007/978-3-030-31019-6_41

phones while their users are executing risky tasks like driving, could reduce the automobile accident rates, play back automatically a song list when the phone detects the start of users physic activity; perform accurate calorie counting in situations of physical activity; identify the interests of a user, among others. Another interest applications mentioned by other authors to use activity detectors on mobile devices are: People fall detection, in [3] an algorithm that can detect when someone fall out, based on data from cellphone accelerometers was designed; detection of drunk drivers, where a cellphone could be used to detect if someone is driving under alcohol effects, or to detect the type of conduction, as well as was proposed in [4] and [5] respectively. This could mean a huge opportunity to correct the way that people do some activities. Nonetheless, to establish the mentioned functions, is necessary to know and tap in a combined way all sensors that intelligent devices incorporates, such as: accelerometers, microphones, gyroscopes, cameras, etc; which could be potentials information sources underutilized on these devices.

This paper presents the design and development of an activity recognition system based on a cellphone and a gesture armband device, in the same way, it provides a comparison of different acquisition schemes and classifiers for seven activities. The paper is organized as follows: next section describes the related work, Sect. 3 explain the used methodology on this work, the obtained results for a validation database predictions and a routine prediction are presented in Sect. 4. Finally, the paper ends with conclusions in Sect. 5, acknowledgments and references.

2   Related Work

A lot of work has been done on the activity recognition based on pure accelerometers like the ones described in [1] and [2]. Despite having different classifiers, some authors have chosen to use simpler methods, which recognize some patterns or behaviors of the signals and take decisions from tuned parameters e.g: Decision tree [3] and pattern matching [4]. Some other works has reported detection of simple activities such as: running, walking and standing by using HHMM (Hierarchical hidden Markov-;Models) which also can predict more complex activities like shopping or taking a bus [6]. Other authors used multilayer perceptron as classifier, getting good scores for predictions [7] and [8]. In [5] the authors used Dynamic Time Warping (DTW) classification, this method is a similarity measuring between two temporal sequences which may vary in speed [9]. In addition, with a greater affinity to our purpose, in [10] and [11] the proposed system used sensors in a wrist or armband, providing different information that performs better recognizing in some activities, in our work we use not only the armband but also the signals provided by the sensors of the cell phone, which allows us to have a greater number of useful variables to calculate the predictions. Finally, the Table 1 summarizes the principal work of different authors that made a great contribution in activity recognition using wearable devices.

Table 1. Related work of activity recognition with wearable technology. Where: W time = window time, acc = accelerometer, mag = magnetometer, gyro:gyroscope and ~ represents no data.

Classifier	#Classes	#Features	Source	App.	W time	Ref.
Multilayer Perceptron	6	6	acc	Activity Recognition	10 s	[7]
Decision Tree	1	3	acc	Fall detection	10 s	[3]
AdaBoost, RF	1	7	acc and gyro	Freezing of gait detection	1 s and 4 s	[12]
DTW	8	1	acc, gyro, mag	Driving style	3 s	[5]
Pattern matching	2	4	acc. and orientation	Drunk detection	5 s	[4]
SVM	18	4	acc	Object and gesture recognition	5 s	[10]
HMM	7	~	acc	training action/activity recognition	5 s	[6]
Multilayer perceptron	9	1	acc	Activity recognition	~	[8]

3   Activity Recognition

This section describes the activity recognition and the process to perform this task, starting with the methodology and ending up with the feature reduction. The activity recognition can be summarized as determining a set of activities (Targets), collecting sensor readings (features), and assigning sensor readings to appropriate activities (Classes). Two acquisition schemes are proposed: using only the cellphone and combining the cellphone with a Myo armband, both evaluated under three combinations of descriptors: All the descriptors (Full features FF), a selected group of descriptors (Best Features BF) and in a tree topology (Hierarchical H). The Fig. 1 shows the steps to achieve the activity recognition in this work, starting with the data collection and ending up with the classification for activity recognition.

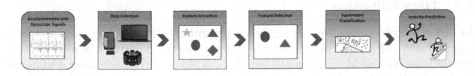

Fig. 1. The used framework for the activity recognition

3.1 Methodology

The scope of the objective of this project contemplates four stages proposed as follows:

1. Configuration of the acquisition system and interest variables, synchronizing the data from an iPhone 7 and a Myo armband.
2. Generation of a detailed database, with signals coming from different users with different age, structure and height; and labelling the real activity as Target in each case.
3. Implementation of five supervised classifiers for seven different activities, comparing the prediction performance of a cellphone respect to a cellphone combined with a Myo armband, as well as, the predictions by using all the features, a selected group of features and a hierarchical scheme.
4. Assessing the prediction variants in two experimental tests: with impersonal data and an user's routine that contents all the activities.

The first stage consisted in the design of procurement experiments and the hardware and software conditioning in a Linux environment with Python programming language, both the commercial measurement elements (smart-phone and wrist wearable device). The appropriate acquisition/transmission interfaces and the appropriate input variables were selected, as well as conditioning to synchronize the information and the activities of interest. During the second stage the experimental tests of acquisition were taken to establish at least one test per activity, each of them in 11 different users with different characteristics of height, weight and age. In addition, information had to be pre-processed in such a way that the known activity was recorded on each sample, as well as the user details that may have an impact on the classification algorithms. The generated database was separated in two parts: 70% (8 users) for training and 30% (3 users) for the first validation test. A second user's database was generated in a continuous routine with all the activities for validation purposes only. During the third stage, the processing algorithms for filtering and data normalization were determined in order to condition the information, to analyze the information and to determinate the features that gave rise to the different classification algorithms. Once the impact of the descriptors on the distinction between classes was evaluated, five supervised classification techniques were implemented to detect the activities. Finally, the trained predictors performance were validated and evaluated. Our code implementation and databases are available online on: https://github.com/HaroldMurcia/wearTECH.

3.2 Data Collection

In order to collect data for the supervised learning task, was necessary to use a smartphone and a wrist device, which read the electrical activity in muscles and includes an Inertial Measurement Unit IMU, in the way to experiment and prove if the classification is better with the band. However, this work only uses the IMU information from the Myo, leaving aside the electromyographic information.

To make reliable the data collection was necessary to implement an acquisition system between the smartphone, the Myo Armband and a computer with Linux Ubuntu 16.04 and Robotic Operating System ROS in Kinetic version (see Fig. 2), this system took real time data and saved it into the computer.

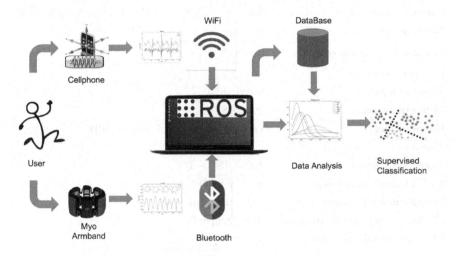

Fig. 2. Synchronized system for data collection and analysis

The acquisition system was divided in 2 important parts, on one hand, the collection of data from the smartphone was done through the use of an application that works on smartphones with operative system iOS called SensorLog, which connects to a computer via wifi with a data-rate up to 100 Hz; on the other hand, the data collection from the Myo armband was performed by using a ROS node, which allowed to get into the information recorded by the sensors in the armband through Bluetooth connection and saved it directly in the computer with a data-rate up to 50 Hz. An acquisition ROS-node was developed to facilitate the recording of fragments of data corresponding to different users and activities, as well as to facilitate the labeling for each case.

3.3 Features and Activity Description

This project considered 7 activities: Walking, running, ascending stairs, descending stairs, standing,driving a car and cycling. Each one presented a different behavior recorded from sensors of cellphone and the armband. When the information collected by these devices is combined each activity has an special pattern making them unique, after a search for information and analysis of the acquired signals the features to describe the pattern where defined, the Table 2 shows the analyzed functions that give rise to the information descriptors.

Table 2. Information of description functions

Function name	Equation
Statistics	
Norm	$\|S\| = \sqrt{s_x{}^2 + s_y{}^2 + s_z{}^2}$
Sum of norms	$Sn = \sum_{i=1}^{n} \|S_i\| = \|S_1\| + \|S_2\| + \ldots + \|S_n\|$
Norm average	$\bar{x} = \frac{Sn}{n}$
Standard deviation of norm	$\sigma = \sqrt{\sum_{i=1}^{n} \frac{\|S_i\|^2}{N} - \bar{x}}$
Kurtosis of norm	$\kappa = \frac{1}{n} \sum_{i=1}^{n} \frac{(x_i - \bar{x})^4}{\sigma^4}$
Maximum norm	$max(\|S\|)$
Minimum norm	$min(\|S\|)$
Range of norm	$range = max(\|S\|) - min(\|S\|)$
Fourier	
Norm with zero mean	$Sf = \|S\| - \bar{x}$
FFT of zero mean norm	$m = \mathscr{F}(Sf)$
Maximum FFT magnitude	$mf = max(m)$
Maximum magnitude frequency	$f = freq(mf)$
FFT-magnitude average	$\bar{x}m = \frac{1}{n} \sum_{i=1}^{n} m_i$
Standard deviation of FFT	$\sigma m = \sqrt{\sum_{i=1}^{n} \frac{m_i{}^2}{N} - \bar{x}m}$
Other cellphone instruments	
Altimeter derivative	$d = \frac{\delta}{\delta t} a(t)$
GPS-speed average	$V = \frac{1}{n} \sum_{i=1}^{n} |v|$
Altimeter average	$\bar{x}d = \frac{1}{n} \sum_{i=1}^{n} d_i$
Altimeter standard deviation	$\sigma d = \sqrt{\sum_{i=1}^{n} \frac{d_i{}^2}{N} - \bar{x}}$

Where m is the norm's Fourier transform, mf is the maximum value after the Fourier transform and f means the position of that maximum value; d means the signal that comes from the altimeter and v means the signal that comes from the GPS.

3.4   Features Reduction

Once the features are extracted from the data is possible to establish the array of Full Features, however, is important to do a preliminary evaluation of the impact of the features on the classes in order to remove the features with a low or null contribution to distinguish the classes. A simple method proposed in [13] based on the assumption of a normal distribution in each descriptor, consists of grouping each descriptor in each class and project its distribution based on the average and variance for each group, according to the Eq. 1.

$$f_{(x|k)} = \frac{1}{\sigma_{(x|k)}\sqrt{2 \times \pi}} \times e^{-\frac{\left(x_{(x|k)} - \mu_{(x|k)}\right)^2}{2\sigma^2_{(x|k)}}} \tag{1}$$

where, $\mu_{(x|k)}$ is the average of $x_{(x|k)}$, $\sigma(x|k)$ is the standard deviation of $x_{(x|k)}$ and $x_{(x|k)}$ is the individual descriptor data corresponding to the class k. Then, is feasible to asses each feature in a graph representation and its individual contribution to differentiate the distributions between them. In this way, the total set of descriptors is reduced by eliminating those that overlap the distributions among themselves, resulting in the space: Best Features. The Fig. 3 illustrates the probability distribution for three descriptors, the seven curves represent the seven classes in a common space. On one hand, the Fig. 3(a) shows a widely overlapped distributions, which means a low contribution to differentiating classes from each other, on the other hand, Fig. 3(b) and (c) show two descriptors with some isolated distribution curves, which represents that the data of these classes presented a sufficient distance to differentiate some of their classes, e.g: upstairs and downstairs for the average of the altimeter derivative or car and run for minimum of the accelerometer norm.

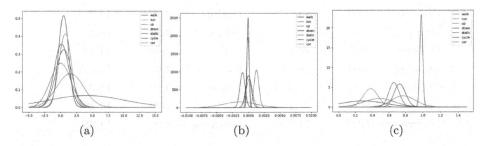

(a)   (b)   (c)

Fig. 3. Distribution of the descriptors to Feature reduction process: (a) kurtosis from smartphone gyroscopes (κ_{ig}), (b) Altimeter mean derivative (σd_{ia}), (c) Minimum of Myo armband accelerations (min_{ma})

Finally, the feature space f can be written as follows:

$$\mathbf{f} = \begin{cases} \bar{x}_{ia}, \kappa_{ia}, min_{ia}, V_{ia}, \bar{x}d_{ia}\sigma d_{ia}, mf_{ia}, f_{ia}, \bar{x}m_{ia}; \\ Sn_{ma}, \kappa_{ma}, min_{ma}, \bar{x}m_{ma}, \sigma m_{ma}; \\ \kappa_{ig}, min_{ig}, ran_{ig}, mf_{ig}, f_{ig}; \\ Sn_{mg}, \kappa_{mg}, min_{mg}, ran_{mg}, f_{mg}, \bar{x}m_{mg}; \end{cases} \tag{2}$$

where sub-index $_{ia}$ corresponds to the signals from smartphone accelerometer, sub-index $_{ig}$ corresponds to the signals from the smartphone gyroscope, and sub-index $_{ma}$ and sub-index $_{mg}$ correspond to the signals from the Myo accelerometer and the Myo gyroscope respectively.

4 Results

This section shows the obtained results, starting with a summary of the collected data and showing the results of the classifiers at different schemes and the prediction on a continuous activity routine.

The process to collect data was the one described in the section data collection. The Table 3 presents the number of samples for the training data set. Note that all the activities contain the same number of examples, mainly because the purpose was to have a fair classification. Once the data set was prepared, five classification techniques were implemented by using the library scikit-learn in Python: Random Forest RF, Support Vector Machine SVM, Neural Network NN, Adaboost and Gaussian Naive Bayes.

Table 3. Number of Samples of each activity in the training database

Training data set					
Smartphone			Smartphone+Myo		
Label	#Samples	Percentage	Label	#Samples	Percentage
Upstairs	2400	14,28%	Upstairs	3600	14,28%
Standing	2400	14,28%	Standing	3600	14,28%
Walking	2400	14,28%	Walking	3600	14,28%
Running	2400	14,28%	Running	3600	14,28%
Cycling	2400	14,28%	Cycling	3600	14,28%
Car	2400	14,28%	Car	3600	14,28%
Downstairs	2400	14,28%	Downstairs	3600	14,28%

4.1 Classification Results

The F1-score was selected as the evaluation indicator, which ranks the prediction from each classifier in a comparison with the Target, based on precision and recall parameters, which in turn are based on a count of True Positives TP, True Negatives TN, False Positives FP and False Negatives FN:

$$F1 = 2 \times \frac{precision \times recall}{precision + recall} \tag{3}$$

It quantify the precision and recall scores in a way that puts the emphasis on having both of them as high as possible (F1 = 0 if either precision or recall is equal to zero, and F1 = 1 implies that both precision and recall are equal to one). The summary results for our activity recognition experiments are presented in the Table 4. This table specifies the predictive accuracy associated with each of the activities, for each of the five learning algorithms, in each class and features groping method. Furthermore, table presents F1-score results for both acquisition schemes: smartphone and smartphone combined with the Myo armband. The obtained results for prediction shows a good performance of the data information showing predictions with percentages close to 100% in most activities. The grouping of features has a notable impact on the prediction, with the Hierarchical scheme getting most of the best results in average, followed by the grouping "Best Features" which reduces the number of descriptors, both in the case of the smartphone acquisition and in the acquisition combined with Myo armband. Regarding the classifiers in the smartphone acquisition, the Random Forest obtained a perfect score in Hierarchical mode, followed by Neural Network in Hierarchical mode. For the combined acquisition with Myo armband the Random Forest Classifier had the Best score with a 85.44% followed by the Adaboost Classifier with a score of 85.30%. Average results also can rank classes according to their ease to distinguish themselves from others, for smartphone acquisition the rank is: Standing, car, cycling, upstairs, running, walking and downstairs; and for combined acquisition with Myo armband the rank is: Standing, car, running, walking, cycling, upstairs and downstairs. Finally, the assessment of the contribution of the Myo, didn't reflect a significant change, given that in most of the cases the score decrease in combined acquisition mode, with the exception of the classes: running and walking, which increase its average scores by adding the data coming from Myo armband. This may be due to the fact that it is these classes that reflect a greater amount of energy in the movements of the arms and therefore a greater variation of information is captured by the Myo band. Therefore, running and walking activities are the only classes that benefit from the additional use of the Myo. However, it is important to highlight that Myo armband has a low sampling frequency, bearing in mind that some studies indicate that raising the acquisition frequencies in wrist devices broadens the prediction possibilities [10].

4.2   Routine Prediction

This section presents a second test for prediction validation. From the results of the Table 5 the Random Forest Classifier was selected to predict the activity from a Routine database that recompiled all the activities, and was compared with the smartphone native prediction, it is important to highlight that was necessary to add a new activity called undefined with the purpose to be more exact with the prediction. The Fig. 4 illustrates the result of this experiment test, in this case the numbers given to each activity are the same for both predictors, native and Random Forest.

Table 4. F1-score results for the first validation database with each activity and classifier in three study cases: FF = Full Features, BF = Best features and H = hierarchical method, ~ represents no data; and F1-score results for native smartphone prediction.

		Smartphone						
		RF	SVM	NN	AdaBoost	Gauss	Average	Native Pred.
Upstairs	FF	0.800	0.000	0.333	0.800	0.000	0.386	~
	BF	0.500	0.571	0.500	0.800	0.000	0.474	~
	H	1.000	0.800	0.800	1.000	0.666	**0.853**	~
Standing	FF	1.000	1.000	1.000	1.000	1.000	0.800	0.854
	BF	1.000	1.000	1.000	1.000	1.000	**1.000**	0.854
	H	1.000	1.000	1.000	1.000	1.000	**1.000**	0.854
Walking	FF	0.857	0.333	0.666	0.800	0.444	**0.620**	0.360
	BF	0.666	0.000	0.333	0.666	0.500	0.433	0.360
	H	1.000	0.000	0.400	0.333	0.571	0.460	0.360
Running	FF	0.800	0.000	0.666	0.666	0.333	0.493	0.000
	BF	0.857	0.857	0.666	1.000	0.666	**0.809**	0.000
	H	1.000	0.666	0.750	0.857	0.400	0.734	0.000
Cycling	FF	1.000	0.000	0.400	0.750	0.000	0.430	0.000
	BF	1.000	1.000	1.000	0.857	0.666	0.904	0.000
	H	1.000	1.000	1.000	0.857	0.800	**0.931**	0.000
Car	FF	1.000	0.800	1.000	0.800	0.666	0.853	0.800
	BF	1.000	0.800	1.000	0.800	1.000	0.920	0.800
	H	1.000	1.000	1.000	0.800	1.000	**0.960**	0.800
DownStairs	FF	0.857	0.000	0.500	0.571	0.000	0.385	~
	BF	0.857	0.500	0.400	0.857	0.000	0.522	~
	H	1.000	0.600	0.666	0.000	0.571	**0.567**	~
		Smartphone+Myo						
		RF	SVM	NN	AdaBoost	Gauss	Average	
Upstairs	FF	0.000	0.400	0.333	0.800	0.000	0.306	~
	BF	0.800	0.285	0.285	0.800	0.666	**0.567**	~
	H	0.666	0.000	0.000	0.800	0.250	0.343	~
Standing	FF	0.857	1.000	0.857	1.000	0.000	0.742	~
	BF	1.000	0.666	1.000	0.800	1.000	0.893	~
	H	1.000	1.000	1.000	1.000	1.000	**1.000**	~
Walking	FF	0.750	0.000	1.000	0.666	0.444	0.572	~
	BF	0.666	0.500	0.750	0.545	0.571	0.606	~
	H	0.857	0.461	0.600	0.857	0.666	**0.088**	~
Running	FF	0.666	0.000	0.666	0.500	0.333	0.433	~
	BF	1.000	0.000	0.857	0.800	0.666	0.664	~
	H	1.000	0.857	0.857	0.857	0.800	**0.874**	~
Cycling	FF	0.800	1.000	0.333	0.750	0.000	0.576	~
	BF	1.000	0.400	0.400	0.666	0.800	**0.653**	~
	H	0.857	0.000	0.666	0.857	0.000	0.476	~
Car	FF	1.000	1.000	0.800	0.800	0.666	0.853	~
	BF	1.000	0.800	0.800	0.800	1.000	**0.880**	~
	H	0.800	1.000	0.800	0.800	0.857	0.851	~
DownStairs	FF	0.666	0.000	0.333	0.400	0.000	0.280	~
	BF	0.571	0.000	0.000	0.400	0.333	0.260	~
	H	0.800	0.000	0.000	0.800	0.285	**0.377**	~

Table 5. Hierarchical Random Forest prediction vs iPhone native prediction for the second validation database; $\sim$ represents no data.

Routine prediction			
	Smartphone	Smartphone+Myo	Native prediction
Upstairs	0.777	0.777	$\sim$
Unknown	0.400	0.444	0.078
Standing	0.941	0.842	0.755
Walking	0.740	0.914	0.480
Running	0.769	0.769	0.000
Cycling	0.857	0.842	0.000
Car	0.976	0.952	0.546
Downstairs	0.631	0.923	$\sim$
Average	0.761	0.807	0.309

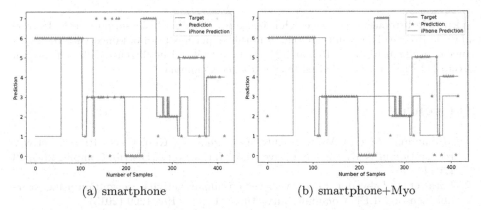

(a) smartphone   (b) smartphone+Myo

Fig. 4. Evaluation of prediction results on second database: Comparing Hierarchical Random Forest Classifier and smartphone prediction in two modes: data from smartphone and data from smartphone and Myo. The assignment of each class by activity is given as follows: $0 =$ Ascending Stairs, $1 =$ undefined, $2 =$ standing, $3 =$ walking, $4 =$ running, $5 =$ cycling, $6 =$ driving a car and $7 =$ Descending stairs

5 Conclusions

An activity recognition system based on wearable devices was implemented and evaluated on different acquisition schemes and different grouping features, and were analyzed with Python language. The results presented an improving on prediction by using a Hierarchical scheme and a feature reduction method. Among five implemented classifiers, Random Forest excelled out in most of the variants used, which achieved a perfect prediction F1-score on a first validation test. Regarding the contribution of a second wrist device, the accelerometers/gyro of a Myo armband were used to asses the possible improvement on activity recognition with 50 hz of sampling rate. In general, at these conditions the adding of Myo information didn't present a significant improvement on the general prediction F1-score, however, some classes (the most common): walking and running increased it average indicator by adding the features coming from the Myo. This fact had a more notable effect on the second validation test where a continuous routine with different activities was used to asses the Random Forest predictor, given that walking activity predictions improved its score by adding the Myo. Finally, regarding validation tests predictions, the proposed system presented best prediction results with respect to the native smartphone prediction, both in assertiveness and number of activities to recognize. The maximum F1-score obtained reached 100% for first validation experiment and 80.7% for second validation experiment respectively.

The results showed that supervised classifiers achieved a good performance predictions in activity recognition based on wearable devices. Future work will focus on recursive implementation of predictors in real time and a higher frequency wrist device such as smart watch for online predictions.

Acknowledgments. This research is being developed with the support of the Universidad de Ibagué. The results presented in this paper has been obtained with the assistance of students from the Research Hotbed on Artificial Intelligence (SI2C), Research Group D+TEC, Universidad de Ibagué, Ibagué-Colombia.

References

1. Muhammad Arshad Awan, S.-D.K., Guangbin, Z., Kim, C.-G.: Human activity recognition in WSN: a comparative study. Int. J. Netw. Distrib. Comput. **2**(4), 10 (2014)
2. Lara, O.D., Labrador, M.A.: A survey on human activity recognition using wearable sensors. IEEE Commun. Surv. Tutor. **15**(3), 1192–1209 (2013)
3. He, Y., Li, Y., Bao, S.D.: Fall detection by built-in tri-accelerometer of smartphone. In: Proceedings of the IEEE-EMBS International Conference on Biomedical and Health Informatics, pp. 184–187. IEEE, January 2012
4. Dai, J., Teng, J., Bai, X., Shen, Z., Xuan, D.: Mobile phone based drunk driving detection. In: Proceedings of the 4th International ICST Conference on Pervasive Computing Technologies for Healthcare (2010)
5. Johnson, D.A., Trivedi, M.M.: Driving style recognition using a smartphone as a sensor platform. In: 2011 14th International IEEE Conference on Intelligent Transportation Systems, pp. 1609–1615. IEEE, October 2011
6. Lee, Y.-S., Cho, S.-B.: Activity recognition using hierarchical hidden Markov models on a smartphone with 3D accelerometer. In: Corchado, E., Kurzyński, M., Woźniak, M. (eds.) HAIS 2011. LNCS (LNAI), vol. 6678, pp. 460–467. Springer, Heidelberg (2011). https://doi.org/10.1007/978-3-642-21219-2_58
7. Kwapisz, J.R., Weiss, G.M., Moore, S.A.: Activity recognition using cell phone accelerometers. ACM SIGKDD Explor. Newsl. **12**, 74 (2011)
8. Song, S., Jang, J., Park, S.: A phone for human activity recognition using triaxial acceleration sensor. In: 2008 Digest of Technical Papers-International Conference on Consumer Electronics, pp. 1–2. IEEE, January 2008

9. Sakoe, H., Chiba, S.: Dynamic programming algorithm optimization for spoken word recognition. IEEE Trans. Acoust. **26**, 43–49 (1978)
10. Laput, G., Xiao, R., Harrison, C.: ViBand. In: Proceedings of the 29th Annual Symposium on User Interface Software and Technology - UIST 2016, pp. 321–333. ACM Press, New York (2016)
11. Maurer, U., Smailagic, A., Siewiorek, D., Deisher, M.: Activity recognition and monitoring using multiple sensors on different body positions. In: International Workshop on Wearable and Implantable Body Sensor Network Systems, pp. 113–116. IEEE (2006)
12. Mazilu, S., et al.: Online detection of freezing of gait with smartphones and machine learning techniques. In: Proceedings of the 6th International Conference on Pervasive Computing Technologies for Healthcare. IEEE (2012)
13. Forero, M.G., Sroubek, F., Cristóbal, G.: Identification of tuberculosis bacteria based on shape and color. Real-Time Imaging **10**, 251–262 (2004)

Approach to Blockchain and Smart Contract in Latin America: Application in Colombia

Luz Angélica Téllez Ordoñez[(✉)], Evelyn Juliana Ruíz Niviayo, and José Ignacio Rodríguez Molano

Universidad Distrital Francisco José de Caldas, Bogotá, Colombia
{latellezo,ejruizn}@correo.udistrital.edu.co,
jirodriguez@udistrital.edu.co

Abstract. Blockchain is a database that allows to develop transactions between two agents without the need of intermediaries, can be public or private under the managements of an organization.

One of the uses of Blockchain is the development of Smart Contracts, known as self-executing programs where responsibilities of the interested parts are established and monitored without human direct participation, what allows them to be simple, unmodifiable, quick and fully automated [10].

In addition, it is worth highlighting that in Latin America the lack of regulation has led to barely incursion in a massive way into the uses of Blockchain. However, the great benefits that this technology can bring to the region are recognized.

In Colombia, particularly, the Blockchain has taken part in the government, health, industry and educative fields, among others. In fact, according to a report by BBC News, Colombia is the third country in Latin America where the purchase and sale of bitcoins grows the most. Nevertheless, in the face of regulations, its reality is not very distant to the one lived by the rest of the continent in general ways, since currently the country does not count with legislation in the area. In spite of this, the legislative power has highlighted the need to define this controls and law projects are currently underway in order to regulate the cryptoactives use and interchange.

Keywords: Blockchain · Smart Contract · Applications · Legislation · Colombia

1 Introduction

Since the introduction of Blockchain in 2009, this technology has grown and taken force rapidly, mainly because of the benefits that it provides, like: decentralization, privacy and security and immutability of data and information.

Due its flexibility and versatility, it is possible to apply Blockchain technologies in various fields, among which its use in finances stands out, however, it has spread to other kind of fields like government, health, science, literacy, art and culture [1].

This article, in addition to provide contextualization about the Blockchain characteristics ant is applications in Latin America, emphasizes in the use of Blockchain in the development of Smart Contracts. And ant the end, deepen in the applications in

© Springer Nature Switzerland AG 2019
J. C. Figueroa-García et al. (Eds.): WEA 2019, CCIS 1052, pp. 500–510, 2019.
https://doi.org/10.1007/978-3-030-31019-6_42

Colombia and in the current state of legislation oriented to the cryptoactives management.

2 State of the Art

2.1 What Is Block Chain?

Blockchain is a database that can be shared by a number of users in a peer-to-peer (P2P) network, generated through an open code software that allows to store information in an orderly an immutable way [2].

This technology began to be known thanks to the Bitcoin, back in 2009, where the unknown author of the article called "Bitcoin: a Peer-to-Peer Electronic Cash System" [3]. Satoshi Nakamoto, explains the transactional technique between two agents, without the need of any intermediary acting as judge in the transaction, this was the first Blockchain network, being one of the infinite uses that can be given to this technology [3].

But, how does Blockchain works? The Blockchain creates networks that allow to share the registration of electronic transactions, by operations through the use of a cryptocurrency or digital asset, subsequently a block packing occurs, that means when the operation happens, the block is built and send across the net to other miners that make part of the chain, in this way, a seal arises, where the operation is recorded with an unmodifiable cryptographic value. Then, there is a verification where the transactions are evaluated, if half of the participants validate the operation, this one is approved and finally it is sent, finalizing the transaction [4].

The main characteristics of Blockchain technology are:

- Decentralized: it does not depend on a single entity, on the contrary, the confidence is distributed across multiple participants.
- Scalability: its blocking rate depends on its algorithm and number of participants.
- Limited privacy: the date provided to the chain are publicly available for all the participants.
- Immutability: the information that has been confirmed and accepted by an enough number of participants, is stored in a permanent an immutable way. Thus, when the information is changed in one block, it is required to do it in the subsequent blocks belonging to this specific chain. [5].

Continuing, the Blockchain is divided in three kinds, according to the authority degree granted to the participants:

- Public Blockchain: anyone can operate and participate. It is used in virtual currency like Bitcoin, although the system can be slow.
- Private Blockchain: an organization is the one in charge of operating the system, it means that only the person that operates the chain is the one in charge of create and approve the content of the transaction. Its main use is in finance entities that do not want to divulge their transactional data.

- Consortium Blockchain: this is a mixed type, where only authorized participants can cooperate, and a consensus is obtained according no its rules. Its main use is in the commercial field or government agencies [6].

2.2   What Is a Smart Contract?

It is a self-executing program or a computational code that is executed in the environment that is going to be deepen, are repeatable and autonomous scripts that are executed in the Blockchain [7], it is destined to implement automated transactions accorded by the parts that intervene, in which exist a set of rules [8], this, added to the inalienable record, offers more security with respect to the traditional contract, and in turn reduces transactional costs associated to the contract execution. Their principal objective is to satisfy contractual conditions created by agreements, whether they are resources to the law, taxes, payment terms and other related activities.

Smart contracts are executed from a set of conditional sentences "if-then" type, accorded between the parts, where the sentences are executed as contractual clauses with real assets associated to given instructions [9]. In addition to the above, the term is used to expose any specification switchable of transaction between two parts, likewise it does not require directly human participation after the contract starts to be part of the Blockchain [10].

Regarding How a Smart Contract is created using Blockchain technology? The developer designs and implements the Smart Contract under a high level programming language like Solidity, Serpent or LLL, then, the contract is compiled in EVM (Ethereum virtual machine) bytecode and is implemented in the Blockchain. When an interested part or another Smart Contract request the contract, this one is executed in EVM, that is a virtual machine based in records [11].

3   Advances in Latin America

The constant globalization in Latin America covers transformations that in some occasions are convergent in different areas, be it political, economic or cultural of the different countries [12] which generate technological changes and the need of adapt to this changes from different positions [13].

While Europe is in the technological frontier [14], the Latin American countries count with short capacities and technological development, similarly the advance and its applications go along with the regulatory framework that is the one who approves its use.

In contrast to the previous, the Blockchain counts with the European Union support [15], who focus on the regulation of the transparency and the cybernetics, [16] countries like the United Kingdom have successfully brought this technology to a national strategic level and have established a development alliance [17, 18]. In the same way, Switzerland counts with specialized campaigns in the use of this technology, like Status, Bancorp and Melonport that make this country an epicenter for the technological and economic development [18].

Nevertheless, the lack of regulation in Latin America, makes that the incursion in the topic is barely starting. It should be noted that this technology will bring multiple benefits to the region, given that, unlike another technological fields, there are not obstacles to face this technology, because the Blockchain logic has gone through the community that builds it [18]. Another point to note is that the implementation does not require big investments in terms of facilities, otherwise it becomes necessary some staff training and human effort, being the principal source for a total success.

Is in that way that is been developing the topic in different forms in each country, for example, in Colombia I created the "Colombia Fintech" organization, that integrates startups and big companies form the finance field. It must be said that the Financial Supervision from this country announced the beginning of the project called Regtech that seeks to use the Blockchain technology for the development of applications that lead to the optimization in the transmission of the entities supervised by this entity.

On the other hand, Chile has developed some initiatives with this technology regarding the incorporation of the information published by the National Energy Commission [17]. At the same time the stock market from Santiago in agreement with IBM incorporates the Blockchain technology in the short sales transactions in the local market, being the first stock market in implement it in Latin America [19].

In an analogous way, the Latin American Bank Federation has recorded significant advances specifically the last years, in technology and finance matters. The access to internet and the constant growing in finance matter makes that Blockchain technology emerge as a vital tool, since it allows costs reduction and greater security [20].

There are not only advances in financial or cadastral issues in Latin America, but also in energy and environment issues, so Endesa, company who belongs to Enel group, launched Endesa Energy Challenge, as a collaborative platform, where both developers and entrepreneurs present proposals in innovation and development matters. This ones is the first Spanish speaking research laboratory that focuses in Blockchain technology [9].

Continuing with the advances in Latin America, there is a company in Argentina made up by argentine technicians and engineers called Rootstock, dedicated to software development for the generation of Smart Contracts, nowadays, the offer different products that work with Blockchain based on Bitcoins [21]. Besides this company, Argentina has dabbled with the Blockchain technology and the traditional payment, allowing the unbanked population and bank services in Latin America (up to 70% in some areas) to buy and sell Bitcoins for the goods and services payment with a simple transfer, direct with their colleagues and merchants, called "Ripio" [19].

Finally, it is important to mention that the European Commission has sponsored the construction of the "EU Blockchain Observatory & Forum" whose objective is to accelerate the innovation and development of the Blockchain ecosystem within the EU, and thus help consolidate Europe as a world leader in this new transforming technology.

This observatory has a map where it is possible to register different interesting initiatives on Blockchain worldwide, not all the projects promoted in each country are registered in this portal, but the information provided there is a good starting point to identify the advances by territory.

From this source, the main projects registered in Latin America were analyzed, the results are shown in the following graphs [33] (Fig. 1).

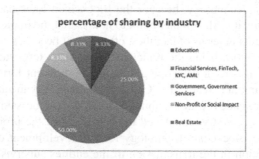

Fig. 1. Percentage of sharing by industry. Source: own work.

In addition, Fig. 2 shows that, in terms of participation by countries, the largest number of initiatives have been developed in Brazil, followed by Argentina and Chile.

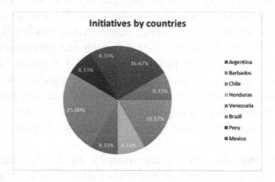

Fig. 2. Initiatives by countries. Source: own work.

4   Applications

In the last years, the use of Blockchain has grown, advantages as the distributed data storage, the point to point transmission and the encryption algorithms have attracted attention from many fields.

One of the main application fields corresponds to the bank industry that facing the emergence of new technologies, changing economic environments and financial innovations, requires new strategies that allow the industry to stay competitive in the market [22]. Various international institutions, including the United Nations have explored the application of Blockchain in different fields. Besides, China, Russia, India, and South Africa have also initiated investigations about the use of this technology, even have created their own laboratories and have established alliances with Blockchain platforms, for the advance in studies on the subject. But what specific scenarios can be addressed with Blockchain? The answer to this question is approached taking into account that the Blockchain is an underlying technology, that allows to transfer value point to point, catching a big quantity of information and therefore mitigating one of the most relevant defects in the commercial banks management, the difficulties that SMEs and natural people face when soliciting credits thanks to the limited knowledge that the financial entities have about their clients [23].

Another interesting field where Blockchain have presence is the education field. Nowadays, some universities have implemented this technology mainly to support the management of academic titles and perform the evaluation of the learning outcomes [1].

Currently, The Nicosia University is using Blockchain in order to manage certificates (Sharples & Domingue 2016). The Massachusetts Institute of Technology (MIT) in cooperation with the company Learning Machine designed a flagship digital system for the online learning, in which the students that finish the projects in the MIT Media Lab get a certification that will be stored in a Blockchain network (Skiba 20017).

Additionally, through Blockchain is possible to record detailed information about the students, including their knowledge and abilities, allowing to transform their achievements into a digital currency that will be stored in the Blockchain. This is known as "learn to win" [1].

5   Applications in Colombia

Although the Blockchain in mainly known for being the cryptocurrencies database, the advantages and attributes that it has allow it to project itself as the future of corporative management [24].

This reality takes place in Colombia, where this technology is expected to keep dabbling in different fields in the short and medium term, not only in the finance filed. Even if it is necessary to recognize that in the world this one is the main application of Blockchain [25], its use has spread to other fields.

But the Blockchain field in Colombia stills counting with flaws, because there are few institutions and professionals that have enough knowledge to evangelize about this topic, even so, Colombia has started a path in order to make known the benefits of this technology through conferences and seminaries [21].

Some fields where the Blockchain technology can be applied are listed and briefly explained next:

- Health: mainly in the archive of clinical histories, in such a way that it is possible to keep and access the information
- Information security: the fact that the access must be approved by the 50% of the users, allows to shield the information from attacks and modifications.
- Government: through the application of Blockchains, the response time in the formalities made in the government entities can be considerably reduced.
- Industry: through the implementation of databases that support the business management [26].

Thereby, one of the possible applications for the Blockchain technology under the use of Smart Contracts in Colombia is the contracting in governmental entities and the participation in public tenders, being this one of the biggest problems that the country faces, since despite there is an entity in charge and there are laws that regulate this topics, there have been cases of corruption, making Colombia to be within the 10 most corrupt countries in Latin America.

The hiring model starts with the public entity need, analyzing clauses, guidelines, scheduling and other requirements needed to generate the offer, as well as the characteristics of the goods, services or works that are being solicited, at the same time the legal, technical and financial conditions are established taking into account the current normativity (law 1150 of 2007), by last, this information enters and parametrize the Blockchain system (Ethereum), being available for the public with the respective "signatures" that endorse it.

On storage issues, each proposal is collected with its attachments which must obligatorily contain common language that makes easier the interaction of the interested parties, and then the proposals are uploaded to the Blockchain platform, that analyzes them in order to make them unique by offer, and validating that they contemplate all the requirements of the offer. At the same time, the registration process for each transaction is a decentralized platform, in which the data is stored and frozen (unmodifiable).

For the closing of the through an award hearing, the evaluation is reviewed and the qualified proponents to continue with the process are determined, and only in this phase is possible to have access to the economic offer document, which presents and evaluation through random mechanisms based on mathematical formulas. This evaluations are encoded in the Blockchain platform (Ethereum) for each specific offer, so it is possible to execute automatically. The interested parties will be notified according to the article number 9 of the law 1150 of 2007.

In order to start with the execution of the bidding process, a Smart Contract is generated, in which the responsibilities and rights of each one of the interested parties are defined. All this is hosted in the Blockchain system guaranteeing the transparency and security of the process.

The Blockchain platform also must permit to the public entities to mold the Smart Contract according to their needs, creating clauses or rules with the purpose of they can work automatically [7] in the Electronic System for Public Contracting (SECOP in Spanish). On the other hand, the opportunity of change in the Colombian education system in regards to fraud in citizen registration is pretty wide, because the country not only presents issues of falsification of university degrees, but also faces problems about registration of fictional people in different educational institutions. This is way the Blockchain technology allows to design a system that manages the register of people in the educational system in Colombia.

For the above, the program "BlockCerts Wallet", from MIT, is taken as a basis. The objective of this program is to generate and verify academic degrees that, together with procedures supported by Blockchain in Bitcoin, allows to control the process without the need of a third party. All this resulted in a set tools that constitute the standard called BlockCerts, which are based in:

- OpenBadges, from IMS GLC
- Verifiable claims, from W3C
- Linked data signatures, from W3C
- Decentralized identifiers, from W3C

That said, the BlockCerts work to generate y verify documents in a quick and orderly manner, creating certificate templates, in which common information of each entity is included. Subsequently, this file saves data from each registered student and generates digital certificates with compacted information through parametrized scripts from the cert-tools component, issues the Bitcoin transaction in the Blockchain with the lot of created certificates. The Bitcoin network performs the computation of the respective hashes and generates the signature.

Having clear the base of the system, the BlockCerts for SIMAT are personalized. SIMAT (in Spanish) it's a platform where the Secretary of Education of Colombia enters and verify the information about enrollments in all the educational establishments in the country.

To obtain the digital enrollment generator system, the main template is personalized. With this template the lot of certificates is generated, including data about the educational institution and the characteristics of the cohesive enrollment process, adding a hash that identifies the set of student records generated, allowing that at the moment of input the data in the cert-tools component, the records are not manipulated and are accurately reflected [27].

The generated certificates are validated by the BlockCerts, because they are built in order to work parametrically with the information included in the certificate. As the template is customized, indications are given to the verification script to validate the information respecting the issuing entity [27].

For that matter, it is possible to recognize the need to develop and explore the capacities that allow to take advantage of all the opportunities that the implementation of the Blockchain technology.

6 Colombian Legislation

As mentioned above, the advantages of Blockchain lead to different countries to be interested in this technology. This reality has not gone unnoticed in Colombia, since ant governmental level has been recognized that Blockchain is a mechanism that besides modernizing the digital economy in the country, can be applied in several fields like innovator rights administration and protection, electoral system security, public services management and off course smart contracting [28].

In fact, an article published by BBC News says that Colombia turned in the third country in Latin America that grown the most in buy and sell of Bitcoins [29]. Notwithstanding, the cryptoactives transactions besides of be a tool for the economic development of a country, can also facilitate the development of illicit activities like money laundering. For this reason the need of work in regulations oriented to the regulation of cryptoactives is latent.

In September of 2018 the national bank of Colombia, Banco de la Republica (BRC), presented a technical document about cryptoactives (CA) by which it was referring to the innovations in cryptocurrencies as Bitcoins, Ether and others, that allow the transfer of digital assets [30].

In this document, the BRC manifest the challenges in policy terms associated to the use of cryptoactives. Among these it is possible to highlight the fact that because of the pseudo anonymous nature of the CA schemes, those can facilitate the movement of resources related to money laundering/terrorism financing (ML/TF). Also, they mention the fact that there is exchange regulation thanks that when operating in internet the participation of agents without being tied to a jurisdiction becomes possible [30].

Given this fact, the legislative power has highlighted the need of define regulatory controls, indeed, nowadays in the Colombian Congress is being processed the law project 028 of 2018, oriented to the regulation of the use of virtual currencies or cryptocurrencies and the transaction ways in the Colombian territory [31].

Additionally, in April of 2019, a template was published in the Republic Congress about a law project leaded by the congressman Mauricio Toro that wants to regulate the cryptoactives interchange services defining general aspects in the operation of the cryptoactives service providers, all this through the creation of a Unique Registry of Cryptoactives Exchange (URCE) that will be managed by the Chambers of Commerce from the country and will count with a database where the Exchanges (operators of CA storage and exchange platforms) that fulfill the requirements established by the law. The inspection, surveillance and control of cryptoactives service providers will be executed by the Ministerio de Tecnologias de la Información y las Comunicaciones (MinTIC) [32].

7   Conclusions

- Blockchain is a technology that has taken great participation worldwide and taking into account that it allows to make decentralized, scalable and immutable operations and provides high level security, is expected that its uses grow in quantity and diversity.
- Smart Contract are self-executing programs that allow to validate the accomplishment of the set of established rules by the involver parties. Its implementation besides of reduce transaction costs provides greater security than the traditional contract.
- The Latin American continent has recognized the need of adequate to the technological changes. This can be evidenced in the different initiatives adopted by some countries. For example, in Chile, Blockchain technology will start to be used to guarantee the security, quality and certainty of the date published from and to the energy sector; in Argentina, the company Rootstock is dedicated to the development of software for the generation of Smart Contracts and in Peru Blockchain is taking presence in the land registration field, looking for connecting the notary and register in order to check the document authenticity.
- In Colombia, Blockchain is being recognized as a great tool and even is being profiled as the future of corporate management. This is why is expected that this

technology takes participation in fields like government, health and industry among others.

- In terms of normativity, Colombia, as well as most countries in the Latin American continent does not count with legislation oriented to the cryptoactives regulation. In this situation, the legislative power has recognized that it must be an answer to this need and nowadays is in curse in the Republic Congress the law project 028 of 2018 and a draft of a law project that intends to regulate the cryptoactives exchange services offered through the platforms.
- The applications in Colombia so far have only been proposed for the use of smart contracts in public tenders in order to reduce corruption. Another field in which it has ventured is in the education system seeking to design a system that allows to manage the records of academic titles.

However, it is necessary to continue making academic contributions that facilitate the implementation of this type of technology in the country.

References

1. Chen, G., Xu, B., Lu, M., Chen, N.-S.: Exploring blockchain technology and its potential applications for education. Smart Learn. Environ. **5**(1), 1–10 (2018)
2. Dolader, C., Bel, J., Muñoz, J.: La blockchain: fundamentos, aplicaciones y relación con otras tecnologías disruptivas. Econ. Ind. **405**, 33–40 (2017)
3. Nakamoto, S.: Bitcoin: A Peer-to-Peer Electronic Cash System, pp. 1–9 (2013)
4. ll Fourier: Blockchain Qué es, p. 1134
5. Knirsch, F., Unterweger, A., Engel, D.: Implementing a blockchain from scratch: why, how, and what we learned. EURASIP J. Inf. Secur. **3**, 2 (2019)
6. Román, J., Fernández, L.: Digital Heritage. Progress in Cultural Heritage: Documentation, Preservation, and Protection, vol. 10059, no. 4 (2018)
7. Guerra, A.G., Roldán, D.F.L.: Método de contratación inteligente para Licitaciones Públicas en Colombia Usando la Tecnologia Blockchain. Director **15**(2), 2017–2019 (2018)
8. Governatori, G., Idelberger, F., Milosevic, Z., Riveret, R., Sartor, G., Xu, X.: On legal contracts, imperative and declarative smart contracts, and blockchain systems. Artif. Intell. Law **26**(4), 377–409 (2018)
9. Altomonte, H.: Volumen I. Número 2. Diciembre 2017 enerLAC, vol. 2 (2017)
10. Treviño, J.A.G.: Blockchain y los 'contratos inteligentes, pp. 26–30 (2017)
11. Wang, C., Castiglione, A., Hutchison, D. (eds.) Network and System Security, vol. 9955 (2016)
12. Superintendencia de Industria y Comercio, "Blockchain, La Revolución de la Confianza Digital" (2018)
13. Kouzinopoulos, C.S., et al.: Security in Computer and Information Sciences, vol. 821. Springer, Heidelberg (2018). https://doi.org/10.1007/978-3-319-95189-8
14. Hess, P.: Cash in East Asia, vol. 44 (2017)
15. Sun, J., Yan, J., Zhang, K.Z.K.: Blockchain-based sharing services: what blockchain technology can contribute to smart cities. Financ. Innov. **2**(1), 26 (2016)
16. Li, X., Cai, Y., Zhu, W.: Cloud Computing and Security Whitepaper (2018)
17. Cabrera, F.: Tecnología Blockchain: elementos aplicaciones y marcos regulatorios, no. 56 (2018)

18. Paso, U.N., El, E., Felipe, D., Ramirez, N., Junco, C.D., Cantor, R.Q.: Blockchain, un paso hacia el desarrollo, pp. 1–5 (2017)
19. Posible, E.L., Generado, I., La, C.O.N., Del, A., Bogotá, D.C.: Al comercio electrónico de medicamentos en Colombia Juan Camilo Vargas Arboleda Trabajo de grado presentado para optar al título de profesional en Negocios Internacionales Andersson S. Parra Castillo Programa Negocios Internacionales (2018)
20. Corredor Higuera, J.A., Díaz Guzmán, D.: Blockchain y mercados financieros: aspectos generales del impacto regulatorio de la aplicación de la tecnología blockchain en los mercados de crédito de América Latina. Derecho PUCP **81**, 405–439 (2018)
21. Cantisani, R.: Trabajo Final de Graduación Maestría en Finanzas UTDT (2017)
22. Lindner, D., Leyh, C.: Organizations in transformation: Agility as consequence or prerequisite of digitization, vol. 320 (2018)
23. Guo, Y.: Blockchain aplicación y las perspectivas en el sector bancario (2016)
24. Pérez, R.L.: 'Blockchain', la tecnología que hace transparentes los negocios|Negocios|Portafolio, portafolio (2018). https://www.portafolio.co/blockchain-la-tecnologia-que-hace-transparentes-los-negocios-516329. Accessed 09 Apr 2019
25. IBM Noticias de IBM, "El 65% de los bancos prevé implementar tecnologías Blockchain en los próximos tres años" (2016). https://www-03.ibm.com/press/es/es/pressrelease/50702.wss. Accessed 09 Apr 2019
26. del Pilar, A.T.M.: Tecnología Blockchain, Univ. Mil. Nueva Granada (2018)
27. Eduardo, S., Urdaneta, M.: Diseño de la arquitectura de un sistema de contratos inteligentes basada en la tecnología Blockchain aplicada al proceso de registro de estudiantes en el sistema de educación colombiano (2018)
28. Isabel Colomna: Colombia le apunta a la economía digital, Senado República de Colombia (2018). http://www.senado.gov.co/mision/item/28084-pie-noticias. Accessed 22 Apr 2019
29. Boris Miranda: Cómo Colombia se convirtió en el país de América Latina en el que más crece la compra y venta de bitcoins, BBC (2018). https://www.bbc.com/mundo/noticias-america-latina-43219365. Accessed 22 Apr 2019
30. Banco de la Republica - Colombia, Criptoactivos, no. 2017 (2018)
31. de Colombia, C.: De las Criptomonedas o menedas virtuales - Proyecto de Ley (2018)
32. Bitcoin.com.mx Colombia da el primer paso para regular Bitcoin, Colombia Fintech (2019). https://www.colombiafintech.co/novedades/colombia-da-el-primer-paso-para-regular-bitcoin. Accessed 22 Apr 2019
33. Comisión Europea: Mapa de la iniciativa (2019). https://www.eublockchainforum.eu/initiative-map. Accessed 1 Jul 2019

Design of an Electronic Voting System Using a Blockchain Network

Carlos A. Ribon[1](✉), Javier M. Leon[1], Oscar F. Corredor[1],
Hermes E. Castellanos[2], Fredy A. Sanz[2], Paola Ariza-Colpas[3],
Vanesa Landero[4], and Carlos Collazos-Morales[2]

[1] Facultad de Ingeniería, Universidad Cooperativa de Colombia,
Bogotá D.C., Colombia
carlos.ribonr@campusucc.edu.co
[2] Vicerrectoría de Investigaciones, Universidad Manuela Beltrán,
Bogotá, Colombia
[3] Departamento de Ciencias de la Computación y Electrónica,
Universidad de la Costa, Barranquilla, Colombia
[4] Universidad Politécnica de Apodaca, Apodaca, Nuevo León, Mexico

Abstract. Design of a scalable electronic voting system, which, based on a generic model designed for this application called voting cell, guarantees the integrity of the information through the use of a private network Blockchain.

For the validation of the system, the implementation of a cell was carried out, for which fifty voters and three voting options were enabled. The stored data was intentionally modified to corroborate the error correction method used by the block chain networks and thus ensure the integrity of the voting system results.

Keywords: Blockchain · Transaction · Hash · Database entity and attributes · Cryptographic algorithm

1 Introduction

In recent years, the term Blockchain has gained popularity as a technology tending to change the world as it is known; mainly due to its wide use in crypto-currency systems such as Bitcoin and Ethereum. However, this technology offers a number of opportunities that go beyond those applications such as: smart contracts, copyright certifications, property certifications and voting systems [1], that is, it can be applied to everyday situations that require guarantee the integrity of the information.

The electoral systems used by nations, be they manual or electronic, generate distrust in the citizenship since the results can be altered if access to the instances that contain the information is obtained; minutes and ballots in case of manual voting and database servers in electronic systems. In addition, with practices of cybernetic espionage and social engineering, you can get to determine the preference of choice of citizens.

© Springer Nature Switzerland AG 2019
J. C. Figueroa-García et al. (Eds.): WEA 2019, CCIS 1052, pp. 511–522, 2019.
https://doi.org/10.1007/978-3-030-31019-6_43

Apply Blockchain to electoral systems, allows maintaining the confidentiality of each person's vote and by its decentralized nature, allows preserving the integrity of the results obtained.

Electronic voting systems backed by Blockchain technology have been developed around the world. One of these cases is the POLYS project launched by the Kaspersky Lab incubator firm based on the Ethereum smart contracts model [2]. *Polys is an online voting platform based on blockchain technology and backed with transparent crypto algorithms. Powered by Kaspersky Lab* [3].

2   Literature Review

2.1   What Is Blockchain?

It is a set of transactions that are registered in a shared database. When using cryptographic keys and being distributed in multiple computers and/or servers, it presents advantages in security against possible manipulations and frauds. Any modification in one of the copies would be useless, since the change should be made in all copies because the database is open and can be audited by anyone who has access to it [4]. For this reason, it is said to be a decentralized system [5].

In Blockchain each block is identified by a hash placed in the header. This is generated using the SHA-256 Secure Hash Algorithm to create a character string of fixed size (256 bits). The SHA-256 will take a flat text of any size as input, and will encrypt it into a 256-bit binary string [6] represented in 64 hexadecimal characters. Each header contains information that links a block to its previous block, in the string that is known as the base. The primary identifier of each block is in its header; is a fingerprint that is constructed by combining two types of information: the information relative to the new block created and the previous block in the chain [7].

2.2   Public and Private Blockchain

The Blockchain can be public or private, according to the permits and accesses granted to it:

A public blockchain network is one in which there are no restrictions to read the string. The data - which can be encrypted - and the sending of transactions for inclusion in the Blockchain can be reviewed by any entity that has access. A private blockchain network is one in which the direct access to the data of the chain of blocks and the sending of the transactions, is limited to a predefined list of users [8].

2.3   Blockchain Components

(1) Miners are dedicated computers to review and validate the transactions that are carried out [9]. Also, they build and write the new data - called blocks - in the Blockchain [4].

(2) The nodes are computers that, using software, store and distribute a copy of the Blockchain [9].

(3) The blocks are records of all transactions that are packaged in blocks that the miners then verify. Then they will be added to the chain once their validation is completed and distributed to all the nodes that make up the network [10].

2.4 Merkle Tree

It is a binary structure based on results of the hash function. It is used to obtain a summary of all transactions included in a block [11].

It is constructed by ordering the transactions in a list and proceeding to count them to check if they are an even number [12], otherwise the last transaction is repeated. Then, hashing of each transaction is performed; the hashes are serialized in pairs and the hashing process becomes recursively until the root of the Merkle tree or root is obtained [13].

3 Voting System Design and Protocols

The design of the system is based on a *private Blockchain network*, that is, the data cannot be accessed from the internet and the system does not need to use any platform. In other words, the information is stored and processed by the system devices. The voting system delivers results when consulting databases whose records - hereinafter called *transactions* - can be audited and corroborated using cryptographic algorithms. For this solution, SHA-256 was used.

3.1 Data Structure

The system is made up of two unrelated databases. The first contains the information of the people authorized to vote in each voting site and the second contains the Blockchain and is made up of two database entities each one with different attributes: first entity stores the transactions, where each vote is represented by one transaction, and the other one stores the blocks that certify transactions (Fig. 1).

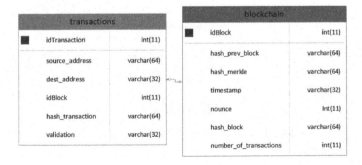

Fig. 1. Blockchain entities

The Transactions Entity has the Following Attributes

- **idTransaction:** it has characteristics of primary key and auto-increment. Its function is to perform the identification of the transaction.
- **source_address:** this attribute contains the identification number of the user. This is got operating the identification number with a random string character of the a finite vector - which is part of characteristic system signature- the result is encrypted with SHA-256. **Thus, this process ensures that the voter identity will be non-obtained** (Fig. 2).

Fig. 2. Voter identification encryption.

For the real application the random string method can be changed for information based in biometric identifiers like fingerprint recognition or facial recognition.

- **dest_adrress:** indicates the option by which the user voted. By counting this attribute, you get the result of the vote.
- **idBlock:** this attribute indicates the number of the block that certifies the transaction. A block can certify one or more transactions; if no block validates the transaction, this field has a null value - these will be called orphan transaction-.
- **hash_transaction:** this string data is calculated by concatenating the attributes source_address and dest_address with a random string character of the finite vector which is part of characteristic system signature; this process guarantees that the valid transactions can be only written by system members. The result is encrypted with SHA-256 (Fig. 3).

Fig. 3. Construction of the transaction hash.

- **Validation:** this attribute is purely informative and is modified each time the Blockchain database is validated. Its value can be "Validated" or "Non-validated".

The Blockchain Entity has the Function to Certify the Groups of Transactions and has the Following Attributes

- **idBlock:** it has characteristics of primary key and auto-increment. Its function is to identify the block.
- **hash_prev_block:** contains the hash of the immediately preceding block. When this is the first block in the chain, this field is zero "0".
- **hash_merkle:** based on the characteristics of the Merkle tree, a single hash is generated that contains information on the orphan transactions that are certified by the block under construction.
- **timestamp:** it is the system's time capture at the moment of generating the block. It is necessary that all the participating nodes are synchronized.
- **nounce:** it is a random number of maximum five digits and it helps to increase the difficulty to alter or rewrite a block.
- **hash_block: is** generated from operating the attributes hash_prev_block, hash_-merkle, timestamp and nounce of this entity. The result is encrypted with SHA-256 and its function is to validate the transactions contained in the block under construction (Fig. 4).

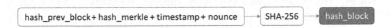

Fig. 4. Construction of the block hash.

- **number_of_transactions:** indicates the number of transactions certified by the block.

3.2 Architecture

To guarantee the reliability of the system, maintaining the secrecy of the vote and protecting the integrity of the results, we have designed **the voting cell system**. The cells represent a generic design implemented in each of the voting sites (Fig. 5).

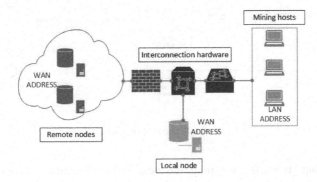

Fig. 5. Voting cell architecture.

The cells are made up of the following components.

- **Mining hosts:** they are the user interfaces. Their function is to validate the registration of the voter, in addition, they are responsible for writing each transaction – vote - and generating the blocks that authenticate the groups of transactions.
- **Local node:** it **stores a database with people authorized to vote on the voting site and a copy of the blockchain** this equipment also executes a JavaScript in order to calculate the hash_merkle, calculate the hash_transaction and calculate the hash_block on the copy of the blockchain which is stored in here.
- **Interconnection hardware:** they are focused on guaranteeing connectivity between cells - voting sites-. Additionally, they allow the implementation of policies that guarantee a reliable network - fault tolerance, scalability, quality of service and security - [14].

The components of the voting cell described so far are the devices that are installed in each voting site.

Taking into account the sensitivity of the information in a actual system application, the use of firewall - such as software or device - is necessary in each voting site in order to implement policies that guarantee the sources and destinations of the traffic of data [15].

Remote Nodes: These are equipment with similar functions to the local node. In practice, they are local nodes of other voting cells, or also, physical and virtual equipment located in places other than voting sites; their function is to store and validate a exactly copy of the Blockchain, therefore, this system is a decentralized one.

3.3   Operation

The system uses two general processes in which different actors participate: *Data processing and Data storage* (Fig. 6).

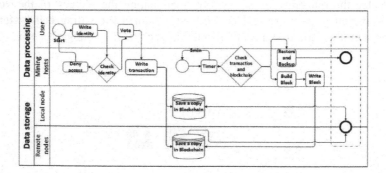

Fig. 6. Processes diagram.

Data Processing. It starts by typing the voter's identification number in the user interface. Here the mining host, through which the system is being accessed, performs the data verification that consists of corroborating if the user is authorized to participate in that voting site or if he has already deposited the vote - denying access in both cases - or if the user can actually deposit his vote. For the last case, the mining host shows the card to the user so that he can make his choice.

When the vote is deposited, the mining team establishes a connection with the nodes that are available and starts the following processes:

- Blockchain verification: in this process, the integrity of the data contained in the two entities of the blockchain is validated in all the nodes with which connection was established. If corrupt database copies are found, the miners updates the database of the affected node using the incremental backup method, that is, only the modified information is replaced [16].

  This verification is done by analyzing the hash_transaction attribute of the transactions entity and the hash_block attribute of the Blockchain entity and this is being carried out all the time both by the miners, who validate any copies of the blockchain with which they have connection, and by the nodes, which validate only the information they have stored.
- Write transaction: once the data has been validated, the attributes of the transaction's entity are written.
- Build block: is activated by a timer in the miner hosts. In this process, the activated miner establishes connection with all the nodes within his reach and blocks the multisession access while performing the verification, that is, during this time the other miners do not have access to the nodes. Once the Blockchain is verified, the remote nodes are unlocked and the block is started on the local node by performing the following sequence.

a. Search orphan transactions: select those transactions whose attribute idBlock in the transactions entity is null. If these types of transactions are not found, the process is finished.
b. Build the hash_merkle attribute: the hash_transaction attributes of the orphan transactions are taken, and a single string data is constructed using the Merkle tree (Fig. 7).

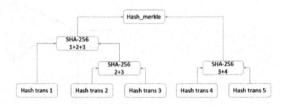

Fig. 7. Merkle hash construction.

If a transaction is altered, the attributes hash_merkle and hash_block in the blockchain entity will be modified. Thus, the system can always identify the transactions – votes- that were altered. This process is persistently carried out by all the nodes on the copy that each one stores.

c. Take the time sample and generate the nounce: in order to obtain the timestamp and nounce attributes of the entity Blockchain.
d. Generate the hash of the block: Concatenates all the attributes of the Blockchain entity and encrypts the result with SHA-256, obtaining the attribute called hash_block.
e. Write the idBlock attribute in the transactions entity.
f. Update the version of the block chain in the other nodes: using the incremental backup method.

Upon completion of this process, the mining host releases the local node, allowing the other miners to write transactions. During the process of building the block, the cell cannot write transactions, in other words, the voting site is disabled. However, the execution time of the process is very short.

Data Storage. Its actors are the local and remote nodes of the whole system. They contain exact copies of the chain of blocks, which are verified by the mining equipment. When corrupt copies are found, that is, copies with altered data or in outdated versions, the miners replace it with the latest version verified in the system - using the incremental backup method-.

4 A Voting Cell Implementation

A voting cell was implemented, in which fifty people are registered to exercise the vote and one card with three possibilities of election; the nodes store databases managed with MySQL Workbench [17] and the mining teams execute a JavaScript developed in NetBeans IDE 8.2 [18].

The cell implemented is shown in the Fig. 8. It is made up of two mining teams, a local server that is a physical team that contains the database of people registered to vote and two remote servers: one physical and the other virtual making use of the Google Cloud Platform.

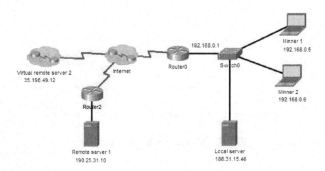

Fig. 8. Voting cell implementation

4.1 Results

The script was executed on the mining equipment. First, the system requests the user's identification number. When the user is authorized, the system provides a digital card so that the voter can choice one of three options. By clicking on any of the options, the user deposits his vote (Table 1).

Table 1. Writing the first transaction.

idTransactions	source_address	dest_adrress	idBlock	hash_transaction	Validation
1	dd28307d6697aa 59d86b530084c0 8ff047d8f8267b4 ab0c156cbb02f0 d09bfd7	Option1	NULL	0a9a603d50f447 6d07b81269eff1e 786a31ef8efdacb 656702537b93ad 0c7f1f	Validated

The identity of the voter cannot be known unless the signature keys of the system are obtained. When the same voting process is repeated through the two mining teams, multiple **orphan transactions** –with idBlock attribute in NULL state- are written (Table 2).

Table 2. Orphan transactions.

idTransactions	source_address,	dest_adrress	idBlock	hash_transaction	Validation
1	dd28307d6697aa 59d86b530084c0 8ff047d8f8267b4 ab0c156cbb02f0 d09bfd7	Option 1	NULL	0a9a603d50f4476d0 7b81269eff1e786a3 1ef8efdacb6567025 37b93ad0c7f1f	Validated
2	4b0e8bd3b5ad09 b06243169a76c3 d86bbb206e689b 2b1b5cea257ffe6 f216414	Option 2	NULL	f1707eb7aa3b34657 f05d466d1ab82a51f 6a29a037151078b9 8360dc88ff800d	Validated
3	70cd531d9a16d1 10523ecb9a15e2 52724e1bc1ea41 f3d819038ac4ae 3926370a	Option 1	NULL	b57e035444da5be7 d4de9b5f5442a6606 09ffa7060fa546a74 d4519f6bc6c488	Validated
4	dc89e5db37ea51 1fceecf49aa2676 12c27e9486b531 f0d6ebd28d849e 3810052	Option 3	NULL	c93163ac4c08fdae6 d226d1136b94be67 e76770139a512e6d 20a143baf604d49	Validated

For the generation of a block, a five-minute timer was programmed. At the end of this time the process of building the block begins with all those orphan transactions existing in the entity (Table 3).

Table 3. Building the first block.

idBlock	hash_prev_block	hash_merkle	Timestamp	nounce	hash_block	number_of_transactions
1	0	2445e0bafe55e7c6b 65e342c4765db825 37b8da3bf23dbfaf8 1c3eafc98f4e51	6/02/2019 16:01	67901	4a16b448cf96280a 02b15e017b45c393 75078bc639f061ba 513b35246e995928	4

The transaction showed in the Table 3 is the first one, therefore, its attribute **hash_prev_block is "0"**. For this case the block construction process took less than **three seconds.**

The blocks building forces a change in the transaction entity specifically in the attribute **idBlock** of the transactions which was certified by the block recently built, therefore, the value NULL in the transactions 1, 2, 3 y 4 is replaced for de number of the block which certificates the transactions, for this case block number one. This process permit that the system can do a relation between block and transactions.

4.2   B. Alteration of Transactions

As an exercise, one of the transactions in the chain of blocks stored on the remote server 1 was altered. The vote registered in the four transaction was changed; "Option 1" was written instead of "Option 3", that is, **a vote was removed for Option 3 and a vote was added for Option 1.** Thus, when the **Remote server 1** recalculates the attributes hash_merkle and hash_block the blockchain is invalidated at that moment, a miner evaluates the blockchain until it finds the block whose hash_merkle attribute is corrupt. Once it is identified, the transactions supported by the corrupt block are invalidated. Then the hash_transaction attributes of the invalidated transactions are recalculated; in this way it is possible to identify specifically the transaction that was altered and proceed to update it using the incremental backup method. So this system manages to maintain the integrity of the information without significantly increasing the traffic between the local and remote nodes.

4.3   Vote Counting

Once the elections are over, the system validates the chain of blocks again and performs the restores or updates of the version of the databases that are necessary, that is, if it finds a corrupt version of the chain of blocks, it is updated or restored. Then the system performs a count of the dest_address attribute of the transaction entity of the blockchain. For the case study, the version of the block chain contained in the local server was exported, from MySQL Workbench to Microsoft Office Excel 2013 and the results obtained were plotted.

5   Conclusions

With the proposed system, by using of the blockchain technology and databases distributed in an electronic voting systems, maintaining the secrecy of the vote and the integrity of the results is possible in an election activity.

The use of Blockchain technology allows easy detection of corrupt data; is achieved by checking the hash attributes of the previous block and merkle hash in the block header. What allows to detect alterations in the chain of blocks quickly and efficiently - with respect to the use of the processor -.

Despite this, there are vulnerabilities in the system. They are basically presence of malware or virus [19] in the mining computers and in the interconnection devices, which can alter the transactions before their registration in the Blockchain, that is, corrupt transactions can be validated and written as long as the information is modified before Your first record in the database. For this reason, it is necessary to establish conventional multilevel security policies, with which, the alteration of transactions is the last security instance of the system.

The use of the scalable model that we called voting cell, reduces the hardware and software requirements in the storage equipment compared with a centralized electronic voting system; the computing capacity is distributed in the mining equipment that is installed in the cells arranged to satisfy the elections. This implies decrease of costs of implementation of the voting system.

References

1. Carmen, O.M.: Blockchain la nueva base de datos no SQL en BIG DATA. Mgr. dissertation, Dept. Sist. Eng. Guadalajara Univ, Libre Univ. Bogotá, Colombia (2017)
2. Rivero, J.: Transparencia electoral: 5 plataformas blockchain para votaciones (2018)
3. Polys. https://polys.me
4. Benjamin, Y.N.: Blockchain y sus aplicaciones. Eng. dissertation, Department of English, Universidad Católica Nuestra Señora de La Asunción. Asunción, PAR (2016)
5. Ayed, A.B.: A conceptual secure blockchain- based electronic voting system (2017). http://aircconline.com/ijnsa/V9N3/9317ijnsa01.pdf
6. Black, J., Rogaway, P., Shrimpton, T.: Black-box analysis of the block-cipher-based hash-function constructions from PGV. In: Yung, M. (ed.) CRYPTO 2002. LNCS, vol. 2442, pp. 320–335. Springer, Heidelberg (2002). https://doi.org/10.1007/3-540-45708-9_21
7. Raval, S.: Decentralized Applications: Harnessing Bitcoin's Blockchain Technology. O'Reilly Media Inc., Sebastopol (2016)
8. BitFuryGroup, Garzik, J.: Public versus private blockchains, 20 October 2015
9. Valeria, B.C., Joel, Z.H.: Implementaciòn de un prototipo de una red descentralizada blockchain para el voto electrónico en la universidad de guayaquil. English dissertation, Fac. Ciencias Matemáticas y Física. Universidad de Guayaquil. Guayaquil, EC (2018)
10. Carlos, da S.D.: ¿Qué es Blockchain y cómo funciona? IBM Systems Blog para Latinoamérica – Español (2017)
11. Merkle, R.C.: A digital signature based on a conventional encryption function. In: Pomerance, C. (ed.) CRYPTO 1987. LNCS, vol. 293, pp. 369–378. Springer, Heidelberg (1988). https://doi.org/10.1007/3-540-48184-2_32

12. Narayanan, A., Boneau, J., Felten, E., Miller, A., Goldfeder, S.: Bitcoin and Cryptocurrency Technologies. Princeton University Press, Princeton (2016)
13. Joffre, A.: Cadena de bloques: potencial aplicación a Historias Clínicas Electrónicas" Esp. dissertation, Fac. Cs. Ecnomicas, exactas, naturales e ingeniería. Uni. De Buenos Aires. Buenos Aires, AR (2017)
14. Odom, W.: CCNA routing and switching official cert guide library, pp. 125–200 (2015)
15. FORTINET NSE institute: FortiGate security study guide for FortiIOS 6.0 (2018)
16. Daniel, B.: Introducción. In: Hacking desde cero 1st ed. Ed. Fox Andina collaboration with Gradi S.A Buenos Aires, AR (2011)
17. MySQL Workbench. https://www.mysql.com/products/workbench/
18. NetBeans IDE. https://netbeans.org/
19. de la Hoz, E., de la Hoz, E.E., Ortiz, A., Ortega, J.: Modelo de detección de intrusiones en sistemas de red, realizando selección de características con FDR y entrenamiento y clasificación con SOM. Revista INGE CUC **8**(1), 85–116 (2012)

Use of Edge Computing for Predictive Maintenance of Industrial Electric Motors

Victor De Leon, Yira Alcazar, and Jose Luis Villa$^{(\boxtimes)}$ (iD)

Universidad Tecnologica de Bolivar, Cartagena de Indias, Colombia
victoroflion@gmail.com, yirapao@outlook.com, jvilla@utb.edu.co
http://www.utb.edu.co/

Abstract. Industrial Internet of Things has become a reality in many kind of industries. In this paper, We explore the case of high quantity of raw data generated by a machine. In the aforementioned case is not viable store and process the data in a traditional Internet of Things architecture. For this case, We use an architecture based on edge computing and Industrial Internet of Things concepts and apply them to a case of machine monitoring for predictive maintenance. The proof of concept shows the potential benefits in real industrial applications.

Keywords: Edge Computing · Industrial Internet of Things ·
Predictive maintenance

1 Introduction

The acceptance of the Internet of Things (IoT) in the industrial field is due to the benefits in the optimization of production and operational efficiency; it means, flexibility and profitability in manufacturing production. This has been achieved thanks to technological movements, which point to the paradigm of connected factories, which consists in the digitization of processes. In this digital age, data represents the relationship between physical and digital elements [1].

It opens the way to intelligent interconnections within the industry with the automation of machines (intelligent objects), coordination and operational convergent technology, and information and communication technology. In this world of intelligent connections are added different types of industries, such as: energy, manufacturing, transport, agriculture, and health [2].

There are different purposes and applications in the Industrial Internet of Things, generally, they are used to connect devices through communications software, with the objective of monitoring, collecting, exchanging, analyzing and acting on information, and thus, changing their behavior or environment [3]. Through the use of sensors to monitor the status of a machine, it is possible to develop advanced and generalized predictive maintenance applications, allowing the reduction of maintenance costs and minimize up-time and make the systems available in one hundred percent and make quick decisions in critical events [4]. However, the amount of data stored, traffic and services (connections between

© Springer Nature Switzerland AG 2019
J. C. Figueroa-García et al. (Eds.): WEA 2019, CCIS 1052, pp. 523–533, 2019.
https://doi.org/10.1007/978-3-030-31019-6_44

users) can affect bandwidth, processing and storage of data in the cloud, as well as data loss and latency.

Two key points to consider in this article are the predictive maintenance and the use of Edge Computing as support for Industrial IoT applications. Quinn defined predictive maintenance as: "Predictive maintenance involves the use of sensing, measuring, or control devices to determine whether there have been significant changes in the physical condition of equipment. Various visual, audio, electronic, pressure, thermal, etc. devices may be used for periodic inspection of equipment in order to determine major change in condition" [5]. Before going into detail with the concept of Edge Computing, it is necessary to give a definition of edge of network or simply edge: "Everything referred to the computing resource and network that is in the path between the data source and the data center in the cloud" [6]. The information caused by Big Data and Internet of Things makes the data agglomerate faster on the edge, than transmitted to its destination. With the help of applications, the border becomes intelligent and can work as a data center on a smaller scale.

There are several source with the same definition of Edge Computing: "cloud computing systems that perform data processing at the edge of the network, near the source of the data" [7]. Basically Edge Computing is a paradigm that decentralizes computing resources and application services are provide throughout the communication path between data source and the cloud.

In particular, We study edge computing architectures to decentralize the power of computing in the data center, acquiring data in real-time of the following parameters: electric current and vibration in a three-phase asynchronous motor, with the intention of processing and analyzing these data; and finally, diagnose the state of the motor and predict anomalies or damages in the motor. The rest of the paper is organized as follows: in Sect. 2 We discus the literature review. In Sect. 3 We describe the architecture for machine monitoring and predictive maintenance using Edge Computing, in Sect. 4 We describe the results of the proof of concept, and finally in Sect. 5 We present some conclusions and future works.

2 Literature Review

In this section We focus on the Edge Computing and applications of IoT to Predictive Maintenance.

2.1 Edge Computing

Schmidt proposes a semantic framework with the use from the ordered point of view in the ontology to allow diagnosis and forecast based on the environment of applications in the cloud for maintenance of manufacturing asset [8]; although, predictive analysis has relevance in intelligent manufacturing; it has not reached fullness, it is still limited, the control of the cycle has not been closed to implement a strategy.

In [9] a multi-layer Edge Computing architecture is presented as follows: (I) Centralized cloud computing, (II) SDN/NFV technologies, (III) Edge Computing, and (IV) IoT objects, sensors or users. Compared to the classic cloud computing model, edge-by-layer computing decreases network traffic, improves application performance, facilitates new load-balancing approaches, awareness of location, network, and network awareness, context information, and finally, minimizes energy consumption.

There are some drawbacks, in terms of implementation in the IIoT, due to the use of devices, costs, invasive infrastructure of devices interconnected with cables, and high energy consumption of devices; Also, other challenges arise in the comparative concentration in accuracy, using a costly computer filter and heuristic iterative algorithms. The objective of the document [13] is to achieve an economic communication in a semantic architecture proposed in IIoT. Intensity in using wireless sensors and a new RSSI/ToF range method.

2.2 Significance of Maintenance

According to mentioned it by Fujishima: "Machine tools are usually used over a long period of more than 10 years, so providing appropriate services are significantly important". Thence, the maintenance of machines take great importance in industrial area. The goal of maintenance, is conservation of machines in good condition or in a certain situation to prevent deterioration. There are two kind of maintenance considered as effective to give solutions before a failure be presented in machines, These are:

- **preventive maintenance:** It's that one maintenance realized periodically agree specifications done by fabricator or experience of machines chief.
- **predictive maintenance:** The maintenance provides a more precise solution, due to the use of sensors that can detect anomalies in the machines. The detection technology is closely related to the functions related to Internet of Think and Industry 4.0, and has acquired great relevance in recent years [10].

Techniques for Maintenance in Current. The following are predictive maintenance techniques, to employ diagnostic strategies:

- **Analysis of the spectrum in influence of motor currents:** This method is used for diagnosis in rotor faults. The components produced by the breakage of bars or rings, f_{b_c}, is given by:

$$f_{b\_c} = (1 \pm 2ks)f, \qquad K = 1, 2, 3 \ldots$$

where s is the slip and f the frequency of feeding.
Breakage of the bars or the ring produces lower sidebands, while the speed oscillations generated by the fault produce the upper sidebands [23]. According to [24] it is possible to define a failure severity factor μ as follows:

$$\mu \approx N \frac{I_n}{I_p}$$

Where N is the rotor bar number, I_n is the amplitude of the component produced by the fault and I_p is the amplitude of the fundamental current. This denotes the number of bars in a row broken approximately.

- **Electrical source faults detected by vibration measurements:** In general, the electrical faults of an engine can produce vibrations, and the failure can be fundamentally due to:
  - Disconnected or short-circuited rotor or stator coils.
  - Cracked rotor bars.
  - Imbalance of phases.
  - Variable air gap.

Vibration Regulations. When information about historic of vibration does not exist, [11] recommends to use the regulations: Evaluation of Vibratory Severity, indicated by ISO 10816. This guide is based on two parameters: amplitude and frequency. To check the machine condition is used vibration speed that has as measures: Revolutions Per Minute (RPM).

Norm ISO 10816-1995. Mechanical vibration. - Evaluation of vibration in a machine by measures in non-rotary parts.

From operative and test monitoring are based to generate the criterion of validation of machines to guarantee a performance reliable for a long-lasting.

Part of this standard applies to machines with 15 KW power and velocity between 120 RPM and 15,000 RPM. The criteria apply to vibrations produced only on the same machine.

Classification According to the Type of Machine, Power or Axis Height

The division of the groups depends on the design, type of rest and support structure of the machine. The machines can have horizontal, vertical or inclined axis and in addition, they can be mounted on rigid or flexible supports [12].

Classification According to the Flexibility of the Support

The system is considered rigid when the first natural frequency of machine-support in the measurement direction is greater than the principal frequency of excitation by at least 25% [12]. The other systems are considered flexible. There are cases in which the machine-support system is rigid in one measurement direction and flexible in the other direction. The Table 1 shows the zone (Table 2):

2.3 IoT Applied to Predictive Maintenance

The Internet initiates a revolution with the change of paradigm, with the need to have connections to the tangible world. There is alternative to use IoT, this article will refer to predictive maintenance with the aim of detecting anomalies and/or defects of machinery in a primary phase, in asynchronous three-phase motors, to prevent failures in the operation.

Table 1. The flexibility of the support according to ISO 10816-1995.

Zone	
A	Vibration values of newly commissioned or reconditioned machines
B	Machines that can work indefinitely without restrictions
C	The condition of the machine is not suitable for continuous operation, but only for a limited period of time
D	The vibration values are dangerous, the machine can be damaged

Table 2. Severity of vibration according to ISO 10816-3.

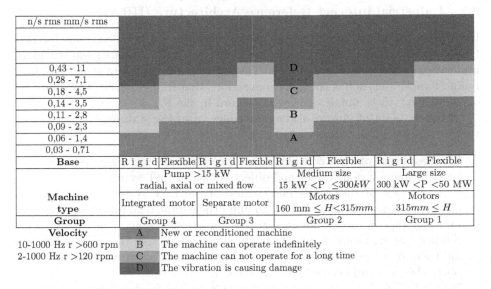

n/s rms mm/s rms								
0,43 - 11				D				
0,28 - 7,1								
0,18 - 4,5				C				
0,14 - 3,5								
0,11 - 2,8				B				
0,09 - 2,3								
0,06 - 1,4				A				
0,03 - 0,71								
Base	R i g i d	Flexible	R i g i d	Flexible	R i g i d	Flexible	R i g i d	Flexible
Machine type	Pump >15 kW radial, axial or mixed flow				Medium size 15 kW <P ≤300kW		Large size 300 kW <P <50 MW	
	Integrated motor		Separate motor		Motors 160 mm ≤ H<315mm		Motors 315mm ≤ H	
Group	Group 4		Group 3		Group 2		Group 1	

Velocity		
10-1000 Hz r >600 rpm	A	New or reconditioned machine
2-1000 Hz r >120 rpm	B	The machine can operate indefinitely
	C	The machine can not operate for a long time
	D	The vibration is causing damage

Predictive maintenance contains different techniques to warn of a possible failure or anomalies in a machine. The technique of "spectrum of lateral bands of currents in phase" is used by [14], to diagnose faults in rotating electrical machines, this research establishes a test system for the verification of magnitudes of the bands, and of this way, identify mechanical and electrical faults. For results obtained, direct current motors-synchronous and induction generators were used.

The induction electric motors are robust machines, which are an essential part in the industrial process; for this reason, predictive maintenance plays a fundamental role in this context. There are different techniques of predictive maintenance, some more effective than others, as shown in [15] in their theoretical analysis supported by the literature for critical review, where three diagnostic techniques for failure in induction motor bars are compared. These techniques are: the analysis of the current, the analysis of the instantaneous angular velocity and the analysis of the vibrations.

3   Reference Architectures Models

There are several reference architectures, of which stand out: IIRA and RAMI 4.0. Both reference architecture aim at the convergence in Information Technology and Operational Technology; the first, focuses on agility and speed, flexibility, cost reduction, business vision and security; and the second is channeled into efficiency, utilization, consistency, continuity and security. The aim is to transform the central mode of connection, data, analysis, optimization and intelligent operations [16]. This article presents IIRA, because it fits the project.

3.1   Industrial Internet Reference Architecture (IIRA)

IIRA is a standards-based guide to design interoperable IIoT systems for IISs (Industrial Internet System), it also functions as a basis to enable and stimulate innovation in an open ecosystem [18]. This reference architecture works with four point of views and each of them are conventions that frame certain characteristics or conditions, these points of view are shown in the Fig. 1.

Business point of view considers the concerns of the stakeholders, as well as their business vision, values and objectives of an IIoT system.

- Business point of view considers the concerns of the stakeholders, as well as their business vision, values and objectives of an IIoT system.
- Point of view of the use details the use of the IIoT system, generally, it is presented as a series of activities, to fulfill the commercial objectives foreseen.
- Functional point of view focuses on those functional components; in the interrelation and structure; in interfaces and interactions, and the relationship and interaction of the system with elements outside the environment, which supports the uses and activities of the system.
- Point of view of the implementation establishes the fundamental technologies to adjust the functional components, communication schemes and life cycle procedures.

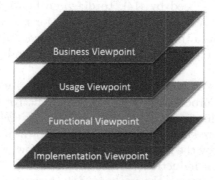

Fig. 1. IIRA model depiction.

4   Architecture for Machine Monitoring Focused on Predictive Maintenance

In industrial systems you can locate a vast amount of data of different parameters produced by a single industrial machine. This can be helpful in maintaining such a machine, for example improving predictive and preventive maintenance decisions. With the new concept of the Internet of Things (IoT), data is acquired in real time, to process, analyze and achieve results quickly and make appropriate decisions [19]. Large companies seek solutions in a pro-active way, monitoring their machines with technologies that are at the forefront, in conjunction with novel data acquisition procedures.

The IoT solution for industrial systems provides real-time monitoring, error detection and anomalies for predictive machine maintenance. A three-phase asynchronous motor generates many parameters; but, the following parameters will be put to tests: vibration and current. However, the reality is that a good amount of the data generated does not need to be stored in the long term, and the usefulness of this data is subject to the information that can be obtained from them. This paper proposes the architecture described in Fig. 2.

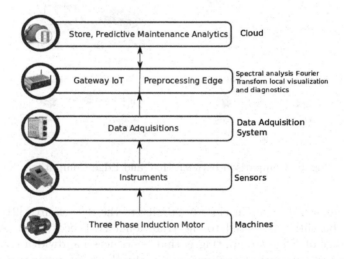

Fig. 2. Architecture.

A system focused on the acquisition of information is proposed, provided by sensors attached to a three-phase asynchronous motor, with the purpose of converging data at the edge of the network, to be processed later, and to send the most relevant information in a spectral form to Cloud In this way, the Edge Computing paradigm contributes with: The performance improvement; compliance, data privacy and data security; and the reduction of the operating cost [7].

5   Proof of Concept

The ecosystem of IIoT, which consists of several layers between hardware and software [20], is shown as follows: First, the acquisition of data (related to the process) by sensors and acquisition systems, then the data is transferred through hubs, gateways and switches like Big Data towards cloud or intranet computing, and finally, they are processed and analyzed through analytical and optimization programs with the aim of increasing the production efficiency of the different tasks in the area of production and service, and make better use of resources [20] Fig. 3a visually describes the ecosystem of IIoT, from the point of view of the predictive maintenance of an industrial electric motor.

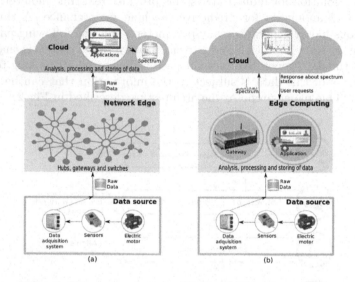

Fig. 3. Comparison between IIoT and Edge Computing.

Edge Computing works in close proximity to the data source [21], and this has several benefits, compared to the traditional IIoT ecosystem. An important advantage of Edge Computing is that it reduces bandwidth consumption and storage and computing requirements in the cloud infrastructure [Medina], because the data is processed close to the source, and the volume of data sent the network is reduced. The other advantage is low latency, the analysis of data near the source, prevents large amounts of data from being transmitted having temporary delay sums within the network [22].

The intention is to implement a system that performs predictive maintenance to an industrial electric motor (SIEMENS 1la7 071-4ya60, Siemens, Berlin), that is, detect the start of anomalies before the engine has a major impact on its system. For this, parameters such as electric current and vibration will be taken.

Three electrical current sensors (SCT-013-010, YHDC, Beijing) are responsible for collecting data, one of each phase of the motor and a vibration sensor

Table 3. Description of devices and applications.

Data Source	
SIEMENS 1la7 071-4ya60. General purpose three-phase motor with alloy housing and increased efficiency, TEFC, VPI insulation (in vacuum), class F.	Two motors of the same characteristics are tested. One partially decomposed and the other in good condition.
SCT-013-010. Current transformers (CT) are sensors that are used to measure alternating current.	Both sensors send electrical pulses to the data acquisition system.
200350 Accelerometer. It's general purpose, case-mounted seismic transducers designed for use with Trendmaster Pro Constant Current Direct Input Card 149811-02 and the Seismic Direct Input Card 164746-01	Note: the current transformers were tested with NI9232 and it works correctly.
NI9232. 3-channel sound and vibration input module of the C series, 102.4 kS/s/ channel, 30 V. The NI-9232 can measure signals from integrated electronic piezoelectric sensors (IEPE) and non-IEPE sensors, such as accelerometers, tachometers and proximity sensors. The NI-9232 incorporates AC / DC coupling	
CDAQ-9191. Chassis CompactDAQ Ethernet and 802.11 Wi-Fi, 1 Slot. The cDAQ-9191 is a bus-powered Wi-Fi chassis, designed for small, remote and distributed sensor systems. The chassis controls the timing, synchronization and data transfer between the C Series I/O modules and an external server.	The data acquisition system receives electrical pulses and they are became in legible data to the NI software and finally sent to the gateway.
Edge Computing	
HPE EL20 Intelligent Edge Gateway. It's rugged performance-optimized edge gateway with additional features and higher compute capabilities to tackle more demanding large data volume deployments at the edge itself. It is optimally configured with CPU, memory, connectivity and an expansion I/O selection, including four (4) port Power over Ethernet (PoE) plus 8-bit digital input/output (DIO), to address a host of IoT needs.	This device has several options for connections, for this project Wi-Fi is used, hence the advantage because the communication is wireless between IoT gateway and CDAQ-9191 chassis. This IoT gateway uses Windows Server 2012 as the operating system.
LabVIEW 2018. It's a graphical programming environment you can use to quickly and efficiently create applications with professional user interfaces. The LabVIEW platform is scalable across different targets and OSs.	An application is created with Labview to obtain data through the Fourier series to obtain frequency spectra.

(200350 Accelerometer, Bently Nevada, Minden-Nevada) is responsible for collecting data on the repetitive movement of the motor around its equilibrium position. Subsequently, through the acquisition system, the data is sent to the edge of the network, for processing, analysis and storage. With the use of an IoT gateway (EL20 Intelligent Edge Gateway, Hewlett Packard Enterprise, San Jose-California) and a processing application (application created with: LabVIEW 2018, National Instruments, Austin-Texas), Edge Computing is performed. With the transformation of the Fourier series, frequency spectra are generated, since, in this way, the visualization of the wave magnitudes and frequencies is facilitated. These frequency spectra are stored in a database within the network device, giving the form of a small data center.

From IoT gateway, the frequency spectra are transferred to the cloud and there are compared with a spectrum pattern (a spectrum historic taken from a similar machine in good state), this is for case of electric current. For case of vibration, the spectra is compared with norm ISO 10816. The spectral information is stored temporary in the cloud, it's not necessary to keep for a long time. Figure 3b visually describes the operation of the project. Below is the Table 3 with the description of the devices and the application to use in the project.

6   Conclusions and Future Works

In this paper We study the use of Industrial Internet of Things methods and tools applied to machine monitoring. In particular, We propose an architecture based on edge computing concepts in order to tackle the case of machine monitoring with high quantity of raw data generated. The results of the proof of concept show the applicability of the implementing this concepts in industry taking a count that We used industrial-like equipment. However, since predictive monitoring requires a large record of historical data, this remains a concept to be tested in this architecture. Our future work is focused in alternatives to feed the database required for predictive monitoring, using both computational simulation and real failure simulation.

Acknowledgments. The authors would like acknowledge the cooperation of all partners within the *Centro de Excelencia y Apropiación en Internet de las Cosas (CEA-IoT)* project. The authors would also like to thank all the institutions that supported this work: the Colombian Ministry for the Information and Communications Technology (*Ministerio de Tecnologías de la Información y las Comunicaciones - MinTIC*) and the Colombian Administrative Department of Science, Technology and Innovation (*Departamento Administrativo de Ciencia, Tecnología e Innovación - Colciencias*) through the *Fondo Nacional de Financiamiento para la Ciencia, la Tecnología y la Innovación Francisco José de Caldas* (Project ID: FP44842-502-2015).

References

1. Gregori, F., Papetti, A., Pandolfi, M., Peruzzini, M., Germani, M.: Improving a production site from a social point of view: an IoT infrastructure to monitor workers condition. Procedia CIRP **72**, 886–891 (2018). https://doi.org/10.1016/j.procir.2018.03.057. http://www.sciencedirect.com/science/article/pii/S2212827118301598. ISSN2212-8271
2. Edge computing consortium. White paper of edge computing consortium (2016)
3. Boyes, H., Hallaq, B., Cunningham, J., Watson, T.: The industrial Internet of Things (IIoT): an analysis framework. Comput. Ind. **101**, 1–12 (2018). https://doi.org/10.1016/j.compind.2018.04.015. http://www.sciencedirect.com/science/article/pii/S0166361517307285. ISSN 0166-3615
4. Civerchia, F., Bocchino, S., Salvadori, C., Rossi, E., Maggiani, L., Petracca, M.: Industrial Internet of Things monitoring solution for advanced predictive maintenance applications. J. Ind. Inf. Integr. **7**, 4–12 (2017). https://doi.org/10.1016/j.jii.2017.02.003. http://www.sciencedirect.com/science/article/pii/S2452414X16300954. ISSN 2452-414X
5. Quinn, J.: The real goal of maintenance engineering, in factory. In: Collins, A.W. (ed.) The Measurement of Naval Facilities Maintenance Effectiveness. Naval Postgraduate School, Monterey CA, p. 90-3 (1964)
6. Cao, J., Zhang, Q., Li, Y., Shi, W., Xu, L.: Edge computing: vision and challenges. IEEE IoT J. **3**(16286981), 637–646 (2016)
7. Industrial Internet Consortium. Introduction to edge computing in IIoT. An Industrial Internet Consortium White Paper, IIC:WHT:IN24:V1.0:PB:20180618. Edge Computing Task Group

8. Schmidt, B., Wang, L., Galar, D.: Semantic framework for predictive maintenance in a cloud environment. Procedia CIRP **62**, 583–588 (2017). https://doi.org/10.1016/j.procir.2016.06.047. ISSN 2212-8271
9. Taherizadeh, S., Jones, A.C., Taylor, I., Zhao, Z., Stankovski, V.: Monitoring self-adaptive applications within edge computing frameworks: a state-of-the-art review. J. Syst. Softw. **136**(Suppl. C), 19–38 (2018)
10. Fujishima, M., Mori, M., Nishimura, K., Takayama, M., Kato, Y.: Development of sensing interface for preventive maintenance of machine tools. Procedia CIRP **61**, 796–799 (2017). https://doi.org/10.1016/j.procir.2016.11.206. http://www.sciencedirect.com/science/article/pii/S2212827116313749. ISSN 2212-8271
11. Cruz, A.M.E.: ESTUDIO DE UN SISTEMA DE MANTENIMIENTO PREDICTIVO BASADO EN ANÁLISIS DE VIBRACIONES IMPLANTADO EN INSTALACIONES DE BOMBEO Y GENERACIÓN (2013)
12. Power-MI, Manual Análisis de Vibraciones. https://power-mi.com/es/content/power-mi-lanza-manual-de-an
13. Pease, S.G., Conway, P.P., West, A.A.: Hybrid ToF and RSSI real-time semantic tracking with an adaptive industrial internet of things architecture. J. Netw. Comput. Appl. **99**, 98–109 (2017)
14. Flores, R., Asiaín, T.I.: Diagnóstico de Fallas en Máquinas Eléctricas Rotatorias Utilizando la Técnica de Espectros de Frecuencia de Bandas Laterales. Información Tecnológica **22**(4), 73–84 (2011). https://doi.org/10.4067/S0718-07642011000400009
15. Talbot, C.E., Saavedra, P.N., Valenzuela, M.A.: Diagnóstico de la Condición de las Barras de Motores de Inducción. Información tecnológica **24**(4), 85–94 (2013). https://doi.org/10.4067/S0718-07642013000400010
16. Lin, S.-W.: Architecture alignment and interoperability (2017)
17. Mourtzis, D., Gargallis, A., Zogopoulos, V.: Modelling of customer oriented applications in product lifecycle using RAMI 4.0. Procedia Manuf. **28**, 31–36 (2019). https://doi.org/10.1016/j.promfg.2018.12.006. http://www.sciencedirect.com/science/article/pii/S2351978918313489. ISSN 2351-9789
18. Lin, S.W., et al.: Industrial internet reference architecture. Technical report, Industrial Internet Consortium (IIC) (2015)
19. Packard, H.: Real-time analysis and condition monitoring with predictive maintenance. Transforming data into value with HPE Edgeline (2017)
20. Gierej, S.: The framework of business model in the context of industrial Internet of Things. Procedia Eng. **182**, 206–212 (2017). https://doi.org/10.1016/j.proeng.2017.03.166. http://www.sciencedirect.com/science/article/pii/S1877705817313024. ISSN 1877-7058
21. Shi, W., Cao, J., Zhang, Q., Li, Y., Xu, L.: Edge computing: vision and challenges. IEEE IoT J. **3**(5), 637–646 (2016)
22. Barroso, M., Dolores, M.: Edge computing para IoT (2019)
23. Bossio, G., De Angelo, C., García, G.: Técnicas de Mantenimiento Predictivo en Máquinas Eléctricas: Diagnóstico de Fallas en el Rotor de los Motores de Inducción. Megavatios, pp. 194–208 (2006)
24. Bellini, A., et al.: On-field experience with online diagnosis of large induction motors cage failures using MCSA. IEEE Trans. Ind. Appl. **38**(4), 1045–1053 (2002). https://doi.org/10.1109/TIA.2002.800591

Power Applications

Integrated Methodology for the Planning of Electrical Distribution System Considering the Continuity of the Service and the Reduction of Technical Losses

Oscar Danilo Montoya[1]([⊠])(iD), Ricardo A. Hincapié[2](iD),
and Mauricio Granada[2](iD)

[1] Programa de Ingeniería Eléctrica e Ingeniería Electrónica,
Universidad Tecnológica de Bolívar, Cartagena, Colombia
`omontoya@utb.edu.co`
[2] Programa de Ingeniería Eléctrica,
Universidad Tecnológica de Pereira, Pereira, Colombia
`{ricardohincapie,magra}@utp.edu.co`

Abstract. This article presents a methodology that allows to obtain an optimal plan of re-configuration of the local distribution system to 13.2 kV, considering the improvement in the continuity of the service to the users and the reduction of technical losses in the network. The methodology consists of two phases: The first deals with the problem of the reconfiguration of primary distribution circuits through permanent measures and temporary measures. The second phase ad-dresses one of the main problems in the planning of the expansion of distribution networks, which consists of the location of the distribution substations, which represent the main link between transmission and distribution systems. The implementation of the methodology allows to simulate different scenarios and constitutes a tool for the planning of the distribution system of the regional operators (OR) of the local distribution systems (LDS).

Keywords: Electric distribution system ·
Optimal expansion planning · Reconfiguration · Substations

1 Introduction

At present, different strategies for the improvement of the reliability of the service are developed and implemented by the Distribution Company (DisCo) according to the requirements of the current regulations and of each one of the companies. These strategies can be classified into two main categories: electric and non-electric. The techniques of the first group have a direct impact on the distribution system and include the addition of: protection and reconnection devices (fuses

J. C. Figueroa-García et al. (Eds.): WEA 2019, CCIS 1052, pp. 537–551, 2019.
https://doi.org/10.1007/978-3-030-31019-6_45

and reclosers), sectioning devices (motorized and manual disconnectors), reconfiguration systems, feeder repowering and integration of distributed generation, among others.

On the other hand, non-electrical strategies can be evaluated from the aspect of reliability exclusively and include mainly information analysis, such as, for example: optimal management of vegetation and optimal location of work groups, among others.

This paper presents a methodology, based on a multi-objective genetic algorithm that allows to obtain an optimal plan of reconfiguration of the local distribution system to 13.2 kV, considering the improvement in the continuity of the service to the users and the reduction of technical losses in the network.

The methodology consists of two phases. The first deals with the problem of the reconfiguration of primary distribution circuits through permanent and temporary measures. The permanent measures refer to the reconfiguration of circuits for loss reduction, that is, modification of the topology of the circuits that will last over time. With regard to temporary measures, the optimal location of protection elements is considered to minimize the effect of faults on the reliability indicators. It is called a temporary measure because it modifies momentarily the operational configuration of the circuits (topology), in order to meet as many users as possible, under contingency conditions. In conclusion, this first phase addresses fundamental aspects of the automation and operation of the LDS.

The second phase addresses one of the main problems in the planning of the expansion of distribution networks, which consists of the location of the distribution substations which represent the main link between the transmission and distribution systems. The availability of places and the sizes of the substations results in restrictions in the planning processes of transmission and distribution. In turn, the design parameters of the substations have a great impact on feeder routes and it is necessary to take into account the need to expand the capacity of the existing substations.

Given that the problems addressed are of non-linear characteristics and with integer and continuous variables, their solution spaces depend exponentially on the size of the problem. For this reason, some strategies are proposed to reduce the solution space and, consequently, its computational complexity. Therefore, the solution technique used corresponds to a metaheuristic based on genetic algorithms.

The proposed methodology integrates the two phases described considering the substitution between substations and between substation circuits of 13.2 kV in order to guarantee the continuity of the service. The implementation of the methodology allows simulating different scenarios and constitutes a tool for the planning of the distribution system of the regional operators (OR) of the LDS.

2   State-of-the-Art Review

One of the most outstanding studies on the theme of reconfiguration of primary circuits was developed in [1], where a methodology for relocation of reclosers is proposed, taking into account the conservation of radiality, the reduction of technical losses and the balance of phases in the network at minimum investment cost.

In the topic of optimal location of recloser devices for improving the reliability indicators, the first work of which there is reference was the one developed in [2], where a methodology is proposed for the optimal location of protection elements in the network, taking into account the cost associated with the unavailability of the system, in addition to the investment and operation costs. The problem is formulated with a mixed integer nonlinear mathematical model and is solved with the metaheuristic technique called Simulated Annealing.

Recently, other studies that incorporate new technological developments in the field of LDS automation and different aspects of what is known as smart networks have been published. In [3] the authors present a methodology to locate switches, transfer elements, fuses and disconnectors, using binary programming (BP), in order to minimize the cost of the devices, in addition to the costs associated with the unused energy and the deterioration of the useful life of the elements of the system, among others. The SAIFI and SAIDI indices are shown, related to the reliability of the system for each one of the proposed solutions. The authors apply binary programming to solve the problem of optimal localization, since the nature of the problem has implicit this characteristic, associated with the appearance or non-appearance of the elements of protection, reason why they discard the application of metaheuristic techniques as a solution tool.

In [4] a methodology is proposed to find the optimal level of automation of medium voltage power distribution networks considering different protection elements (switches, reclosers, auto-sectionalizers and switches). Likewise, within the electrical system planning group of the University Tecnológica of Pereira, agreements have been developed with Colciencias [5] and the Commission for Energy and Gas Regulation CREG [6], in order to advance studies for the reduction of technical losses in distribution systems using different circuit reconfiguration strategies.

In [7] an explicit mathematical model is developed for the minimization of the SAIDI and SAIFI indicators, in addition to the investment cost associated with the protection elements, it is proposed to locate reclosers, switches and fuses as a mono-objective optimization model using the GAMS commercial optimization package with the Baron solver, and a comparison is made with answers obtained through the implementation of genetic algorithms.

The planning of the distribution substations is considered one of the most important steps in the power system planning process. This is because they represent the main link between the transmission and distribution systems. The availability of places and the sizes of the substations results in restrictions in both planning processes in the transmission and distribution and in turn the design parameters of the substations have a great impact on the routes of the feeders. Additionally, the need to expand the capacity of the existing substations must be taken into account.

The planning of the substations involves the following aspects [8,9]: construction site, size, service areas, associated equipment, construction time and entry into operation. It is common to direct the analysis with the interests of minimizing construction and operation costs, reducing technical losses and maintaining voltage regulation at the permitted levels during the pre-established planning horizon. In some cases, reliability restrictions are taken into account in terms of guaranteeing the service provision of continuous electrical power to the final user.

In [10] a first approach is developed to deal with the problem of dimensioning and construction time of the substations, where size and time are effectively decoupled using a pseudo-dynamic approach. The method requires the sequential application of different optimization models, such as linear and integer programming, to the static planning model in a single period. The question of whether or not to build a new substation is based entirely on the consideration of voltage drop from the substation to the point of charge (voltage regulation). The main disadvantage of this method lies in the voltage prediction, in which it is assumed that the load densities are uniform in the service area of the substation, which is not entirely true in most cases. Additionally, the team's locations are not taken into account.

In [11] a model to determine the location of the equipment, its size and its service area for distribution substations is presented. The model is based on solving the transport model where the objective function pretends to carry power over long distances. In this model it is assumed that the total demand is equal to the total supply and the objective is to determine a feasible flow pattern that minimizes the total cost of transporting the energy. This approach does not include the costs of the equipment in its objective function, and in turn models all the substations (potential and existing) as source nodes, which generates an optimal solution with all the substations being used, even though some of them deliver a small amount of charge. On the other hand, this method does not consider any restrictions, such as voltage restrictions in its final solution. Additionally, voltage regulation calculations are not included.

A model of fixed load transfer between circuits for the selection of an optimal lo-cation of a substation is developed in [8]. The objective function represents both the fixed and variable costs associated with the substation and the problem is solved with an integer branch-and-bound optimization technique. This model is considered static, since it does not consider the variation of the demands over time. However, restrictions for voltage limits are not included.

In [12] a flexible model is introduced for the optimal planning of distribution stations and/or primary feeders using a fixed branch-and-bound algorithm, which includes an explicit modeling of the fixed and variable cost components. However, no restriction for voltage limits is included in this technique.

Finally, in [13] a state of the art in the planning of the distribution is presented, where all the aspects that are taken into account in regards to model and method of solution that have been presented in the specialized literature are included. In addition, aspects such as the optimal location of substations and reclosers are included. In this reference a structure of three levels is developed to classify the different approaches or methods. At level 1, the classification is made based on the planning models that have or do not have reliability characteristics. At level 2, two distinctive categories are presented: planning with and without uncertainty modeling. The third classification shows the different mathematical formulations of the objective functions and their corresponding solution strategies.

3   General Formulation of the Reconfiguration Problem

The problem of optimal localization of normally open (RNA) and normally closed (RNC) reclosers in electric power distribution systems is the fundamental basis of the LDS automation process and is formulated as a multi-objective optimization problem, where the objectives under study are: the minimization of fixed costs (equipment costs, construction of sections, installation, etc.) and the minimization of the level of average unserved energy (NENS).

The integrated operation of these devices allows considering two main functions for the OR: (i) the isolation of zones under faults and (ii) the restoration of the service of said zones. The above originates a set of areas or operational zones in the LDS originated by the location of the RNC and the RNA. Each one of these zones is characterized by its NENS, which remains constant and is independent of the section in which the failure event occurs, since the same protection devices associated with the zone will always operate. Therefore, each set of possible RNA and RNC locations will define the number of operating zones that appear in the set of circuits analyzed, as well as their size. The definition of the zones generates a new problem consisting of the determination of the NENS associated to each area in the presence of a fault phenomenon in one of the circuit elements that are contained therein.

The distribution system presented in Fig. 1 corresponds to a set of independent circuits, each fed by substations A, B, and C respectively. This system presents a possible configuration for the cutting and reconnecting elements, where the reclosers at the head of each circuit exist by regulation and the remaining set of RNC (2, 3, 4, 6, 7 and 9) is the subset of possible location alternatives. In addition to this the set of reconnection keys between circuits is made up of the group of RNA (1, 2, 3 and 4) that considers those points that can be transferred to another circuit at the occurrence of an event. It should be noted that the operational zones are those formed by the groups of RNA and RNC, which allow to isolate the areas under the influence of the fault and transfer loads to other sources of supply during the time the interruption lasts, thus, the areas that are formed for the system are shown in Fig. 1.

To visualize the behavior of the operative zones at the occurrence of permanent failures, suppose a failure in ZONE 5. It is evident that the first maneuver to be performed to clear the fault, is to change the operative state of the RNC (5, 6 and 7).), with which the entire circuit corresponding to substation C is taken out of operation. However, it is observed that areas outside the fault are affected, which should not suffer service interruptions for long periods of time, so the strategy for recovering load centers, after having isolated the zone in fault, consists of changing the operational state of the RNAs (3 and 4) in order to supply the ZONES (6 and 7), through the sub-stations A and B, respectively.

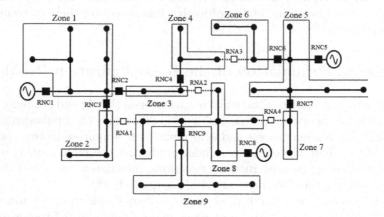

Fig. 1. Conformation of operative zones based on the location of RNA and RNC

The process of isolation and recovery of loading areas through the coordinated operation of RNA and RNC is an effective strategy to reduce the impact of faults and allows to reduce the NENS. However, it is highly dependent on the location of the protection devices on the network, for which it is necessary to develop a methodology that allows evaluating all the possible scenarios of location of elements and determining those sets that guarantee the maximum reduction of the level of energy not served at minimum cost.

The problem is formulated as a multi-objective model according to (1)–(6).
Objective functions:

$$\min \quad \text{NENS}_z = \sum_{i \in Z} \lambda_i f_i^p \left(Tp_i, I_z \right), \tag{1}$$

$$\min \quad C_f = \sum_{j=1}^{ND} C_j x_j, \tag{2}$$

Set of constraints:

$$|I_l| \leq \bar{I}_l, \tag{3}$$

$$V_k^{\min} \leq V_k \leq V_k^{\max}, \tag{4}$$

$$\sum_{j=1}^{ND} x_j \leq ND_{\max}, \tag{5}$$

$$\sum_{j=1}^{ND} C_j x_j \leq RF_{\max}, \tag{6}$$

where, NENS_z is the average unserviced energy level of zone z, λ_i is the average failure rate of line i contained in zone z, Tp_i corresponds to the average time duration of the failure in section i belonging to zone z, I_z is the amount of interrupted power in zone z, $f_i^p(Tp_i, I_z)$ corresponds to the function that quantifies the cost of permanent interruption, by type of consumer connected to the receipt node i, with non-supplied demand value I_z and duration T_{pi}, C_f is the fixed cost of installing protection devices over the network, C_j represents the cost of installing a device in section j, x_j is the decision variable of installation or not of an RNA or RNC device in section j. It is a decision variable of binary type, which means that if the value is one (1), the device is installed, otherwise if its value is zero (0), it is not installed; I_l represents the magnitude of the current that flows through line l, V_k is the magnitude of the tension in the node k, ND corresponds to the number of possible reclosing elements to be located, $ND_{\max}$ represents the maximum number of reclosers available, and $RF_{\max}$ is the maximum financial resource for the realization of the project.

Since it is a multi-objective problem, the objective function is divided into two parts. The first objective function corresponds to the average NENS, which takes into account analytically the level of reliability of the network. To quantify this objective, the contingency simulation criterion $n-1$ is used through the evaluation of a fault in each section of the circuit and the energy not served is evaluated, taking into account the possibility of restoring operational zones through the RNA. At the time the contingency is made, the RNC are considered to isolate the fault. That is, from a contingency in a network section, the level of energy not served for the whole system is evaluated, adding the value of the level of each zone. Therefore, the total NENS of the system will be the sum of all the contributions of unprovided energy from each zone, as presented in (7).

$$\text{NENS}_T = \sum_{Z=1}^{NZ} \text{NENS}_z, \tag{7}$$

where NENS_T is the total average of unserved energy level and NZ is the total number of operational zones for an RNA and RNC configuration. When a contingency is simulated using criterion $n-1$, two types of sweeps are incorporated into the algorithm in order to calculate the objective function: downstream of the fault location (look for the RNCs to isolate the fault and the RNAs to restore the areas without service), and upstream of the fault location (look for the RNC to isolate the fault).

At the moment in which it is evaluated if a zone without service can be fed through another zone by means of the RNA, the regulation of the network and the capacity of load transfer (chargeability) is verified. If the location of an RNA in a place causes that an area cannot be fed through this element, due to the violation of one of the two criteria mentioned above (regulation and chargeability), then it is considered that this area has a demand not attended, so when calculating its NENS, the value of the objective function increases.

The second objective function is basically a cost function that quantifies the investment value necessary for a configuration of proposed protection devices, considering labor, cost of equipment, structures, among other costs.

If all the protection devices (RNA and RNC) considered were located in the system, the value of the objective function defined in (7) would decrease, as there would be a smaller number of areas with unattended load because there would be a greater quantity of possibilities of interconnection with other zones. If this happens, it is clear that the value of the function given by (2) would increase considerably, since we would have a much higher value associated with the installation of all the devices. Otherwise, if you only intend to connect a reduced group of devices, for example, an RNA and an RNC, the cost function would have a very low value, however, this would necessarily involve a small number of operational zones, which would limit to a greater extend the possibility of reconnection between circuits, which consequently would raise the total NENS of the network.

According to the above, it can be observed that the improvement of the objective function defined by (7) worsens the objective function (2), and vice versa. Due to this, it is concluded that both objectives are in conflict, so it is not necessary to search only one solution proposal, in such a way that different system conditions can be evaluated.

Note that the set of restrictions (3) to (6) obey, respectively, the following characteristics:

✓ Chargeability sections: ensures that the flowing current in all the sections of the network do not exceed a permitted limit; it influences the calculation of the average NENS, since it verifies if, by flowing capacity, an operative zone can be restored or not.

✓ Voltage regulation: defines the limits of voltage allowed for the nodes of the network, and is specified as an input parameter of the algorithm. This restriction evaluates that, if a load is restored by means of an RNA, the nodes contained in it are within the limits of voltage allowed by regulations; if so the energy of that area can be recovered, otherwise, this sums to the average NENS.

✓ Maximum number of reclosers: in the event that the location of RNA and RNC devices is limited by a maximum number of elements to be located, it ensures that all location proposals never exceed this limit.

✓ Financial resource: like the previous restriction, it limits any proposed location of RNA and RNC to a maximum of available investment resources.

4 General Formulation of the Substation Planning Problem

The problem that is addressed in this project is one of mathematical optimization where it is intended to find a final solution that yields one or more of the following results:

✓ The optimal location of new power substations (33/13.2 kV), starting from some probable locations, established a priori using certain criteria such as electrical moment.
✓ The expansion in capacity (MVA) of the existing substations, presetting some possible increment ranges for each substation.
✓ The improvement of the reliability of the system, by reducing the NENS.
✓ The incorporation of auxiliary circuits.

In order to establish the location of the substations in a DisCo, taking into account the existing units, the growth of the demand and guaranteeing the reliability of the system, a strategy based on the sectorization of the area of DisCo influence is proposed, by means of its delimitation in square areas of dimension 1.2×1.2 km^2 denominated micro-areas. Additionally, the projected substations (candidates) and the existing ones are located in georeferenced points of the area as shown in Fig. 2. It is important to establish that the proposed methodology does not project the replacement of existing substations, but the location of new units and/or the expansion of the existing ones.

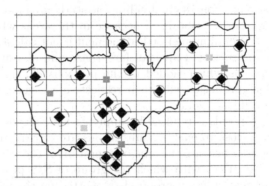

Fig. 2. Quadrants of the area operation

In each micro-area the load density value is calculated by its location in the central point of the established micro-area (load center). The charge density consists of the accumulation of charge within it, said value is determined from the following equation:

$$D_i = \sum_{j=1}^{t_i} \frac{C_{ij}}{A}, \quad \forall j \in i \tag{8}$$

where, D_i is the load density of the micro-area i [kVA/km^2], C_{ij} represents the load given in kVA of the transformer j that belongs to the micro-area i, t_i is the total number of transformers that are in the micro-area i, and A represents the micro-area conformed by the geographical location of the loads, i.e., 1.44 km^2.

Initially, the monthly billing information of each transformer in the system is known and it is considered that there are no substations located. Then the system is divided into m grids grouping n micro-areas, these divisions are called areas. In each area q the electric moment is calculated as shown in (9) with respect to each micro-area j, where D_j corresponds to the load density value calculated in (8) and X_{ij} is the Euclidean distance from the central point of the micro-area i to the central point of the micro-area j. For each area, the micro-area with the minimum electrical moment is selected (this position determines the location of a proposed substation).

$$M_{iq} = \sum_{j=1}^{n} D_j X_{ij}, \quad \forall i,j \in q \tag{9}$$

Equation (9) must be evaluated for each of the n micro-areas that belong to the area. The density of charge in each micro-area is discretized, by means of a grouping technique (k-means), in the ranges of low, medium and high load.

Through the methodology proposed above, the substation proposals for the DisCo are calculated. For this case the construction of the areas is carried out in two stages, the first stage consists in dividing the study area into 120 equal areas, with which 86 proposals are obtained, because in the areas where there are no sectors with loads, the minimum electrical moment is not calculated. The second stage consists of constructing 4 areas of larger size and of equal dimensions to obtain 4 new proposals which, added to the previous 86, make up a total of 90 initial substations proposals with their respective XY geographical positions within the system influence zone.

This set of 90 proposals is reduced by applying the following filters. Substations (S/S) that are close to existing substations are discarded from the group of substations proposed because the area of operation of these is already covered by the existing substations, with which the group of S/S proposals is initially reduced to 72. The new group of proposals is plotted on the map that contains voltage level circuits equal to 33 kV where the distance from each one of the S/S to the closest network section is calculated; based on the above, substations that have a distance greater than 10 km are discarded from the proposals, with which the group of proposals is reduced to 33, as shown in Fig. 3.

The dimensioning of the S/S is determined from a percentage of load transfer (%tc) of the circuits that are in the vicinity of each one of the proposals and additionally the totality of the load of the largest associated circuit, with the objective of allowing the total transfer of any of the circuits in a fault scenario in some of the neighboring substations.

In other words, each circuit involved was partitioned into two: the first partition or topology is associated with the existing substation and the second partition is associated with the new substation proposal (Fig. 4). It is highlighted that the demands of the circuits involved were projected to 10 years using the percentage of growth given by UPME.

In Fig. 4 the connection point is given by the shortest feasible distance between the proposed substation and the neighboring circuit. The word feasible

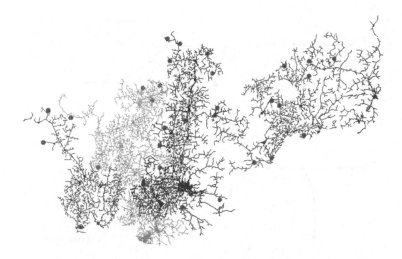

Fig. 3. Location of the proposed substations

means that the connection point must belong to the main branch, in order to allow the transfer of the load. The cutoff point is determined by a sensitivity criterion, which consists in determining which part of the existing topology is transferred to the new substation according to a pre-established percentage of load. The percentage of final load with which the modified circuit remains is around 40 % or 60 % depending on the load of the base circuit.

5   Integrated Methodology

Here, we present the necessary stages to carry out the integrated process of substation planning and reconfiguration. The first stage consists in the location and dimensioning of the candidate substations. Once the new substations are located, the reconfiguration is carried out in order to improve the reliability of the system.

Stage 1: Locate and size substations.
Stage 2: Determine the groups that are affected by the new substations.
Stage 3: Locate RNA at the cut points.
Stage 4: Perform the optimization process in order to determine the location of the reclosers.
Stage 5: In each proposal generated add the cost of the RNA and the cost of the proposed substations.
Stage 6: In each generation proposal add the benefit obtained due to the reduction of technical losses of each substation involved.

From the previous process of substations, it must be taken into account that some proposals are exclusive. This occurs because some of the proposed substations share the same circuit, but the proposed cut in each of them is

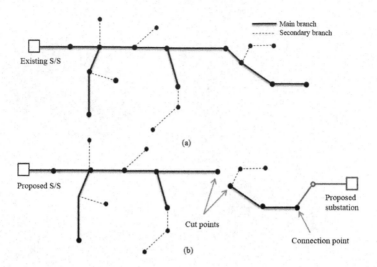

Fig. 4. Example circuit partition: (a) Original topology, (b) new topologies

different, which entails selecting one of the 2 possible substations. This selection criterion is determined by the benefit-cost ratio provided by the installation of the substations, selecting the one with the highest B/C ratio. This reduces the set of 33 to 19 substations to enter the reconfiguration process. It is emphasized that the groups formed for the study of reconfiguration are constituted only by circuits that show closeness or physical connection (cut/connect elements).

With the set of candidate positions for the installation of RNA and RNC, the recloser devices already installed and the cutoff points defined as points with RNA installed in the system, the optimization process is proceeded to be executed to optimize the location of reclosers. For this, the NSGA-II [14] solution technique is applied, which is based on the meta-heuristic genetic algorithm technique, applying the logic proposed by Chu and Beasley in [15], to evaluate the possible locations of new recloser elements and the economic viability. Finally, the last two stages correspond to the financial analysis of the plans and the analysis of the benefit/cost relationships, respectively.

6   Obtained Results

This section presents a description of the results that can be obtained from the tool developed and the main impacts and aspects observed in the results obtained with the LDS. The specific information of the plans and the detailed values are not presented in this document by confidentiality clauses of the DisCo, due to limitation in the number of pages of this article and mainly because for a proper interpretation it is required to know large volumes of information related to topological and billing characteristics of the different LDS of DisCo circuits and substations.

Among the results obtained in the reconfiguration phase, the percentage of annual energy loss reduction, the restored energy and the maximum profits of each group created in year 0 and with the respective 10 and 30 year projections are highlighted.

Said gain is related to the energy recovered due to the optimal location of reclosers in the system. It is also possible to obtain a report of the groups formed for the reconfiguration and the S/S new proposals that impact each one of them. Each group has associated values which correspond to the 30-year earnings for the reduction of technical losses and energy level not served. These gain values are distributed in a weighted manner depending on the number of circuits present in said group.

The new S/S that present circuits in each conformed group and the construction cost of the S/S are reported, which are distributed in a weighted manner according to the number of circuits and their input energy value present in said group. The total gain of each group is obtained by adding the gain caused by the recovery of energy with respect to the base case and the gain obtained by the reduction of technical losses. In addition, the total gain of each group for a period of thirty years is shown. This allows obtaining the benefit-cost relation for each of the groups over a period of thirty years.

The methodology allows to visualize and propose additional strategies for the construction of new circuits in order to reduce technical losses, improve reliability and protect the market by guaranteeing service to potential customers. In addition, it allows to propose different strategies that permit to maintain in function substations with greater impact in the specified area. For example, at the moment of failure of the transformer of a specific substation, part or all of the circuits of said the S/S are fed by means of a neighboring S/S making use of the network section at 33 kV and performing the appropriate operational maneuvers. In the new scenario the network section at 33 kV is temporarily energized at 13.2 kV from the backup S/S supplying temporarily the transformation 33 kV–13.2 kV.

Another strategy for a 33 kV power failure scenario for a specific S/S, is to supply the energy deficit by using an express circuit at 33 kV, which is energized from a neighboring S/S. In the moment of failure of the transformer of a specific S/S, considering that all of its circuits cannot be fed by any neighboring S/S. It is proposed to feed the special circuits or a small group of circuits belonging to the S/S in fault by means of an express circuit at 13.2 kV, which is fed from any neighboring S/S with sufficient capacity for the transfer.

A quartile analysis allows to conclude the following, regarding the percentage of NENS reduction: 25% of the groups present a reduction of NENS less than or equals to 11.93%, 50% of the data has a reduction of NENS less or equals to 20.45% and 75% of the data shows a reduction of NENS less than or equal to 28.72%.

For a period of 30 years, 27 of the reconfiguration plans are attractive to be implemented and the rest of the groups have a benefit/cost ratio of less than 1. This is because the cost of the NENS reduction is not enough to recover the investment made in the reclosers proposed for these groups. In order to calculate the relationship between the current ITAD of the system and the ITAD of the study, the level of energy not served (NENS) is used, before and after each of the study measures was carried out, as shown in (10).

$$\frac{\text{ITAD}_{New}}{\text{ITAD}_{Base}} = \frac{\frac{\text{NENS}_{New}}{VT}}{\frac{\text{NENS}_{Base}}{VT}}, \tag{10}$$

where NENS_{New} is the non-served energy level after applied the methodology, NENS_{Base} corresponds to the non-served energy level before applied the methodology, and VT represents the energy sales.

7   Conclusions and Recommendations

As an additional benefit, the proposed reconfiguration plans include all zones served by the DisCo which is equivalent to say that it covers all quality groups (1 to 4); that is, the values of unserved energy NTG1 to NTG4 are reduced and consequently, the quarterly indexes of discontinuity ITG1 to ITG4 are reduced, as a consequence, it is barely obvious that the quarterly indexes of ITAD grouped in discontinuity will be improved, making likewise that the annual grouped index of discontinuity (IAAD) will improve. Regarding the worst-served index (IPS), the processors (and users), to whom compensation for this concept will be paid, will be reduced.

The proposed methodology to determine the optimal location of substations presents a good sensitivity since about 20% of the proposals correspond to S/S located in the current system of the regional operator.

The conformation of each one of the substations proposed through the transfer of load of circuits near its location, allows to diminish the technical losses around 54.83% in relation to the current state of the system, besides improving the quality of the energy and the continuity of the service, which is evidenced in the percentage of voltage regulation in each of the final circuits.

According to the results obtained for the selected proposals (small power), it is observed that the impact of the cost of the 33 kV network on the final cost is significant, even though the distances between the proposals and the 33 kV networks were intended to be the shortest possible. This allows us to conclude that the costs associated with the construction of new networks have a considerable influence on the decision to build new substations.

The capacity assigned to each proposed substation was foreseen in function of the amount of load that will attend; additionally, it is considered that said capacity will be sufficient to attend at least one of the circuits that is related to it. This is feasible if you want to perform a substitution before a contingency of type $n-1$ between the adjacent substations; However, it is important to bear in mind that this capacity can be modified depending on the reliability requirements that are to be met, for example, if a complete substitution of a neighboring substation is desired, then said substation will have its own capacity for the attention of its own demand plus the capacity of the substation or the substations that need to be supplied.

Acknowledgments. This work was supported by the MSc Program in Electrical Engineering of Universidad Tecnologica de Pereira. The authors also thank the Research Group "Desarrollo en Investigacion de Operaciones - DINOP".

References

1. Baran, M.E., Wu, F.F.: Network reconfiguration in distribution systems for loss reduction and load balancing. IEEE Trans. Power Del. **4**(2), 1401–1407 (1989)
2. Billinton, R., Jonnavithula, S.: Optimal switching device placement in radial distribution systems. IEEE Trans. Power Del. **11**(3), 1646–1651 (1996)
3. Darabi, F., Shooshtari, A.T., Babaei, E., Darabi, S.: Reliability cost allocation of protective devices using binary programming. In: 2011 IEEE Symposium on Business, Engineering and Industrial Applications, pp. 469–474, September 2011
4. Popovic, D.S., Glamocic, L.R., Nimrihter, M.D.: The optimal automation level of medium voltage distribution networks. Int. J. Electr. Power Energy Syst. **33**(3), 430–438 (2011)
5. UTP-Colciencias: Reducción de pérdidas por etapas en sistemas de distribución. Technical report, Universidad Tecnológica de Pereira (2006)
6. UTP-CREG: Medidas para la reducción de pérdidas técnicas en los sistemas de distribución. Technical report, Universidad Tecnológica de Pereira (2010)
7. Ferreira, G., Bretas, A.: A nonlinear binary programming model for electric distribution systems reliability optimization. Int. J. Electr. Power Energy Syst. **43**(1), 384–392 (2012)
8. Thompson, G.L., Wall, D.L.: A branch and bound model for choosing optimal substation locations. IEEE Trans. Power App. Syst. **PAS–100**(5), 2683–2688 (1981)
9. Temraz, H., Salama, M.: A planning model for siting, sizing and timing of distribution substations and defining the associated service area. Electr. Power Syst. Res. **62**(2), 145–151 (2002)
10. Masud, E.: An interactive procedure for sizing and timing distribution substations using optimization techniques. IEEE Trans. Power App. Syst. **PAS–93**(5), 1281–1286 (1974)
11. Crawford, D.M., Holt, S.B.: A mathematical optimization technique for locating and sizing distribution substations, and deriving their optimal service areas. IEEE Trans. Power App. Syst. **94**(2), 230–235 (1975)
12. Sun, D.I., Farris, D.R., Cote, P.J., Shoults, R.R., Chen, M.S.: Optimal distribution substation and primary feeder planning via the fixed charge network formulation. IEEE Trans. Power App. Syst. **PAS–101**(3), 602–609 (1982)
13. Ganguly, S., Das, N.C.S.D.: Recent advances on power distribution system planning: a state-of-the-art survey. Energy Syst. **4**(2), 165–193 (2013)
14. Deb, K., Pratap, A., Agarwal, S., Meyarivan, T.: A fast and elitist multiobjective genetic algorithm: NSGA-II. IEEE Trans. Evol. Comput. **6**(2), 182–197 (2002)
15. Chu, P., Beasley, J.: A genetic algorithm for the multidimensional knapsack problem. J. Heuristics **4**(1), 63–86 (1998)

Determination of the Voltage Stability Index in DC Networks with CPLs: A GAMS Implementation

William Tadeo Amin[1], Oscar Danilo Montoya[1]([✉])[iD],
and Luis Fernando Grisales-Noreña[2][iD]

[1] Programa de Ingeniería Eléctrica e Ingeniería Electrónica,
Universidad Tecnológica de Bolívar, Cartagena, Colombia
witambu@gmail.com, omontoya@utb.edu.co
[2] Departamento de Electromecánica y Mecatrónica,
Instituto Tecnológico Metropolitano, Medellín, Colombia
luisgrisales@itm.edu.co

Abstract. This paper addresses the voltage collapse analysis in direct-current (DC) power grids via nonlinear optimization approach. The formulation of this problem corresponds to an optimization problem, where the objective function is the maximization of the loadability consumption at all the constant power loads, subject to the conventional power flow balance equations. To solve this nonlinear non-convex optimization problem a large-scale nonlinear optimization package known as General Algebraic Modeling System (GAMS) is employed. Different nonlinear solvers available in GAMS are used to confirm that the optimal solution has been reached. A small 4-node test system is used to illustrate the GAMS implementation. Finally, two test systems with 21 and 33 nodes respectively, are used for simulation purposes in order to confirm both the effectiveness and robustness of the nonlinear model, and the proposed GAMS solution methodology.

Keywords: Direct-current networks ·
General algebraic modeling system · Nonlinear optimization ·
Optimal power flow analysis · Voltage stability margin

1 Introduction

Historically, the electricity generation has been carried out on a large scale in places close to the primary source of energy, then, this energy is transmitted

This work was supported in part by the Administrative Department of Science, Technology, and Innovation of Colombia (COLCIENCIAS) through the National Scholarship Program under Grant 727-2015, in part by the Universidad Tecnológica de Bolívar under Project C2018P020 and in part by the Instituto Tecnológico Metropolitano under the project P17211.

© Springer Nature Switzerland AG 2019
J. C. Figueroa-García et al. (Eds.): WEA 2019, CCIS 1052, pp. 552–564, 2019.
https://doi.org/10.1007/978-3-030-31019-6_46

to large consumption centers [1]. This model shows benefits at the moment of establishing a consolidated electricity market. However, the transportation of large amounts of energy implies a higher and robust infrastructure with considerable losses, leading to a decrease in service quality due to the constant growth in demand [2,3].

Currently, power systems are always submitted under huge changes, due to advances in power electronics, as some parts of the system are becoming of direct current, for both low and high power applications. This is motivated in the first case, by the penetration increase of renewable resources [4,5]. DC electric networks have emerged in recent years as part of economic alternatives to provide electric service to urban and rural areas by integrating multiple distributed energy resources [6,7].

Conventional alternating current power networks usually integrate these resources through the use of DC-AC and AC-AC converters [8]; furthermore, to operate directly in DC power networks, the conversion from AC to DC is reduced, therefore, some indicators such as power losses and voltage regulation can be improved [9,10].

Advances and cost reduction of electronic power converters, together with the concept of micro-grid, make possible the construction, operation, management and control of electric networks under the DC paradigm [11,12]. In the stability problem, the loadability factor permits to know the lines capacity and the variation of voltage in order to guarantee the system operation in stable conditions [13–15].

In all contexts, the stability and capacity of transmission lines in power grids, have been studied in depth using heuristic approaches [16–18]. In the stability problem, the capacity of the generators is defined by optimization algorithms that solves the classical optimal power flow problem for electrical networks [19–21].

This new reality of electrical networks requires an improvement of the technical operational characteristics, such as voltage stability [22], control of distributed energy resources [9], and optimal power flow analysis [17], among others. These requirements represent a challenge since the system is highly nonlinear due to the presence of power loads [23–25].

Based on the literature review mentioned above, in this paper, a nonlinear programming formulation to determine the voltage stability index in DC power grids is proposed, in terms of a tutorial to introduce undergraduate and graduate engineering students for solving nonlinear optimization problems in GAMS [13, 19]. It is necessary to point out that there is no evidence of this type of studies in the literature (i.e., tutorial style researches in this area), which creates a research opportunity for this work.

The remain of this document is organized as follows: Sect. 2 shows the nonlinear programming (NLP) model to determine the voltage stability margin for DC networks by maximizing the loadability index. Section 3 presents the proposed solution methodology using the GAMS optimization package, which is illustrated with a 4-nodes test system. Section 4 shows the main characteristics of the 21-nodes and 33-nodes test feeders employed for validating the applicability of the proposed NLP model. Section 5 presents the numerical solution of the voltage stability margin determination for both test systems after using GAMS in conjunction with the nonlinear large scale BARON and KNITRO solvers. Finally, Sect. 6 presents the main conclusions derived from this research work.

2   Mathematical Model

The problem to determine the stability margin in DC power grids corresponds to a nonlinear non-convex optimization problem [11]. It is composed by a single objective function and the set of conventional power flow equations [13,19]. The complete mathematical formulation of the stability index determination in DC power grids can be formulated as follows.

Objective function

$$z = \max \sum_{i=1}^{n} (1 + \lambda_i) p_i^d \tag{1}$$

where z corresponds to the objective function value, λ_i represents the loadability index, i.e., the maximization variable, and p_i^d is the power consumption at each constant power node i. Notice that n corresponds to the total number of nodes of the network, i.e., it is the cardinality of the set that contains all the nodes $\mathcal{N}$.

Set of constraints

$$p_i^g - (1 + \lambda_i) p_i^d = v_i \sum_{j=1}^{n} G_{ij} v_j; \quad \forall i \in \mathcal{N} \tag{2}$$

$$v_i^{\min} \leq v_i \leq v_i^{\max}; \quad \forall i \in \mathcal{N} \tag{3}$$

$$\lambda_i \geq 0; \quad \forall i \in \mathcal{N} \tag{4}$$

where p_i^g corresponds to the power generation at each slack node, v_i is the voltage profile at each node, while $v_i^{\min}$ and $v_i^{\max}$ are the lower and upper voltage bounds. Note that G_{ij} is the ij^{th} component of the conductance matrix.

The mathematical model in (1) to (4) corresponds the nonlinear optimization model that represents the voltage stability margin determination in DC power grids. Equation (1) calculates the objective function value associated with the maximum loadability of the DC network, (2) is the power balance equation, i.e., combination of the Kirchhoff's laws in power form (first Tellegen theorem); (3) helps to determine the solution space bounds in terms of the voltage variables (regulation constraints), and (4) defines the positiveness of the optimization variable.

3   Solution Methodology

GAMS is a power modeling toolbox used to solve multiple mono-objective optimization problems, which include linear programming models and nonlinear, non-convex and mixed-integer optimization models. The model presented in the previous section corresponds to a NLP problem. In the following, the main commands on GAMS and a brief implementation example are presented.

3.1 Main Commands to Solve Optimization Using GAMS

Solution of any optimization problem using GAMS requires basic programming skills. In general terms, the main window of GAMS provides plain texts to formulate the optimization problem in the following steps [26]:

1. Define decision variables using some of these definitions: variables, integer variables, positive variables or binary variables. Notice that the choice of a subset of variables depends on the nature of the optimization problem under analysis.
2. Define set of necessary equations using the reserved word equations. First, names of the equations are defined and then the corresponding mathematical formulas are written.
3. Select the name of the model using reserved word: an arbitrary name for the model.
4. Solve the mathematical model using the next commands: solve arbitrary name using model type maximizing or minimizing objective function variable.
5. Use the reserve word display to present the solution of the interest variables.

A complete description of the GAMS reserved words, commands and syntax is available in [27].

3.2 An Illustrative Example

Considering a circuit interconnection of ideal voltage source (slack node), resistive lines and loads into a DC network. This research proposes a system stability analysis for DC power grids, so, an algorithm is proposed to provide a solution to the stability problem formulated in the previous mathematical model.

This is a 4-node test system, with an ideal power source located at node 1 which operates with 1.0 p.u. The test system configuration and parameters are presented in Fig. 1. Note that all these values are calculated considering 1 kV and 100 kW as voltage and power bases, respectively.

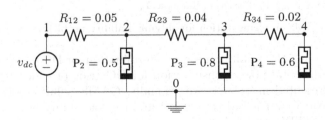

Fig. 1. Electrical configuration for the 4-nodes test system

Algorithm 1 shows the implementation of the stability problem in DC power grids in GAMS via sets formulation. This formulation allows expanding any mathematical problem only by modifying input data, without changing the mathematical structure of the problem. This condition is achieved because the sets permit going through all the variables of the problem regardless the size.

```
1:  SETS
2:  i set of nodes /N1*N4/
3:  g set of nodes /G1/
4:  map(g,i) Relation nodes-generators /G1.N1/
5:  alias(i,j);
6:  Table Gbus(i,j)
7:        N1    N2    N3    N4
8:  N1    20   -20    0     0
9:  N2   -20    45   -25    0
10: N3    0    -25    75   -50
11: N4    0     0    -50    50;
12: Table Load(i,*)
13:       vmin   vmax   Pot
14: N1    0.00   1.05   0
15: N2    0.00   1.05   0.50
16: N3    0.00   1.05   0.80
17: N4    0.00   1.05   0.60;
18: Variables
19: Pmaxd Maximum Load Power
20: v(i) Nodal Voltages
21: Pg(g) Power of Generators
22: Lambda loadability index;
23: v.lo(i) = Load(i,'vmin');
24: v.fx('N1') = 1.00;
25: Lambda.lo = 0;
26: Equations
27: FO Objetive function
28: Balance(i) Power balance;
29: FO.. Pmaxd=E=sum(i,(1+Lambda)*Load(i,'Pot'));
30: Balance(i).. sum(g$map(g,i),Pg(g))-(1+Lambda)*Load(i,'Pot')=E=v(i)*
                 sum(j,Gbus(i,j)*v(j));
31: Model OPF_Clase /all/;
32: solve OPF_Clase using NLP maxmizing Pmaxd;
33: display v.l, Pg.l, Pmaxd.l, Lambda.l;
```

Algorithm 1: GAMS implementation for solving stability problem.

The solution of the stability margin determination for DC networks via maximization of the total power consumption for DC grids provided by GAMS for voltages is presented in Table 1. Additionally, GAMS Solution shows that the Maximum Load Power is PMaxd $= 3.184$ and the loadability index is $\lambda = 0.676$.

Solvers KNITRO and BARON were executed to compare the CPU time and the number of iterations needed to achieve the solution of the problem,

Table 1. GAMS solution for the stability index problem in DC power grids with a 4-nodes test feeder

Node	Voltage [p.u]	Node	Voltage [p.u]
1	1.000	3	0.503
2	0.697	4	0.459

these solvers allow to solve nonlinear programming problems such as the model mathematical proposed [26].

Table 2. Parameters of solvers for the 4-nodes test system

Solver	CPU time [s]	Number of iterations
KNITRO	0.031	10
BARON	0.380	1

Table 2 shows the characteristics based on time and the number of iterations for the two solvers tested. For both cases the same responses were obtained for the loadability index, the voltages in all the nodes, the maximum load power and the powers in all the generators; however, even though the BARON solver only had one iteration, the CPU time used was 12.258 times greater than the KNITRO solver.

This illustrative example showed the possibility to solve mono-objective optimization problems in GAMS by only implementing their mathematical models, without using heuristic or metaheuristic approaches commonly adopted in specialized literature. The following sections present the GAMS solution of the stability index calculation problem in DC power grids for power load maximization in well known literature test feeders.

4   Test Systems

The applicability of the GAMS package to solve the voltage stability index determination in DC power grids is performed using two test feeders with 21 and 33 nodes respectively. Both systems were adapted to evaluate the stability problem shown. The main characteristics of these systems are described below:

4.1   21-Nodes Test Feeder

This test system is formed by 21 nodes and 20 lines with multiple constant power loads, which is an adaptation of the system originally presented in [6,12].

Besides, the test system includes two ideal voltage generators at nodes 1 and 21. The electrical configuration of the test system is illustrated in Fig. 2, and the power consumption is listed in Table 3.

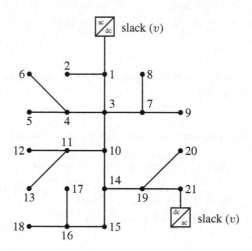

Fig. 2. Electrical configuration for the 21-nodes test system

Table 3. Electrical parameters for the 21-nodes test system

From (i)	To (j)	$R_{ij}[\Omega]$	P_j [kW]	From (i)	To (j)	$R_{ij}[\Omega]$	P_j [kW]
1	2	0.0053	0.70	11	12	0.0079	0.68
1	3	0.0054	0.00	11	13	0.0078	0.10
3	4	0.0054	0.36	10	14	0.0083	0.00
4	5	0.0063	0.04	14	15	0.0065	0.22
4	6	0.0051	0.36	15	16	0.0064	0.23
3	7	0.0037	0.00	16	17	0.0074	0.43
7	8	0.0079	0.32	16	18	0.0081	0.34
7	9	0.0072	0.80	14	19	0.0078	0.09
3	10	0.0053	0.00	19	20	0.0084	0.21
10	11	0.0038	0.45	19	21	0.0082	0.21

The test system voltage and power bases are 1 kV and 100 kW, respectively. Notice that the generator located at node 1 is operated with a voltage of 1.0 p.u, while generator located at node 21 operates at a voltage of 1.05 p.u.

4.2   33-Nodes Test Feeder

This test system corresponds to an adaptation of the classical ac 33-nodes test system employed for distributed generation integration [28]. To transform this system to a DC network, we used 12.66 kV and 100 kW as voltage and power bases; in addition to this, reactance component in all branches and reactive power consumption in all nodes are neglected. Figure 3 presents the 33-node test feeder configuration. Table 4 presents the real parameters of the system.

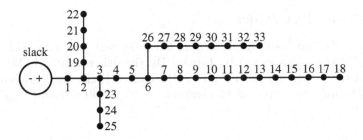

Fig. 3. Electrical configuration for the 33-nodes test system

Table 4. Electrical parameters for the 33-nodes test system

From (i)	To (j)	R_{ij} [Ω]	P_j [kW]	From (i)	To (j)	R_{ij} [Ω]	P_j [kW]
1	2	0.0922	100	17	18	0.7320	90
2	3	0.4930	90	2	19	0.1640	90
3	4	0.3660	120	19	20	1.5042	90
4	5	0.3811	60	20	21	0.4095	90
5	6	0.8190	60	21	22	0.7089	90
6	7	0.1872	200	3	23	0.4512	90
7	8	1.7114	200	23	24	0.8980	420
8	9	1.0300	60	24	25	0.8900	420
9	10	1.0400	60	6	26	0.2030	60
10	11	0.1966	45	26	27	0.2842	60
11	12	0.3744	60	27	28	1.0590	60
12	13	1.4680	60	28	29	0.8042	120
13	14	0.5416	120	29	30	0.5075	200
14	15	0.5910	60	30	31	0.9744	150
15	16	0.7463	60	31	32	0.3105	210
16	17	1.2890	60	32	33	0.3410	60

5   Simulation and Results

The computational analysis was carried out in a desk computer with an INTEL(R) Core(TM) i5 - 3550 processor at 3.50 GHz, 8 GB RAM, running a

64-bits Windows 7 Professional operating system and GAMS with version 21.2. Some versions of GAMS contain restricted solvers for a certain number of equations or variables, so if you do not have the solvers mentioned here, you can use GAMS in any way in the NLP mode.

For the solution of these systems KNITRO solver was used, which permits to solve NLP problems and, in comparison with BARON solver, it has a shorter CPU time to obtain the solution shown in Table 2. NLP models allow solving different nonlinear functions as long as they do not contain discrete variables.

5.1   21-Nodes Test Feeder

The solution for the stability problem in 21-nodes test feeder for Voltage, provided by GAMS, is presented in Table 5. By the other hand, GAMS solution shows that the Maximum Load Power is $PMaxd = 41.935$, the loadability index is $\lambda = 6.569$ and the Power of Generators are $P_{G1} = 40.110$ and $P_{G2} = 24.192$ respectively.

Table 5. Voltage behavior in the 21-nodes test system

Node	Voltage [p.u]	Node	Voltage [p.u]	Node	Voltage [p.u]
1	1.000	8	0.743	15	0.599
2	0.971	9	0.708	16	0.491
3	0.813	10	0.732	17	0.436
4	0.772	11	0.676	18	0.444
5	0.770	12	0.610	19	0.873
6	0.754	13	0.667	20	0.858
7	0.769	14	0.726	21	1.050

The loadability index shows a relationship between the total demand of the system and the growth it can have in order for the system to maintain stability. In this case, $\lambda = 6.569$ is the maximum possible index to this system, with an inverse relation between loadability index and the minimum voltage, to raise the minimum voltage of the system, loadability index would decrease.

Notice that in this DC grid, the voltage at node 17 decreased to 0.436 p.u and the system remains stable. This situation is mainly important, since it implies that the decrease in voltage is a clear evidence that the system is lead to the voltage collapse point. This can be avoided by defining a secure voltage margin zone; which also can be determined by using voltage constraint (3) and maximum secure operating limitation, e.g., $v_{min} = 0.8$ p.u. Nevertheless, this value depends exclusively on the operative consigns of each utility manager.

5.2   33-Nodes Test Feeder

The solution for the stability problem in 33-nodes test feeder for voltages, provided by GAMS, is presented in Table 6. Further, GAMS solution shows that the Maximum Load Power is $PMaxd = 184.815$, the loadability index is $\lambda = 3.975$ and the Power of Generator is $P_{G1} = 274.917$.

Table 6. GAMS solution of stability problem in DC power grids for 33-nodes test feeder

Node	Voltage [p.u]	Node	Voltage [p.u]	Node	Voltage [p.u]
1	1.000	12	0.496	23	0.891
2	0.904	13	0.446	24	0.864
3	0.906	14	0.430	25	0.850
4	0.862	15	0.417	26	0.714
5	0.817	16	0.406	27	0.701
6	0.723	17	0.389	28	0.658
7	0.711	18	0.384	29	0.627
8	0.612	19	0.982	30	0.610
9	0.564	20	0.970	31	0.589
10	0.518	21	0.968	32	0.584
11	0.510	22	0.966	33	0.583

The minimum voltage occurs at node 18 and decreased to 0.384 p.u keeping the system stability, which is lower compared with the results obtained for the 21-nodes test feeder. However, although the system has a lower voltage in some nodes, it has a lower loadability index, i.e., $\lambda = 3.975$.

According to the results mentioned above, it is important to design a structure of a microgrid to maintain a reliable system, without failures due to overloads in the lines or a critical decrease in voltages at the nodes, due to the growth in demand system.

5.3   Comparison with Reported Methods

In order to observe the efficiency of the proposed nonlinear optimization model and its solution using the GAMS package, we compare the proposed approach with two recent approaches in this line. The first method corresponds to a semidefinite programming (SDP) approach solved in CVX for MATLAB [19], while the second approach is an heuristic methodology based on a recursive evaluation of the Newton-Raphson (NR) method [13]. Table 7 shows the comparison results among GAMS, SDP and the NR approaches for the 21- and 33-node test feeders.

Table 7. Comparison of the proposed approach with conventional methods in the calculation of the loadability parameter

System	GAMS	SDP	NR
21-node	6.569 (0.16)	6.569 (0.53)	6.569 (7.19)
33-node	3.975 (0.25)	3.963 (0.91)	3.967 (7.86)

From results presented in Table 7, we can observed that: the three methods enhance the same global optimum for this problem (e.g., 6.569) in the case of the 21-node test system, being the GAMS package the fastest approach with 0.16 s, followed by the SDP method with 0.53 s; in the 33-node test feeder, the solution reported by GAMS enhance a better solution with 3.975 of loadability factor, while the SDP and the NR methods only reach 3.963 and 3.967, respectively. It is important to mention, that in the case of the 33-node test system, the time tendency remains equal to the 21-node test feeder, i.e., the GAMS approach is the fastest method and the NR is the slowest approach.

6   Conclusions

A NLP model for stability margin determination in DC power grids was described. This model was processed using the commercial optimization package GAMS to obtain the maximum load power and the loadability index in a DC power grid.

The stability in a DC electric network was analyzed taking into account the variation of the loads, the capacity of the lines and the voltage fluctuation of the maximum points in which the system remains stable. This model was solved using the KNITRO optimizer available for GAMS.

The results confirmed that power load maximization in DC power grids follows a nonlinear relation between the total power injected and the loadability at the nodes of the system, as well as the existence of a nonlinear relation with the voltage impair and the loadability index.

This type of analysis will help designers to develop efficient and stable DC microgrids. Moreover, such problems require to include renewable energy sources and the variability of the power generation, which is a subject that needs further investigation.

References

1. Parhizi, S., Lotfi, H., Khodaei, A., Bahramirad, S.: State of the art in research on microgrids: a review. IEEE Access **3**, 890–925 (2015)
2. Georgilakis, P.S., Hatziargyriou, N.D.: Optimal distributed generation placement in power distribution networks: models, methods, and future research. IEEE Trans. Power Syst. **28**(3), 3420–3428 (2013)

3. Samper, M.E., Reta, R.A.: Regulatory analysis of distributed generation installed by distribution utilities. IEEE Lat. Am. Trans. **13**(3), 665–672 (2015)
4. Elsayed, A.T., Mohamed, A.A., Mohammed, O.A.: DC microgrids and distribution systems: an overview. Electr. Power Syst. Res. **119**, 407–417 (2015)
5. Planas, E., Andreu, J., Gárate, J.I., Martínez De Alegría, I., Ibarra, E.: AC and DC technology in microgrids: a review. Renew. Sustain. Energy Rev. **43**, 726–749 (2015)
6. Montoya, O.D., Grisales-Noreña, L., González-Montoya, D., Ramos-Paja, C., Garces, A.: Linear power flow formulation for low-voltage DC power grids. Electr. Power Syst. Res. **163**, 375–381 (2018)
7. Montoya, O.D., Gil-González, W., Garces, A.: Optimal power flow on DC microgrids: a quadratic convex approximation. IEEE Trans. Circuits Syst. II **66**(6), 1018–1022 (2019)
8. Justo, J.J., Mwasilu, F., Lee, J., Jung, J.-W.: AC-microgrids versus DC-microgrids with distributed energy resources: a review. Renew. Sustain. Energy Rev. **24**, 387–405 (2013)
9. Nasirian, V., Moayedi, S., Davoudi, A., Lewis, F.L.: Distributed cooperative control of DC microgrids. IEEE Trans. Power Electron. **30**(4), 2288–2303 (2015)
10. Papadimitriou, C., Zountouridou, E., Hatziargyriou, N.: Review of hierarchical control in DC microgrids. Electr. Power Syst. Res. **122**, 159–167 (2015). http://www.sciencedirect.com/science/article/pii/S0378779615000073
11. Velasquez, O.S., Montoya, O.D., Garrido, V.M., Grisales-Noreña, L.F.: Optimal power flow in direct-current power grids via black hole optimization. AEEE Adv. Electr. Electron. Eng. **17**(1), 24–32 (2019). http://advances.utc.sk/index.php/AEEE/article/view/3069
12. Garcés, A.: On the convergence of newton's method in power flow studies for DC microgrids. IEEE Trans. Power Syst. **33**(5), 5770–5777 (2018)
13. Montoya, O.D., Gil-González, W., Garrido, V.M.: Voltage stability margin in DC grids with CPLs: a recursive newton-raphson approximation. IEEE Trans. Circuits Syst. **II**, 1–1 (2019)
14. Simpson-Porco, J.W., Dörfler, F., Bullo, F.: On resistive networks of constant-power devices. IEEE Trans. Circuits Syst. II **62**(8), 811–815 (2015)
15. Barabanov, N., Ortega, R., Griñó, R., Polyak, B.: On existence and stability of equilibria of linear time-invariant systems with constant power loads. IEEE Trans. Circuits Syst. I **63**(1), 114–121 (2016)
16. Niazi, G., Lalwani, M.: PSO based optimal distributed generation placement and sizing in power distribution networks: a comprehensive review. In: 2017 International Conference on Computer, Communications and Electronics (Comptelix), pp. 305–311, July 2017
17. Rajalakshmi, J., Durairaj, S.: Review on optimal distributed generation placement using particle swarm optimization algorithms. In: 2016 International Conference on Emerging Trends in Engineering, Technology and Science (ICETETS), pp. 1–6, Feburary 2016
18. Grisales-Noreña, L.F., Gonzalez-Montoya, D., Ramos-Paja, C.A.: Optimal sizing and location of distributed generators based on PBIL and PSO techniques. Energies **11**(1018), 1–27 (2018)
19. Montoya, O.D.: Numerical approximation of the maximum power consumption in DC-MGs with CPLs via an SDP model. IEEE Trans. Circuits Syst. II **66**(4), 642–646 (2019)

20. Vatani, M., Solati Alkaran, D., Sanjari, M.J., Gharehpetian, G.B.: Multiple distributed generation units allocation in distribution network for loss reduction based on a combination of analytical and genetic algorithm methods. IET Gener. Transm. Distrib. **10**(1), 66–72 (2016)

21. Yuan, H., Li, F., Wei, Y., Zhu, J.: Novel linearized power flow and linearized OPF models for active distribution networks with application in distribution LMP. IEEE Trans. Smart Grid **9**(1), 438–448 (2018)

22. Salomonsson, D., Soder, L., Sannino, A.: Protection of low-voltage DC microgrids. IEEE Trans. Power Del. **24**(3), 1045–1053 (2009)

23. Montoya, O.D., Gil-González, W., Grisales-Noreña, L.F.: Optimal power dispatch of DGs in DC power grids: a hybrid gauss-seidel-genetic-algorithm methodology for solving the OPF problem. WSEAS Trans. Power Syst. **13**(33), 335–346 (2018). http://www.wseas.org/multimedia/journals/power/2018/a665116-598.pdf

24. Li, J., Liu, F., Wang, Z., Low, S.H., Mei, S.: Optimal power flow in stand-alone DC microgrids. IEEE Trans. Power Syst. **33**(5), 5496–5506 (2018)

25. Montoya, O.D., Gil-González, W., Garces, A.: Sequential quadratic programming models for solving the OPF problem in DC grids. Electr. Power Syst. Res. **169**, 18–23 (2019)

26. Montoya, O.D.: Solving a classical optimization problem using GAMS optimizer package: economic dispatch problem implementation. ing. cienc. **13**(26), 39–63 (2017)

27. GAMS Development Corp.: Gams free demo version, March 2019. https://www.gams.com/download/

28. Nordman, B., Christensen, K.: DC local power distribution: technology, deployment, and pathways to success. IEEE Electrific. Mag. **4**(2), 29–36 (2016)

Analysis of Power Losses in Electric Distribution System Using a MATLAB-Based Graphical User Interface (GUI)

Luis Alejandro Rojas[1], Oscar Danilo Montoya[2]([⊠]), and Javier Campillo[2]

[1] Facultad de Diseño e Ingeniería, Fundación Universitaria Antonio de Arévalo,
Cartagena, Colombia
luis.rojas@unitecnar.edu.co
[2] Programa de Ingeniería Eléctrica e Ingeniería Electrónica,
Universidad Tecnológica de Bolívar, Cartagena, Colombia
{omontoya,jcampillo}@utb.edu.co

Abstract. This paper describes a graphical user interface (GUI) developed in MATLAB that provides a user-friendly environment for analyzing the power loss behavior in distribution networks with radial configurations. This GUI allows power systems analysts an easier understanding of the effect of the power dissipation in conductors. The implementation of this GUI implements three radial test feeders using 10, 33 and 69 nodes. As power flow methodology, the successive approximation power flow method was employed. The proposed GUI interface allows identifying the power loss performance in the distribution networks by including a distributed generator (DG) into the grid, operating with unity power factor. This DG is connected to each node to determine which connection provides with the optimal power loss minimization. Numerical results supported by the graphical analysis validate the applicability and importance of user-friendly GUI interfaces for analyzing power systems.

Keywords: Distribution systems · Distributed generators ·
Graphical interface · Radial power flow · Successive approximations

1 Introduction

Medium and high voltage electrical distribution networks, play an essential role in the economic and social development of any country or region [1]; since these,

This work was supported in part by the Administrative Department of Science, Technology, and Innovation of Colombia (COLCIENCIAS) through the National Scholarship Program under Grant 727-2015 and, in part by the Universidad Tecnológica de Bolívar under Project C2018P020.

© Springer Nature Switzerland AG 2019
J. C. Figueroa-García et al. (Eds.): WEA 2019, CCIS 1052, pp. 565–576, 2019.
https://doi.org/10.1007/978-3-030-31019-6_47

allow providing a reliable and efficient electricity supply to end-users [2]. Designing those networks, however, pose a complex optimization problem with multiple solutions due to the non-linearities and non-convexities presented in its formulation [3]. Specialized literature often proposes metaheuristic optimization algorithms, such as tabu-search [4], simulated annealing [5,6], and genetic algorithms [3], among others, to solve this formulation. Note that all of these optimization methods use power flow as essential toolboxes for determining the electrical performance of the proposed expansion planes [7].

Another important issue in distribution systems analysis refers to the mixed-integer nonlinear programming (MINLP) problem associated to the optimal location and dimensioning of distributed generators in radial distribution networks. This problem is complex to solve and it is typically addressed using metaheuristic methods [3]. This MINLP formulation aims at identifying the best location for the DGs, in order to reduce power losses [8], which implies that the power flow analysis is again, the most important toolbox in this process.

In that sense, the analysis of the power losses in large systems, requires different computational methods and toolboxes for studying these grids under different optimization approaches. To do so, here, we propose a sequential power flow analysis procedure in order to identify the most sensible nodes in distribution networks that are suitable for locating DGs, in order to minimize the total grid power losses.

In this work, we present a GUI developed in MATLAB that allows the end-user to analyze graphically, the behavior of the power losses in three radial systems [9]. Using this tool, the user can evaluate the behavior of these three systems at the same time to make optimal decisions based on power flow analysis.

To develop the GUI, three widely used radial test feeders were included. These feeders are composed by 10 nodes and 9 lines [10]; 33 nodes and 32 lines [11]; and 69 nodes and 68 lines [12]; respectively. For each one of these systems, the radial flow is calculated and plotted in order to obtain the exact point where the system begins to show signs of power losses when DGs are located and dispatched. To achieve this, a vector of power increments, each one with 100 samples is used until 10000 samples are reached.

This paper is organized as follows: Sect. 2 presents the mathematical formulation of the classical power flow problem in the complex domain, as well as the successive approximation method for solving it. Section 3 presents the GUI detailed development process. On Sect. 4, the main results and its respective analysis are presented. Section 5 shows the main conclusions derived from this work.

2 Mathematical Model

In this section, the complete formulation of the power flow equations for electrical networks in the complex domain, followed by the successive approximation method for power flow analysis is presented [18].

2.1 Power Flow Formulation

A steady-state representation was used in the complex domain to provide a solution to the mathematical model and load the YBUS of each of the radial distribution systems [7]. The formulation is represented in the following Eqs.: (1) and (2):

$$\mathbf{I} = \mathbb{Y}\mathbf{V}, \tag{1}$$

$$\mathbf{S} = \mathbb{D}\left(\mathbf{V}\right)\mathbf{I}^{\star} \Leftrightarrow \mathbf{S}^{\star} = \mathbb{D}\left(\mathbf{V}^{\star}\right)\mathbf{I}, \tag{2}$$

where:

- $\mathbf{I} \in \mathcal{C}^n$: Nodal Currents.
- $\mathbf{V} \in \mathcal{C}^n$: Voltages Vector.
- $\mathbb{Y} \in \mathcal{C}^{n \times n}$: Nodal Admittance Matrix.
- $\mathbb{D}\left(\mathbf{V}\right)$: Diagonal Positive Definitive Matrix.
- $\mathbb{D}_{ii} = \mathbf{V}_i$, $i = 1, 2, ..., n$ and $\mathbb{D}_{ij} = 0$, $i \neq j$.
- $\mathbf{S} \in \mathcal{C}^n$: Net Power Injection Vector.
- n: Total Nodes of the Distribution.

When Eqs. (1) and (2), are solved together and therefore, Eq. (3) can be obtained.

$$\mathbf{S}^{\star} = \mathbb{D}\left(\mathbf{V}^{\star}\right)\mathbb{Y}\mathbf{V}, \tag{3}$$

Since the main objective is to calculate the power flow, the equation (3) should be rewritten in the same form as (1) and (2).

$$\mathbf{S}_g^{\star} = \mathbb{D}\left(\mathbf{V}_g^{\star}\right)\left[\mathbb{Y}_{gg}\mathbf{V}_g + \mathbb{Y}_{gd}\mathbf{V}_d\right], \tag{4}$$

$$-\mathbf{S}_d^{\star} = \mathbb{D}\left(\mathbf{V}_d^{\star}\right)\left[\mathbb{Y}_{dg}\mathbf{V}_g + \mathbb{Y}_{dd}\mathbf{V}_d\right], \tag{5}$$

where:

- $\mathbf{S}_g \in \mathcal{C}^s$: Power generation in the slack nodes.
- $\mathbf{S}_d \in \mathcal{C}^{n-s}$: Complex power consumed at load nodes.
- $\mathbf{V}_g \in \mathcal{C}^s$: Voltage output in the slack nodes.
- $\mathbf{V}_d \in \mathcal{C}^{n-s}$: Unknown voltages at load nodes.
- $\mathbb{D}\left(\mathbf{V}_s^{\star}\right) \in \mathbb{C}^{s \times s}$: Diagonal matrix that contains all the slack voltages across its diagonal.
- $\mathbb{D}\left(\mathbf{V}_d^{\star}\right) \in \mathbb{C}^{(n-s) \times (n-s)}$: Diagonal matrix that contains all the load voltages across its diagonal.
- n: Number of nodes in the network.

– s: Number of ideal generators (i.e., slack nodes $s \geq 1$).

Additionally:

$$\mathbb{Y} = \begin{pmatrix} \mathbb{Y}_{gg} & \mathbb{Y}_{gd} \\ \mathbb{Y}_{dg} & \mathbb{Y}_{dd} \end{pmatrix},$$

It must be taken into account that:

– $\mathbb{Y}_{dg} = \mathbb{Y}_{gd}^{T}$.

Different methods are used to analyze radial electrical distribution systems. Some of these methods use sweep backward/forward power flow methods [13, 14], classical approaches based on Newton-Raphson or Gauss-Seidel formulations [15] or linear approximations based on Laurent's series expansion [16, 17]. For the development of the calculations in the graphical interface, a numerical method for solving power flow equation using successive approximations was used [18, 19].

2.2   Power Flow Solution Based on Successive Approximations

The method of successive approximations [18, 19] presents optimal yields and results, unlike methods such as Gauss-Jacobi or Gauss-Seidel that develop in the complex field and present optimal flows. However, improvements can be observed when the Newton-Raphson method is applied [15]. In the development of the graphical interface, the method of successive approximations [18, 19] is used as a base, which requires rearranging the following equations in the following way:

$$\mathbb{Y}_{dd}\mathbf{V}_d = -\mathbb{D}_d^{-1}\left(\mathbf{V}_d^\star\right)\mathbf{S}_d^\star - \mathbb{Y}_{dg}\mathbf{V}_g. \tag{6}$$

Observing Eq. (6) and knowing that $\mathbb{Y}_{dd}$ is positively defined, this can be reversed by generating the following equation.

$$\mathbf{V}_d = -\mathbb{Y}_{dd}^{-1}\mathbb{D}_d^{-1}\left(\mathbf{V}_d^\star\right)\mathbf{S}_d^\star - \mathbb{Y}_{dd}^{-1}\mathbb{Y}_{dg}\mathbf{V}_g. \tag{7}$$

The equation shown in (7) represents the typical structure of fixed point theorems for solving roots in nonlinear problems. It is emphasized that the solution of this equation is solved with iterative processes like the one shown below:

$$\mathbf{V}_d^{t+1} = -\mathbb{Y}_{dd}^{-1}\mathbb{D}_d^{-1}\left(\left(\mathbf{V}_d^\star\right)^t\right)\mathbf{S}_d^\star - \mathbb{Y}_{dd}^{-1}\mathbb{Y}_{dg}\mathbf{V}_g. \tag{8}$$

It must be taken into account that the Eq. (8) is developed in the complex field in order to solve the radial flow in the electrical distribution system and only the inversion of the constant parameter matrix is required. This, undoubtedly offers a great advantage in comparison with other solver methods. The variable t represent the time.

3   Graphical User Interface Design

The development of the graphic interface will be shown in steps, as follows:

- In the first step, the function used to calculate the YBUS of each of the systems will be described.
- In the second step, the function created for calculating the RadialFlow of each of the systems will be described.
- In the third step, the general description of the development of the GUI in MATLAB will be presented.

3.1   YBUS Function

For calculating YBUS for the radial system of 10, 33 and 69 nodes, the functions FormationYBUS1, FormationYBUS and FormationYBUS2 were created.

The code to execute the YBUS function of each system can be found in the GitHub repository:

- https://github.com/alejandrorojas030917/Analysis-of-Power-Losses..-in-Electric-Distribution-System-using-a-MATLAB-GUIDE

To start the YBUS, YBUS1 and YBUS2 functions, the database *Data* should be called. In this database, the data to load the YBUS of each of the tables is stored.

The information for the tables is available at:

- https://github.com/alejandrorojas030917/Analysis-of-Power-Losses..-in-Electric-Distribution-System-using-a-MATLAB-GUIDE

3.2   RadialFlow Function

To calculate the radial flow of the radial system for 10, 33 and 69 nodes, the functions RadialFlow1, RadialFlow and RadialFlow2 were created. The functions are available at:

- https://github.com/alejandrorojas030917/Analysis-of-Power-Losses..-in-Electric-Distribution-System-using-a-MATLAB-GUIDE

3.3   GUI General Description

The GUI focuses on presenting a clean interface for analyzing the losses in the radial distribution systems. A graphics window presents the visual analysis in a range of 0 to 10000 samples. This range represents the increase in power to analyze the losses in each of these moments.

Additionally, the user can introduce the the nominal power of the system and the base power for the analysis of the systems in the parameters box. Furthermore, three radio buttons are available for the user to select which of the three systems the losses analysis will be performed on, StartTF10, StartTF33 and StartTF69. If the user would like to run the test across the three systems at the same time, the "Keep Graph" option should be selected, otherwise, only the radial node system selected will be analyzed and visualized. A sample screenshot of the GUI is shown in Fig. 1.

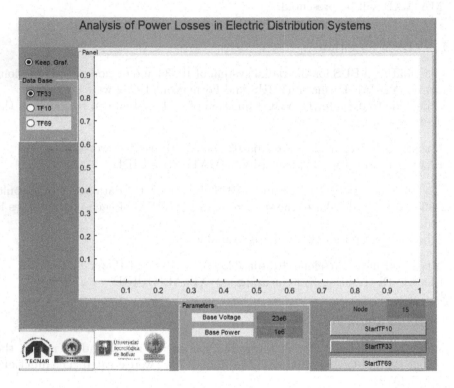

Fig. 1. Analysis of power losses in electric distribution system using MATLAB GUI

In Fig. 2, the analysis for each of the systems analyzed, is shown. The graphical tool pin-points the location of the coordinate where the lowest power losses are obtained. Results for the 10-node system are shown in Fig. 2a, for the 33 nodes in Fig. 2b and for the 69 nodes in Fig. 2c.

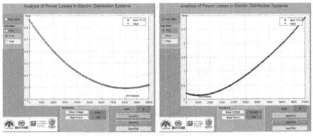

(a) Location coordinate mi- (b) Location coordinate minor power losses TF10. nor power losses TF33.

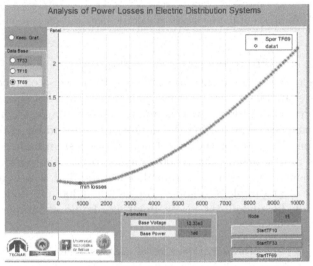

(c) Location coordinate minor power losses TF69.

Fig. 2. Location power losses.

4 Analysis and Results

In this section, results of the analysis for power losses on each of the systems will be presented. Special emphasis will be placed upon the advantages offered by the successive approximations algorithm used for the calculation of radial flow presented in Sect. 2.

4.1 Power Losses Analysis TF10

Power losses for the system of 10 nodes and 9 lines are shown in Fig. 3.

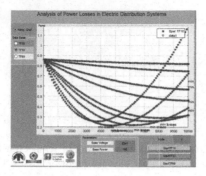

Fig. 3. Analysis of power losses in electric distribution system TF10

In the case of TF10, all the nodes were taken and it is noticeable that there are points where it is unnecessary to continue with power-step increments since it also increases the losses once the focal point (the black dot that represent the lowest losses) have been found. At this point, the user can decide if carrying out a one-to-one analysis or increasing the number of nodes to be analyzed.

As shown on Table 1, for the first 4 nodes, the system had to optimize the whole process until reaching the 10000 samples to find the point at which the minimum amount of losses were obtained. For node 5, it was found at sample 8100; On node 6, at sample; On node 7, on sample 6300; On node 8; at sample 4700; and finally, for node 9 the lowest point was found at sample 3800.

Table 1. Power losses analysis TF10

Node	Sper Real	Sper Imag	Sample
1	0.8175	0.9145	10000
2	07470	0.7556	10000
3	0.5679	0.4826	10000
4	0.4609	0.3892	10000
5	0.3176	0.2667	8100
6	0.3195	0.2704	7400
7	0.3897	0.3107	6300
8	0.7257	0.5042	4700
9	1.1834	0.7704	3800

It was concluded that for this system the smallest losses were found on nodes 5 and 6.

4.2   Power Losses Analysis TF33

For the analysis of power losses in the system of 33 nodes and 32 lines, 8 random nodes were taken as shown in Fig. 4. The point where the minimum losses were obtained, is marked as a green dot for each node.

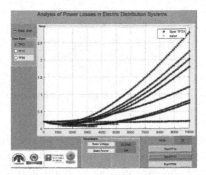

Fig. 4. Analysis of power losses in electric distribution system TF33

As presented on Table 2, minimum losses for node 1were obtained at sample 4100; for node 5, on sample 2600; at node 10, on sample 1400; at node 15; on sample 1000; at node 20, on sample 400; and finally, at node 30, on sample 1400.

Table 2. Power losses analysis TF33

Node	Sper Real	Sper Imag	Sample
1	0.2207	0.1477	4100
5	0.7473	0.4991	2600
10	2.0721	1.5857	1400
15	3.0271	2.3835	1000
20	1.2179	1.1051	400
25	0.8227	0.5327	2500
30	2.0239	1.5574	1400
32	2.2512	1.8883	1200

It was concluded that for this system in the nodes analyzed, the smallest losses were found at nodes 1 and 5.

4.3   Power Losses Analysis TF69

Power losses analysis plots for the system of 69 nodes and 68 lines are shown in Fig. 5. The point where the minimum losses were obtained, is marked in cyan color for each node.

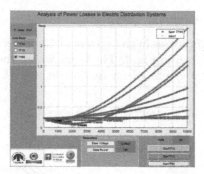

Fig. 5. Analysis of power losses in electric distribution system TF69

As shown in Table 3. at node 1; the lowest power loss point was found on sample 4400; at node 7, on sample 3000; at node 14, on sample 90; at node 21, on sample 800; at node 28, on sample 100; at node 40, on sample 200 and finally, at the nodes 59 and 60 the lowest power loss point was found on sample 1900.

Table 3. Power losses analysis TF69

Node	Sper Real	Sper Imag	Sample
1	0.2301	0.1044	4400
7	0.4275	0.2118	3000
14	2.0824	0.7408	900
21	2.4359	0.8541	800
28	0.2718	0.2065	100
40	0.7363	0.7426	200
45	0.9643	1.0129	200
59	1.5117	0.6059	1900
60	1.6238	0.6673	1900

It was concluded that for this system, at the nodes analyzed, the smallest losses were found in nodes 1 and 28.

5   Conclusions

The developed GUI used as a power loss analysis tool in electrical distribution systems, proved great usefulness to help deciding where to place DGs to reduce losses, when considering different system under the same conditions. It is worth highlighting that the losses for the system of 10 nodes were smaller in comparison with the nodes analyzed for the systems of 33 and 69 nodes.

If a comparison is made between the three radial distribution systems. The 10 node system showed a better performance than the other ones. However, if the comparison were carried out only between the systems of 33 and 69 nodes, the system of 69 nodes offers fewer losses at the points analyzed. One of the reasons for this refers to the size of the system.

Future improvements will be implemented on the GUI, for instance, combinatorial and well known optimization methods such as Genetic Algorithms, Tabu Search and Particle Swarm Optimization for optimal placement and dimensioning of DGs in electrical grids as a tool for introducing engineering students with optimization will be added to the tool.

References

1. Osman, T., Mohammad, S.: Power distribution asset management. In: 2006 IEEE Power Engineering Society General Meeting, pp. 7–14 (2006). https://doi.org/10.1109/PES.2006.1709234
2. Renani, Y.K., Ehsan, M., Shahidehpour, M.: Optimal transactive market operations with distribution system operators. IEEE Trans. Smart Grid 9(6), 6692–6701 (2018). https://doi.org/10.1109/TSG.2017.2718546
3. Ghasemi, H., Aghaei, J., Babamalek Gharehpetian, G., Safdarian, A.: MILP model for integrated expansion planning of multi-carrier active energy systems. IET Gener. Transm. Distrib. 13(7), 1177–1189 (2019). https://doi.org/10.1049/iet-gtd.2018.6328
4. Baydar, B., Gozde, H., Taplamacioglu, M.C., Kucuk, A.O.: Resilient optimal power flow with evolutionary computation methods: short survey. In: Mahdavi Tabatabaei, N., Najafi Ravadanegh, S., Bizon, N. (eds.) Power Systems Resilience. PS, pp. 163–189. Springer, Cham (2019). https://doi.org/10.1007/978-3-319-94442-5_7
5. Koziel, S., Landeros Rojas, A., Moskwa, S.: Power loss reduction through distribution network reconfiguration using feasibility-preserving simulated annealing. In: 2018 19th International Scientific Conference on Electric Power Engineering (EPE), pp. 1–5 (2018). https://doi.org/10.1109/EPE.2018.8396016
6. Zhangab, W., Malekic, A., RosendJingqingLiu, M.A.: Optimization with a simulated annealing algorithm of a hybrid system for renewable energy including battery and hydrogen storage. Energy 163, 191–207 (2018). https://doi.org/10.1016/j.energy.2018.08.112
7. Zhang, X., Shahidehpour, M., Alabdulwahab, A., Abusorrah, A.: Optimal expansion planning of energy hub with multiple energy infrastructures. IEEE Trans. Smart Grid 6(5), 2302–2311 (2015). https://doi.org/10.1109/TSG.2015.2390640
8. Novajan, S., Jalali, M., Zare, K.: An MINLP approach for optimal DG unit's allocation in radial/mesh distribution systems take into account voltage stability index. Iran. J. Sci. Technol. 39(2), 155–165 (2015). https://doi.org/10.22099/IJSTE.2015.3488
9. Frances, J., Perez-Molina, M., Bleda, S., Fernandez, E., Neipp, C., Belendez, A.: Educational software for interference and optical diffraction analysis in Fresnel and Fraunhofer regions based on MATLAB GUIs and the FDTD method. IEEE Trans. Educ. 55(1), 118–125 (2012). https://doi.org/10.1109/TE.2011.2150750
10. Siddiqui, A.S., Rahman, F.: Optimal capacitor placement to reduce losses in distribution system. WSEAS Trans. Power Syst. 7(1), 12–17 (2012)

11. Askarzadeh, A.: Capacitor placement in distribution systems for power loss reduction and voltage improvement: a new methodology. IET Gener. Transm. Distrib. **10**(14), 3631–3638 (2016). https://doi.org/10.1049/iet-gtd.2016.0419
12. Sultana, S., Roy, P.K.: Krill herd algorithm for optimal location of distributed generator in radial distribution system. Appl. Soft Comput. **40**, 391–404 (2016). https://doi.org/10.1016/j.asoc.2015.11.036
13. Garces, A.: A linear three-phase load flow for power distribution systems. IEEE Trans. Power Syst. **31**(1), 827–828 (2016). https://doi.org/10.1109/TPWRS.2015.2394296
14. Samal, P., Ganguly, S.: A modified forward backward sweep load flow algorithm for unbalanced radial distribution systems. In: 2015 IEEE Power Energy Society General Meeting, pp. 1–5 (2015). https://doi.org/10.1109/PESGM.2015.7286413
15. Faisal, M., Al Hosani, S.M.H., Mohamed, HH, Z.: A novel approach to solve power flow for islanded microgrids using modified newton Raphson with droop control of DG. IEEE Trans. Sustain. Energy **7**(2), 493–503 (2016). https://doi.org/10.1109/TSTE.2015.2502482
16. Montoya, O.D., Grisales-Noreña, L.F., Gonzalez-Montoya, D., Ramos-Paja, C.A., Garces, A.: Linear power flow formulation for low-voltage DC power grids. Electr. Power Syst. Res. **163**(A), 375–381 (2018). https://doi.org/10.1016/j.epsr.2018.07.003
17. Garces, A.: A quadratic approximation for the optimal power flow in power distribution systems. Electr. Power Syst. Res. **130**, 222–229 (2016). https://doi.org/10.1016/j.epsr.2015.09.006
18. Montoya, O.D., Garrido, V.M., Gil-González, W., Grisales-Noreña, L.: Power flow analysis in DC grids: two alternative numerical methods. In: IEEE Transactions on Circuits and Systems II: Express Briefs, pp 1–5 (2019). https://doi.org/10.1109/TCSII.2019.2891640
19. Garces, A.: Uniqueness of the power flow solutions in low voltage direct current grids. Electr. Power Syst. Res. **151**, 149–153 (2017). https://doi.org/10.1016/j.epsr.2017.05.031

Design and Characterization of Graphite Piezoresistors in Paper for Applications in Sensor Devices

Luiz Antonio Rasia[1]([✉]) [iD], Patricia Carolina Pedrali[1] [iD],
Humber Furlan[2] [iD], and Mariana Amorim Fraga[3] [iD]

[1] Regional University of the Northwest of the State of Rio Grande do Sul,
Ijuí, Brazil
{rasia,patricia.pedrali}@unijui.edu.br
[2] Faculty of Technology of São Paulo - CEETEPS, São Paulo, Brazil
humber@fatecsp.br
[3] ITA – Technological Institute of Aeronautics, São Paulo, Brazil
mafraga@ieee.org

Abstract. This paper discusses the process of manufacturing and performance analysis of piezoresistive graphite sensors in paper substrate and encapsulated with epoxy resin. Graphite in thin paper films have been investigated for a wide range of applications due to their excellent electrical and mechanical properties. The processing of graphite sensor elements using mechanical exfoliation in paper, GoP method, does not generate considerable environmental impacts, does not demand complex processes and equipment that generate high costs and have controllable functionalities. In the last decade, several research and development activities have been conducted on the use of these thin films as piezoresistors in MEMS sensors. The sensor was designed from the analytical formulas found in the literature and the analysis of the results was obtained with the SciDAVis free software. Graphite sensors on flexible polymer substrates can be applied to portable wearable devices, as well as sensors for the Internet of things, bioengineering and applications in various areas of science and technology.

Keywords: Piezoresistive sensor · Graphite on paper (GoP) ·
Wearable devices · Analytical solution

1 Introduction

In this work pencil graphite is used for the production of piezoresistors and paper as a substrate in order to obtain low cost manufacturing processes when compared to the processes used for silicon.

Traditionally known equations for monocrystalline and polycrystalline silicon are used to determine the value of piezoresistive coefficients, πs, of amorphous DLC - Diamond Like Carbon films [1]. Monocrystalline and polycrystalline silicon is a material that has been characterized by [2] for the manufacture of piezoresistive sensor devices.

© Springer Nature Switzerland AG 2019
J. C. Figueroa-García et al. (Eds.): WEA 2019, CCIS 1052, pp. 577–583, 2019.
https://doi.org/10.1007/978-3-030-31019-6_48

It is currently necessary to study new materials (semiconductors, polymers and metals) to replace silicon in different application areas and MEMS devices – micro-electromechanical systems [3–8]. Silicon involves very complex process steps and is generally costly in addition to producing many environmentally hazardous wastes.

In the last decade graphite has been attracting the attention of the international scientific community to the development of new electronic products due to the low cost, lightness, flexibility and biocompatibility presented by Kanaparthi [9].

These characteristics above provide a good indication for the development of piezoresistive sensors elements using graphite films of pencil 2B deposited on flexible A4 paper. This process is known as GoP - Graphite on Paper as shown Fig. 1.

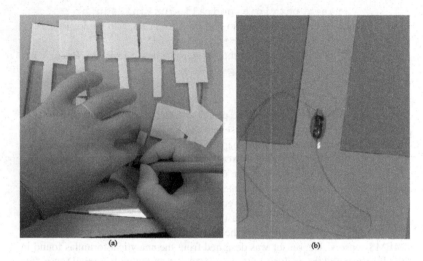

Fig. 1. (a) Deposition of graphite on paper substrate and (b) encapsulated piezoresistor.

Graphite is composed of carbon atoms that are linked by covalent bonds. Each carbon atom is bonded to three other carbon atoms. Therefore, graphite is composed of infinite layers of carbon atoms hybridized with sp^2 bonds. This type of hybridization occurs when the carbon has a double bond and two single bonds or a pi (π) bond and three sigma bonds (σ). In fact, the sp^2 hybridization is caused between the atoms that establish the double bond.

In each layer, called graphene sheet, one carbon atom is attached to three other atoms, forming a planar array of fused hexagons [4].

The often quoted resistivity values are 3000×10^{-6} Ω m in the c direction and 2.5–5.0×10^{-6} Ω m the ab direction. The specific gravity is 2.26 g/cm^3 and electron mobility varies between 20000–100 cm^2/V s and hole mobility between 15000–90 cm^2/V s with directions. The band gap is considered 0.04 eV according to [10].

The graphite characteristics described above are important for an optimized sensor device design.

1.1   Piezoresistor Mathematical Model and Processing Steps

The resistance, R, of a piezoresistor is determined by the Eq. (1):

$$R = \frac{\rho \ell}{A} = \frac{\rho \ell}{wt} \tag{1}$$

where, $\rho = \rho_0$, is the resistivity of the graphite, $\ell = L$, length, w, the width and, t, thickness of the sensor element.

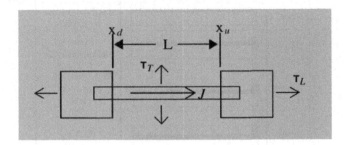

Fig. 2. Piezoresistor model

The resistance, R, of a piezoresistor, shown in Fig. 2, can be calculated according to [11] by Eq. (2):

$$R = R_{ref} + \rho_o \pi_l \int_{xd}^{xu} T_l(x)dx + \rho_0 \pi_t \int_{xd}^{xu} T_t(x)dx \tag{2}$$

where, R_{ref}, represents the value of the piezoresistor value without applying mechanical stresses, π_l, π_t, are the longitudinal and transverse piezoresistive coefficients, respectively. The mechanical stress applied to the crimped beam is given by, T_l (x), and, T_t (x), longitudinally and transversely.

The piezoresistive effect can be described expressing the change of electrical resistance, $\Delta R/R$, of macroscopic form in function of mechanical stress, mechanical deformation, ε, and the sensitivity factor or gauge factor, GF, [9] given by Eq. (3):

$$GF = \frac{\Delta R/R}{\varepsilon} \tag{3}$$

Hooke's law relates the strain mechanical longitudinal to the stress mechanical by Eq. (4):

$$\sigma = E \varepsilon_L \tag{4}$$

where, E, is the Young's modulus or the modulus of elasticity of the material [12]. The Young's modulus of elasticity of the graphite crystal varies up to two orders of magnitude with the directions 1060–36.5 GPa.

For the fabrication of the sensor elements a few steps were followed presented by Renan [4]: polymer substrate sizing, GoP deposition, copper contact fixation and encapsulation, shown in Fig. 3.

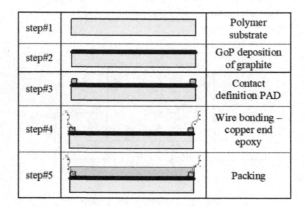

Fig. 3. Description of the processing steps of graphite sensor elements

Using the manufacturing steps described in Fig. 3, in a clean environment, air temperature of 26 °C and humidity of 59%, the sensor elements were made accordance with to the model shown in Fig. 2.

1.2   Material and Method of Characterization of Piezoresistor

The experimental arrangement is based on the cantilever method with the application of a mechanical stress at the free end of the beam using small "weights", with mass ranging from 0.104 g to 1.23 g are used as shown in Fig. 4.

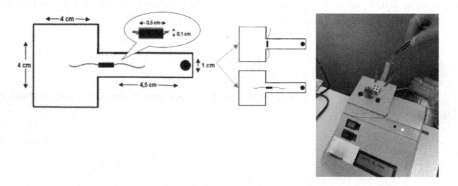

Fig. 4. Experimental arrangement and photograph of measuring equipment

The experimental bench works as an ohmmeter to measure piezoresistance in the Giga Ohms scale [5]. The results are shown with seven decimal places and stored on a memory card. The data can be used in other software for plotting graphs.

The electrical contacts were made with fine copper wires the deposition uniformity of the film was inspected through an AM-313T digital microscope as shown in Fig. 5.

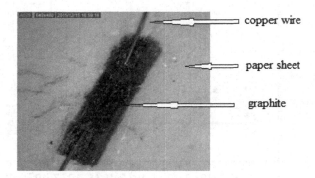

copper wire

paper sheet

graphite

Fig. 5. Photograph of piezoresistor on paper

2   Results and Discussions

The results presented for fifteen samples of piezoresistors positioned longitudinally and transversely on the crimped beam indicate that it is necessary to characterize individually each of the sensing elements. Otherwise, our analysis indicates that both tend to approximate the theoretical model given by the dotted black line.

The piezoresistive coefficient is an intrinsic microscopic property of the material used for sensing devices and indicates the sensitivity of the material to the effects of mechanical stress and deformation. The average longitudinal piezoresistive coefficient found was 5.03271×10^{-10} m^2/N and 3.04394×10^{-10} m^2/N for transversely positioned sensor elements.

Graphite presents excellent sensitivity to mechanical stresses, as can be seen in Figs. 6 and 7 obtained using the SciDAVis free software.

The results shown for the longitudinal piezoresistive coefficients in Fig. 6 and transverse in Fig. 7 differ in magnitude because the transverse mechanical stress is divided by the Poisson coefficient although it respects Hooke's Law.

In this work all piezoresistors analyzed are shown indicating the need for individual characterization of each sensor manufactured to guarantee an efficient functional device.

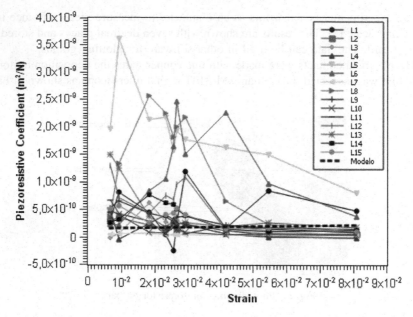

Fig. 6. Piezoresistive coefficient as a function of mechanical deformation of encapsulated sensor devices longitudinal

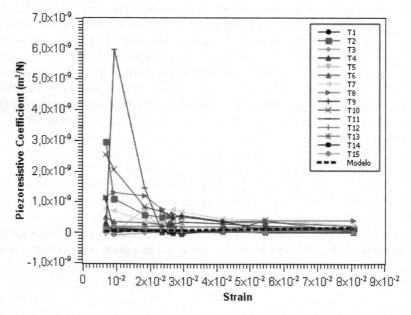

Fig. 7. Piezoresistive coefficient as a function of mechanical deformation of encapsulated sensor devices transversal

3   Conclusions

Graphite is a viable alternative for the substitution of conventional materials, such as silicon in polymeric devices, due to its performance in relation to the gage factor presented and the processing facilities of the sensor elements. This work is important for the manufacture of different types of sensors which can be applied to wearable devices as well as sensors for the internet of things since they are produced using flexible and polymeric materials.

Acknowledgments. The authors thank the Regional University of the Northwest of the State of Rio Grande do Sul and the Foundation for Research Support – FAPERGS and CNPq for financial support.

References

1. Rasia, L.A., Mansano, R.D., Damiani, L.R., Viana, C.E.: Piezoresistive response of ITO films deposited at room temperature by magnetron sputtering. J. Mater. Sci. **45**, 4224–4228 (2010). https://doi.org/10.1007/s10853-010-4517-1
2. Kanda, Y., Yasukawa, A.: Optimum design considerations for silicon piezoresistive pressure sensors. Sens. Actuators, A **62**, 539–542 (1997)
3. Geremias, M., Moreira, R.C., Rasia, L.A., Moi, A.: Mathematical modeling of piezoresistive elements. J. Phys: Conf. Ser. **648**, 012012 (2015)
4. Gabbi, R., Rasia, L.A., Valdiero, A.C., Gabbi, M.T.T.: An approach for computational simulation of the elements piezoresistive of graphite. Int. J. Dev. Res. **8**, 19150–19155 (2018)
5. Valdiero, C.A., Rasia, L.A., Valdiero, A.C.: Experimental development of low cost equipment for electrical characterization of graphite sensor elements. In: Kowalski, V.A., Acosta, A.M., Enriquez, H.D. (eds.) X Simposio Internacional de Ingeniería Industrial: Actualidad y Nuevas Tendencias, pp. 1106 – 1111, Oberá Argentina (2017)
6. Mahadeva, S.K., Walus, K., Stoeber, B.: Paper as a platform for sensing applications and other devices: a review. ACS Appl. Mater. Interfaces (2015). https://doi.org/10.1021/acsami.5b00373
7. Dinh, T., Phan, H.P., Dao, D.V., Woodfield, P., Qamar, A., Nguyen, N.T.: Graphite on paper as material for sensitive thermoresistive sensors. J. Mater. Chem. C **3**, 8776–8779 (2015)
8. Liu, H., et al.: Paper: a promising material for human-friendly functional wearable electronics (2017). https://doi.org/10.1016/j.mser.2017.01.001
9. Kanaparthi, S., Badhulika, S.: Low cost, flexible and biodegradable touch sensor fabricated by solvent-free processing of graphite on cellulose paper. Sens. Actuators B: Chem. **242**, 857–864 (2017)
10. Zabel, H., Solin, S.: Graphite Intercalation Compounds I Structure and Dynamics. Spring Series in Materials Science, vol. 14. Springer, Berlin (1990). https://doi.org/10.1007/978-3-642-75270-4. Fed. Rep. of Germany
11. Gniazdowski, Z., Kowalski, P.: Practical approach to extraction of piezoresistance coefficient. Sens. Actuators, A **68**, 329–332 (1998)
12. Rasia, L.A., Leal, G., Kobertein, L.L., Furlan, H., Massi, M., Fraga, M.F.: Design and analytical studies of a DLC thin-film piezoresistive pressure microsensor. In: Figueroa-García, J., López-Santana, E., Villa-Ramírez, J., Ferro-Escobar, R. (eds.) WEA 2017. CCIS, vol. 742, pp. 433–443. Springer, Cham (2017). https://doi.org/10.1007/978-3-319-66963-2_39

A Remote Monitoring System
for Charging Stations with Photovoltaic
Generation

Santiago Sánchez, Isabel Cárdenas-Gómez$^{(\boxtimes)}$, Ricardo Mejía-Gutiérrez,
and Gilberto Osorio-Gómez

Design Engineering Research Group (GRID), Universidad EAFIT,
Carrera 49 No 7 Sur–50, Medellín, Colombia
{ssanch30,icardenasg,rmejiag,gosoriog}@eafit.edu.co
http://www.eafit.edu.co

Abstract. This work aims to develop a prototype of a monitoring system for a Photovoltaic Charging Station (PVCS) installed in *Universidad Eafit*. The design is proposed according to the context of remote areas, which are off-grid or where utility grid's quality is low, and considering the possibility of having standalone charging stations installed in such places. The proposed system integrates several hardware components and communication protocols by making use of Internet of Things (IoT) and Cloud Platform technology. The presented solution is a low-cost infrastructure and enables real-time monitoring and data storing for future analysis.

Keywords: Charging station · Monitoring · Internet of Things · Bosch XDK · Photovoltaic

1 Introduction

Photovoltaic (PV) energy can be considered as one of the Renewable Energies (REs) with higher potential in the future, thanks to its capacity to supply the worldwide energy demand [17]. This technology has great relevance in particular for rural or remote areas, which are not connected to the grid and, usually located away from electricity networks. This condition is commonly found in developing countries and corresponds to living conditions of approximately one third of society [8].

The so-called standalone or off-grid PV systems, as its name implies, have the capability of operating and generating electricity independently from the utility grid. This characteristic converts them into a suitable energy source in remote areas [14]. Some applications have been implemented, such as the case of *Isla Fuerte*, Córdoba, a Colombian island off-grid, where the government has installed 709 solar panels, which provide the energy for about six hours per day [3].

© Springer Nature Switzerland AG 2019
J. C. Figueroa-García et al. (Eds.): WEA 2019, CCIS 1052, pp. 584–595, 2019.
https://doi.org/10.1007/978-3-030-31019-6_49

Other applications of standalone PV systems can be found in the field of electric mobility; specifically, in charging infrastructure. Standalone PVCS incorporate a battery storage unit in the architecture, used between the PV system and the Electric Vehicle (EV), in order to lever intermittence of the solar irradiance and to store PV energy for future use [4].

Despite the benefits of such systems, having off-grid installations leads to some challenges for the system's owner or supervisor (Utility, Community or Person). For a proper management and control, it is necessary to frequently check the systems' variables involved during operation. Those variables may be related to external factors (such as atmospheric conditions) or to internal and technical aspects (e.g. current, voltage, solar panel temperature, among others).

In order to be able to track a set of variables, PV systems should be complemented with a "monitoring" infrastructure. This add-on to traditional PV systems includes interconnected sensors, data transfer, data storage and analytics, where Internet of Things (IoT) and Cloud Platform technologies turns out to be a feasible architecture alternative.

2   State of the Art

2.1   Renewable Charging Stations

The integration of REs such as PV in charging infrastructure for EV, has gained attention as an alternative energy source than using only the utility grid in the charging process. This has been prompted by looking for solutions to the strain on the grid caused by EV [16], as well as by the purpose of making EV a more sustainable technology by reducing their Greenhouse Gas (GHG) emissions when being charged from clean energy sources [9].

PVCS can be classified in two main categories according to the interaction with the grid, these are PV-standalone and PV-grid [4]. Both configurations provide advantages for different scenarios, the first one is suitable for remote areas which are off-grid or where utility grid's quality is low. However, PV adds uncertainty on the station's performance. External factors such as weather conditions, affect and cause intermittence in the PV generation. Thus, there are some developments regarding simulations tools and mathematical models that analyze the performance of PV systems. The system's monitoring and performance's data acquisition can be helpful to improve the accuracy of such models [12].

2.2   Monitoring Systems Background

Literature about monitoring Charging Station (CS) differs, not only on technical aspects (such as measurement devices and communication protocols), but also on the purpose of the monitoring task itself. Some authors propose a smart charging infrastructure [15], where the goal of the monitoring process is to use real time data as input for charging scheduling algorithms. They gather data of both CS and EVs, and the data transmission is based on a ZigBee network and

3G connection. The first protocol is chosen due to the advantages it offers for low transmission rate, low power consumption and low cost. The work presented in [13] introduces a monitoring system to analyze the grid power quality, the load demand and the impact on the grid caused by EV charging. They use distributed acquisition terminals, installed in the stations, to collect electrical data, such as power, harmonics, voltage and frequency of the charging point. This information is then sent to another system using Ethernet communication, whereas EV charging characteristics data is collected through GPRS protocol. On the other hand, authors in [6] focus the monitoring task on the storage subsystem of the CS. They track variables related to batteries' status (e.g State of Charge (SoC), voltage and time remaining), using a Data Acquisition Card with USB connection to computer, where values are stored and analyzed.

As shown in previous works, monitoring is useful to efficiently manage and control systems, but it also helps on their proper planning. Accordingly, some authors record opened access real-time operation data from 49 DC chargers spread over the city, with the objective to predict the charging demand [10]. The data saved consists of charger id, timestamp and working status (on-off). Using this information along with Artificial Neural Networks, allowed them to predict the occupancy probability for the chargers and to establish new possible chargers' locations.

As evidenced in the aforementioned references, there is a diversity on technologies found among monitoring projects, derived from the particular conditions and context of each application. For example, the type of communication to use, which can be either wired or wireless, will depend on different characteristics of the network such as network size, traffic volume, type of data and communication requirements [1]. To deal with this heterogeneity among elements, an IoT infrastructure becomes a good alternative to create a proper integration. It offers several options for wireless technologies, including from RFID, that is useful for proximity networks, to Cellular networks, employed in Wireless Wide Area Networks. The adoption of IoT is growing and gaining popularity, it is expected that by 2021 there will be approximately 28 billion devices connected [11].

This IoT scheme, could facilitate the installation and operation of PV systems in remote non-connected areas, by informing to the institution in charge of the system's operation, about its current state through wireless communication architecture.

3   Case Study: Monitoring Implementation in a CS

By 2015, as a result of a research project, *Universidad Eafit* developed a Charging Station, under a Solar Tree shape, to recharge electric bicycles. The prototype was called "Ceiba Solar"[1]. This prototype was the first stand-alone PVCS in the campus, with a generation capacity of 1.5 kW and including a solar tracking system (see Fig. 1). This CS allows students to charge different devices, such as

---

[1] *Ceiba* is one of the most relevant Trees in Latin-America and Colombia.

Fig. 1. The Solar-Tree, so-called "Ceiba Solar" at *Universidad EAFIT*

laptops, mobiles, electric bicycles, among others, and it can also provide power for 15 parking luminaries around it.

Since the installation's date, due to a lack of a monitoring system, the University does not have relevant operation data about it, neither about consumption nor generation. Thus, addressing the importance of recording data, the core motivation of this research is the implementation of a monitoring system for the Ceiba Solar.

Given its off-grid characteristic, which implies not having either aerial or terrestrial wiring, wireless communication shows up as the best alternative to transfer data. Along the communication system, all signals involved during the station's operation have to be converted into readable data, have to be stored and should be analyzed in order to get useful information. Hence, to successfully achieve these tasks, an IoT architecture is considered.

According to the five layer architecture for an IoT system presented in [2], Fig. 2 shows different options for the Objects, Object Abstraction and Application layers. First layer includes sensors to gather data and actuators; then, in the Object Abstraction layer, through different communication protocols, occurs the data transfer process between sensors and the Service layer, which is hosted in a Gateway. A convenient way to store and process all these collected data is making use of Cloud Platforms [2]. Ubidots, ThingWorx and Amazon AWS are considered among the possible options for the project. Multiple application protocols to exchange data between Gateway and Cloud Platform can be implemented, including MQTT, XMPP, HTTP, CoAP, REST and Light-weight M2M (LWM2M).

With the multiple options of devices and technology, as well as the amount of variables that could be monitored, this project is divided into three phases that guide the decisions making process about the parameters of the system.

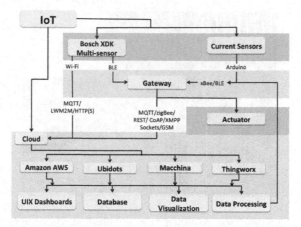

Fig. 2. Options for IoT architecture

3.1 Phase I: Debugging and Selection of Variables to Monitor

Numerous variables are involved during the station's operation; however, not all of them must be considered into the monitoring process. To determine the importance of each variable and to establish the ones to be recorded, a Function to Data Matrix (FDM) method is used. As explained in [7], it allows to compare and determine the most relevant variables for the system's performance.

The first step of the FDM, consists of building a Functions Tree (FT) taking into account the main goal of the system and the necessary sub-functions to accomplish it. As shown in Fig. 3, the first node of the tree is the principal objective, *to improve energy generation and consumption on Eafit's CS*. To achieve this, three other sub-functions must be performed, they are: to transform PV energy into AC/DC energy, to get data, and to perform actions. These three functions are then divided in other sub-tasks needed for their fulfillment.

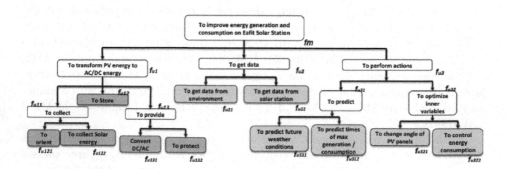

Fig. 3. Functions Tree of Eafit's PVCS

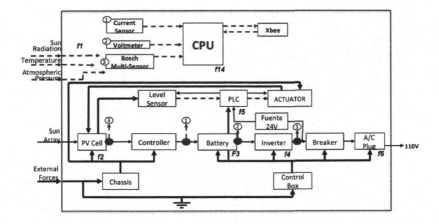

Fig. 4. Functional Diagram structure of Eafit's PVCS

After this step, the process continues with the Functional Diagram structure, presented in Fig. 4. It includes the system's principal components, that are represented in blocks, and the flows of matter, energy and signal among them.

Considering previous structures, the next step is to create the FDM selection matrix presented in Table 1. It indicates the correlation between the flows of the Functional Diagram, that are described in the first column of the table, and the basic functions established in the FT, which are specified in the first row of the table. The correlation consists on giving a number, which can be 0, 1, 3 or 9, according to the level of impact that a variable has in the fulfillment of a basic function. For example, Solar Irradiance is considered to have a high impact on $f_{u_{321}}$ (to change angle of PV panels), whereas it does not have effect in $f_{u_{32}}$ (to optimize inner variables). This numeric evaluation, allows then to compute the most relevant variables and functions.

The highest scored functions correspond to $f_{u_{322}}$: *to control energy consumption*, $f_{u_{312}}$: *to predict times of maximum generation and consumption* and $f_{u_{22}}$: *to get data from solar station*. The most relevant variables are battery SoC, PV array tilt angle, solar irradiance, battery voltage, inverter current and device consumption. Hence, this is the set of variables considered for the monitoring system. However, these variables can be measured either directly or indirectly, e.g to calculate battery SoC, the input current to the battery can be recorded over a period of time and then integrated.

3.2 Phase II: Components Selection and Communication Protocols

After defining the set of variables, Phase II presents the selection of devices and technology. As shown in Fig. 2, there are diverse options for the main layers.

Hardware and Components Analysis. Considering the monitoring variables and the technical aspects of the CS, Table 2 provides information about the

Table 1. Funtion to Data Matrix (FDM) for Eafit's solar station

Flow	Variable Name	Attributes			Basic Functions											V.Rel
		α	β	γ	fu121	fu122	fu12	fu131	fu32	fu21	fu22	fu311	fu312	fu321	fu322	
f1 - f2	Solar Irradiance	0.0	W/m2	[100,1200]	3	3	3	0	0	3	0	3	3	9	1	3,11
	Wind Speed	0.0	Km/h	[0,30]	0	0	1	0	0	3	0	3	1	1	0	1,00
	Wind Direction	0.0	°	[0,360]	0	0	0	0	0	3	0	1	1	1	0	0,67
	Temperature	0.0	°C	[0,50]	0	0	0	0	0	3	0	3	1	0	0	0,78
	Atmospheric Pressure	0.0	atm	[0,1]	0	0	1	0	0	3	0	3	3	0	1	1,22
	Rain	0.0	mm	[0,1000]	0	0	1	0	0	3	0	3	3	1	1	1,33
-f2 - f3	PV Angle	0.0	°	[0,360]	9	9	3	0	0	1	3	0	3	9	3	4,44
	Input Voltage	0.0	V	[0,72]	3	3	0	0	0	1	3	0	0	3	0	1,44
	MPPT Current	0.0	A	[0,32]	3	3	1	0	0	0	3	0	0	0	0	1,11
	MPPT Voltage	0.0	V	12	3	3	1	0	0	0	3	0	0	0	0	1,11
f3 - f4	Battery Voltage	0.0	V	[6,12]	3	3	9	1	0	0	1	0	0	1	3	2,33
	Battery Current State	0.0	Ah	200	0	3	9	1	0	0	9	0	9	3	9	4,78
f4 - f5	Inverter Current	0.0	A	[0,32]	0	0	1	9	0	3	3	0	3	0	3	2,44
	Inverter Voltage	0.0	V	[100,130]	0	0	1	9	0	3	1	0	0	0	0	1,56
f5	Actuator Current	0.0	A	[0,10]	0	0	0	0	3	0	3	0	0	0	3	1,00
f6	Device Consumption	0.0	Wh	[0,32]	0	0	0	0	9	0	3	0	3	0	9	2,67
	Device State of Charge	0.0	V	[0,5]	0	0	0	0	0	0	0	0	3	0	3	0,67
	Function Relevance				2,67	3,00	3,44	2,22	1,33	2,89	3,56	1,78	3,67	3,11	4,00	

Table 2. Components selection

Variable	Technical need	Value	Unit	Selection
Generation Current	To measure current up to 100 A	≤100	A	Allegro DC 100 A
Consumption Current	To measure current up to 200 A	≤200	A	Shunt resistance
Battery Voltage	To measure voltage of CS battery	≤12	V	Analog sensor resistance
Solar Panel's inclination	To measure tilt degree of solar panels array	≤180°	°	Bosch XDK Multisensor

selection of sensors and other devices for each measurement. All sensors were connected, Fig. 5 shows the installation of Allegro DC and Shunt resistance.

Most of the sensors selected work with analog signals, but in the case of Bosch XDK, it can work with various communication protocols, such as WiFi, Bluetooth Low Energy (BLE), I2C and UART. The XDK, which was chosen for tilt measurement, allows to track more variables through the 7 sensors included, i.e accelerometer, acoustic, digital light, gyroscope, humidity, magnetometer, pressure and temperature.

Communication Protocols. For the integration among network's components, it is necessary to use different communication interfaces that consider the operation conditions of the station. Currently, Eafit's CS does not have a wired communication network. Besides, it is desired to keep the concept of building this kind of stations in remote areas for future work; thus, installing a wireless communication protocol could bring more benefits and a more interesting analysis than having a wired one.

Considering the possibility that CS in remote locations could not have an internet connection, the idea is to have a network composed by a set of nodes and a central controller. In this network, each node, i.e stations, will include a micro-controller in charge of collecting sensors' data and sending it to the central controller through long distances. And the central controller acts as the Gateway in the communication network.

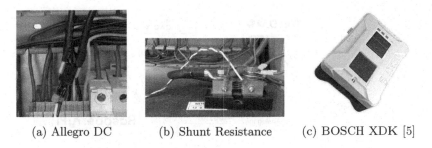

(a) Allegro DC   (b) Shunt Resistance   (c) BOSCH XDK [5]

Fig. 5. Sensors employed in the present development

The signals coming from the sensors can be transmitted through wired and/or wireless communication. In this project, the device selected for collecting all data from sensors is an Arduino 101 board, thanks to its availability of analog inputs and compatibility with BLE. The board is in charge of transmitting collected data to a Raspberry Pi Gateway located some meters away, which finally sends all information to an IoT platform for its future visualization and analysis. The configuration scheme with these main components is shown in Fig. 6.

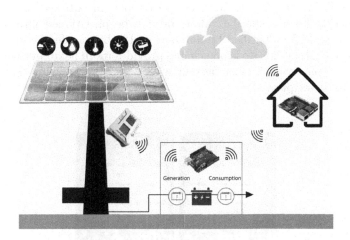

Fig. 6. Final configuration

Regarding technical and operation aspects indicated above, the diagram presented in Fig. 7 illustrates the detailed communication network finally implemented. From these communications, there is a specially interested in the connection between BOSCH XDK and Arduino 101. The communication between these nodes is made with BLE. This protocol is relatively new and was created specifically for IoT, offering the possibility to simultaneously communicate multiple sensors and/or peripheral devices with a central one.

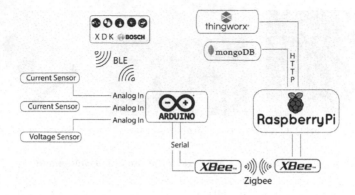

Fig. 7. Communications scheme

Two kinds of devices exist in BLE: central and peripheral. Each of them has different possibilities for interacting with others. For example, a peripheral device can notify the change on a value to the central device, without being permanently connected. This helps to decrease its energy consumption. Furthermore, BLE devices allow to organize information in packets or folders, called services, as illustrates Fig. 8. Services are divided in sub-folders named characteristics, that have a specific value and can be partitioned into descriptors. Each service folder is identified by numbers of 128 bits, called Unique Universal Identifiers (UUIDs). This division scheme provides more flexibility when sharing data because some values must be sent with a higher frequency than others or using certain descriptors.

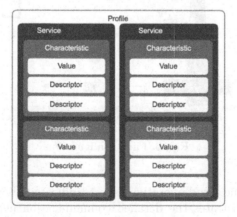

Fig. 8. BLE scheme

The XDK includes multiples services, but only some of them are in charge of transmitting sensors' data. The services required in this project, with their

Table 3. XDK services

	XDK Control Service *UUID* 55b741d0-7ada-11e4-82f8-0800200c9a66	High Data Rate Service *UUID* c2967210-7ba4-11e4-82f8-0800200c9a66
Services		
Characteristics	Start Sensor Sampling and Notification *UUID* 55b741d1-7ada-11e4-82f8-0800200c9a66	High Priority Array *UUID* c2967211-7ba4-11e4-82f8-0800200c9a66
	XDK Fusion Sensor *UUID* 55b741d5-7ada-11e4-82f8-0800200c9a66	Low Priority Array *UUID* c2967212-7ba4-11e4-82f8-0800200c9a66

respective characteristic are described in Table 3. The XDK Control Service is the only one that can be discovered by Arduino.

These characteristics provide sensors' data, which is then configured with JSON format in order to transmit it to a server. Data is sent with certain period of time, which varies according to the type of information.

3.3 Phase III: Database Structure and Graphical User Interface (GUI)

Since one of the goals of system monitoring is to further analyze data, either for simple tasks like verifying system performance or for artificial intelligence projects like developing prediction models; the Gateway is in charge of transmitting data for visualization, storing and future processing. For the present system, the platform ThingWorx is used for both, storing and visualization.

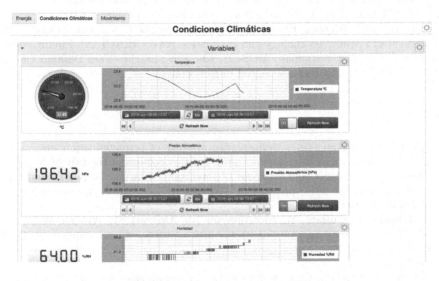

Fig. 9. Remote monitoring GUI

The design proposed for the GUI, consisted in building customizable dashboards on ThingWorx, with the purpose to allow that the user access the different panels in the order he/she preferred. Thus, an independent graph interface, called Gadget, was created for each sensor. The initial proposal for the dashboards' distribution and some charts are shown in Fig. 9.

4   Conclusions and Future Work

The entire monitoring system was installed and tested, including all devices, wireless communication and cloud platform. It was possible to combine the benefits of IoT and Cloud Platform. The architecture implemented, can be seen as a low cost and easy-to-adapt solution for monitoring standalone PVCS.

In addition to the selected set of variables, other information that could be integrated into the monitoring system to perform better data analytics could be the user's variables. This could include, for example, the type of device connected by the user, connection time, its consumption, etc. Hence, it would be possible to get not only generation models but also for consumption.

Future work is mainly oriented to analyze and apply machine learning to the data stored through this monitoring system. Besides, it considers adding several features, such as system's failures detection and alerts, in order to have a more robust monitoring system.

Acknowledgements. Authors would like to thank Universidad EAFIT to support this research through the Research Assistantship grant from project 828-000134, which is also developed in the framework of the "ENERGETICA 2030" Scientific Ecosystem (code 58667) funded by The World Bank (contract No. FP44842-210-2018) through the call "778-2017 Scientific Ecosystems" managed by the Colombian Administrative Department of Science, Technology and Innovation (COLCIENCIAS). Finally, authors would like to thank the company BOSCH, who provides the Cross Domain Development Kit (XDK) that was implemented in this analysis.

References

1. Ahmed, M.A., Kim, Y.C.: Performance analysis of communication networks for EV charging stations in residential grid. In: Proceedings of the 6th ACM Symposium on Development and Analysis of Intelligent Vehicular Networks and Applications, DIVANet 2017, pp. 63–70. ACM, New York (2017). https://doi.org/10.1145/3132340.3132352
2. Al-Fuqaha, A., Guizani, M., Mohammadi, M., Aledhari, M., Ayyash, M.: Internet of things: a survey on enabling technologies, protocols, and applications. IEEE Commun. Surv. Tutor. **17**(4), 2347–2376 (2015). https://doi.org/10.1109/COMST.2015.2444095
3. Álvarez, R.D.: Isla fuerte cumplió un año sin energía eléctrica. El Universal, October 2018. https://www.eluniversal.com.co/cartagena/isla-fuerte-cumplio-un-ano-sin-energia-electrica-288924-AUEU406350

4. Bhatti, A.R., Salam, Z., Aziz, M.J.B.A., Yee, K.P., Ashique, R.H.: Electric vehicles charging using photovoltaic: status and technological review. Renew. Sustain. Energy Rev. **54**, 34–47 (2016). https://doi.org/10.1016/j.rser.2015.09.091. http://www.sciencedirect.com/science/article/pii/S1364032115010618

5. BOSCH: XDK cross domain development kit. https://xdk.bosch-connectivity. com/hardware. Accessed 02 June 2018

6. Chowdhury, F., Shabnam, F., Islam, F., Azad, A.: Software implementation of the central solar battery charging station (CSBCS). In: 2013 International Conference on Power, Energy and Control (ICPEC), pp. 746–750, February 2013. https://doi. org/10.1109/ICPEC.2013.6527754

7. Fernández-Montoya, M., Mejía-Gutiérrez, R., Osorio-Gómez, G.: A function to data matrix (FDM) approach for mission variables consideration, vol. 108, p. 10008 (2017)

8. International Energy Agency: Renewable Energy Services for Developing Countries, December 2008. http://www.iea-pvps.org/index.php?id=368

9. Karmaker, A.K., Ahmed, M.R., Hossain, M.A., Sikder, M.M.: Feasibility assessment & design of hybrid renewable energy based electric vehicle charging station in Bangladesh. Sustain. Cities Soc. **39**, 189–202 (2018). https://doi.org/10.1016/j.scs.2018.02.035. http://www.sciencedirect.com/science/ article/pii/S221067071731661X

10. Lee, J., Park, G.L.: Temporal data stream analysis for EV charging infrastructure in Jeju. In: Proceedings of the International Conference on Research in Adaptive and Convergent Systems, RACS 2017, pp. 36–39. ACM, New York (2017). https:// doi.org/10.1145/3129676.3129717

11. Mahmoud, M.S., Mohamad, A.A.: A study of efficient power consumption wireless communication techniques/modules for internet of things (IoT) applications. Comput. Sci. Commun. **06**(02), 19–29 (2016)

12. Mondol, J.D., Yohanis, Y.G., Norton, B.: Comparison of measured and predicted long term performance of grid a connected photovoltaic system. Energy Convers. Manag. **48**(4), 1065–1080 (2007). https://doi.org/10.1016/j.enconman.2006. 10.021. http://www.sciencedirect.com/science/article/pii/S0196890406003372

13. Nie, X., et al.: Online monitoring and integrated analysis system for EV charging station. In: 2013 IEEE PES Asia-Pacific Power and Energy Engineering Conference (APPEEC), pp. 1–6, December 2013. https://doi.org/10.1109/APPEEC. 2013.6837206

14. Qazi, S.: Chapter 2 - fundamentals of standalone photovoltaic systems. In: Qazi, S. (ed.) Standalone Photovoltaic (PV) Systems for Disaster Relief and Remote Areas, pp. 31–82. Elsevier (2017). https://doi.org/10.1016/B978-0-12-803022-6.00002-2. http://www.sciencedirect.com/science/article/pii/B9780128030226000022

15. Shepelev, A., Chung, C., Gadh, R.: Mesh network design for smart charging infrastructure and electric vehicle remote monitoring. In: 2013 International Conference on ICT Convergence (ICTC), pp. 250–255, October 2013. https://doi.org/10.1109/ ICTC.2013.6675352

16. Yang, L., Ribberink, H.: Investigation of the potential to improve DC fast charging station economics by integrating photovoltaic power generation and/or local battery energy storage system. Energy **167**, 246–259 (2019). https://doi. org/10.1016/j.energy.2018.10.147. http://www.sciencedirect.com/science/article/ pii/S0360544218321431

17. Zobaa, A.F., Bansal, R.C.: Handbook of Renewable Energy Technology. World Scientific, Singapore (2011). https://doi.org/10.1142/7489. https://www.worlds cientific.com/doi/abs/10.1142/7489

Kinetic Model of Magnetic Nanoparticles in the Bloodstream Under the Influence of an External Magnetic Field

Laura María Roa Barrantes$^{(\boxtimes)}$ (ID), Diego Julián Rodríguez Patarroyo$^{(\boxtimes)}$ (ID), and Jaime Francisco Pantoja Benavides$^{(\boxtimes)}$ (ID)

Research group Ingeniería y Nanotecnología para la vida INVID,
Universidad Distrital Fracisco José de caldas, Bogotá, Colombia
lmroab@correo.udistrital.edu.co,
djrodriguezp,jfpantojab}@udistrital.edu.co

Abstract. A mathematical model was developed to describe the trajectories of magnetic nanoparticles in a blood vessel under the influence of an external magnetic field, by the direction of the magnetic drug (MDT). The equations of motion were solved by the technique of molecular dynamics. The nanoparticles are injected near the target region, along the blood vessel in the z direction and their trajectory is controlled by means of an external magnetic field produced by a cylindrical magnet (NdFeB) located outside the body, the orientation of the field lines are perpendicular to the blood flow, that is, in the ϱ direction. For this case, the blood vessel is assumed as a cylindrical tube with radial symmetry and constant laminar flow, with a magnetic nanoparticle inside it. All the forces that can significantly influence the trajectory of the nanoparticle are taken into account, such as the magnetization force, the drag force and the external magnetic field. The results show that the particles that are within the influence of the magnetic field will be captured and attracted by it when it is strong, which happens while the magnet is near the blood vessel, however, as the distance becomes larger the magnetic nanoparticle are released from the magnetic field and flow to the blood vessels in the z direction due of the force of drag.

Keywords: Nanoparticles trajectories · Magnetic drug targeting · Magnetic nanoparticles

1 Introduction

The supply of drugs by magnetic nanoparticles through the bloodstream is a technique known as magnetic drugs targeting (MDT), its use allows to avoid the dispersion of drugs in undesirable places [14] being directed to the target regions so that its release is more efficient, thereby reducing side effects, thus improving the quality of life of the patient. The size, shape and surface chemistry of the nanoparticles have important characteristics about their binding and elimination

© Springer Nature Switzerland AG 2019
J. C. Figueroa-García et al. (Eds.): WEA 2019, CCIS 1052, pp. 596–604, 2019.
https://doi.org/10.1007/978-3-030-31019-6_50

upon contact with the human body. In general, particles of more than 200 nm are efficiently eliminated by the reticle-endothelial system (liver, spleen and bone marrow), while particles of less than 10 nm can be rapidly eliminated by renal clearance, monomuclear response or by extravasation [9, 16].

The MDT technique has been a subject of research very mentioned in several articles [1, 10, 17]. Previous works such as those by Ruiz et. al [12] experimentally synthesized iron oxide nanoparticles (Fe_3O_4) of up to 10 nm in diameter, homogeneous spherical with a biocompatible coating, in their study of toxicity in mice they found that the materials are safe for biomedical applications. On another hand, Haverkort et al. [5] who apply the MDT technique in large human arteries taking into account the characteristics of the blood fluid, by means of simulations of capture of magnetic nanoparticles in 3D, finding that 50% of them manage to be captured by the magnetic field. Lunnoo et al. [9] computationally studied the efficiency of capture based on the size of iron, magnetite and maghemite nanoparticles, as well as the effects of different types of coating on a drug-carrying structure. In their findings, they describe that the coating does not significantly influence the magnetization of the nanoparticle, and that the appropriate size is between 10–200 nm, but the capture efficiency of nanoparticles decreases as their size decreases. Furlani et al. [3] developed an analytical method to predict the transport and capture of nanoparticles using a magnetic field; as a result they claim that the malignant tissue can be located within the body several centimeters away. Later, Furlani and Furlani [2] mathematically predict, by analytical methods, the transport and capture of nanoparticles, taking into account the external magnetic field, the drag force and the magnetization of the particle. Finally, they suggest that the developed theory can be used to optimize the particle size as well as the parameters of the external magnet. Sharma et al. [15] They develop a mathematical model that predicts the trajectories of a group of nanoparticles, solving by means of the Runge-Kutta of order 4 method. They affirm that the total of the nanoparticles were captured in the center of the magnet when it is very near to the human body, and that, as it moves away, the capture diminishes until it is null.

In this paper, we present the mathematical modeling and an analysis by computer simulation that describes the trajectory of a magnetic nanoparticle injected close to the target tissue and upstream of the blood flow, along the blood vessel in the z direction and is directed to the target zone by means of a cylindrical magnet (NdFeB) located outside the body, which generates a constant magnetic field of 0.4 T whose lines are perpendicular to the blood flow in the direction ϱ. In the Fig. 1 you can see the blood vessel and the magnet that generates the magnetic field. The molecular dynamics technique solves the differential equations of order 2 non-linear (Eqs. 9 and 10), that predict the trajectory of a magnetic nanoparticle in the blood flow in the presence of an external magnetic field, taking into account characteristics such as magnetization, magnetic saturation, geometry and size of the magnet, nanoparticle and blood vessel; additionally the continuous laminar blood flow is assumed [18].

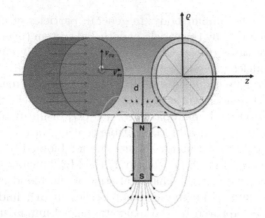

Fig. 1. Schematic of the transport system of the magnetic nanoparticle in a blood vessel and the magnetic field is applied outside the blood vessel.

2   Methodology

For the computational simulation, the description of the conditions to determine the equations of movement that interact in the model was taken into account, then the programming in C++ making use of the technique of molecular dynamics by Verlet; Finally, for the analysis and interpretation, all forces that influence the trajectory of the nanoparticle were taken into account, modifying the intensity of the magnetic field due to changes in the magnet distance.

The nanoparticles are injected upstream, near the target tissue, along the direction of the blood vessel z and are directed by means of an external magnetic field, located outside the body, the orientation of the lines of the magnetic field are perpendicular to blood flow. For this case, the blood vessel is assumed as a cylindrical tube with radial symmetry and constant laminar flow, with a magnetic nanoparticle inside it. The forces that influence these trajectories are the external magnetic field, the magnetization of the nanoparticle and the force of the blood flow drag [15]. The blood vessel model is naturally in 3D, but due to the radial symmetry of the vessel, the equations of motion can be formulated in terms of the radial axis ϱ and the direction of blood flow. The parameters used are based on the bibliography [3,5,7–9,15], in some cases, they were adjusted to the system.

The equations were solved using the computational technique The molecular dynamics that allows the study of particles or systems at atomic scale. This technique allows to calculate trajectories of the atoms or particles that form the matter, which makes it possible to simulate the microscopic behavior of a system. Knowing the trajectories of the parcels allows obtaining information about the forces acting in a system allowing not only the characterization and monitoring of the same but also the control; in this case the Verlet algorithm, also known as the cellular method, is based on numerical methods that allow solving the numerical integration of ordinary second-order differential equations with known initial values, serves as a basis and algorithm to describe the uniform rectilinear motion [4,6].

2.1 Model Formulation

For the formulation of the system, the following were taken into account: External magnetic field (H), Magnetic forces (F_m) and drag (F_f), the equations of movement and the parameters of values constants and variables for magnet, nanoparticle, flow and blood vessel in the Table 1 shows parameters and features to the system.

Table 1. Parameters and features

Parameter	Value	Unit	References
Permanent magnet			
Material	Rare earths	NdFeB	[3]
Diameter	$4 \leq d \leq 6$	cm	[15]
Magnetic saturation	10^6	A/m^1	[5]
Magnetic nanoparticle			
Material	Fe_3O_4	Magnetite	[15]
Diameter	$75 \leq d \leq 200$	nm	[9]
Susceptibility	$\chi \gg 1$	-	[15]
Density	$5000 \geq rho \geq 6450$	Kg/m^3	[8,15]
Vessel and blood flow			
Radio	$50 \leq R \leq 75$	μm	[2]
Viscosity	$3.2 * 10^{-3}$	Ns/m^2	[15]
Density	1060	Kg/m^3	[5,15]
Average speed	10	mm/s	[15]

External Magnetic Field

The transport of the nanoparticle is due to the influence of the external magnetic field, since while it is present, it magnetizes each nanoparticle as a superparamagnetic monodomain that responds kinetically in the direction of said field [11,13], and, once it is removed from the system, the nanoparticle loses its magnetization. Which makes it less harmful to biological use. Equations 1 and 2 correspond to the magnetic field produced by the external magnet on the axes ϱ y z. In the Table 1 the assumed characteristics for the permanent magnet are described.

$$\mathbf{H}(\mathbf{z}, \varrho)_\varrho = \frac{M_s R_m^2}{2} \left[\frac{(\varrho + d)^2 - z^2}{[(\varrho + d)^2 + z^2]^2} \right] \tag{1}$$

$$\mathbf{H}(\mathbf{z}, \varrho)_z = \frac{M_s R_m^2}{2} \left[\frac{2(\varrho + d)z}{[(\varrho + d)^2 + z^2]^2} \right] \tag{2}$$

where, $\mathbf{H}_\varrho$ and $\mathbf{H}_z$ corresponds to the intensity of the magnetic field of the permanent magnet in the axes ϱ and z respectively, M_s, is the magnetic saturation, R_m, is the Radius of the permanent magnet and d, is the distance between the center of the permanent magnet and the perpendicular in the center of the Blood vessel with the axis z.

Magnetic Force on the Nanoparticle
Equations 3 and 4 represent the magnetic force in each of the axes (z and ϱ). Due to magnetite (Fe_3O_4) has a high magnetic susceptibility, nanoparticles present an attractive response upon entering the magnetic field produced by the external magnet. In the Table 1, the parameters used to predict the trajectories of the nanoparticle are displayed.

$$\mathbf{F}(\mathbf{z}, \varrho)_{m\varrho} = K_1 \frac{d}{2[d^2 + z^2]^3} \tag{3}$$

$$\mathbf{F}(\mathbf{z}, \varrho)_{mz} = k_1 \frac{z}{2[d^2 + z^2]^3} \tag{4}$$

where, $\mathbf{F}_{m\varrho}$ and $\mathbf{F}_{mz}$ corresponds to the magnetic force experienced by the nanoparticle in the axes ϱ and z respectively, K_1 corresponds to the constant: $3\mu_0 v_p M_s^2 R_m^4$ (μ_0 the magnetic permeability in the vacuum, v_p is the volume of the particle, M_s the magnetization of the magnet and R_m the radius of the magnet) and d is the distance between the magnet and the perpendicular to the axis z of the blood vessel.

Drag Force
A laminar fluid parallel to the z axis with constant viscosity is assumed in a cylindrical blood vessel of $50\,\mu m$ radius. In the Table 1 are the parameters considered for both the flow and the blood vessel. Likewise the drag force on the nanoparticle can be expressed as shown in the Eq. 5, where, $\mathbf{F}_0$ corresponds to $6\pi\eta R_p$ and the velocities of the nanoparticle and the fluid are $\mathbf{V}_p$ and $\bar{\mathbf{V}}_f$ respectively.

$$\mathbf{F}_f = -\mathbf{F}_0(\mathbf{V}_p - \bar{\mathbf{V}}_f) \tag{5}$$

The final velocity of the nanoparticle depends on the velocity of the fluid ($\bar{\mathbf{V}}_f$) and the velocity profile given in this case, as shown in Eq. 6.

$$\mathbf{V}_f = 2\bar{\mathbf{V}}_f \left[1 - \left(\frac{\varrho}{R_v}\right)^2\right] \tag{6}$$

replacing 6 in 5, you get the drag force on the nanoparticle in each of the addresses ϱ y z, as you can see in Eqs. 7 and 8 respectively.

$$\mathbf{F}_{f\varrho} = -\mathbf{F}_0 \mathbf{V}_{p\varrho} \tag{7}$$

$$\mathbf{F}_{fz} = -\mathbf{F}_0 \left[\mathbf{V}_{pz} - 2\bar{\mathbf{V}}_f \left[1 - \left(\frac{\varrho}{R_v}\right)^2\right]\right] \tag{8}$$

Motion Equations

From Eqs. 1–4, 7 and 8 arise the equations of motion that predict the trajectories of the nanoparticles (9 and 10).

$$\left(\frac{d\mathbf{V}_{p\varrho}}{dt}\right) = \left(\frac{K_2}{m}\right)\frac{d}{2(d^2+z^2)^3} - \frac{\mathbf{F}_0}{m}\mathbf{V}_\varrho \qquad (9)$$

$$\left(\frac{d\mathbf{V}_{pz}}{dt}\right) = \frac{2\mathbf{F}_0\bar{\mathbf{V}}_f}{m}\left[1 - \left(\frac{\varrho}{R_v}\right)^2\right] + \left(\frac{K_2}{m}\right)\frac{z}{(d^2+z^2)^3} - \frac{\mathbf{F}_0}{m}\mathbf{V}_z \qquad (10)$$

where, K_2, corresponds to the following constant $\frac{1}{3\eta}\mu_0 R_p^2 M_s^2 R_m^4$ where the viscosity of the blood (η), the permeability in vacuum (μ_0), the radii of both the particle (R_p) and the permanent magnet (R_m) and the magnetization thereof are taken into account, $\mathbf{F}_0$ corresponds to the drag force of the fluid, determined by $6\pi\eta R_p\mathbf{V}_{p\varrho}$.

3   Results and Analysis

The mathematical model allows to predict, by computer simulation, the trajectory described by a magnetic nanoparticle that travels through a cylindrical blood vessel under the influence of an external magnetic field. The forces that act and significantly influence the nanoparticle including the magnetization force of the nanoparticle caused by the influence of the external magnetic field whose components described in Eqs. 1 and 2 are considered constant throughout the simulation. Velocities and trajectories are analyzed, following the nanoparticle when the intensity of the magnetic field changes as the distance of the magnet changes to the center of the blood vessel.

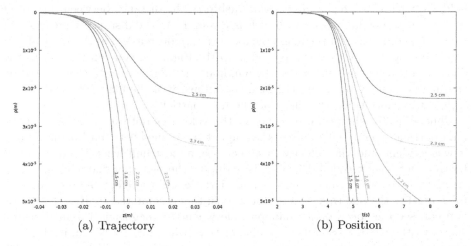

(a) Trajectory   (b) Position

Fig. 2. Magnetic nanoparticle trajectory and position in ϱ, changing the distance of the magnet between 1.5 cm and 2.5 cm

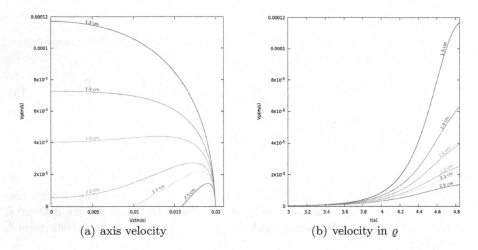

(a) axis velocity   (b) velocity in ϱ

Fig. 3. Velocity of nanoparticles changing the distance of the magnet between 1.5 cm and 2.5 cm

The radial ϱ and horizontal z components of the magnetic force ($\mathbf{F_{m\varrho}}$ and $\mathbf{F_{mz}}$) along the axis of the blood vessel allow show in Fig. 2(a), the trajectory of the nanoparticles by varying the distance (d) between the magnet and the blood vessel. In the curves, it is observed that when increasing the intensity of the magnetic field the nanoparticle changes its trajectory almost immediately upon entering the magnetic field, therefore, the nanoparticles located in the center of the blood vessel are captured when the distance between the magnet and blood vessel is between 1.5, 2.0 and 2.2 cm, from 2.3 cm the influence of magnetic force is not enough, which causes the nanoparticle to be released and continue their trajectory on directed z, along the blood vessel. This is because the magnetic field strength (H_m) has a direct relationship to the distance between the blood vessel and the magnet, as shown in Eqs. 3 and 4. As the distance increases (d), the radial component of the magnetic force ($\mathbf{F_{m\varrho}}$), decreases and therefore allows the free movement of the nanoparticles. In the Fig. 2(b), you can see how as the distance of the magnet increases, the nanoparticle takes longer to be captured by the magnetic field, even above 2.2 cm the intensity of the magnetic field begins to lose the capacity of attraction on the nanoparticle.

The Fig. 3(a) shows the behavior of the velocities both in ϱ and in z of the nanoparticle when the distance of the magnet is modified between 1.5 and 2.5 cm, it was evident that the velocity in ϱ decrease, almost null when the distance of the magnet has exceeded 2.4 cm, this is due to the fact that the magnetic field strength is too weak to capture the nanoparticle and therefore the predominant force on it is the one that acts on the z axis; this is reinforced with Fig. 3(b), as you can see the speed of the nanoparticle when the magnet is 1.5 cm from the center of the blood vessel, increases faster than when it is to 2.5 cm, in this case the nanoparticle reaches a maximum speed below 20 μm/s, which is not enough to modify its trajectory and go to the target region.

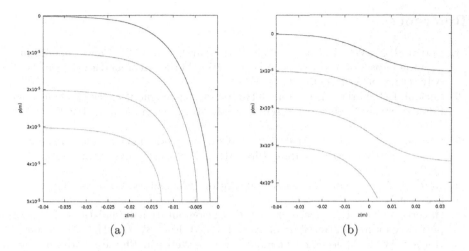

Fig. 4. Trajectory of the nanoparticle varying the position in the axis ϱ

In the Fig. 4, the position of the nanoparticle along the axis ϱ was varied and leaving the magnet fixed in case (a) it is located at a distance of 1.5 cm from the center of the blood vessel, it can be seen that the nearer the nanoparticle of the magnet is, the stronger the change in the trajectory of the magnet will be; This is because the intensity of the magnetic field is much higher. In the Fig. 4(b) the distance of the magnet is fixed at 3.0 cm, it can be seen that even if the nanoparticle is near the lower edge of the blood vessel the position of the nanoparticle in the axis ϱ does not change much since the magnetic force is not enough to draw it towards the center of the magnet.

4   Conclusions

In summary, a mathematical model has been presented that allows us to predict, by computational simulation, the transport of magnetic nanoparticles in blood vessels by the action of an external magnetic field. The model incorporates all the forces that significantly influence the kinetics of nanoparticles, including the magnetic field caused by an external magnet, magnetic force and drag force. The nonlinear partial differential equations obtained, which model the system, have been solved by means of the molecular dynamics technique. The results show that the nanoparticle will be captured and attracted by the influence of the magnetic field towards the desired target zone, as long as the intensity of the field is sufficiently strong, when distance d increases, the intensity of the magnetic field decreases and, therefore, the magnetic force as well. It can also be evidenced that the nanoparticle subjected to the influence of an external magnetic field will be captured between 4 and 8 s, after this time, it can be affirmed that the trajectory of a nanoparticle depends on the drag force of the fluid blood.

References

1. Bertrand, N., Wu, J., Xu, X., Kamaly, N., Farokhzad, O.C.: Cancer nanotechnology: the impact of passive and active targeting in the era of modern cancer biology. Adv. Drug Deliv. Rev. **66**, 2–25 (2014)
2. Furlani, E.J., Furlani, E.P.: A model for predicting magnetic targeting of multifunctional particles in the microvasculature. J. Magn. Magn. Mater. **312**(1), 187–193 (2007)
3. Furlani, E.P., Ng, K.C.: Analytical model of magnetic nanoparticle transport and capture in the microvasculature. Phys. Rev. E - Stat. Nonlinear Soft Matter Phys. (2006)
4. Haile, J.M.: Molecular Dynamics Simulation: Elementary Methods. Wiley, Hoboken (1992)
5. Haverkort, J.W., Kenjereš, S., Kleijn, C.R.: Computational simulations of magnetic particle capture in arterial flows. Ann. Biomed. Eng. **37**(12), 2436–2448 (2009)
6. Hoover, W.G.: Molecular Dynamics. Lecture Notes in Physics. Springer, Berlin (1986)
7. Kayal, S., Bandyopadhyay, D., Mandal, T.K., Ramanujan, R.V.: The flow of magnetic nanoparticles in magnetic drug targeting. RSC Adv. **1**(2), 238–246 (2011)
8. Kenjereš, S.: On recent progress in modelling and simulations of multi-scale transfer of mass, momentum and particles in bio-medical applications. Flow Turbul. Combust. **96**(3), 837–860 (2016)
9. Lunnoo, T., Puangmali, T.: Capture efficiency of biocompatible magnetic nanoparticles in arterial flow: a computer simulation for magnetic drug targeting. Nanoscale Res. Lett. **10**, 1 (2015)
10. Maity, A.R., Stepensky, D.: Delivery of drugs to intracellular organelles using drug delivery systems: analysis of research trends and targeting efficiencies. Int. J. Pharm. **496**(2), 268–274 (2015)
11. Mohammed, L., Gomaa, H.G., Ragab, D., Zhu, J.: Magnetic nanoparticles for environmental and biomedical applications: a review. Particuology **30**, 1–14 (2017)
12. Ruiz, A., Mancebo, A., Beola, L., Sosa, I., Gutiérrez, L.: Dose-response bioconversion and toxicity analysis of magnetite nanoparticles. IEEE Magn. Lett. **7**, 1–5 (2016)
13. Rukshin, I., Mohrenweiser, J., Yue, P., Afkhami, S.: Modeling superparamagnetic particles in blood flow for applications in magnetic drug targeting. Fluids **2**(2), 29 (2017)
14. Russo, F., Boghi, A., Gori, F.: Numerical simulation of magnetic nano drug targeting in patient-specific lower respiratory tract. J. Magn. Magn. Mater. **451**, 554–564 (2018)
15. Sharma, S., Gaur, A., Singh, U., Katiyar, V.: Capture efficiency of magnetic nanoparticles in a tube under magnetic field. Procedia Mater. Sci. **10**, 64–69 (2015). Cnt 2014
16. Tan, J., Thomas, A., Liu, Y.: Influence of red blood cells on nanoparticle targeted delivery in microcirculation. Soft Matter **8**, 1934–1946 (2011)
17. Tietze, R., et al.: Magnetic nanoparticle-based drug delivery for cancer therapy. Biochem. Biophys. Res. Commun. **468**(3), 463–470 (2015)
18. Vijayaratnam, P.R., O'Brien, C.C., Reizes, J.A., Barber, T.J., Edelman, E.R.: The impact of blood rheology on drug transport in stented arteries: steady simulations. PLoS ONE **10**, 6 (2015)

Battery State of Charge Estimation Error Comparison Across Different OCV-SOC Curve Approximating Methods

Rafael Sanín[✉], Mauricio Fernández-Montoya,
Maria Alejandra Garzón-Vargas, and Alejandro Velásquez-López

Design Engineering Research Group (GRID), EAFIT University, Medellín, Colombia
{rsanine,mferna21,mgarzon8,avelasq9}@eafit.edu.co
http://www.eafit.edu.co/grid

Abstract. Accurate estimation of Rechargeable Batteries Parameters, such as State Of Charge (SOC), contributes to their safety and reliable operation in a wide variety of applications (e.g. automotive, stationary energy storage, medical equipment, among others). Due to variations in environmental and load conditions, battery cells and their instrumentation devices can experience deviations from their standard operation values, leading to an imprecise measurement of State Of Charge (SOC) indicator variables. Then, SOC estimation models are required. These estimations developed through analytical models consider intrinsic battery chemistry variables and operation cycle conditions are taken from charge and discharge testing; where hysteresis phenomena, measurement, and theoretical adjustment errors can be identified over Open Circuit Voltage (OCV)-SOC curves.

This study compares the model adjustment errors of several estimation methods, taken from literature to approximate the OCV-SOC curves of a rechargeable battery pack.

Keywords: SOC · Rechargeable battery · OCV-SOC curve · Estimation model · Sigma Point Kalman Filter (SPKF)

1 Introduction

The social and industrial interest to contribute to environmental sustainability is growing progressively, which is especially relevant over transportation, with an estimated consumption of 14 million barrels per day (71%) only in the US. The migration of fossil fuel-based transportation to Electric Vehicles (EVs) along with renewable energy sources would lead to drastic improvements in air quality and reduction of greenhouse gases, the main cause of global warming [1]. Although EVs could significantly reduce Greenhouse Gas (GHG) emissions [2,3] and fossil fuel dependence, they still represent a small market share of vehicles in service, with 1.10% of new registrations in 2016 [4]. The refusal of the market to migrate to Electric Vehicle (EV) is based on the high cost of battery packs

© Springer Nature Switzerland AG 2019
J. C. Figueroa-García et al. (Eds.): WEA 2019, CCIS 1052, pp. 605–615, 2019.
https://doi.org/10.1007/978-3-030-31019-6_51

(nearly 30 % of the total purchase cost of a BEV [5]), their limited stored energy capacity, and lifespan [6]. However, the potential of increasing specific energy density relies on the adoption of more sophisticated monitoring strategies.

Although high energy-density batteries have seen their development more widespread in consumer electronics (such as cell phones and laptops), the high availability of recharging points and relatively constant power consumption of these devices allows flexibility in terms of State Of Charge (SOC) estimation. Conversely, EV batteries require high power delivery and energy storage capacities (~ 100KWh) within constrained spaces, tight weight limits and still required to be sold for an affordable price [7]. Their charging schedules are tied by the owner's specific requirements and access to charging stations, being mostly public facilities out of customer reach. This implies that the EV must be able to take full advantage of each watt-hour of energy from its battery pack. Therefore knowing or estimating the SOC of the battery is essential, these specific conditions lead the need to improve and validate the SOC estimation models in an EV battery pack.

There are different steps in the construction of SOC estimation models in which improvements can be made. There are improvements focused on: (i) the characterization tests of the rechargeable batteries, (ii) parametrization of the models and (iii) robustness of the same models.

This study seeks to identify if there are statistically significant differences between the different methods proposed in the literature to approximate the OCV-SOC curve, used to parameterize the models for SOC, in this case, the Sigma Point Kalman Filter (SPKF) model proposed by [8].

2   Battery State of Charge Estimation

SOC is a fundamental parameter during operative states of the battery (charging and discharging). The estimation of the SOC is performed automatically by the Battery Management System (BMS), since it measures and processes variables related to the current state of the battery, such as pack voltage, cell voltage, pack current and temperature of the cells.

In that sense, SOC is defined as the current remaining releasable energy $Q_{Releasable}$ expressed as a portion of its total rated energy capacity Q_{Rated}, within safe operative limits [9,10]:

$$SOC = \frac{Q_{Releasable}}{Q_{Rated}} \cdot 100\% \tag{1}$$

By measuring the energy storage decay, based on SOC estimations during battery lifespan, State Of Health (SOH) estimation can be performed by relating the maximum releasable battery capacity for each charging/discharging cycle, Q_{Max}, to the rated battery capacity Q_{Rated} [10–12].

$$SOH = \frac{Q_{Max}}{Q_{Rated}} \cdot 100\% \tag{2}$$

By measuring individual cell (module) voltages, dangerous conditions of Overvoltage or Undervoltage can be avoided [13]. Cell equalization algorithms guarantee to obtain as much energy as possible from the battery pack, close to the Q_{Rated} capacity, even if the internal Equivalent Series Resistance (ESR) from cells or modules were unmatched [14]. Battery temperature and parasitic capacitance can also affect the estimation of SOC [15]. SOC is a non-linear function of battery parameters [16].

There have been developments about estimation methods to determine SOC, including Discharge Tests, Coulomb count, Open Circuit Voltage (OCV) curves, impedance spectroscopy, artificial neural network (ANN), Fuzzy Logic, Kalman Filters, among others [17].

2.1 SOC Estimation Methods based on Equivalent Circuit Models

OCV vs SOC Curve: OCV vs SOC curve is a conventional method constructed from successive charging and discharging tests performed at different Deep of Discharge (DOD) and temperature scenarios. From raw data, look-up tables for each operative conditions serve as a guide to link each OCV chart point to the corresponding SOC value. As this method relies on measurements, it does not work well with cell chemistry's where voltage change rate is significantly smaller than the change rate in capacity (i.e., flat regions in the OCV-SOC curve that represent complex transient response dynamics in Lithium-based chemistry's) [18].

Coulomb Counting: Conventional method used as a reference for the comparison of SOC estimation methods.

Coulomb counting calculates the remaining portion of $Q_{Releasable}$ by accumulating the input or output charge for a time t. This method requires long monitoring times and accurate integration algorithms. Although Coulomb counting is easy to implement, has shown to be impractical for real time monitoring due to vast memory resources required and well known cumulative errors, which are tied to instrumentation fluctuations, bias, temperature [18], sampling period variations and discretization [10].

On its continuous form, SOC estimation by Coulomb counting is shown below, being $SOC_{(t)}$ State of Charge at given time t, $SOC_{(0)}$ State of Charge at time $t = 0$, Q_{Rated} as battery rated capacity in Coulombs or Ampere-hours, η: Coulombic efficiency as a relationship between discharge capacity $Q_{Discharge}$ and charge capacity Q_{Charge}, and $i(t)$: Measured input current at time t.

$$SOC_{(t)} = SOC_{(0)} - \frac{1}{Q_{Rated}} \int_0^t \eta . i(t) dt \qquad (3)$$

$$\eta = \frac{Q_{Discharge}}{Q_{Charge}} x100\% \qquad (4)$$

Kalman Filter: Model-based state estimation method belonging to recursive adaptive filters. Widely used in dynamic applications. Based on the combination of measured pair of Current-Voltage parameters for a given sample k, For this purpose, a faithfull mathematical model is required to represent the battery behaviour, usually represented as a states space model shown in the following equations:

Linear Kalman filter assumes the following state space model, where x_{k-1}: State, u_{k-1}: Input, w_{k-1}: Process noise, y_{k-1}: Output and v_{k-1}: Sensor noise.

$$x_k = A_{k-1}x_{k-1} + B_{k-1}u_{k-1} + w_{k-1} \tag{5}$$

$$y_k = C_k x_k + D_k u_k + v_k \tag{6}$$

Also, for Nonlinear Kalman filtering, state space model representation considers embedded system dynamics representation as shown below:

$$x_k = f(x_{k-1}, u_{k-1}, w_{k-1}) \tag{7}$$

$$y_k = h(x_k, u_k, v_k) \tag{8}$$

where:

- $f(\cdot, \cdot, \cdot)$: Time varying function that depends on state, input and process noise.
- $h(\cdot, \cdot, \cdot)$: Time varying function that depends on state, input and sensor noise.

The main requirement for implementing adaptative filters is that the battery cell model has to be linearized. For analytical linearization, (Extended Kalman Filter (EKF)) method is preferred. If statistical or empirical linearization is performed, (Sigma-Point Kalman Filter (SPKF)) is used instead [18].

3   Approximating the OCV-SOC Curve

The relationship between the cell's voltage and its SOC during charging and discharging operations differs because of cell hysteresis phenomena, directly related to cell Coulombic efficiency. Some authors have proposed different ways to approximate the OCV - SOC curves to obtain the parameters of the mathematical model from the cell. There are some of the methods proposed to approximate the OCV curve, which will be discussed below. Chen et al. compared different approximation OCV-SOC curve methods and evaluated their effect over the error in the estimation of SOC. For each experiment the estimated SOC and terminal voltage were calculated using the respective $OCV(SOC_{(k)})$ function and the sgn_k value. In order to make a comparison about the impact of battery hysteresis on the accuracy of SOC estimation in the model, they presented 4 different experiments, where Extended Kalman Filter (EKF) parameters were obtained using different sets of OCV curves as it follows [19].

Method 1. Use only OCV_Charge curve to get the $OCV(SOC_{(k)})$ function and fit the whole procedure [19].

$$OCV(SOC_{(k)}) = OCV\_Charge(SOC_{(k)}),$$

$$\begin{cases} 1, \text{ when } i_k > \varepsilon \\ 0, \text{ when } i_k < -\varepsilon \\ sgn_{k-1}, \text{when } |i_k| \leq \varepsilon \end{cases} \tag{9}$$

Where $i_{(k)}$ is the measured input current and $sgn_{(k)}$ is the hysteresis effect model.

Method 2. Use only $OCV\_Discharge$ curve to get the $OCV(SOC_{(k)})$ function and fit the whole procedure [19].

$$OCV(SOC_{(k)}) = OCV\_Discharge(SOC_{(k)}),$$

$$\begin{cases} 0, \text{ when } i_{(k)} > \varepsilon \\ -1, \text{ when } i_{(k)} < -\varepsilon \\ sgn_{(k-1)}, \text{when } |i_{(k)}| \leq \varepsilon \end{cases} \tag{10}$$

Method 3. Use only OCV_Mean curve to get the $OCV(SOC_{(k)})$ function and fit the whole procedure [19].

$$OCV(SOC_{(k)}) = OCV\_Mean(SOC_{(k)}),$$

$$\begin{cases} 1/2, \text{ when } i_{(k)} > \varepsilon \\ -1/2, \text{ when } i_{(k)} < -\varepsilon \\ sgn_{k-1}, \text{when } |i_{(k)}| \leq \varepsilon \end{cases} \tag{11}$$

Method 4. Split charge and discharge stages with OCV_Charge curve and $OCV\_Discharge$ curve respectively. Find the $OCV(SOC_{(k)})$ function for the charge and discharge stage, and set [19].

$$OCV(SOC_{(k)}) = \begin{cases} OCV\_Discharge(SOC_{(k)}), \text{ when } i_{(k)} > \varepsilon \\ OCV\_Charge(SOC_{(k)}), \text{ when } i_{(k)} < -\varepsilon \\ OCV(SOC_k)_{(k-1)}, \text{when } |i_{(k)}| \leq \varepsilon \end{cases}$$

$$sgn_{(k)} = 0$$

Thele et al. [20] proposed a hysteresis model of a cell that was later used by other authors as Gagneur et al. [21].

Method 5. use the OCV discharge curve as a reference, including a hysteresis factor taking values within charging-discharging hysteresis window.

$$E_{eq}(SOC) = U_{discharge}(SOC) + U_{(hys)}(SOC)$$

$$\begin{cases} H_{(hys,k)} = H_{(hys,k-1)} + \dfrac{i_{(k-1)}T_{(s)}}{Q_{Hys}} \\ 0 < H_{(hy,k)} < 1 \end{cases} \tag{12}$$

Method 6. Plett et al. proposed a more sophisticated method to approximate the OCV-SOC curve using 50% SOC value as a reference, and using a blending factor to determine the weight of both the OCV-SOC discharge and charge curve when approximating the OCV-SOC curve [8].

4   OCV Curve Fitting Methods Comparison

After a brief presentation of each approximation method, based on OCV-SOC curves (and including hysteresis effects) each one was replicated using the "ESC model toolbox" from MATLAB®. Which were presented as supplementary files available in the article of Prof. Gregory Plett [8]. This toolbox is capable to generate cell models that consider the dependence of the OCV concerning SOC, Ohmic resistance, diffusion voltages and hysteresis phenomena.

It is of interest to this study, to evaluate each of the OCV-SOC models with the same Enhanced Self Correcting cell model. In addition, using charge and discharge datasets from LiFePO4 A123 cell also included in the same toolbox. Table 1 shows A123 Lithium-iron cell technical parameters considered in the MATLAB®Toolbox.

Table 1. Partial Lithium Iron Phosphate A123 cell technical characteristics

Cell chemistry	LiFePO4
Capacity rating	2230 mAh
Minimum voltage	2 v
Nominal voltage	3.3 v
Maximum voltage	3.75 v
Weight (with safety circuit removed)	76 g
Dimensions (mm)	25.4 mm
Length	65 mm

A model was generated using linear interpolation for each of the OCV-SOC curves approximation methods proposed on the literature. Then, using least squares method (LS), the root mean square error (RMS error) was calculated between the OCV-SOC approximation curve and its prediction model.

Figure 1 shows the approximated OCV-SOC curve for each authors method and its corresponding prediction model.

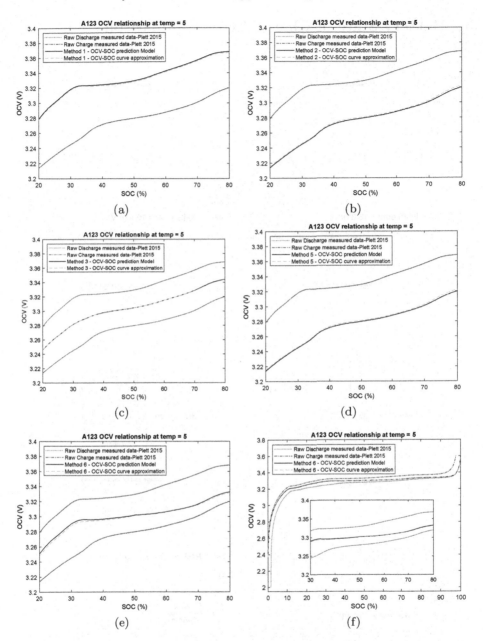

Fig. 1. SOC - OCV curve approximating methods for A123 LiFePO4 Cell data. (a) Method 1. (b) Method 2. (c) Method 3. (d) Method 6. (f) Method 6

5   Battery State of Charge Error Comparison

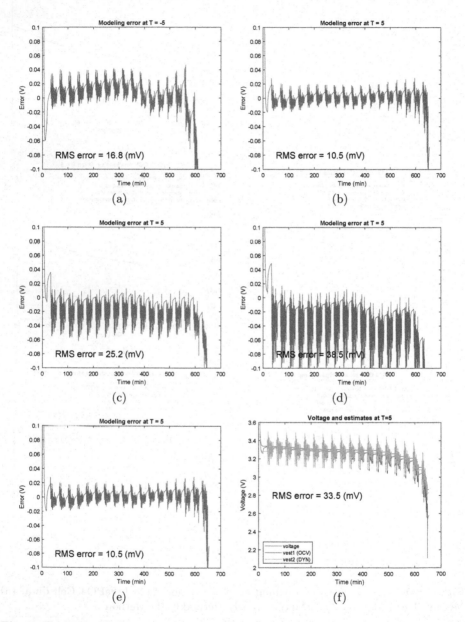

Fig. 2. Dynamic SOC estimation error with different methods parametrization. (a) Method 1 estimation error. (b) Method 2 estimation error. (c) Method 3 estimation error. (d) Method 4 estimation error. (e) Method 5 estimation error. (f) Method 6 voltage estimation

To perform the comparison, SPKF method was used via the "ESC model toolbox" to estimate the SOC RMS error for a dynamic test based on the successive runs over the Urban Dynamometer Driving Schedule (UDDS) load profile. This SPKF method is a variation of the EKF based on statistical/empirical linearization for every data point. Each one of the models previously discussed was used to feed the SPKF SOC estimation method. Figure 2 shows how the SPKF performed using each of the methods and the corresponding SOC RMS estimation errors.

Data Analysis. For each parameteized models taken from evaluated methods, the absolute error between the experimental measurements and the voltage estimations between 5% and 95% of SOC was calculated.

When assessing the mean variance across methods, the residuals assumptions of normality, homoscedasticity and statistical independence were not met. In that sense, A non-parametric Kruskal-Wallis test was performed to assess mean difference across methods, followed by a Wilcoxon rank sum test with the Bonferroni correction.

A $p-value$ of 2.2^{-16} with $df = 5$ resulted from the non-parametric Kruskalwalis test. Table 2 shows the Wilcoxon rank sum test.

Table 2. Post hoc Wilcoxon-bonferroni rank sum test

	Method 1	Method 2	Method 3	Method 4	Method 5
Method 2	$< 2.0^{-16}$	-	-	-	-
Method 3	$< 2.0^{-16}$		-	-	-
Method 4	1	$< 2.0^{-16}$	$< 2.0^{-16}$	-	-
Method 5	$< 2.0^{-16}$	1	$< 2.0^{-16}$		-
Method 6	$< 2.0^{-16}$	$< 2.0^{-16}$	$< 2.0^{-16}$	$< 2.0^{-16}$	$< 2.0^{-16}$

Based on the results shown in Table 2, there is a statistically significant difference between the average errors from method 6 and the other methods. On the other hand, it was found that there is no statistically significant difference between the average error values from methods 1 and 4, as well as in methods 2 and 5. The confidence interval was set to 95%.

6   Conclusions

Although the overall prediction models studied fits closely the OCV-SOC curve and SOC estimation methods yields acceptable results, It is widely accepted by authors that they are still improvements to be made to have a faithful representation from the internal phenomena of a battery cell, especially when charge and discharge cycles are performed.

Furthermore, several SOC curve estimations were obtained using experimental datasets provided by the literature. By inspection, they seem to have returned satisfactory results. After applying a non-parametric statistical test (Kruskal-Wallis), statistically significant differences between the issued methods were found with a 95% confidence.

This leads us to think that conclusive statistical values could be obtained by feeding evaluated models based on OCV-SOC curves from different lithium-based cells, so that the estimation effectiveness of the methods can be identified under specific conditions of DOD or SOH. Now, preliminarily, different methods can be applied simultaneously to estimate a single OCV-SOC in different SOC intervals, so a combination of estimation methods will be evaluated in the future.

It is also important keep in track of computational cost and mathematical simplicity, as it prevails when performing an estimation in real-time applications. So, the accuracy of the estimation must be balanced against the processing time and required instrumentation - sampling - and the processing of the signals, until a superior method is found.

Acknowledgments. We would like to thank Universidad EAFIT as the sponsor of this work, through the Research Assistantship grant from project 828-000134. This research has also been developed in the framework of the "ENERGÉTICA 2030" Research Program, code number 58667, framed in the initiative "Colombia Científica", funded by The World Bank through the call 778-2017 Scientific Ecosystems", managed by the Colombian Administrative Department of Science, Technology and Innovation (COLCIENCIAS).

References

1. Hawkins, T., Singh, B., Majeau-Bettez, G., Strømman, A.: Comparative environmental life cycle assessment of conventional and electric vehicles. J. Ind. Ecol. **17**(1), 53–64 (2012). https://doi.org/10.1111/j.1530-9290.2012.00532.x
2. Wu, Y., Zhang, L.: Can the development of electric vehicles reduce the emission of air pollutants and greenhouse gases in developing countries? Transp. Res. Part D: Transp. Environ. **51**, 129–145 (2017). https://doi.org/10.1016/j.trd.2016.12.007
3. Manzetti, S., Mariasiu, F.: Electric vehicle battery technologies: from present state to future systems. Renew. Sustain. Energy Rev. **51**, 1004–1012 (2015). https://doi.org/10.1016/j.rser.2015.07.010
4. Cazzola, P., Gorner, M., Schuitmaker, R., Maroney, E.: Global EV outlook 2016. International Energy Agency, France (2016)
5. Nykvist, B., Nilsson, M.: Rapidly falling costs of battery packs for electric vehicles. Nat. Clim. Change **5**(4), 329–332 (2015). https://doi.org/10.1038/nclimate2564
6. Martinez-Laserna, E., et al.: Battery second life: hype, hope or reality? A critical review of the state of the art. Renew. Sustain. Energy Rev. **93**, 701–718 (2018). https://doi.org/10.1016/j.rser.2018.04.035
7. Fernàndez-Montoya, M., Arias-Rosales, A., Osorio-Gómez, G., Mejía-Gutiérrez, R.: Nominal energy optimisation method of constrained battery packs through the iteration of the series-parallel topology. Int. J. Energy Res. **41**(12), 1709–1729 (2017). https://doi.org/10.1002/er.3734
8. Plett, G.: Extended Kalman filtering for battery management systems of LiPB-based HEV battery packs. J. Power Sources **134**(2), 262–276 (2004). https://doi.org/10.1016/j.jpowsour.2004.02.032

9. Cheng, K., Divakar, B., Wu, H., Ding, K., Ho, H.: Battery-Management System (BMS) and SOC development for electrical vehicles. IEEE Trans. Veh. Technol. **60**(1), 76–88 (2011). https://doi.org/10.1109/tvt.2010.2089647
10. Ng, K., Moo, C., Chen, Y., Hsieh, Y.: Enhanced coulomb counting method for estimating state-of-charge and state-of-health of lithium-ion batteries. Appl. Energy **86**(9), 1506–1511 (2009). https://doi.org/10.1016/j.apenergy.2008.11.021
11. Moura, S., Chaturvedi, N., Krstic, M.: PDE estimation techniques for advanced battery management systems – Part I: SOC estimation. In: 2012 American Control Conference (ACC) (2012). https://doi.org/10.1109/acc.2012.6315019
12. Berecibar, M., Gandiaga, I., Villarreal, I., Omar, N., Van Mierlo, J., Van den Bossche, P.: Critical review of state of health estimation methods of Li-ion batteries for real applications. Renew. Sustain. Energy Rev. **56**, 572–587 (2016). https://doi.org/10.1016/j.rser.2015.11.042
13. Haq, I., et al.: Development of battery management system for cell monitoring and protection. In: 2014 International Conference on Electrical Engineering and Computer Science (ICEECS) (2014). https://doi.org/10.1109/iceecs.2014.7045246
14. Speltino, C., Stefanopoulou, A., Fiengo, G.: Cell equalization in battery stacks through state of charge estimation polling. In: Proceedings of the 2010 American Control Conference (2010). https://doi.org/10.1109/acc.2010.5530710
15. Chiasson, J., Vairamohan, B.: Estimating the state of charge of a battery. In: Proceedings of the 2003 American Control Conference (2003). https://doi.org/10.1109/acc.2003.1243757
16. Abu-Sharkh, S., Doerffel, D.: Rapid test and non-linear model characterisation of solid-state Lithium-ion batteries. J. Power Sources **130**(1–2), 266–274 (2004). https://doi.org/10.1016/j.jpowsour.2003.12.001
17. Pop, V., Bergveld, H., Notten, P., Regtien, P.: State-of-the-art of battery state-of-charge determination. Meas. Sci. Technol. **16**(12), R93–R110 (2005). https://doi.org/10.1088/0957-0233/16/12/r01
18. Fotouhi, A., Auger, D., Propp, K., Longo, S., Wild, M.: A review on electric vehicle battery modelling: from Lithium-ion toward Lithium-Sulphur. Renew. Sustain. Energy Rev. **56**, 1008–1021 (2016). https://doi.org/10.1016/j.rser.2015.12.009
19. Chen, Z., Qiu, S., Masrur, M., Murphey, Y.: Battery state of charge estimation based on a combined model of Extended Kalman Filter and neural networks. In: The 2011 International Joint Conference on Neural Networks (2011). https://doi.org/10.1109/ijcnn.2011.6033495
20. Thele, M., Bohlen, O., Sauer, D., Karden, E.: Development of a voltage-behavior model for NiMH batteries using an impedance-based modeling concept. J. Power Sources **175**(1), 635–643 (2008). https://doi.org/10.1016/j.jpowsour.2007.08.039
21. Gagneur, L., Forgez, C., Franco, A.: Lithium-ion state of charge observer with open circuit voltage hysteresis model. In: 2013 15th European Conference on Power Electronics and Applications (EPE) (2013). https://doi.org/10.1109/epe.2013.6631974
22. Xiong, R., Yu, Q., Wang, L., Lin, C.: A novel method to obtain the open circuit voltage for the state of charge of lithium ion batteries in electric vehicles by using H infinity filter. Appl. Energy **207**, 346–353 (2017). https://doi.org/10.1016/j.apenergy.2017.05.136

Computation of Electromagnetic Fields for 220 kV Power Line in Cartagena de Indias

Luis Eduardo Rueda$^{(\boxtimes)}$ ⓘ, Jorge Eliecer Duque$^{(\boxtimes)}$ ⓘ, Enrique Vanegas$^{(\boxtimes)}$ ⓘ, and Eduardo Gomez$^{(\boxtimes)}$ ⓘ

Universidad Tecnológica de Bolívar, Cartagena de Indias, Colombia
{lrueda,jduque,evanegas,egomez}@utb.edu.co
http://www.utb.edu.co

Abstract. The growth of the cities towards the suburban areas has caused that the buildings are construct near the lines of high voltage. This has led to detailed studies of the electric and magnetic fields generated by these lines to determine the potential impact on the health of people within their area of influence. Therefore, it is necessary to calculate the profiles of the electric and magnetic fields, near the high voltage lines as a function of the distance to the center of the same and determine if the values are within the exposure limits accepted by national and international organizations. To achieve this, a program was written in Matlab that performs the calculation of the electric and magnetic field profiles under the power transmission lines based on fundamental laws. The results were validated by measurements made in accordance with the procedures established by IEEE in a 220 kV electric transmission line located in the city of Cartagena de Indias.

Keywords: Electric and magnetic fields · Computation · Matlab toolbox · Public health · Power lines

1 Introduction

The location of lines of transmission of energy in urban areas generates a rejection in the affected communities due to the preoccupation that exists on the possible effects in the health that can produce the electromagnetic fields of industrial frequency. Several international organizations have established the limits of exposure to electromagnetic fields in work and public places. Among these organizations are the International Commission on Protection against Non-Ionizing Radiation (ICNIRP) [1] and the Institute of Electrical and Electronic Engineers (IEEE) [2] that have set a limit of exposure to the electric field of 5 kV/m and a limit of exposure to the magnetic field $100 \, \mu T$ for the general public at a frequency of 60 Hz. In Colombia, the Reglamento Técnico de Instalaciones

Supported by UTB.

Eléctricas (RETIE) [3] has established the exposure values to the electric field of 4.16 kV/m and 200 μT for exposure of the general public up to 8 continuous hours.

The construction of a high-voltage power line that surrounded a suburban area of Cartagena de Indias caused concern and rejection among the population near the area of influence of the line, due to the possible effects on public health. Given the importance of the city as Historical Heritage of Humanity, tourist place of Colombia, and knowing the problem that could cause in its image at national and international level, it was decided to carry out a study of the electric and magnetic fields produced by the line, to verify that the exposure levels were within the established limits. In order to facilitate this study, a toolbox was developed in Matlab to model and simulate electromagnetic fields in high voltage transmission lines, in order to verify whether existing transmission lines or new projects meet the permissible exposure limit.

2   Methods and Materials

2.1   Measurement of the Electromagnetic Fields

An Aaronia Spectran NF 5035 was used for measure the electromagnetic fields. This equipment records the magnetic field in μ T and the electric field strengths in V/m. Figure 1 shows the 220 kV transmission line used in the study.

Fig. 1. The 220 kV power line.

For the measurement of the fields, the procedure described in the IEEE 644-1994 [2] standard complied with as follows:

1. The measuring device was placed in an insulating element, as measurements at ground level can significantly influence the value measured.
2. The electric and magnetic fields were measured at 1 m above ground level.
3. The meter sensor was oriented to read the components of the electromagnetic fields.
4. To ensure an error of less than 3% in all cases, the operator of the measuring equipment was placed more than 3 m from the sensor.
5. The lateral profile of the magnetic and electric fields ware taken at selected points of interest along a section of the transmission line. In the middle of the section between towers, the data is record at intervals of 5 m, from the center of the line up to a distance of 30 m, in the normal direction of the line at 1 m above ground level.

2.2   Calculation of the Electric Field

The Gauss's Law applied to an infinitely long conductor calculates the maximum electric field at a point near an energy transmission line. The Image Method is use to take into account the effect of soil proximity, in this case applied to a series of equivalent loads, as shown in Fig. 2. In order to determine equivalent electrical loads per unit of length, the Load Simulation Method is apply, starting with the calculation of the distances between the conductors and phase voltages of the transmission line. For practical purposes, it is assume that the permittivity of the air is independent of the climatic conditions and is equal to the permittivity of the free space: $\epsilon_0 = 8,854 * 10^{-12}$ F/m. Another assumption is neglected the influence of the support structures of the conductors and any other object in the vicinity.

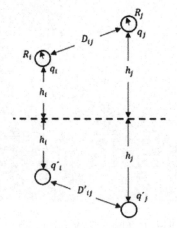

Fig. 2. Conductors i and j with their corresponding images.

In transmission lines with N conductors, the charges induced in each of them are calculate through potential's coefficients [5,6]. For a three-phase transmission line, the equivalent electric charges of each conductor can be calculate by inverting the following matrix equation:

$$\mathbf{V} = \mathbf{P}.\mathbf{Q} \tag{1}$$

Where $\mathbf{V}$ the column vector of known potentials, $\mathbf{Q}$ is the column vector of fictitious simulation charges, and $\mathbf{P}$ is the potential coefficients matrix.

For an conductor of infinite length, the potential coefficients are given in next equations:

$$P_{ij} = \frac{\lambda}{2\pi\epsilon_0} \frac{D'_{ij}}{D_{ij}} \tag{2}$$

$$P_{ii} = \frac{\lambda}{2\pi\epsilon_0} \frac{2h_i}{R_i} \tag{3}$$

Where: D'_{ij} is the distance between the conductor i and j, D'_{ii} is the distance between the conductor i and the image of conductor j, and R_i is the radius of the conductor i.

The charge vector is:

$$\mathbf{Q} = \mathbf{P}^{-1}.\mathbf{V} \tag{4}$$

The electric field due to a conductor considering the effect of the earth [6] is based on the Gauss's Law, obtaining that the field for the real charge and the image charge are respectively:

$$E_r = \frac{\lambda}{2\pi\epsilon_0 R} \tag{5}$$

$$E_i = \frac{\lambda}{2\pi\epsilon_0 R_i} \tag{6}$$

The distances from the real conductor and the image conductor to any point are respectively, as shows in Fig. 3:

$$R = \sqrt{(x_r - x_p)^2 + (h - y_p)^2} \tag{7}$$

$$R' = \sqrt{(x_r - x_p)^2 + (h + y_p)^2} \tag{8}$$

The horizontal and vertical components of the electric field are:

$$E_x = |E_r|cos\theta_1 - |E_i|cos\theta_2 \tag{9}$$

$$E_y = -|E_r|sin\theta_1 - |E_i|sin\theta_2 \tag{10}$$

Where:

$$cos\theta_1 = \frac{x_p - x_r}{R} \tag{11}$$

$$cos\theta_2 = \frac{x_p - x_r}{R'} \tag{12}$$

$$sin\theta_1 = \frac{h - y_p}{R} \tag{13}$$

$$sin\theta_2 = \frac{h + y_p}{R'} \tag{14}$$

For N conductors the electric field is:

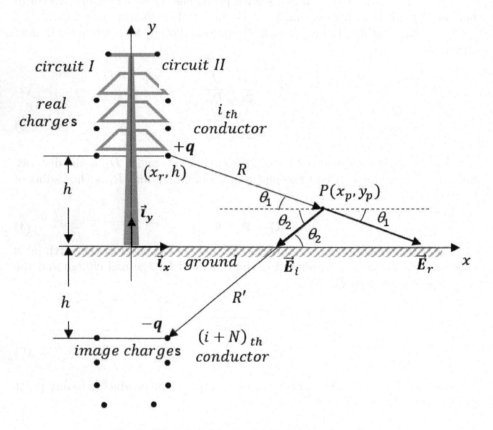

Fig. 3. Electric field at point P due to power line.

$$E_x = \frac{q_i}{2\pi\epsilon_0} \sum_{i=1}^{N} \left\{ \frac{(x - x_i)}{(x_i - x)^2 + (y_i - y)^2} - \frac{(x - x_i)}{(x_i - x)^2 + (y_i + y)^2} \right\} \tag{15}$$

$$E_y = \frac{-q_i}{2\pi\epsilon_0} \sum_{i=1}^{N} \left\{ \frac{(y_i - y)}{(x_i - x)^2 + (y_i - y)^2} - \frac{(y_i + y)}{(x_i - x)^2 + (y_i + y)^2} \right\} \tag{16}$$

The total electric field is:

$$E = \sqrt{E_x{}^2 + E_y{}^2} \tag{17}$$

2.3 Calculation of the Magnetic Field

The low frequency magnetic field in a power line depends on the electrical currents in its conductors [8–14]. Generally, if the currents are known, the magnetic field can be calculated with Ampere's law, assuming that the conductors are infinite and that the magnetic permeability of the air is equal to $\mu_0 = 4\pi*10^{-7}\,\mathrm{H/m}$. The superposition principle will apply to take into account the influence of multiple conductors.

For an infinite conductor carrying a current I, the magnetic flux density B, according to the Ampere Law, is:

$$B = \frac{\mu_0 I}{2\pi R} \tag{18}$$

The Fig. 4 shows the distance from the conductor at (x_i, y_i) to point (x_p, y_p):

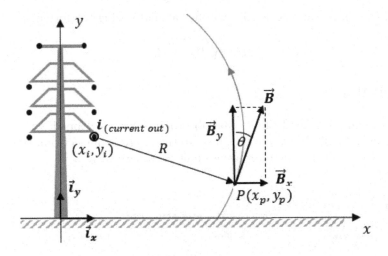

Fig. 4. Lateral profile of the electric field form the 220 kV power line.

$$R = \sqrt{(x_p - x_i)^2 + (y_p - y_i)^2} \tag{19}$$

The magnetic field to any point (x_p, y_p) is:

$$B = \frac{\mu_0 I}{2\pi\sqrt{(x_p - x_i)^2 + (y_p - y_i)^2}} \tag{20}$$

Now, the horizontal and vertical components of B:

$$B_x = -\frac{\mu_0 I_0 sin\theta}{2\pi\sqrt{(x_p - x_i)^2 + (y_p - y_i)^2}} \tag{21}$$

$$B_y = -\frac{\mu_0 I_0 cos\theta}{2\pi\sqrt{(x_p - x_i)^2 + (y_p - y_i)^2}} \tag{22}$$

622   L. E. Rueda et al.

Where:

$$sin\theta = \frac{y_p - y_i}{\sqrt{(x_p - x_i)^2 + (y_p - y_i)^2}} \qquad (23)$$

$$cos\theta = \frac{x_p - x_i}{\sqrt{(x_p - x_i)^2 + (y_p - y_i)^2}} \qquad (24)$$

For N conductors the magnetic field is:

$$B_x = -\frac{\mu_0 I_0}{2\pi} \sum_{i=1}^{N} \left\{ \frac{(y_p - y_i)}{(x_p - x_i)^2 + (y_p - y_i)^2} \right\} \qquad (25)$$

$$B_y = -\frac{\mu_0 I_0}{2\pi} \sum_{i=1}^{N} \left\{ \frac{(x_p - x_i)}{(x_p - x_i)^2 + (y_p - y_i)^2} \right\} \qquad (26)$$

Finally, the magnetic flux density will be calculate using the formula:

$$B = \sqrt{B_x^2 + B_y^2} \qquad (27)$$

3   Results

From Mathematical modeling, a Matlab program was developed with functions and graphics to provide a quick solution in the analysis of electromagnetic fields in transmission lines. The interface graphic showing in Fig. 5.

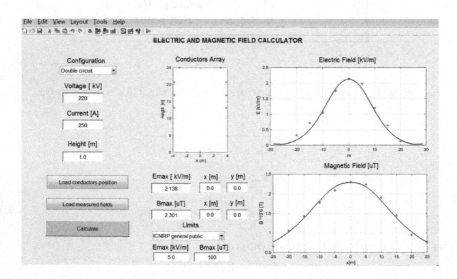

Fig. 5. Software interface for computation of electric and magnetic field

The input data for the program are the coordinates of each conductor, the diameter of the conductor, the phase voltages, the currents of each conductor and the height above ground level. The position of the conductors in the line is obtain from the structure of the pylon as shown in Fig. 6.

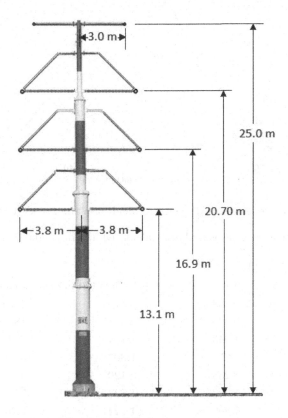

Fig. 6. 220 kV tower geometry

The measurements made in the 220 kV power line of the Bolívar-Bosque circuit in the city of Cartagena de Indias were compared with the profiles of the electric and magnetic fields generated by the program. The accuracy of these results was verified taking into account a series of calculations published in [5, 9, 12].

Figure 7 shows the profile of the electric field obtained at a height of 1 m according to the IEEE standard 644-1994. The measured data show a tendency to continue the profile of the calculated electric field. As seen in the experimental results shown in Table 1, the electric field strength measured at the center of the 220 kV line is 2.238 kV/m and the calculated one is 2.120 kV/m, which results in an error of 5.27%.

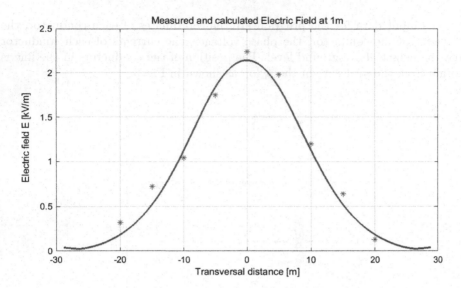

Fig. 7. Lateral profile of the electric field form the 220 kV power line

Table 1. Electric field measured and calculated at 1 m height from the ground

Electric field			
Distance [m]	Measured [kV/m]	Calculated [kV/m]	Error [%]
−20	0.223	0.172	22.86
−15	0.620	0.507	18.22
−10	1.043	1.124	7.76
−5	1.75	1.807	3.28
0	2.238	2.120	5.27
5	1.980	1.834	7.3
10	1.203	1.124	6.56
15	0.587	0.508	13.4
20	0.132	0.151	12,5
25	0.034	0.029	14,7

Figure 8 shows the profile of the magnetic field obtained at a height of 1 m according to the IEEE standard 644-1994. The measured data show a tendency to continue the profile of the calculated magnetic field. As seen in the experimental results shown in Table 2, the magnetic flux density measured at the center of the 220 kV line is 2.305 μT and the calculated one is 2.229 μT, which results in an error of 0.65%.

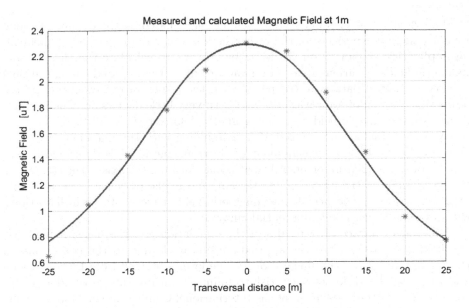

Fig. 8. Lateral profile of the magnetic field form the 220 kV power line

Table 2. Magnetic field measured at 1 m height from the ground

Magnetic field			
Distance [m]	Measured field [μT]	Calculated field [μT]	Error [%]
−25	0.651	0.7653	14.93
−20	1.053	0.992	5.79
−15	1.432	1.397	2.44
−10	1.784	1.837	2.97
−5	2.088	2.162	3.44
0	2.305	2.229	0.65
5	2.236	2.187	2.19
10	1.911	1.837	3.87
15	1.452	1.397	3.78
20	0.953	1.03	8.079
25	0.765	0.5671	25.86

4   Conclusions

The procedure based on the IEEE-Std 644-1994 standard was followed for the measurement of electric and magnetic fields generated by a 220 kV transmission line, compatible with a vertical double electric circuit structure, height of 25 m and a length of 2 km, bordering a salty swamp in the suburbs of the city of Cartagena de Indias.

The 220 kV transmission system was modeled, based on the documentation, regulations and experience of the researchers in order to design and implement an application supported on the Matlab software, to calculate the electric and magnetic fields in various space points according to the required configuration.

The measured data were compared with the results of the program and an admissible margin of error was obtained with very little dispersion. The average errors for the electric field and the magnetic field were 6% and 2.76% respectively, values that do not exceed 10%, complying with the maximum value of the global error for the measurement of electromagnetic fields described in the regulations. The measurements taken at points far from the axis of the structure, due to changes in the profile of the terrain, and in the presence of natural and artificial obstacles, the electric and magnetic field yielded data with distortions that altered the map of equipotential curves.

Differences between the results of the simulation and the measurements of the fields are attribute to the approximations made due to the conditions of the terrain and the environmental ones. The levels obtained from Electric Field and Magnetic Field do not show risk to human health in the area under study, complying with the regulations of the International Commission on Non-Ionizing Radiation Protection, ICNIRP and RETIE.

The toolbox developed in Matlab represents an effective tool for the characterization of exposure levels to 60 Hz electromagnetic fields for any power line configuration.

References

1. International Commission on Non Ionizing Radiation Protection: Guidelines for limiting exposure to time-varying electric, magnetic and electromagnetic fields (1 Hz to 100 kHz). Health Phys. **99**(6), 818–836 (2010). https://doi.org/10.1097/HP.0b013e3181f06c86
2. IEEE Standard Procedures for Measurement of Power Frequency Electric and Magnetic Fields From AC Power Lines, Std. 644-1994
3. Ministerio de Minas y Energía: Reglamento Técnico de Instalaciones Eléctricas (RETIE), Colombia (2013). https://www.minenergia.gov.co. Accessed 6 Jan 2019
4. Xiao, L., Holbert, K.: Development of software for calculating electromagnetic fields near power lines. In: North American Power Symposium, NAPS 2014, pp. 1–6. IEEE Press (2014). https://doi.org/10.1109/NAPS.2014.6965378
5. Sahbudin, R., Fauzi, S., Hitam, S., Mokhtar, M.: Investigation of electrical potential and electromagnetic field for overhead high voltage power lines in Malaysia. J. Appl. Sci. (2010). https://doi.org/10.3923/jas.2010.2862.2868
6. Himadri, D.: Implementation of basic charge configurations to charge simulation method for electric field calculations. Int. J. Adv. Res. Electr. Electron. Instrum. Eng. **3**(5), 9607–9611 (2014)
7. Djekidl, R., Bessedik, S., Abdechafik, H.: Electric field modeling and analysis of EHV power line using improved calculation method. Facta Universitatis Series Electronics and Energetics (2018). https://doi.org/10.2298/FUEE1803425D

8. Lunca, E., Istrate, M., Salceanu, A., Tibuliac, S.: Computation of the magnetic field exposure from 110 kV overhead power lines. In: International Conference and Exposition on Electrical and Power Engineering, Iasi, pp. 628–631 (2012). https://doi.org/10.1109/ICEPE.2012.6463803

9. Milutinov, M., Prsa, M., Juhas, A.: Electromagnetic field underneath overhead high voltage power line. In: 4th International Conference on Engineering Technologies - ICET 2009, Novi Sad, Serbia (2009)

10. Miodrag, M., Anamarija, J., Miroslav, P.: Electric and magnetic fields in vicinity of overhead multi-line power system. In: 2nd International Conference on Modern Power Systems MPS, Romania, vol. 313, pp. 12–14 (2008)

11. Qabazard: A survey of electromagnetic field radiation associated with power transmission lines in the state of Kuwait. In: International Conference on Electromagnetics in Advanced Applications, Torino 2007, pp. 795–797 (2007). https://doi.org/10.1109/ICEAA.2007.4387423

12. Ahmadi, H., Mohseni, S., Shayegani, A.: Electromagnetic fields near transmission lines - problems and solutions. Iran. J. Environ. Health Sci. Eng. **7**(2), 181–188 (2010)

13. Braicu, S.F., Czumbil, L., Stet, D., Micu, D.D.: Evaluation of the electric and magnetic field near high voltage power lines. International Conference on Advancements of Medicine and Health Care through Technology; 12th–15th October 2016, Cluj-Napoca, Romania. IP, vol. 59, pp. 141–146. Springer, Cham (2017). https://doi.org/10.1007/978-3-319-52875-5_32

14. Tourab, W., Babouri, A.: Measurement and modeling of personal exposure to the electric and magnetic fields in the vicinity of high voltage power lines. Saf. Health Work **7**, 102–110 (2016). https://doi.org/10.1016/j.shaw.2015.11.006

Modal Analysis for a Power System Benchmark with Topological Changes

Julian Patino[1]([✉])(iD), Carlos A. Ramirez[2,3](iD), and Jairo Espinosa[3](iD)

[1] Departamento de Electrónica, Facultad de Ingeniería,
Institución Universitaria Pascual Bravo, Medellín, Colombia
julian.patino@pascualbravo.edu.co
[2] Centro de Automatización industrial, Regional Caldas, SENA,
Magdalena, Colombia
alramirezgo@sena.edu.co
[3] Departamento de Ingeniería Eléctrica y Automática, Facultad de Minas,
Universidad Nacional de Colombia, Medellín, Colombia
jespinov@unal.edu.co

Abstract. This work studies voltage stability of power systems through modal analysis technique. A summary of voltage stability methods is also presented. This paper illustrates several aspects of the modal analysis through simulation over an IEEE benchmark, including the extraction of nodal participation factors. Also, simulation explores the effects of disturbances and the implementation of an HVDC transmission line. Results show the impact of the combination of load variations and network topological changes in system modes, especially for the cases including HVDC links.

Keywords: Voltage stability · Modal analysis · Participation factors

1 Introduction

In recent years, the problem of the voltage instability has evolved into one of the main dynamical constraints in power system operation [21]. Several power outages and voltage collapse events over broad areas have been attributed to some degree of voltage instability problems [4,5]. This situation has impulsed the development of several analysis techniques, powered by the use of computer-aided programs, in order to properly evaluate and design control actions to maintain voltage stability [3,15]. In this sense, the identification of the power system elements generating the instability phenomena constitutes a critical task when dealing with voltage stability [22].

The behavior of power systems is studied through dynamic system analysis techniques [18], and many sensitivity analysis [10,19,20] could be found in literature. For the topic of voltage stability, there are techniques based on modal analysis, singular value decomposition, optimal power flows, and the extraction of the associated stability indexes [7,11]. Despite the high number of methods

© Springer Nature Switzerland AG 2019
J. C. Figueroa-García et al. (Eds.): WEA 2019, CCIS 1052, pp. 628–639, 2019.
https://doi.org/10.1007/978-3-030-31019-6_53

developed for voltage stability analysis, their practical application is restricted by the assumptions required about the power system model, and the lack of information about the voltage instability mechanism [14]. The modal analysis appears as a valuable solution, offering information about both the generating elements and the proximity to voltage instability for power systems [13].

Many works using modal analysis have been presented in the literature, ranging from the daily operation of power systems [23] to grid congestion management [12]. In [8], an evaluation of voltage stability is performed over a system with 3700 nodes, where the analysis included calculation of participation factors for nodes, branches, and generators, using the state-space model employed for conventional power flow analysis.

The work in [17] performs voltage stability analysis for a power system employing both static and dynamic techniques. This work highlights the computational advantages of the modal analysis and the extensive information extracted from dynamic studies. Reference [1] applies modal analysis to HVDC multi-radial systems, highlighting the importance of the eigenvectors in disturbance evaluation. Reference [7] reports a comparison of the main techniques for voltage stability analysis, illustrating the implementation of different load models into the modal analysis. Also, the work in [13] shows the application of modal analysis for instability control of large power systems, improving the stability margins in post-contingency mode.

In this context, the objective of this work is the application of modal analysis for voltage stability evaluation in power systems with both load and topological variations (HVDC transmission lines). The study case is the IEEE One Area RTS-96 benchmark [9] for reliability analysis, with some minor modifications. The employed computational tool is PSAT [16]. This work is divided as follows: Sect. 2 presents a brief review of voltage stability analysis in power systems. Section 3 shows the theoretical derivation of the modal analysis of power systems. Section 4 describes the studied simulation scenarios, with the discussion of results in Sect. 5. Finally, some conclusions are provided.

2   Voltage Stability Analysis in Power Systems

Voltage stability has become one of the most restrictive factors for planning and operation stages of electrical power systems [4]. The analysis techniques to study voltage stability can be classified as dynamic or static methods [14].

2.1   Dynamic Analysis Methods

These methods are based on the time-domain solution of the non-linear equations for the power system model [14] by using power flow analysis and numerical integration methods. These techniques are used mainly for small signal stability analysis. Dynamical tools allow the recreation of different scenarios, including regular operation and contingencies, and they are employed to determine the response time and the performance of the elements under different conditions.

They are essential for post-mortem studies, analysis and coordination of protections and controls, and the benchmarking of simplified (steady-state) analyses.

2.2 Static Analysis

These approaches capture some snapshots of system behavior to different operational conditions at several frames over the time-domain response trajectory. Due to the consideration of the derivatives of the state variables of the system as zero-valued, the equations of the system model reduce to merely algebraic expressions. Static analysis is commonly employed for the bulk of planning and operating studies through many system conditions and contingencies. It is also used for on-line analysis and the identification of causes of instability and the selection of remedial measures. There are many proposed techniques in this category, and the following subsections describe some of the more widely employed ones. See references [2, 6, 14] for more in-depth analysis of the techniques.

1. **Conventional power flows.** These are the static power flows representing the nodal voltage variation to the load power changes. These techniques calculate the states, limits, and voltage stability margins for the power systems. The results are used to plot voltage versus power curves, and to determine the proximity to instability and the critical nodes, branches, or areas in the system. Some of the main techniques are:
   - Sensitivity analysis: this method studies the voltage variation with power changes ($\frac{dV}{dP}$ and $\frac{dV}{dQ}$).
   - Jacobian matrix singularity: it uses the reduction of the Jacobian matrix of power flow to determine model singularity points. These points define the stability limits for the system nodes.
   - Modal analysis: this method finds system eigenvalues and eigenvectors from the reduction of the Jacobian matrix of power flow. See Sect. 3 for the detailed explanation of this technique.
   - Network equivalent: This technique obtains system equivalent circuits in order to compare them with nodal load equivalents.
   - Tangent vector: These methods employ the phasor difference of the variables associated with voltage stability, which were previously determined through power flow analysis under regular and critical operation.
2. **Progressive power flows.** Methods based on continuous power flows designed to determine voltage stability limits of the system accurately [14].

3   Modal Analysis

This section briefly describes the modal analysis technique for voltage stability assessment. See references [8, 14] for more details.

3.1 $V - Q$ Sensitivity Analysis

At first, the power flow Jacobian matrix is obtained to include linearized dynamics of generators, static loads, induction motors, SVC, and HVDC links. Let ΔP, ΔQ, $\Delta \theta$ and ΔV denote the incremental variations in a given bus for active power, reactive power, voltage angle and voltage magnitude. The steady-state Jacobian matrix is:

$$\begin{bmatrix} \Delta P \\ \Delta Q \end{bmatrix} = \begin{bmatrix} J_{P\theta} & J_{PV} \\ J_{Q\theta} & J_{QV} \end{bmatrix} \cdot \begin{bmatrix} \Delta \theta \\ \Delta V \end{bmatrix} \tag{1}$$

Letting $\Delta P = 0$, and solving Eq. (1) for ΔQ,

$$\Delta Q = \left[J_{QV} - J_{Q\theta} J_{P\theta}^{-1} J_{PV} \right] = J_R \Delta V \tag{2}$$

and

$$\Delta V = J_R^{-1} \Delta Q \tag{3}$$

The term J_R is representing the linearized relationship between bus reactive power injection (ΔQ) and voltage magnitude (ΔV). J_R is known as the reduced steady-state Jacobian matrix. Although incremental changes in active power P are ignored ($\Delta P = 0$), variations in power transferences or system load are considered by the analysis of ΔV and ΔQ relationship at different operating conditions. The ith diagonal element of i_R^{-1} is denominated the $V\,Q$ sensitivity at bus i; stable operation is indicated by a positive $V\,Q$ sensitivity value.

3.2 $Q - V$ Modal Analysis

Eigenvalues and eigenvectors of J_R must be computed to analyze the voltage stability characteristic of the system. Let ξ be the right eigenvector matrix, Λ the diagonal eigenvalue matrix, and η the left eigenvector matrix of J_R. According to the definition of these matrices and vectors,

$$J_R^{-1} = \xi \Lambda^{-1} \eta \tag{4}$$

From Eqs. (3) and (4),

$$\Delta V = \xi \Lambda^{-1} \eta \Delta Q = \sum_i (\frac{\xi_i \eta_i}{\lambda_i}) \Delta Q \tag{5}$$

In this last equation, the term $v = \eta \Delta V$ is called the vector of modal voltage variations. The vector of modal reactive power variations is $q = \eta \Delta Q$. Contrary to the case for J_R^{-1} in Eq. (3), Λ^{-1} is always a diagonal matrix. In consequence, Eq. (5) is representing uncoupled first-order equations. Thus, for the ith mode,

$$v_i = \frac{1}{\lambda_i} q_i \tag{6}$$

If eigenvalue $\lambda_i > 0$, the ith modal reactive power change results in the ith modal voltage change in the same direction, indicating a stable mode. In general terms, $\lambda > 0$ represents a stable mode, and $\lambda < 0$ and unstable mode. The magnitude of eigenvalue can be an approximate measurement of the system "distance" to instability, as the original problem is non-linear.

3.3   Bus Participation Factors

The participation of buses, branches, and generators in the system modes offers an indication of the mechanism of potential voltage instability [14]. Calculation of the participation factors relies on the eigenvectors of J_R, to represent the degree of association of each element with a given system mode. From Eq. 7, the bus participation factor denoting the relative participation of bus k in mode i is given by:

$$P_{ki} = \xi_{ki}\eta_{ki} \tag{7}$$

Bus participation factors allow the determination of the regions associated with each system mode. As the left and right eigenvectors are normalized, the sum of all bus participation factors for each given mode corresponds to unity. The impact of the corrective actions applied at a given bus for stabilization of a mode is determined by the size of bus participation at that mode. A *localized mode* has a small number of buses with significant participation and the remaining buses with almost zero-valued participation factors. A *not localized mode* has many buses with a small but similar degree of participation, and the rest of the buses with close to zero participation.

4   Case of Study

The selected benchmark is the enhanced test system IEEE One Area RTS-96 [9] proposed for use in power system reliability evaluation. The benchmark is composed of 24 buses with two voltage zones of 138 kV and 230 kV, as shown

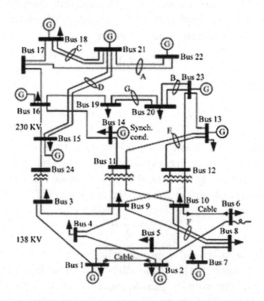

Fig. 1. The IEEE reliability test system 1996

in Fig. 1. The system also contains four transformers with constant tap ratio and one phase-shifting transformer (between buses 110 and 112). The longest line has a length of about 117 km. For every simulation scenario considered, the slack node is bus 113. To perform the modal analysis to the selected benchmark, we study the simulation scenarios described below.

4.1 Scenario A

For this simulation scenario, we use the IEEE RTS-96 benchmark as seen in Fig. 1. The description of the analysis procedure is listed below.

1. Run power flow, and perform modal analysis.
2. Identify the unstable modes. If all the modes are stable, select the closest mode to instability (closest to zero).
3. Using nodal participation factors, identify the node (or nodes) with the most participation in the mode selected in the last step.
4. Increase the load (variations of 1%) in the node selected in the last step. Rerun the power flow, perform a new modal analysis, and store the values of the modes and participation factors for the closest node to instability.
5. Repeat the previous step until the power flow convergence stops.

4.2 Scenario B

For this scenario, we modify the benchmark configuration. We change the transmission line between buses 102 and 106 for a High-Voltage Direct Current (HVDC) link, using the parameters listed in Table 1. After this change, we perform the same analysis of scenario A, increasing the load on the bus of most participation in the mode closest to instability.

Table 1. HVDC link parameters.

Parameter	Value [unit]	Parameter	Value [unit]
Power	100 MVA	Frequency	100 Hz
Voltage at terminal buses	138 kV	DC ratings	[138 2.5] [kV kA]
Transformer reactants	[0.135 0.126] [p.u]	Tap ratios	[1.25 1.25] [p.u/p.u]
PI Regulator constants	[20 25]	DC line	[0.0652 0.20] [p.u]
Rectifier angles	[120 5] [deg]	Ref. DC limits	[1.0 0.1 0.9 0.0] [p.u]
Current and active power	[0.5 0.5] [p.u]	DC voltage order	[1.0] [p.u]

4.3 Scenario C

We start from the benchmark with the HVDC link, and proceed in the same way as the Scenario A. However, after the initial modal analysis, we increase the load of other node in the network, instead of the node with the most participation in the mode closer to instability.

4.4 Scenario E

For this scenario, we return to the original benchmark configuration for studying the effects of the phase-shifting transformer in the modal analysis of the system. The procedure is described in the next list:

1. Run power flow for the benchmark system.
2. Perform modal analysis and calculate the participation factors.
3. Apply a phase shift of 10° to the phase-shifting transformer. Then, rerun the power flow and perform modal analysis.
4. Increase the load (variations of 1%) in the bus of more significant participation for the mode closest to instability. Run again, the power flow, and then perform a new modal analysis. Store the values of the modes and participation factors for the node closest to instability.
5. Repeat previous step until the power flow stops converging.

5 Results and Discussion

Modal values were computed before making load variations or phase-shifts for the three studied topologies: the original benchmark, the case with HVDC link and the case with phase-shift. For all the scenarios, the mode λ_4 is the closest mode to instability (see Table 2). For this reason, this mode is the center of the remaining analysis. As seen in Table 2, the topological changes of the HVDC link and the phase-shift did not affect the initial modal analysis of the benchmark system significantly. So, in order to perform a more in-depth study, the introduction of more variations in the system is required. Notably, we want to increase the load in determined points of the network. In this way, we need to calculate the participation factors to find the most sensitive nodes.

Consequently, we extract the participation factors for mode 4, as shown in Table 3, for every node with participation greater than zero. Following the procedure explained in the previous section, we can identify bus 6 as the node with the most significant contribution to mode 4 for all the considered scenarios. So, node 6 load will be increased for Scenarios A, C, and E. Arbitrarily, bus 4 is selected as the alternative node for load variations in Scenarios B and D.

Table 2. Eigenvalues for each of the analyzed IEEE RTS-96 Benchmark configurations.

Node	Benchmark	With HVDC	Phase-shift
λ_1	180,2	180,2	180,2
λ_2	121,6	121,7	121,6
λ_3	83,7	121,7	121,6
λ_4	8,9	7,4	9,3
λ_5	11,7	11,2	12,2
λ_6	15,8	15,8	16,1
λ_7	22,1	21,0	40,7
λ_8	25,6	25,4	35,6
λ_9	35,8	35,7	25,6
λ_{10}	41,0	40,8	22,6
λ_{11}	57,1	56,4	56,8
λ_{12}	61,8	61,3	61,8
λ_{13}	63,5	63,5	63,5
from λ_{14} to λ_{24}	999,0	999,0	999,0

Table 3. Participation factors for mode 4 for the analyzed benchmark configurations.

Node	Benchmark	With HVDC	Phase-shift
4	0,11	0,04	0,11
5	0,16	0,31	0,16
6	0,58	0,49	0,57
7	0,02	0,01	0,02
8	0,05	0,06	0,05
9	0,07	0,05	0,07
10	0,00	0,02	0,00
11	0,02	0,02	0,02

5.1   IEEE RTS-96 Original Benchmark Scenarios

These are the simulation Scenarios A and B. Incremental load variations were applied in nodes 6 and 4 until the power flow stopped converging. Figure 2 shows the evolution of the modes closer to instability for both scenarios A and B. For both cases, a variation in the mode values as the load increases can be observed, especially for Scenario A. In both cases, modes 4, 5 and 6 alternate figure bottom. As we can see from Table 2, these three nodes are the modes closer to zero, confirming the tendency shown for the initial modal analysis.

Figure 3 shows the evolution of the participation factors of the nodes with incremental load in mode 4 for Scenarios A and B. For Scenario A, we expected the participation factor of node 6 to rise, as we are stressing the more sensitive

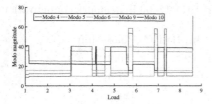
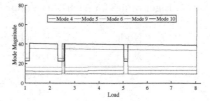

Fig. 2. Mode evolution comparison for base benchmark case. Scenario A (left); Scenario B (right).

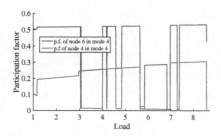
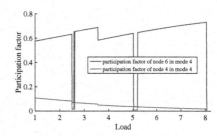

Fig. 3. Evolution of participation factor values for buses 4 and 6 in mode 4 for base benchmark case. Scenario A (left); Scenario B (right).

point of the mode. However, this node decreased the value of its participation factor drastically for determined load intervals. This behavior could be related to the mode evolution shown in Fig. 2 because the more significant variations in the participation factors of the nodes seem to occur when mode 4 changes its value. Confirming this idea, Scenario B presents more constant participation factors, as mode changes are less frequent for this scenario.

5.2   HDVC Link Related Scenarios

The simulation scenarios involved with the HVDC link are Scenarios C and D. Incremental variations of one unit of the load in nodes 6 and 4 were performed until the power flow stopped convergence. Figure 4 shows the evolution of the modes closer to instability for both scenarios C and D. The inclusion of the HVDC link seems to have a stabilizing effect for the evolution of the modes. For scenario C, the modes remain almost constant. However, variations in node 4 make mode 6 the closest to instability at the start of the analysis, changing the patterns of Table 2. This changes when mode 6 elevates its value, and mode 4 retakes its spot at the bottom of the graphic.

As seen in Fig. 5, participation factors remain almost constant for Scenario C. The participation factors for Scenario D mirror the tendency of the modes, as the value for node 6 rises as the same time than mode 4 becomes the mode closer to zero. This behavior evidences the relationship between the mode occurrence and the change of the weak point of the system. The system is weaker than the other cases, as the scenarios with HVDC link stopped power flow convergence with load increments of around 40% of the initial value.

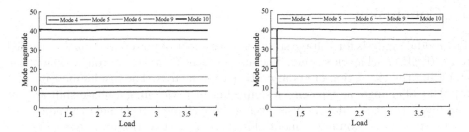

Fig. 4. Mode evolution comparison for benchmark with HVDC link. Scenario C (left); Scenario D (right).

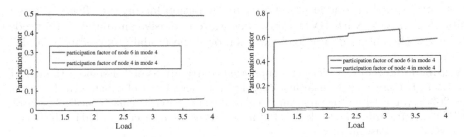

Fig. 5. Evolution of participation factor values for buses 4 and 6 in mode 4 for benchmark with HVDC link. Scenario C (left); Scenario D (right).

5.3 Phase-Shifting Scenario

The only scenario here is Scenario E. Figure 6 shows both the evolution of the modes closer to instability, and the evolution of the participation factors of the nodes 4 and 6 with incremental load (in node 6 only) in mode 4. The analysis is very similar to Scenario A. This could suggest that a phase-shift of only 10 degrees is inconsequential for the system, as the tendencies of both mode evolution and participation factors behave in the same way as Scenario A.

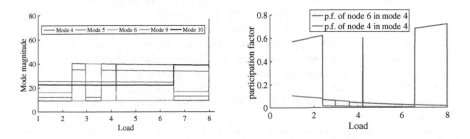

Fig. 6. Results for Scenario E. Mode evolution with incremental load in node 6 (left); evolution of participation factor values for buses 4 and 6 in mode 4 (right).

6 Conclusion

The modal analysis for voltage stability assessment of power systems was applied to an IEEE benchmark system. The method was illustrated through simulation, including the extraction of nodal participation factors. The results indicate that topological changes as replacing a simple line or performing a phase-shift are not significant for the modal analysis, even if those changes occur near the node with the most participation in the mode closest to instability. However, system modes change when the topological changes combined with load variations. Also, variations in the modal values affect the nodes closest to instability because of the corresponding changes in the nodal participation factors. When load increments were performed in a node with minor participation factor, the effects were sensible for the case with HVDC link only. More extensive simulations are needed to assess the effects of any load variation over the modal analysis in general.

Acknowledgement. Colciencias supported contributions of J. Espinosa through the project "Estrategia de transformación del sector energético Colombiano en el horizonte de 2030", financed by the program "Convocatoria 778 Ecosistema Científico", contract FP44842-210-2018. The work of J. Patino is part of the project IN201904 of Institución Universitaria Pascual Bravo.

References

1. Aik, D.L.H., Andersson, G.: Use of participation factors in modal voltage stability analysis of multi-infeed HVDC systems. IEEE Transact. Power Deliv. **13**(1), 203–211 (1998)
2. Ajjarapu, V., Lee, B.: Bibliography on voltage stability. IEEE Transact. Power Syst. **13**(1), 115–125 (1998)
3. Alvarez, S.R., Mazo, E.H.L., Oviedo, J.E.: Evaluation of power system partitioning methods for secondary voltage regulation application. In: 2017 IEEE 3rd Colombian Conference on Automatic Control (CCAC), pp. 1–6, October 2017. https://doi.org/10.1109/CCAC.2017.8276463
4. Andersson, G., et al.: Causes of the 2003 major grid blackouts in North America and Europe, and recommended means to improve system dynamic performance. IEEE Transact. Power Syst. **20**(4), 1922–1928 (2005)
5. Ángel Zea, A.: Amortiguamiento de oscilaciones de muy baja frecuencia usando PSSs multibanda con señales globales = Very low frequency oscillations damping using multiband PSSs with global signals. Master's thesis, Universidad Nacional de Colombia - Sede Manizales (2012). http://bdigital.unal.edu.co/5980/
6. Chowdhury, B.H., Taylor, C.W.: Voltage stability analysis: VQ power flow simulation versus dynamic simulation. IEEE Transact. Power Syst. **15**(4), 1354–1359 (2000)
7. Committee I.P.S.E.: Suggested Techniques for Voltage Stability Analysis (1993)
8. Gao, B., Morison, G.K., Kundur, P.: Voltage stability evaluation using modal analysis. IEEE Transact. Power Syst. **7**(4), 1529–1542 (1992)
9. Grigg, C., et al.: The IEEE reliability test system-1996. A report prepared by the reliability test system task force of the application of probability methods subcommittee. IEEE Transact. Power Syst. **14**(3), 1010–1020 (1999)

10. Hiskens, I.A., Pai, M.A.: Trajectory sensitivity analysis of hybrid systems. IEEE Transact. Circuits Syst. I: Fundam. Theory Appl. **47**(2), 204–220 (2000)
11. Horta, R., Espinosa, J., Patiño, J.: Frequency and voltage control of a power system with information about grid topology. In: 2015 IEEE 2nd Colombian Conference on Automatic Control (CCAC), pp. 1–6. IEEE (2015). https://doi.org/10.1109/CCAC.2015.7345203
12. Kopcak, I., da Silva, L.C.P., da Costa, V.F., Naturesa, J.S.: Transmission systems congestion management by using modal participation factors. In: 2003 IEEE Bologna Power Tech Conference Proceedings, vol. 2, pp. 6-pp. IEEE (2003)
13. Kundur, P., Gao, B., Morison, G.K.: Practical application of modal analysis for increasing voltage stability margins. In: Joint International Power Conference Athens Power Tech 1993, APT 1993, vol. 1, pp. 222–227. IEEE (1993)
14. Kundur, P.: Power System Stability and Control. McGraw-Hill, New York (1994)
15. Kundur, P., et al.: Definition and classification of power system stability. IEEE Transact. Power Syst. **19**(2), 1387–1401 (2004)
16. Milano, F.: An open source power system analysis toolbox. IEEE Transact. Power Syst. **20**(3), 1199–1206 (2005)
17. Morison, G.K., Gao, B., Kundur, P.: Voltage stability analysis using static and dynamic approaches. IEEE Transact. Power Syst. **8**(3), 1159–1171 (1993)
18. Patiño, J., López, J.D., Espinosa, J.: Analysis of control sensitivity functions for power system frequency regulation. In: Figueroa-García, J.C., López-Santana, E.R., Rodriguez-Molano, J.I. (eds.) WEA 2018. CCIS, vol. 915, pp. 606–617. Springer, Cham (2018). https://doi.org/10.1007/978-3-030-00350-0_50
19. Patiño, J., López, J.D., Espinosa, J.: Sensitivity analysis of frequency regulation parameters in power systems with wind generation. In: Precup, R.-E., Kamal, T., Zulqadar Hassan, S. (eds.) Advanced Control and Optimization Paradigms for Wind Energy Systems. PS, pp. 67–87. Springer, Singapore (2019). https://doi.org/10.1007/978-981-13-5995-8_3
20. Patino, J., Valencia, F., Espinosa, J.: Sensitivity analysis for frequency regulation in a two-area power system. Int. J. Renew. Energy Res. (IJRER) **7**(2), 700–706 (2017)
21. Patiño, J.A.: Frequency regulation for power systems with renewable energy sources (2018). http://bdigital.unal.edu.co/71344/. tesis o trabajo de grado presentada(o) como requisito parcial para optar al título de: Doctor en Ingeniería - Ingeniería Automática. - Línea de Investigación: Modelamiento, Simulación y Control de Sistemas Dinámicos
22. Ruiz, S., Patino, J., Marquez, A., Espinosa, J.: Optimal design for an electrical hybrid microgrid in Colombia under fuel price variation. Int. J. Renew. Energy Res. **7**(24), 1535–1545 (2017). http://ijrer.com/index.php/ijrer/article/view/6128/pdf
23. Weichao, W., Jianli, N., Ngan, H.W.: Small-disturbance voltage stability study on shaanxi power system. In: 2005 IEEE/PES Transmission and Distribution Conference and Exhibition: Asia and Pacific, pp. 1–5. IEEE (2005)

Simulation Systems

Areas with the Highest Use of Simulator for Health Education in Colombia

Maria Bernarda Salazar-Sánchez[1](✉)(iD),
Alher Mauricio Hernández-Valdivieso[1](iD),
Carolina Rodríguez-López[1](iD), Juan Camilo Mesa-Agudelo[1](iD),
Isabel Cristina Muñoz-Ortega[1](iD), Leidy Yaneth Serna-Higuita[2],
and Luis Felipe Buitrago-Castro[1](iD)

[1] Bioinstrumentation and Clinical Engineering Research Group - GIBIC,
Bioengineering Department, Universidad de Antioquia UdeA,
Calle 70 No. 52-21, A.A. 1226, Medellín, Colombia
{bernarda.salazar, alher.hernandez,
carolina.rodriguezl, camilo.mesa, isabelc.munoz,
luis.buitragoc}@udea.edu.co
[2] Department of Automatic Control (ESAII), Biomedical Engineering Research
Center (CREB) and Biomedical Research Networking Center in Bioengineering,
Biomaterials, and Nanomedicine, CIBER-BBN, Universitat Politècnica de
Catalunya, Barcelona, Spain
leidy.yanet.serna@upc.edu

Abstract. One of the most causes of adverse events in the healthcare institutions is the lack of training of the assistance staff, therefore the use of simulators in medical education has begun to be part of the curriculums of some programs, however, there are areas, that still do not have some kind of tool for interactive training. This paper aim is to identify these areas in higher education institutions in Colombia. The review consisted of seeks the medical simulation centers and simulators used in the teaching-learning process, identifying specific healthcare areas. 192 programs in health sciences are reported in the information system of education in Colombia, and at least 120 Centers and/or Simulation Laboratories for medical education are assigned to the Colombian Association of Simulation in Health Sciences. The areas with the highest use of simulators in the training are pre-hospital care, cardiology, and gynecology, which addresses a small percentage of the health sciences. The above may be due to the high cost of the most used simulators, task-trainers and mannequins, which suggests that the development of tools or another kind of simulator like computer-based is necessary, specifically to areas like critical care where it has been demonstrated, that occurs the most adverse events in the world.

Keywords: Simulators · Software applications · Health education

1 Introduction

The main objective of health professionals is to assure the well-being and safety of the patient and optimize their quality of life. Therefore during the professional training phase they must acquire a set of structural elements, processes, tools, and methodologies

© Springer Nature Switzerland AG 2019
J. C. Figueroa-García et al. (Eds.): WEA 2019, CCIS 1052, pp. 643–652, 2019.
https://doi.org/10.1007/978-3-030-31019-6_54

that allow them to minimize or mitigate the risks associated with the health care process [1]. The lack of professional experience can increase not only the morbidity of the patient but also decrease the confidence in the care and treatment received from the care personnel [2].

Recent studies conducted by Institutions in Latin America [2, 3] indicate that 36.5% of the errors in the treatment of patients were due to the lack of skills of the healthcare personnel. This demonstrates the need both to strengthen the current training strategies and to provide new approaches that promote the use of new technologies, in order to ensure and protect patient safety [4]. In recent years, one of the strategies that have generated the greatest impact in continuing professional training is the clinical simulation, which is defined as a set of techniques that allow learning from the experience obtained in environments that reproduce the reality.

The main advantage of medical simulation is that it has a place in controlled environments that ensure safety both for the patient and for the clinician. In addition, such a technique allows varying patient's conditions and observing their effect in real time, as many times as the student requires it [5]. The majority of the clinical simulation is based on the use of high fidelity physical simulators, which require physical space for their proper use and involve high costs for Educational Institutions [6]. Due to this and to the growth in access to technology, the strategy of addressing medical education and simulation through Information and Communication Technologies (ICTs) has emerged. These new tools can be developed to improve the acquisition of clinical skills and knowledge at different levels of learning both in their undergraduate and graduate training, as well as during their professional activities. Furthermore to increasing access to learning materials, providing greater opportunities for asynchronous learning and offering students access to multiple resources to explore topics [7].

There is recent evidence of the importance of the use of simulators and medical applications in training both undergraduate and postgraduate, as well as professionally. As examples, we find the study conducted by Gunn et al. [8] where a virtual reality tool was used for the training of undergraduate students-radiology and medical imaging technology. The study conducted by Lee et al. [9] where a surgery simulator was used for the training of residents in urology, and the study conducted by Rosenblatt et al. [10] where a patient simulator was used to evaluate the technical and non-technical skills of anesthesiologists within the institution, in order to establish needs for retraining.

The most common use of task simulators and mannequins is the management of emergencies, traumas, endotracheal intubation and resuscitation, tasks with more emphasis in nursing and prehospital care [11, 12], being Lacrdal Medical Corporation [13] and Cae Healthcare [14] some of the producers of simulators of this type, with simulators of adult and child patients. In the case of virtual reality simulators, the use is focused on laparoscopic surgery training, neurosurgery training, and echocardiography training [15]. Some of its producers are Surgical Science, Laparo and Medical X [16–18]. While in the case of computer-based simulators or mobile applications, its use has been focused on drug guides, medical calculators, and pregnancy wheels, among others [19].

For the specific case of Colombia, the use of simulators for medical education has been accepted in areas such as gynecology and obstetrics with the use of mannequin simulators [20], diagnosis of pathologies with task simulators [21, 22] and laparoscopic surgery with virtual reality simulators [23]. However, no evidence was found of the official use of application-type simulators in health programs, especially in Colombia [24].

Therefore, knowing the current need for continuing education in all areas, this paper aims to identify the areas of health sciences in which there is greater use of tools that support the acquisition of knowledge and skills within a multidisciplinary environment, identifying the areas in which it might be more relevant to focus development efforts, either because of the high cost of the simulators or because of the lack of possible equipment adapted to the training needs.

2   Methods

This research has a mixed approach of descriptive type, which seeks to characterize an interesting phenomenon to the academic communities of the health sciences. For it, two reviews have been carried out. The first one is a review of medical simulation centers and laboratories, and human simulators used in the teaching-learning process in Colombian health academic programs [25]. Undergraduate and postgraduate programs have been grouped as shown in Table 1.

Table 1. Undergraduate and postgraduate programs grouping in some areas of health sciences in Colombia [25].

Areas of health sciences	Academic programs
Medicine	Medicine
Nursing	Nursing
Veterinary	Veterinary Medicine; Zoological Medicine
Respiratory and Cardiorespiratory Therapy	Respiratory Therapy; Cardiorespiratory Therapy
Anesthesiology Specialization	Anesthesiology; Anesthesiology and resuscitation; Anesthesiology and perioperative medicine; Cardiothoracic anesthesia; Cardiovascular anesthesiology; Cardiovascular and thoracic anesthesia
Pneumology Specialization	Clinical pneumology; Pneumology; Pediatric pulmonology
Surgery Specialization	General surgery; Pediatric surgery; Neurosurgery; Cardiovascular surgery; Vascular surgery and angiology; Reconstructive surgery and hip joint replacement; Oncological surgery; Gastrointestinal surgery and digestive endoscopy; Spine surgery; Head and neck surgery; Vascular surgery; Otorhinolaryngology and head- neck surgery; Transplant surgery Dermatology and dermatologic surgery; Trauma and emergency surgery; Stomatology and oral surgery; Thorax surgery; Surgery of transplants of abdominal organs; Breast and soft tissue surgery; Gynecological endoscopic surgery; Advanced laparoscopic surgery
Critical Medicine and Intensive Care Specialization	Critical and intensive care medicine; Nursing in adult care; Nursing in child care; Nursing in pediatric critical care; Nursing care in critical care; Critical patient's nursing care; Nursing for the care of the patient in a critical state; Critical medicine and pediatric intensive care; Physiotherapy in critical care

The second review was carried out by looking for areas in which simulators are used, taking as a primary source the curricula description in academic programs, published articles, Colombian Association of Clinical Simulation and Institutional websites.

We grouped the simulators according to the classification proposed by Lopreiato [26] and Dudding et al. [23]. They classified these into five large groups, such as can be observed in Table 2. These categories allow describing how faithful the simulator is with respect to the real characteristics of clinical practice. Finally, the data collected will be analyzed.

Table 2. Definitions and examples of levels fidelity of simulators used in healthcare simulation [23, 26].

Type de simulators	Definition	Example
Standardized patients	A patient with a specific condition in a realistic, standardized, and repeatable way	A full-body simulator characterized by its great realism and designed to enhance individual skills in the airway, breathing, cardiac and circulation management [13]
Task trainers	A model that represents a part or region of the human body such as an arm, or an abdomen	Airway trainer allows to practice oral, digital, and nasal intubation, may also be practiced and evaluated suction techniques, and proper cuff inflation [27]
Mannequins	A real-sized human like simulator representing a patient for health care simulation and education that may be controlled using computers and software	A mannequin programmed to reproduce 32 heart sounds, 21 lung sounds, 20 peristaltic sounds and 4 types of carotid murmurs, to teach cardiovascular, pulmonary and abdominal auscultation [28]
Computer-based	A simulation represented on a computer screen, often based on interactive gaming technologies	Global 3D medical application with an anatomy visualization system for anatomical education, combined with a recognized radiology software and great clinical content [28]
Immersive virtual reality	A real-life situation three-dimensional representation that deeply involves the participants' senses, emotions, thinking, and behavior; that has the feeling of immersion	A laparoscopic surgery simulator gives students the opportunity to improve their psychomotor performance through standardized and measurable training, provided only by virtual reality simulators [18]

3 Results and Discussion

Table 3 shows the number of undergraduate and postgraduate programs of some health sciences areas in Colombia. According to National Information System of Higher Education (SNIES), Colombia has approximately one hundred ninety-two (192) programs in health sciences, of which one hundred thirty-seven (137) are undergraduate and fifty-five (55) postgraduate programs. Moreover, 100% of the programs involve traditional classroom or face-to-face methodology but there is no evidence in the curricula the use of simulators [25].

Table 3. Number of undergraduate and postgraduate programs of some areas of health sciences in Colombia. The type of learning methodology of the academic program is mentioned: Traditional/Face-To-Face or Virtual/Online [25].

Academic programs	Universities (Public and private)	Average number of students (per year)	Education	
			Traditional	Virtual
Medicine	49	47771	49	0
Nursing	56	24468	56	0
Veterinary	27	15727	27	0
Respiratory and Cardiorespiratory Therapy	5	1560	5	0
Anesthesiology Specialization	15	331	26	0
Pneumology Specialization	3	11	6	0
Surgery Specialization	19	519	19	0
Critical Medicine and Intensive Care Specialization	18	267	18	0
Total	192	90654	192	0

On the other hand, a maximum clinical practice activity of 66 h per week (hospital practice) is performed by students both from undergraduate programs (since the second year of the studies) and from postgraduate programs (at the beginning of the studies), as established by Law 1917 of 2018 [29]. These hospital practices, which are frequently carried out following high-quality standards, seek to make easier the student's process learning. However, they often depend on the number of clinical cases and exposure time to each clinical case that can be given to a concerned student, both undergraduate and graduate programs [30]. Additionally, Colombian legislation also establishes restrictions on the participation of students in the care of patients within the hospital entities [31], which also reduces the number of hours during their training period [32, 33].

The limited exposure time that a student can have during their hospital practice, as well as legislation restrictions, has recently promoted the creation of Simulation

Centers and Laboratories with high standards in both public and private entities and Universities. Currently, there are at least 120 Centers and/or Simulation Laboratories for medical education assigned to the Colombian Association of Simulation in Health Sciences [34]. The main purpose of these centers and laboratories is provide physical spaces for the healthcare professionals training. For this, they often incorporate simulation equipment and software platforms, as shown in Table 4, which are focused mainly on training for specific areas in Health Clinic Sciences and according to the categories specified in Table 2, so much for undergraduate and postgraduate programs.

Table 4. The number of used simulators in undergraduate and postgraduate programs. Focused on training for specific areas in Health Clinic Sciences.

Areas	Type of simulators				
	Standardized patients	Task trainers	Mannequins	Computer-based	Immersive virtual reality
Surgery	0	1	0	0	4
Respiratory Therapy	0	7	0	0	0
Pre-hospital care	8	14	27	0	0
Cardiology	1	0	21	0	0
Semiology, anatomy, and physiology	8	18	18	9	0
Internal Medicine	0	5	2	1	0
Gynecology	5	20	3	0	0
Traumatology	0	7	0	0	0
Total (%)	12.29	40.22	39.66	5.59	2.23

Table 5 shows the average cost range of this kind of simulators and software. It can seen that their acquisition requires high investment costs, mainly in immersive virtual reality simulators. This is consistent with the low number of related simulators used in Colombia (see Table 4), where only four (4) immersive virtual reality simulators are

Table 5. Average range cost of simulators and software used in the Health Clinic Sciences. The prices were provided by supplier companies. References about suppliers [13, 17, 18, 35–40].

Cost (USD)	Type of simulators				
	Standardized patients	Task trainers	Mannequins	Computer-based	Immersive virtual reality
Cheapest	5,100.00	325.00	1,695.00	0.00	159.00
Most expensive	10,000.00	60,000.00	80,000.00	79,026.00	100,000.00

currently used in the training of surgery areas, mainly for laparoscopic surgery, which is close to 3% of the country's simulators in health clinical sciences. Karim Qayumil et al. found that despite the great interest and needs of these specific training spaces, the use of simulation in health care education is limited to specific areas and is not a budgeted item in many institutions [34].

Of the five large groups in which the simulators are presented in Table 4, it can be seen that in Colombia the most implemented are those in the categories of task trainers with 40.22% and the mannequins with 39.66%, however, some areas in health clinic sciences only have one simulator even when the number of students in both undergraduate and postgraduate programs is higher than 25000 per year (see Table 3). However, the simulators and software are now in widespread use in medical education and medical student evaluations, Isserberg et al. showed that, educational feedback is the most important feature of simulation-based medical education and identified repetitive practice as a key feature involving the use of high-fidelity simulations in medical education [41]. Although in Colombia these new learning approaches are being implemented, more efforts are necessary. The current growing and implementation of simulation centers as well as the development of tools for both teaching and learning process, like e-learning applications, are still not enough to cover the needs of several fields related to healthcare.

The above can be evidenced from the point of view of adverse events, as mentioned in the introduction, an average of 36% of adverse events occur due to the lack of personnel training. Furthermore, it has been shown that the highest risk occurs in the intensive care unit (ICU), due to the use of the technology, the type and number of interventions, and the severity of the patients [42]. In ICU the areas of nursing, critical care, and respiratory therapy predominate, especially in the management of mechanical ventilation. According to the Table 5 the area related to ICU that has some kind of simulator in Colombia, is the respiratory therapy with seven simulators in the country. The research reports that are mostly related to training in endotracheal intubation, a minimum percentage of services provided in ICU. Therefore, it is possible to analyze that in Colombia it is necessary the development and use of tools, simulators, and applications, to provide more training and continuous education in the areas related to the critical patients.

4   Conclusions

This paper provides an overview of how clinical simulation has penetrated the health training processes in Colombia during the latest years. Particularly, simulation has become a very important tool both for learning and for training processes of clinicians and students in several areas of health. We proposed that clinical simulation has considerable potential because it adapts to the learning needs and rhythms of each individual. It makes easier the acquisition of skills necessary for professional development such as analytical and clinical thinking for problem solving, decision making, leadership, communication, among other skills. Additionally, simulation allows testing hypothesis and reproducing the complex and rare situation in controlled environments that, otherwise, could involve a certain risk both for the patient and for participants.

However, the high cost of simulation centers suggests that simulation based on computational systems, i.e. e-learning applications, and immersive virtual reality, could be solutions to such limitations, particularly in areas like surgery, respiratory therapy, internal medicine and traumatology, where the availability of simulation tools looks scant. These computers based solutions take advantage of ubiquitous technology and information to support and to improve the competencies of the concerned clinical professional.

Acknowledgments. This work was partially supported by COLCIENCIAS under Grant "CT 450-2018 - Desarrollo de aplicaciones móviles para el aprendizaje del sistema respiratorio: Conceptos básicos, diagnóstico de enfermedades, terapia y rehabilitación - recursos provenientes del Sistema General de Regalías fondos de CTeI de la Gobernación de Antioquia, administrados a través del patrimonio autónomo fondo nacional de financiamiento para la ciencia, la tecnología y la innovación Francisco José de Caldas" (Colombia); and by Universidad de Antioquia under Grant 2018-20133 (Medellín, Antioquia, Colombia).

Conflict of Interest. The author(s) declare(s) that there is no conflict of interest regarding the publication of this paper.

References

1. Pinilla, A.E.: Educación en ciencias de la salud y en educación médica. Acta Médica Colomb. **43**(2), 61–65 (2018)
2. Zárate-Grajales, R., Olvera-Arreola, S., Hernández-Cantoral, A., Hernández Corral, S., Sánchez-Angeles, S., Valdez Labastida, R.: Factores relacionados con eventos adversos reportados por enfermería en unidades de cuidados intensivos. Proyecto multicéntrico. Enfermería Univ., **12**(2), 63–72 (2015)
3. Achury Saldaña, D., et al.: Study of adverse events, factors and periodicity in hospitalized patients in ICU. Enfermería Glob., **15**(42), 324–340 (2016)
4. Amoore, J.N.: A structured approach for investigating the causes of medical device adverse events. J. Med. Eng. **2014**(1), 1–13 (2014)
5. Lamé, G., Dixon-Woods, M.: Using clinical simulation to study how to improve quality and safety in healthcare. BMJ Simul. Technol. Enhanc. Learn. (2018). https://doi.org/10.1136/bmjstel-2018-000370
6. Padilha, J.M., Machado, P.P., Ribeiro, A.L., Ramos, J.L.: Clinical Virtual Simulation in Nursing Education. Clin. Simul. Nurs. **15**, 13–18 (2018)
7. Schifferdecker, K.E., Berman, N.B., Fall, L.H., Fischer, M.R.: Adoption of computer-assisted learning in medical education: The educators' perspective. Med. Educ. **46**(11), 1063–1073 (2012)
8. Gunn, T., Jones, L., Bridge, P., Rowntree, P., Nissen, L.: The use of virtual reality simulation to improve technical skill in the undergraduate medical imaging student. Interact. Learn. Environ. **26**(5), 613–620 (2018)
9. Lee, J.Y., et al.: Laparoscopic warm-up exercises improve performance of senior-level trainees during laparoscopic renal surgery. J. Endourol. **26**(5), 545–550 (2011)
10. Rosenblatt, M.A., Abrams, K.J., Levine, A.I., Sugarman, M., Vitkun, S., Yudkowitz, F.S.: The use of a human patient simulator in the evaluation of and development of a remedial prescription for an anesthesiologist with lapsed medical skills. Anesth. Analg. **94**(1), 149–153 (2002)

11. Aebersold, M.: The history of simulation and its impact on the future. AACN Adv. Crit. Care **27**(1), 56–61 (2016)
12. Braga, M.S., et al.: Effect of just-in-time simulation training on provider performance and patient outcomes for clinical procedures: a systematic review. BMJ Simul. Technol. Enhanc. Learn. **1**(3), 94–102 (2015)
13. Laerdal Medical Corporation, Laerdal Medical (2018). https://www.laerdal.com/. Accessed 12 Apr 2019
14. Cae Healthcare products, CAE Healthcare (2019). https://caehealthcare.com/products/. Accessed 12 Apr 2019
15. Barsom, E.Z., Graafland, M., Schijven, M.P.: Systematic review on the effectiveness of augmented reality applications in medical training. Surg. Endosc. **30**(10), 4174–4183 (2016)
16. Laparo, Laparo – Laparoscopic training of future (2019). https://laparo.pl/en/. Accessed 10 Apr 2019
17. Medical X, LAP-X, Laparoscopic surgical simulator (2017). https://www.medical-x.com/products/lap_x/. Accessed 09 Apr 2019
18. Surgical Science, LapSim - The proven training system, (2009). https://surgicalscience.com/systems/lapsim/. Accessed 09 Apr 2019
19. Franko, O.I., Tirrell, T.F.: Smartphone app use among medical providers in ACGME training programs. J. Med. Syst. **36**(5), 3135–3139 (2012)
20. Cardona-Arias, J.A., Cordoba, J.P., Velasquez Ibarra, A.A.: Efficacy of obstetric simulation in the learning of skills related to birthing care in medical students, Medellin-Colombia. Transl. Biomed., **09**(03), 1–7 (2018)
21. Fernández-Ávila, D.G., et al.: The effect of an educational intervention, based on clinical simulation, on the diagnosis of rheumatoid arthritis and osteoarthritis. Musculoskeletal Care **16**(1), 147–151 (2018)
22. Angarita, F.A., Price, B., Castelo, M., Tawil, M., Ayala, J.C., Torregrossa, L.: Improving the competency of medical students in clinical breast examination through a standardized simulation and multimedia-based curriculum. Breast Cancer Res. Treat. **173**(2), 439–445 (2019)
23. Dudding, C.C., Nottingham, E.E.: A national survey of simulation use in university programs in communication sciences and disorders. Am. J. Speech-Lang. Pathol. **27**(1), 71–81 (2018)
24. Marín, F.V., Inciarte, A.J., Hernández, H.G., Pitre, R.C.: Strategies of institutions of higher education for the integration of information and communication technologies and of innovation in the teaching process. a study in the district of Barranquilla, Colombia | Estrategias de las instituciones de educación s. Form. Univ. **10**(6), 29–38 (2017)
25. Ministerio de Educación de Colombia, SNIES: Sistema Nacional de Información de Educación Superior (2019). https://www.mineducacion.gov.co/sistemasinfo/snies/. Accessed 10 Apr 2019
26. Lopreiato, J.O.: Healthcare simulation Dictionary. Society for Simulation in Healthcare Associate (2016)
27. GT Simulators, Ultrasound training model (2019). https://www.gtsimulators.com/. Accessed 12 Apr 2019
28. TecnoSim, Sam-ii-the-student-auscultation-manikin (2018). http://www.tecnosim.com.mx/producto/sam-ii-the-student-auscultation-manikin/. Accessed 12 Apr 2019
29. Congreso de la República de Colombia, "Ley 1917 de 2018 - Reglamentación del sistema de residencias médicas en Colombia," Bogotá, Colombia (2018)
30. Duque, G.R., Monsalve, L.C.O.: Sistema de Residencias Médicas en Colombia: Marco conceptual para una propuesta de regulación (2013)

31. Ministerio de la Protección Social, "Decreto 2376 del 1 Julio 2010 - Regula la relación docencia - servicio en Colombia," Bogotá, Colombia (2010)
32. Bermudez, C., Monroy, A., Torreglosa, L., Henao, F.: Estado actual de la formacion de residentes de cirugía general en Colombia. Rev. Colomb. Cirugía 21(4), 225–239 (2006)
33. Castro, A.: Necesidad de evaluar los programas de formación de cirugía en Colombia Oración Maestros de la Cirugía Colombiana 2016. Rev Colomb Cir. 31(161), 4 (2016)
34. Camacho, H.M.: La simulación clínica: Nueva herramienta para enseñar medicina. Medicina (B. Aires). 34(3), 242–246 (2012)
35. Universidad de Antioquia, Mesa de Anatomía Digital, nueva herramienta didáctica en el Centro de Simulación. https://bit.ly/2vo9yuT. Accessed 11 Apr 2019
36. Universidad Politécnica de Cataluña, Virtual laboratories (2011). https://bioart.upc.edu/en/virtual-laboratories. Accessed 10 Apr 2019
37. Tecnomed 2000 electromedicina, Simuladores - Material Didáctico archivos (2000). https://tecnomed2000.com/categoria-producto/simuladores-mat-didac/. Accessed 11 Apr 2019
38. Cardionics, The heart of auscultation (1969). https://www.cardionics.com/. Accessed 10 Apr 2019
39. 3B Scientific, Simuladores Médicos (2019). https://www.a3bs.com/. Accessed 12 Apr 2019
40. MedicalExpo, El salón online del sector médico (2019). http://www.medicalexpo.es/. Accessed 12 Apr 2019
41. Issenberg, S.B., McGaghie, W.C., Petrusa, E.R., Gordon, D.L., Scalese, R.J.: Features and uses of high-fidelity medical simulations that lead to effective learning: a BEME systematic review. Med. Teach. 27(1), 10–28 (2005)
42. Zárate-Grajales, R., Olvera-Arreola, S., Hernández-Cantoral, A., Hernández-Corral, S., Sánchez-Angeles, S., Valdez Labastida, R.: Factores relacionados con eventos adversos reportados por enfermería en unidades de cuidados intensivos. Proyecto multicéntrico. Enfermería Univ., 12(2), 63–72 (2015)

Simulation in the Farsite of a Forest Fire Presented in the Eastern Hills of the Town of San Cristóbal in Bogotá

Leidy Yolanda López Osorio$^{(\boxtimes)}$, Giovanni Bermúdez Bohórquez,
and Evy Fernanda Tapias

University Francisco José de Caldas, Bogotá, Colombia
{lylopezo,eftapiasf}@correo.udistrital.edu.co,
gbermudez@udistrital.edu.co

Abstract. This article presents the simulation of a forest fire in the Eastern hills in the town of San Cristóbal in Bogotá, for which case an event presented in 2016 is taken as a case study, of which data provided by the Official Fire Department, the satellite images of the area and meteorological information are available. As a result, fire propagation characteristics are obtained, such as the shape of the fire, the area and perimeter of fuel consumed, and the length of the flames.

Keywords: Forest fire · Simulation · Spread of fire

1 Introduction

Forest fires are events that cause damage to the environmental dynamics, water, flora, fauna and soil, and have caused the deterioration of air quality in Bogota and the environment. Additionally, when fires occur near homes, there is a deterioration in the quality of life of the people living there, due to emissions during combustion, loss of equipment, crops and domestic animals [1]. In the last four years, plant cover fires in the eastern hills of the San Cristóbal locality have consumed more than 350 hectares of vegetation, which is equivalent to about three times the Simón Bolívar park [2, 3].

Therefore, the protection of the eastern hills of Bogotá is a very important issue due to the complexity of its Andean forest ecosystems, with species that are fundamental for water collection given the connection between the Chingaza and Sumapaz massifs, besides being a protector and natural regulator of the rains and winds that arrive in the city [4].

Bogota has an integrated system of emergency attention and having constituent specialized attention agencies for the attention of forest fire events such as the Official Fire Department, the Civil Defense, the Metropolitan Police and the Colombian Air Force, which have designed procedures to react to emergency, but due to the lack of technologies to identify the characteristics of fire propagation, they must use the previous experience to design an extinction plan.

This article presents the simulation of a forest fire in the town of San Cristóbal in Farsite, with the aim of identifying the characteristics of fire propagation in the area, taking into account the topography, climate and fuels.

© Springer Nature Switzerland AG 2019
J. C. Figueroa-García et al. (Eds.): WEA 2019, CCIS 1052, pp. 653–663, 2019.
https://doi.org/10.1007/978-3-030-31019-6_55

2 Simulation of Forest Fires

Due to the level of detail of the models of forest fire propagation of theoretical type, and the limited availability of information about the land; the development of models of empirical type is a trend, which has allowed scientific advances in the field of pre-dicting the behavior of fire in vegetable fuels [5].

In order to overcome the difficulties that arise with theoretical models, computa-tional tools have been developed that offer a visual representation of landscapes, and the development of fires on them [6, 7]. The simulators take part of the theoretical models, and according to the meteorological, topographic and fuel conditions, they present a prediction of the fire propagation, dispersion and intensity, depth and length of the flames, intensity of the reaction, amid others. Among the models used by the simulators, elliptical propagation, cellular automata, arrangement propagation, Marcov chains, percolation models and stochastic and chaotic techniques are the most renowned [5, 8].

- Elliptical propagation: with this model, in a continuous terrain where the fire grows taking into account the mathematical properties of the ellipses, and the aspects of fire behavior. The perimeter of the line of fire is represented is represented with small ellipses [9].
- Cellular Automata: this simulation technique also assumes a continuous terrain, which is represented by cells, which have a value according to the conditions of the surface, for each cell the probability of propagating the fire through governed rules is evaluated by physical aspects [9].
- Percolation model: in this case the terrain is divided by a mesh, in which fire is propagated taking into account the fuel of the cells, that is flames advance if it can be burned. The propagation also depends on the topography and fuel [9].

The use of vital tools for the analysis of the behavior of forest fires contributes to the planning and development of extinction and prevention plans, to make the work of the attention agencies diminish the damage caused to the environment and in addition to reduce the costs of resources allocated to recover housing, machinery and crops [10].

3 Farsite

It is a simulation software for forest fires which uses the information related to the topography, fuels and the meteorological conditions of the land, to determine the behavior and progress of the fire for long periods of time, considering a continuous distribution of the vegetation [11].

Farsite uses the Rothermel fire propagation model, the Van Wagner crown fire initiation model, the Rothermel crown fire propagation model, an Albini post-frontal combustion model, and the moisture model of the dead fuel of Nelson 2000 [11–13].

The program uses the technique of elliptical propagation, so the fire is represented as a polygon that expands continuously, in certain time spaces. The propagation is carried out using vertices, equidistant points that represent the point of ignition of a flame that moves outwards [14] (Fig. 1-a). The points in two dimensions X and Y, represent the growth of the perimeter, the number of points will increase while the polygon grows. The fire perimeter is represented by small ellipses, which are joined from the vertices as shown in Fig. 1-b [5].

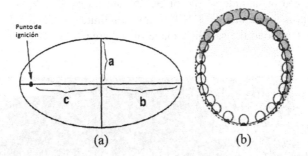

Fig. 1. Propagation of the fire in Farsite (a) Vertexes to represent the ignition point (b) polygon of fire propagation in Farsite [5, 14].

The simulation is built by importing GIS data (geographical information system) from a specific area, and then Farsite issues the information of the fire perimeters, the intensity of the fire line, the length of the flame, the speed of propagation and the direction, the fire activity of the crown, etc. Although it usually consumes a lot of time in the calculation, the results are accurate and reliable to simulate the spread of forest fires [15].

The entrance of Farsite requires five digital maps in ASCII format, fuel map, elevation map, slope map, aspects map and canopy coverage or shade map (Fig. 2), additionally data regarding the temperature, speed data, wind direction, precipitation, the date and time of the event and the duration thereof are required; this last information can be loaded in a flat file or entered directly into the program.

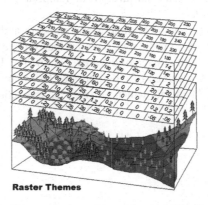

Raster Themes

Fig. 2. Representation of input layers in Farsite [14].

4 Study Area

The simulation of the forest fire was made in the eastern hills area of Bogotá in the town of San Cristóbal, Fig. 3 shows the area delineated in Google Maps [16], the upper left point is located at latitude 4° 34, 56'56" N and longitude: 74° 4' 55" W and the lower right point is at latitude 4° 31'19" N and longitude 74° 2' 23" W; These points are required to download the satellite image of the area.

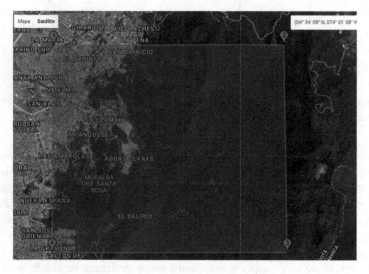

Fig. 3. Locality of San Cristóbal [16].

The download of the satellite image was made through the USGS Earth Explorer site, developed by the United States Geological Survey, which allows access to high resolution images of the Earth's surface, from LandSat, ASTER, MODIS sensors, LiDAR and AVHRR [17].

USGS Earth Explorer uses the Google Maps platform and allows you to establish search criteria related to site coordinates, date and percentage of cloudiness [18].

Figure 4 shows the satellite image of the area, obtained by USGS Earth Explorer on March 15, 2015 with a percentage of cloudiness of less than 15%, from the LandSat satellite, which contains 11 layers, which allowed the extraction of the vegetation and topography of the area.

Fig. 4. Satellite image of the area of the Eastern Hills in the town of San Cristóbal [18].

After obtaining the satellite image of the study area, the software QGis version 2.18 was used for the generation of the input raster for the Farsite, these layers are matrices where each cell has a value that translates into certain information [19].

Fuel Map
This layer provides information related to the type of vegetation present in the field, Farsite has reserved the numbers from 1 to 13 for the standard fuel model, some numbers between 101–219 are used for the extended set of models, water is represented by the number 98 and the rock is 99 [11]. In the area of San Cristóbal fine and dry grass and grass (1 and 2), forest (3), páramo (4), crops (5), urban area (6) and rock can be found.

Slope Map
The raster slope can have units of degrees or percentages of inclination with respect to the horizontal. The slope is necessary to calculate the effects of the slope on the propagation of fire and solar radiation [11].

Map of Aspects
It contains values for the topographic aspect that depend on the GIS application that provides the data. If the appearance data comes from a GRASS ASCII file, all the values are oriented counterclockwise from the east. The aspect values in a raster file in ARC / GRID ASCII format (ArcInfo, ArcView, ArcGIS) must be azimuth values, clockwise degrees from the north [11].

Elevation Map
It can have units of meters or feet above sea level. The elevation is necessary for the adiabatic adjustment of temperature and humidity and for the conversion of fire propagation between horizontal and slope distances [11].

Canopy Coverage Map

The canopy cover is used to calculate the shading and wind reduction factors for all fuel models, it is the horizontal percentage of the ground surface that is covered by treetops.

The canopy is measured as the horizontal fraction of the land that is covered directly above the canopy of the tree. The coverage units can be categories (1–4) or percentage values (0–100) [11].

In Fig. 5 the landscape corresponding to the area where the fire will develop, the colors correspond to the fuels mentioned above are displayed.

Fig. 5. Landscape of the San Blas area in Farsite. Own source

5 Case Study

Table 1 shows the data of the forest fire event, which occurred in the town of San Cristóbal, which was registered and attended by the Official Bogota Fire Department, the information was supplemented with the Information System reports for Risk Management and Climate Change - SIRE.

The incident was selected taking into account the spread of burned vegetable fuel and the time of the fire.

Table 1. Incident data [2, 20, 21].

Information	Incident
Date	01/02/2016
Approximate location	Aguas Claras 1 – El Delirio
Hectares consumed	157,6
Combustible material	Native vegetation and prickly broom
Report time NUSE - 123	9:31 a.m.
Time of arrival in the area	9:40 a.m.
Work time (hours)	13,3
Ending time	11:48 p.m.
Duration of the incident (hours)	14,17

5.1 Simulation of the Event

To simulate the incident that occurred in the clear water zone 1, in addition to knowing the extent of the fuel consumed, the duration of the incident and the hours of occurrence, it is necessary to have information on the seasonal regime of the area on the day of the fire, given by the temperature, the humidity, the elevation of the land, the precipitations and the winds.

Table 2 shows the seasonal regime of Aguas Claras 1, for the day of the incident. This data is entered into Farsite as part of the landscape, along with raster elevation, shadow, fuel, aspects and slopes.

Table 2. Aguas Claras 1 seasonal regime for the day of the event [22–24].

Rainfall (mm)	6,09				
Minimum temperature (°C)	9,2				
Maximum temperature (°C)	22				
Average humidity (%)	65				
Elevation (m)	2800				

Winds					
Hour	Speed (Km/h)	Direction (degrees)	Hour	Speed (Km/h)	Direction (degrees)
00:00	6	33	12:00	11	92
01:00	6	25	13:00	11	187
02:00	6	31	14:00	12	227
03:00	5	31	15:00	13	247
04:00	6	32	16:00	12	252
05:00	7	33	17:00	10	257
06:00	6	25	18:00	12	271
07:00	7	32	19:00	10	255
08:00	9	44	20:00	10	26
09:00	10	45	21:00	9	33
10:00	10	71	22:00	6	31
11:00	10	80	23:00	6	19

With the information in Table 2, the time and wind files in Farsite [25, 26] are loaded, which determine the configuration options for incident duration and simulation parameters, such as the time intervals in the that you will obtain information related to the area and the perimeter consumed by the fire.

Figure 6 shows the result of the simulation of the incident, in the area of Aguas Claras 1. The burned area is represented with a white border, inside this is the ignition point that was set according to the information of the consumed fuel delivered by the Official Fire Department.

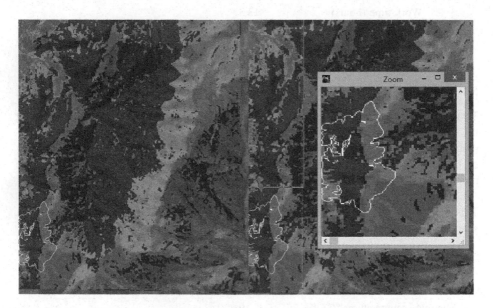

Fig. 6. Result of the simulation of the incident 1. Own source

It is observed that the fire took an irregular shape, due to the variable wind, the irregular topography of the area and the heterogeneous fuel, represented by the colors on the map, blue for type 3 forest, green for type 4, paramo fuel, and light blue for type 5, crops.

Another result delivered by the simulator is the area and the horizontal and topographic perimeter, the first takes into account a homogeneous soil and the second the elevations of the area [27]; the latter will always be greater for the field of study, since it is a mountainous area. Figure 7 shows the area and perimeter consumed, these images were generated by Farsite.

According to the results of the simulation, fuel burned after 13.3 h of fire, 170,041 horizontal hectares and 185,426 hectares were consumed taking into account the topography. The irregular shape of the incident had a horizontal perimeter of 11,021 k.

The difference with respect to the information registered by the firemen is 12.4 Ha, which can be attributed to the fact that no extinction actions were programmed, so that

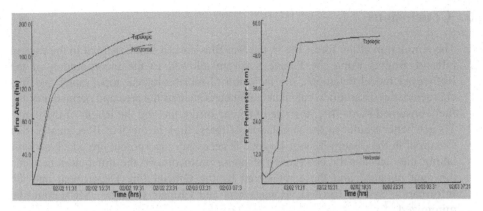

Fig. 7. Area and perimeter of fuel consumed by the fire in the incident. Own source. (Color figure online)

the fire propagated uncontrollably, besides that the ignition point is arbitrarily set in the Aguas Claras area 1, since the exact location is not available.

Another result that was obtained from the simulation was the rate of propagation of the fire (speed), with respect to heat per unit area (heat density), the product of the axes gives information on the length of the flame (Fig. 8). The red dots indicate active fire fronts [27].

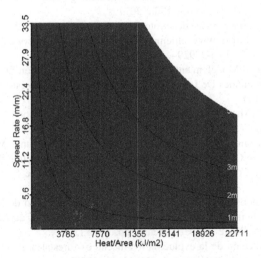

Fig. 8. Length of the flame in the incident. Own source (Color figure online)

It is observed that flames up to 5 m long with a heat density of up to 22711 JK/m^2, also active fires of up to one meter in length.

6   Conclusions

1. The simulation of the forest fire in the San Blas area of San Cristóbal in the eastern hills of Bogotá using the Farsite software allowed to the incorporation of the Rothermel model equations, the inclusion of meteorological topography and fuel characteristics, in addition calculate parameters such as the area and perimeter of the fuel consumed by the fire, the rate of spread of the fire and the length of the flame.
2. To get better results in the simulation of forest fires in the San Blas area of San Cristóbal in the eastern hills of Bogotá, is necessary incorporate fire attack actions, taking into account the emergency response protocols, So the differences between the data obtained and those registered by the Official Fire Department and the Information System for Risk Management and Climate Change - SIRE could be minimized.

References

1. I. D. de G. del R. Y. cambio C. IDIGER: «Marco de actuación estrategia distrital para la respuesta a emergencias» , Bogotá - Colombia (2017)
2. U.A.E.C.O.B. dem B. UAE Bomberos de Bogotá: «Base De Datos», Bogotá - Colombia (2017)
3. Secretaría Distrital de Ambiente, S.: «Incendios forestales en Bogota» (2017). http://www. ambientebogota.gov.co/c/journal/view_article_content?groupId=10157&articleId= 5789101&version=1.2. Accedido 28 dic 2017
4. El Tiempo: «La importancia de proteger a los cerros orientales de Bogotá» (2019). Disponible en: https://www.eltiempo.com/vida/ciencia/la-importancia-de-proteger-a-los-cerros-orientales-de-bogota-279294. Accessed 21 abr 2019
5. Velásquez, D.F.V.: «Modelamiento Y Simulación De Propagación De Incendios Forestales En Los Cerros Orientales De La Ciudad De Bogotá D.C Usando Farsite», Repos. Univ. los Andes, p. 68 (2013)
6. McCormick, P.S., Ahrens, J.P.: Visualization of wildfire simulations. IEEE Comput. Graph. Appl. 18(2), 17–19 (1998)
7. Herrera, O.A., Levano, M.A., Moreno, M., Aldunate, R.G., Bruno, M.: «Realistic Terrain Model in a Wildfire Context for El Yali Reserve: Serious Videogame Simulation». In: 2014 33rd International Conference of the Chilean Computer Science Social, pp. 54–56. IEEE (2014)
8. Moreno, F.L., Mateos, J.J., Moya, M.: «Determinación del riesgo de Incendio y propuestas de prevención en la interfaz urbano-forestal de Descargamaría - Cáceres». In: Wildfire 2007 4th International Wildlife Fire Conference, pp. 1–12 (2007)
9. Malen, M.: «Predicción de la evolución los incendios forestales guiada dinámicamente por los datos», Universidad Autónoma de Barcelona (2009)
10. Bermúdez, A., Casado, R., García, E.M., Gómez, Á., Quiles, F.J., Ruiz-gallardo, J. R.: «Empleo de una red de sensores en el reajuste de modelos de comportamiento del fuego en incendios forestales». Wildfire, p. 12 (2007)
11. U.S.F.S. USDA: «FARSITE | Programa de Ciencia de Fuego, Combustible y Humo» (2012). Disponible en: https://www.firelab.org/project/farsite. Accessed 17 abr 2019

12. Pérez-Aranda Romero, J.: Aplicación de técnicas gráficas al estudio y evolución de incendios forestales. Almería: Editorial Universidad de Almería (2015)
13. Torraza, A.: «Desarrollo del motor de cálculo de un simulador de incendios forestales». Universidad Nacional de Cordoba (2014)
14. Finney, M.A.: «Mechanistic modeling of landscape fire patterns». Fire.org, p. 26 (1999)
15. Yun, S., Chen, C., Li, J., Tang, L.: «Wildfire Spread Simulation and Visualization in Virtual Environments», p. 5. IEEE (2011)
16. Google: «Google Maps» (2019). Disponible en: https://www.google.es/maps/@4.5527715,-74.1063775,15z. Accessed 17 abr 2019
17. Asociación Geoinnova, «Imágenes satelitales gratuitas: principales sitios web de descarga» (2016). [En línea]. Disponible en: https://geoinnova.org/blog-territorio/imagenes-satelitales-gratuitas/. Accessed 17 abr 2019
18. Departament of the interior U.S: «USGS EarthExplorer» (2017). Disponible en: https://earthexplorer.usgs.gov/. Accessed 17 abr 2019
19. Qgis: «Lesson: Trabajando con Datos Ráster» (2019). Disponible en: https://docs.qgis.org/2.14/es/docs/training_manual/rasters/data_manipulation.html. Accessed 17 abr 2019
20. S. de I. para la G. del R. y C. C.- SIRE: «Base de datos sire - Incendios forestales», Bogotá - Colombia (2017)
21. D.N. de B. de C.- DNBC: «Eventos Atendidos por Bomberos Colombia» (2018). Disponible en: https://bomberos.mininterior.gov.co/sala-de-prensa/noticias/eventos-atendidos-por-bomberos-colombia. Accessed 14 Mar 2019
22. I. de H. M. y E. A. IDEAM: «Atlas Interactivo - Vientos - IDEAM» (2016). Disponible en: http://atlas.ideam.gov.co/visorAtlasVientos.html. Accessed 26 Mar 2019
23. I. de H. M. y E. A. A. M. de B. IDEAM: «Estudio de la Caracterización Climática de Bogotá y Cuenca Alta del Río Tunjuelo» , Bogota (2016)
24. I. de H. M. y E. A. IDEAM: «Medición, procesamiento de la información y red de estaciones que miden viento en colombia» , en *Atlas de Viento y Energía Eólica de Colombia*, Bogotá, p. 12 (2017)
25. Farsite: «Weather File» . http://www.fire.org/downloads/farsite/WebHelp/referenceguide/pop_ups/pu_weather_file.htm. Accessed 26 Mar 2019
26. Farsite: «Wind File» . http://fire.org/downloads/farsite/WebHelp/referenceguide/pop_ups/pu_wind_file.htm. Accessed 26 Mar 2019
27. Farsite: «Output Tutorial», Fire.org (2019). http://fire.org/downloads/farsite/WebHelp/tutorial/tutorial11_output.htm. Accessed 30 Mar 2019

Systemic Model of the Rice Chain. Plateau of Ibagué Case

Harold Alexander Cuellar-Molina[1] ⒾⒹ, José Fidel Torres-Delgado[1] ⒾⒹ, and Nelson Javier Tovar-Perilla[2](✉) ⒾⒹ

[1] Universidad de Los Andes, Bogotá, Colombia
{ha.cuellar, ftorres}@uniandes.edu.co
[2] Facultad de Ingeniería, Universidad de Ibagué, Ibagué, Colombia
nelson.tovar@unibague.edu.co

Abstract. The rice supply chain in Colombia has low competitiveness, which happens mainly in the echelon of farmers. The problems are related to production costs, yield and paddy rice prices that impact farmers' profitability. In this work, a dynamic simulation model is proposed, which combines elements of several authors. It follows the line that worked [1], it is incorporated the inventories of each of the echelons of the supply chain proposed by [2, 3] and the formulation of pricing described by [4]; to identify the actors and relevant variables of the chain, analyze the behavior of the rice chain in different situations and propose improvements. From analysis of scenarios, it was concluded that the cultivated area and yield are the variables that allow to achieve a greater impact on the profitability of the farmer.

Keywords: Rice · Supply chain · System dynamics model

1 Introduction

The agricultural sector has a strategic importance in the process of economic and social development in Colombia [5]. However, the participation of this sector in total GDP has been decreasing from a share of close to 8% in 2000, to 6% in 2016.

It is interesting to analyze the rice chain because rice is a fundamental product for labor market in the agricultural sector. Due to the opening of the country to international markets, in the medium term the rice sector will be faced with international competition. According to this situation, it is essential to increase productivities [6].

Tolima is the second department with the largest share in harvested area and production of mechanized rice nationwide. The chain of rice - milling consists of three echelons: agricultural, industrial and marketing [7].

The area known as Plateau of Ibagué has some agronomic and climatic characteristics that gives the rice a specific quality, this allowed it to obtain the Certificate of Origin for the rice that occurs in this area. However, in this area there are several problems such as high leasing costs that affect production costs, lack of articulation in the chain and the use of certified seed, causing variations in prices and yield in the crop, and turn problems in the farmer's profitability. Because of the problems described above, the aim of this degree work is to design a simulation model for the rice chain in

© Springer Nature Switzerland AG 2019
J. C. Figueroa-García et al. (Eds.): WEA 2019, CCIS 1052, pp. 664–675, 2019.
https://doi.org/10.1007/978-3-030-31019-6_56

Plateau of Ibagué that will improve the decision-making process of the actors in the chain. This article is organized as follows: a literature review of simulation models applied to agricultural supply chains in Sect. 2. In Sect. 3, there is a description of the methodology used. In the following section we present the proposal of a model of the rice chain. The results of the research in Sect. 5. Finally, the conclusions and future work in Sects. 6 and 7 respectively.

2 Literature Review

In the improvement of the agricultural sector, different techniques have been implemented, such as system dynamics, discrete event simulation and agents-based simulation, which serve as decision support tools for different actors in the chain. In the study carried out by Meadows, a system dynamics model for "commodity" supply chains is proposed. This structure is made up of two negative feedback cycles with the presence of delays, which causes the oscillatory behavior of the chain variables [1].

Additional works that use systems dynamics with objectives and contributions such as: study the behavior of agricultural supply chains [8–13], identification of policies [14], value analysis [15, 16], costs [17], transport and storage [18, 19], and integration of decision making [20]. In the study of [2] a simulation model is proposed with a systems dynamics approach that allows exploring different improvement scenarios to increase profits in agrifood supply chains.

Studies on the rice chain have been limited. They have focused on designing policies for efficient and sustainable management, [3], investigate the willingness to buy rice [21], better understanding of the factors that affect the supply and demand [22] and analyze self-sufficiency [23].

On the other hand, simulation of discrete events was used with the purpose of modeling the behavior of food supply chains [24], study the effect of changing the quantity of the order [25], the decision making in logistics [26] and transport [27].

[28] Makes a literature review on simulation models based on agents applied in the agrifood supply chain and [29] presents a simulation of multiple agents to study the market competition.

According to the exposed thing in this section it is possible to be appreciated that the tools of dynamics of systems, the simulation of discreet events and the simulation based on agents, can approach different levels from decision. However, for the problems addressed in this paper, it is considered that agricultural supply chains are a complex system, which presents decision rules that create important feedbacks among the partners of the chain, the system dynamics is suitable for modeling the supply chains and for policy design [3, 4].

Therefore, it is proposed to design a model of the rice chain in Plateau of Ibagué, which allows to understand which are the relevant actors and variables. The main difference of this degree work regarding the literature review, is that it combines elements of several authors. It follows the line that worked [1], in addition, it incorporates the inventories of each of the echelons of the supply chain proposed by [2, 3] and finally, the formulation of pricing is taken into account described by [4].

3 Methodology

The development of the research proposal will be carried out in four stages. The first stage was a review of the simulation models used in agricultural supply chains and information gathering on the rice chain of Plateau of Ibagué and Center Zone (Tolima). In the next stage, it proceeded to determine the important variables related to the rice supply chain. The third stage consists of carrying out the process of modeling the rice supply chain, based on the models proposed by [1–4]. Finally, different scenarios were analyzed to understand the rice supply chain and determine which variables generate the greatest benefit to the actors in the chain.

4 Model of the Rice Chain

In the approach of the model of the rice chain in which the different echelons of the chain are contemplated and the relationships that exist among them, the following activities were developed [4]: problematic, information sources, relevant actors, conceptual model of rice chain, variables and assumptions.

4.1 Problematic

In the work carried out by Sarmiento, it was identified that the low competitiveness of the rice chain is found mainly in the agricultural echelon [30]. This echelon presents problems related to production costs, yield and prices of paddy rice that impact the famers' profitability [31]. In the country, there are five (5) rice areas that have different agro-ecological characteristics: Center, Llanos Orientales, Bajo Cauca, Costa Norte and Santanderes [32]. The Plateau of Ibagué belongs to the Center Zone, where several problems are presented, which are described below:

The rent is a cost that is related to paddy rice prices [33]. According to Fedearroz data, the cost of leasing represents on average 19.6% of the total cost per hectare. Additionally, in the Center zone, the cost of leasing has a positive correlation with paddy rice prices (see Fig. 1). Likewise, Tables 1 and 2 show a high presence of tenants in the rice cultivation in the center zone in 2007 and 2016, which not only affects the cost of the producers, but also hinders the adoption of technology and the increase of production efficiency in the zone [34].

Figure 1 shows the price behavior of paddy rice, where there are increases and decreases in prices, indicating an instability of the variables associated with the price, such as the area planted and the inventories [34] which is a consequence of the lack of articulation between the actors of the chain. The instability of the prices, the high cost of production and added to the variations in the yield in the crop (see Fig. 2), causes a low competitiveness of the producers that can be reflected in the performance of the producer's profitability (see Fig. 3). Both price and cost of production determine the profitability that affects the permanence of the producers in the agricultural activity [35].

Table 1. Area and production of rice mechanized by holding, first semester, Colombia, Center zone, 2007. Source: [36]

Tenure	Area (ha)	Production (t)
Owner	32.097	253.890
Lessee	37.375	292.417
Other	584	4.583
Total	70.056	550.890

Table 2. Harvested area and production of mechanized rice by holding, second semester, Colombia, Center zone, 2016. Source: [37]

Tenure	Area (ha)	Production (t)
Owner	36.428	274.834
Lessee	42.283	308.055
Other	174	1.293
Total	78.885	584.182

Fig. 1. Cost of lease and sale price of paddy rice. Constant prices: 2008. Source: [38]

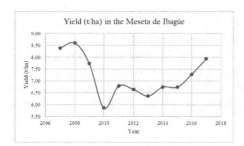

Fig. 2. Performance of the producers of the Plateau of Ibagué. Source: [39].

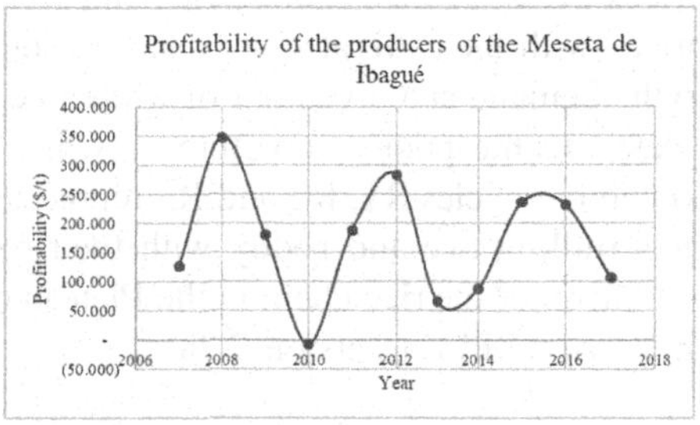

Fig. 3. Profitability of the producers of the Plateau of Ibagué. Constant prices: 2008. Source: [38–40]. Elaboration: authors.

4.2 Information Sources

To develop the research work different sources of information were used:

- Cultivated area, yield and paddy rice production in the Plateau of Ibagué, based on [39], humidity and impurities, from the study of [35] and piling index, of research carried out by Fedearroz [41, 42].
- Price of paddy rice, rice grinding, white rice, costs per hectare and consumption per capita, from the rice statistics of Fedearroz [38, 40, 43].

- To understand the dynamics of the rice chain and understand the point of view of different actors in the chain, we reviewed several studies carried out by different institutions [7, 31, 32, 34, 35, 44, 45] and follow-up to national newspapers.

4.3 Relevant Actors

To determine the relevant actors, the heuristic proposed by [46], was used, which consists of answering a set of answers, in a thorough and careful manner, that manage to guide the process of identifying the relevant actors of the problematic situation. In conclusion the relevant actors of the problem are: Government, MADR (Ministry of Agriculture and Rural Development), merchants, Induarroz, Mills, Fedearroz, producers and consumers.

4.4 Conceptual Model of Rice Chain

The model of the rice chain is made up of the echelons of farmers, milling and marketing [45], taking into account the models developed by [1–3], the conceptual model of the rice chain was proposed, presented in Fig. 4. In this model, prices, inventories of each echelon in the chain, cultivated area and demand are considered. The conceptual model consists of 7 cycles of negative feedback or balance cycle and 3 cycles of positive feedback or reinforcement cycle.

In Fig. 4 there are 4 balance cycles (B4, B5, B6 and B7, each represented by a different color). The feedback cycles B4, B5 and B6 are in charge of balancing the prices of paddy rice, milling rice and white rice respectively, due to the relationship of prices with the cultivated area and inventories. Cycle B7 relates the price of white rice to the demand and inventory of white rice. On the other hand, cycles B1, B2 and B3 are related to the pricing structure of white rice, milling rice and paddy rice. The reinforcement cycles R1, R2 and R3 represent the relationship between the prices of white rice, milling rice and paddy with their respective costs. The model diagram of levels and flows of the rice chain in the Plateau of Ibagué, presented in Fig. 5, was developed in Vensim®PLE (Version 7.2a).

4.5 Variables

According to the definition of relevant variables [46], in each echelon in the chain, quantitative variables that interact with each other through the system were defined to affect the performance variable of this degree work that is: "Farmer profitability". The main variables that are related to the chain are listed below:

- Cultivated area: number of hectares cultivated in the semester [ha] = INTEG (Rate of area planted - Rate of area harvested, 7395)
- Paddy R price: The price per ton of paddy rice [$/t] = INTEG (Paddy R price change, 850000)
- Producer cost: It is the cost per ton of paddy rice [$/t] = (Cost per hectare /Yield)
- Profitability Farmer: The profitability obtained by the farmer per ton of paddy rice [$/t] = Paddy R price - Producer cost

- Paddy R inventory: Inventory of dry paddy rice in the semester [t] = INTEG (Buy paddy rice - paddy for milling - LostPR, 25215)
- Milling R inventory: Semiannual milling rice inventory [t] = INTEG (Increase - Decrease -LostMR, 18910)
- Milling R price: It is the milling rice price [$/kg] = INTEG (Milling R price change, 1800)
- White R inventory: White rice inventory [t] = INTEG (Buy - lostWR- Sale, 18910)
- White R price: Price of white rice per kilogram [$/kg] = INTEG (White R price change, 2215)
- Population: Number of people who demand the product. Source: was determined from the cultivated area [39] and consumption per capita [43], taking into account the recommendations of experts [hab/sem] = 680000
- Demand: Tons of White Rice demanded [t/sem] = Consumption per capita * Population /Conversion Kgton.

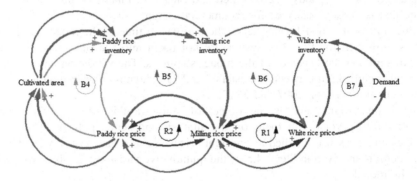

Fig. 4. Conceptual model of the rice chain in the Plateau of Ibagué. Elaboration: authors. (Color figure online)

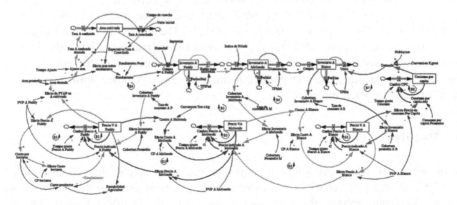

Fig. 5. Diagram of levels and flows of the rice chain in the Plateau of Ibagué. Elaboration: authors.

4.6   Assumptions

The model has the following assumptions:

- The numbers of the prices of white rice, milling, paddy and costs per hectare correspond to the center zone, since the Plateau of Ibagué belongs to the center zone, these data are of reference for the Plateau of Ibagué.
- Inventory information is difficult to access and the information available is not disaggregated. That is why it was estimated from the sources of the satellite account of the rice agroindustry, the report of "Commercial Policy for Rice" by Fedesarrollo and the sectoral numerals of the rice of MADR. Taking into account, the proportion represented by the production of the Plateau of Ibagué regarding the national production, the corresponding level of inventory that would be handled in each echelon of the chain was estimated. In addition, with this information the coverage and the rate of consumption of all the echelons were estimated.
- Paddy rice refers to rice that has a shell, milling rice corresponds to the rice that is obtained after the paddy rice is milled and bleached. Finally, white rice is milling rice that is already packaged for commercialization.
- Time unit of the model: semesters. The simulation time of the model is 32 semesters; however, the first 9 semesters are not taken into account because after the ninth semester the behavior of the model stabilizes. The validation analysis of the model is carried out between semesters 9 and 31, which is compared with respect to the behavior between 2007 and 2017.
- The main variable that is the object of study in this paper is the "Farmer Profitability", which will focus on the analysis and action policies. The data on prices and costs was handled as constant prices and as a base year it was 2008 and the definitions given in literal 4.5 of the quantitative variables are also assumptions of the model.

4.7   Validation

To validate the model, the paired t-test was carried out between the real data and the simulated data for the variables cultivated area, paddy rice price and farmer's profitability between the semesters 2007A and 2017B. The model was made in Vensim, and with Python support, 1,000 runs of the model were made and later, the RStudio software was used to perform the respective statistical analysis of the results. Additionally, with the run data, the prediction interval was calculated with a confidence level of 95% for each semester.

5   Results

In the model, scenarios that affect the farmer profitability were evaluated, the modified variables were applied as of the semester 31. The future analysis of the scenarios was made taking into account the information from semester 41 to 60, because between semester 32 and 40 it is a transition period while the model adjusts to the new conditions, after this period it stabilizes the behavior of the model.

Scenario 1, fixing paddy rice price: with this scenario a great beneficiary would be the producer, since a price setting would allow him to improve his profitability. Between semesters 41 to 60 it went from obtaining an average profitability of $165.978/t to $309.700/t, an improvement of 86.6%. However, there are other variables of interest in the chain that are affected such as the cultivated area and paddy rice inventory.

When fixing the price, it motivates the increase in the cultivated area that causes the average inventory of paddy rice to increase from 30,870 tons to 37,450 tons (representing an increase of 21,3%) between the semesters 41 to 60. A scenario that benefits the farmer but harms the next echelon (milling), because it will have an inventory of paddy rice elevated and besides a high price that affects their costs.

Scenario 2, increase crop yield: in the period analyzed (between semesters 41 to 60), despite the change in average yield, the profitability of the producer went from $165.970/t to $174.910/t, which represented an increase of 5,38%. This variation is due to the increase in yield, which generates an increase in the average levels of paddy rice inventory, since it went from 30.876 tons to 31.831 tons (increase of 3,09%), which causes the price of paddy rice decreased as it went from $881.835/t to $843.432/t (a decrease of 4,35%). All this leads to the farmer's profitability is not improved.

Scenario 3, reduce moisture and impurity in paddy rice: in the analyzed period, the variables such as the cultivated area and paddy rice inventory did not vary. The paddy rice price went from $881.835/t to $888.860/t, a small variation, however, profitability increased by 20,74%, as it went from a profit of $165.970/t to $200.398/t. Then it can be concluded that this is a scenario that benefits the farmer and also, does not generate any damage to inventories or prices.

Scenario 4, increase the consumption per capita of rice: the increase in consumption does not generate an increase in the producer's profitability, however, it has negative consequences for consumers because the price of white rice increased by 13% (between the semester 41 and 60) due to that the price went from $2.224/kg to $2.513/kg. This was caused because the levels of white rice inventory decreased by 25.9%.

Scenario 5, use variables modified in scenarios 2,3, and 4 together: the farmer's profitability between semester 41 and 60, went from $165.980/ton to $195.690/t representing an increase of 17,9%. However, in order to achieve this increase, it was necessary to make improvements in yield, and in the quality characteristics of paddy rice, additionally it was necessary to increase the cultivated area and the storage capacity of paddy rice in order to meet the increase in demand.

Scenario 6, fixing of cultivated area and increase in crop yield: between semesters 41 and 60, the average inventory of paddy rice went from 30.876 t to 29.411 t, however, the average price of paddy rice increased by 10%. As the cultivated area was controlled and the yield increased, it allowed the average profitability of the farmer to go from $165.970/t to $237.650/t (an increase of 43,2%).

Scenario 7, create paddy rice collection center and increase yield in the crop: a storage center with an average storage capacity of 50,000 t was simulated, in addition, the farmer's yield was 7,8 t/ha as of the 31st semester. In semester 41 and 60, the producer's profitability went from $165.970/t to $171.350/t, an increase of 3,24%, however, it is highlighted that the variation in profitability decreased and tends to stabilize. By controlling the production that is delivered to the milling echelon, a stabilization of the inventories is generated, which in turn allows the stabilization of the prices and the cultivated area.

5.1 Analysis of Results

With the simulation of the scenarios described above, the comparison was made to determine which scenario allows improving the variable "Farmer Profitability". In the analysis scenario 1 was not taken into account, since this scenario benefits the producers but harms the milling echelon. An ANOVA test and its respective post ANOVA analysis were performed.

Table 3 presents the mean and the standard deviation of the scenarios. Scenarios 6 and 7 present the smallest standard deviation (see Fig. 6). From the analysis, it was concluded that scenario 6 allows greater benefits to farmers.

Table 3. Mean and standard deviation of the scenarios

Scenario	Mean ($/t)	Standard deviation ($/t)
Initial	$165.978	$70.235
2	$174.910	$77.602
3	$185.578	$98.010
4	$166.017	$70.363
5	$195.688	$88.904
6	$237.650	$23.698
7	$178.643	$10.611

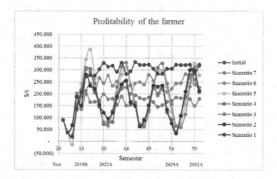

Fig. 6. Farmer's profitability in each scenario. Elaboration: authors.

6 Conclusions

The systemic approach in which the problem was addressed allowed the identification of the main actors in the rice supply chain. With the help of the conceptual model of the productive chain it was possible to identify the feedback cycles of the variables.

Based on the simulation model, different scenarios were presented that show which variables will improve the farmer's profitability. From the comparison of the scenarios, it was possible to identify that the best scenario is the control of the cultivated area and an increase in crop yield (scenario 6), since it allows the farmer's profitability to increase by 43.2%.

The scenarios of control of the cultivated area (scenario 6) and the creation of collection centers (scenario 7), are the scenarios that allow to stabilize the producer's profitability, under normal conditions the deviation equals $70,235/t a difference from the scenarios 6 and 7 that generate a deviation of profitability of $23,700/t and $10,611/t respectively; However, the scenario of control of the cultivated area generates better results in the variable farmer's profitability. Scenario 6 generates a 43.2% increase in profitability while scenario 7 generates an increase of 3.24%.

From the variables analyzed in the scenarios, it can be seen that the cultivated area and yield are the variables that allow a greater impact on the farmer's profitability. Because the cultivated area and the yield affect the inventories, which in turn affects the prices and finally, the profitability is affected.

7   Future Work

As future work the following researches can be carried out:

Elaborate an interface that facilitates the use of the model, to the actors of the rice supply chain.

Propose a model that allows to build cooperation between the different echelons in the chain, since at present, it can be seen that in the rice production chain, there is confrontation among producers, industrialists, traders and the government, which causes the planning problem that occurs in the rice chain.

Analyze the rice supply chain taking into account variables related to climate change, in order to propose measures for farmers to face this problem.

Study how the economic opening of the country, such as import and export, affects the behavior of the rice chain.

Model the rice supply chain, which allows analyzing the influence of technology on the efficiency of the chain.

References

1. Meadows, D.L.: The dynamics of commodity production cycles (1969)
2. Tovar Perilla, N.J., Torres Delgado, J.F., Ignacio Gómez, M.: Diseño de un modelo para la intervención logística de cadenas de suministro agroalimentarias (2018)
3. Bala, B.K., Bhuiyan, M.G.K., Alam, M.M., Mohamed Arshad, F., Sidique, S.F., Alias, E.F.: Modelling of supply chain of rice in Bangladesh. Int. J. Syst. Sci. Oper. Logist. **2674**, 1–17 (2016)
4. Sterman, J.D.: Business Dynamics: Systems Thinking and Modeling for a Complex World. McGraw-Hill, London (2000)
5. Consejo Privado de Competitividad: Informe Nacional de Competitividad 2008–2009. Bogotá (2008)

6. FINAGRO: Perspectiva del sector agropecuario Colombiano., Bogotá (2014)
7. Tovar Perilla, N.J., Bermeo Andrade, H.P., Torres Delgado, J.F., García León, A.A., Linares Vanegas, A.I.: El potencial logístico en las agrocadenas del Tolima (2011)
8. Minegishi, S., Thiel, D.: System dynamics modeling and simulation of a particular food supply chain. Simul. Pract. Theory. **8**, 321–339 (2000)
9. Kumar, S., Nigmatullin, A.: A system dynamics analysis of food supply chains - case study with non-perishable products. Simul. Model. Pract. Theory **19**, 2151–2168 (2011). https://doi.org/10.1016/j.simpat.2011.06.006
10. Teimoury, E., Nedaei, H., Ansari, S., Sabbaghi, M.: A multi-objective analysis for import quota policy making in a perishable fruit and vegetable supply chain: a system dynamics approach. Comput. Electron. Agric. **93**, 37–45 (2013)
11. Arshad, F.M., Bala, B.K., Alias, E.F., Abdulla, I.: Modelling boom and bust of cocoa production systems in Malaysia. Ecol. Modell. **309–310**, 22–32 (2015)
12. Orjuela Castro, J.A., Adarmes Jaimes, W.: Dynamic impact of the structure of the supply chain of perishable foods on logistics performance and food security. J. Ind. Eng. Manag. **10**, 687–710 (2017)
13. Tsaples, G., Tarnanidis, T.: A system dynamics model and interface for the simulation and analysis of milk supply chains. In: Driving Agribusiness With Technology Innovations, pp. 311–335 (2017)
14. Georgiadis, P., Vlachos, D., Iakovou, E.: A system dynamics modeling framework for the strategic supply chain management of food chains. J. Food Eng. **70**, 351–364 (2005)
15. Atamer Balkan, B., Meral, S.: Olive oil industry dynamics : the case of Turkey. In: Proceeding of the 35th International Conference of the System Dynamics Society, pp. 1–26. Cambridge (2017)
16. Schepers, H., Van Kooten, O.: Profitability of 'ready-to-eat' strategies: towards model assisted negotiation in a fresh-produce chain. In: Quantifying the Agri-Food supply Chain, pp. 117–132 (2006)
17. Sachan, A., Sahay, B.S., Sharma, D.: Developing Indian grain supply chain cost model: a system dynamics approach. Int. J. Product. Perform. Manag. **54**, 187–205 (2005)
18. Orjuela-castro, J.A., Sepulveda-Garcia, D.A., Ospina-Contreras, I.D.: Effects of using multimodal transport over the logistics performance of the food chain of Uchuva. In: Third Workshop on Engineering Applications, WEA 2016, pp. 165–177 (2016)
19. Figueroa-García, J.C., Diaz Gamez, G.L., Bernal Celemín, M.P.: Applied computer sciences in engineering: 4th workshop on engineering applications, WEA 2017 Cartagena, Colombia, 27–29 September 2017 proceedings. In: 4th Workshop on Engineering Applications, WEA 2017. pp. 225–237 (2017)
20. Piewthongngam, K., Vijitnopparat, P., Pathumnakul, S., Chumpatong, S., Duangjinda, M.: System dynamics modelling of an integrated pig production supply chain. Biosyst. Eng. **127**, 24–40 (2014)
21. Hu, S., Wu, H., Cai, Y.: Prediction and Simulation on the Consumers Purchase Intention of Rice based on System Dynamics Modeling. Rev. Ibérica Sist. e Tecnol. Informação. **E5**, 136–145 (2016)
22. Rahim, F.H.A., Hawari, N.N., Abidin, N.Z.: Supply and Demand of Rice in Malaysia : a system dynamics approach. Int. J. Supply Chain Manag. **6**, 234–240 (2017)
23. Sulistyo, S.R., Alfa, B.N., Subagyo, S.: Modeling Indonesia's rice supply and demand using system dynamics. In: 2016 International Conference on Industrial Engineering and Engineering Management, IEEM 2016, 04–07 December 2016, pp. 415–419 (2016)
24. Van Der Vorst, J.G.A.J., Beulens, A.J.M., Van Beek, P.: Modelling and simulating multi-echelon food systems. Eur. J. Oper. Res. **122**, 354–366 (2000)

25. Galal, N.M., El-Kilany, K.S.: Sustainable agri-food supply chain with uncertain demand and lead time. Int. J. Simul. Model. **15**, 485–496 (2016)
26. Tako, A.A., Robinson, S.: The application of discrete event simulation and system dynamics in the logistics and supply chain context. Decis. Support Syst. **52**, 802–815 (2012)
27. Borodin, V., Hnaien, F., Labadie, N.: A discrete event simulation model for harvest operations under stochastic conditions. In: 10th IEEE International Conference on Networking, Sensing and Control (ICNSC), pp. 708–713. Francia (2013)
28. Sarwo, D., Stephan, B., Eldridge, S.: Applications of agent-based modelling and simulation in the agri-food supply chains. Eur. J. Oper. Res. **269**, 1–12 (2017)
29. Mejía, G., García-Díaz, C.: Market-level effects of firm-level adaptation and intermediation in networked markets of fresh foods : a case study in Colombia. Agric. Syst. **160**, 132–142 (2017)
30. Sarmiento Hernández, G.E.: Lineamientos para el diseño políticas públicas para mejorar la competitividad de los productores de arroz de la zona centro de Colombia (2016)
31. Chica, L.J., Tirado, O.Y.C., Barreto, O.J.M.: Indicadores de competitividad del cultivo del arroz en Colombia y Estados Unidos. Rev. Ciencias Agrícolas. **33**, 16–31 (2016)
32. Fedearroz: IV Censo Nacional Arrocero 2016., Bogotá D.C (2017)
33. Centro de Productividad del Tolima: Convenio regional para la competitividad de la cadena arroz - molineria del Tolima (zona arrocera centro) (2000)
34. Fedearroz: Dinámica del sector arrocero de los Llanos Orientales de Colombia, 1999–2011. Bogotá D.C (2011)
35. Espinal, G.C.F., Martínez Covaleda, H.J., Acevedo Gaitán, X.: La cadena del arroz en Colombia: Una mirada de su estructura y dinámica 1991–2005 (2005)
36. Fedearroz: III Censo Nacional Arrocero - Zona Centro., Bogotá D.C (2008)
37. Fedearroz: IV Censo Nacional Arrocero 2016 - Zona Centro., Bogotá D.C (2017)
38. Fedearroz: Serie Históricas – Precios. http://www.fedearroz.com.co/new/precios.php
39. Agronet: Estadísticas Agrícolas - Área, producción, rendimiento y participación. http://www.agronet.gov.co/estadistica/Paginas/default.aspx
40. Fedearroz: Series Históricas – Costos. http://www.fedearroz.com.co/new/costos.php
41. Preciado Pérez, L.G.: Época oportuna de cosecha y calibración de cosechadoras para el cultivo del arroz. In: Curso internacional sobre el manejo del cultivo de arroz., Ibagué (2014)
42. Salamanca Grosso, G., Osorio Tangarife, M.P., Alvarez Laverde, H.R., Rodriguez Barragán, O.A.: Valoración de los indices de pilada de algunas variedades de arroz colombiano. Fac. Ciencias Dep. Química. Univ. del Tolima. 2–5 (2007)
43. Fedearroz: Series Históricas – Consumo. http://www.fedearroz.com.co/new/consumo.php
44. Centro de Productividad del Tolima: Convenio Regional para la competitividad de la Cadena del Arroz - Molineria del Tolima (Zona Arrocera Centro). Papel House Group, Ibagué (2000)
45. Linares Vanegas, A.I.: Caracterización de la red logística de las cadenas productivas del Tolima., Ibagué (2009)
46. Aldana Valdés, E., Reyes Alvarado, A.: Disolver Problemas: Criterio para Formular Proyectos Sociales. Universidad de los Andes (Colombia). Facultad de Ingeniería. Departamento de Ingeniería Industrial, Bogotá D.C (2004)

Using Text Mining Tools to Define Trends in Territorial Competitiveness Indicators

David Ovallos-Gazabon[1]([✉]), Nataly Puello-Pereira[2],
Farid Meléndez-Pertuz[2], Jaime Vélez-Zapata[2],
Emiro De-La-Hoz-Franco[2], Joaquín F. Sanchez[3], Claudia Caro-Ruiz[3],
César A. Cárdenas[3], and Carlos Collazos-Morales[3]

[1] Vicerrectoría de Investigaciones, Universidad Simón Bolivar,
Barranquilla, Colombia
david.ovallos@unisimonbolivar.edu.co
[2] Departamento de Ciencias de la Computación y Electrónica,
Universidad de la Costa, Barranquilla, Colombia
[3] Vicerrectoría de Investigaciones, Universidad Manuela Beltrán,
Bogotá, Colombia

Abstract. For this study, articles from the fields of Social Sciences; Economics; Econometrics and Finance; Business and Management; and Accounting have been monitored for the period from 1979 to 2019. VOSviewer® was used to create, visualize and explore bibliometric information from Scopus scientific database, for the identification of trends about indicators that have not been frequently considered, compared to competitiveness regional indexes territorial competitiveness indicators. It has generated preliminary conclusions using citation relationships between journals, collaborative relationships between researchers, and coexistence relationships between scientific terms from the identified target literature. The identified trends are related to Renewable energy, Sustainability, Higher Education, Destination Competitiveness, Knowledge Management, Cross Borders Regions and Small and Medium-sized Entrepreneurship.

Keywords: Text mining · Vosviewer · Competitiveness measurement ·
Indicator · Territorial

1 Introduction

The functionality of text mining tools provides support for creating term maps based on a corpus of documents. A term map is a two-dimensional map in which terms are located in such a way that the distance between two terms can be interpreted as an indication of the relatedness of those terms. In general, the smaller the distance between two terms, the stronger the terms are related to each other. The relatedness of terms is determined based on co-occurrences in documents. These documents can be for instance scientific publications (either titles and abstracts or full texts), patents, or newspaper articles [1].

© Springer Nature Switzerland AG 2019
J. C. Figueroa-García et al. (Eds.): WEA 2019, CCIS 1052, pp. 676–685, 2019.
https://doi.org/10.1007/978-3-030-31019-6_57

Territorial competitiveness is defined on the types of legitimate spatial delimitations established by the current society, and their convergence in the global space, influencing the strategic positioning of their economies through the use of capital, territorial resources, and institutional agents [2, 3]. In addition, it seeks to increasingly integrate all activity sectors promoting a global coherence with the cooperation of all territories, and articulating policies oriented to the social, productive and economic growth in each territorial space [4, 5].

Measures of territorial competitiveness are relevant tools for identifying and analysing current problems, establishing effective strategies for territorial improvement and life quality population [6–8]. However, there is no a consensus about which indicators should be used for this purpose, on account of the diversity of existing models and of the analysis context that may be country, regional, urban centres and rural areas.

The main indicators of territorial competitiveness develop the quantification of current economic, political and social conditions [9]. A literature review indicates that the smaller the territory, more specific are its measurements towards the sectors of the territory that have lower levels of competitiveness. It is found measurement levels of global, macro, meso, national and rural type [3, 10–13].

Using VOSviewer® [14–17], it is an initial exercise to identify territorial competitiveness indicators that can be implemented in the municipal context, and that are aligned to indicators systems currently used in the Colombian context in order to strengthen its policies of technological innovation, and productive growth, envisaging to be more internationally competitive [18–22].

2 Methodology

In this study, the worldwide scientific production about territorial competitiveness indicators is analysed using the information from 5233 articles identified in SCOPUS, built on the period from 1979 to 2019. The methodology pretends to identify certain trends in scientific production worldwide on the subject analysed; and from there, selecting recent or novel indicators that have not been frequently considered. Besides, it is important to define authors, institutions, journals and networks in order to ameliorate the analysis. The methodology of this work demands to minimize possible biases of the observer in the systematic review of literature on territorial competitiveness, and it consists of four phases. Definition of guiding questions, Search in specialized databases, Download of bibliographic records and Consolidation and analysis of the information.

2.1 Definition of Guiding Questions

The guiding questions have been defined as: What is territorial competitiveness? What are the main models and indicators for measuring competitiveness at the territorial level? Who are the most important authors, institutions and countries in the field? From these questions the search equation was developed and defined as:

TITLE-ABS-KEY (territorial AND competitiveness) AND (LIMIT-TO (SUB-JAREA, "SOCI") OR LIMIT-TO (SUBJAREA, "ECON") OR LIMIT-TO (SUB-JAREA, "BUSI") OR LIMIT-TO (SUBJAREA, "ENGI") OR LIMIT-TO (SUBJAREA, "MATH")).

2.2   Search in Specialized Databases

SCOPUS database was selected and the exploration generated 5233 records. SCOPUS compile results from other bibliographic databases and independent scientific publications.

2.3   Download of Bibliographic Records

once the records were identified, they were downloaded using the tools offers by SCOPUS. For this stage, the CSV format was used which facilitates its subsequent processing using EXCEL® 2016.

2.4   Consolidation and Analysis of the Information

It was used tools as dynamic tables and macros in EXCEL® 2016. It were created different tables and queries as Author vs Author, Country vs Country, Institutions vs Institutions, journals vs journals, and Keywords vs Keywords, among others. This process generates the input for the graphics elaboration in VOSviewer®.

3   Results

3.1   Countries Relationship

Three clusters were identified related to the origin of the publications country: Cluster number one, identified with blue colour, has as core in England with roughly 1100 publications and the largest number of interactions, this is because some of the major journals and publishing companies related to this topic are based in the UK (Emerald Group Publishing, Blackwell Publishing Inc., Oxford University Press, SAGE Publications, among others). It is interesting to observe that main relationships in this cluster are between European countries, without implying a disconnection with other countries. See Fig. 1.

The cluster number two, identified with red colour, has the United States as the country with the highest number of interactions along with Germany, China and the Netherlands; these countries are the location of some of the biggest publishing companies in the world (Taylor & Francis, Elsevier, Blackwell Publishing Inc., Springer, Routledge, among others). Cluster number three, underlined in blue colour, is mainly the group of countries with Latin languages which evidences the tendency to send works to publishing houses in the origin language (OmniaScience, Universia Holding, among others), but also includes countries like Egypt, Israel and Turkey.

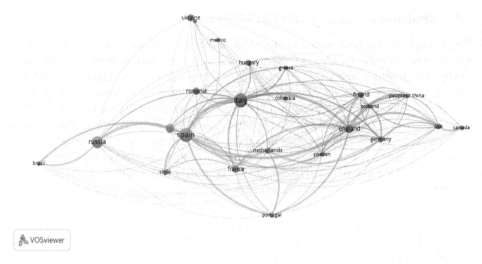

Fig. 1. Countries relationship (Color figure online)

3.2 Authors Relationship

This visualization permits to identify the relationships between authors. Results are presented with authors with at least three works in conjunction with other authors from the list obtained. Besides, it is identified two clusters. On the whole, a high prevalence of Europeans authors is evidenced, being Camagni, European Commission and OECD who develop more interaction or collaborations. An element to emphasize is that these authors are not in the group of authors or works most cited, according to the information identified in Scopus. See Fig. 2.

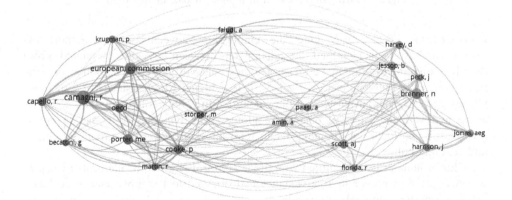

Fig. 2. Relations between authors (Color figure online)

3.3   Relationship Among Institution

The liaison among institutions in the study topic it is shown in Fig. 3. The cluster number one, in red colour, shows important levels of cooperation among universities in European Countries like Italy (Polytechnic of Milan) and Spain (University of Vigo, Universidad Autonoma de Madrid). The cluster number two, identified with green colour is composed mainly by North American universities (Harvard University, UCL and Oregon University). Cluster tree in blue colour, groups universities from Italy as Università degli Studi di Messina, università roma Sapienza and Università Catania. Finally, the four cluster in yellow colour group institutions as University of the Basque Country and Deusto University in Spain, and Pontificia Universidad Catolica de Chile. See Fig. 3.

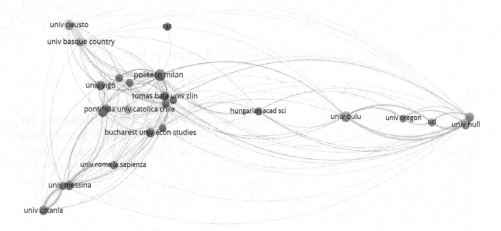

Fig. 3. Relationship between institutions (Color figure online)

Co-occurrence of Keywords: Once the relationship between countries, authors and institutions have been identified, the relationship between keywords is studied. From this, it is identified the thematic areas or topics that will guide the definition of territorial competitiveness indicators. Besides, it is evidenced the existence of four inter-related clusters. The cluster number one, identified in yellow colour, contains elements associated with the effect of business agglomeration dynamics on competitiveness, positioning and local development. Other relevant elements in this group are cluster and regional policy. See Fig. 4.

Cluster number two, identified with green colour, is formed by elements related to the generation of competitive advantages and oriented to the urban and rural development through regional innovation systems and industrial districts. The cluster

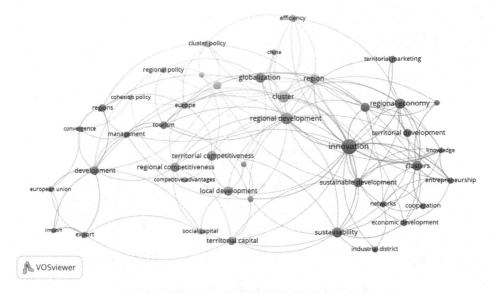

Fig. 4. Result for co-occurrence of keywords (Color figure online)

number three, identified with blue colour, is mainly related to aspects of context analysis for competitiveness. The cluster number four, identified with red, refers to elements or strategies of innovation and territorial specialization such as the development of a business environment, business empowerment, development of specialized production systems that are constituted in points of competitiveness and especially, the development of regional policies for the capacity improvement of human capital.

3.4 Emerging Areas for the Definition of Regional Competitiveness Indicators

An analysis of the terms found allows identifying emerging trends or concepts in the literature on territorial competitiveness. The existing models do not have a theoretical approach such as resources based view (RBV); moreover, not all models consider the firm performance as an element of analysis. Elements related to renewable energy, sustainability and energy are not common in the literature on territorial competitiveness. The exercise also evidenced the important role that has been taken in the analysis, the higher education to overcome barriers and build up a destination competitiveness to generate welfare. Other emerging terms are related to the role of tourism, the generation of efficient markets, the knowledge management, cross borders regions, and crisis. See Fig. 5.

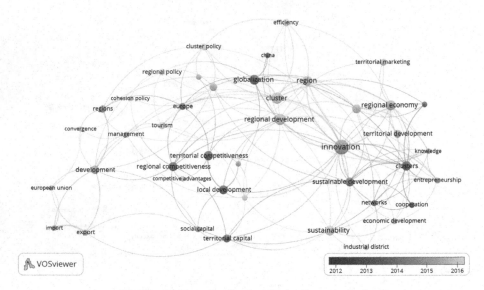

Fig. 5. Overlay visualization (Color figure online)

From the Overlay Visualization, it is possible to identify current theoretical elements in the literature, and that according to the preliminary review, they have not been used in models of competitiveness measurement such as [3, 8, 11–13, 25, 29, 42]. The Table 1 gives a summary of topics recognized.

Table 1. Topics identified for construction of competitiveness indicators.

Topic	References
Renewable energy	[23–26]
Sustainability	[27–29]
Higher Education	[30–35]
Barriers	[36, 37]
Destination competitiveness	[28, 38, 39]
Knowledge management	[40]
Cross borders regions	[41]
Crisis	[42–45]
Driven forces	[46–48]
Small and medium-sized entrepreneurship	[49, 50]

4   Conclusion

The use of text mining tools has proved to be a very useful technique in the identification of territorial competitiveness indicators. It was possible to recognize elements that have not been considered by other measurement models; thus, it is considered an important contribution in the development of indicators and instruments for the measurement of territorial competitiveness. Some of the main findings are related to resources based view (RBV) and the firm performance approach, as well as, to elements associated with renewable energy and sustainability.

Each element could be considerate as a starting point for a new research in order to generate all necessary information to develop indicators of competitiveness in the territorial context. Competitiveness measure is an important tool that can determine those factors that influence in the growth of an economy in order to expand the opportunities for its populations; and in the Colombian context, it permit to strength its policies of technological innovation and productive growth.

References

1. van Eck, N.J., Waltman, L.: Text mining and visualization using VOSviewer. ISSI Newsl. **7**(3), 50–54 (2011)
2. Fajnzylber, F.: Competitividad internacional: evolución y lecciones. Rev. la CEPAL (1988)
3. Porter, M.E.: The Competitive Advantage of Nations. Harvard Business Review, Boston (1990)
4. Smith, A.: The Wealth of Nations. W. Strahan T. Cadell, London (1776)
5. Chorianopoulos, I., Pagonis, T., Koukoulas, S., Drymoniti, S.: Planning, competitiveness and sprawl in the Mediterranean city: the case of Athens. Cities **27**(4), 249–259 (2010)
6. Fagerberg, J.: International Competitiveness. Econ. J. **98**(391), 355–374 (2009)
7. Scott, A.J.: Global City Regions: Trends, Theory, Policy. Oxford University Press (2001)
8. Mortimore, M., Bonifaz, J.L., de Oliveira, J.L.D.: La Competitividad Internacional: Un Canálisis De Las Experiencias De Asia En Desarrollo Y América Latina (1998)
9. De Guzmán, M., Pantoja, K.R.: Indicadores de competitividad. Proyecto Andino de Competitividad (2001)
10. Lombana, J., Rozas Gutiérrez, S.: Marco analítico de la competitividad: Fundamentos para el estudio de la competitividad regional. Pensam. y Gestión **26**, 1–38 (2009)
11. World Economic Forum. The global competitiveness report 2015–2016, vol. 5, no. 5 (2015)
12. Lall, S.: Competitiveness indices and developing countries: an economic evaluation of the global competitiveness report. World Dev. **29**(9), 1501–1525 (2001)
13. Araoz, M., Carrillo, C., van Gihhoven, S.: Indicadores de competitividad para los países andinos (2011)
14. van Eck, N.J., Waltman, L.: Measuring Scholarly Impact, no. 1982 (2014)
15. Jeong, D., Koo, Y.: Analysis of trend and convergence for science and technology using the VOSviewer. Int. J. Contents **12**(3), 54–58 (2016)
16. Van Eck, N.J., Waltman, L.: Software survey: VOSviewer, a computer program for bibliometric mapping. Scientometrics **84**(2), 523–538 (2010)
17. Zahedi, Z., Van Eck, N.J.: Visualizing readership activity of Mendeley users using VOSviewer. In: altmetrics14: Expanding impacts and metrics, Workshop at Web Science - Conference, pp. 23–26 (2014)
18. Barrios Vásquez, J., Angulo-Cuentas, G.: Prioritizing STI initiatives: towards a methodological framework. In: IAMOT 2016 - 25th International Association for Management of Technology Conference, Proceedings: Technology - Future Thinking (2016)
19. Schwab, K., et al.: The Global Competitiveness Report (2014)

20. Velasques, M.I.: Comision economica para america latina y el caribe., and Departamento administrativo nacional de Estadistica. Indicadores de competitividad y productividad para america latina y el caribe. p. 43 (1995)
21. Consejo Privado de Competitividad. Informe nacional de competitividad 2015–2016, p. 271 (2015)
22. Consejo Privado de Competitividad., Centro de pensamiento de Estrategias Competitivas., and Universidsad Del Rosario., Indice Departamental De competitividad 2015 (2015)
23. Roh, S., Kim, D.: Evaluation of perceptions on economic feasibility of energy sources. Energy Sources Part B Econ. Plan. Policy 12, 1–4 (2017)
24. Mezősi, A., Kácsor, E., Beöthy, Á., Törőcsik, Á., Szabó, L.: Modelling support policies and renewable energy sources deployment in the Hungarian district heating sector. Energy Environ. 28(1–2), 70–87 (2017)
25. Ligus, M.: An analysis of competitiveness and potential of renewable energy technologies in Poland. Energy Environ. 26(8), 1247–1269 (2015)
26. Caspary, G.: Gauging the future competitiveness of renewable energy in Colombia. Energy Econ. 31(3), 443–449 (2009)
27. Tan, Y., Ochoa, J.J., Langston, C., Shen, L.: An empirical study on the relationship between sustainability performance and business competitiveness of international construction contractors. J. Clean. Prod. 93, 273–278 (2015)
28. Cucculelli, M., Goffi, G.: Does sustainability enhance tourism destination competitiveness? Evidence from Italian Destinations of Excellence. J. Clean. Prod. 111, 370–382 (2016)
29. Monfaredzadeh, T., Berardi, U.: Beneath the smart city: dichotomy between sustainability and competitiveness. Int. J. Sustain. Build. Technol. Urban Dev. 6(3), 140–156 (2015)
30. Stonkiene, M., Matkeviciene, R., Vaiginiene, E.: Evaluation of the national higher education system's competitiveness: Theoretical model. Compet. Rev. 26(2), 116–131 (2016)
31. Lopez-Leyva, S., Rhoades, G.: Country competitiveness relationship with higher education indicators. J. Technol. Manag. Innov. 11(4), 47–55 (2016)
32. Aleksejeva, L.: Country's competitiveness and sustainability: higher education impact. J. Secur. Sustain. Issues 5(3), 355–363 (2016)
33. Svobodova, L.: Technological readiness and higher education in the Czech Republic. In: IEEE Global Engineering Education Conference, EDUCON 2016, 10–13 April 2016, pp. 874–882 (2016)
34. Ovallos-Gazabon, D.A., De La Hoz-Escorcia, S.M., Maldonado-Perez, D.J.: Creatividad, innovación y emprendimiento en la formación de ingenieros en Colombia. Un estudio prospectivo. Rev. Educ. en Ing. 10(19), 90–104 (2015)
35. Ovallos Gazabón, D., Villalobos Toro, B., De La Hoz Escorcia, S., Maldonado Perez, D.: Gamification for innovation management at organizational level. A state of the art review. Espacios 37(8), 2 (2016)
36. Kreneva, S.G., Halturina, E.N., Nurmuhametov, I.M., Bakhtina, T.B.: Forming estimation cluster structures from the point of view of competitiveness of potential of Republic Mary El with the influence of economic sanctions of the West. Mediterr. J. Soc. Sci. 6(3), 245–252 (2015)
37. 16th International Multidisciplinary Scientific GeoConference, SGEM 2016. In: International Multidisciplinary Scientific GeoConference Surveying Geology and Mining Ecology Management, SGEM 2016, vol. 3, pp. 1–1100 (2016). https://www.sgem.org/sgemlib/spip.php?rubrique276
38. Cánovas, E.R., Castiñeira, C.B.: The role of the cultural heritage in the renovation of coastal tourism areas: the case study of the Costa Blanca tourism destination. Cuadernos Geograficos, vol. 55, no. 2. Instituto Universitario de Investigaciones Turísticas, Universidad de Alicante, Spain, pp. 299–319 (2016)

39. Silvestrelli, P.: Tourism development through heritage enhancement and hospitality innovation. Int. J. Glob. Small Bus. 5(1–2), 20–33 (2013)
40. Rhéaume, L., Gardoni, M.: Strategy-making for innovation management and the development of corporate universities. Int. J. Interact. Des. Manuf. 10(1), 73–84 (2015)
41. Rutherford, T.D., Holmes, J.: (Small) Differences that (Still) Matter? Cross-border regions and work place governance in the southern Ontario and US Great Lakes automotive industry. Reg. Stud. 47(1), 116–127 (2013)
42. Capello, R., Caragliu, A., Fratesi, U.: Modeling regional growth between competitiveness and austerity measures: the MASST3 model. Int. Reg. Sci. Rev. 40(1), 38–74 (2017)
43. Camagni, R., Capello, R.: Rationale and design of EU cohesion policies in a period of crisis. Reg. Sci. Policy Pract. 7(1), 25–47 (2015)
44. Sebastián, M.C., García, A.M.M., López, F.G.: Europe 2020 Strategy and the Information society as tools of cohesion and integration in time of crisis: Utopia or reality? Investig. Bibl. 28(64), 101–115 (2014)
45. De Rosa, S., Salvati, L.: Beyond a 'side street story'? Naples from spontaneous centrality to entropic polycentricism, towards a 'crisis city'. Cities 51, 74–83 (2016)
46. Camisón, C., Forés, B.: Is tourism firm competitiveness driven by different internal or external specific factors?: New empirical evidence from Spain. Tour. Manag. 48, 477–499 (2015)
47. Thomé, K.M., Medeiros, J.J.: Drivers of successful international business strategy: insights from the evolution of a trading company. Int. J. Emerg. Mark. 11(1), 89–110 (2016)
48. Builes, P.: Tendencias tecnológicas que influyen en el aumento de la productividad empresarial. INGE CUC 11(2), 84–96 (2015)
49. Arend, R.J.: Entrepreneurship and dynamic capabilities: how firm age and size affect the 'capability enhancement-SME performance' relationship. Small Bus. Econ. 42(1), 33–57 (2014)
50. Ericson, J.H., Wenngren, J., Kaartinen, H., Solvang, W.D.: SMEs' challenges and needs in relation to innovation agendas and strategies. In: 2016 International Symposium on Small-Scale Intelligent Manufacturing Systems, SIMS 2016, pp. 13–17 (2016)

Interval Simulator of the Glucose-Insulin System

Maira García-Jaramillo[1]([✉]) [iD], Fabian León-Vargas[2][iD], Nicolás Rosales[3][iD], Andrés Molano[2][iD], and Fabricio Garelli[3][iD]

[1] Facultad de Ingeniería, Universidad EAN, Bogotá, Colombia
magarcia@universidadean.edu.co
[2] Facultad de Ing. Mecánica, Electrónica y Biomédica, Universidad Antonio Nariño,
Bogotá, Colombia
{fabianleon,andres.molano}@uan.edu.co
[3] Facultad de Ingeniería, Instituto LEICI (UNLP-CONICET),
Universidad Nacional de La Plata, La Plata, Argentina
{nicolas.rosales,fabricio}@ing.unlp.edu.ar

Abstract. In this paper, an interval simulator that considers different sources of uncertainty to estimate the blood glucose level of type 1 diabetes patients is presented. In particular, this study examines a model that includes the dynamics from the insulin delivery input to the subcutaneous-glucose concentration output, and a model that estimates the insulin-on-board considering uncertainty. Each model is studied using modal interval analysis to achieve an optimal computation. The simulator includes several interval models that can be combined with each other in order to expand possibilities in the design and assessment of the glucose regulation algorithms and insulin therapies for diabetes patients. The main features of the interval simulator are shown in this work.

Keywords: Interval simulation · Glucose-insulin system · Diabetes · Insulin-on-board · Uncertainty

1 Introduction

Diabetes mellitus (DM) is a metabolic disease characterized by elevated plasma glucose levels (hyperglycemia), which can lead to long-term micro- or macrovascular complications. Because of these complications, diabetes is one of the most common causes of death in most countries. In the last study of 221 countries and territories, the International Diabetes Federation concluded that close to four million deaths in the age group ranging from 20 to 79 years of age could be attributed to diabetes in 2017. The same study shows that the number of people with diabetes worldwide will increase from 425 million in 2017 to 628.6 million in 2045 [1].

There are two types of diabetes: (a) type 2 diabetes (T2D), which involves a reduction in the efficiency of insulin for promoting the transport of plasma glucose into the cells due to a resistance to insulin, resulting in the eventual

© Springer Nature Switzerland AG 2019
J. C. Figueroa-García et al. (Eds.): WEA 2019, CCIS 1052, pp. 686–695, 2019.
https://doi.org/10.1007/978-3-030-31019-6_58

loss of insulin production and (b) type 1 diabetes (T1D), in which the insulin-producing cells of the pancreas are destroyed, ultimately leading to a total loss of insulin production; therefore, exogenous insulin administration is required in order to replace its physiological secretion.

For this purpose, different insulin dosage regimens, such as the multiple daily injection (MDI) therapy or the continuous subcutaneous insulin infusion (CSII) therapy through an external pump are used. However, these insulin therapies can produce hypoglycemia (low glucose levels) events and the associated clinical complications.

In order to avoid the risks that are related to the therapies required by the patients, different rules and tools to calculate the insulin dose have been developed. In recent years, the development of the artificial pancreas (AP) has addressed most of the challenges related to the patients' insulin therapy. Such development is based on a closed-loop control scheme that involves a continuous glucose monitoring system (CGMS) and an insulin pump.

One of the most relevant contributions leading to several AP developments around the world has been the simulator created by the University of Virginia (UVa) and, approved by the Food and Drug Administration (FDA), which is considered as the pre-clinical test phase for glucose regulation algorithms [2]. The UVa simulator provides a set of virtual subjects based on real individual data, a simulated sensor that replicates typical errors in continuous glucose monitoring, and a simulated insulin pump. The UVa simulator is a substitute for animal trials in the preclinical testing of closed-loop control strategies. However, carbohydrate counting, capillary glucose measurements, CGMS accuracy, inter-patient and intra-patient variability and other sources of uncertainty are not considered in this simulator nor in other simulators with similar purposes. These simulators incorporate one model for each subsystem integrating the glucose-insulin system, which can be seen as a limiting condition for the design of control systems or identification purposes. A comparison of the main diabetes simulations tools, including the UVa simulator, was presented by Colmegna [3].

This work presents a simulator that allows considering multi-factor uncertainty in parameters, initial conditions, and inputs of several glucose-insulin dynamic models. This simulator uses the Modal Interval Analysis (MIA) [4] method in order to generate the interval version of glucose-insulin models most used in a pre-clinical test phase. Each interval model provides an envelope that includes all possible model responses. New models, used for designing and testing closed-loop control algorithms, were integrated to this simulator as interval versions, in order to support novel AP control systems.

2 Methodology

Diabetes simulators are used to improve clinical designs and the performance of control algorithms prior to application. A diabetes simulation tool requires a mathematical model to predict the dynamics of the glucose-insulin system. Different mathematical models for glucose regulation systems have been proposed over the past 50 years [5]; most of them used for glucose prediction in decision-aid systems for the optimization of insulin therapies and glucose control strategies for T1D patients. In general, each model is composed of different subsystems describing processes whose final interaction allows obtaining an estimate of the glucose-insulin dynamics. They are grouped as the glucose subsystem, the insulin subsystem, and the insulin action subsystem [2,6]. Several models of the glucose-insulin dynamics used for glucose prediction were studied in [7], to include different sources of uncertainty and intra-patient variability. As a result, interval model versions from different authors' subsystems were developed: three insulin action and glucose kinetics models, two subcutaneous insulin absorption models, and two gastric emptying, digestion, and absorption models. A preliminary version of the interval simulator that includes some of these models was presented in [8].

The scheme of the interval simulator that is proposed here, is showed in Fig. 1.

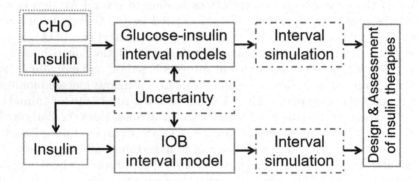

Fig. 1. Interval simulator scheme. Uncertainty may affect several components related to glucose-insulin dynamics, for example, insulin and carbohydrates (CHO) inputs, parameters of the glucose-insulin models, and the insulin-on-board (IOB) estimation.

In this scheme, uncertainty is represented by interval models whose parameters, inputs, and/or initial states can take interval values. In order to yield an exact computation of the range, each model included here was automatically analyzed and put in its optimal form using MIA [4]. MIA is used to reduce the impact of multiple instances of the same variable in the expression to be evaluated, avoiding overestimation.

Here, two additional models to the ones presented in previous works [4,7, 8] have been studied in order to achieve an optimal computation, where the corresponding interval model is evaluated using MIA to avoid multi-incident variables, i.e. multiple instances of the same variable in the expression leading to the overestimation of the interval simulation.

Interval models in Sect. 2.1 were selected due to their applications in the design of closed-loop controllers for artificial pancreas systems.

2.1 Interval Models

Each model was analyzed according to parameters, inputs, and initial conditions with uncertainty, and rewritten in such a way that the exact range was obtained. In cases where it was required, the theorem of coercion to optimality was applied, taking into account the definition of dual operator as $Dual([a_1, a_2]) = [a_2, a_1]$ to obtain an optimal rational computation (ORC). The reader can find details about this procedure with MIA in [4,9].

Glucose-Insulin Low Order Model. The first model is a discrete average representation of the Linear Parameter-Varying (LPV) model presented by Colmegna et al. [10], which captures dynamics from the insulin delivery input to the subcutaneous-glucose concentration output. This model was developed to be part of the closed-loop control strategies, also known as artificial pancreas systems, and can be tuned for each patient by means of the parameter k according to the "1800" rule, which relates the insulin sensitivity with the total-daily-insulin (TDI) of the patient.

The model by Colmegna et al. was studied in this document considering the intra-patient variability and the different sources of uncertainty; that is, the food intake, the insulin dose, the preprandial blood glucose, the insulin sensitivity, and the initial states. Parameters and initial states related to these uncertainties were evaluated using the MIA to obtain an ORC.

The insulin to subcutaneous glucose concentration deviation model is then given by Eq. 1:

$$x_1(t+1) = \Delta t x_2(t) + x_1(t)$$
$$x_2(t+1) = \Delta t x_3(t) + x_2(t)$$
$$x_3(t+1) = \Delta t (p_1(-p_2 p_3 Dual(x_1(t))) - (p_2 + p_3) + Dual(x_2(t)) - Dual(x_3(t)))$$
$$\qquad - p_2 p_3 Dual(x_2(t)) - (p_2 + p_3) Dual(x_3(t))) + (x_3(t))$$
$$\qquad + \Delta t (Basal + Bolus)$$
$$x_4(t+1) = x_4(t) - \frac{\Delta t Dual(x_4(t))}{t_{max,G}} + \Delta t D$$

$$x_5(t+1) = x_5(t) + \frac{(x_4(t) - Dual(x_5(t)))\Delta t}{t_{max,G}}$$
$$G_e(t) = k(z x_1(t) + x_2(t)) + \frac{k_{ra} x_5(t)}{t_{max,G}}$$

$$\tag{1}$$

where p_1, p_2 and p_3 and z are parameters that correspond to the three poles and zero, respectively, in the Laplace representation of the model by Colmegna et al. [10]. *Basal* and *Bolus* (IU) correspond to inputs related to the insulin delivery. The model was expandend considering a glucose absorption model, where states x_4 and x_5 were adapted from the Hovorka et al. model [6] to estimate the glucose absorption rate. The D (mg) input is related to the amount of ingested CHO, $t_{max,G}$ (min) is the time-of-maximum appearance of glucose in plasma, and k_{ra} (dimensionless) is the carbohydrate bioavailability. Finally, the plasma glucose estimation is given by $G_e(t)$. The time step Δt is defined such that $\Delta t < 1/(p_1 + p_2 + p_3)$ in order to satisfy the monotonicity conditions that are required.

IOB Model. The second new model studied and included in the interval simulator scheme (Fig. 1), is a discrete version of the IOB model presented by León-Vargas et al. [11]. This IOB model allows estimating how much insulin must still act in the body, and it depends on the patient's glucose-insulin dynamics. This estimation can help prevent an excess of insulin and therefore hypoglycemia events since once the insulin enters the body it is not possible to extract it.

The IOB estimate requires knowing with certainty the duration-of-insulin-action (DIA) of the patient, which is not individually analyzed and defined by physicians when setting up the insulin pump therapy [12]. Here, we consider uncertainty in the DIA by means of the K_{DIA} parameter. The rational computation of the interval IOB model proposed in this document can be performed from Eq. (2).

$$
\begin{aligned}
C_1(t+1) &= C_1(t)(1 - \Delta t K_{DIA}) + \Delta t u(t) \\
C_{12}(t+1) &= C_{12}(t)(1 - \Delta t K_{DIA}) + \Delta t u(t) + \Delta t Dual(K_{DIA})C_1(t) \\
C_2(t+1) &= C_{12}(t+1) - Dual(C_1(t+1)) \\
IOB &= C_1(t) + C_2(t)
\end{aligned}
\tag{2}
$$

subject to $\Delta t < 1/C_2(t)$, where $C_1(t)$ and $C_2(t)$ are two compartments, $u(t)$ is the insulin dose, and $C_{12} = C_1 + C_2$ is an additional state created to avoid multi-incident variables.

3 Results

3.1 Simulation Environment

The interval simulator was implemented using the Matlab software R2018b. A class named *vector interval arithmetic* [13], which incorporates the so-called extended interval arithmetic (Kaucher arithmetic) and allows using the MIA theory, was used in order to obtain the envelope of glucose (i.e. the range of the trajectories) for the interval models above.

Figure 2 shows the user interface of the interval simulator. It requires selecting the model of each subsystem, the (%) uncertainty associated with each parameter or input, the virtual patient, the food and insulin scenario, and the outputs to plot. According to the option selected, a new window will open to enter or choose additional information. It is important to highlight that the use of the user interface is optional, as the simulation scenario can be configured directly in a text file (m file) in Matlab. The parameters and the inputs considered uncertain in each of the interval models that are included in the interval simulation are presented in Table 1.

In addition, the interval simulator offers obtaining a risk index outcome that quantifies the risk of experiencing different grades of hypo- or hyperglycemia in the postprandial state of the interval simulation. This outcome was presented in [8].

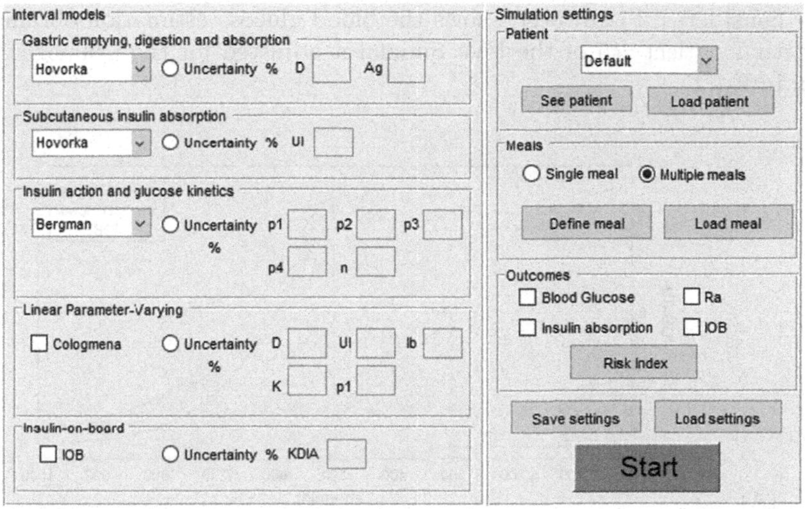

Fig. 2. Interval simulator: user interface. Parameters of uncertainty options appear according to the interval model selected. Scenario simulation settings can be customized.

Table 1. Model parameters with uncertainty of each subsystem.

Subsystem	Model	Parameter uncertainty
Carbohydrate digestion and absorption	Hovorka et al. (2014)	D, A_G, $t_{max,G}$
	Dalla Man et al. (2006)	D
Subcutaneous insulin absorption	Hovorka et al. (2004)	u
	Dalla Man et al. (2007)	u
Insulin action and glucose kinetics	Bergman et al. (1981)	p_1, p_2, p_3, p_4, n
	Colmegna et al. (2015)	D, $Basal$, $Bolus$, p_1, k
Insulin-on-board	León-Vargas et al. (2013)	K_{DIA}

3.2   Simulation Results

Figure 3 shows the output of the interval simulation for a scenario using the models explained in Sect. 2.1 and the simulation environment detailed in Sect. 3.1. An example of the IOB estimation based on Eq. 2 is presented in the Fig. 3(A). The blue solid line corresponds to the upper and lower bound performed by the interval simulator, while the green dotted line corresponds to the IOB without uncertainty. Boundaries represent the worst cases obtained from the prediction of glucose excursions derived from the interval simulation according to the uncertainty considered. Figure 3(B) shows the blood glucose estimation obtained for the virtual patient #5 of the UVa Simulator adjusted for the Colmegna et al. model in Eq. 1.

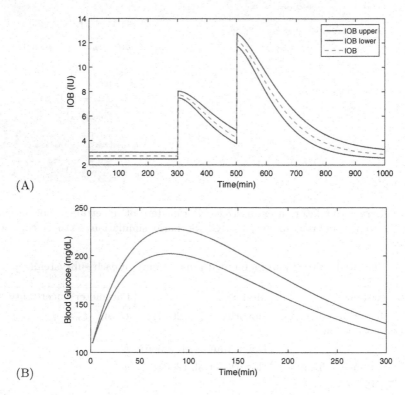

(A)

(B)

Fig. 3. (A) Envelope of IOB obtained with 10% uncertainty in K_{DIA} for 1 IU/h of basal insulin, with 5 and 8 IU of bolus insulin at 300 and 500 min, respectively. The green dotted line corresponds to the IOB without uncertainty. (B) Envelope of blood glucose obtained with 10% uncertainty for a single meal (40 g of carbs), 5% in the bolus insulin (6 IU), 3% in p_1 and 2% in p_2. (Color figure online)

The interval blood glucose traces obtained from the combination of different interval models corresponding to several subsystems in two test scenarios are shown in Fig. 4. In this case, the glucose rate of appearance and insulin absorption models from Dalla Man et al., and the interval insulin action and glucose kinetics models from Bergman et al., were used to demonstrate the functionality that the interval simulator has when interacting with glucose-insulin dynamics models from different authors. The intervals models that were implemented can be found in [14]. A digital copy of this simulator can be requested to the authors.

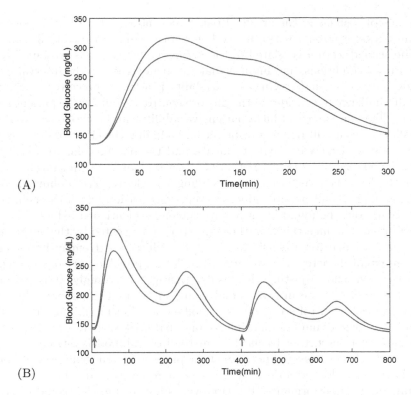

Fig. 4. (A) Envelopes of blood glucose obtained for virtual patient #2 (adjusted from the UVa simulator) for a single meal (100 g of carbs) with 10% uncertainty, bolus insulin (10 IU) with 5%, and 3% and 2% in parameters related with insulin sensitivity, p_1 and p_2, respectively. (B) Virtual patient #5 (adjusted from the UVa simulator) considering two meals (100 gr and 50 gr) with 10% uncertainty. The red arrows indicate the food intake timing. Additionally, two insulin bolus (6 and 5 IU) were delivered simultaneously with corresponding food intake. Uncertainty of 3% and 2% in parameters p_1 and p_2 respectively, were also included.

4   Discussion

The interval simulator presents two features to highlight. The first one is related to the use of different models by different authors in order to estimate the output of each subsystem of the glucose-insulin dynamics, which at the best of our knowledge, no simulators of the glucose-insulin system allow this functionality so far, either for designing or testing purposes. The integration of these models was achieved by homogenizing the units of the input and outputs signals as required by the corresponding models combination. Additionally, a cohort of virtual patients from the UVa simulator adjusted in [7] was included.

This feature allows to include more complex dynamics for a particular virtual patient, which can be used, for example, for designing or evaluating the closed-loop control systems in the artificial pancreas context, where it is important to obtain a good controller performance before proceeding with clinical trials.

The second feature is related to the different sources of uncertainty (parameters, initial conditions, and inputs) that can be assigned to the interval models included in this simulator. Glucose variability is actually perceived as the most difficult challenge to consider in the glucose control design for the patient's daily life [15]. This physiological intra-patient variability can be explained from a set of challenges that still remains to be faced, including the effect of exercise, concurrent illness, large carbohydrate meals, and the pharmacokinetics of current subcutaneous insulin. The simulation of interval models with uncertainty yields upper and lower bounds, instead of providing a single response, defining an envelope that includes all possible glucose excursions, within which the behavior of the patient could be found by means of challenges mentioned before.

An integrated uncertainty in the simulation, represented by the output envelope, may be used for a worst-case analysis, which is extremely important in the context of diabetes. For example, predicting possible episodes of hypo or hyperglycemia and adjusting the insulin therapy accordingly. It is important to understand that the interval simulation can be used to support the design of novel glucose control strategies, as it offers an efficient estimation of all the possible response dynamics allowing to anticipate risk scenarios for the patient.

Finally, it is important to clarify that the interval models introduced in this work, Sect. 2.1, were selected because of the purpose for automatic control design they have, and also because they have been recently tested in clinical trials obtaining a good performance [16]. However, additional models could be considered in future versions.

5   Conclusion

An interval models simulator to estimate the dynamics of the glucose-insulin system and the insulin-on-board considering different sources of uncertainty was presented in this paper. In particular, two new models were studied and integrated as interval models in this simulator. The first one is a glucose-insulin system model developed by Colmegna et al. intended to design glycemic control strategies due to of its simplicity and easy tuning. The second one is a model that estimates the insulin-on-board, that has been used as part of safety schemes for glycemic control strategies.

This simulator includes several interval models that can be combined with each other in order to expand possibilities in the design and assessment of glucose regulation algorithms and insulin therapies for T1D patients.

Acknowledgments. M. García-Jaramillo was supported by Colciencias Project 110180763081 and Universidad EAN. F. León-Vargas and A. Molano were supported by Universidad Antonio Nariño Project #2018222 and Colciencias Project #110180763081. F. Garelli and N. Rosales were supported by Agencia Nacional de Promoción Científica y Tecnológica (PICT 2017-3211), CONICET (PIP 2015-0837), Universidad Nacional de La Plata (I216) of Argentina.

References

1. International Diabetes Federation: IDF Diabetes Atlas, 8th edn. International Diabetes Federation, Brussels (2017)
2. Dalla, M.C., Raimondo, D., Rizza, R., Cobelli, C.: GIM, simulation software of meal glucose-insulin model. J. Diabetes Sci. Technol. **1**(3), 323–330 (2007)
3. Colmegna P.: Simulation & control in type 1 diabetes. Ph.D. thesis, Instituto Tecnologico de Buenos Aires (2015)
4. Calm, R., García-Jaramillo, M., Bondia, J., Sainz, M.A., Vehí, J.: Comparison of interval and Monte Carlo simulation for the prediction of postprandial glucose under uncertainty in type 1 diabetes mellitus. Comput. Methods Programs Biomed. **104**(3), 325–332 (2011)
5. Cobelli, C., Dalla, M.C., Sparacino, G., Magni, L., De Nicolao, G., Kovatchev, B.: Diabetes: models, signals and control. IEEE Rev. Biomed. Eng. **2**, 54–96 (2009)
6. Hovorka, R., Canonico, V., Chassin, L.J., et al.: Nonlinear model predictive control of glucose concentration in subjects with type 1 diabetes. Physiol. Meas. **25**, 905–920 (2004)
7. García-Jaramillo, M., Calm, R., Bondia, J., Vehí, J.: Prediction of postprandial blood glucose under uncertainty and intra-patient variability in type 1 diabetes: a comparative study of three interval models. Comput. Methods Programs Biomed. **108**(1), 224–233 (2012)
8. García-Jaramillo, M., Delgado, J.S., León-Vargas, F.: Glu4Pred: a computational tool for design and testing of insulin therapies for patients with type 1 diabetes based on interval simulation. In: Torres, I., Bustamante, J., Sierra, D. (eds.) VII Latin American Congress on Biomedical Engineering CLAIB 2016, Bucaramanga, Santander, Colombia, October 26th–28th, 2016. IP, vol. 60, pp. 337–340. Springer, Singapore (2017). https://doi.org/10.1007/978-981-10-4086-3_85
9. Sainz, M., Armengol, J., Calm, R., Herrero, P., Jorba Jorba, L., Vehi, J.: Modal Interval Analysis: New Tools for Numerical Information. Springer, Cham (2013). https://doi.org/10.1007/978-3-319-01721-1
10. Colmegna, P., Sánchez-Peña, R.S., Gondhalekar, R: Control-oriented linear parameter-varying model for glucose control in type 1 diabetes. In: IEEE Conference on Control Applications (CCA), Buenos Aires, pp. 410–415 (2016)
11. León-Vargas, F., Garelli, F., De Battista, H., Vehí, J.: Postprandial blood glucose control using a hybrid adaptive PD controller with insulin-on-board limitation. Biomed. Signal Process. Control **8**(6), 724–732 (2013)
12. Walsh, J., Roberts, R.: Pumping Insulin: Everything You Need for Success on a Smart Insulin Pump. Torrey Pines Press, San Diego (2006)
13. Herrero, P., Georgiou, P., Toumazou, C., Delaunay, B., Jaulin, L.: An efficient implementation of the SIVIA algorithm in a high-level numerical programming language. Reliable Comput. **16**, 239–251 (2012)
14. García-Jaramillo, M.: Prediction of postprandial blood glucose under intra-patient variability and uncertainty and its use in the design of insulin dosing strategies for type 1 diabetic patients. Ph.D. thesis, Universitat de Girona (2013)
15. Peyser, T., Dassau, E., Breton, M., Skyler, J.S.: The artificial pancreas: current status and future prospects in the management of diabetes. Ann. N. Y. Acad. Sci. **1311**, 102–123 (2014). https://doi.org/10.1111/nyas.12431
16. Sánchez-Peña, R., et al.: Artificial pancreas: clinical study in Latin America without premeal insulin boluses. J. Diabetes Sci. Technol. **12**(5), 914–925 (2018)

Optimization

Adapting the Archetype "Accidental Adversaries" in Humanitarian Operations

Diana C. Guzmán-Cortés[1] and Carlos Franco[2]([⊠])

[1] Research Group in Logistics Systems,
Universidad de la Sabana, Chía, Colombia
dianaguco@unisabana.edu.co
[2] Innovation Center, School of Management,
Universidad del Rosario, Bogotá, Colombia
carlosa.franco@urosario.edu.co

Abstract. The present work is focused on the involuntary obstruction problem between stakeholders in humanitarian operations, specifically in search and rescue operations. The archetype of accidental adversaries is used to represent this situation. First, this works presents a brief introduction related to humanitarian logistics and collaboration or coordination problems. Then, the archetype of accidental adversaries is described and adapted for humanitarian operations. Finally, a dynamic model is presented, and the performance was evaluated in two scenarios, the first one considers operations obstruction and the second one considers resources shared between stakeholders as a collaborative strategy. As a conclusion, was found that the establishment of alliances or collaborative strategies between humanitarian organizations at the same level enhances the performance of rescue operations increasing the rescue rate.

Keywords: Humanitarian operations · System dynamics ·
Accidental adversaries

1 Introduction

A disaster is defined as a non-routine event that exceeds the response capacity of the affected area to save lives, preserve property and maintain the social, ecological, economic and political stability of the affected region [1]. Also, a disaster is defined as a disorder that affects a physical system as a whole and endangers your priorities and goals [2]. Thus, a natural event can be characterized as a natural disaster when it occurs in populated areas, causing the destruction of local infrastructure and leaving the population in a state deprivation and suffering [3].

According to [4] in the annual report of the Centre for Research on the Epidemiology of Disasters (CRED), in 2017, 318 natural disasters occurred, affecting 122 countries. The number of deaths caused were 9.503, 96 million people were affected, and economic damages were reported for US$314 billion. Although 2017 had lower mortality, this was the second most costly year after 2011 when the earthquake and tsunami in Japan were presented.

All the operations and stakeholders necessary to satisfy the needs of the affected population constitute the humanitarian supply chain. Hence, humanitarian logistics

© Springer Nature Switzerland AG 2019
J. C. Figueroa-García et al. (Eds.): WEA 2019, CCIS 1052, pp. 699–708, 2019.
https://doi.org/10.1007/978-3-030-31019-6_59

corresponds to the processes and systems involved in the mobilization of people, resources, skills, and knowledge to help vulnerable people affected by disasters [2].

Humanitarian logistics implies a complex interaction of a great variety and quantity of actors (NGOs, governments, military forces, private companies, among others) [5] who come together to assist to the population, generating problems of collaboration and coordination in the humanitarian supply chain. The multiplicity of stakeholders could obstruct humanitarian actions [6–8].

Also, this situation could generate competition for funding or media attention between similar organizations with the common objective of providing relief goods or services to the affected population [9].

Hence, this highlights the collaboration and coordination between actors in the humanitarian supply chain as an essential aspect for the failure or success of humanitarian operations [10].

Coordination refers to the cooperation of two or more independent organizations with the purpose of sharing their information or resources [11]. Coordination also refers to centralized decision-making, the realization of joint projects and division of tasks or clustering [12].

Related to collaboration, in the commercial supply chain it has been defined as a function of seven components [13]: information exchange, congruence of objectives, synchronized decisions, aligned incentives, shared resources, team communication, creation of joint knowledge. These components are also essential in the humanitarian supply chain with particular adaptations considering the own objectives [14].

The lack of collaboration and coordination between stakeholders in humanitarian logistics can generate significant losses of human lives and material resources [11], high logistics cost, and attention times.

For reducing negative impacts, it is essential to design collaborative logistics strategies that contemplate joint and voluntary work between humanitarian organizations and consider sharing information, resources, infrastructure, personnel to provide the best possible response to the affected people [14].

Since the complexity inherent to humanitarian operations and the need to evaluate the impacts and effects of different strategies or decisions in the system performance, system dynamics (SD) is an appropriated and useful tool for decision makers in this context [15]. Moreover, system dynamics has been few used in the context of humanitarian operations, according to the literature reviews made by the authors [16] and [17].

[18] used SD to model vehicle supply chains in humanitarian operations considering centralized, decentralized, and hybrid procurement strategy. [14] present a collaborative approach for aid delivering in the immediate response considering infrastructure and information sharing between stakeholders and evaluate the impact in the response time, using SD.

Thus, the present work uses systems dynamics to represent and understand situations of competition between organizations of the same level, considering involuntary obstructions in the development of their activities due to lack of collaboration and coordination among actors involved.

This paper is organized as follows: first, the Accidental Adversaries archetype and its adaptation for search and rescue operations in humanitarian relief are presented. Then, the dynamic model is presented followed by the results. Finally, some conclusions are established.

2 Humanitarian Logistics and the Archetype "Accidental Adversaries"

2.1 Archetype "Accidental Adversaries"

According to [19] in the Escalation archetype there are two parties. One part takes actions that are perceived by the other as a threat. The other part takes actions to reduce the generated gap and both parties keep taking actions with the aim to improve their own situation, creating a reinforcing process.

The archetype "Accidental Adversaries" is similar to the archetype "Escalation" [20] in terms of the pattern of behavior that develops over time. "Accidental Adversaries" archetype begins its relationships with win-win goals and objectives between the adversaries, generally taking advantage of their respective strengths and minimizing the weaknesses. The main goal is to achieve together what they cannot achieve separately.

Involuntarily, one adversary (denoted by part A) performs an action that the other adversary (denoted by part B) interprets as an offense, that is, outside of its cooperation agreements. Instead of communicating and maintaining a dialogue, the offended part assumes that the action was hostile and considers that it has anything to discuss with Part A and resorts to retaliation. Therefore, when Part B makes his actions, Part A is surprised feeling offended and beginning a circle of retaliatory actions between the two parts. Once the adversary's relationship is established, the pattern of behavior that develops over time is very similar to the archetype named "Escalation".

However, an external reinforcement loop is available to the adversaries in case they suspend their mental models and choose to dialogue, starts a new beginning in their association, as shown in the causal loop diagram presented in Fig. 1.

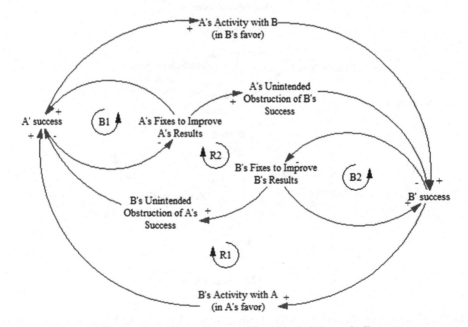

Fig. 1. Causal loop diagram "Accidental Adversaries"

As can be seen in Fig. 1, the archetype is composed of two balance loops and two positive loops. The loops of balance are presented between the actions performed by each adversary to improve their performance and the individual success, that is, the greater the adjustment or action of the adversary, the greater the success and therefore the greater the success achieved, needing less adjustment to achieve their goal. For the positive loops, the first loop occurs between the actions that unintentionally affect the performance of the other part, the greater the action performed by part A to reach its goal, the greater involuntary obstruction occurs in the success of part B and vice versa. The second, as mentioned above, occurs when the parties decide to cooperate again, that is, to carry out joint activities that provide mutual benefit.

2.2   Adaptation of the Archetype

Adapting the previous causal loop diagram into the humanitarian logistic system, the behavior presented in the previous section can be observed among humanitarian organizations of different support systems. Search and rescue organizations could obstruct their operations between themselves to get better results, and funding or media attention.

In the case of search and rescue, the larger the affected or missing population, the greater the rescue personnel required and therefore, the greater the amount of population rescued. This situation occurs for both part A and B, as it can be seen in the causal diagram presented in Fig. 2, identified by the two balance loops (B1, B2).

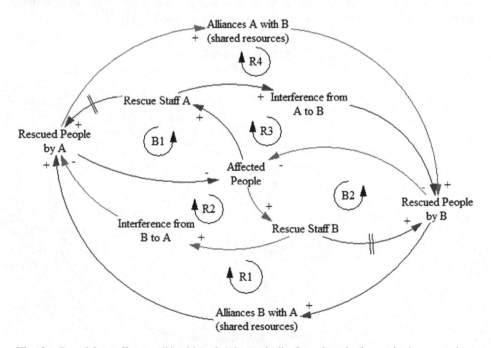

Fig. 2. Causal loop diagram "Accidental Adversaries" adapted to the humanitarian operations

In addition, in Fig. 2 it can be identified the two positive loops defined in the archetype (R2, R3). Involuntary obstruction occurs due to the rescue capacity of each part: a greater rescue capacity of part A, the greater number of people rescued by A and therefore the greater obstruction of A in the operations of B, and vice versa.

The positive loop (R1) related to the joint activities is represented by the interaction of the two actors, which can be established by sharing resources that facilitate them to reach their objective, such as the means of transportation of search and rescue personnel to the affected area in order to rescue as much of the population affected as possible.

And finally, the positive loop (R4) connects the interferences with the possible alliances or partnerships between actors.

3 Simulation Model

For modeling and simulating the behavior explained before, we have built a model using the Forrester representation and simulated using the Vensim® software. In Fig. 3, the model is presented.

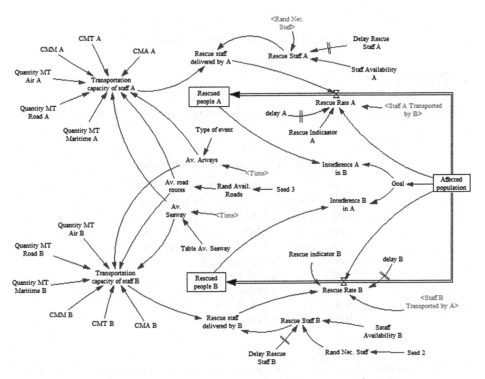

Fig. 3. Forrester diagram – search and rescue operations

704 D. C. Guzmán-Cortés and C. Franco

To determine the quantity of search and rescue staff of an organization transported by the other one, given the partnership alliances established between them, we have considered the option of sharing resources, in this case, the capacity to mobilize staff. This second view is presented in Fig. 4.

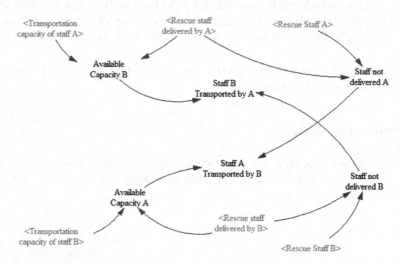

Fig. 4. Forrester diagram – view 2, shared resources

4 Results

The following are the initial conditions considered by our simulation (see Table 1):

Table 1. Initial conditions of the model

Name - Value	Name - Value	Name - Value
$NPA = 5000$	$CMTAA = 7$	$CMTA = 10$
$NPRA = 0$	$CMTAB = 3$	$CMTB = 8$
$NPRB = 0$	$CMTTA = 100$	$CMAA = 5$
$DPA = 500$	$CMTTB = 78$	$CMAB = 5$
$DPB = 300$	$CMTAgA = 20$	
$DPRA = 1$	$CMTAgB = 15$	
$DPRB = 1$	$CMTAB = 3$	
$IRA = 1.4$	$CMAgA = 8$	
$IRB = 0.82$	$CMAgB = 3$	

The simulation of the model was carried out in two scenarios. In the first scenario, no alliances between parts A and B were considered to observe the behavior of interference or obstructions in the operations of one part in the other one. It is assumed that the performance of part A has been greater over the years, that's why part A is capable to get more funds that let them to have more resources and capacity. Figures 5 and 6 shows the behavior of some system variables.

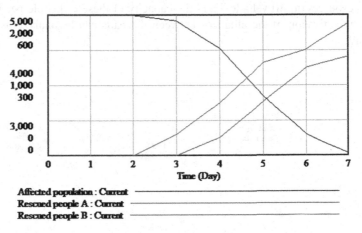

Fig. 5. Results – affected population and rescued people by A and B

Figure 5 shows the decrease of the affected population, which decrease from 5000 people disappeared at the beginning of 2512 on the seventh day. Consistent with the initial conditions, the population rescued by part A is significantly greater than the rescued by part B, that is considered as an interference in the operations of B, the greater number of people rescued by A the smaller number of susceptible disappeared persons of being rescued by B.

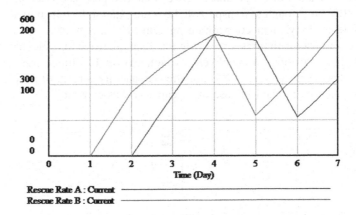

Fig. 6. Results – rescue capacities A and B

Figure 6 shows a considerable difference between the rescue rates of the two competitors, affected by the necessities of personnel, the personnel available, the capacities for mobilization, and the rescue rate of each part. According to the initial favorable conditions of part A, it has a more efficient rescue rate than part B, which directly affects the number of people rescued.

On the other hand, the second scenario is evaluated. If the availability transportation resources (to 40 vehicles) and the capacity of these (7 people per vehicle) is reduced, the activation of the alliances between the parts can be analyze as shown in Figs. 7 and 8.

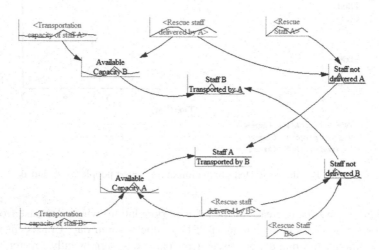

Fig. 7. Results – second view, shared resources for establishing alliances

Figure 7 shows the behavior of the variables used in the second view of the model. In Fig. 8 the activation of the alliances between the two parts is observed. Because the capacity of B is not enough to transport all the rescue staff to be transported, and Part A has available capacity, then cooperation agreements are activated. In this case, the agreements consider sharing resources with the main objective of achieving their goals. At the fifth time, a quantity of undelivered personnel from B is transported by A, which contributes that the rescue rate of B is not affected, and the number of people rescued is equal to the number reached in case of its capacity was enough.

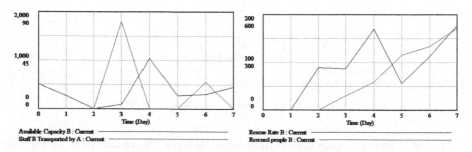

Fig. 8. Results – Available capacity B, Staff B transported by A, Rescue Rate B, Rescue people B.

5 Conclusions

In this work, we have shown how two humanitarian organizations that share the same objective, in this case search and rescue organizations, unwittingly become rivals during the performance of their relief operations.

These obstructions can be solved through the implementation of collaboration and/or coordination strategies where organizations of the same level choose to share resources and/or information or act together to provide the best possible attention to the population affected by the disaster.

In [21] a strategy of coordination and collaboration to provide a platform of resources and capacities to work jointly among the actors is proposed. This policy has been considered in the model with the second scenario. When capacities of rescue are not enough to attend the affected population, but there is another organization with enough capacity to share, the agreements are activated with the main purpose to increase their rescue rates.

References

1. Holguín-Veras, J., Jaller, M., Aros-Vera, F., Amaya, J., Encarnación, T., Wachtendorf, T.: Disaster response logistics: chief findings of fieldwork research. In: Zobel, C., Altay, N., Haselkorn, M. (eds.) Advances in Managing Humanitarian Operations. ISOR, pp. 33–57. Springer, Cham (2016). https://doi.org/10.1007/978-3-319-24418-1_3
2. Van Wassenhove, L.N.: Humanitarian aid logistics: supply chain management in high gear. J. Oper. Res. Soc. 57(5), 475–489 (2006)
3. Da Costa, S.R.A., Campos, V.B.G., Bandeira, R.A.D.M.: Supply chains in humanitarian operations: cases and analysis. Procedia - Soc. Behav. Sci. 54, 598–607 (2012)
4. Wallemacq, P.: Natural disasters in 2017: lower mortality, higher cost (2018)
5. Heaslip, G., Sharif, A.M., Althonayan, A.: Employing a systems-based perspective to the identification of inter-relationships within humanitarian logistics. Int. J. Prod. Econ. 139(2), 377–392 (2012)
6. Balcik, B., Beamon, B.M., Krejci, C.C., Muramatsu, K.M., Ramirez, M.: Coordination in humanitarian relief chains: practices, challenges and opportunities. Int. J. Prod. Econ. 126(1), 22–34 (2010)
7. Carroll, A., Neu, J.: Volatility, unpredictability and asymmetry: an organising framework for humanitarian logistics operations? Manag. Res. News 32(11), 1024–1037 (2009)
8. Chandes, J., Paché, G.: Pensar la acción colectiva en el contexto de la logística humanitaria: las lecciones del sismo de Pisco. J. Econ. Finance Adm. Sci. 14, 47–62 (2009)
9. Moshtari, M., Gonçalves, P.: Factors influencing interorganizational collaboration within a disaster relief context. Voluntas 28(4), 1673–1694 (2017)
10. Dorasamy, M., Raman, M., Kaliannan, M.: Knowledge management systems in support of disasters management: a two decade review. Technol. Forecast. Soc. Chang. 80, 1834–1853 (2013)
11. Kaynak, R., Tuğer, A.T.: Coordination and collaboration functions of disaster coordination centers for humanitarian logistics. Procedia - Soc. Behav. Sci. 109, 432–437 (2014)
12. Balcik, B., Beamon, B.M., Krejci, C.C., Muramatsu, K.M., Ramirez, M.: Coordination in humanitarian relief chains: practices, challenges and opportunities. Int. J. Prod. Econ. 126, 22–34 (2010)

13. Cao, M., Zhang, Q.: Supply chain collaboration: impact on collaborative advantage and firm performance. J. Oper. Manag. **29**(3), 163–180 (2011)
14. Guzmán Cortés, D.C., González Rodríguez, L.J., Franco, C.: Collaborative strategies for humanitarian logistics with system dynamics and project management. In: Villa, S., Urrea, G., Castañeda, J.A., Larsen, E.R. (eds.) Decision-making in Humanitarian Operations, pp. 249–273. Springer, Cham (2019). https://doi.org/10.1007/978-3-319-91509-8_11
15. Besiou, M., Stapleton, O., Van Wassenhove, L.N.: System dynamics for humanitarian operations. J. Humanit. Logist. Supply Chain Manag. **1**(1), 78–103 (2011)
16. Altay, N., Green, W.G.: OR/MS research in disaster operations management. Eur. J. Oper. Res. **175**(1), 475–493 (2006)
17. Galindo, G., Batta, R.: Review of recent developments in OR/MS research in disaster operations management. Eur. J. Oper. Res. **230**(2), 201–211 (2013)
18. Besiou, M., Pedraza-Martinez, A.J., Van Wassenhove, L.N.: Vehicle supply chains in humanitarian operations: decentralization, operational mix, and earmarked funding. Prod. Oper. Manag. **23**(11), 1950–1965 (2014)
19. Kim, D.H., Anderson, V.: Systems Archetype Basics: From Story to Structure (1998)
20. Braun, W.: The System Archetypes (2002)
21. Akhtar, P., Marr, N.E., Garnevska, E.V.: Coordination in humanitarian relief chains: chain coordinators. J. Humanit. Logist. Supply Chain Manag. **2**(1), 85–103 (2012)

Modeling for the Evaluation of Public Policy Alternatives in the Supply Chain of Natural Gas in Colombia

Mauricio Becerra-Fernandez[1,3](✉) (iD), Danny Ibarra-Vega[2](✉) (iD),
Johan Manuel Redondo[1](✉) (iD), and Isaac Dyner[3](✉)

[1] Catholic University of Colombia, Bogota D.C., Colombia
{mbecerra,jmredondo}@ucatolica.edu.co
[2] International Research Center for Applied Complexity Sciences, Bogota D.C., Colombia
ingdanny09@hotmail.com
[3] Jorge Tadeo Lozano University, Bogota D.C., Colombia
{mauricio.becerraf,isaac.dynerr}@utadeo.edu.co
https://www.ucatolica.edu.co,
https://www.ircacs.org, https://www.utadeo.edu.co

Abstract. Natural gas is considered the fuel of the transition of fossil sources and renewable energies. This is why demand levels have increased worldwide, which requires the intervention of public and private actors to meet these requirements. Participation in the supply of diverse interconnected actors of the provider-client form, a supply chain for natural gas, in which the effects of the application of the policies that can be analyzed in time, through the use of a Model Based on Systems Dynamics for the Colombian case. The results of the model show the behavior of reserve levels, production, and transport against the levels of implementation of the policies formulated by the national government, which allows recommending actions to decision makers in the planning of policies aimed at a guarantee the uninterrupted supply of this resource.

Keywords: Supply chain · Natural gas · Energy policy ·
System dynamics · Modeling

1 Introduction

Natural gas is demanded by different sectors, such as transportation, industry, residential, commercial and electric power generation. The processing of natural gas requires a few stages from the source of extraction until delivery to the final consumer. It is transported safely and efficiently around the world, generating low environmental impacts either in the form of liquefied natural gas (LNG) using methane tankers or through various regions through gas pipelines [1,3].

Supported by Catholic University of Colombia.

J. C. Figueroa-García et al. (Eds.): WEA 2019, CCIS 1052, pp. 709–721, 2019.
https://doi.org/10.1007/978-3-030-31019-6_60

In the generation of conventional energy, natural gas is one of the most efficient fossil fuels compared to other fuels, with a market share of at least 22% in this generation, with low costs, greater flexibility and speed in the construction of power plants. Natural gas helps reduce the greenhouse effect since it has a lower CO_2 emission factor than other fossil fuels [19].

In Colombia, natural gas is consumed by two large groups classified into sectors of generation and non-generation of electricity. Within the non-generation group are refineries, petrochemicals, general industry, vehicular consumption, and residential consumption. In the period between 1997 and 2017, the total consumption of natural gas in Colombia grew by 43%, going from 567 to 812 MMSCFD (Million Cubic Feet per Day) in that period. The non-power generation group grew by 127%, while the electricity generation group decreased by 52%. The main increases in consumption are in the vehicular sector with an increase of 757% and in the residential sector with an increase of 286%, all in the same period mentioned [2].

Modeling with System Dynamics has been used to investigate the energy supply, within these works the one by Cai et al. who applies a model to provide alternatives in the production of helium [7]. North et al. use an integrated model (system dynamics and agents) for the analysis of energy security, which describes two alternative methods used to study conflicts in energy supply [14]. Howells et al. apply a model of system optimization and dynamics that includes some economic interactions with the energy system, in the implementation of measures that impact the reduction of emissions to the environment [12]. Horschig et al. make a model in the energy market of Germany showing that without plans of incentives and financing in R & D, penetration in the country's market of substitutes substitute to natural gas is not achieved [11]. Recent research on natural gas in Colombia, evaluate the policies for the supply of this resource using the AHP methodology, the supply chain management approach and the systems dynamics modeling [4–6].

For Schroeder et al. the supply chain is the network comprised of the manufacturing and service operations, through which raw materials are supplied and transformed until the delivery of a final product to the consumer [16]. The supply chain considers the physical flow of materials, money, and information throughout the purchasing, production and distribution operations. On the other hand, for Sterman the objective of systemic thinking through modeling with systems dynamics, is to improve the understanding of the ways in which the performance of an organization is related to its internal structure and its operational policies, including relationships with customers, competitors, and suppliers, to subsequently use that knowledge in the design of leverage policies for success [18].

Considering the above, modeling with systems dynamics contributes to the analysis of supply chains, in this case, applied to the analysis of policies that guarantee the supply of a service such as natural gas, so that they can be integrated into this analysis. Main actors that participate in the attention of the demand of this resource.

This article is organized as follows: in the modeling section of the supply chain, the hypothesis surrounding this research is presented, based on the analysis of the causal and Forrester diagrams. Subsequently, the variables and parameters used in the modeling are presented, as well as the verification and validation of the developed model. In the policy scenarios section, the policies defined by the national government and their effect on the natural gas supply chain are analyzed. Finally, conclusions are presented regarding the main contributions of studying the policies for the supply of natural gas as a dynamic supply chain.

2   Natural Gas Supply Chain Model

The supply chain model for natural gas supply is based on the following modeling approaches. In terms of supply chain management presented by Sterman, see [17], modeling the natural gas supply chain by Becerra et al., see [4,5], modeling of the energy system developed by Cardenas et al., see [8], modeling of national energy market by Redondo et al., see [15], and analysis of natural gas production and exploitation status by Eker et al., see [9].

2.1   Causal Loop Diagram

The dynamic hypothesis considered for the construction of the model is based on previous approaches. This can be seen in Fig. 1 and is explained as follows: By combining the policies in the supply chain, better supply performance is achieved through the improvement in the reserve margin, the increase in capacity generation and the reduction of wellhead and consumer prices.

In Fig. 1 there are five negative feedback loops, which are explained with the following sentences E_i:

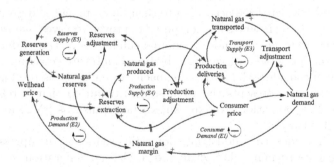

Fig. 1. Causal loop diagram for the natural gas supply model in Colombia.

$\mathbf{E}_1$ *Consumer demand feedback loop*: an increase in the consumer price causes a decrease in the demand for natural gas. If the demand increases, the natural gas margin will also do so, generating an increase in the consumer price.

E₂ *Production demand feedback loop*: an increase in the wellhead price of the well causes an increase in the requirements for the development of reserves and the production of natural gas. If natural gas reserves increase, the natural gas margin decreases, generating an increase in the wellhead price.

E₃ *Transport supply feedback loop*: the increase in demand for natural gas by the final consumption sectors, causes an increase in the need for natural gas to be transported, which after adjusting the current transport capacity with respect to the expected coverage to avoid shortages, generates the need for transport capacity and considering a delay for its construction.

E₄ *Production supply feedback loop*: the increase in the requirement of natural gas to transport, causes an increase in the need for natural gas to be produced, which after adjusting the current production capacity with respect to the expected coverage to avoid shortages, generates the need for production capacity and considering a delay for its construction.

E₅ *Reserves supply feedback loop*: the increase in the requirement of natural gas to produce, causes an increase in the need to develop natural gas reserves, which after the adjustment of the current generation capacity of reserves with respect to the expected coverage to avoid shortages, generates the need of capacity in the generation of these reserves and considering a delay for their development.

2.2 Model and Forrester Diagram

The Forrester diagram developed from Fig. 1 can be seen in the Fig. 2. Within the supply chain modeling of natural gas in Colombia, the main actors that intervene in the supply are integrated as described below [13]:

- Reserves: reserves are classified according to the level of certainty associated with the projections and are categorized based on the maturity of the project and characterized according to their development and production status. Therefore, the reserves are composed of proven reserves (whose profitability has been established under economic conditions at the evaluation date), probable and possible reserves (may be based on future economic conditions).
- Production: considers the national capacity of natural gas production.
- Transportation: represents the volume of distribution that is related to the National Transportation System (known in Spanish as SNT) and its interconnected networks.
- Demand: includes the industrial, domestic, refineries, compressed natural vehicle gas, petrochemical, electric and residential generation sectors.

Based on the Forrester diagram and within the design of the supply chain model, four interconnected level variables are considered, which represent changes in the state of natural gas from generation of reserves to delivery to the final consumer and in which the demand of the previous link (actor), corresponds to the requirements of the following link, all this expressed in Giga Cubic Feet [GCF]. In the Table 1 the equations are presented.

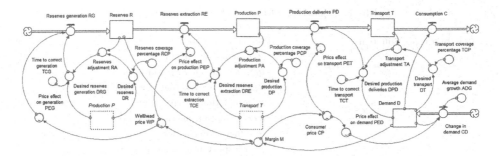

Fig. 2. Forrester diagram (Stocks and Flows) for the natural gas supply chain model.

Similarly, from historical data, the effects of the wellhead price WP on generation PEG (see Eq. 1) and on natural gas production PEP (see Eq. 2) were defined. Likewise, the effects of the price to the consumer CP were defined on the transport PET (see Eq. 3) and on the demand of natural gas PED (see Eq. 4).

$$PEG = 0.9333 - 0.0161WP + 0.0105WP^2 \qquad (1)$$
$$PEP = 0.7771 + 0.1605WP - 0.0197WP^2 \qquad (2)$$
$$PET = 1.0451 - 0.0022CP + 0.0005CP^2 \qquad (3)$$
$$PED = 1.0395 - 0.0117CP + 0.0021CP^2 \qquad (4)$$

3   Calibration and Validation of the Model

For the calibration and validation of the model, historical data was taken of the levels of reserves, production, transport and demand in Giga Cubic Feet GCF, of the main Colombian state institutions responsible for managing the supply of natural gas, which are UPME (Energy Mining Planning Unit) and Ecopetrol (Colombian Petroleum Company). The calibration consisted mainly of observing the behavior of the levels of reserves, production, transport and demand, each one as a link in the supply chain of natural gas, this according to the influence of the margin on the wellhead and consumer price. In the case of validation and based on historical information. The comparison made between these historical data and the simulated values for the variables of reserves, production, transport, demand, margin, the price at the wellhead and consumer price, are shown in Fig. 6.

In summary, to guarantee the adequate representation of the simulation model, the mean squared error (MSE), the mean square root deviation (RMSE), the average absolute error (MAD) and the percentage error absolute (MAPE) were calculated for the variables mentioned above, see Table 2. Based on this, it can be seen that the average MAPE is 16.84%, which shows that the way to represent the variables in the model is adequate.

Table 1. Equations of the levels and flows diagram.

Equation type	Equation	Symbolic meaning
Level	$\dfrac{dR}{dt} = RG - RE$	R: reserves of natural gas
		RG: flow of generation of reserves
		RE: flow of extraction of reserves
Level	$\dfrac{dP}{dt} = RE - PD$	P: production of natural gas
		PD: flow of production deliveries
		RE: flow of extraction of reserves
Level	$\dfrac{dT}{dt} = PD - C$	T: transportation of natural gas
		PD: flow of production deliveries
		C: national consumption of natural gas
Level	$\dfrac{dD}{dt} = CD$	D: natural gas demand
		CD: changes in demand
Flow	$RG = DRG \cdot PEG$	RG: flow of generation of reserves
		DRG: desired generation of reserves
		PEG: price effect on generation
Flow	$RE = DRE \cdot PEP$	RE: flow of extraction of reserves
		DRE: extraction of desired reserves
		PEP: price effect on production
Flow	$PD = DPD \cdot PET$	PD flow of production deliveries
		DPD: desired production deliveries
		PET: price effect on transport
Flow	$CD = D \cdot ADG \cdot PED$	CD: changes in demand
		ADG: average growth of generation
		PED: effect of the consumer price
Auxiliar	$Dvs_i = D_{i+1} + Ad_i / Dl_i$	Dvs_i: desired values to be supplied in the natural gas supply chain
		D_{i+1}: level of demand of the next link $(i + 1)$
		Dl_i: tlme to make the adjustment to the demand in link i, given the delay in the generation of capacity
		i: subscript indicating the links in the supply chain (1 = reserve level, 2 = production level, 3 = transport level)
Auxiliar	$Ad_i = Dvd_{i+1} - Lv_i$	Ad_i: adjusted value of supply requirements of link i
		Lv_i: current level of the link i
Auxiliar	$Dvd_{i+1} = D_{i+1} \cdot (1 + CP_i)$	Dvd_{i+1}: desired values demanded by the following link $(i + 1)$
		CP_i: percentage of coverage (security stock) of link i
Auxiliar	$M = D/R$	M: reserve margin
		D: natural gas demand
		R: reserves of natural gas
Auxiliar	$WP = 0.857 e^{21.799M}$	WP: wellhead price
		M: reserve margin
Auxiliar	$CP = 4.447 e^{19.895M}$	CP: consumer price
		M: reserve margin

Table 2. Validation of the model (Summary).

Variable	MSE	RMSE	MAD	MAPE
Reserves	1027232.5	1013.5	847.7	12.47%
Production	4593.6	67.8	41.3	10.12%
Transport	2347.1	48.4	33.7	9.72%
Demand	596.7	24.4	18.7	5.97%
Margin	0.0002	0.012	0.010	19.20%
Wellhead price	1.2	1.1	0.9	36.31%
Consumer price	24.4	4.9	2.9	24.07%

4 Policy Scenarios

The Colombian government through Decree 2345 of 2015 and the Resolution of the Ministry of Mines and Energy 40052 of 2016, seeks to identify the necessary actions to guarantee in a timely manner the security of natural gas supply in the medium and long term, in addition to the reliability in the provision of the service in case of failures in the infrastructure, through the development of expansion works. That is why, through the Transitory Natural Gas Supply Plan developed by the Energy Mining Planning Unit (UPME), it presents an instrument for the evaluation of the availability and demand of natural gas in the short and medium term, providing certainty about infrastructure projects in the country, as well as elements for investment decision making [13]. As a result of the plan mentioned above, the increase in the demand for the resource and the implementation date of the infrastructure projects are estimated in terms of reserve development, production capacity and transportation, see Table 3.

Through this article, we seek to evaluate the implementation of infrastructure works defined by the national government, which allows us to analyze the behavior over time of the impact of this "bottom-up" implementation of natural gas supply, in a that elements are provided for the design of solid supply policy. For this, four scenarios are defined that go from a weak or no policy implementation, to a strong policy implementation (policy integration), which are explained below:

- No policy implementation **S1**: in this scenario, none of the proposed policies for the chain actors in the supply of natural gas are implemented.
- Reserve policies **S2**: in this scenario, projects related to the development of possible reserves, resources to be discovered (YTF) and implementation of unconventional resources in the extraction of the resource is implemented.
- Production policy **S3**: in this scenario, the projects related to the implementation of imported natural gas regasification plants are considered, which facilitate this process by both the Caribbean Sea (Cartagena regasification plant) and the Pacific Ocean (Buenaventura regasification plant).

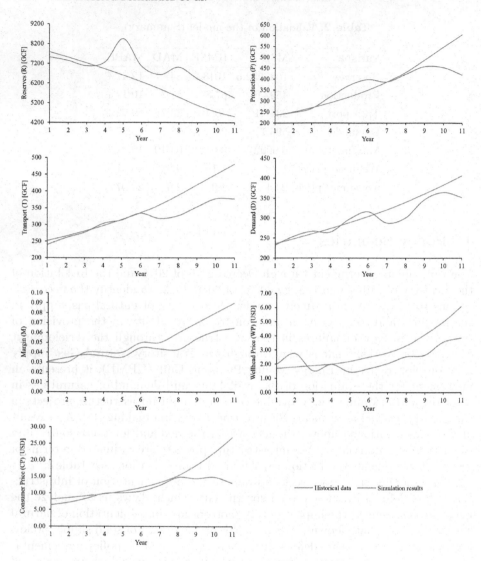

Fig. 3. Consumer and wellhead price effects

- Transportation policy **S4**: in this scenario, the projects related to the expansion of transport capacity are implemented, using gas pipelines, new sections, and flows (Fig. 3).

5 Results and Discussion

For the scenarios presented above, the behavior of the following variables is analyzed in the model and they are explained below:

Table 3. Infrastructure development planning.

Supply chain links	Policy project	Increase in capacity (GCF)	Implementation year
Reserves	Possible	1040	Through 20 years
	YTF (Yet to Find)	3000	
	No conventional	2000	
Production	Cartagena Regasification Plant	160.6	2023
	Buenaventura Regasification Plant	146	2021
Transport	Jobo-Sahagún (Córdoba) stretch	60.225	2019
	Sincelejo – Cartagena stretch	94.9	2019
	Cartagena – Barranquilla stretch	160.6	2019
	Barranquilla-La Guajira stretch	73	2017
	Cusiana – La Belleza pipeline	166.075	2019
	La Belleza – Vasconia pipeline	103.66	2019
	El Porvenir – Apiay pipeline stretch	23.36	2017
	Buenaventura – Yumbo pipeline	164.25	2023
	Yumbo y Cerrito flow	109.5	2023
	Sebastopol y Medellín flow	24.455	2018
	El Cerrito – Popayán pipeline	3.285	2018

- Levels of demand D, transport T, production P and reserves R.
- Reserve generation RG flows, reserve extraction RE and production deliveries PD.
- Auxiliary margin variables M, wellhead price WP and consumer price CP.

5.1   Demand, Transport, Production and Reserves

The demand presents an approximate growth of 1150%, passing $236GCF$ in the year 2005 to an average of $2,946GCF$ in the year 2050. In the proposed scenarios, this variable is not affected because the demand for the resource must always be attended to, see Fig. 4a. The transport, production and reserve levels fall without the intervention of the supply policies, as the implementation of the policies mentioned above increases, there is a greater supply of the resource along the chain in the simulation time. In the scenario that combines all supply policies **S4**, an increase in these levels is observed to meet the demand of the next link or customer. If the supply chain is observed backward, that is, from the client to the suppliers, there is an increase in the discrepancy of transport, production and reserve levels for the scenarios analyzed, which is known in logistics as "the bullwhip effect" [10], see Fig. 4b, c, and d.

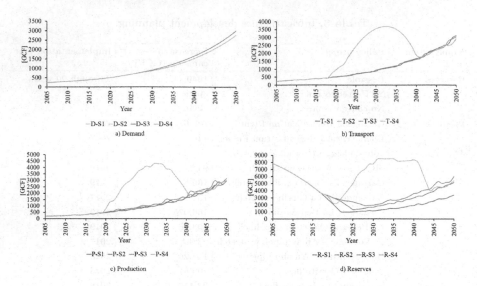

Fig. 4. Behavior of level variables by scenario

5.2 Generation of Reserves, Extraction of Reserves and Production Deliveries

The inflows respond to the requirements of the next link in the chain, considering delays in the generation of the necessary capacity to meet said requirements, a greater oscillation is generated in a greater degree of implementation of the policies analyzed (see Fig. 5a, b, and c).

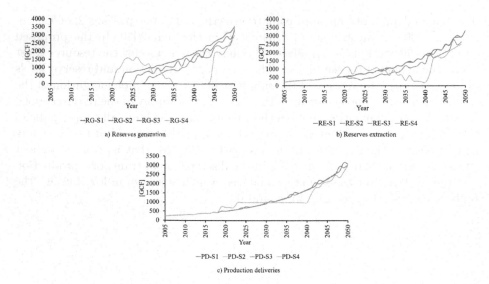

Fig. 5. Behavior of auxiliary variables by scenario

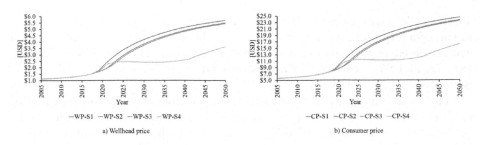

a) Wellhead price

b) Consumer price

Fig. 6. Accumulative average prices

5.3 Margin, the Price at the Wellhead and Consumer Price

As measures of the performance of the implementation of the policies analyzed, the average accumulated wellhead and consumer price are calculated. By this, it is observed that utilizing the integration of supply policies in all the links of the supply chain (transport, reserves, and production), lower prices are achieved. In the case of the wellhead price it is 52% lower, see Fig. 6a, and for the consumer price at 47% lower, see Fig. 6b, in the scenario that considers the aforementioned integration **S4**, in front of the scenarios where the implementation is null or partial (**S1, S2** and **S3**).

6   Conclusions

In this article, the supply of natural gas has been modeled as a supply chain, in which the actors involved interconnect to meet the demand of the resource by various sectors. For the development of this model, the system dynamics methodology was used, through which it is possible to observe the supply-demand relationship of the actors involved in the supply, concerning the related prices and against various government policies that they seek to avoid shortages in the supply.

The proposed model represents the actors of the supply chain through levels interconnected by incoming and outgoing flows, which regulate the exchanges between one and another actor, by means of the requirements of the demand and considering the margin of reserves, which in turn, they affect the prices of the resource and the generation of supply capacity, making the analysis appear in an integrated manner. These effects (effects) can be defined using historical data from the natural gas market, as well as being useful in the definition of current levels and parameters, which may provide greater consistency in the process of verification and validation of the model.

The demand for natural gas in the country is expected to grow in the coming years, mainly as a response to the low price compared to other energy alternatives, ease in the development of infrastructure for processing and supply, safety and less impact on the environment. Make it an ideal fuel for the transition to unconventional and/or renewable energy. Through the scenario that combines all the policies proposed by the national government (S4), there is a stimulus in the generation of capacity at all levels in the supply chain, contrary to what was observed in the partial implementation scenarios of the policies analyzed. (S1, S2, and S3), in which the actors respond to the demand but with a lower performance in terms of prices.

The reserve margin is reduced as a greater degree of policy implementation is generated, going from an average of 54% in the scenario without policy intervention (S1) to an average of 18% in the scenario where all the supply policies (S4) are combined, derived from the stimulus to the generation of capacity in the actors involved and contributing to the goal in the development of the supply chains, with respect to avoiding shortages at competitive prices for the market.

For this reason, the regulator (national government) must determine the mechanisms for the integration of the actors or organizations that are part of the supply of natural gas, in the planning of investment projects in the generation of infrastructure in the various links, which it results in a better performance in the levels of supply and the prices (wellhead and consumer). This is a confirmation of the hypothesis proposed in this research, which considers the benefits of the integration of supply chain actors in the planning of policies aimed at improving performance in the supply of the resource.

References

1. British Petroleum Statistical Review of World Energy 2017 (2017). https://www.bp.com/content/dam/bp-country/dech/PDF/bp-statistical-review-of-world-energy-2017-full-report.pdf. Accessed 10 Apr 2019
2. Colombian Oil and Gas Information System (2017). http://www.sipg.gov.co/Inicio/GasNatural/Estadisticas/Demanda/tabid/122/. Accessed 10 Apr 2019
3. British Petroleum Statistical Review of World Energy 2018 (2018). https://www.bp.com/content/dam/bp/business-sites/en/global/corporate/pdfs/energy-economics/statistical-review/bp-stats-review-2018-full-report.pdf. Accessed 10 Apr 2019
4. Becerra Fernández, M., González La Rotta, E.C., Cosenz, F., Dyner Rezonzew, I.: Demand and supply model for the natural gas supply chain in Colombia. In: Li, L., Hasegawa, K., Tanaka, S. (eds.) AsiaSim 2018. CCIS, vol. 946, pp. 220–231. Springer, Singapore (2018). https://doi.org/10.1007/978-981-13-2853-4_17
5. Becerra Fernández, M., González La Rotta, E.C., Cosenz, F., Dyner Rezonzew, I.: Supporting the natural gas supply chain public policies through simulation methods: a dynamic performance management approach. In: Figueroa-García, J.C., López-Santana, E.R., Rodriguez-Molano, J.I. (eds.) WEA 2018. CCIS, vol. 915, pp. 363–376. Springer, Cham (2018). https://doi.org/10.1007/978-3-030-00350-0_31
6. Becerra-Fernandez, M., Yee, R.R.: Selection of alternatives for the natural gas supply in Colombia using the analytic hierarchy process. Ingenieria 22(2), 190–210 (2017)
7. Cai, Z., Clarke, R.H., Glowacki, B.A., Nuttall, W.J., Ward, N.: Ongoing ascent to the helium production plateau-insights from system dynamics. Resour. Policy 35(2), 77–89 (2010)

8. Cardenas, L.M., Franco, C.J., Dyner, I.: Assessing emissions-mitigation energy policy under integrated supply and demand analysis: the Colombian case. J. Clean. Prod. **112**, 3759–3773 (2016)
9. Eker, S., Van Daalen, E.: Investigating the effects of uncertainties in the upstream gas sector. Int. J. Syst. Syst. Eng. **4**(2), 99 (2013)
10. Forrester, J.W.: Industrial dynamics. J. Oper. Res. Soc. **48**(10), 1037–1041 (1997)
11. Horschig, T., Billig, E., Thrän, D.: Model-based estimation of market potential for Bio-SNG in the German biomethane market until 2030 within a system dynamics approach. Agron. Res. **14**(3), 754–767 (2016)
12. Howells, M., Jeong, K., Langlois, L., Lee, M.K., Nam, K.Y., Rogner, H.H.: Incorporating macroeconomic feedback into an energy systems model using an IO approach: evaluating the rebound effect in the Korean electricity system. Energy Policy **38**(6), 2700–2728 (2010)
13. Mining and Energy Planning Unit of Colombia, UPME: Indicative Plan of Natural Gas Supply - 2016 (2016). http://www1.upme.gov.co/Hidrocarburos/Estudios %202014-2016/Plan_Transitorio_Absatecimiento_Gas_Natural_Abril_2016.pdf. Accessed 10 Apr 2019
14. North, M.J., Murphy, J.T., Sydelko, P., Martinez-Moyano, I., Sallach, D.L., Macal, C.M.: Integrated modeling of conflict and energy. In: 2015 Winter Simulation Conference (WSC), pp. 2499–2510 (2015)
15. Redondo, J.M., Olivar, G., Ibarra-Vega, D., Dyner, I.: Modeling for the regional integration of electricity markets. Energy Sustain. Dev. **43**, 100–113 (2018)
16. Schroeder, R.G., Goldstain, S.M., Rungutusanatham, J.M.: Operations Management Concepts and Contemporary Cases. McGraw-Hill, Mexico D.F. (2011)
17. Sterman, J.: Booms, busts, and beer: understanding the dynamics of supply chains. In: Bendoly, E., van Wezel, W., Bachrach, D. (eds.) Handbook of Behavioral Operations Management: Social and Psychological Dynamics in Production and Service Settings, pp. 203–237. Oxford University Press, New York (2015)
18. Sterman, J.: Business Dynamics Systems Thinking and Modeling for a Complex World. McGraw-Hill, New York (2000)
19. International Gas Union, Eurogas: The Role of Natural Gas in a Sustainable Energy Market (2010). http://www.utilitypost.com/wp-content/uploads/ 2015/05/THE-ROLE-OF-NATURAL-GAS-IN-A-SUSTAINABLE-ENERGY-MARKET.pdf. Accessed 10 Apr 2019

Design of Distribution Network of a Fresh Egg Producing and Commercializing Company in Colombia

Adriana Isabel Linares Vanegas[1] (ID)
and Nelson Javier Tovar-Perilla[2](✉) (ID)

[1] Departamento Nacional de Planeación, Ibagué, Colombia
adrisli86@hotmail.com
[2] Facultad de Ingeniería, Universidad de Ibagué, Ibagué, Colombia
nelson.tovar@unibague.edu.co

Abstract. This paper describes the process to design a distribution network of a company of production and commercialization of fresh egg. The aim is showing methodological aspects, variables analyzed, mathematical model proposed and the results obtained for the design of the distribution network. The proposed network allows increasing the level of customer service and reducing the logistic cost. Methodology for development of work focused on three phases: First, the analysis of variables that influence the operation of the company's distribution system. Second, a mixed integer linear programming (MIP) mathematical model was developed with the current distribution network and with the addition of new distribution centers. Finally, different scenarios were proposed to evaluate the variability and uncertainty of relevant variables of the system.

Keywords: Distribution network · Location-allocation model ·
Mixed integer linear programming

1 Introduction

The adequate management supply chain is a necessity of companies to survive in the business environment. It is important that companies have tools to adapt to change. Logistics is considered as a determinant factor for continuous improvement and a differentiating element of the environment [1]. It is a decisive factor for companies' competitiveness, since it efficiently manages and controls the flows along the supply chain to satisfy customers' requirements [2].

According to International Monetary Fund, average costs of logistics are around 12% of the world's gross national product, occupying the second position behind the purchase costs. In Colombia, National Logistics Survey showed that logistics costs represent 18% of total sales in the country, a higher value compare with Andean countries (13.9%) [3, 4]. On the overall of these costs, distribution costs represent approximately 60% of total [5]. Distribution logistics relates to a direct contact with the customer, and it becomes a critical aspect in logistics processes, it must answer effectively to a wide variety of specific criteria and guaranteeing levels of suitable service, that lead to satisfy the customers [6].

© Springer Nature Switzerland AG 2019
J. C. Figueroa-García et al. (Eds.): WEA 2019, CCIS 1052, pp. 722–734, 2019.
https://doi.org/10.1007/978-3-030-31019-6_61

The importance of distribution process shows the need of efficient distribution networks designing, guarantying the competitiveness of companies. One of the most important aspects in the distribution networks design is location of facilities, since it generates annual savings between 5% and 10% of the total logistics costs [7].

In Colombia, the industrial sector of production of fresh eggs produced 7376 million of unities in 2018, and in 2017 registered incomes for 1.6 billons of COP. The eggs' consumption has grown significantly in recent years, from 242 to 293 eggs per capita between 2014 and 2018, which is seen as a potential growth and expansion opportunity for companies of sector [8].

The ABC company of fresh eggs analyzed in this work (name is reserved for confidentiality purposes) determined to attend new customers located all around the country as a new trade strategy in order to increase its market. This decision involved a new production plant with a capacity of 5,000,000 eggs per day, 5 times more than its current production. This scenario required the redesign of distribution network that allows it to support the Company's expansion plan and guarantee its operational efficiency. For this reason, this work was aimed at designing the distribution network of the Company, in order to determine the optimal location of new distribution centers (DC) and determine allocation of DC to satisfy the customer's demand, through a formulation and analysis of a MILP mathematical model to solve location-allocation problem (LAP).

2 Distribution Problem – Review of Literature

The trend towards the globalization of industry involves coordination of complex flows of materials and information from a multitude of agents throughout the supply chain, fact that has highlighted the inadequate organizational structures to satisfy customer requirements [9].

The high costs associated with the distribution process has generated that decisions related to distribution and transport are considered strategic, not only because of financial and economic impact, but because of the implications in service's levels. Distribution involves activities related to transport of goods from production to the final points of sale and consumption. It covers functions of movement, handling of goods, transport, transshipment, storage services (shipping, storage and inventory management) and wholesale and retail [9].

The objective of designing a distribution network is to optimize the flow of goods through the network, from points where the merchandise is produced to demand points in order to reduce costs and increases service's levels. Distribution network's analysis can be carried out from two perspectives: (a) Optimization of the flows of goods: with existing distribution network is sought to optimize the flows of merchandise through the network. (b) Improvement of the existing network: it is sought to choose the best configuration of the facilities of the network in order to reach the objectives and minimize total costs in companies [10].

Strategic decisions such as location of facilities, transportation and inventory management, affect the cost of the distribution system and the quality of the level of customer service. For this reason, a good network design is determined by the influence of location, allocation, routing, and inventory [11]. Among tools to address the problems of distribution, the most commonly used is modeling through mixed-integer programming (MIP) taken into account (a) Level of aggregation of demand [12]; (b) Type of product in the supply chain [13]; (c) Number of stages within SC to be modeled [14]; (d) Uncertainty of the variables to be analyzed [15] and; (e) Modeling approach (discrete or continuous) [16].

Authors have been used this technique to address the problem of designing the distribution network. Works include location of production plants and distribution warehouses, to determine the best distribution strategy among plants - ware-houses – customers. The objective of this design is to satisfy customer demands and minimize the total costs of distribution network [12].

This paper describes procedure to design distribution network of a company dedicated to production and commercialization of fresh egg in Colombia to solve the LAP by the application of MIP model. The objective of model was to determine location of new distribution centers to determine the amount of egg to be transported from production plants - DC - customers. Table 1 shows the methodology employed.

Table 1. Methodology employed

Phases	Activities
Identification of variables that influence in distribution process	Direct observation of the process/field visits
Formulation, execution of model based on mixed integer linear programming (MIP)	Execution of model with the current situation of the company Execution of model with the addition of new distribution centers
Evaluation of variability and uncertainty of relevant variables of the system	Analysis of results for the distribution network with the different proposed scenarios

2.1 Description of Company

ABC is a company dedicated to the production and commercialization of eggs; it distributes more than 1.5 million unities daily. ABC's supply chain is composed by four main links: Concentrate feed factory, Poultry farms, Productions farms and Distribution centers (DC). Hens are taken from poultry farms to production farms at week 16. Eggs are taken from production farms to distribution center, where the eggs are classified according to its weight in six types. Eggs are packing in cardboard trays at DCs and finally, distributed to customers located in more than 10 cities in the country. The transport is carried out in vehicles with capacity between 70,000 to 402,000 eggs. Customers are served from DC's in a 1-day lead-time.

2.2 Identification of the Problem and Solution Proposed

Identified problem in ABC's distribution system was a location-allocation problem (LAP). To solve this problem a MIP was proposed. This model was developed in GAMS® software using Solver CPLEX and solved using NEOS Server platform.

Construction of model seeks to be a support for planning of supply chain, in which three levels can be distinguished (strategic, tactical and operational) [17]. Taking into account that level of decision depends on the scope of the model; proposed model is at strategic level, since locations of storage and distribution will be identified. Input data will be taken based on a year of time.

2.3 Models Construction

In this study two MIP models were applied. In both models a growth of eggs' consumption was assumed. One of them was developed with the currently situation of the company and the second one was developed including new distribution centers to evaluate the need of construction of them. Table 2 shows the proposed scenarios in each model developed. The scenarios make changes in relevant variables of the system, such as demand, production capacity and opening of new distribution centers. Demand projections in sceneries were calculated taking into account per capita consumption at the national level, which is 250 eggs per year, with an annual increase of 5% [8].

Table 2. Proposed scenarios in the construction of models

Model with currently situation company	Model with new DC
Direct scenario: Distribution system was modeled as it currently works, without change demand pattern	*S6.* Distribution system was modeled as it currently works, without change demand pattern, but LAP was modeled. This scenario was modeled to determine if new distribution centers are required to operate in ABC Company
S1. Increase of 5% of demand in all current customers. Increase in capacity of production plant SP with a new automated shed. Increase of 5% in capacity of distribution center SP	
S2. Increase of 10% of demand in all current customers. Increase in capacity of production plant SP with two new automated sheds. Increase of 10% in capacity of distribution center SP	
S3. Increase of 15% of demand in all current customers. Increase in capacity of production plant SP with two new automated sheds. Increase of 15% in capacity of distribution center SP	*S7.* Increase in capacity of distribution center SP in 350,000,000 eggs per year. Increase in production capacity of production plant SP with eight automated sheds. Increase of 20% of demand in all current customers, but LAP was modeled. This scenario was modeled to determine if new distribution centers are required to operate in ABC Company
S4. Increase of 20% of demand in all current customers. Increase in capacity of production plant SP with three new automated sheds. Increase of 20% in capacity of distribution center SP	
S5. Increase in capacity of distribution center SP in 350,000,000 eggs per year. Increase in production capacity of production plant SP with eight automated sheds. Increase of 20% of demand in all current customers	

Table 3 shows the notation used to formulate the model to analyze direct delivery scenario and scenarios 1–5 for currently situation of the company.

Table 3. Index, parameters and decision variables of proposed model in the currently situation

Index			Parameters	
	Name	Values		Name
I	Set of production plants	C, BA, NA, T, SP	c_{ij}	Unit cost of transport from production plant at site i to distribution center at site j
J	Set of DC	C, SP, P	h_{jlt}	Unit cost of transport from distribution center at site j to customer zone at site l by means of transport t
L	Set of customer zones	B, I, M, N, V, T, CH, E, G, L	w_j	Storage capacity of distribution center at site j
K	Set of type of eggs	B, A, AA, AAA, J	v_j	Unit cost of material handling in distribution center at site j
T	Set of means of transport	T, S, P, M	c_{ij}	Unit cost of transport from production plant at site i to distribution center at site j
			d_{ki}	Availability of product k in the production plant at site i
			e_{kl}	Demand for product k in customer zone at site l
			di_{lt}	Days of inventory in customer zone at site l by means of transport t
Decision variables				
s_{ijk}	Quantity of product k that is distributed from production plant at site i to distribution center at site j			
x_{jlkt}	Quantity of product k that is distributed from distribution center at site j to customer zone at site l by means of transport t			
y_{jlt}	1 if means of transport t is selected to deliver product from distribution center at site j to customer zone at site l; 0 otherwise			

Objective function is total logistics cost of ABC's distribution process. The first term is total transport cost from production plants to distribution centers, the second term is total material handling cost in distribution centers and, third term is total transport cost from distribution centers to customer zones:

$$Min\, Z = \sum_i \sum_j \sum_k c_{ij} s_{ijk} + \sum_i \sum_j \sum_k s_{ijk} \times v_j + \sum_j \sum_l \sum_k \sum_t h_{jlt} \times x_{jlkt}$$

Table 4 shows the constraints, equations and the scope of the constrain use to develop the model with the currently situation of the company:

Table 4. Constraints, equations and the scope of the constrain (model with currently situation of the company)

Constrain	Equation	Scope of the constrain
Availability of product k in production plant at site i	$\sum_j s_{ijk} \leq d_{ki} \quad \forall i,k$	It guarantees that all egg production that is sent from production plant at site i to distribution centers at site j does not exceed production capacity in production plant at site i
Capacity of distribution center at site j	$\sum_{ik} S_{ijk} \leq w_j \quad \forall j$	It guarantees that egg production that is sent from production plants at site i to distribution center at site j does not exceed storage capacity of the distribution center at site j
Supply of product k at customer zone at site l	$\sum_{jt} X_{jlkt} \geq e_{kl} \quad \forall k,l$	It guarantees that quantity of egg sent from distribution centers at site j to customer zone at site l does not exceed demand of customer zone at site l
Flow conservation of product k in distribution center j	$\sum_i s_{ijk} = \sum_{lt} X_{jlkt} \quad \forall j,k$	It guarantees that quantity of egg transported from productions plants at site i to distribution center at site j is equal to quantity of egg transported from distribution center at site j to customer zones at site l
Relation 1 of variables for selection of means of transport	$\sum_k X_{jlkt} \geq y_{jlt} \quad \forall j,l,t$	Constraints set that relate binary variable of transportation means selection with variable of quantity sent of product k to customer zones at site l
Relation 2 of variables for selection of means of transport	$\sum_k X_{jlkt} \leq 1.000.000.000 \times y_{jlt} \quad \forall j,l,t$	
Selection of a single means of transport	$\sum_t y_{jlt} = 1 \quad \forall j,l$	Constraints set that guarantees that quantity of egg distributed from distribution center at site j to customer zones at site l is served in a single transport type t
Selection of means of transport per days of inventory	$y_{jlt} \times di_{lt} \leq 4 \quad \forall j,l,t$	Constraints set that guarantees that quantity of egg sent from distribution center at site j to customer zone at site l by means of transport t does not exceed days of inventory allowed for storage in customer zones at site l

Table 5 shows the notation used to formulate the model to analyze scenarios 6–7 for model with the addition of distribution centers.

Table 5. Index, parameters and decision variables of proposed model with the addition of distribution centers

Index			Parameters	
	Name	Values		Name
I	Set of production plants	C, BA, NA, T, SP	c_{ij}	Unit cost of transport from production plant at site i to distribution center at site j
J	Set of DC	C, SP, P	h_{jmt}	Unit cost of transport from distribution center at site j to new distribution center at site m by means of transport t
L	Set of customer zones	B, I, M, N, V, T, CH, E, G, L	g_{mlt}	Unit cost of transport from new distribution center at site m to customer zone at site l by means of transport t
K	Set of type of eggs	B, A, AA, AAA, J	w_j	Storage capacity of distribution center at site j
T	Set of means of transport	T, S, P, M	wm_m	Storage capacity of new distribution center at site m
M	Set of new DC	B, I, M, N, V, T, CH, E, G, L	v_j	Unit cost of material handling in distribution center at site j
			vm_m	Unit cost of material handling in new distribution center at site m
			f_m	Opening cost of new distribution center at site m
			d_{ki}	Availability of product k in the production plant at site i
			e_{kl}	Demand for product k in customer zone at site l
			di_{lt}	Days of inventory in customer zone at site l by means of transport t
			dim_{mt}	Days of inventory in new distribution center at site m by means of transport t

Decision variables	
s_{ijk}	Quantity of product k that is distributed from production plant at site i to distribution center at site j
x_{jmkt}	Quantity of product k that is distributed from distribution center at site j to new distribution center at site m by means of transport t
o_m	Quantity of product that output from new distribution center at site m
DM_m	Demand served by new distribution center at site m without counting demand of himself (variable without sign constraint)
u_m	Variable of conversion of negative values to positive ones of variable DM
y_{jmt}	1 if means of transport t is selected to deliver product from distribution center at site j to new distribution center at site m; 0 otherwise
r_{mlt}	1 if means of transport t is selected to deliver product from new distribution center at site m to customer zone at site l; 0 otherwise
A_m	1 if new distribution center at site m is opened; 0 otherwise
q_{mlt}	1 if new distribution center at site m attends customer zone at site l by means of transport t; 0 otherwise

Objective function is total logistics cost of ABC's distribution process. The first term is total transport cost from production plants to existing distribution centers; the second term is total material handling cost in existing distribution centers; the third term is total transport cost from existing distribution centers to new distribution centers; the fourth term is total opening cost of new distribution centers; the fifth term is total material handling cost in new distribution centers and; the sixth term is total transport cost from new distribution centers to customer zones.

$$Min\ Z = \sum_i \sum_j \sum_k c_{ij} s_{ijk} + \sum_i \sum_j \sum_k S_{ijk} v_j + \sum_j \sum_m \sum_k \sum_t h_{jmt} x_{jmkt}$$

$$+ 4/360 \sum_m f_m u_m + \sum_m vm_m u_m + \sum_m \sum_l \sum_k \sum_t g_{mlt} q_{mlt} e_{kl}$$

Table 6 shows the constraints, equations and the scope of the constrain use to develop the model with the addition of new distribution centers.

Table 6. Constraints, equations and the scope of the constrain (model with the addition of new distribution centers)

Constrain	Equation	Scope of the constrain
Availability of product k in production plant at site i	$\sum_j s_{ijk} \leq d_{ki}$ $\forall i, k$	It guarantees that all egg production that is sent from production plant at site i to distribution centers at site j does not exceed production capacity in production plant at site i
Capacity of distribution center at site j	$\sum_{ik} S_{ijk} \leq w_j$ $\forall j$	It guarantees that egg production that is sent from production plants at site i to distribution center at site j does not exceed storage capacity of the distribution center at site j
Supply of product k at customer zone at site l	$\sum_{mt} q_{mlt} \geq 1$ $\forall l$	It guarantees that quantity of egg distributed from distribution center at site m to customer zones at site l is served in a single transport type t
Flow conservation of product k in distribution center j	$\sum_i s_{ijk} = \sum_{mt} x_{jmkt}$ $\forall j, k$	It guarantees that quantity of egg transported from productions plants at site i to distribution center at site j is equal to quantity of egg transported from distribution center at site j to distribution center at site m
Flow conservation of product k in distribution center m	$\sum_{jtk} x_{jmkt} = \sum_{lkt} q_{mlt} e_{kl}$ $\forall m$	It guarantees that quantity of egg transported from distribution centers at site j to distribution center at site m is equal to quantity of egg transported from distribution center at site m to customer zones at site l

(continued)

Table 6. (*continued*)

Constrain	Equation	Scope of the constrain
Relation 1 of variables for selection of means of transport	$\sum_k x_{jmkt} \geq y_{jmt}$ $\forall j, m, t$	Constraints set that relate binary variable of transportation means selection with variable of quantity sent of product k from distribution centers at site j to distribution centers at site m
Relation 2 of variables for selection of means of transport	$\sum_k x_{jmkt} \leq 1.000.000.000 \times y_{jmt}$ $\forall j, m, t$	
Selection of means of transport t by inventory days between distribution centers j and m	$y_{jmt} dim_{mt} \leq 4$ $\forall jmt$	It guarantees that quantity of egg sent from distribution center at site j to distribution centers at site m by means of transport t does not exceed days of inventory allowed for storage in distribution centers at site m
Selection of means of transport t by inventory days from distribution centers m to customer zones l	$q_{mlt} \times di_{lt} \leq 4$ $\forall m, l, t$	It guarantees that quantity of egg sent from distribution center at site j to customer zone at site l by means of transport t does not exceed days of inventory allowed for storage in customer zones at site l
Constraint 1 of opening distribution center m	$o_m \geq A_m$ $\forall m$	Constraints set that relates quantity variable that leaves distribution center m with opening binary variable of a distribution center m
Constraint 2 of opening distribution center m	$o_m \leq 1.000.000.000 \times A_m$ $\forall m$	
Delivery from distribution center m to customer zone l	$\sum_{jkt} x_{jmkt} = o_m$ $\forall m$	It guarantees that quantity of egg transported from distribution centers at site m to customer zones at site l is equal to quantity of egg that leaves of distribution centers at site m
Demand to be served by each distribution center m	$\sum_{lkt} q_{mlt} e_{kl} -$ $\sum_{kl} \$(ord_m \, eq \, ord_l) e_{kl} = DM_m$ $\forall m$	It determines quantity of egg in customer zones l to serve by the distribution center at site m
Conversion equation from negative values to positive values	$u_m \geq DM_m$ $\forall m$	Constraints set that guarantees that quantity of demand served by the distribution center m is positive
Conversion equation from negative values to positive values	$u_m \geq -DM_m$ $\forall m$	

2.4   Results and Discussions

Current Situation of the Company

The ABC's total costs of distribution for each scenario analyzed as well as the increases in cost and demand and quantity of product that is distributed from production plant at site i to distribution center at site j for each scenario analyzed are shown in Tables 7 and 8.

Table 7. Total cost for different scenarios analyzed

Scenario	Total cost (millions COP per year)	Cost increase	Demand increase
Direct	2,193	–	–
1	2,340	6.7%	5%
2	2,506	14.3%	10%
3	2,683	22.3%	15%
4	2,859	30.4%	20%
5	2,025	−7.6%	20%

Table 8. Results of S_{ijk} variables in scenarios modeled

i-j	Direct	Scenario 1	Scenario 2	Scenario 3	Scenario 4	Scenario 5
C-C	244,672,034	244,672,034	244,672,034	244,672,034	244,672,034	244,672,034
BA-C	38,314,353	38,314,353	38,314,353	38,314,353	38,314,353	38,314,353
NA-C	52,559,512	52,559,512	52,559,512	52,559,512	52,559,512	50,738,077
T-C	55,182,987	55,182,987	55,182,987	55,182,987	55,182,987	0
SP-C	0	747,630	26,537,000	52,316,387	78,101,000	0
SP-SP	43,200,395	45,360,000	47,520,000	49,679,556	51,840,790	336,944,,889
SP-P	124,962,666	149,999,762	149,999,427	149,995,845	150,000,916	0

In scenario 5, there is a significant saving in the total logistics cost of network compared to scenarios proposed, since transport costs between distribution centers and material handling costs are eliminated. On the other hand, in direct scenario, distribution center C is not used to storage egg produced of production plant SP, however when increase demand, scenarios 1–4, this DC is used because of capacity of others DCs is totally used. This fact increases total cost because transport between DCs is increased. Another important result is fact that means of transport of greater capacity are used for long shipments and those of smaller capacity for near shipments.

Given constraints of inventory time in customers, the highest demand customers are given daily deliveries, while those with less demand, the delivery times range from 3 to days (See Table 9).

Table 9. Inventory days in scenarios modeled

Customer	Direct	Scenario 1	Scenario 2	Scenario 3	Scenario 4	Scenario 5
B	0,18	0,12	0,07	0,03	0,47	0,47
I	0,08	0,03	0,11	0,06	0,02	0,02
M	4,00	4,00	4,00	4,00	4,00	4,00
N	3,27	3,07	2,88	2,71	2,56	2,56
V	3,46	3,24	3,05	2,87	2,71	2,71
T	1,93	3,93	3,71	3,50	3,32	3,32
CH	2,06	1,91	4,00	3,78	3,58	3,58
E	4,00	4,00	4,00	4,00	4,00	4,00
G	1,93	3,94	3,72	3,51	3,32	3,32
L	4,00	4,00	4,00	4,00	4,00	4,00

From above Table, it can be determined that for customer B case, due to demand and high inventory turnover. There is a very low indicator of inventory days, which decreases as demand increases in each scenario, with exception of scenario 4 and 5. In those scenarios where an increase occurs, because number of trips required increases from 2 to 3 leaving more inventory in this customer. It also happens in case of customer I, that number of trips increases in scenario 2, going from 8 to 9 trips per day. Customers N and V do not suffer variations in types of transport used, therefore days of inventory are reduced when demand increases. Customers T, CH and G, when increasing demand, need to change type of transport to another with greater capacity to cover it, which means that meaningful changes are showed in scenario 1. For customers T and G and in scenario 2 for customer CH. Customers M, E and L do not present changes among the scenarios.

Additionally, an analysis of capacity of the system to absorb increases in demand was made. This analysis showed that customers with a higher level of demand, such as B and I, could increase demand by up to 14% on average without affecting the system and those with lower demand up to 30% on average (See Table 10).

Table 10. Maximum variation of daily demand

Customer	Direct	Scenario 1	Scenario 2	Scenario 3	Scenario 4	Scenario 5
B	18%	12%	7%	3%	47%	47%
I	8%	3%	11%	6%	2%	2%
M	65%	57%	50%	43%	37%	37%
N	7%	2%	29%	24%	19%	19%
V	11%	6%	1%	29%	24%	24%
T	46%	23%	18%	13%	8%	8%
CH	2%	46%	25%	20%	15%	15%
E	77%	69%	61%	54%	48%	48%
G	47%	24%	18%	13%	8%	8%
L	60%	52%	45%	39%	33%	33%

Finally, an analysis of the frequency of deliveries that must be made to cover demand was developed. Table 11 shows the frequency of deliveries of each client according to the evaluated scenario. This analysis showed that for customers with higher demand, such as B and I, it is necessary to make deliveries on a daily basis to meet demand and keep the level of service. For other customers, frequency of deliveries varies according to rotation of the inventory of each zone from 1 to 4 days, maximum time of egg durability in customer.

Addition of New Distribution Centers
The results of total distribution costs for 6th scenario was 2,193 million COP per year same obtained in the direct scenario. It means, in current operating conditions, it is better to continue with the current distribution system, without opening new distribution centers. That is why the opening a new distribution center, the transport cost is

Table 11. Delivery frequency in scenarios modeled

Customer	Direct	Scenario 1	Scenario 2	Scenario 3	Scenario 4	Scenario 5
B	Daily	Daily	Daily	Daily	Daily	Daily
I	Daily	Daily	Daily	Daily	Daily	Daily
M	4 days	4 days	4 days	4 days	4 days	4 days
N	3 days	3 days	2 days	2 days	2 days	2 days
V	3 days	3 days	3 days	2 days	2 days	2 days
T	1 day	3 days	3 days	3 days	3 days	3 days
CH	2 days	1 day	4 days	3 days	3 days	3 days
E	4 days	4 days	4 days	4 days	4 days	4 days
G	1 day	3 days	3 days	3 days	3 days	3 days
L	4 days	4 days	4 days	4 days	4 days	4 days

reduced due to cheaper means of transport are used. However, it is important to take into account that it causes increases of costs related to the opening and handling, making this scenario not feasible in economics terms.

The results of 7th scenario show that to meet the increase in demand it is necessary to open a distribution center in zone I. This distribution center would serve customers located in I, M, CH, E, G and L; the other zones are served from the current distribution centers. The ABC's total costs of distribution for 7th scenario was 2,118 million COP per year, with an increase over the cost of scenario 5 due to the cost of opening a new distribution center.

3   Conclusions

The distribution system modelling and the mathematical representation of variables included in that system is an image of current behavior of the company distribution in a year. This fact allows the model defining tactical and strategic strategies about storage and transportation of eggs and type of vehicle in order to attend the current clients at lower cost. With model results the company will determine which decision make regarding capital increase and vehicles based on the claim's forecast.

Company has a limited storage capacity in the distribution center SP near production plant SP, which has an important production capacity. This fact indicates that this production plant needs to be expanded to increase its production potential. Therefore, in distribution center SP, the company needs to focus their decisions on the plant infrastructure enlargement making accurate investment with the aim of reducing the total operating costs. Investment will ensure the attention of client's requirements.

In current operating system, there is not a distribution and deliveries programming plan to define the client's requirements. These decisions are in charge of the logistic department, which makes the decision based on product availability on the different production plants and the transportation means availability. It reflects the necessity of a redesign in the distribution net in the company.

This research is a first step towards the distribution system study to operating level, it allows the company knowing amount of travels, attention of specific's clients, stock's levels, production of and infrastructure capacity, and distribution channels.

References

1. Mora, L.A.: Gestión Logística integral, Bogotá: Ecoediciones (2008)
2. Acero, M.: El diseño de las cadenas de suministro ¿Qué tanto necesitamos administrar una cadena? (2006)
3. Rey, M.F.: Competitividad nacional en logística medida a través del desempeño logístico de las empresas, Latin American Logistics Center, Atlanta (2008)
4. Álvarez, C., Pabón, C., Ortiz, J.F.: Logística en Colombia: camino hacia la competitividad, Supestos Económicos (2010)
5. World Bank: Índice de Desempeño Logístico. World Bank, Washington DC (2014)
6. Cámara Colombiana de la Infraestructura: Ingeniería y TLC, Foro (2006)
7. Robusté, F.: Logística del transporte. Ediciones de la Universidad Politécnica de Cataluña, Barcelona (2005)
8. FENAVI, Producción del huevo en Colombia, Programa de estudios económicos, Bogotá (2018)
9. Christopher, M.: Logistics and Supply Chain Management, 4th edn. Prentice Hall, Londres (2010)
10. Ambrosino, D., Swtella, M.G.: Distribution network design: new problems and related models. Eur. J. Oper. Res. **165**, 610–624 (2005)
11. Georgiadis, M., Tsiakis, P., Longinidis, P., Sofioglou, M.: Optimal design of supply chain networks under uncertain transient demand variations. Omega **39**, 254–272 (2011)
12. Amiri, A.: Designing a distribution network in a supply chain system: Formulation and efficient solution procedure. Eur. J. Oper. Res. **171**(2), 567–576 (2006)
13. Zhou, G., Min, H., Genc, M.: The balanced allocation of customers to multiple distribution centers in the supply chain network: a genetic algorithm approach. Comput. Ind. Eng. **43**(1–2), 251–261 (2002)
14. Lu, Z., Bostel, N.: A facility location model for logistics systems including reverse flows: the case of remanufacturing activities. Comput. Oper. Res. **34**(2), 299–323 (2007)
15. Max Shen, Z., Qi, L.: Incorporating inventory and routing costs in strategic location models. Eur. J. Oper. Res. **179**, 372–389 (2007)
16. Melo, M., Nickel, S., Saldanha-da-Gama, F.: Facility location and supply chain management - a review. Eur. J. Oper. Res. **196**, 401–412 (2009)
17. Dasci, A., Verter, V.: A continuous model for production–distribution system design. Eur. J. Oper. Res. **129**(2), 287–298 (2001)

Mixed-Integer Linear Programming Models for One-Commodity Pickup and Delivery Traveling Salesman Problems

Juan D. Palacio[ID] and Juan Carlos Rivera[✉][ID]

Grupo de investigación en Modelado Matemático,
Departamento de Ciencias Matemáticas, Escuela de Ciencias, Universidad EAFIT,
Medellín, Colombia
{jpalac26,jrivera6}@eafit.edu.co

Abstract. This article addresses two different pickup and delivery routing problems. In the first one, called the one-commodity pickup and delivery traveling salesman problem, a known amount of a single product is supplied or demanded by a set of two different types of locations (pickup or delivery nodes). Therefore, a capacitated vehicle must visit each location once at a minimum cost. We also deal with the relaxed case where locations can be visited several times. In the last problem, the pickup or delivery operation can be split into several smaller pickups or deliveries, and also locations can be used as temporal storage points with the aim of reducing the cost of the route. To solve these problems, we present two mixed-integer linear programming models and we solve them via commercial solver. We analyze how several visits to a single location may improve solution quality and we also show that our simple strategy has a good performance for instances with up to 60 locations.

Keywords: Pickup and delivery · Traveling salesman problem ·
Mixed-integer linear programming · Split delivery

1 Introduction

The *vehicle routing problem* (VRP) is one of the most popular problems in combinatorial optimization [6]. The number of applications of the VRP has been growing since 1959 when a first article on the *truck dispatching problem* was published [8]. For services and goods distribution, the VRP aims to design a set of routes for a collection of capacitated vehicles. These vehicles visit customers with a previously known demand and, generally, the total cost associated to the routes must be minimized. Actually, a vast number of variants based on different objective functions and conditions are reported: VRP with time windows [10], VRP with heterogeneous fleet [5, 23], periodic VRP [24, 28], selective VRP [12, 22], multi-trip VRP [3, 26], and the multi-depot VRP [20], is just a small subset of the VRP variations. A special case of the VRP also arises if only one vehicle is available, the well-known *traveling salesman problem* (TSP).

© Springer Nature Switzerland AG 2019
J. C. Figueroa-García et al. (Eds.): WEA 2019, CCIS 1052, pp. 735–751, 2019.
https://doi.org/10.1007/978-3-030-31019-6_62

In this paper, we study two TSPs variants that include pickup and delivery operations. In the literature, these problems are well-known as *pickup and delivery traveling salesman problems* (PDTSPs). Particularly, we first analyze the *one-commodity* case (1–PDTSP) in which a single product is allowed to be transported from some locations (i.e., customers) to others. In this problem, there are two types of locations: pickup points that supply the commodity and delivery points which demand the product. Therefore, in the 1–PDTSP, the vehicle takes commodity units from the pickup locations to the delivery destinations with the aim to minimize the total cost (e.g., distance) of the route. Contrary to most of TSP variants, in 1–PDTSP the vehicle has a limited capacity. Needless to say, the capacity constraints for the vehicle must be satisfied and each location is visited once. We also deal with another 1–PDTSP variant where several visits are allowed for each location. Generally, in the vehicle routing literature, the use of this condition leads to split delivery problems. In our case, with a single vehicle, the *split demand one-commodity* TSP (SD1PDTSP) arises [27]. The SD1PDTSP is a special case of the 1–PDTSP that allows to partially serve demands on delivery locations or load a partial amount of commodity in pickup locations in each visit. At the end of the route, all pickup and delivery requests must be completely performed.

To deal with the 1–PDTSP, we present a mixed-integer linear programming (MILP) model and we show how it can be adapted in order to find a mathematical formulation for the SD1PDTSP. Taking advantage of the MILP structure for the SD1PDTSP, we also describe how this model allows not only to split the demand on locations but also, to store temporally some units of the commodity if necessary. In this case, it is possible to load or unload more than the required number of units in locations, and then in a later visit, the vehicle is allowed to take back or load the temporally stored units. The study of the split demand process and the temporal storage capability of our SD1PDTSP model relies on a possible reduction of the route cost. This reduction is based on a larger number of visits that avoid to traverse longer arcs as in the 1–PDTSP. Note that split demand has three alternatives in the SD1PDTSP: (i) the demand of a node (delivery or pickup) can be split in several smaller deliveries or pickups, (ii) a location can be used to storage an amount of units that are picked up later, and (iii) a location can be used to lend an amount of units that are replaced later.

Our motivation to study the 1–PDTSP and the SD1PDTSP is twofold since these problems are interesting from a theoretical and practical point of view. Firstly, the 1–PDTSP and the SD1PDTSP are $\mathcal{NP}$-hard because the problems can be reduced to a TSP if the vehicle capacity is large enough [15,17]. Moreover, as mentioned in [16], checking if there is a feasible solution of a 1–PDTSP instance is a strongly $\mathcal{NP}$-complete problem. Therefore, to design and report efficient solution strategies for the problems become relevant in the vehicle routing optimization literature. On the other hand, many applications for the 1-PDTSP have been reported so far. The *bicycle repositioning problem* (BRP) for bicycle sharing systems (BSSs) is probably the most studied application of one-commodity PDTPSs. In the BRP, a vehicle must visit all the BSS stations picking up or delivering an optimal number of bicycles in order to satisfy the demand of available parking slots and bikes. Performing this repositioning operation during the night, when the demand for services is negligible (e.g. bikes are not available for users) is referred to as the *static repositioning problem* [11]. In this case, it is possible to assume that demands are fixed and also, since traffic flow is minimal, travel times between stations may be considered as deterministic data in real scenarios. The BRP has become a relevant problem since BSSs have emerged as a new mobility mode and a way to reduce mobility and environmental issues in urban areas [7].

In spite of the previous work on 1–PDTSP and its applications, only [27] and [17] have tackled the SD1PDTSP. In this paper, we address these problems by providing three main contributions: (i) new mathematical formulations for the 1–PDTSP and the SD1PDTSP, (ii) a numerical analysis of the benefits on split demand and temporal storage in PDTSPs, (iii) a set of computational experiments solving instances with up to 60 locations, showing a competitive performance based on results in [27]. The remainder of this paper is structured as follows. Section 2 summarizes the main contributions on 1–PDTSPs reported in the literature and some applications of the problem as the reposition operations in BSSs. Section 3 describes our proposed MILPs to deal with the 1–PDTSP and the SD1PDTSP. In Sect. 4, we report the main results of our approach and finally, in Sect. 5 we outline some conclusions and future research opportunities.

2   Literature Review

In this section we first summarize the most relevant literature based on the 1–PDTSP and the SD1PTSP. Then, from a practical perspective, we also provide some of the related work on the 1–PDTSP as a BRP in the bike sharing context. As mentioned before, the BRP in BSSs is one of the most relevant application of the studied problems.

The 1–PDTSP is formally presented in [15]. In their work, authors describe an integer linear programming formulation for the problem and a solution strategy based on *branch-and-cut* (B&C). They describe a set of valid inequalities to strength the linear relaxation as well as an adaptation of the *nearest insertion* heuristic to provide feasible solutions. To test the performance of their B&C algorithm, authors generate similar instances to those presented in [21]. The size of the instances vary from 20 to 50 locations, each one with a demand (pickup or delivery quantity) randomly generated in $[-10, 10]$. In the computational experiments, the vehicle capacity also varies starting from 10. As it was expected, the difficulty of the instances is not only related to the number of locations but to the vehicle capacity. Authors prove that computational times increase significantly as the vehicle capacity decreases.

Given the $\mathcal{NP}$-hard nature of the 1–PDTSP, it is also been tackled via heuristic procedures. In [16], authors propose two heuristic approaches. The first one is based on a greedy algorithm. A solution, not necessarily feasible, is built using an adaptation of the *nearest neighbor* algorithm. Then, local search procedures (i.e., *2-opt* and *3-opt*) are applied to the constructive solution. The second heuristic procedure uses an adaptation of the B&C proposed in [15] in order to find optimal solutions locally. This adaptation of the B&C explores tighter sections of the feasible space by adding a constraint on the number of edges that differ from a previously known solution. The B&C finds neighbors that could improve the quality of the initial solution. Authors test these heuristic procedures with instances up to 500 locations and different values for vehicle capacity in [10, 1000]. When the value of vehicle capacity is large enough (i.e., 1000), the 1–PDTSP solution coincided with the TSP solution. As a benchmark study, authors also solve the PDTSP using these heuristics and prove that their results outperforms a *tabu search* (TS) proposed in [13].

The 1–PDTSP is also addressed in [14] via metaheuristic algorithms. In this case, the solution approach is based on a *greedy randomize adaptive search procedure* (GRASP) and *variable neighborhood descent* (VND). The constructive phase of the GRASP may end up with an unfeasible solution but the improvement phase in which the local search is replaced by a VND, is able to repair the unfeasibility. This improvement phase is composed by *2-opt* and *3-opt* procedures. At the end of the algorithm, a second VND is applied to the best solution found. This post-optimization stage includes *move forward* and *move backward* operators. The performance of the hybrid metaheuristic is tested on the small and large size instances previously used in [16] with up to 500 locations. Similar to [14], in [29] a metaheuristic procedure is described. To solve the 1–PDTSP, authors propose a *genetic algorithm* (GA) with an embedded local search procedure. This GA includes a particular pheromone-based method that helps to estimate pheromone trails on the edges of the 1–PDTSP network as in the *ant colony optimization* (ACO) algorithm. While the local search procedure is based on *2-opt*, the mutation operator in the GA uses a *3-exchange* operator.

As mentioned before, in the 1–PDTSP exactly one visit to each location is mandatory. Nevertheless it is possible to split the pickup or delivery quantity if multiple visits are allowed. This problem, the SD1PDTSP, is introduced in [27] as a generalization of the 1–PDTSP and the *split delivery traveling salesman problem* (SDTSP). Since the main problem addressed on this paper is not the SDTSP, we refer the reader to [2] and [1] for a detailed description of the problem. Authors in [27] propose a mixed-integer lineal programming model to deal with the SD1PDTSP in which the maximum number of visit to locations is a parameter. Therefore, the MILP is also able to deal with the 1–PDTSP. As a solution strategy, the authors adapt the B&C algorithm in [15] to solve also SD1PDTSP instances up to 50 locations. While results are not competitive with other strategies to deal with the 1–PDTSP, this exact approach provides good results for the split delivery case. Apart from the exact approaches, the SD1PDTP is also study in [17] with a matheuristic algorithm that apply a constructive procedure and then, a refinement phase to improve solution quality. The constructive procedure is based on a graph in which nodes represent potential visits to locations (i.e., each location is represented by several nodes). Then, the refinement phase uses an adaptation of the MILP presented in [27] to improve the quality of route pieces. This matheuristic approach is used to solve instances with up 500 locations. To the best of our knowledge, only the strategies presented in [27] and [17] deal with the SD1PDTSP showing a promising research field.

Let us remark that one of the most studied applications for 1–PDTSPs is the BRP. This problem has been tackled via exact, heuristic and matheuristic approaches. Since this work is not devoted to the BRP, we briefly describe the most representative research in this problem. In [25], authors formulate two MILPs in which the cost of the routes number of bike shortages in each station of the system are minimized. The mathematical models are tested on instances with up to 60 stations based on certain locations of Velib (BSS in Paris) and then, with a complete real instance of 104 stations and one or two vehicles. The procedure in [4] is a B&C algorithm for the BRP. This algorithm is based on a MILP relaxation for the problem and provides lower bounds when several visits to each station are allowed. On the other hand, a TS with four different neighborhoods is also designed to find upper bounds. The evaluated instances vary from 20 to 100 stations. In [11], the authors propose a 3-step matheuristic based on a clustering process supported on savings heuristic and two MILPs to deal with the routing decisions though clusters and the repositioning operation in a reduced network (i.e., each cluster). For instances up to 150 stations, the matheuristic outperforms the one of the formulations presented in [25].

The B&B proposed in [19] solves the BRP when minimizing the total waiting time of stations. While lower bounds are computed via *lagrangian relaxation*, the upper bounds can be calculated by means of a GA, a *greedy search* or a *nearest neighbor procedure*. Next, authors in [9] describe an iterated *destroy and repair metaheuristic* (D&R) for the BRP. Initially, the D&R algorithm starts with a variant of savings heuristic in order to find an initial solution. Next, after some nodes are removed from routes, the solution is repaired via insertion moves or the adapted savings algorithm. Authors also use local search procedures within a VND framework. Finally, [18] describe an *hybrid large neighborhood search* (HLNS) algorithm. This metaheuristic includes five removal operators, five insertion (repair) operators and a TS applied to the most promising solutions. Testing instances with up to 518 stations, the HLNS is able to outperform a proposed MILP coded on CPLEX and the matheuristic described in [11].

3   Problem Formulation

Firstly, this section presents mathematical formulations for a family of problems related to the Pickup and Delivery TSP. We first describe a MILP for the 1–PDTSP and then, we show how to model the SD1PDTSP by including new constraints to the 1–PDTSP formulation. Next, we describe graphically the split delivery and the temporally storage and show their impacts in two small instances.

3.1   Mathematical Model for the 1–PDTSP

To introduce the basic notation for the MILPs, we define a set of locations $\mathcal{N}$ in which the depot (hereafter represented as location 0) and all customers are included. Therefore, the family of pickup problems is defined under a complete graph $\mathcal{G} = (\mathcal{N}, \mathcal{A})$ where $\mathcal{A}$ is the set of arcs connecting pairs of locations.

For each arc (i, j) in $\mathcal{A}$, we define c_{ij} as the distance from going from i to j. The parameter q_i denotes the demand on the location i ($i \in \mathcal{N}$). Without loss of generality, a positive value of q_i represents a shortage of units. Then, if $q_i > 0$, a delivery operation of q_i units is performed in location i. On the other hand, $q_i < 0$ means a surplus. Then, the vehicle must pickup $|q_i|$ units when visiting location i. The value Q denotes the capacity of the vehicle. To state our mathematical formulation, we define the binary decision variable y_{ij} where $(i, j) \in \mathcal{A}$. This variable takes the value of one if the vehicle uses the arc (i, j) in the solution and the zero otherwise. The variable x_{ij} denotes the load of the vehicle if the arc (i, j) is traversed. Finally, a variable z_{ij} is defined to keep track of the sequence of arcs used in the solution. Formally, z_{ij} indicates the order in which the arc (i, j) is traversed in the solution. The mathematical model for the 1–PDTSP, from now referred as MILP_{PD}, is as follows:

$$\min F = \sum_{(i,j) \in \mathcal{A}} c_{ij} \cdot y_{ij} \tag{1}$$

subject to,

$$\sum_{\substack{j \in \mathcal{N} \\ i \neq j}} y_{ij} = 1, \quad \forall\, i \in \mathcal{N} \tag{2}$$

$$\sum_{i \in \mathcal{N}} y_{ij} = \sum_{i \in \mathcal{N}} y_{ji}, \quad \forall\, j \in \mathcal{N} \tag{3}$$

$$x_{ij} \leq Q \cdot y_{ij}, \quad \forall\, (i, j) \in \mathcal{A} \tag{4}$$

$$\sum_{j \in \mathcal{N}} x_{ji} - \sum_{j \in \mathcal{N}} x_{ij} = q_i, \quad \forall\, i \in \mathcal{N} \tag{5}$$

$$\sum_{j \in \mathcal{N}} z_{ji} - \sum_{j \in \mathcal{N}} z_{ij} = 1, \quad \forall\, i \in \mathcal{N} \setminus \{0\} \tag{6}$$

$$z_{ij} \leq |\mathcal{N}| \cdot y_{ij}, \quad \forall\, (i, j) \in \mathcal{A} \tag{7}$$

$$y_{ij} \in \{0, 1\}, \quad \forall\, (i, j) \in \mathcal{A} \tag{8}$$

$$z_{ij}, x_{ij} \geq 0, \quad \forall\, (i, j) \in \mathcal{A} \tag{9}$$

Equation (1) represents the objective function in which total traveled distance is minimized. Expressions in (2) and (3) are the routing constraints: equations in (2) ensure that each location is visited exactly once, while constraints in (3) enforce to leave a location once it is visited. Constraints in (4) force the model to find loads that not exceed the vehicle capacity while those in (5) model the flow of units along the used arcs. Equations (6) and (7) limit arc coefficients and prevent subtours on the solution. Note that in classical TSP and VRP formulations, constraints (4) and (5) prevent subtours. Nevertheless, as q_i can be negative in the 1–PDTSP, (4) and (5) are not enough. Equations (8) and (9) define the domain of decision variables. Needless to say, variables x_{ij} and

z_{ij} could be integer, but given the structure of our formulation, a continuous domain will lead to integer values.

3.2 Mathematical Model for the SD1PDTSP

As mentioned before, it is possible to model the SD1PDTSP by introducing new constraints on MILP$_{PD}$. In the split delivery scenario, the vehicle can visit a location i several times in order to meet the total pickup or delivery quantity (i.e., q_i). Let q_i^v be the number of units to pickup or deliver in location i on visit v. Then, a feasible solution must satisfy that $\sum_v q_i^v = q_i$. In MILP$_{PD}$, the total demand of each location is described by equations in (5). Therefore, to allow multiple visits to i ($i \in \mathcal{N}$), constraints in (2) can be replaced by:

$$\sum_{\substack{j \in \mathcal{N} \\ i \neq j}} y_{ij} \geq \left\lceil \frac{|q_i|}{Q} \right\rceil, \quad \forall\, i \in \mathcal{N} \tag{10}$$

Additionally, if vehicle visits several times a subset of locations, the number of arcs in the solution is greater than $|\mathcal{N}|$. Then, we replace equations in (7) for a similar set of constraints:

$$z_{ij} \leq 2 \cdot |\mathcal{N}| \cdot y_{ij}, \quad \forall\, (i,j) \in \mathcal{A} \tag{11}$$

The expression $2 \cdot |\mathcal{N}|$ is an upper bound for variables z_{ij}. Let us comment that given the continuous nature of these variables, the value of the upper bound does not affect the performance of our MILPs. Replacing equations in (2) by expression in (10) and updating the upper bound for z_{ij} as in (11), we define a set of constraints Ω where Ω is given by expressions in (3) to (6), and (8) to (11). Then, the SD1PDTSP (from now MILP$_{SD}$) can be modeled as follows:

$$\min f = \sum_{(i,j) \in \mathcal{A}} c_{ij} \cdot y_{ij}$$

$$\text{subject to,} \quad \Omega$$

Finally, if multiple visits can be performed to location i, note that expressions in (5) allow to a couple of variables x_{ij} and x_{ji} to take values not necessarily equal to q_i. This would lead to take location i as a temporal storage point where units can be picked up in a later visit or some units can be taken away from i temporally until a future visit occurs.

3.3 A Split Delivery and Temporal Storage Example

In this section, we present two graphical examples for the 1–PDTPSP and the SD1TSP. As mentioned in Sect. 3.2, it is important to remember that if several visits are performed, then $\sum_v q_i^v = q_i$ must be satisfied. Nonetheless, conceptually speaking, if $\sum_v |q_i^v| = |q_i|$, the set of operations correspond to split, which means that a delivery (or a pickup) is divided into several smaller deliveries (or pickups); on the contrary, if $\sum_v |q_i^v| \neq |q_i|$, the set of operations correspond to temporary storage, which means that a delivery (or a pickup) is the result of several deliveries and pickups. In the second case, q_i and each q_i^v do not have the same sign.

Figure 1 depicts the optimal solution of an instance (from now called Instance 1) with 20 locations if multiple visits are not allowed (i.e., the instance is solved as a 1–PDTSP). The first value near to each location represents the number of units to pick up or deliver and the second one, is the load of the vehicle when entering to such location. As an example, location 19 has a request of four units and the vehicle arrives there with a load of six. The total cost of this route is 4963. In Fig. 2, we represent the optimal solution of Instance 1 if it is solved as a SD1PDTSP. Note that in this new solution, location 4 is visited twice. Firstly, the vehicle goes from location 2 to location 4 with a load of nine which is not enough to supply the demand of ten units. Secondly, a split delivery is performed; the vehicle delivers all the load in location 4. Thirdly, it visits location 7 picking up five units. Fourthly, it goes back to location 4 with a load of five and as a second delivery, supply the pending demand (i.e., one last unit). Finally, the vehicle leaves location 4 with four units. The total cost of this route is 4759.

In a similar way, we depict in Fig. 3 the optimal solution of a different instance (Instance 2) solved as a 1–PDTSP. The total cost of this route 4976. If Instance 2 is solved as a SD1PDTSP, the total cost of the route is 4787. In this case, there are two locations visited twice (i.e., locations 18 and 15). Firstly, as in Instance 1, the demand on location 18 is split. Initially, with a load of 9 units, the vehicle visits 18, it leaves all the load and pickup eight units in location 13. Then, it goes back to 18, complete the supply and it moves to 15 with a load of seven. Although the vehicle arrives in 15 with seven units, an optimal decision is to supply the demand (one unit), store five there and then going to location 2 with a load of one. After location 16 is visited, the vehicle goes back to 15 completely empty and pickup the five units stored previously. The route continues visiting location 10 (Fig. 4).

4   Computational Experiments

In this section, we firstly present results on MILPs performance for the 1–PDTSP and SD1PDTSP. Next, we analyze how split delivery, temporal storage and vehicle capacity affect objective function values. Lastly, we compare briefly the performance of our MILPs with those previously presented in [27]. To test the performance of the models described in Sect. 3, we solved a set of well-known 1–PDTSP instances available at http://hhperez.webs.ull.es/PDsite/. We use instances with $|\mathcal{N}| = \{20, 30, 40, 50, 60\}$. The location demand vary from -10 to 10 (i.e., $q_i \in [-10, 10] \; \forall \; i \in \mathcal{N}$). We define three different values for the vehicle capacity: $Q = \{10, 20, 40\}$. For each size of the problems and each value of Q, 10 instances are available. Therefore, 150 instances were solved for each problem. For a detailed description about the instances generation, we refer the

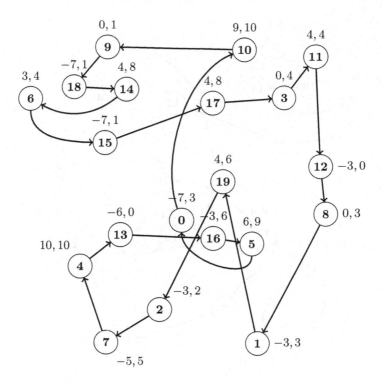

Fig. 1. Instance 1 solved as 1-PDTSP with $f^* = 4963$

reader to [15] and [16]. All the experiments reported in this section have been conducted using Gurobi optimizer 8.1.1 in an Intel Core i7 with 64 gigabytes of RAM running under Ubuntu 18.04 (x86-64). For each running of the models, we set a maximum computational time of one hour (3600 s).

4.1 Results on 1–PDTSP and SD1PDTSP

Tables 1 and 2 summarize the computational results when solving the set of instances with $MILP_{PD}$ and $MILP_{SD}$, respectively. We report the number of times that each MILP is able to provide the optimal solution for each size of the instances and the three tested values for the vehicle capacity. We compute an average gap (Avg. gap) as $Avg.gap = \frac{UB-LB}{UB}$ where UB and LB are the best solution and the final lower bound reported by the optimizer. The average computational time in seconds required to find the solution (Avg. time) is also included in the tables.

In particular, as Table 1 shows, for the 1–PDTSP it is possible to find the optimal solution for all the instances with up to 40 locations. For larger instances with 50 and 60 locations, the number of optimal solutions increases and computation time decreases as the vehicle capacity is extended. This is an expected

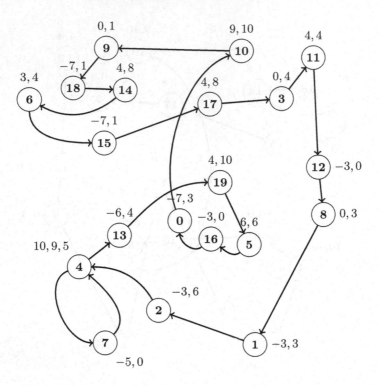

Fig. 2. Instance 1 solved as SD1PDTSP with $f^* = 4759$

result since large values of Q leads to a classical TSP. Note that for the largest instances (60 locations) and the smallest value for the vehicle capacity (the hardest case), solutions obtained with MILP_{PD} do not deliver more than 5.64% of gap on average.

When solving the MILP_{SD}, the optimizer is also able to find the optimal solution for all the instances up to 40 locations (see Table 2). Moreover, if split delivery and temporal storage are allowed, the optimal solution is found for an additional instance with 50 locations and the tightest value for Q. Let us also note that average gaps decrease for hardest instances (with 50 and 60 locations and $Q = 10$) if locations may be visited more than once. In this particular case, the average gap decrease from 5.64% (see Table 1) to 2.17%. A similar behavior is obtained for larger values of vehicle capacity. When split delivery and storage are allowed, notice that computational times for small instances are larger when they are compared with the 1–PDTSP case. For example, while MILP_{PD} requires 59.42 s, the MILP_{SD} is solved in 120.74 s on average for $|\mathcal{N}| = 30$ and $Q = 10$. On the contrary, for instances with more than 30 locations in which split delivery and storage are allowed, computational times are always less than the reported in Table 1 for 1–PDTSP.

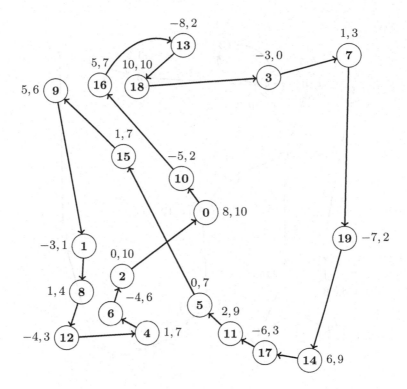

Fig. 3. Instance 2 solved as 1-PDTSP with $f^* = 4976$

4.2 Analysis on Split Delivery, Temporal Storage and Vehicle Capacity

Since Table 2 evidences that split delivery or temporal storage help to decrease gaps and computing times, we also analyze how these properties affect the objective function quality. Table 3 shows the main results for those instances with an optimal solution delivered by Gurobi when solving $MILP_{PD}$ and $MILP_{SD}$. We report the number of times that $MILP_{SD}$ delivers a solution with split delivery or storage in at least one location and we compute the average and maximum cost saving (Avg. cost saving and Max. cost saving, respectively) for those instances in which $f_{MILP_{SD}} < f_{MILP_{PD}}$. Saving for one instance is computed as follows:

$$\text{cost saving} = \frac{f_{MILP_{PD}} - f_{MILP_{SD}}}{f_{MILP_{SD}}} \cdot 100\% \tag{12}$$

Note that if the vehicle capacity is 10, then at least in 80% of the instances (4 out of 5 when $|\mathcal{N}| = 40$) is better to visit more than once at least one location. Similarly, for $Q = 10$, average cost improvements vary from 2.59% to 3.58% as the number of locations decreases. For instances with $|\mathcal{N}| = 20$ it is possible to find cost improvements up to 9.10%. As the value for Q increases, the vehicle may not need to visit several times a location if its capacity is large

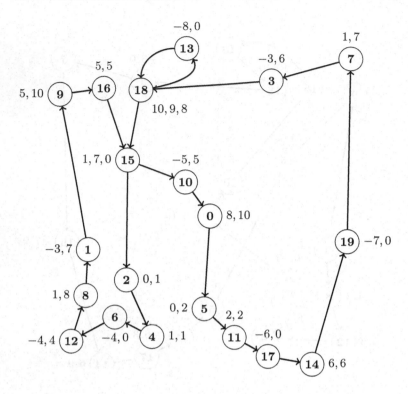

Fig. 4. Instance 2 solved as SD1PDTSP with $f^* = 4787$

enough. Notice that if $Q = 20$, the number of instances in which split delivery or temporal storage is recommended as well as the average and maximum cost savings, decrease. For the largest Q value, several visits to a location do not improve objective function value.

Table 1. MILP$_{PD}$ results for the 1–PDTSP

$|\mathcal{N}|$	$Q = 10$			$Q = 20$			$Q = 40$		
	# Optimal solutions	Avg. gap	Avg. time (s)	# Optimal solutions	Avg. gap	Avg. time (s)	# Optimal solutions	Avg. gap	Avg. time (s)
20	10/10	0.00%	3.46	10/10	0.00%	0.49	10/10	0.00%	0.17
30	10/10	0.00%	59.42	10/10	0.00%	61.19	10/10	0.00%	0.96
40	10/10	0.00%	989.57	10/10	0.00%	53.52	10/10	0.00%	1.81
50	5/10	1.73%	2368.12	9/10	0.20%	1133.59	10/10	0.00%	13.80
60	1/10	5.64%	3569.99	8/10	0.38%	1201.49	10/10	0.00%	18.44

Table 2. MILP$_{SD}$ results for the SD1PDTSP

$\mathcal{N}$	$Q = 10$			$Q = 20$			$Q = 40$		
	# Optimal solutions	Avg. gap	Avg. time (s)	# Optimal solutions	Avg. gap	Avg. time (s)	# Optimal solutions	Avg. gap	Avg. time (s)
20	10/10	0.00%	3.82	10/10	0.00%	0.90	10/10	0.00%	0.21
30	10/10	0.00%	120.74	10/10	0.00%	10.84	10/10	0.00%	1.52
40	10/10	0.00%	655.45	10/10	0.00%	25.82	10/10	0.00%	2.54
50	6/10	0.81%	2070.46	9/10	0.12%	821.88	10/10	0.00%	18.85
60	2/10	2.17%	3313.65	8/10	0.23%	1128.40	10/10	0.00%	26.56

Table 3. Split delivery and temporal storage impact on objective function

$\mathcal{N}$	$Q = 10$			$Q = 20$			$Q = 40$		
	Split or storage	Avg. cost saving	Max. cost saving	Split or- storage	Avg. cost saving	Max. cost saving	Split or storage	Avg. cost saving	Max. cost saving
20	9/10	3.58%	9.10%	0/10	0.00%	0.00%	0/10	0.00%	0.00%
30	9/10	3.01%	5.44%	3/10	0.99%	2.00%	0/10	0.00%	0.00%
40	10/10	2.74%	6.83%	2/10	0.78%	1.44%	0/10	0.00%	0.00%
50	4/5	2.50%	3.47%	4/9	0.71%	1.24%	0/10	0.00%	0.00%
60	1/1	2.59%	2.59%	1/8	0.18%	0.18%	0/10	0.00%	0.00%

Let us remark that values in Table 3 are computed with instances in which the optimal solution is found when solving MILP$_{PD}$ and MILP$_{SD}$. Nevertheless, there exits a small subset of instances in which optimal solutions are not reported by the solver but an objective function improvement can be expected if split delivery or storage is allowed. Table 4 shows for each one of these instances that the solver provides a final lower bound (LB) for MILP$_{PD}$ greater than the upper bound (UB) found by MILP$_{SD}$. Then, similarly to Eq. (12), we also compute a minimum expected cost saving as follows:

$$\text{Min. expected cost saving} = \frac{LB_{MILP_{PD}} - UB_{MILP_{SD}}}{UB_{MILP_{SD}}} \cdot 100\%$$

For the nine instances reported in Table 4, a minimum cost improvement equal to 2.06% is expected on average. Moreover, for these instances, we also remark that final gaps obtained with MILP$_{SD}$, are tighter than those computed when solving MILP$_{PD}$.

Once we prove that split delivery or temporal storage improve the quality of our objective function. We also analyze briefly how an increase on vehicle capacity reduces the total cost of the route. To do so, we only consider again those instances with optimal solution when solving our both MILPs. Table 5 reports the average cost improvement as a percentage if the vehicle capacity is doubled when Q takes the value of 10 and 20 and a single or multiple visits are allowed to locations. Table 5 shows that if only one visit per location is allowed, then an increase on vehicle capacity leads to a higher improvement on the objective function values. As we expected, in presence of split delivery or temporal storage, cost saving are lower since the vehicle is able to use shorter arcs in the optimal solution with a tighter capacity.

Table 4. Expected cost improvement for instances with non-optimal solution

$|\mathcal{N}|$	Q	Instance	MILP$_{PD}$			MILP$_{SD}$			Min. expected cost saving
			UB	LB	gap	UB	LB	gap	
50	10	n50q10C	9221	8896	3.52%	8842	8706	1.54%	0.61%
50	10	n50q10D	10,275	10,052	2.17%	9944	9819	1.26%	1.09%
50	10	n50q10E	9492	9492	0.00%	9238	9154	0.91%	2.75%
50	10	n50q10F	8684	8374	3.57%	7716	7716	0.00%	8.53%
50	10	n50q10I	8329	8227	1.22%	8000	8000	0.00%	2.84%
60	10	n60q10B	8514	8406	1.27%	8384	8313	0.85%	0.26%
60	10	n60q10D	11,112	10,663	4.04%	10,626	10,482	1.36%	0.35%
60	10	n60q10F	9507	8441	11.21%	8335	8025	3.72%	1.27%
60	10	n60q10J	9302	8296	10.81%	8226	8226	0.00%	0.85%
Average					4.20%			1.07%	2.06%

Table 5. Cost improvements for Q variations

$|\mathcal{N}|$	From $Q = 10$ to $Q = 20$		From $Q = 20$ to $Q = 40$	
	MILP$_{PD}$	MILP$_{SD}$	MILP$_{PD}$	MILP$_{SD}$
20	27.50%	23.52%	6.53%	6.53%
30	31.07%	28.02%	8.96%	8.57%
40	30.71%	27.50%	6.95%	6.77%
50	23.78%	21.07%	8.89%	8.54%
60	24.05%	20.95%	6.74%	6.71%
Average	27.42%	24.21%	7.62%	7.43%

4.3   MILPs Benchmark

As mentioned before and to the best of our knowledge, only the B&C strategy described in [27] deals with the SD1PDTSP. In that article, authors use a subset of the instances we solve to test our MILPs. Particulary, when $|\mathcal{N}| = 30$. Therefore, we compare our MILP's performance with the solution strategy proposed in [27]. Table 6 shows the results reported in [27]: lower and upper bounds as well as computational times in seconds for the 1–PDTSP and the SD1PDTSP. In particular, for the 1–PDTSP, while the B&C is able to deliver four out of ten optimal solutions as upper bounds, the MILP$_{PD}$ closes the gap for the whole set of instances. If split deliveries are allowed, while the strategy described in [27] reports upper bounds equal to the optimal solution for nine out of ten instances, our MILP reports a 0.00% of gap for all of them. Finally, let us comment that our objective function values and computational times required to solve the tested instances outperform those reported in [27].

Table 6. Benchmark results based on [27]

Instance	Q	1–PDTSP					SD1PDTSP				
		B& C [27]			MILP$_{PD}$		B& C [27]			MILP$_{SD}$	
		LB	UB	time (s)	f*	time (s)	LB	UB	time (s)	f*	time (s)
n30q10A	10	5724.8	6727	1253.9	6403	111.96	5654.1	6256	2266.4	6256	55.65
n30q10A	10	6193.2	6603	165.8	6603	14.65	5478.6	6603	591.1	6603	168.51
n30q10C	10	5215.5	6486	1197.9	6486	60.89	5149.3	6348	2278.5	6348	281.18
n30q10D	10	5450	6577	2698.4	6652	19.34	5279.2	6380	3811.8	6380	12.13
n30q10E	10	5691.2	6070	588.1	6070	4.25	5402.5	6052	942.6	6052	18.35
n30q10F	10	5392.5	5737	600.4	5737	7.48	5225	5727	1008.4	5727	18.99
n30q10G	10	8705.8	9305	2135.1	9371	311.63	8641.7	9005	3994.7	9005	549.31
n30q10H	10	5191.5	6433	457.9	6431	8.52	5020.4	6164	4598.6	6164	15.85
n30q10I	10	5156.2	5864	310.4	5821	28.14	4969.5	5596	4839.8	5596	71.96
n30q10J	10	5865.7	6192	224.8	6187	27.35	5601.4	6090	1712.5	5868	15.42

5   Concluding Remarks

In this paper, we present new mathematical formulations based on mixed-integer lineal programming for the 1–PDTSP and the SD1PTSP. The MILP proposed for the 1–PDTSP can be easily adapted to deal with split delivery and temporal storage operations. These models are able to deal with instances up to 60 locations in decent computational times finding optimal solutions for all the instances up to 40 locations. We run experiments with different values for the vehicle capacity and we show the benefits of split delivery and storage when such capacity is tight. We also compare our main results with a reported exact approach concluding that our models are competitive outperforming computational times and solution quality.

As future research directions, we propose to study different valid inequalities in order to improve the performance of our MILPs. For practical purposes, we believe there are opportunities exploring multi-vehicle formulations and develop study cases based on BSSs. Finally, given the $\mathcal{NP}$-hardness nature of the studied problems, we are motivated to combine our mathematical formulations within matheuristic algorithms in order to deal with larger instances.

References

1. Archetti, C., Bianchessi, N., Speranza, M.G.: Branch-and-cut algorithms for the split delivery vehicle routing problem. Eur. J. Oper. Res. **238**(3), 685–698 (2014)
2. Archetti, C., Speranza, M.G.: Vehicle routing problems with split deliveries. Int. Trans. Oper. Res. **19**(1–2), 3–22 (2012)
3. Brandao, J., Mercer, A.: The multi-trip vehicle routing problem. J. Oper. Res. Soc. **49**(8), 799–805 (1998)
4. Chemla, D., Meunier, F., Wolfler Calvo, R.: Bike sharing systems: Solving the static rebalancing problem. Discrete Optim. **10**(2), 120–146 (2013)

5. Coelho, V.N., Grasas, A., Ramalhinho, H., Coelho, I.M., Souza, M.J., Cruz, R.C.: An ILS-based algorithm to solve a large-scale real heterogeneous fleet VRP with multi-trips and docking constraints. Eur. J. Oper. Res. **250**(2), 367–376 (2016)
6. Cordeau, J.F., Laporte, G., Savelsbergh, M.W., Vigo, D.: Vehicle routing. In: Handbooks in Operations Research and Management Science, vol. 14, pp. 367–428 (2007)
7. Cruz, F., Subramanian, A., Bruck, B.P., Iori, M.: A heuristic algorithm for a single vehicle static bike sharing rebalancing problem. Comput. Oper. Res. **79**, 19–33 (2017)
8. Dantzig, G.B., Ramser, J.H.: The truck dispatching problem. Manage. Sci. **6**(1), 80–91 (1959)
9. Dell'Amico, M., Iori, M., Novellani, S., Stützle, T.: A destroy and repair algorithm for the bike sharing rebalancing problem. Comput. Oper. Res. **71**, 149–162 (2016)
10. Dixit, A., Mishra, A., Shukla, A.: Vehicle routing problem with time windows using meta-heuristic algorithms: a survey. In: Yadav, N., Yadav, A., Bansal, J.C., Deep, K., Kim, J.H. (eds.) Harmony Search and Nature Inspired Optimization Algorithms. AISC, vol. 741, pp. 539–546. Springer, Singapore (2019). https://doi.org/10.1007/978-981-13-0761-4_52
11. Forma, I.A., Raviv, T., Tzur, M.: A 3-step math heuristic for the static repositioning problem in bike-sharing systems. Transp. Res. Part B Methodol. **71**, 230–247 (2015)
12. Franca, L.S., Ribeiro, G.M., Chaves, G.D.L.D.: The planning of selective collection in a real-life vehicle routing problem: a case in Rio de Janeiro. Sustain. Cities Soc. **47**, 101488 (2019)
13. Gendreau, M., Laporte, G., Vigo, D.: Heuristics for the traveling salesman problem with pickup and delivery. Comput. Oper. Res. **26**(7), 699–714 (1999)
14. Hernández-Pérez, H., Rodríguez-Martín, I., Salazar-González, J.J.: A hybrid GRASP/VND heuristic for the one-commodity pickup-and-delivery traveling salesman problem. Comput. Oper. Res. **36**(5), 1639–1645 (2009)
15. Hernández-Pérez, H., Salazar-González, J.J.: A branch-and-cut algorithm for a traveling salesman problem with pickup and delivery. Discrete Appl. Math. **145**(1), 126–139 (2004)
16. Hernández-Pérez, H., Salazar-González, J.J.: Heuristics for the one-commodity pickup-and-delivery traveling salesman problem. Transp. Sci. **38**(2), 245–255 (2004)
17. Hernández-Pérez, H., Salazar-González, J.J., Santos-Hernández, B.: Heuristic algorithm for the split-demand one-commodity pickup-and-delivery travelling salesman problem. Comput. Oper. Res. **97**, 1–17 (2018)
18. Ho, S.C., Szeto, W.Y.: A hybrid large neighborhood search for the static multi-vehicle bike-repositioning problem. Transp. Res. Part B Methodol. **95**, 340–363 (2017)
19. Kadri, A.A., Kacem, I., Labadi, K.: A branch-and-bound algorithm for solving the static rebalancing problem in bicycle-sharing systems. Comput. Ind. Eng. **95**, 41–52 (2016)
20. Laporte, G., Nobert, Y., Taillefer, S.: Solving a family of multi-depot vehicle routing and location-routing problems. Transp. Sci. **22**(3), 161–172 (1988)
21. Mosheiov, G.: The travelling salesman problem with pick-up and delivery. Eur. J. Oper. Res. **79**(2), 299–310 (1994)
22. Posada, A., Rivera, J.C., Palacio, J.D.: A mixed-integer linear programming model for a selective vehicle routing problem. In: Figueroa-García, J.C., Villegas, J.G., Orozco-Arroyave, J.R., Maya Duque, P.A. (eds.) WEA 2018. CCIS, vol. 916, pp. 108–119. Springer, Cham (2018). https://doi.org/10.1007/978-3-030-00353-1_10

23. Prins, C.: Two memetic algorithms for heterogeneous fleet vehicle routing problems. Eng. Appl. Artif. Intell. **22**(6), 916–928 (2009)
24. Prodhon, C., Prins, C.: A memetic algorithm with population management (MA—PM) for the periodic location-routing problem. In: Blesa, M., et al. (eds.) HM 2008. LNCS, vol. 5296, pp. 43–57. Springer, Heidelberg (2008). https://doi. org/10.1007/978-3-540-88439-2_4
25. Raviv, T., Tzur, M., Forma, I.: Static repositioning in a bike-sharing system: models and solution approaches. EURO J. Transp. Logist. **2**(3), 187–229 (2013)
26. Rivera, J.C., Afsar, H.M., Prins, C.: Mathematical formulations and exact algorithm for the multitrip cumulative capacitated single-vehicle routing problem. Eur. J. Oper. Res. **249**(1), 93–104 (2016)
27. Salazar-González, J.J., Santos-Hernández, B.: The split-demand one-commodity pickup-and-delivery travelling salesman problem. Transp. Res. Part B: Methodol. **75**, 58–73 (2015)
28. Vidal, T., Crainic, T.G., Gendreau, M., Lahrichi, N., Rei, W.: A hybrid genetic algorithm for multidepot and periodic vehicle routing problems. Oper. Res. **60**(3), 611–624 (2012)
29. Zhao, F., Li, S., Sun, J., Mei, D.: Genetic algorithm for the one-commodity pickup-and-delivery traveling salesman problem. Comput. Ind. Eng. **56**(4), 1642–1648 (2009)

A Bi-objective Model for the Humanitarian Aid Distribution Problem: Analyzing the Trade-off Between Shortage and Inventory at Risk

Julián Alberto Espejo-Díaz[1(✉)] and William J. Guerrero[2]

[1] Master of Design and Process Management, Universidad de La Sabana,
Chía, Colombia
julianesdi@unisabana.edu.co
[2] Faculty of Engineering, Universidad de La Sabana, Chía, Colombia
william.guerrerol@unisabana.edu.co

Abstract. Avoiding shortages or lowering the amount of humanitarian aid in risk of being lost due to geological hazards, the repetition of a disaster or security issues are two conflictive objectives faced by humanitarian logistics planners. This paper presents a multi-objective mathematical formulation which analyzes the trade-off between these objectives in delivery operations of humanitarian aid. To do so, an epsilon-constraint method is used to find the pareto front for the problem, providing the decision-maker the necessary information to see the overall performance of the operation and to decide how much inventory would be at risk based on the maximum level of shortage in the operation. A real-case study inspired by the 2017 Mocoa-Colombia landslide is presented to use in conjunction with the proposal. Results show that for the case study a clear Pareto front is found obtaining the optimal routes and quantities of the non-dominated solutions and the guidance for the operational decisions.

Keywords: Humanitarian logistics · Inventory routing problem ·
Disaster relief · ε-constraint

1 Introduction

Over the last years, several disasters have drawn the world attention because of the vast number of casualties and the big economic losses. Disasters such as the earthquake in Haiti in 2010, the earthquake and the subsequent tsunami in Japan in 2011, the Mexico and Ecuador earthquakes in 2016 and 2017 and more recently the catastrophe in Indonesia in 2018 have claimed thousands of lives and have left millions of people homeless. Disaster databases such as [1] or yearly reports on the topic [2] indicate that the frequency of disasters has grown in the last decades along with its magnitude and impact. Additionally, some forecasts strongly state that this trend will continue and the number and effect of both natural and human-made disasters in the next decades might be more significant than before [3]. Given the previous context, it can clearly be seen that the communities must work towards being better prepared to mitigate and respond to any disaster situation. During a disaster, there are a high level of unpredictability, pressure of response, destroyed infrastructure which difficult rescue and response

© Springer Nature Switzerland AG 2019
J. C. Figueroa-García et al. (Eds.): WEA 2019, CCIS 1052, pp. 752–763, 2019.
https://doi.org/10.1007/978-3-030-31019-6_63

operations, multiple actors trying to help without coordination and an urgent need to make accurate decisions [4]. To deal with these challenges, humanitarian logistics represents an opportunity to better prepare and respond to these events. Its main objective is to minimize casualties and human suffering by providing supplies to the affected population while making an efficient and effective allocation of scarce resources [5].

One of the crucial decisions humanitarian logistics decision makers should face is the delivery of the collected humanitarian aid (mostly donations). To do so, the routes of the available vehicles should be planned while considering the quantity to deliver in these vehicles. The decisions regarding the routes can be seen as a vehicle routing problem (VRP) and it's formally defined as the problem of finding optimal routes from one or multiple depots to a number of geographically disperse customers [6]. When the quantity of humanitarian aid carried by the vehicles is considered to be optimized, the problem is extended to the inventory routing problem (IRP) which in its basic version consists in finding the optimum lot sizes to deliver a set of customers while minimizing the distribution and holding inventory costs [7]. Some authors also stated that the IRP can be seen as the integration of the vehicle routing problem (VRP), and the inventory management problem (IM) [8], where there are different orders specified by a set of customers and the supplier has the objective of satisfying the customer while minimizing distribution and holding inventory costs. While the VRP aims to find the delivery routes, in the IRP the quantity delivered and the time of the delivery are considered along with the routes [9]. A complete review with the IRP objectives, variants and solution methodologies are presented in [8] and [10].

The IRP version in humanitarian logistics enhances the classical problem considering multiple disaster features. Number of depots and shelters to be opened, disruptions in the road network, demand variability, shortages, inventory and routing decisions, deprivation costs, uncertainties and less frequently the safety in depots and shelters regarding the risk of inventory losses or shelter destruction are the frequent disaster features studied. This risk level is associated to the persistence of the thread regarding localization of shelters, some of them may be in risky zones with geological hazards (e.g., landslide points or flood areas), near dangerous facilities (e.g. gas stations, chemical warehouses), in unsafe zones with probability of riots or located in facilities with no evacuation plans [11]. The previous factors in the worst-case scenario would cause entire shelters to become useless or being destroyed and consequently, large amounts of humanitarian aid would be unusable causing even more shortages increasing the suffering of the affected population.

This paper addresses the distribution of humanitarian aid considering simultaneously the shortage in shelters as well as the risk of inventory losses given by the persistence of the threat (aftershocks or new disaster events). These two objectives are opposites or are in conflict, since a shelter with high levels of inventory there would has less shortages but, there would be more risk of humanitarian aid being destroyed. On the other hand, if there is less inventory the shortages would be more significant. The minimization of the previous objectives is made using an epsilon constraint methodology obtaining the Pareto efficiency front of the problem. The paper is organized as follows. Section 2 presents a brief literature review on the inventory routing problems in humanitarian logistics and related work. Section 3 defines formally the problem, the multi-objective model formulation for the problem is presented in Sect. 4. Section 5 contains the epsilon constraint methodology for the problem, in Sect. 6 a real-case study inspired in the 2017 Mocoa-Colombia is presented to use with the approach and, finally Sect. 7 shows some conclusions and future work.

2 Literature Review

There have been several research studies aimed at building decision-making tools in humanitarian logistics specifically in the distribution of humanitarian aid. Among relevant authors who have worked on this specific topic, Pérez-Rodríguez and Holguín-Veras [12] developed an inventory routing model for allocation and supply routing decisions that minimize deprivation costs. Another relevant contribution is found in [13], the authors proposed a multi-objective stochastic programming model in which the criteria for selecting the shelters to be opened is the safety of them concerning the risk of destruction or stealing. Tofighi et al. [5] proposed a mathematical model for localization and relief distribution plan wherein the first stage of the model the locations of warehouses are proposed and in the second stage, the distribution plan and the prepositioned inventory for each location is planned incorporating stochastic parameters with the use of fuzzy programming to represent the uncertainties. In [14] the authors introduced the Covering tour Location Routing Problem with Replenishment (CLRPR), and create a mathematical model to solve it which is tested for small-size instances in a humanitarian logistics context. Moreno et al. [15] presented an integrated relief distribution model under uncertainty with deprivation costs.

A practical application of an inventory routing model is found in [16]. In this paper the authors applied and adapted an IRP model to a real case scenario in Marikina City, Philippines. The model aims to minimize the routing cost while minimizing unsatisfied demands through penalties. Another recent relevant contribution is in [17], the authors proposed a mixed integer problem to find the optimal route for drones to deliver packages to certain nodes and solved the model by column generation. A related work which also considers two objectives in its approach is presented in [18], the authors introduced a mathematical model for tackling the distribution of materials and injured people and proposed a bi-objective stochastic model to solve the problem. In [19] a decision-support system (DSS) with simulation and optimization is proposed to determine potential transfer points in a disaster event. The approach introduced agent-based modeling, search heuristics and tabu search for better choosing transfer points. According to the literature review, most of the previous work tackles the humanitarian delivery aid problem with inventory routing models which considers transportation costs, social costs, operational costs, location decisions, uncertainties in the supply or demand. These works do not consider the risks of inventory losses associated with the likelihood of the locations being struck by a natural or man-made disaster or security issues. To the best of our knowledge, the related works which consider inventory losses risk do no take inventory routing decisions, the consideration was only made at facility location level.

3 Problem Definition

Inventory and routing decisions in the aftermath of a catastrophe is a complex activity mostly made manually in which multiple criteria and factors must be considered. The purpose of this activity is to establish the quantities and the routes the available vehicles must follow to deliver humanitarian aid to the opened shelters. It is proposed a multi-objective multi vehicle inventory routing problem for the delivery of humanitarian aid in the form of kits. To do so, the problem is formally stated as follows.

It is considered a set of shelters $N = \{1, 2, \ldots, m\}$ which are geographically distributed over an affected area and must be served in multiple $T = \{1, 2, \ldots, t\}$ periods with different quantities of humanitarian aid in form of kits from a single depot. Thus, the inventory routing problem for delivering humanitarian aid can be defined in a non-directed graph $G = (V, A)$ with a set of nodes $V = N \cup \{0\}$, where N are the shelter locations and $\{0\}$ the depot. The set of arcs is defined by $A = \{(i, j) : i, j \in V, i \neq j\}$ and each arc (i, j) has associated a non-negative value c_{ij} which represents the travel cost between nodes i and j and the total cost of the routes should not be higher that an established budget P.

Each shelter $i \in N$ has a demand D_{nt} which must be fulfilled in the period $t \in T$. The shelters have a maximum capacity U_n for receiving humanitarian kits and have an initial inventory level II_n, the depot has also an initial inventory level ID. Additionally, the shelters have a level of risk associated with the probability of being destroyed or its inventory being lost. This risk R_n is parametrized in a scale from 1 to 5 being 5 the higher risk level. Finally, to deliver the humanitarian aid from the depot to the different shelters a fleet of vehicles $K = \{1, 2, \ldots, k\}$ are available which have a maximum load capacity Q_k. Next Section shows the mathematical model for the problem presented before.

4 Bi-objective Mixed Integer Model

In this section the mathematical formulation for the problem is presented. First, the sets, parameters and variables are defined and finally Eqs. (1)–(22) presents the objective functions and constraints of the model.

Sets

M: Shelters set $N = \{1, \ldots, n\}$
K: Vehicles set $K = \{1, \ldots, k\}$
V = Vertex set (Shelters and Depot) $N' = N \cup \{0\}$
A: Set of arcs $(i, j) \in V, i > j$
T: Time set $T = \{1, \ldots, t\}$
T': Time set $T' = T \cup \{t + 1\}$

Parameters

Q_k: Capacity of vehicle k
C_{ij}: Transportation cost from node i to j.
U_n: Maximum inventory level at shelter n.

D_{nt}: Demand of shelter n in period t

II_n: Initial inventory level at shelter n

ID: Initial inventory level at depot

R_n Risk level at shelter n. [1 Lowest risk, 5 higher].

HD_t: Humanitarian aid donations available at depot in period t

P: Total budget for transportation cost

Variables

Y_{ijkt}: 1 if vehicle k uses the arc $(i - j)$ in period t, 0 otherwise.

X_{nkt}: Quantity of humanitarian aid delivered to shelter n in vehicle k in period t

Z_{nkt} 1 if shelter n is served by vehicle k in period t, 0 otherwise.

B_t Inventory Level at Depot in period t

I_{nt} Inventory Level at Shelter n in period t

S_{nt} Shortage level at shelter n in period t

The two objectives in our model are indicated by Eqs. (1) and (2) and described as follows: Objective function 1 minimizes shortage or stock-out at shelters and objective function 2 minimizes the level of inventory at risk in shelters.

$$Minimize\ FO1 = \sum_{n \in M} \sum_{t \in T} S_{nt} \tag{1}$$

$$Minimize\ FO2 = \sum_{n \in M} \sum_{t \in T'} I_{nt} R_n \tag{2}$$

Subject to:

$$B_t = B_{t-1} + HD_{kt-1} - \sum_{n \in M} \sum_{k \in K} X_{nkt-1} \quad \forall t \in T' | t > 1 \tag{3}$$

$$B_1 = ID \tag{4}$$

$$B_t \geq \sum_{n \in M} \sum_{k \in K} X_{nkt} \quad \forall t \in T \tag{5}$$

$$I_{nt} = I_{nt-1} + \sum_{k \in K} X_{nkt-1} - D_{nt-1} + S_{nt-1} \quad \forall t \in T', n \in M | t > 1 \tag{6}$$

$$I_{n1} = II_n \quad \forall n \in M \tag{7}$$

$$I_{nt} \leq U_n \quad \forall t \in T, n \in M \tag{8}$$

$$\sum_{k \in K} X_{nkt} \leq U_n - I_{nt} \quad \forall t \in T, n \in M, k \in K \tag{9}$$

$$\sum_{k \in K} X_{nkt} \leq U_n Z_{nt} \quad \forall t \in T, n \in M, k \in K \tag{10}$$

$$X_{nkt} \geq Z_{nt} \quad \forall t \in T, n \in M, k \in K \tag{11}$$

$$\sum_{n \in M} X_{nkt} \leq Q_k \qquad \forall t \in T, k \in K \tag{12}$$

$$\sum_{(0,i) \in A} Y_{0ikt} \geq Z_{0kt} \qquad \forall t \in T, k \in K \tag{13}$$

$$\sum_{(0,i) \in A} Y_{0ikt} \leq 1 \qquad \forall t \in T, k \in K \tag{14}$$

$$\sum_{n \in M} X_{nkt} \leq Q_k Z_{0kt} \qquad \forall t \in T, k \in K \tag{15}$$

$$\sum_{j \in V} Y_{ijkt} + \sum_{e \in V} Y_{eikt} = 2Z_{ikt} \qquad \forall t \in T, i \in M, k \in K \tag{16}$$

$$Y_{ijkt} = 0 \qquad \forall t \in T, k \in K, (i-j) \in M | i = j \tag{17}$$

$$\sum_{j \in V} Y_{ijkt} \leq 1 \qquad \forall t \in T, i \in M, k \in K \tag{18}$$

$$\sum_{i \in V} Y_{ijkt} \leq 1 \qquad \forall t \in T, i \in M, k \in K \tag{19}$$

$$\sum_{i \in L} \sum_{j \in L | j < i} Y_{ijkt} \leq \sum_{i \in L} Z_{ikt} - Z_{hkt} \qquad L \subseteq M, \forall t \in T, \forall h \in L, k \in K \tag{20}$$

$$\sum_{(i-j) \in A} \sum_{t \in T} \sum_{k \in K} C_{ij} Y_{ijkt} \leq P \tag{21}$$

$$B_t, X_{nkt}, S_{nt}, I_{nt} \geq 0, Z_{nkt}, Y_{ijkt} \in \{0, 1\} \tag{22}$$

Constraints (3) calculates the inventory level at depot, (4) establishes the initial inventory level for the depot, (5) ensures that the depot is not allowed to send more than its existences, inventory definition and initial inventory for shelters are calculated in (6) and (7). In (8), (9) and (10) the observation of shelters' capacity is made. Constraints (11) considers vehicles capacities, (12) guarantees each vehicle visiting a shelter must deliver humanitarian aid, (13), (14) and (15) assures each vehicle must start its route from the depot, flow conservation constraints are presented in (16) where each vehicle visiting a depot must leave, in (17) vehicles are forbidden to visit a shelter and the go to the same shelter again. In (18) and (19) it is contemplated that each vehicle can visit only one time per period the same shelter, (20) are the subtours elimination constraints, (21) are the budget constraints for travel costs and finally (22) are the nonnegativity and binary constraints for the decision variables.

5   ϵ-Constraint Methodology

There are several methods of multi-objective optimization that have been successfully tested in the literature and in real life problems where there is no single optimal solution that optimizes all the objective functions at once. Methodologies such as goal programming (GP), constraint programming (CP), epsilon (ϵ) - constraint method and the Reference Point Method (RPM) are among the most used multi-objective methodologies [20]. In this paper, the ϵ-constraint method is used to solve our multi-objective optimization problem. To do so, first we optimize one objective function using the other as constraints and incorporating them in the constraint part of the mathematical model. Finally, the parametrical variations in the right-hand side (RHS) of the constrained objective functions e_i give efficient solutions which are in the pareto frontier. In this problem, the objective function of shortage is minimized as seen in Eq. (23), while the inventory at risk objective is considered as constraint and defining the highest acceptable limit for that objective e_2 as shown in (24). This process is done multiple times obtaining the non-dominated solutions and the pareto efficiency front for the problem.

$$Minimize\ FO1 = \sum_{n \in M} \sum_{t \in T} S_{nt} \tag{23}$$

$$FO2: \sum_{n \in M} \sum_{t \in T} I_{nt} R_n \le e_2 \tag{24}$$

6 Results

6.1 Description of the Case-Study

On the night of 31 March 2017 heavy rain in Mocoa-Colombia caused the Mulata, Mocoa and Sangoyaco rivers to overflow originating in the first hours of 1 April a landslide which affected the urban area of Mocoa heavily, killing more than 300 persons, an approximate of 330 persons were injured and more than one hundred disappeared [21]. The flood and debris rushed multiple infrastructures such as streets, residential buildings, and streets affecting 17 neighborhoods and approximately 45000 people [22]. In the period of 12-04-2017 to 15-04-2017 eight shelters were used to serve the affected people and were established in schools, universities, coliseums and other locations. Additionally, there was no information available of a depot, so it is assumed to be in the transport terminal at the center of the city, the previous locations are depicted in Fig. 1. The risk of inventory losses at shelters were estimated based on the shelters' closeness to the affected areas as shown in Fig. 2 concerning the persistence of the threat (another landslide).

The data of demand was collected based on the Colombian Red Cross SITREP an information bullet available in [23] as seen in Table 1, initial inventory levels for all depots are 50 kits and its maximum capacity is 1000 kits. On the other hand, humanitarian donations are assumed to be high in the first period (2500 kits), but it decreased over time allowing shortage at shelters with 500 and 700 kits respectively, also an initial inventory level for the depot was considered (1700 kits). Additionally, two vehicles are assumed to be available for performing the routes and delivering the humanitarian kits to shelters with a capacity of 1000 kits.

Finally, using the Haversine formula with the georeferentiation of shelters and depot from Table 1 the distance from the nodes were calculated and the costs were estimated proportionally.

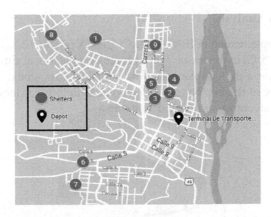

Fig. 1. Localization of shelters and depot

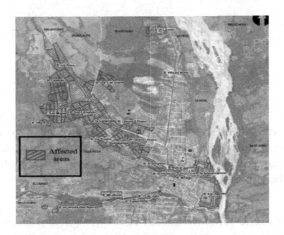

Fig. 2. Affected areas of the 2017 Mocoa-Colombia Landslide source [24]

Table 1. Shelters' parameters for the case-study

	Name	Geospatial information		Demand			Risk level
		Latitude	Longitude	1	2	3	
1	Instituto Tecnológico del Putumayo	1.156705	−76.652341	398	350	302	4
2	INDER	1.151616	−76.646039	381	316	250	2
3	I.E. Pio XII	1.151050	−76.647303	102	82	62	3
4	Coliseo Olímpico el Jardín	1.152832	−76.645638	251	231	211	2
5	Organización Zonal Indígena del Putumayo	1.152442	−76.647652	200	200	200	2
6	I.E. Fray Plácido	1.145214	−76.653422	110	55	0	1
7	Coliseo Las Américas	1.143125	−76.654044	242	276	213	1
8	La Esmeralda	1.157034	−76.656072	245	224	203	5

6.2 Results and Analysis

The approach is implemented in IBM ILOG CPLEX Version: 12.8.0.0 in a laptop with 6 GB RAM and 2.5 GHz processor with average computational times for each run of 200 s. Figure 3 shows the optimal pareto front for the case study, it can be seen the conflictive behavior of the two objective functions, with lower values of shortage there are high levels of inventory at risk and vice versa.

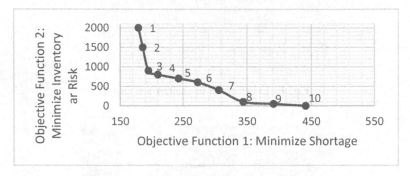

Fig. 3. Optimal Pareto Front for the case study

Table 2 presents the objective function values for the points of the Fig. 3. To measure the performance of the pareto front, the Spacing metric is used, and it represents how evenly distributed are the found non-dominated solutions along the pareto front. The metric gave a value of 154.1 which indicates that the solutions are not evenly distributed over the pareto front.

Table 2. Objective function values with pareto solutions

Solution	Objective function 1 (Shortage)	Objective function 2 (Inventory at risk)
1	179	1998
2	186	1500
3	195	900
4	210	800
5	243	700
6	273	600
7	306	400
8	344	100
9	391	50
10	441	0

Furthermore, each solution gives the optimal distribution scheme for the humanitarian aid operation. Tables 3 and 4 present the routes and quantities delivered to each shelter in two solutions with shortage levels of 344 and 194 respectively. It's worth noting that the routes and the quantity delivered by each vehicle change based on the solution. Even though in the first period the routes for both vehicles are similar, the quantities changed, but in the second and third period the routes vary significantly as well as the quantities delivered. For instance, the solution of Table 3 visited more frequently the shelters delivering less quantities of humanitarian aid, therefore, the inventory at risk was lower and the shortage higher. On the contrary, the solution of Table 4 uses less arcs, visits less shelters delivering higher quantities of humanitarian aid, risking more inventory but lowering shortages. It's worth noting that exists a balance between the two objective functions, in other words, if the decision maker wants to avoid shortages, he/she will send more humanitarian aid to the shelters with lower risk and allow some shortage at the shelter with higher risk of inventory losses.

Table 3. Routes and quantities with a Shortage level of 344

Period	Vehicle	Route	Quantity delivered to shelters							
			1	2	3	4	5	6	7	8
1	1	0-4-2-0	–	331	–	201	–	–	–	–
	2	0-3-5-1-8-6-7-0	348	–	52	–	150	60	195	195
2	1	0-3-5-4-2-0	–	316	81	231	200	–	–	–
	2	0-6-7-8-1-3-0	350	–	1	–	–	55	370	224
3	1	–	–	–	–	–	–	–	–	–
	2	0-3-5-1-4-2-0	302	225	62	211	200	–	–	–

Table 4. Routes and quantities with a Shortage level of 195

Period	Vehicle	Route	Quantity delivered to shelters							
			1	2	3	4	5	6	7	8
1	1	0-7-6-1-5-3-0	348	–	52	–	150	115	256	–
	2	0-2-4-0	–	387	–	201	–	–	–	–
2	1	0-3-5-4-2-0	–	277	81	442	200	–	–	–
	2	0-3-1-8-7-0	350	–	1	–	–	–	425	224
3	1	0-3-8-1-5-2-0	302	233	62	–	200	–	–	203
	2	–	–	–	–	–	–	–	–	–

7 Conclusions and Future Work

In this paper, a bi-objective mathematical model for the delivery of humanitarian aid considering shortage and inventory at risk was presented. The proposal can give both tactical and operational view of the delivery operations in the aftermath of a catastrophe. The decision-maker has the routes and quantities to deliver in any optimal solution he/she chooses. In other words, if the humanitarian logistics decision-maker wants to avoid as much as possible shortage putting at risk inventory, the proposal will give him/her the distribution plan. On the other hand, if the decision-maker is more conservative and allow some shortage risking less inventory, the proposal will also provide him/her the delivery scheme with the routes and quantities. In the case-study inspired in the Mocoa-Colombia 2017 landslide, a clear Pareto front was found, showing the extreme values of the objective functions and the others non-dominated solutions, showing that the epsilon-constraint methodology tackled efficiently the bi-objective model and found a balance between shortage and inventory at risk. To the best of our knowledge, similar works do not consider inventory at risk (caused by the persistence of the threat) in inventory and routing decisions. The literature review suggests that this consideration is only made at location decisions (shelters or ware-houses) and not when shelters are already opened. Future work should be directed at developing methodologies to parametrize the inventory at risk level, considering more factors such as security issues or including experts' choices. Additionally, although the computational times are not an obstacle in the case-study, bigger problems with more locations or vehicles would require developing procedures such as heuristics or metaheuristics which will speed up finding the model solutions. Finally, in this approach it is considered a known demand which does not change over time, in the aftermath of the disaster the demand is unknown and vary over time. Therefore, future efforts should be focused to developing a methodology which considers dynamic demands or supply, for instance a multi-agent simulation model or discrete simulation events, Finally, future works should include uncertainty in parameters such as demand, travel times, supply etc.

Acknowledgements. We thank Universidad de La Sabana for supporting financially this work, also, the authors thank the comments of the anonymous referees that improved our paper.

References

1. Centre for Research on the Epidemiology Database CRED: EM-DAT The international disaster database (2018). https://www.emdat.be/
2. SwissRe: Natural catastrophes and man-made disasters in 2017: a year of record-breaking losses (2018)
3. Global Facility for Disaster Reduction and Recovery: The making of a riskier future: How our decisions are shaping future disaster risk (2016)
4. Kunz, N., Van Wassenhove, L.N., Besiou, M., Hambye, C., Kovács, G.: Relevance of humanitarian logistics research: best practices and way forward. Int. J. Oper. Prod. Manag. **37**(11), 1585–1599 (2017)
5. Tofighi, S., Torabi, S.A., Mansouri, S.A.: Humanitarian logistics network design under mixed uncertainty. Eur. J. Oper. Res. **250**(1), 239–250 (2016)
6. Laporte, G.: The vehicle routing problem: an overview of exact and approximate algorithms. Eur. J. Oper. Res. **59**(3), 345–358 (1992)
7. Coelho, L.C., Laporte, G.: A branch-and-cut algorithm for the multi-product multi-vehicle inventory-routing problem. Int. J. Prod. Res. **51**(23–24), 7156–7169 (2013)
8. Coelho, L.C., Cordeau, J.-F., Laporte, G.: Thirty years of inventory routing. Transp. Sci. **48** (1), 1–19 (2014)

9. Moin, N.H., Salhi, S.: Inventory routing problems: a logistical overview. J. Oper. Res. Soc. **58**(9), 1185–1194 (2007)
10. Andersson, H., Hoff, A., Christiansen, M., Hasle, G., Løkketangen, A.: Industrial aspects and literature survey: combined inventory management and routing. Comput. Oper. Res. **37** (9), 1515–1536 (2010)
11. Chen, W., Zhai, G., Ren, C., Shi, Y., Zhang, J.: Urban resources selection and allocation for emergency shelters: In a multi-hazard environment. Int. J. Environ. Res. Public Health **15**(6), 1261 (2018)
12. Pérez-Rodríguez, N., Holguín-Veras, J.: Inventory-allocation distribution models for postdisaster humanitarian logistics with explicit consideration of deprivation costs. Transp. Sci. **50**(4), 1261–1285 (2016)
13. Bozorgi-Amiri, A., Jabalameli, M.S., Mirzapour Al-e-Hashem, S.M.J.: A multi-objective robust stochastic programming model for disaster relief logistics under uncertainty. OR Spectr. **35**(4), 905–933 (2013)
14. Nedjati, A., Izbirak, G., Arkat, J.: Bi-objective covering tour location routing problem with replenishment at intermediate depots: formulation and meta-heuristics. Comput. Ind. Eng. **110**, 191–206 (2017)
15. Moreno, A., Alem, D., Ferreira, D., Clark, A.: An effective two-stage stochastic multi-trip location-transportation model with social concerns in relief supply chains. Eur. J. Oper. Res. **269**(3), 1050–1071 (2018)
16. Putong, L.L., De Leon, M.M.: A modified Balcik last mile distribution model for relief operations using open road networks. Procedia Eng. **212**, 133–140 (2018)
17. Rabta, B., Wankmüller, C., Reiner, G.: A drone fleet model for last-mile distribution in disaster relief operations. Int. J. Disaster Risk Reduct. **28**(February), 107–112 (2018)
18. Najafi, M., Eshghi, K., Dullaert, W.: A multi-objective robust optimization model for logistics planning in the earthquake response phase. Transp. Res. Part E Logist. Transp. Rev. **49**(1), 217–249 (2013)
19. Fikar, C., Gronalt, M., Hirsch, P.: A decision support system for coordinated disaster relief distribution. Expert Syst. Appl. **57**, 104–116 (2016)
20. Mavrotas, G.: Effective implementation of the e-constraint method in multi-objective mathematical programming problems. Appl. Math. Comput. **213**(2), 455–465 (2009)
21. Reliefweb: Colombia – Inundaciones en Mocoa, Putumayo - Reporte de Situación No. 03 (al 11.04.2017) (2017)
22. Cheng, D., Cui, Y., Su, F., Jia, Y., Choi, C.E.: The characteristics of the Mocoa compound disaster event, Colombia. Landslides **15**(6), 1223–1232 (2018)
23. Cruz Roja Colombiana: SITREP #9 - EMERGENCIA MOCOA PUTUMAYO (2017)
24. UN Office for the Coordination of Humanitarian Affairs (OCHA), Colombia: Putumayo - Mocoa Zonas de afectación (2017). https://www.humanitarianresponse.info/es/operations/colombia/infographic/colombia-municipio-de-mocoa-putumayo-afectación-por-avalancha

A General Local Search Pareto Approach with Regular Criteria for Solving the Job-Shop Scheduling Problem Multi-resource Resource Flexibility with Linear Routes

Andrés Alberto García-León[(✉)] [ID]
and William Fernando Torres Tapia[ID]

Facultad de Ingeniería Programa de Ingeniería Industrial, Universidad de Ibagué,
Ibagué, Colombia
andres.garcia@unibague.edu.co,
williamindustrial2014@gmail.com

Abstract. The Job-shop Scheduling problem Multi-resource Resource flexibility with linear routes is an extension of the classical Job-shop Scheduling problem "JSMRFLR" where an operation needs several resources (machines) simultaneously to be processed and each machine is selected from a given set. Linear route indicates that an operation is exclusively performed for a job. Publications related to this problem are really scarce and they are dedicated to minimize makespan criterion, which aims to minimize the use of the machines. In the modern scenery of the Operations Management, the exclusive minimization of the makespan does not allow to analyze aspects of the customer service to ensure high levels of competitiveness such as the consideration of due-date and the importance between jobs. In this paper, we propose a general Pareto approach to solve the JSMRFLR with regular criteria, which operates by an efficient local search at using a fast estimation function for the criteria considering the conjunctive graph. During the search, the set of non-dominated solutions is updated. The efficiency of our approach is illustrated on instances of literature at performing three sets of criteria. The first set considers makespan and maximum tardiness. In the second total flow time is added and in the third the total tardiness. As a product of our approach, a reference of results is proposed by future research.

Keywords: Scheduling theory ·
Extension of the Job-shop scheduling problem · Regular criteria · Local search ·
Pareto optimization

1 Introduction

For the Operations Management, the success of the production programming depends on the scheduling decisions. These decisions lead to determine the sequence of activities and the assignment of resources to optimize an objective function. In the literature of scheduling, the highest rigor of the decisions have been focused on

© Springer Nature Switzerland AG 2019
J. C. Figueroa-García et al. (Eds.): WEA 2019, CCIS 1052, pp. 764–775, 2019.
https://doi.org/10.1007/978-3-030-31019-6_64

configurations derived of the classical flow-shop and Job-shop problems such as parallel machines, sequence dependent set up times, maintenance activities and others. Concerning to the minimization of criteria, makespan, that is the maximum completion time of jobs has been the most studied. Minimizing makespan does not consider relevant aspects for the customer service like the due-date of jobs that represents the delivery date agreed with customers and the importance between them. Therefore, minimizing regular criteria different than the makespan leads to identify key aspects to improve the customer service.

One of the extensions of the Job-shop problem is the Multi-resource and Resource flexibility with linear routes. This extension was proposed by [1]. The Multi-resource considers that an operation needs several resources simultaneously to be performed and resource flexibility determines that a resource (machine) is chosen from a given set. Linear route means that each operation is performed exclusively for a job. To best of our knowledge, it is scarce the level of publications at solving this problem even considering makespan.

This paper is oriented to improve the level of customer service and the productivity in a more realistic industrial environment such as the Job-shop Scheduling Problem Multi-resource Resource Flexibility with linear routes "JSMRFLR". To reach the goal, a fast local search algorithm that uses the properties of a conjunctive graph adapted to regular criteria is designed to solve the JSMRFLR in Pareto manner at minimizing a combination of regular criteria. The solutions that belong to the Pareto front are gotten iteratively. In each iteration, a random criterion is selected and the move is determined by an estimation function that considering the evaluation simultaneous of reversing a critical arc (x, y) that belongs to the critical path of a job that affects a criterion and the reassignment of x and y at maintaining the level of operations into the conjunctive graph (maximum number of arcs from the start dummy node) between operations j and k.

During the search, the set of non-dominated solutions is updated at removing the dominated solutions and adding of a new one if it is necessary. The proposed approach is validated in instances of the literature proposed by [1] at solving three different sets of criteria. In the first set, makespan and maximum tardiness are solved. The second set adds the total flow time, and the third adds the total tardiness. As a contribution of our experiments a benchmark of results is proposed for future research. The paper is detailed as follows. Section 2 describes and models the problem with the considerations of the front of Pareto. In Sect. 3, the algorithm that solves the problem is described. Finally, Sect. 4 illustrates some computational experiments.

2 The Problem and Pareto Optimization

The objective of this Section is to illustrate the problem with its components and the guidelines to obtain the Pareto front at minimizing a set of regular criteria.

2.1 Problem Description and Modeling

To describe the problem, it is necessary to consider the Job-shop Scheduling Problem "JSP". In the JSP, a set of n jobs $J = \{J_1, \ldots J_n\}$ are processed on a set $M =$

$\{M_1, \ldots, M_m\}$ of m machines that are available. Each machine can only process one job at a time. A job J_i is obtained at performing sequentially n_i operations in a fix route. Preempting operations is not allowed. It means that an operation cannot be interrupted once started. Each job J_i has a due-date d_i. The JSP Multi-resource Resource Flexibility with linear routes "JSMRFLR" considers that an operation needs several resources simultaneously to be performed and resource flexibility indicates that a resource may be selected in a given set.

A model of the disjunctive graph for the Multi-resource shop scheduling with resource flexibility considering linear and non-linear routes is proposed in [1]. This model is used for minimizing makespan. To minimize regular criteria in the JSMRFLR, we have added the properties of linear routes from the JSP, which were validated in [2] and adapted for the flexible Job-shop scheduling problem in [3]. In the conjunctive graph for minimizing regular criteria for the JSMRFLR, the n nodes ϕ_i that represents the finalization of the jobs, the concept of maximum number of arcs between node 0 and an operation x (l_x) and the tail from a node x to the dummy node $\phi_i(q_x^i)$ have been added.

In the JSMRFLR, the disjunctive graph is noted $G = (V, A, E)$, where V is the set of nodes, A is the set of conjunctive arcs and E is the set of disjunctive arcs. The nodes in E represent operations of jobs (set O), plus a dummy node 0 that corresponds to the start of each job, and n dummy nodes ϕ_i. A contains conjunctive arcs which connect two consecutive operations on the routing of jobs, the node 0 to every first operation of each job, and the last operation of J_i to a dummy node ϕ_i. The set E contains disjunctive arcs between every pair of operations assigned to the same resource. Let E_k be the set of disjunctive arcs between pairs of operations that must be processed on k, $E = \cup E_k$.

The set of operations O has to be processed on a set of machines (resources) M. To be processed an operation $x \in O$ requires $R(x)$ resources simultaneously and M_x^k is the resource subset in which the kth resource $(1 \leq k \leq R(x))$ must be selected. The M_x^k subsets are not necessarily disjoint, for example, a resource could belong to several subsets. To obtain a feasible schedule in the JSMRFLR, assignment and sequencing decisions have to be made to solve the conflict in E. In each operation, the assignment decision consists on determining which machine or resource must be selected from each subset to perform it. However, it is mandatory to ensure of not assigning a resource twice or more to the same operation, additionally the processing time of an operation x (p_x) is determined by the maximum time of the resource where it is assigned. The sequencing decision deals with determining a sequence of operations on each selected resource k to minimize any regular criterion. It is important to highlight that the sequence of operations on resources does not lead to create cycles in the conjunctive graph. As soon as a solution is obtained, it is possible to extract information to identify the properties to create moves which lead to improve any criterion. The arc from 0 to the first operation of J_i has a length equal to the release date r_i of j_i. Any remaining arc has a length equal to the processing time of the operation from which it starts. The starting time of x, $h_x = L(0, x)$ called head, that corresponds to the length of the longest path from 0 to x. The tail from a node x to the dummy node $\phi_i(q_x^i)$ is equal to $[L(x, \phi_i) - p_x]$ if a path exists from x to ϕ_i and $-\infty$ otherwise. A path from 0 to ϕ_i is called critical if its length is equal to C_i, and every node x belonging to this critical path is critical according to job J_i. A critical node x for job J_i satisfies $h_x + p_x + q_x^i = C_i$. The level l_x of a node x in G denotes the maximum number of arcs in a path from 0 to x. After obtaining the heads of the nodes of the graph, the criterion of a feasible schedule represented by the selection can be determined in $O(n)$ from the starting times of the dummy nodes. For instance, the makespan is obtained using the formula $C_{max} = \max C_i$. Additionally the tardiness (T_i), $T_i = \max(0, C_i - d_i)$. Then, the maximum tardiness is $T_{max} = \max T_i$, total tardiness (T) is the sum of the tardiness of jobs $(\sum_1^n T_i)$ and the total flow time is the sum of the completion time of jobs $(\sum_1^n C_i)$.

2.2 Pareto Optimization

Pareto optimization aims to find a set of non-dominated solutions at optimizing a set of criteria (often conflicting). In our case, for optimizing regular criteria, all objectives lead to be minimized. The set of non-dominated solutions Q represents the Pareto front and its comprehension requires to check the dominance between solutions, and the conditions that a solution s must satisfy to be included in Q. Concerning to the dominance between solutions, solutions A and B are considered. To determine if A dominates to B or B is dominated by A, the following conditions must be true: (1) A is not worse than B for all objectives, and (2) A is strictly better than B for at least one objective. To know if a solution s must be included in Q, two conditions must be ensured: (1) Any two solutions of Q must be non-dominated with respect to each other and, (2) Any solution not in Q is dominated by at least one solution in Q.

The Fig. 1 helps to illustrate two non-dominated solutions of an instance with three jobs, seven operations and six machines or resources (M_1, M_2, M_3, M_4, M_5 and M_6) at minimizing makespan and maximum tardiness simultaneously. Besides, the due dates for jobs are determined. They are $d_1 = 6$, $d_2 = 12$ and $d_3 = 6$ (see column d_i). The solution in Fig. 1(a) aims to minimize makespan, and in the Fig. 1(b) the maximum tardiness. The solution in the Fig. 1(a) can be used to explain some properties of the conjunctive graph and some remarks can be extracted. The first job has two operations (see the first route for a job). The first operation of the first job requires two resources simultaneously (see dashed rectangle). The first resource is selected between M_1 and M_4. If M_1 is selected 3 is the processing time, otherwise 2. The second resource is selected between M_2 and M_4. In this example, M_4 and M_2 are assigned respectively (they are highlighted in yellow and blue color) and the processing time is 2. Note that a resource was not assigned twice. Considering the same operation, it starts at time 0 and finishing at time 2 (see 0/2), since the processing time is 2 (see 0 + 2 = 2). Considering that one operation cannot start before finishing all its predecessors, the completion time of all jobs (see column C_i) and the tardiness of all jobs are calculated (see column T_i).

The solutions illustrated in the Fig. 1 are non-dominated solutions. If for example makespan and maximum tardiness are considered, in the Fig. 1(a) the values for the criteria are 12 and 4 respectively, and in the Fig. 1(b) these values are 14 and 2. It means that for a decision maker without considering importance between criteria both solutions are equivalent and they satisfy the conditions of non-dominance between solutions.

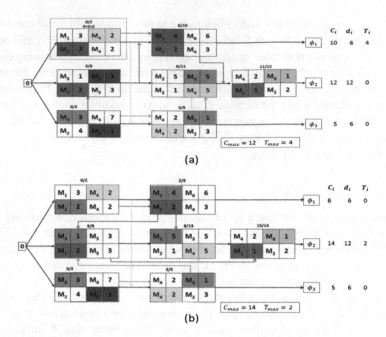

Fig. 1. Examples of two non-dominated solutions with makespan and maximum tardiness

2.3   Quality of the Pareto Front

There is not any consensus to establish the quality of the Pareto Front. Different approaches have been proposed (see for example [4] and [5]). However, two aspects are mandatory to consider: convergence and diversity. Convergence implies that the set of non-dominated solutions must be located closest to the origin of coordinates. Diversity is related to the solutions in sparsely space to ensure that the decision maker has several and representative trade-off solutions among conflicting criteria. To determine the quality of the front, the set of metrics employed in [5] are analyzed. In this case, for the convergence the hypervolume (HV), elite solutions and the Mean Ideal Distance (MID) are measured. HV is the volume covered by the solutions of the front and respect to the worst solution, since regular criteria are minimized. Elite solutions are the best values of the criteria. MID is the average Euclidean distance obtained between each non-dominated solution and the origin. Concerning to the diversity, the maximum spread (D) and spacing (SP) are analyzed. D is the longest diagonal of the hyper box formed by the extreme values of the criteria, and SP is the average distance between consecutive solutions.

The Fig. 2 is an image of the results generated by our algorithm, which will be explained in the next section at minimizing in Pareto manner makespan, maximum tardiness and total flow time (TFT) at performing the instance *mjs07* during five minutes from [1]. This Figure is divided in two parts. The part a represents a txt file with the results. For example, the algorithm gets eight non-dominated solutions. Each solution shows the value of the criteria. Additionally, the metrics are separated by diversity and convergence. In the part b, the eight non-dominated solutions are plotted on a three dimensional plane.

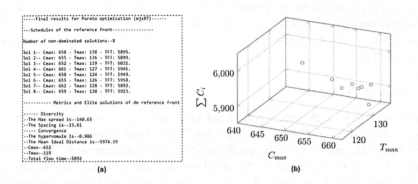

```
·······Final results for Pareto optimization (mjs07)·······
:---Schedules of the reference front···············
:Number of non-dominated solutions--8
:Sol 1-- Cmax: 658 - Tmax: 138 - TFT: 5895.
:Sol 2-- Cmax: 655 - Tmax: 136 - TFT: 5899.
:Sol 3-- Cmax: 652 - Tmax: 119 - TFT: 6031.
:Sol 4-- Cmax: 661 - Tmax: 127 - TFT: 5945.
:Sol 5-- Cmax: 658 - Tmax: 124 - TFT: 5949.
:Sol 6-- Cmax: 655 - Tmax: 126 - TFT: 5958.
:Sol 7-- Cmax: 662 - Tmax: 128 - TFT: 5892.
:Sol 8-- Cmax: 659 - Tmax: 130 - TFT: 5923.

:·········· Metrics and Elite solutions of de reference front:
:····· Diversity
:--The Max spread is--140.65
:--The Spacing is--23.61
:····· Convergence
:--The hypervolume is--0.986
:--The Mean Ideal Distance is--5974.19
:--Cmax--652
:--Tmax--119
:--Total flow time--5892
```

(a)   (b)

Fig. 2. Results for the instance *mjs07* at minimizing C_{max}, T_{max} and $\sum C_i$

3 Description of the Algorithm

In Sect. 2 were defined the components of the problem JSMRFLR and the guidelines of Pareto optimization, which are used to describe the proposed algorithm. Basically, our algorithm is a local search process that uses the properties of the conjunctive graph, a test of feasibility conditions, an estimation function and a procedure to update the set of non-dominated solutions.

3.1 Feasibility Conditions and Estimation Functions

Feasibility conditions aim to check if a critical operation could be moved without performing any transformation in the conjunctive graph. For this problem, two types of moves are considered: reversing critical arc (x, y) and the reassignment of a critical operation performed on resource L to resource L' between j and k. Respect to reverse critical arcs, the conditions validated in [2] for minimizing regular criteria have been extended to this problem. However, it is important to clarify that if several arcs connect x and y, all arcs must be reversed, since they are critical, and x and y must belong to different jobs.

In the reassignment, moving an operation ε ($\varepsilon = x$ or $\varepsilon = y$) between operations j and k from resource L to L', it is necessary to check that there are no paths from $b(\forall b \in B)$ to j, and simultaneously from k to $c(\forall c \in C)$. Here, B (resp. C) is the set formed for all immediate successors (resp. predecessors) of ε without considering the successor (resp. predecessor) linked to the resource L. To ensure it, two expressions considering the number of arcs must be satisfied: (1) $l_j \leq \min_{b \in B}\{l_b\}$ and (2) $l_k \geq \max_{c \in C}\{l_c\}$. These expressions are validated, since there is not possible to get a path from a node u to v if $l_v \leq l_u$. To estimate the value of any regular criterion, the completion time of a job must be estimated. It means to determine the completion time of each node ϕ_i. To determine it, two sets of functions based on the type of move.

Concerning to swap a critical arc, the three expressions to L_1, L_2 and L_3 from [2] have been extended to the JSMRFLR problem. Those expressions aim to maintain the same values for the heads or start time for operations and the tails to nodes ϕ_i at reversing a critical arc. At reassigning an operation ε between j and k, we want to maintain the same conditions (heads and tails) to reach a better precision of the estimation. In this case the condition for C_1, C_2 from [1] and L_3 from [6] have been adapted at considering regular criteria.

3.2   Steps of the Search

The search starts with an initial solution, which is the first solution added to the set of non-dominated solutions. Then, iteratively two steps (improvement and diversification) according to the conditions of the graph are executed. Simultaneously the set of non-dominated solutions is updated. In the initial solution, the jobs are sorted in increasing way according to their due-date. Then, for the assignment and sequence of operations on machines (resources) is solved at considering the operation in route of the order jobs. It means that, if there exist and ordering of jobs, the assignment and sequence decisions solve the first operation of all them, then, the second and so on. The objective of the assignment and sequence decisions aim to obtain the lowest completion time per operation at evaluating the capacity of machines. The initial solution is general and it does not make any distinction between criteria.

To transform the conjunctive graph, all critical arcs that belong to the critical paths of jobs that affect the criterion are referenced to create a move at selecting the best neighbor. The algorithm aims to optimize a Pareto approach and iteratively a random criterion is selected to create a move. Selecting the best neighbor implies determine the feasibility of all moves, and then on each feasible move the evaluation of the estimation function which were described in Sect. 3.1. To clarify the functioning of the search, let **CRT** be a set of k criteria to minimize, $Crt_i \in \textbf{CRT}$ a criterion i to minimize; besides, let C_{Sel} be a random chosen criterion to optimize from **CRT**. Let $CFOR \subset CRT$ be a subset of **CRT** that contains the forbidden criteria, which means that in case of a random selection of a criterion, a forbidden criterion cannot be selected. A criterion becomes forbidden when, in the improvement step, it is selected to create a move, and it cannot be generated.

The Fig. 3 illustrates the algorithm for the improvement step. In each iteration, a random criterion C_{Sel} is selected to create a move. If it is not possible to create a move using C_{Sel}, C_{Sel} becomes forbidden and it is added to **CFOR**. The search selects a new criterion that belongs to CRT-CFOR. However, when a move is performed, all criteria are authorized to be selected or the set **CFOR** is emptied. If it is not possible to create a move, the search goes to the diversification step considering the neighborhood of the last forbidden criterion. In this step, when a move is performed the criteria with its local and global optimal are updated.

When, it is not possible to create a move considering the random criterion, a new criterion is selected until the move can be performed. If an improvement move cannot be created, the diversification step starts. It consists on performing iteratively b random moves (b $\in$ [2, 5]) considering the last selected criterion. After that, the search returns to the improvement phase. The set of non-dominated solutions is updated as follows.

Algorithm	Improvement phase in local search process

```
1:  Input: current solution
2:  CFOR = ∅
3:  repeat
4:       Csel ← random(Crtᵢ ∈ {CRT − CFOR})
5:       if it is possible to create an improving move using Csel then
6:            Perform the move and generate the new solution
7:            Update the value for the k criteria
8:            Update the set of non-dominated solutions
9:            Update the local optimal for the k criteria
10:           Update the global optimal for the k criteria
11:           CFOR = ∅
12:      else
13:           Add Csel to CFOR
14:      end if
15: until (CRT − CFOR = ∅)
16: Go to the diversification step with Csel
```

Fig. 3. Algorithm for the improvement step

When a solution s is gotten, it is checked to determine its addition in Q at applying the conditions described in Sect. 2.2. If s were added in Q, s could dominate other solutions, which must be removed from Q. The set of non-dominated solutions is updated at validating simultaneously the addition of the new solution and the elimination of the dominated solutions.

4 Computational Experiments

To validate and evaluate the efficiency of our approach, the instances with linear routing studied in [1] have been considered. Our algorithm was developed in Java language. The experiments were conducted on a PC with 3.40 GHz and 8 GB RAM for each set of criteria on each instance during ten minutes. To calculate the maximum tardiness and the total tardiness, it is necessary to determine the due-date d_i of the jobs. They were generated by introducing a parameter f equals to 1.1, which is inspired from [7]. d_i is determined by multiplying the sum of the average processing times of operations belong to J_i by f. To determine the average processing time of an operation, it is calculated at considering the highest processing time per subset of resources. It is important to mention that d_i was rounded to the next integer number.

The results are presented in three steps. In the first step the efficiency of makespan criterion is evaluated at considering the best known values determined in [1]. In the second step, the elite solutions are analyzed to determine the best combination of criteria to optimize and finally, with the best combination of criteria the results for the metrics of the front of Pareto are calculated.

4.1 Evaluating Makespan

Makespan criterion is the only benchmark to determine the quality of our results at evaluating its convergence. It means the nearest distance respect to a known value. The Table 1 illustrates the best known values (see column BKV) and the best values at considering the three sets of criteria. Additionally, column $DP(\%)$ determines the percentage difference between the best result and the best known value. Besides, if a better known value is gotten, it is underlined and an asterisk is written in column $DP(\%)$. The best makespan of our experiment are written in **bold**.

Table 1. Results for the best makespan in the three sets

Instance	BKV	Set A	Set B	Set C	DP(%)	Instance	BKV	Set A	Set B	Set C	DP(%)
mjs01	361	361	362	362	0.0	mjs35	265	266	269	269	0.4
mjs02	384	321	376	376	*	mjs36	225	246	269	257	9.3
mjs03	378	382	379	379	0.3	mjs37	207	229	261	242	10.6
mjs04	394	404	399	399	1.3	mjs38	241	254	271	262	5.4
mjs05	643	680	682	682	5.8	mjs39	210	231	262	246	10.0
mjs06	585	556	573	573	*	mjs40	241	241	264	242	0.0
mjs07	644	648	673	659	0.6	mjs41	218	248	276	237	8.7
mjs08	575	582	597	597	1.2	mjs42	250	250	282	257	0.0
mjs09	568	572	578	578	0.7	mjs43	219	228	267	242	4.1
mjs10	928	932	965	965	0.4	mjs44	258	268	324	280	3.9
mjs11	1057	1047	1040	1040	*	mjs45	296	333	464	456	12.5
mjs12	859	843	862	862	*	mjs46	300	384	491	413	28.0
mjs13	827	884	902	909	6.9	mjs47	333	377	490	481	13.2
mjs14	946	1026	1020	1020	7.8	mjs48	327	368	469	436	12.5
mjs15	1469	1467	1457	1447	*	mjs49	356	390	470	466	9.6
mjs16	1312	1380	1352	1352	3.0	mjs50	327	430	516	472	31.5
mjs17	1572	1567	1582	1582	*	mjs51	373	452	536	509	21.2
mjs18	1544	1571	1628	1601	1.7	mjs52	317	387	434	415	22.1
mjs19	1572	1553	1598	1566	*	mjs53	353	419	546	495	18.7
mjs20	1033	1075	1068	1068	3.4	mjs54	311	407	467	454	30.9
mjs21	916	918	922	922	0.2	mjs55	493	797	819	819	61.7
mjs22	924	964	956	956	3.5	mjs56	508	789	873	715	40.7
mjs23	957	969	990	990	1.3	mjs57	500	788	973	948	57.6
mjs24	918	893	890	890	*	mjs58	530	802	884	814	51.3
mjs25	1513	1541	1568	1548	1.9	mjs59	490	916	1024	881	79.8
mjs26	1481	1448	1474	1414	*	mjs60	268	299	421	395	11.6
mjs27	1566	1649	1693	1602	2.3	mjs61	303	332	452	374	9.6
mjs28	1395	1530	1631	1545	9.7	mjs62	284	306	426	357	7.7
mjs29	1336	1444	1502	1455	8.1	mjs63	289	317	398	344	9.7
mjs30	218	239	247	231	6.0	mjs64	240	277	346	306	15.4
mjs31	218	250	281	281	14.7	mjs65	381	508	622	622	33.3
mjs32	219	250	266	255	14.2	mjs66	423	558	652	652	31.9
mjs33	224	241	254	246	7.6	mjs67	408	558	639	639	36.8
mjs34	213	229	238	232	7.5	mjs68	400	554	754	667	38.5

At observing the Table 1, it is possible to infer that our approach evidences a significant performance at minimizing the makespan combined with other criteria. For example, our approach leads to a better makespan than the best known value in nine of 68 instances (*mjs02, 06, 11, 12, 15, 17, 19, 24* and *26*). Besides, the best known value is reached in three instances: *mjs01, mjs40* and *mjs42*, since, the percentage difference is 0.0 (see column *DP*). Additionally, in 16 instances the *DP* is less or equal than 5.0% and in six of them is less than 1.0%. Respect to each set, *SetA* Performs better than *SetB* and *SetC* in 52 instances. *SetC* performs better in 16 instances and *SetB* in eight without a superiority level. Since, in the eight instances *SetB* gets the same performance than *SetC*. As conclusion, at evaluating the convergence of the makespan in the consolidation of the set of non-dominated solutions *SetB* is not efficient and the better combination is the maximum tardiness.

4.2   Evaluating Maximum Tardiness and Total Flow Time

The Table 2 illustrates the elite solutions for both criteria. Again, the best value for the criteria is written in bold. Analyzing the results for maximum tardiness, in 32 instances, optimal solution ($T_{max} = 0$) is gotten, and in 25 of them is gotten in the three sets for the three sets. Concerning to the performance of the sets, Set A presents the best performance in 29 instances, Set B in 5 and Set C in 15. Respect to the total flow time, only Sets B and C are analyzed. At observing the results, Set C leads to better results, since, it is evidenced in 58 instances. At evaluating the performance of the three sets, it is evident the superiority of the *SetB* when a bi-criteria analysis (Makespan and Tmax) is performed. However, if some criteria are added, the best results are gotten in *SetC*.

Table 2. Results for the best T_{max} and $\sum C_i$ in the three sets

Instance	T_{max}			$\sum C_i$		Instance	T_{max}			$\sum C_i$	
	Set A	Set B	Set C	Set B	Set C		Set A	Set B	Set C	Set B	Set C
mjs01	19	23	19	3132	3125	mjs35	0	0	0	2382	2211
mjs02	57	53	54	3295	3329	mjs36	0	0	0	2368	2146
mjs03	14	19	17	3331	3331	mjs37	0	0	0	2291	1948
mjs04	67	65	65	3328	3306	mjs38	0	0	0	2458	2192
mjs05	112	116	119	6062	5795	mjs39	0	0	0	2273	1984
mjs06	58	70	72	5367	5267	mjs40	0	0	0	2194	1935
mjs07	123	136	128	6043	5921	mjs41	0	0	0	2460	2067
mjs08	88	89	89	5135	5226	mjs42	0	0	0	2206	2009
mjs09	76	80	80	5065	4952	mjs43	0	0	0	2011	1863
mjs10	601	608	601	8613	8437	mjs44	0	0	0	2758	2149
mjs11	695	706	690	9165	8936	mjs45	0	0	0	4331	3765
mjs12	482	498	502	7964	7674	mjs46	0	0	0	4606	3941
mjs13	530	550	545	8144	8198	mjs47	0	0	0	4491	3854
mjs14	653	647	629	9490	8939	mjs48	0	0	0	4522	3508
mjs15	928	916	885	13447	13561	mjs49	0	0	0	4274	3785
mjs16	874	855	873	12625	12825	mjs50	0	74	26	4975	4221
mjs17	1082	1064	1094	15017	15331	mjs51	2	95	50	5032	4524
mjs18	1037	1079	1041	15370	15091	mjs52	0	2	0	4034	3539
mjs19	1040	1094	1047	15281	14461	mjs53	0	103	28	5067	4518
mjs20	702	705	711	9351	9400	mjs54	0	0	0	4304	3806
mjs21	547	547	557	8036	8121	mjs55	159	166	181	7999	8036
mjs22	621	614	609	8723	8694	mjs56	116	220	59	8494	6888
mjs23	592	641	619	8892	8638	mjs57	88	308	242	9391	8895
mjs24	545	549	548	8216	7923	mjs58	108	174	121	8294	7633
mjs25	997	1033	1015	14776	14597	mjs59	240	359	163	9872	7926
mjs26	940	962	902	14485	13003	mjs60	0	0	0	3954	3655
mjs27	1113	1157	1048	15887	14675	mjs61	0	10	0	4000	3383
mjs28	998	1103	958	14936	13670	mjs62	0	0	0	3834	3226
mjs29	911	969	902	14264	13545	mjs63	0	0	0	3757	3207
mjs30	0	0	0	2228	1980	mjs64	0	0	0	3208	2823
mjs31	0	0	0	2473	2148	mjs65	0	0	0	6075	5933
mjs32	0	0	0	2492	2180	mjs66	0	18	0	6358	5949
mjs33	0	0	0	2323	2173	mjs67	0	0	69	6124	6840
mjs34	0	0	0	2087	1995	mjs68	0	60	0	7177	6539

4.3   Results for Set A and Set C

The main conclusion of the last sub Sections is that the best results are reached for *Sets A and C*. In this Section the results of the metrics are calculated and written in Tables 3 and 4, where column Sol means the number of non-dominated solutions generated by the search. Additionally, in Table 4 the total tardiness criterion is recorded. The results of these Tables can be used as benchmark to determine the quality of a Pareto front. However, different combination of criteria must be performed to determine the performance mainly of the makespan at trying to reduce the distance from the origin.

Table 3. Quality metrics for *Set A*

Instance	Sol	HV	D	SP	MID	Instance	Sol	HV	D	SP	MID
mjs01	5	0.996	53.2	14.7	380.5	mjs35	1	0.997	0.0	0.0	266.0
mjs02	7	0.995	50.7	4.4	408.8	mjs36	1	0.997	0.0	0.0	246.0
mjs03	3	0.996	15.3	4.4	391.7	mjs37	1	0.998	0.0	0.0	239.0
mjs04	5	0.995	62.2	2.2	450.5	mjs38	1	0.997	0.0	0.0	271.0
mjs05	2	0.992	12.2	2.7	704.0	mjs39	1	0.998	0.0	0.0	236.0
mjs06	4	0.993	47.9	11.1	603.4	mjs40	1	0.998	0.0	0.0	241.0
mjs07	2	0.992	32.0	4.1	686.2	mjs41	1	0.997	0.0	0.0	257.0
mjs08	1	0.993	0.0	0.0	616.4	mjs42	1	0.997	0.0	0.0	250.0
mjs09	1	0.993	0.0	0.0	578.4	mjs43	1	0.997	0.0	0.0	238.0
mjs10	1	0.983	0.0	0.0	1256.7	mjs44	1	0.997	0.0	0.0	270.0
mjs11	1	0.983	0.0	0.0	1258.1	mjs45	1	0.996	0.0	0.0	372.0
mjs12	3	0.985	33.1	10.4	1061.5	mjs46	1	0.996	0.0	0.0	429.0
mjs13	1	0.986	0.0	0.0	1057.8	mjs47	1	0.997	0.0	0.0	383.0
mjs14	4	0.983	39.0	11.0	1253.0	mjs48	1	0.996	0.0	0.0	373.0
mjs15	1	0.975	0.0	0.0	1808.9	mjs49	1	0.996	0.0	0.0	430.0
mjs16	1	0.976	0.0	0.0	1741.5	mjs50	1	0.995	0.0	0.0	467.2
mjs17	1	0.97	0.0	0.0	2167.5	mjs51	2	0.994	12.0	2.6	517.9
mjs18	1	0.97	0.0	0.0	1995.2	mjs52	1	0.996	0.0	0.0	421.0
mjs19	1	0.97	0.0	0.0	2070.7	mjs53	3	0.995	17.0	2.4	466.6
mjs20	1	0.981	0.0	0.0	1374.6	mjs54	1	0.996	0.0	0.0	407.0
mjs21	1	0.985	0.0	0.0	1086.3	mjs55	2	0.990	2.8	1.4	879.9
mjs22	2	0.984	26.0	3.7	1185.2	mjs56	3	0.990	29.1	2.4	864.6
mjs23	1	0.984	0.0	0.0	1151.5	mjs57	1	0.990	0.0	0.0	904.9
mjs24	1	0.985	0.0	0.0	1097.1	mjs58	2	0.990	19.7	3.7	875.6
mjs25	1	0.974	0.0	0.0	1886.0	mjs59	1	0.990	0.0	0.0	1043.6
mjs26	1	0.974	0.0	0.0	1829.4	mjs60	1	0.997	0.0	0.0	332.0
mjs27	1	0.971	0.0	0.0	2077.0	mjs61	1	0.996	0.0	0.0	359.0
mjs28	1	0.973	0.0	0.0	1970.6	mjs62	1	0.997	0.0	0.0	342.0
mjs29	1	0.975	0.0	0.0	1801.4	mjs63	1	0.997	0.0	0.0	341.0
mjs30	1	0.997	0.0	0.0	252.0	mjs64	1	0.997	0.0	0.0	297.0
mjs31	1	0.997	0.0	0.0	255.0	mjs65	1	0.994	0.0	0.0	569.0
mjs32	1	0.997	0.0	0.0	258.0	mjs66	1	0.994	0.0	0.0	591.0
mjs33	1	0.997	0.0	0.0	253.0	mjs67	1	0.994	0.0	0.0	628.0
mjs34	1	0.997	0.0	0.0	241.0	mjs68	1	0.994	0.0	0.0	626.0

Table 4. Quality metrics for *Set C*

Instance	Sol	$\sum T_i$	HV	D	SP	MID	Instance	Sol	$\sum T_i$	HV	D	SP	MID
mjs01	31	61	0.992	216.7	15.7	3329.3	mjs35	5	0	0.995	95.6	13.3	2284.3
mjs02	18	179	0.992	145.2	22.1	3454.3	mjs36	1	0	0.995	0.0	0.0	2201.1
mjs03	12	42	0.992	141.7	10.4	3425.1	mjs37	5	0	0.995	112.8	24.4	2115.3
mjs04	20	241	0.990	184.3	13.7	3479.5	mjs38	4	0	0.995	74.2	2.5	2293.9
mjs05	9	1022	0.984	251.4	17.3	6445.7	mjs39	3	0	0.995	110.3	42.4	2221.5
mjs06	6	434	0.987	95.6	6.9	5541.1	mjs40	2	0	0.996	34.8	4.7	1994.9
mjs07	3	882	0.985	84.9	50.0	6145.8	mjs41	3	0	0.996	34.4	5.2	2174.0
mjs08	2	534	0.987	23.8	4.4	5462.3	mjs42	2	0	0.995	20.1	3.3	2035.4
mjs09	13	399	0.987	292.3	30.7	5359.3	mjs43	1	0	0.996	0.0	0.0	1924.3
mjs10	5	5315	0.970	432.8	136.0	10433.6	mjs44	3	0	0.995	101.5	2.4	2223.4
mjs11	2	5634	0.968	35.3	5.6	10652.4	mjs45	1	0	0.991	0.0	0.0	4127.3
mjs12	9	4358	0.973	50.3	52.4	9362.4	mjs46	1	0	0.992	0.0	0.0	3962.6
mjs13	3	4887	0.972	107.0	18.9	9800.6	mjs47	3	0	0.991	48.4	19.8	4191.7
mjs14	5	5523	0.968	348.6	27.6	10798.3	mjs48	1	0	0.992	0.0	0.0	4005.8
mjs15	2	8557	0.955	97.7	9.1	16230.3	mjs49	3	0	0.991	24.4	11.8	4120.5
mjs16	1	8114	0.957	0.0	0.0	15560.4	mjs50	4	49	0.990	247.7	88.1	4419.4
mjs17	6	10904	0.950	457.8	107.4	19429.9	mjs51	2	334	0.990	51.1	6.7	4764.9
mjs18	4	9972	0.950	166.5	72.7	18246.6	mjs52	2	0	0.992	74.6	6.7	3824.0
mjs19	3	9492	0.950	355.9	197.5	17542.5	mjs53	8	113	0.990	132.5	14.4	4590.2
mjs20	3	5851	0.970	287.6	25.5	11308.6	mjs54	2	18	0.990	22,0	4,4	4262.1
mjs21	9	4980	0.971	322.9	51.2	9925.7	mjs55	1	1428	0.980	0.0	0.0	8303.3
mjs22	5	5376	0.970	612.0	77.8	10573.6	mjs56	2	251	0.985	21.3	4.1	6939.3
mjs23	2	5856	0.968	65.6	7.4	11045.3	mjs57	3	2188	0.977	109.1	23.1	9261.0
mjs24	1	4993	0.970	0.0	0.0	9763.5	mjs58	1	847	0.982	0.0	0.0	7723.8
mjs25	7	9466	0.950	290.6	36.8	17645.6	mjs59	1	1779	0.979	0.0	0.0	8686.5
mjs26	1	8306	0.956	0.0	0.0	15682.4	mjs60	1	0	0.992	0.0	0.0	3676.3
mjs27	4	10180	0.949	74.4	15.0	18405.6	mjs61	2	0	0.993	6.4	2.1	3445.6
mjs28	1	9537	0.951	0.0	0.0	17405.0	mjs62	2	0	0.993	34.0	4.9	3259.4
mjs29	6	8535	0.954	489.2	75.3	16364.6	mjs63	2	0	0.993	30.7	4.4	3273.7
mjs30	1	0	0.996	0.0	0.0	2018.3	mjs64	1	0	0.994	0.0	0.0	2839.5
mjs31	1	0	0.994	0.0	0.0	3123.1	mjs65	1	0	0.988	0.0	0.0	6119.4
mjs32	7	0	0.995	56.8	7.3	2324.8	mjs66	3	483	0.984	173.6	121.6	7116.2
mjs33	2	0	0.995	7.2	2.2	2190.1	mjs67	2	618	0.983	246.4	13.9	7346.4
mjs34	3	0	0.996	21.2	8.5	2029.2	mjs68	3	0	0.987	7.8	1.4	6576.2

5 Conclusion

This paper illustrates a local search algorithm to solve the job shop scheduling Multi resource Resource flexibility with linear routes at minimizing different combinations of regular criteria in Pareto manner. We have presented results for three sets of criteria. To best of our knowledge, there is not any reference about of this extension of the job-shop scheduling problem to calculate regular criteria different than the makespan. The algorithm is supported in the adaptation of estimation functions as extensions of the classical problem and the proposition of a conjunctive graph. In its formulation, the properties of heads, tails and levels of operations have been considered. Computational results show the efficiency of our algorithm at getting some best known values and better values in some instances for the makespan. Additionally optimal solutions are gotten by the maximum tardiness and the total tardiness.

As perspective of the proposed approach, we will study two extensions. The first is the formulation of new estimation function for non-linear route problem (for example, in assembly process), and the second is the solution considering weighted objective functions for improving the making decision process. This research is supported by the project "Formulation and validation of heuristics for optimizing the customer service in flexible configurations in the Tolima region", identified with the code 17-465-INT, which is financed by the Universidad de Ibagué (Colombia).

References

1. Dauzère-Pérès, S., Roux, W., Lasserre, J.: Multi-resource shop scheduling with resource flexibility. Eur. J. Oper. Res. **107**(2), 289–305 (1998)
2. Mati, Y., Dauzère-Pérès, S., Lahlou, C.: A general approach for optimizing regular criteria in the job-shop scheduling problem. Eur. J. Oper. Res. **212**(1), 33–42 (2011)
3. García-León, A., Dauzère-Pérès, S., Mati, Y.: Minimizing regular criteria in the flexible job-shop scheduling problem. In: 7th Multidisciplinary International Scheduling Conference: Theory and Applications, pp. 443–456 (2015)
4. Zitzler, E., Thiele, L., Laumanns, M., Fonseca, C.M., da Fonseca, V.G.: Performance assessment of multiobjective optimizers: an analysis and review. IEEE Trans. Evol. Comput. **7**, 117–132 (2003)
5. García-León, A., Dauzère-Pérès, S., Mati, Y.: An efficient Pareto approach for solving the multi-objective flexible job-shop scheduling problem with regular criteria. Comput. Oper. Res. **108**, 187–200 (2019)
6. Dauzère-Pérès, S., Paulli, J.: An integrated approach for modeling and solving the general multiprocessor job-shop scheduling problem using tabu search. Ann. Oper. Res. **70**, 281–306 (1997)
7. Singer, M., Pinedo, M.: A computational study of branch and bound techniques for minimizing the total weighted tardiness in job shops. IIE Trans. **30**(2), 109–118 (1998)

Author Index

Printed in the United States
By Bookmasters